W9-ARM-136

Today's most **popular authors** have collaborated on this exciting new series, which combines **great literature** with remarkably **effective instruction,** bringing real writers and real tools together for real results.

Give your students

Real writers

unprecedented access
to award-winning authors
(see page T2)

Real tools

remarkably effective tools
for differentiated instruction
(see page T4)

Real results

built-in benchmarking to guarantee
standards mastery and learning
success   (see page T6)

"**This project is what I wish I'd had when I was in school . . . a resource where I could not only read really good writing, but also get a sense about how the authors actually felt!**"

—Cornelius Eady
featured unit author

TEACHER'S EDITION CONTENTS

TEACHER'S EDITION

PRENTICE HALL
LITERATURE

PENGUIN EDITION

THE BRITISH TRADITION

VOLUME I

Copyright © 2007 by Pearson Education, Inc., publishing as Pearson Prentice Hall, Boston, Massachusetts 02116. All rights reserved. Printed in the United States of America. This publication is protected by copyright, and permission should be obtained from the publisher prior to any prohibited reproduction, storage in a retrieval system, or transmission in any form or by any means, electronic, mechanical, photocopying, recording, or likewise. For information regarding permission(s), write to: Rights and Permissions Department, One Lake Street, Upper Saddle River, New Jersey 07458.

Pearson Prentice Hall™ is a trademark of Pearson Education, Inc.
Pearson® is a registered trademark of Pearson plc.
Prentice Hall® is a registered trademark of Pearson Education, Inc.

Boston, Massachusetts
Upper Saddle River, New Jersey

ISBN 0-13-131761-X

3 4 5 6 7 8 9 10   10 09 08 07 06

Real writers

Fifty-three of today's most popular writers have collaborated on this extraordinary new program.

Now your students can learn about reading, writing, and literature from the authors themselves, as they share their personal experiences, insights, and expertise while presenting key instructional concepts.

> " It's a little bit like having you, the students, come backstage with Tim O'Brien, a writer. "
>
> **—Tim O'Brien**
> Grade 11, Unit 5 author

From the Scholar's Desk

JUDITH ORTIZ COFER INTRODUCES
"Ithaka" by Constantine Cavafy

An Interview with Judith Ortiz Cofer
Conducted by Prentice Hall

What aspect of the ancient Greek epic the *Odyssey* would most help someone reading Cavafy's "Ithaka"? The *Odyssey* contains worlds. It's a love story. It's a story of a man trying to get back home to his wife after fighting and suffering in a long war. It's a story of a king and a story of loyalty. But to Cavafy, I think it was especially a story of the journey in between here and there. He shows you how the journey becomes a symbolic journey, standing for your life and goals

......oem is so often recited at graduations ......nies? Yes, the theme is that, when you go

Judith Ortiz Cofer has won numerous awards for her work as a poet, an essayist, and a novelist. In 1994, she won the O. Henry Prize for short story. Or......

Each **unit** in *Prentice Hall Literature* is hosted by one of the featured **authors**. Each author serves as a **guide** for your students, taking them on an unforgettable journey through the writer's world and introducing them to a universe of great literature.

Give your students unprecedented access to award-winning authors!

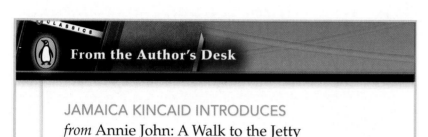

From the Author's Desk

JAMAICA KINCAID INTRODUCES

from Annie John: A Walk to the Jetty

Making Memories and Stories

I come from a small island in the Caribbean that was part of the British Empire until the early 1970s when it gained political independence. Everyone I knew was literate and everyone I knew told stories.

My mother, in particular, not only knew how to read, she did so for sheer pleasure. At the time, she was the only person I ever saw do this, sit and read just for the sake of reading.

She also told me stories but these stories were not folk tales or stories about revered ancestors; they were stories about what she was like as a child, what her mother and father did, what had happened to her before I was born, what the world into which I was born was like before I was born, what the day was like when I took my first steps, the first words I said, the things I liked to eat. I was too young then to make proper memories for myself and so the memory I have of that time are the memories she created for me.

It was at that time, the time before I could make my own memories, that she taught me to read. I believe now that this set of circumstances, my mother telling me stories and teaching me to read, led to my own obsession with literature and writing and especially writing about her.

The Influence of Autobiography

Walk to the Jetty
novel traces the

Jamaica Kincaid

Jamaica Kincaid won the Morton Dauwen Zabek Award for *At the Bottom of the River* (1983) and she was a finalist for the PEN Faulkner Award for *The Autobiography of My Mother* (1995). Kincaid's stories often focus on the development of relationships between women, especially between mothers and daughters.

Each author

- hosts a unit in *Prentice Hall Literature*
- introduces a literary genre or historical period
- provides insight into the "story behind the story"
- answers questions about writing and literature from real students
- shares his or her expertise as scholars or translators of great works of literature

From the Author's Desk DVD

A corresponding video program brings your students into the writer's world, as the authors explain how their personal experiences shaped their writing and how they use the world around them to create the stories that inform, engage, and entertain readers around the world.

Real tools

Presenting: QuickTake™
instant progress monitoring
as easy as 1, 2, 3!

1 Pose questions
to the entire class

2 Students answer via
response pads

3 Results are recorded
and displayed instantly

eInstruction.com

Deliver differentiated instruction easily and seamlessly.

For every selection:

- **Leveled Reading Warm-ups**
  Brief reading passages comprising high-interest
  text and low-level Lexile™ vocabulary preteach
  essential reading skills.

- **Leveled Vocabulary Warm-ups**
  Lexiled™ word lists and activities prepare
  students for reading selections.

- **Leveled Assessment**
  Two levels of selection tests allow you to provide
  assessment targeted for different ability levels.

- **Reader's Notebook series**
  Three levels of interactive readers support
  every selection.

Technology to help you Plan, Teach, and Assess:

- **TeacherEXPRESS™**
  Powerful lesson-planning, resource management,
  and standards-aligned assessment tools, all in one
  place, make class preparation quick and easy!

- **StudentEXPRESS™**
  An interactive textbook, electronic worksheets,
  and links to online activities make this the perfect
  student tool for studying or test review.

- **Exam*View*™ Test Generator**
  Create standards-aligned tests in seconds or
  customize tests to suit individual student's needs.

Reader's Notebook

Differentiated Instruction
Solutions for All Learners

Adapted Version

PRENTICE HALL
LITERATURE

PENGUIN EDITION

Support for every selection in the student text, including:
- Selections with adapted and authentic text
- Enhanced design for easier readability
- Customized, interactive reading, literary analysis, and vocabulary support
- Text and visual selection summaries
- Sentence starters for expressive vocabulary
- "Turbo" vocabulary building tools
- Complete text also available on audio CD

Three levels of Reader's Notebooks ensure that all students get the help they need.

The Reader's Notebook is an interactive companion to the student text that provides additional support for the skills presented. The Adapted version provides additional scaffolding through the use of modified text summaries and partially filled-in graphic organizers, while the English Learner's version provides additional language and vocabulary support.

Accessibility at a Glance charts help you find the best fit for your students.

These charts, at the beginning of each selection grouping, provide a quick way to determine which selections will be more accessible—and more challenging—for your students.

Differentiated Instruction Solutions for All Learners

Accessibility at a Glance

	Creation Hymn	Night
Context	Hindu speculations about the world's origin	Hindu belief in nature's protective forces
Language	Abstract nouns and several series of short questions	Concrete nouns and different personal pronouns referring to a goddess
Concept Level	Accessible (The origin of the world is mysterious.)	Accessible (Think of night as a protective goddess.)
Literary Merit	Vedic hymn from the *Rig Veda*	Vedic hymn from the *Rig Veda*
Lexile	590	590
Overall Rating	Average	Average

Differentiated Instruction Solutions for All Learners

Strategy for Less Proficient Readers
Have students identify three of the four short story elements—main characters, setting, and main events of the plot. Have them use these three elements to try to establish the story's theme or themes.

Strategy for English Learners
Have students diagram the story's plot. Remind them that plot consists of exposition, rising action, climax, falling action, and resolution. Can students find all five stages in this story, or do they think it is missing one or more stages? Which ones?

Strategy for Advanced Readers
Have students discuss which narrative element—plot, character, setting, or theme—is most important to this story. Have them explain their answers in brief essays.

Differentiated instruction for every selection.

These notes provide specific strategies you can use to tailor instruction for all students, including English language learners, gifted students, and less proficient readers.

Real results

Catch small learning problems <u>before</u> they become big ones!

Diagnose Readiness

Brief assessments at the beginning of each part determine student readiness to learn new skills.

Monitor Progress

Assessment Practice features after each selection group check skills proficiency and make sure students are on track.

Benchmark Mastery

Frequent benchmark tests gauge standards mastery and determine whether intervention is needed.

Online Reading Intervention

Introducing: Prentice Hall Success Tracker™

Help your students make real progress!

This fully automated, interactive online diagnostic and remediation system provides:

- Diagnosis and benchmarking of skills
- Customized skills practice
- At-a-glance standards reporting

See page T80 for more information.

Built-in benchmarking ensures success.

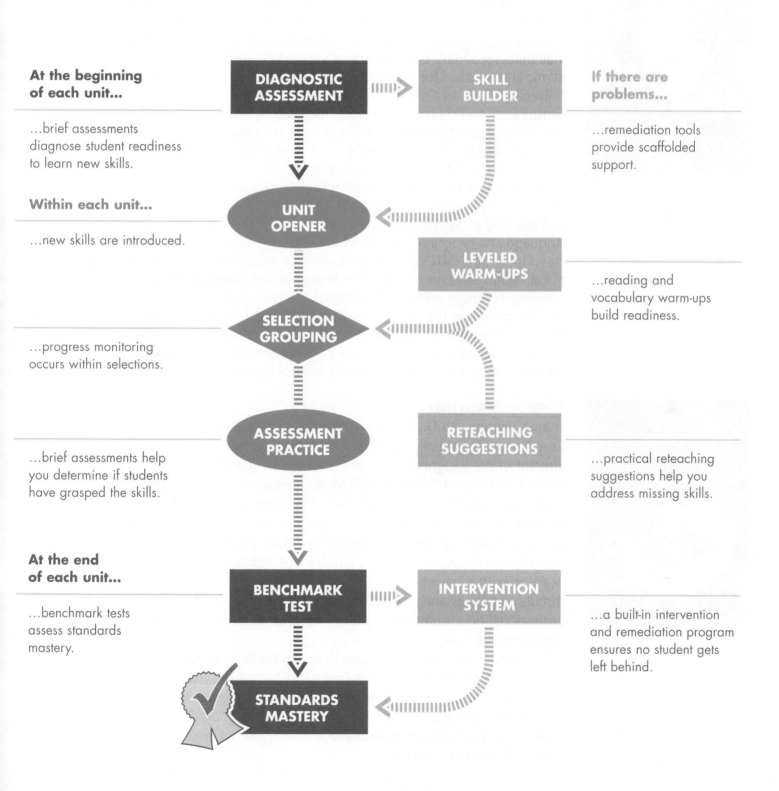

At the beginning of each unit...

...brief assessments diagnose student readiness to learn new skills.

Within each unit...

...new skills are introduced.

...progress monitoring occurs within selections.

...brief assessments help you determine if students have grasped the skills.

At the end of each unit...

...benchmark tests assess standards mastery.

DIAGNOSTIC ASSESSMENT

SKILL BUILDER

UNIT OPENER

LEVELED WARM-UPS

SELECTION GROUPING

ASSESSMENT PRACTICE

RETEACHING SUGGESTIONS

BENCHMARK TEST

INTERVENTION SYSTEM

STANDARDS MASTERY

If there are problems...

...remediation tools provide scaffolded support.

...reading and vocabulary warm-ups build readiness.

...practical reteaching suggestions help you address missing skills.

...a built-in intervention and remediation program ensures no student gets left behind.

CONTRIBUTING AUTHORS

The contributing authors guided the direction and philosophy of *Prentice Hall Literature, Penguin Edition.*
Working with the development team, they helped to build the pedagogical integrity of the program and to
ensure its relevance for today's teachers and students.

Kate **Kinsella**

Kate Kinsella, Ed.D., is a teacher educator in the Department of
Secondary Education at San Francisco State University. She teaches
coursework addressing academic language and literacy development in linguistically and culturally diverse classrooms. Dr. Kinsella
maintains secondary classroom involvement by teaching an academic literacy class for adolescent English learners through the
University's Step to College Program. She publishes and provides
consultancy and training nationally, focusing upon responsible
instructional practices that provide second language learners and
less proficient readers in grades 4–12 with the language and
literacy skills vital to educational mobility.

Dr. Kinsella is the program author for *Reading in the Content
Areas: Strategies for Reading Success,* published by Pearson Learning,
and the lead program author for the 2002 Prentice Hall secondary
language arts program *Timeless Voices: Timeless Themes.* She is the
co-editor of the *CATESOL Journal* (California Association of Teachers
of ESL) and serves on the editorial board for the *California Reader.*
A former Fulbright scholar, Dr. Kinsella has received numerous
awards, including the prestigious Marcus Foster Memorial Reading
Award, offered by the California Reading Association in 2002 to a
California educator who has made a significant statewide impact
on both policy and pedagogy in the area of literacy.

Sharon **Vaughn**

Sharon Vaughn, Ph.D., is the H.E. Hartfelder/The Southland
Corporation Regents Professor at the University of Texas and also
director of the Vaughn Gross Center for Reading and Language Arts
at the University of Texas (VGCRLA). As director of the VGCRLA, she
leads more than five major initiatives, including The Central
Regional Reading First Technical Assistance Center; the Three-Tier
Reading Research Project; a bilingual-biliteracy (English/Spanish)
intervention research study; the Grades 1–4 Teacher Reading
Academies that have been used for teacher education
throughout Texas and the nation; and the creation of online
professional development in reading for teachers and other interested professionals.

Dr. Vaughn has published more than ten books and over one
hundred research articles. She is Editor in Chief of the *Journal of
Learning Disabilities* and serves on the editorial boards of more than
ten research journals, including the *Journal of Educational
Psychology,* the *American Educational Research Journal,* and the
Journal of Special Education.

Kevin **Feldman**

Kevin Feldman, Ed.D., is the Director of Reading and Intervention for the Sonoma County Office of Education and an independent educational consultant. He publishes and provides consultancy and training nationally, focusing upon improving school-wide literacy skills as well as targeted interventions for struggling readers, special needs students, and second language learners. Dr. Feldman is the co-author of the California Special Education Reading Task Force report and the lead program author for the 2002 Prentice Hall secondary language arts program *Timeless Voices: Timeless Themes.* He serves as technical consultant to the California Reading and Literature Project and the CalSTAT State Special Education Improvement Project. Dr. Feldman has taught for nineteen years at the university level in Special Education and Masters' level programs for University of California, Riverside, and Sonoma State University.

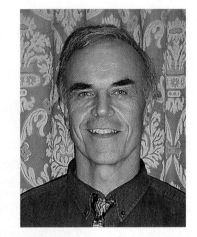

Dr. Feldman earned his undergraduate degree in Psychology from Washington State University and has a Master's Degree from UC Riverside in Special Education, Learning Disabilities, and Instructional Design. He has an Ed.D. from the University of San Francisco in Curriculum and Instruction.

Differentiated Instruction Advisor

Don **Deshler**

Don Deshler, Ph.D, is the Director of the Center for Research on Learning (CRL) at the University of Kansas. Dr. Deshler's expertise centers on adolescent literacy, learning strategic instruction, and instructional strategies for teaching content-area classes to academically diverse classes. He is the author of *Teaching Content to All: Evidence-Based Inclusive Practices in Middle and Secondary Schools,* a text which presents the instructional practices that have been tested and validated through his research at CRL.

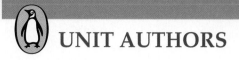

UNIT AUTHORS

An award-winning, contemporary author hosts each unit in each level of *Prentice Hall Literature: Penguin Edition*. In the upper-level courses, some of these authors are renowned scholars or translators, while others are famous for their own contributions to literature. All of these authors serve as guides for your students, helping to introduce the period or culture covered in a unit, discussing the work of a traditional author or their own work or translation, and revealing their own writing processes. Following are the featured unit authors who guide students for *The British Tradition*.

Burton **Raffel (b.1928)**

Unit 1: From Legend to History (A.D. 449–1485)

Burton Raffel is ideally suited to introduce this unit and his own translation of *Beowulf*. In addition to that highly praised translation, his numerous books include *Poems From the Old English* and *The Forked Tongue: A Study of the Translation Process*. Professor Raffel has taught English, Classics, and Comparative Literature at many universities.

Seamus **Heaney (b. 1939)**

Unit 1: From Legend to History (A.D. 449–1485)

Seamus Heaney, winner of the 1995 Nobel Prize in Literature, provides his own perspective on translating *Beowulf*. In 1999, his translation of this Old English epic won the Whitbread Book Award, one of the most prestigious literary prizes in the United Kingdom.

Frank **Kermode (b. 1919)**

Unit 2: Celebrating Humanity (1485–1625)

Frank Kermode, knighted in 1991 for his contributions to literary scholarship, is a perfect choice for introducing this unit and Shakespeare's *Macbeth*. A Fellow of the British Academy and of the Royal Society of Literature, he has written or edited more than forty books. These include *Shakespeare, Shakespeare's Language,* and *The Age of Shakespeare*.

Richard **Rodriguez (b. 1944)**

Unit 3: A Turbulent Time (1625–1798)

Premier American essayist Richard Rodriguez provides a fascinating view of this era and of the work of Joseph Addison. Mr. Rodriguez, who traces some of his literary roots to eighteenth-century London, won The Christopher Prize for his autobiography, *Hunger of Memory,* and the George Foster Peabody Award for his television essays.

Elizabeth **McCracken (b. 1966)**

Unit 4: Rebels and Dreamers (1798–1832)

Acclaimed American novelist Elizabeth McCracken is well suited to comment on Romantic literature in general and Mary Shelley's *Frankenstein* in particular. Ms. McCracken's own novel *The Giant's House,* a finalist for the National Book Award, offers a contemporary take on such Romantic themes as the extraordinary in everyday life, the nature of the grotesque, and the fated love of two soulmates.

James **Berry (b. 1925)**

Unit 5: Progress and Decline (1833–1901)

James Berry, who received the Order of the British Empire (OBE) for services to poetry, grew up in Jamaica and came to Britain in 1948. He provides an interesting, contemporary perspective on nineteenth-century British colonialism by discussing his experiences growing up in a colonized country. He also comments on his own poetry in relation to the imperial assumptions of Rudyard Kipling's verse.

Anita **Desai (b. 1937)**

Unit 6: A Time of Rapid Change (1901–Present)

The Indian novelist Anita Desai, winner of the Winifred Holtby Memorial Prize and a Fellow of the Royal Society of Literature, reveals how the breakup of the British Empire affected postcolonial Indian literature. She also introduces her story "A Devoted Son," which focuses on the conflicts between new and traditional values in contemporary India, and she provides valuable insights into her writing process.

PROGRAM ADVISORS

The program advisors provided ongoing input throughout the development of *Prentice Hall Literature: Penguin Edition*. Their valuable insights ensure that the perspectives of the teachers throughout the country are represented within this literature series.

Sherice Alford
Language Arts Instructor
Cape Fear Senior High School
Fayetteville, North Carolina

Leslie Ballard
State Director
North Central Association CASI
Indiana State University
Terre Haute, Indiana

Heather Barnes
Language Arts Instructor
Central Crossing High School
Grove City, Ohio

Kathryn Shelley-Barnes
District Support Specialist
Traverse City Central High School
Traverse City, Michigan

Karen C. Lilly-Bowyer
Instructional Services Assessment Team
Winston-Salem Forsyth County Schools
Winston-Salem, North Carolina

Lee Bromberger
English Department Chairperson
Mukwonago High School
Mukwonago, Wisconsin

Shawn L. Brumfield
Literacy Coach
Horace Mann Middle School
Los Angeles Unified School District
Local 3
Los Angeles, California

Susanne Buttrey
Librarian
Sycamore Middle School
Pleasant View, Tennessee

Denise Campbell
K-12 Literacy Content Coordinator
Cherry Creek School District
Centennial, Colorado

Patricia A. Cantrowitz
Language Arts Instructor (Retired)
Union-Endicott High School
Endicott, New York

Holly Carr
Language Arts Instructor
Central Crossing High School
Grove City, Ohio

Melody Renee Chalmers
Language Arts Instructor
E. E. Smith High School
Fayetteville, North Carolina

Susan Cisna
Language Arts Instructor
East Prairie Junior High School
Tuscola, Illinois

Barbra Evans-Thompson
English Department Chairperson
Westover High School
Fayetteville, North Carolina

Ebony Forte
Language Arts Instructor
Pine Forest Senior High School
Fayetteville, North Carolina

Linda Fund
Reading Specialist
Ezra L. Nolan Middle School #40
Jersey City, New Jersey

Karen Gibson, Ph.D.
Communication Arts Program Leader
Appleton Area School District
Appleton, Wisconsin

Gail Hacker
Language Arts Instructor (Retired)
North Charleston High School
North Charleston, South Carolina

Kimberly Hartman
Language Arts Instructor
Franklin Heights High School
Columbus, Ohio

Doris Sue Hawkins
Language Arts Instructor
C. W. Otto Middle School
Lansing, Michigan

Darby Holley
Language Arts Instructor
Henry L. Sneed Middle School
Florence, South Carolina

Helen Hudson
Language Arts Instructor
Crawfordsville High School
Crawfordsville, Indiana

Kathleen Keane
English Department Chairperson
Foxborough High School
Foxborough, Massachusetts

John Kiser
English Curriculum Specialist (Retired)
Charlotte-Mecklenburg Schools
Charlotte, North Carolina

Cheryl W. Lee
Language Arts Instructor
Douglas Byrd High School
Fayetteville, North Carolina

Carrie Lichtenberg
Language Arts Instructor
Highlands High School
Ft. Thomas, Kentucky

Catherine Linn
Language Arts Instructor
Palm Springs High School
Palm Desert, California

Agathaniki Locklear
District Technology Resource Teacher
Kenton County Schools
Ft. Wright, Kentucky

John Ludy
Language Arts Instructor
Fremont High School
Fremont, Indiana

Louise R. Matthewson
Language Arts Instructor
Albuquerque Public Schools
Albuquerque, New Mexico

Sherrie McDowell
Language Arts Instructor
Central High School
Cheyenne, Wyoming

Suzanne Mitoraj
English/Language Arts Consultant
Berlin, Connecticut

Nancy Monroe
Language Arts Instructor
Bolton High School
Alexandria, Louisiana

Gail Phelps
Language Arts Instructor
Northwood Middle School
North Little Rock, Arkansas

Matthew Scanlon
K-12 Humanities Supervisor
Hackettstown Public Schools
Hackettstown, New Jersey

John Scott
Language Arts Instructor (Retired)
Hampton City Schools
Hampton City, Virginia

Jean Shope
Language Arts Instructor
Grant Middle School
Albuquerque, New Mexico

Margaret St. Sauver
Staff Development-English/Language Arts
St. Paul Public Schools
St. Paul, Minnesota

Steve Thalheimer
Language Arts Instructor
Lawrenceburg High School
Lawrenceburg, Indiana

Cathy Robbs Turner
Director of Academies
Chattanooga Central High School
Harrison, Tennessee

Sandra VanBelois
Language Arts Instructor
Jack Britt High School
Fayetteville, North Carolina

Martha Lee Wildman
Language Arts Instructor
Lynn Middle School
Las Cruces, New Mexico

Melissa Williams
Language Arts Instructor
Delsea Regional High School
Franklinville, New Jersey

Charles Youngs
HS Language Arts Curriculum Facilitator
Bethel Park High School
Bethel Park, Pennsylvania

CONTENTS IN BRIEF

Contents ■ *vii*

Unit 1

From Legend to History
The Old English and Medieval Periods (A.D. 449–1485)

From the Translator's Desk
Burton Raffel

Part One Earthly Exile, Heavenly Home

Part Two Focus on Literary Forms: The Epic 33

Part Three A National Spirit

SELECTION GROUPINGS
These groupings allow you to compare a variety of literary works.

SAT PREP ACT

Unit 2

Celebrating Humanity
The English Renaissance Period (1485–1625)

From the Scholar's Desk
Frank Kermode

Part One Lovers and Their Lines

SAT PREP ACT

Unit 3

A Turbulent Time
The Seventeenth and Eighteenth Centuries (1625–1798)

From the Author's Desk

Richard Rodriquez

Part One The War Against Time

Part Two A Nation Divided

Rebels and Dreamers:
The Romantic Period (1798–1832)

From the Scholar's Desk
Elizabeth McCracken

Part One Fantasy and Reality

Part Two Focus on Literary Forms: Lyric Poetry

Part Three The Reaction to Society's Ills

Unit 5

Progress and Decline:
The Victorian Period (1833–1901)

From the Author's Desk
James Berry

Part One Relationships

Comparing Literary Works

Comparing Literary Works

Part Two Focus on Literary Forms: The Novel

Comparing Literary Works

Connections: Literature Around the World

SAT
PREP
ACT

Unit 6

A Time of Rapid Change
The Modern and Postmodern Periods (1901–Present)

From the Author's Desk
Anita Desai

Part One Waking From the Dream

Part Four From the National to the Global

INFORMATIONAL TEXTS AND OTHER NONFICTION

■ Reading Informational Materials—Instructional Workshops

■ Additional Nonfiction—Selections by Type

Primary Sources:
History, Political Texts, and Speeches

Primary Sources:
Diaries, Journals, and Letters

Essays and Articles

Autobiography and Biography

■ Historical and Literary Background

INFORMATIONAL MATERIALS AND OTHER NONFICTION
(continued)

SKILLS WORKSHOPS

■ Writing Workshops

■ Vocabulary Workshops

■ Assessment Workshops

■ Communications Workshops

■ Connections to Literature

Literature Around the World

American Literature

PRENTICE HALL LITERATURE: A RICH TRADITION OF LEARNING SUCCESS

The Research Process

Since 1988, *Prentice Hall Literature* has been at the forefront of language arts instruction, providing teachers and their students with quality instruction and assessment tools to ensure success. Each successive edition builds on the strong heritage of *Prentice Hall Literature*.

To develop the current edition of *Prentice Hall Literature*, we conducted a variety of research studies, yielding three key elements of an effective language arts program: clean, clear, non-distracting design with considerate text; systematic, consistent skills instruction; and built-in benchmarking to ensure learning success. Our research comprised these three design stages:

1 EXPLORATORY NEEDS ASSESSMENT

In conjunction with Prentice Hall authors, we conducted research to explore proven educational reading methodologies. The results of this research were incorporated into our instructional strategy and pedagogy to create a more effective literature program. This stage included

- Reading research
- Review of state standards
- Teacher interviews

2 FORMATIVE RESEARCH, DEVELOPMENT, AND FIELD-TESTING

During this phase of the research, we developed and field-tested prototype material with students and teachers. Results informed revisions to the final design and pedagogy. Formative research included

- Field testing of prototypes in classroom pilots
- Classroom observations
- Teacher reviews
- Supervisor reviews
- Educator advisory panels

3 SUMMATIVE RESEARCH, VALIDATION RESEARCH

Finally, we have conducted and will continue to conduct longer-term research under actual classroom conditions. Research at this phase includes:

- Pilot-testing
- Prepublication learner verification research
- Postpublication validation studies, including validation of test questions
- Evaluation of results on standardized tests

RESEARCH BIBLIOGRAPHY

Reading

Alexander, Patricia A., and Tamara Jetton. "Learning from Text: A Multidimensional and Developmental Perspective." *Handbook of Reading Research*, vol. 3, ed. M. L. Kamil, P. B. Mosenthal, P. D. Pearson, and R. Barr. Mahwah, NJ: Lawrence Erlbaum Associates, 2000. 285–310.

Finders, Margaret J., and Susan Hynds. *Literacy Lessons: Teaching and Learning with Middle School Students.* Upper Saddle River, NJ: Merrill, 2003.

Guthrie, John T., and Allan Wigfield. "Engagement and Motivation in Reading." *Handbook of Reading Research,* vol. 3, ed. M. L. Kamil, P. B. Mosenthal, P. D. Pearson, and R. Barr. Mahwah, NJ: Lawrence Erlbaum Associates, 2000. 403–422.

Harvey, Stephanie, and Anne Goudvis. "Determining Importance in Text: The Nonfiction Connection." *Strategies That Work: Teaching Comprehension to Enhance Understanding.* Portland, ME: Stenhouse Publishers, 2000.

Langer, Judith. "Beating the Odds: Teaching Middle and High School Students to Read and Write Well," 1999. Center on English Learning and Achievement. May 2003. <http://cela.albany.edu/eie2/main.html>

National Reading Panel. *Teaching Children to Read: An Evidence-Based Assessment of the Scientific Research on Reading and Its Implications for Reading Instruction.* NIH Publication 00-4769. Bethesda, MD: U.S. Department of Health and Human Services, 2000.

Pressley, Michael. "What Should Comprehension Instruction Be the Instruction Of?" *Handbook of Reading Research*, vol. 3, ed. M. L. Kamil, P. B. Mosenthal, P. D. Pearson, and R. Barr. Mahwah, NJ: Lawrence Erlbaum Associates, 2000. 545–562.

Vocabulary

Baumann, J.F., and E.J. Kame'enui. *Vocabulary Instruction: From Research to Practice.* New York: Guilford Press, 2004.

Blachowicz, Camille, and Peter Fisher. *Teaching Vocabulary in All Classrooms*, 2nd Ed. Upper Saddle River, NJ: Merrill, 2002.

Coxhead, Averil. "A New Academic Word List." *TESOL Quarterly*, 2000.

Kinsella, Kate. "Strategies to Teach Academic Vocabulary." Strategies to Promote Academic Literacy for Second Language Learners Within the English Language Arts Classroom, 2005.

Kinsella, Kate, and Kevin Feldman. *Narrowing the Language Gap: The Case for Explicit Vocabulary Instruction.* New York: Scholastic, Inc., 2005.

Marzano, Robert J. "The Developing Vision of Vocabulary Instruction." *Vocabulary Instruction: From Research to Practice.* New York: Guilford Press, 2004

Differentiated Instruction

Allington, Richard L. *What Really Matters for Struggling Readers: Designing Research-Based Programs.* New York: Longman, 2001.

Armbruster, Bonnie, and Thomas H. Anderson. "On Selecting 'Considerate' Content Area Textbooks." *Remedial and Special Education*, vol. 9 (1): 47–52.

Carnine, Douglas, Jerry Silbert, and Edward J. Kame'enui. *Direct Instruction Reading. 3rd ed.* Upper Saddle River, NJ: Prentice Hall, 1997.

Deshler, Donald D., Keith B. Lenz, and Brenda R. Kissam. *Teaching Content to All: Evidence-Based Inclusive Practices in Middle and Secondary Schools.* Boston: Allyn and Bacon, 2004.

Moore, David. W., and Kathleen A. Hinchman. *Starting Out: A Guide to Teaching Adolescents Who Struggle with Reading.* Boston: Allyn and Bacon, 2003.

Vaughn, Sharon, Candace S. Bos, and Jeanne Shay Schumm. *Teaching Exceptional, Diverse, and At-Risk Students in the General Education Classroom.* Boston: Allyn and Bacon, 2002.

FIELD-TESTING OF PRENTICE HALL LITERATURE, PENGUIN EDITION

Background In May 2004, six Language Arts teachers and 133 students field-tested Grade 7 and Grade 9 prototypes. Each teacher taught the prototype with one or more classes for three weeks. The students involved in the study represented a wide range of backgrounds and ability levels.

Prentice Hall researchers and editors used a variety of tools to gather information, including classroom observation and weekly debriefings with teachers who kept weekly lesson logs to note their experiences and observations about the prototype. In addition, we reviewed the results of pre-tests and post-tests to assess students' knowledge of the skills addressed in the prototypes.

Key Findings Reaction to the prototype from both teachers and students was highly favorable. The most highly-praised features of the program included the following:

Paired Selections: Teachers liked choosing which selection to teach. They agreed that this organization was useful for differentiated instruction.

Skills Instruction: Teachers praised the systematic skills instruction in the prototype. Classroom observation, teacher lesson logs, and student post-test results confirmed student mastery of the skills taught in the prototype.

Literature Selections: Students praised the selections as "interesting" and "fun-to-read," while teachers also noted that the content of the prototype was appropriate for their students' grade and ability levels.

Unit Authors: Teachers felt the featured unit authors added value by providing the writers' insights into their works.

Program Design and Organization: Both students and teachers enjoyed the bright, vibrant pictures. Teachers also commended the ratio of text to visuals, the consistent organization, and the ease of navigation.

How Field-Testing Informed Development

Pacing The prototype included more material than could be taught in a three-week cycle.	The final product includes fewer part-level features and provides suggestions for revised pacing.
Reading Informational Materials Students and teachers commented that the prototype selection was not age-appropriate.	Editors identified selections for the feature that would be more relevant to students' everyday lives, such as articles, recipes, applications, and schedules.
Practice and Assess Questions Students and teachers told us that some questions were too complicated.	Questions in the final product are direct, clear, and concise.
Vocabulary Instruction Teachers told us that they wanted to see more vocabulary development.	We expanded the part vocabulary preview and review. For each selection, we developed Vocabulary Warm-ups to increase the number of words taught per selection.

PRENTICE HALL LITERATURE: PROVEN TO GET RESULTS

National Effect-Size Study: Student Performance of *Prentice Hall Literature*, Users vs. Non-Users

This quasi-experimental study examined longitudinal test results of 976 closely matched user and non-user districts as a point of comparison across the same time periods and achievement tests.

Prentice Hall users performed as well or better than their counterparts, achieving approximately a 56 percent gain in the percentage of students meeting or exceeding state reading/ELA standards and a 62 percent gain in national percentile ranking after one or more years of program implementation. A sustained gain was noted in districts that have implemented the program for two or more years.

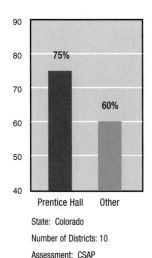

State: Colorado

Number of Districts: 10

Assessment: CSAP

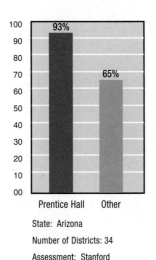

State: Arizona

Number of Districts: 34

Assessment: Stanford

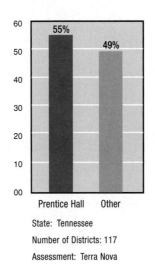

State: Tennessee

Number of Districts: 117

Assessment: Terra Nova

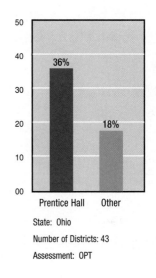

State: Ohio

Number of Districts: 43

Assessment: OPT

Learner Verification Research

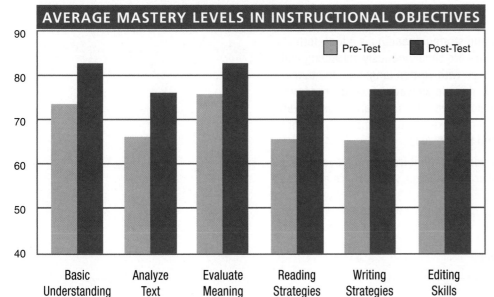

AVERAGE MASTERY LEVELS IN INSTRUCTIONAL OBJECTIVES

In a yearlong learner verification study, students using *Prentice Hall Literature* increased their mastery levels in several diagnostic skill areas for reading/language arts.

All students were tested at the start of the year with a nationally normed standardized test, the TerraNova™ Complete Battery Plus exam. At the end of the study period, students were retested with the same standardized test. Only students who completed both the pre- and post-tests were included in this analysis. All tests were scored by CTB/McGraw Hill, publisher of the TerraNova™.

PROFESSIONAL DEVELOPMENT GUIDEBOOK

The Prentice Hall contributing authors and advisors guided the pedagogical design and content of Prentice Hall Literature Penguin Edition. *Their expertise informed the development of instruction and support. In these pages, we share the authors' expertise on some of the key issues in language arts education.*

BECOMING A STRATEGIC READING TEACHER

"It's not what you say or do that ultimately matters. It is what you get the students to do as a result of what you said and did that counts."

Kate Kinsella Ed.D.

Strategic Reading

Recent research suggests that skillful and strategic reading is a long-term developmental process in which "readers are simultaneously extracting and constructing meaning" through interaction with written language. In other words, successful readers know how to decode all types of words, read with fluency and expression, have well-developed vocabularies, and possess various comprehension strategies such as note-taking and summarizing to employ as the reading task demands (Snow and Sweet, 2003).

Research illustrates that virtually all students benefit from direct, systematic, and explicit instruction in reading (Baker and Gersten, 2000). There are three stages to the instructional process:

- **Instructional Frontloading** (before reading)
- **Guided Instruction** (during reading)
- **Reflection and Study** (after reading)

Instructional Frontloading

If teachers emphasize preteaching, or frontloading instruction, they will help structure learning to ensure student success. Frontloading instruction is especially critical in mixed-ability classrooms with English language learners, students with special needs, and other students performing below grade level in terms of literacy. Before reading, prepare students with the following prereading activities and instruction:

- Introduce the big concepts.
- Provide direct teaching of vocabulary necessary to comprehend key ideas.
- Build academic vocabulary.
- Build, activate, and elaborate on background knowledge.
- Pique curiosity and guide students to generate questions.
- Use launch activities that incorporate key vocabulary.

Guided Instruction

In guided instruction, the teacher models approaches for how to actively engage with the text to gain meaning. The teacher guides the students through the text using reading strategies and then guides discussion about the content using participation strategies.

Structured Accountable Responses

During the instructional frontloading and the guided instruction, it is important to ensure participation by all students in a nonthreatening environment. The following strategies are ways to structure your instruction so that all students are accountable and prepared to participate.

Use partners. Partner response increases active language use, attention, and higher order thinking during instruction.

- Choose partners, alternating ranking based on literacy/social skills.
- Assign roles—such as *A* and *B*. *"A's tell B's two things we have learned about. . . ."*
- Give a specific topic. *"What do you predict. . . ?" "What are two things we have learned about. . . . ?"*
- Allow a brief time of exchange: *"A's tell B's two things we have learned about. . . ."*
- Call on students to share with the class after they have practiced with a partner.

Write first. Writing first increases thinking, accountability, and focus. It provides you as the teacher with concrete formative feedback. Having students write before responding connects written language to oral language, and it provides an opportunity for students to target academic language.

Nominate volunteers. Choosing volunteers based on your observations during partner work or written work allows you to ensure that all students participate and succeed. Circulate and observe as students discuss or write about the topic. Ask students to share their responses with you. Then, "nominate" the students you will ask to share with the class—that is, alert the student that he or she will be sharing with the class, so that the student can practice with a partner or with you before sharing with the larger group.

PRENTICE HALL LITERATURE

Putting Research Into Practice

You can introduce the big concepts for each selection using the **Connecting to the Selection** feature in the **Student Edition**.

You will find teaching plans for instructional frontloading in the *General Resources* including plans and student pages for the following activities:

- Anticipation Guide
- KWL Chart
- Idea Wave

PRENTICE HALL LITERATURE

Putting Research Into Practice

You can use questions and prompts provided in the **Student Edition** and the **Teacher's Edition** as prompts for structured accountable responses.

Language for Active Classroom Participation

Explicitly teach students ways to express themselves in class discussions. Model the use of these phrases, and encourage students to use them in responding.

Expressing an Opinion
I think that _____
I believe that _____
In my opinion _____

Asking for Clarification
What do you mean?
Will you explain that again?
I have a question about that.

Soliciting a Response
What do you think?
Do you agree?

Individual Reporting
I discovered from _____ that ____
I found out that _____
_____ pointed out that

Disagreeing
I don't agree with you because
I got a different answer than you.
I see it a different way.

Affirming
That's an interesting idea.
I hadn't thought of that.
I see what you mean.

Predicting
I predict that _____
I imagine that _____
Based on _____ I predict that ____

Paraphrasing and Clarifying
So you are saying that _____
In other words, you think that _____
What I hear you saying is _____

Acknowledging Ideas
My idea is related to _____'s idea.
My idea is similar to _____'s idea.
My idea builds on _____'s idea.

Partner and Group Reporting
We agreed that _____
We decided that _____
We had a different approach.
We had a similar idea.

Offering a Suggestion
Maybe we could _____
What if we _____
Here's something we might try.

Holding the Floor
As I was saying _____
What I was trying to say was _____

PRENTICE HALL LITERATURE

Putting Research Into Practice

- Questions and notes in the **Student Edition** provide frequent, regular opportunities for applying the strategies.
- In the Reading and Vocabulary Preview, in the **Student Edition**, students learn the academic vocabulary needed to write and speak about the concepts taught in the parts of the unit.

- The **Teachers' Edition** provides strategies for ensuring student participation.
- You will find teaching plans and student pages in the *General Resources* for participation strategies, including
  - Oral Cloze
  - Choral Reading
  - ReQuest

Works Cited

Gersten, Russell and Scott K. Baker. "What We Know About Effective Instructional Practices for English-Language Learners." *Exceptional Children,* Vol. 66(4), 2000. 454-470.

Snow, Catherine E. and Anne Polselli Sweet. "Reading for Comprehension." *Rethinking Reading Comprehension.* New York: Guilford Press, 2003.

ENERGIZING VOCABULARY INSTRUCTION

"Educators need to make robust intentional vocabulary instruction a high priority."

Kevin Feldman Ed.D.

Vocabulary Instruction

There is a clear consensus among literacy researchers that accelerating vocabulary growth is a vital and often neglected component of comprehensive language arts instruction (Baumann and Kame'enui, 2004). Numerous studies have documented the strong and reciprocal relationship between vocabulary knowledge and reading comprehension. Research focused on school-age second language learners similarly concludes that vocabulary knowledge is the single best predictor of their academic achievement across subject matter domains. Therefore, educators need to make robust intentional vocabulary instruction a high priority. Intensive instruction should focus on words related to central lesson concepts and high-use academic words. Academic word lists developed by researchers can help educators determine appropriate high-use academic words (Coxhead, 2000; Xue and Nation, 1984).

Big Ideas in Vocabulary Teaching

Connect
Assess students' current knowledge of the target lesson vocabulary.
Give explanations before definitions.
Use student friendly explanations.
Use language students already know.
Use examples from students' experiential realm.
Use synonyms.

Process
Have students give examples and images.
Have students use "Show you know" sentences.
Have students generate synonyms and antonyms.

Practice
Have students use graphic organizers and webs.
Have students use the words in new contexts.

Rationale for Direct Vocabulary Instruction

Over the past two decades, mounting research has challenged traditional views regarding the role of direct teaching in vocabulary development. Numerous studies have documented the positive impact of direct, explicit vocabulary instruction on both immediate word learning and longer-term reading comprehension (Baker, Simmons, and Kame'enui, 1995; Beck, McKeown, and Kucan, 2002; Biemiller, 2004; Marzano, 2004).

Putting Research Into Practice

- You can preteach academic vocabulary in the **Reading and Vocabulary Preview** at the beginning of each part of the **Student Edition**.

- All vocabulary activities in the **Student Edition** are structured to be generative, "show you know" types of activities.

- You can develop students expressive vocabulary for talking about the big concepts and themes of the literature with the **Connecting to the Literature** feature that precedes every selection in the **Student Edition**.

- The **Teacher's Edition** provides consistent support for introducing vocabulary at the beginning of every selection.

- The *Unit Resources* provide generative activities for all vocabulary instruction and activities.

A Powerful Teaching Routine

The following steps can be elaborated and adapted, depending on the relative importance of the words in question and the students' background knowledge.

1) **Pronounce** The first step in teaching a new term is guiding students in correctly pronouncing the word. This will support learners in decoding the word confidently, while also supporting both auditory and muscle memory (Shaywitz, 2003).

2) **Explain** Understanding a new term requires a clear explanation of the meaning, using language familiar to the students (Beck et al., 2002; Stahl, 1999). Provide a synonym to solidify the connection between the new vocabulary term and students' prior knowledge.

3) **Provide examples** Students will usually need at least two or three examples of a new term to firmly grasp the meaning of it. Moreover, these examples should be drawn from a variety of contexts, not only the one used in the reading or lesson.

4) **Elaborate** Research in cognitive psychology consistently indicates that learners understand and remember information better when they elaborate on it themselves (Marzano et al., 2001). Thus, students' understanding of new vocabulary terms is strengthened when they are given opportunities to elaborate word meanings by generating their own examples.

5) **Assess** Research, such as Baker et al., (1995) and Marzano (2004), have documented the importance of incorporating regular informal assessment into the instructional process, especially with academically diverse learners. Assessment of vocabulary involves both formative evaluation (quick checks for understanding) and summative evaluation (formal quizzes or tests).

PRENTICE HALL LITERATURE

Putting Research Into Practice

- Use the Vocabulary notes in the **Teacher's Edition** for consistent, predictable vocabulary instruction structure.

- Use the **Vocabulary Knowledge Rating Sheet** in **General Resources** to assess students' current knowledge.

- Use the **Academic Vocabulary** lessons in the **Vocabulary Preview and Review** to introduce high-frequency words.

- Use the sample sentences in the **Vocabulary Builder** feature with each selection in the **Student Edition** to preteach words.

Works Cited

Baker, Scott, Deborah C. Simmons, and Edward J. Kame'enui. *Vocabulary Acquisition: Synthesis of the Research.* (Tech. Report No. 13). Eugene: University of Oregon, National Center to Improve the Tools of Educators, 1995.

Baumann, James F., and Edward J. Kame'enui. Eds. *Vocabulary Instruction: From Research to Practice.* New York: Guilford Press, 2004.

Beck, Isabel L., Margaret G. McKeown, and Linda Kucan. *Bringing Words to Life: Robust Vocabulary Instruction Solving Problems in the Teaching of Literacy.* New York: Guilford Publications, 2002.

Biemiller, Andrew. "Teaching Vocabulary in the Primary Grades: Vocabulary Instruction Needed." Eds. J.F. Baumann and Edward J. Kame'enui. *Vocabulary Instruction: From Research to Practice.* New York: Guilford Press, 2004.

Coxhead, Averil. "A New Academic Word List." *TESOL Quarterly,* 2000.

Marzano, Robert J., Debra J. Pickering, and Jane E. Pollock. *Classroom Instruction That Works: Research-Based Strategies for Increasing Student Achievement.* Alexandria, Virginia: Association for Supervision and Curriculum Development, 2001.

Marzano, Robert J. "The Developing Vision of Vocabulary Instruction." Eds. J.F. Baumann and E.J. Kame'enui. *Vocabulary Instruction: From Research to Practice.* New York: Guilford Press, 2004.

Shaywitz, Sally E. *Overcoming Dyslexia: A New and Complete Science-Based Program for Reading Problems at Any Level.* New York: Knopf, 2003.

Stahl, Steven A. *Vocabulary Development.* Cambridge: Brookline, 1999.

Xue, Guoyi, and I. S. P. Nation. "A University Word List." *Language Learning and Communication.* Vol. 3(2), 1984, 215-229.

GIVING HOPE TO STRUGGLING READERS

"Students with reading difficulties are very aware that they struggle. What is amazing is that despite these challenges, students are motivated to improve when given stimulating text, good instruction, and opportunities."

Sharon Vaughn, Ph.D.

Middle and high school students are expected to read at proficient levels and possess vocabularies and comprehension skills for understanding complex reading material. However, despite reading intervention programs during the primary grades, many students continue to experience learning problems well into their adolescent years. Many of these students experience difficulty in word recognition skills, decoding, reading fluency, and vocabulary development (Biancarosa and Snow, 2004). Moreover, besides their scant word recognition skills and poor reading fluency, students with low reading skills may demonstrate significant deficits in reading comprehension. Unfortunately, findings from previous research indicate that adolescents with reading-related learning disabilities become further behind in reading each year in school and risk losing the skills they acquired during elementary school.

Older students with reading disabilities need explicit and systematic instruction in reading. In addition, their instruction in reading is enhanced by experiences that are designed explicitly to foster vocabulary development, background knowledge, the ability to detect and comprehend relationships among verbal concepts, and the ability to actively use strategies to ensure understanding and retention of material.

Attitudes Toward Reading

In general, students with low reading skills perceive reading as a difficult, unsuccessful, and unappealing activity (McKenna, Kear, and Ellsworth, 1995). Increasingly, researchers have used qualitative studies to describe middle and high school students' reading opportunities and reader characteristics. Kos (1991), for example, explores the reasons why middle school students reading problems persist. Using a case study approach, Kos identified three reasons why middle school students make limited progress in reading.

PRENTICE HALL LITERATURE

Putting Research Into Practice

- **The Vocabulary and Reading Warm-ups** in the *Unit Resources* are explicitly designed to foster vocabulary development and build background knowledge.

- Use the *Reader's Notebook* series to enhance students' ability to actively use reading strategies taught in the **Student Edition**.

- First, although students are cognizant of their deficiencies in reading and in the instruction they have received and are motivated to improve their reading, they feel hopeless to do so in their current school situations.

- Second, reading problems may manifest themselves in stress-related behaviors and distraction from instruction.

- Third, even when students attempt to use reading strategies, they often fail to use them efficiently.

Bintz (1993) examined reasons for declining interest in reading during the middle and high school years. According to Bintz, although students' interest in school reading declines, they do not necessarily lose interest in pleasure reading and informational reading outside of school. Second, students are not nonstrategic in their approach to reading, nor do they use dysfunctional strategies. Rather, Bintz maintains, middle and high school students use different strategies for in-school and out-of-school reading. For instance, in school, students were observed using shortcut strategies to assist them in completing assignments. Outside of school, however, these students were more inclined to use higher-level strategies because the material was personally interesting. Third, students do not fit into developmental categories such as avid, passive, or reluctant readers, but instead demonstrate different literate behaviors depending on the tasks they perform, the texts they read, and the interpretive stances they adopt.

Likewise, Worthy and McKool (1996), through analysis of student interviews of sixth-grade students who were good readers but who also had negative attitudes toward reading, suggested that students' negative attitudes toward reading may be related to their limited opportunities in reading instruction. Students who indicated negative attitudes toward reading also indicated that they had limited opportunities to read independently, select reading materials, or read personally interesting materials in school. Moreover, their feelings about reading instruction and materials used in school might have distorted their opinion about reading in general and thus their willingness to read.

PRENTICE HALL LITERATURE

Putting Research Into Practice

- Use the **On Your Own** feature and the **For Further Reading** pages in the **Student Edition** to encourage independent reading.

Works Cited

Biancarosa, Gina, and Catherine E. Snow. "Reading Next—A Vision for Action and Research in Middle and High School Literacy: A Report to Carnegie Corporation of New York." Washington, DC: Alliance for Excellent Education, 2004.

Bintz, William P. "Resistant Readers in Secondary Education: Some Insights and Implications." *Journal of Reading.* Vol. 36(8), May 1993. 604-615.

Kos, Raylene. "Persistence of Reading Disabilities: The Voices of Four Middle School Students." *American Educational Research Journal.* Vol. 28(4), Winter 1991, 875-895.

McKenna, Michael C., Dennis J. Kear, and R. A. Ellsworth. "Children's Attitudes Toward Reading: A National Survey." *Reading Research Quarterly,* Vol. 30(4), 1995, 934-956.

Worthy, Jo, and S. McKool. "Students Who Say They Hate to Read: The Importance of Opportunity, Choice, and Access." Eds. Donald J. Leu, Charles K. Kinzer, and Kathleen Hinchman, *Literacies for the 21st Century: Research and Practice.* Chicago: National Reading Conference, 1996, 245-256.

MAKING THE DIFFERENCE MATTER

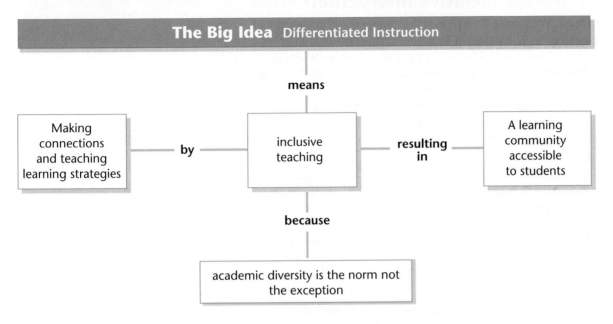

The Big Idea Differentiated Instruction

means

Making connections and teaching learning strategies

by

inclusive teaching

resulting in

A learning community accessible to students

because

academic diversity is the norm not the exception

Why do we need differentiated instruction?

The wide range of academic diversity in schools today presents both a challenge and an opportunity to all teachers. Because the challenge is so great and the need to accommodate all students so urgent, we need to think about the problem of planning and teaching to include all learners in a new way.

Diversity is the norm. Thinking about diversity among students as the norm rather than as something out of the ordinary is the first step in building inclusive teaching practices. Diane Ferguson (1995) has noted that "Meaningful change will require nothing less than a joint effort to reinvent schools to be more accommodating to all dimensions of human diversity" (282). She argues that we must change our view of the school's role from one of providing educational services to one of providing educational support for learning:

> Valuing diversity and difference, rather than trying to change or diminish it so that everyone fits some ideal of similarity, leads to the realization that we can support students in their efforts to become active members of their communities....Perhaps the most important feature of support as a concept for schooling is that it is grounded in the perspective of the person receiving it, not the person providing it.

This is not to say, however, that differences should be ignored. It is important to respect differences and to incorporate them into the classroom and the curriculum, so that learning is grounded in what is familiar to students.

Don Deshler, Ph.D.

Works Cited

Ferguson, Diane L. "The Real Challenge of Inclusion: Confessions of a 'Rabid Inclusionist.'"
Phi Delta Kappan. Vol. 77(4), 1995, 281-87.

How do we provide inclusive instruction?

Make connections. What does it mean to make connections? It means that as a teacher you need to be as concerned about understanding your students and what is important and meaningful to them as you are about understanding your content and how to teach it. Making connections means that students need to believe that what you want to teach is important and relevant to them and that you can and will help them learn. Making connections also means that you as the teacher need to believe it is worthwhile to build a learning community in your classroom, to know and understand your students well enough to make choices about content and instruction so that all students have an opportunity to learn. Every good teacher aspires to these goals, and many teachers successfully realize them. But as academic diversity among students grows in secondary schools, teachers need more support and more tools to be effective with all learners. Support can be gained, we believe, by thinking about a classroom as a learning community where teacher and students work together to ensure that everyone is learning. More tools become available with the implementation of teaching routines and learning strategies that make learning more accessible to more learners.

Understand what students already know. What students already know, or their "prior knowledge," comes not only from what students have previously learned in school, but also from their lived experiences. Lived experience includes all the differences that students bring with them into the schools, such as culture, language, ethnic background, as well as previous learning successes or failures. Valuing and using the prior knowledge of students allows teachers to link new knowledge to what students already know, thereby making learning more meaningful for students. It also allows students to construct new knowledge for themselves.

Teach learning strategies. Finally, students are more likely to make connections in learning the content in your class if they know how to learn. All good listeners use strategies to learn new things. Some students are better than others at developing strategies to learn. Inclusive teaching means that you have to take into account whether all your students are good strategic learners, and the only way to do this is to teach them—explicitly—how to use and develop learning strategies.

What is the result of differentiated instruction?

A learning community. Making connections and building a learning community in your classroom will establish an environment where learning, cooperation, and respect for differences are all valued. The "work" of this community is learning. Everyday practices and routines are based on cooperation in accomplishing this work, and the interests and learning needs of everyone in the community are taken seriously.

PROGRAM CONSULTANTS

The Prentice Hall national language arts consultants advised on many aspects of this program, particularly the professional development strand. The professional development notes in this textbook represent successful strategies acquired and applied during their many years of experience in classrooms.

Yvonne R. Cadiz
Language Arts, ESOL, and Spanish teacher
Curriculum Specialist for ESOL
Hillsborough County, Tampa, FL
Director of the MERIT Program (Multilingual Educational Resource Information and Training Program), University of South Florida

Anita Clay
District Coordinator, Gateway Institute of Technology
St. Louis, MO

Nancy McDonald
K-12 Reading Specialist
Waterloo School District, Waterloo, WI
Belleville School District, Belleville, WI
Title I Language Arts Teacher, 6-8
Beloit Turner Middle School, Beloit, WI
Grade 8 Language Arts Teacher
Olson Junior High School, Woodstock, IL

Jean Ripple
Language Arts Teacher, 1-10
Model Classroom for Inclusion
Pennsylvania

John R. Scannell
Teacher, 9-12 English, Writing, Acting and Drama, Debate and Public Address
Newport HS, Bellevue, WA
Lykens Jr. HS, Lykens, PA
Nazareth HS, Nazareth, PA

Kathryne Lewis Stewart
Director of Humanities Instruction
Tomball Independent School District
Tomball, TX
Teacher/GT Specialist
Burleson High School
Burleson Independent School District
Burleson, TX

Joseph A. Wieczorek, Ph.D.
Instructor, Georgetown University
College of Notre Dame
University of Maryland, Baltimore County
Howard County Public Schools, MD
Language Specialist, FBI

LITERATURE REVIEW PANEL

These teachers helped develop the Penguin Edition of *Prentice Hall Literature* by testing new selections by contemporary authors and gathering student questions for these authors to answer. The work of these teachers helped ensure that the program would be truly interactive, with a built-in dialogue between authors and students.

Sherry Abner
Two Rivers Middle School
Covington, KY

Heather Barnes
Central Crossing High School
Grove City, OH

Bonnie Bellows
Humboldt Senior High School
St. Paul, MN

Shawn L. Brumfield
Los Angeles Unified School District
Los Angeles, CA

Donna Burch
Southern Middle School
Somerset, KY

Susanne Buttrey
Sycamore Middle School
Pleasant View, TN

Denise Campbell
Cherry Creek School District
Centennial, CO

Holly Carr
Central Crossing High School
Grove City, OH

Vanessa Carroll
LBJ High School
Austin, TX

Joanne Chambers
Swiftwater Intermediate School
Swiftwater, PA

Susan Cisna
East Prairie Junior High School
Tuscola, IL

Nancy DiGasso
Pine Bush High School
Pine Bush, NY

Karen Gibson
Appleton North High School
Appleton, WI

Margaret Jan Graham
Cobb Middle School
Tallahassee, FL

Doris Sue Hawkins
C. W. Otto Middle School
Lansing, MI

Deanna Hilliard
Soddy Daisy Middle School
Soddy Daisy, TN

Helen Hudson
Crawfordsville High School
Crawfordsville, IN

Gisele Le Duc
East Lyme Middle School
Niantic, CT

Greg MacAvoy
Pine Bush High School
Pine Bush, NY

Deb Madej
Norris Middle School
Omaha, NE

Nancy Mast
Hobart Middle School
Hobart, IN

Nancy Monroe
Bolton High School
Alexandria, LA

Suzanne Moore
Sunrise Middle School
Clackamas, OR

Paul Putnoki
Torrington Middle School
Torrington, CT

Herb Ranlose
Zion Benton High School
Zion, IL

Robert Rarrick
Union Endicott Senior High
Endicott, NY

Margaret St. Sauver
St. Paul Public Schools
St. Paul, MN

Denise Greer Wallace
Western Valley Middle School
Phoenix, AZ

Debbie Watts
Jacobs Fork Middle School
Newton, NC

Melissa Williams
Delsea Regional High School
Franklinville, NJ

Charles Youngs
Bethel Park High School
Bethel Park, PA

1 WHERE DO I START?

Right here! These pages will guide you through the program's organization and describe the resources you have available to enrich your teaching. *Prentice Hall Literature, Penguin Edition,* is carefully designed to make pacing, lesson planning, teaching, and assessment easier.

2 HOW DO I INTRODUCE THE UNIT?

Each unit in this book presents the literature of a specific time period. The unit is hosted by a featured contemporary author, scholar, or translator who introduces a literary trend or theme in the **Setting the Scene** essay.

> The *From the Author's Desk* orange banner appears throughout the unit when the featured author appears.

Use the unit **Introduction** to develop students' understanding and appreciation for literature in its broader context.

> The timeline shows the literature in the context of key world events and other literary milestones.

Technology

From the Author's Desk

Stimulate students' interest with this engaging DVD featuring in-depth interviews with unit authors discussing unit concepts, literature, history, reading, and writing.

Use the **History of the Period** and the **Literature of the Period** essays to introduce the major events, influential people, critical themes, and important trends of the time period. This background information will build a strong foundation for the literary exploration to follow in the unit selections.

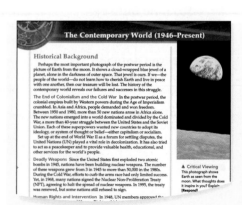

3 WHAT SHOULD I USE TO PLAN AND PREPARE?

Start your planning with the **Time and Resource Manager** before every selection or selection grouping. This guide provides these tools:

- a detailed lesson plan
- suggestions for incorporating program resources into your instruction
- recommendations for pacing each element of your lesson
- information about lesson objectives

Meeting Your Standards
Standards coverage information

Step-by-Step Teaching Guide
A systematic approach to teaching the literature

Pacing Guide
Suggested pacing information

Resources
Suggested resources for differentiated instruction

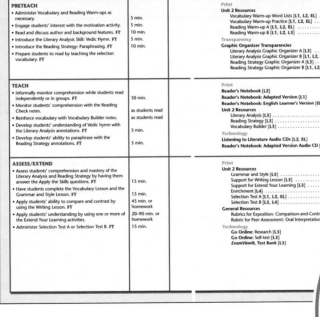

| TIME AND RESOURCE MANAGER | *from the* Rig Veda |

✓ Meeting Your Standards

Students will

1. analyze and respond to literary elements.
   - Literary Analysis: Vedic Hymn
2. read, comprehend, analyze, and critique hymns.
   - Reading Strategy: Paraphrasing
   - Reading Check questions
   - Apply the Skills questions
   - Assessment Practice (ATE)
3. develop vocabulary.
   - Vocabulary Lesson: Latin Prefix: *im- / in-*
4. understand and apply written and oral language conventions.
   - Spelling Strategy
   - Grammar and Style Lesson: Concrete and Abstract Nouns
5. develop writing proficiency.
   - Writing Lesson: Comparison-and-Contrast Essay
6. develop appropriate research strategies.
   - Extend Your Learning: Culture Spreadsheet
7. understand and apply listening and speaking strategies.
   - Extend Your Learning: Oral Interpretation

Block Scheduling: Use one 90-minute class period to preteach the skills and have students read the selection. Use a second 90-minute class period to assess students' mastery of skills, extend their learning, and monitor their progress.

Homework Suggestions
Following are possibilities for homework assignments.
- Support pages from *Unit 2 Resources:*
  - Literary Analysis
  - Reading Strategy
  - Vocabulary Builder
  - Grammar and Style
- An Extend Your Learning project and the Writing Lesson for this selection may be completed over several days.

Step-by-Step Teaching Guide | Pacing Guide

PRETEACH
- Administer Vocabulary and Reading Warm-ups as necessary. — 5 min.
- Engage students' interest with the motivation activity. — 5 min.
- Read and discuss author and background features. FT — 10 min.
- Introduce the Literary Analysis Skill: Vedic Hymn. FT — 5 min.
- Introduce the Reading Strategy: Paraphrasing. FT — 10 min.
- Prepare students to read by teaching the selection vocabulary. FT

TEACH
- Informally monitor comprehension while students read independently or in groups. FT — 30 min.
- Monitor students' comprehension with the Reading Check notes. — as students read
- Reinforce vocabulary with Vocabulary Builder notes. — as students read
- Develop students' understanding of Vedic hymn with the Literary Analysis annotations. FT — 5 min.
- Develop students' ability to paraphrase with the Reading Strategy annotations. FT — 5 min.

ASSESS/EXTEND
- Assess students' comprehension and mastery of the Literary Analysis and Reading Strategy by having them answer the Apply the Skills questions. FT — 15 min.
- Have students complete the Vocabulary Lesson and the Grammar and Style Lesson. FT — 15 min.
- Apply students' ability to compare and contrast by using the Writing Lesson. FT — 45 min. or homework
- Apply students' understanding by using one or more of the Extend Your Learning activities. — 20–90 min. or homework
- Administer Selection Test A or Selection Test B. FT — 15 min.

Resources

Print
Unit 2 Resources
Vocabulary Warm-up Word Lists [L1, L2, EL] .... p. 6
Vocabulary Warm-up Practice [L1, L2, EL] .... p. 7
Reading Warm-up A [L1, L2, EL] .... p. 8
Reading Warm-up B [L1, L2, L3] .... p. 9

Transparency
Graphic Organizer Transparencies
Literary Analysis Graphic Organizer A [L3] .... p. 36
Literary Analysis Graphic Organizer B [L1, L2, EL] .... p. 37
Reading Strategy Graphic Organizer A [L3] .... p. 34
Reading Strategy Graphic Organizer B [L1, L2, EL] .... p. 35

Print
Reader's Notebook [L2]
Reader's Notebook: Adapted Version [L1]
Reader's Notebook: English Learner's Version [EL]
Unit 2 Resources
Literary Analysis [L3] .... p. 10
Reading Strategy [L3] .... p. 11
Vocabulary Builder [L3] .... p. 12

Technology
Listening to Literature Audio CDs [L2, EL]
Reader's Notebook: Adapted Version Audio CD [L1, L2]

Print
Unit 2 Resources
Grammar and Style [L3] .... p. 13
Support for Writing Lesson [L3] .... p. 14
Support for Extend Your Learning [L3] .... p. 15
Enrichment [L4] .... p. 16
Selection Test A [L1, L2, EL] .... pp. 17
Selection Test B [L3, L4] .... p. 17
General Resources
Rubrics for Exposition: Comparison-and-Contrast Essay [L3]
Rubric for Peer Assessment: Oral Interpretation ....

Technology
Go Online: Research [L3]
Go Online: Self-test [L3]
ExamView®, Test Bank [L3]

Choosing Resources for Differentiated Instruction

[L1] Special Needs Students
[L2] Below-Level Students
[L3] All Students
[L4] Advanced Students
[EL] English Learners

For Vocabulary and Reading Warm-ups and for Selection Tests, A signifies "less challenging" and B "more challenging." For Graphic Organizer transparencies, A signifies "not filled in" and B "filled in."

FT Fast Track Instruction: To move the lesson more quickly, use the strategies and activities identified with FT.

Scaffolding for Less Proficient and Advanced Students
The leveled Critical Thinking questions after selections progress in the levels of thinking required to answer them. To address the needs of your different students, you may use the (a) level questions for your less proficient students and the (b) level questions with your on-level and advanced students. The occasional (c) level questions are appropriate for your advanced students.

TeacherEXPRESS Use this complete suite of powerful teaching tools to make lesson planning and testing quicker and easier.

StudentEXPRESS Use the interactive textbook (online and on CD-ROM) to make selections and activities come alive with audio and video support and interactive questions.

Technology

PRENTICE HALL
TeacherEXPRESS Plan · Teach · Assess Use this complete suite of powerful teaching tools to make lesson planning and testing quicker and easier.

PRENTICE HALL
StudentEXPRESS Learn · Study · Succeed Use the interactive textbook (online and on CD-ROM) to make selections and activities come alive with audio and video support and interactive questions.

Go Online For: Information about Lex...
Professional Visit: www.PHSchool.cc...
Development Web Code: eue-11...

4 HOW DOES THE PROGRAM HELP ME WITH PACING?

The **Diagnostic and Benchmark Tests** divide the program into three-week instructional blocks, with each segment focusing on core skills and standards. This consistent organization ensures thorough skills coverage presented in manageable chunks. A benchmark test is provided for each part, allowing you to administer assessment at 3-, 6-, or 9-week intervals. This systematic, logical organization with built-in progress monitoring allows you to make sound instructional choices for your class without missing any skills or standards.

5 HOW DO I TEACH EACH UNIT?

A Start each unit with the **Introduction** featuring the unit author and providing key literary and historical background.

B Teach literary analysis with representative literature of the period. (See p. T53 for more information.)

C Develop student mastery of literary elements with the instruction in **Focus on Literary Forms** and the selections that follow.

D Use **A Closer Look** features for an in-depth exploration of trends in literature.

E Teach **Comparing Literary Works** groupings to help students analyze literary elements in two or more selections. (See p. T53 for more information.)

F Present **Connections** features to show the thematic relationship among works from different literary heritages.

G Show students how to apply reading skills to real-life reading situations with the **Reading Informational Materials** features.

H Use the Skills Workshops to provide opportunities for skills practice and high-stakes test preparation.

SAT PREP ACT

Every selection is supported by these resources:

- Skills Development Workbook
- Graphic Organizers on Transparency
- Selection Tests
- Reader's Notebook series
- Listening to Literature audio program
- Student Express
- Teacher Express

6 HOW DO I TEACH A SELECTION?

Each selection or selection grouping follows a consistent pattern. This allows you and your students to appreciate significant works of literature by developing essential literary analysis and critical reading skills.

Check the **Accessibility at a Glance** chart in the Teacher's Edition for an analysis of the factors influencing accessibility, and choose the most appropriate literature for your students.

Use the **Build Skills** pages to present a full author biography and instruction on literary analysis, reading strategy, and vocabulary. Build context with the **Background** notes that appear at the beginning of each selection.

After completing the selection, use the **Critical Reading** and **Apply the Skills** pages to assess students' understanding. For grammar, vocabulary skills, and writing practice, use the **Build Language Skills** pages.

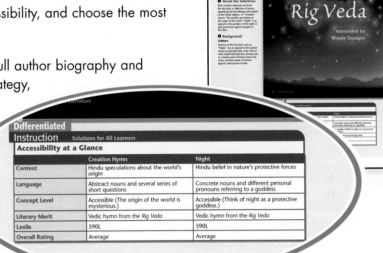

Differentiated Instruction — Solutions for All Learners

Accessibility at a Glance

	Creation Hymn	Night
Context	Hindu speculations about the world's origin	Hindu belief in nature's protective forces
Language	Abstract nouns and several series of short questions	Concrete nouns and different personal pronouns referring to a goddess
Concept Level	Accessible (The origin of the world is mysterious.)	Accessible (Think of night as a protective goddess.)
Literary Merit	Vedic hymn from the *Rig Veda*	Vedic hymn from the *Rig Veda*
Lexile	590L	590L
Overall Rating	Average	Average

mk ■ 37

7 HOW DO I DIFFERENTIATE INSTRUCTION?

Prentice Hall Literature provides unprecedented opportunities for differentiated instruction:

- **Teacher's Edition:** Use the strategies and techniques geared toward different reading levels and learning styles.
- **Reader's Notebooks:** Customize instruction for every selection with reading support for struggling readers and English learners.
- **Leveled Vocabulary and Reading Warm-ups:** For each selection, build background, fluency, and vocabulary.
- **Leveled Selection Tests:** Choose from two tests for each selection, according to your students' ability levels.
- **Graphic Organizers:** Give struggling readers additional support with completed versions of all organizers in the Student Edition.

Differentiated Instruction — Solutions for All Learners

Support for Special Needs Students
Students may have difficulty understanding that the dialogue between Jean and Priscilla is imaginary. Make certain that they understand the purpose of the note at the bottom of the previous page. Then remind students that the Pilgrims were the first people from Europe to move to America and that some of them arrived on the *Mayflower*. Explain that when Jean opens the book, she imagines the Pilgrims are with her and on their way to America just as she will be one day soon.

Enrichment for Gifted/Talented Students
Ask students to consider why Jean probably relates to Priscilla. Have them think of story characters with whom they identify or admire. Have them create an imaginary discussion with the character of their choice. Their discussion should consider an issue or solve a problem. Encourage students to choose their individual tone (e.g., serious, formal, humorous) and perform the dialogue for the class.

8 WHEN DO I TEACH WRITING?

This program incorporates opportunities in every unit for both process writing and writing for assessment.

Process Writing In each unit, a **Writing Workshop** with step-by-step instruction guides students to develop their ideas into full-length compositions, addressing these key stages in the writing process:

- Prewriting
- Drafting
- Revising
- Editing and Proofreading
- Publishing and Presenting

In addition, a **Writing About Literature** workshop in each unit provides practice in analytical writing, guiding students through the key areas of writing a thesis statement, gathering evidence, and drafting a response to a specific literature-based prompt.

Timed Writing To address the growing call for on-demand writing and to prepare students for college entrance exams, the program provides many opportunities in each unit to help students practice writing for assessment. Timed Writing prompts ask students to produce brief expository or persuasive writing relating to the literature they have read.

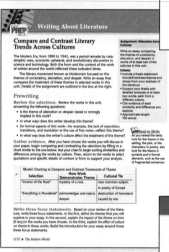

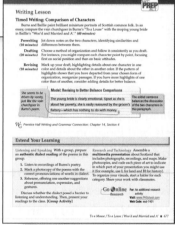

Technology

Score student essays in seconds.

Finally, to facilitate your teaching of writing, the Prentice Hall **Online Essay Scorer** provides instant scoring and feedback, plus tips for revision. You save time and your students become better writers!

9 HOW DO I MONITOR STUDENT PROGRESS?

Prentice Hall makes progress monitoring easy with frequent opportunities to evaluate student progress and to reteach material.

- Use the **Diagnostic Tests** as indicated to determine readiness. You will find frequent reading checks and suggestions in the Teacher's Edition for monitoring student progress during reading.
- After reading the selections, use the **Selection Tests** to assess comprehension and mastery of the reading and literary analysis skills.
- As you teach the unit, use the **Monitor Your Progress** pages in standardized-test format. These appear after the Reading Informational Materials section and in unit workshops to give students practice in applying specific skills under test-taking conditions.
- Use the **Benchmark Tests** to monitor progress at regular, frequent intervals. For your convenience, tests are provided at 3-week intervals.

Technology

Monitor student progress instantly in an interactive format.

Access companion Web sites for self-tests.

Use the electronic test generator to customize assessment.

10 HOW DOES PRENTICE HALL LITERATURE HELP ME DEVELOP AS A TEACHER?

The Teacher's Edition provides built-in professional development. Look for these special features:

- **Step-by-Step Teaching:** Margin notes provide strategies, tips, and examples for teaching skills.
- **Differentiated Instruction:** Notes provide support, strategies, and enrichment for learners of varied abilities.
- **Professional Development:** Pedagogical explanations of specific techniques enhance your effectiveness as a teacher.

Unit	From the Author's Desk	Focus on Literary Forms	A Closer Look	Connections	Reading Informational Materials
1 **From Legend to History** A.D. 449–1485	Burton Raffel, Seamus Heaney, *from* **Beowulf** pp. 36–37, 66–67	The Epic pp. 34–35	Chaucer's Guided Tour of Medieval Life and Literature pp. 94–95	**Gilgamesh;** *from the* **Iliad** pp. 68–74 Alex Haley, *from* **My Furthest-Back Person** pp. 204–207	Maps: Using Maps for Verification and Interpretation pp. 90–93
2 **Celebrating Humanity** 1485–1625	Frank Kermode pp. 300–301	Drama pp. 292–293	The Elizabethan Theater, Shakespeare on Stage, Shakespeare on Film pp. 294–299	Petrarch and Neruda, **Sonnets** pp. 266–268 *from* **Mary Chesnut's Civil War** pp. 402–403	Newspaper Articles: Evaluating Information pp. 398–401
3 **A Turbulent Time** 1625–1798	Richard Rodriguez, *from* **Days of Obligation** pp. 604–606	The Essay pp. 590–591	Making "Darkness Visible": Milton's Epic Ambition pp. 470–471	Confucius, *from* **The Analects** and Thomas Jefferson, *from* **The Declaration of Independence** pp. 586–588 Anna Quindlen, "Homeless" pp. 626–629	Online Search Engines: Evaluating the Appropriateness of a Search Result pp. 630–633
4 **Rebels and Dreamers** 1798–1832	Elizabeth McCracken pp. 688–689	Lyric Poetry pp. 704–705	Poetry and Friendship in the Romantic Age pp. 726–727	Edgar Allan Poe, **"Oval Portrait"** pp. 700–702 Heine, Basho, Buson, Issa, **Poems** pp. 804–808	Guidebooks: Interpreting and Using Diagrams pp. 722–725
5 **Progress and Decline** 1833–1901	James Berry, **"From Lucy: Englan' Lady," "Freedom," "Time Removed"** pp. 940–942	The Novel pp. 897–899	The Curiosity Workshop of Charles Dickens: Making Myths pp. 900–901	Leo Tolstoy, *from* **War and Peace** pp. 922–926 E.E. Cummings, **"anyone lived in a pretty how town"** pp. 988–989	Web Sites: Evaluating Credibility of Sources pp. 960–964
6 **A Time of Rapid Change** 1901–Present	Anita Desai, **"A Devoted Son"** pp. 1294–1295	The Short Story pp. 1156–1157	Critical Commentary on "The Hollow Men" pp. 1044–1045	Borges **"Book of Sand"** pp. 1224–1228 Tom Wolfe, *from* **The Right Stuff** pp. 1325–1327	Mission Statements: Interpreting the Organization of a Mission Statement pp. 1070–1073

Technology

Go Online PHSchool.com • Author Biography • Self-tests • Research Activities	**From the Author's Desk DVD** Bring real writers into your classroom				**ExamView QuickTake** Monitor student progress instantly

PRENTICE HALL **StudentEXPRESS** Learn · Study · Succeed

PRENTICE HALL **TeacherEXPRESS** Plan · Teach · Assess

Instant access to all program resources with the click of a mouse

Writing About Literature	Writing Workshop	Vocabulary Workshop	Assessment Workshop	Communications Workshop
Analyzing Literary Periods pp. 208–209	Narration: Autobiographical Narrative pp. 210–217	Define, Identify, Label p. 218	Critical Reading Sequential Order p. 219	Delivering Autobiographical Presentations p. 220
Compare and Contrast Literary Trends pp. 404–405	Persuasion: Persuasive Essay pp. 406–413	Recall, Predict, Summarize p. 414	Critical Reading: Forms of Propaganda p. 415	Analyzing Advertising p. 416
Compare and Contrast Literary Themes pp. 634–635	Narration: Reflective Essay pp. 636–643	Differentiate, Analyze, Infer p. 644	Critical Reading: Writer's Point of View p. 645	Analyzing Persuasive Techniques p. 646
Evaluate Literary Trends pp. 834–835	Workplace Writing: Job Portfolio and Résumé: pp. 836–843	Illustrate, Apply, Demonstrate p. 844	Critical Reading: Critical Reasoning p. 845	Critiquing Persuasive Devices p. 846
Analyze Literary Periods pp. 990–991	Research: Research Paper pp. 992–1001	Compare and Contrast, Conclude, Deduce p. 1002	Critical Reading: Paired Passages p. 1003	Delivering a Persuasive Speech p. 1004
Evaluate Literary Trends pp. 1328–1329	Exposition: Multimedia Report pp. 1330–1337	Interpret, Evaluate, Judge p. 1338	Critical Reading: Strategy, Organization, and Style p. 1339	Analyzing Bias in News Media p. 1340
	PH Online Essay Scorer: electronic essay grader	Monitor student progress instantly.	Monitor student progress instantly.	Monitor student progress instantly.

  Instant access to all program resources with the click of a mouse

	Selection	Reading Strategy	Literary Analysis	Vocabulary
PART 1	**"The Seafarer"** (A), translated by Burton Raffel, SE, p. 18; **"The Wanderer"** (MA), translated by Charles W. Kennedy, SE, p. 23; **"The Wife's Lament"** (MC), translated by Ann Stanford, SE, p. 27	**Connecting to Historical Context**, SE, p. 17; *UR1*, p. 12; **Reading Warm-ups A and B**, *UR1*, pp. 9–10; **Reading Strategy Graphic Organizers A and B**, *GOT*, pp. 1–2	**Anglo-Saxon Lyrics**, SE, p. 17; *UR1*, p. 11; **Literary Analysis Graphic Organizers A and B**, *GOT*, pp. 3–4	**Vocabulary Builder**, SE, p. 17: *admonish, sentinel, fervent, rancor, compassionate, grievous, winsomeness, rapture, redress, blithe* **Anglo-Saxon Suffix:** *-ness*, SE, p. 31; *UR1*, p. 13
PART 2 **FOCUS ON EPIC**	from *Beowulf* (A), translated by Burton Raffel, SE, p. 40	**Paraphrasing**, SE, p. 39; *UR1*, p. 31; **Reading Warm-ups A and B**, *UR1*, pp. 28–29; **Reading Strategy Graphic Organizers A and B**, *GOT*, pp. 5–6	**The Epic**, SE, p. 39; *UR1*, p. 30; **Literary Analysis Graphic Organizers A and B**, *GOT*, pp. 7–8	**Vocabulary Builder**, SE, p. 39: *reparation, solace, purge, writhing, massive, loathsome* **Latin Root:** *-sol-*, SE, p. 64; *UR1*, p. 32
PART 3	from *A History of the English Church and People* (MC), Bede, translated by Leo Sherley-Price, SE, p. 78; **from *The Anglo-Saxon Chronicle*** (A), translated by Anne Savage, SE, p. 83	**Breaking Down Sentences**, SE, p. 77; *UR1*, p. 48; **Reading Warm-ups A and B**, *UR1*, pp. 45–46; **Reading Strategy Graphic Organizers A and B**, *GOT*, pp. 9–10	**Historical Writing**, SE, p. 77; *UR1*, p. 47; **Literary Analysis Graphic Organizers A and B**, *GOT*, pp. 11–12	**Vocabulary Builder**, SE, p. 77: *promontories, innumerable, stranded, barricaded, ravaged* **Latin Suffix:** *-ade*, SE, p. 88; *UR1*, p. 49
	from *The Canterbury Tales:* **"The Prologue"** (A), Geoffrey Chaucer, translated by Neville Coghill, SE, p. 98	**Analyzing Difficult Sentences**, SE, p. 97; *UR1*, p. 74; **Reading Warm-ups A and B**, *UR1*, pp. 71–72; **Reading Strategy Graphic Organizers A and B**, *GOT*, pp. 13–14	**Characterization**, SE, p. 97; *UR1*, p. 73; **Literary Analysis Graphic Organizers A and B**, *GOT*, pp. 15–16	**Vocabulary Builder**, SE, p. 97: *solicitous, garnished, absolution, commission, sanguine, avouches, prevarication* **Latin Suffix:** *-tion*, SE, p. 121; *UR1*, p. 75
	from *The Canterbury Tales:* **"The Pardoner's Tale"** (A), Geoffrey Chaucer, translated by Neville Coghill, SE, p. 123	**Rereading for Clarification**, SE, p. 122; *UR1*, p. 90; **Reading Warm-ups A and B**, *UR1*, pp. 87–88; **Reading Strategy Graphic Organizers A and B**, *GOT*, pp. 17–18	**Allegory**, SE, p. 122; *UR1*, p. 89; **Literary Analysis Graphic Organizers A and B**, *GOT*, pp. 19–20	**Vocabulary Builder**, SE, p. 122: *pallor, hoary, prating, tarry, apothecary* **Greek Prefix:** *apo-*, SE, p. 135; *UR1*, p. 91
	from *The Canterbury Tales:* **"The Wife of Bath's Tale"** (A), Geoffrey Chaucer, translated by Neville Coghill, SE, p. 137	**Using Context Clues**, SE, p. 136; *UR1*, p. 106; **Reading Warm-ups A and B**, *UR1*, pp. 103–104; **Reading Strategy Graphic Organizers A and B**, *GOT*, pp. 21–22	**Frame**, SE, p. 136; *UR1*, p. 105; **Literary Analysis Graphic Organizers A and B**, *GOT*, pp. 23–24	**Vocabulary Builder**, SE, p. 136: *implored, relates, misalliance, contemptuous, bequeath, prowess, esteemed, rebuke* **Multiple-Meaning Words**, SE, p. 157; *UR1*, p. 107
PART 4	from *Sir Gawain and the Green Knight* (A), translated by Marie Borroff, SE, p. 162; **from Morte d'Arthur** (A), Sir Thomas Malory, SE, p. 176	**Summarizing**, SE, p. 161; *UR1*, p. 123; **Reading Warm-ups A and B**, *UR1*, pp. 120–121; **Reading Strategy Graphic Organizers A and B**, *GOT*, pp. 25–26	**Medieval Romance**, SE, p. 161; *UR1*, p. 122; **Literary Analysis Graphic Organizers A and B**, *GOT*, pp. 27–28	**Vocabulary Builder**, SE, p. 161: *assay, adjure, feigned, adroitly, largesse, righteous, entreated, peril, interred* **Word Root:** *-droit-*, SE, p. 186; *UR1*, p. 124

Key to Program References:
SE: Student Edition **UR:** Unit Resources **GOT:** Graphic Organizer Transparencies **GR:** General Resources **WG:** Writing and Grammar
MA: More Accessible **A:** Average **MC:** More Challenging. See Accessibility at a Glance chart on selection pages.

Grammar	Writing	Extend Your Learning	Assessment
Compound Predicates, SE, p. 31; *UR1*, p. 14; *WG*, Ch. 18, Section 1	**Writing Lesson:** Timed Writing: Analysis of a Literary Theme, SE, p. 32; *UR1*, p. 15; *WG*, Ch. 14, Section 3	**Listening and Speaking:** Oral Interpretation, SE, p. 32; *UR1*, p. 16 **Research and Technology: Help Wanted** Page, SE, p. 32	**Diagnostic Test 1**, *UR1*, pp. 2–4; **Selection Tests A and B**, *UR1*, pp. 18–23; **Rubrics for Response to Literature**, *GR*, pp. 65–66; **Rubric for Peer Assessment:** Oral Interpretation, *GR*, p. 130
Appositives and Appositive Phrases, SE, p. 64; *UR1*, p. 33; *WG*, Ch. 19, Section 1	**Writing Lesson:** Timed Writing: Response to Criticism, SE, p. 65; *UR1*, p. 34; *WG*, Ch. 14, Section 4	**Listening and Speaking: Dramatic Reading**, SE, p. 65; *UR1*, p. 35 **Research and Technology:** Dictionary of Epic Heroes, SE, p. 65	**Selection Tests A and B**, *UR1*, pp. 37–42; **Rubrics for Response to Literature**, *GR*, pp. 65–66; **Rubric for Peer Assessment:** Dramatic Performance, *GR*, p. 131
Compound Sentences, SE, p. 88; *UR1*, p. 50; *WG*, Ch. 19, Section 4	**Writing Lesson:** Timed Writing: Critical Comparison of Historical Sources, SE, p. 89; *UR1*, p. 51; *WG*, Ch. 13, Section 4	**Listening and Speaking:** Radio Interview, SE, p. 89; *UR1*, p. 52 **Research and Technology:** Museum Exhibit, SE, p. 89	**Selection Tests A and B**, *UR1*, pp. 54–59; **Rubrics for Exposition:** Comparison-and-Contrast Essay, *GR*, pp. 69–70; **Rubric for Peer Assessment:** Dramatic Performance, *GR*, p. 131; **Benchmark Test 1**, *UR1*, pp. 60–65
Past and Past Perfect Tenses, SE, p. 121; *UR1*, p. 76; *WG*, Ch. 21, Section 2		**Listening and Speaking:** Dialogue, SE, p. 121 **Writing:** Critical Response, SE, p. 121; *UR1*, p. 77	**Diagnostic Test 2**, *UR1*, pp. 66–68; **Selection Tests A and B**, *UR1*, pp. 79–84; **Rubrics for Response to Literature**, *GR*, pp. 65–66
Clauses with *who* and *whom*, SE, p. 135; *UR1*, p. 92; *WG*, Ch. 22, Section 2		**Writing:** Summary, SE, p. 135 **Research and Technology:** Multimedia Report, SE, p. 135; *UR1*, p. 93	**Selection Tests A and B**, *UR1*, pp. 95–100
Correcting Run-On Sentences, SE, p. 157; *UR1*, p. 108; *WG*, Ch. 27, Section 3	**Writing Lesson:** Allegory, SE, p. 158; *UR1*, p. 109; *WG*, Ch. 5, Section 4	**Listening and Speaking:** Critical Talk, SE, p. 158; *UR1*, p. 110 **Research and Technology:** Poster, SE, p. 158	**Selection Tests A and B**, *UR1*, pp. 112–117; **Rubrics for Narration:** Short Story, *GR*, pp. 57–58; **Rubric for Peer Assessment:** Speech, *GR*, p. 129
Comparative and Superlative Forms, SE, p. 186; *UR1*, p. 125; *WG*, Ch. 24, Section 1	**Writing Lesson:** Interior Monologue, SE, p. 187; *UR1*, p. 126; *WG*, Ch. 5, Section 2	**Listening and Speaking:** Proposal for a Multimedia Presentation, SE, p. 187; *UR1*, p. 127 **Research and Technology:** Oral Report, SE, p. 187	**Selection Tests A and B**, *UR1*, pp. 129–134; **Rubrics for Response to Literature**, *GR*, pp. 65–66; **Rubric for Speaking:** Presenting a Proposal, *GR*, p. 91

All selections are supported in the Reader's Notebooks.

From Legend to History (A.D. 449–1485) (continued)

	Selection	Reading Strategy	Literary Analysis	Vocabulary
PART 4 *(continued)*	*Letters of Margaret Paston* (A), Margaret Paston, SE, p. 190; **"Twa Corbies"** (MA), SE, p. 194; **"Lord Randall"** (MA), SE, p. 195; **"Get Up and Bar the Door"** (MA), SE, p. 196; **"Barbara Allan"** (MA), SE, p. 198	**Understanding Dialect,** SE, p. 189; *UR1*, p. 140; **Reading Warm-ups A and B,** *UR1*, pp. 137–138; **Reading Strategy Graphic Organizers A and B,** *GOT*, pp. 29–30	**Letter and Folk Ballad,** SE, p. 189; *UR1*, p. 139; **Literary Analysis Graphic Organizers A and B,** *GOT*, pp. 31–32	**Vocabulary Builder,** SE, p. 189: *aldermen, enquiry, succor, certify, remnant, ransacked, asunder, assault* **Latin Root:** *-cert-*, SE, p. 202; *UR1*, p. 141

Celebrating Humanity (1485–1625)

	Selection	Reading Strategy	Literary Analysis	Vocabulary
PART 1	**"Sonnet 1"** (MC), Edmund Spenser, SE, p. 240; **"Sonnet 35"** (MC), Edmund Spenser, SE, p. 241; **"Sonnet 75"** (MC), Edmund Spenser, SE p. 242; **"Sonnet 31"** (MA), Sir Philip Sidney, SE, p. 243; **"Sonnet 39"** (MA), Sir Philip Sidney, SE, p. 244	**Paraphrasing,** SE, p. 239; *UR2*, p. 12; **Reading Warm-ups A and B,** *UR2*, pp. 9–10; **Reading Strategy Graphic Organizers A and B,** *GOT*, pp. 34–35	**The Sonnet,** SE, p. 239; *UR2*, p. 11; **Literary Analysis Graphic Organizers A and B,** *GOT*, pp. 36–37	**Vocabulary Builder,** SE, p. 239: *deign, assay, devise, wan, languished, balm* **Forms of** *languished*, SE, p. 246; *UR2*, p. 13
	"The Passionate Shepherd to His Love" (A), Christopher Marlowe, SE, p. 250; **"The Nymph's Reply to the Shepherd"** (MC), Sir Walter Raleigh, SE, p. 251	**Identifying with the Speaker of a Poem,** SE, p. 249; *UR2*, p. 29; **Reading Warm-ups A and B,** *UR2*, pp. 26–27; **Reading Strategy Graphic Organizers A and B,** *GOT*, pp. 38–39	**Pastoral,** SE, p. 249; *UR2*, p. 28; **Literary Analysis Graphic Organizers A and B,** *GOT*, pp. 40–41	**Vocabulary Builder,** SE, p. 249: *melodious, madrigals, move, reckoning, wither* **Word origins:** *wither*, SE, p. 254; *UR2*, p. 30
	"Sonnet 29" (MC), William Shakespeare, SE, p. 258; **"Sonnet 106"** (MC), William Shakespeare, SE, p. 260; **"Sonnet 116"** (A), William Shakespeare, SE, p. 261; **"Sonnet 130"** (A), William Shakespeare, SE, p. 262	**Relating Structure to Theme,** SE, p. 257; *UR2*, p. 46; **Reading Warm-ups A and B,** *UR2*, pp. 43–44; **Reading Strategy Graphic Organizers A and B,** *GOT*, pp. 42–43	**The Shakespearean Sonnet,** SE, p. 257; *UR2*, p. 45; **Literary Analysis Graphic Organizers A and B,** *GOT*, pp. 44–45	**Vocabulary Builder,** SE, p. 257: *scope, sullen, chronicle, prefiguring, impediments, alters* **Greek Root:** *-chron-*, SE, p. 264; *UR2*, p. 47
PART 2	**from** *Utopia* (MC), Sir Thomas More, SE, p. 272; **"Speech Before Her Troops"** (MA), Queen Elizabeth I, SE, p. 274	**Summarizing,** SE, p. 271; *UR2*, p. 63; **Reading Warm-ups A and B,** *UR2*, pp. 60–61; **Reading Strategy Graphic Organizers A and B,** *GOT*, pp. 46–47	**The Monarch as Hero,** SE, p. 271; *UR2*, p. 62; **Literary Analysis Graphic Organizers A and B,** *GOT*, pp. 48–49	**Vocabulary Builder,** SE, p. 271: *confiscation, sloth, subsequently, abrogated, forfeited, fraudulent, treachery, stead* **Latin Root:** *-sequent-*, SE, p. 278; *UR2*, p. 64
	from *The King James Bible* (A), SE, p. 282	**Inferring Meaning,** SE, p. 281; *UR2*, p. 80; **Reading Warm-ups A and B,** *UR2*, pp. 77–78; **Reading Strategy Graphic Organizers A and B,** *GOT*, pp. 50–51	**Psalm, Sermon, and Parable,** SE, p. 281; *UR2*, p. 79; **Literary Analysis Graphic Organizers A and B,** *GOT*, pp. 52–53	**Vocabulary Builder,** SE, p. 281: *righteousness, stature, prodigal, entreated, transgressed* **Latin Root:** *-stat-*, SE, p. 289; *UR2*, p. 81

Key to Program References:
SE: Student Edition **UR:** Unit Resources **GOT:** Graphic Organizer Transparencies **GR:** General Resources **WG:** Writing and Grammar
MA: More accessible **A:** Average **MC:** More Challenging. See Accessibility at a Glance chart on selection pages.

Grammar	Writing	Extend Your Learning	Assessment
Direct Address, SE, p. 202; *UR1,* p. 142; *WG,* Ch. 27, Section 2	**Writing Lesson:** Investigative Report, SE, p. 203; *UR1,* p. 143; *WG,* Ch. 13, Section 4	**Listening and Speaking:** Phone Conversation, SE, p. 203 **Research and Technology:** Holidays Chart, SE, p. 203; *UR1,* p. 144	**Selection Tests A and B,** *UR1,* pp. 146–151; **Rubrics for Research:** Research Report, *GR,* pp. 51–52; **Rubric for Speaking:** Delivering a Research Presentation, *GR,* p. 91; **Benchmark Test 2,** *UR1,* pp. 159–164

Grammar	Writing	Extend Your Learning	Assessment
Capitalization of Proper Nouns, SE, p. 246; *UR2,* p. 14; *WG,* Ch. 26	**Writing Lesson:** Introduction to a Sonnet Sequence, SE, p. 247; *UR2,* p. 15; *WG,* Ch. 14, Section 2	**Listening and Speaking:** Scene with Dialogue, SE, p. 247; *UR2,* p. 16 **Research and Technology:** Biographical Report, SE, p. 247	**Diagnostic Test 3,** *UR2,* pp. 2–4; **Selection Tests A and B,** *UR2,* pp. 18–23; **Rubrics for Response to Literature,** *GR,* pp. 65–66; **Rubric for Peer Assessment:** Dramatic Performance, *GR,* p. 131
Adjective and Adverb Phrases, SE, p. 254; *UR2,* p. 31; *WG,* Ch. 19, Section 1	**Writing Lesson:** Timed Writing: Compare-and-Contrast Essay, SE, p. 255; *UR2,* p. 32; *WG,* Ch. 8, Section 4	**Listening and Speaking:** Oral Interpretation, SE, p. 255; *UR2,* p. 33 **Research and Technology:** Display Poster, SE, p. 255	**Selection Tests A and B,** *UR2,* pp. 35–40; **Rubrics for Exposition:** Comparison-and-Contrast Essay, *GR,* pp. 69–70; **Rubric for Peer Assessment:** Oral Interpretation, *GR,* p. 130
Participles as Adjectives, SE, p. 264; *UR2,* p. 48; *WG,* Ch. 19, Section 2	**Writing Lesson:** Timed Writing: Analysis of a Sonnet's Imagery, SE, p. 265; *UR2,* p. 49; *WG,* Ch. 14, Section 3	**Listening and Speaking:** Sonnet Recital, SE, p. 265; *UR2,* p. 50 **Research and Technology:** Multimedia Report, SE, p. 265	**Selection Tests A and B,** *UR2,* pp. 52–57; **Rubrics for Response to Literature,** *GR,* pp. 65–66; **Rubric for Peer Assessment:** Oral Interpretation, *GR,* p. 130
Complex Sentences, SE, p. 278; *UR2,* p. 65; *WG,* Ch. 19, Section 4	**Writing Lesson:** Letter to an Editor, SE, p. 279; *UR2,* p. 66; *WG,* Ch. 7, Section 4	**Listening and Speaking:** Debate, SE, p. 279, *UR2,* p. 67 **Research and Technology:** Illustrated Timeline, SE, p. 279	**Selection Tests A and B,** *UR2,* pp. 69–74; **Rubrics for Persuasion:** Persuasive Essay, *GR,* pp. 45–46; **Rubric for Speaking:** Delivering a Persuasive Speech *GR,* p. 89
Infinitive Phrases, SE, p. 289; *UR2,* p. 82; *WG,* Ch. 19, Section 2	**Writing Lesson:** Parable in King James Style, SE, p. 290; *UR2,* p. 83; *WG,* Ch. 5, Section 3	**Listening and Speaking:** Retelling, SE, p. 290; *UR2,* p. 84 **Research and Technology:** Evaluative Report, SE, p. 290	**Selection Tests A and B,** *UR2,* pp. 86–91; **Rubrics for Narration:** Short Story, *GR,* pp. 57–58; **Rubric for Peer Assessment:** Dramatic Performance, *GR,* p. 131

All selections are supported in the Reader's Notebooks.

Celebrating Humanity (1485–1625) *(continued)*

	Selection	Reading Strategy	Literary Analysis	Vocabulary
PART 3 / **FOCUS ON DRAMA**	*The Tragedy of Macbeth: Act I* (MC), William Shakespeare, SE, p. 306	**Using Text Aids**, SE, p. 305; *UR2*, p. 99; **Reading Warm-ups A and B**, *UR2*, pp. 96–97	**Elizabethan Drama**, SE, p. 305; *UR2*, p. 98; **Literary Analysis Graphic Organizers A and B**, *GOT*, pp. 54–55, 56–57	**Vocabulary Builder**, SE, p. 305: *valor, reasons, imperial, liege, sovereign* **Power Words**, SE, p. 325; *UR2*, p. 100
	The Tragedy of Macbeth: Act II (MC), William Shakespeare, SE, p. 327	**Reading Verse for Meaning**, SE, p. 326; *UR2*, p. 115; **Reading Warm-ups A and B**, *UR2*, pp. 112–113; **Reading Strategy Graphic Organizers A and B**, *GOT*, pp. 58–59	**Blank Verse**, SE, p. 326; *UR2*, p. 114; **Literary Analysis Graphic Organizers A and B**, *GOT*, pp. 60–61	**Vocabulary Builder**, SE, p. 326: *augment, palpable, stealthy, multitudinous, equivocate, predominance* **Latin Root**: *-voc-*, SE, p. 341; *UR2*, p. 116
	The Tragedy of Macbeth: Act III (MC), William Shakespeare, SE, p. 343	**Reading Between the Lines**, SE, p. 342; *UR2*, p. 140; **Reading Warm-ups A and B**, *UR2*, pp. 137–138; **Reading Strategy Graphic Organizers A and B**, *GOT*, pp. 62–63	**Conflict**, SE, p. 342; *UR2*, p. 139; **Literary Analysis Graphic Organizers A and B**, *GOT*, pp. 64–65	**Vocabulary Builder**, SE, p. 342: *indissoluble, dauntless, jocund, infirmity, malevolence* **Latin Prefix**: *mal-*, SE, p. 359; *UR2*, p. 141
	The Tragedy of Macbeth: Act IV (MC), William Shakespeare, SE, p. 361	**Using Your Senses**, SE, p. 360; *UR2*, p. 156; **Reading Warm-ups A and B**, *UR2*, pp. 153–154; **Reading Strategy Graphic Organizers A and B**, *GOT*, pp. 66–67	**Imagery**, SE, p. 360; *UR2*, p. 155; **Literary Analysis Graphic Organizers A and B**, *GOT*, pp. 68–69	**Vocabulary Builder**, SE, p. 360: *pernicious, judicious, sundry, intemperance, avarice, credulous* **Latin Root**: *-cred-*, SE, p. 379; *UR2*, p. 157
	The Tragedy of Macbeth: Act V (MC), William Shakespeare, SE, p. 381	**Inferring Beliefs of the Period**, SE, p. 380; *UR2*, p. 172; **Reading Warm-ups A and B**, *UR2*, pp. 169–170; **Reading Strategy Graphic Organizers A and B**, *GOT*, pp. 70–71	**Shakespearean Tragedy**, SE, p. 380; *UR2*, p. 171; **Literary Analysis Graphic Organizers A and B**, *GOT*, pp. 72–73	**Vocabulary Builder**, SE, p. 380: *perturbation, pristine, clamorous, harbingers* **Latin Root**: *-turb-*, SE, p. 396; *UR2*, p. 173

A Turbulent Time (1625–1798)

	Selection	Reading Strategy	Literary Analysis	Vocabulary
PART 1	"Song" (MC), John Donne, SE, p. 436; "A Valediction: Forbidding Mourning" (A), John Donne, SE, p. 438; "Holy Sonnet 10" (MC), John Donne, SE p. 440; "Meditation 17" (A), John Donne, SE, p. 442	**Recognizing the Speaker's Situation and Motivation**, SE, p. 435; *UR3*, p. 12; **Reading Warm-ups A and B**, *UR3*, pp. 9–10; **Reading Strategy Graphic Organizers A and B**, *GOT*, pp. 75–76	**Metaphysical Poetry**, SE, p. 435; *UR3*, p. 11; **Literary Analysis Graphic Organizers A and B**, *GOT*, pp. 77–78	**Vocabulary Builder**, SE, p. 435: *profanation, laity, trepidation, breach, contention, piety, intermit, covetousness* **Latin Prefix**: *inter-*, SE, p. 446; *UR3*, p. 13
	"On My First Son" (A), Ben Jonson, SE, p. 450; "Still to Be Neat" (A), Ben Jonson, SE, p. 452; "Song: To Celia" (A), Ben Jonson, SE, p. 454	**Hypothesizing**, SE, p. 449; *UR3*, p. 29; **Reading Warm-ups A and B**, *UR3*, pp. 26–27; **Reading Strategy Graphic Organizers A and B**, *GOT*, pp. 79–80	**Epigrams**, SE, p. 449; *UR3*, p. 28; **Literary Analysis Graphic Organizers A and B**, *GOT*, pp. 81–82	**Vocabulary Builder**, SE, p. 449: *thou, thy, thine, wast, wert, hast, hath, dost, doth* **Archaic Words**, SE, p. 456; *UR3*, p. 30

Key to Program References:
SE: Student Edition **UR:** Unit Resources **GOT:** Graphic Organizer Transparencies **GR:** General Resources **WG:** Writing and Grammar
MA: More accessible **A:** Average **MC:** More Challenging. See Accessibility at a Glance chart on selection pages.

Grammar	Writing	Extend Your Learning	Assessment
Action Verbs and Linking Verbs, SE, p. 325; *UR2,* p. 101; *WG,* Ch. 17, Section 2		**Writing:** Speech of Welcome, SE, p. 325 **Research and Technology:** Oral Report, SE, p. 325; *UR2,* p. 102	**Selection Tests A and B,** *UR2,* pp. 104–109
Commonly Confused Words: *Lie* and *Lay,* SE, p. 341; *UR2,* p. 117; *WG,* Ch. 25, Section 2		**Listening and Speaking:** Debate, SE, p. 341; *UR2,* p. 118 **Writing:** Investigational Journal, SE, p. 341	**Selection Tests A and B,** *UR2,* pp. 120–125; **Rubric for Speaking:** Delivering a Persuasive Speech, *GR,* p. 89; **Benchmark Test 3,** *UR2,* pp. 126–131
Subject and Verb Agreement, SE, p. 359; *UR2,* p. 142; *WG,* Ch. 23, Section 1		**Writing:** Diary Entry, SE, p. 359 **Research and Technology:** Annotated Bibliography, SE, p. 359; *UR2,* p. 143	**Diagnostic Test 4,** *UR2,* pp. 132–134; **Selection Tests A and B,** *UR2,* pp. 145–150
Possessive Forms, SE, p. 379; *UR2,* p. 158; *WG,* Ch. 27, Section 6		**Writing:** Motivational Flyer, SE, p. 379 **Listening and Speaking:** Interview, SE, p. 379; *UR2,* p. 159	**Selection Tests A and B,** *UR2,* pp. 161–166
Pronouns and Antecedents, SE, p. 396; *UR2,* p. 174; *WG,* Ch. 23, Section 2	**Writing Lesson:** Timed Writing: Response to Criticism, SE, p. 397; *UR2,* p. 175; *WG,* Ch. 14, Section 2	**Listening and Speaking:** Battlefield Report, SE, p. 397; *UR2,* p. 176 **Research and Technology:** Annotated Bibliography, SE, p. 397	**Selection Tests A and B,** *UR2,* pp. 178–183; **Rubrics for Response to Literature,** *GR,* pp. 65–66; **Benchmark Test 4,** *UR2,* pp. 191–196

Grammar	Writing	Extend Your Learning	Assessment
Active and Passive Voice, SE, p. 446; *UR3,* p. 14; *WG,* Ch. 21, Section 4	**Writing Lesson:** Persuasive Speech Based on Donne's Work, SE, p. 447; *UR3,* p. 15; *WG,* Ch. 7, Section 4	**Listening and Speaking:** Dramatic Reading, SE, p. 447; *UR3,* p. 16 **Research and Technology:** Science Report, SE, p. 447	**Diagnostic Test 5,** *UR3,* pp. 2–4; **Selection Tests A and B,** *UR3,* pp. 18–23; **Rubrics for Persuasion:** Persuasive Essay, *GR,* pp. 45–46
Modifiers: Placement of *only,* SE, p. 456; *UR3,* p. 31; *WG,* Ch. 20, Section 5	**Writing Lesson:** Timed Writing: Critical Response, SE, p. 457; *UR3,* p. 32; *WG,* Ch. 14, Section 4	**Listening and Speaking:** Debate, SE, p. 457; *UR3,* p. 33 **Research and Technology:** Biographical Report, SE, p. 457	**Selection Tests A and B,** *UR3,* pp. 35–40; **Rubrics for Response to Literature,** *GR,* pp. 65–66

All selections are supported in the Reader's Notebooks.

A Turbulent Time (1625–1798) *(continued)*

	Selection	Reading Strategy	Literary Analysis	Vocabulary
PART 1 *(continued)*	**"To His Coy Mistress"** (MC), Andrew Marvell, SE, p. 460; **"To the Virgins, to Make Much of Time"** (MC), Robert Herrick, SE, p. 463; **"Song"** (A), Sir John Suckling, SE, p. 464	**Inferring the Speaker's Attitude**, SE, p. 459; *UR3*, p. 46; **Reading Warm-ups A and B**, *UR3*, pp. 43–44; **Reading Strategy Graphic Organizers A and B**, *GOT*, pp. 83–84	*Carpe Diem* **Theme**, SE, p. 459; *UR3*, p. 45; **Literary Analysis Graphic Organizers A and B**, *GOT*, pp. 85–86	**Vocabulary Builder**, SE, p. 459: *coyness, amorous, languish, prime, wan* **Related Forms of** *prime*, SE, p. 467; *UR3*, p. 47
PART 2	**Sonnet VII: "How Soon Hath Time"** (MC), John Milton, SE, p. 474; **Sonnet XIX: "When I Consider"** (MC), John Milton, SE, p. 476; **from** *Paradise Lost* (MC), John Milton, SE, p. 478	**Breaking Down Sentences**, SE, p. 473; *UR3*, p. 63; **Reading Warm-ups A and B**, *UR3*, pp. 60–61; **Reading Strategy Graphic Organizers A and B**, *GOT*, pp. 87–88	**The Italian Sonnet; Epic Poetry**, SE, p. 473; *UR3*, p. 62; **Literary Analysis Graphic Organizers A and B**, *GOT*, pp. 89–90	**Vocabulary Builder**, SE, p. 473: *semblance, illumine, transgress, guile, obdurate, tempestuous, transcendent, suppliant, ignominy* **Latin Root:** *-lum-*, SE, p. 488; *UR3*, p. 64
	from *Eve's Apology in Defense of Women* (A), Amelia Lanier, SE, p. 492; **"To Lucasta, on Going to the Wars"** (MA), Richard Lovelace, SE, p. 494; **"To Althea, from Prison"** (A), Richard Lovelace, SE, p. 496	**Using Historical Context**, SE, p. 491; *UR3*, p. 80; **Reading Warm-ups A and B**, *UR3*, pp. 77–78; **Reading Strategy Graphic Organizers A and B**, *GOT*, pp. 91–92	**Tradition and Reform**, SE, p. 491; *UR3*, p. 79; **Literary Analysis Graphic Organizers A and B**, *GOT*, pp. 93–94	**Vocabulary Builder**, SE, p. 491: *breach, discretion, inconstancy* **Terms With** *breach*, SE, p. 499; *UR3*, p. 81
PART 3	**from** *The Diary* (A), Samuel Pepys, SE, p. 504; **from** *A Journal of the Plague Year* (A), Daniel Defoe, SE, p. 511	**Drawing Conclusions**, SE, p. 503; *UR3*, p. 97; **Reading Warm-ups A and B**, *UR3*, pp. 94–95; **Reading Strategy Graphic Organizers A and B**, *GOT*, pp. 95–96	**Diaries and Journals**, SE, p. 503; *UR3*, p. 96; **Literary Analysis Graphic Organizers A and B**, *GOT*, pp. 97–98	**Vocabulary Builder**, SE, p. 503: *apprehensions, abated, lamentable, combustible, malicious, discoursing, distemper importuning, prodigious* **Latin Prefix:** *dis-*, SE, p. 518; *UR3*, p. 98
	from *Gulliver's Travels* (A), Jonathan Swift, SE, p. 522	**Interpreting**, SE, p. 521; *UR3*, p. 123; **Reading Warm-ups A and B**, *UR3*, pp. 120–121; **Reading Strategy Graphic Organizers A and B**, *GOT*, pp. 99–100	**Satire**, SE, p. 521; *UR3*, p. 122; **Literary Analysis Graphic Organizers A and B**, *GOT*, pp. 101–102	**Vocabulary Builder**, SE, p. 521: *conjecture, expostulate, schism, expedient, habituate, odious* **Latin Root:** *-jec-*, SE, p. 534; *UR3*, p. 124
	from *An Essay on Man* (MC), Alexander Pope, SE, p. 538; **from** *The Rape of the Lock* (MC), Alexander Pope, SE, p. 540	**Recognizing Author's Purpose**, SE, p. 537; *UR3*, p. 140; **Reading Warm-ups A and B**, *UR3*, pp. 137–138; **Reading Strategy Graphic Organizers A and B**, *GOT*, pp. 105–106	**Mock Epic**, SE, p. 537; *UR3*, p. 139; **Literary Analysis Graphic Organizers A and B**, *GOT*, pp. 103–104	**Vocabulary Builder**, SE, p. 537: *stoic, disabused, obliquely, plebeian, destitute, assignations* **Words From Political Science**, SE, p. 552; *UR3*, p. 141
	from *A Dictionary of the English Language* (MA), Samuel Johnson, SE, p. 556; **from the** *Life of Samuel Johnson* (A), James Boswell, SE, p. 562	**Establishing a Purpose**, SE, p. 555; *UR3*, p. 157; **Reading Warm-ups A and B**, *UR3*, pp. 154–155; **Reading Strategy Graphic Organizers A and B**, *GOT*, pp. 107–108	**Dictionary; Biography**, SE, p. 555; *UR3*, p. 156; **Literary Analysis Graphic Organizers A and B**, *GOT*, pp. 109–110	**Vocabulary Builder**, SE, p. 555: *recompense, caprices, adulterations, propagators, risible, abasement, credulity, malignity, pernicious, inculcated* **Latin Root:** *-dict-*, SE, p. 570; *UR3*, p. 158
	"Elegy Written in a Country Churchyard" (MC), Thomas Gray, SE, p. 574; **"A Nocturnal Reverie"** (MC), Anne Finch, Countess of Winchilsea, SE, p. 580	**Paraphrasing**, SE, p. 573; *UR3*, p. 174; **Reading Warm-ups A and B**, *UR3*, pp. 171–172; **Reading Strategy Graphic Organizers A and B**, *GOT*, pp. 111–112	**Pre–Romantic Poetry**, SE, p. 573; *UR3*, p. 173; **Literary Analysis Graphic Organizers A and B**, *GOT*, pp. 113–114	**Vocabulary Builder**, SE, p. 573: *penury, circumscribed, ingenuous, ignoble, nocturnal, temperate, venerable, forage* **Latin Prefix:** *circum-*, SE, p. 584; *UR3*, p. 175

Key to Program References:
SE: Student Edition   **UR:** Unit Resources   **GOT:** Graphic Organizer Transparencies   **GR:** General Resources   **WG:** Writing and Grammar
MA: More accessible   **A:** Average   **MC:** More Challenging. See Accessibility at a Glance chart on selection pages.

Skills Navigator

Grammar	Writing	Extend Your Learning	Assessment
Irregular Forms of Adjectives, SE, p. 467; *UR3*, p. 48; *WG*, Ch. 24, Section 1	**Writing Lesson:** Witty Poem, SE, p. 468; *UR3*, p. 49; *WG*, Ch. 6, Connected Assignment	**Listening and Speaking:** Phone Skit, SE, p. 468; *UR3*, p. 50 **Research and Technology:** Comparative Biographical Essay, SE, p. 468	**Selection Tests A and B,** *UR3*, pp. 52–57; **Rubrics for Poem (Rhyming)**, *GR*, pp. 73–74
Usage: *Who* and *Whom*, SE, p. 488; *UR3*, p. 65; *WG*, Ch. 22, Section 2	**Writing Lesson:** Critical Analysis of a Literary Theme, SE, p. 488; *UR3*, p. 66; *WG*, Ch. 14, Section 4	**Listening and Speaking:** Speech, SE, p. 489 **Research and Technology:** Documentary, SE, p. 489; *UR3*, p. 67	**Selection Tests A and B,** *UR3*, pp. 69–74; **Rubrics for Response to Literature**, *GR*, pp. 65–66
Correlative Conjunctions, SE, p. 499; *UR3*, p. 82; *WG*, Ch. 17, Section 4	**Writing Lesson:** Essay Connecting Literature With Experience, SE, p. 500; *UR3*, p. 83; *WG*, Ch. 4, Section 2	**Listening and Speaking:** Ballad, SE, p. 500, *UR3*, p. 84 **Research and Technology:** Report with Spreadsheets, SE, p. 500	**Selection Tests A and B,** *UR3*, pp. 86–91; **Rubrics for Writing for Assessment**, *GR*, pp. 67–68; **Rubrics for Poem (Rhyming)**, *GR*, pp. 73–74
Gerunds, SE, p. 518; *UR3*, p. 99; *WG*, Ch. 19, Section 2	**Writing Lesson:** Timed Writing: Response to Criticism, SE, p. 519; *UR3*, p. 100; *WG*, Ch. 14, Section 3	**Listening and Speaking:** Performance as a Town Crier, SE, p. 519; *UR3*, p. 101 **Research and Technology:** Fact-Check Report, SE, p. 519	**Selection Tests A and B,** *UR3*, pp. 103–108; **Rubrics for Response to Literature**, *GR*, pp. 65–66; **Benchmark Test 5**, *UR3*, pp. 109–114
Usage: *between* and *among*, SE, p. 534; *UR3*, p. 125; *WG*, Ch. 25, Section 2	**Writing Lesson:** Descriptive Satire, SE, p. 535; *UR3*, p. 126; *WG*, Ch. 14, Section 4	**Listening and Speaking:** Special-Effects Plan, SE, p. 535; *UR3*, p. 127 **Research and Technology:** Research Report, SE, p. 535	**Diagnostic Test 6**, *UR3*, pp. 115–117; **Selection Tests A and B,** *UR3*, pp. 129–134; **Rubrics for Descriptive Essay**, *GR*, pp. 63–64
Inverted Word Order, SE, p. 552; *UR3*, p. 142; *WG*, Ch. 18, Section 2	**Writing Lesson:** Imitating an Author's Style, SE, p. 553; *UR3*, p. 143; *WG*, Ch. 20, Section 6	**Listening and Speaking:** Graduation Speech, SE, p. 553; *UR3*, p. 144 **Research and Technology:** Glossary, SE, p. 553	**Selection Tests A and B,** *UR3*, pp. 146–151; **Rubrics for Poem (Rhyming)**, *GR*, pp. 73–74
Parenthetical Expressions, SE, p. 570; *UR3*, p. 159; *WG*, Ch. 27, Section 2	**Writing Lesson:** Comparative Analysis of Dictionaries, SE, p. 571; *UR3*, p. 160; *WG*, Ch. 9, Sections 3 and 4	**Listening and Speaking:** Reenactment, SE, p. 571; *UR3*, p. 161 **Research and Technology:** Biographical Sketch, SE, p. 571	**Selection Tests A and B,** *UR3*, pp. 163–168; **Rubrics for Exposition:** Comparison-and-Contrast Essay, *GR*, pp. 69–70
Pronoun–Antecedent Agreement, SE, p. 584; *UR3*, p. 176; *WG*, Ch. 23, Section 2	**Writing Lesson:** Timed Writing: Reflective Essay, SE, p. 585; *UR3*, p. 177; *WG*, Ch. 6, Section 2	**Listening and Speaking:** Group Reading, SE, p. 585; *UR3*, p. 178 **Research and Technology:** Daydream Report, SE, p. 585	**Selection Tests A and B,** *UR3*, pp. 180–185; **Rubrics for Reflective Essay**, *GR*, pp. 47–48

All selections are supported in the Reader's Notebooks.

	Selection	Reading Strategy	Literary Analysis	Vocabulary
PART 4 / **FOCUS ON ESSAY**	"On Spring" (A), Samuel Johnson, SE, p. 594; *The Aims of the Spectator* (A), Joseph Addison, SE, p. 598	**Drawing Inferences**, SE, p. 593; *UR3*, p. 191; **Reading Warm-ups A and B**, *UR3*, pp. 188–189; **Reading Strategy Graphic Organizers A and B**, *GOT*, pp. 115–116	**Essay**, SE, p. 593; *UR3*, p. 190; **Literary Analysis Graphic Organizers A and B**, *GOT*, pp. 117–118	**Vocabulary Builder**, SE, p. 593: *procured, divert, speculation, transient, affluence, contentious, trifles, embellishments* **Latin Root:** *-spec-*, SE, p. 602; *UR3*, p. 192
	"A Modest Proposal" (A), Jonathan Swift, SE, p. 614	**Recognizing Author's Purpose**, SE, p. 613; *UR3*, p. 210; **Reading Warm-ups A and B**, *UR3*, pp. 207–208; **Reading Strategy Graphic Organizers A and B**, *GOT*, pp. 119–120	**Satirical Essay**, SE, p. 613; *UR3*, p. 209; **Literary Analysis Graphic Organizers A and B**, *GOT*, pp. 121–122	**Vocabulary Builder**, SE, p. 613: *sustenance, commodity, collateral, deference, censure, encumbrance, contrive, incur* **Word Parts:** Prefix: *en-*, SE, p. 624; *UR3*, p. 211

UNIT 4
Rebels and Dreamers (1798–1832)

	Selection	Reading Strategy	Literary Analysis	Vocabulary
PART 1	"To a Mouse" (MC), Robert Burns, SE, p. 666; "To a Louse" (MC), Robert Burns, SE, p. 669; "Woo'd and Married and A' " (A), Joanna Baillie, SE, p. 672	**Translating Dialect**, SE, p. 665; *UR4*, p. 12; **Reading Warm-ups A and B**, *UR4*, pp. 9–10; **Reading Strategy Graphic Organizers A and B**, *GOT*, pp. 124–125	**Dialect**, SE, p. 665; *UR4*, p. 11; **Literary Analysis Graphic Organizers A and B**, *GOT*, pp. 126–127	**Vocabulary Builder**, SE, p. 665: *dominion, impudence, winsome, discretion, inconstantly* **Anglo-Saxon Suffix:** *-some*, SE, p. 676; *UR4*, p. 13
	"The Lamb" (MA), William Blake, SE, p. 680; "The Tyger" (MA), William Blake, SE, p. 681; "The Chimney Sweeper" (A), William Blake, SE, p. 683, "Infant Sorrow" (MA), William Blake, SE, p. 684	**Using Visuals as Key to Meaning**, SE, p. 679; *UR4*, p. 29; **Reading Warm-ups A and B**, *UR4*, pp. 26–27; **Reading Strategy Graphic Organizers A and B**, *GOT*, pp. 130–131	**Symbols**, SE, p. 679; *UR4*, p. 28; **Literary Analysis Graphic Organizers A and B**, *GOT*, pp. 128–129	**Vocabulary Builder**, SE, p. 679: *vales, symmetry, aspire* **Latin Root:** *-spir-*, SE, p. 686; *UR4*, p. 30
	Introduction to *Frankenstein* (MC), Mary Shelley, SE, p. 692	**Predicting**, SE, p. 691; *UR4*, p. 48; **Reading Warm-ups A and B**, *UR4*, pp. 45–46; **Reading Strategy Graphic Organizers A and B**, *GOT*, pp. 132–133	**The Gothic Tradition**, SE, p. 691; *UR4*, p. 47; **Literary Analysis Graphic Organizers A and B**, *GOT*, pp. 134–135	**Vocabulary Builder**, SE, p. 691: *appendage, ungenial, acceded, platitude, phantasm, incitement* **Related Words:** *phantasm* and *fantasy*, SE, p. 698; *UR4*, p. 49

Key to Program References:
SE: Student Edition **UR:** Unit Resources **GOT:** Graphic Organizer Transparencies **GR:** General Resources **WG:** Writing and Grammar
MA: More accessible **A:** Average **MC:** More Challenging. See Accessibility at a Glance chart on selection pages.

Skills Navigator

Grammar	Writing	Extend Your Learning	Assessment
Adjective Clauses, SE, p. 602; *UR3*, p. 193; *WG*, Ch. 19, Section 3	**Writing Lesson:** Essay on Human Behavior, SE, p. 603; *UR3*, p. 194; *WG*, Ch. 6, Section 4	**Listening and Speaking:** Monologue, SE, p. 603; *UR3*, p. 195 **Research and Technology:** Analysis of the Audience, SE, p. 603	**Selection Tests A and B,** *UR3*, pp. 199–204; **Rubrics for Reflective Essay,** *GR*, pp. 47–48
Vary Sentence Beginnings, SE, p. 624; *UR3*, p. 212; *WG*, Ch. 11, Section 2	**Writing Lesson:** Satirical Essay, SE, p. 625; *UR3*, p. 213; *WG*, Ch. 11, Section 2	**Listening and Speaking:** Interview, SE, p. 625 **Research and Technology:** Timeline, SE, p. 625; *UR3*, p. 214	**Selection Tests A and B,** *UR3*, pp. 216–221; **Rubrics for Response to Literature,** *GR*, pp. 65–66; **Benchmark Test 6,** *UR3*, pp. 229–234

Grammar	Writing	Extend Your Learning	Assessment
Interjections, SE p. 676; *UR4*, p. 14; *WG* Ch. 17, Section 4	**Writing Lesson:** Timed Writing: Comparison of Characters, SE, p. 677; *UR4* p. 15; *WG* Ch. 14, Section 4	**Listening and Speaking:** Authentic Dialect Reading, SE, p. 677; *UR4*, p. 16 **Research and Technology:** Multimedia Presentation, SE, p. 677	**Diagnostic Test 7,** *UR3*, pp. 2–4; **Selection Tests A and B,** *UR4*, pp. 18–23; **Rubrics for Exposition: Comparison-and-Contrast Essay,** *GR*, pp. 69–70
Commonly Confused Words: *rise* and *raise*, SE, p. 686; *UR4*, p. 31; *WG* Ch. 25, Section 2	**Writing Lesson:** Timed Writing: Comparative Literary Analysis, SE, p. 687; *UR4*, p. 32; *WG* Ch. 14, Section 4	**Listening and Speaking:** Musical Reading, SE, p. 687 **Research and Technology:** Advertisement, SE, p. 687; *UR4*, p. 33	**Selection Tests A and B,** *UR4*, pp. 35–40; **Rubrics for Response to Literature,** *GR*, pp. 65–66
Past Participial Phrases, SE, p. 698; *UR4*, p. 50; *WG* Ch. 19, Section 2	**Writing Lesson:** Timed Writing: Essay Comparing and Contrasting Impressions of a Work, SE, p. 699; *UR4*, p. 51; *WG* Ch. 9, Section 3	**Listening and Speaking:** Radio Play, SE, p. 699 **Research and Technology:** Science Report, SE, p. 699; *UR4*, p. 52	**Selection Tests A and B,** *UR4*, pp. 54–59; **Rubrics for Exposition: Comparison-and-Contrast Essay,** *GR*, pp. 69–70

All selections are supported in the Reader's Notebooks.

	Selection	Reading Strategy	Literary Analysis	Vocabulary
PART 2 *FOCUS ON LYRIC POETRY*	**"Lines Composed a Few Miles Above Tintern Abbey"** (MC), William Wordsworth, SE, p. 708; **from "The Prelude"** (MC), William Wordsworth, SE, p. 714; **"The World Is Too Much With Us"** (A), William Wordsworth, SE, p. 717; **"London, 1802"** (A), William Wordsworth, SE, p. 718	**Using Literary Context,** SE, p. 707; *UR4*, p. 65; **Reading Warm-ups A and B,** *UR4*, pp. 62–63; **Reading Strategy Graphic Organizers A and B,** *GOT*, pp. 136–137	**Romanticism and the Lyric,** SE, p. 707; *UR4*, p. 64; **Literary Analysis Graphic Organizers A and B,** *GOT*, pp. 138–139	**Vocabulary Builder,** SE, p. 707: *recompense, roused, presumption, anatomize, confounded, sordid, stagnant* **Forms of** *anatomize*, SE, p. 720; *UR4*, p. 66
	"The Rime of the Ancient Mariner" (A), Samuel Taylor Coleridge, SE, p. 730; **"Kubla Khan"** (MA), Samuel Taylor Coleridge, SE, p. 754	**Analyzing Poetic Effects,** SE, p. 729; *UR4*, p. 91; **Reading Warm-ups A and B,** *UR4*, pp. 88–89; **Reading Strategy Graphic Organizers A and B,** *GOT*, pp. 140–141	**Poetic Sound Devices,** SE, p. 729; *UR4*, p. 90; **Literary Analysis Graphic Organizers A and B,** GOT, pp. 142–143	**Vocabulary Builder,** SE, p. 729: *averred, sojourn, expiated, reverence, sinuous, tumult* **Latin Root:** *-journ-*, SE, p. 758; *UR4*, p. 92
	"She Walks in Beauty" (MA), George Gordon, Lord Byron, SE, p. 762; **from "Childe Harold's Pilgrimage: Apostrophe to the Ocean"** (A), George Gordon, Lord Byron, SE, p. 764; **from** *Don Juan* (MA), George Gordon, Lord Byron, SE, p. 768	**Questioning,** SE, p. 761; *UR4*, p. 108; **Reading Warm-ups A and B,** *UR4*, pp. 105–106; **Reading Strategy Graphic Organizers A and B,** *GOT*, pp. 144–145	**Figurative Language,** SE, p. 761; *UR4*, p. 107; **Literary Analysis Graphic Organizers A and B,** *GOT*, pp. 146–147	**Vocabulary Builder,** SE, p. 761: *arbiter, tempests, torrid, fathomless, retort, insensible, credulous, copious, avarice* **Latin Suffix** *-ous*, SE, p. 772; *UR4*, p. 109
	"Ozymandias" (A), Percy Bysshe Shelley, SE, p. 776; **"Ode to the West Wind"** (MC), Percy Bysshe Shelley, SE, p. 778; **"To a Skylark"** (MA), Percy Bysshe Shelley, SE, p. 781	**Responding to Imagery,** SE, p. 775; *UR4*, p. 125; **Reading Warm-ups A and B,** *UR4*, pp. 122–123; **Reading Strategy Graphic Organizers A and B,** *GOT*, pp. 148–149	**Imagery,** SE, p. 775; *UR4*, p. 124; **Literary Analysis Graphic Organizers A and B,** *GOT*, pp. 150–151	**Vocabulary Builder,** SE, p. 775: *visage, verge, sepulcher, impulse, blithe, profuse, vernal, satiety* **Latin Root:** *-puls-*, SE, p. 786; *UR4*, p. 126
	"On First Looking into Chapman's Homer" (A), John Keats, SE, p. 790; **"When I Have Fears That I May Cease to Be"** (A), John Keats, SE, p. 792; **"Ode to a Nightingale"** (MC), John Keats, SE, p. 794; **"Ode on a Grecian Urn"** (MC), John Keats, SE, p. 798	**Paraphrasing,** SE, p. 789; *UR4*, p. 142; **Reading Warm-ups A and B,** *UR4*, pp. 139–140; **Reading Strategy Graphic Organizers A and B,** *GOT*, pp. 152–153	**The Ode,** SE, p. 789; *UR4*, p. 141; **Literary Analysis Graphic Organizers A and B,** *GOT*, pp. 154–155	**Vocabulary Builder,** SE, p. 789: *ken, surmise, gleaned, teeming, vintage, requiem* **Latin Suffix** *-age*, SE, p. 802; *UR4*, p. 143
PART 3	**Speech to Parliament: "In Defense of the Lower Classes"** (MC), George Gordon, Lord Byron, SE, p. 812; **A Song: "Men of England"** (A), Percy Bysshe Shelley, SE, p. 815; **"On the Passing of the Reform Bill"** (A), Thomas Babington Macaulay, SE, p. 816	**Setting a Purpose for Reading,** SE, p. 811; *UR4*, p. 159; **Reading Warm-ups A and B,** *UR4*, pp. 156–157; **Reading Strategy Graphic Organizers A and B,** *GOT*, pp. 156–157	**Political Commentary,** SE, p. 811; *UR4*, p. 158; **Literary Analysis Graphic Organizers A and B,** *GOT*, pp. 158–159	**Vocabulary Builder,** SE, p. 811: *impediments, decimation, efficacious, emancipate, balm, inauspicious* **Latin Root** *-dec-*, SE, p. 820; *UR4*, p. 160
	"On Making an Agreeable Marriage" (A), Jane Austen, SE, p. 824; **from** *A Vindication of the Rights of Woman* (A), Mary Wollstonecraft, SE, p. 828	**Determining the Writer's Purpose,** SE, p. 823; *UR4*, p. 176; **Reading Warm-ups A and B,** *UR4*, pp. 173–174; **Reading Strategy Graphic Organizers A and B,** *GOT*, pp. 160–161	**Social Commentary,** SE, p. 823; *UR4*, p. 175; **Literary Analysis Graphic Organizers A and B,** *GOT*, pp. 162–163	**Vocabulary Builder,** SE, p. 823: *scruple, amiable, vindication, solicitude, fastidious, specious, fortitude, preponderates, gravity* **Latin Root** *-fort-*, SE, p. 832; *UR4*, p. 177

Key to Program References:
SE: Student Edition **UR:** Unit Resources **GOT:** Graphic Organizer Transparencies **GR:** General Resources **WG:** Writing and Grammar
MA: More accessible **A:** Average **MC:** More Challenging. See Accessibility at a Glance chart on selection pages.

Skills Navigator

Grammar	Writing	Extend Your Learning	Assessment
Present Participial Phrases, SE, p. 720; *UR4,* p. 67; *WG* Ch. 19, Section 2	**Writing Lesson:** Timed Writing: Response to Criticism, SE, p. 721; *UR4,* p. 68; *WG* Ch. 14, Section 3	**Listening and Speaking:** Photo Essay Presentation, SE, p. 721; *UR4,* p. 69 **Research and Technology:** Cultural Analysis, SE, p. 721	**Selection Tests A and B,** *UR4,* pp. 71–76; **Rubrics for Response to Literature,** *GR,* pp. 65–66; **Benchmark Test 7,** *UR4,* pp. 77–82
Inverted Word Order, SE, p. 758; *UR4,* p. 93; *WG* Ch. 18, Section 2	**Writing Lesson:** Timed Writing: Analysis of a Symbol, SE, p. 759; *UR4,* p. 94; *WG* Ch. 14, Section 4	**Listening and Speaking:** Dramatic Reading, SE, p. 759; *UR4,* p. 95 **Research and Technology:** Evaluation of a Literary Friendship, SE, p. 759	**Diagnostic Test 8,** *UR4,* pp. 83–85; **Selection Tests A and B,** *UR4,* pp. 97–102; **Rubrics for Response to Literature,** *GR,* pp. 65–66
Subject and Verb Agreement, SE, p. 772; *UR4,* p. 110; *WG* Ch. 23, Section 1	**Writing Lesson:** Monologue; SE, p. 773; *UR4,* p. 111; *WG* Ch. 5, Section 4	**Listening and Speaking:** Eulogy, SE, p. 773; *UR4,* p. 112 **Research and Technology:** Proposal for a Portrait, SE, p. 773	**Selection Tests A and B,** *UR4,* pp.114–119; **Rubrics for Autobiographical Narrative,** *GR,* pp. 43–44
Subjunctive Mood, SE, p. 786; *UR4,* p. 127; *WG* Ch. 21, Section 3	**Writing Lesson:** Introductory Background on a Poem, SE, p. 787; *UR4,* p. 128; *WG* Ch. 13, Section 3	**Listening and Speaking:** Weather Report, SE, p. 787; *UR4,* p. 129 **Research and Technology:** Cultural Report, SE, p. 787	**Selection Tests A and B,** *UR4,* pp.131–136; **Rubrics for Research Report,** *GR,* pp. 51–52
Direct Address, SE, p. 802; *UR4,* p. 144; *WG* Ch. 27, Section 2	**Writing Lesson:** Timed Writing: Response to Criticism, SE, p. 803; *UR4,* p. 145; *WG* Ch. 14, Section 2	**Listening and Speaking:** Oral Report, SE, p. 803; *UR4,* p. 146 **Research and Technology:** Science Display, SE, p. 803	**Selection Tests A and B,** *UR4,* pp.148–153; **Rubrics for Response to Literature,** *GR,* pp. 65–66; **Rubric for Oral Summary,** *GR,* p. 90
Correlative Conjunctions, SE, p. 820; *UR4,* p. 161; *WG* Ch. 17, Section 4	**Writing Lesson:** Editorial on a Political Issue, SE, p. 821; *UR4,* p. 162; *WG* Ch. 7, Section 4	**Listening and Speaking:** Speech, SE, p. 821 **Research and Technology:** Report, SE, p. 821; *UR4,* p. 163	**Selection Tests A and B,** *UR4,* pp. 165–170; **Rubrics for Persuasion: Persuasive Essay,** *GR,* pp. 45–46
Commas in a Series, SE, p. 832; *UR4,* p. 178; *WG* Ch. 27, Section 2	**Writing Lesson:** Letter to an Author, SE, p. 833; *UR4,* p. 179; *WG* Ch. 14, Section 2	**Listening and Speaking:** Telephone Call, SE, p. 833; *UR4,* p. 180 **Research and Technology:** Annotated Illustrated Timeline, SE, p. 833	**Selection Tests A and B,** *UR4,* pp. 182–187; **Rubrics for Response to Literature,** *GR,* pp. 65–66; **Benchmark Test 8,** *UR4,* pp. 195–200

All selections are supported in the Reader's Notebooks.

	Selection	Reading Strategy	Literary Analysis	Vocabulary
PART 1	from "In Memoriam, A. H. H." (A), Alfred, Lord Tennyson, SE, p. 866; "The Lady of Shalott" (A), Alfred, Lord Tennyson, SE, p. 869; from The Princess: "Tears, Idle Tears" (A), Alfred, Lord Tennyson, SE, p. 875; "Ulysses" (MA), Alfred, Lord Tennyson, SE, p. 876	**Judging a Poet's Message**, SE, p. 865; *URS*, p. 12; **Reading Warm-ups A and B**, *URS*, pp. 9–10; **Reading Strategy Graphic Organizers A and B**, *GOT*, pp. 165–166	**The Speaker in Poetry**, SE, pp. 865; *URS*, p. 11; **Literary Analysis Graphic Organizers A and B**, *GOT*, pp. 167–168	**Vocabulary Builder**, SE, p. 865: *diffusive, churls, waning, furrows* **Medieval Words**, SE, p. 880; *URS*, p. 13
	"My Last Duchess" (A), Robert Browning, SE, p. 884; "Life in a Love" (A), Robert Browning, SE, p. 887; "Love Among the Ruins" (A), Robert Browning, SE, p. 888; "Sonnet 43" (MA), Elizabeth Barrett Browning, SE, p. 893	**Making Inferences About the Speaker**, SE, p. 883; *URS*, p. 29; **Reading Warm-ups A and B**, *URS*, pp. 26–27; **Reading Strategy Graphic Organizers A and B**, *GOT*, pp. 169–170	**Dramatic Monologue**, SE, p. 883; *URS*, p. 28; **Literary Analysis Graphic Organizers A and B**, *GOT*, pp. 171–172	**Vocabulary Builder**, SE, p. 883: *countenance, officious, munificence, dowry, eludes, vestige, sublime, minions* **Latin Suffix** *-ence*, SE, p. 895; *URS*, p. 30
PART 2 FOCUS ON THE NOVEL	from Hard Times (A), Charles Dickens, SE, p. 904; from Jane Eyre (MA), Charlotte Brontë, SE, p. 911	**Recognizing the Writer's Purpose**, SE, p. 903; *URS*, p. 46; **Reading Warm-ups A and B**, *URS*, pp. 43–44; **Reading Strategy Graphic Organizers A and B**, *GOT*, pp. 173–174	**The Novel and Social Criticism**, SE, p. 903; *URS*, p. 45; **Literary Analysis Graphic Organizers A and B**, *GOT*, pp. 175–176	**Vocabulary Builder**, SE, p. 903: *monotonous, obstinate, adversary, indignant, approbation, obscure, comprised, sundry* **Greek Prefix:** *mono-*, SE, p. 920; *URS*, p. 47
PART 3	"Dover Beach" (A), Matthew Arnold, SE, p. 930; "Recessional" (A), Rudyard Kipling, SE, p. 932; "The Widow at Windsor" (MC), Rudyard Kipling, SE, p. 935	**Drawing Conclusions**, SE, p. 929; *URS*, p. 63; **Reading Warm-ups A and B**, *URS*, pp. 60–61; **Reading Strategy Graphic Organizers A and B**, *GOT*, pp. 177–178	**Mood as a Key to Theme**, SE, p. 929; *URS*, p. 62; **Literary Analysis Graphic Organizers A and B**, *GOT*, pp. 179–180	**Vocabulary Builder**, SE, p. 929: *tranquil, cadence, turbid, dominion, contrite* **Latin Root:** *-domi-*, SE, p. 938; *URS*, p. 64
	"Condition of Ireland" (A), *The Illustrated London News*, SE, p. 950; "Progress in Personal Comfort" (MA), Sydney Smith, SE, p. 954	**Distinguishing Emotive and Informative Language**, SE, p. 949; *URS*, p. 82; **Reading Warm-ups A and B**, *URS*, pp. 79–80; **Reading Strategy Graphic Organizers A and B**, *GOT*, pp. 181–182	**Journalistic Essay**, SE, p. 949; *URS*, p. 81; **Literary Analysis Graphic Organizers A and B**, *GOT*, pp. 183–184	**Vocabulary Builder**, SE, p. 949: *requisites, sanction, exonerate, melancholy, indolence, depredation* **"Humor" Words**, SE, p. 958; *URS*, p. 83
PART 4	"Remembrance" (A), Emily Brontë, SE, p. 968; "The Darkling Thrush" (MA), Thomas Hardy, SE, p. 971; "Ah, Are You Digging on My Grave?" (MA), Thomas Hardy, SE, p. 973	**Reading Stanzas as Units of Meaning**, SE, p. 967; *URS*, p. 99; **Reading Warm-ups A and B**, *URS*, pp. 96–97; **Reading Strategy Graphic Organizers A and B**, *GOT*, pp. 185–186	**Stanza Structure and Irony**, SE, p. 967; *URS*, p. 98; **Literary Analysis Graphic Organizers A and B**, *GOT*, pp. 187–188	**Vocabulary Builder**, SE, p. 967: *languish, rapturous, gaunt, terrestrial* **Latin Root** *-terr(a)-*, SE, p. 976; *URS*, p. 100
	"God's Grandeur" (A), Gerard Manley Hopkins, SE, p. 980; "Spring and Fall: To a Young Child" (A), Gerard Manley Hopkins, SE, p. 982; "To an Athlete Dying Young" (MA), A.E. Housman, SE, p. 983; "When I Was One-and-Twenty" (MA), A.E. Housman, SE, p. 984	**Applying Biography**, SE p. 979; *URS*, p. 116; **Reading Warm-ups A and B**, *URS*, pp. 113–114; **Reading Strategy Graphic Organizers A and B**, *GOT*, pp. 189–190	**Rhythm and Meter**, SE, p. 979; *URS*, p. 115; **Literary Analysis Graphic Organizers A and B**, *GOT*, pp. 191–192	**Vocabulary Builder**, SE, p. 979: *grandeur, blight, rue* **Coined Words**, SE, p. 986; *URS*, p. 117

SE: Student Edition **UR:** Unit Resources **GOT:** Graphic Organizer Transparencies **GR:** General Resources **WG:** Writing and Grammar
MA: More accessible **A:** Average **MC:** More Challenging. See Accessibility at a Glance chart on selection pages.

Grammar	Writing	Extend Your Learning	Assessment
Parallel Structure, SE, p. 880; *URS*, p. 14; *WG* Ch. 20, Section 6	**Writing Lesson:** Biographical Essay, SE, p. 881; *URS*, p. 15; *WG* Ch. 10, Section 3	**Listening and Speaking:** Videotaped News Report, SE, p. 881; *URS*, p. 16 **Research and Technology:** Sketches of a Set, SE, p. 881	**Diagnostic Test 9**, *URS*, pp. 2–4; **Selection Tests A and B**, *URS*, pp. 18–23; **Rubrics for Exposition:** Cause-and-Effect Essay, *GR*, pp. 55–56; **Rubric for Listening: Evaluation of the News**, *GR*, p. 86
Usage: *like* and *as*, SE, p. 895; *URS*, p. 31; *WG* Ch. 25, Section 2	**Writing Lesson:** Written Recommendation About the Duke's Proposal, SE, p. 896; *URS*, p. 32; *WG* Ch. 11, Section 4	**Listening and Speaking:** Oral Interpretation, SE, p. 896; *URS*, p. 33 **Research and Technology:** Guided Tour, SE, p. 896	**Selection Tests A and B**, *URS*, pp. 35–40; **Rubrics for Persuasion: Persuasive Essay**, *GR*, pp. 45–46; **Rubric for Peer Assessment: Oral Interpretation**, *GR*, p. 130
Punctuation of Dialogue, SE, p. 920; *URS*, p. 48; *WG* Ch. 27, Section 4	**Writing Lesson:** Annotated Bibliography on Victorian Education, SE, p. 921; *URS*, p. 49; *WG* Ch. 31, Section 2	**Listening and Speaking:** Debate, SE, p. 921; *URS*, p. 50 **Research and Technology:** Biography of Charles Dickens's Childhood, SE, p. 921	**Selection Tests A and B**, *URS*, pp. 52–57; **Rubrics for Research: Research Report**, *GR*, pp. 51–52; **Rubric for Speaking: Delivering a Research Presentation**, *GR*, p. 92
Present Tense, SE, p. 938; *URS*, p. 65; *WG* Ch. 21, Section 1	**Writing Lesson:** Timed Writing: Response to Criticism, SE, p. 939; *URS*, p. 66; *WG* Ch. 14, Section 2	**Listening and Speaking:** Oral Interpretation, SE, p. 939; *URS*, p. 67 **Research and Technology:** Film Review, SE, p. 939	**Selection Tests A and B**, *URS*, pp. 71–76; **Rubrics for Response to Literature**, *GR*, pp. 65–66; **Rubric for Listening: Analysis of the News**, *GR*, p. 86
Coordinating Conjunctions, SE, p. 958; *URS*, p. 84; *WG* Ch. 17, Section 4	**Writing Lesson:** Timed Writing: Comparison and Contrast of Viewpoints, SE, p. 959; *URS*, p. 85; *WG* Ch. 9, Section 2	**Listening and Speaking:** Comic Monologue, SE, p. 959; *URS*, p. 86 **Research and Technology:** Report, SE, p. 959	**Selection Tests A and B**, *URS*, pp. 88–93; **Rubrics for Exposition: Comparison-and-Contrast Essay**, *GR*, pp. 69–70; **Rubric for Peer Assessment: Dramatic Performance**, *GR*, p. 131
Pronoun Case Following *Than* or *As*, SE, p. 976; *URS*, p. 101; *WG* Ch. 22, Section 1	**Writing Lesson:** Comparative Analysis of Literary Sources, SE, p. 977; *URS*, p. 102; *WG* Ch. 31, Section 2	**Research and Technology:** Biography, SE, p. 977; *URS*, p. 103 **Listening and Speaking:** Dramatic Reading, SE, p. 977	**Selection Tests A and B**, *URS*, pp. 105–110; **Rubrics for Exposition: Comparison-and-Contrast Essay**, *GR*, pp. 69–70; **Rubrics for Biographical Essay**, *GR*, pp. 77–78
Capitalization of Compass Points, SE, p. 986; *URS*, p. 118; *WG* Ch. 26	**Writing Lesson:** Timed Writing: Analytical Essay, SE, p. 987; *URS*, p. 119; *WG* Ch. 14, Section 4	**Listening and Speaking:** Victorian Poetry Contest, SE, p. 987; *URS*, p. 120 **Research and Technology:** Multimedia Presentation, SE, p. 987	**Selection Tests A and B**, *URS*, pp. 122–127; **Rubrics for Response to Literature**, *GR*, pp. 65–66; **Rubric for Peer Assessment: Oral Interpretation**, *GR*, p. 130; **Benchmark Test 9**, *URS*, pp. 135–140

All selections are supported in the Reader's Notebooks.

UNIT 6 — A Time of Rapid Change (1901–Present)

	Selection	Reading Strategy	Literary Analysis	Vocabulary
PART 1	**"When You Are Old"** (MA), William Butler Yeats, SE, p. 1024; **"The Lake Isle of Innisfree"** (MA), William Butler Yeats, SE, p. 1026; **"The Wild Swans at Coole"** (MA), William Butler Yeats, SE, p. 1027; **"The Second Coming"** (A), William Butler Yeats, SE, p. 1029; **"Sailing to Byzantium"** (MC), William Butler Yeats, SE, p. 1031	**Applying Literary Background**, SE, p. 1023; *UR6*, p. 12; **Reading Warm-ups A and B**, *UR6*, pp. 9–10; **Reading Strategy Graphic Organizers A and B**, *GOT*, pp. 194–195	**Symbolism**, SE, pp. 1023; *UR6*, p. 11; **Literary Analysis Graphic Organizers A and B**, *GOT*, pp. 196–197	**Vocabulary Builder**, SE, p. 1023: *clamorous, conquest, anarchy, conviction, paltry, artifice* **Latin Root:** *-ques-*, SE, p. 1034; *UR6*, p. 13
	"Preludes" (A), T.S. Eliot, SE, p. 1040; **"Journey of the Magi"** (MA), T.S. Eliot, SE, p. 1042; **"The Hollow Men"** (MC), T.S. Eliot, SE, p. 1047	**Interpreting**, SE, p. 1039; *UR6*, p. 29; **Reading Warm-ups A and B**, *UR6*, pp. 26–27; **Reading Strategy Graphic Organizers A and B**, *GOT*, pp. 198–199	**Modernism**, SE, p. 1039; *UR6*, p. 28; **Literary Analysis Graphic Organizers A and B**, *GOT*, pp. 200–201	**Vocabulary Builder**, SE, p. 1039: *galled, refractory, dispensation, supplication, tumid* **Latin Root:** *-fract-*, SE, p. 1052; *UR6*, p. 30
	"In Memory of W. B. Yeats" (A), W.H. Auden, SE, p. 1056; **"Musée des Beaux Arts"** (A), W. H. Auden, SE, p. 1060; **"Carrick Revisited"** (MC), Louis MacNiece, SE, p. 1062; **"Not Palaces"** (MC), Stephen Spender, SE, p. 1065	**Paraphrasing**, SE, p. 1055; *UR6*, p. 46; **Reading Warm-ups A and B**, *UR6*, pp. 43–44; **Reading Strategy Graphic Organizers A and B**, *GOT*, pp. 202–203	**Theme**, SE, p. 1055; *UR6*, p. 45; **Literary Analysis Graphic Organizers A and B**, *GOT*, pp. 204–205	**Vocabulary Builder**, SE, p. 1055: *sequestered, topographical, affinities, prenatal, intrigues* **Greek Root:** *-top-*, SE, p. 1068; *UR6*, p. 47
	"Shooting an Elephant" (A), George Orwell, SE, p. 1076	**Recognizing the Writer's Attitude**, SE, p. 1075; *UR6*, p. 63; **Reading Warm-ups A and B**, *UR6*, pp. 60–61; **Reading Strategy Graphic Organizers A and B**, *GOT*, pp. 206–207	**Irony**, SE, p. 1075; *UR6*, p. 62; **Literary Analysis Graphic Organizers A and B**, *GOT*, pp. 208–209	**Vocabulary Builder**, SE, p. 1075: *prostrate, imperialism, despotic, squalid, dominion, senility* **Words About Politics**, SE, p. 1086; *UR6*, p. 64
	"The Demon Lover" (A), Elizabeth Bowen, SE, p. 1090	**Responding to the Story**, SE, p. 1089; *UR6*, p. 80; **Reading Warm-ups A and B**, *UR6*, pp. 77–78; **Reading Strategy Graphic Organizers A and B**, *GOT*, pp. 212–213	**The Ghost Story**, SE, p. 1089; *UR6*, p. 79; **Literary Analysis Graphic Organizers A and B**, *GOT*, pp. 210–211	**Vocabulary Builder**, SE, p. 1089: *spectral, dislocation, arboreal, circumscribed, aperture* **Latin Root:** *-loc-*, SE, p. 1099; *UR6*, p. 81
PART 3	**"The Soldier"** (MA), Rupert Brooke, SE, p. 1104; **"Wirers"** (MA), Siegfried Sassoon, SE, p. 1106; **"Anthem for Doomed Youth"** (A), Wilfred Owen, SE, p. 1107; **"Birds on the Western Front"** (A), Saki, SE, p. 1108	**Making Inferences**, SE, p. 1103; *UR6*, p. 106; **Reading Warm-ups A and B**, *UR6*, pp. 103–104; **Reading Strategy Graphic Organizers A and B**, *GOT*, pp. 214–215	**Tone**, SE, p. 1103; *UR6*, p. 105; **Literary Analysis Graphic Organizers A and B**, *GOT*, pp. 216–217	**Vocabulary Builder**, SE, p. 1103: *stealthy, desolate, mockeries, pallor, laudable, requisitioned, disconcerted* **Latin Root:** *-laud-*, SE, p. 1114; *UR6*, p. 107
	"Wartime Speech" (MC), Sir Winston Churchill, SE, p. 1118; **"Defending Nonviolent Resistance"** (A), Mohandas K. Gandhi, SE, p. 1122	**Identifying Main Points and Support**, SE, p. 1117; *UR6*, p. 123; **Reading Warm-ups A and B**, *UR6*, pp. 120–121; **Reading Strategy Graphic Organizers A and B**, *GOT*, pp. 218–219	**Speech**, SE, p. 1117; *UR6*, p. 122; **Literary Analysis Graphic Organizers A and B**, *GOT*, pp. 220–221	**Vocabulary Builder**, SE, p. 1117: *intimidated, endurance, formidable, invincible, retaliate, disaffection, diabolical, extenuating, excrescence* **Latin Root:** *-dur-*, SE, p. 1128; *UR6*, p. 124

Key to Program References:
SE: Student Edition **UR:** Unit Resources **GOT:** Graphic Organizer Transparencies **GR:** General Resources **WG:** Writing and Grammar
MA: More accessible **A:** Average **MC:** More Challenging. See Accessibility at a Glance chart on selection pages.

Grammar	Writing	Extend Your Learning	Assessment
Noun Clauses, SE, p. 1034; *UR6,* p. 14; *WG* Ch. 19, Section 3	**Writing Lesson:** Timed Writing: Response to Criticism, SE, p. 1035; *UR6,* p. 15; *WG* Ch. 14, Section 4	**Listening and Speaking:** Oral Interpretation, SE, p. 1035; *UR6,* p. 16 **Research and Technology:** Visual Display, SE, p. 1035	**Diagnostic Test 10,** *UR6,* pp. 2–4; **Selection Tests A and B,** *UR6,* pp. 18–23; **Rubrics for Self-Assessment: Critique,** *GR,* pp. 75–76; **Rubric for Peer Assessment: Oral Interpretation,** *GR,* p. 130
Adjectival Modifiers, SE, p. 1052; *UR6,* p. 31; *WG* Ch. 19, Sections 1-3	**Writing Lesson:** Timed Writing: Response to Criticism, SE, p. 1053; *UR6,* p. 32; *WG* Ch. 14, Section 4	**Listening and Speaking:** Debate on Modernism, SE, p. 1053; *UR6,* p. 33 **Research and Technology:** Cultural Report, SE, p. 1053;	**Selection Tests A and B,** *UR6,* pp. 35–40; **Rubrics for Critique,** *GR,* pp. 75–76; **Rubric for Listening: Evaluating Persuasive Techniques,** *GR,* p. 83
Parallel Structure, SE, p. 1068; *UR6,* p. 48; *WG* Ch. 20, Section 6	**Writing Lesson:** Poem About an Artwork, SE, p. 1069; *UR6,* p. 49; *WG* Ch. 6, Section 4	**Listening and Speaking:** Group Reading, SE, p. 1069; *UR6,* p. 50 **Research and Technology:** Art Exhibition, SE, p. 1069	**Selection Tests A and B,** *UR6,* pp. 52–57; **Rubrics for Poem (Rhyming),** *GR,* pp. 73–74; **Rubric for Peer Assessment: Dramatic Performance,** *GR,* p. 131
Participial Phrases: Restrictive and Nonrestrictive, SE, p. 1086; *UR6,* p. 65; *WG* Ch. 19, Section 2	**Writing Lesson:** Essay in Orwell's Style, SE, p. 1087; *UR6,* p. 66; *WG* Ch. 4, Section 4	**Listening and Speaking:** Audiovisual Presentation, SE, p. 1087 **Research and Technology:** Biography, SE, p. 1087; *UR6,* p. 67	**Selection Tests A and B,** *UR6,* pp. 69–74; **Rubrics for Narration: Autobiographical Narrative,** *GR,* pp. 43–44; **Rubrics for Biographical Essay,** *GR,* pp. 77–78
Sentence Beginnings: Participial Phrases, SE p. 1099; *UR6,* p. 82; *WG* Ch. 19, Section 2	**Writing Lesson:** Sequel, SE, p. 1100; *UR6,* p. 83; *WG* Ch. 5, Section 3	**Listening and Speaking:** Story Reading, SE, p. 1100; *UR6,* p. 84 **Research and Technology:** History Report, SE, p. 1100	**Selection Tests A and B,** *UR6,* pp. 86–91; **Rubrics for Narration,** *GR,* pp. 57–58; **Rubric for Speaking,** *GR,* pp. 88; **Benchmark Test 10,** *UR6,* pp. 92–97
Adjective Clauses with *Who* and *Whom,* SE, p. 1114; *UR6,* p. 108; *WG* Ch. 22, Section 2	**Writing Lesson:** Timed Writing: Critical Response, SE, p. 1115; *UR6,* p. 109; *WG* Ch. 14, Section 3	**Listening and Speaking:** Debate, SE, p. 1115 **Research and Technology:** Report, SE, p. 1115; *UR6,* p. 110	**Diagnostic Test 11,** *UR6,* pp. 98–100; **Selection Tests A and B,** *UR6,* pp. 112–117; **Rubrics for Response to Literature,** *GR,* pp. 65–66; **Rubric for Research: Research Report,** *GR,* pp. 51–52
Parallel Structure, SE, p. 1128; *UR6,* p. 125; *WG* Ch. 20, Section 6	**Writing Lesson:** Persuasive Speech, SE, p. 1129; *UR6,* p. 126; *WG* Ch. 7, Section 4	**Listening and Speaking:** Panel Discussion, SE, p. 1129 **Research and Technology:** Critique, SE, p. 1129; *UR6,* p. 127	**Selection Tests A and B,** *UR6,* pp. 129–134; **Rubrics for Persuasion: Persuasive Essay,** *GR,* pp. 45–46; **Rubrics for Self-Assessment:** Critique, *GR,* pp. 75–76

All selections are supported in the Reader's Notebooks.

	Selection	Reading Strategy	Literary Analysis	Vocabulary
PART 2 *(continued)*	"**Follower**" (MA), Seamus Heaney, SE, p. 1132; "**Two Lorries**" (A), Seamus Heaney, SE, p. 1135; "**Outside History**" (A), Eavan Boland, SE, p. 1137	**Summarizing**, SE, p. 1131; *UR6*, p. 140; **Reading Warm-ups A and B**, *UR6*, pp. 137–138; **Reading Strategy Graphic Organizers A and B**, *GOT*, pp. 222–223	**Diction and Style**, SE, p. 1131; *UR6*, p. 139; **Literary Analysis Graphic Organizers A and B**, *GOT*, pp. 224–225	**Vocabulary Builder**, SE, p. 1131: *furrow, nuisance, inklings, mortal, ordeal* **Latin Root:** *-mort-*, SE, p. 1140; *UR6*, p. 141
	"**No Witchcraft for Sale**" (MA), Doris Lessing, SE, p. 1144	**Analyzing Cultural Differences**, SE, p. 1143; *UR6*, p. 157; **Reading Warm-ups A and B**, *UR6*, pp. 154–155; **Reading Strategy Graphic Organizers A and B**, *GOT*, pp. 226–227	**Cultural Conflict**, SE, p. 1143; *UR6*, p. 156; **Literary Analysis Graphic Organizers A and B**, *GOT*, pp. 228–229	**Vocabulary Builder**, SE, p. 1143: *reverently, defiantly, efficacy, incredulously, skeptical* **Forms of** *skeptical*, SE, p. 1153; *UR6*, p. 158
PART 3 — **FOCUS ON SHORT STORY**	"**The Lagoon**" (MC), Joseph Conrad, SE, p. 1160; "**Araby**" (A), James Joyce, SE, p. 1173	**Picturing the Action and Situation**, SE, p. 1159; *UR6*, p. 174; **Reading Warm-ups A and B**, *UR6*, pp. 171–172; **Reading Strategy Graphic Organizers A and B**, *GOT*, pp. 230–231	**Plot Devices**, SE, p. 1159; *UR6*, p. 173; **Literary Analysis Graphic Organizers A and B**, *GOT*, pp. 232–233	**Vocabulary Builder**, SE, p. 1159: *portals, invincible, propitiate, conflagration, august, imperturbable, litanies, garrulous, derided* **Latin Root:** *-vinc-*, SE, p. 1180; *UR6*, p. 175
	"**The Lady in the Looking Glass: A Reflection**" (MC), Virginia Woolf, SE, p. 1184; "**The First Year of My Life**" (A), Muriel Spark, SE, p. 1190	**Questioning**, SE, p. 1183; *UR6*, p. 191; **Reading Warm-ups A and B**, *UR6*, pp. 188–189; **Reading Strategy Graphic Organizers A and B**, *GOT*, pp. 234–235	**Point of View: Modern Experiments**, SE, p. 1183; *UR6*, p. 190; **Literary Analysis Graphic Organizers A and B**, *GOT*, pp. 236–237	**Vocabulary Builder**, SE, p. 1183: *suffused, transient, upbraidings, evanescence, reticent, omniscient, authenticity, discerned* **Latin Prefix:** *-trans-*, SE, p. 1198; *UR6*, p. 192
	"**The Rocking-Horse Winner**" (A), D.H. Lawrence, SE, p. 1202; "**A Shocking Accident**" (A), Graham Greene, SE, p. 1216	**Identifying With a Character**, SE, p. 1021; *UR6*, p. 208; **Reading Warm-ups A and B**, *UR6*, pp. 205–206; **Reading Strategy Graphic Organizers A and B**, *GOT*, pp. 238–239	**Theme and Symbol**, SE, p. 1201; *UR6*, p. 207; **Literary Analysis Graphic Organizers A and B**, *GOT*, pp. 240–241	**Vocabulary Builder**, SE, p. 1021: *discreet, brazening, careered, obstinately, uncanny, remonstrated, apprehension, embarked, intrinsically* **Latin Prefix:** *ob-*, SE, p. 1222; *UR6*, p. 209
PART 4	"**Do Not Go Gentle Into That Good Night**" (A), Dylan Thomas, SE, p. 1232; "**Fern Hill**" (A), Dylan Thomas, SE, p. 1234; "**The Horses**" (A), Ted Hughes, SE, p. 1236; "**The Rain Horse**" (MA), Ted Hughes, SE, p. 1239	**Judging the Writer's Message**, SE, p. 1231; *UR6*, p. 234; **Reading Warm-ups A and B**, *UR6*, pp. 231–232; **Reading Strategy Graphic Organizers A and B**, *GOT*, pp. 242–243	**Voice**, SE, p. 1231; *UR6*, p. 233; **Literary Analysis Graphic Organizers A and B**, *GOT*, pp. 244–245	**Vocabulary Builder**, SE, p. 1231: *grieved, transfiguring, exasperated, nondescript, malevolent* **Latin Root:** *-vol-*, SE, p. 1248; *UR6*, p. 235
	"**An Arundel Tomb**" (MC), Philip Larkin, SE, p. 1252; "**The Explosion**" (A), Philip Larkin, SE, p. 1254; "**On the Patio**" (A), Peter Redgrove, SE, p. 1256; "**Not Waving but Drowning**" (MA), Stevie Smith, SE, p. 1258	**Reading in Sentences**, SE, p. 1251; *UR6*, p. 251; **Reading Warm-ups A and B**, *UR6*, pp. 248–249; **Reading Strategy Graphic Organizers A and B**, *GOT*, pp. 246–247	**Free Verse and Meter**, SE, p. 1251; *UR6*, p. 250; **Literary Analysis Graphic Organizers A and B**, *GOT*, pp. 248–249	**Vocabulary Builder**, SE, p. 1251: *effigy, supine, fidelity, larking* **Latin Root:** *-fid-*, SE, p. 1260; *UR6*, p. 252

Key to Program References:
SE: Student Edition **UR:** Unit Resources **GOT:** Graphic Organizer Transparencies **GR:** General Resources **WG:** Writing and Grammar
MA: More accessible **A:** Average **MC:** More Challenging. See Accessibility at a Glance chart on selection pages.

Skills Navigator

Grammar	Writing	Extend Your Learning	Assessment
Concrete and Abstract Nouns, SE, p. 1140; *UR6*, p. 142; *WG* Ch. 17, Section 1	**Writing Lesson:** Poem With a Strong Central Image, SE, p. 1141; *UR6*, p. 143; *WG* Ch. 6, Connected Assignment	**Listening and Speaking:** Interpretive Reading, SE, p. 1141; *UR6*, p. 144 **Research and Technology:** Conflict Report, SE, p. 1141	**Selection Tests A and B,** *UR6*, pp. 146–151; **Rubrics for Poem (Rhyming),** *GR*, pp. 73–74; **Rubric for Peer Assessment: Dramatic Performance,** *GR*, p. 131
Correct Use of *like* and *as*, SE, p. 1153; *UR6*, p. 159; *WG* Ch. 25, Section 2	**Writing Lesson:** Timed Writing: Problem-and-Solution Essay, SE, p. 1154; *UR6*, p. 160; *WG* Ch. 11, Section 3	**Listening and Speaking:** Debate on Colonialism, SE, p. 1154 **Research and Technology:** Oral Report on Medical Botany, SE, p. 1154; *UR6*, p. 161	**Selection Tests A and B,** *UR6*, pp. 163–168; **Rubrics for Exposition: Problem-and-Solution Essay,** *GR*, pp. 59–60; **Rubrics for Research:** Research Report, *GR*, pp. 51–52
Adverb Clause, SE, p. 1180; *UR6*, p. 176; *WG* Ch. 19, Section 3	**Writing Lesson:** Timed Writing: Literary Essay, SE, p. 1181; *UR6*, p. 177; *WG* Ch. 14, Section 4	**Listening and Speaking:** Literary Trial, SE, p. 1181; *UR6*, p. 178 **Research and Technology:** Research Presentation, SE, p. 1181	**Selection Tests A and B,** *UR6*, pp. 180–185; **Rubrics for Response to Literature,** *GR*, pp. 65–66; **Rubric for Listening:** Analyzing Persuasive Techniques, *GR*, p. 83
Subject-Verb Agreement in Inverted Sentences, SE, p. 1198; *UR6*, p. 193; *WG* Ch. 20, Section 3	**Writing Lesson:** Timed Writing: Essay on a Literary Theme, SE, p. 1199; *UR6*, p. 194; *WG* Ch. 14, Section 2	**Listening and Speaking:** Discussion Group, SE, p. 1199 **Research and Technology:** Report on Cultural Trends, SE, p. 1199; *UR6*, p. 195	**Selection Tests A and B,** *UR6*, pp. 197–202; **Rubrics for Response to Literature,** *GR*, pp. 65–66; **Rubrics for Research: Research Report,** *GR*, pp. 51–52
Subjunctive Mood, SE, p. 1222; *UR6*, p. 210; *WG* Ch. 21, Section 3	**Writing Lesson:** Product Description, SE, p. 1223; *UR6*, p. 211; *WG* Ch. 8, Section 2	**Listening and Speaking:** Soliloquy, SE, p. 1223; *UR6*, p. 212 **Research and Technology:** Multimedia Travelogue, SE, p. 1223	**Selection Tests A and B,** *UR6*, pp. 214–219; **Rubrics for Descriptive Essay,** *GR*, pp. 63–64; **Rubric for Peer Assessment: Dramatic Performance,** *GR*, p. 131; **Benchmark Test 11,** *UR6*, pp. 220–225
Sentence Beginnings: Adverb Clauses, SE, p. 1248; *UR6*, p. 236; *WG* Ch. 19, Section 3	**Writing Lesson:** Parody of a Poet's Voice, SE, p. 1249; *UR6*, p. 237; *WG* Ch. 14, Section 2	**Listening and Speaking:** Oral Interpretations, SE, p. 1249; *UR6*, p. 238 **Research and Technology:** Panel Presentation, SE, p. 1249	**Diagnostic Test 12,** *UR6*, pp. 226–228; **Selection Tests A and B,** *UR6*, pp. 240–245; **Rubrics for Poem (Rhyming),** *GR*, pp. 73–74; **Rubric for Peer Assessment: Oral Interpretation,** *GR*, p. 130
Sequence of Tenses, SE, p. 1260; *UR6*, p. 253; *WG* Ch. 21, Section 2	**Writing Lesson:** Timed Writing: Reflective Essay, SE, p. 1261; *UR6*, p. 254; *WG* Ch. 6, Section 3	**Listening and Speaking:** Eulogy, SE, p. 1261; *UR6*, p. 255 **Research and Technology:** Slide Show, SE, p. 1261	**Selection Tests A and B,** *UR6*, pp. 257–262; **Rubrics for Reflective Essay,** *GR*, pp. 47–48; **Rubric for Peer Assessment: Speech,** *GR*, p. 129

All selections are supported in the Reader's Notebooks.

PART 4 *(continued)*

Selection	Reading Strategy	Literary Analysis	Vocabulary
"B. Wordsworth" (A), V. S. Naipaul, SE, p. 1264	**Responding to Characters**, SE, p. 1263; *UR6*, p. 268; **Reading Warm-ups A and B**, *UR6*, pp. 265–266; **Reading Strategy Graphic Organizers A and B**, *GOT*, pp. 250–251	**First-Person Narrator**, SE, p. 1263; *UR6*, p. 267; **Literary Analysis Graphic Organizers A and B**, *GOT*, pp. 252–253	**Vocabulary Builder**, SE, p. 1263: *rogue, patronize, distill, keenly* **Forms of *patron***, SE, p. 1272; *UR6*, p. 269
"The Train from Rhodesia" (MA), Nadine Gordimer, SE, p. 1276	**Reading Between the Lines**, SE, p. 1275; *UR6*, p. 285; **Reading Warm-ups A and B**, *UR6*, pp. 282–283; **Reading Strategy Graphic Organizers A and B**, *GOT*, pp. 254–255	**Conflict and Theme**, SE, p. 1275; *UR6*, p. 284; **Literary Analysis Graphic Organizers A and B**, *GOT*, pp. 256–257	**Vocabulary Builder**, SE, p. 1275: *impressionistic, elongated, segmented, splaying, atrophy* **Greek Prefix:** *a-*, SE, p. 1282; *UR6*, p. 286
from "Midsummer, XXIII" (MC), Derek Walcott, SE, p. 1286; from "Omeros" from Chapter XXVIII (MC), Derek Walcott, SE, p. 1288	**Applying Background Information**, SE, p. 1285; *UR6*, p. 302; **Reading Warm-ups A and B**, *UR6*, pp. 299–300; **Reading Strategy Graphic Organizers A and B**, *GOT*, pp. 258–259	**Theme and Context**, SE, p. 1285; *UR6*, p. 301; **Literary Analysis Graphic Organizers A and B**, *GOT*, pp. 260–261	**Vocabulary Builder**, SE, p. 1285: *antic, rancor, eclipse, inducted* **Latin Root:** *-duc-*, SE, p. 1292; *UR6*, p. 303
"A Devoted Son" (A), Anita Desai, SE, p. 1298	**Evaluating Characters' Decisions**, SE, p. 1297; *UR6*, p. 321; **Reading Warm-ups A and B**, *UR6*, pp. 318–319; **Reading Strategy Graphic Organizers A and B**, *GOT*, pp. 262–263	**Static and Dynamic Characters**, SE, p. 1297; *UR6*, p. 320; **Literary Analysis Graphic Organizers A and B**, *GOT*, pp. 264–265	**Vocabulary Builder**, SE, p. 1297: *exemplary, filial, encomiums, complaisant, fathom* **Latin Root:** *-fil-*, SE, p. 1310; *UR6*, p. 322
from "We'll Never Conquer Space" (A), Arthur C. Clarke, SE, p. 1314	**Challenging the Text**, SE, p. 1313; *UR6*, p. 338; **Reading Warm-ups A and B**, *UR6*, pp. 335–336; **Reading Strategy Graphic Organizers A and B**, *GOT*, pp. 266–267	**Prophetic Essay**, SE, p. 1313; *UR6*, p. 337; **Literary Analysis Graphic Organizers A and B**, *GOT*, pp. 268–269	**Vocabulary Builder**, SE, p. 1313: *ludicrous, irrevocable, instantaneous, enigma, inevitable, zenith* **Latin Suffixes:** *-ible* and *-able*, SE, p. 1322; *UR6*, p. 339

Key to Program References:
SE: Student Edition **UR:** Unit Resources, **GOT:** Graphic Organizer Transparencies, **GR:** General Resources, **WG:** Writing and Grammar, **MA:** More accessible **A:** Average **MC:** More Challenging. See Accessibility at a Glance chart on selection pages.

Grammar	Writing	Extend Your Learning	Assessment
Pronoun Case in Compound Constructions, SE, p. 1272; *UR6*, p. 270; *WG* Ch. 22, Section 1	**Writing Lesson:** Account of a Remarkable Person, SE, p. 1273; *UR6*, p. 271; *WG* Ch. 6, Section 2	**Listening and Speaking:** Multimedia Tour, SE, p. 1273; *UR6*, p. 272 **Research and Technology:** Classroom Exhibit, SE, p. 1273	**Selection Tests A and B,** *UR6*, pp. 274–279; **Rubrics for Biographical Essay**, *GR*, pp. 77–78; **Rubrics for Multimedia Report**, *GR*, pp. 53–54
Nominative Absolutes, SE, p. 1282; *UR6*, p. 287; *WG* Ch. 19, Section 2	**Writing Lesson:** Timed Writing: Analysis of Storytelling Technique, SE, p. 1283; *UR6*, p. 288; *WG* Ch. 14, Section 3	**Listening and Speaking:** Debate, SE, p. 1283; *UR6*, p. 289 **Research and Technology:** Historical Report, SE, p. 1283	**Selection Tests A and B,** *UR6*, pp. 291–296; **Rubrics for Response to Literature**, *GR*, pp. 65–66; **Rubric for Listening: Analyzing Persuasive Techniques**, *GR*, p. 83
Commonly Confused Words: *affect* and *effect*, SE, p. 1292; *UR6*, p. 304; *WG* Ch. 25, Section 2	**Writing Lesson:** Script for the Multimedia Presentation of a Poem, SE, p. 1293; *UR6*, p. 305; *WG* Ch. 28, Section 3	**Listening and Speaking:** Recitation, SE, p. 1293; *UR6*, p. 306 **Research and Technology:** Caribbean Culture Festival, SE, p. 1293	**Selection Tests A and B,** *UR6*, pp. 308–313; **Rubrics for Multimedia Report**, *GR*, pp. 53–54; **Rubric for Peer Assessment: Oral Interpretation**, *GR*, p. 130
Sentence Variety, SE, p. 1310; *UR6*, p. 323; *WG* Ch. 19, Section 4	**Writing Lesson:** Proposal for a Program for the Elderly, SE, p. 1311; *UR6*, p. 324; *WG* Ch. 7, Section 4	**Listening and Speaking:** Role Play, SE, p. 1311; *UR6*, p. 325 **Research and Technology:** Social Services Report, SE, p. 1311	**Selection Tests A and B,** *UR6*, pp. 327–332; **Rubrics for Problem-and-Solution Essay**, *GR*, pp. 59–60; **Rubric for Peer Assessment: Dramatic Performance**, *GR*, p. 131
Linking Verbs and Subject Complements, SE, p. 1322; *UR6*, p. 340; *WG* Ch. 18, Section 3	**Writing Lesson:** Timed Writing: Analysis of an Argument, SE, p. 1323; *UR6*, p. 341; *WG* Ch. 14, Section 4	**Listening and Speaking:** Panel Discussion, SE, p. 1323; *UR6*, p. 342 **Research and Technology:** Museum Exhibit, SE, p. 1323	**Selection Tests A and B,** *UR6*, pp. 344–349; **Rubrics for Response to Literature**, *GR*, pp. 65–66; **Rubric for Speaking: Delivering a Research Presentation**, *GR*, p. 92; **Benchmark Test 12**, *UR6*, pp. 357–362

All Selections are supported in the Reader's Notebooks.

Language Arts Standards-at-a-Glance

This chart provides an overview of where you'll find the general Language Arts standards addressed in *Prentice Hall Literature: The Penguin Edition*. Prentice Hall developed this list of standards based on a review of state standards across the country. For more detailed information regarding skills coverage, see the **Skills Navigator**, beginning on page T52, which provides an overview of the skills by selection. The **Time and Resource Managers** show the skills for each selection or selection group.

Standard Course of Study for Language Arts

	UNIT 1				UNIT 2			UNIT 3				UNIT 4			UNIT 5				UNIT 6			
PART	1	2	3	4	1	2	3	1	2	3	4	1	2	3	1	2	3	4	1	2	3	4

Reading—Reflection and Response: Students will reflect upon and respond to print and non-print text.

	1	2	3	4	1	2	3	1	2	3	4	1	2	3	1	2	3	4	1	2	3	4
Compose texts that reflect complex thoughts and feelings.		●			●						●					●			●			●
Compose reflective texts that give a sense of socio-political implications.	●				●	●	●			●	●						●		●	●		
Compose texts that encourage self-reflection among audiences.								●		●		●	●	●					●			●
Give written responses that elicit audience empathy with text.						●	●						●									●
Give written responses that encourage audiences to connect with text.		●																			●	
Give written responses that encourage audiences to consider cultural/historical influences on text.		●	●						●				●		●				●		●	
Give written responses that encourage audiences to compare their responses to their peers'.		●				●																
Give written responses that encourage audiences to relate textual features to their own writing.		●			●			●		●		●			●	●						●
Select and modify reading strategies when reading complex texts.		●				●	●	●		●	●	●										
Analyze text components and evaluate their impact on text.		●						●	●	●					●		●		●			●
Support understanding of complex texts by providing textual evidence.					●				●		●	●				●						
Show understanding of main idea and supporting details.	●				●		●								●				●	●		
Summarize key textual events.	●	●	●		●				●				●						●	●		
Infer, predict, and draw conclusions based on text.			●							●		●	●		●		●		●	●		
Identify and analyze influences, contexts, or biases.	●	●	●		●	●	●		●	●		●							●			●
Connect works to self and related topics.	●							●		●			●									

● *Supports standard mastery*

Standard Course of Study for Language Arts

Standard	U1·1	U1·2	U1·3	U1·4	U2·1	U2·2	U2·3	U2·4	U3·1	U3·2	U3·3	U3·4	U4·1	U4·2	U4·3	U4·4	U5·1	U5·2	U5·3	U5·4	U6·1	U6·2	U6·3	U6·4
Analyze and evaluate the effects of the author's style.					●					●	●	●	●	●								●	●	●
Analyze and evaluate connections among concepts, characters, and experiences.	●	●	●	●			●						●	●	●	●		●						●
Identify and analyze elements of environment found in text.		●	●				●		●	●	●		●					●	●		●			●

Research/Analysis: Students will conduct research and analyze text in order to inform an audience.

Standard	U1·1	U1·2	U1·3	U1·4	U2·1	U2·2	U2·3	U2·4	U3·1	U3·2	U3·3	U3·4	U4·1	U4·2	U4·3	U4·4	U5·1	U5·2	U5·3	U5·4	U6·1	U6·2	U6·3	U6·4
Process texts that relate issues from various critical stances.	●		●	●	●	●		●	●		●						●							
Compare texts that propose different ideas about similar concepts.						●			●	●		●		●				●						
Define principles at work in personal experience and in literature.						●								●					●					
Predict future events on the basis of principles expressed in life and literature.										●				●				●						
Compose texts that explicate literary or life principles through research.				●	●																			
Present and support a thesis that considers alternative perspectives.			●						●					●										●
Compose texts that adjust tone and method of presentation to audience.																			●					
Select, monitor, and modify reading strategies appropriate to reader's purpose.							●						●	●	●		●							
Identify and analyze text components and evaluate their impact on text.			●			●					●	●		●	●		●	●				●		
Provide textual evidence to support reader's understanding of and response to text.			●				●										●					●		
Demonstrate comprehension of main idea and support in grade appropriate texts.							●														●	●		●
Summarize key events and points.						●																		
Infer, predict, and draw conclusions from text.		●				●	●	●					●											
Identify and analyze influences, contexts, and biases.	●		●			●	●				●													
Connect works, self, and related topics.																			●		●			
Analyze and evaluate effects of author's craft and style.																	●		●					
Analyze and evaluate relationships among concepts, characters, and experiences.			●		●	●	●		●													●	●	●

Standard Course of Study for Language Arts

	UNIT	1				2			3				4			5				6			
	PART	1	2	3	4	1	2	3	1	2	3	4	1	2	3	1	2	3	4	1	2	3	4
Identify and analyze informational elements in text in light of purpose and context.										●	●			●			●						
Critical Reading—Evaluation: Students will use critical thinking skills to analyze and evaluate text structures and develop and support arguments.																							
Use varied resources to research and define issues of public concern.								●									●						
Specify claims and support made for issues of public concern.							●										●						●
Word claim of an argument clearly in order to gain audience respect.							●																●
Specify convincing support when delivering an argumentative claim.							●	●									●						●
Use an appropriate tone and stance when delivering an argument.							●											●					
Monitor and modify reading strategies appropriate to readers' purpose.														●			●						
Identify and analyze text components and evaluate their impact on text.			●										●				●	●		●			
Provide textual evidence to support reader's understanding of and response to text.													●										
Demonstrate comprehension of main idea and support in grade appropriate texts.		●				●			●				●				●						
Summarize key events and points.		●				●			●							●					●		
Infer, predict, and draw conclusions from text.									●														
Identify and analyze influences, contexts, and biases.		●					●						●										
Connect works, self, and related topics.													●										
Analyze and evaluate effects of author's craft and style.																●		●					●
Analyze and evaluate relationships among concepts, characters, and experiences.			●				●										●						
Identify and analyze informational elements in text in light of purpose and context.													●										
Critical Reading—Analysis: Students will analyze text to gain meaning and synthesize ideas.																							
Establish and apply credible criteria enabling an audience to judge claims.		●					●							●						●			
Support assessments of claims with reasons and evidence.														●		●							

Standard Course of Study for Language Arts

	Unit 1				Unit 2			Unit 3				Unit 4			Unit 5				Unit 6			
PART	1	2	3	4	1	2	3	1	2	3	4	1	2	3	1	2	3	4	1	2	3	4
Develop critiques that show an audience how themes relate among texts.						●		●	●				●									
Develop critiques that show audiences how authors' assumptions, backgrounds, and values affect texts.					●							●										
Develop critiques that show an audience how more than one critical approach affects interpretation.										●			●			●						
Select, monitor, and modify reading strategies appropriate to reader's purpose.	●			●		●			●				●								●	
Identify and analyze text components and evaluate their impact on text.																	●					●
Provide textual evidence to support reader's understanding of and response to text.								●	●													
Demonstrate comprehension of main idea and support in grade appropriate texts.																				●	●	
Summarize key events and points.																						●
Infer, predict, and draw conclusions from text.													●									
Identify and analyze influences, contexts, and biases.			●		●																	
Connect works, self, and related topics.		●															●					●
Analyze and evaluate effects of author's craft and style.													●						●		●	●
Analyze and evaluate relationships among concepts, characters, and experiences.										●							●			●	●	●
Identify and analyze informational elements in text in light of purpose and context.							●			●						●			●		●	●

Literary Analysis: Students will analyze and interpret British Literature.

	Unit 1				Unit 2			Unit 3				Unit 4			Unit 5				Unit 6			
Recognize common themes in British literature and support ideas with textual evidence.	●									●			●			●			●		●	●
Relate cultural and historical events to British literature and identify ambiguity, prejudice, and complexity therein.		●				●			●	●			●							●	●	
Make associations between historical and current viewpoints in British literature.			●						●	●			●				●			●	●	
Understand how literary movements influence writers in British literature.						●						●					●					
Observe how selected British literary works broaden imaginative experiences and enrich real life.						●	●									●	●				●	
Relate style, meaning, and genre in works of British literature.					●	●		●	●			●	●				●			●		●

Standard Course of Study for Language Arts

	UNIT 1				UNIT 2				UNIT 3				UNIT 4				UNIT 5				UNIT 6			
PART	1	2	3	4	1	2	3	4	1	2	3	4	1	2	3	4	1	2	3	4	1	2	3	4
Apply literary, grammatical, and rhetorical terms to British literature.													•				•							•
Demonstrate the significance of selected British literature using print and non-print media.									•															•
Discern the effect of interpreting British literature from critical perspectives.	•					•	•			•	•		•				•				•			
Select, monitor, and modify reading strategies appropriate to reader's purpose.										•	•								•					
Identify and analyze text components and evaluate their impact on text.	•										•							•	•	•	•	•		
Provide textual evidence to support reader's understanding of and response to text.																		•						
Demonstrate comprehension of main idea and support in grade appropriate texts.									•	•											•			•
Summarize key events and points.																								•
Infer, predict, and draw conclusions from text.						•													•					
Identify and analyze influences, contexts, and biases.						•			•				•						•		•			
Connect works, self, and related topics.		•				•	•	•																
Analyze and evaluate effects of author's craft and style.									•							•		•	•	•		•	•	
Analyze and evaluate relationships among concepts, characters, and experiences.	•								•										•					•
Identify and analyze informational elements in text in light of purpose and context.					•		•		•		•	•	•					•			•			

Language—Vocabulary, Grammar, Usage, and Mechanics: Students will apply conventions of grammar and language usage.

	UNIT 1				UNIT 2				UNIT 3				UNIT 4				UNIT 5				UNIT 6			
Use vocabulary strategies to determine meaning of words in order to write clearly.	•		•	•		•	•	•	•		•	•	•	•			•		•		•	•	•	•
Understand use and application of grammatical, metaphorical, and rhetorical devices.	•		•	•		•	•	•	•		•	•	•		•									
Recognize how to use different language conventions.		•		•			•	•			•						•				•	•	•	
Revise writing to enhance style and nuance when considering questions, purpose, and audience.		•		•						•		•												•

Standard Course of Study for Language Arts

	1				2			3				4			5				6			
UNIT / PART	1	2	3	4	1	2	3	1	2	3	4	1	2	3	1	2	3	4	1	2	3	4
Contrast language use by British authors in different eras.		●						●									●					
Analyze power of standard usage over nonstandard usage in formal settings.													●									
Review and refine various sentence structures in speech and writing.		●						●		●			●								●	●
Edit for punctuation, spelling, mechanics, and standard American English.		●			●							●	●		●							
Use appropriate transitional words and phrases.												●	●									

Catch small problems *before* they become big ones.

How it works:
Success Tracker diagnoses student readiness to learn new skills and benchmarks their progress towards standards mastery.

1 AT THE BEGINNING OF EACH UNIT OR PART:

- Students take Diagnostic Tests online.
- Tests measure skills necessary to successfully complete the unit.
- Tests are scored instantly and results trigger one of three levels:

  High Score = No remediation required

  Medium Score = Level B remediation

  Low Score = Level A remediation
- Success Tracker provides a list of recommended remediation assignments to students automatically.

2 AT THE END OF EACH UNIT OR PART:

- Students take Benchmark Tests online.
- Tests measure mastery of skills covered in the unit.
- Tests are scored instantly, and a list of "mastered" and "unmastered" skills are reported to the teacher.
- Remediation activities are automatically assigned, based on "unmastered" Skills.
- Benchmark retests can be assigned online to students by the teacher, if needed.

3 AS YOU DOCUMENT ADEQUATE YEARLY PROGRESS (AYP):

Success Tracker's easy-to-use reporting system lets you see at a glance where students may be having trouble mastering standards. These reports give you the kind of data you need to make decisions that will positively affect student performance on high-stakes tests.

Welcome to your new classroom!

PRENTICE HALL
LITERATURE

THE BRITISH TRADITION

Big Ben by Andre Derain (1880–1954) shows the clock tower of the Palace of Westminster, a famous landmark in London, England. The clock tower is nicknamed Big Ben because of its large bell. Derain's choppy brush strokes, informal structures, and vivid colors earned him a reputation among a group of painters called the *fauves,* a French term meaning "wild beasts." His style was influenced by the impressionist painter Vincent van Gogh, and he had a friendship with another famous painter, Pablo Picasso.

PENGUIN **EDITION**

PEARSON
Prentice Hall

Upper Saddle River, New Jersey
Boston, Massachusetts

ISBN 0-13-131720-2

1 2 3 4 5 6 7 8 9 10   09 08 07 06 05

Cover: Big Ben, Andre Derain, ©2005 Artists Rights Society (ARS), New York/ADAGP, Paris, Giraudon/Art Resource, NY

ACKNOWLEDGMENTS

Grateful acknowledgment is made to the following for copyrighted material:

Gillon Aitken Associates Limited
"B. Wordsworth" from *Miguel Street* by V. S. Naipaul. Copyright © 1959 by V. S. Naipaul.

G. Bell and Sons, Ltd. "A Modest Proposal" by Jonathan Swift from *The Prose Works Of Jonathan Swift, D.D., Vol. VII.*

Georges Borchardt, Inc. c/o Muriel Spark
"The First Year of My Life" from *The Stories Of Muriel Spark.* Copyright © 1995 by Copyright Administration.

Curtis Brown London "Be Ye Men of Valor" (retitled Wartime Speech), BBC London, May 19, 1940, from *Blood, Toil, Tears and Sweat: The Speeches of Winston Churchill* edited and with an introduction by David Cannadine. Speeches Copyright © 1989 by Winston Churchill MP.

Cambridge University Press Excerpt from "Letter to Thomas Flower Ellis from Thomas Babington Macaulay on the Passing of the Reform Bill" written in 1831, from *The Selected Letters of Thomas Babington Macaulay,* ed. Thomas Pinney, 5 vols.

The Citadel Press "The Lorelei" by Heinrich Heine from *The Poetry and Prose of Heinrich Reine,* edited by Frederic Ewen. Copyright © 1948, 1976 by The Citadel Press.

Doubleday "Haiku" from *An Introduction To Haiku* by Harold G. Henderson, copyright © 1958 by Harold G. Henderson.

Encyclopaedia Britannica, Inc. "Encyclopedia Britannica Online: Cavalier Poets." Copyright © 2004 by Encyclopaedia Britannica, Inc.

Faber and Faber Limited "The Rain Horse" by Ted Hughes from *Wodwo.* Copyright © 1967. "Not Palaces" by Stephen Spender. In the UK, from *Collected Poems 1928-1985.* Copyright © 1986 by Stephen Spender. Copyright © 1934 by The Modern Library, Inc. and renewed 1962, 1964, 1986 by Stephen Spender. "The Horses" from *New Selected Poems* by Ted Hughes. Copyright © 1957, 1960 by Ted Hughes. Published in

the UK in *The Hawk in the Rain* by Ted Hughes. "The Hollow Men" from *Collected Poems 1909-1962* by T. S. Eliot, copyright 1936 by Harcourt, Inc. and renewed 1964, 1963 by T. S. Eliot. "Journey of the Magi" from *Collected Poems 1909-1962* by T. S. Eliot, copyright 1936 by Harcourt Brace & Company, copyright © 1964, 1963 by T. S. Eliot.

Farrar, Straus & Giroux, LLC "An Arundel Tomb" from *Collected Poems by Philip Larkin.* Copyright © 1988, 1989 by the Estate of Philip Larkin. Excerpt from Omeros by Derek Walcott. Copyright © 1990 by Derek Walcott. "Two Lorries" from *The Spirit Level* by Seamus Heaney. Copyright © 1996 by Seamus Heaney. "The Explosion" from *Collected Poems by Philip Larkin.* Copyright © 1988, 1989 by the Estate of Phi. Excerpt from "Midsummer" from *Collected Poems 1948-1984* by Derek Walcott. Copyright © 1986 by Derek Walcott. "Follower" from *Poems 1965-1975* by Seamus Heaney. Copyright © 1980 by Seamus Heaney. From *The Right Stuff* by Tom Wolfe.

Harcourt, Inc. "The Lady in the Looking Glass: A Reflection" from *A Haunted House And Other Short Stories* by Virginia Woolf, copyright 1944 and renewed 1972 by Harcourt, Inc.

Harlan Davidson/Forum Press, Inc. Excerpt from *Book I of Utopia* by Thomas More, edited and translated by H.V.S. Ogden, pp. 21, 22 (Crofts Classics Series). Copyright © 1949 by Harlan Davidson, Inc.

HarperCollins Publishers, Inc. "A Devoted Son" from *Games At Twilight And Other Stories* by Anita Desai. Copyright © 1978 by Anita Desai.

A M Heath & Company Limited, Authors' Agents "Shooting an Elephant" from *Shooting An Elephant And Other Essays* by George Orwell (copyright © George Orwell, 1936).

David Higham Associates Limited "A Shocking Accident", copyright © 1957 by Graham Greene, from *Collected Stories Of Graham Greene* by Graham Greene. "On the Patio" from *Poems 1954-1987* by Peter Redgrove. Copyright © Peter Redgrove, 1959, 1961, 1963, 1966, 1972, 1973, 1975, 1977, 1979, 1981, 1985, 1986, 1987.

(Continued on page R64, which is hereby considered an extension of this copyright page.)

PRENTICE HALL
LITERATURE

PENGUIN EDITION

THE BRITISH TRADITION
VOLUME I

Students will

1. read selections in different genres from the beginnings of the British literary tradition through the Middle Ages.

2. apply a variety of reading strategies, particularly literal comprehension, appropriate for reading these selections.

3. analyze literary elements.

4. use a variety of strategies to build vocabulary.

5. learn elements of grammar, usage, and style.

6. use recursive writing processes to write in a variety of forms.

7. develop listening and speaking skills.

8. express and support responses to various types of texts.

9. prepare, evaluate, and critique oral presentations.

Unit 1
From Legend to History
A.D. 449–1485

Unit Instructional Resources

In **Unit 1 Resources,** you will find materials to support students in developing and mastering the unit skills and to help you assess their progress.

▶ **Vocabulary and Reading**

Additional vocabulary and reading support, based on Lexile scores of vocabulary words, is provided for each selection or grouping.

• **Word Lists A and B** and **Practices A and B** provide vocabulary-building activities for students reading two grades or one grade below level, respectively.

• **Reading Warm-ups A and B,** for students reading two grades or one grade below level, respectively, consist of short readings and activities that provide a context and practice for newly learned vocabulary.

▶ **Selection Support**

• **Reading Strategy**
• **Literary Analysis**
• **Vocabulary Builder**
• **Grammar and Style**
• **Support for Writing**
• **Support for Extend Your Learning**
• **Enrichment**

Assessment Resources

Skills Assessment

Unit 1 Resources
  Selection Tests A and B

TeacherExpress™
  ExamView® Test Bank
    Software

Adequate Yearly Progress Assessment

Unit 1 Resources
  Diagnostic Tests 1 and 2
  Benchmark Tests 1 and 2

Standardized Assessment

Standardized Test
Preparation Workbook

The Old English and Medieval Periods

Miniature of Gawain leaving Arthur's court and arriving at the White Abbey in search of Lancelot. Ms. Douce 199, fol. 151v, Bodleian Library, University of Oxford

"Who pulleth out this sword of this stone and anvil, is rightwise king born of all England."

—Sir Thomas Malory, from *Morte d'Arthur*

◁ This illustration from a manuscript of *Sir Gawain and the Green Knight* illuminates the text with art, ornate borders, and letters.

From Legend to History (A.D. 449–1485) ■ 1

Unit Features

Introduce Burton Raffel

- Burton Raffel introduces the unit and provides insights into Britain's early settlers. His introduction to *Beowulf* appears later in the unit on pages 36–37.

- Have students read the introductory paragraph about Burton Raffel. Tell them that Raffel has taught at universities in the United States, Israel, and Canada. He practiced law on Wall Street, and besides writing numerous translations, he has written poetry and critical studies.

- Use the *From the Author's Desk DVD* to introduce Burton Raffel. Show Segment 1 to provide insight into his writing career. After students have watched the segment, discuss the role of a translator.

With Rain Comes Life

- Have students read Raffel's commentary on early life in Britain.

- Raffel explains the hierarchical structure of the time period. **Ask:** Do you think that society during this time period needed this structure? Why?
Possible response: During this time period, it was necessary to have a hierarchical structure. It helped form some sort of law and stability in a society that was mainly uneducated. Those who were educated were leaders in the Church and the nobility; the hierarchical structure was a natural solution.

- Tell students that Burton Raffel will provide insights into *Beowulf* in Part 2 of this unit.

Setting the Scene

The literature in Unit 1 introduces the rich cultural heritage that lays the foundations for *The British Tradition*. The following essay by translator Burton Raffel describes the people who first called England their home. Later, the unit introduction and the literature that follows present the writing that these early settlers contributed to the immense canon, or collection, of works called British Literature.

 From the Translator's Desk
Burton Raffel Talks About the Time Period

Burton Raffel

Introducing Burton Raffel (b. 1928) Born in New York, poet and scholar Burton Raffel has translated such classics as *Beowulf, Don Quixote,* and Rabelais' *Gargantua and Pantagruel.* He is currently a professor of English at the University of Louisiana.

With Rain Comes Life

We tell jokes about the rainy English climate. A warm ocean current brings that moisture, and makes England the green, fertile land it still is. When the last ice age ended, some three thousand years ago, all across Europe easy hunting ended with it, and people without rich pasturage and easy farming went hungry. The English Channel was not as broad as it is today, and wave after wave of immigrants came pouring across.

Daily Life Life for England's earliest settlers was in many ways much like that still lived in England, as recently as the early nineteenth century. Cities were, for the most part, a thing of the future, though London was even then beginning to become a rich, bustling port. People lived on and by the land, which was worked by both men and women. Sheep were kept for their wool, pigs for their meat, chickens for their eggs. Most people raised a large percentage of the food they ate. There were no shops where one could buy such necessities as clothing (woven and sewn by hand), though artisans like blacksmiths made tools and other metallic items. Most of the land was owned by nobles, both hereditary and newly created aristocrats, having been made counts and earls as kingly rewards. There were many kingdoms on the island now called England and a good deal of quarreling between and among them.

Kings, Lords, Knights, and Peasants Society was hierarchical—that is, very little moved upward from the peasant level, and virtually everything proceeded downward from the nobility. No one imagined questioning the necessity for these largely fixed relationships. Without leadership, no community would function, and no stability would have been possible. These were matters as much taken for granted as, today, automobiles and television sets. Most of what we would call "work" was performed by those at the lower levels of society. We have no direct testimony from them, but

Teaching Resources

The following resources can be used to enrich or extend the instruction for the Unit 1 Introduction.

From the Author's Desk DVD
   Burton Raffel, Segment 1

Unit 1 Resources
   Names and Terms to Know, p. 5
   Focus Questions, p. 6
   Listening and Viewing: Burton Raffel, p. 25

from drawings and paintings, and surviving documents written by clergy or the minority of aristocrats who could read and write, there is a sense of relatively prosperous busyness. England was a rich habitat, as its inhabitants well knew. What overseas trading there was usually involved costly goods that only a few could afford. There was a good deal of local trading, most of which was conducted on the barter principle. Aristocrats dressed elaborately and expensively; most others dressed very plainly, both men and women wearing loose-fitting garments very like what we today call "smocks."

People not only worked, but they played. There was a good deal of group dancing: the songs we call "carols" in fact began as dance music. There were harvest and other agricultural festivals, and there were more solemn religious festivals. For both the secular and the holy festivities, there were other entertainments, from storytelling to dramatic presentations.

From Many Kingdoms to One Nation By the ninth century, some unification of the country's many kingdoms had occurred. Alfred the Great was the most notable English ruler, though still not entirely in control. Immigrants and Anglo-Saxon "natives" pulled and tugged at one another, and continued to fight over the prosperous green land. It was William of Brittany (in France) who finally created as much unity as England was to know for almost another five hundred years. In 1066, at the Battle of Hastings, William the Conqueror defeated an Anglo-Saxon opponent and became the increasingly powerful king of England. The kind of feudal structure he enforced was based on a close accounting of wealth, as reported, at William's direction, by the famous Domesday Book. William's England, now a Norman French "colony," was officially a French-speaking land: indeed, English law courts employed French until the sixteenth century.

But toward the end of the Anglo-Saxon period, we do not know exactly when, someone, somewhere, produced a poetic narrative, probably meant as a guide to proper kingship. This famous book is known as *Beowulf*.

▲ Critical Viewing
What items of value might be listed in the Domesday Book, shown here? **[Speculate]**

Go Online
—Author Link

For: A video clip of Burton Raffel
Visit: www.PHSchool.com
Web Code: ese-8101

For: More about Burton Raffel
Visit: www.PHSchool.com
Web Code: ese-9101

Tell students that the terms and questions listed here are the key points in this introductory material. This information provides a context for the selections in the unit. Students should use the terms and questions as a guide to focus their reading of the unit introduction. When students have completed the unit introduction, they should be able to identify or explain each of these terms and answer or discuss the Focus Questions.

To provide students with additional help in reading the Unit 1 introduction, give them pages 5 and 6 from *Unit 1 Resources*.

Concept Connector ➡

After students have read the unit introduction, return to the Focus Questions to review the main points. For key points, see p. 13.

Go Online
—Author Link — Typing in the Web Codes when prompted will bring students to a video clip and more information on Burton Raffel.

Reading the Unit Introduction

Reading for Information and Insight Use the following terms and questions to guide your reading of the unit introduction on pages 6–14.

Names and Terms to Know
Celts and Anglo-Saxons
Alfred the Great
Norman Conquest
William, Duke of Normandy
Magna Carta
Feudal System
Gutenberg

Focus Questions As you read this introduction, use what you learn to answer these questions:
- What impact did Alfred the Great have on the development of England?
- In what ways did literature keep history alive in Anglo-Saxon and medieval England?

Using the Timeline

The Timeline can serve a number of instructional purposes, as follows:

Getting an Overview

Use the Timeline to help students get a quick overview of themes and events of the period. This approach will benefit all students but may be especially helpful for visually oriented students, English-language learners, and those less proficient in reading. (For strategies in using the Timeline as an overview, see the bottom of this page.)

Thinking Critically

Questions are provided on the facing page. Use these questions to have students review the events, discuss their significance, and examine the *so what* behind the *what happened.*

Connecting to Selections

Have students refer to the Timeline when beginning to read individual selections. By consulting the Timeline regularly, they will gain a better sense of the period's chronology. In addition, they will appreciate the world events that gave rise to these works of literature.

Projects

Students can use the Timeline as a launching pad for projects such as these:

- **Customized Timeline** Have students create a period timeline in their notebooks, adding key dates as they read new selections. They can use dates from this Timeline as a starting framework.
- **Special Report** Have students scan the Timeline for items that interest them, research these further, and report on them to the class.

British and World Events

449   600   900

BRITISH EVENTS

- 449 Anglo-Saxon invasion. ▼

- 597 St. Augustine founds Christian monastery at Canterbury, Kent.
- 653 Celtic church begins to spread Christianity among people living in Severn Valley.

- 664 Synod of Whitby establishes Roman Church in England.
- 731 **Bede** completes *A History of the English Church and People.*
- c. 750 Surviving version of *Beowulf* composed.
- 793 Vikings attack Lindisfarne.
- 871 Alfred the Great becomes King of Wessex. ▼

- c. 975 Saxon monks copy Old English poems into *The Exeter Book.*
- 991 English defeated by Danes at Battle of Maldon.
- 1040 Macbeth kills Duncan I.
- 1042 Edward the Confessor becomes king of Saxons.
- 1066 Normans defeat Saxons at Hastings; William the Conqueror becomes king of England. ▲

WORLD EVENTS

- 476 Western Europe: Fall of Western Roman Empire.
- 496 France: Clovis, king of Franks, converts to Christianity.
- 542 Byzantine Empire: Plague kills half the population of the capital, Constantinople.
- 552 Japan: Buddhism introduced. ▶
- 591 China: Beginning of book printing.

- 637 Middle East: Jerusalem conquered by Arabs.
- 712 Spain: Seville conquered by Moors.
- 732 France: Charles Martel defeats Moors.
- 771 France: Charlemagne becomes king.
- 800 Peru: Incas build city of Machu Picchu.
- c. 810 Baghdad: Algebra devised.
- 861 North Atlantic: Vikings discover Iceland.

- c. 900 Western Europe: Feudalism develops.
- 911 France: Normans establish Normandy.
- 982 Greenland: Eric the Red establishes first Viking colony.
- c. 1020 America: Viking explorer Leif Ericson explores Canadian coast.
- 1045 Spain: Birth of El Cid, national hero who fought Moors.
- 1053 Italy: Normans conquer Sicily.
- 1096 Europe and Middle East: First Crusade begins.

4 ■ From Legend to History (A.D. 449–1485)

Getting an Overview of the Period

Introduction To give students an overview of the period, indicate the span of dates along the top of the Timeline. Next, point out that the Timeline is divided into specifically British Events (on the top) and World Events (on the bottom). Have students practice scanning the Timeline across, looking at both the British Events and the World Events. Finally, point out that the events in the Timeline often represent beginnings, turning points, and endings.

Key Events Have students identify key political events, such as invasions.
Answer: In 449, Anglo-Saxons invaded; in 1066, the Normans invaded.
Then, have students trace cultural developments.
Possible responses: In 597, Christianity was introduced; in 871, Alfred the Great became king; and in 1215, the Magna Carta was signed.

- 1073 Canterbury becomes England's religious center.
- c. 1130 Oxford becomes a center for learning.
- 1170 Thomas Becket, Archbishop of Canterbury, murdered. ▼
- 1215 King John forced to sign Magna Carta.

- 1233 First coal mined at Newcastle.
- 1258 First commoners allowed in Parliament.
- 1272 Edward I becomes king.
- 1277 England conquers Wales.
- 1295 Edward I assembles Model Parliament.
- 1337 Beginning of the Hundred Years' War with France.
- 1348 Black Death begins sweeping through England.
- c. 1375 Surviving version of *Sir Gawain and the Green Knight* written.

- 1381 Bible first translated into English.

- 1381 Peasants' Revolt.
- 1386 **Chaucer** begins writing *The Canterbury Tales.* ▲
- 1455–1485 The Wars of the Roses.
- c. 1470 Thomas Malory writes *Morte d'Arthur.*

- c. 1100 France: *Song of Roland* written.
- 1139 Portugal: Afonso I defeats Moors and assumes title of king.
- c. 1150 Spain: First paper made.
- 1192 Austria: Duke Leopold imprisons Richard I of England.
- 1194 Iceland: *Elder Edda*, a collection of Norse myths and legends, first appears.
- 1214 China: Mongol leader Genghis Khan captures Peking.

- 1275 China: Marco Polo visits court of Kublai Khan.
- 1291 Europe and Middle East: End of Crusades.
- 1307 Italy: Dante begins writing *The Divine Comedy.*
- 1325 Mexico: Aztecs establish Mexico City and create a dating system with a solar year of 365 days. ▶
- 1341 Italy: Petrarch crowned poet laureate of Rome.

- 1429 France: Joan of Arc leads French in breaking siege of Orléans.
- 1453 France: Hundred Years' War with England ends.
- 1453 Germany: First Gutenberg Bible printed.
  - 1461 France: François Villon writes *Grand Testament.*
  - 1484 Italy: Botticelli paints *Birth of Venus.*
  - 1485 Peru: Incan Empire reaches its zenith.

Introduction ■ 5

---

for the introduction of Christianity to England? (b) Why is this date important? **[Hypothesize]**
Answer: (a) In 597, St. Augustine founded a monastery at Canterbury. (b) Britain eventually became a Christian nation.

2. (a) When did the Vikings attack a site in Britain? (b) What may have happened to this seafaring, warlike people? **[Infer]**
Answer: (a) They attacked Lindisfarne in 793. (b) **Possible responses:** The Vikings were defeated by the settled peoples of the area to which they sailed and gave up raiding; the Vikings settled down in the places to which they traveled and were assimilated by the local people.

3. (a) What important military campaign occurred in France a year after Bede completed his *History*? (b) If those who lost the battle had won it, how might the history of Britain have been different? **[Speculate]**
Answer: (a) Charles Martel defeated the Moors. (b) Britain, too, might have fallen to Moorish invaders.

4. (a) When did the Normans conquer England? (b) Does the Timeline suggest that they were eventually expelled or that they were assimilated (married local people and eventually lost their distinct identity)? Explain. **[Hypothesize]**
Answer: (a) The Normans conquered England in 1066. (b) There is no mention of a battle or revolt after 1066; the Timeline suggests that they assimilated.

5. (a) What two dramatic events occurred in Britain in the 1330s and 1340s? (b) How might these events have affected the population of the British Isles? **[Infer]**
Answer: (a) In 1337, the Hundred Years' War with France began. In 1348, the Black Death swept across England. (b) They probably decreased the population dramatically.

Critical Viewing

1. Why might the invaders of Britain in 449 have decorated their helmets with horns? **[Infer]**
Possible response: The invaders wore horns to frighten their enemies.

Answers continued

2. Describe the style in which the artist portrays the murder of Archbishop Thomas Becket of Canterbury. What does this style suggest about reaction to his death? **[Interpret]**
Possible response: The artist uses gestures to show the forcefulness of the assassins and the vulnerability of Thomas Becket, suggesting that he was wrongfully killed.

3. Look at the picture of Chaucer's pilgrim (1386). What would it have been like to travel on horseback from London to Canterbury? **[Speculate]**
Possible response: Students may mention exposure to the elements and the need to stop at inns.

Literature of the Period

- "The Seafarer," p. 18, and "The Wanderer," p. 23, offer piercing, first-person accounts of the loneliness and alienation that sea-roving and warfare could prompt.

- *Beowulf*, p. 40, sets forth the stoic credo of the Anglo-Saxon invaders mentioned in the historical accounts.

- The excerpt from Bede's *The History of the English Church and People*, p. 78, will acquaint students with a work that was translated into English and was made more accessible under the sponsorship of King Alfred the Great.

- The excerpt from *The Anglo-Saxon Chronicle*, p. 83, details some of the events from the Danish invasion up to the death of Alfred the Great.

Critical Viewing

Answer: Church-going would have become part of people's weekly routines; people may have turned to priests and monks for advice or for help in settling disputes; traditional pagan rituals accompanying planting, harvesting, and other work may have been banned by the Church.

Historical Background

The Conquest of Britain Between 800 and 600 B.C., two groups of Celts from southern Europe invaded the British Isles. One group, who called themselves Brythons (now spelled "Britons"), settled on the largest island, Britain. The other, known as Gaels, settled on the second largest island, known to us as Ireland.

The Celts were farmers and hunters. They organized themselves into tightly knit clans, each with a fearsome loyalty to its chieftain. When these clans fell into disagreement with one another, they often looked to a class of priests known as Druids to settle their disputes.

The next conquerors of Britain were the far more sophisticated Romans. In 55 B.C. and again the next year, the Roman general Julius Caesar made hasty invasions. The true conquest of Britain, however, occurred nearly one hundred years later. Disciplined Roman legions spread over the island, establishing camps that soon grew into towns. The Roman rule of Britain lasted for more than 300 years. It ended only when northern European tribes invaded Italy and increased pressure on Rome itself. The last Roman legions departed from Britain to defend Rome in A.D. 407. By that time, the Britons faced a new set of invaders.

These invaders were the Anglo-Saxons, from what is now Germany. Some Anglo-Saxons appear to have been deep-sea fishermen; others seem to have been farmers, perhaps seeking soil richer than the sandy or marshy land at home. Gradually, the newcomers took over more and more of what today is England.

The Coming of Christianity By the fourth century, the Romans had accepted Christianity and had introduced it to Britain. A century later, when the Celts fled the Anglo-Saxons, they took their Christian faith with them. Although Rome fell to barbarian tribes in A.D. 476, the Celtic Christian Church continued to thrive.

In the late sixth century, a soldier and abbot named Columba, along with some monks, gained converts to Christianity and established monasteries in the north. In 597, the Roman cleric Saint Augustine (not the early Christian Church father) arrived in southeast England and converted King Ethelbert of Kent to Christianity. Augustine set up a monastery at Canterbury in Kent and began preaching his faith to other rulers as well.

Spread of Christianity in Europe, 476–1050

- Christian areas, 476
- Christian areas added by 1050
- Muslim areas, 1050

▲ **Critical Viewing**
This map shows the spread of Christianity throughout Europe. What effects might this religious conversion have had on daily life? **[Analyze Causes and Effects]**

6 ■ From Legend to History (A.D. 449–1485)

Enrichment

The Meaning of Roman Rule
To help students understand the importance of Roman rule, ask them whether they have ever visited another city in the United States. How did they find their way there? Where did they eat and, if they paid for accommodations, where did they spend the night? Point out factors enabling Americans to leave their homes and travel hundreds of miles with confidence: a uniform currency, restaurant franchises, hotel chains, similar laws.

Explain to students that Rome provided some of the same things. It built roads, fortifications, and aqueducts. Its military forces defended Britain against alien invasion. Its laws enabled the English to enjoy some of the protections enjoyed by other citizens. Also, the use of Latin throughout the empire guaranteed that traders could be at home in many places around the world. Have students speculate whether our world is moving in the direction of a universal language and currency. Discuss the advantages and disadvantages of such a system.

By providing counsel to quarreling rulers, the Church promoted peace and helped unify the English people.

Danish Invasion In the ninth century, the Norse of Norway and the Danes of Denmark were pressured by their own rising populations and took to the seas. These Vikings carried their piracy to the British Isles. The Norse set their sights on Northumbria, Scotland, Wales, and Ireland, whereas the Danes targeted eastern and southern England.

The Viking invaders sacked and plundered monasteries, destroyed manuscripts, and stole sacred religious objects. They burned entire communities and put villagers to the sword. Although the English fought back valiantly, the Danes made broad inroads. By the middle of the ninth century, most of northern, eastern, and central England had fallen to the invaders.

In 871, a king ascended to the Wessex throne who would become the only ruler in England's history ever to be honored with the epithet "the Great." This king was Alfred, and he earned the title partly by resisting further Danish encroachment. Under a truce concluded in 886, England was formally divided: The Saxons acknowledged Danish rule in the east and north, and the Danes agreed to respect Saxon rule in the south. Alfred the Great became a national hero.

Alfred's achievements went far beyond the field of battle, however. Not only was he instrumental in preserving the remnants of pre-Danish civilization in Britain, but he encouraged a rebirth of learning and education.

Toward the close of the tenth century, however, more Danes from Europe attempted to recapture and widen the Danelaw, the eastern and northern sections of England under Danish control. Once they succeeded, they forced the Saxons to select Danish kings. Then, in 1042, the line of succession returned to a descendant of Alfred the Great. This king, Edward, had acquired the title "the Confessor" because he was a deeply religious Christian. His death in 1066 led to the end of the Anglo-Saxon period of history.

The Norman Conquest The Normans, or "north men," were descendants of Vikings who had invaded the coast of France in the ninth century. William, Duke of Normandy, had family ties to Edward the Confessor, the English king. When Edward died in 1066, the Saxon council of elders chose Harold II to be king. William of Normandy, however, claimed that Edward had promised the throne to him, and he crossed the English Channel to assert his claim by force. At the Battle of Hastings, near a seaside village in southern England, Harold was killed, and William emerged victorious.

Over the next five years, William suppressed the Anglo-Saxon nobility and confiscated their lands. He saw to it that Normans controlled the government and that business was conducted in Norman French or in Latin. The Normans gradually remade England along feudal lines. Feudalism had taken root on the European continent at a time when no central

▲ **Critical Viewing**
What can you infer about Viking society and technology by studying this sword? [**Make an Inference**]

ments more accessible, Alfred oversaw translations of Bede's *History* and other works from Latin into Anglo-Saxon, the everyday language of the people. In this way he fostered the growth of the English language and its literature. He also began to keep records of English history in *The Anglo-Saxon Chronicle,* one of our principal sources of information on early English life.

Humanities

Use the illustrations in this section to introduce students to illuminated manuscripts. (Excerpts from manuscripts appear on the unit opener spread and on p. 5.)

Explain how monks, dedicated to copying over precious manuscripts, would devote days to working with paints and gold leaf to adorn the pages of illuminated manuscripts.

Tasks were divided: Some provided paintings to illustrate the story; others adorned with clever designs the borders of the page or the capital letters. (The latter are the original illuminators.)

Before the invasions of the Danes, English manuscript art at Lindisfarne, Weymouth, and Jarrow was dominated by the decorative techniques brought by Irish monks.

Critical Viewing

Answer: The Vikings were metal workers. The sword is long and broad, not thin like a rapier; it is designed for long crosscuts, not thrusts. This indicates that the Vikings valued physical strength.

Strategy for Less Proficient Readers
Have students preview the art and illustrations in this section and answer the questions about them before reading "From Legend to History."

Strategy for English Learners
Have these students use the illustrations and photographs in "From Legend to History" to speculate about the era. Also, have them glance at the bold headings in the text in this section. Have them formulate questions that the sections introduced by these heads might answer.

Strategy for Advanced Readers
Challenge more advanced students to use the illustrations and photographs along with the information in "From Legend to History" to draw conclusions about the daily life of teenagers during this period.

Vikings, the Normans had adopted many French ways over the years. They had become devout Christians. They had accustomed themselves to speaking a dialect of the French language. They had also organized themselves according to the French political and economic system of the times—feudalism.

Critical Viewing

Answer: The Normans who arrived in England came prepared to camp, since they brought with them cooking implements such as the tongs and grill shown at the right. This suggests that they were used to military campaigns away from home.

Fine Art Transparencies

Use Art Transparency 2, *Harold Brings News to William*, to give students more of a sense of the Bayeux Tapestry. The transparency is accompanied by an Enrichment Note on the tapestry and additional activities.

Humanities
Bayeux Tapestry

Using colored thread, medieval French needleworkers stitched the story of William the Conqueror's invasion of England—from the precipitating events through the Battle of Hastings—in more than seventy scenes on a long (231 feet), narrow (19½ inches) strip of linen. Their work, known as the Bayeux Tapestry (after the French town in which it was hung), has served as a valuable source of information about these events. Though the tapestry's pictorial style is simple, details are rendered precisely and accurately.

government was strong enough to keep order. The feudal system involved an exchange of property for personal service. In theory, all the land belonged to the king, who parceled it out among his powerful supporters. He gave these supporters noble titles—usually "Baron"—and special privileges. As a vassal of his overlord, each baron paid certain fees, or taxes, and supplied a specified number of knights—professional soldiers—should the king require them. In return for their services, knights usually received smaller parcels of land, called manors. The peasants who worked these manors were the lowest class in the feudal system, the serfs.

The Reign of the Plantagenets Although Norman influence continued for centuries, Norman rule ended in 1154 when Henry Plantagenet, Count of Anjou, came to the throne as Henry II. Henry founded the royal house of Plantagenet and established a record as one of England's ablest kings.

Henry's concern with legal matters led him into direct conflict with the Church. When the archbishop's seat at Canterbury fell vacant, he appointed his friend Thomas Becket to the position, expecting Becket to go along with royal policy. Instead, Becket defied the king and appealed to the Pope. The Pope sided with Becket, provoking Henry to rage.

Some of Henry's knights misunderstood the royal wrath. In 1170, four of them murdered Becket in his cathedral. Henry quickly condemned the crime and tried to atone for it by making a holy journey, or pilgrimage, to Becket's tomb. Thereafter, a pilgrimage to Becket's shrine at Canterbury became a common English means of showing religious devotion.

The Magna Carta The next king, Richard I, spent most of his reign staging military expeditions overseas. His activities proved costly, and his successor, King John, inherited the debts. John tried to raise money by ordering new taxes on the barons. The barons resisted these measures, bringing England to the brink of civil war. To avert further trouble, King John at last agreed to certain of the barons' conditions by putting his seal on the Magna Carta (Latin for "Great Charter").

In the Magna Carta, the king promised not to tax land without first meeting with the barons. Although the document produced no radical changes in government, many historians believe its restrictions on royal power marked the beginning of constitutional government in England.

Lancasters, Yorks, and Tudors In 1399, the House of Lancaster replaced the Plantagenets on the throne. The Lancastrian kings were Henry IV, Henry V, and Henry VI, all of whom later became central figures in the

▲ **Critical Viewing** The Bayeux Tapestry is a piece of embroidered linen (231 feet by 19 ½ inches) that tells the story of King Harold's defeat at Hastings in 1066. This small section of the tapestry shows the Normans preparing a meal after their Channel crossing. What conclusions can you draw from this scene about the Normans and their way of life? **[Draw Conclusions]**

Enrichment

Watching the Sky

During the Middle Ages, observing the sky was an important activity. Determining weather and seasons was vital, but the sky was also searched for stars, planets, and such phenomena as comets and eclipses. These phenomena were studied both as a matter of curiosity and because many were viewed as omens.

In the spring of 1066, only a few months after Harold's coronation, a comet appeared. It was seen as a bad omen. We now know, based on the date and the comet's cycle, that it was

Halley's comet. Its appearance was recorded on the Bayeux Tapestry and was mentioned in *The Anglo-Saxon Chronicle*.

Ask students how our current study of the sky compares with that of the Middle Ages. Encourage students to find a picture of Halley's Comet as rendered on the Bayeux Tapestry and as shown in a modern astronomical photograph. (Books and the Internet are both good sources.)

historical dramas of Shakespeare. Through the fifteenth century, however, the House of York contested Lancastrian rule. The conflicts known as the Wars of the Roses (1455–1485) pitted York against Lancaster. First one house, then the other ruled as they fought over the throne. Eventually, Henry Tudor, a distant cousin and supporter of the Lancastrian kings, led a rebellion against the unpopular Yorkist king Richard III and killed him in battle. Tudor, crowned Henry VII, later married Richard's niece, uniting the houses of York and Lancaster and ending the Wars of the Roses.

Decline of the Feudal System While royal families struggled for supremacy, the social structure of England was changing. After the great plague, called the Black Death, swept across England in 1348 and 1349, a massive labor shortage increased the value of a peasant's work. Landowners began paying their farmers in cash, giving these workers a greater sense of freedom. Along with freedom went frustration, as peasants began to complain about discriminatory laws and heavy taxes. In 1381, peasants in England staged a revolt against serfdom. The revolt was crushed, but many of its causes continued, and so did the peasants' discontent. Gradually, a free peasantry replaced the serfs of the Middle Ages. However, the question of social justice for the lower classes would arise again.

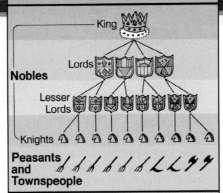

▲ **Critical Viewing**
(a) What aspects of feudal society, as diagrammed here, are similar to aspects of modern-day America? (b) What class of modern people is equivalent to the class of knights in feudal society? [Relate]

The British Tradition — Point/Counterpoint

The Middle Ages: 1000 Years of Darkness?
The Middle Ages are sometimes pictured as a glittering time of chivalrous knights and daring deeds. Were they actually centuries of brutality and chaos? Two historians express opposing points of view.

YES! "It says much about the Middle Ages that in the year 1500, after a thousand years of neglect, the roads built by the Romans were still the best on the continent: . . . The level of everyday violence—deaths in alehouse brawls, during bouts with staves, or even in playing football or wrestling— was shocking. Tournaments were really occasions for . . . mayhem."

—from *A World Lit Only by Fire* by William Manchester

NO! "In the development of single communities and groups of communities there occurs now and again a moment of equilibrium, when institutions are stable and adapted to the needs of those who live under them; when the minds of men are filled with ideas which they find completely satisfying. . . . Such a period were the Middle Ages. . . ."

—from *Medieval Europe* by H.W.C. Davis

Introduction ■ 9

POINT/COUNTERPOINT

Underscore that the period known as the Middle Ages stretches over 1,000 years and covers many countries. Then, ask the following questions.

1. Why are the two viewpoints so different?
   Answer: The two historians are looking at different aspects of the era.

2. Is it possible that both historians are correct? Explain.
   Answer: Answers should include the concept that any era has both good and bad elements.

3. What are some aspects of current culture that future historians might view as positive or negative? Is there anything that the first historian might describe as "everyday violence" today?
   Possible responses: Answers might include modern medicine and space exploration in the positive column and crime and war in the negative. As for violence, some might point to gangs or violent video games and movies, or they might note that violence is more common in some countries.

Explain to students that a peasant's diet was limited to bread and vegetables; meat was a luxury. After 1000, trade began to flourish, agriculture expanded, and money began to circulate. By the 1300s, peasants were renting their land or being paid for their labor. Their old bondage to the land was loosening.

Critical Viewing

Possible response:

(a) In medieval society, like today, few people occupied places of extreme privilege. (b) Modern-day equivalents to the knights of feudal society might include professional soldiers. Those who own or have important managerial authority over a large business could be compared to lords or lesser lords. Today's workers, with the freedom to move from job to job, are not really equivalent to medieval serfs.

Literature of the Period

- The ties binding king to lord and lord to peasant in medieval society gave people a firm sense of their place in the social order. For an affecting lament on the loss of this sense—the plight of the exile— refer students to "The Wanderer," beginning on p. 23.

- The chart of Feudal Society suggests that medieval society was rigidly hierarchical. However, let students know that Chaucer's *The Canterbury Tales: The Prologue* (p. 98) reveals a colorful diversity of occupations and social classes.

Background
Music

Monastic culture, preserver of the Anglo-Saxon epics and histories, also produced the distinctive music of the period: the Gregorian chant. Named for Pope Gregory I (c. A. D. 540–604), these chants are musical settings for the texts used in masses and prayer services. The chants, or plainsongs, feature only one melody line and rarely use more than ten pitches, yet they encompass a variety of styles and structures.

ing of the Anglo-Saxons?
Answer: The Celts and, later, the Romans ruled Britain before the coming of the Anglo-Saxons.

2. What important cultural development occurred in Britain during the late sixth century?
Answer: Roman missionaries began to convert the Anglo-Saxons to Christianity.

3. Which Anglo-Saxon king is remembered for making peace with the Danes?
Answer: Alfred the Great is the Anglo-Saxon king who made peace with the Danes.

4. Briefly describe the social system the Normans imposed on England.
Answer: The Normans imposed feudalism on England. Feudalism was a hierarchical society with distinct classes, based on landownership and loyalty.

Critical Thinking

1. How was the concept of property under feudalism different from today's ideas of property? [Compare and Contrast]
Answer: In feudalism, all land was owned, in theory, by the king. In return for the loyalty of his barons, he granted them its use. In the modern idea of property, land is owned by whoever has bought it.

2. How was the Magna Carta a step on the way to Britain's constitutional monarchy of power? [Infer]
Answer: It lessened the monarchy's power, making it more dependent on the monarch's subjects' consent.

3. How did the plague contribute to the birth of capitalism? [Generalize]
Answer: It led to the introduction of money as the link between lord and serf.

Critical Viewing

Possible responses: The Anglo-Saxons may have buried such items with their royal dead to show them honor and because these things were appropriate for kings. There may also have been some thought of needing these things in an afterlife.

Literature of the Period

Anglo-Saxon Literature Anglo-Saxon literature began not with books, but with spoken verse and incantations. The reciting of poems often occurred on ceremonial occasions, such as the celebration of military victories.

Anglo-Saxon Poetry This early verse falls mainly into two categories: heroic poetry, recounting the achievements of warriors, and elegiac poetry, lamenting the deaths of loved ones and the loss of the past. The long poem *Beowulf* is the most famous example of heroic poetry, whereas a famous elegiac poem is "The Wanderer."

Beowulf This epic, or long heroic poem, is the story of a great legendary warrior renowned for his courage, strength, and dignity. Because it is the first such work known to have been composed in the English language, it is considered the national epic of England.

Like most Anglo-Saxon poets, the author of *Beowulf* is unknown. Although versions of the poem were likely recited as early as the sixth century, the text that we have today was composed in the eighth century and not written down until the eleventh. Thus, the poem includes many references to Christian ideas and Latin classics. Clearly evident in *Beowulf*, however, are the values of a warrior society, especially those of dignity, bravery, and prowess in battle.

Anglo-Saxon Prose Before the reign of Alfred the Great, all important prose written in the British Isles was composed in Latin. The monks who transcribed these works regarded the vernacular, the language of the common people, as a "vulgar tongue." The greatest of England's Latin scholars was the Venerable Bede (673–735), whose *History of the English Church and People* gives an account of England from the Roman invasion to his own time.

Another great work of prose from this time is *The Anglo-Saxon Chronicles,* the name given to a group of historical journals written and compiled in monasteries. Unlike Bede's *History,* these records were written in Old English, the earliest form of our own language.

Literature of the English Middle Ages During this period, the first true dramas emerged, the poet Geoffrey Chaucer created a vivid picture of medieval life, romances portrayed the deeds of knights, and anonymous balladeers sang of love and deeds of outlaws.

▲ **Critical Viewing**
This gold shoulder clasp comes from the site of a seventh-century grave or commemorative tomb for an Anglo-Saxon king. It is comparable to items buried with Beowulf. Why do you think Anglo-Saxons buried such items with their royal dead? [Infer]

Enrichment

Invention in the Middle Ages

Though people sometimes describe the Middle Ages as a time of intellectual darkness and superstition, it was an era that saw significant advances in the technology of agriculture. In at least some parts of western Europe, the plow was no longer a simple blade to scratch the earth. It rode on wheels, and a new arrangement of parts ensured that it would actually turn over the soil as it passed. Windmills began to appear, harnessing the power of the wind to grind grain into flour. Even hand tools such as axes were improved during this time.

Medieval Drama During early Norman times, the Church often sponsored plays as part of religious services. In time, these plays moved from the church building to the churchyard and then to the marketplace. The earliest dramas were miracle plays, or mystery plays, that retold stories from the Bible or dealt with aspects of the lives of saints.

During the turbulent fifteenth century, a new kind of drama arose: the morality play. Morality plays depicted the lives of ordinary people and taught moral lessons.

An Emerging National Identity In 1454, a German silversmith, Johann Gutenberg, perfected a process of printing from movable type. Printing then spread rapidly throughout Europe, and, in 1476, William Caxton set up the first movable-type press in England. English literature no longer needed to be hand-copied by church scribes.

One of Caxton's first projects was the printing of Geoffrey Chaucer's work. Chaucer wrote in Middle English, a language quite close to English as it is spoken today. After centuries of the ebb and flow of conquerors and their languages, the island of England had finally settled on a national identity of its own.

Geoffrey Chaucer Poet Geoffrey Chaucer was born into the merchant class that was adding to the wealth of London and the nation. Chaucer's father was a wine merchant, and young Geoffrey grew up amid the bustle of a successful international business. As a teenager, he entered an aristocratic household as a servant. This apprenticeship led to a career in which he served the nobility as a capable administrator. Chaucer's perch in society, just below the aristocracy, gave him a perfect vantage point for observing all kinds of people.

Nowhere does Chaucer display his keen powers of observation better than in *The Canterbury Tales*. This work, planned as an exchange of tales among pilgrims journeying to the shrine of martyr Thomas Becket at Canterbury, gave Chaucer the opportunity to show a cross section of medieval society. In doing so, he moved literature beyond the themes of courtly love and knightly adventure that dominated the many medieval tales called romances. His compassionate humor and lively realism make him one of the first modern writers.

Although Chaucer completed only 22 of the 120 tales that scholars think he planned to write, these 22 exhibit a great variety. They include the tale of chivalry told by the Knight, the *fabliaux* (French for "short stories")

▲ Critical Viewing
In the late fifteenth century, the movable-type press began to play an important role in society. This set of letters and its designed border were produced by William Caxton's printing device. Speculate about the effect this device had on English society. **[Speculate]**

might have been the audience for such poems? **[Infer]**
Answer: Anglo-Saxon nobles and warriors were a likely audience for these heroic poems.

2. Monks originally wrote in Latin. What conclusions can you draw from the fact that *The Anglo-Saxon Chronicle* was written in Old English? **[Draw Conclusions]**
Answer: The English began to take their own, native tradition more seriously.

3. (a) How is a morality play different from a mystery play? (b) Why might morality plays have emerged during the turmoil of the fifteenth century? **[Analyze Causes and Effects]**
Answer: (a) Morality plays had ordinary people as their main characters. Mystery plays used Bible characters or saints.
(b) Perhaps during times of trouble, people looked to see their own uncertainties and troubles dramatized on stage.

Critical Viewing

Answer: Books were easier to make, so they became more widespread; it became easier to acquire knowledge; more people could learn to read.

told by the Miller and the Reeve, the animal fable told by the Nun's Priest, and the story based on a fairy tale told by the Merchant. The highly moral Parson, when asked to contribute a tale, declines to tell an "idle story" like those of the other pilgrims. This passage shows how Chaucer introduces a greater dimension of realism by having his fictional storytellers describe their tales and react to previous ones.

Romances, Lyrics, and Ballads Medieval romances were tales describing the adventures of knights. The most popular romances told about King Arthur. For centuries after their defeat by the Anglo-Saxons, the Celts had told stories of this great Celtic hero. Inasmuch as historians cannot say for certain whether Arthur actually lived or not, tales about him are considered legends, a blend of fact and fiction. When the Normans were battling the Anglo-Saxons, they became interested in the old Celtic legends. Because of the Normans' French ties, the tales of Arthur spread not only in England but also in France. In the fifteenth century, Sir Thomas Malory collected these tales in his book *Morte d'Arthur* ("The Death of Arthur").

Europeans of the Middle Ages had a fondness for a harplike instrument called the lyre. In palaces and castles, poets often strummed lyres as they recited their verse. From this custom, English lyric poetry developed. Lyric poems of this period fall into two main categories: secular and religious. The usual topics of secular poetry are love and nature. Religious lyrics might consist of a hymn praising God or a prayer of supplication.

Another popular poetic form was the ballad, a folk song that told a story. Experts find most surviving ballads impossible to date. One series concerns Robin Hood, a legendary hero who may have existed around the turn of the thirteenth century. An outlaw, Robin lives in the woods with his band of "merrye" men, robbing from the rich and helping the poor.

▲ **Critical Viewing**
(a) Which of these two figures is probably Robin Hood? Why? (b) What does the artist's portrayal of Robin Hood suggest about his way of life, his abilities, and his motives? **[Analyze]**

The British Tradition

Close-Up on History

Two Funerals

To get an overview of British literature, you might begin with two funerals. These ceremonies occur 1,500 years apart, but each honors a person of great importance. Between these two solemn public events—one real and one fictional—the story of British literature unfolds.

One occurred on Saturday, September 6, 1997. It was the funeral of Diana, Princess of Wales. You yourself might have been among the estimated 2.5 billion people worldwide to watch the services for Diana, killed in a tragic auto accident.

The other funeral, from the beginnings of British history and literature, honored Beowulf. He was the king of a Germanic tribe living in southern Sweden, probably during the early sixth century A.D. His death came, after a glorious lifetime of killing enemies and monsters, in a desperate battle with a dragon.

from **Beowulf**
Translated by Seamus Heaney

The Geat people built a pyre for Beowulf,
stacked and decked it until it stood four-square,
hung with helmets, heavy war-shields
and shining armor, just as he had ordered.
5 Then his warriors laid him in the middle of it,
mourning a lord far-famed and beloved.
On a height they kindled the hugest of all
funeral fires; fumes of woodsmoke
billowed darkly up, the blaze roared
10 and drowned out their weeping, wind died down
and flames wrought havoc in the hot bone-house,
burning it to the core. They were disconsolate
and wailed aloud for their lord's decease.

from "A Farewell to the 'People's Princess'"
by Dan Balz (The Washington Post)

LONDON, Sept. 6—In precedent-shattering ceremonies that were at once sorrowful and uplifting, Diana, Princess of Wales, was remembered today as a woman of ì natural nobility" whose life of compassion and style transcended sometimes abusive press coverage and even the royal family itself. Later she was laid to rest on her family's estate, concluding one of the most extraordinary weeks in the modern history of Britain. . . .

A Story Told in Literature A comparison of these funerals shows that in 1,500 years, warring male-centered tribes that valued physical courage and loyalty became a nation of male and female citizens who valued concern for all those in need and the honest expression of feelings as much as physical courage. British literature both recorded and influenced this dramatic change.

crash on September 6, 1997, was met by a tremendous outpouring of grief in Britain and abroad. Musicians such as Elton John composed songs in her honor, many of the charities she represented around the world honored her in special ceremonies, and her funeral service was broadcast around the world. In Paris, near the tunnel where her car crashed, a golden torch was erected in her memory. Throughout Britain, a moment of silence was observed as the country mourned the death of its beloved princess.

- Have students discuss funerals of other famous people and ways in which they were honored. **Ask** students what kinds of literature keep records of these occurrences. **Possible responses:** Students may suggest newspaper/magazine articles, poems, or nonfiction books.

Introduction ■ 13

Concept Connector

Have students return to the Focus Questions on p. 3. Ask them to use these questions to orally summarize the main points in the unit introduction. Students' summaries should include the following points:

Impact of Alfred the Great on England:

- His achievements in battle helped stop further Danish invasions.

- He supported education and learning.

Literature as historical records in Anglo-Saxon and medieval England:

- Heroic poems detailed the achievements of warriors in battle.

- Anglo-Saxon prose, such as *A History of the English Church and People* and *The Anglo-Saxon Chronicle* served as historical records of the time period.

- Geoffrey Chaucer's *The Canterbury Tales* are observations of medieval society.

The Changing English Language

Critical Thinking

1. What kinds of events caused important changes in early English? **[Generalize]**
   Answer: Conquest and invasion contributed to the development of early English.

2. Review the examples of English words with Norman roots. What areas of life do you think the English words adapted from the Normans mostly concern? **[Draw Conclusions]**
   Answer: Normans dominated the upper strata of society. They influenced the vocabulary of courtly behavior and etiquette.

Critical Viewing

1. Use the map to determine what type of language the Danes brought to England. **[Interpret a Map]**
   Answer: The Danes brought a Germanic language to England.

2. Use the map to determine which people who contributed to the English language did not come from the European continent. **[Interpret a Map]**
   Answer: The Celts, who came from Ireland, did not come from the Continent.

Answer to the Activity

Students can find the first eighteen lines of "The Prologue" to *The Canterbury Tales* in Chaucer's original Middle English on p. 98. The subject of a Middle English sentence, like that of a modern English sentence, generally precedes and adjoins the verb. Common nouns are generally preceded by articles. "Little" words, such as *the* and *and,* appear in identical form in both languages. Many Middle English words, such as *melodyë,* are almost exactly like their modern forms but include a final *e.* Middle English used the verb *hath,* no longer current in modern English. In some forms, verbs that otherwise resemble their modern equivalents end in *-en.* A *y* appears at the beginning of some verbs.

The Beginnings of English

BY RICHARD LEDERER

ENGLISH

The rise of English as a planetary language is an unparalleled success story that began long ago, in the middle of the fifth century A.D. Several large tribes of sea rovers—the Angles, Saxons, and Jutes—lived along the continental North Sea coast, from Denmark to Holland. Around A.D. 449, these Teutonic plunderers sailed across the water and invaded the islands then known as Britannia. They found the land pleasant and the people easy to conquer, so they remained there. They brought with them a Low Germanic tongue that, in its new setting, became Anglo-Saxon, or Old English. In A.D. 827, King Egbert first named Britannia *Englaland,* "land of the Angles."

The language came to be called *Englisc.* Old Englisc differs so much from modern English that it is harder for us to learn than German is. Still, we can recognize a number of Anglo-Saxon words: *bedd, candel, eorth, froendscipe, mann, moder,* and *waeter.* Anglo-Saxon words such as these concern the unchanging basics of life. They survived subsequent social upheavals nearly unmodified. English was to gain its more sophisticated words from other languages, as in the case of the multitude of scientific terms that derive from Latin and Greek.

MIDDLE ENGLISH

A dramatic evolution in the language came after yet another conquest of England, this one by the Norman French two centuries after the rule of Egbert. The new conquerors came from Normandy, a province of France. These Normans (shortened from *Northmen*) had originally been Viking freebooters from Scandinavia, but they now spoke French and had taken to French customs.

In 1066, under William, Duke of Normandy, the Normans invaded England. In a bloody battle at Hastings they conquered the Saxons and Danes who resisted them, killed the Saxon king, Harold, and forced the nobles to choose Duke William as king of England.

One result was that Old Englisc was flooded by the French spoken by the Normans. Examples of French influence include the words *sir, madam, courtesy, honor, chivalry, dine, table, roast, court,* and *royal.* From this infusion of French words emerged a tongue that today we call Middle English.

Celts brought Gaelic.
Danes brought a Germanic language.
IRELAND
DENMARK
Baltic Sea
Angles brought a Germanic language.
ATLANTIC OCEAN
ENGLAND
Normans brought French.
GERMANY
HOLY ROMAN EMPIRE
FRANCE (Normandy)
Romans brought Latin.
ITALY
Papal States
0 150 300
0 150 300 km
N

Languages Brought Into England

Activity

Read the opening verse of the Prologue to Geoffrey Chaucer's *Canterbury Tales* and look for the words *March, shires,* and *martyr.* Research the origins of these words to gain a fuller understanding of their meanings. Then, write briefly about what their diverse origins suggest about the history of the English language itself.

Enrichment

Listening to Old and Middle English

Have students listen to the readings in Old English (from *Beowulf*) and in Middle English (from "The Prologue" to *The Canterbury Tales*) on the **Listening to Literature Audio CDs.**

Before playing the reading from *Beowulf,* have students read lines 530–542 of the poem. Knowing the basic meaning of the passage may help them identify words.

Have students listen to the Middle English. After they hear the recording, ask them how much they understood, and have them use dictionaries to identify words with Anglo-Saxon and French roots. **Possible responses:** An Anglo-Saxon word is *droghte* (drought); a word with a French root is *vertu* (virtue).

Earthly Exile, Heavenly Home

Arrival of Williams at Penvesy, (detail from Bayeux Tapestry)

Earthly Exile, Heavenly Home 15

The selections in this section explore the theme of exile in Anglo-Saxon poetry. "The Seafarer" tells the tale of a sailor whose passion for the sea causes him to undertake dangerous, lonely voyages. The plight of a warrior who must find a new place in the world after his lord dies is described in "The Wanderer." In "The Wife's Lament," a woman whose husband has sent her away describes her misfortune.

Humanities

Arrival of William at Penvesy, (detail from Bayeux Tapestry)

The Bayeux Tapestery commemorates the conquest of England by William the Conquerer in 1066 and was probably commissioned by William's half brother, Odo, the bishop of Bayeux.

Have your students link the art to the focus of this part, "Earthly Exile, Heavenly Home," by answering these questions.

1. The Bayeux Tapestry shows over seventy details from a historical event. What historical event might be commemorated in such an art-work today?
   Possible responses: A contemporary Bayeux Tapestry might show the conquest of space, beginning with the first airplanes; it might show a presidential campaign, beginning with earlier events in the candidate's career.

2. This great work about a non-religious subject was probably commissioned by a bishop and displayed in his cathedral. What do these facts tell you about the role of the Church in the Middle Ages?
   Answer: These facts suggest that the Church was actively involved in political and international events in the Middle Ages.

Monitoring Progress

Before students read the selections in Part 1, administer **Diagnostic Test 1** (*Unit 1 Resources,* pp. 2–4). This test will determine students' level of readiness for the reading and vocabulary skills.

Differentiated
Instruction   Solutions for All Learners

Accessibility at a Glance

More Accessible	Average	More Challenging
The Wanderer	The Seafarer	The Wife's Lament

Meeting Your Standards

Students will

1. **analyze and respond to literary elements.**
   - Literary Analysis: Anglo-Saxon Lyrics

2. **read, comprehend, analyze, and critique a poem.**
   - Reading Strategy: Connecting to Historical Context
   - Reading Check questions
   - Apply the Skills questions
   - Assessment Practice (ATE)

3. **develop vocabulary.**
   - Vocabulary Lesson: Anglo-Saxon Suffix: *-ness*

4. **understand and apply written and oral language conventions.**
   - Spelling Strategy
   - Grammar and Style Lesson: Compound Predicates

5. **develop writing proficiency.**
   - Writing Lesson: Analysis of a Literary Theme

6. **develop appropriate research strategies.**
   - Extend Your Learning: Help Wanted Page

7. **understand and apply listening and speaking strategies.**
   - Extend Your Learning: Oral Interpretation

Block Scheduling: Use one 90-minute class period to preteach the skills and have students read the selection. Use a second 90-minute class period to assess students' mastery of skills, extend their learning, and monitor their progress.

Homework Suggestions

Following are possibilities for homework assignments:

- Support pages from *Unit 1 Resources:*
    Literary Analysis
    Reading Strategy
    Vocabulary Builder
    Grammar and Style

- An Extend Your Learning project and the Writing Lesson for this selection grouping may be completed over several days.

Step-by-Step Teaching Guide	Pacing Guide
PRETEACH	
• Administer Vocabulary and Reading Warm-ups as necessary.	5 min.
• Engage students' interest with the motivation activity.	5 min.
• Read and discuss author and background features. **FT**	10 min.
• Introduce the Literary Analysis Skill: Anglo-Saxon Lyrics. **FT**	5 min.
• Introduce the Reading Strategy: Connecting to Historical Context. **FT**	10 min.
• Prepare students to read by teaching the selection vocabulary. **FT**	
TEACH	
• Informally monitor comprehension while students read independently or in groups. **FT**	30 min.
• Monitor students' comprehension with the Reading Check notes.	as students read
• Reinforce vocabulary with Vocabulary Builder notes.	as students read
• Develop students' understanding of Anglo-Saxon lyrics with the Literary Analysis annotations. **FT**	5 min.
• Develop students' ability to connect to historical context with the Reading Strategy annotations. **FT**	5 min.
ASSESS/EXTEND	
• Assess students' comprehension and mastery of the Literary Analysis and Reading Strategy by having them answer the Apply the Skills questions. **FT**	15 min.
• Have students complete the Vocabulary Lesson and the Grammar and Style Lesson. **FT**	15 min.
• Apply students' knowledge of analyzing themes by using the Writing Lesson. **FT**	45 min. or homework
• Apply students' understanding by using one or more of the Extend Your Learning activities.	20–90 min. or homework
• Administer Selection Test A or Selection Test B. **FT**	15 min.

Resources

PRINT

Unit 1 Resources

TRANSPARENCY

Graphic Organizer Transparencies

PRINT

Reader's Notebook [L2]
Reader's Notebook: Adapted Version [L1]
Reader's Notebook: English Learner's Version [EL]

Unit 1 Resources

TECHNOLOGY

Listening to Literature Audio CDs [L2, EL]
Reader's Notebook: Adapted Version Audio CD [L1, L2]

PRINT

Unit 1 Resources

General Resources

TECHNOLOGY

Go Online: Research [L3]
Go Online: Self-test [L3]
ExamView® Test Bank [L3]

Choosing Resources for Differentiated Instruction

[L1] Special Needs Students

[L2] Below-Level Students

[L3] All Students

[L4] Advanced Students

[EL] English Learners

For Vocabulary and Reading Warm-ups and for Selection Tests, **A** signifies "less challenging" and **B** "more challenging." For Graphic Organizer Transparencies, **A** signifies "not filled in" and **B** "filled in."

FT Fast Track Instruction: To move the lesson more quickly, use the strategies and activities identified with **FT**.

Scaffolding for Less Proficient and Advanced Students

The leveled Critical Thinking questions after selections progress in the levels of thinking required to answer them. To address the needs of your different students, you may use the (a) level questions for your less proficient students and the (b) level questions with your on-level and advanced students. The occasional (c) level questions are appropriate for your advanced students.

PRENTICE HALL
Teacher EXPRESS™
Plan • Teach • Assess
Use this complete suite of powerful teaching tools to make lesson planning and testing quicker and easier.

PRENTICE HALL
Student EXPRESS™
Learn • Study • Succeed
Use the interactive textbook (online and on CD-ROM) to make selections and activities come alive with audio and video support and interactive questions.

Monitoring Progress

Before students read "The Seafarer," administer **Diagnostic Test 1** (*Unit 1 Resources,* pp. 2–4).

Go Online
Professional Development
For: Information about Lexiles
Visit: www.PHSchool.com
Web Code: eue-1111

Motivation

To make the theme of exile more concrete for students, have them imagine that they are sent away forever from their home, friends, and community. Ask each student to imagine a place of exile, such as a foreign country, the wilderness, the sea, or space. Then, have students imagine themselves in this place permanently—and without contact with those they love. Ask students to list, in order of importance, things and people they would yearn for and feelings they might have. Then, ask students to name the kinds of hopes and dreams that might sustain them.

❶ Background
More About the Authors

No one knows the names of the authors of these poems, but we do know much about the era in which they were collected. Alfred the Great, King of Wessex, was a brilliant soldier and wise ruler, but his greatest legacy was his passion for learning and literacy, which he actively promoted. He directed all young freemen to learn to read English. He learned Latin and translated many works into English. He had learned his love of English poetry from his mother and had once hoped to be a literary scholar. The poems in this grouping, collected during this era, are found in *The Exeter Book,* the largest collection of Old English poetry in existence and one of only four collections from the period to survive to present day. Exeter, in the southwest of England, was an important city during the Middle Ages, defended twice by Alfred the Great against invading Danes. Around 975, this collection was copied, and the manuscript was given by Bishop Leofric to Exeter Cathedral, where the book remains to this day.

❶ The Seafarer • The Wanderer • The Wife's Lament

The Exeter Book

Imagine what life would be like if there were no television sets and if movies played in theaters only on important occasions. On the day a movie was to be shown, the air would crackle with anticipation. People would gather beforehand, chatting excitedly. The next day, everyone would discuss the film, quoting dialogue and reenacting scenes.

Telling the Story This scenario may seem as if it belongs in a movie of its own, but it captures the nature of entertainment during Britain's Anglo-Saxon period, from the fifth to the eleventh century. Few people of the time were able to read, and movies lay centuries in the future. Instead, people turned to traveling storytellers, known as *scops,* who memorized, adapted, and passed along an oral tradition of stories and songs. Through the years, many of these works were lost. Others, however, were eventually written down.

An Early Anthology *The Exeter Book* is a collection of manuscripts that includes pieces of this oral tradition. The book was probably compiled by monks during the reign of Alfred the Great, between A.D. 871 and 899. The later history of *The Exeter Book* is a mystery to scholars, but it has evidently survived some rough treatment. The book has a large burn, several stains from a drinking mug, and marks that suggest it was once used as a cutting board! The book survived this abuse, though, which is fortunate—without *The Exeter Book,* many stories that came out of the oral tradition would have been lost to us forever. "The Seafarer," "The Wanderer," and "The Wife's Lament" were all discovered in this collection.

Guests Who Came to Stay Those who recited and listened to the tales recorded in *The Exeter Book*—the Anglo-Saxons—were not native to Britain. In the 400s, Roman soldiers stationed in Britain had abandoned the island to defend Rome. The native inhabitants of England were soon threatened by Picts from Scotland and Scots from Ireland. One British king invited warlike Germanic tribes from Europe to help him defend Britain. These "guests" proved to be the most dangerous invaders of them all. By the 500s, Angles, Saxons, and other Germanic peoples had settled England themselves, driving out most of the Britons.

A Growing Culture The Angles and Saxons who conquered Britain brought with them a warrior culture, a seafaring tradition, and pagan beliefs, including a grim, fatalistic view of the world. They were followed by missionaries sent by Rome. Eventually, these missionaries converted Britain to Christianity. During this period, various literary forms flourished, including historical and religious prose written by monks as well as the oral poetry of scops. Anglo-Saxon culture at the time of *The Exeter Book* was a blend of traditions, mixing pagan ideas of fate with Christian faith in heaven, the boasts of proud warriors with lessons about humility. Preserved by scops and monks, this culture gave Britain its first literature.

A Quick Look at Anglo-Saxon Culture
- The Anglo-Saxons were expert seafarers who sailed the ocean to raid or settle other lands.
- After the Anglo-Saxons settled England in the 500s, many converted to Christianity. They retained, though, a pagan conviction in the power of fate, and retold Germanic and Scandinavian tales of heroes and monsters.
- Men dominated Anglo-Saxon society, and women had few rights.

Preview

Connecting to the Literature

As you read these poems about people in exile, think about what it would be like to live away from home, unsure of whether you will ever return.

Literary Analysis

Anglo-Saxon Lyrics

A lyric poem expresses the thoughts and feelings of a single speaker. **Anglo-Saxon lyrics** were composed for easy memorization and recitation. They contain these elements:

- Lines with regular rhythms, usually with four strong beats
- **Caesuras,** rhythmic breaks in the middle of lines, where the reciter could pause for breath
- **Kennings,** two-word poetic renamings of people, places, and things, such as the kenning *whales' home* for the sea
- **Assonance,** the repetition of vowel sounds in unrhymed, stressed syllables (for example, "b<u>a</u>tter these <u>ra</u>mp<u>a</u>rts")
- **Alliteration,** the repetition of initial consonant sounds in accented syllables.

Notice how these elements add a unique flavor to Anglo-Saxon lyrics.

Comparing Literary Works

Each of the lyrics in this grouping is an **elegy,** a lyric poem mourning the loss of someone or something. Though their circumstances vary greatly, each speaker may be said to have lost a home. As you read, notice the similarities and differences among the speakers' experiences.

Reading Strategy

Connecting to Historical Context

Knowing about the period in which a work originated will help you understand it better. Apply the information on the previous page as you read the poems in this grouping. Use a diagram like the one shown.

Vocabulary Builder

admonish (ad män′ ish) *v.* advise; caution (p. 20)

sentinel (sen′ ti nəl) *n.* person or animal that guards (p. 20)

fervent (fʉr′ vənt) *adj.* having or showing great warmth of feeling (p. 21)

rancor (raŋ′ kər) *n.* ill will (p. 21)

compassionate (kəm pash′ ən it) *adj.* sympathizing; pitying (p. 23)

grievous (grēv′ əs) *adj.* causing sorrow; hard to bear (p. 23)

winsomeness (win′ səm nis) *n.* charm; delightfulness (p. 23)

rapture (rap′ chər) *n.* joy; great pleasure (p. 25)

redress (ri dres′) *n.* compensation, as for a wrong (p. 26)

blithe (blīth) *adj.* cheerful (p. 27)

Event/Idea
The speaker is exiled when his lord dies.

↑

Historical Background
Anglo-Saxon warriors depended on the protection of a powerful lord.

❷ Literary Analysis
Anglo-Saxon Lyrics

- Tell students that as they read "The Seafarer," they will focus on aspects of the poem characteristic of Anglo-Saxon lyrics, such as kennings, caesuras, regular rhythms, assonance, and alliteration.
- Read the instruction about Anglo-Saxon lyrics together as a class. Call students' attention to the examples from the poem.
- Use the instruction for Comparing Literary Works to compare the Anglo-Saxon lyrics in this selection.

❸ Reading Strategy
Connecting to Historical Context

- Remind students that authors of the poems in this grouping were Anglo-Saxons, Germanic tribes who settled England in the 400s.
- Review with students the box on aspects of Anglo-Saxon culture.
- Point out the example that shows how one event from "The Wanderer" is clarified by historical context.
- Encourage students to keep this historical context in mind when reading poems in this grouping.
- Give students a copy of **Reading Strategy Graphic Organizer A, p. 1** in *Graphic Organizer Transparencies,* to use as they read the selections.

Vocabulary Builder

- Pronounce each vocabulary word for students, and read the definitions as a class. Have students identify any words with which they are already familiar.

Differentiated Instruction   Solutions for All Learners

Support for Special Needs Students
Have students use the support pages for these selections in the *Reader's Notebook: Adapted Version.* Completing these pages will prepare students to read the selections in the Student Edition.

Support for Less Proficient Readers
Have students use the support pages for these selections in the *Reader's Notebook.* After students finish the pages in the *Reader's Notebook,* have them complete the questions and activities in the Student Edition.

Support for English Learners
Have students use the support pages for these selections in the *Reader's Notebook: English Learner's Version.* Completing these pages will prepare students to read the selections in the Student Edition.

Learning Modalities
Musical/Rhythmic Learners

Have small groups of students interpret, practice, and perform lines 1–26 of "The Seafarer." Ask students to re-create not only the rhythm and tone but also some of the background sounds that the seafarer would have experienced.

❶ About the Selection

Who could be more wretched than the lonely seafarer, drifting in icy waters, far from human companionship? Yet, though the seafarer is "drowning in desolation" at sea, he returns to it again and again, for life itself, no matter where it is spent, is exile: The only home is heaven.

❷ Humanities

Ships With Three Men, Fish, illuminated manuscript

Three men in a boat are confronted by a whale. Although the whale is busy eating fish, the men seem intent on getting out of its reach.

The illustration lacks perspective and also lacks realism. The sea is interpreted as an abstract shape. Yet the size of the whale and its proximity to the boat convey that this is a fearful moment. Use these questions for discussion:

1. Does the illustration help you to visualize what the seafarer relates?
Possible responses: The illustration suggests the dangers of life at sea, as does the speaker. However, the speaker emphasizes the solitude of seafaring, while the illustration shows a group of sailors.

2. Do the sailors seem to share the seafarer's feelings?
Possible response: The seated sailor, like the seafarer, appears to accept his fate.

❸ Critical Viewing

Answer: Students may observe that the perspective is flat and that the boat, rigging, whale, and waves are stylized. The sailors' clothing, the rudder, and sail may be true to the seafarer's experience.

Ships with Three Men, Fish, Fish, The Bodleian Library, University of Oxford

❸ ⏶ **Critical Viewing** Which elements in this picture are true to the seafarer's experience? Which elements are stylized? **[Classify]**

18 ■ From Legend to History (449–1485)

Differentiated Instruction
Solutions for All Learners

Accessibility at a Glance

	The Seafarer	The Wanderer	The Wife's Lament
Context	Anglo-Saxon oral tradition	Anglo-Saxon oral tradition	Anglo-Saxon oral tradition
Language	Sensory details; long and short sentences	Formal diction; footnoted period language	Poetic diction and syntax
Concept Level	Challenging (both physical experiences and abstract truths)	Challenging (accepting one's fate)	Accessible (personal observations and feelings)
Literary Merit	Classic	Classic	Classic
Lexile	NP	NP	NP
Overall Rating	Average	More accessible	More challenging

The Seafarer

Translated by Burton Raffel

Background Each of the poems in this grouping is about exile—
a prolonged stay away from home that is forced upon the exiled person. To
the Anglo-Saxon people of Britain, *home* meant something different from
what it means for people today. An Anglo-Saxon warrior viewed himself as
the follower of a particular lord or king, not as a citizen of a nation. In
exchange for a warrior's sworn loyalty, a lord dispensed goods—bread, fruit,
riches won in raids—and guaranteed security in a dangerous world.
Gathering in the mead-hall, a building dedicated to their feasts, a lord and
his warriors would share food, drink, entertainment, and fellowship. Smoky,
noisy, smelly, and crowded, the mead-hall was home.

   This tale is true, and mine. It tells
   How the sea took me, swept me back
   And forth in sorrow and fear and pain,
   Showed me suffering in a hundred ships,
5 In a thousand ports, and in me. It tells
   Of smashing surf when I sweated in the cold
   Of an anxious watch, perched in the bow
   As it dashed under cliffs. My feet were cast
   In icy bands, bound with frost,
10 With frozen chains, and hardship groaned
   Around my heart. Hunger tore
   At my sea-weary soul. No man sheltered
   On the quiet fairness of earth can feel
   How wretched I was, drifting through winter
15 On an ice-cold sea, whirled in sorrow,
   Alone in a world blown clear of love,
   Hung with icicles. The hailstorms flew.

Reading Strategy
**Connecting to Historical
Context** What Anglo-
Saxon ideas of home and
community explain why
the speaker feels so
strongly about his exile?

Reading Check
What sufferings has the
speaker endured at sea?

The Seafarer ■ 19

**❹ Reading Strategy
Connecting to Historical
Context**

- Call on a volunteer to read aloud
the bracketed passage.

- Then, **ask** the Reading Strategy
question: What Anglo-Saxon ideas
of home and community explain
why the speaker feels so strongly
about his exile?
Possible response: Anglo-Saxons
had a very strong sense of community. Home represented warmth,
compared to the sea's cold; love,
compared to the sea's loneliness;
and safety, compared to the sea's
dangers. Also, the fellowship and
community of the mead-hall would
be missed. All that seemed good,
and that gave a man his identity,
was tied up with home and community.

**❺ Critical Thinking
Support**

- **Ask** students what things in this
first stanza can be "heard" or
"seen" based on the author's
descriptions.
Possible responses: A ship being
tossed in the waves, different ships,
different ports, and the roar of the
pounding surf can be seen and
heard in the first stanza.

- Based on what they've read, **ask**
students to predict what might
happen to the seafarer.

❻ Reading Check

Answer: The speaker has endured
smashing surf, danger, anxiety, cold,
hunger, hardship, weariness, sorrow,
hailstorms, and a loveless world.

Britain, Seafaring Nation

The ocean has long protected the British Isles. In fact, since the Norman Conquest in 1066, no one has succeeded in invading Britain. The ocean has also provided Britain with an income. From the explorers and merchants who made the country powerful to the fishermen who still work along her coasts, the British people have long benefited from the sea. For centuries, ships were the best and fastest way to move goods from one country to another, and the British had the best ships and the finest seamen. It was said that "Britain ruled the waves." Merchant ships came in from the Mediterranean, Africa, India, and, eventually, North America. During the Age of Exploration, Captain John Cook, an explorer and scientist, peacefully changed the map of the world more than any other man in history. The English involvement with the sea is still reflected in the country's literature, and can be enjoyed in such exciting works as the Horatio Hornblower novels and Patrick O'Brian's Aubrey-Maturin books.

Connect to the Literature

Encourage students to use details from the text to support their answers.
Possible response: The speaker is drawn back to the sea by its promise of freedom and adventure.

❽ Literary Analysis
Anglo-Saxon Lyrics

▶ **Monitor Progress:** Ask a volunteer to define the literary term *alliteration*. Then, ask the student to provide an example.
Answer: The repetition of initial consonant sounds in accented syllables.

- **Ask** students the Literary Analysis question: How does the alliteration of words beginning with *w, r,* and *s* affect the sound and meaning of lines 59–62?
Possible Response: The alliteration of words beginning with *w, r,* and *s* makes the passage, at first, slightly mesmerizing like the waves, but it also propels the passage— "solitary, screaming, exciting" has great energy.

- Have students continue to look for alliteration as they read.

The only sound was the roaring sea,
The freezing waves. The song of the swan
20 Might serve for pleasure, the cry of the sea-fowl,
The death-noise of birds instead of laughter,
The mewing of gulls instead of mead.[1]
Storms beat on the rocky cliffs and were echoed
By icy-feathered terns and the eagle's screams;
25 No kinsman could offer comfort there,
To a soul left drowning in desolation.
　　　And who could believe, knowing but
The passion of cities, swelled proud with wine
And no taste of misfortune, how often, how wearily,
30 I put myself back on the paths of the sea.
Night would blacken; it would snow from the north;
Frost bound the earth and hail would fall,
The coldest seeds. And how my heart
Would begin to beat, knowing once more
35 The salt waves tossing and the towering sea!
The time for journeys would come and my soul
Called me eagerly out, sent me over
The horizon, seeking foreigners' homes.
　　　But there isn't a man on earth so proud,
40 So born to greatness, so bold with his youth,
Grown so brave, or so graced by God,
That he feels no fear as the sails unfurl,
Wondering what Fate has willed and will do.
No harps ring in his heart, no rewards,
45 No passion for women, no worldly pleasures,
Nothing, only the ocean's heave;
But longing wraps itself around him.
Orchards blossom, the towns bloom,
Fields grow lovely as the world springs fresh,
50 And all these <u>admonish</u> that willing mind
Leaping to journeys, always set
In thoughts traveling on a quickening tide.
So summer's <u>sentinel</u>, the cuckoo, sings
In his murmuring voice, and our hearts mourn
55 As he urges. Who could understand,
In ignorant ease, what we others suffer
As the paths of exile stretch endlessly on?
　　　And yet my heart wanders away,
My soul roams with the sea, the whales'
60 Home, wandering to the widest corners
Of the world, returning ravenous with desire,
Flying solitary, screaming, exciting me
To the open ocean, breaking oaths

---

1. **mead** liquor made from fermented honey and water.

❼ Britain, Seafaring Nation

Britain is an island, and its inhabitants have always had a complex relationship with the sea. Throughout British history, the ocean has been both an avenue to new lands and a mighty barrier to strangers, both a gateway to trade and conquest and a scene of terrifying isolation.

From its very beginning, the literature of Britain reflects this complicated connection. "The Seafarer," one of the earliest known British poems, explores the intense hold of the sea on the speaker's heart, an enduring theme. The theme of exile found in this ninth-century poem reappears, for instance, in the twentieth century in Joseph Conrad's sea tales.

Connect to the Literature

What draws the speaker of "The Seafarer" back to the ocean time and again?

Vocabulary Builder

admonish (ad män´ ish) *v.* advise; caution

sentinel (sen´ ti nəl) *n.* person or animal that guards

Literary Analysis
Anglo-Saxon Lyrics

How does the alliteration of words beginning with *w, r,* and *s* affect the sound and meaning of lines 59–62?

Enrichment

Fate

Explain to students that different cultures have different opinions about the role of fate in people's lives. These opinions can be seen as running along a continuum. At one end are those who believe that there is no free choice whatsoever; at the other end are those who believe that people have responsibility for everything that happens in their lives.

The Greeks believed that human life was subject to the whims of the gods, whereas Chaldean Egyptians, who introduced astrology, believed that planetary position had a direct influence on people's lives.

The Catholic Church maintains that people have free will. Hinduism combines fate with free will in the concept of karma, the belief that life in the present is determined by actions in past lives but that people are free to improve their character for future lives.

On the curve of a wave.
          Thus the joys of God
65 Are <u>fervent</u> with life, where life itself
Fades quickly into the earth. The wealth
Of the world neither reaches to Heaven nor remains.
No man has ever faced the dawn
Certain which of Fate's three threats
70 Would fall: illness, or age, or an enemy's
Sword, snatching the life from his soul.
The praise the living pour on the dead
Flowers from reputation: plant
An earthly life of profit reaped
75 Even from hatred and <u>rancor</u>, of bravery
Flung in the devil's face, and death
Can only bring you earthly praise
And a song to celebrate a place
With the angels, life eternally blessed
80 In the hosts of Heaven.
          The days are gone
When the kingdoms of earth flourished in glory;
Now there are no rulers, no emperors,
No givers of gold, as once there were,
When wonderful things were worked among them
85 And they lived in lordly magnificence.
Those powers have vanished, those pleasures are dead.
The weakest survives and the world continues,
Kept spinning by toil. All glory is tarnished.
The world's honor ages and shrinks,
90 Bent like the men who mold it. Their faces
Blanch as time advances, their beards
Wither and they mourn the memory of friends.
The sons of princes, sown in the dust.
The soul stripped of its flesh knows nothing
95 Of sweetness or sour, feels no pain,
Bends neither its hand nor its brain. A brother
Opens his palms and pours down gold
On his kinsman's grave, strewing his coffin
With treasures intended for Heaven, but nothing
100 Golden shakes the wrath of God
For a soul overflowing with sin, and nothing
Hidden on earth rises to Heaven.
    We all fear God. He turns the earth,
He set it swinging firmly in space,
105 Gave life to the world and light to the sky.
Death leaps at the fools who forget their God.
He who lives humbly has angels from Heaven
To carry him courage and strength and belief.
A man must conquer pride, not kill it,

Vocabulary Builder
fervent (fur' vənt) *adj.*
having or showing great
warmth of feeling

Vocabulary Builder
rancor (raŋ' kər) *n.* ill will

Literary Analysis
**Anglo-Saxon Lyrics
and the Elegy** What
does the speaker mourn
in lines 81–90?

❿ **Reading Check**
Why does the seafarer
return to the sea time and
again?

The Seafarer ■ 21

**❾ Literary Analysis
Anglo-Saxon Lyrics and the
Elegy**

▶ **Reteach:** Remind students that an
elegy is a lament for the loss of
someone or something.

• Read aloud the bracketed passage.
Ask students to answer the Literary
Analysis question: What does the
speaker mourn in lines 81–90?
Answer: The speaker mourns the
end of the era of prosperity and
empire, when gold was freely given
by rulers whose power was magnificent and inspiring.

• **Ask** students to explain how these
lines function as an elegy.
Answer: An elegy laments the loss
of something or someone. These
lines are an elegy for the now vanished "good old days."

❿ Reading Check

Answer: The seafarer returns to the
sea time and time again because he
is drawn to the adventure and the
excitement of travel into unknown
lands.

1. **Possible response:** I agree that "Fate is stronger. . . than any man's mind," because free will can only accomplish so much; eventually, the course of events will bring about a series of events that the best mind could not predict or anticipate.

2. (a) **Possible responses:** Three images related to weather in the first stanza include "the winter on an ice-cold sea," a world "hung with icicles," and hailstorms. (b) They convey the misery and desolation of the speaker's experiences at sea.

3. (a) The speaker's heart "begin[s] to beat" when he is reunited with the salt waves and the towering sea. (b) **Possible response:** Many things that are valued have high "price tags." People such as astronauts, mountain climbers, or war correspondents risk great danger to pursue what they feel are worthwhile passions or exciting endeavors. Almost nothing important comes without some work or difficulty.

4. (a) The seafarer does not respond to the pleasures of life on land. (b) The seafarer is more attached to life at sea than on land.

5. (a) The speaker means that wandering and the ocean are in his heart; they are part of who he is. As a result, he cannot resist the call of the sea. (b) The speaker is not fully at home on land, because he always wants to be at sea, and he is not fully at home at sea, because he feels himself in exile. Also, he views heaven as his true home.

6. (a) Our home is in Heaven with God. (b) The seafarer's ideas about God and heaven seem to suggest that life on Earth is not as important as the heavenly home; when the seafarer dies, his exile will be over.

7. **Possible response:** Like the seafarer, most people will always have a longing for something that they don't have, whether that is a different location, or a different job or life, or even Heaven.

---

110 Be firm with his fellows, chaste for himself,
　　Treat all the world as the world deserves,
　　With love or with hate but never with harm,
　　Though an enemy seek to scorch him in hell,
　　Or set the flames of a funeral pyre
115 Under his lord. Fate is stronger
　　And God mightier than any man's mind.
　　Our thoughts should turn to where our home is,
　　Consider the ways of coming there,
　　Then strive for sure permission for us
120 To rise to that eternal joy,
　　That life born in the love of God
　　And the hope of Heaven. Praise the Holy
　　Grace of Him who honored us,
　　Eternal, unchanging creator of earth. Amen.

Critical Reading

1. **Respond:** Do you agree that "Fate is stronger . . . than any man's mind"? Why or why not?

2. (a) **Recall:** Identify three images related to weather in the first stanza. (b) **Interpret:** What does each convey about the speaker's experiences at sea?

3. (a) **Recall:** What causes the speaker's heart to "begin to beat"? (b) **Generalize:** How can someone dislike something as much as the seafarer dislikes life at sea and yet be drawn to it?

4. (a) **Recall:** What is the seafarer's response to "harps," "rewards," "passion," and the other pleasures of life on the land (lines 44–47)? (b) **Interpret:** Judging from his response to these things, explain whether he is more attached to life on land than he is to life at sea.

5. (a) **Interpret:** What does the speaker mean when he says in lines 58–61 "And yet my heart wanders away, / My soul roams with the sea, . . . / . . . returning ravenous with desire, . . ."? (b) **Draw Conclusions:** Is the speaker fully at home on land, on the sea, or in neither place? Explain.

6. (a) **Interpret:** According to the last section of the poem, where is our home? (b) **Synthesize:** Explain the connection between the poem's concluding message and its depiction of the seafarer's wandering existence.

7. **Evaluate:** Can people find a way of life in which they are fully happy, or, like the seafarer, will they always have longings for another place? Explain.

The WANDERER

Translated by Charles W. Kennedy

⓫

Oft to the wanderer,   weary of exile,
Cometh God's pity,   <u>compassionate</u> love,
Though woefully toiling   on wintry seas
With churning oar   in the icy wave,
5 Homeless and helpless   he fled from fate.
Thus saith the wanderer   mindful of misery,
<u>Grievous</u> disasters,   and death of kin:
    "Oft when the day broke, oft at the dawning,
Lonely and wretched   I wailed my woe.
10 No man is living,   no comrade left,
To whom I dare fully   unlock my heart.
I have learned truly   the mark of a man
Is keeping his counsel   and locking his lips,
Let him think what he will!   For, woe of heart
15 Withstandeth not fate: a failing spirit
Earneth no help.   Men eager for honor
Bury their sorrow   deep in the breast.
    "So have I also,   often in wretchedness
Fettered[1] my feelings,   far from my kin,
20 Homeless and hapless,[2]   since days of old,
When the dark earth covered   my dear lord's face,
And I sailed away   with sorrowful heart,
Over wintry seas,   seeking a gold-lord,
If far or near   lived one to befriend me
25 With gift in the mead-hall   and comfort for grief.
    "Who bears it, knows   what a bitter companion,
Shoulder to shoulder,   sorrow can be,
When friends are no more.   His fortune is exile,
Not gifts of fine gold;   a heart that is frozen,
30 Earth's <u>winsomeness</u> dead.   And he dreams of the hall-men,
The dealing of treasure,   the days of his youth,

---

1. **fettered** (fet´ ərd) chained; restrained.
2. **hapless** (hap´ lis) unlucky.

Vocabulary Builder

compassionate (kəm pash´ ən it) *adj.* sympathizing; pitying

grievous (grēv´ əs) *adj.* causing sorrow; hard to bear

Literary Analysis

Anglo-Saxon Lyrics How does the kenning "gold-lord" help you understand the wanderer's goal?

Vocabulary Builder

winsomeness (win´ səm nis) *n.* charm; delightfulness

⓮ 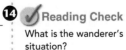 Reading Check

What is the wanderer's situation?

The Wanderer ■ 23

⓫ **About the Selection**
The wanderer in this poem has experienced the complete collapse of his entire world: His lord has died. That means he has no more purpose, no more friends, no more hopes of enjoying treasures, no one to feast with, and no one's knee upon which to lay his hand and promise loyalty. He is alone, cast out, left to wander in search of a new lord.

⓬ **Literary Analysis**
Anglo-Saxon Lyrics

▶ **Reteach:** Remind students that a kenning is a metaphorical phrase used in place of a concrete noun.

• Call on a volunteer to read the bracketed passage aloud. Have students **identify** the kenning.

▶ **Monitor Progress:** Then **ask** the Literary Analysis question: How does the kenning "gold-lord" help you understand the wanderer's goal?
Answer: The kenning suggests that the wanderer's livelihood is intimately connected with his having a lord, or one who will provide him with gold, or money.

⓭ **Vocabulary Builder**
The Anglo-Saxon Suffix -ness

• Call students' attention to the word *winsomeness* and its definition. Tell students that the suffix *-ness* means "quality or condition of being." So winsomeness is the quality of being winsome.

• Explain that nouns are created when *-ness* is added to adjectives. For example, *winsome* is an adjective that has been turned into the noun *winsomeness*.

• Point out that, if an adjective ends in *-y*, the *-y* changes to *-i* before *-ness* is added. **Ask** students to think of familiar words that end with the suffix *-ness* and determine the adjectives from which they were formed—or have them think of an adjective and add *-ness*.
Possible responses: dark/darkness; happy/happiness; lonely/loneliness.

⓮ **Reading Check**
Answer: The wanderer is bereft because his lord has died, and he is left lonely and without means to support himself or hope of enjoying himself in his lord's company.

Enrichment

"The Wanderer"

"The Wanderer" is considered the most nearly perfect in form and feeling of all Old English lyrics because of its intensity of emotion. In manuscript, it shows the fewest signs of accidental mutilation or of deliberate tamperings by later copyists.

"The Wanderer" probably dates to the 700s or earlier, at a time when Scandinavia was in upheaval and many sailors fled ancestral homes there to settle finally in England. The poem might have reminded its northern English audience of the struggles their forebears met before reaching England.

Point out to students that immigrants throughout history have found ways to remind themselves of the past. Even modern immigrants often recite poems, tell stories, or sing songs about their former land.

The Wreck of a Transport Ship,
1810, by J.M.W. Turner

The talent of Joseph Mallord William Turner (1775–1851) was recognized early and encouraged. He was educated at the Royal Academy of Arts and had his first exhibition of paintings at the age of 15. His varied interests and wide travels are often reflected in his work. The painting that appears on this page dates to the first period of his mature work (1800–1820). During this period, he focused on mythological and historical scenes. He often painted epic scenes of catastrophe that underscored humanity's frailty in the face of natural forces. As his career progressed, his paintings were characterized more and more by diffused light and color. This created an effect that, as painter John Constable noted, looked as if Turner painted "with tinted steam." Turner is considered by many to be the greatest of all landscape painters. During his life he created approximately 280 oil paintings and 19,000 drawings and watercolors, most of which are now in the collection of the Tate Gallery in London.

16 **Critical Viewing**

Possible answer: While the picture does not show the events of the poem, it does reflect the poem's mood, which is bleak, desperate, and filled with sorrow over the death of friends and family.

15

16 ▲ **Critical Viewing** Does the scene in this painting match the mood of the poem? Explain. **[Connect]**

When his lord bade welcome   to wassail[3] and feast.
But gone is that gladness,   and never again
Shall come the loved counsel   of comrade and king.
35   "Even in slumber   his sorrow assaileth,
And, dreaming he claspeth   his dear lord again,
Head on knee, hand on knee,   loyally laying,
Pledging his liege[4]   as in days long past.
Then from his slumber   he starts lonely-hearted,
40   Beholding gray stretches   of tossing sea.
Sea-birds bathing,   with wings outspread,
While hailstorms darken,   and driving snow.
Bitterer then   is the bane of his wretchedness,

---

3. **wassail** (wäs´ əl) a toast in drinking a person's health, or a celebration at which such toasts are made.
4. **liege** (lēj) lord; sovereign.

24 ■ From Legend to History (449–1485)

Enrichment

The Homily
Point out to students that the passage in lines 58–65 interrupts an intensely concrete and dramatic scene with a homily, a passage that gives general advice pertaining to morals and conduct.

Some critics have argued that the homiletic passages in "The Wanderer" must be later additions to a poem that is otherwise remarkably terse, lyrical, intense, and dramatic.

Other critics assert that the homilies are perfectly in character, even when they contradict attitudes expressed in other parts of the poem. In this view, they serve as an ironic device, showing the wanderer's belief in justice at those moments when he is most overcome by grief.

The longing for loved one: his grief is renewed.
45 The forms of his kinsmen   take shape in the silence:
In <u>rapture</u> he greets them;   in gladness he scans
Old comrades remembered.   But they melt into air
With no word of greeting   to gladden his heart.
Then again surges   his sorrow upon him;
50 And grimly he spurs   his weary soul
Once more to the toil   of the tossing sea.
        "No wonder therefore,   in all the world,
If a shadow darkens   upon my spirit
When I reflect   on the fates of men—
55 How one by one   proud warriors vanish
From the halls that knew them,   and day by day
All this earth ages   and droops unto death.
No man may know wisdom   till many a winter
Has been his portion.   A wise man is patient,
60 Not swift to anger,   nor hasty of speech,
Neither too weak,   nor too reckless, in war,
Neither fearful nor fain,[5]   nor too wishful of wealth,
Nor too eager in vow—   ere he know the event.
A brave man must bide[6]   when he speaketh his boast
65 Until he know surely   the goal of his spirit.
        "A wise man will ponder   how dread is that doom
When all this world's wealth   shall be scattered and waste
As now, over all,   through the regions of earth,
Walls stand rime-covered[7]   and swept by the winds.
70 The battlements crumble,   the wine-halls decay;
Joyless and silent   the heroes are sleeping
Where the proud host fell   by the wall they defended.
Some battle launched   on their long, last journey;
One a bird bore   o'er the billowing sea:
75 One the gray wolf slew;   one a grieving earl
Sadly gave   to the grave's embrace.
The Warden of men   hath wasted this world
Till the sound of music   and revel is stilled,
And these giant-built structures   stand empty of life.
80   "He who shall muse   on these moldering ruins,
And deeply ponder   this darkling life,
Must brood on old legends   of battle and bloodshed,
And heavy the mood   that troubles his heart:
'Where now is the warrior?   Where is the war horse?
85 Bestowal of treasure,   and sharing of feast?
Alas! the bright ale-cup,   the byrny-clad[8] warrior,

---

5. **fain** (fān) archaic word meaning "eager." In this context it means "too eager."
6. **bide** (bīd) wait.
7. **rime** (rīm)-**covered** covered with frost.
8. **byrny** (bər′ nē)-**clad** dressed in a coat of chain-mail armor.

The Wanderer ■ 25

---

⑰ Critical Thinking
Analyze

• Read aloud the bracketed passage. Then, **ask** students to explain what the wanderer imagines.
Answer: He imagines his comrades before him. The wanderer greets them, but they disappear without returning the greeting.

• Remind students what they learned about an *elegy*. **Ask** them to explain how this passage is elegiac.
Answer: The passage is elegiac in that it deals with sorrow over that which is lost.

⑱ Reading Strategy
Connecting to Historical Context

▶ **Reteach:** Remind students that historical context concerns more than events. It also concerns beliefs and ideas—what is called "worldview."

• Have students review what they know about the Anglo-Saxon worldview after they read this stanza. Suggest that they review the introductory material at the beginning of the selection.

• Then, **ask** students to answer the Reading Strategy question: How does your knowledge of Anglo-Saxon life help you appreciate the mood of these lines?
Possible response: The wanderer expresses a contentment with fate and an appreciation for the wisdom that comes through experience, which are in keeping with Anglo-Saxon values of accepting one's destiny and proving oneself in acts of courage and bravery.

⑲ Reading Check

Answer: The wanderer reflects on the passage of time and of all the things and people that have been lost to death and decay.

Differentiated Instruction   Solutions for All Learners

Support for Special Needs Students
The unusual line breaks may make this poem difficult to read. Pick a section or stanza and summarize it for students. Then have students rewrite it as normal sentences, without line breaks, using punctuation as a guideline. Monitor progress to ensure accuracy, or do it as a group. Then, have them break the sentences into phrases. Discuss the phrases, helping students determine meaning. Point out how the meaning of a phrase contributes to the meaning of the sentence, section, or stanza.

Support for Gifted/Talented Students
In order to help them better understand the images in the poem, have students look for pictures of the things described in "The Wanderer." This may include people in period dress, castles, weapons, ceremonies, monuments, or anything else appropriate to the period and the poem. Have students create a brief presentation for the class that combines pictures they have found with an interpretive reading of lines that might be illustrated by the pictures.

⑳ Literary Analysis
Anglo-Saxon Lyrics

- Remind students that alliteration and assonance are effective for making the poem entertaining and memorable, but they are also often used to connect ideas.

- **Ask** students what images and ideas alliteration and assonance bind together in lines 87–92.
Possible response: Alliteration binds together images such as a "wall wondrous high," "serpent shapes," "carnage" and "conquering fate," and assonance binds together words such as "warriors" with "memorials."

㉑ Literary Analysis
Anglo-Saxon Lyrics

- Remind students that a caesura is a pause.

- Have students **answer** the Literary Analysis question: How are caesuras indicated on the page?
Answer: Caesuras are indicated by a space mid-line.

ASSESS

Answers

1. Students may relate to the wanderer's search for belonging or his concern about being a good person.

2. (a) The speakers in the poem are the narrator and the wanderer.
(b) The narrator describes what the wanderer experiences from an omniscient point of view; the wanderer describes his experiences from his own point of view.
(c) It makes it possible to see things from both outside and inside his personal experiences.

3. (a) The wanderer goes into exile because his lord died and he is searching for a new gold-lord.
(b) Students' responses may include such images as darkness, winter, wind-tossed seas, and crumbling walls.

4. (a) The wanderer reflects on the fact that death claims everyone.
(b) His grief at the death of his lord causes him to ponder the deaths of all men.

5. The wanderer believes that wisdom comes from contemplating things that last, because life is short.

continued

26

---

⑳

90

The prince in his splendor—   those days are long sped
In the night of the past,   as if they never had been!'
And now remains only,   for warriors' memorial,
A wall wondrous high   with serpent shapes carved.
Storms of ash-spears   have smitten the earls,
Carnage of weapon,   and conquering fate.
      "Storms now batter   these ramparts of stone;
Blowing snow   and the blast of winter

95

㉑

Enfold the earth;   night-shadows fall
Darkly lowering,   from the north driving
Raging hail   in wrath upon men.
Wretchedness fills   the realm of earth,
And fate's decrees   transform the world.

100

Here wealth is fleeting,   friends are fleeting,
Man is fleeting,   maid is fleeting;
All the foundation of earth   shall fail!"
      Thus spake the sage   in solitude pondering.
Good man is he   who guardeth his faith.

105

He must never too quickly   unburden his breast
Of its sorrow, but eagerly   strive for redress;
And happy the man   who seeketh for mercy
From his heavenly Father,   our fortress and strength.

Literary Analysis
Anglo-Saxon Lyrics
How are caesuras indicated on the page?

Vocabulary Builder
redress (ri dres´) *n.* compensation, as for a wrong

Critical Reading

1. **Respond:** In what ways is the wanderer someone with whom you can sympathize?

2. **(a) Recall:** Who are the speakers in the poem? **(b) Analyze:** What is the relationship between the two? **(c) Analyze:** What effect does the use of two speakers have on the reader's picture of the wanderer?

3. **(a) Recall:** Why does the wanderer go into exile?
(b) Analyze: What images does the poet use to convey his isolation and despair?

4. **(a) Recall:** What are "the fates of men" on which the wanderer reflects?
(b) Connect: Why might the wanderer's own experiences have led him to such brooding thoughts?

5. **Synthesize:** According to the poem, how might reflection on "the fates of men" lead to wisdom?

6. **Evaluate:** Do you think dwelling on the sorrowful, painful side of life can give a person wisdom and a valuable perspective on life, or do you think it can be harmful? Explain.

Answers continued

6. Students may say that reflecting on the difficult aspects of life can prepare someone for difficulties they might face. Others might think that dwelling on sorrow will not have positive effects. Students may note that the wanderer's life was difficult and required such thoughts.

The Wife's Lament

Translated by Ann Stanford

Susanna in Bath, (detail), Albrecht Altdorfer, *Wasserholendes Mädchen,* München, Alte Pinakothek

I make this song   about me full sadly
my own wayfaring.   I a woman tell
what griefs I had   since I grew up
new or old   never more than now.
5 Ever I know   the dark of my exile.

First my lord went out   away from his people
over the wave-tumult.   I grieved each dawn
wondered where my lord   my first on earth might be.
Then I went forth   a friendless exile
10 to seek service   in my sorrow's need.
My man's kinsmen   began to plot
by darkened thought   to divide us two
so we most widely   in the world's kingdom
lived wretchedly   and I suffered longing.

15 My lord commanded me   to move my dwelling here.
I had few loved ones   in this land
or faithful friends.   For this my heart grieves:
that I should find the man   well matched to me
hard of fortune   mournful of mind
20 hiding his mood   thinking of murder.

Blithe was our bearing   often we vowed
that but death alone   would part us two
naught else.   But this is turned round
now . . .   as if it never were
25 our friendship.   I must far and near

---

22 About the Selection

The speaker of this poem has been sent into exile by her husband. Although she still longs for him, she is bitter and angry about the friendless, lonely, joyless fate she must endure.

23 Humanities

Susanna Fetching Water (detail from **Susanna in Bath**), 1526, by Albrecht Altdorfer

One of the most important artists of the German Renaissance, Albrecht Altdorfer was a painter, draftsman, and printmaker.

Although everything he painted seems highly detailed, Altdorfer aimed for the coordination of all details within the space of the picture. Use this question for discussion:

How does this picture express the idea of sadness? Would you use it to illustrate the theme of exile? Explain.
Answer: Students may say that despite the beauty of the details, the dark colors and the shadows create a dominant impression of detachment. All of these impressions help evoke a state of exile.

24 Critical Viewing

 Critical Viewing
Compare the woman in this picture with the speaker in the poem.
[Compare and Contrast]

Answer: The woman in this painting is alone, like the speaker in the poem, and may even seem sad or pensive. However, the speaker appears to live in some wretched, lonely, dark place, whereas the woman in the painting lives in or approaches a civilized dwelling.

Vocabulary Builder
blithe (blīth) *adj.* cheerful

25 Reading Check

Reading Check
What has happened between the speaker and her husband?

Answer: The speaker and her husband have become alienated from each other, because his kinsmen convinced him to believe lies about her, and he sent her into exile.

Differentiated Instruction   Solutions for All Learners

Enrichment for Advanced Readers

This era offers a wealth of fascinating topics for students who wish to study further. Not only will delving into the early Middle Ages be interesting, but it will deepen students' appreciation of the period's poetry and make connecting with historical context both easier and richer.

Students might consider further research into the poetry of the era. Alternatively, they may wish to study such related topics as the life and times of Alfred the Great; the seafaring traditions of the Anglo-Saxons; day-to-day life in this era, and how war and disease may have contributed to a focus on the eternal; or the impact of an early emphasis on literacy on the development of literature and education in England.

If time permits, you may wish to encourage students to share some of what they learn with the class.

26 Humanities

***Shipping off a Coastline in Rough Sea*, Petrus Johannes Schotel (1808-1865)**

Petrus Johannes Schotel was born in Dordrect on August 19, 1808. His father, Johannes Christiaan Schotel, was a famous maritime painter.

Schotel inherited his father's love of nautical art and became a drawing instructor for the Royal Naval Academy in Medemblik. After a time teaching, he moved his family and became a full-time artist. He produced mainly paintings, but he also made lithographs and etches. Schotel's series of 45 lithographs entitled "Dutch Heroism at Sea" portray important naval battles throughout Dutch history. These pictures are a tribute to the navy and are on exhibit at the Naval Museum. Use this question for discussion:

• How do the details in this painting show the artist's love of maritime scenes?

  Possible answer: He captures the power of the sea over the human condition. His detailed rendering of the waves emphasizes their power.

27 Critical Viewing

Possible response: The speaker may imagine her husband, who was lost at sea, tossed by the ocean like the ship in this painting. Lines 7, 48, and 49 support these imaginings.

27 ▲ **Critical Viewing** Do you think this painting reflects the imaginings of the speaker? Why or why not? **[Analyze]**

bear the anger   of my beloved.
The man sent me out   to live in the woods
under an oak tree   in this den in the earth.
Ancient this earth hall.   I am all longing.

30 The valleys are dark   the hills high
the yard overgrown   bitter with briars
a joyless dwelling.   Full oft the lack of my lord
seizes me cruelly here.   Friends there are on earth
living beloved   lying in bed
35 while I at dawn   am walking alone
under the oak tree   through these earth halls.
There I may sit   the summerlong day
there I can weep   over my exile
my many hardships.   Hence I may not rest
40 from this care of heart   which belongs to me ever
nor all this longing   that has caught me in this life.

May that young man   be sad-minded always
hard his heart's thought   while he must wear
a blithe bearing   with care in the breast
45 a crowd of sorrows.   May on himself depend
all his world's joy.   Be he outlawed far
in a strange folk-land—   that my beloved sits
under a rocky cliff   rimed with frost
a lord dreary in spirit   drenched with water
50 in a ruined hall.   My lord endures
much care of mind.   He remembers too often
a happier dwelling.   Woe be to them
that for a loved one   must wait in longing.

**Literary Analysis
Anglo-Saxon Lyrics and
the Elegy** What does the
wife mourn in this elegy?

Critical Reading

1. **(a) Recall:** Why was the wife commanded to leave her home?
   (b) Interpret: What do lines 25–26 suggest about her reaction to this event?

2. **Interpret:** How do the setting and her daily life reinforce the idea expressed in the line "I am all longing"?

3. **(a) Generalize:** How might a listener feel about his or her griefs after hearing the wife's lament? **(b) Draw Conclusions:** Explain why the poem presents the wife as an image of pure longing, rather than as a person who will one day move on.

4. **Evaluate:** Is the wife justified in her anger and sorrow? Explain.

The Wife's Lament ■ 29

1. **Possible response:** Regular rhythms, the alliteration and assonance that contribute to the poems' sound, the caesuras, and logical order of images would make it easier to perform these poems aloud.

2. (a) In "The Wife's Lament," "wave-tumult" is used to mean the ocean. In "The Wanderer," "gold-lord" is used to mean new lord. (b) The kennings make common things more poetic.

3. (a) Alliteration: he, who; muse, moldering; deeply, darkling; brood, battle, bloodshed; heavy, heart. (b) The meaning reinforced is of lost identity (he, who), thoughts on death and the transience of life (muse–moldering, brood–battle, bloodshed), and sorrow (deep, darkling; heavy, heart).

4. (a) Assonance: I, find; fortune, mournful; that, man, matched; mind, hiding. Alliteration: man, matched, me, mournful, mind, mood, murder. (b) The repeating sounds make it possible to hear and see connections between words that build the image.

5. (a) Each reflects on something lost or absent. (b) **Possible response:** "The Wanderer" is moving because the speaker's whole world is gone.

6. "Seafarer," feeling like an exile at home and at sea; insight: we are exiles on earth, heaven is home. "Wanderer," his lord is dead and he is exiled; insight: life is short and hard, look to God for mercy and strength. "The Wife's Lament," banished by husband; insight: longing and waiting.

7. Beauty is created by the evocative and melodic way that sorrow is portrayed. Value is found in sharing common human feelings, and in "Seafarer" and "Wanderer" in directing the listener's thoughts to God.

8. The wanderer's situation would be impossible to understand without knowing that the sense of purpose and identity of a warrior, were tied to his lord.

9. Without knowing that the husband had the right to banish his wife, and that the wife had little recourse, it would be difficult to understand the situation in "The Wife's Lament."

continued

Apply the Skills

The Seafarer • *The Wanderer* • *The Wife's Lament*

Literary Analysis

Anglo-Saxon Lyrics

1. Find one example in each poem of a feature that could help a story-teller recite that poem, and explain why it would help.

2. (a) Find two examples of **kennings** in the poems, and explain the meaning of each. (b) Explain how these kennings added to the enjoyment of the poems.

3. (a) Find four uses of **alliteration** in lines 80–83 of "The Wanderer." (b) Explain how each reinforces the meaning.

4. (a) Identify two uses each of **assonance** and alliteration in lines 18–20 of "A Wife's Lament." (b) Explain how these effects link words to form strong images.

Comparing Literary Works

5. (a) What makes each of these poems an **elegy**? (b) Which one do you find most moving? Why?

6. Use a graphic organizer like the following to compare the lesson that each poem teaches about suffering.

Poem	Cause of Suffering	Insight Gained

7. Using one example from each poem, compare the ways in which the poems find artistic value, even beauty, in sorrow and longing.

Reading Strategy

Connecting to Historical Context

8. Why is understanding a warrior's relationship to his lord important to appreciating "The Wanderer"?

9. How does understanding the position of Anglo-Saxon women help you understand "A Wife's Lament"?

Extend Understanding

10. **Geography Connection:** The sea is important in British literature. Describe a geographic feature that might be crucial in the literature of another nation. Explain what it might represent.

30 ■ From Legend to History (449–1485)

Quick Review

A **lyric poem** expresses the thoughts and feelings of a single speaker.
Anglo-Saxon lyrics feature the following devices:

- caesuras
- kennings
- alliteration
- assonance

An **elegy** is a lyric poem mourning a loss.

To **connect literature to historical context**, use information about the period in which the work was written to help you understand its meaning.

For: Self-test
Visit: www.PHSchool.com
Web Code: esa-6102

Answers continued

10. **Possible response:** A desert offers images of desolation and physical and spiritual isolation. Deserts might feature in the tales of North Africa or Australia.

Go **Online**
Assessment Students may use the **Self-test** to prepare for **Selection Test A** or **Selection Test B**.

Build Language Skills

Vocabulary Lesson

Word Analysis:
Anglo-Saxon Suffix *-ness*

"The Wanderer" uses the word *winsomeness,* which contains the Anglo-Saxon suffix *-ness,* meaning "the state of being or quality of." Though most English science and math words are formed from Latin or Greek word parts, *-ness* is used in a few. Use your knowlege of the suffix to define these words:

1. obliqueness **2.** handedness **3.** randomness

Spelling Strategy

When adding a suffix that begins with a consonant to a word that ends in *e,* retain the final *e:* blithe + -ly = blithely. Add the suffix in parentheses to each word.

1. irate (*-ly*) **3.** replace (*-ment*)
2. price (*-less*) **4.** spite (*-ful*)

Vocabulary Builder: Synonyms

Synonyms are words that are close to each other in meaning. Replace each italicized word below with a synonym from the vocabulary list on page 17. You may need to change the form of the word.

1. Before being exiled by the king, we were *carefree* and known for our *charm;* we looked forward to the future with *joy.*

2. Being left with nothing, my husband and I sought *compensation.*

3. Our *caring* queen was sympathetic when she learned of our *distressing* situation.

4. The queen *advised* the king to end his *spite* and repeal our banishment.

5. A *spirited* believer in justice, the queen appointed a *guard* to watch over our home.

Grammar and Style Lesson

Compound Predicates

A predicate is the part of a sentence that contains the main verb and states the action or condition of the subject. A **compound predicate** has two or more verbs or verb phrases that relate to the same subject. In this example from "The Seafarer," the subject is *sea.* The three verbs in the compound predicate are underlined.

> **Example:** . . . the sea <u>took</u> me, <u>swept</u> me back / And forth in sorrow and fear and pain, / <u>Showed</u> me suffering in a hundred ships, . . .

As you can see in the example above, compound predicates can be used to create an effect of movement or drama by "piling up" events.

WG *Prentice Hall Writing and Grammar Connection: Chapter 18, Section 1*

Practice Identify the verbs or verb phrases in the following compound predicates.

1. The world's honor ages and shrinks, . . .

2. The soul . . . knows nothing / Of sweetness or sour, feels no pain, / Bends neither its hands nor its brain. . . .

3. A brother / Opens his palms and pours down gold / On his kinsman's grave. . . .

4. "All this earth ages and droops. . . ."

5. He must never too quickly unburden his breast / Of its sorrow, but eagerly strive for redress. . . .

Writing Application Write a paragraph about a change in the wife's fate in "A Wife's Lament." Use a compound predicate in each sentence.

---

❶ Vocabulary Lesson
Word Analysis

1. Obliqueness is the state or quality of being roundabout or circuitous.

2. Handedness is a tendency to use one hand more than the other.

3. Randomness is the state or quality of being irregular.

Spelling Strategy

1. irately   3. replacement
2. priceless   4. spiteful

Vocabulary Builder

1. blithe, winsomeness, rapture
2. redress
3. compassionate, grievous
4. admonished, rancor
5. fervent, sentinel

❷ Grammar and Style Lesson

1. ages, shrinks
2. knows, feels, Bends
3. Opens, pours
4. ages, droops
5. unburden, strive

Writing Application

Possible response: The wife's husband pondered and questioned his heart about his actions. He recognized and understood that the way in which he treated her was unkind. He feared that she hated and resented him. He resolved to apologize and ask her for forgiveness.

WG **Writing and Grammar, Diamond Level**

Students will find further instruction and practice on compound predicates in Chapter 18, Section 1.

Assessment Practice

Sequential Order   (For more practice, see *Standardized Test Preparation Workbook,* p. 1.)

Some tests require students to identify the order in which events have occurred. Use this sample test item:

Blithe was our bearing often we vowed/that but death alone would part us two/naught else. But this is turned round/now . . . as if it never were/our friendship. I must far and near/bear the anger of my beloved. /The man sent me out to live in the woods/under an oak tree in this den in the earth.

Which of the following happens last according to the speaker in "The Wife's Lament"?

A The beloved sent the speaker into the woods.

B The two vowed that only death would part them.

C The speaker must bear the beloved's anger.

D The man sent the speaker into the woods.

Have students use verb tenses and signal words such as *now* to help them determine that C is the correct answer.

❸ Writing Lesson

You may use this Writing Lesson as timed-writing practice, or you may allow students to develop the essay as a writing assignment over several days.

- To guide students in writing this literary analysis, give them the **Support for Writing Lesson** page (*Unit 1 Resources*, p. 15).

- Review with students their understanding of elegies. Remind students of the centrality of mourning to the elegy.

- Tell students that in preparing their essays on the appearance of exile, they should look for passages in each poem that introduce the themes of exile and suffering.

- Use the Writing Lesson to guide students in developing their essays.

- Use the Response to Literature rubrics, pp. 65–66 in *General Resources*, to evaluate student work.

❹ Research and Technology

- Have students work in small groups to do Internet research on Anglo-Saxon professions.

- Encourage students to consult "Help Wanted" ads in their local newspapers or online.

- Remind students to create ads that would be appropriate for men and women from the Anglo-Saxon era.

- Encourage students to share their Help Wanted pages with their classmates.

- The **Support for Extend Your Learning** page (*Unit 1 Resources*, p. 16) provides guided note-taking opportunities to help students complete the Extend Your Learning activities.

- Use the Oral Interpretation rubric, p. 130 in *General Resources*, to evaluate student's interpretations.

Go Online — Research   Have students type in the Web Code for another research activity.

---

❸ Writing Lesson

Timed Writing: Analysis of a Literary Theme

Each of the elegies in this grouping speaks movingly on the theme of exile. In an essay, analyze the appearance of the theme of exile in each poem. Compare the ways in which each poem creates beauty out of a painful experience. *(40 minutes)*

Prewriting *(10 minutes)*	Reread the selections, taking notes on the theme of exile. Then, write a one- or two-sentence summary of the feelings and imagery associated with exile in each.
Drafting *(20 minutes)*	As you draft, use examples showing how each poem creates rich imagery and powerful feelings from the sufferings of exile.
Revising *(10 minutes)*	Review your draft, examining the flow of ideas. Consider adding transitions such as *for instance* and *as a result* to clarify the connections between ideas.

> **Model: Revising to Clarify Connection of Ideas**
>
> Even depressing thoughts can have a kind of gloomy
>
> ~~For instance, when~~
>
> grandeur. When the Wanderer uses images like "Walls
>
> stand rime-covered and swept by the winds…," he
>
> creates a kind of splendor out of destruction.

Adding the transition words *for instance* clarifies the connection between a general statement and a specific example.

*W*G *Prentice Hall Writing and Grammar Connection: Chapter 14, Section 3*

❹ Extend Your Learning

Listening and Speaking In the role of a scop, or traveling storyteller, give an **oral interpretation** of an Anglo-Saxon poem for the class. Use these rehearsal strategies:

1. Mark up a copy of the poem to indicate which words you will emphasize.
2. Add performance notes to the copy as you rehearse.

During your reading, consult your notes. Speak slowly enough so that your audience can follow.

Research and Technology The speakers in these poems had ordinary occupations—wife, sailor, and soldier. With a group, create an Anglo-Saxon **Help Wanted page.** First, investigate Anglo-Saxon occupations. Next, write ads listing the requirements for each job, and assemble them into a Help Wanted page. **[Group Activity]**

Go Online Research   **For:** An additional research activity   **Visit:** www.PHSchool.com   **Web Code:** esd-7101

Assessment Resources

The following resources can be used to assess students' knowledge and skills.

Unit 1 Resources
   Selection Test A, pp. 18–20
   Selection Test B, pp. 21–23

General Resources
   Rubrics for Response to Literature, pp. 65–66
   Rubric for Oral Interpretation, p. 130

Go Online Assessment   Students may use the **Self-test** to prepare for **Selection test A** or **Selection Test B.**

Focus on Literary Forms: The Epic

Beowulf on the Funeral Pyre, Rockwell Kent

Focus on Literary Forms: The Epic ■ 33

**Differentiated
Instruction**   Solutions for All Learners

Accessibility at a Glance

Average
from Beowulf

Selection Planning Guide

The selections in this part provide insight into the nature of the epic hero and the conventions of the epic. The primary selection consists of excerpts from *Beowulf,* the most famous epic in the British tradition, and includes the battles with Grendel, Grendel's mother, and the dragon. Epics from ancient times are represented by excerpts from *Gilgamesh* and the *Iliad.* These reveal how the qualities prized in a hero vary across cultures. Gilgamesh is celebrated for his construction of cities and temples. Although the heroes of *The Iliad* have human failings, they are regarded as heroes for their skill as warriors.

Humanities

Beowulf on the Funeral Pyre, by Rockwell Kent

This work depicts the epic hero Beowulf being cremated in a hero's funeral. Tell students that they will read about Beowulf, an Anglo-Saxon hero who helped the Danish king by slaying the monster Grendel and Grendel's mother, but who was himself fatally wounded when he killed a fire-breathing dragon. Point out the contrast between the stylized, shimmering flames in the background and the dark, solid pyre upon which Beowulf's body rests.

Have students link the painting to Part 2 by answering the following question:

• Even if you did not know the title of this art, what details and elements in the work would lead you to realize that this man is viewed as a hero?

Possible response: Heroic elements in this work include the unearthly light above the body, the way the pyre is carefully arranged and decorated with shields, the sword and garlands at the man's feet, and the position of the man—sitting up, holding his sword as if undefeated and ready to fight again.

Students will

1. recognize and appreciate the types and features of epics.
2. apply strategies for reading epics.

❶ Elements of the Epic

- Review the definition of an epic with the class. Emphasize to students that an epic is more than just a long narrative poem. To be an epic, a poem needs to include elements that set it apart from other narratives.

- Read through the elements of the epic with the class. Point out that the first three elements described—the epic hero, the quest, and valorous deeds—are essential elements of the form.

- Explain to students that an epic hero, who is larger-than-life, can be understood as a symbol of goodness, heroism, and strength for the people of a culture.

- Tell students that divine intervention and great historical events are often, but not always, part of epics. For example, while the *Iliad* is set during the Trojan War, *Beowulf* does not have a backdrop of such historical importance.

❷ Types of Epic

- Point out to students that the two types of epics are closely related; the style and conventions of literary epics come from the older folk epics.

- Point out that *Beowulf* is a folk epic. Be sure that students understand that this means *Beowulf* existed as a story, handed down orally from generation to generation, long before it was written down. You may also want to point out that the version in this unit is a translation, removed one step further from the original oral source.

Defining the Epic

One of the earliest forms of literature is the epic. An *epic* is a long narrative poem that recounts the adventures of a legendary hero in pursuit of a goal of national importance. The hero's accomplishments reflect the values of his culture and usually figure prominently in the history or mythology of his people.

... THE EPIC IMPARTS
SOLEMNITY TO HISTORY....

— *Victor Hugo*

❶ **Elements of the Epic**

Certain key elements set the epic narrative apart from other types of stories.

- **Epic hero:** The epic hero is the central character of an epic. This character is a larger-than-life figure, typically of noble or semidivine birth, who pits his courage, skill, and virtue against opposing, often evil, forces. In the early English epic *Beowulf,* for example, the hero Beowulf is a young warrior of high standing who battles a brutal and bloodthirsty monster.

- **Quest:** A quest is a long, dangerous journey or mission undertaken by the epic hero. The quest is the hero's opportunity to prove his heroism and win honor and undying renown. Beowulf embarks on a quest to aid a neighboring kingdom by defeating the hideous monster Grendel.

- **Valorous deeds:** These actions demonstrate the hero's courage, strength, or virtue and make up most of the action in the narrative. For example, Beowulf's superhuman strength is shown when he fights the savage Grendel with his bare hands—and wins!

- **Divine intervention:** In many epics, the hero receives help from a god or another supernatural force who takes an interest in his quest. In the ancient Greek epic the *Iliad,* for example, the goddess Athene helps the hero Achilleus.

- **Great events:** Important events from the history or mythology of a nation or culture often provide the backdrop for the epic narrative. The *Iliad,* for example, takes place during the Trojan War, a war in which the Greeks invaded and conquered the city of Troy.

34 ■ *From Legend to History (449–1485)*

Enrichment

An epic hero is courageous, valiant, virtuous, and larger-than-life, sometimes even god-like. Not only are epic heroes more than human, they are also more than individuals. Epic heroes embody the values and ideals of a nation or culture. For example, the hero Beowulf is a mighty warrior with supernatural powers, but he is more than a superhero. He represents the strength, love, and loyalty to which the Anglo-Saxon England that produced the folk epic *Beowulf* aspired.

Epics express national and cultural ideals in other ways as well. Through its exciting story of war and heroics, Homer's *Iliad* presents ancient Greece during a critical historical moment, the Trojan War.

For students, the narrative heroics may be the most compelling aspect of an epic like *Beowulf.* Encourage them, however, to look beyond the level of narrative and consider the meaning the poem might have had to the people who first heard it recited.

❷ Types of Epics

The epic genre is often divided into two categories.

Folk Epics

In ancient times, stories about heroes were recited or sung as entertainment and passed down orally from one generation to the next. These stories were eventually unified into *folk epics* and written down long after they were first composed. Examples of the folk epic include the following:

- **Beowulf** (Anglo-Saxon)
- **Mahabharata** (Indian)
- **Gilgamesh** (Sumerian)
- **Sundiata** (West African)

Literary Epics

Literary epics are written by individual authors, drawing on the style and conventions of the folk epic. Examples of literary epics include the following:

- **Iliad** and **Odyssey** by Homer
- **Divine Comedy** by Dante Alighieri
- **Aeneid** by Virgil
- **Paradise Lost** by John Milton

❸ Epic Conventions

Most epics share certain literary or formal characteristics called *epic conventions.*

- An epic opens by stating the subject or purpose, followed by an invocation of a muse (a spirit thought to inspire an artist) or supernatural force who would help to tell the story.
- The plot begins *in medias res*—Latin for "in the middle of things." In other words, the reader joins the story in the thick of the action.
- Most epics are serious in tone and lofty in style, a technique meant to convey the importance of the events. Long speeches by the characters suggest an impressive formality, as do the lists (or catalogs) of battles, weapons, and royal gifts.

❹ Strategies for Reading Poetry

Use these strategies as you read an epic.

Rereading the Action The lists, or catalogs, in epics often interrupt the action to provide colorful descriptions of a character or a scene. After reading a list, reread the surrounding action before continuing. This strategy helps you follow the action in the epic.

Picturing the Action and Situation Epic poetry is filled with rich, descriptive language about exciting action. As you read these vivid descriptions, picture what is happening, visualizing each scene as if it were a scene in a movie. Forming a mental picture of what you are reading helps bring the epic to life.

Focus on Literary Forms: The Epic ■ 35

...ventions are characteristics of epics that go beyond the characters and plot. Epic conventions are concerned with structure and style and how epic stories are told.

- When reviewing the conventions with the class, explain that the Muses of Greek mythology were goddesses that presided over the arts and sciences, including poetry. To invoke a Muse was to ask for divine inspiration.

- Point out to students that sometimes they will need background information before beginning an epic poem so that starting in the middle of the action does not confuse them.

- Explain to students that the lengthy speeches and lists in epics relate back to the oral tradition of epics. In a time when many people did not read and these stories were not written down, the elevated style of the epics was likely impressive to listeners and held their attention.

❹ Strategies for Reading an Epic

- Explain to students that the characteristics of epics—their length, their larger-than-life heroes and actions, and their conventions—can make them challenging to read. Tell students that the strategies on this page will help them focus on and follow the narrative of epics.

- Point out that epics have been translated from other languages, which results in the absence of regular, rhyming lines of poetry. As with any other difficult-to-understand poetry, encourage students to follow punctuation and focus on one sentence at a time.

- In addition to the suggestion on the page, explain to students that before they read a lengthy speech or list, they may also want to skip ahead and preview the action that follows it. This previewing technique may help students to place the speech or list in importance compared to the action surrounding it.

- To make visualizing an epic's action easier, encourage students to make lists of sensory details—what the characters see, touch, smell, hear and taste. Tell students that by picturing the character, scenes, and events, they can use rich descriptions to bring the epic to life.

35

Meeting Your Standards

Students will

1. **analyze and respond to literary elements.**
   - Literary Analysis: The Epic

2. **read, comprehend, analyze, and critique an epic.**
   - Reading Strategy: Paraphrasing
   - Reading Check questions
   - Apply the Skills questions
   - Assessment Practice (ATE)

3. **develop vocabulary.**
   - Vocabulary Lesson: Latin Word Root: -sol-

4. **understand and apply written and oral language conventions.**
   - Spelling Strategy
   - Grammar and Style Lesson: Appositives and Appositive Phrases

5. **develop writing proficiency.**
   - Writing Lesson: Response to Criticism

6. **develop appropriate research strategies.**
   - Extend Your Learning: Dictionary of Epic Heroes

7. **understand and apply listening and speaking strategies.**
   - Extend Your Learning: Dramatic Reading

Block Scheduling: Use one 90-minute class period to preteach the skills and have students read the selection. Use a second 90-minute class period to assess students' mastery of skills, extend their learning, and monitor their progress.

Homework Suggestions

Following are possibilities for homework assignments.

- Support pages from *Unit 1 Resources:*
  Literary Analysis
  Reading Strategy
  Vocabulary Builder
  Grammar and Style

- An Extend Your Learning project and the Writing Lesson for this selection may be completed over several days.

Step-by-Step Teaching Guide	Pacing Guide
PRETEACH	
• Administer Vocabulary and Reading Warm-ups as necessary.	5 min.
• Engage students' interest with the motivation activity.	5 min.
• Read and discuss author, background, and From the Translator's Desk features. **FT**	10 min.
• Introduce the Literary Analysis Skill: The Epic. **FT**	5 min.
• Introduce the Reading Strategy: Paraphrasing. **FT**	10 min.
• Prepare students to read by teaching the selection vocabulary. **FT**	
TEACH	
• Informally monitor comprehension while students read independently or in groups. **FT**	30 min.
• Monitor students' comprehension with the Reading Check notes.	as students read
• Reinforce vocabulary with Vocabulary Builder notes.	as students read
• Develop students' understanding of the epic with the Literary Analysis annotations. **FT**	5 min.
• Develop students' ability to paraphrase with the Reading Strategy annotations. **FT**	5 min.
ASSESS/EXTEND	
• Assess students' comprehension and mastery of the Literary Analysis and Reading Strategy by having them answer the Apply the Skills questions. **FT**	15 min.
• Have students complete the Vocabulary Lesson and the Grammar and Style Lesson. **FT**	15 min.
• Apply students' knowledge of revising to clarify connections by using the Writing Lesson. **FT**	45 min. or homework
• Apply students' understanding by using one or more of the Extend Your Learning activities.	20–90 min. or homework
• Administer Selection Test A or Selection Test B. **FT**	15 min.

Resources

Choosing Resources for Differentiated Instruction

[**L1**] Special Needs Students
[**L2**] Below-Level Students
[**L3**] All Students
[**L4**] Advanced Students
[**EL**] English Learners

For Vocabulary and Reading Warm-ups and for Selection Tests, **A** signifies "less challenging" and **B** "more challenging." For Graphic Organizer Transparencies, **A** signifies "not filled in" and **B** "filled in."

FT Fast Track Instruction: To move the lesson more quickly, use the strategies and activities identified with **FT**.

Scaffolding for Less Proficient and Advanced Students

The leveled Critical Thinking questions after selections progress in the levels of thinking required to answer them. To address the needs of your different students, you may use the (a) level questions for your less proficient students and the (b) level questions with your on-level and advanced students. The occasional (c) level questions are appropriate for your advanced students.

PRENTICE HALL
TeacherEXPRESS™ Use this complete
Plan · Teach · Assess suite of powerful
teaching tools to make lesson planning and testing quicker and easier.

PRENTICE HALL
StudentEXPRESS™ Use the interac-
Learn · Study · Succeed tive textbook
(online and on CD-ROM) to make selections and activities come alive with audio and video support and interactive questions.

Go Online **For:** Information about Lexiles
Professional **Visit:** www.PHSchool.com
Development **Web Code:** eue-1111

Burton Raffel

- Tell students that Burton Raffel is well known as a scholar and translator. He has taught literature and classics at universities around the world, from the United States to Canada to Israel. In addition to translating *Beowulf*, he has translated French, Spanish, Greek, and Russian literature. He has even translated the literature of Indonesia.

- Show students Segment 2 on Burton Raffel on the *From the Author's Desk DVD* for insight into Raffel's perspective on *Beowulf*. After students have watched the segment, encourage them to discuss the qualities that make the epic difficult for contemporary readers, as well as the qualities that are still appealing.

- **Ask** students if, based on the DVD segment, they think they would enjoy reading *Beowulf*. Press students to explain their answers with references to the DVD segment. **Possible response:** Students may say they will enjoy *Beowulf* because, in addition to being an important early work of English literature, it is an exciting adventure story. Some students may find the challenge of the cultural difference intriguing.

A Legendary Tale, Larger than Life

- Have students read Raffel's commentary on pages 36–37. Point out that Raffel's first task is to introduce the epic and offer a preview of its plot.

- **Ask** students what qualities make Beowulf such an extraordinarily heroic figure. **Possible response:** He has great courage and magical powers, such as the ability to breathe underwater. His name suggests that he is superhuman, part bear and part wolf.

- Explain to students that the first section of *Beowulf*—the struggle between the hero and the monster Grandel—is especially suspenseful and exciting. Point out such dramatic events as the arrival of Grendel, Beowulf's journey to Hrothgar's court, and the battle between hero and monster. Use Raffel's summary to build students' anticipation for the epic.

BURTON RAFFEL INTRODUCES
Beowulf

Burton Raffel

Burton Raffel has won the Frances Steloff Poetry Prize and the French-American Foundation's Translation Prize. He is the author of numerous poems, screenplays, and novels.

A Legendary Tale, Larger Than Life

Beowulf is a sweeping, action-packed narrative. Written in highly dramatic language, it has characters who are almost all kings, princes, and their heroic followers. The plot is energized by a pair of powerful man-eating monsters and, at the end, a greedy, fire-spouting dragon. All three are killed by the poem's principal character, Beowulf, who possesses magical qualities of his own. He can swim for days on end; he can breathe for extended periods underwater; his very name tells us in three ways that he is no mere human. He is Beo, or "bear." He is also Wulf, or "wolf." And most important of all, his name does not begin exactly as his father's name, Edgetho: for everyone in Anglo-Saxon England, this break in tradition would have been a dead giveaway of Beowulf's extraordinary character.

A Grand Beginning The story crackles with wonderfully calculated suspense. The hero himself is not introduced at the start. Man-eating Grendel takes the stage, emerging out of the kind of darkness and terror in which Anglo-Saxon life was steeped. Beowulf comes to help the besieged king Hrothgar. (His exciting travel over the deep waves was the first part of the poem I read, over fifty years ago.) The poem carefully explains his heroic, profoundly social motives. Offering himself as a potential sacrifice to Grendel, he fights with and tears an arm off the monster, who flees back into darkness.

Everyone is overjoyed, there is much celebrating—until Grendel's mother enters the scene, hungry (literally) for revenge. Beowulf promptly accepts the challenge, diving far down into the water, finding the lady demon, and in the end killing her in a very close fight. Loaded with praise and gifts, he returns to his own king, to whose throne he succeeds.

The Passage of Time Fifty years later, the old Beowulf's land is terrorized by a fire-breathing dragon. Unlike a good king, and like some of the bad kings in the poem, the dragon fiercely guards and never shares its treasures. Beowulf does not hesitate. But he is old and not as strong as he was. Significantly, he must have help, and is so badly burned that, after the dragon is dead, Beowulf too dies. His people give him a royal burial, and a monument, and sing the praises due to a fearless ruler who so totally embodied the virtues of a warrior king.

Teaching Resources

The following resources can be used to enrich or extend the instruction for From the Translator's Desk.

Unit 1 Resources
> From the Translator's Desk: Burton Raffel, p. 24
> Listening and Viewing, p. 25

From the Author's Desk DVD
> **Burton Raffel,** Segment 2

The Spirit of *Beowulf*

Beowulf is not a pagan poem. There are no pagan gods, no idols, no wanton human sacrifices. Anglo-Saxon England had long since been Christianized when *Beowulf* was composed, but the epic is primarily concerned with social, not religious issues. Still, if not overtly Christian, *Beowulf*'s close identification with ancient Hebraic ways of life marks it as very much an Old Testament poem. "Almighty God," clearly and repeatedly evoked, operates ethically and holds humans to high moral standards. The creation story of Genesis is beautifully paraphrased. Hell is cited as the home of evil; the Abel and Cain tale is mentioned explicitly. And just as evil is punished, good prevails. The message is that men must learn to behave responsibly, and to love and be faithful to one another, exactly as *Beowulf* has shown that they can.

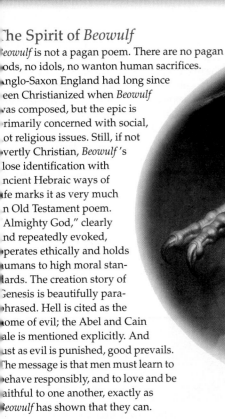

▲ **Critical Viewing**
Which of the dragon's characteristics might a storyteller share with an audience? **[Connect]**

Thinking About the Commentary

1. **(a) Recall:** What was the first part of *Beowulf* that Burton Raffel read?
   (b) Speculate: Based on Raffel's introduction, what aspects of the poem do you think led to his lifelong interest in *Beowulf*?

2. **(a) Recall:** What details of the poem allow Raffel to say so definitely that *Beowulf* is not a pagan poem? **(b) Analyze:** What might the religious dimension of *Beowulf* tell us about the culture that produced it?

As You Read *Beowulf* . . .

3. Be ready to compare and contrast your reaction to the poem with Raffel's.

4. Think about how Raffel's passion for the poem is revealed in his translation.

From the Translator's Desk: Burton Raffel ■ 37

The Passage of Time

- Call students' attention to Raffel's summary of the final struggle between Beowulf and the dragon.
- **Ask** students to describe the contrast Raffel suggests between the hero and the fire-breathing beast. **Possible response:** Raffel suggests that Beowulf represents the virtues of a great king, while the dragon embodies the destructiveness and greed of a bad king.

The Spirit of *Beowulf*

Explain to students that although *Beowulf* is the oldest existing work of literature in English, it does not predate the arrival of Christianity in England. According to Raffel, the epic has a Judeo-Christian perspective on the social issues at its core. Encourage students to look for these social themes as they read.

ASSESS

Answers

1. (a) The first part Raffel read was the description of Beowulf's journey over deep waves to King Hrothgar's court. (b) **Possible response:** Raffel seems to be interested in *Beowulf* because it deals with social issues, establishing moral standards and telling readers that they must be responsible and faithful towards one another. He is also drawn to the poem's excitement and suspense.

2. (a) *Beowulf* includes references to the Judeo-Christian God, the creation story of Genesis, Hell, and the story of Abel and Cain.
   (b) **Possible response:** The poem was produced by a Christian culture that had moved away from the old gods. It was also a culture concerned with moral and ethical standards of behavior.

3. Students are not likely to embrace *Beowulf* as whole-heartedly as Raffel does. They do not have his academic background, so they will not be familiar with the culture the poem reflects. But the action and excitement to which Raffel responds so strongly should be gripping for students as well.

4. Students may point to the flow of Raffel's translation, and its dramatic building of tension and suspense. They are likely to find that Raffel's translation captures the excitement he first found in *Beowulf*.

37

Motivation

Explain to students that the epic poem *Beowulf* contains many features common in action movies—a super-hero possessing amazing strength and courage, a ruthless villain, suspense, and sustained action. To demonstrate each of these action movie elements, read the following dramatic passages aloud: *superhero*, lines 506–511; *villain*, lines 19–29; *suspense*, lines 285–302; *sustained action*, lines 682–688. Then, ask students to speculate on what sort of ratings a current film of *Beowulf* might receive.

❶ Background
More About the Author

Anglo-Saxons were the descendants of three different Germanic peoples—the Angles, Saxons, and Jutes. These groups migrated to England from Northern Germany in the 5th century. The author of *Beowulf* is unknown, but it seems likely that he was from one of the Anglian settlements. Recent discoveries in this region include burial sites with grave goods that are similar to those in the poem, and that are closely linked to Beowulf's homeland, Sweden. While there is no evidence that Beowulf himself ever existed (in fact, no reference is made to *Beowulf* in any other source), there are people and events in the poem that are true. Higlac really was king of the Geats. He died in battle sometime in the 520s—which is one reason we know that *Beowulf* was composed after that decade, because the poem mentions Higlac's death. Hrothgar, too, is among many historical characters in the work. The interweaving of characters and legends from the 500s and 600s argues for composition in the 600s or 700s, when audiences would still be familiar with the events.

Build Skills Epic

from Beowulf ❶

About Beowulf

At the dawn of English literature stands *Beowulf*. Like the epics of other cultures—the *Iliad* and the *Odyssey* of ancient Greece and the *Sundiata* of Mali—*Beowulf* is the self-portrait of a culture. In this adventure-packed poem, the Anglo-Saxons of eighth-century Britain embodied the traditions that shaped their world in one towering figure—Beowulf, sword-wielding slayer of monsters, upholder of the right, warrior-chieftain. The Anglo-Saxons left us few factual records of their life and history. In *Beowulf*, however, they vividly recorded their dreams, aspirations, and fears.

The Stuff of Legend Although the action takes place in sixth-century Scandinavia, *Beowulf* was originally told in Old English, the language spoken by the Anglo-Saxons of England during the years 500 to 1100. Beowulf, a Geat from a region that is today southern Sweden, sets sail to aid the Danish King Hrothgar in his fight against the monster Grendel. A terrifying swampland creature whose eyes burn "with gruesome light," Grendel has been terrorizing Hrothgar's great banquet hall, Herot, for twelve years. The battle between Beowulf, a young warrior of great strength and courage, and Grendel, his bloodthirsty foe, is the first of three mortal battles in this long poem.

Forging an Epic The tales in *Beowulf* originate from a time when stories and poems were passed along by word of mouth. In Anglo-Saxon England, traveling minstrels, called *scops*, captivated audiences with long narrative poems. These poems changed and grew as they were passed from one scop to another. *Beowulf* was told and retold in this fashion throughout England for hundreds of years. In the eleventh century, the epic was finally written down.

Beowulf grew out of other, earlier traditions. The monsters and dragons of the tale, the brave warriors steadfastly loyal to their heroic chief, the descent into the eerie regions below the earth—these were familiar elements of Scandinavian or Celtic folk tales. Even a detail as specific as Beowulf's seizure of Grendel's arm can be traced to earlier tales.

A Guide to Life By forging these various traditions into one unified tale and by adding the later influence of Christianity, the Anglo-Saxon scops created a central reference point for their culture. Listening to *Beowulf*, an Anglo-Saxon could learn of bravery and loyalty, of the monsters that spite and hatred could be, and of the heroism needed to conquer them.

From Oral Tradition to Cyberspace and Beyond The only original manuscript of the complete 3,182-line poem comes to us from Sir Robert Cotton's (1571–1631) collection of medieval manuscripts. In 1731, the manuscript was saved from a fire but did not escape damage—2,000 letters crumbled away from the edges of the manuscript. Thanks to an initiative called the Electronic *Beowulf* Project, the manuscript has now been preserved and made available electronically.

Although much of the attention given to the poem is scholarly, *Beowulf* is far from a museum piece. The adventuresome tale, clanging with blood-curdling battles and the noble ring of bold oaths, continues to thrill readers. In 2000, the celebrated Irish poet Seamus Heaney published his translation of *Beowulf* to public acclaim. Preserved in song, then in writing, then on a hard drive, the memory of Beowulf has stood strong through the ages, finally calling on a modern poet to renew the sounds and spirit of Britain's first epic.

Preview

Connecting to the Literature

It is a familiar but stirring scene: A brave hero battles his archenemy, an evildoer who will stop at nothing to win. The theme of hero and villain goes back more than twelve hundred years, to a time when Anglo-Saxon storytellers sang of the battles of Beowulf, legendary warrior.

Literary Analysis

The Epic

An **epic** is a long narrative poem, sometimes developed orally, that celebrates the deeds of a legendary or heroic figure. Epics are among the earliest forms of literature. Early epics, such as Homer's *Iliad* from ancient Greece, capture the cultural and religious values of the peoples who created and retold them. Common features of epics include the following:

- The hero battles forces that threaten the order of his world.
- The story is told in a serious manner, often in special, elevated language.

Beowulf, the epic of the Anglo-Saxons, uses elements of Anglo-Saxon poetry such as the **kenning** and **caesura**. (For more about these elements, see p. 17.)

Connecting Literary Elements

A **legendary hero** is a larger-than-life character whose accomplishments are celebrated in traditional tales. Beowulf's boastful self-confidence, his feats of strength, and his victories in battle make him a classic legendary hero. Upholding the values of his culture—loyalty, bravery, honor—he can teach modern readers a great deal about the Anglo-Saxon view of the world.

Reading Strategy

Paraphrasing

Although *Beowulf* has been translated into modern English, its long, involved sentences may still be difficult to follow. To aid your understanding, **paraphrase** complex passages—identify the key details in a passage and restate them in your own words. Use a graphic organizer like the one shown.

Original

High on a wall a Danish watcher / Patrolling along the cliffs saw / The travelers crossing to the shore, their shields / Raised and shining....

Key Details

guard

saw people

come ashore

Paraphrase

A Danish guard saw strangers come ashore, holding up their shields.

Vocabulary Builder

reparation (rep′ ə rā′ shən) *n.* something making up for a wrong or an injury (p. 43)

solace (säl′ is) *n.* comfort; relief (p. 43)

purge (pʉrj) *v.* purify; cleanse (p. 47)

writhing (rīth′ iŋ) *adj.* making twisting or turning motions (p. 49)

massive (mas′ iv) *adj.* big and solid; bulky (p. 54)

loathsome (lōth′ səm) *adj.* disgusting (p. 54)

from *Beowulf* ■ 39

---

❷ Literary Analysis
The Epic

- Tell students that, as they read *Beowulf*, they should focus on the epic qualities of the poem, such as elevated language and a hero who struggles against evil to restore order.

- Read the definition of the epic together as a class. Ask students to rephrase the definition in their own words. Make sure students understand that a poem is not characterized as an epic by its length alone.

- Use the instruction for Connecting Literary Elements to connect the heroism of Beowulf's character to the epic tradition.

❸ Reading Strategy
Paraphrasing

- Remind students that when you *paraphrase*, you restate another person's words or ideas using your own words.

- Then, review the example of paraphrasing that appears in the graphic organizer. Explain to students that the act of paraphrasing can help them better understand a confusing or difficult passage.

- Instruct students to use a graphic organizer like the one shown to help them reword complicated passages from *Beowulf*.

- Give students a copy of **Literary Analysis Graphic Organizer A**, p. 5 in *Graphic Organizer Transparencies*, to use as they read the selection.

Vocabulary Builder

- Pronounce each vocabulary word for students, and read the definitions as a class. Have students identify any words with which they are already familiar.

Differentiated Instruction   Solutions for All Learners

Support for Special Needs Students
Have students use the support pages for *Beowulf* in the *Reader's Notebook: Adapted Version.* Completing these pages will prepare students to read the selections in the Student Edition.

Support for Less Proficient Readers
Have students use the support pages for *Beowulf* in the *Reader's Notebook.* Completing these pages will prepare students to read the selection in the Student Edition.

Support for English Learners
Have students use the support pages for *Beowulf* in the *Reader's Notebook: English Learner's Version.* Completing these pages will prepare students to read the selections in the Student Edition.

Learning Modalities
Visual/Spatial Learners Encourage students to find illustrated books that portray Grendel, the creation story outlined in these first lines, or some aspect of the time and places in which *Beowulf* takes place. If appropriate, have them share these pictures with the class.

❶ About the Selection

Familiarity with the epic formula of *Beowulf* is a prerequisite for reading major works by Milton and Tennyson, as well as lighthearted mock epics by Chaucer and Pope. However, because of the stirring language and compelling action, *Beowulf* stands on its own merits, drawing readers into the adventures of another time and place. In *Beowulf,* students witness a character who transforms himself from a hero who uses strength to ensure his own fame to a leader who dies for the sake of his people.

❷ Humanities

Grendel, by Patten Wilson

This portrait of Grendel was commissioned for an edition of *Beowulf.* After students have read the selection, use these questions for discussion:

1. Which details in the drawing are mentioned in the poem? Which are implied but not specifically mentioned?
   Possible responses: Details mentioned include Grendel's claws (lines 33–35), gleaming eyes (lines 300–302), and "powerful jaws" and "great teeth" (lines 316–319). The opening, especially lines 15–29, implies a demonic appearance, reflected in the horns and pointed ears.

2. What moment in the narrative is suggested by this drawing?
   Possible response: Grendel appears to be stalking victims.

❸ Critical Viewing

Answer: Details include the horns, pointed ears, and goatlike beard that are often used in representations of demons, as well as fangs, fur, and claws. Also, the dark colors give the illustration a threatening mood.

❶

❷

Grendel (Frontispiece from *Beowulf*), Patten Wilson, The British Library

❸ ▲ Critical Viewing What details of this painting make Grendel look fearsome? [**Analyze**]

40 ■ *From Legend to History (449–1485)*

Differentiated
Instruction   Solutions for All Learners

Accessibility at a Glance

	from **Beowulf**
Context	Anglo-Saxon epic
Language	Long complex sentences
Concept Level	Accessible (description of heroic figure and deeds)
Literary Merit	Heroic/epic
Overall rating	Average

from Beowulf

Translated by Burton Raffel

Background When *Beowulf* was composed, England was changing from a pagan to a Christian culture. Pagan Anglo-Saxons told grim tales of life ruled by fate, tales in which people struggled against monsters for their place in the world. The missionaries who converted them to Christianity taught them that human beings and their choices of good or evil were at the center of creation. *Beowulf* reflects both pagan and Christian traditions.

The selection opens during an evening of celebration at Herot, the banquet hall of the Danish king Hrothgar (hroth´ gär). Outside in the darkness, however, lurks the murderous monster Grendel.

The Wrath of Grendel

     A powerful monster, living down
In the darkness, growled in pain, impatient
As day after day the music rang
Loud in that hall,[1] the harp's rejoicing
5 Call and the poet's clear songs, sung
Of the ancient beginnings of us all, recalling
The Almighty making the earth, shaping
These beautiful plains marked off by oceans,
Then proudly setting the sun and moon
10 To glow across the land and light it;
The corners of the earth were made lovely with trees
And leaves, made quick with life, with each
Of the nations who now move on its face. And then
As now warriors sang of their pleasure:
15 So Hrothgar's men lived happy in his hall
Till the monster stirred, that demon, that fiend,
Grendel, who haunted the moors, the wild
Marshes, and made his home in a hell
Not hell but earth. He was spawned in that slime,
20 Conceived by a pair of those monsters born

---

1. **hall** Herot.

❺ Burton Raffel
Translator's Insight
The reference at line 4 is not to the large, full-stringed harp we know, but something more like a lute or a small Spanish guitar.

Literary Analysis
The Epic What does the story of Grendel's origins suggest about the beliefs of Anglo-Saxon culture?

❼ Reading Check
What does Grendel resent about Hrothgar and his men?

from Beowulf ■ 41

---

❹ Critical Thinking
Compare and Contrast
- **Ask** students to contrast the description of Herot with the dwelling of the monster Grendel found in the first four lines of the poem. **Answer:** Herot is filled with music and rejoicing, while the monster lives down in the darkness and growls with pain.
- Based on these differences in dwellings, discuss in class the contrasts students might expect to find between the personalities of the inhabitants of these different dwellings.

❺ Translator's Insight
- Draw students' attention to Raffel's note on the meaning of *harp*. Tell students that a lute is a small pear-shaped stringed instrument. Discuss how this knowledge creates a clearer vision of the celebration.

❻ Literary Analysis
The Epic
▶ **Monitor Progress:** Read aloud the bracketed passage. Then, have students identify any details of epic poetry they find. Record students' responses on the chalkboard. **Answer:** Details include: serious, elevated language; forces of evil and good clearly defined; evil forces that threaten order.
- **Ask** students the Literary Analysis question: What does the story of Grendel's origins suggest about the beliefs of Anglo-Saxon culture? **Answer:** The existence of a monster shows the mythological, Germanic influences on the poem. Christian influences are evident in the passage, which contrasts "the Almighty" and the light and beauty of his creation with the "demon" or "fiend," who inhabits the darkness. Hence, the beliefs of Anglo-Saxon culture were primarily Christian but retained elements of the pagan.

❼ Reading Check
Answer: Grendel resents the ease and pleasure that Hrothgar and his men experience in their hall compared with his own dark, painful existence.

41

- **Ask** students to focus on lines 34–40 to themselves and think about what is occurring here.

- Then, **ask** students to answer the Reading Strategy question: What are the main ideas in the sentences in lines 34–40?
Answer: The monster thinks quickly, moves, and kills quickly. His victims are asleep, peaceful, unaware of their danger. Grendel kills them as they sleep and carries their bodies off. Killing makes Grendel happy.

- Point out to students that this passage combines the Christian elements of the battle between good and evil, as well as the biblical characters of Cain and Abel with Germanic myths about swamp-dwelling monsters that change form.

❾ Literary Analysis
The Epic

- Have students pause in their reading to **discuss** and answer the Literary Analysis question: How does the length of Hrothgar's suffering increase the epic feeling of this tale?
Possible response: The long period of suffering gives the tale a feeling of epic proportion and underscores the seriousness of the problem.

- **Ask** students what other element of the epic tradition is identified in lines 59–60.
Answer: The battle between good and evil is highlighted in the line "Grendel ruled, fought with the righteous."

Of Cain,[2] murderous creatures banished
By God, punished forever for the crime
Of Abel's death. The Almighty drove
Those demons out, and their exile was bitter,
25 Shut away from men; they split
Into a thousand forms of evil—spirits
And fiends, goblins, monsters, giants,
A brood forever opposing the Lord's
Will, and again and again defeated.
30   Then, when darkness had dropped, Grendel
Went up to Herot, wondering what the warriors
Would do in that hall when their drinking was done.
He found them sprawled in sleep, suspecting
Nothing, their dreams undisturbed. The monster's
35 Thoughts were as quick as his greed or his claws:
He slipped through the door and there in the silence
Snatched up thirty men, smashed them
Unknowing in their beds and ran out with their bodies,
The blood dripping behind him, back
40 To his lair, delighted with his night's slaughter.
    At daybreak, with the sun's first light, they saw
How well he had worked, and in that gray morning
Broke their long feast with tears and laments
For the dead. Hrothgar, their lord, sat joyless
45 In Herot, a mighty prince mourning
The fate of his lost friends and companions,
Knowing by its tracks that some demon had torn
His followers apart. He wept, fearing
The beginning might not be the end. And that night
50 Grendel came again, so set
On murder that no crime could ever be enough,
No savage assault quench his lust
For evil. Then each warrior tried
To escape him, searched for rest in different
55 Beds, as far from Herot as they could find,
Seeing how Grendel hunted when they slept.
Distance was safety; the only survivors
Were those who fled him. Hate had triumphed.
    So Grendel ruled, fought with the righteous,
60 One against many, and won; so Herot
Stood empty, and stayed deserted for years,
Twelve winters of grief for Hrothgar, king
Of the Danes, sorrow heaped at his door
By hell-forged hands. His misery leaped
65 The seas, was told and sung in all

---

2. **Cain** oldest son of Adam and Eve, who murdered his brother Abel.

Enrichment

Nautical Technology

The Geats were excellent sailors whom "the wind hurried . . . over the waves" and "through the sea like a bird." Acquiring such sailing skill is not a simple matter; it requires an understanding of the forces of wind, water, and the capabilities of your ship. This is especially true when your destination lies directly into the wind.

Have interested students research the forces at work and the techniques required to sail a vessel against the wind. The process of sailing can be diagrammed and demonstrated to the class using a hypothetical island destination that lies a prescribed number of miles upwind from one's present location. The diagram should show the angle of the wind, the position of the sail, and the direction of the various forces that result in forward movement.

Men's ears: how Grendel's hatred began,
How the monster relished his savage war
On the Danes, keeping the bloody feud
Alive, seeking no peace, offering
70 No truce, accepting no settlement, no price
In gold or land, and paying the living
For one crime only with another. No one
Waited for <u>reparation</u> from his plundering claws:
That shadow of death hunted in the darkness,
75 Stalked Hrothgar's warriors, old
And young, lying in waiting, hidden
In mist, invisibly following them from the edge
Of the marsh, always there, unseen.
    So mankind's enemy continued his crimes,
80 Killing as often as he could, coming
Alone, bloodthirsty and horrible. Though he lived
In Herot, when the night hid him, he never
Dared to touch King Hrothgar's glorious
Throne, protected by God—God,
85 Whose love Grendel could not know. But Hrothgar's
Heart was bent. The best and most noble
Of his council debated remedies, sat
In secret sessions, talking of terror
And wondering what the bravest of warriors could do.
90 And sometimes they sacrificed to the old stone gods,
Made heathen vows, hoping for Hell's
Support, the Devil's guidance in driving
Their affliction off. That was their way,
And the heathen's only hope, Hell
95 Always in their hearts, knowing neither God
Nor His passing as He walks through our world, the Lord
Of Heaven and earth; their ears could not hear
His praise nor know His glory. Let them
Beware, those who are thrust into danger,
100 Clutched at by trouble, yet can carry no <u>solace</u>
In their hearts, cannot hope to be better! Hail
To those who will rise to God, drop off
Their dead bodies and seek our Father's peace!

The Coming of Beowulf

    So the living sorrow of Healfdane's son[3]
105 Simmered, bitter and fresh, and no wisdom
Or strength could break it: that agony hung
On king and people alike, harsh
And unending, violent and cruel, and evil.

---

3. **Healfdane's** (hä´ alf den´ nez) **son** Hrothgar.

Burton Raffel
Translator's Insight
A normal feud involves two sides: it takes two to tangle. Literary lore suggests that monsters are interested in fights they know they will win.

Vocabulary Builder
reparation (rep´ ə rā´ shən) *n.* something making up for a wrong or an injury

Vocabulary Builder
solace (säl´ is) *n.* comfort; relief

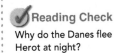

Reading Check
Why do the Danes flee Herot at night?

from Beowulf ■ 43

Differentiated Instruction — Solutions for All Learners

Strategy for Less Proficient Readers
Have students work together in small groups, rewriting difficult passages in their own words. Have students use the paraphrase chart on p. 39 to break down the progress of the plot on p. 41.

Strategy for Gifted/Talented Students
Have students work in small groups to recreate a scene from *Beowulf* for the stage. Some students may wish to do a dramatic reading, others may wish to use **Listening to Literature Audio CDs**, as narration for their performance.

Strategy for Advanced Readers
Have students write character analyses for Grendel and Hrothgar based on what they have read. Ask students to address how the poet aligns these characters with good and evil based on their behavior.

⑩ Translator's Insight
• Point out Raffel's insight note about literary lore to students. **Ask** students what this information reveals about Grendel.
Possible response: Students may suggest that Grendel only fights the weak. He does not possess any worthy heroic qualities.

⑪ Critical Thinking
Analyze
• Read aloud the bracketed passage, and **ask** students how the poem establishes that the coming battle is not just a battle between a hero and a monster, but a battle between good and evil.
Answer: Hrothgar's throne is untouched because it is protected by God, who is unknown to Grendel.
• Point out that this passage also comments on the belief, held about kings and queens for most of Europe's history, that rulers have their positions by divine right.

⑫ Vocabulary Builder
The Latin Word Root -sol-
• Call students' attention to the word *solace* and its definition. Tell students that the Latin word root -sol- is derived from the word *solari*, which means "to console or comfort, to soothe."
• Point out that, as with other roots, meaning is built with prefixes and suffixes. For example, *disconsolate* would describe someone who lacks (*dis*-) that which gives solace. **Ask** students what they think *inconsolable* would mean.
Answer: Not able to be comforted.
• Explain to students that Latin has many other words that, like *solari*, contain the letters -sol-, so it is important to check the meanings of words with which they are unfamiliar.

⑬ Reading Check
Answer: The Danes flee Herot at night because Grendel hunts at night, while they sleep.

14 Literary Analysis
The Epic

14 Literary Analysis
The Epic

▶ **Reteach** Remind students that an epic hero embodies the values and the ideals of the culture that produces him.

- **Ask** students, on the basis of the description of Beowulf in lines 109–122, what qualities they think were valued by Anglo-Saxons.
  Answer: They valued strength, leadership, willingness to help others, and bravery.

15 Reading Strategy
Paraphrasing

- Have students follow the Reading Strategy prompt and paraphrase lines 125–131.

- **Ask** volunteers to share their paraphrases.
  Possible response: The Geats loaded their armor into a strong boat. They felt ready for whatever might happen. Following their hearts, they set sail, traveling safely past cliffs and through ocean currents.

16 Background
History

The Oseberg Ship, Viking artifact, c. A.D. 850

This ship is an important relic of Viking times. Though it was built in the ninth century, its design is so elegant that it has interested modern shipbuilders. (Recent replicas of this type of ship have actually crossed the Atlantic.) The wooden, sail- and oar-powered boat is more than seventy-two feet long. The rudder was at the side, rather than in the stern. Use these questions for discussion:

1. Does this ship look as though it could cross the sea?
   Possible response: The boat must be seaworthy because a replica traveled across the Atlantic.

2. How is the Oseberg ship similar to or different from modern ships?
   Possible responses: Modern ships retain the streamlined hull, but not the elaborate decorations. Modern ships are made of steel, are powered by engines, and have rudders in the stern. The Viking ship is made of wood, is powered by sail and oar, and has its rudder at the side.

In his far-off home Beowulf, Higlac's[4]
110 Follower and the strongest of the Geats—greater
And stronger than anyone anywhere in this world—
Heard how Grendel filled nights with horror
And quickly commanded a boat fitted out,
Proclaiming that he'd go to that famous king.

14 115 Would sail across the sea to Hrothgar,
Now when help was needed. None
Of the wise ones regretted his going, much
As he was loved by the Geats: the omens were good,
And they urged the adventure on. So Beowulf
120 Chose the mightiest men he could find,
The bravest and best of the Geats, fourteen
In all, and led them down to their boat;
He knew the sea, would point the prow
Straight to that distant Danish shore.

125   Then they sailed, set their ship
Out on the waves, under the cliffs.
15 Ready for what came they wound through the currents,
The seas beating at the sand, and were borne
In the lap of their shining ship, lined
130 With gleaming armor, going safely
In that oak-hard boat to where their hearts took them.
The wind hurried them over the waves,
The ship foamed through the sea like a bird
Until, in the time they had known it would take,
135 Standing in the round-curled prow they could see
Sparkling hills, high and green
Jutting up over the shore, and rejoicing
In those rock-steep cliffs they quietly ended
Their voyage. Jumping to the ground, the Geats
140 Pushed their boat to the sand and tied it
In place, mail[5] shirts and armor rattling
As they swiftly moored their ship. And then
They gave thanks to God for their easy crossing.
        High on a wall a Danish watcher
145 Patrolling along the cliffs saw
The travelers crossing to the shore, their shields
Raised and shining; he came riding down,
Hrothgar's lieutenant, spurring his horse,
Needing to know why they'd landed, these men

---

4. Higlac's (hig´ laks) Higlac was the king of the Geats (gā´ ats) and Beowulf's feudal lord and uncle.
5. mail flexible body armor made of metal.

44 ■ *From Legend to History (449–1485)*

Reading Strategy
Paraphrasing Paraphrase lines 125–131. Remember that your paraphrase need not follow the word order of the original.

16

The Oseberg Ship (Viking artifact, c. A.D. 850) Viking Ship Museum, Bygdoy, Oslo

Differentiated
Instruction Solutions for All Learners

Enrichment for Advanced Readers
Suggest that students read additional sections from *Beowulf*. Provide students with copies of *Grendel* by John Gardner and *The Legacy of Heorot* by Larry Niven, Jerry Pournelle, and Steven Barnes. You may also wish to use **Authors In Depth, The British Tradition**, which contains the following selections from Beowulf:

- Celebration at Herot (epic, p. 5)
- Beowulf Returns Home (epic, p. 7)
- Beowulf and the Dragon (epic, p. 16)

After students have read these or other works by the author of *Beowulf*, have them form discussion groups in which they compare and contrast the selections they have read. Suggest criteria for comparison, such as setting, theme, and characters. To extend the activity, have volunteers present to the class brief oral reports on their favorite *Beowulf* selections.

150 In armor. Shaking his heavy spear
In their faces he spoke:
                    "Whose soldiers are you,
You who've been carried in your deep-keeled ship
Across the sea-road to this country of mine?
Listen! I've stood on these cliffs longer
155 Than you know, keeping our coast free
Of pirates, raiders sneaking ashore
From their ships, seeking our lives and our gold.
None have ever come more openly—
And yet you've offered no password, no sign
160 From my prince, no permission from my people for your landing
Here. Nor have I ever seen,
Out of all the men on earth, one greater
Than has come with you; no commoner carries
Such weapons, unless his appearance, and his beauty,
165 Are both lies. You! Tell me your name,
And your father's; no spies go further onto Danish
Soil than you've come already. Strangers,
From wherever it was you sailed, tell it,
And tell it quickly, the quicker the better,
170 I say, for us all. Speak, say
Exactly who you are, and from where, and why."
        Their leader answered him, Beowulf unlocking
Words from deep in his breast:
                    "We are Geats,
Men who follow Higlac. My father
175 Was a famous soldier, known far and wide
As a leader of men. His name was Edgetho.
His life lasted many winters;
Wise men all over the earth surely
Remember him still. And we have come seeking
180 Your prince, Healfdane's son, protector
Of this people, only in friendship: instruct us,
Watchman, help us with your words! Our errand
Is a great one, our business with the glorious king
Of the Danes no secret; there's nothing dark
185 Or hidden in our coming. You know (if we've heard
The truth, and been told honestly) that your country
Is cursed with some strange, vicious creature
That hunts only at night and that no one
Has seen. It's said, watchman, that he has slaughtered
190 Your people, brought terror to the darkness. Perhaps
Hrothgar can hunt, here in my heart,
For some way to drive this devil out—
If anything will ever end the evils
Afflicting your wise and famous lord.
195 Here he can cool his burning sorrow.

Literary Analysis
The Epic How do word choice and other stylistic features of the watchman's speech add a serious, epic tone to his question?

Literary Analysis
The Epic and the Legendary Hero What does Beowulf's way of identifying himself suggest about the values of a warrior culture?

 Reading Check
Why does Beowulf sail to Denmark?

from *Beowulf* ■ 45

⓱ Literary Analysis
The Epic

▶ **Reteach** Remind students that telling the story in a serious manner is one of the characteristics of an epic, and that special, elevated language is often used.

• Have students focus on lines 151–171. **Ask** them the Literary Analysis question: How do word choice and stylistic features of the watchman's speech add an epic tone to his question?
Possible answer: The watchman's speech is filled with serious concerns—his care in doing his job, the presence of pirates and raiders—and these are addressed in a serious tone. The style of his delivery is formal and elevated—for example, in lines 152–153. The watchman also works as a device of the epic, to let us know that Beowulf is bigger, better looking, and more beautifully outfitted with armor than anyone the watchman has ever seen, so the speech furthers the epic ideal of the legendary hero being the obvious superior of all around him.

⓲ Literary Analysis
The Epic and the Legendary Hero

• Have students look at lines 173–179 and **identify** the details of Beowulf's response to the watchman's challenge.

• Then, **ask** the Literary Analysis question: What does Beowulf's way of identifying himself suggest about the values of a warrior culture?
Answer: They valued military prowess, leadership, having a respected father, and wisdom.

⓳ Reading Check

Answer: Beowulf sails to Denmark to help Hrothgar defend his people against the monster, Grendel.

45

Pre-Viking Scandinavia (that is, pre-ninth century) produced many artifacts highly decorated with carving and ornamentation. This so-called barbarian art may have been influenced by forms and patterns of Near Eastern origin; for example, snake forms have been traced to ancient Mesopotamia. Decorated metalwork, like the gilt-silver brooch here, was carried westward to England and Ireland by traders and invaders. Use the following questions for discussion:

1. How do you think sunlight might have enhanced the appearance of objects like this brooch?
   Answer: It probably caused the intricate designs to sparkle as they reflected the light in many directions.

2. What can we infer about ancient Scandinavian society based on decorative objects like this one?
   Possible responses: People valued beauty even in utilitarian objects. The society was advanced and wealthy enough to support artisans.

Or else he may see his suffering go on
Forever, for as long as Herot towers
High on your hills."

           The mounted officer
Answered him bluntly, the brave watchman:
200   "A soldier should know the difference between words
And deeds, and keep that knowledge clear
In his brain. I believe your words, I trust in
Your friendship. Go forward, weapons and armor
And all, on into Denmark. I'll guide you
205 Myself—and my men will guard your ship,
Keep it safe here on our shores,
Your fresh-tarred boat, watch it well,
Until that curving prow carries
Across the sea to Geatland a chosen
210 Warrior who bravely does battle with the creature
Haunting our people, who survives that horror
Unhurt, and goes home bearing our love."
      Then they moved on. Their boat lay moored,
Tied tight to its anchor. Glittering at the top
215 Of their golden helmets wild boar heads gleamed,
Shining decorations, swinging as they marched,
Erect like guards, like sentinels, as though ready
To fight. They marched, Beowulf and his men
And their guide, until they could see the gables
220 Of Herot, covered with hammered gold
And glowing in the sun—that most famous of all dwellings,
Towering majestic, its glittering roofs
Visible far across the land.
Their guide reined in his horse, pointing
225 To that hall, built by Hrothgar for the best
And bravest of his men; the path was plain,
They could see their way. . . .

❖——◆——❖

Beowulf and his men arrive at Herot and are called to see the King.

❖——◆——❖

          Beowulf arose, with his men
230 Around him, ordering a few to remain
With their weapons, leading the others quickly
Along under Herot's steep roof into Hrothgar's
Presence. Standing on that prince's own hearth,
Helmeted, the silvery metal of his mail shirt
235 Gleaming with a smith's high art, he greeted
The Danes' great lord:

Gilt silver brooch from Gotland (Pre-Viking Scandinavia)
Statens Historiska Museet, Stockholm

Enrichment

Heroic Tradition in World Cultures

Literary historians have pointed out that the themes and style of *Beowulf* owe much to the Germanic heroic tradition. The writers of *The New Encyclopedia Britannica* state the following:

"Beowulf himself seems more altruistic than other Germanic heroes or the heroes of the *Iliad*. It is significant that his three battles are not against men, which would entail the retaliation of the blood feud, but against evil monsters, enemies of the whole community,

and civilization itself. Many critics have seen the poem as a Christian allegory, with Beowulf as the champion of goodness and light against the forces of evil and darkness. His sacrificial death is not seen as tragic but as the fitting end of a good (some would say 'too good') hero's life."

"Hail, Hrothgar!
Higlac is my cousin[6] and my king; the days
Of my youth have been filled with glory. Now Grendel's
Name has echoed in our land: sailors
240 Have brought us stories of Herot, the best
Of all mead-halls,[7] deserted and useless when the moon
Hangs in skies the sun had lit,
Light and life fleeing together.
My people have said, the wisest, most knowing
245 And best of them, that my duty was to go to the Danes'
Great king. They have seen my strength for themselves,
Have watched me rise from the darkness of war,
Dripping with my enemies' blood. I drove
Five great giants into chains, chased
250 All of that race from the earth. I swam
In the blackness of night, hunting monsters
Out of the ocean, and killing them one
By one; death was my errand and the fate
They had earned. Now Grendel and I are called
255 Together, and I've come. Grant me, then,
Lord and protector of this noble place,
A single request! I have come so far,
O shelterer of warriors and your people's loved friend,
That this one favor you should not refuse me—
260 That I, alone and with the help of my men,
May purge all evil from this hall. I have heard,
Too, that the monster's scorn of men
Is so great that he needs no weapons and fears none.
Nor will I. My lord Higlac
265 Might think less of me if I let my sword
Go where my feet were afraid to, if I hid
Behind some broad linden[8] shield: my hands
Alone shall fight for me, struggle for life
Against the monster. God must decide
270 Who will be given to death's cold grip.
Grendel's plan, I think, will be
What it has been before, to invade this hall
And gorge his belly with our bodies. If he can,
If he can. And I think, if my time will have come,
275 There'll be nothing to mourn over, no corpse to prepare
For its grave: Grendel will carry our bloody
Flesh to the moors, crunch on our bones
And smear torn scraps of our skin on the walls

---

6. **cousin** here, used as a general term for relative.
7. **mead-halls** To reward his thanes, the king in heroic literature would build a hall
   where mead (a drink made from fermented honey) was served.
8. **linden** very sturdy type of wood.

from Beowulf ■ 47

Literary Analysis
The Epic and the Legendary Hero How do Beowulf's boasts of great deeds and his announcement of his plan establish him as a hero?

Vocabulary Builder
purge (pʉrj) *v.* purify; cleanse

Reading Strategy
Paraphrasing Paraphrase Beowulf's plans in lines 264–279.

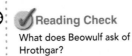Reading Check
What does Beowulf ask of Hrothgar?

㉑ Literary Analysis
The Epic and the Legendary Hero

- Remind students that the legendary hero is larger than life and has a track record of battles and adventures that reinforces both his confidence and his reputation.

▶ **Monitor Progress:** After students have read Beowulf's speech, **ask** students the Literary Analysis question: How do Beowulf's boasts of past deeds and his announcement of his plan establish him as a hero?
Possible response: Beowulf relates the type of larger-than-life accomplishments one would expect from a legendary hero, including the defeat of giants, and also establishes that he is famous for his deeds (his people have seen him in battle, and that is why they sent him).

- Point out that, in epics, the boasting of heroes such as Beowulf is never empty. They have always accomplished what they say they have. Also, their skills in battle are always matched with great virtues, such as loyalty and the desire to help others. In addition, there is a kind of humility in these heroes, in that they generally acknowledge that the skills they possess are gifts from a higher power.

㉒ Reading Strategy
Paraphrasing

- Have students paraphrase Beowulf's plans in lines 264–279.
Possible response: Beowulf plans to wait for Grendel in the hall, where he will fight the monster with his bare hands. He realizes that he may be killed and eaten.

- **Ask** students what Beowulf gives as his reason for fighting barehanded.
Answer: He is afraid that it would be less honorable to use a sword and hide behind a shield. Besides, the battle is in God's hands.

㉓ Reading Check

Answer: Beowulf asks Hrothgar to grant him the single request that he alone, and with the help of his men, may purge all evil from the hall.

Differentiated Instruction   Solutions for All Learners

Strategy for Less Proficient Readers
Have students review the list of Beowulf's accomplishments on p. 47. Encourage students to use this list to summarize all that they have learned about Beowulf's character so far. Then, ask volunteers to share and discuss their summaries.

Enrichment for Gifted/Talented Students
Have each student create a single-panel cartoon that illustrates one of Beowulf's accomplishments listed on p. 47. Encourage students to use sentences from the selection as captions for their cartoons.

Support for Advanced Readers
Lead a discussion in which students consider the tone, style, and language in the selection from *Beowulf*. During the discussion, have students recall what qualifies as epic in the writing of *Beowulf*.

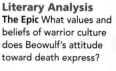

↑
       Of his den. No, I expect no Danes
280 Will fret about sewing our shrouds, if he wins.
       And if death does take me, send the hammered
24 Mail of my armor to Higlac, return
       The inheritance I had from Hrethel, and he
       From Wayland.[9] Fate will unwind as it must!"

That night Beowulf and his men stay inside Herot. While his men sleep, Beowulf lies awake, eager to meet with Grendel.

The Battle with Grendel

285   Out from the marsh, from the foot of misty
       Hills and bogs, bearing God's hatred,
       Grendel came, hoping to kill
       Anyone he could trap on this trip to high Herot.
       He moved quickly through the cloudy night,
290 Up from his swampland, sliding silently
       Toward that gold-shining hall. He had visited Hrothgar's
       Home before, knew the way—
25 But never, before nor after that night,
       Found Herot defended so firmly, his reception
295 So harsh. He journeyed, forever joyless,
       Straight to the door, then snapped it open,
       Tore its iron fasteners with a touch
       And rushed angrily over the threshold.
       He strode quickly across the inlaid
300 Floor, snarling and fierce: his eyes
       Gleamed in the darkness, burned with a gruesome
       Light. Then he stopped, seeing the hall
       Crowded with sleeping warriors, stuffed
       With rows of young soldiers resting together.
305 And his heart laughed, he relished the sight,
       Intended to tear the life from those bodies
       By morning; the monster's mind was hot
       With the thought of food and the feasting his belly
       Would soon know. But fate, that night, intended
310 Grendel to gnaw the broken bones
       Of his last human supper. Human
       Eyes were watching his evil steps,
       Waiting to see his swift hard claws.
       Grendel snatched at the first Geat
315 He came to, ripped him apart, cut

26
Medieval Viking Warrior

---

9. Wayland from Germanic folklore, an invisible blacksmith.

Enrichment

Kennings in Anglo-Saxon Verse

There are many kennings in "The Battle with Grendel." Kennings are descriptive, poetical expressions used instead of the simple name of a person or thing. The word comes from the Scandinavian words *kenna vith,* which mean "to name after."

In *Beowulf,* the kennings include "shepherd of evil" and "guardian of crime" (line 325), "Higlac's follower" (line 333), "infamous killer" (line 337), "Almighty's enemy" (line 360), and "hell's captive" (line 363).

In the original Old English, the primary purpose of kennings was to maintain the alliteration required by Anglo-Saxon verse. According to convention, one of the accented syllables after the caesura (a pause in a line of verse) has to alliterate with at least one of the accented syllables in the first half of the line.

His body to bits with powerful jaws,
Drank the blood from his veins and bolted
Him down, hands and feet; death
And Grendel's great teeth came together,
320   Snapping life shut. Then he stepped to another
Still body, clutched at Beowulf with his claws,
Grasped at a strong-hearted wakeful sleeper
—And was instantly seized himself, claws
Bent back as Beowulf leaned up on one arm.
325   That shepherd of evil, guardian of crime,
Knew at once that nowhere on earth
Had he met a man whose hands were harder;
His mind was flooded with fear—but nothing
Could take his talons and himself from that tight
330   Hard grip. Grendel's one thought was to run
From Beowulf, flee back to his marsh and hide there:
This was a different Herot than the hall he had emptied.
But Higlac's follower remembered his final
Boast and, standing erect, stopped
335   The monster's flight, fastened those claws
In his fists till they cracked, clutched Grendel
Closer. The infamous killer fought
For his freedom, wanting no flesh but retreat,
Desiring nothing but escape; his claws
340   Had been caught, he was trapped. That trip to Herot
Was a miserable journey for the <u>writhing</u> monster!
       The high hall rang, its roof boards swayed,
And Danes shook with terror. Down
The aisles the battle swept, angry
345   And wild. Herot trembled, wonderfully
Built to withstand the blows, the struggling
Great bodies beating at its beautiful walls;
Shaped and fastened with iron, inside
And out, artfully worked, the building
350   Stood firm. Its benches rattled, fell
To the floor, gold-covered boards grating
As Grendel and Beowulf battled across them.
Hrothgar's wise men had fashioned Herot
To stand forever; only fire,
355   They had planned, could shatter what such skill had put
Together, swallow in hot flames such splendor
Of ivory and iron and wood. Suddenly
The sounds changed, the Danes started
In new terror, cowering in their beds as the terrible
360   Screams of the Almighty's enemy sang
In the darkness, the horrible shrieks of pain
And defeat, the tears torn out of Grendel's
Taut throat, hell's captive caught in the arms

Literary Analysis
The Epic How do the "renamings" of Grendel in line 325 emphasize the weighty significance of the battle that is about to begin?

28 *Burton Raffel*
Translator's Insight
Like bullies, monsters immediately think of running, as soon as they find themselves in what might be a fair fight.

Vocabulary Builder
writhing (rīth̲ iɴ) *adj.* making twisting or turning motions

30 ✓ Reading Check
What advantage does Beowulf have in his fight with Grendel?

from Beowulf ■ 49

27 **Literary Analysis**
The Epic

• Have students **identify** phrases used to describe Grendel in line 325.
Answer: "shepherd of evil," "guardian of crime"

• Then, **ask** them the Literary Analysis question: How do the "renamings" of Grendel in line 325 emphasize the weighty significance of the battle that is about to begin?
Answer: These kennings show that the battle is not just between man and monster, but between forces of good and evil. Grendel is not just evil himself, but is a source and caretaker of evil.

28 **Translator's Insight**

• Direct students' attention to the translator's insight note. Beowulf forces Grendel to finally fight a fair fight. **Ask** students to predict who will win the battle.
Possible answer: Students may suggest that Beowulf will win because good always conquers evil.

29 **Critical Thinking**
Relate

• Have students review lines 347–357, focusing on the description of the building.

• **Ask** students to relate the loving description of Herot to the photographs of Scandinavian artifacts that illustrate this section.
Possible responses: Even everyday objects are decorated; objects are valued for their beauty as well as their functionality.

30 **Reading Check**

Possible responses: Beowulf's advantage over Grendel is his superior strength. Grendel is moved to fear at the hardness of Beowulf's hands.

Differentiated
Instruction   Solutions for All Learners

Background for Gifted/Talented Students
Review kennings with students, and point out examples on these pages. Discuss how kennings poetically describe the things or people they name. Then, have students create kennings for people, things, or places from everyday life—for example, sports heroes, cars, highways, school, or home. If they wish, they may create a short story using some of these kennings. Alternatively, you might have them share their kennings with the class and have students try to guess what they describe.

Enrichment for Advanced Readers
Have students consider what they have read about Grendel and Beowulf. They should examine how different situations and passions (evil and murder for Grendel and honor and virtue for Beowulf) would affect how each viewed the events of the poem. How, for example, might Grendel view the battle that appears on these pages? Ask students to write a few paragraphs relating what might have been going through Grendel's mind as he approached Herot, killed and ate the first Geat, and battled Beowulf.

49

③ Literary Analysis
The Epic

- Have students read the description of the battle between Beowulf and Grendel to themselves. Encourage students to record their impressions of the battle as they read.

- Then, **ask** them the Literary Analysis question: Which details from the description of the battle between Beowulf and Grendel add realism? Which details add epic grandness?
  Possible answers: The descriptions of Grendel's screams, shrieks, and tears, combined with those of Beowulf's secure hold on the monster, add realism. Epic grandness is suggested by the description of how Grendel has bewitched the weapons of Beowulf's men as well as the descriptions of Beowulf as the strongest of all men on earth and the "mighty protector of men" and of Grendel as "afflictor of men, tormentor of their days."

- **Ask** students to consider Grendel's recognition that he is feuding with God. How might this change his perspective?
  Possible responses: It might increase his fear, and in the poem it increases his hatred, to realize that his real enemy is not just a mortal man.

② Reading Strategy
Paraphrasing

- Have students follow the Reading Strategy prompt: **Paraphrase** the sentence in lines 392–397.
  Possible responses: The battle between Grendel and Beowulf ended. Beowulf is more famous than before. Grendel escaped, wounded, and fled to his den at the bottom of the marsh, where he would wait to die.

- **Discuss** how this episode shows Beowulf accomplishing his goals.
  Possible response: Beowulf wanted victory, but glory seemed even more important to him, and he has gained this with Grendel's defeat.

Of him who of all the men on earth
365 Was the strongest.
                    That mighty protector of men
Meant to hold the monster till its life
Leaped out, knowing the fiend was no use
To anyone in Denmark. All of Beowulf's
Band had jumped from their beds, ancestral
370 Swords raised and ready, determined
To protect their prince if they could. Their courage
Was great but all wasted: they could hack at Grendel
From every side, trying to open
A path for his evil soul, but their points
375 Could not hurt him, the sharpest and hardest iron
Could not scratch at his skin, for that sin-stained demon
Had bewitched all men's weapons, laid spells
That blunted every mortal man's blade.
And yet his time had come, his days
380 Were over, his death near; down
To hell he would go, swept groaning and helpless
To the waiting hands of still worse fiends.
Now he discovered—once the afflictor
Of men, tormentor of their days—what it meant
385 To feud with Almighty God: Grendel
Saw that his strength was deserting him, his claws
Bound fast, Higlac's brave follower tearing at
His hands. The monster's hatred rose higher,
But his power had gone. He twisted in pain,
390 And the bleeding sinews deep in his shoulder
Snapped, muscle and bone split
And broke. The battle was over, Beowulf
Had been granted new glory: Grendel escaped,
But wounded as he was could flee to his den,
395 His miserable hole at the bottom of the marsh,
Only to die, to wait for the end
Of all his days. And after that bloody
Combat the Danes laughed with delight.
He who had come to them from across the sea,
400 Bold and strong-minded, had driven affliction
Off, purged Herot clean. He was happy,
Now, with that night's fierce work; the Danes
Had been served as he'd boasted he'd serve them; Beowulf,
A prince of the Geats, had killed Grendel,
405 Ended the grief, the sorrow, the suffering
Forced on Hrothgar's helpless people
By a bloodthirsty fiend. No Dane doubted
The victory, for the proof, hanging high
From the rafters where Beowulf had hung it, was the monster's
410 Arm, claw and shoulder and all.

50 ■ From Legend to History (449–1485)

Literary Analysis
The Epic Which details from this description of the battle between Beowulf and Grendel add realism? Which details add epic grandeur?

Reading Strategy
Paraphrasing Paraphrase the sentence in lines 392–397.

Enrichment

Mythical Monsters

Most of us are familiar with monsters from books, movies, and games. However, monsters go far back in history, and almost all cultures tell stories of fantastic creatures.

The chimera of Greek myth is a combination of a lion, a goat, and a snake; the Aztec god Quetzalcoatl is represented by a winged serpent. The Arabian roc is an immense eagle, the Hawaiian *mo'o* is a giant lizard, and the Norse Midgaard Serpent is a snake big enough to encircle the world. In Jacarilla Apache folk tales, the hero Killer-of-Enemies slays a giant elk and a monster eagle.

Monsters like Grendel may be used to symbolize evil. In medieval Christian art, for example, several saints appear as dragon-slayers. Present-day Balinese, who believe that life is a struggle between good and evil spirits, perform sacred dances in which the good, lionlike *Barong* clashes with the evil witch *Rangda*.

The Danes celebrate Beowulf's victory. That night, though, Grendel's mother kills Hrothgar's closest friend and carries off her child's claw. The next day the horrified king tells Beowulf about the two monsters and their underwater lair.

The Monsters' Lair

"I've heard that my people, peasants working
In the fields, have seen a pair of such fiends
Wandering in the moors and marshes, giant
Monsters living in those desert lands.
415 And they've said to my wise men that, as well as they could see,
One of the devils was a female creature.
The other, they say, walked through the wilderness
Like a man—but mightier than any man.
They were frightened, and they fled, hoping to find help
420 In Herot. They named the huge one Grendel:
If he had a father no one knew him,
Or whether there'd been others before these two,
Hidden evil before hidden evil.
They live in secret places, windy
425 Cliffs, wolf-dens where water pours
From the rocks, then runs underground, where mist
Steams like black clouds, and the groves of trees
Growing out over their lake are all covered
With frozen spray, and wind down snakelike
430 Roots that reach as far as the water
And help keep it dark. At night that lake
Burns like a torch. No one knows its bottom,
No wisdom reaches such depths. A deer,
Hunted through the woods by packs of hounds,
435 A stag with great horns, though driven through the forest
From faraway places, prefers to die
On those shores, refuses to save its life
In that water. It isn't far, nor is it
A pleasant spot! When the wind stirs
440 And storms, waves splash toward the sky,
As dark as the air, as black as the rain
That the heavens weep. Our only help,
Again, lies with you. Grendel's mother
Is hidden in her terrible home, in a place
445 You've not seen. Seek it, if you dare! Save us,
Once more, and again twisted gold,
Heaped-up ancient treasure, will reward you
For the battle you win!"

33

Golden horn, National Museet, Copenhagen

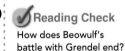

34 ✓ **Reading Check**
How does Beowulf's battle with Grendel end?

from Beowulf ■ 51

Relate

- Tell students that works that share a common cultural context often have elements or themes that are related.

- If students have read "The Wanderer" 23–26, **ask** them to discuss how this passage connects to that poem.
  Answer: Both reveal how important it was in Anglo-Saxon culture for a warrior to have a lord. Beowulf ensures that his men do not meet the fate of the wanderer by asking Hrothgar to become their lord should Beowulf be killed.

36 **Background**

Artifact

Silver pendant showing the helmet of the Vendel, tenth century

The Vikings celebrated courage and skill in battle. However, Viking culture was sophisticated in many ways and enriched the countries they invaded. Vikings were noted for daring exploration, an emphasis on individual freedom, a tradition of storytelling, and skill in carving.

This silver pendant bears a face that is similar to faces found on Viking helmets, buckles, and other articles of clothing. Use these questions for discussion:

1. How does the helmet on the pendant compare to the way you imagine Beowulf's helmet to be?
   Possible response: Beowulf's helmet might be similar to this or might be even more elaborate.

2. Who do you think might have worn a pendant like this one? Why?
   Possible response: It may have been worn by a warrior as a memento or for luck in battle.

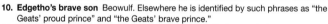

Beowulf resolves to kill Grendel's monstrous mother. He travels to the lake in which she lives.

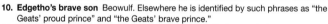

The Battle With Grendel's Mother

Then Edgetho's brave son[10] spoke:

"Remember,

450 Hrothgar, O knowing king, now
When my danger is near, the warm words we uttered,
And if your enemy should end my life
Then be, O generous prince, forever
The father and protector of all whom I leave
455 Behind me, here in your hands, my beloved
Comrades left with no leader, their leader
Dead. And the precious gifts you gave me,
My friend, send them to Higlac. May he see
In their golden brightness, the Geats' great lord
460 Gazing at your treasure, that here in Denmark
I found a noble protector, a giver
Of rings whose rewards I won and briefly
Relished. And you, Unferth,[11] let
My famous old sword stay in your hands:
465 I shall shape glory with Hrunting, or death
Will hurry me from this earth!"

As his words ended

He leaped into the lake, would not wait for anyone's
Answer; the heaving water covered him
Over. For hours he sank through the waves;
470 At last he saw the mud of the bottom.
And all at once the greedy she-wolf
Who'd ruled those waters for half a hundred
Years discovered him, saw that a creature
From above had come to explore the bottom
475 Of her wet world. She welcomed him in her claws,
Clutched at him savagely but could not harm him,
Tried to work her fingers through the tight
Ring-woven mail on his breast, but tore
And scratched in vain. Then she carried him, armor
480 And sword and all, to her home; he struggled
To free his weapon, and failed. The fight
Brought other monsters swimming to see

Silver pendant showing the helmet of the Vendel (Early Viking period, 10th century) Statens Historiska Museet, Stockholm

---

10. **Edgetho's brave son** Beowulf. Elsewhere he is identified by such phrases as "the Geats' proud prince" and "the Geats' brave prince."
11. **Unferth** Danish warrior who had questioned Beowulf's bravery before the battle with Grendel.

Enrichment

Pagan and Christian Influences

The popularity of pagan and almost-pagan legends like *Beowulf* was a source of concern and irritation to early Christian leaders. The scholar and monk Alcuin, who was taught at Bede's school and who created a system of universal education for Charlemagne, wrote a famous letter home in 797. In it, he criticized the English bishop for allowing Christian priests, while dining, to listen to poetry about the pagan king Ingeld—one of the characters in *Beowulf*. Alcuin argued that the poem was inappropriate for the priests, who needed to be learning the Scripture they would be teaching. Eventually, Christian influences began to filter into the pagan stories. Two centuries later, it was the clergy who recorded *Beowulf*, saving the legend so that we can still enjoy it today.

Her catch, a host of sea beasts who beat at
His mail shirt, stabbing with tusks and teeth
485 As they followed along. Then he realized, suddenly,
That she'd brought him into someone's battle-hall,
And there the water's heat could not hurt him,
Nor anything in the lake attack him through
The building's high-arching roof. A brilliant
490 Light burned all around him, the lake
Itself like a fiery flame.
                    Then he saw
The mighty water witch and swung his sword,
His ring-marked blade, straight at her head;
The iron sang its fierce song,
495 Sang Beowulf's strength. But her guest
Discovered that no sword could slice her evil
Skin, that Hrunting could not hurt her, was useless
Now when he needed it. They wrestled, she ripped
And tore and clawed at him, bit holes in his helmet,
500 And that too failed him; for the first time in years
Of being worn to war it would earn no glory;
It was the last time anyone would wear it. But Beowulf
Longed only for fame, leaped back
Into battle. He tossed his sword aside,
505 Angry; the steel-edged blade lay where
He'd dropped it. If weapons were useless he'd use
His hands, the strength in his fingers. So fame
Comes to the men who mean to win it
And care about nothing else! He raised
510 His arms and seized her by the shoulder; anger
Doubled his strength, he threw her to the floor.
She fell, Grendel's fierce mother, and the Geats'
Proud prince was ready to leap on her. But she rose
At once and repaid him with her clutching claws,
515 Wildly tearing at him. He was weary, that best
And strongest of soldiers; his feet stumbled
And in an instant she had him down, held helpless.
Squatting with her weight on his stomach, she drew
A dagger, brown with dried blood, and prepared
520 To avenge her only son. But he was stretched
On his back, and her stabbing blade was blunted
By the woven mail shirt he wore on his chest.
The hammered links held; the point
Could not touch him. He'd have traveled to the bottom of the earth,
525 Edgetho's son, and died there, if that shining
Woven metal had not helped—and Holy
God, who sent him victory, gave judgment
For truth and right, Ruler of the Heavens,
Once Beowulf was back on his feet and fighting.

Literary Analysis
The Epic How does the setting of this battle add to its epic significance? (Consider what it shows about the realms in which Beowulf has power.)

Reading Strategy
Paraphrasing Paraphrase the sentence describing the combat in lines 498–502.

38

Burton Raffel
Translator's Insight
True warriors are totally dedicated and fight for fame (honor), not for tangible rewards.

40

Reading Check
Why does Beowulf toss aside his sword in the fight?

from *Beowulf* ■ 53

37 Literary Analysis
The Epic

• Tell students to pay attention to details about the setting as they read about Beowulf's pursuit of Grendel's mother to her lair.

▶ **Monitor Progress: Ask** students the Literary Analysis question: How does the setting of this battle add to its epic significance?
Possible responses: The fact that this takes place underwater, in an obviously mythological setting, underscores the fact that this is a battle against forces of evil. As with the rulers in the land of men, there is a great battle hall, a fit setting for an epic battle. Also, the fact that Beowulf's powers are not lessened and that he can even function in the monster's lair adds to his status as legendary hero.

38 Translator's Insight

• Draw students' attention to Raffel's comment about true warriors. How does the motivation for honor alone amplify the character of Beowulf?
Possible answer: Fighting for honor alone adds to Beowulf's status as a hero. This pure, non-secular motivation helps exemplify that he represents good and is battling true evil.

39 Reading Strategy
Paraphrasing

• Have students follow the Reading Strategy prompt: **Paraphrase** the sentence describing the combat in lines 498–502.
Answer: Beowulf wrestled with Grendel's mother. She used her claws and her teeth to fight. She bit through his helmet. That helmet had served him for years, but it was ruined.

• Point out that even the helmet was considered something that could earn glory. Unlike the sword, Hrunting, the helmet was not named, but those items on which a warrior's life depended were often held in high regard.

40 Reading Check

Answer: Beowulf tosses his sword aside because no sword can slice the skin of Grendel's mother.

Point out that this passage under-scores once again the pagan-Christian blend in the poem. The Christian God is said to give Beowulf victory, and yet the sword Beowulf finds on the wall was "blessed" with the magic of giants. This is not a blending that is limited to this story. In the tales of King Arthur and Merlin, we see another legendary hero who relies on a found sword, magic, and God. You may want to explain to students that, in many countries, when Christianity arrived, it was often the leaders and the educated who became Christians, while the common folk clung to many of their pagan traditions—even if they nominally became Christians. Encourage students to look for this type of blending of traditions—for example, in lines 579 and following.

42 Reading Strategy

Paraphrasing

- Have students follow the Reading Strategy prompt: **Paraphrase** lines 543–562.
  Possible responses: The den of Grendel's mother became bright, and Beowulf carried the sword to find the dead Grendel, to dishonor the corpse because of the evil deeds against Hrothgar and his men. When he found Grendel, dead in a corner, Beowulf beheaded him.

- **Ask** students what they think the significance of the bright light might be.
  Possible response: Because evil was destroyed, darkness was banished.

---

530 Then he saw, hanging on the wall, a heavy
       Sword, hammered by giants, strong
       And blessed with their magic, the best of all weapons
       But so <u>massive</u> that no ordinary man could lift
       Its carved and decorated length. He drew it
535 From its scabbard, broke the chain on its hilt,
       And then, savage, now, angry
       And desperate, lifted it high over his head
       And struck with all the strength he had left,
       Caught her in the neck and cut it through,
540 Broke bones and all. Her body fell
       To the floor, lifeless, the sword was wet
       With her blood, and Beowulf rejoiced at the sight.
            The brilliant light shone, suddenly,
       As though burning in that hall, and as bright as Heaven's
545 Own candle, lit in the sky. He looked
       At her home, then following along the wall
       Went walking, his hands tight on the sword,
       His heart still angry. He was hunting another
       Dead monster, and took his weapon with him
550 For final revenge against Grendel's vicious
       Attacks, his nighttime raids, over
       And over, coming to Herot when Hrothgar's
       Men slept, killing them in their beds,
       Eating some on the spot, fifteen
555 Or more, and running to his <u>loathsome</u> moor
       With another such sickening meal waiting
       In his pouch. But Beowulf repaid him for those visits,
       Found him lying dead in his corner,
       Armless, exactly as that fierce fighter
560 Had sent him out from Herot, then struck off
       His head with a single swift blow. The body
       jerked for the last time, then lay still.
            The wise old warriors who surrounded Hrothgar,
       Like him staring into the monsters' lake,
565 Saw the waves surging and blood
       Spurting through. They spoke about Beowulf,
       All the graybeards, whispered together
       And said that hope was gone, that the hero
       Had lost fame and his life at once, and would never
570 Return to the living, come back as triumphant
       As he had left; almost all agreed that Grendel's
       Mighty mother, the she-wolf, had killed him.
       The sun slid over past noon, went further
       Down. The Danes gave up, left
575 The lake and went home, Hrothgar with them.
       The Geats stayed, sat sadly, watching,
       Imagining they saw their lord but not believing

Vocabulary Builder
massive (mas´ iv) *adj.* big and solid; bulky

Reading Strategy
Paraphrasing Paraphrase lines 543–562.

Vocabulary Builder
loathsome (lōth´ səm) *adj.* disgusting

They would ever see him again.
                              —Then the sword
Melted, blood-soaked, dripping down
580 Like water, disappearing like ice when the world's
Eternal Lord loosens invisible
Fetters and unwinds icicles and frost
As only He can, He who rules
Time and seasons, He who is truly
585 God. The monsters' hall was full of
Rich treasures, but all that Beowulf took
Was Grendel's head and the hilt of the giants'
Jeweled sword; the rest of that ring-marked
Blade had dissolved in Grendel's steaming
590 Blood, boiling even after his death.
And then the battle's only survivor
Swam up and away from those silent corpses;
The water was calm and clean, the whole
Huge lake peaceful once the demons who'd lived in it
595 Were dead.
        Then that noble protector of all seamen
Swam to land, rejoicing in the heavy
Burdens he was bringing with him. He
And all his glorious band of Geats
600 Thanked God that their leader had come back unharmed;
They left the lake together. The Geats
Carried Beowulf's helmet, and his mail shirt.
Behind them the water slowly thickened
As the monsters' blood came seeping up.
They walked quickly, happily, across
605 Roads all of them remembered, left
The lake and the cliffs alongside it, brave men
Staggering under the weight of Grendel's skull,
Too heavy for fewer than four of them to handle—
Two on each side of the spear jammed through it—
610 Yet proud of their ugly load and determined
That the Danes, seated in Herot, should see it.
Soon, fourteen Geats arrived
At the hall, bold and warlike, and with Beowulf,
Their lord and leader, they walked on the mead-hall
615 Green. Then the Geats' brave prince entered
Herot, covered with glory for the daring
Battles he had fought; he sought Hrothgar
To salute him and show Grendel's head.
He carried that terrible trophy by the hair,
620 Brought it straight to where the Danes sat,
Drinking, the queen among them. It was a weird
And wonderful sight, and the warriors stared.

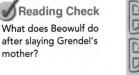

from *Beowulf* ■ 55

55

After being honored by Hrothgar, Beowulf and his fellow Geats return home, where he eventually becomes King. Beowulf rules Geatland for fifty years. When a dragon menaces his kingdom, Beowulf, now an old man, determines to slay the beast. Before going into battle, he tells his men about the royal house and his exploits in its service.

The Last Battle

And Beowulf uttered his final boast:
"I've never known fear, as a youth I fought
625 In endless battles. I am old, now,
But I will fight again, seek fame still,
If the dragon hiding in his tower dares
To face me."
                    Then he said farewell to his followers,
Each in his turn, for the last time:
630   "I'd use no sword, no weapon, if this beast
Could be killed without it, crushed to death
Like Grendel, gripped in my hands and torn
Limb from limb. But his breath will be burning
Hot, poison will pour from his tongue.
635 I feel no shame, with shield and sword
And armor, against this monster: when he comes to me

46 ▼ **Critical Viewing**
What characteristics do this dragon and Grendel have in common?
[Compare and Contrast]

45

I mean to stand, not run from his shooting
Flames, stand till fate decides
Which of us wins. My heart is firm,
640 My hands calm: I need no hot
Words. Wait for me close by, my friends.
We shall see, soon, who will survive
This bloody battle, stand when the fighting
Is done. No one else could do
645 What I mean to, here, no man but me
Could hope to defeat this monster. No one
Could try. And this dragon's treasure, his gold
And everything hidden in that tower, will be mine
Or war will sweep me to a bitter death!"
650   Then Beowulf rose, still brave, still strong,
And with his shield at his side, and a mail shirt on his breast,
Strode calmly, confidently, toward the tower, under
The rocky cliffs: no coward could have walked there!
And then he who'd endured dozens of desperate
655 Battles, who'd stand boldly while swords and shields
Clashed, the best of kings, saw
Huge stone arches and felt the heat
Of the dragon's breath, flooding down
Through the hidden entrance, too hot for anyone
660 To stand, a streaming current of fire
And smoke that blocked all passage. And the Geats'
Lord and leader, angry, lowered
His sword and roared out a battle cry,
A call so loud and clear that it reached through
665 The hoary rock, hung in the dragon's
Ear. The beast rose, angry,
Knowing a man had come—and then nothing
But war could have followed. Its breath came first.
A steaming cloud pouring from the stone,
670 Then the earth itself shook. Beowulf
Swung his shield into place, held it
In front of him, facing the entrance. The dragon
Coiled and uncoiled, its heart urging it
Into battle. Beowulf's ancient sword
675 Was waiting, unsheathed, his sharp and gleaming
Blade. The beast came closer; both of them
Were ready, each set on slaughter. The Geats'
Great prince stood firm, unmoving, prepared
Behind his high shield, waiting in his shining
680 Armor. The monster came quickly toward him,
Pouring out fire and smoke, hurrying
To its fate. Flames beat at the iron
Shield, and for a time it held, protected
Beowulf as he'd planned; then it began to melt,

Literary Analysis
The Epic What does Beowulf's speech in lines 630–649 suggest to you about Anglo-Saxon values?

47

Detail of a dragon head on the Mammen horse collar (Viking artifact, 10th century), National Museum, Denmark

49 ✓ **Reading Check**
How does Beowulf plan to fight the dragon?

from Beowulf ■ 57

Analyze

- **Explain** that lines 645–692 present a turning point.
- **Ask** students how this battle is different from the others that Beowulf has fought.

    Answer: Fate is against the hero for the first time, and Beowulf knows he is going to lose.

51 **Background**

Artifact

Gilt bronze winged dragon, eighth century

This example of eighth-century gilt-bronze craftsmanship comes from Sweden, but it is representative of works by other Scandinavian artists who also preferred designs of real or mythical animals to the human figure or plant forms. They were less concerned with accurate representation than with creating complex, abstract, patterns. Dragons like this one eventually appeared in Christian art as well. Use these questions for discussion:

1. How does this artifact suggest that eighth-century Scandinavians were interested in abstract designs?

    Possible responses: The artifact is not strongly representational; in fact, it is difficult to tell what it is. The artist was more interested in creating beautiful, flowing lines than in depicting a plausible creature.

2. **Compare** the dragon to the one on the previous page.

    Answer: This dragon is far more abstract than the one on p. 57.

52 **Literary Analysis**

The Epic

- **Ask** students the Literary Analysis question: What do these lines reveal about the values of warrior culture?

    Possible responses: Good swords and armor are valuable and highly prized, making them a gift of honor. Weapons and armor were among the most important items a son inherited from his father. The pedigree of a warrior's sword and armor was important.

Gilt bronze winged dragon (Swedish artifact, 8th century).
Staters Historiska Museet, Stockholm

---

685 And for the first time in his life that famous prince
        Fought with fate against him, with glory
        Denied him. He knew it, but he raised his sword
        And struck at the dragon's scaly hide.
        The ancient blade broke, bit into
690 The monster's skin, drew blood, but cracked
        And failed him before it went deep enough, helped him
        Less than he needed. The dragon leaped
        With pain, thrashed and beat at him, spouting
        Murderous flames, spreading them everywhere.
695 And the Geats' ring-giver did not boast of glorious
        Victories in other wars: his weapon
        Had failed him, deserted him, now when he needed it
        Most, that excellent sword. Edgetho's
        Famous son stared at death,
700 Unwilling to leave this world, to exchange it
        For a dwelling in some distant place—a journey
        Into darkness that all men must make, as death
        Ends their few brief hours on earth.
            Quickly, the dragon came at him, encouraged
705 As Beowulf fell back; its breath flared,
        And he suffered, wrapped around in swirling
        Flames—a king, before, but now
        A beaten warrior. None of his comrades
        Came to him, helped him, his brave and noble
710 Followers; they ran for their lives, fled
        Deep in a wood. And only one of them
        Remained, stood there, miserable, remembering,
        As a good man must, what kinship should mean.

            His name was Wiglaf, he was Wexstan's son
715 And a good soldier; his family had been Swedish,
        Once. Watching Beowulf, he could see
        How his king was suffering, burning. Remembering
        Everything his lord and cousin had given him,
        Armor and gold and the great estates
720 Wexstan's family enjoyed, Wiglaf's
        Mind was made up; he raised his yellow
        Shield and drew his sword—an ancient
        Weapon that had once belonged to Onela's
        Nephew, and that Wexstan had won, killing
725 The prince when he fled from Sweden, sought safety
        With Herdred, and found death.[12] And Wiglaf's father
        Had carried the dead man's armor, and his sword,

---

12. Onela's / Nephew . . . found death When Onela seized the throne of Sweden, his two nephews sought shelter with the king of Geatland, Herdred. Wiglaf's father, Wexstan, killed the older nephew for Onela.

Literary Analysis
The Epic What do these lines reveal about the values of warrior culture?

Enrichment

Death of a Hero

Explain to students that mythographers such as Joseph Campbell (in his book *The Hero With a Thousand Faces*) point out that heroes are usually described in terms of life's peak moments. For example, young Beowulf's early triumphs are dramatized—he slays both Grendel and Grendel's mother. His death fighting the dragon is also featured in the epic. However, nothing of his fifty-year reign as king is shown in the poem.

To Onela, and the king had said nothing, only
Given him armor and sword and all,
730 Everything his rebel nephew had owned
And lost when he left this life. And Wexstan
Had kept those shining gifts, held them
For years, waiting for his son to use them,
Wear them as honorably and well as once
735 His father had done; then Wexstan died
And Wiglaf was his heir, inherited treasures
And weapons and land. He'd never worn
That armor, fought with that sword, until Beowulf
Called him to his side, led him into war.
740 But his soul did not melt, his sword was strong;
The dragon discovered his courage, and his weapon,
When the rush of battle brought them together.
    And Wiglaf, his heart heavy, uttered
The kind of words his comrades deserved:
745   "I remember how we sat in the mead-hall, drinking
And boasting of how brave we'd be when Beowulf
Needed us, he who gave us these swords
And armor: all of us swore to repay him,
When the time came, kindness for kindness
750 —With our lives, if he needed them. He allowed us to
        join him,
Chose us from all his great army, thinking
Our boasting words had some weight, believing
Our promises, trusting our swords. He took us
For soldiers, for men. He meant to kill
755 This monster himself, our mighty king,
Fight this battle alone and unaided,
As in the days when his strength and daring dazzled
Men's eyes. But those days are over and gone
And now our lord must lean on younger
760 Arms. And we must go to him, while angry
Flames burn at his flesh, help
Our glorious king! By almighty God,
I'd rather burn myself than see
Flames swirling around my lord.
765 And who are we to carry home
Our shields before we've slain his enemy
And ours, to run back to our homes with Beowulf
So hard-pressed here? I swear that nothing
He ever did deserved an end
770 Like this, dying miserably and alone,
Butchered by this savage beast: we swore
That these swords and armor were each for us all!"
    Then he ran to his king, crying encouragement
As he dove through the dragon's deadly fumes.

Literary Analysis
The Epic and the Legendary Hero
According to Wiglaf, what is Beowulf's relationship with his followers like?

Literary Analysis
The Epic and the Legendary Hero What does Wiglaf's decision suggest about the way in which a legendary hero can inspire heroism in others?

 Reading Check
How do Beowulf's companions react when the dragon breathes flame on him?

from *Beowulf* ■ 59

56

Background

Artifact

Oseberg Dragon, c. 850

This spectacular carved wooden artifact is one of the most impressive finds from the ship burial at Oseberg. The Oseberg Dragon is a post head found among the furniture on the ninth-century Oseberg ship, a royal barge used for the burial of a Norwegian queen. The post is covered with an intricate profusion of "gripping beasts," a classic Viking decorative pattern. Use these questions for discussion:

1. Where might carving like this be seen in *Beowulf?*
   Possible responses: Elaborate carvings may have been found in Herot, in Beowulf's mead-hall, or in the dragon's lair among his other collected treasures.

2. What do this artifact and the description of Beowulf's funeral tell you about funerary practices in Scandinavian culture?
   Answer: Important people were often buried with treasure.

57 Reading Strategy

Paraphrasing

- Tell students that in almost all legends of dragons, the dragons had huge hoards of valuable treasure. Dragons were proverbial for greed and acquisitiveness.

- Have students follow the Reading Strategy prompt: What is the main idea in the sentence in lines 779–785?
  Possible response: These things were made for use, not hoarding, and rotted with disuse.

Wiglaf and Beowulf kill the dragon, but the old king is mortally wounded. As he dies, Beowulf asks Wiglaf to bring him the treasure that the dragon was guarding.

The Spoils

775   Then Wexstan's son went in, as quickly
As he could, did as the dying Beowulf
Asked, entered the inner darkness
Of the tower, went with his mail shirt and his sword.
Flushed with victory he groped his way,
780 A brave young warrior, and suddenly saw
Piles of gleaming gold, precious
Gems, scattered on the floor, cups
And bracelets, rusty old helmets, beautifully
Made but rotting with no hands to rub
785 And polish them. They lay where the dragon left them;
It had flown in the darkness, once, before fighting
Its final battle. (So gold can easily
Triumph, defeat the strongest of men,
No matter how deep it is hidden!) And he saw,
790 Hanging high above, a golden
Banner, woven by the best of weavers
And beautiful. And over everything he saw
A strange light, shining everywhere,
On walls and floor and treasure. Nothing
795 Moved, no other monsters appeared;
He took what he wanted, all the treasures
That pleased his eye, heavy plates
And golden cups and the glorious banner,
Loaded his arms with all they could hold.
800 Beowulf's dagger, his iron blade,
Had finished the fire-spitting terror
That once protected tower and treasures
Alike; the gray-bearded lord of the Geats
Had ended those flying, burning raids
805 Forever.
      Then Wiglaf went back, anxious
To return while Beowulf was alive, to bring him
Treasure they'd won together. He ran,
Hoping his wounded king, weak
And dying, had not left the world too soon.
810 Then he brought their treasure to Beowulf, and found
His famous king bloody, gasping
For breath. But Wiglaf sprinkled water

60 ■ From Legend to History (449–1485)

57
Reading Strategy
Paraphrasing What is the main idea in the sentence in lines 779–785?

56

Head of carved post from the ship burial at Oseberg (Viking, c. A.D. 850). Viking Ship Museum, Bygdoy, Oslo

---

Enrichment

Epics

Because epics have been used the world over to preserve values and traditions, they are a rich resource for exploring world cultures.

Have interested students gather information on these epics and share their findings with the class.
- Finland: *Kalevala*
- France: *Chanson de Roland*
- India: *Ramayana* and *Mahabharata*

- Italy: *Orlando Furioso*
- Japan: *Heike Monogatari*
- Mali: *Sundiata*
- Norway: *Volsunga Saga*
- Polynesia: *Maui*
- Rome: *The Aeneid*
- Ancient Greece: the *Odyssey,* the *Iliad*
- Spain: *Poema del Cid*

Over his lord, until the words
Deep in his breast broke through and were heard.
815 Beholding the treasure he spoke, haltingly:
        "For this, this gold, these jewels, I thank
Our Father in Heaven, Ruler of the Earth—
For all of this, that His grace has given me,
Allowed me to bring to my people while breath
820 Still came to my lips. I sold my life
For this treasure, and I sold it well. Take
What I leave, Wiglaf, lead my people,
Help them; my time is gone. Have
The brave Geats build me a tomb,
825 When the funeral flames have burned me, and build it
Here, at the water's edge, high
On this spit of land, so sailors can see
This tower, and remember my name, and call it
Beowulf's tower, and boats in the darkness
830 And mist, crossing the sea, will know it."
        Then that brave king gave the golden
Necklace from around his throat to Wiglaf,
Gave him his gold-covered helmet, and his rings,
And his mail shirt, and ordered him to use them well:
835   "You're the last of all our far-flung family.
Fate has swept our race away,
Taken warriors in their strength and led them
To the death that was waiting. And now I follow them."
        The old man's mouth was silent, spoke
840 No more, had said as much as it could;
He would sleep in the fire, soon. His soul
Left his flesh, flew to glory.

⟡—◈—⟡

Wiglaf denounces the warriors who deserted Beowulf. The Geats burn their king's
body on a funeral pyre and bitterly lament his death.

⟡—◈—⟡

The Farewell

        Then the Geats built the tower, as Beowulf
Had asked, strong and tall, so sailors
845 Could find it from far and wide; working
For ten long days they made his monument,
Sealed his ashes in walls as straight
And high as wise and willing hands
Could raise them. And the riches he and Wiglaf
850 Had won from the dragon, rings, necklaces,
Ancient, hammered armor—all

Literary Analysis
The Epic In Beowulf's death scene, what is shown about the importance in warrior culture of the commemoration of individuals after death?

59

60 Reading Check
What is Beowulf's last request?

---

58 Literary Analysis
The Epic

- Remind students that when Beowulf first landed in Denmark, he identified himself in terms of his father being remembered still (lines 174–179).
- Have students **answer** the Literary Analysis question: In Beowulf's death scene, what is shown about the importance of the commemoration of individuals after death? **Answer:** Being remembered was important to the individual; a father's glory could aid his son, and undying fame was a way of overcoming death.
- Have students consider how this scene compares to the ways in which the dead are commemorated in our age.

59 Reading Strategy
Paraphrasing

- Have students read lines 823–830 to themselves.
- Then, **ask** students to paraphrase the main idea in the sentence in these lines. **Answer:** Build a tomb for my ashes. Place it where sailors will see it and remember me.

60 Reading Check

Answer: Beowulf's last request is for Wiglaf to lead his people and to erect a tower in Beowulf's name.

Differentiated
Instruction   **Solutions for All Learners**

Strategy for Less Proficient Readers
Have students reread Beowulf's death scene and his requests to Wiglaf. Then, have them make a list of the many accomplishments Beowulf has achieved in his life, based on what they have read. Read one or two obituaries from the newspaper or encyclopedia yearbook, so students understand what they are like. Finally, have them write an obituary to Beowulf in which they incorporate all that they have learned.

Support for Special Needs Students
Have students analyze the requests Beowulf makes regarding his burial. Have them note the following and decide what their purpose might be:
- The tower is built on the water's edge, high on a spit of land so sailors can see it.
- Beowulf's ashes are sealed inside.
Ask students to compose an inscription to be written on the tomb that sums up Beowulf's legacy to the Geats.

① **Translator's Insight**

① **Translator's Insight**

- Point out Raffel's comment to students. Tell students that mild is not always used in a religious sense. However, pairing the term with prince does create some Christian allusions. **Ask** students what Christian figure would be described as Beowulf is in lines 867–869. **Possible answer:** Students may suggest Jesus Christ, who is often referred to as a mild prince in the New Testament.

ASSESS

Answers

1. Students may say Beowulf's battles with Grendel, Grendel's mother, or the dragon.

2. (a) Grendel is annoyed by the happiness and singing of the warriors. (b) **Possible response:** The universal conflict behind the attack is the battle between good and evil, or between God and Satan.

3. (a) He travels to Herot to rid the Danes of Grendel. (b) It shows that he is brave, cares about others, and hates evil and suffering. (c) Grendel is the opposite of Beowulf, hating others and loving evil and suffering. Beowulf is the ideal of goodness; Grendel is the personification of evil.

4. (a) Beowulf's speech suggests that he defined his identity in terms of his bravery, strength, and courage. (b) Beowulf and Grendel are each convinced of his own individual invincibility. Their battle occurs because of their pride in their abilities.

5. By conquering Grendel, Beowulf has not only ended the life of the menace that has plagued the Danes, but he has eradicated the presence of evil from the world, including its existence in his own life.

6. (a) At the end of the poem, when Wiglaf thinks of Beowulf's great deeds, he is inspired to battle the dragon. (b) Beowulf embodied the values of the age in which he lived. The poem reminds readers that his culture valued a man who was strong, brave, wise, aware of duty, compassionate, and God-fearing.

continued

The treasures they'd taken were left there, too,
Silver and jewels buried in the sandy
Ground, back in the earth, again
855 And forever hidden and useless to men.
And then twelve of the bravest Geats
Rode their horses around the tower,
Telling their sorrow, telling stories
Of their dead king and his greatness, his glory,
860 Praising him for heroic deeds, for a life
As noble as his name. So should all men
Raise up words for their lords, warm
With love, when their shield and protector leaves
His body behind, sends his soul
865 On high. And so Beowulf's followers
Rode, mourning their beloved leader,
Crying that no better king had ever
Lived, no prince so mild, no man
So open to his people, so deserving of praise.

① *Burton Raffel*
Translator's Insight
"Mild" is not a description of Beowulf as we have seen him. But it is a description often used in the New Testament, more evidence that *Beowulf* is not a pagan poem.

Critical Reading

1. **Respond:** Which episode in the epic did you find most thrilling? Why?

2. **(a) Recall:** At the opening of the poem, what annoys Grendel and leads to his attacks? **(b) Interpret:** What universal conflict lies behind his war with the Danes?

3. **(a) Recall:** Why does Beowulf travel to Herot? **(b) Infer:** What do his motives for the trip tell you about his character? **(c) Analyze:** How does the contrast between Grendel and Beowulf turn their conflict into a fight between good and evil?

4. **(a) Infer:** What does Beowulf's speech in lines 246–255 show about how he defines his identity? **(b) Compare and Contrast:** Although Beowulf is brave and Grendel is spiteful, both might be said to act out of pride. Explain.

5. **Synthesize:** Beowulf's defeat of Grendel might be described as the defeat of the "dark side" of the warrior's life. Explain.

6. **(a) Support:** Identify an example from the epic in which the memory of Beowulf's deeds inspires someone. **(b) Synthesize:** Explain how the poem, by keeping Beowulf's memory alive, keeps a culture's values alive.

7. **Evaluate:** Do you think Beowulf's deeds make him a good role model? Explain.

Answers continued

7. **Possible response:** Students may say that Beowulf's deeds make him a good role model because he helped the Danes and vanquished evil. Also, he acted out of a sense of duty and worked to help others.

Apply the Skills

from *Beowulf*

Literary Analysis

The Epic

1. **Epics** often center on a battle between good and evil. Find evidence in lines 173–198 to indicate that Beowulf is battling for the good.

2. An epic reflects the values of the culture that produced it. Use a chart like the one shown to identify three specific features of *Beowulf* that probably pleased its original audience. For each, draw a conclusion about Anglo-Saxon tastes and values.

Feature	Why Pleasing	Values Reflected
boastful speeches	makes hero seem superhuman	

3. **(a)** What details show the importance of Christian beliefs in the epic? **(b)** What details reveal the importance of pagan warrior values, such as a belief in fate, a taste for boasting, a pride in loyalty, and a desire for fame?

4. Frustrated pride may lead to spite, just as a loyalty may lead to vengeance, and eagerness for glory may turn into greed. Explain how each creature Beowulf battles represents an extreme and dangerous form of warrior values and behavior.

Connecting Literary Elements

5. **(a)** List two heroic characteristics of Beowulf. **(b)** Find a passage that shows the hero's more human side. Explain your choice. **(c)** Identify each main character and the traits that make him heroic.

6. **(a)** Is Beowulf a believable character, or is he "too heroic"? Explain. **(b)** How does his believability affect your sympathy for him?

Reading Strategy

Paraphrasing

7. **Paraphrase** lines 843–861 from *Beowulf*.

8. **(a)** Explain which details you did not understand before paraphrasing. **(b)** Compare your paraphrase to the original, citing poetic effects that were lost in your paraphrase.

Extend Understanding

9. **Cultural Connection:** Compare the way the epic commemorates Beowulf with the way our culture celebrates its heroes.

QuickReview

An **epic** is an extended narrative poem that celebrates the deeds of a legendary or heroic figure.

A **legendary hero** is a larger-than-life character whose accomplishments reflect a people's values and way of life.

To **paraphrase**, identify key ideas and details in a text and restate them in your own words.

Go Online
Assessment

For: Self-test
Visit: www.PHSchool.com
Web Code: esa-6103

from *Beowulf* ■ 63

63

❶ Vocabulary Lesson

Word Analysis

1. Beowulf; *consolation* is something that eases grief.

2. Grendel's mother; *inconsolable* means not easily comforted.

Spelling Strategy

1. raising   3. inquiring
2. enraging

Vocabulary Builder

1. c   4. c
2. a   5. c
3. a   6. b

❷ Grammar and Style Lesson

1. The appositive phrase is "Men who follow Higlac," and "Geats" is what is being described.

2. The appositive phrases are "Healfdane's son" and "protector/Of this people," and "Your prince" is what is being described.

3. The appositive phrase is "His miserable hole at the bottom of the marsh," and "Grendel's den" is what is being described.

4. The appositive phrase is "the she wolf," and "Grendel's mother" is what is being described.

5. The appositive phrase is "Their lord and leader," and "Beowulf" is who is being described.

Writing Application

Possible answer: Grendel, misery's stepchild, a minister of evil, wandered into the den.

W︎G Writing and Grammar, Diamond Level

Students will find further instruction and practice on appositives and appositive phrases in Chapter 19, Section 1.

Build Language Skills

❶ Vocabulary Lesson

Word Analysis: Latin Root -sol-

The Latin root *-sol-* means "to comfort." The root appears in the word *solace*, "an easing of grief, loneliness, or discomfort." With the meaning of *-sol-* in mind, answer the following questions. Provide a definition of each italicized word.

1. Which character in the epic might receive a *consolation* prize?

2. Which character is *inconsolable*?

Spelling Strategy

For words ending in *e*, drop the final *e* when adding the suffix *-ing*: writhe + *-ing* = writhing. Add the suffix *-ing* to these words.

1. raise   2. enrage   3. inquire

Vocabulary Builder: Antonyms

Choose the letter of the word that is the antonym, the word opposite in meaning, of the first word.

1. reparation: **(a)** reimbursement, **(b)** renewal, **(c)** theft

2. solace: **(a)** aggravation, **(b)** resentment, **(c)** comfort

3. purge: **(a)** pollute, **(b)** purify, **(c)** complete

4. writhing: **(a)** valor, **(b)** churning, **(c)** still

5. massive: **(a)** average, **(b)** tremendous, **(c)** flimsy

6. loathsome: **(a)** disgusting, **(b)** delightful, **(c)** angry

❷ Grammar and Style Lesson

Appositives and Appositive Phrases

An **appositive** is a noun or pronoun placed next to another noun or pronoun to identify or explain it. An **appositive phrase** is an appositive with modifiers. The underlined appositive phrase below gives additional information about Beowulf:

> In his far-off home Beowulf, <u>Higlac's</u>
> <u>Follower and the strongest of the Geats—</u>

If an appositive is necessary to identify who or what is being spoken about, it is not set off with commas. If an appositive is not essential to the meaning of the sentence, it should be set off with commas.

Appositive phrases are a key element of epic style, in which naming and renaming things and people is an important poetic act.

Practice In each item, identify the appositive phrase and name what is being described.

1. "We are Geats, / Men who follow Higlac. My father / Was a famous soldier, . . ."

2. "And we have come seeking / Your prince, Healfdane's son, protector / Of this people, only in friendship: instruct us, . . ."

3. . . . Grendel escaped, / But wounded as he was could flee to his den, / His miserable hole at the bottom of the marsh, . . .

4. . . . almost all agreed that Grendel's / Mighty mother, the she-wolf, had killed him.

5. . . . with Beowulf, / Their lord and leader, they walked on the mead-hall / Green.

Writing Application Write a description of Gendel, using two appositive phrases.

W︎G *Prentice Hall Writing and Grammar Connection: Chapter 19, Section 1*

Assessment Practice

Sequential Order   (For more practice, see *Standardized Test Preparation Workbook*, p. 2.)

Some tests require students to identify sequential order. Use this sample test item:

> The monster's/Thoughts were as quick as his greed or his claws:/He slipped through the door and there in the silence/Snatched up thirty men, smashed them/ Unknowing in their beds and ran out with their bodies,/ The blood dripping behind him, back/To his lair, delighted with his night's slaughter.

Of the four actions described, which did Grendel perform third?

A He happily went back to his lair.

B He came up with an idea quickly.

C He smashed thirty men in their beds.

D He slipped through the door.

The correct answer is *C*. Choices *A*, *B*, and *D* are all activities that Grendel performs, but they are not the third activity Grendel performs.

Writing Lesson

Timed Writing: Response to Criticism

Burton Raffel, a translator of *Beowulf*, remarks that "of all the many-sided excellences" of the poem, one of the most satisfying "is the poet's insight into people." In a brief essay, agree or disagree. Your response should clearly set out your position and develop support for it by analyzing scenes from the poem. *(40 minutes)*

Prewriting *(10 minutes)* — Begin by taking notes on passages that show either an insight or a lack of insight into people. Concentrate on descriptions of characters' motives or notable actions. Then, take your own position on Raffel's statement.

Drafting *(20 minutes)* — In your introduction, state your response to Raffel's comment. Then, discuss scenes from the poem, clearly showing how each supports your point.

Revising *(10 minutes)* — Review your draft, placing a star next to each important reference you make to the poem. For each star, make sure you have explained the significance of the passage and its connection to your main point.

> **Model: Revising to Clarify Connections**
>
> ☆ When Wiglaf runs back to show Beowulf the treasure, the poet puts the finishing touch on his portrayal of this young warrior. *It is clear from this action how eager Wiglaf is to win his dying lord's approval and to console him. The episode demonstrates the poet's insight into people and their behavior.*
>
> With this revision, the writer clarifies the example and shows how it supports the main point.

W̲G *Prentice Hall Writing and Grammar Connection: Chapter 14, Section 4*

Extend Your Learning

Listening and Speaking Give a **dramatic reading** of a passage from *Beowulf*, such as the suspenseful battle with Grendel's mother.

1. Rehearse your reading with a partner, guiding each other about the pace and expressiveness of your reading.
2. Jot down reminders about pacing and expression on a performance copy of the passage.

Present your reading to the class.

Research and Technology Work with a group to prepare a **dictionary** of epic heroes. Include facts about each hero's culture of origin, ancestry, identifying characteristics, accomplishments, and fate. **[Group Activity]**

Go Online
Research

For: An additional research activity
Visit: www.PHSchool.com
Web Code: esd-7102

from *Beowulf* ■ 65

---

❸ Writing Lesson

You may use this Writing Lesson as timed-writing practice, or you may allow students to develop the essay as a writing assignment over several days.

- To guide students in writing this response to criticism, give them the **Support for Writing Lesson** page (*Unit 1 Resources,* p. 34).
- Model a passage from *Beowulf* for students in which the poet offers insight into people.
- Use the Writing Lesson to guide students in developing their essays.
- Tell students that when they write essays in which they support or defend an observation, they need a clear thesis statement that indicates their position and it must be backed up with evidence.
- Use the Response to Literature rubric in *General Resources,* pp. 65–66, to evaluate students' essays.

❹ Listening and Speaking

- Have students work in small groups to decide on the passage in *Beowulf* that they will read.
- Encourage students to practice pronouncing any difficult words or unusual names, so that their readings can flow smoothly.
- Remind students to guide the pace and expressiveness of their readings using inflection and eye contact.
- The **Support for Extend Your Learning** page (*Unit 1 Resources,* p. 35) provides guided note-taking opportunities to help students complete the Extend Your Learning activities.
- To evaluate students' dramatic readings use the rubric for Peer Assessment: Dramatic Performance, p. 131 in *General Resources.*

Go Online
Research
Have students type in the Web Code for another research activity.

Assessment Resources

The following resources can be used to assess students' knowledge and skills.

Unit 1 Resources
  Selection Test A, pp. 37–39
  Selection Test B, pp. 40–42

General Resources
  Rubrics for Response to
    Literature, pp. 65–66
  Rubric for Peer Assessment: Dramatic
    Performance, p. 131

Go Online
Assessment
Students may use the **Self-test** to prepare for **Selection Test A** or **Selection Test B.**

Seamus Heaney

Tell students that Seamus Heaney is much more than just a translator. He is among the world's most renowned poets. He began writing poetry in the 1960s while he was teaching in Ireland. Early on, his work was marked by the heavy rhythms of Anglo-Saxon English—a linguistic interest that is reflected in Heaney's translation of *Beowulf*. In 1995, Heaney was awarded the Nobel Prize for Literature.

Giving Shape to Poetry

- After students read Heaney's commentary, point out that his focus is on *Beowulf's* language and the linguistic tradition that produced it, rather than the epic's plot and themes.

- Call students' attention to Heaney's literal translation of the Old English word for poet, *scop*. **Ask** students to explain the question Heaney raises about this term, and the answer he offers.
Possible response: The question Heaney poses is whether *Beowulf* was composed orally or in its written form. Heaney's answer is that both the oral and written traditions were likely involved.

- Explain to students that studies have been done to prove that listening to certain types of music while studying aids the memory. Discuss with students how this idea can be related to Heaney's description of the *scop*.

The Original Beowulf

- Call students' attention to the Old English lines from *Beowulf*. Review Heaney's commentary on the Old English lines with the class. Guide them to recognize the evidence of alliteration in the original text.

SEAMUS HEANEY
Discusses *Beowulf*

Giving Shape to Poetry

A poet in Old English was called a *scop,* pronounced "shop" and meaning "a shaper." But did he do his shaping with a pen on parchment or with sound-patterns in the ear? Was he a scribe or was he a singer? Was *Beowulf* the result of mouth and ear work, or pen and paperwork?

The answer has to be that it was both. We have evidence that the *scop* chanted his poems to the accompaniment of a harp, so the notes he struck with his voice and his instrument were designed to fasten his words into the ear and the memory. But the intricacy of the patterning suggests that over time his live performance developed into a written score, so the heard melody has come down to us as a manuscript, a word which basically means handwritten marks.

The Original *Beowulf*

In the original, for example, three lines of one passage of *Beowulf* look like this:

Him ðā gegiredan Gēata lēode
ād on eorðan unwāclīcne,
helmum behongen, hilde-bordum.

Look again and you can see words and traces of words that we still use. "Him," obviously, in line 1; "helmets" and "hung" and "boards" in line 3; and once you realize that the strange letter ð is the symbol that Anglo-Saxon scribes used for the "th," you can see "earth" in line 2. But the words were meant to be heard rather than seen, and if you keep looking you can find alliteration that the first audience listened for in every line.

Seamus Heaney

Seamus Heaney's poetry focuses on the cities and farms of his homeland in Northern Ireland and the political and religious strife that he has witnessed. Among his translations are *Beowulf* (2000) and Sophocles' drama *Antigone* (2004).

▼ **Critical Viewing**
Why do historians preserve documents like this page from *Beowulf*? **[Speculate]**

The Music of Storytelling

Translating an old poem means keeping time, in both the musical and historical sense; it means staying faithful to the original, but not to the point of sounding out of tune. I wanted my version to be a score for performance and tried, therefore, to tune my voice not only to the movement of the Anglo-Saxon lines but to the other voices that had been familiar to me in Northern Ireland. I wrote for my first local accent, imagining the poetry being spoken by old neighbors who always gave their storytelling a natural pace and stress. When I tried out a line, the test would be: do these words sound sure and true if I pretend to be one of those big-voiced elders?

Take, for example, the third line: it tolls like a bell that has been rung four times, and when I translated it I wanted to keep the heavy downbeat of the original alliterating words, so it came out as "hung with helmets, heavy war-shields." I was after a similar effect in later lines such as "funeral fires; fumes of woodsmoke" and "and wailed aloud for their lord's decease."

Still, there is epic pride in the lines as well as elegy, so I wanted them to sound not only mournful but elevated. Ideally, the translator of *Beowulf* will construct something in words that is the equivalent of the burial mound constructed by the Geats, something to make us feel both their hero's greatness and their grief at his loss.

▲ **Critical Viewing**
In what ways does the burial mound pictured here convey both greatness and serenity? **[Interpret]**

Thinking About the Commentary

1. **(a) Recall:** According to Heaney's essay, was the original Old English scop a writer or a musician? **(b) Speculate:** In what ways do you think details in this translation of *Beowulf* were influenced by the manner in which the tale was originally told?

2. **(a) Recall:** On what voices does Heaney model his translation? **(b) Infer:** Why might it have helped Heaney to have specific voices in mind as he translated?

As You Think About *Beowulf* . . .

3. **Generalize:** Many translators have produced versions of *Beowulf*. In what ways might translators' decisions affect your experience with the epic?

From the Translator's Desk: Seamus Heaney ■ 67

The Music of Storytelling

- Have students compare the Old English line from *Beowulf* to Heaney's translation. **Ask** them what the elements of the original rhythm they can see in the translation.
Possible response: The translation shares the heavy stresses of the original, replicating the four beats of the Old English version.

- Call students' attention to Heaney's comments on keeping *Beowulf's* Old English rhythm in his translation. Be sure students understand that maintaining the rhythm was a primary concern for the poet and translator. **Ask** students if, based on the examples here, they think Heaney achieved this goal.
Possible response: Most students will agree that he has achieved his goal.

ASSESS

Answers

1. (a) Heaney believes the *scop* was both writer and musician.
(b) **Possible response:** The rhythms of the translation seem to have grown from oral recitations with musical accompaniment. The drama and excitement of the poem may have also grown from its storytelling roots.

2. (a) Heaney models his translation on the voices of Northern Ireland.
(b) **Possible response:** Heaney used the voices he had in mind to structure the rhythms of his translation. Keeping specific voices in mind gave the translation a consistency it might have otherwise lacked.

3. **Possible response:** Students are likely to observe that the translators create rhythms that can either enhance or impede their enjoyment of *Beowulf*. Students may also note that the choices translators make can change the plot's focus, its pacing, and even the words of the poem and their connotations.

Differentiated Instruction   Solutions for All Learners

Enrichment for Gifted/Talented Students
Students may be interested in the rhythms of Seamus Heaney's translation of *Beowulf*. Encourage them to stage a dramatic reading of Heaney's translation of the epic. Remind students that, in his translation, Heaney attempted to keep the poem's original musical rhythms. Have students read Heaney's translation of *Beowulf* and select sections to read. Performers should find recordings to use as musical accompaniment. Have students perform their reading for the class.

Enrichment for Advanced Readers
Students may be particularly struck by the difference in rhythm between Burton Raffel and Seamus Heaney's translations of *Beowulf*. Encourage students to read Heaney's *Beowulf* independently. Students should select scenes from each translation of the epic to compare, looking closely at the impact the translators have on the poem. Have students write an essay comparing and contrasting the two translations. Which do they find more exciting and dramatic?

Background
Literature

As is typical of the *Iliad,* this excerpt is filled with contradictions. Although Homer is himself a Greek, he portrays both sides as equally likely to include heroes, villains, and scoundrels. Moreover, even a hero like Achilleus can behave badly, first sulking in his tent, then needlessly desecrating the memory of Hektor by dragging his body through the dust. Our sympathies are mixed: We feel for Achilleus, who has lost his friend, but we also feel for Andromache when she loses her husband. And the gods, of course, take both sides and interfere with the humans in ways that seem both helpful and unfair. In Homer's world, there are many heroic deeds but no easy answers.

Critical Viewing

Answer: The ancient Greeks celebrated equestrian sports and valued horsemanship in battle.

Then looking darkly at him swift-footed Achilleus answered:
"Hektor, argue me no agreements. I cannot forgive you.
As there are no trustworthy oaths between men and lions,
25 nor wolves and lambs have spirit that can be brought
    to agreement
but forever these hold feelings of hate for each other,
so there can be no love between you and me, nor
    shall there be
oaths between us, but one or the other must fall
    before then
to glut with his blood Ares the god who fights under
    the shield's guard.
30 Remember every valor of yours, for now the need comes
hardest upon you to be a spearman and a bold warrior.
There shall be no more escape for you, but Pallas Athene
will kill you soon by my spear. You will pay in a lump for
    all those
sorrows of my companions you killed in your spear's fury."
35 So he spoke, and balanced the spear far shadowed, and threw it;
but glorious Hektor kept his eyes on him, and avoided it,
for he dropped, watchful, to his knee, and the bronze spear
    flew over his shoulder
and stuck in the ground, but Pallas Athene snatched it, and gave it
back to Achilleus, unseen by Hektor shepherd of the people.
40 But now Hektor spoke out to the blameless son of Peleus:
"You missed; and it was not, O Achilleus like the immortals,
from Zeus that you knew my destiny; but you thought so; or rather
you are someone clever in speech and spoke to swindle me,
to make me afraid of you and forget my valor and war strength.
45 You will not stick your spear in my back as I run away from you
but drive it into my chest as I storm straight in against you;
if the god gives you that; and now look out for my brazen
spear. I wish it might be taken full length in your body.
And indeed the war would be a lighter thing for the Trojans
50 if you were dead, seeing that you are their greatest affliction."
    So he spoke, and balanced the spear far shadowed, and threw it,
and struck the middle of Peleïdes' shield, nor missed it,
but the spear was driven far back from the shield, and Hektor
    was angered
because his swift weapon had been loosed from his hand in a
    vain cast.
55 He stood discouraged, and had no other ash spear; but lifting
his voice he called aloud on Deïphobos of the pale shield,
and asked him for a long spear, but Deïphobos was not near him.
And Hektor knew the truth inside his heart, and spoke aloud:
"No use. Here at last the gods have summoned me deathward.
60 I thought Deïphobos the hero was here close beside me,
but he is behind the wall and it was Athene cheating me,

▲ **Critical Viewing**
From this vase painting, what can you deduce about ancient Greek attitudes towards horsemanship and other battle skills? **[Deduce]**

Thematic Connection

Possible response: Students may say that the battle between Hektor and Achilleus is even more intense than that between Beowulf and Grendel's mother because the two warriors appear to know each other well, and the description of the sword penetrating Hektor's throat is so brutal and bloody.

and now evil death is close to me, and no longer far away,
and there is no way out. So it must long since have been pleasing
to Zeus, and Zeus' son who strikes from afar, this way; though
    before this

65 they defended me gladly. But now my death is upon me.
Let me at least not die without a struggle, inglorious,
but do some big thing first, that men to come shall know of it."

    So he spoke, and pulling out the sharp sword that was slung
at the hollow of his side, huge and heavy, and gathering

70 himself together, he made his swoop, like a high-flown eagle
who launches himself out of the murk of the clouds on the flat land
to catch away a tender lamb or a shivering hare; so
Hektor made his swoop, swinging his sharp sword, and Achilleus
charged, the heart within him loaded with savage fury.

75 In front of his chest the beautiful elaborate great shield
covered him, and with the glittering helm with four horns
he nodded; the lovely golden fringes were shaken about it
which Hephaistos[4] had driven close along the horn of the helmet.
And as a star moves among stars in the night's darkening,

80 Hesper,[5] who is the fairest star who stands in the sky, such
was the shining from the pointed spear Achilleus was shaking
in his right hand with evil intention toward brilliant Hektor.
He was eyeing Hektor's splendid body, to see where it might best
give way, but all the rest of the skin was held in the armour,

85 brazen and splendid, he stripped when he cut down the strength
    of Patroklos;[6]
yet showed where the collar-bones hold the neck from
    the shoulders,
the throat, where death of the soul comes most swiftly; in this place
brilliant Achilleus drove the spear as he came on in fury,
and clean through the soft part of the neck the spearpoint
    was driven.

90 Yet the ash spear heavy with bronze did not sever the windpipe,
so that Hektor could still make exchange of words spoken.
But he dropped in the dust, and brilliant Achilleus vaunted
    above him:
"Hektor, surely you thought as you killed Patroklos you would be
safe, and since I was far away you thought nothing of me,

95 O fool, for an avenger was left, far greater than he was,
behind him and away by the hollow ships. And it was I;
and I have broken your strength; on you the dogs and the vultures
shall feed and foully rip you; the Achaians will bury Patroklos."

    In his weakness Hektor of the shining helm spoke to him:

100 "I entreat you, by your life, by your knees, by your parents,

---

4. Hephaistos (hē fes′ təs) god of fire and the forge. He made Achilleus' armor.
5. Hesper (hes′ pər) the evening star.
6. Patroklos (pə träk′ lōs) companion and henchman to Achilleus.

Thematic Connection
Compare the intensity and suspense of this battle scene with that of Beowulf's battle with Grendel's mother.

Reading Check
Which hero wins the combat?

Connections: from the *Iliad* ■ 73

Enrichment

The Real Trojan War

For years, scholars were skeptical about the existence of an actual city of Troy. Then, the German archaeologist Heinrich Schliemann (1822–1890) discovered the ruins of four cities, one on top of the other, which were indeed Troy, also known as Ilion. The city was located on a mound in Asian Turkey known as Hissarlik. Eventually, Troy was established as a city whose culture dated back to the Bronze Age (3500 B.C.).

Scholars now believe that the events in Homer's epic reflect an actual war that took place around 1200 B.C. over control of trade in the Dardanelles, a long, narrow body of water known in ancient times as the Hellespont, which links the Sea of Marmara to the Mediterranean Sea. Schliemann also engaged in excavations at Mycenae, Ithaca (home of Homer's hero Odysseus), and Tiryns.

1. The Prologue to *Gilgamesh* suggests that a Sumerian king was expected to build cities and temples, dig wells so that his people had water, and open roads between his kingdom and the outside world.

2. (a) Hektor asks Achilleus not to let the dogs feed on his corpse and to allow his body to be returned to his people. (b) Achilleus's response—that no amount of ransom will be enough to grant Hektor's request—seems vindictive. Hektor's request and Achilleus' response suggest that family was important to the ancient Greeks, and that in the case of war, all is fair.

3. **Possible responses:** Answers will vary. Students should offer evidence to support their claims.

---

do not let the dogs feed on me by the ships of the Achaians,
but take yourself the bronze and gold that are there in abundance,
those gifts that my father and the lady my mother will give you,
and give my body to be taken home again, so that the Trojans
105 and the wives of the Trojans may give me in death my rite of
　　burning."
　　But looking darkly at him swift-footed Achilleus answered:
"No more entreating of me, you dog, by knees or parents.
I wish only that my spirit and fury would drive me
to hack your meat away and eat it raw for the things that
110 you have done to me. So there is no one who can hold the dogs off
from your head, not if they bring here and set before me ten times
and twenty times the ransom, and promise more in addition,
not if Priam son of Dardanos should offer to
weigh out your bulk in gold; not even so shall the lady your mother
115 who herself bore you lay you on the death-bed and mourn you:
no, but the dogs and the birds will have you all for their feasting."
　　Then, dying, Hektor of the shining helmet spoke to him:
"I know you well as I look upon you, I know that I could not
persuade you, since indeed in your breast is a heart of iron.
120 Be careful now; for I might be made into the gods' curse
upon you, on that day when Paris and Phoibos Apollo[7]
destroy you in the Skaian gates,[8] for all your valor."
　　He spoke, and as he spoke the end of death closed in
　　upon him,
and the soul fluttering free of the limbs went down into
　　Death's house
125 mourning her destiny, leaving youth and manhood behind her.
Now though he was a dead man brilliant Achilleus spoke to him:
"Die: and I will take my own death at whatever time
Zeus and the rest of the immortals choose to accomplish it."

---

7. **Paris and Phoibus Apollo** (par′ is; fē′ bəs ə pôl′ ō) Paris, son of King Priam, and Apollo, the archer god of light and of healing who protects the Trojans.
8. **Skaian gates** (skē′ ən) the main gates of Troy.

Connecting Literature Around the World

1. What does the Prologue to *Gilgamesh* suggest about the duties of a Sumerian king?

2. **(a)** What does Hektor ask of Achilleus after he is mortally wounded? **(b)** What conclusions about the values of ancient Greece can you draw from this request and Achilleus' response?

3. Compare and contrast a modern leader with Gilgamesh, Achilleus, and Beowulf. Consider both their deeds and their values

Homer

One of the most powerful influences on British and European literature has been the ancient Greek epics the *Iliad* and the *Odyssey*. The Greeks ascribed these poems to the blind, half-legendary poet Homer, whom they called "The Poet." Although his birth and death dates are uncertain, he probably composed the *Iliad* late in the eighth century B.C.

The epic tells about the legendary Trojan War, set hundreds of years earlier, in which Greek forces attacked the city of Troy in Asia Minor in quest of the return of the beautiful Helen, wife of their chieftain Menelaus. At the center of the *Iliad* is the wrath of the mighty Achilleus, the greatest of the Greek warriors. Slighted by Menelaus, Achilleus withdraws his help from the Greek cause—until the Trojan Hektor slays his best friend, Patroklos, and provokes him into a ferocious rage.

Enrichment

Funeral Rites in Ancient Greece
One of the worst threats in the *Iliad,* and among the worst fears people express, is that a corpse will be left unburied, to be eaten by vultures and dogs. In fact, this never actually happens in the poem. The ancient Greeks' great concern about proper burial is also seen in the *Odyssey,* in which the ghost of one of Odysseus' men begs for proper burial, and, most famously, in Sophocles's *Antigone,* in which Antigone defies a royal edict in order to bury her brother.

A National Spirit

Selection Planning Guide

The selections in this section reveal the development of an English national identity. Excerpts from two medieval histories, *A History of the English Church and People* and *The Anglo-Saxon Chronicle,* describe events of the early Middle Ages. The excerpts from *The Canterbury Tales* reveal much about the structure of fourteenth-century society and also show the development of a national language.

Humanities

Four Kings of England, 1250–1259

This page from an illuminated manuscript depicts four successive English kings. Henry II (upper left) ruled from 1154 to 1189. He expanded royal authority throughout his reign. Henry was succeeded by his son, Richard I (upper right). Richard the Lionheart was king until 1199, but he spent most of his reign outside of England, fighting in the Crusades. In his absence, the country was ruled by his brother, John (lower left), who succeeded him in 1199 and is most famous for signing the Magna Carta in 1215. Henry III (lower right), John's son, ascended to the throne in 1216, at age nine. He ruled until 1272.

Ask students the following:

• Why might the use of English (rather than Latin) for important documents enhance national identity?
Possible response: It would imply that England was developing an established language and culture distinct from Roman models.

Benchmark

After students have completed the excerpt from the *Anglo-Saxon Chronicle,* administer **Benchmark Test 1.** If the Benchmark Test reveals that some of the students need further work, use the **Interpretation Guide** to determine the appropriate reteaching page in the **Reading Kit** and on **Success Tracker.**

Monitoring Progress

Before students read *The Canterbury Tales: The Prologue,* administer **Diagnostic Test 2.** This test will determine students' level of readiness for the reading and vocabulary skills.

Differentiated Instruction   Solutions for All Learners

Accessibility at a Glance

Average

from The Anglo-Saxon Chronicle

from The Canterbury Tales:
  The Prologue
  The Pardoner's Tale
  The Wife of Bath's Tale

More Challenging

from A History of the English Church and People

75

TIME AND RESOURCE MANAGER

 Meeting Your Standards

Students will

1. **analyze and respond to literary elements.**
   - Literary Analysis: Historical Writing

2. **read, comprehend, analyze, and critique nonfiction.**
   - Reading Strategy: Breaking Down Sentences
   - Reading Check questions
   - Apply the Skills questions
   - Assessment Practice (ATE)

3. **develop vocabulary.**
   - Vocabulary Lesson: Latin Suffix: *-ade*

4. **understand and apply written and oral language conventions.**
   - Spelling Strategy
   - Grammar and Style Lesson: Compound Sentences

5. **develop writing proficiency.**
   - Writing Lesson: Critical Comparison of Historical Sources

6. **develop appropriate research strategies.**
   - Extend Your Learning: Museum Exhibit

7. **understand and apply listening and speaking strategies.**
   - Extend Your Learning: Radio Interview

Block Scheduling: Use one 90-minute class period to preteach the skills and have students read the selection. Use a second 90-minute class period to assess students' mastery of skills, extend their learning, and monitor their progress.

Homework Suggestions

Following are possibilities for homework assignments.

- Support pages from *Unit 1 Resources:*
  Literary Analysis
  Reading Strategy
  Vocabulary Builder
  Grammar and Style

- An Extend Your Learning project and the Writing Lesson for this selection group may be completed over several days.

Step-by-Step Teaching Guide	Pacing Guide
PRETEACH	
• Administer Vocabulary and Reading Warm-ups as necessary.	5 min.
• Engage students' interest with the motivation activity.	5 min.
• Read and discuss author and background features. **FT**	10 min.
• Introduce the Literary Analysis Skill: Historical Writing. **FT**	5 min.
• Introduce the Reading Strategy: Breaking Down Sentences. **FT**	10 min.
• Prepare students to read by teaching the selection vocabulary. **FT**	
TEACH	
• Informally monitor comprehension while students read independently or in groups. **FT**	30 min.
• Monitor students' comprehension with the Reading Check notes.	as students read
• Reinforce vocabulary with Vocabulary Builder notes.	as students read
• Develop students' understanding of historical writing with the Literary Analysis annotations. **FT**	5 min.
• Develop students' ability to break down sentences with the Reading Strategy annotations. **FT**	5 min.
ASSESS/EXTEND	
• Assess students' comprehension and mastery of the Literary Analysis and Reading Strategy by having them answer the Apply the Skills questions. **FT**	15 min.
• Have students complete the Vocabulary Lesson and the Grammar and Style Lesson. **FT**	15 min.
• Apply students' ability to elaborate on critical insights by using the Writing Lesson. **FT**	45 min. or homework
• Apply students' understanding by using one or more of the Extend Your Learning activities.	20–90 min. or homework
• Administer Selection Test A or Selection Test B. **FT**	15 min.

Resources

Choosing Resources for Differentiated Instruction

[L1] Special Needs Students

[L2] Below-Level Students

[L3] All Students

[L4] Advanced Students

[EL] English Learners

For Vocabulary and Reading Warm-ups and for Selection Tests, **A** signifies "less challenging" and **B** "more challenging." For Graphic Organizer Transparencies, **A** signifies "not filled in" and **B** "filled in."

FT Fast Track Instruction: To move the lesson more quickly, use the strategies and activities identified with **FT**.

Scaffolding for Less Proficient and Advanced Students

The leveled Critical Thinking questions after selections progress in the levels of thinking required to answer them. To address the needs of your different students, you may use the (a) level questions for your less proficient students and the (b) level questions with your on-level and advanced students. The occasional (c) level questions are appropriate for your advanced students.

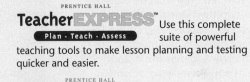

PRENTICE HALL
Teacher EXPRESS™ Use this complete
Plan · Teach · Assess suite of powerful
teaching tools to make lesson planning and testing
quicker and easier.

PRENTICE HALL
Student EXPRESS™ Use the interac-
Learn · Study · Succeed tive textbook
(online and on CD-ROM) to make selections and
activities come alive with audio and video support
and interactive questions.

Benchmark

After students have completed these selections, administer **Benchmark Test 1** (*Unit 1 Resources,* pp. 60–65). If the Benchmark Test reveals that some of the students need further work, use the **Interpretation Guide** to determine the appropriate reteaching page in the **Reading Kit** and on **Success Tracker.**

Go **Online**
Professional
Development

For: Information about Lexiles
Visit: www.PHSchool.com
Web Code: eue-1111

Motivation

Ask students what movies or TV shows they have seen that involved time travel. Then, ask them where and when, if time travel really did exist, they would like to go. Ask what they would like to discover about these places, people, or times. Point out that, in a way, they can travel in their minds. Though Hollywood's version of history is rarely accurate, movies and TV still offer images of dress, architecture, and other aspects of the past. Archaeologists make new discoveries routinely. But our main source for information from the past is the writing of people who actually lived during the times that fire our imaginations. Tell students that the selections they are about to read will carry them back more than a thousand years into the past.

❶ Background
More About the Author

In addition to histories and biographies, Bede wrote treatises on spelling, hymns, figures of speech, poetry, theology, and reckoning time. A diligent scholar, he anxiously assessed the accuracy of his sources and recorded only what he regarded as trustworthy evidence. His work remains an indispensable source for many of the facts and much of the feel of early Anglo-Saxon history. Bede's knowledge, insights, and scholarly enthusiasm were perpetuated at a school founded by Bede's pupil, Archbishop Egbert of York, and were carried to the continent by one of the school's students, Alcuin, who became master of Charlemagne's palace school.

The renaissance of scholarship that produced *The Anglo-Saxon Chronicle* was fired by the passion of King Alfred, also called Alfred the Great, who considered literacy one of the foremost goals of his rule.

❶ History of the English Church and People • The Anglo-Saxon Chronicle

Bede
(673–735)

It was as if the lights had gone out. In the fifth century, the Roman Empire abandoned Britain. Rome was the center of the most advanced civilization in the West. As part of the Roman Empire, Britain had been connected with a larger world of trade and culture. Roman missionaries taught reading and writing as they preached Christianity. Roman soldiers patrolled Britain's borders. Once Rome withdrew, however, Britain was isolated, threatened by invasion from without and by strife from within.

Keeping Learning Alive Monasteries, particularly in Ireland, kept knowledge alive during these dark times. Monks studied Latin, the language of the Roman Empire. They laboriously copied books. The more scholarly wrote new works.

Much of what we know about England before A.D. 700 is based on the work of one such monk, Bede. A contemporary of the unknown author of *Beowulf,* Bede was the most learned scholar of his day. Although he wrote forty books on various subjects, his reputation would be secure on the basis of one—*A History of the English Church and People,* for which Bede is called the father of English history.

A Daily Reminder Bede was born in Wearmouth (now Sunderland) in northeastern England. At age seven, he entered the nearby monastic school of Jarrow. A diligent student, he stayed on as a priest and scholar. Although Bede lived his whole life at Jarrow, he wrote in Latin, so his work was accessible to scholars throughout the West. His pupils carried his writings to Europe. Famous in his own lifetime for its scholarship, his work has become a part of daily life—Bede helped originate the dating of events from the birth of Christ, a cornerstone of the Western calendar.

A Scholarly Work In the *History,* Bede describes the conquest of Britain by the Anglo-Saxon tribes after the departure of the Romans. His main concern, however, was the expansion of Christianity in England. Bede gathered information from many kinds of documents, interviewed knowledgeable monks, and, in general, proceeded very much like a modern historian.

In the century after his death, Bede's history was translated from Latin into English for King Alfred. In the same century, Bede was honored with the title "the Venerable [respected] Bede."

The Anglo-Saxon Chronicle

In ninth-century Britain, the story of the past existed only in fragments: a poem passed from one person to another; a parchment that listed the names of old kings; a soldier's memories of a battle. Bede's *History* was an exception, but the work was available only in Latin.

During the renaissance of scholarship in King Alfred's reign (A.D. 871–899), a group of monks decided to knit together this fragmentary story. Their efforts resulted in *The Anglo-Saxon Chronicle,* a unique English historic record.

Putting the Pieces Together In writing the *Chronicle,* these monks pulled together parts of Bede's *History,* existing chronologies, royal genealogies (family trees), and other historic documents. They wrote their new manuscript by hand and sent copies to several other monasteries.

A Letter to the Future For the following two centuries, monks added news to the *Chronicle*—ranging from gossip about a local baron to the battles of kings. *The Anglo-Saxon Chronicle* became a kind of chain letter from one generation to the next.

76 ■ *From Legend to History (449–1485)*

Preview

Connecting to the Literature

When the authors of these selections wrote, there was no videotape or computer disk. The memory of the past took only the most fragile forms—a memorized song, a rare manuscript. These selections are among the few records we have from the time.

Literary Analysis

Historical Writing

Historical writing tells the story of past events using evidence, such as documents from the period, that the writer has evaluated for reliability. Examining the evidence is one way that writers of history take a step back from the shared beliefs of those around them. You can sense this historical "step back" in a sentence from Bede's *History:* "Britain, formerly known as Albion, is an island in the ocean. . . ." The moment Bede wrote that sentence, he left behind his tiny corner of England for a wider world, one that knew little about Britain.

Comparing Literary Works

Both of these selections are accounts from Anglo-Saxon times of early British history. However, the kinds of details they include differ. Bede provides a general background on Britain, while the selection from *The Anglo-Saxon Chronicle* focuses on wars between the Anglo-Saxons and the Danes. In addition, the authors make decisions that may surprise you about what details to include. These selections model the following characteristics:

- Down-to-earth facts
- Fanciful details
- Traces of the author's own loyalties.

As you read, compare the types of details the authors include.

Reading Strategy

Breaking Down Sentences

Bede sometimes writes in long, complicated sentences. To help you interpret them, **break down long sentences** into main and related parts. First, identify the part expressing the main action or actions. Then, identify details that answer *who, what, when, where,* or *why* about these actions. Use a chart like this one to break down long sentences.

Highlighted Main Idea

The same year, the forces in East Anglia and Northumbria greatly harassed Wessex along the south coast with raiding bands. . . .

When:	**Where:**
The same year	(the forces from) East Anglia and Northumbria

Vocabulary Builder

promontories (präm′ ən tôr′ ēz) *n.* peaks of high land sticking out into the water (p. 78)

innumerable (i n<del>oo</del>′ mer ə bəl) *adj.* too many to count (p. 80)

stranded (stran′ did) *v.* forced into shallow water or onto a beach; left helpless (p. 84)

barricaded (bar′ i kād′ id) *v.* blocked (p. 85)

ravaged (rav′ ijd) *v.* destroyed (p. 85)

from *A History of the English Church and People* / from *The Anglo-Saxon Chronicle*   77

❷ **Literary Analysis**
Historical Writing

- Explain to students that, in this lesson, they will focus on historical writing, works that tell the story of past events drawing on such evidence as documents from the period.

- Explain that early English history writers often reveal the shared beliefs of those around them in their accounts.

- Use the instruction for Comparing Literary Works to review with students how historical writing can include different kinds of facts that alter the nature of the work.

❸ **Reading Strategy**
Breaking Down Sentences

- Explain that long, complicated sentences can be more easily understood if students break them into their main ideas and pieces.

- Encourage students to ask questions such as *who, what, when, where,* or *why* of any sentences they find difficult.

- Provide students with a copy of **Reading Strategy Graphic Organizer A,** p. 9 in *Graphic Organizer Transparencies,* to use as they read the selections.

Vocabulary Builder

- Pronounce each vocabulary word for students and read the definitions as a class. Have students identify any words with which they are already familiar.

Differentiated Instruction   Solutions for All Learners

Support for Special Needs Students
Have students complete the **Preview** and **Build Skills** pages for these selections in the *Reader's Notebook: Adapted Version.* Completing these pages will prepare students to read the selections in the Student Edition.

Support for Less Proficient Readers
Have students complete the **Preview** and **Build Skills** pages for these selections in the *Reader's Notebook.* After students finish the pages in the *Reader's Notebook,* have them complete the questions and activities in the Student Edition.

Support for English Learners
Have students complete the **Preview** and **Build Skills** pages for these selections in the *Reader's Notebook: English Learner's Version.* Completing these pages will prepare students to read the selections in the Student Edition.

Learning Modalities
Verbal/Linguistic Learners
Have students work in pairs to create and answer *who? what? where? why? when?* and *how?* questions about each paragraph or section. Explain that this is one way to rephrase information and check comprehension.

❶ About the Selection
Bede's work, which traced English history from the time of the Roman Invasion (54 B.C.) until A.D. 731, was written in Latin but later translated into English, so it could be read by a wider audience. This excerpt describes the geography and early peoples of Britain.

Bede has been called the father of English history, because he was among the first to use the methods of a historian: He consulted written records, interviewed knowledgeable people, studied letters and documents, and cited sources.

❶

from A History of the English Church and People

Bede *Translated by Leo Sherley–Price*

Background Although the majority of British people in Bede's day were illiterate and written records were scarce, monasteries such as the one to which Bede belonged were dedicated to continuing a tradition of learning. Through the monastery, Bede had access to books and other documents, as well as contact with other learned monks. Using these sources, he was able to generate his history of Britain. His fellow Britons may have been illiterate, but Bede had in mind a larger world of readers for his work—the Church to which he belonged and the Roman civilization in which it participated. Bede wrote his account of Britain for such readers, starting at the beginning with the basics.

The Situation of Britain and Ireland: Their Earliest Inhabitants

Britain, formerly known as Albion, is an island in the ocean, facing between north and west, and lying at a considerable distance from the coasts of Germany, Gaul, and Spain, which together form the greater part of Europe. It extends 800 miles northwards, and is 200 in breadth, except where a number of <u>promontories</u> stretch farther, the coastline round which extends to 3,675 miles. To the south lies Belgic Gaul,[1] from the nearest shore of which travelers can see the

Vocabulary Builder
promontories (präm′ ən tôr′ ēz) *n.* peaks of high land sticking out into the water

1. **Belgic Gaul** France.

Differentiated Instruction   Solutions for All Learners

Accessibility at a Glance

	from **A History of the English Church and People**	*from* **The Anglo-Saxon Chronicle**
Context	Medieval history	Medieval history
Language	Explanatory, factual detail	Narrative
Concept Level	Challenging (history)	Average
Literary Merit	Historical	Historical
Lexile	NP	NP
Other	Early scholarly writing	Unique historical record
Overall Rating	More challenging	Average

❷

Monks, The Bodleian Library, University of Oxford

❸ ▲ **Critical Viewing** The picture includes two events that occurred at different times. In what sense is time like a straight line for Bede? In what sense is it a series of events that all belong to one picture? **[Connect]**

from *A History of the English Church and People* ■ 79

❷ **Humanities**

Monks

Bede wrote two accounts of Cuthbert's life, one in verse and one in prose. Saint Cuthbert (634?–687), one of the most venerated of English saints, began life as a shepherd. He entered the monastery of Melrose in Northumbria when he felt called to ministry. He spent many years aiding plague victims, and was largely responsible for the spread of Christianity among the Celtic people of Northumbria. Cuthbert's reputation for devotion and holiness grew. In addition to his care for people, Cuthbert worked diligently (and successfully) to protect birds, which made him one of the earliest wildlife conservationists.

Cuthbert was eventually (685) made Bishop of Lindisfarne. Hence, it is to Saint Cuthbert's successor that the life of the saint is being presented in this illustration.

Use these questions for discussion:

1. What do you think was the purpose of the illustration?
Possible response: The illustration showed the importance of the book and explained the book's history. It served a purpose similar to the photograph of the author and the blurb on the dust jacket of a modern book.

2. What does this illustration tell you about the attitude of later generations toward Bede?
Answer: Bede and his writing were held in high regard centuries after his death.

❸ **Critical Viewing**

Possible response: In this illustration, as in Bede's work, events happen one after the other, in a straight line that moves from past to present to future. However, in both works, it is also evident that events are interconnected, with each one related to others.

❹ Literary Analysis
Historical Writing

- Remind students that writing from any era, including our own, will include information that might later be disproved. However, even things that are later disproved tell us about the era. For example, the statement that burning jet drives away snakes indicates that snakes were a problem.

- Point out that Bede quotes his source when he is not sure of the evidence, as when he attributes the theory of heated water to Saint Basil.

- Have students **respond** to the Literary Analysis prompt: Find two facts, and identify one claim for which you might need more evidence.
Possible responses: Facts include: Cockles are abundant, a scarlet dye is obtained from cockles, the country has salt and hot springs, the land has metals, jet and amber carry a static charge. The claims about how water is heated and that burning jet drives away snakes need more evidence.

❺ Reading Strategy
Breaking Down Sentences

- Suggest that students rewrite a long sentence as several shorter sentences.

- Have students **follow** the Reading Strategy prompt: Break down the sentence beginning "Cockles" to find the core ideas.
Answer: Cockles are plentiful. A scarlet dye is extracted from them. The dye is used on cloth. The color doesn't fade but becomes more beautiful.

❻ Critical Thinking
Analyze

- Remind students that Bede was (as were most literate people in his day) a priest.

- **Ask** them how Bede's religious background is revealed in the paragraph that begins "At the present time . . ."
Answer: Bede refers to divine law and the study of God's truth.

---

❹ city known as Rutubi Portus, which the English have corrupted to Reptacestir.[2] The distance from there across the sea to Gessoriacum,[3] the nearest coast of the Morini, is 50 miles or, as some write it, 450 furlongs.[4] On the opposite side of Britain, which lies open to the boundless ocean, lie the isles of the Orcades.[5] Britain is rich in grain and timber; it has good pasturage for cattle and draft animals,[6] and vines are cultivated in various localities. There are many land and sea birds of various species, and it is well known for its plentiful springs and rivers abounding in fish. There are salmon and eel fisheries, while seals, dolphins, and sometimes whales are caught. There are also many varieties of shellfish, such as mussels, in which are often found excellent pearls of several colors: red, purple, violet, and green, but mainly white. Cockles[7] are abundant, and a beautiful scarlet dye is extracted from them which remains unfaded by sunshine or rain; indeed, the older the cloth, the more beautiful its color. The country has both salt and hot springs, and the waters flowing from them provide hot baths, in which the people bathe separately according to age and sex. As Saint Basil says: "Water receives its heat when it flows across certain metals, and becomes hot, and even scalding." The land has rich veins of many metals, including copper, iron, lead, and silver. There is also much black jet[8] of fine quality, which sparkles in firelight. When burned, it drives away snakes, and, like amber, when it is warmed by friction, it clings to whatever is applied to it. In old times, the country had twenty-eight noble cities, and <u>innumerable</u> castles, all of which were guarded by walls, towers, and barred gates.

Since Britain lies far north toward the pole, the nights are short in summer, and at midnight it is hard to tell whether the evening twilight still lingers or whether dawn is approaching; for in these northern latitudes the sun does not remain long below the horizon at night. Consequently both summer days and winter nights are long, and when the sun withdraws southwards, the winter nights last eighteen hours. In Armenia,[9] Macedonia,[10] and Italy, and other countries of that latitude, the longest day lasts only fifteen hours and the shortest nine.

❻ At the present time there are in Britain, in harmony with the five books of the divine law, five languages and four nations—English, British, Scots, and Picts. Each of these have their own language, but all are united in their study of God's truth by the fifth, Latin, which

---

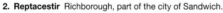

2. **Reptacestir** Richborough, part of the city of Sandwich.
3. **Gessoriacum** Boulogne, France.
4. **furlongs** units for measuring distance; a furlong is equal to one eighth of a mile.
5. **Orcades** Orkney Isles.
6. **draft animals** animals used for pulling loads.
7. **Cockles** edible shellfish with two heart-shaped shells.
8. **jet** *n.* type of coal.
9. **Armenia** region between the Black and the Caspian seas, now divided between the nations of Armenia and Turkey.
10. **Macedonia** region in the eastern Mediterranean, divided among Greece, Yugoslavia, and Bulgaria.

80 ■ *From Legend to History (449–1485)*

Literary Analysis
Historical Writing Find two facts in this paragraph. Then, identify one claim for which you might need more evidence.

Reading Strategy
❺ **Breaking Down Sentences** Break down the sentence beginning "Cockles" to find the core ideas.

Vocabulary Builder
innumerable (i nōō′ mər ə bəl) *adj.* too many to count

Enrichment

Illustrating History
Societies have many ways of recording history, and some methods depend primarily on illustrations rather than on text. For example, Native Americans, the Hmong, and the ancient Mayans used pictures on skins, cloth, or carved into stone. Incas kept records with quipus, knotted colored threads. Many modern alphabets developed from pictographs. Have students discuss advantages and disadvantages of using pictures instead of written words.

has become a common medium through the study of the scriptures. The original inhabitants of the island were the Britons, from whom it takes its name, and who, according to tradition, crossed into Britain from Armorica,[11] and occupied the southern parts. When they had spread northwards and possessed the greater part of the islands, it is said that some Picts from Scythia[12] put to sea in a few long ships and were driven by storms around the coasts of Britain, arriving at length on the north coast of Ireland. Here they found the nation of the Scots, from whom they asked permission to settle, but their request was refused. Ireland is the largest island after Britain, and lies to the west. It is shorter than Britain to the north, but extends far beyond it to the south towards the northern coasts of Spain, although a wide sea separates them. These Pictish seafarers, as I have said, asked for a grant of land to make a settlement. The Scots replied that there was not room for them both, but said: "We can give you good advice. There is another island not far to the east, which we often see in the distance on clear days. Go and settle there if you wish; should you meet resistance, we will come to your help." So the Picts crossed into Britain, and began to settle in the north of the island, since the Britons were in possession of the south. Having no women with them, these Picts asked wives of the Scots, who consented on condition that, when any dispute arose, they should choose a king from the female royal line rather than the male. This custom continues among the Picts to this day. As time went on, Britain received a third nation, that of the Scots, who migrated from Ireland under their chieftain Reuda, and by a combination of force and treaty, obtained from the Picts the settlements that they still hold. From the name of this chieftain, they are still known as Dalreudians, for in their tongue *dal* means a division.

Ireland is broader than Britain, and its mild and healthy climate is superior. Snow rarely lies longer than three days, so that there is no

---

11. **Armorica** Brittany, France.
12. **Scythia** ancient region in southeastern Europe.

▲ Critical Viewing
Bede's fellow monks spent years creating books filled with pages such as this one. What can you infer about the values of the society that produced such work? **[Infer]**

✓ Reading Check
What are the four nations of England?

from A History of the English Church and People ■ 81

---

❼ Humanities

A Page of Bede's History, c. ninth century.

This page is from an illuminated, or decorated, manuscript. Such manuscripts were entirely handcrafted by scribes, who worked in monasteries called *scriptoriums,* where they spent day after day copying pages from books. Originally, they copied religious works, but later they copied other types of work as well.

Copying a book required a great deal of work. Before scribes could even begin, they had to cut pens from quills or reeds, grind ink, mix paints, and prepare parchment from calf- or lambskin.

In manuscripts such as the one shown, the scribes often created large ornate letters called *versals.* Versals marked the beginnings of books, chapters, verses, and paragraphs. In some manuscripts, real gold was applied to the versals as well as to other parts of the page. Many pages were miniature works of art.

Use the following discussion questions:

1. Why do you think this artist worked so hard to produce this image?
   Answer: The artist wanted to show the importance of the written word by making it beautiful.

2. What can you infer about the history of the English people from the artwork?
   Possible response: The knotwork and animal forms suggest the influence of Anglo-Saxon settlers and Viking invaders.

❽ Critical Viewing

Possible response: Students may say that the society valued learning, literacy, and art; they were willing to invest large amounts of time and resources to preserve knowledge.

❾ Reading Check

Answer: The four nations of England are the English, British, Scots, and the Picts.

Differentiated Instruction — Solutions for All Learners

Support for Special Needs Student
Students may benefit from reading along with the recorded version of this selection on the **Listening to Literature Audio CDs.** Stop the recording every one or two paragraphs to discuss what has been covered. Be aware of words or ideas that might give students trouble, and help them discover the meanings. For example, in the first paragraph, the word *corrupted* does not mean evil when it relates to language, but simply means changed (though it implies a lower form of language).

Enrichment for Gifted/Talented Students
Illuminated manuscripts ranged from simply handsome to incredibly and gorgeously elaborate. Encourage students to find illustrations of such work to share with the class. Then, encourage them to create a *versal*—an ornate capital letter—to start either this selection or a favorite story. Remind students that illumination always related in some way to the story, as illustrations do today, and suggest that they try to include elements appropriate to the story they choose when they create their versals.

- Point out that good writers have a reason for including certain details they use—usually to support or illustrate the main idea of a paragraph or to supply information.

- Remind students that the claim that burning jet drives away snakes was an indication that snakes were a problem in England. Point out that this paragraph confirms this conclusion.

- **Ask** students the Literary Analysis question: What purpose guides Bede's choice of details in this selection?
  Possible response: Students may say that Bede's details illuminate his statement that Ireland has a mild, healthy, superior climate.

ASSESS

Answers

1. **Possible responses** may include the color of pearls, the use of cockles for dye, the qualities of jet, and the Pictish custom of inheritance.

2. (a) Britain is an island in the ocean. Britain has a 3,675-mile coastline. (b) This information suggests Britain's isolation from other countries and its reliance on the ocean for its economy and lifestyle.

3. (a) He says the scarlet dye is extracted from cockles and used in cloth. (b) **Possible response:** This information suggests that the society is highly evolved, and possibly wealthy.

4. (a) Latin unites Britain because it is the common language of the educated in all four nations. (b) The most important factor is the "study of God's truth": that is, the shared religion of Christianity.

5. (a) Factors dividing England are its different populations; factors uniting England include its Christian faith and its use of Latin as the common language of the educated. The factors uniting England seem stronger. (b) Bede creates an overall impression of a prosperous, flourishing England characterized by ethnic diversity.

6. **Possible responses:** Yes, Bede offers a highly detailed account of Great Britain at the time.

---

need to store hay in summer for winter use or to build stables for beasts. There are no reptiles, and no snake can exist there, for although often brought over from Britain, as soon as the ship nears land, they breathe its scented air and die. In fact, almost everything in this isle enjoys immunity to poison, and I have heard that folk suffering from snakebite have drunk water in which scrapings from the leaves of books from Ireland had been steeped, and that this remedy checked the spreading poison and reduced the swelling. The island abounds in milk and honey, and there is no lack of vines, fish, and birds, while deer and goats are widely hunted. It is the original home of the Scots, who, as already mentioned, later migrated and joined the Britons and Picts in Britain. There is a very extensive arm of the sea, which originally formed the boundary between the Britons and the Picts. This runs inland from the west for a great distance as far as the strongly fortified British city of Alcuith.[13] It was to the northern shores of this firth[14] that the Scots came and established their new homeland.

13. **Alcuith** Dumbarton, Scotland.
14. **firth** narrow arm of the sea.

Critical Reading

1. **Respond:** List three details you found interesting in Bede's history of England.

2. **(a) Recall:** List two pieces of geographical information Bede gives about Britain. **(b) Analyze:** How does this information help explain the nature of life there?

3. **(a) Recall:** What background does Bede give about British scarlet dye? **(b) Infer:** What does this information suggest about the lifestyle or economy of the country?

4. **(a) Interpret:** In what way does Latin unite England? **(b) Interpret:** According to Bede, what factor is most important in uniting people and giving them a common identity?

5. **(a) Compare and Contrast:** Contrast factors in Bede's account that are dividing England with those uniting it. Which seem stronger? **(b) Draw Conclusions:** What overall impression of England does Bede create?

6. **Evaluate:** Does Bede do a good job answering readers' questions about England? Explain, giving three examples of questions a reader would have.

Go Online
Author Link
For: More about Bede
Visit: www.PHSchool.com
Web Code: ese-9102

Answers continued

He explains why Ireland is believed to repulse snakes, he explains Britain's location in the world, and he explains the nature of the relationship among the four nations of Britain.

Go Online For additional informa-
Author Link tion about Bede, have students type in the Web Code, then select B from the alphabet, and then select Bede.

from The ANGLO-SAXON CHRONICLE

Translated by
Anne Savage

The Anglo-Saxon Kingdoms

- ▨ Under Danish rule
- ▢ Subject to Anglo-Saxons
- ♛ Kingdoms

896 In the summer of this year, the force[1] split up, one part in East Anglia,[2] one part in Northumbria;[3] and those who were without property got themselves ships and went south over the sea to the Seine.

The force had not, by the grace of God, utterly broken down the English; but they were more greatly broken in those three years by the slaughter of cattle and men, most of all by the fact that many of the

---

1. **the force** Danish settlers in England; Vikings.
2. **East Anglia** kingdom of Anglo-Saxon England in the East, including modern Norfolk and Suffolk.
3. **Northumbria** kingdom of Anglo-Saxon England in the North, including the city of York.

 ▲ **Critical Viewing**
Using the map, explain the relative locations of East Anglia, Wessex, and Kent. **[Interpret]**

☑ **Reading Check**
Identify one problem that has weakened the English.

from *The Anglo-Saxon Chronicle* ■ 83

⑪ About the Selection
The Anglo-Saxon Chronicle went on to cover the period until 1154. Because the documents in it were written over several centuries, they provide more than just a history of certain events; they also give insight into the development of the English language.

⑫ Critical Viewing
Answer: East Anglia is in the east, below the compass rose; Wessex is near the center of the southern coast, and Kent is in the southeasternmost area of the island.

⑬ Reading Check
Answer: The English have been weakened by the attacks of the Danes.

Differentiated Instruction   Solutions for All Learners

Support for Less Proficient Readers
Before students read this selection review difficult vocabulary with them and identify critical concepts that they should notice in the readings. This will help students master key concepts of this selection.

Vocabulary for English Learners
So that students can hear the names pronounced, play the **Listening to Literature Audio CDs** and have them follow along in their texts. Help them differentiate between words that are simply interesting historically and those which might be useful for them to know.

Enrichment for Advanced Students
Students may enjoy learning more about Anglo-Saxon names, including what they mean. Encourage them to use the Internet or library resources to research this era and its people. Students can present their findings to the class.

Though Anglo-Saxon included influences from all the cultures that settled or invaded England, including the Jutes, Angles, Saxons, Vikings, and Romans, the language we call Old English comes from the West Saxon dialect. This is so largely because of Alfred the Great's passion for literacy, and his translation of so many works from Latin, Northumbrian, and Mercian into what became standard Old English.

Though Old English is in many ways a very foreign language to those of us who know Modern English, there are still clear connections between old and new. For example, though *ic* doesn't look much like *I, we* has not changed at all. *Thaet* and *theos* can be recognized as *that* and *this,* and the verb forms for *sing* aren't that unfamiliar: *singan, singth, sang.*

In fact, in many respects, the pronunciation was more different than the words. Letters that are now silent were pronounced (for example, they would pronounce the *k* in *knee*). However, though ties to the languages from which it arose were still evident, by the time Alfred was king, English was taking shape as a separate language—just waiting for the next great linguistic influx, which came with the Norman Conquest, and the adding of Norman French to the mix.

Encourage students to try to pronounce some of the names featured in *The Anglo-Saxon Chronicle,* using the guidelines in the student text.

Connect to the Literature
Encourage students to sound out the words and practice pronunciation with a partner.

---

king's best thanes[4] in the land had died in those three years. One of them was Swithulf, bishop of Rochester; also Ceolmund, ealdorman[5] in Kent, Beorhtulf, ealdorman in Essex, Wulfred, ealdorman in Hampshire, Ealhheard, bishop of Dorchester, Eadulf, king's thane in Sussex, Beornulf, reeve[6] of Winchester, Ecgulf, king's horse-thane, and many others also, though I have named the most distinguished.

The same year, the forces in East Anglia and Northumbria greatly harassed Wessex along the south coast with raiding bands, most of all with the ash-ships[7] they had built many years before. Then King Alfred commanded longships to be built against the ash-ships. They were nearly twice as long as the others; some had sixty oars, some more. They were both swifter and steadier, also higher than the others; nor were they in the Frisian[8] manner or the Danish, but as he himself thought might be most useful.

As it fell out, at a certain time in the same year, six ships came to the Isle of Wight and did much evil there, both in Devon and everywhere along the sea-coast. Then the king commanded men to go there with nine of the new ships, and they went in front of them at the river's mouth in the open sea. The Danes went out with three ships against them, and three stood higher up the river's mouth, beached on dry land; the men from them had gone inland. The English took two of their three ships at the river's mouth, further out, killed the men, and one ship got away—and also on that all the men were killed but five. They got away because the other ships ran aground. They were very awkwardly aground: three were stranded on the same side of the deep water as the Danish ships, and the others all on the other side. But when the tide had ebbed many furlongs[9] from the ships, the Danes went out from their three ships to the other three that were <u>stranded</u> on their side and there fought with them. There were killed Lucumon the king's reeve, Wulfheard the Frisian, Aebbe the Frisian, Aethelhere the Frisian, Athelferth of the king's household, and in all, Frisians and English, sixty-two, and one hundred and twenty of the Danes.

The tide, however, came to the Danish ships before the Christians[10] could shove out, and in this way they rowed out. They were all so damaged that they could not row around Sussex; but there

---

4. **thanes** lords in Anglo-Saxon society, ranking below the members of a king's family.
5. **ealdorman** official who managed specific areas of a kingdom.
6. **reeve** official who collected taxes for the king.
7. **ash-ships** ships used by Vikings, propelled by oar and sail.
8. **Frisian** relating to people originally from Frisia, a region now divided between the Netherlands and Germany.
9. **furlongs** units for measuring distance; a furlong is equal to one eighth of a mile.
10. **the Christians** referring here to the English and Frisian forces, in contrast to the unconverted Danes.

84 ■ *From Legend to History (449–1485)*

⓮ **Cultural Connection**

Anglo-Saxon Pronunciations

There are no silent letters in Old English. Most consonants are pronounced as in modern English. For example, *Eadulf* can be pronounced a′ əd oolf′.

H before a vowel is pronounced as it is in modern English. Before a consonant or at the end of a word, it has a "throat-clearing" sound, as in the word *loch* (läkh). For example, *Beorhtulf* was probably pronounced bā′ ōrkh toolf′.

Vowels and Consonants

- *ae = a* in *ash*
- *c* before or after *i* and *e*, or after *a = ch*; otherwise, *c = k*
- *cg = j*
- *ea = a* in *ash* + ə
- *f* between two vowels = *v*
- *g* before or after *i* or *e*, or after *ae = y* as in *year*; otherwise, *g = g* in *get*
- *sc = sh* in *ship*
- *y = ew*

Connect to the Literature

Use the pronunciation guide to say the names Ealhheard, Ecgulf, and Aethelhere.

Vocabulary Builder
stranded (stran′ did) *v.* forced into shallow water or onto a beach; left helpless

---

Enrichment

Anglo-Saxons

An Anglo-Saxon was any member of the Germanic peoples who inhabited and ruled England from the 400s to the time of the Norman Conquest. The Venerable Bede relates that Anglo-Saxons were descended from three different groups—the Angles, Saxons, and Jutes. A British chieftain, Vortigern, invited them to come to help him defend his country against Pictish and Irish invaders. Ethnically, the Anglo-Saxons included all these people, plus England's original Celtic inhabitants and subsequent Viking and Danish invaders.

Actually, when Bede wrote about these people, he called them "Old Saxons." It was probably writers on the continent who coined the term *Anglo-Saxon,* to differentiate between the Saxons living in England and those still in Europe. When the Normans invaded in 1066, *Anglo-Saxon* came to mean "the English"—that is, anyone who wasn't Norman.

the sea threw two of them to land, and the men were led to Winchester, to the king. He commanded them to be hanged. The men who were on the one ship badly wounded came to East Anglia. The same summer no less than twenty ships perished with men and all along the south coast. The same year Wulfric the king's horse-thane died; he was also the Welsh-reeve.

900 Alfred, son of Aethelwulf, passed away, six nights before All Saints' Day. He was king over all the English, except for that part which was under Danish rule; and he held that kingdom for one and a half years less than thirty. Then his son Edward received the kingdom. Aethelwald, his father's brother's son, took over the manors at Wimbourne and at Christchurch, without the leave of the king and his counsellors. Then the king rode with the army until he camped at Badbury Rings near Wimbourne, and Aethelwald occupied the manor with those men who were loyal to him, and had <u>barricaded</u> all the gates against them; he said that he would stay there, alive or dead. Then he stole himself away under the cover of night, and sought the force in Northumbria. The king commanded them to ride after, but he could not be overtaken. They captured the woman he had seized without the king's leave and against the bishop's command, because she was hallowed[11] as a nun.

In the same year, Aethelred passed away, who was an ealdorman in Devon, four weeks before King Alfred.

902 Athelwald came here over the sea with all the ships he could get, and in Essex they submitted to him.

903 Aethelwald lured the East Anglian force into breaking the peace, so that they <u>ravaged</u> over the land of Mercia, until they came to Cricklade, went over the Thames there, seized all they could carry off both in and around Braydon and then went homeward again. Then King Edward went after them, as quickly as he could gather his army, and ravaged all their land between Devil's Dyke and Fleam Dyke and the Ouse, and everything up to the northern fens.[12] When he meant to leave there, he had it announced to the army that they would all leave together. The Kentish[13] stayed on there against his command and [the] seven messages he had sent to them. The force came upon them there, and they fought; ealdorman Sigulf was killed there, ealdorman Sigelm, Eadwold the king's thane, abbot[14] Cenulf, Sigebriht son of Sigulf, Eadwald son of Acca, and many besides them although I have named the most distinguished. On the Danish side were killed Eohric their king, atheling[15] Aethelwald, who had lured them into peacebreaking, Byrhtsige son of the atheling Beornoth,

---

11. **hallowed** made holy; given over, in a ceremony, to religious purposes.
12. **Dyke . . . fens** Dykes are barriers made of earth; fens are areas of peaty land covered with water.
13. **The Kentish** inhabitants of Kent, an English kingdom ruled by the kings of Wessex after 825.
14. **abbot** leader of a monastery; chief monk.
15. **atheling** Anglo-Saxon noble, especially one related to the kings of Wessex.

Literary Analysis
Historical Writing Why might the tone of the second sentence in this paragraph suggest the writer is proud of Alfred?

Vocabulary Builder
barricaded (barʹ i kādʹ id) v. blocked

ravaged (ravʹ ijd) v. destroyed

Reading Strategy
Breaking Down Sentences Break down this sentence about Edward into smaller details to clarify its meaning.

**Reading Check**
What new conflict troubles England under Edward?

from The Anglo-Saxon Chronicle ■ 85

---

⑮ Literary Analysis
Historical Writing

- Tell students to think about the turmoil that England had experienced up until the point of Alfred's rule.

- **Ask** students the Literary Analysis question: Why might the tone of the second sentence in this paragraph suggest that the writer is proud of Alfred?
  Possible response: This writer is recording the history of his own people, which he must think is worth recording. Alfred was the first great king of England, and so would be admired by someone who thought English history was important.

⑯ Vocabulary Builder
Latin Suffix -ade

- Call students' attention to the word *barricaded* and its definition. Point out that this is a verb form of the noun *barricade*. *Barricade* includes the Latin noun suffix *-ade*, which means "the act of," "the result of," or "a gathering of." For example, *promenade* is the act of walking—*walking* in the original French being *promener*.

- Have students **suggest** other words that contain this suffix, and list them on the chalkboard.
  Possible responses: *lemonade, motorcade, cavalcade, ambuscade, serenade, arcade, comrade.*

- Have students look up any unfamiliar words in a dictionary.

⑰ Reading Strategy
Breaking Down Sentences

- Have students **respond** to the Reading Strategy prompt: Break down this sentence about Edward into smaller details to clarify its meaning.
  Answer: King Edward pursued Aethelwald and his East Anglian force. He followed as quickly as he could gather his own army. He destroyed their land between Devil's Dyke and Fleam Dyke and the Ouse, and northward to the fens.

⑱ Reading Check
Answer: Edward and Aethelwald, cousins, fight with each other.

1. Students' responses should address the era's attractions or the disadvantages of invasions, wars, and rebellions that plagued the era.

2. (a) The Anglo-Saxons of Alfred's time faced the threat of invasion by the Danes. (b) English opposition to that threat seems fairly united under Alfred, who ruled over all of England except the part controlled by the Danes.

3. (a) Aethelwald takes over the manors of Wimbourne and at Christchurch without the king's permission, and he lures the East Anglians into breaking the peace. (b) Under Edward, the unity of the English was not strong.

4. (a) Edward plans to leave the battle zone. (b) The Kentish refused to obey Edward, suggesting that he could not enforce his authority. (c) Factors such as differences in language, culture, and ethnicity made it difficult for one ruler to control all of Britain, as did the distance between the main areas, and the lack of a uniform system of government.

5. (a) The inclusion of such information shows that this was considered to be of universal (that is, national) importance. (b) The *Chronicle* is a sign of national unity because it suggests that this is the history of one nation.

6. (a) **Possible responses:** Most students will probably say that this excerpt succeeds in answering a reader's questions about Anglo-Saxon England. They may cite such questions as "Who ruled over Anglo-Saxon England?" "Who were the principal enemies of the Anglo-Saxons?" and "What were some important events during this time?" (b) **Possible response:** *Chronicle* does succeed in creating pictures of important figures by describing their relationships, challenges, and accomplishments.

hold[16] Ysopa, hold Oscytel, and very many besides them we might not now name. On either hand much slaughter was made, and of the Danes there were more killed, though they had the battlefield. Ealhswith passed away. That same year was the fight at The Holme between the Kentish and the Danes. Ealdorman Aethelwulf died, brother of Ealhswith, King Alfred's mother; and abbot Virgilus of the Scots; and the mass-priest Grimbold. In the same year a new church in Chester was hallowed, and the relics of St. Judoc[17] brought there.

904 The moon darkened.

905 A comet appeared on October 20th.

906 Alfred died, who was town-reeve at Bath; and in the same year the peace was fastened at Tiddingford, just as King Edward advised, both with the East Anglians and the Northumbrians.

---

16. **hold** the equivalent in the Danelaw of a reeve, an official who collected taxes for the king.
17. **relics of St. Judoc** objects associated with Saint Josse, patron of harvests and ships

Critical Reading

1. **Respond:** Do you think you would have liked living in the era described in the *Chronicle*? Why or why not?

2. **(a) Recall:** What threat did the Anglo-Saxons of Alfred's time face? **(b) Draw Conclusions:** How united does the English opposition to that threat appear to be during his reign? Explain.

3. **(a) Recall:** List two actions Aethelwald takes after Edward becomes king. **(b) Interpret:** What do these actions suggest about the unity of the English under Edward?

4. **(a) Recall:** What does Edward plan to do after pursuing the East Anglian force? **(b) Infer:** What does the Kentish response to this plan and to his commands suggest about Edward's authority? **(c) Draw Conclusions:** What factors made it difficult for one ruler to control all of Britain?

5. **(a) Summarize:** The *Chronicle* lists the deaths of important Anglo-Saxons. Explain how the inclusion of this information creates the sense that the Anglo-Saxons are a nation. **(b) Draw Conclusions:** Explain how the *Chronicle* itself is a sign of national unity.

6. **(a) Evaluate:** Does this excerpt succeed in answering a reader's questions about Anglo-Saxon England? Explain, giving three examples of such questions. **(b) Evaluate:** Does it succeed in creating a picture of important figures such as Alfred? Explain.

Apply the Skills

History of the English Church and People •
The Anglo-Saxon Chronicle

Literary Analysis

Historical Writing

1. What kinds of details indicate that Bede's work is **historical writing,** intended for a wider audience than just inhabitants of Britain?

2. **(a)** Give an example of evidence Bede offers for a claim he makes. **(b)** How convincing is this evidence?

3. **(a)** What knowledge of Anglo-Saxon times does the *Chronicle* assume readers have? **(b)** Give an example of background information offered by the *Chronicle* that a later reader might not have.

4. Evaluate Bede's *History* and the *Chronicle* as pieces of historical writing. Using a chart like the following, give examples of points where the authors give enough or too little background information or evidence, or where the organization aided or impeded understanding.

Necessary Background	Evidence	Clear Organization

Comparing Literary Works

5. **(a)** Compare the topics of the two selections. **(b)** Compare the kinds of details the selections include that a modern historian might consider unsupported or extraneous. **(c)** Compare the writers' purposes in offering such details.

6. Compare and contrast the impression of England that each selection conveys.

Reading Strategy

Breaking Down Sentences

Read the sentence in Bede that begins "As time went on, Britain received a third nation, . . ." (p. 81). Then, answer these questions:

7. Which words in this sentence state the main action?

8. Answer the questions *who, what, where,* and *how* about the main action.

Extend Understanding

9. **History Connection:** Name three facts in the *Chronicle* and describe the methods a modern historian might use to verify each.

from *A History of the English Church and People* / from *The Anglo-Saxon Chronicle* ■ 87

QuickReview

Historical writing tells the story of past events, using evidence from the period.

Breaking down a sentence into the main action and the details that tell more about it helps you better understand the sentence.

Go Online
Assessment

For: Self-test
Visit: www.PHSchool.com
Web Code: esa-6104

Answers continued

9. **Possible response:** Alfred's death, Edward's ascension, and the comet's appearance. Historians could search historical records to verify the events.

Go Online
Assessment   Students may use the **Self-test** to prepare for
Selection Test A or **Selection Test B**.

Answers

1. **Possible response:** Bede includes such details as Britain's former name, its location in relation to other countries, and information about resources.

2. (a) **Possible response:** Bede says Ireland's climate is superior to Britain's, and he offers as evidence that snow doesn't last, hay doesn't need to be stored for winter, and there are no reptiles. (b) These are convincing proofs. However, Bede attributes Ireland's lack of reptiles to the fragrant air, which sounds more like legend.

3. (a) **Possible response:** It assumes that readers know that the Danes are the chief rival of the Anglo-Saxons. (b) **Possible response:** It explains that Edward and Aethelwald were cousins.

4. **History:** Necessary Background: "Five languages and four nations"; Evidence: "English, British, Scots, Picts & Latin"; Clear Organization: organization helped understanding; **Chronicle:** Necessary Background: Danes and English at war; Evidence: "one part in East Anglia, one part in Northumbria . . ."; Clear Organization: organization is clear, but background information is needed to know that the Danes and English are enemies.

5. (a) Bede's work is more a complete, detailed narrative; the *Chronicle* reads more like a timeline. (b) **Possible response:** Modern historians might not have included the details about snakes in Ireland or the detail of the nun's capture. (c) Bede may have included his detail to enhance his remarks; the *Chronicle* may have included the detail about the nun to discredit Aethelwald.

6. **Possible response:** Bede's account of England suggests a country in harmony; the *Chronicle* suggests greater turmoil.

7. The main action of the sentence is stated in the words, "Britain received a third nation."

8. **Possible responses:** *Who:* The Scots, a third nation; *What:* became part of Britain; *Where:* from Ireland to settlements obtained from the Picts; *How:* migrated, and by a combination of force and treaty.

❶ Vocabulary Lesson

Word Analysis

1. *Lemonade* means "the result of preparing lemons as a beverage."

2. *Motorcade* means "a gathering of automobiles."

3. *Cannonade* means "the act of firing cannons."

4. *Cavalcade* means "a gathering of horses."

Spelling Strategy

1. cities   3. treaties

2. boundaries

Vocabulary Builder

1. promontories   4. stranded

2. ravaged   5. barricaded

3. innumerable

❷ Grammar and Style Lesson

1. The Anglo-Saxons referred to them as Danes, but we call them Vikings.

2. No snakes exist in Ireland; the air there is said to kill them.

3. Alfred did not set out to rule England, but events dictated otherwise.

4. The Dane may have gone to Northumbria, or he may have settled in East Anglia.

5. Aethelwald conquered East Anglia in 902, and the next year, he lured the East Anglians into breaking the peace.

Writing Application

Possible responses: Alfred was a beloved king, and England suffered when he died. Life was difficult, but the nation prevailed against the invading Danes. Edward and his cousin fought each other, but eventually life settled down.

Build Language Skills

❶ Vocabulary Lesson

Word Analysis: Latin Suffix -ade

The Latin suffix *-ade* means "the act of," "the result of," or "a gathering of." Knowing the meaning of the suffix can help you see that *barricade* means "the result of barring the way." Use this information to define these words:

1. lemonade   3. cannonade
2. motorcade   4. cavalcade

Spelling Strategy

If a word ends with a consonant and *y*, change the *y* to *ies* to form the plural. *Promontory* becomes *promontories*. Pluralize these words:

1. city   2. boundary   3. treaty

Vocabulary Builder: Sentence Completion

Choose words from the vocabulary list on page 77 to complete the following sentences.

1. High on the ___?___, the king could see his ships entering the firth.

2. Suddenly, a fleet of Viking ships appeared and savagely ___?___ the king's boats.

3. The fierceness of the attack made it seem there were ___?___ ships.

4. Several of the king's ships ended up ___?___ on the beach.

5. Others tried to sail back out to sea, but the Vikings had ___?___ the harbor.

❷ Grammar and Style Lesson

Compound Sentences

A **compound sentence** is a sentence with two or more independent clauses, clauses that can each stand alone as a sentence.

> IND.CLAUSE
> There are many land and sea birds of various
> IND.CLAUSE
> species, and it is well known for its plentiful springs and rivers abounding in fish.

The conjunction or punctuation that joins the parts of a compound sentence expresses the relationship between the parts:

- *and, for, so,* or a semicolon: addition; further details or support; sequence; explanation
- *but, yet:* contrast; opposition; exception
- *or, nor:* alternative

WG Prentice Hall Writing and Grammar Connection: Chapter 19, Section 4

88 ■ *From Legend to History (449–1485)*

Practice Rewrite each pair of sentences below as compound sentence. Use the conjunction that suggests the indicated relationship between idea:

1. The Anglo-Saxons referred to them as Dane We call them Vikings. (contrast)

2. No snakes exist in Ireland. The air there is said to kill them. (further support)

3. Alfred did not set out to rule England. Events dictated otherwise. (contrast)

4. The Dane may have gone to Northumbria. He may have settled in East Anglia. (alternative)

5. Athelwald conquered East Anglia in 902. Th next year, he lured the East Anglians into breaking the peace. (addition)

Writing Application Write three compound sen tences on Anglo-Saxon life.

Assessment Practice

Sequential Order   (For more practice, see *Standardized Test Preparation Workbook*, p. 3.)

Many tests require students to identify the sequence of events. Have students take notes to identify the sequence of events.

"The English took two of their [Danes'] three ships, . . . killed the men, and one ship got away . . . on that all the men were killed but five. They got away because the other ships ran aground. . . . But when the tide had ebbed many furlongs from the ships, the Danes went out from their three ships to the other three . . . and there fought with them."

What happened immediately after the Danish ship with five survivors escaped?

A The tide ebbed and the remaining Danes attacked three of the English ships.

B The other three Danish ships got away.

C The English ships ran aground.

D The tide came in to the Danish side, and the Danish ships rowed out first.

By using their notes, students should be able to determine that choice *A* is correct.

Writing Lesson

Timed Writing: Critical Comparison of Historical Sources

Both Bede and the writers of *The Anglo-Saxon Chronicle* help build a national identity for Britain. By presenting diverse customs, events, and geographical facts as parts of one story, they portray Britain as a unified entity. Write an essay analyzing the vision of national identity in each work. *(40 minutes)*

Prewriting
(10 minutes)
Take notes on the aspects of Britain covered by each selection. Next, summarize the ingredients, such as geography or political control, that each work includes in its picture of Britain. Then, identify the factors uniting these ingredients in one story.

Drafting
(20 minutes)
Begin by posing the question your essay answers and stating your conclusions. Develop your points in logical order.

Revising
(10 minutes)
Highlight each example you use. For each marked passage, ask yourself, In what other way might the writer have treated this information? Consider adding your answers to clarify your insights.

Model: Revising to Elaborate on Critical Insights

Bede is guided by geography when he includes the

The Picts are a separate people, and he could have

treated their story as separate from the story of Anglo-

Saxon England.

settling of the Picts in Scotland in his story. In addition to geography, though, Bede is thinking of language and religion.

The added sentence clarifies the insight by answering the question, *What are the alternative possibilities?*

Prentice Hall Writing and Grammar Connection: Chapter 13, Section 4

Extend Your Learning

Listening and Speaking Develop a short **radio interview** between Bede and a reporter. Adjust the language you use as follows:

- Use informal language for friendly talk.
- Switch to technical language when discussing historical or geographical details.

Tape your interview. **[Group Activity]**

Research and Technology Produce a **museum exhibit** on medieval seafaring technology. Use research to draw a set of diagrams of a Viking ship. Include images that illuminate Viking life.

 **Go Online**
Research

For: An additional research activity
Visit: www.PHSchool.com
Web Code: esd-7103

from *A History of the English Church and People* / from *The Anglo-Saxon Chronicle* ■ 89

Assessment Resources

The following resources can be used to assess students' knowledge and skills.

Unit 1 Resources
  Selection Test A, pp. 54–56
  Selection Test B, pp. 57–59
  Benchmark Test 1, pp. 60–65

General Resources
  Rubrics for Exposition: Comparison-and-Contrast Essay, pp. 69–70
  Rubric for Peer Assessment: Dramatic Performance, p. 131

Go Online
Assessment Students may use the **Self-test** to prepare for **Selection Test A** or **Selection Test B**.

Benchmark
Administer **Benchmark Test 1.** If some students need further work, use the **Interpretation Guide** to determine the appropriate reteaching page in the **Reading Kit** and on **Success Tracker.**

---

❸ Writing Lesson

You may use this Writing Lesson as timed-writing practice, or you may allow students to develop the essay as a writing assignment over several days.

- To guide students in writing this critical comparison, give them the **Support for Writing Lesson** page (*Unit 1 Resources*, p. 51).
- Tell students that, in this lesson, they will make a critical comparison of historical sources.
- Remind students that a critical comparison requires them to consider the way in which two or more sources present their evidence in their historical accounts.
- Read the Writing Lesson with students and use it to guide them in developing their understandings of each selection.
- Use the rubric for Exposition: Comparison-and-Contrast Essay, pp. 69–70 in *General Resources,* to evaluate student work.

❹ Listening and Speaking

- Read the Listening and Speaking lesson as a class, and then encourage students to reread Bede's work before they proceed.
- Remind students that radio interviews require careful planning; they should base interview questions on timely material that Bede would be able to answer.
- Encourage students to use language appropriate to the types of the questions in the interview.
- The **Support for Extend Your Learning** page (*Unit 1 Resources,* p. 52) provides guided note-taking opportunities to help students complete the Extend Your Learning activities.
- Have students use the rubric for Peer Assessment: Dramatic Performance, p. 131 in *General Resources,* to evaluate one another's interviews.

Go Online
Research Have students type in the Web Code for another research activity.

Reading Informational Materials

Students will

1. use maps for verification and interpretation.

2. interpret keys, symbols, and cardinal directions on maps.

3. draw conclusions based on geographical information provided on a map.

See Teacher Express™/Lesson View for a detailed lesson plan for Reading Informational Materials.

About Maps

- Have students read "About Maps." Then, discuss elements of maps students have seen or used.
  Possible responses: Students might mention keys, legends, or symbols.

- **Ask** students what kinds of things maps enable people to do.
  Possible responses: Maps help people determine their location, calculate the distance between two or more places, and explain the geographical features that separate regions.

- Discuss how knowing one's location on a map might aid one's ability to interpret the map.

Reading Strategy
Using Maps for Verification and Interpretation

- Have students read the information about the Reading Strategy.

- Discuss why understanding geographical location is useful in the analysis of texts.

- **Ask** students to name different kinds of maps that focus on specific kinds of information.
  Possible responses: Political maps show political divisions such as nations, without showing topographical features. Physical maps show the geographical features of an area, such as land masses, bodies of water, and mountain ranges. Relief maps are three-dimensional models of an area's terrain.

Maps

About Maps

The general purpose of a **map** is to present geographical information in a convenient graphic form. To use a map effectively, you should be familiar with the following basic map components:

- A legend or key defines the symbols used on the map.
- A compass rose shows cardinal directions (north, south, east, west).
- A scale shows the ratio between distances on the map and actual distances on the Earth.

Reading Strategy
Using Maps for Verification and Interpretation

To **verify and interpret** information is to check whether it is true and to explore its significance and implications. To verify and interpret textual information using a map, follow the steps below. (The chart shows how these steps might apply to *The Anglo-Saxon Chronicle,* p. 83.)

1. Identify claims in the text for which geographical information is relevant.

2. Formulate geographical questions based on the text.

3. Obtain a map of the region referenced in the text. Consider whether you need a map that focuses on a specific kind of information.

4. Use the map to answer your questions. Note any discrepancies or additional questions and consult other sources for answers.

Sample Geographical Claims
The Anglo-Saxon Chronicle: Both Anglo-Saxons and Danes, who were enemies, ruled parts of England in the 800s.
Sample Geographical Questions
Which group controlled the most territory?
Type of Map Needed
Historical: should show England in the 800s with political borders.
Answers / Additional Questions
Who controlled the regions of Cornwall and Wales?

Scan the map on the next page. Note regions and facts on the map that are relevant to the selections in this part.

Differentiated Instruction   Solutions for All Learners

Reading Support
Give students reading support with the appropriate version of the **Reader's Notebooks:**

Reader's Notebook **[L2, L3]**

Reader's Notebook: Adapted Version **[L1, L2]**

Reader's Notebook: English Learner's Version **[EL]**

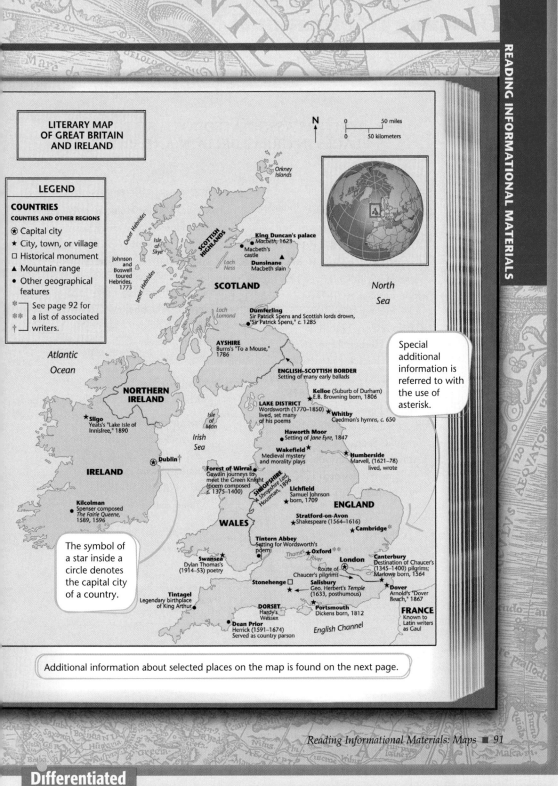

LITERARY MAP
OF GREAT BRITAIN
AND IRELAND

LEGEND

COUNTRIES
COUNTIES AND OTHER REGIONS

⊛ Capital city
★ City, town, or village
□ Historical monument
▲ Mountain range
• Other geographical
  features

* ⎤ See page 92 for
** ⎟ a list of associated
† ⎦ writers.

N

0 ____ 50 miles
0 ____ 50 kilometers

Orkney
Islands

Outer Hebrides

Isle
of
Skye

Inner Hebrides

SCOTTISH
HIGHLANDS

King Duncan's palace
Macbeth, 1623
• Macbeth's
  castle
Loch
Ness
▲ Dunsinane
  Macbeth slain

Johnson
and
Boswell
toured
Hebrides,
1773

SCOTLAND

North
Sea

Loch
Lomond
Dumferling
Sir Patrick Spens and Scottish lords drown,
"Sir Patrick Spens," c. 1285

Atlantic
Ocean

AYRSHIRE
Burns's "To a Mouse,"
1786

ENGLISH–SCOTTISH BORDER
Setting of many early ballads

Kelloe (Suburb of Durham)
E.B. Browning born, 1806

**NORTHERN
IRELAND**

Isle
of
Man

LAKE DISTRICT
Wordsworth (1770–1850)
lived, set many
of his poems

• Whitby
Caedmon's hymns, c. 650

★ Sligo
Yeats's "Lake Isle of
Innisfree," 1890

Irish
Sea

Haworth Moor
Setting of Jane Eyre, 1847

Wakefield ★
Medieval mystery
and morality plays

★ Humberside
Marvell, (1621–78)
lived, wrote

⊛ Dublin †

IRELAND

Forest of Wirral
Gawain journeys to
meet the Green Knight
(poem composed
c. 1375–1400)

SHROPSHIRE
A Shropshire Lad,
Housman, 1896

• Lichfield
Samuel Johnson
born, 1709

ENGLAND

• Kilcolman
Spenser composed
The Faïrie Queene,
1589, 1596

Stratford-on-Avon
★Shakespeare (1564–1616)

★ Cambridge ⁂

WALES

Tintern Abbey
Setting for Wordsworth's
poem
•

The symbol of
a star inside a
circle denotes
the capital city
of a country.

★ Oxford **

Thames
River

London
Route of
Chaucer's pilgrims

Canterbury
Destination of Chaucer's
(1345–1400) pilgrims;
Marlowe born, 1564

Swansea
Dylan Thomas's
(1914–53) poetry

Stonehenge □

Salisbury
Geo. Herbert's Temple
(1633, posthumous)

★ Dover
Arnold's "Dover
Beach," 1867

★ Tintagel
Legendary birthplace
of King Arthur

DORSET
Hardy's
Wessex

• Portsmouth
Dickens born, 1812

FRANCE
Known to
Latin writers
as Gaul

• Dean Prior
Herrick (1591–1674)
Served as country parson

English Channel

Special
additional
information is
referred to with
the use of
asterisk.

The symbol of
a star inside a
circle denotes
the capital city
of a country.

Additional information about selected places on the map is found on the next page.

Reading Maps

- Explain that students might find this map in an anthology of European or British literature.
- Point out that this map focuses exclusively on the significance of geographical location as it relates to literary works and authors.
- Have students read the map and the notes that identify the elements of the map.
- **Ask** students why the following items are included in the map, and what the items signify.
  Asterisk: Signifies that special additional information, such as the author's association with a particular university, is denoted.
  The symbol of a star inside a circle: Signifies the capital city of a country.

continued on page 92

Differentiated
Instruction   Solutions for All Learners

Strategy for
Special Needs Students
Encourage students to consult the legend on the map before they begin to read it. Direct their attention to the call-out boxes as well. Ask them to name the number of countries on the map, and to indicate bodies of water before they begin analyzing the map for literary content.

Enrichment for
Gifted/Talented Students
Have students work in groups to create a literary map of a city in America, using the Internet or encyclopedias to choose a city and gather information. Students may want to create maps for cities such as New York or Boston, which are notable centers for art.

Enrichment for
Advanced Students
Have each student design a quiz to test a classmate's knowledge of the Literary Map of Great Britain. Have students write questions to accompany the map, based on the list of authors on p. 92, or on information they have gleaned from examining the map. Then, have each student exchange his or her quiz with a partner, and take the partner's quiz.

91

- Have students turn back to p. 91 and locate Cambridge, Oxford, and Dublin on the map.

- Point out that the authors in the lists labeled "Cambridge" and "Oxford" are affiliated with universities there, but those in the "Dublin" list are associated with the city.

- **Ask** students why they think the information on this page was included as a separate feature, rather than as part of the map. **Answer:** The list of authors would have cluttered the map and made the geographical distinctions difficult to see.

WRITERS ASSOCIATED WITH SELECTED PLACES IN GREAT BRITAIN AND IRELAND

*Cambridge
Authors who studied here include:

Francis **Bacon** 1561–1626
Rupert **Brooke** 1887–1915
George Gordon, Lord **Byron** 1788–1824
Samuel Taylor **Coleridge** 1772–1834
John **Dryden** 1631–1700
E.M. **Forster** 1879–1970
Thomas **Gray** 1716–1771
George **Herbert** 1593–1633
Robert **Herrick** 1591–1674
Christopher **Marlowe** 1564–1593
Andrew **Marvell** 1621–1678
Samuel **Pepys** 1633–1703
Siegfried **Sassoon** 1886–1967
Edmund **Spenser** 1552?–1599
Alfred, Lord **Tennyson** 1809–1892
William **Wordsworth** 1770–1850
Sir Thomas **Wyatt** 1503–1542

T. S. **Eliot** 1888–1965
Gerard Manley **Hopkins** 1844–1889
A.E. **Housman** 1859–1936
Samuel **Johnson** 1709–1784
Richard **Lovelace** 1618–1657
Louis **MacNeice** 1907–1963
Sir Walter **Raleigh** 1552–1618
Percy Bysshe **Shelley** 1792–1822
Sir Philip **Sidney** 1554–1586
Richard **Steele** 1672–1729

†Dublin
Authors associated with the city include:

James **Joyce** 1882–1941
George Bernard **Shaw** 1856–1950
Sir Richard **Steele** 1672–1729
Jonathan **Swift** 1667–1745
Oscar **Wilde** 1854–1900
William Butler **Yeats** 1865–1939

**Oxford
Authors who studied here include:

Joseph **Addison** 1672–1719
Matthew **Arnold** 1822–1888
John **Donne** 1572–1631

Devices such as double asterisks link the information on this page to the map on the previous page.

Differentiated Instruction   Solutions for All Learners

Enrichment for Gifted/Talented Students
Have students select a writer listed on p. 92. Then, have students research the writer and create a poster displaying their information. Posters should be imaginative and contain graphics to enhance the presentation. Give students guidelines as to the minimum number of facts to be displayed on their posters.

Enrichment for Advanced Students
Have students research some of the writers listed on p. 92 in the library or on the Internet. Students can research background on the writers and create a list of their literary work. If students choose writers associated with Dublin, have them discover why the writers are associated with the city. Pose questions such as: Did they live there? Did they write about Dublin?

Assessment Practice

Reading: Using Maps for Verification and Interpretation

Directions: *Read the excerpt from* A History of the English Church and People *on page 78. Then, choose the letter of the best answer to each question about the literary map.*

1. By approximately how many miles does Bede overestimate the distance that England extends northward from its southernmost point?
   A about 100 miles
   B about 250 miles
   C about 450 miles
   D about 600 miles

2. According to the general route described by Bede, which place on the map would the Picts have passed after leaving Ireland?
   A Loch Lomond
   B Thames River
   C Outer Hebrides
   D Shropshire

3. Bede says that the original Britons crossed into Britain from what is now France. Where in Britain would they have likely landed, according to the literary map?
   A Dorset
   B Dover
   C Dumferling
   D Dublin

Reading: Comprehension and Interpretation

Directions: *Write your answers on a separate sheet of paper.*

4. What is the purpose of the Literary Map of Great Britain and Ireland?

5. Given the distance and the time period, is it likely that an average citizen would travel from Stratford-on-Avon to Northern Scotland for pleasure? Explain your answer.

6. Based on the map and the accompanying list, which island seems to have a richer literary history, Great Britain or Ireland? Explain your response.

Timed Writing: Persuasive Essay

Choose an area on the map that might be of interest to a literary historian. Then, write an essay persuading the historian to visit the area, using points of interest on the map to support your argument. *(20 minutes)*

Reading: Using Maps for Verification and Interpretation

1. B
2. A
3. B

Reading: Comprehension and Interpretation

4. The purpose of the map is to show the relationship between geographical location and literary works and authors.

5. It is not likely that a citizen would have traveled for pleasure because the distance is too great without the convenience of modern travel.

6. Great Britain has the greater literary history because it has more authors that studied in the area and more locations of famous writers.

Timed Writing

- Encourage students to create a strong thesis statement for their essays. Tell them to organize their main points in order of importance.

- Suggest that students plan their time to give 5 minutes to planning, 10 minutes to writing, and 5 minutes to reviewing and revising.

Extend the Lesson

Creating Maps from Textual Descriptions

Have students read the excerpt from *The Anglo-Saxon Chronicle,* page 83. Then, students should trace the outlines of the British Isles and of the Anglo-Saxon kingdoms from a map of the period. Next, referring only to the selections, ask students to fill in the geographical features and regions described in the text. Tell them to use a special color to fill in features the locations of which they can only guess at. Finally, have them compare their maps to a map of England at the time (you will find one on page 83). Ask students to explain what errors they made, and what additional information in the text might have helped them avoid these errors.

Background
Thomas à Becket, Archbishop of Canterbury

The pilgrims in *The Canterbury Tales* are on their way to the shrine of Thomas à Becket at the cathedral in Canterbury. Becket was appointed by Henry II as Archbishop of Canterbury and became famous for his struggle to keep the English church free from royal control.

In the 1160s, a series of conflicts ensued between Becket and Henry II over Henry's attempt to control the church. After fleeing to France in 1164, Becket returned to England in 1170 and quickly revived his struggle with Henry. In earshot of his knights, Henry questioned if there was anyone who might get rid of Becket. Four knights interpreted Henry's words as a request and went off to Canterbury, where they killed Becket while he was at evening prayers.

Pope Alexander III made Becket a saint in 1173, and Becket's tomb at Canterbury soon became a popular place for pilgrims. Later, however, King Henry VIII destroyed the shrine that had been dedicated to Becket at Canterbury.

Chaucer's Guided Tour of Medieval Life and Literature

Rich people, poor people, stock brokers, artists, farmers, street vendors . . . with all of the different lifestyles in our culture, you may wonder what single event could gather together people from all parts of society. Geoffrey Chaucer found in his own society an orderly, even joyous event that gathered people from diverse backgrounds and occupations—a pilgrimage, or journey to a sacred spot. It is such a pilgrimage that gathers together the diverse characters in his masterpiece, *The Canterbury Tales.*

The Journey Begins Like modern travelers, medieval pilgrims must have been eager to while away their time traveling. Chaucer uses this fact to set his story in motion. *The Canterbury Tales* begins with a Prologue, in which the Narrator, presumably Chaucer himself, meets 29 other pilgrims at the Tabard Inn, located in a suburb of London. As the pilgrims prepare for their journey, the host of the Inn, Harry Bailey, sets a challenge. To make the journey more entertaining, he suggests that each pilgrim tell two stories on the way to Canterbury and two stories on the return trip. The person who tells the best tale will be treated to a feast hosted by the other pilgrims. The pilgrims accept the challenge, and Bailey himself decides to join them and judge the competition.

> **❝** *Canterbury Tales is actually a story about stories....* **❞**

Each of the following sections of the work consists of one of the pilgrim's tales. Brief transitions, as one storyteller finishes and another begins, link the stories. In this way, the work is actually a story about stories, twenty-four different tales set within the overarching tale of the pilgrimage.

Snapshots of an Era In the Prologue, Chaucer sketches a brief but vivid portrait of each pilgrim, creating a lively sense of medieval life. In itself, the Prologue is a great literary achievement. As critic Vincent Hopper notes,

> The description of the various pilgrims turn in rapid sequence from an article of clothing to a point of character and back again with no apparent organization or desire for it. Yet so effective is this artful artlessness that each pilgrim stands out sharply as a type of medieval personality and also as a highly individualized character. . . .

Chaucer begins his survey of medieval society with the courtly world, which centered around the nobility. Medieval nobles such as Chaucer's Knight held land granted them by a lord or king, for whom they fought in times of war. In the middle ranks of medieval society were learned professionals, such as Chaucer's Doctor, and wealthy businessmen. The lower

orders included craftsmen, storekeepers, and minor administrators, such as the Reeve and the Manciple. The various ranks of the Church, a cornerstone of medieval society, are represented by characters from the Prioress to the Summoner.

However, as Chaucer writes about character ranks and types, he presents them as real people, individuals who defy categorizing. For example, though all outward appearances suggest that the Merchant is wealthy, he is, in fact, deeply in debt—a secret he keeps from some of his fellow travelers. Such breaks in stereotype provide readers with an even greater insight into the daily lives of medieval people.

A Literary Tour The popular genres in Chaucer's day included romances (tales of chivalry), *fabliaux* (short, bawdy, humorous stories), the stories of saint's lives, sermons, and allegories (narratives in which characters represent abstractions such as Pride or Honor). Each pilgrim chooses to tell a type of tale consistent with his or her character, and each of the major forms of medieval literature is represented. Chaucer wrote much of the *Tales* using his own form, the heroic couplet, a pair of rhyming lines with five stressed syllables each. For this important innovation, along with his other achievements, he is known as the father of English poetry.

The Endless Road Traveling with Chaucer's pilgrims, a reader may feel that the world is a big place but that, somehow, all of its pieces fit together. *The Canterbury Tales* reminds us that every journey from here to there is filled with stories, waiting to be told.

⋀ Critical Viewing
For what reasons might someone choose to leave a homestead like the one pictured to go on a pilgrimage? **[Speculate]**

Activity

Modern Day Travelers

Imagine taking a long bus or plane trip. With a group, discuss the types of people traveling with you. Come up with your own cast of characters for a modern-day version of *The Canterbury Tales*. Use these questions to guide your discussion:
- What different kinds of people make up our society today? Identify six types and build a character that matches each.
- In what ways might many of these individuals break the stereotype they outwardly appear to fit?
- What kind of tale might each character tell?
Choose a point person to share your ideas with the class.

Differentiated Instruction   Solutions for All Learners

Strategy for Less Proficient Readers
Have students read A Closer Look. As they read Chaucer's Prologue, p. 98, have them take notes on the social status and ethical qualities of each character. Guide them in a discussion about their findings.

Enrichment for Gifted/Talented Students
Have students read A Closer Look. As they read Chaucer's Prologue, p. 98, have them take notes on the social status and ethical qualities of each character. Then, have them draw a scene of the pilgrims en route, drawing on Chaucer's descriptions and conveying a sense of the event and the times.

Enrichment for Advanced Readers
Have students read A Closer Look. As they read Chaucer's Prologue, p. 98, have them take notes on the social status and ethical qualities of each character. Then, have them choose a pilgrim and read the tale he or she tells. They should write an essay explaining how the tale reflects the pilgrim's character.

Background
The Three Estates
Social stratification in medieval Europe consisted primarily of three social classes, or "estates." The first estate comprised the clergy, the second comprised nobility, and the third workers and peasants. However, this traditional division began to break down during the late Middle Ages as a new "middle class" began to form, consisting of trained urban workers and merchants.

In *The Canterbury Tales*, Chaucer is highly conscious of the social divisions known as the "estates." The Prologue to *The Canterbury Tales* is an example of "estates satire," a genre that satirizes the abuses that occur within the three traditional Estates—in particular, the clergy.

Critical Thinking
1. What does Chaucer's description of a pilgrimage indicate about society in his day?
   Possible response: On the one hand, it shows the clear division of society into defined groups and roles; on the other, it shows that there were occasions when people of different classes would mix together.

2. In what ways does Chaucer indicate a strong new sense of English cultural identity?
   Possible response: Chaucer developed new verse forms reflecting the nature of spoken English in his day; he "sums up" English society in the characters of the pilgrims and English literature in the genres of the tales. In these ways, he expresses a new, strong sense of an English cultural identity.

Activity
Form students into groups. Encourage students to brainstorm the six stereotypes together, and then individually build the characters. Once individuals have created their characters, they can all create the tales together.

TIME AND RESOURCE MANAGER

from **The Canterbury Tales: The Prologue**

 Meeting Your Standards

Students will

1. **analyze and respond to literary elements.**
   - Literary Analysis: Characterization

2. **read, comprehend, analyze, and critique a poem.**
   - Reading Strategy: Analyzing Difficult Sentences
   - Reading Check questions
   - Apply the Skills questions
   - Assessment Practice (ATE)

3. **develop vocabulary.**
   - Vocabulary Lesson: Latin Suffix: *-tion*

4. **understand and apply written and oral language conventions.**
   - Spelling Strategy
   - Grammar and Style Lesson: Past and Past Perfect Tenses

5. **develop writing proficiency.**
   - Writing Lesson: Allegory (after "The Wife of Bath's Tale ")

6. **develop appropriate writing strategies.**
   - Extend Your Learning: Critical Response

7. **understand and apply listening and speaking strategies.**
   - Extend Your Learning: Dialogue

Block Scheduling: Use one 90-minute class period to preteach the skills and have students read the selection. Use a second 90-minute class period to assess students' mastery of skills, extend their learning, and monitor their progress.

Homework Suggestions

Following are possibilities for homework assignments.

- Support pages from *Unit 1 Resources:*
  Literary Analysis
  Reading Strategy
  Vocabulary Builder
  Grammar and Style

- An Extend Your Learning project and the Writing Lesson for this selection may be completed over several days.

Step-by-Step Teaching Guide	Pacing Guide
PRETEACH	
• Administer Vocabulary and Reading Warm-ups as necessary.	5 min.
• Engage students' interest with the motivation activity.	5 min.
• Read and discuss author and background features. **FT**	10 min.
• Introduce the Literary Analysis Skill: Characterization **FT**	5 min.
• Introduce the Reading Strategy: Analyzing Difficult Sentences **FT**	10 min.
• Prepare students to read by teaching the selection vocabulary. **FT**	
TEACH	
• Informally monitor comprehension while students read independently or in groups. **FT**	30 min.
• Monitor students' comprehension with the Reading Check notes.	as students read
• Reinforce vocabulary with Vocabulary Builder notes.	as students read
• Develop students' understanding of characterization with the Literary Analysis annotations. **FT**	5 min.
• Develop students' ability to analyze difficult sentences with the Reading Strategy annotations. **FT**	5 min.
ASSESS/EXTEND	
• Assess students' comprehension and mastery of the Literary Analysis and Reading Strategy by having them answer the Apply the Skills questions. **FT**	15 min.
• Have students complete the Vocabulary Lesson and the Grammar and Style Lesson. **FT**	15 min.
• Apply students' understanding by using one or more of the Extend Your Learning activities.	20–90 min. or homework
• Administer Selection Test A or Selection Test B. **FT**	15 min.

Resources

Choosing Resources for Differentiated Instruction

[**L1**] Special Needs Students

[**L2**] Below-Level Students

[**L3**] All Students

[**L4**] Advanced Students

[**EL**] English Learners

For Vocabulary and Reading Warm-ups and for Selection Tests, **A** signifies "less challenging" and **B** "more challenging." For Graphic Organizer Transparencies, **A** signifies "not filled in" and **B** "filled in."

FT Fast Track Instruction: To move the lesson more quickly, use the strategies and activities identified with **FT**.

Scaffolding for Less Proficient and Advanced Students

The leveled Critical Thinking questions after selections progress in the levels of thinking required to answer them. To address the needs of your different students, you may use the (a) level questions for your less proficient students and the (b) level questions with your on-level and advanced students. The occasional (c) level questions are appropriate for your advanced students.

PRENTICE HALL
Teacher EXPRESS™ Use this complete
Plan · Teach · Assess   suite of powerful
teaching tools to make lesson planning and testing quicker and easier.

PRENTICE HALL
Student EXPRESS™ Use the interac-
Learn · Study · Succeed   tive textbook
(online and on CD-ROM) to make selections and activities come alive with audio and video support and interactive questions.

Monitoring Progress

Before students read *The Prologue,* administer **Diagnostic Test 2** (*Unit 1 Resources,* pp. 66–68).

Go Online
Professional
Development
For: Information about Lexiles
Visit: www.PHSchool.com
Web Code: eue-1111

Motivation

Many teenagers enjoy fantasy role-playing games or computer adventure games. Have students discuss strategies for winning such games. Elicit the idea that it is vital to pay attention to the surroundings and to the other characters.

Have students imagine that they have just started a new medieval adventure game. Ask what first impressions they might form of these strangers:

- A nun who feeds her dogs meats, milk, and fresh bread
- A well-fed monk wearing fine clothing and riding an excellent horse with a fancy bridle
- A skinny young man in tattered clothing carrying books
- A large, brawny man telling off-color stories and jokes.

❶ Background
More About the Author

The name Chaucer is derived from the French word *chaussier,* meaning a maker of footwear. The family had, in fact, made its fortune from leather, as well as wine. Chaucer spoke French, Latin, and Italian, in addition to Middle English, and his work shows evidence of his having read widely. It is likely that, for his government work, he would have studied law, too. Chaucer was no mere clerk—he was sufficiently important within the government to attain a guaranteed income for life.

Chaucer was appointed a justice of the peace for Kent in 1385, and in 1386 he became a knight for the shire of Kent, to attend Parliament. He was a courtier, diplomat, civil servant, and trusted aide to three kings; his contribution to the management of public affairs in the second half of the fourteenth century would have been noteworthy even if he hadn't become the age's greatest poet.

Build Skills   *Poem*

❶ *from* The Canterbury Tales: The Prologue

Geoffrey Chaucer
(1343?–1400)

Son of a merchant, page in a royal house, soldier, diplomat, and royal clerk, Geoffrey Chaucer saw quite a bit of the medieval world. His varied experiences helped prepare him to write *The Canterbury Tales.* This masterpiece provides the best contemporary picture we have of fourteenth-century England. Gathering characters from different walks of life, Chaucer takes the reader on a journey through medieval society.

The Poet's Beginning The exact date of Geoffrey Chaucer's birth is unknown, but official records furnish many details of his active life. Born into a middle-class family, Chaucer was sent in his early teens to work as page to the wife of Lionel of Antwerp, a son of the reigning monarch, Edward III. Through this position, middle-class Chaucer was introduced to the aristocratic society of England. In 1359, while serving in the English Army in France, Chaucer was captured and held prisoner. King Edward paid a £16 (sixteen-pound) ransom for his release—a sum that was eight times what a simple laborer might make in a year. In 1366, Chaucer married Philippa Pan, a lady-in-waiting to the queen. Their eldest child, Thomas, continued his father's rise in the world, marrying a noblewoman and acquiring great wealth.

The Poet Matures Chaucer began writing in his twenties, practicing and honing his skills as a poet as he rose through the ranks of medieval society. His early poems were based on the works of European poets. These were followed by various translations of French poetry. His first major work, *The Book of the Duchess,* was probably completed in early 1369, almost one year after the death of Blanche of Lancaster, for whose grieving husband, John of Gaunt, he wrote the poem. As Chaucer grew older, he developed a mature style of his own. In *Troilus and Criseyde,* a later poem drawn from the Greek legend of the Trojan War, Chaucer displays penetrating insight into human character.

The Canterbury Tales Chaucer wrote *The Canterbury Tales* in his later years. No one knows for certain what prompted him to begin this work. Chaucer's inspiration may have come from his own participation in the pilgrimage to Canterbury. A pilgrimage is a long journey to a shrine or holy site, taken by people who wish to express their devotion. Chaucer certainly had the opportunity to observe many pilgrims starting their journeys—a window of his London home overlooked the pilgrim road that led to Canterbury.

In this masterwork, each character tells a tale on the way to Canterbury. Just as the tellers of *The Canterbury Tales* come from the length and breadth of medieval society, the tales encompass medieval literature—from romance to comedy, from rhyme to prose, from crude humor to religious mysteries. Only 24 of the projected 120 tales were finished, but they stand together as a complete work.

The Father of English Poetry In his own lifetime, Geoffrey Chaucer was considered the greatest English poet. Recognized as a shrewd storyteller, he was also praised by a contemporary as the first to "rain the gold dewdrops of speech and eloquence" into English literature. Throughout history, new generations of poets writing in English have studied his work for inspiration and insight.

Chaucer lies buried in Westminster Abbey. In recognition of his unique position in England's literary tradition, Westminster's honorary burial area for distinguished writers, the Poets' Corner, was established around his tomb.

Preview

Connecting to the Literature

It may have been a class trip you took to a museum or a visit to a famous person's birthplace. Trips taken for inspiration or renewal, even if they are not religious, can loosely be termed pilgrimages. The pilgrims who gather in the Prologue are about to depart on such a journey.

Literary Analysis

Characterization

As you read the Prologue, look for these forms of **characterization**—techniques of revealing character:

- **Direct characterization** presents direct statements about a character, such as Chaucer's statement that the Knight "followed chivalry, / Truth, honor. . . ."
- **Indirect characterization** uses actions, thoughts, and dialogue to reveal a character's personality. By saying "he was not gaily dressed," for instance, Chaucer suggests that the Knight is not vain and perhaps takes the pilgrimage seriously enough to rush to join it straight from battle.

Connecting Literary Elements

Each character in *The Canterbury Tales* represents a different segment of society in Chaucer's time. By noting the virtues and faults of each, Chaucer provides **social commentary,** writing that offers insight into society, its values, and its customs. While reading, draw conclusions from the characters about Chaucer's views on English society.

Reading Strategy

Analyzing Difficult Sentences

Chaucer's Prologue begins with an eighteen-line sentence. To **analyze difficult sentences** such as this one, use the questions *when, who, where, what,* and *how* to identify the essential information each conveys. Use a chart like the one shown to finish analyzing Chaucer's first sentence.

When?	in April
Who?	people; palmers
Where?	
What?	
Why?	
How?	

Vocabulary Builder

solicitous (sə lis′ ə təs) *adj.* showing care or concern (p. 102)

garnished (gär′ nisht) *adj.* decorated; trimmed (p. 103)

absolution (ab′ sə lōō′ shən) *n.* act of freeing someone of a sin or criminal charge (p. 104)

commission (kə mish′ ən) *n.* authorization; act of giving authority to an individual (p. 106)

sanguine (saŋ′ gwin) *adj.* confident; cheerful (p. 107)

avouches (ə vouch′ ez) *v.* asserts positively; affirms (p. 108)

prevarication (pri var′ i kā′ shən) *n.* evasion of truth (p. 116)

from *The Canterbury Tales: The Prologue* ■ 97

❷ Literary Analysis
Characterization

- Tell students that, in this lesson, they will focus on characterization in the work of Chaucer.
- Review with students direct characterization, or direct descriptions of a character, and indirect characterization, development of a character through descriptions of appearance, actions, thoughts, and words.
- Tell students that, by looking for these kinds of characterization in Chaucer's poem, they will be able to discover the pilgrims' characters.
- Use the instruction for Connecting Literary Elements to explain how Chaucer uses characterization to provide social commentary.

❸ Reading Strategy
Analyzing Difficult Sentences

- Remind students that difficult sentences can be simplified by breaking them down into their essential parts.
- Encourage students to ask questions of difficult sentences, such as *who, what, when, where* and *how.*
- Provide students with a copy of **Reading Strategy Graphic Organizer A**, p. 13 in *Graphic Organizer Transparencies*, to use as they read the selection.

Vocabulary Builder

- Pronounce each vocabulary word for students, and read the definitions as a class. Have students identify any words with which they are already familiar.

Differentiated Instruction   Solutions for All Learners

Support for Special Needs Students
Have students read the adapted version of The Prologue in the *Reader's Notebook: Adapted Version*. This version provides basic-level instruction in an interactive format with questions and write-on lines. Completing these pages will prepare students to read the selection in the Student Edition.

Support for Less Proficient Readers
Have students read The Prologue in the *Reader's Notebook.* This version provides basic-level instruction in an interactive format with questions and write-on lines. After students finish the selection in the *Reader's Notebook,* have them complete the questions and activities in the Student Edition.

Support for English Learners
Have students read The Prologue in the *Reader's Notebook: English Learner's Version.* This version provides basic-level instruction in an interactive format with questions and write-on lines. Completing these pages will prepare students to read the selection in the Student Edition.

Learning Modalities
Visual/Spatial Learners Have
these students preview the illustrations accompanying this selection
prior to reading it. Encourage them
to share their impressions of the
characters based on the illustrations.

❶ About the Selection

Chaucer's collection of fourteenth-
century heroes and rogues offers a
rare snapshot of medieval life and
values. Moreover, it provides enduring evidence that human nature
changes very little. In Chaucer's characters, we see something of ourselves
and the people around us.

❶ *from* **The Canterbury Tales**
The Prologue

Geoffrey Chaucer
Translated by Nevill Coghill

Background In medieval Christianity, pilgrimages—long, annual
trips to holy places—were a popular way to express religious devotion.
Canterbury, a town 55 miles southeast of London, was a major destination
for English pilgrims. The cathedral in Canterbury was the site of Archbishop
Thomas à Becket's murder in 1170. Days after the murder and three years
before Becket was made a saint, people began flocking to the cathedral to
pay their respects.

The first eighteen lines of the Prologue are presented here in Chaucer's
original Middle English, followed by the entire Prologue in a modern
translation.

> Whan that Aprill with his shourës sootë
> The droghte of March hath percëd to the rootë,
> And bathëd every veyne in swich licour
> Of which vertu engendrëd is the flour;
> 5 Whan Zephirus eek with his sweetë breeth
> Inspirëd hath in every holt and heeth
> The tendrë croppës, and the yongë sonnë
> Hath in the Ram his halvë cours yronnë,
> And smalë fowelës maken melodyë,
> 10 That slepen al the nyght with open ye
> (So priketh hem nature in hir corages);
> Thanne longen folk to goon on pilgrimages,
> And palmeres for to seken straungë strondës,
> To fernë halwës, kowthe in sondry londës;
> 15 And specially from every shirës endë
> Of Engelond to Caunterbury they wendë,
> The hooly blisful martir for to seke,
> That hem hath holpen whan that they were seekë.

Differentiated
Instruction   Solutions for All Learners

Accessibility at a Glance

	from **The Canterbury Tales: The Prologue**
Context	Medieval literature
Language	Vocabulary footnotes
Concept Level	Average (human nature)
Literary Merit	Classic
Lexile	NP
Other	Social comments/satire
Overall Rating	Average

When in April the sweet showers fall
And pierce the drought of March to the root, and all
The veins are bathed in liquor of such power
As brings about the engendering of the flower,
5 When also Zephyrus¹ with his sweet breath
Exhales an air in every grove and heath
Upon tender shoots, and the young sun
His half-course in the sign of the Ram² has run,
And the small fowl are making melody
10 That sleep away the night with open eye
(So nature pricks them and their heart engages)
Then people long to go on pilgrimages
And palmers³ long to seek the stranger strands⁴
Of far-off saints, hallowed in sundry lands,
15 And specially, from every shire's end
In England, down to Canterbury they wend
To seek the holy blissful martyr,⁵ quick
To give his help to them when they were sick.
        It happened in that season that one day
20 In Southwark,⁶ at The Tabard,⁷ as I lay
Ready to go on pilgrimage and start
For Canterbury, most devout at heart,
At night there came into that hostelry
Some nine and twenty in a company
25 Of sundry folk happening then to fall
In fellowship, and they were pilgrims all
That towards Canterbury meant to ride.
The rooms and stables of the inn were wide;
They made us easy, all was of the best.
30 And shortly, when the sun had gone to rest,
By speaking to them all upon the trip
I soon was one of them in fellowship
And promised to rise early and take the way
To Canterbury, as you heard me say.
35   But nonetheless, while I have time and space,
Before my story takes a further pace,
It seems a reasonable thing to say
What their condition was, the full array
Of each of them, as it appeared to me
40 According to profession and degree,

1. **Zephyrus** (zef′ ə rəs) the west wind.
2. **Ram** Aries, the first sign of the zodiac. The pilgrimage began on April 11, 1387.
3. **palmers** pilgrims who wore two crossed palm leaves to show that they had visited the Holy Land.
4. **strands** shores.
5. **martyr** St. Thomas à Becket, the Archbishop of Canterbury, who was murdered in Canterbury Cathedral in 1170.
6. **Southwark** (suth′ ərk) suburb of London at the time.
7. **The Tabard** (ta′ bərd) an inn.

Literary Analysis
Characterization In these lines, what does the narrator suggest about the pilgrims' motives for going to Canterbury?

Reading Strategy
Analyzing Difficult Sentences *What* does Chaucer say he will do in lines 35–42? *How,* or *in what manner,* will he do it?

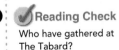

Reading Check
Who have gathered at The Tabard?

from The Canterbury Tales: The Prologue ■ 99

❷ Literary Analysis
Characterization

- You may wish to introduce *The Prologue* by playing the **Listening to Literature Audio CD** of the Middle English version while students follow along in their texts.

- Point out that there are both differences and similarities in language. Also note that the meter and rhyme scheme have been preserved in the modern English version.

- Remind students to look for details that will help them get to know the characters and understand their beliefs, ideas, and position.

- **Ask** students the Literary Analysis question: What does the narrator suggest about the pilgrims' motives for going to Canterbury?
Answer: They want to visit the saint's shrine and ask for his help and healing.

❸ Reading Strategy
Analyzing Difficult Sentences

- Remind students that by asking questions such as *when, who, how, where,* and *why* of a passage, they can analyze its meaning and identify the essential information it conveys.

- Point out that *condition* in line 38 refers to social position or rank.

- Then, **ask** students the Reading Strategy question: *What* does Chaucer say he will do in lines 35–42? *How,* or *in what manner,* will he do it?
Answer: Chaucer says that, before he tells more of the story, he is going to describe the people who are going along with him on the pilgrimage. He will include their social position, how they are dressed, their professions, and whatever else he can determine from what he has seen so far.

❹ Reading Check
Answer: Pilgrims *en route* to Canterbury are gathered at The Tabard in Southwark.

- **Ask** students why they think Chaucer started with the Knight. **Possible response:** He possessed the highest social standing among the pilgrims.

- Explain to students that, when Chaucer describes the Knight as the epitome of chivalry, he is talking about an ideal from the past. By the 1380s, when Chaucer began *The Canterbury Tales,* feudalism and chivalry had nearly disappeared from England.

- Remind students that some characterization is direct and some is indirect.

- **Ask** students the Literary Analysis question: What do lines 54–65 indirectly suggest about the Knight's character?
  Answer: He is brave, loves action and adventure, really believes in the ideals of chivalry—and must be an excellent fighter to have survived so many battles.

- **Ask** students which lines use direct characterization, and what details are added about the Knight's character.
  Answer: Lines 70–74 describe his character directly, stating that he is wise, modest, true, and a perfect gentle-knight.

❻ Literary Analysis
Characterization

- Remind students that the details that help characterize someone in this work (as well as in others) are not always obvious—and not always part of the individual's description.

- Point out that the comment in line 80 shows that the Knight has just returned from another battle.
  Ask students what additional information we gain about the Knight in the first few lines of the description of the Squire.
  Answer: We learn that the Knight has a son, the Squire, and we learn that the Knight is no youngster, if his son is already twenty.

And what apparel they were riding in;
And at a Knight I therefore will begin.
There was a *Knight*, a most distinguished man,
Who from the day on which he first began
45 To ride abroad had followed chivalry,
Truth, honor, generousness and courtesy.
He had done nobly in his sovereign's war
And ridden into battle, no man more,
As well in Christian as heathen places,
50 And ever honored for his noble graces.
    When we took Alexandria,[8] he was there.
He often sat at table in the chair
Of honor, above all nations, when in Prussia.
In Lithuania he had ridden, and Russia,
55 No Christian man so often, of his rank.
When, in Granada, Algeciras sank
Under assault, he had been there, and in
North Africa, raiding Benamarin;
In Anatolia he had been as well
60 And fought when Ayas and Attalia fell,
For all along the Mediterranean coast
He had embarked with many a noble host.
In fifteen mortal battles he had been
And jousted for our faith at Tramissene
65 Thrice in the lists, and always killed his man.
This same distinguished knight had led the van[9]
Once with the Bey of Balat,[10] doing work
For him against another heathen Turk;
He was of sovereign value in all eyes.
70 And though so much distinguished, he was wise
And in his bearing modest as a maid.
He never yet a boorish thing had said
In all his life to any, come what might;
He was a true, a perfect gentle-knight.
75 Speaking of his equipment, he possessed
Fine horses, but he was not gaily dressed.
He wore a fustian[11] tunic stained and dark
With smudges where his armor had left mark;
Just home from service, he had joined our ranks
80 To do his pilgrimage and render thanks.
    He had his son with him, a fine young *Squire*,
A lover and cadet, a lad of fire

---

8. **Alexandria** site of one of the campaigns fought by Christians against groups who posed a threat to Europe during the fourteenth century. The place names that follow refer to other battle sites in these campaigns, or crusades.
9. **van** the part of the army that goes before the rest (short for *vanguard*).
10. **Bey of Balat** pagan leader.
11. **fustian** (fus´ chən) *n.* coarse cloth of cotton and linen.

100 ■ From Legend to History (449–1485)

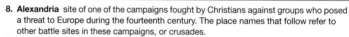

Enrichment

The Knight
The Knight is said to have done nobly in "his sovereign's war." Scholars suggest that this is a reference to the campaigns of the Hundred Years' War between England and France. However, based on the other references, the Knight must have served some forty years in northeastern Europe, the western Mediterranean, the Turkish empire of the eastern Mediterranean, and North Africa.

Have students trace the travels of the Knight and report on the culture and customs of the people occupying those regions today.

With locks as curly as if they had been pressed.
He was some twenty years of age, I guessed.
85 In stature he was of a moderate length,
With wonderful agility and strength.
He'd seen some service with the cavalry
In Flanders and Artois and Picardy[12]
And had done valiantly in little space
90 Of time, in hope to win his lady's grace.
He was embroidered like a meadow bright
And full of freshest flowers, red and white.
Singing he was, or fluting all the day;
He was as fresh as is the month of May.
95 Short was his gown, the sleeves were long and wide;
He knew the way to sit a horse and ride.
He could make songs and poems and recite,
Knew how to joust and dance, to draw and write.
He loved so hotly that till dawn grew pale
100 He slept as little as a nightingale.
Courteous he was, lowly and serviceable,
And carved to serve his father at the table.
    There was a *Yeoman*[13] with him at his side,
No other servant; so he chose to ride.
105 This Yeoman wore a coat and hood of green,
And peacock-feathered arrows, bright and keen
And neatly sheathed, hung at his belt the while
—For he could dress his gear in yeoman style,
His arrows never drooped their feathers low—
110 And in his hand he bore a mighty bow.
His head was like a nut, his face was brown.
He knew the whole of woodcraft up and down.
A saucy brace[14] was on his arm to ward
It from the bow-string, and a shield and sword
115 Hung at one side, and at the other slipped
A jaunty dirk,[15] spear-sharp and well-equipped.
A medal of St. Christopher[16] he wore
Of shining silver on his breast, and bore
A hunting-horn, well slung and burnished clean,
120 That dangled from a baldric[17] of bright green.
He was a proper forester I guess.
    There also was a *Nun*, a Prioress.[18]
Her way of smiling very simple and coy.

---

12. **Flanders . . . Picardy** regions in Belgium and France.
13. *Yeoman* (yōˊ mən) *n.* attendant.
14. **brace** bracelet.
15. **dirk** *n.* dagger.
16. **St. Christopher** patron saint of travelers.
17. **baldric** *n.* belt worn over one shoulder and across the chest to support a sword.
18. **Prioress** *n.* in an abbey, the nun ranking just below the abbess.

❽ ▼ Critical Viewing
Compare this portrait with Chaucer's description of the Yeoman. What details did the artist choose to change or omit? **[Compare and Contrast]**

❼

The Yeoman, Arthur Szyk for *The Canterbury Tales*

❾ Reading Check
What is the relationship among the Knight, the Squire and the Yeoman?

from *The Canterbury Tales: The Prologue* ■ 101

❼ Humanities

The Yeoman, 1946, by Arthur Szyk
In this miniature, painted in 1946 for *The Canterbury Tales*, the artist shows a fully equipped medieval yeoman. He appears ready for any occurrence in the forest, from the appearance of game to an attack by a highwayman. He is portrayed as a sturdy fellow with a serious expression on his face. In painting these miniatures, Arthur Szyk, with patience and meticulous care, imitates monkish manuscript painters. Through this painstaking effect, he succeeds in capturing the charm and medieval flavor of that art.

Use these questions for discussion:

1. How does Szyk's depiction of the Yeoman compare with your image of him?
   Possible responses: Some students may say that the art matches their image of the Yeoman. Other students may point out ways in which the artist's depiction differs from what they imagine. For many students, the Yeoman will match their images of Robin Hood.

2. What details of this illustration would you like to change?
   Possible response: Students may suggest ways to make the illustration match Chaucer's description more closely, such as changing the Yeoman's jacket to green, or putting a brace on his arm.

❽ Critical Viewing

Possible response: The Yeoman's arrows are slung over his shoulder rather than hanging at his belt as in Chaucer's description. The artist has also chosen to omit the arm brace, the medal of St. Christopher, and the hunting horn. Some students may dispute whether the coat and hood are green, as only the lining appears to be green. Students may also identify elements in the portrait that Chaucer does not mention, such as the purse and feathered cap.

❾ Reading Check

Answer: The Knight's son is the squire, and the squire's servant is the Yeoman.

Differentiated Instruction   Solutions for All Learners

Strategy for Less Proficient Readers
To help students keep track of details, write the titles of the various characters being described on the board or an overhead transparency. Then, as students read one description at a time, have them suggest character traits and descriptive elements, and list these beneath the appropriate title.

Background for English Learners
Use illustrations in the text to point out items described—for example, the Yeoman's bow, dirk, and arrows. For characters not illustrated, you may wish to bring in more pictures. In addition, students may benefit from seeing images of horses, a medieval town, and even of Canterbury Cathedral. Also, review footnotes with students, to make certain they understand the words in the definitions. For example, defining Prioress in terms of an abbey helps only if students know what an abbey is.

❿ Reading Strategy
Analyzing Difficult Sentences

- Remind students to break down any difficult or confusing sentences by asking questions of it, beginning with *who, what, how, when* and *where*.

- Then, **ask** students the Reading Strategy question: What two basic qualities does the sentence in lines 141–145 attribute to the Nun?
Answer: On the one hand, the Nun is friendly and entertaining, on the other hand, she is working very hard at pretending to be elegant.

⓫ Literary Analysis
Characterization

- Review with students how indirect and direct characterization reveal something about a character (p. 97 of text).

- Then, **ask** students the Literary Analysis question: What can you infer about the Prioress based on this detailed description of her jewelry?
Possible response: Most students will realize that the jewelry indicates wealth. Students may also suggest that it indicates a degree of worldliness.

- Point out the reference to Eglantyne in line 125, and explain that Eglantyne is a type of wild rose whose long, thorny stems readily entangle passersby. Eglantyne was also the name of several "clinging-vine" heroines in medieval romances.

- **Ask** students what Chaucer is saying about the Prioress by calling her Madam Eglantyne.
Possible response: He is saying that she is clinging, helpless, and perhaps a bit too dainty.

- Have students **identify** other elements of the description that show that the Prioress was excessively dainty, in Chaucer's view.
Possible response: Comments about her wiping "her upper lip so clean," and about being reduced to tears by seeing a mouse in a trap, suggest that Chaucer thinks her daintiness is extreme.

Her greatest oath was only "By St. Loy!"[19]
125 And she was known as Madam Eglantyne.
And well she sang a service,[20] with a fine
Intoning through her nose, as was most seemly,
And she spoke daintily in French, extremely,
After the school of Stratford-atte-Bowe;[21]
130 French in the Paris style she did not know.
At meat her manners were well taught withal;
No morsel from her lips did she let fall,
Nor dipped her fingers in the sauce too deep;
But she could carry a morsel up and keep
135 The smallest drop from falling on her breast.
For courtliness she had a special zest,
And she would wipe her upper lip so clean
That not a trace of grease was to be seen
Upon the cup when she had drunk; to eat,
140 She reached a hand sedately for the meat.
She certainly was very entertaining,
Pleasant and friendly in her ways, and straining
To counterfeit a courtly kind of grace,
A stately bearing fitting to her place,
145 And to seem dignified in all her dealings.
As for her sympathies and tender feelings,
She was so charitably <u>solicitous</u>
She used to weep if she but saw a mouse
Caught in a trap, if it were dead or bleeding.
150 And she had little dogs she would be feeding
With roasted flesh, or milk, or fine white bread.
And bitterly she wept if one were dead
Or someone took a stick and made it smart;
She was all sentiment and tender heart.
155 Her veil was gathered in a seemly way,
Her nose was elegant, her eyes glass-gray;
Her mouth was very small, but soft and red,
Her forehead, certainly, was fair of spread,
Almost a span[22] across the brows, I own;
160 She was indeed by no means undergrown.
Her cloak, I noticed, had a graceful charm.
She wore a coral trinket on her arm,
A set of beads, the gaudies[23] tricked in green,
Whence hung a golden brooch of brightest sheen
165 On which there first was graven a crowned *A*,

19. **St. Loy** St. Eligius, patron saint of goldsmiths and courtiers.
20. **service** daily prayer.
21. **Stratford-atte-Bowe** nunnery near London.
22. **span** nine inches.
23. **gaudies** large green beads that marked certain prayers on a set of prayer beads.

Reading Strategy
Analyzing Difficult Sentences What two basic qualities does the sentence in lines 141–145 attribute to the Nun?

Vocabulary Builder
solicitous (sə lis′ ə təs) *adj.* showing care or concern

Literary Analysis
Characterization What can you infer about the Prioress based on this detailed description of her jewelry?

And lower, *Amor vincit omnia.*[24]
    Another *Nun*, the chaplain at her cell,
Was riding with her, and *three Priests* as well.
    A *Monk* there was, one of the finest sort
170 Who rode the country; hunting was his sport.
A manly man, to be an Abbot able;
Many a dainty horse he had in stable.
His bridle, when he rode, a man might hear
Jingling in a whistling wind as clear,
175 Aye, and as loud as does the chapel bell
Where my lord Monk was Prior of the cell.
The Rule of good St. Benet or St. Maur[25]
As old and strict he tended to ignore;
He let go by the things of yesterday
180 And took the modern world's more spacious way.
He did not rate that text at a plucked hen
Which says that hunters are not holy men
And that a monk uncloistered is a mere
Fish out of water, flapping on the pier,
185 That is to say a monk out of his cloister.
That was a text he held not worth an oyster;
And I agreed and said his views were sound;
Was he to study till his head went round
Poring over books in cloisters? Must he toil
190 As Austin[26] bade and till the very soil?
Was he to leave the world upon the shelf?
Let Austin have his labor to himself.
    This Monk was therefore a good man to horse;
Greyhounds he had, as swift as birds, to course.
195 Hunting a hare or riding at a fence
Was all his fun, he spared for no expense.
I saw his sleeves were <u>garnished</u> at the hand
With fine gray fur, the finest in the land,
And on his hood, to fasten it at his chin
200 He had a wrought-gold cunningly fashioned pin;
Into a lover's knot it seemed to pass.
His head was bald and shone like looking-glass;
So did his face, as if it had been greased.
He was a fat and personable priest;
205 His prominent eyeballs never seemed to settle.
They glittered like the flames beneath a kettle;
Supple his boots, his horse in fine condition.
He was a prelate fit for exhibition,
He was not pale like a tormented soul.

---

24. **Amor vincit omnia** (ä′ môr′ vin′ chit ôm′ nē ä′) "love conquers all" (Latin).
25. **St. Benet or St. Maur** St. Benedict, author of monastic rules, and St. Maurice, one of his followers. Benet and Maur are French versions of Benedict and Maurice.
26. **Austin** English version of St. Augustine, who criticized lazy monks.

⑬ ▼ Critical Viewing
What can you infer from this picture about the Monk's style of living? List three details supporting your conclusion. **[Infer]**

The Monk, Arthur Szyk for *The Canterbury Tales*

Vocabulary Builder
garnished (gär′ nisht) *adj.*
decorated; trimmed

⑭ ✔ Reading Check
What is the Monk's main interest?

from The Canterbury Tales: The Prologue ■ 103

Reteach: Remind students that social commentary is writing that provides insights into society, its values, and its customs. By helping us understand the era of a work, social commentary helps us understand the motives and lives of the individuals who lived in that society.

- Have students **identify** key elements of the description of the Monk.
  Possible response: He loves to hunt, rides a horse well, likes to eat (he's fat, and he "liked a fat swan best"); he ignores any doctrine he doesn't like.

Monitor Progress: Ask students the first Literary Analysis question: What do the details about the Monk indirectly suggest about religious institutions of the time?
Possible response: It seems likely that the religious institutions of the time provided a comfortable lifestyle for some without requiring special devotion from them.

16 Vocabulary Builder
Latin Suffix -tion

- Call students' attention to the word *absolution* and its definition. Explain that the suffix *-tion* is derived from Latin and means "the act or process of."

- Have students **suggest** other words and phrases that contain this Latin suffix, and list them on the chalkboard.
  Possible responses: *solution, illustration, assignation, motivation, illumination*

- Have students look up any unfamiliar words in a dictionary.

17 Literary Analysis
Characterization

- Review with students the differences between indirect and direct characterization.

- Then, **ask** students the second Literary Analysis question: In lines 244–254, is Chaucer using direct characterization or indirect characterization? Explain.
  Answer: Chaucer is using an indirect method of characterization: He describes who the Friar knew and where he spent his time.

104

---

15 210　He liked a fat swan best, and roasted whole.
　　　His palfrey[27] was as brown as is a berry.
　　　　　There was a *Friar*, a wanton[28] one and merry
　　　A Limiter,[29] a very festive fellow.
　　　In all Four Orders[30] there was none so mellow
215　So glib with gallant phrase and well-turned speech.
　　　He'd fixed up many a marriage, giving each
　　　Of his young women what he could afford her.
　　　He was a noble pillar to his Order.
　　　Highly beloved and intimate was he
220　With County folk[31] within his boundary,
　　　And city dames of honor and possessions;
　　　For he was qualified to hear confessions,
　　　Or so he said, with more than priestly scope;
　　　He had a special license from the Pope.
225　Sweetly he heard his penitents at shrift[32]
16　　　With pleasant <u>absolution</u>, for a gift.
　　　He was an easy man in penance-giving
　　　Where he could hope to make a decent living;
　　　It's a sure sign whenever gifts are given
230　To a poor Order that a man's well shriven,[33]
　　　And should he give enough he knew in verity
　　　The penitent repented in sincerity.
　　　For many a fellow is so hard of heart
　　　He cannot weep, for all his inward smart.
235　Therefore instead of weeping and of prayer
　　　One should give silver for a poor Friar's care.
　　　He kept his tippet[34] stuffed with pins for curls,
　　　And pocket-knives, to give to pretty girls.
　　　And certainly his voice was gay and sturdy,
240　For he sang well and played the hurdy-gurdy.[35]
　　　At sing-songs he was champion of the hour.
　　　His neck was whiter than a lily-flower
　　　But strong enough to butt a bruiser down.
　　　He knew the taverns well in every town
17　245　And every innkeeper and barmaid too
　　　Better than lepers, beggars and that crew,
　　　For in so eminent a man as he
　　　It was not fitting with the dignity

---

27. **palfrey** *n.* saddle horse.
28. **wanton** *adj.* jolly.
29. **Limiter** friar who is given begging rights for a certain limited area.
30. **Four Orders** There were four orders of friars who supported themselves by begging: Dominicans, Franciscans, Carmelites, and Augustinians.
31. **County folk** The phrase refers to rich landowners.
32. **shrift** *n.* confession.
33. **well shriven** *adj.* absolved of his sins.
34. **tippet** *n.* hood.
35. **hurdy-gurdy** stringed instrument played by cranking a wheel.

Literary Analysis
Characterization and Social Commentary What do the details about the Monk's habits and tastes indirectly suggest about religious institutions of the time?

Vocabulary Builder
absolution (ab′ sə lo͞o′ shən) *n.* act of freeing someone of a sin or of a criminal charge

Literary Analysis
Characterization In lines 244–254, is Chaucer using direct characterization or indirect characterization? Explain.

Enrichment

The Clergy

In the Middle Ages, some people entered the clergy because they felt called to a life of devotion. However, this was not always the case. Because inheritance laws gave all land and titles to first-born sons, other sons had to make their own fortunes. Generally, second sons became knights, seeking glory in battle, while third sons went into the church. In those days, the church held power that was second only to the crown's—and was often even greater.

As a result, it was common for members of the clergy to be wealthy, because they came from wealthy, noble families. It was also common for them to have only as much interest in religion as was necessary to get ahead. While there were still honorable and devoted people within the church, they were often outnumbered by those who were in it for the power. This situation resulted in many abuses, some of which were not addressed until the Reformation.

Of his position, dealing with a scum
250 Of wretched lepers; nothing good can come
Of dealings with the slum-and-gutter dwellers,
But only with the rich and victual-sellers.
But anywhere a profit might accrue
Courteous he was and lowly of service too.
255 Natural gifts like his were hard to match.
He was the finest beggar of his batch,
And, for his begging-district, payed a rent;
His brethren did no poaching where he went.
For though a widow mightn't have a shoe,
260 So pleasant was his holy how-d'ye-do
He got his farthing from her just the same
Before he left, and so his income came
To more than he laid out. And how he romped,
Just like a puppy! He was ever prompt
265 To arbitrate disputes on settling days
(For a small fee) in many helpful ways,
Not then appearing as your cloistered scholar
With threadbare habit hardly worth a dollar,
But much more like a Doctor or a Pope.
270 Of double-worsted was the semi-cope[36]
Upon his shoulders, and the swelling fold
About him, like a bell about its mold
When it is casting, rounded out his dress.
He lisped a little out of wantonness
275 To make his English sweet upon his tongue.
When he had played his harp, or having sung,
His eyes would twinkle in his head as bright
As any star upon a frosty night.
This worthy's name was Hubert, it appeared.
280   There was a *Merchant* with a forking beard
And motley dress, high on his horse he sat,
Upon his head a Flemish[37] beaver hat
And on his feet daintily buckled boots.
He told of his opinions and pursuits
285 In solemn tones, and how he never lost.
The sea should be kept free at any cost
(He thought) upon the Harwich-Holland range,[38]
He was expert at currency exchange.
This estimable Merchant so had set
290 His wits to work, none knew he was in debt,
He was so stately in negotiation,
Loan, bargain and commercial obligation.

---

36. **semi-cope** cape.
37. **Flemish** from Flanders.
38. **Harwich-Holland range** the North Sea between England and Holland.

 Reading Strategy
**Analyzing Difficult
Sentences** What is the
main thought in the
sentence in lines 259–263?
What question about this
main idea (*who, what,
where, when, why,* or *how*)
do the other parts of the
sentence help answer?

**Reading Check**
How does the Friar earn
his living?

from *The Canterbury Tales: The Prologue* ■ 105

⑱ Reading Strategy
Analyzing Difficult Sentences

• Explain to students that, unlike monks, whose work lay within a monastery, friars were itinerant clergymen whose begging supported schools, hospitals, the poor, and other church-related institutions—or it was supposed to. The Friar exemplifies the corruption to which many of these people had sunk by Chaucer's time.

• **Ask** students the Reading Strategy question: What is the main thought in the sentence in lines 259–263? **Possible response:** The *who* in the sentence is both the Friar (the sentence's subject) and the widow; *what* is the farthing (money); *when* is before he leaves; *why* is because he wants an income; *how* is he is such a skillful beggar. The main idea is that he gets money even from the poor to supplement his own income.

• The Friar's job was supposed to include helping the poor, and the teachings of Christianity include protecting widows and helping the poor. **Ask** students, with this in mind, what they can deduce about the Friar's beliefs. **Possible response:** It is evident that the Friar cares nothing about what he is supposed to be doing or what he says he believes. He is in it for the money, and possibly for the good opinion being a member of the clergy might gain him.

⑲ Reading Check

Answer: The Friar earns his living by skillful begging.

**Differentiated
Instruction**   Solutions for All Learners

**Strategy for
Less Proficient Readers**
To help students appreciate the rhythm of the language in the selection, read selected passages aloud as students follow along in their textbooks. Hearing the poetry will also help students understand that they should not stop at the end of a line unless a punctuation mark indicates that they should do so.

**Vocabulary for
Gifted/Talented Students**
Students may enjoy creating the kind of brief, vivid description that Chaucer uses to introduce us to the characters in his tale. Encourage students to think of a character from a story or movie, and write a description of him or her that uses specific, revealing images. Rhyming is optional.

**Enrichment for
Advanced Readers**
Some students who read *The Prologue* may be fascinated by the actual travel involved in making a pilgrimage. You may want to direct these students to a travel agency for a further look at planning a journey, and a connection to a career in travel.

⑳ Humanities

The Student, 1946, by Arthur Szyk

In the miniature, *The Student,* Szyk cleverly shows the Oxford Cleric's preference for intellectual attainment over worldly matters. His drab tunic and patched knees contrast with his intent expression as he reads his book. He absently gestures with his left hand as if in conversation with himself, unaware of the picture he presents to others. Although not as decorative as the other, more richly dressed characters illustrated by Szyk, the student is detailed with care and skill.

Use these questions for discussion:

1. Do you think Szyk's miniature captures the personality of the Oxford Cleric as Chaucer has portrayed him?
   Possible responses: Students will probably say that the miniature captures the Oxford Cleric's "unworldly," studious personality.

2. Does Szyk's student remind you of any young scholar you have ever seen?
   Answer: Students may be reminded of classmates or acquaintances whom they characterize as bookworms or nerds.

㉑ Critical Viewing

Possible responses: Students may conclude that the student likes to read and lives rather frugally. These characteristics are suggested by the following details: He is reading; his hose are patched at the knees; and he lacks the more luxurious purses, swords, and adornment seen in the pictures of the other pilgrims.

He was an excellent fellow all the same;
To tell the truth I do not know his name.

295   An *Oxford Cleric,* still a student though,
One who had taken logic long ago,
Was there; his horse was thinner than a rake,
And he was not too fat, I undertake,
But had a hollow look, a sober stare;

300   The thread upon his overcoat was bare.
He had found no preferment in the church
And he was too unworldly to make search
For secular employment. By his bed
He preferred having twenty books in red

305   And black, of Aristotle's[39] philosophy,
To having fine clothes, fiddle or psaltery.[40]
Though a philosopher, as I have told,
He had not found the stone for making gold.[41]
Whatever money from his friends he took

310   He spent on learning or another book
And prayed for them most earnestly, returning
Thanks to them thus for paying for his learning.
His only care was study, and indeed
He never spoke a word more than was need,

315   Formal at that, respectful in the extreme,
Short, to the point, and lofty in his theme.
The thought of moral virtue filled his speech
And he would gladly learn, and gladly teach.
    A *Sergeant at the Law* who paid his calls,

320   Wary and wise, for clients at St. Paul's[42]
There also was, of noted excellence.
Discreet he was, a man to reverence,
Or so he seemed, his sayings were so wise.
He often had been Justice of Assize

325   By letters patent, and in full <u>commission</u>.
His fame and learning and his high position
Had won him many a robe and many a fee.
There was no such conveyancer[43] as he;
All was fee-simple[44] to his strong digestion,

330   Not one conveyance could be called in question.
Nowhere there was so busy a man as he;
But was less busy than he seemed to be.

---

39. Aristotle's (ar´ is tät´ əlz) referring to the Greek philosopher (384–322 B.C.).
40. psaltery (sôl´ tər ē) ancient stringed instrument.
41. stone . . . gold At the time, alchemists believed that a "philosopher's stone" existed that could turn base metals into gold.
42. St. Paul's London cathedral near the center of legal activities in the city. Lawyers often met near there to discuss cases.
43. conveyancer one who draws up documents for transferring ownership of property.
44. fee-simple unrestricted ownership.

⑳

The Student, Arthur Szyk for *The Canterbury Tales*

㉑ ▲ **Critical Viewing**
What can you infer from this picture about the Oxford Cleric's style of living? List three details supporting your conclusion. **[Infer]**

Vocabulary Builder
commission (kə mish´ ən)
n. authorization; act of giving authority to an individual

Enrichment

Chaucer's Travels

Considering that Chaucer's characters have traveled as widely as they have and experienced the ups and downs of fortune, it is interesting to trace the advances and reversals of the author himself. In a book entitled *The History of English Literature,* Peter Quennell reports the following:

Between 1370 and 1386, Chaucer undertook a variety of important diplomatic missions. Thus he made an official journey to Italy toward the end of 1372, when he visited Genoa, Pisa, and Florence, and remained for over ten months; in 1377 he was dispatched to Flanders and France; in 1378 he was returned to France and, soon afterwards, set forth on another errand to Italy. His activities were well rewarded—not only with such minor privileges as the right to demand a jug of wine from the pantry of the royal butler, but with the comptrollership of the duties of wool and skins and, later, the comptrollership of the Petty Customs.

He knew of every judgment, case and crime
Recorded, ever since King William's time.
335 He could dictate defenses or draft deeds;
No one could pinch a comma from his screeds,[45]
And he knew every statute off by rote.
He wore a homely parti-colored coat
Girt with a silken belt of pin-stripe stuff;
340 Of his appearance I have said enough.
       There was a *Franklin*[46] with him, it appeared;
White as a daisy-petal was his beard.
A <u>sanguine</u> man, high-colored and benign,
He loved a morning sop[47] of cake in wine.
345 He lived for pleasure and had always done,
For he was Epicurus'[48] very son,
In whose opinion sensual delight
Was the one true felicity in sight.
As noted as St. Julian[49] was for bounty
350 He made his household free to all the County.
His bread, his ale were the finest of the fine
And no one had a better stock of wine.
His house was never short of bake-meat pies,
Of fish and flesh, and these in such supplies
355 It positively snowed with meat and drink
And all the dainties that a man could think.
According to the seasons of the year
Changes of dish were ordered to appear.
He kept fat partridges in coops, beyond,
360 Many a bream and pike were in his pond.
Woe to the cook whose sauces had no sting
Or who was unprepared in anything!
And in his hall a table stood arrayed
And ready all day long, with places laid.
365 As Justice at the Sessions[50] none stood higher;
He often had been Member for the Shire.[51]
A dagger and a little purse of silk
Hung at his girdle, white as morning milk.
As Sheriff he checked audit, every entry.
370 He was a model among landed gentry.
       A *Haberdasher*, a *Dyer*, a *Carpenter*,
A *Weaver* and a *Carpet-maker* were

---

45. **screeds** long, boring speeches or pieces of writing.
46. *Franklin* wealthy landowner.
47. **sop** piece.
48. **Epicurus'** (ep´ i kyoor´ əs) referring to a Greek philosopher (341–270 B.C.) who believed that happiness is the most important goal in life.
49. **St. Julian** patron saint of hospitality.
50. **Sessions** court sessions.
51. **Member . . . Shire** Parliamentary representative for the county.

Vocabulary Builder
sanguine (saŋ´ gwin) *adj.*
confident; cheerful

Reading Strategy
**Analyzing Difficult
Sentences** What question
do lines 346–348 answer
about the main idea in
line 345?

Literary Analysis
Characterization What
are the Franklin's
interests?

Reading Check
What are the Cleric's
interests?

from *The Canterbury Tales: The Prologue* ■ 107

㉒ Reading Strategy
Analyzing Difficult Sentences

• Tell students to check the footnotes regularly as they read and to think about what the information provided adds to the descriptions.

• Remind students that, as with most poetry, a line end does not mean the end of a sentence. Encourage students to be guided by punctuation, rather than by line breaks, as they read.

• **Ask** students the Reading Strategy question: What question do lines 346–348 answer about the main idea in line 345?
Possible response: The lines answer the question *why,* revealing why the Franklin lived for pleasure.

㉓ Literary Analysis
Characterization

• Tell students that the word *franklin* comes from a Middle English word, *frankelein,* which means *free man.* It is related to the Old French of *franc,* which meant *free.*

• Explain that, in Chaucer's day, the social position of franklin was a relatively new one. The middle class was just emerging. During most of the Middle Ages, a free landowner who was not part of the nobility simply did not exist.

• **Ask** students the Literary Analysis question: What are the Franklin's interests?
Possible response: He loves food and drink. He loves to entertain and has a reputation for hospitality. He is also involved in community affairs and has been a judge, sheriff, and Parliamentary representative.

• You may wish to **discuss** with students why someone like the Franklin, who is a member of a class of free men which did not exist until recently, might have the interests the Franklin has.
Possible response: It seems natural that people who had been locked out of both government and the possibility of wealth and landownership for so long would eagerly exercise these options once they were free to do so.

㉔ Reading Check
Answer: The Cleric likes books of philosophy.

- **Point out** that this group of successful, affluent, skilled workers would be part of the new, rising middle class, perhaps even achieving, and certainly desiring, the status of upper class.

- **Ask** students the first Literary Analysis question: What point is Chaucer making about the relationship between these men and their wives?
Possible response: It seems that their wives are eager social climbers who urge their husbands to run for office. The fact that the men are stylishly dressed and successful shows that they either agree with their wives or are motivated by their wives' wishes (prodding, nagging).

26 Literary Analysis
Characterization

- **Ask** students what they can infer from line 400.
Answer: The Skipper probably rides badly, because he lives at sea.

- **Point out** that the places named in Chaucer's description were as far as anyone was sailing in those days, and suggest the Skipper's considerable experience. In fact, the name Finisterre means "end of the earth."

- **Ask** students the second Literary Analysis question: What picture of the Skipper is created by the mixture of details about his heartlessness with details about his competence?
Possible response: He is ruthless with enemies but is very competent. He is able to withstand hardship and is a careful, judicious planner. He probably thinks of things in terms of results.

- **Point out** that the name of his barge, *The Maudelayne,* is the word from which we get *maudlin,* which means either "weepy sentimentality" or "tearful and silly due to drunkenness." You may wish to discuss with students why Chaucer may have chosen this name.
Possible responses: Irony, because the Skipper seems unsentimental, or a reference to the drinking noted in lines 406–407.

Among our ranks, all in the livery
Of one impressive guild-fraternity.[52]
375 They were so trim and fresh their gear would pass
For new. Their knives were not tricked out with brass
But wrought with purest silver, which <u>avouches</u>
A like display on girdles and on pouches.
Each seemed a worthy burgess,[53] fit to grace
380 A guild-hall with a seat upon the dais.
Their wisdom would have justified a plan
To make each one of them an alderman;
They had the capital and revenue,
Besides their wives declared it was their due.
385 And if they did not think so, then they ought;
To be called "*Madam*" is a glorious thought,
And so is going to church and being seen
Having your mantle carried like a queen.
       They had a *Cook* with them who stood alone
390 For boiling chicken with a marrow-bone,
Sharp flavoring-powder and a spice for savor.
He could distinguish London ale by flavor,
And he could roast and seethe and broil and fry,
Make good thick soup and bake a tasty pie.
395 But what a pity—so it seemed to me,
That he should have an ulcer on his knee.
As for blancmange,[54] he made it with the best.
       There was a *Skipper* hailing from far west;
He came from Dartmouth, so I understood.
400 He rode a farmer's horse as best he could,
In a woolen gown that reached his knee.
A dagger on a lanyard[55] falling free
Hung from his neck under his arm and down.
The summer heat had tanned his color brown,
405 And certainly he was an excellent fellow.
Many a draught of vintage, red and yellow,
He'd drawn at Bordeaux, while the trader snored.
The nicer rules of conscience he ignored.
If, when he fought, the enemy vessel sank,
410 He sent his prisoners home; they walked the plank.
As for his skill in reckoning his tides,
Currents and many another risk besides,
Moons, harbors, pilots, he had such dispatch
That none from Hull to Carthage was his match.

---

52. **guild-fraternity** In the Middle Ages, associations of men practicing the same craft or trade, called guilds, set standards for workmanship and protected their members by controlling competition.
53. **burgess** member of a legislative body.
54. **blancmange** (blə mänzh´) at the time, the name of a creamy chicken dish.
55. **lanyard** loose rope around the neck.

Enrichment

The Skilled Trades

Chaucer includes several skilled tradesmen in his tale. Some, like the Carpenter, practice trades still well known today. Others, like the Miller, a person who operates a grain mill, practice trades that have all but disappeared, having been made obsolete by technology.

Chaucer heaps praise on the Cook for seven of the nine lines he devotes to this pilgrim. Students may want to analyze the importance of the food preparer in medieval society.

Have interested students investigate which skilled trades have disappeared or come into being over the years. You might help them get started by having them look up what a fletcher did for a living and when welding became an important skill.

415   Hardy he was, prudent in undertaking;
      His beard in many a tempest had its shaking,
      And he knew all the havens as they were
      From Gottland to the Cape of Finisterre,
      And every creek in Brittany and Spain;
420   The barge he owned was called *The Maudelayne.*

      A *Doctor* too emerged as we proceeded;
      No one alive could talk as well as he did
      On points of medicine and of surgery,
      For, being grounded in astronomy,
425   He watched his patient's favorable star
      And, by his Natural Magic, knew what are
      The lucky hours and planetary degrees
      For making charms and magic effigies.
      The cause of every malady you'd got
430   He knew, and whether dry, cold, moist or hot;[56]
      He knew their seat, their humor and condition.
      He was a perfect practicing physician.
      These causes being known for what they were,
      He gave the man his medicine then and there.
435   All his apothecaries[57] in a tribe
      Were ready with the drugs he would prescribe,
      And each made money from the other's guile;
      They had been friendly for a goodish while.
      He was well-versed in Aesculapius[58] too
440   And what Hippocrates and Rufus knew
      And Dioscorides, now dead and gone,
      Galen and Rhazes, Hali, Serapion,
      Averroes, Avicenna, Constantine,
      Scotch Bernard, John of Gaddesden, Gilbertine.[59]
445   In his own diet he observed some measure;
      There were no superfluities for pleasure,
      Only digestives, nutritives and such.
      He did not read the Bible very much.
      In blood-red garments, slashed with bluish-gray
450   And lined with taffeta,[60] he rode his way;
      Yet he was rather close as to expenses
      And kept the gold he won in pestilences.
      Gold stimulates the heart, or so we're told.
      He therefore had a special love of gold.
455   A worthy *woman* from beside Bath[61] city

---

56. The cause . . . hot It was believed that the body was composed of four "humors" (cold and dry, hot and moist, hot and dry, cold and moist) and that diseases resulted from a disturbance of one of these "humors."
57. apothecaries (ə päth′ə ker′ ēz) persons who prepared medicines.
58. Aesculapius (es′ kyoo lā′ pē əs) in Roman mythology, the god of medicine and healing.
59. Hippocrates . . . Gilbertine famous physicians and medical authorities.
60. taffeta (taf′ i tə) fine silk fabric.
61. Bath English resort city.

**Reading Strategy
Analyzing Difficult Sentences** In the sentence in lines 421–428, what is said about *how* the Doctor practices medicine?

27

 28 **Reading Check**

What are two characteristics of the Skipper?

from The Canterbury Tales: The Prologue ■ 109

---

27 **Reading Strategy**
Analyzing Difficult Sentences

- Explain that *astronomy* in line 424 really means *astrology* in this context. Astronomy is the scientific study of the universe; astrology is the divination of the supposed influence of the stars on human events.

- Tell students that people didn't know about germs until the nineteenth century. Point out the footnote about humors, and explain that some of the ways in which humors were "balanced" were through purging or bleeding patients.

- Explain that an effigy (line 428) was usually a human figure, and **ask** students why they think an effigy might have been used to "treat" a disease.
Possible responses: Students may be reminded of voodoo, where pins are stuck in a doll to hurt the person the doll represents. This would be the reverse, using the doll to heal the person represented. They may also be aware of the practice of burning enemies in effigy, which also might relate to the magic and charms of destroying the disease.

- Students may be interested to know that the line (448) about not reading the Bible very much probably has two applications for this character: the Bible has clear instruction about washing thoroughly before and after caring for the sick, which would relate to his medical practice, and the Bible also states that "the love of money is the root of all kinds of evil," which would connect to line 454 and the Doctor's "special love of gold."

- To help students learn more about the Doctor's practices, **ask** them the Reading Strategy question: In the sentence in lines 421–428, what is said about *how* the Doctor practices medicine?
Answer: The Doctor watches people's stars (rather than their illnesses) and makes charms and magic images based on "lucky hours," rather than on any diagnosis of disease.

28 **Reading Check**

Possible response: The Skipper is a skilled navigator but is ruthless in dealing with enemies.

109

The Wife of Bath, 1946, by
Arthur Szyk

In this miniature the artist shows the good Wife of Bath to be an imposing and decorative figure. The provocative posture and bold eyes are in keeping with Chaucer's description of her. The tiny details of dress, such as the gold buttons and the heart pattern on her belt, show the extreme skill of the artist in executing a painting on such a small scale. When discussing this painting with your class, point out similarities between Szyk's portrait of the Wife of Bath and Chaucer's written account of her.

Use these questions for discussion:

1. What impression of the Wife's personality does the painting express?
   Possible response: She is bold, saucy, and outspoken.

2. What does Chaucer's description of her convey that the painting does not?
   Possible response: Students may point out physical details that the artist chose not to include, such as her wimple or gap-teeth. Chaucer's description also includes details that cannot be shown in the portrait, such as her deafness, her skill at clothmaking, her anger when others do not defer to her, and her love of traveling.

30 **Critical Viewing**

Possible response: Students may say that the Wife's self-assured, bold stance suggests confidence, independence, and even superiority to others on the journey. Her cane, gold buttons, and fur-trimmed attire imply a degree of wealth. Her hat and smile could be evidence of a flamboyance that is reinforced by Chaucer's poem.

31 **Reading Strategy**
Analyzing Difficult Sentences

- Suggest that students break the sentence into smaller sections.

- Then, **ask** them the Reading Strategy question: What is the main idea in lines 493–500?
  Answer: The Parson is a good, kind, patient man. He is poor because he gives away his belongings to his parishioners.

110

Was with us, somewhat deaf, which was a pity.
In making cloth she showed so great a bent
She bettered those of Ypres and of Ghent.[62]
In all the parish not a dame dared stir
460 Towards the altar steps in front of her,
And if indeed they did, so wrath was she
As to be quite put out of charity.
Her kerchiefs were of finely woven ground;[63]
I dared have sworn they weighed a good ten pound,
465 The ones she wore on Sunday, on her head.
Her hose were of the finest scarlet red
And gartered tight; her shoes were soft and new.
Bold was her face, handsome, and red in hue.
A worthy woman all her life, what's more
470 She'd had five husbands, all at the church door,
Apart from other company in youth;
No need just now to speak of that, forsooth.
And she had thrice been to Jerusalem,
Seen many strange rivers and passed over them;
475 She'd been to Rome and also to Boulogne,
St. James of Compostella and Cologne,[64]
And she was skilled in wandering by the way.
She had gap-teeth, set widely, truth to say.
Easily on an ambling horse she sat
480 Well wimpled[65] up, and on her head a hat
As broad as is a buckler[66] or a shield;
She had a flowing mantle that concealed
Large hips, her heels spurred sharply under that.
In company she liked to laugh and chat
485 And knew the remedies for love's mischances,
An art in which she knew the oldest dances.
       A holy-minded man of good renown
There was, and poor, the *Parson* to a town,
Yet he was rich in holy thought and work.
490 He also was a learned man, a clerk,
Who truly knew Christ's gospel and would preach it
Devoutly to parishioners, and teach it.
Benign and wonderfully diligent,
And patient when adversity was sent
495 (For so he proved in great adversity)
He much disliked extorting tithe[67] or fee,

---

62. **Ypres** (ē′ prə) **and of Ghent** (gent) Flemish cities known for wool making.
63. **ground** composite fabric.
64. **Jerusalem . . . Rome . . . Boulogne . . . St. James of Compostella . . . Cologne** famous pilgrimage sites at the time.
65. **wimpled** wearing a scarf covering the head, neck, and chin.
66. **buckler** small round shield.
67. **tithe** (tīth) one tenth of a person's income, paid as a tax to support the church.

30 ▲ **Critical Viewing**
What does the Wife of Bath's pose convey about her character? [Analyze]

Reading Strategy
Analyzing Difficult Sentences What is the main idea in lines 493–500?

Enrichment

Plague

Plague, which is caused by the bacterium *Yersinia pestis,* is primarily a disease of rats and the fleas that feed upon them. Under certain conditions, the fleas bite humans, transmitting the plague-causing bacterium.

There are three forms of plague in humans: bubonic, pneumonic, and septicemic. Bubonic plague is characterized by swellings (buboes) of the lymph nodes, and is transmitted from person to person only by fleas. Pneumonic plague is a severe infection of the lungs that can be transmitted directly from one person to another. Pneumonic plague is extremely contagious and is usually fatal. Septicemic plague causes a massive infection of the blood that causes death before bubonic or pneumonic signs appear. Because of the way plague is transmitted, the most severe epidemics occur in crowded, unsanitary urban areas where people live in close proximity to rats—such as medieval cities.

Nay rather he preferred beyond a doubt
Giving to poor parishioners round about
From his own goods and Easter offerings
500 He found sufficiency in little things.
Wide was his parish, with houses far asunder,
Yet he neglected not in rain or thunder,
In sickness or in grief, to pay a call
      On the remotest, whether great or small,
505 Upon his feet, and in his hand a stave.
This noble example to his sheep he gave,
First following the word before he taught it,
And it was from the gospel he had caught it.
This little proverb he would add thereto
510 That if gold rust, what then will iron do?
For if a priest be foul in whom we trust
No wonder that a common man should rust;
And shame it is to see—let priests take stock—
A soiled shepherd and a snowy flock.
515 The true example that a priest should give
Is one of cleanness, how the sheep should live.
He did not set his benefice to hire[68]
And leave his sheep encumbered in the mire
Or run to London to earn easy bread
520 By singing masses for the wealthy dead,
Or find some Brotherhood and get enrolled.
He stayed at home and watched over his fold
So that no wolf should make the sheep miscarry.
He was a shepherd and no mercenary.
525 Holy and virtuous he was, but then
Never contemptuous of sinful men,
Never disdainful, never too proud or fine,
But was discreet in teaching and benign.
His business was to show a fair behavior
530 And draw men thus to Heaven and their Savior,
Unless indeed a man were obstinate;
And such, whether of high or low estate,
He put to sharp rebuke to say the least.
I think there never was a better priest.
535 He sought no pomp or glory in his dealings,
No scrupulosity had spiced his feelings.
Christ and His Twelve Apostles and their lore
He taught, but followed it himself before.
      There was a *Plowman* with him there, his brother.
540 Many a load of dung one time or other
He must have carted through the morning dew.
He was an honest worker, good and true,

---

68. **set . . . hire** pay someone else to perform his parish duties.

32

**Literary Analysis
Characterization and
Social Commentary**
How does Chaucer use
his characterization of the
Parson to comment on
the way priests ought to
behave?

33  **Reading Check**
What is the Parson's main
characteristic?

from *The Canterbury Tales: The Prologue* ■ 111

32 **Literary Analysis
Characterization and Social
Commentary**

- Encourage students to list specific things that Chaucer identifies as either actions or traits of the Parson.

- You may want to discuss in class which of these traits have already been shown to be lacking in other members of the clergy in the group. For example, the Parson gives to the poor, while the Friar was described as taking the farthing from the poor widow (lines 259–263).

- **Ask** students the Literary Analysis question: How does Chaucer use his characterization of the Parson to comment on the way priests ought to behave?
  Answer: He shows that the Parson not only knows well what he says he believes, he lives out his beliefs. He leads by example. Most of the virtues he exhibits are in direct contrast to traits of others in the group, from the hypocrisy of the clergy to the vanity and greed of the merchants to the ruthlessness of the Skipper.

- Because Chaucer says that the Parson is "an example to his sheep," what can we assume that Chaucer feels about how others ought to behave, even if they are not in the clergy?
  Answer: It is evident that Chaucer feels that others should share the traits of integrity, kindness, and generosity exhibited by the Parson.

33 **Reading Check**

Possible response: The Parson's main characteristic is that he lives out what he professes to believe.

**Differentiated
Instruction** Solutions for All Learners

Enrichment for Advanced Readers
Suggest that students read additional works by Geoffrey Chaucer, such as *Book of Duchess, House of Fame,* and *Troilus and Criseyde.* You may also wish to use **Authors In Depth,** The British Tradition, which contains the following additional selection:
- *from* The Knight's Tale
  Additional tales from *The Canterbury Tales* can also be found by going to www.PHSchool.com and following the hot links for this selection.

After students have read additional works by Chaucer, have them form discussion groups in which they compare and contrast the selections they have read. Suggest criteria for comparison, such as characterization, lessons or morals to stories, sentiment, social commentary, or ideas. To extend that activity, have volunteers present to the class brief oral reports on their favorite Chaucer selections.

111

34 Literary Analysis
Characterization and Social Commentary

- **Ask** students the Literary Analysis question: What social commentary does the description of the Plowman provide?

Answer: The plowman is a good citizen, and Chaucer suggests his virtues by indicating how he helps the poor, pays his tithes on time, and loves God and his neighbor heartily.

35 Literary Analysis
Characterization

- **Ask** students the second Literary Analysis question: What does the comparison of the Miller's hair color to that of a sow or a fox indirectly suggest about his character?

Answer: Students should recognize that by associating the Miller's hair with that of a sow and a fox, Chaucer links him to common characteristics of those animals—slovenliness and cunning.

Living in peace and perfect charity,
And, as the gospel bade him, so did he,
545 Loving God best with all his heart and mind
And then his neighbor as himself, repined
At no misfortune, slacked for no content,
For steadily about his work he went
To thrash his corn, to dig or to manure
550 Or make a ditch; and he would help the poor
For love of Christ and never take a penny
If he could help it, and, as prompt as any,
He paid his tithes in full when they were due
On what he owned, and on his earnings too.
555 He wore a tabard[69] smock and rode a mare.
There was a *Reeve*,[70] also a *Miller*, there,
A College *Manciple*[71] from the Inns of Court,
A papal *Pardoner*[72] and, in close consort,
A Church-Court *Summoner*,[73] riding at a trot,
560 And finally myself—that was the lot.
    The *Miller* was a chap of sixteen stone,[74]
A great stout fellow big in brawn and bone.
He did well out of them, for he could go
And win the ram at any wrestling show.
565 Broad, knotty and short-shouldered, he would boast
He could heave any door off hinge and post,
Or take a run and break it with his head.
His beard, like any sow or fox, was red
And broad as well, as though it were a spade;
570 And, at its very tip, his nose displayed
A wart on which there stood a tuft of hair.
Red as the bristles in an old sow's ear.
His nostrils were as black as they were wide.
He had a sword and buckler at his side,
575 His mighty mouth was like a furnace door.
A wrangler and buffoon, he had a store
Of tavern stories, filthy in the main.
His was a master-hand at stealing grain.
He felt it with his thumb and thus he knew
580 Its quality and took three times his due—
A thumb of gold, by God, to gauge an oat!
He wore a hood of blue and a white coat.
He liked to play his bagpipes up and down
And that was how he brought us out of town.

---

69. **tabard** loose jacket.
70. *Reeve* estate manager.
71. *Manciple* buyer of provisions.
72. *Pardoner* one who dispenses papal pardons.
73. *Summoner* one who serves summonses to church courts.
74. **sixteen stone** 224 pounds. A stone equals 14 pounds.

Literary Analysis
Characterization and Social Commentary What social commentary does the description of the Plowman provide?

Literary Analysis
Characterization What does the comparison of the Miller's hair color to that of a sow or fox indirectly suggest about his character?

Enrichment

Thomas à Becket

The murder of Thomas à Becket is a well-known, if somewhat mysterious event in English history. A close friend of Henry II, Thomas was Archbishop of Canterbury and Chancellor of England. However, Thomas and the King became engaged in a bitter quarrel over the right of the courts to try members of the clergy accused of crimes. On December 29, 1170, four of the King's knights killed the archbishop in his cathedral at Canterbury. Thomas was canonized in 1173, and the pope took the unusual step of forcing Henry to do public penance. Historians dispute whether Henry gave orders for the assassination. Nevertheless, Thomas à Becket is considered a martyr to the faith.

    T.S. Eliot's poetic drama *Murder in the Cathedral* was first performed in 1935 in the Chapter House of the Cathedral, just a few yards from the spot where Becket was murdered more than 700 years earlier.

585   The *Manciple* came from the Inner Temple;
    All caterers might follow his example
    In buying victuals; he was never rash
    Whether he bought on credit or paid cash.
    He used to watch the market most precisely
590   And go in first, and so he did quite nicely.
    Now isn't it a marvel of God's grace
    That an illiterate fellow can outpace
    The wisdom of a heap of learned men?
    His masters—he had more than thirty then—
595   All versed in the abstrusest legal knowledge,
    Could have produced a dozen from their College
    Fit to be stewards in land and rents and game
    To any Peer in England you could name,
    And show him how to live on what he had
600   Debt-free (unless of course the Peer were mad)
    Or be as frugal as he might desire,
    And they were fit to help about the Shire
    In any legal case there was to try;
    And yet this Manciple could wipe their eye.
605   The *Reeve* was old and choleric and thin;
    His beard was shaven closely to the skin,
    His shorn hair came abruptly to a stop
    Above his ears, and he was docked on top
    Just like a priest in front; his legs were lean,
610   Like sticks they were, no calf was to be seen.
    He kept his bins and garners[75] very trim;
    No auditor could gain a point on him.
    And he could judge by watching drought and rain
    The yield he might expect from seed and grain.
615   His master's sheep, his animals and hens,
    Pigs, horses, dairies, stores and cattle-pens
    Were wholly trusted to his government.
    And he was under contract to present
    The accounts, right from his master's earliest years.
620   No one had ever caught him in arrears.
    No bailiff, serf or herdsman dared to kick,
    He knew their dodges, knew their every trick;
    Feared like the plague he was, by those beneath.
    He had a lovely dwelling on a heath,
625   Shadowed in green by trees above the sward.[76]
    A better hand at bargains than his lord,
    He had grown rich and had a store of treasure
    Well tucked away, yet out it came to pleasure
    His lord with subtle loans or gifts of goods,

75. **garners** *n.* buildings for storing grain.
76. **sward** *n.* turf.

Reading Strategy
Analyzing Difficult Sentences What are the two subjects of the comparison in lines 594–604?

 Reading Check
What is the Miller like?

38 **Reading Strategy**
Analyzing Difficult Sentences

- Remind students to ask questions of the passage to help them break down difficult sentences.

- Then, **ask** them the Reading Strategy question: In the sentence in lines 647–650, what could not be cured?

Answer: The Summoner's pimples could not be cured.

39 **Literary Analysis**
Characterization

▶ **Reteach:** Remind students that indirect characterization uses details to suggest a character's personality, whereas direct characterization specifically describes a character's personality.

▶ **Monitor Progress:** Then, **ask** them the Literary Analysis question: In lines 652–659, is the characterization of the Summoner direct or indirect? Explain.

Answer: Students should recognize that the characterization of the Summoner in this passage is indirect—the passage describes how he behaves—drunkenly and unintelligently—and encourages the reader to extend that description to his character.

630 To earn his thanks and even coats and hoods.
When young he'd learnt a useful trade and still
He was a carpenter of first-rate skill.
The stallion-cob he rode at a slow trot
Was dapple-gray and bore the name of Scot.

635 He wore an overcoat of bluish shade
And rather long; he had a rusty blade
Slung at his side. He came, as I heard tell,
From Norfolk, near a place called Baldeswell.
His coat was tucked under his belt and splayed.

640 He rode the hindmost of our cavalcade.
     There was a *Summoner* with us in the place
Who had a fire-red cherubinnish face,[77]
For he had carbuncles.[78] His eyes were narrow,
He was as hot and lecherous as a sparrow.

645 Black, scabby brows he had, and a thin beard.
Children were afraid when he appeared.
No quicksilver, lead ointments, tartar creams,
Boracic, no, nor brimstone,[79] so it seems,
Could make a salve that had the power to bite,

650 Clean up or cure his whelks[80] of knobby white.
Or purge the pimples sitting on his cheeks.
Garlic he loved, and onions too, and leeks,
And drinking strong wine till all was hazy.
Then he would shout and jabber as if crazy,

655 And wouldn't speak a word except in Latin
When he was drunk, such tags as he was pat in;
He only had a few, say two or three,
That he had mugged up out of some decree;
No wonder, for he heard them every day.

660 And, as you know, a man can teach a jay
To call out "Walter" better than the Pope.
But had you tried to test his wits and grope
For more, you'd have found nothing in the bag.
Then "*Questio quid juris*"[81] was his tag.

665 He was a gentle varlet and a kind one,
No better fellow if you went to find one.
He would allow—just for a quart of wine—
Any good lad to keep a concubine
A twelvemonth and dispense it altogether!

670 Yet he could pluck a finch to leave no feather:

Reading Strategy
Analyzing Difficult Sentences In the sentence in lines 647–650, what could not be cured?

Literary Analysis
Characterization In lines 652–659, is the characterization of the Summoner direct or indirect? Explain.

---

77. **fire-red . . . face** In the art of the Middle Ages, the faces of cherubs, or angels, were often painted red.
78. **carbuncles** (kär′ buŋ′ kəlz) *n.* pus-filled boils resulting from a bacterial infection under the skin.
79. **quicksilver . . . brimstone** various chemicals and chemical compounds, used as remedies. *Quicksilver* is a name for mercury. *Brimstone* is a name for sulfur.
80. **whelks** *n.* pustules; pimples.
81. **"Questio quid juris"** "The question is, What is the point of law?" (Latin).

114 ■ *From Legend to History (449–1485)*

Enrichment

Local Historic Site
Point out that the pilgrims set out to visit the site of an important event in their religious and civic history. Perhaps there are places in your area that people come to visit because of a well-known event that occurred there. Tell students that it does not have to be something that changed history. It might be something known primarily to people in the area.

Have students decide on such a place in your area and have them create a sign or similar marker to place on the site. The sign should summarize what happened and why it is significant.

And if he found some rascal with a maid
He would instruct him not to be afraid
In such a case of the Archdeacon's curse
(Unless the rascal's soul were in his purse)
575 For in his purse the punishment should be.
"Purse is the good Archdeacon's Hell," said he.
But well I know he lied in what he said;
A curse should put a guilty man in dread,
For curses kill, as shriving brings, salvation.
580 We should beware of excommunication.
Thus, as he pleased, the man could bring duress
On any young fellow in the diocese.
He knew their secrets, they did what he said.
He wore a garland set upon his head
585 Large as the holly-bush upon a stake
Outside an ale-house, and he had a cake,
A round one, which it was his joke to wield
As if it were intended for a shield.

    He and a gentle *Pardoner* rode together,
590 A bird from Charing Cross of the same feather,
Just back from visiting the Court of Rome.
He loudly sang "*Come hither, love, come home!*"
The Summoner sang deep seconds to this song,
No trumpet ever sounded half so strong.
595 This Pardoner had hair as yellow as wax,
Hanging down smoothly like a hank of flax.
In driblets fell his locks behind his head
Down to his shoulder which they overspread;
Thinly they fell, like rat-tails, one by one.
700 He wore no hood upon his head, for fun;
The hood inside his wallet had been stowed,
He aimed at riding in the latest mode;
But for a little cap his head was bare
And he had bulging eyeballs, like a hare.
705 He'd sewed a holy relic on his cap;
His wallet lay before him on his lap,
Brimful of pardons come from Rome all hot.
He had the same small voice a goat has got.
His chin no beard had harbored, nor would harbor,
710 Smoother than ever chin was left by barber.
I judge he was a gelding, or a mare.
As to his trade, from Berwick down to Ware
There was no pardoner of equal grace,
For in his trunk he had a pillowcase
715 Which he asserted was Our Lady's veil.
He said he had a gobbet[82] of the sail

82. **gobbet** piece.

The Pardoner, Arthur Szyk for *The Canterbury Tales*

▲ **Critical Viewing**
How well does this picture of the Pardoner match Chaucer's description of him in lines 695–710? **[Assess]**

✔ **Reading Check**
How does the Summoner turn religion to personal profit?

from The Canterbury Tales: The Prologue ■ 115

Saint Peter had the time when he made bold
To walk the waves, till Jesu Christ took hold.
He had a cross of metal set with stones
720 And, in a glass, a rubble of pigs' bones.
And with these relics, any time he found
Some poor up-country parson to astound,
On one short day, in money down, he drew
More than the parson in a month or two,
725 And by his flatteries and <u>prevarication</u>
Made monkeys of the priest and congregation.
But still to do him justice first and last
In church he was a noble ecclesiast.
How well he read a lesson or told a story!
730 But best of all he sang an Offertory,[83]
For well he knew that when that song was sung
He'd have to preach and tune his honey-tongue
And (well he could) win silver from the crowd.
That's why he sang so merrily and loud.
735   Now I have told you shortly, in a clause,
The rank, the array, the number and the cause
Of our assembly in this company
In Southwark, at that high-class hostelry
Known as *The Tabard*, close beside *The Bell*.
740 And now the time has come for me to tell
How we behaved that evening; I'll begin
After we had alighted at the inn,
Then I'll report our journey, stage by stage,
All the remainder of our pilgrimage.
745 But first I beg of you, in courtesy,
Not to condemn me as unmannerly
If I speak plainly and with no concealings
And give account of all their words and dealings,
Using their very phrases as they fell.
750 For certainly, as you all know so well,
He who repeats a tale after a man
Is bound to say, as nearly as he can,
Each single word, if he remembers it,
However rudely spoken or unfit,
755 Or else the tale he tells will be untrue,
The things invented and the phrases new.
He may not flinch although it were his brother,
If he says one word he must say the other.
And Christ Himself spoke broad[84] in Holy Writ,
760 And as you know there's nothing there unfit,
And Plato[85] says, for those with power to read,

Literary Analysis
Characterization What facts in lines 719–726 indirectly characterize the Pardoner?

Vocabulary Builde
prevarication (pri var′ i kā′ shən) *n.* evasion of truth

Reading Strategy
Analyzing Difficult Sentences Why does Chaucer apologize in the sentence starting with line 745?

---

83. **Offertory** song that accompanies the collection of the offering at a church service.
84. **broad** bluntly.
85. **Plato** Greek philosopher (427?–347? B.C.)

"The word should be as cousin to the deed."
Further I beg you to forgive it me
If I neglect the order and degree
765 And what is due to rank in what I've planned.
I'm short of wit as you will understand.
    Our *Host* gave us great welcome; everyone
Was given a place and supper was begun.
He served the finest victuals you could think,
770 The wine was strong and we were glad to drink.
A very striking man our Host withal,
And fit to be a marshal in a hall.
His eyes were bright, his girth a little wide;
There is no finer burgess in Cheapside.[86]
775 Bold in his speech, yet wise and full of tact,
There was no manly attribute he lacked,
What's more he was a merry-hearted man.
After our meal he jokingly began
To talk of sport, and, among other things
780 After we'd settled up our reckonings,
He said as follows: "Truly, gentlemen,
You're very welcome and I can't think when
—Upon my word I'm telling you no lie—
I've seen a gathering here that looked so spry,
785 No, not this year, as in this tavern now.
I'd think you up some fun if I knew how.
And, as it happens, a thought has just occurred
And it will cost you nothing, on my word.
You're off to Canterbury—well, God speed!
790 Blessed St. Thomas answer to your need!
And I don't doubt, before the journey's done
You mean to while the time in tales and fun.
Indeed, there's little pleasure for your bones
Riding along and all as dumb as stones.
795 So let me then propose for your enjoyment,
Just as I said, a suitable employment.
And if my notion suits and you agree
And promise to submit yourselves to me
Playing your parts exactly as I say
800 Tomorrow as you ride along the way,
Then by my father's soul (and he is dead)
If you don't like it you can have my head!
Hold up your hands, and not another word."
    Well, our consent of course was not deferred,
805 It seemed not worth a serious debate;
We all agreed to it at any rate
And bade him issue what commands he would.

---

86. **Cheapside** district in London.

The British Tradition

45 *The Literature of Social Observation*

Chaucer was just one author in a long tradition of British writers who detailed ironic observations of social types. Four centuries later, for instance, eighteenth-century writers such as Joseph Addison held up a mirror to middle-class society, describing the typical characters of the day and their follies.

The tradition of social commentary bloomed with the invention of the novel, a form built around keen observations of character and society. Yet the novel emphasized the individual in a way that earlier literature often did not. The characters of nineteenth-century novelist Charles Dickens, for instance, take on their social roles with extravagant, individual style. In a sense, though, Dickens was only following Chaucer. In pilgrims such as the Wife of Bath, the Skipper, and the Host, you can already detect a spark of vital individuality, deeper than any social role.

Connect to the Literature

Identify three ways in which the Wife of Bath both fits and defies the stereotype of a woman of her time.

  Reading Check
What concern does the Host raise?

from The Canterbury Tales: The Prologue ■ 117

45 The British Tradition
The Literature of Social Observation Students should think about works they've read that involve extensive social observation. Explain that not all works of social observation are critical of society, but many of them are. Students may want to look at the cartoons in local newspapers, many of which are well known for their social commentary and observation. Have them consider in what ways Chaucer's social commentary was a springboard for the types of social observation in contemporary publications.

Connect to the Literature
Encourage students to reread the description of the Wife of Bath before answering the question.
Possible responses She travelled alone. She knew how to dance, make cloth, and observe the religious conventions of her time. She was a good conversationalist.

46 Reading Check

Answer: The Host raises the concern that they'll be riding without much to amuse them.

Differentiated
Instruction   Solutions for All Learners

Support for Less Proficient Readers
To help reinforce what they have learned, have students work through the interactive review of this selection with the **Got It! Assessment Videotapes**, Tape 1. Encourage students to note any concepts that are unclear or any questions that they miss, and then review with them where the answers are found in the selection.

Vocabulary for English Learners
Review with students the vocabulary list from p. 97. Then, have them go through the lesson to find the words in context, and have them read aloud the sentence or phrase in which the word appears. Discuss how the definition of the word contributes to understanding the sentence.

Enrichment for Advanced Readers
Encourage students to pick a topic suggested by this selection (for example, medieval medicine, the rise of the middle class, or life at sea) and do further research. Have them write a brief report relating something they discover that sheds additional light on the lives and times of Chaucer's characters.

- **Ask** students the Literary Analysis question: What does the Host's decision to accompany the pilgrims suggest about him?
Possible response: The Host is a generous, curious fellow.

"My lords," he said, "now listen for your good,
And please don't treat my notion with disdain.
810 This is the point. I'll make it short and plain.
Each one of you shall help to make things slip
By telling two stories on the outward trip
To Canterbury, that's what I intend,
And, on the homeward way to journey's end
815 Another two, tales from the days of old;
And then the man whose story is best told,
That is to say who gives the fullest measure
Of good morality and general pleasure,
He shall be given a supper, paid by all,
820 Here in this tavern, in this very hall,
When we come back again from Canterbury.
And in the hope to keep you bright and merry
I'll go along with you myself and ride
All at my own expense and serve as guide.
825 I'll be the judge, and those who won't obey
Shall pay for what we spend upon the way.
Now if you all agree to what you've heard
Tell me at once without another word,
And I will make arrangements early for it."
830   Of course we all agreed, in fact we swore it
Delightedly, and made entreaty too
That he should act as he proposed to do,
Become our Governor in short, and be
Judge of our tales and general referee,
835 And set the supper at a certain price.
We promised to be ruled by his advice
Come high, come low; unanimously thus
We set him up in judgment over us.
More wine was fetched, the business being done;
840 We drank it off and up went everyone
To bed without a moment of delay.
     Early next morning at the spring of day
Up rose our Host and roused us like a cock,
Gathering us together in a flock,
845 And off we rode at slightly faster pace
Than walking to St. Thomas' watering-place;[87]
And there our Host drew up, began to ease
His horse, and said, "Now, listen if you please,
My lords! Remember what you promised me.
850 If evensong and matins will agree[88]

Literary Analysis
Characterization What does the Host's decision to accompany the pilgrim suggest about him?

---

87. **St. Thomas' watering-place** a brook two miles from the inn.
88. **If evensong . . . agree** "if what you said last night holds true this morning."

Let's see who shall be first to tell a tale.
And as I hope to drink good wine and ale
I'll be your judge. The rebel who disobeys,
However much the journey costs, he pays.
855 Now draw for cut[89] and then we can depart;
The man who draws the shortest cut shall start."

---

89. **draw for cut** draw lots, as when pulling straws from a bunch; the person who pulls the short straw is "it."

Critical Reading

1. **Respond:** Which of the pilgrims would you most like to meet? Why?

2. **(a) Recall:** List three characteristics of the Nun. **(b) Deduce:** What details does Chaucer include in his description of the Nun to make gentle fun of her? Explain.

3. **(a) Recall:** Identify two of the main characteristics of the Friar and the Parson. **(b) Compare and Contrast:** What are some of the ways in which the Friar and the Parson differ?

4. **Infer:** Judging from the descriptions of the two, what does Chaucer think can cause a religious person to fail in his or her duty?

5. **Compare and Contrast:** How does Chaucer's attitude towards the Monk differ, if at all, from his attitude towards the Friar? Explain.

6. **(a) Infer:** What does Chaucer seem to dislike about the Skipper? **(b) Infer:** What does he seem to admire about this character? **(c) Draw Conclusions:** Describe Chaucer's overall attitude toward him.

7. **Draw Conclusions:** Judging from his pilgrims, do you think Chaucer believes people are basically good, basically evil, or often a mix of the two? Give examples to support your answer.

8. **(a) Apply:** What modern character types match the characters in the Prologue? **(b) Apply:** What types would Chaucer not have anticipated?

9. **(a) Analyze:** From what segments of medieval society do the pilgrims come? **(b) Draw Conclusions:** What does their participation in a common pilgrimage suggest about the times?

10. **Evaluate:** Do you think Chaucer's view of people is justified? Explain.

Go Online
Author Link

For: More about Geoffrey Chaucer
Visit: www.PHSchool.com
Web Code: ese-9103

from The Canterbury Tales: The Prologue ■ 119

Go Online
Author Link For additional information about Geoffrey Chaucer, have students type in the Web Code, then select C from the alphabet, and then select Geoffrey Chaucer.

Answers

1. Students may name any pilgrim, but should give reasons for their choices.

2. (a) The Nun's voice is too nasal, her French is not fluent, and she is trying too hard to be graceful. (b) These three details seem designed to poke fun at her; they undermine the soberness of her role.

3. (a) The Friar does not take his religious vows seriously; he prefers worldly pleasures. The Parson is virtuous and helps the poor parishioners. (b) The Friar is corrupt and the Parson is good. The Friar takes advantage of people, and the Parson helps them.

4. **Possible response:** Chaucer seems to think that when people become too attached to wealth, they can become corrupt.

5. The Monk's worldly pursuits are similar to those of the Friar, but Chaucer seems to think the Monk is more noble and less corrupt than the Friar.

6. (a) Chaucer dislikes the Skipper's stealing wine and forcing prisoners to walk the plank. (b) He seems to admire his abilities as a navigator. (c) Chaucer seems mildly disapproving of the Skipper.

7. **Possible responses:** Students' choices of details should support their answers. Chaucer applauds the goodness of the Parson and is scandalized by the Friar's and Summoner's corruptness. Though Chaucer exposes folly and vice in many of the pilgrims, he seems to accept imperfection as part of humanity's fate.

8. (a) **Possible responses:** Students might, for example, compare the Parson to Mother Teresa or the Cleric to a bookish classmate. (b) **Possible responses:** Chaucer might not have anticipated Wall Street brokers or computer techies.

9. (a) The pilgrims come from all levels of medieval society. (b) It suggests that class divisions in their society did not extend to religious faith.

10. **Possible response:** Students may say his view is justified and give examples of good and bad qualities they've seen in people.

119

Answers

1. The Doctor cares more about gold than about his patients (direct); he and his apothecaries worked together selling drugs at inflated prices (indirect); He does not read the Bible (indirect).

2. **Possible responses:** (a) The Plowman is "an honest worker, good and true"—direct statement. The Reeve is "old and choleric and thin"—use of physical description. The Nun "used to weep if she but saw a mouse/caught in a trap"—use of action. (b) In the case of the Reeve, the description suggests that he is shrewd and tough. The Nun's action shows she is foolishly sentimental.

3. **Possible responses:** (a) Chaucer's description of the Nun's poor French. (b) Chaucer's tone undermines the Nun's efforts at seeming refined.

4. **Possible response:** Students may say that the description of the Miller is vivid because it incorporates physical description and actions.

5. **Possible response:** (a) Pardoner: holy relic sewn on his hat, wallet bulging with pardons. Implication: corruption was rampant in the giving of pardons. (b) Knight: truth, honor, generosity, courtesy. Implication: society promoted civility and virtuous behavior.

6. In medieval society, people may have been defined by their profession or their social role.

7. *Who:* A Knight; *what:* he rode to battle; *how much:* more than anyone else; *how well:* very well.

8. The Parson was an exemplary figure in order to draw people to God; if a man was difficult, he rebuked him no matter what his social status.

9. Responses will vary but should identify the major points of the sentence selected.

10. **Possible responses:** an airplane pilot, a mechanic, a computer programmer, or a movie actor.

 Students may use the **Self-test** to prepare for **Selection Test A** or **Selection Test B**.

Apply the Skills

from *The Canterbury Tales: The Prologue*

Literary Analysis

Characterization

1. Give three details that Chaucer uses to **characterize** the Doctor. For each, note whether the characterization is **direct** or **indirect**.

2. **(a)** Find one example of each of the following kinds of details in Chaucer's characterizations: direct statement, physical description, character's action. **(b)** Explain how your examples of physical description and action indirectly characterize that pilgrim.

3. **(a)** Identify an example in which Chaucer uses mild sarcasm in describing a character. **(b)** Explain how his tone changes the meaning of the description.

4. Choose the character sketch you find most effective. Explain the method Chaucer uses to make the sketch so vivid.

Connecting Literary Elements

5. Use a chart like the one below to reflect on the **social commentary** in the Prologue. **(a)** What social comment does Chaucer make in his sketch of the Pardoner? **(b)** What does the sketch of the Knight suggest were some of the excellences promoted by medieval society?

Character	Detail		Implication About Society
		→	

6. Most of Chaucer's characters are named after a profession. What does this emphasis on social roles suggest about medieval society?

Reading Strategy

Analyzing Difficult Sentences

7. Analyze the sentence in lines 47–50 answering the questions *who, what, how much,* and *how well.*

8. Analyze the sentence in lines 529–533.

9. Find and analyze another long sentence from the Prologue.

Extend Understanding

10. **Cultural Connection:** If Chaucer were writing today, what three kinds of pilgrims might he consider adding to the group?

120 ■ From Legend to History (449–1485)

QuickReview

Characterization is the technique a writer uses to create and develop the personality of a character. Characterization may be **direct**—stated outright—or **indirect**—suggested through details of appearance or action or by the character's statements.

Social commentary is writing that offers insight into a society, its values, and its customs.

Analyze difficult sentences by applying the questions *who, what, where, when, why,* and *how* to them.

Go Online Assessment
For: Self-test
Visit: www.PHSchool.com
Web Code: esa-6105

Assessment Practice

Signal Words (For more practice, see *Standardized Test Preparation Workbook*, p. 4.)

Many tests require students to identify sequence of events. Have students note the signal words that clue the order of events.

". . . on homeward way to journey's end
Another two, tales from the days of old;
And then the man whose story is best told
. . . shall be given a supper, paid by all . . .
when we come back again from Canterbury."

What does the Host say will happen at the *end* of the pilgrims' journey?

A Each pilgrim will tell two stories from the "days of old."

B The pilgrims will treat the person who told the best story to supper.

C The person who does not obey rules will pay for all the journey's expenses.

D The host will treat the pilgrim who told the best story to supper.

Responses *A, C,* and *D* are inaccurate. The word *when* signals a later time. The correct answer is *B*.

120

Build Language Skills

Vocabulary Lesson

Word Analysis: Latin Suffix -tion

The Latin suffix -tion means "the act or process of" or "the result of the act or process of." To prevaricate means "to distort the truth." Prevarication is the act of distorting the truth. Use your knowledge of -tion to define the words below.

1. narration 2. elevation 3. oration

Spelling Strategy

Usually, the ending pronounced shun is spelled tion, as in prevarication. It can also be spelled sion, ssion, and, in a few cases, cion. Fill in the blanks below to spell the shun sound correctly.

1. ten__ion 2. expre__ion 3. man__ion

Grammar and Style Lesson

Past and Past Perfect Tenses

The **past tense** is a verb form showing an action or a condition that began and ended in the past. The **past perfect tense** indicates an action or a condition that ended before another past action began.

> PAST PERFECT TENSE
> This estimable Merchant so <u>had set</u> / His wits
> PAST TENSE
> to work, none <u>knew</u> he was in debt. . . .

W/G *Prentice Hall Writing and Grammar Connection: Chapter 21, Section 2*

Vocabulary Builder: Synonyms

Review the vocabulary list on page 97. Then, match each numbered word with its synonym.

1. solicitous   a. asserts
2. garnished   b. authorization
3. sanguine   c. an act freeing from sin
4. avouches   d. confident
5. commission   e. caring
6. absolution   f. decorated
7. prevarication   g. lying

Practice Recount each pair of events. Show sequence by using the past and the past perfect.

1. Narrator meets pilgrims / stays at inn
2. Nun plans trip / wears nice clothing
3. Cleric is poor / finds no preferment
4. Wife goes to Rome / joins the group
5. Pardoner sells relic / lies about its origin

Writing Application Using verbs in both the past and past perfect tenses, describe a modern pilgrim.

Extend Your Learning

Writing Write a **critical response** to the poet William Blake's assertion that the "characters of Chaucer's pilgrims are the characters which compose all ages and nations." Use examples from the Prologue to explain why you agree or disagree with Blake's idea that Chaucer's characterizations can apply to people today.

Listening and Speaking With two partners, perform a **dialogue** for three of the pilgrims, discussing the trip you are about to take. Prepare by rereading the sections of the Prologue describing your characters. Use language and expressions appropriate to each character. **[Group Activity]**

from *The Canterbury Tales: The Prologue* ■ 121

Assessment Resources

The following resources can be used to assess students' knowledge and skills.

Unit 1 Resources
  Selection Test A, pp. 79–81
  Selection Test B, pp. 82–84

General Resources
  Rubrics for Response to Literature,
  pp. 65–66

Go Online Students may use the **Self-test**
Assessment to prepare for **Selection Test A**
or **Selection Test B.**

❶ Vocabulary Lesson
Word Analysis

1. *Narration* is the act or process of speaking or telling a story.
2. *Elevation* is the act or process of raising or lifting up.
3. *Oration* is the act or process of speaking formally.

Spelling Strategy

1. tension   3. mansion
2. expression

Vocabulary Builder

1. e   3. d   5. b   7. g
2. f   4. a   6. c

❷ Grammar and Style Lesson
Possible responses:

1. met, had stayed
2. had planned, wore
3. was, had found
4. had gone, joined
5. sold, had lied

Writing Application

Possible response: The pilgrim went to Lourdes to see the miracles that had occurred there.

W/G **Writing and Grammar, Diamond Level**

Students will find further instruction and practice on past and past perfect tense in Chapter 21, Section 2.

❸ Extension Activities

• Read the Listening and Speaking Lesson with students.

• Have students work together in groups of three to prepare a dialogue for three of the pilgrims.

• Encourage each group to reread the passages that describe the characters they have chosen.

• Then, have students write scripts appropriate to their characters.

• Use the Response to Literature rubric, pp. 65–66 in *General Resources,* to evaluate student work.

• The **Support for Extend Your Learning** page (*Unit 1 Resources,* p. 77) provides guided note-taking opportunities to help students complete the Extend Your Learning activities.

Meeting Your Standards

Students will

1. **analyze and respond to literary elements.**
   - Literary Analysis: Allegory

2. **read, comprehend, analyze, and critique a poem.**
   - Reading Strategy: Rereading for Clarification
   - Reading Check questions
   - Apply the Skills questions
   - Assessment Practice (ATE)

3. **develop vocabulary.**
   - Vocabulary Lesson: Greek Prefix: *apo-*

4. **understand and apply written and oral language conventions.**
   - Spelling Strategy
   - Grammar and Style Lesson: Clauses With *who* and *whom*

5. **develop writing proficiency.**
   - Writing Lesson: Allegory (after "The Wife of Bath's Tale)

6. **develop appropriate research strategies.**
   - Extend Your Learning: Multimedia Report

7. **develop writing strategies.**
   - Extend Your Learning: Summary

Block Scheduling: Use one 90-minute class period to preteach the skills and have students read the selection. Use a second 90-minute class period to assess students' mastery of skills, extend their learning, and monitor their progress.

Homework Suggestions

Following are possibilities for homework assignments.

- Support pages from *Unit 1 Resources:*
  Literary Analysis
  Reading Strategy
  Vocabulary Builder
  Grammar and Style

- An Extend Your Learning project and the Writing Lesson for this selection may be completed over several days.

Step-by-Step Teaching Guide	Pacing Guide
PRETEACH	
• Administer Vocabulary and Reading Warm-ups as necessary.	5 min.
• Engage students' interest with the motivation activity.	5 min.
• Read and discuss author and background features. **FT**	10 min.
• Introduce the Literary Analysis Skill: Allegory. **FT**	5 min.
• Introduce the Reading Strategy: Rereading for Clarification. **FT**	10 min.
• Prepare students to read by teaching the selection vocabulary. **FT**	
TEACH	
• Informally monitor comprehension while students read independently or in groups. **FT**	30 min.
• Monitor students' comprehension with the Reading Check notes.	as students read
• Reinforce vocabulary with Vocabulary Builder notes.	as students read
• Develop students' understanding of exemplum (anecdote) with the Literary Analysis annotations. **FT**	5 min.
• Develop students' ability to reread for clarification with the Reading Strategy annotations. **FT**	5 min.
ASSESS/EXTEND	
• Assess students' comprehension and mastery of the Literary Analysis and Reading Strategy by having them answer the Apply the Skills questions. **FT**	15 min.
• Have students complete the Vocabulary Lesson and the Grammar and Style Lesson. **FT**	15 min.
• Apply students' understanding by using one or more of the Extend Your Learning activities.	20–90 min. or homework
• Administer Selection Test A or Selection Test B. **FT**	15 min.

Resources

Choosing Resources for Differentiated Instruction

[**L1**] Special Needs Students

[**L2**] Below-Level Students

[**L3**] All Students

[**L4**] Advanced Students

[**EL**] English Learners

For Vocabulary and Reading Warm-ups and for Selection Tests, **A** signifies "less challenging" and **B** "more challenging." For Graphic Organizer Transparencies, **A** signifies "not filled in" and **B** "filled in."

FT Fast Track Instruction: To move the lesson more quickly, use the strategies and activities identified with **FT**.

Scaffolding for Less Proficient and Advanced Students

The leveled Critical Thinking questions after selections progress in the levels of thinking required to answer them. To address the needs of your different students, you may use the (a) level questions for your less proficient students and the (b) level questions with your on-level and advanced students. The occasional (c) level questions are appropriate for your advanced students.

PRENTICE HALL

Teacher EXPRESS™ Use this complete
Plan · Teach · Assess suite of powerful
teaching tools to make lesson planning and testing quicker and easier.

PRENTICE HALL

Student EXPRESS™ Use the interac-
Learn · Study · Succeed tive textbook
(online and on CD-ROM) to make selections and activities come alive with audio and video support and interactive questions.

Go Online
Professional
Development

For: Information about Lexiles
Visit: www.PHSchool.com
Web Code: eue-1111

Motivation

Explain that this tale takes place during a plague. The pestilence, we know now, was not one disease but two occurring simultaneously: bubonic plague and the far more contagious and usually fatal pneumonic plague. A plague death is the impetus that begins the tale.

❶ Literary Analysis
Allegory

- Explain to students that in this lesson they will focus on the exemplum, an anecdote or brief story that teaches a lesson.

- Use the instruction for Connecting Literary Elements to review with students how a good exemplum uses archetypal narrative elements.

- Review the archetypal elements of a good exemplum: characters, events, and things in threes; test of characters' moral fiber; a mysterious guide who points the way; a just ending that rewards the good or punishes evil.

❷ Reading Strategy
Rereading for Clarification

- Tell students that by rereading they can learn things that they missed in a first reading.

- Explain that when they reread, students can approach the text already knowing how characters act or what they do.

- Provide students with a copy of **Reading Strategy Graphic Organizer A**, p. 17 in *Graphic Organizer Transparencies*, to use as they read the selection.

Vocabulary Builder

- Pronounce each vocabulary word for students, and read the definitions as a class. Have students indentify any words with which they are already familiar.

Build Skills   *Poem*

The Pardoner's Tale

❶ Literary Analysis
Allegory

Allegories are narratives that have both literal and deeper, symbolic meanings. "The Pardoner's Tale" is a type of allegory called an *exemplum*, Latin for "example." The tale is an exemplum against the sin of greed, and the Pardoner uses the tale to illustrate the point of one of his sermons, "Love of money is the root of all evil." As you read the tale, consider how it illustrates this point—and aids the Pardoner in his swindles.

Connecting Literary Elements

To teach its lesson effectively, an allegory must be easily understood and remembered by the listeners. For this reason, an allegory may use certain basic storytelling patterns, or **archetypal narrative elements,** found in folk literature around the world. These elements include the following:

- Characters, events, and other things that come in threes
- A test of characters' moral fiber leading to their destiny
- A mysterious guide who helps point the way
- A just ending that rewards good or punishes evil

Because it includes such elements, the basic story in "The Pardoner's Tale" was able to survive retelling after retelling as it traveled from ancient India to Persia (present-day Iran) across the Middle East to Europe, finally coming to England. Note the elements in the tale that make the story and its moral memorable and clear.

❷ Reading Strategy
Rereading for Clarification

Rereading passages in a work can clarify characters' identities, the sequence or causes of events, and even puzzling language. As you read "The Pardoner's Tale," reread earlier passages to clarify any lines that puzzle you. Use a diagram like the one shown to clarify difficult passages.

Vocabulary Builder

pallor (paľ ər) *n.* unnatural lack of color; paleness (p. 128)

hoary (hôr′ ē) *adj.* white or gray with age (p. 128)

prating (prāt′ iŋ) *n.* chatter (p. 128)

tarry (tar′ ē) *v.* to delay or linger (p. 130)

apothecary (ə päth′ ə ker′ ē) *n.* pharmacist; druggist (p. 130)

> **Passage**
>
> ìHe g athered lots and hid them in his hand.

> **Reread Earlier Passage**
>
> "'We draw for lots an‹ see the way it goes; / The one who draws tł longest, lucky man, .

> **Clarification**
>
> "Drawing lots" must be like drawing straw The one who draws the longest is ìit. "

122 ■ From Legend to History (449–1485)

Differentiated Instruction   Solutions for All Learners

Support for Special Needs Students
Have students complete the **Preview** and **Build Skills** pages for "The Pardoner's Tale" in the *Reader's Notebook: Adapted Version*. These pages provide a selection summary, an abbreviated presentation of the reading and literary skills, and the graphic organizer on the **Build Skills** page in the student book.

Support for Less Proficient Readers
Have students complete the **Preview** and **Build Skills** pages for "The Pardoner's Tale" in the *Reader's Notebook*. These pages provide a selection summary, an abbreviated presentation of the reading and literary skills, and the graphic organizer on the **Build Skills** page in the student book.

Support for English Learners
Have students complete the **Preview** and **Build Skills** pages for the selection in the *Reader's Notebook: English Learner's Version*. These pages provide a selection summary, an abbreviated presentation of the skills, additional contextual vocabulary, and the graphic organizer on the **Build Skills** page in the student book.

from The Pardoner's Tale

Geoffrey Chaucer
Translated by Nevill Coghill

Review and Anticipate   In the Prologue, Chaucer describes the Pardoner as a cleric full of "flatteries and prevarication." By selling pardons—documents officially forgiving the purchaser's sins—and supposedly holy relics, the swindling Pardoner earns more in one short day than a poor country parson earns in a month or two. Even while exposing the Pardoner's dishonesty, Chaucer praises the Pardoner's persuasive skills: "How well he read a lesson or told a story!" Now, when it is the Pardoner's turn to tell a story, he himself explains his methods: All his sermons illustrate the biblical text *Radix malorum est cupiditas* ("Love of money is the root of all evil"). He finds that preaching against the sin of avarice, or greed, is the best way to get people to pay him large sums of money for his pardons and relics! After providing this boastful explanation, he then proceeds to tell one of the stories from his sermons. As you read, think of answers to the question, What effect would the Pardoner's story have on an audience of poorly educated country folk?

from *The Pardoner's Tale* ■ 123

Differentiated Instruction   Solutions for All Learners

Accessibility at a Glance

	The Pardoner's Tale
Context	Social/Religious commentary
Language	Vocabulary footnotes
Concept Level	Average (greed)
Literary Merit	Classic
Lexile	NP
Other	Morality tale/Allegory
Overall Rating	Average

123

❷ **Reading Strategy**
Rereading for Clarification

- Explain to students that, in a work with so much description and so many details, it is sometimes helpful to reread to find out to what a later comment refers.

- **Ask** students the Reading Strategy question: Reread lines 14–15 for an example of the "antics" to which the Pardoner refers in line 17.
Answer: The "antics" involve the Pardoner stretching his neck, craning from side to side, and pecking like a pigeon.

The Pardoner's Prologue

"My lords," he said, "in churches where I preach
I cultivate a haughty kind of speech
And ring it out as roundly as a bell;
I've got it all by heart, the tale I tell.
5 I have a text, it always is the same
And always has been, since I learnt the game,
Old as the hills and fresher than the grass,
Radix malorum est cupiditas."[1]

—————◆◆◆◆—————

The Pardoner explains how he introduces himself to a congregation, showing official documents and offering relics as cures for various problems. Next, he explains how he preaches.

—————◆◆◆◆—————

"Then, priestlike in my pulpit, with a frown,
10 I stand, and when the yokels[2] have sat down,
I preach, as you have heard me say before,
And tell a hundred lying mockeries[3] more.
I take great pains, and stretching out my neck
To east and west I crane about and peck
15 Just like a pigeon sitting on a barn.
My hands and tongue together spin the yarn
And all my antics[4] are a joy to see.
The curse of avarice and cupidity[5]
Is all my sermon, for it frees the pelf.[6]
20 Out come the pence, and specially for myself,
For my exclusive purpose is to win
And not at all to castigate[7] their sin.
Once dead what matter how their souls may fare?
They can go blackberrying, for all I care!
25   "Believe me, many a sermon or devotive
Exordium[8] issues from an evil motive.
Some to give pleasure by their flattery
And gain promotion through hypocrisy,
Some out of vanity, some out of hate;

---

1. *Radix malorum est cupiditas* Latin for "Greed is the root of all evil."
2. **yokels** (yō′ kəlz) *n.* unsophisticated people living in a rural area.
3. **mockeries** (mäk′ ər ēz) *n.* stories that are untrue.
4. **antics** (an′ tiks) *n.* playful, silly, or ludicrous acts.
5. **avarice** (av′ ə ris) **and cupidity** (kyōō pid′ ə tē) *n.* desire to gain wealth; greed (synonyms).
6. **pelf** (pelf) *n.* ill-gotten gains of money or wealth.
7. **castigate** (kas′ ti gāt′) *v.* to punish severely.
8. **Exordium** (eg zôr′ dē əm) *n.* the opening part of an oration.

Enrichment

Religious Corruption and Reform

Chaucer's characterization of the Pardoner as a rapacious figure out for personal gain is a satire of the religious state of affairs in his era. Before the Reformation in the sixteenth century, religious abuses were fairly common. The Pardoner's lack of concern for the souls of his parishioners, and his willingness to rob them of their small personal reserves of cash, suggest his level of villainy.

Relic-dealers profited at the expense of the faithful, and sinecures—cushy jobs funded by the coffers of the church—were available to people connected with religious corruption. The Reformation, led by Martin Luther, John Calvin, Ulrich Zwingli and John Knox, originated as a protest against these religious abuses. These reformers broke away from the Roman Catholic Church to found various denominations of Protestantism.

30 Or when I dare not otherwise debate
    I'll put my discourse into such a shape,
    My tongue will be a dagger; no escape
    For him from slandering falsehood shall there be,
    If he has hurt my brethren[9] or me.
35 For though I never mention him by name
    The congregation guesses all the same
    From certain hints that everybody knows,
    And so I take revenge upon our foes
    And spit my venom forth, while I profess
40 Holy and true—or seeming holiness.
        "But let me briefly make my purpose plain;
    I preach for nothing but for greed of gain
    And use the same old text, as bold as brass,
    Radix malorum est cupiditas.
45 And thus I preach against the very vice
    I make my living out of—avarice.
    And yet however guilty of that sin
    Myself with others I have power to win
    Them from it, I can bring them to repent;
50 But that is not my principal intent.
    Covetousness[10] is both the root and stuff
    Of all I preach. That ought to be enough.
        "Well, then I give examples thick and fast
    From bygone times, old stories from the past.
55 A yokel mind loves stories from of old,
    Being the kind it can repeat and hold.
    What! Do you think, as long as I can preach
    And get their silver for the things I teach,
    That I will live in poverty, from choice?
60 That's not the counsel of my inner voice!
    No! Let me preach and beg from kirk[11] to kirk
    And never do an honest job of work,
    No, nor make baskets, like St. Paul, to gain
    A livelihood. I do not preach in vain.
65 There's no apostle I would counterfeit;
    I mean to have money, wool and cheese and wheat
    Though it were given me by the poorest lad
    Or poorest village widow, though she had
    A string of starving children, all agape.
70 No, let me drink the liquor of the grape
    And keep a jolly wench in every town!
        "But listen, gentlemen; to bring things down
    To a conclusion, would you like a tale?

---

9. **brethren** (breth′ rən) *n.* brothers.
10. **covetousness** (kuv′ ət əs nis) *n.* greed, especially for what belongs to others.
11. **kirk** *n.* church.

❸

The Pardoner, Arthur Szyk for The Canterbury Tales, The George Macy Companies

❹ ⚠ **Critical Viewing** Do the Pardoner's garments in the illustration support his claims about his success? Explain. [Connect]

❺ ✓ **Reading Check**
What vice does the Pardoner admit to having, even though he preaches against it?

from *The Pardoner's Tale* ■ 125

- Remind students that an exemplum is a brief anecdote that teaches a lesson.

- Then, **ask** them the Literary Analysis question: Which details in the opening sentence enable the audience to form a quick opinion of the main characters?
  Answer: Students should say that the characters are "rioters," and that they're drinking before nine in the morning.

❼ Reading Strategy
Rereading for Clarification

- Read line 102 aloud to students.

- Then, **ask** students the Reading Strategy question: What earlier line explains the reference to the "adversary" in line 102?
  Answer: Either line 95 or 98—both of which mention Death—explain the reference to the "adversary."

Now as I've drunk a draught of corn-ripe ale,
75 By God it stands to reason I can strike
On some good story that you all will like.
For though I am a wholly vicious man
Don't think I can't tell moral tales. I can!
Here's one I often preach when out for winning;
80 Now please be quiet. Here is the beginning."

The Pardoner's Tale

It's of three rioters I have to tell
❻ Who, long before the morning service bell,[12]
Were sitting in a tavern for a drink.
And as they sat, they heard the hand-bell clink
85 Before a coffin going to the grave;
One of them called the little tavern-knave[13]
And said "Go and find out at once—look spry!—
Whose corpse is in that coffin passing by;
And see you get the name correctly too."
90 "Sir," said the boy, "no need, I promise you;
Two hours before you came here I was told.
He was a friend of yours in days of old,
And suddenly, last night, the man was slain,
Upon his bench, face up, dead drunk again.
95 There came a privy[14] thief, they call him Death,
Who kills us all round here, and in a breath
He speared him through the heart, he never stirred.
And then Death went his way without a word.
He's killed a thousand in the present plague.[15]
100 And, sir, it doesn't do to be too vague
If you should meet him; you had best be wary.
Be on your guard with such an adversary,
❼ Be primed to meet him everywhere you go,
That's what my mother said. It's all I know."
105   The publican[16] joined in with, "By St. Mary,

---

12. **long before . . . bell** long before 9:00 A.M.
13. **tavern-knave** serving boy.
14. **privy** secretive.
15. **plague** the Black Death, which killed over a third of the population of Europe from 1347–1351. The plague reached England in 1348.
16. **publican** innkeeper.

Literary Analysis
Allegory Which details in the opening sentence enable the audience to form a quick opinion of the main characters?

Reading Strategy
Rereading for Clarification What earlier line explains the reference to the "adversary" in line 102?

Enrichment

Morality Plays

Allegorical dramas of the late Middle Ages were known as *morality plays.* Many of them were presented as popular pageants, and they always included abstract personifications, such as Charity, Mercy, Truth, Pity, Church, rather than figures from history or individuals. Morality plays are dramatic presentations of sermons. The most famous morality play is *Everyman,* written around 1500. When Everyman receives a summons from Death, he tries in vain to convince his friends Fellowship, Kindred, Worldly Goods, and Beauty to journey with him. Only Good Deeds remains faithful.

In "The Pardoner's Tale," Death is personified, but the other figures remain anonymous—three rioters and an old man. Shaped as an exemplum, or moral anecdote, the tale also functions as a less dramatic version of a morality play.

What the child says is right; you'd best be wary,
This very year he killed, in a large village
A mile away, man, woman, serf at tillage,[17]
Page in the household, children—all there were.
110 Yes, I imagine that he lives round there.
It's well to be prepared in these alarms,
He might do you dishonor." "Huh, God's arms!"
The rioter said, "Is he so fierce to meet?
I'll search for him, by Jesus, street by street.
115 God's blessed bones! I'll register a vow!
Here, chaps! The three of us together now,
Hold up your hands, like me, and we'll be brothers
In this affair, and each defend the others,
And we will kill this traitor Death, I say!
120 Away with him as he had made away
With all our friends. God's dignity! Tonight!"
       They made their bargain, swore with appetite,
These three, to live and die for one another
As brother-born might swear to his born brother.
125 And up they started in their drunken rage
And made towards this village which the page
And publican had spoken of before.
Many and grisly were the oaths they swore,
Tearing Christ's blessed body to a shred;[18]
130 "If we can only catch him, Death is dead!"
       When they had gone not fully half a mile,
Just as they were about to cross a stile,
They came upon a very poor old man
Who humbly greeted them and thus began,
135 "God look to you, my lords, and give you quiet!"
To which the proudest of these men of riot
Gave back the answer, "What, old fool? Give place!
Why are you all wrapped up except your face?
Why live so long? Isn't it time to die?"
140   The old, old fellow looked him in the eye
And said, "Because I never yet have found,
Though I have walked to India, searching round
Village and city on my pilgrimage,
One who would change his youth to have my age.
145 And so my age is mine and must be still
Upon me, for such time as God may will.
       "Not even Death, alas, will take my life;
So, like a wretched prisoner at strife
Within himself, I walk alone and wait

---

17. **tillage** plowing.
18. **Tearing . . . shred** their oaths included such expressions as "God's arms" and "God's blessed bones."

Literary Analysis
Allegory and Archetypal Elements What details of the publican's comments build the danger of the situation?

Reading Strategy
Rereading for Clarification What lines explain the "bargain" the rioters are said to have made in line 122?

10 Reading Check
What do the three rioters swear to do?

from The Pardoner's Tale ■ 127

⓫ **Reading Strategy**
Rereading for Clarification

- **Ask** students the Reading Strategy question: Who is the "she" in line 159? What earlier lines give you the answer?
  Answer: Students should know that "she" refers to the old man's mother, mentioned in lines 152 and 156.

⓬ **Literary Analysis**
Allegory and Archetypal Elements

- Read aloud the bracketed passage to students.
- Review with them the many possible archetypal narrative elements in an exemplum.
- Then, **ask** them the Literary Analysis question: What archetypal role does the old man play?
  Answer: The old man is the mysterious guide who helps point the way.

150 About the earth, which is my mother's gate,
Knock-knocking with my staff from night to noon
And crying, 'Mother, open to me soon!
Look at me, mother, won't you let me in?
See how I wither, flesh and blood and skin!
155 Alas! When will these bones be laid to rest?
Mother, I would exchange—for that were best—
The wardrobe in my chamber, standing there
So long, for yours! Aye, for a shirt of hair[19]

⓫ | To wrap me in!' She has refused her grace,
160 Whence comes the <u>pallor</u> of my withered face.
    "But it dishonored you when you began
To speak so roughly, sir, to an old man,
Unless he had injured you in word or deed.
It says in holy writ, as you may read,
165 'Thou shalt rise up before the <u>hoary</u> head
And honor it,' And therefore be it said
'Do no more harm to an old man than you,
Being now young, would have another do
When you are old'—if you should live till then.
170 And so may God be with you, gentlemen,
For I must go whither I have to go.'
    "By God," the gambler said, "you shan't do so,
You don't get off so easy, by St. John!
I heard you mention, just a moment gone,
175 A certain traitor Death who singles out
And kills the fine young fellows hereabout.
And you're his spy, by God! You wait a bit.
Say where he is or you shall pay for it,
By God and by the Holy Sacrament!
180 I say you've joined together by consent
To kill us younger folk, you thieving swine!"
    "Well, sirs," he said, "if it be your design
To find out Death, turn up this crooked way
Towards that grove, I left him there today
⓬ 185 Under a tree, and there you'll find him waiting.
He isn't one to hide for all your <u>prating</u>.
You see that oak? He won't be far to find.
And God protect you that redeemed mankind,
Aye, and amend you!" Thus that ancient man.
190   At once the three young rioters began
To run, and reached the tree, and there they found
A pile of golden florins[20] on the ground,
New-coined, eight bushels of them as they thought.
No longer was it Death those fellows sought,

---

19. **shirt of hair** here, a shroud.
20. **florins** coins.

Reading Strategy
Rereading for Clarification
Who is "she" in line 159? What earlier lines give you the answer?

Vocabulary Builder
pallor (pal′ ər) *n.* unnatural lack of color; paleness

hoary (hôr′ ē) *adj.* white or gray with age

Literary Analysis
Allegory and Archetypal Elements What archetypal role does the old man play?

Vocabulary Builder
prating (prāt′ iŋ) *n.* chatter

195 For they were all so thrilled to see the sight,
The florins were so beautiful and bright,
That down they sat beside the precious pile.
The wickedest spoke first after a while.
"Brothers," he said, "you listen to what I say.
200 I'm pretty sharp although I joke away.
It's clear that Fortune has bestowed this treasure
To let us live in jollity and pleasure.
Light come, light go! We'll spend it as we ought.
God's precious dignity! Who would have thought
205 This morning was to be our lucky day?

"If one could only get the gold away,
Back to my house, or else to yours, perhaps
For as you know, the gold is ours, chaps—
We'd all be at the top of fortune, hey?
210 But certainly it can't be done by day.
People would call us robbers—a strong gang,
So our own property would make us hang.
No, we must bring this treasure back by night
Some prudent way, and keep it out of sight.
215 And so as a solution I propose
We draw for lots and see the way it goes;
The one who draws the longest, lucky man,
Shall run to town as quickly as he can
To fetch us bread and wine—but keep things dark—
220 While two remain in hiding here to mark
Our heap of treasure. If there's no delay,
When night comes down we'll carry it away,
All three of us, wherever we have planned."

He gathered lots and hid them in his hand
225 Bidding them draw for where the luck should fall.
It fell upon the youngest of them all,
And off he ran at once towards the town.

As soon as he had gone, the first sat down
And thus began a parley[21] with the other:
230 "You know that you can trust me as a brother;
Now let me tell you where your profit lies;
You know our friend has gone to get supplies
And here's a lot of gold that is to be
Divided equally amongst us three.
235 Nevertheless, if I could shape things thus
So that we shared it out—the two of us—
Wouldn't you take it as a friendly act?"

"But how?" the other said. "He knows the fact
that all the gold was left with me and you;
240 What can we tell him? What are we to do?"

---

21. **parley** discussion.

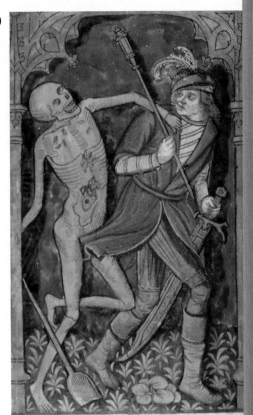

 ▲ **Critical Viewing**
What moral might a medieval illustration like this one have served to teach? [Hypothesize]

Literary Analysis
Allegory Into what new sin does greed lead the rioters?

16 ✓ **Reading Check**
What does the old man say the rioters will find under the tree? What do they find there?

La Danse Macabre

This French painting dates to the 1400s. *La Danse Macabre*, also called the Dance of Death, was a common medieval allegory that represented the all-conquering power of death. The concept originated in the late thirteenth or early fourteenth century, and became one of the most common images during the Middle Ages, as the Black Death in the mid-fourteenth century and the Hundred Years' War (1337–1453) devastated Europe. Generally, there is a procession in the image, with people arranged in order of rank, from popes and kings down through children, clerks, and hermits. In the image shown here (which is half of a painting—the second half is on p. 131), a wealthy young man is approached by Death.

Use the following questions for discussion:

1. Why would this allegory include images of people from all levels of society?
   Possible response: It illustrates that death does not respect titles or wealth, but comes to everyone.

2. Why might people surrounded by death include it in their art?
   Possible response: To remind the evil or vain that death is inevitable. They considered it such a common, inescapable part of life that it seemed natural to include it in their art.

14 **Critical Viewing**

Possible response: Students may say that the medieval illustration may have served to teach that death could come to anyone, even the young, strong, and rich.

15 **Literary Analysis**
Allegory

- **Ask** students the Literary Analysis question: Into what new sin does greed lead the rioters?
  Answer: Greed leads the rioters into plotting the murder of the third rioter.

16 **Reading Check**

Answer: The old man says the rioters will find Death under the tree. They find a pile of golden florins.

129

⓱ Reading Strategy
Rereading for Clarification

- **Ask** students the Reading Strategy question: What does the first rioter mean by "as in game"? Which earlier lines explain the meaning?
Answer: Students should say that lines 248–249 explain the phrase. They will act as if the attack is all in fun, like a game of wrestling.

⓲ Literary Analysis
Allegory

- Read the bracketed passage aloud to students.

- Then, **ask** them the Literary Analysis question: What new sin does greed lead the youngest rioter to contemplate?
Answer: The youngest rioter contemplates poisoning his two comrades.

⓳ Vocabulary Builder
Greek Prefix: apo-

- Call students' attention to *apothecary,* a word that means "pharmacist," or "druggist." Explain to students that *apothecary* contains the Greek prefix *apo-,* which means "away; off; separate." An *apothecary* is someone who "puts away" prescriptions (that is, he stores them).

- Have students **suggest** other words that contain this Greek prefix, and list them on the chalkboard.
Possible responses: *apostrophe, apology, apostle, apostasy*

- Have students look up any unfamiliar words in dictionaries.

"Is it a bargain," said the first, "or no?
For I can tell you in a word or so
What's to be done to bring the thing about."
"Trust me," the other said, "you needn't doubt
245 My word. I won't betray you, I'll be true."
     "Well," said his friend, "you see that we are two,
And two are twice as powerful as one.
Now look; when he comes back, get up in fun
To have a wrestle; then, as you attack,
250 I'll up and put my dagger through his back
While you and he are struggling, as in game;
Then draw your dagger too and do the same.
Then all this money will be ours to spend,
Divided equally of course, dear friend.
255 Then we can gratify our lusts and fill
The day with dicing at our own sweet will."
Thus these two miscreants[22] agreed to slay
The third and youngest, as you heard me say.
     The youngest, as he ran towards the town,
260 Kept turning over, rolling up and down
Within his heart the beauty of those bright
New florins, saying, "Lord, to think I might
Have all that treasure to myself alone!
Could there be anyone beneath the throne
265 Of God so happy as I then should be?"
     And so the Fiend,[23] our common enemy,
Was given power to put it in his thought
That there was always poison to be bought,
And that with poison he could kill his friends.
270 To men in such a state the Devil sends
Thoughts of this kind, and has a full permission
To lure them on to sorrow and perdition;[24]
For this young man was utterly content
To kill them both and never to repent.
275   And on he ran, he had no thought to tarry,
Came to the town, found an apothecary
And said, "Sell me some poison if you will,
I have a lot of rats I want to kill
And there's a polecat too about my yard
280 That takes my chickens and it hits me hard;
But I'll get even, as is only right,
With vermin that destroy a man by night."
     The chemist answered, "I've a preparation
Which you shall have, and by my soul's salvation

---

22. **miscreants** villains.
23. **Fiend** Satan.
24. **perdition** damnation.

130 ■ From Legend to History (449–1485)

Reading Strategy
Rereading for Clarification
What does the first rioter mean by "as in game"? Which earlier lines explain this meaning?

Literary Analysis
Allegory What new sin does greed lead the youngest rioter to contemplate?

Vocabulary Builder
tarry (tar´ ē) v. to delay or linger

apothecary (ə päth´ ə ker´ ē) n. pharmacist; druggist

Enrichment

The Apothecary

Though apothecaries in Chaucer's time were essentially the pharmacists of their era, their roles were actually considerably greater. Unlike pharmacists, they could prescribe cures themselves, and they could care for humans and animals alike. Also, because there were no prepackaged medicines, they had to be able to formulate everything themselves.

Because doctors in this era had so little to offer, and often offered worse than nothing (bleeding, leeches), an apothecary was often a more popular choice when one was ill. Though some apothecaries were "quacks," many were very knowledgeable about useful medicinal herbs, poisons and antidotes, the limited number of mixtures that did have some effect, and symptoms of various diseases.

Because apothecaries could compound poisons for dealing with pests, they became a source not only of lethal draughts, but also of plot twists. In Shakespeare's *Romeo and Juliet,* for example, Romeo goes to an apothecary to buy the poison with which he will end his life.

▲ **Critical Viewing** Compare this illustration to the one on page 129. What point might the artist make by depicting contrasting individuals being taken by death? [Compare and Contrast]

from *The Pardoner's Tale* ■ 131

⟨20⟩ Humanities
La Danse Macabre

This is the second half of the fifteenth-century image found on p. 129. Though French, this painting is now in the collection of the Lambeth Palace Library in London. Here, the artist shows death coming for a priest.

In addition to being common in paintings, the allegorical theme of the Dance of Death was also represented in drama, poetry, music, and dance. Death is viewed as the great equalizer—both inevitable and impartial. The paintings often adorned churches and were meant to remind people that repentance and loving God would be wise before death—represented then as now by a skeleton—came to escort them to their final destination.

Use the following questions for discussion:
• Why do you think the priest looks so calm, when the young man looked so surprised by death's arrival?
Possible responses: Perhaps the priest is more at peace and better prepared for death. Perhaps he was simply more aware that it comes to everyone.

⟨21⟩ Critical Viewing

Possible response: Students may say that the contrast emphasizes the inescapable fact of death, which comes to the man devoted to religion as well as to the young man bent on pleasure.

Differentiated Instruction   Solutions for All Learners

Strategy for Less Proficient Readers	**Strategy for English Learners**	**Enrichment for Advanced Readers**
Students may benefit from a review of the Literary Analysis and Reading Strategy skills. Model these skills by walking them through examples.	Give a brief overview of the story, and have students look for supporting elements as they read. Help students define and pronounce unfamiliar words. However, guide students away from worrying about place names or obscure terms, such as *florins* and *publican*.	Encourage students to choose an element from this tale, or from the art that accompanies it, and do further study. Abuses of pardon-selling, the Dance of Death, or the knowledge of apothecaries of the era are among the possibilities. Have students share with the class any interesting facts they discover.

❻ Humanities

King Arthur,

1903, Charles Ernest Butler

London-based artist Charles Ernest Butler (1864–c.1918) was best known for his paintings of landscapes and mythological figures. Although he was born after the height of the Pre-Raphaelite movement, Butler admired that style. As this painting shows, Butler felt a deep reverence for bygone days of kings and knights. His painting depicts a powerful and physically flawless King Arthur bathed in pure light. Use these questions for discussion:

1. What is the painter's attitude toward the subject, King Arthur?
Answer: The king's stature and action of crowning himself show his power. The lighting in the painting is clear and flattering. It makes the king look physically perfect.

2. What does the painting suggest about the days of King Arthur?
Answer: It suggests that bravery and valor were highly admired.

❼ Critical Viewing

Answer: Both knights would wear similar attire, and both would likely be armed. The painting, however, suggests a worthy knight who protects and serves his king, whereas the knight in the tale seems self-serving, careless, and brutish.

140   *From Legend to History (449–1485)*

❻

❼ ◄ **Critical Viewing**
Compare and contrast this painting of a knight to the impression you have of the knight in the Wife's tale.
[Compare and Contrast]

Enrichment

The Changing Meaning of *Chivalry*
People sometimes say that chivalry is dead—meaning that men no longer hold doors open for women or practice other forms of polite behavior. Originally, however, chivalry had little to do with politeness; it had to with codes of conduct and ideal qualities such as bravery and honor. Men who were chivalrous were knights who rode horses and fought on behalf of their kings. Knights who practiced chivalry were loyal to God, their temporal master or king, and their love (which was usually platonic). This system of ideals experienced its height in the twelfth and thirteenth centuries.

Whether to show him mercy or refuse.
45   The queen returned him thanks with all her might,
And then she sent a summons to the knight
At her convenience, and expressed her will:
"You stand, for such is the position still,
In no way certain of your life," said she,
50 "Yet you shall live if you can answer me:
What is the thing that women most desire?
Beware the axe and say as I require.
     "If you can't answer on the moment, though,
I will concede you this: you are to go
55 A twelvemonth and a day to seek and learn
Sufficient answer, then you shall return.
I shall take gages[4] from you to extort
Surrender of your body to the court."
     Sad was the knight and sorrowfully sighed,
60 But there! All other choices were denied,
And in the end he chose to go away
And to return after a year and day
Armed with such answer as there might be sent
To him by God. He took his leave and went.
65   He knocked at every house, searched every place,
Yes, anywhere that offered hope of grace.
What could it be that women wanted most?
But all the same he never touched a coast,
Country or town in which there seemed to be
70 Any two people willing to agree.
     Some said that women wanted wealth and treasure,
"Honor," said some, some "Jollity and pleasure,"
Some "Gorgeous clothes" and others "Fun in bed,"
"To be oft widowed and remarried," said
75 Others again, and some that what most mattered
Was that we should be cossetted[5] and flattered.
That's very near the truth, it seems to me;
A man can win us best with flattery.
To dance attendance on us, make a fuss,
80 Ensnares us all, the best and worst of us.
     Some say the things we most desire are these:
Freedom to do exactly as we please,
With no one to reprove our faults and lies,
Rather to have one call us good and wise.
85 Truly there's not a woman in ten score
Who has a fault, and someone rubs the sore,
But she will kick if what he says is true;
You try it out and you will find so too.

---

4. **gages** guarantees.
5. **cossetted** pampered.

The Canterbury Tales: The Wife of Bath's Tale ■ 141

---

❽

Reading Strategy
Using Context Clues
Use line 53 to determine
a synonym for the word
concede in line 54.

❾

Reading Strategy
Using Context Clues
Which context clues
might help you figure out
the meaning of *ensnares*
in line 80?

❿  **Reading Check**

What punishment does
the queen demand of
the knight?

---

❽ Reading Strategy
Using Context Clues

• Point out that the meanings of
some words can be determined
fairly accurately by using context
clues.

• **Ask** students to summarize lines
50–58.
Answer: The queen tells the
knight that he shall live if he can
correctly answer what it is that
women desire most. She tells him
that if he cannot answer now, he
can have a year and a day to find
an answer.

• **Ask** students to respond to the first
Reading Strategy prompt: Use line
53 to determine a synonym for the
word *concede* in line 54. Mention
to students that they can use the
context through line 58 to determine the meaning of *concede*.
Possible response: Beginning in
line 53, the Queen tells the knight
that if he cannot answer the question now she will give him a grace
period in which to find an answer.
Students may suggest *grant* or *give*
as a synonym for *concede*.

• If possible, have students confirm
their meaning in a dictionary or
thesaurus.

❾ Reading Strategy
Using Context Clues

• **Ask** students to summarize the
answers the knight finds in
lines 71–80.
Answer: Some women want
wealth, and some want honor;
some want pleasure; some want
nice clothes; and others want fun
in bed. Others want to be married
and widowed. Most want to be
flattered because men who flatter
women often catch them.

• **Ask** students the second Reading
Strategy question: Which context
clues might help you figure out the
meaning of *ensnares* in line 80?
Possible response: Line 78 talks
about the best way for a man to
"win" a woman. Lines 79–80 further expand on how flattery works
on all women. Therefore, *ensnares*
must mean *catches* or *traps*.

❿ Reading Check

Answer: The queen demands that
the knight find the answer to the
question "What do women most
desire?"

Differentiated Instruction   Solutions for All Learners

Support for Less Proficient Readers
Help students understand that the tale of the
Wife of Bath has a moral or lesson. A lesson,
like a theme, is often expressed through the
characters' words and actions. Ask students to
consider the lesson that the knight is about to
learn during his punishment. Help students
understand that the knight learns women
should be treated with respect, something he
did not know at the beginning of the story.
Have students pay attention to how the knight
treats women at different points in the story.

Enrichment for Gifted/Talented Students
Have students create a comic strip of the
knight's quest. Ask them to depict his encounters with people and the answers they provide.
Students can elaborate on the story by men-
tioning places the knight travels to or even creating new scenes or scenarios for the knight in
his journey. Have students address the knight's
attitude toward women. Does he get annoyed
on his journey, or does he become more
respectful?

However vicious we may be within
90 We like to be thought wise and void of sin.
Others assert we women find it sweet
When we are thought dependable, discreet
And secret, firm of purpose and controlled,
Never betraying things that we are told.
95 But that's not worth the handle of a rake;
Women conceal a thing? For Heaven's sake!
Remember Midas?[6] Will you hear the tale?
　　　Among some other little things, now stale,
Ovid <u>relates</u> that under his long hair
100 The unhappy Midas grew a splendid pair
Of ass's ears; as subtly as he might,
He kept his foul deformity from sight;
Save for his wife, there was not one that knew.
He loved her best, and trusted in her too.
105 He begged her not to tell a living creature
That he possessed so horrible a feature.
And she—she swore, were all the world to win,
She would not do such villainy and sin
As saddle her husband with so foul a name;
110 Besides to speak would be to share the shame.
Nevertheless she thought she would have died
Keeping this secret bottled up inside;
It seemed to swell her heart and she, no doubt,
Thought it was on the point of bursting out.
115 　　Fearing to speak of it to woman or man,
Down to a reedy marsh she quickly ran
And reached the sedge. Her heart was all on fire
And, as a bittern[7] bumbles in the mire,
She whispered to the water, near the ground,
120 "Betray me not, O water, with thy sound!
To thee alone I tell it: it appears
My husband has a pair of ass's ears!
Ah! My heart's well again, the secret's out!
I could no longer keep it, not a doubt."
125 And so you see, although we may hold fast
A little while, it must come out at last,
We can't keep secrets; as for Midas, well,
Read Ovid for his story; he will tell.
　　This knight that I am telling you about
130 Perceived at last he never would find out
What it could be that women loved the best.
Faint was the soul within his sorrowful breast

---

6. Midas In mythology, King Midas had the magic touch that turned everything to gold. Here, Chaucer makes reference to Ovid's *Metamorphosis*.
7. bittern small wading bird.

Vocabulary Builder
relates (ri lāts´) *v.* tells

Literary Analysis
Frame What clues signal the beginning and ending of a tale-within-a-tale here?

❷ ▼ Critical Viewing
Which details in this illustration of the Wife of Bath suggest she is a wealthy, confident woman? [Interpret]

Enrichment

The Tale of King Midas

The figure of King Midas appears in several ancient Greek myths. The story that the Wife of Bath cites is a lesser known one.

King Midas sprouted the ears of an ass because he had offended the god Apollo. While serving as a judge in a musical contest between Apollo and the satyr Marsyas, Midas judged in favor of the satyr. The angry god took his revenge by changing the king's ears into those of a donkey. Different versions exist of what happened next.

According to some versions, only King Midas' barber knew the truth about his ears. Unlike in "The Wife of Bath's Tale," it is the barber, not Midas' wife, who cannot keep a secret. The barber whispers the secret into a hole where reeds will soon grow. Wind blowing through the reeds releases the barber's secret so everyone can hear it.

142

14

As home he went, he dared no longer stay;
His year was up and now it was the day.
135   As he rode home in a dejected mood
Suddenly, at the margin of a wood,
He saw a dance upon the leafy floor
Of four and twenty ladies, nay, and more.
Eagerly he approached, in hope to learn
140 Some words of wisdom ere he should return;
But lo! Before he came to where they were,
Dancers and dance all vanished into air!
There wasn't a living creature to be seen
Save one old woman crouched upon the green.
145 A fouler-looking creature I suppose
Could scarcely be imagined. She arose
And said, "Sir knight, there's no way on from here.
Tell me what you are looking for, my dear,
For peradventure that were best for you;
150 We old, old women know a thing or two."
    "Dear Mother," said the knight, "alack the day!
I am as good as dead if I can't say
What thing it is that women most desire;
If you could tell me I would pay your hire."
155 "Give me your hand," she said, "and swear to do
Whatever I shall next require of you
—If so to do should lie within your might—
And you shall know the answer before night."
"Upon my honor," he answered, "I agree."
160 "Then," said the crone, "I dare to guarantee
Your life is safe; I shall make good my claim.
Upon my life the queen will say the same.
Show me the very proudest of them all
In costly coverchief or jewelled caul[8]
165 That dare say no to what I have to teach.
Let us go forward without further speech."
And then she crooned her gospel in his ear
And told him to be glad and not to fear.
    They came to court. This knight, in full array,
170 Stood forth and said, "O Queen, I've kept my day
And kept my word and have my answer ready."
    There sat the noble matrons and the heady
Young girls, and widows too, that have the grace
Of wisdom, all assembled in that place,
175 And there the queen herself was throned to hear
And judge his answer. Then the knight drew near
And silence was commanded through the hall.

---

8. **coverchief. . .caul** kerchief, and a decorative cap, both worn as headgear by medieval women.

Reading Strategy
Using Context Clues
What clues in context hint at the meaning of *crone* in line 160?

15 **Reading Check**
Where did the knight discover the old woman who would answer his question?

The Canterbury Tales: The Wife of Bath's Tale ■ 143

14 Reading Strategy
Using Context Clues

• **Ask** students to state what is happening in lines 130–135.
Answer: The knight understands that he will never find the answer to the question, and he prepares to go home to receive his punishment.

• Tell students to think about how they would feel if they were in the knight's position—having failed at their quest and facing certain punishment.
Possible response: Students may say that they would feel sad, despairing, or full of dread.

• Then, have students **find** clues to the knight's mood or emotional state in lines 130–135.
Answer: The words *faint, sorrowful,* and *dejected* describe his mood.

• **Ask** the Reading Strategy question: What clues in context hint at the meaning of *crone* in line 160?
Answer: Lines 143–146 provide the best description of the old woman. As she is the only woman speaking here, a *crone* must be a very old woman.

• As students continue to read, have them notice how the knight's mood completely reverses from dejection to hope as he eagerly approaches a group of women who may provide him with an answer.

15 Reading Check

Answer: He discovered her at the edge of the woods.

16 Humanities

Fairies at a Window, c. 1864,
John Anster Fitzgerald

Fairies were a popular subject among
English painters during the Victorian
era. Artists such as John Anster
Fitzgerald (1819–1906) used fairies
to depict a world that was far away
from the gritty, industrialized London
in which he lived.

Use these questions for discussion:

1. How does the artwork capture the
   spirit of the scene in which the
   knight meets the old woman?
   Answer: Both scenes have mystical elements to them. In the
   painting, fairies hover in the air. In
   the tale, a group of dancing
   women disappears.

2. What details in the artwork suggest magic and fantasy?
   Answer: The creatures are shiny,
   and they hover or fly. They seem
   tiny and sprite-like, not at all
   human.

16

Enrichment

Fairy Tales and Folk Tales

Fairy tales are often confused with folk tales, in
part because both have been taken from their
original contexts and presented as tales for children. Fairy tales, however, were originally tales
about small, magical, often mischievous creatures. In medieval times, people believed that
fairies were real and lived in forest kingdoms.

"The Wife of Bath's Tale" contains elements
of a fairy Tale. For example, the wife discusses
fairies as if they were real. In addition, like
most fairy tales, her tale is set in a time
steeped in legend and lore. Finally, her story,

like every fairy tale, has a happy ending.

The Wife's tale veers off into the realm of
folk tale or folklore when it presents its lesson.
Folk tales, like fables and unlike fairy tales,
were told to children as warnings, and they
contained clear lessons about proper behavior.
When the Wife tells how the old woman lectures the errant knight about the meaning of
gentility, she has departed from the traditional
fairy tale. In that way, "The Wife of Bath's Tale"
is a modern story, blending elements of traditional tales and creating something new.

⑰ Critical Viewing

Answer: The painting is mysterious and somewhat mystical, even dream-like. The tale, which mentions fairies and mystical characters, shares these qualities.

⑱ Reading Check

Answer: Women want to master their husbands as they master their lovers.

The queen then bade the knight to tell them all
What thing it was that women wanted most.
180 He stood not silent like a beast or post,
But gave his answer with the ringing word
Of a man's voice and the assembly heard:
    "My liege and lady, in general," said he,
"A woman wants the self-same sovereignty
185 Over her husband as over her lover,
And master him; he must not be above her.
That is your greatest wish, whether you kill
Or spare me; please yourself. I wait your will."
    In all the court not one that shook her head
190 Or contradicted what the knight had said;
Maid, wife and widow cried, "He's saved his life!"

⑰ ⚠ Critical Viewing
In what way is the mood of this painting similar to the mood in the tale? **[Compare]**

⑱ Reading Check
According to the knight, what do women most want?

The Canterbury Tales: The Wife of Bath's Tale ■ 145

Differentiated Instruction   Solutions for All Learners

Enrichment for Gifted/Talented Students
Invite students to go on a quest of their own. Have students ask the knight's question to their female family members, friends, and acquaintances, and then make a list of all the answers. Challenge students to tally the answers and write a short essay that analyzes their results. Students should compare the answers from modern women to the answers the knight received in "The Wife of Bath's Tale." Ask volunteers to share the results of their research with the class.

Enrichment for Advanced Readers
Point out that a scene in which someone receives judgment at court is a plot device that even today causes suspense. Have students relate this device to courtroom scenes they have read (a classic example is the courtroom scenes in *To Kill a Mockingbird*) or seen in crime dramas on screen or on television. Have students reread or view a modern courtroom scene and then write a short essay in which they compare it with the scene in which the knight appears before the queen and her court.

Portrait of an Old Woman,
Pietro Bellotti

Pietro Bellotti (1627–1700) was a renowned Venetian portrait painter. Unlike many portrait painters of his time, he did not idealize his subjects. Instead, he depicted them as realistically as possible. He preferred to paint people from the working classes but made his living from painting members of foreign courts visiting in Venice.

Use these questions for discussion:

1. What details in the portrait tell you that the figure is not idealized?
   Answer: The lines on the woman's face, the misshapen area around her mouth, and the natural looking folds on her neck give the woman a realistic appearance.

2. Do you think it is likely that the woman in the painting, like the old woman in the story, is poor? Explain your answer.
   Answer: The fact that the woman appears so plain suggests she is poor. Her clothing is simple, and her face is worn and tired. She does not wear jewelry and does not smile or seem happy or content.

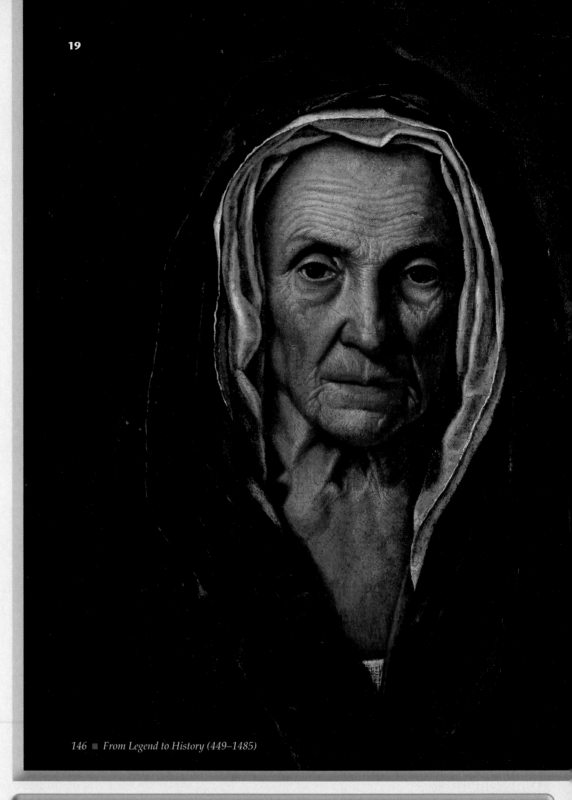

19

146 ■ *From Legend to History (449–1485)*

Enrichment

Ranks and Titles in "The Wife of Bath's Tale"
The ranks and titles mentioned in "The Wife of Bath's Tale" are remnants of a feudalistic society. Many of them are still in use, although few of them provide the bearer any significant power, other than social standing. Below are the definitions of some of the ranks and titles that appear in "The Wife of Bath's Tale," with their original and modern meanings.

liege: This is a feudal term; it is the lord to whom a knight or peasant owed loyalty and service.

sovereign: The term for the chief or leader with highest rank—the king or queen; the term still refers to the ruler of England.

duke: In medieval times it referred to a prince who ruled his own independent territory; today, it is the rank of someone who is born royal but is not a prince.

knight: In the Middle Ages, it meant a military servant of the king; today it is an honorary rank.

And on the word up started the old wife,
The one the knight saw sitting on the green,
And cried, "Your mercy, sovereign lady queen!
195 Before the court disperses, do me right!
'Twas I who taught this answer to the knight,
For which he swore, and pledged his honor to it,
That the first thing I asked of him he'd do it,
So far as it should lie within his might.
200 Before this court I ask you then, sir knight,
To keep your word and take me for your wife:
For well you know that I have saved your life.
If this be false, deny it on your sword!"
　　　"Alas!" he said, "Old lady, by the Lord
205 I know indeed that such was my behest,
But for God's love think of a new request,
Take all my goods, but leave my body free."
"A curse on us," she said, "if I agree!
I may be foul, I may be poor and old,
210 Yet will not choose to be, for all the gold
That's bedded in the earth or lies above,
Less than your wife, nay, than your very love!"
　　　"My love?" said he. "By Heaven, my damnation!
Alas that any of my race and station
215 Should ever make so foul a <u>misalliance</u>!"
Yet in the end his pleading and defiance
All went for nothing, he was forced to wed.
He takes his ancient wife and goes to bed.
　　　Now peradventure some may well suspect
220 A lack of care in me since I neglect
To tell of the rejoicings and display
Made at the feast upon their wedding-day.
I have but a short answer to let fall;
I say there was no joy or feast at all,
225 Nothing but heaviness of heart and sorrow.
He married her in private on the morrow
And all day long stayed hidden like an owl,
It was such torture that his wife looked foul.
　　　Great was the anguish churning in his head
230 When he and she were piloted to bed;
He wallowed back and forth in desperate style.
His ancient wife lay smiling all the while;
At last she said "Bless us! Is this, my dear,
How knights and wives get on together here?
235 Are these the laws of good King Arthur's house?
Are knights of his all so <u>contemptuous</u>?
I am your own beloved and your wife,

20 ◄ **Critical Viewing**
What life experiences
might the woman pictured
here and the old woman in
the tale have in common?
[Speculate]

Vocabulary Builder
misalliance (misəli´ əns) *n.*
mismatch

contemptuous (kəntemp´
chōōəs) *adj.* scornful

Reading Strategy
Using Context Clues
What is the meaning
of *anguish* in line 229?
Identify the context
clues that helped you to
determine the meaning.

22 **Reading Check**
In addition to becoming
the knight's wife, what
more does the old woman
demand?

The Canterbury Tales: The Wife of Bath's Tale ■ 147

20 **Critical Viewing**
Answer: Both women have probably worked hard in their day, married
and borne children, and endured the
hardships of daily medieval life,
including household chores and rav-
aging illnesses.

21 **Reading Strategy**
Using Context Clues
• Have students reread lines 226–231
and **summarize** them.
Possible response: The knight
marries the old woman in a private
ceremony, and he stays inside all
day because he does not want anyone to see how ugly she is. On his
wedding night, he is miserable and
desperate.

• **Ask** students the Reading Strategy
question: What is the meaning of
anguish in line 229? Identify the
context clues that helped you to
determine the meaning.
Answer: Students should identify
the words *torture, churning, wallow-
ing,* and *desperate* as clues to the
meaning of *anguish,* which means
"deep distress." All the words suggest that the knight is suffering.

22 **Reading Check**
Answer: She wants to become his
"very love."

147

㉓ Literary Analysis
Frame

- Point out to students that this is the part of the tale where the Wife describes the meaning of gentility, or moral behavior.

- Remind students that the Wife of Bath is aware of her audience, the other pilgrims in the frame story. As good Christians, they will definitely have clear ideas about how people should treat one another.

- **Ask** students the Literary Analysis question: What comparison might the Wife's listeners make between the old gentility and their riding companion, the Knight?
  Answer: The listeners would believe that the Knight possesses true gentility. He believes gentility is not inherited because of title or birth. His actions show his gentility.

㉔ Critical Thinking
Evaluate

- Explain that pp. 148–153 are essentially a monologue in which the old woman lectures the knight on the true meaning of gentility and counters his objections to her as a wife. Point out that the old woman refers to time-honored sources, such as the writings of Dante and the Bible, to back up her ideas.

- **Ask** students what the old woman's debating techniques say about her.
  Answer: Students may suggest that the woman is clearly knowledgeable and well read. She can also formulate and deliver a solid argument.

- Have students reread lines 271–278. **Ask** them to explain how the quotation from Dante supports the woman's argument.
  Answer: The woman uses Dante to support her argument that gentility or nobility requires more than just being from a good family. Dante says that God, not one's family, provides each human with a sense of gentleness.

And I am she, indeed, that saved your life;
And certainly I never did you wrong.
240 Then why, this first of nights, so sad a song?
You're carrying on as if you were half-witted
Say, for God's love, what sin have I committed?
I'll put things right if you will tell me how."
    "Put right?" he cried. "That never can be now!
245 Nothing can ever be put right again!
You're old, and so abominably plain,
So poor to start with, so low-bred to follow;
It's little wonder if I twist and wallow!
God, that my heart would burst within my breast!"
250   "Is that," said she, "the cause of your unrest?"
    "Yes, certainly," he said, "and can you wonder?"
    "I could set right what you suppose a blunder,
That's if I cared to, in a day or two,
If I were shown more courtesy by you.
255 Just now," she said, "you spoke of gentle birth,
Such as descends from ancient wealth and worth.
If that's the claim you make for gentlemen
Such as arrogance is hardly worth a hen.
Whoever loves to work for virtuous ends,
260 Public and private, and who most intends
To do what deeds of gentleness he can,
Take him to be the greatest gentleman.
Christ wills we take our gentleness from Him,
Not from a wealth of ancestry long dim,
265 Though they <u>bequeath</u> their whole establishment
By which we claim to be of high descent.
Our fathers cannot make us a bequest
Of all those virtues that became them best
And earned for them the name of gentleman,
270 But bade us follow them as best we can.
    "Thus the wise poet of the Florentines,
Dante[9] by name, has written in these lines,
For such is the opinion Dante launches:
'Seldom arises by these slender branches
275 <u>Prowess</u> of men, for it is God, no less,
Wills us to claim of Him our gentleness.'
For of our parents nothing can we claim
Save temporal things, and these may hurt and maim.
    "But everyone knows this as well as I;
280 For if gentility were implanted by
The natural course of lineage down the line,

Literary Analysis
Frame What comparison might the Wife's listeners make between the old gentility and their riding companion, the Knight?

Vocabulary Builder
bequeath (bē kwēth´) v. hand down as an inheritance

Vocabulary Builder
prowess (prou´ is) n. heroism; distinction

9. **Dante** Dante Alighieri (dän´ tā al əg yer´ ē) (1265–1321) Italian poet who wrote the *Divine Comedy.*

Enrichment

The Literary Influence of Dante

Dante Alighieri (1265–1321) was and remains among the most important European poets of all time. Dante's best-known work is the *Divine Comedy,* a narrative poem that describes one man's excursion from Hell to Heaven. Chaucer was a great admirer of Dante's works.

However, it is Dante's *Il Convivio (The Banquet)* that the Wife of Bath cites in her tale. Dante wrote it between 1304 and 1307 during the time he was in exile from his native Florence, having been cast out by the political party with whom he did not agree. Essentially,

The Banquet is a four-book series in which Dante sets forth commentary and poetry that argues in favor of using Italian, not Latin, as the language of art and literature.

The Banquet has several similarities to Chaucer's *The Canterbury Tales.* Like the *Tales,* it uses a frame device to provide structure for a series of long poems. Both works combine poetry and moral arguments in an enduring way. Finally, *The Banquet,* like Chaucer's masterpiece, was written in the vernacular language and served to champion its use in literature.

26 ◄ Critical Viewing
Predict the end of the Wife's tale using details from this painting to support your answer. [Predict]

Public or private, could it cease to shine
In doing the fair work of gentle deed?
No vice or villainy could then bear seed.
285   "Take fire and carry it to the darkest house
Between this kingdom and the Caucasus,[10]
And shut the doors on it and leave it there,
It will burn on, and it will burn as fair
As if ten thousand men were there to see,
290 For fire will keep its nature and degree,
I can assure you, sir, until it dies.
    "But gentleness, as you will recognize,
Is not annexed in nature to possessions,

28 ✓ Reading Check

For what four reasons does the knight find the old woman objectionable?

---

10. **Caucuses** (kô′ kə səs) mountain range between southeastern Europe and western Asia.

The Canterbury Tales: The Wife of Bath's Tale ■ 149

Differentiated Instruction   Solutions for All Learners

Strategy for Less Proficient Readers
Students may benefit from some guidance as they read the old woman's arguments on pp. 148–153. Draw a three-column chart on the board and label the columns *Gentility* (lines 271–310), *Poverty* (lines 311–352), and *Old Age/Beauty* (lines 353–373). Have students work in pairs or small groups to identify key ideas and phrases for each topic the woman addresses. After students complete their analysis, discuss the three ideas as a class. Work together to analyze students' findings, and then, generate statements that reflect what the old woman says about each idea.

Enrichment for Gifted/Talented Students
Challenge students to translate the old woman's arguments about gentility, poverty, and beauty into modern language. Ask students to work in pairs or small groups to imagine a modern version of the woman's arguments for a relationship between an older woman and a younger man. Students can condense and modernize the ideas and language. Have students stage a scene in which the knight and the old woman argue their cases. Afterwards, as a class, discuss the merits of the old woman's arguments and their updated version.

---

25 **Humanities**

The End of the Quest, 1921, by Sir Frank Dicksee

Sir Frank Dicksee (1853–1928) was a portrait painter and illustrator who contributed artwork to some of the most influential magazines of the Victorian period. He also painted biblical and allegorical scenes, using rich colors and costumes to bring a long-lost world to life. His paintings were well liked by the public.

Use this question for discussion:

• What word or phrase best describes the scene in Dicksee's painting? **Possible response:** Students may suggest words such as *devotion, love, admiration, respect,* or *parting.*

26 **Critical Viewing**

Possible response: The painting implies that the knight will learn to respect the old woman and will give in to her. Some students may predict that the old woman is really a young woman in disguise.

27 **Critical Thinking**
Analyze

• Have students read the analogy the woman makes between a burning fire and gentility in lines 285–295. **Ask** them to restate those lines in their own words. **Possible response:** If you take fire and let it burn in the darkest house, it burns whether someone sees it or not. Gentility, or gentleness, is not a result or reflection of one's wealth or birth. It is a quality that, like fire, exists whether you can see it or not.

• Finally, **ask** students what point the woman is trying to make. **Possible response:** People who possess true gentility are always gentle. The quality of gentility is expressed in one's actions and cannot be inherited or bought.

28 **Reading Check**

Answer: He claims she is old, abominably plain, poor, and low-bred.

- Have a volunteer read aloud lines 296–304. **Ask** students to summarize the ideas expressed in these lines.
Possible response: Being of noble birth does not make one a gentleman. If a person does not act nobly or follow a creed or code, then he is a churl.

- **Ask** the Reading Strategy question: From the context, can you guess the meaning of *churl* in line 304? Which words serve as clues?
Possible response: The words that provide clues are *vice* and *bad manners*. A churl is a boor or obnoxious person. The text makes it clear that a churl is not a gentleman.

30 **Literary Analysis**
Frame

- **Ask** a volunteer to read aloud lines 323–352. Challenge students to summarize the old woman's views on poverty.
Answer: Poverty is no cause for shame because God himself chose a life of poverty. People who are materially poor may be rich in spirit and wisdom.

- **Ask** students the Literary Analysis question: Which characters from the General Prologue might disagree with the hag's view on poverty? Would the Wife agree with them, or with the hag? Explain.
Possible response: The Merchant, the Pardoner, and the Monk would disagree with the old woman. Their rich attire and love of material possessions demonstrate their disagreement. Some students may suggest that the Wife herself would disagree with them. She wears fine clothing and likes having been married to rich men.

31 **Critical Viewing**

Answer: Lines 323–332 are illustrated in the painting.

Men fail in living up to their professions;
295 But fire never ceases to be fire.
God knows you'll often find, if you enquire,
Some lording full of villainy and shame.
If you would be <u>esteemed</u> for the mere name
Of having been by birth a gentleman
300 And stemming from some virtuous, noble clan,
And do not live yourself by gentle deed
Or take your fathers' noble code and creed,
You are no gentleman, though duke or earl.
Vice and bad manners are what make a churl.
305   "Gentility is only the renown
For bounty that your fathers handed down,
Quite foreign to your person, not your own;
Gentility must come from God alone.
That we are gentle comes to us by grace
310 And by no means is it bequeathed with place.
    "Reflect how noble (says Valerius)[11]
Was Tullius surnamed Hostilius,
Who rose from poverty to nobleness.
And read Boethius, Seneca no less,
315 Thus they express themselves and are agreed:
'Gentle is he that does a gentle deed.'
And therefore, my dear husband, I conclude
That even if my ancestors were rude,
Yet God on high—and so I hope He will—
320 Can grant me grace to live in virtue still,
A gentlewoman only when beginning
To live in virtue and to shrink from sinning.
    "As for my poverty which you reprove,
Almighty God Himself in whom we move,
325 Believe and have our being, chose a life
Of poverty, and every man or wife
Nay, every child can see our Heavenly King
Would never stoop to choose a shameful thing.
No shame in poverty if the heart is gay,
330 As Seneca and all the learned say.
He who accepts his poverty unhurt
I'd say is rich although he lacked a shirt.
But truly poor are they who whine and fret
And covet what they cannot hope to get.
335 And he that, having nothing, covets not,

---

11. **Valerius . . . Seneca** Valerius (və lir′ ē əs) Maximus was a first-century A.D. Roman author who collected historical anecdotes. Tullios Hostilius rose from humble beginnings to become a legendary king of Rome. Boethius (bō ē′ thē əs) was a Roman philosopher whose *The Consolation of Philosophy* is a recognized source for Chaucer's writings. Seneca was a Roman philosopher and dramatist.

Vocabulary Builder
esteemed (ə stēmd′) *v.* highly respected

Reading Strategy
Using Context Clues
From the context, can you guess the meaning of *churl* in line 304? Which words serve as clues?

Literary Analysis
Frame Which characters from the General Prologue might disagree with the hag's view on poverty? Would the Wife agree with them, or with the hag? Explain.

31 ▶ **Critical Viewing**
Which lines from the old woman's speech does this painting best illustrate? **[Interpret]**

The Charity of St. Eloi and the Healing of the Ill, Anonymous

St. Eloi was born in France in c. 590. He was a talented goldsmith, who eventually gained notice of the king, Clotaire II. After the king's death, he was made chief councilor. St. Eloi used his position to obtain alms for the poor and to ransom captives. He also founded several monasteries and had churches built.

This work captures all of the elements of medieval art. First, it depicts a religious event—a saint healing the sick. Second, the figures are dressed and depicted as real people who lived at the time. Third, the church, with its curved Romanesque arches, serves as a background for the action. Students should also notice the shadows cast by the figures in the foreground. The shadows add a three-dimensional element, an innovation during the Middle Ages with its two-dimensional art.

Use these questions for discussion:

1. How can you tell from the painting that St. Eloi is a role model for gentility?
   Answer: His gentility is visible in his actions. He kindness to the poor shows this virtue.

2. How does the appearance of the halo above the saint's head fit with the Wife of Bath's ideas about gentility?
   Answer: The Wife of Bath says that gentility comes from God.

The Canterbury Tales: The Wife of Bath's Tale ■ 151

Differentiated
Instruction   **Solutions for All Learners**

Vocabulary for English Learners
Point out to students that today the word *gentle* usually means "not harsh or rough," but the original meaning of the word is "of high birth." Provide students with the words below, all of which have the same root—*gentil.* Discuss how the words are generally used today and how these uses are different from the words' original meanings.

gentility
genteel
gentle
gentleman/gentlewoman

Enrichment for Gifted/Talented Students
Ask students to consider the ways that sound effects and music contribute to video games, movies, and television shows. Then, challenge students to think of background music and sound effects that would be appropriate to accompany scenes from "The Wife of Bath's Tale." Have students create a storyboard that identifies scenes from the story and annotate each scene with ideas about sounds and music. Ask students to share their storyboards with the class and explain their choices.

33 Humanities

Angel at the Door, by Eleanor Fortescue-Brickdale (1871–1945)

Eleanor Fortescue-Brickdale, like most middle class girls, was educated at home. At the age of 17, however, she went to study at the Crystal Palace School of Art. Then, after several unsuccessful attempts she was admitted to the Royal Academy of Art in 1897. Fortescue-Brickdale was a Pre-Raphaelite painter, and she mainly worked in stained glass, oil, and watercolor. She achieved success in her oil paintings of historical themes and in her illustrations for Tennyson's "Poems."

Use this question for discussion:

• How does this painting support the old woman's belief that there is no shame in poverty?
Answer: The beggar in the painting is actually an angel in disguise.

34 Critical Viewing

Possible response: The old woman may believe that beggars are angels in disguise. She believed that her words would change the knight's behavior, and she knows that she is not what she appears to be.

33

152 ■ *From Legend to History (449–1485)*

34 ◄ **Critical Viewing**
Might the old woman in the tale believe that all beggars are angels in disguise, as implied in this image? Explain. **[Speculate]**

Enrichment

Chaucer's Influence

Seventeenth-century poet and dramatist John Dryden called Chaucer "the father of English poetry." Dryden admired Chaucer in the same way that the Greeks admired Homer or the Romans admired Virgil. He found in Chaucer's work "a perpetual fountain of good sense."

A century later, the poet and essayist Samuel Taylor Coleridge wrote:

[I find] unceasing delight in Chaucer. His cheerfulness is especially delicious to me in my old age. How exquisitely tender he is,

and yet how perfectly free from the least touch of sickly melancholy or morbid drooping. The sympathy of the poet with the subjects of his poetry is particularly remarkable in Shakespeare and Chaucer; but what Shakespeare effects by a strong act of imagination and mental changing, Chaucer does without any effort, merely by the inborn kindly joyousness of his nature. How well we seem to know Chaucer! How absolutely nothing do we know of Shakespeare!

Is rich, though you may think he is a sot.[12]
    "True poverty can find a song to sing.
Juvenal says a pleasant little thing:
'The poor can dance and sing in the relief
340 Of having nothing that will tempt a thief.'
Though it be hateful, poverty is good,
A great incentive to a livelihood,
And a great help to our capacity
For wisdom, if accepted patiently.
345 Poverty is, though wanting in estate,
A kind of wealth that none calumniate.[13]
Poverty often, when the heart is lowly,
Brings one to God and teaches what is holy,
Gives knowledge of oneself and even lends
350 A glass by which to see one's truest friends.
And since it's no offence, let me be plain;
Do not <u>rebuke</u> my poverty again.
    "Lastly you taxed me, sir, with being old.
Yet even if you never had been told
355 By ancient books, you gentlemen engage
Yourselves in honor to respect old age.
To call an old man 'father' shows good breeding,
And this could be supported from my reading.
    "You say I'm old and fouler than a fen.
360 You need not fear to be a cuckold, then.
Filth and old age, I'm sure you will agree,
Are powerful wardens upon chastity.
Nevertheless, well knowing your delights,
I shall fulfil your worldly appetites.
365   "You have two choices; which one will you try?
To have me old and ugly till I die,
But still a loyal, true and humble wife
That never will displease you all her life,
Or would you rather I were young and pretty
370 And chance your arm what happens in a city
Where friends will visit you because of me,
Yes, and in other places too, maybe.
Which would you have? The choice is all your own."
    The knight thought long, and with a piteous groan
375 At last he said, with all the care in life,
"My lady and my love, my dearest wife,
I leave the matter to your wise decision.
You make the choice yourself, for the provision
Of what may be agreeable and rich

---

12. Sot fool.
13. calumniate (kə lum′ ne āt′) slander.

Reading Strategy
Using Context Clues
Which context clues help clarify the meaning of *incentive* in line 342?

Vocabulary Builder
rebuke (ri byook′) *v.*
criticize strongly

Reading Check
Identify two benefits that the old woman says can come with poverty.

35 Reading Strategy
Using Context Clues

- Review with students that context clues are words and phrases in a surrounding passage that shed light on the meaning of an unfamiliar word.

- Ask a volunteer to read aloud lines 341–344. Then **ask** the Reading Strategy question: Which context clues help clarify the meaning of *incentive* in line 342?
Answer: The phrase "great help" is the closest context clue. It should suggest to students that an incentive is something that makes a person work harder or feel motivated.

- Once students figure out the meaning of the word *incentive,* **ask** a volunteer to paraphrase the sentence. **Possible response:** Poverty helps you work harder, and it helps make you wise.

36 Reading Check

Answer: Benefits include having nothing worth stealing, self-knowledge, and greater spirituality.

Differentiated Instruction   Solutions for All Learners

Enrichment for Gifted/Talented Students
Students may enjoy turning the ending of the story into an episode of a talk show. Have several students act out the last section of the story, in which the old woman outlines the benefits and drawbacks of having an old and ugly wife or a young and beautiful wife. Have the knight be present on the stage along with a young mystery woman. Students should act out the interaction between the three people. Which woman does the knight choose?

Enrichment for Advanced Readers
Students may enjoy writing alternative endings to the tale. Organize students into small groups. Have some groups rewrite the ending on the basis of the knight's choosing a new, young, and beautiful wife. Have the other groups rewrite the ending on the basis of the knight's choice of an old but loyal wife. Ask students to share their endings with the class. Talk about how the alternative endings compare with the actual surprise ending of the tale.

Since the days of the Norman Conquest in the eleventh century, English law held that a woman was the subordinate partner in a marriage. The legal term that described the relationship was *coverture*. The word literally means "cover." In other words, a woman was under the protection or cover of her husband. When a woman married, coverture caused a woman to lose her own rights, individuality, and property in the eyes of the law. It relieved a woman of all legal responsibilities. For example, a woman could not be sued and did not have to pay taxes. On the other hand, a woman's property was entirely controlled by her husband, and she had no rights when it came to her income, her property, or her children during marriage or in the event of a divorce.

Coverture was in effect in the United States until 1839, when married women obtained some of their legal rights. Women argued that they needed to control their money and property while their men were away for long periods fighting in wars or pioneering new lands.

Connect to the Literature
Encourage students to review the tale and the Wife's description in the Prologue before answering the question.

Answer: Unlike the women of her day, the Wife of Bath exerted control over the men she had married and confidently told a tale in which a woman triumphed over her husband. She was independent and was traveling to Canterbury as an equal among men.

380　In honor to us both, I don't care which;
　　　Whatever pleases you suffices me."
　　　　　"And have I won the mastery?" said she,
　　　"Since I'm to choose and rule as I think fit?"
　　　"Certainly, wife," he answered her, "that's it."
385　"Kiss me," she cried. "No quarrels! On my oath
　　　And word of honor, you shall find me both,
　　　That is, both fair and faithful as a wife;
　　　May I go howling mad and take my life
　　　Unless I prove to be as good and true
390　As ever wife was since the world was new!
　　　And if to-morrow when the sun's above
　　　I seem less fair than any lady-love,
　　　Than any queen or empress east or west,
　　　Do with my life and death as you think best.
395　Cast up the curtain, husband. Look at me!"
　　　　　And when indeed the knight had looked to see,
　　　Lo, she was young and lovely, rich in charms.

37 Literature in Context

Cultural Connection

Selfsame Sovereignty

The Wife of Bath uses the story of the knight and the old woman to express her own belief in *selfsame sovereignty*, or equality in marriage between a husband and wife. Whether such an idea meant that women shared ownership of property and family wealth, or whether it meant they had an equal share in decision-making, such a belief was definitely well ahead of the times.

In medieval England, women could inherit property only if there were no male heirs in the family. Usually, property was entailed, or assigned to the male survivors, the women being left under the men's care until marriage or death. Moreover, at marriage a woman was often required to renounce any further claims to her father's property. Often, any property she did bring to the marriage was immediately forfeited to her husband, leaving her with virtually no further claim to it. Only in the late 1800s did Great Britain's Married Women's Property Acts first allow a woman the right to property in her own name.

That such laws did not exist in medieval England reinforced the perception that women held the subordinate role in society, a social expectation that the Wife of Bath refused to obey.

Connect to the Literature

In what ways does Chaucer's description of the Wife of Bath, as well as her tale, suggest that she was an unusual woman for her time?

In ecstasy he caught her in her arms,
His heart went bathing in a bath of blisses
400 And melted in a hundred thousand kisses,
And she responded in the fullest measure
With all that could delight or give him pleasure.
    So they lived ever after to the end
In perfect bliss; and may Christ Jesus send
405 Us husbands meek and young and fresh in bed,
And grace to overbid them when we wed.
And—Jesu hear my prayer!—cut short the lives
Of those who won't be governed by their wives;
And all old, angry niggards of their pence,[14]
410 God send them soon a very pestilence!

14. **niggards** (nig′ ərdz) **of their pence** misers stingy with their money.

Critical Reading

1. **Respond:** Were you surprised by the outcome of this story? Why or why not?

2. **(a) Compare and Contrast:** According to the Wife of Bath, in what way does life in her day differ from life in King Arthur's time? **(b) Deduce:** What does the Wife think of this change? How do you know?

3. **(a) Recall:** What punishment does the king initially issue to the knight? **(b) Speculate:** Why might the king willingly allow his wife to effect a different punishment instead? **(c) Apply:** What philosophy about relationships do the king and queen share with the Wife of Bath?

4. **(a) Recall:** What character flaw is the tale-within-a-tale of Midas's wife meant to illustrate? **(b) Evaluate:** In your opinion, does this inner story undercut the main point of the Wife's tale? Explain.

5. **(a) Recall:** What bargain does the knight make with the old woman? **(b) Analyze:** Why do you think the queen forces the knight to keep his part of the bargain?

6. **(a) Recall:** How does the old woman define true gentility? **(b) Evaluate:** How effective are her arguments about gentility, poverty and old age? **(c) Apply:** Do her arguments still relate to today's world? Explain.

7. **(a) Recall:** What final choice does the old woman offer the knight? **(b) Infer:** In what way does his response show that he has finally learned his lesson about the nature of women? **(c) Make a Judgment:** Has the knight experienced sufficient punishment and redemption for his crime? Explain.

8. **Speculate:** In today's society, where might you find individuals who would agree with the Wife and the philosophy she illustrates with her story? Who might argue against such opinions?

Go Online
Author Link

For: More about Geoffrey Chaucer
Visit: www.PHSchool.com
Web Code: ese-9103

The Canterbury Tales: The Wife of Bath's Tale ■ 155

Answers continued

7. (a) The old woman offers the knight a choice between an old, ugly, loyal, humble wife and an unfaithful, young, beautiful wife. (b) By letting his wife make the decision, the knight shows that he has understood her lesson. (c) **Possible response:** The knight has experienced sufficient punishment and redemption; he has worked hard to find the answer to save his life, and he has honored his promise to the old woman. He learned his lesson about

respecting his wife, and he receives his reward.

8. **Possible response:** Many modern women would probably agree with the Wife of Bath. People with old-fashioned ideas about women's roles might disagree with the Wife of Bath.

Go Online For additional information about
Author Link Geoffrey Chaucer, have students type in the Web Code, then select C from the alphabet, and then select Geoffrey Chaucer.

---

38 **Literary Analysis**
Frame

- **Ask** students the Literary Analysis question: Which words serve as a clue that the interior story is finished and that the Wife has turned her attention toward her riding companions?
  Answer: Students should recognize the traditional tale-ending words "So they lived ever after to the end in perfect bliss" as the clue that the story is finished. She also gives a last prayer for all women.

ASSESS

Answers

1. Students may be surprised by the old woman's transformation.

2. (a) According to the Wife of Bath, people do not see fairies as they did during King Arthur's time because friars have purged them all. (b) The Wife thinks that the change is not positive. She suggests that friars have swarmed the countryside and are likely to take a woman's virtue.

3. (a) The king sentences the knight to death. (b) **Possible response:** The king might be an excellent husband who defers to his wife's decisions. (c) The king and queen understand equality in marriage.

4. (a) The tale illustrates the Wife's point that women are incapable of keeping secrets. (b) Students may respond that the inner story does not undercut the main point; it simply shows that the Wife is aware that women have faults.

5. (a) The knight agrees to do what the old woman wants after she tells him the secret to what women desire most. (b) **Possible response:** The queen believes the knight should marry the woman to keep his honor.

6. (a) True gentility is not inherited or based on one's possessions; it is a gift from God and a moral goodness. (b) **Possible response:** The arguments are effective; they cause the knight to change his behavior and defer to his wife's decision. (c) Students may respond that the arguments are still valid. Although gentility is an old-fashioned concept, moral behavior is not.

Answers

1. (a) Unlike the old woman in the story, the Wife of Bath is well off, well dressed, and well traveled. Like the old woman, the Wife is wise and confident in her abilities. (b) The Wife certainly identifies with the old woman who is wise, just, articulate, and persuasive.

2. (a) **Good Morality/Lesson:** knight receives merciful punishment; he is forced to marry old woman; gentility is defined as gift from God and the exercise of good values; poverty is not shameful; knight rewarded for deferring to wife's judgment **General Pleasure/ Entertainment Value:** ridicule of friars; description of the court and the knight's journey; story of King Midas; magical characters; knight's anguish at marrying old woman; twists and turns of plot. (b) **Final Judgment:** The host would probably be entertained by the tale, although he might disagree with the Wife's idea that women should master their husbands.

3. Although the frame story's setting is contemporary with the author, the Wife's story is set centuries before during the age of King Arthur. The frame story begins in the English town of Southwark; the Wife's tale takes place in the countryside and in the royal court.

4. (a) Both scenes are set in the countryside and contain magical dancing creatures. (b) The rural setting and the magical creatures suggest that a happy, fairy-tale ending will follow.

5. (a) The clues include the knight's perception that he will never find the answer he needs and his decision to return to the Queen. (b) Possible synonyms include *brokenhearted, despondent,* and *melancholy.*

6. *Suffices* means "satisfies, is enough, is adequate." Students should understand that the knight's insistence that he does not care and will be pleased by whatever his wife decides is a context clue.

7. **Possible response:** The fairy-tale nature of the story suggests that women in medieval times had little autonomy or influence over their husbands. Also, the Wife of Bath's comments about women's lack of safety among friars and the

156

Apply the Skills

The Wife of Bath's Tale

Literary Analysis

Frame

1. Reread the description of the Wife of Bath in the General Prologue, or the **frame** for the Wife's tale. **(a)** Compare the characteristics of the Wife to those of the old woman in the Wife's tale. **(b)** Do you think the Wife identifies with the old woman? Why or why not?

2. In the frame, the Host declares he will judge the pilgrims' tales on their "good morality and general pleasure" (lines 818–825), their ability to teach a moral or lesson, and the entertainment value for the listeners. If you were the Host, how would you respond to the Wife's tale? **(a)** Use the first chart below to note details from the tale. **(b)** Then, use the details to determine a final judgment.

Good Morality/ Lesson	General Pleasure/ Entertainment Value		Final Judgment
		⇨	

Connecting Literary Elements

3. In what ways does the **setting** of "The Wife of Bath's Tale" compare or contrast with the setting of the frame story the pilgrimage to Canterbury?

4. **(a)** In what ways do the details of setting in lines 135–144 echo the description of "ancient days" in lines 3–7? **(b)** Describe the way these details hint at, or foreshadow, the happy ending of the tale.

Reading Strategy

Using Context Clues

5. **(a)** What **context clues** in the inner story help to define the word *dejected* in line 135? **(b)** Identify three words you might use instead of *dejected* that would retain the meaning of the lines surrounding the word.

6. Define the word *suffices* as it is used in line 381, explaining which context clues enabled you to determine its meaning.

Extend Understanding

7. **Social Studies Connection:** In what way is a story like "The Wife of Bath's Tale" an important commentary on the lives of medieval women?

156 ■ From Legend to History (449–1485)

QuickReview

A **frame** is a story that brackets, or frames, another story or group of stories.

A story's **setting** is the time and place in which the characters live.

When you use **context clues,** you determine the meaning of a word by using nearby words or phases that shed light on its meaning.

Go Online
Assessment
For: Self-test
Visit: www.PHSchool.com
Web Code: esa-6107

Answers continued

knight's rough treatment of the young maiden suggest that life for medieval women could be difficult or dangerous.

Go Online   Students may use the **Self-test**
Assessment   to prepare for **Selection Test A**
or **Selection Test B**.

Build Language Skills

Vocabulary Lesson

Word Analysis: Multiple-Meaning Words

Many words in English have more than one meaning. For example, the word *bear* as a noun refers to a large, shaggy animal. As a verb, *bear* can mean "to carry," "endure," or "give birth to." Usually, the meaning of the word changes according to its part of speech.

Explain how each of the following words has more than one meaning. Use a dictionary to check your work.

1. relate   2. act   3. might

Spelling Strategy

To form a noun from an adjective that ends with the suffix *-ent,* use the suffix *-ence: different* becomes *difference.* Use the suffix *-ance* for adjectives ending in *-ant: important* becomes *importance.* Complete each word below using *-ence* or *-ance.*

1. elig ___   3. compet___
2. magnific ___   4. compli ___

Grammar and Style Lesson

Correcting Run-On Sentences

Using a **semicolon** to join closely related independent clauses is one way to correct a run-on. In some cases, the second clause may need a conjunctive adverb, such as *however, nonetheless,* or *furthermore,* followed by a comma.

> **Semicolon with conjunctive adverb:** No one knows why Chaucer wrote *The Canterbury Tales;* <u>however</u>, his inspiration may have come from his own pilgrimage to Canterbury.

Practice   Correct the following run-on sentences, adding semicolons and conjunctive adverbs where needed.

1. The Wife of Bath is a vivid character she does not hesitate to voice her opinions.

W̸G   *Prentice Hall Writing and Grammar Connection: Chapter 27, Section 3*

Vocabulary Builder: Synonyms and Antonyms

Review the vocabulary words on page 136. Then, for each numbered item below, use an S to identify the word pair as synonyms, or words with similar meanings. Use an A to identify the word pair as antonyms, or words opposite in meaning.

1. implored; pleaded

2. relates; suppresses

3. misalliance; match

4. contemptuous; praiseworthy

5. bequeath; hand down

6. prowess; cowardice

7. esteemed; despised

8. rebuke; scold

2. The tale begins with a description of King Arthur's time the Wife quickly contrasts that bygone age with her own time.

3. The king favors putting the knight to death the queen devises a different punishment.

4. The old woman's arguments on gentility and poverty are indisputable the knight is compelled to yield to her.

5. The Wife's riding companions listen attentively to her story she may win the competition.

Writing Application   Write four sentences describing the Wife of Bath. Use a semicolon and a conjunctive adverb in each sentence.

The Canterbury Tales: The Wife of Bath's Tale ■ 157

---

❶ Vocabulary Lesson
Word Analysis
1. *Relate* means "to tell," "to make connections," and "to have a relationship."
2. The noun *act* means "a deed," "an action," "a decision," "a formal legal document," "a section of a play," and "a show of feelings that may not be true." The verb *act* means "to perform," "to behave," "to take action," "to have an effect," and "to pretend."
3. The noun *might* means "great strength." The verb *might* is used to express possibility.

Spelling Strategy
1. elegance   3. competence
2. magnificence   4. compliance

Vocabulary Builder
1. S   3. A   5. S   7. A
2. A   4. A   6. A   8. S

❷ Grammar and Style Lesson
1. character; she
2. time; however, the Wife
3. death; however, the queen
4. indisputable; the knight
5. her story; she

Writing Application Possible Answers:
1. The Wife of Bath had been married five times; consequently, she knew something about marriage.
2. The Wife of Bath invented the character of the knight; however, she based him largely on her husband.
3. She was cynical toward the clergy; thus, she mistrusted friars who roamed the woods.
4. According to the Wife of Bath, gentility came from God; therefore, poverty and gentility were not mutually exclusive.

✓ Meeting Your Standards

Students will

1. **analyze and respond to literary elements.**
   - Literary Analysis: Medieval Romance

2. **read, comprehend, analyze, and critique a poem and a work of fiction.**
   - Reading Strategy: Summarizing
   - Reading Check questions
   - Apply the Skills questions
   - Assessment Practice (ATE)

3. **develop vocabulary.**
   - Vocabulary Lesson: Word Root: *-droit-*

4. **understand and apply written and oral language conventions.**
   - Spelling Strategy
   - Grammar and Style Lesson: Comparative and Superlative Forms

5. **develop writing proficiency.**
   - Writing Lesson: Interior Monologue

6. **develop appropriate research strategies.**
   - Extend Your Learning: Oral Report

7. **understand and apply listening and speaking strategies.**
   - Extend Your Learning: Proposal for a Multimedia Presentation

Block Scheduling: Use one 90-minute class period to preteach the skills and have students read the selection. Use a second 90-minute class period to assess students' mastery of skills, extend their learning, and monitor their progress.

Homework Suggestions

Following are possibilities for homework assignments:

- Support pages from *Unit 1 Resources:*
  - **Literary Analysis**
  - **Reading Strategy**
  - **Vocabulary Builder**
  - **Grammar and Style**

- An Extend Your Learning project and the Writing Lesson for this selection group may be completed over several days.

Step-by-Step Teaching Guide	Pacing Guide
PRETEACH	
• Administer Vocabulary and Reading Warm-ups as necessary.	5 min.
• Engage students' interest with the motivation activity.	5 min.
• Read and discuss author and background features. **FT**	10 min.
• Introduce the Literary Analysis Skill: Medieval Romance. **FT**	5 min.
• Introduce the Reading Strategy: Summarizing. **FT**	10 min.
• Prepare students to read by teaching the selection vocabulary. **FT**	
TEACH	
• Informally monitor comprehension while students read independently or in groups. **FT**	30 min.
• Monitor students' comprehension with the Reading Check notes.	as students read
• Reinforce vocabulary with Vocabulary Builder notes.	as students read
• Develop students' understanding of medieval romance with the Literary Analysis annotations. **FT**	5 min.
• Develop students' ability to summarize with the Reading Strategy annotations. **FT**	5 min.
ASSESS/EXTEND	
• Assess students' comprehension and mastery of the Literary Analysis and Reading Strategy by having them answer the Apply the Skills questions. **FT**	15 min.
• Have students complete the Vocabulary Lesson and the Grammar and Style Lesson. **FT**	15 min.
• Apply students' knowledge of how reactions enhance action by using the Writing Lesson. **FT**	45 min. or homework
• Apply students' understanding by using one or more of the Extend Your Learning activities.	20–90 min. or homework
• Administer Selection Test A or Selection Test B. **FT**	15 min.

Pre

Con

M
tresse
you a
select

Lit

Med

R
times
adve
tell o
conce
them

Con

T
base
the p

M
leger
izatic
read
litera

Re

Sun

T
As yo

Voc

assay

adjur
appe

feign
of; p

adro
or m

large
(p. 1

Resources

PRINT
Unit 1 Resources

TRANSPARENCY
Graphic Organizer Transparencies

PRINT
Reader's Notebook [L2]
Reader's Notebook: Adapted Version [L1]
Reader's Notebook: English Learner's Version [EL]
Unit 1 Resources

TECHNOLOGY
Listening to Literature Audio CDs [L2, EL]
Reader's Notebook: Adapted Version Audio CD [L1, L2]

PRINT
Unit 1 Resources
General Resources

TECHNOLOGY
Go Online: Research [L3]
Go Online: Self-test [L3]
ExamView® Test Bank **[L3]**

Choosing Resources for Differentiated Instruction

[L1] Special Needs Students
[L2] Below-Level Students
[L3] All Students
[L4] Advanced Students
[EL] English Learners

For Vocabulary and Reading Warm-ups and for Selection Tests, A signifies "less challenging" and B "more challenging." For Graphic Organizer Transparencies, A signifies "not filled in" and B "filled in."

FT Fast Track Instruction: To move the lesson more quickly, use the strategies and activities identified with **FT**.

Scaffolding for Less Proficient and Advanced Students

The leveled Critical Thinking questions after selections progress in the levels of thinking required to answer them. To address the needs of your different students, you may use the (a) level questions for your less proficient students and the (b) level questions with your on-level and advanced students. The occasional (c) level questions are appropriate for your advanced students.

PRENTICE HALL
Teacher EXPRESS Use this complete
Plan · Teach · Assess suite of powerful
teaching tools to make lesson planning and testing quicker and easier.

PRENTICE HALL
Student EXPRESS Use the interac-
Learn · Study · Succeed tive textbook
(online and on CD-ROM) to make selections and activities come alive with audio and video support and interactive questions.

Go Online
Professional Development
For: Information about Lexiles
Visit: www.PHSchool.com
Web Code: eue-1111

Learning Modalities
Musical/Rhythmic Learners
Direct students to examine the rhythmic structure of the stanzas in *Sir Gawain and the Green Knight*. Have them identify reasons for the shorter quatrains at the end of each stanza.

❶ About the Selection

The story of the green knight who tests the honesty and bravery of Arthur's knight Gawain still remains one of the most popular of the Arthurian legends. Its vivid descriptions, lively language, and dramatic picture of life in medieval times have a timeless appeal for students, and its skillful use of alliteration and rhyme makes it an excellent introduction to Arthurian legends.

In the story, an enormous green knight bursts into Arthur's hall and challenges King Arthur to strike the first blow in a duel, provided that in a year's time he seek out the Green Knight and allow him to deal the first blow. Gawain takes the challenge on Arthur's behalf and promptly chops off the intruder's head. To his astonishment, the intruder picks up his head, repeats his challenge, and leaves. A year later, Gawain sets off on his adventure in the course of which his loyalty, honesty, and bravery undergo various tests.

❶ from Sir Gawain and the Green Knight

Translated by Marie Borroff

Background The legend of King Arthur is probably based on the life of a Celtic warrior who fought the Anglo-Saxon invaders of England in the late fifth and early sixth centuries. His role as a defender of England made him a hero to the Britons, the island's Celtic inhabitants. They told stories celebrating his just rule and championship of the oppressed and abused.

By the time the Arthurian legends were transformed into written literature, the Britons had long since been defeated by the Anglo-Saxons. The fact that the tales came from a vanished world only fueled their power as literature. The Arthurian stories set an ideal for knights, and ideals are never fully realized in the present. Their true home may be the legendary past, or a future yet to come.

The selection begins at the start of a New Year's Eve feast at King Arthur's Court in Camelot. Before anyone has started eating, the festivities are interrupted by an immense green knight who suddenly appears at the hall door. The knight rides a green horse and is armed with a gigantic ax.

This horseman hurtles in, and the hall enters;
Riding to the high dais,[1] recked he no danger;
Not a greeting he gave as the guests he o'erlooked,
Nor wasted his words, but "Where is," he said,
5 "The captain of this crowd? Keenly I wish
To see that sire with sight, and to himself say my say."
    He swaggered all about
    To scan the host so gay;
    He halted, as if in doubt
10   Who in that hall held sway.

---

1. dais (dā′ is) *n.* platform.

162 ■ From Legend to History (449–1485)

Differentiated
Instruction   Solutions for All Learners

Accessibility at a Glance

	Sir Gawain and Green Knight	Morte d'Arthur
Context	Arthurian legend; courtly love	Arthurian legend
Language	Vocabulary footnotes	Medieval vocabulary; long sentences
Concept Level	Accessible (medieval romance)	Accessible (King Arthur and his knights)
Literary Merit	Classic	Classic
Lexile	NP	1200L
Overall rating	Average	Average

There were stares on all sides as the stranger spoke,
For much did they marvel what it might mean
That a horseman and a horse should have such a hue,
Grow green as the grass, and greener, it seemed.
15 Then green fused on gold more glorious by far.
All the onlookers eyed him, and edged nearer,
And awaited in wonder what he would do,
For many sights had they seen, but such a one never,
So that phantom and fairy the folk there deemed it,
20 Therefore chary[2] of answer was many a champion bold,
And stunned at his strong words stone-still they sat
In a swooning silence in the stately hall.
As all were slipped into sleep, so slackened their speech apace.
     Not all, I think, for dread,
25   But some of courteous grace
     Let him who was their head
     Be spokesman in that place.

Then Arthur before the high dais that entrance beholds,
And hailed him, as behooved, for he had no fear.
30 And said "Fellow, in faith you have found fair welcome;
The head of this hostelry Arthur am I;
Leap lightly down, and linger, I pray,
And the tale of your intent you shall tell us after."
"Nay, so help me," said the other, "He that on high sits,
35 To tarry here any time, 'twas not mine errand;
But as the praise of you, prince, is puffed up so high,
And your court and your company are counted the best,
Stoutest under steel-gear on steeds to ride,
Worthiest of their works the wide world over,
40 And peerless to prove in passages of arms,
And courtesy here is carried to its height,
And so at this season I have sought you out.
You may be certain by the branch that I bear in hand
That I pass here in peace, and would part friends,
45 For had I come to this court on combat bent,
I have a hauberk[3] at home, and a helm beside,
A shield and a sharp spear, shining bright,
And other weapons to wield, I ween well, to boot,
But as I willed no war, I wore no metal.
50 But if you be so bold as all men believe,
You will graciously grant the game that I ask by right."
     Arthur answer gave
     And said, "Sir courteous knight,
     If contest here you crave,
55   You shall not fail to fight."

---

2. **chary** (cher´ ē) *adj.* not giving freely.
3. **hauberk** (hô´ bərk) *n.* coat of armor.

Reading Strategy
Summarizing What are three main points of the Green Knight's speech in lines 34–51?

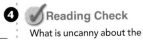
Reading Check
What is uncanny about the Knight who enters Arthur's court?

from Sir Gawain and the Green Knight ■ 163

---

❷ Literary Analysis
Medieval Romance

- **Ask** students what aspect of medieval romance is introduced in lines 11–19.
  Answer: The elements of strange events and fantasy are introduced here.

- Have students identify other elements of medieval romance that are mentioned on these pages.
  Answer: Elements of medieval romance include a king (King Arthur), knights, ladies, banquet hall, courtesy, bravery, armor, weapons, contest/fight.

❸ Reading Strategy
Summarizing

- Have students read lines 34–51.

- **Ask** students to name key words or phrases that reveal the Green Knight's purpose.
  Possible response: The knight mentions an errand (line 35) and that he sought out king Arthur specifically (line 42).

- Then, **ask** students the Reading Strategy question: What are three main points of the Green Knight's speech in lines 34–51?
  Answer: The Green Knight has heard glowing reports of King Arthur and his knights, he comes in peace, and he would enter into a contest with Sir Arthur.

❹ Reading Check

Answer: Both the great size of the Knight and the fact that he is green are uncanny (mysterious and weird).

Differentiated Instruction   Solutions for All Learners

Support for Special Needs Students
Have students read along as they listen to the **Listening to Literature Audio CD.** Play only one stanza at a time, allowing students time to digest what they have heard and read. Have students tell what action has taken place in each session.

Vocabulary for English Learners
Relate the general events of a section (stanza, page) of the story. Then, have students read that section and note unfamiliar words. Help them understand these words, both by assisting them in finding definitions and by discussing meanings in context. Then, have them reread and paraphrase the section.

Enrichment for Gifted/Talented Students
Students may enjoy reading the poem aloud, dramatizing the events. Assign the roles of Arthur, Gawain, and the Green Knight, and allow other students to rotate the role of the narrator. These students may also enjoy learning about other Arthurian legends at www.PHSchool.com.

163

⑤ Background

Literature Explain to students that the Beheading Game, described here, is a traditional plot element in early medieval romances. Many authorities believe that the ritual beheadings were originally related to crops. Beheading seed pods is one way of ensuring strong plant growth for the next year, and perhaps this is what the custom reflects.

⑥ Reading Strategy
Summarizing

- Explain to students that Arthur initially believes that the Green Knight has come to challenge someone to a fight—the sort of "game" one finds in medieval tournaments.

- After students have read the Green Knight's challenge in lines 60–76, **ask** them to summarize what he is proposing.
Answer: The Green Knight wants someone to play his game. He will allow anyone who is brave enough to strike a blow with his ax. Then, in one year and a day, the Green Knight gets to do the same.

⑦ Literary Analysis
Medieval Romance

- **Ask** students the Literary Analysis question: What aspects of medieval romances does the Green Knight's appearance illustrate?
Answer: The description combines realistic and supernatural elements.

▶ **Monitor Progress:** Ask students to point out specific words and phrases that helped them answer the question.

▶ **Reteach:** If students have difficulty recognizing important words, work with them to find synonyms that may be more accessible.

"Nay, to fight, in good faith, is far from my thought;
There are about on these benches but beardless children,
Were I here in full arms on a haughty[4] steed,
For measured against mine, their might is puny.
60 And so I call in this court for a Christmas game,
For 'tis Yule, and New Year, and many young bloods about;
If any in this house such hardihood claims,
Be so bold in his blood, his brain so wild,
As stoutly to strike one stroke for another,
65 I shall give him as my gift this gisarme[5] noble,
This ax, that is heavy enough, to handle as he likes,
And I shall bide the first blow, as bare as I sit.
If there be one so wilful my words to assay,
Let him leap hither lightly, lay hold of this weapon;
70 I quitclaim it forever, keep it as his own,
And I shall stand him a stroke, steady on this floor,
So you grant me the guerdon to give him another, sans blame.[6]
    In a twelvemonth[7] and a day
    He shall have of me the same;
75   Now be it seen straightway
    Who dares take up the game."

If he astonished them at first, stiller were then
All that household in hall, the high and the low;
The stranger on his green steed stirred in the saddle,
80 And roisterously his red eyes he rolled all about,
Bent his bristling brows, that were bright green,
Wagged his beard as he watched who would arise.
When the court kept its counsel he coughed aloud,
And cleared his throat coolly, the clearer to speak:
85 "What, is this Arthur's house," said that horseman then,
"Whose fame is so fair in far realms and wide?
Where is now your arrogance and your awesome deeds,
Your valor and your victories and your vaunting words?
Now are the revel and renown of the Round Table
90 Overwhelmed with a word of one man's speech,
For all cower and quake, and no cut felt!"
With this he laughs so loud that the lord grieved;
The blood for sheer shame shot to his face, and pride.
    With rage his face flushed red,
95   And so did all beside.
    Then the king as bold man bred
    Toward the stranger took a stride.

---

4. **haughty** (hôt´ ē) *adj.* lofty.
5. **gisarme** (gi zärm´) *n.* battle-ax.
6. **I shall . . . blame** "I will stand firm while he strikes me with the ax provided that you reward me with the opportunity to do the same to him without being blamed for it."
7. **twelvemonth** a year.

Vocabulary Builder
assay (as´ ā) *v.* prove or test

Literary Analysis
Medieval Romance What aspect of medieval romances does the Green Knight's appearance illustrate?

Enrichment

New Year's Celebrations
The Green Knight has arrived at a New Year's celebration, at which people are feasting. Although not everyone celebrates the New Year on the same date, cultures throughout the world do celebrate it on some day.

Many New Year's festivities involve traditional foods. Most foods eaten on New Year's are chosen because they are associated with some combination of good luck, wealth, or fertility. The foods are thought to help ensure these in the coming year.

Celebrants in some cultures enjoy sweet foods, such as challah or honey cakes eaten by the Jews, and sweet cakes made from rice eaten by Cambodians. Other cultures feature savory foods, such as noodles in Japan, lentils in Italy, and a combination of black-eyed peas and rice eaten by African Americans. Some families avoid meat on New Year's, whereas other families emphasize it.

Three Knights Returning from a Tournament. French miniature from "Recueil de Traites de Devotion."

9 ◀ **Critical Viewing**
From this picture, what can you infer about a knight's readiness for challenges of skill, such as tournaments? **[Infer]**

And said, "Sir, now we see you will say but folly,
Which whoso has sought, it suits that he find.
100 No guest here is aghast of your great words.
Give to me your gisarme, in God's own name,
And the boon you have begged shall straight be granted."
He leaps to him lightly, lays hold of his weapon;
The green fellow on foot fiercely alights.
105 Now has Arthur his ax, and the haft[8] grips,
And sternly stirs it about, on striking bent.
The stranger before him stood there erect,
Higher than any in the house by a head and more;
With stern look as he stood, he stroked his beard,
110 And with undaunted countenance drew down his coat,
No more moved nor dismayed for his mighty dints
Than any bold man on bench had brought him a drink of wine.
    Gawain by Guenevere
    Toward the king doth now incline:
115   "I beseech, before all here,
    That this melee may be mine."

"Would you grant me the grace," said Gawain to the king,
"To be gone from this bench and stand by you there,
If I without discourtesy might quit this board,

10 ✓ **Reading Check**
What challenge does the Green Knight make to Arthur's court?

8. **haft** *n.* handle of a weapon or tool.

from *Sir Gawain and the Green Knight* ■ 165

---

8 **Humanities**

Three Knights Returning From a Tournament

Medieval art often depicts events from real life, such as this scene of three knights returning from a tournament. In fact, information about customs, clothing, food, and relationships in the Middle Ages often comes from art of the times.

Use these questions for discussion:

1. How do the knights in this illustration compare with the popular image of knights seen in movies and television?
Possible response: Knights in movies are often glamourized. Also, early medieval chain mail, as is seen here, is not as commonly portrayed as the solid armor worn slightly later. However, many directors now make an effort to show knights in armor authentic to the period of a story.

2. **Ask** students what they might learn from looking at the picture's details. For example, the armor looks the same on all three, but the tunics are different. What might this signify?
Possible responses: Students may guess (correctly) that the different tunics would be similar to uniforms in identifying who you are or for whom you are fighting. The horses, too, wear colors, perhaps to identify the owner. Students may also observe that armor goes head to toe; the knights feared and protected themselves from injury at the tournament. Also, only swords are seen, so it seems likely that this was not a jousting tournament (a contest involving long spears called lances).

9 **Critical Viewing**

Possible response: With armor head to toe, helmets on, and swords at the ready, it seems that knights were eager and ready to take on challenges of skill.

10 **Reading Check**

Answer: The knight will allow Arthur to strike him with an ax, provided that in a year and a day, Arthur will allow the Green Knight to strike him one blow with the same weapon.

165

- Depending on students' familiarity with the chivalric ideal, you may wish to review the material in the Enrichment box below before asking them the Literary Analysis question.

- Remind students that chivalry—the code of knighthood during the Middle Ages—is at the heart of medieval romance.

- **Ask** students the Literary Analysis question: In what way are Gawain's words in lines 128–134 consistent with the ideals of chivalry?
  Answer: Gawain's words reflect the ideal qualities of humility, respect for the king, and courtesy.

❶❷ **Reading Strategy**
Summarizing

- Point out that the Green Knight is chivalrous in his reply, but also emphasizes the importance of Gawain's chivalry. Words such as *covenant, upon oath, oath,* and *swear upon oath* (lines 161–175) underscore the importance of a knight's word.

- Have students **summarize** the key points and conditions of the challenge, as described in lines 150–184.
  Possible response: Whatever happens, Gawain must seek out the knight in a year. He can bring any weapon he wants, but he must come alone. Gawain asks the Green Knight's name. The knight says he will tell his name, and where he lives, after he has received Gawain's blow—but if he can't speak, Gawain can drop the matter.

120 And if my liege lady⁹ misliked it not,
I would come to your counsel before your court noble.
For I find it not fit, as in faith it is known,
When such a boon is begged before all these knights,
Though you be tempted thereto, to take it on yourself
125 While so bold men about upon benches sit,
That no host under heaven is hardier of will,
Nor better brothers-in-arms where battle is joined;
I am the weakest, well I know, and of wit feeblest;
And the loss of my life would be least of any;
130 That I have you for uncle is my only praise;
My body, but for your blood, is barren of worth;
And for that this folly befits not a king,
And 'tis I that have asked it, it ought to be mine,
And if my claim be not comely let all this court judge in sight."
135　　　The court assays the claim,
　　　And in counsel all unite
　　　To give Gawain the game
　　　And release the king outright.

Then the king called the knight to come to his side,
140 And he rose up readily, and reached him with speed,
Bows low to his lord, lays hold of the weapon,
And he releases it lightly, and lifts up his hand,
And gives him God's blessing, and graciously prays
That his heart and his hand may be hardy both.
145 "Keep, cousin," said the king, "what you cut with this day,
And if you rule it aright, then readily, I know,
You shall stand the stroke it will strike after."
Gawain goes to the guest with gisarme in hand,
And boldly he bides there, abashed not a whit.
150 Then hails he Sir Gawain, the horseman in green:
"Recount we our contract, ere you come further.
First I ask and adjure you, how you are called
That you tell me true, so that trust it I may."
"In good faith," said the good knight, "Gawain am I
155 Whose buffet befalls you,¹⁰ whate'er betide after,
And at this time twelvemonth take from you another
With what weapon you will, and with no man else alive."
　　　The other nods assent:
　　　"Sir Gawain, as I may thrive,
160　　　I am wondrous well content
　　　That you this dint¹¹ shall drive."

---

9. **liege** (lēj) **lady** Guenevere, the wife of the lord, Arthur, to whom Gawain is bound to give service and allegiance.
10. **Whose . . . you** "whose blow you will receive."
11. **dint** *n.* blow.

166 ■ From Legend to History (449–1485)

Enrichment

Chivalry

The connection between knighthood and a code of behavior is not incidental. In the 11th century, Viking invaders had no concept of sparing civilians, women, or captured enemies. However, in the Middle Ages, Christianity dramatically altered attitudes.

The desire to protect civilians made it necessary to clearly distinguish them from combatants. This led to the development of distinctive uniforms for the military and the adoption of a code of chivalry. Actions considered unchivalrous would lead to censure from fellow soldiers.

Though few could maintain all the virtues all the time, the ideal was seriously pursued by knights of the age. The virtues of chivalry included humility, loyalty to God, king, and country, courage, honor, being true to one's word, protection of the weak, respect for women, generosity, fairness to enemies, courtesy, developing one's skills, and determination to fight evil.

"Sir Gawain," said the Green Knight, "By God, I rejoice
That your fist shall fetch this favor I seek,
And you have readily rehearsed, and in right terms,
165 Each clause of my covenant with the king your lord,
Save that you shall assure me, sir, upon oath,
That you shall seek me yourself, wheresoever you deem
My lodgings may lie, and look for such wages[12]
As you have offered me here before all this host."
170 "What is the way there?" said Gawain, "Where do you dwell?
I heard never of your house, by Him that made me,
Nor I know you not, knight, your name nor your court.
But tell me truly thereof, and teach me your name,
And I shall fare forth to find you, so far as I may,
175 And this I say in good certain, and swear upon oath."
"That is enough in New Year, you need say no more,"
Said the knight in the green to Gawain the noble,
"If I tell you true, when I have taken your knock,
And if you handily have hit, you shall hear straightway
180 Of my house and my home and my own name;
Then follow in my footsteps by faithful accord.
And if I spend no speech, you shall speed the better:
You can feast with your friends, nor further trace my tracks.[13]
      Now hold your grim tool steady
185   And show us how it hacks."
      "Gladly, sir; all ready,"
      Says Gawain; he strokes the ax.

The Green Knight upon ground girds him with care:
Bows a bit with his head, and bares his flesh:
190 His long lovely locks he laid over his crown,
Let the naked nape for the need be shown
Gawain grips to his ax and gathers it aloft—
The left foot on the floor before him he set—
Brought it down deftly upon the bare neck,
195 That the shock of the sharp blow shivered the bones
And cut the flesh cleanly and clove it in twain,[14]
That the blade of bright steel bit into the ground,
The head was hewn off and fell to the floor;
Many found it at their feet, as forth it rolled;
200 The blood gushed from the body, bright on the green,
Yet fell not the fellow, nor faltered a whit,
But stoutly he starts forth upon stiff shanks,
And as all stood staring he stretched forth his hand,

---

12. **wages** *n.* payment; that is, a strike with the ax.
13. **If I tell you . . . tracks** The Green Knight tells Gawain that he will let him know where he
lives after he has taken the blow. If he is unable to speak following the blow, there will be
no need for Gawain to know.
14. **clove it in twain** split it in two.

Reading Strategy
Summarizing How would
you summarize the event
in lines 188–213?

 Reading Check
What does Gawain do to
the Green Knight?

from Sir Gawain and the Green Knight ■ 167

⓭ Reading Strategy
Summarizing

• Suggest that, to make summarizing
easier, students break the longer
passage into individual events.
Noting where one action or event
ends and another begins will make
it easier to identify which are the
main ones.

▶ **Monitor Progress: Ask** students
to summarize what has happened
in the story to this point.
Answer: Arthur's celebration is
interrupted by a large green
knight, who issues a challenge to
Arthur. Gawain, one of Arthur's
knights, asks permission to accept
the challenge in Arthur's place, and
permission is granted.

• **Ask** students the Reading Strategy
question: How would you summarize the event in lines 188–213?
Answer: The Green Knight bows
his head and bares his neck.
Gawain picks up the ax and deals a
sharp blow, cutting off the Green
Knight's head. The head rolls across
the floor. To everyone's surprise,
the knight reaches out with one
arm, grabs the head, and mounts
his horse.

• Have students **identify** the details
in this stanza that are realistic and
those that are supernatural.
Answer: Details from the beheading are realistic; what follows is
supernatural.

▶ **Reteach:** If students have difficulty summarizing, help them
locate relevant details in the text
and ask them to make notes to
help with their summaries.

⓮ Reading Check

Answer: Gawain cuts off the Green
Knight's head.

⑮ Literary Analysis
Medieval Romance

- **Ask** students what is happening in this stanza (line 214 and following). **Answer:** The Green Knight is holding his severed head, and the head is talking.

- Point out that the listeners were probably pretty stunned by this sight. You may want to discuss with students how people today might react to this, and what they think is going through Gawain's mind during this speech.

- Remind students that this poem was intended to be fun. While it upholds the ideas of the era, it also contains a lot of humor.

- Point out the alliteration in lines 226–231. Explain that poems such as this were often presented in dramatic readings. The alliteration made it more memorable, but also added to the action, energy, and sense of fun.

- **Ask** students the Literary Analysis question: What two characteristics of a medieval romance are reflected in lines 214–231? **Answer:** Sir Gawain's honor is being put to the test. The dramatic language and supernatural actions are also characteristics of medieval romance.

⑯ Reading Strategy
Summarizing

- Remind students that a summary restates only the main ideas of a passage. Have students read lines 236–254 and identify the main points in this description of Arthur's reaction to the Green Knight.

- Then, **ask** students the Reading Strategy question: Sum up Arthur's reaction to the Green Knight's visit. **Answer:** Arthur was uneasy about the whole event, but held his true feelings in check. He then urged all to dance and eat, and watch the entertainment.

- **Ask** students why Arthur might behave in such a casual manner after witnessing such a scene. **Possible responses:** Some students might suggest that it's part of his bravery, or that he does not want to spoil the festivities. Others may think he does not want to upset Gawain.

Laid hold of his head and heaved it aloft,
205 Then goes to the green steed, grasps the bridle,
Steps into the stirrup, bestrides his mount,
And his head by the hair in his hand holds,
And as steady he sits in the stately saddle
As he had met with no mishap, nor missing were his head.
210   His bulk about he haled,
   That fearsome body that bled;
   There were many in the court that quailed
   Before all his say was said.

For the head in his hand he holds right up;
215 Toward the first on the dais directs he the face,
And it lifted up its lids, and looked with wide eyes,
And said as much with its mouth as now you may hear:
"Sir Gawain, forget not to go as agreed,
And cease not to seek till me, sir, you find,
220 As you promised in the presence of these proud knights.
To the Green Chapel come, I charge you, to take
Such a dint as you have dealt—you have well deserved
That your neck should have a knock on New Year's morn.
The Knight of the Green Chapel I am well-known to many,
225 Wherefore you cannot fail to find me at last;
Therefore come, or be counted a recreant[15] knight."
With a roisterous rush he flings round the reins,
Hurtles out at the hall door, his head in his hand,
That the flint fire flew from the flashing hooves.
230 Which way he went, not one of them knew
Nor whence he was come in the wide world so fair.
   The king and Gawain gay
   Make a game of the Green Knight there,
   Yet all who saw it say
235   'Twas a wonder past compare.

Though high-born Arthur at heart had wonder,
He let no sign be seen, but said aloud
To the comely queen, with courteous speech,
"Dear dame, on this day dismay you no whit;
240 Such crafts are becoming at Christmastide,
Laughing at interludes, light songs and mirth,
Amid dancing of damsels with doughty knights.
Nevertheless of my meat now let me partake,
For I have met with a marvel, I may not deny."
245 He glanced at Sir Gawain, and gaily he said,
"Now, sir, hang up your ax, that has hewn enough,"
And over the high dais it was hung on the wall

---

15. recreant *adj.* cowardly.

168 ■ From Legend to History (449–1485)

Literary Analysis
Medieval Romance
What two characteristics of a medieval romance are reflected in lines 214–231?

Reading Strategy
Summarizing Sum up Arthur's reaction to the Green Knight's visit.

Enrichment

Knights

As populations grew and wealth increased, it was possible for people to specialize. No longer did a family have to defend their own property. They could rely on the local lord and his knights. A knight was, in essence, a professional soldier.

One development in the eighth century reinforced this trend—the stirrup. Because mounted men could now concentrate on fighting, rather than simply staying on the horse, they were suddenly much more powerful. The cavalry became the most important element of medieval armies.

Knighthood originally included only those men who could afford the high cost of a horse and armor. During the eleventh century, most knights were nobles, landowners, or free men with money. But the boundaries were fluid, and anyone who managed to get the training and equipment to be a knight could eventually enter that class.

That men in amazement might on it look,
And tell in true terms the tale of the wonder.
250 Then they turned toward the table, those two together,
The good king and Gawain, and made great feast,
With all dainties double, dishes rare,
With all manner of meat and minstrelsy both,
Such happiness wholly had they that day in hold.
255 　　Now take care, Sir Gawain,
　　That your courage wax not cold
　　When you must turn again
　　To your enterprise foretold.

The following November, Sir Gawain sets out to fulfill his promise to the Green Knight. For weeks, he travels alone through the cold, threatening woods of North Wales. Then, after he prays for shelter, he comes upon a wondrous castle on Christmas Eve, where he is greeted warmly by the lord of the castle and his lady. The lord assures Sir Gawain that the Green Chapel is nearby and promises to provide him with a guide to lead him there on New Year's Day. Before the lord and Sir Gawain retire for the night, they agree to exchange whatever they receive during the next three days. Sir Gawain keeps his pledge for the first two days, but he fails to give the lord the magic green girdle that the lady gives him on the third day, because she gives it with the promise that it will protect him from harm. The next day, Gawain sets out for the Green Chapel. His guide urges him not to proceed, but Gawain feels that it would be dishonorable not to fulfill his pledge. He is determined to accept his fate; however, he wears the magic green girdle that the lady has given him.

He puts his heels to his horse, and picks up the path;
260 Goes in beside a grove where the ground is steep,
Rides down the rough slope right to the valley;
And then he looked a little about him—the landscape was wild,
And not a soul to be seen, nor sign of a dwelling,
But high banks on either hand hemmed it about,
265 With many a ragged rock and rough-hewn crag;
The skies seemed scored by the scowling peaks.
Then he halted his horse, and hoved there a space,
And sought on every side for a sight of the Chapel,

Gawain Receiving the Green Girdle, Fritz Kredel, Woodcut, From John Gardner's *The Complete Works of the Gawain Poet,* © 1965, The University of Chicago.

❶❽ ▲ **Critical Viewing**
Does the simple, stylized look of this woodcut suit the style of the selection? Explain. [**Assess**]

❶❾ ✔ **Reading Check**
What happens after Gawain chops off the Green Knight's head?

from Sir Gawain and the Green Knight ■ 169

Differentiated
Instruction　　Solutions for All Learners

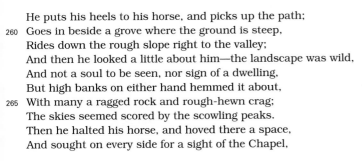

Support for Special Needs Students	**Strategy for Less Proficient Readers**	**Enrichment for Gifted/Talented Students**
Have students follow along as they listen to the selection on the **Listening to Literature Audio CD.** Play each stanza, and then stop and discuss what has occurred. Have students write one or two sentences about what has happened in the story. They can keep a running summary of all the action in this manner.	Assign each student several lines, or as many lines as describe a single event or action in the story. Help students interpret the action in their lines, and then have them draw a picture of the action and label it with a simple sentence. The pictures can be placed in order on the bulletin board or in a notebook.	Have students write and produce a dramatic interpretation of the challenge of the Green Knight, the blow of the ax delivered by Gawain, the Green Knight's subsequent actions, and the reaction of King Arthur. Such a dramatization can be produced for the class.

❶❼ **Humanities**

Gawain Receiving the Green Girdle, by Fritz Kredel.

Fritz Kredel (1900–1973) was a German-born American artist. Kredel worked chiefly in woodcut, prints made from designs cut into wooden blocks. He won many awards both in the United States and in Europe for his book illustrations.

Kredel used medieval techniques to make this woodcut. If Kredel's illustration were compared to a medieval woodcut, it would be difficult to tell, from style alone, which was done in this century.

Kredel made a point of thoroughly studying a text before he illustrated it. He felt that in illustration the artist should strive to glorify the author's work, not to overshadow it. In *Gawain,* the simple lines and sparse detail give an accurate portrayal of the characters without distracting our focus of attention from the poem.

Use these questions for discussion:
1. What details of the era in general are present in the woodcut?
   Possible response: The woodcut shows the clothing of the era but also highlights such elements of chivalry as the sword, armor, courtesy, and respect for women.

2. Are highly realistic oil or watercolor paintings usually preferable to line drawings or woodcuts such as this? Explain.
   Possible response: In some cases, a more realistic painting might help one visualize elements of the story, but in the case of this poem, the woodcut seems to be more consistent with the stylized narrative.

❶❽ **Critical Viewing**

Answer: Yes, the style suits the selection. It evokes the era of tales and gives just enough detail to enhance, but not overwhelm, the story.

❶❾ **Reading Check**

Answer: After Gawain chops off the Green Knight's head, the knight gathers his head and mounts his horse. He then reminds Gawain that he must find him in a year, reveals that he is the Knight of the Green Chapel, and gallops off.

169

- Have a volunteer read aloud lines 262–286. Ask students to pay careful attention to the details about the setting described in this passage.

- **Ask** students to relate how the setting in this passage adds to the story.
  Possible response: The setting mirrors Gawain's mental state and creates suspense.

- **Ask** students the Reading Strategy question: How would you summarize the description of the setting in lines 262–286?
  Answer: The area is wild and rugged. It is not what Gawain expected. Instead of a formal church, he finds a grass mound with entrance holes, much like a cave.

21 Literary Analysis
Medieval Romance and Legend

- Remind students that knighthood arose only as a result of the growing influence of Christianity, so mentions of heaven and hell are not concepts new to Malory's audience.

- Suggest that students think about prose tales of adventure stories, and then consider how this speech differs from how they might retell an adventurous scene from a movie.

- **Ask** students the Literary Analysis question: In what way does Gawain's speech in lines 287–294 add a dimension to the story that might not have been present in the original legend?
  Possible response: There is more imagery and alliteration here than would normally be found in the telling of an adventure tale. The bleakness of the place reflects the bleakness of Gawain's feelings and situation. The alliteration is a tool used throughout this poem to make it memorable and entertaining.

But no such place appeared, which puzzled him sore,
270 Yet he saw some way off what seemed like a mound,
     A hillock high and broad, hard by the water,
     Where the stream fell in foam down the face of the steep
     And bubbled as if it boiled on its bed below.
     The knight urges his horse, and heads for the knoll;
275 Leaps lightly to earth; loops well the rein
     Of his steed to a stout branch, and stations him there.
     He strides straight to the mound, and strolls all about,
     Much wondering what it was, but no whit the wiser;
     It had a hole at one end, and on either side,
280 And was covered with coarse grass in clumps all without,
     And hollow all within, like some old cave,
     Or a crevice of an old crag—he could not discern aright.
         "Can this be the Chapel Green?
         Alack!" said the man, "Here might
285   The devil himself be seen
         Saying matins[16] at black midnight!"

     "Now by heaven," said he, "it is bleak hereabouts;
     This prayer house is hideous, half covered with grass!
     Well may the grim man mantled in green
290 Hold here his orisons,[17] in hell's own style!
     Now I feel it is the Fiend, in my five wits,
     That has tempted me to this tryst,[18] to take my life;
     This is a Chapel of mischance, may the mischief take it!
     As accursed a country church as I came upon ever!"
295 With his helm on his head, his lance in his hand,
     He stalks toward the steep wall of that strange house.
     Then he heard, on the hill, behind a hard rock,
     Beyond the brook, from the bank, a most barbarous din:
     Lord! it clattered in the cliff fit to cleave it in two,
300 As one upon a grindstone ground a great scythe!
     Lord! it whirred like a mill-wheel whirling about!
     Lord! it echoed loud and long, lamentable to hear!
     Then "By heaven," said the bold knight, "That business up there
     Is arranged for my arrival, or else I am much misled.
305   Let God work! Ah me!
         All hope of help has fled!
         Forfeit my life may be
         But noise I do not dread."

     Then he listened no longer, but loudly he called,
310 "Who has power in this place, high parley to hold?

---

16. **matins** *n.* morning prayers.
17. **orisons** *n.* prayers.
18. **tryst** (trist) *n.* meeting.

Enrichment

Sir Gawain

Sir Gawain and the Green Knight is only one of many tales in which Gawain appears. Gawain was the greatest knight of the Round Table long before Lancelot was introduced into Arthurian legend. The handsome, chivalrous Gawain enjoyed centuries of popularity with an astonishing variety of audiences. His adventures were recited publicly throughout the Middle Ages and Renaissance.

In many of the Gawain romances, the knight responds to the challenge of a strange intruder (a shape-shifting monster, a Turk, the Green Knight) at a lavish Arthurian feast.

Because France and England had strong cultural ties, Gawain appears in both traditions. However, while Gawain is pure in English tales, he is definitely a ladies' man in the French versions. But in all tales, he is brave, loyal, and true to his word—and the most skilled fighter of all the knights.

For none greets Sir Gawain, or gives him good day;
If any would a word with him, let him walk forth
And speak now or never, to speed his affairs."
"Abide," said one on the bank above over his head,

315 "And what I promised you once shall straightway be given."
Yet he stayed not his grindstone, nor stinted its noise,
But worked awhile at his whetting before he would rest,
And then he comes around a crag, from a cave in the rocks,
Hurtling out of hiding with a hateful weapon,

320 A Danish ax[19] devised for that day's deed,
With a broad blade and bright, bent in a curve,
Filed to a fine edge—four feet it measured
By the length of the lace that was looped round the haft.
And in form as at first, the fellow all green,

325 His lordly face and his legs, his locks and his beard,
Save that firm upon two feet forward he strides,
Sets a hand on the ax-head, the haft to the earth;
When he came to the cold stream, and cared not to wade,
He vaults over on his ax, and advances amain

330 On a broad bank of snow, overbearing and brisk of mood.
        Little did the knight incline
        When face to face they stood;
        Said the other man, "Friend mine,
        It seems your word holds good!"

335 "God love you, Sir Gawain!" said the Green Knight then,
"And well met this morning, man, at my place!
And you have followed me faithfully and found me betimes,
And on the business between us we both are agreed:
Twelve months ago today you took what was yours,

340 And you at this New Year must yield me the same.
And we have met in these mountains, remote from all eyes:
There is none here to halt us or hinder our sport;
Unhasp your high helm, and have here your wages;
Make no more demur[20] than I did myself

345 When you hacked off my head with one hard blow."
"No, by God," said Sir Gawain, "that granted me life,
I shall grudge not the guerdon[21] grim though it prove;
And you may lay on as you like till the last of my part be paid."
        He proffered, with good grace,
350   His bare neck to the blade,
        And feigned a cheerful face:
        He scorned to seem afraid.

---

19. **Danish ax** long-bladed ax.
20. **demur** (dē muŗ) protest; delay.
21. **guerdon** n. reward.

Literary Analysis
Medieval Romance and Legend Which details in lines 309–334 strike you as belonging to the legend retold by the poem? Which details sound more literary?

Vocabulary Builder
feigned (fānd) v. made a false show of; pretended

 **Reading Check** ㉓

What is the Green Knight doing when Gawain arrives at the Green Chapel?

from Sir Gawain and the Green Knight ■ 171

㉒ **Literary Analysis**
Medieval Romance and Legend

- Remind students that authors often change fictional accounts to accomplish different things. Their purposes might include instructing, inspiring, entertaining, focusing on an ideal, mocking that same ideal, relating common human experiences, or relating a moral—singly or in any combination.

- Explain that a legend frequently begins as a simpler story that is then altered and embellished over time.

- Tell them that without knowing the original legend, it can be difficult to say with certainty where the changes are made, but one can usually tell what is an added "flourish" as opposed to an element of a straightforward story.

- With this in mind, have students examine lines 309–334. Suggest that they record the details in this passage in a chart similar to the one shown.

Details from the legend	Details Added in the Retelling

- Then, **ask** students the Literary Analysis question: Which details in lines 309–334 strike you as belonging to the legend retold by the poem? Which details sound more literary?

Possible response: Gawain's calling out, the Green Knight sharpening his ax, and the knight coming out to greet Gawain all seem to be likely elements of the original legend. The considerable amount of detail about the process of sharpening the ax, as well as its appearance, may have been added to increase suspense. More details about the Green Knight also add to the suspense, by reminding us how large and powerful he is, and may have been added. Some students may mention that the alliteration is an added literary detail.

㉓ **Reading Check**

Answer: The Green Knight is grinding, or sharpening, his ax in preparation for dealing Gawain a blow.

171

- **Ask** students which of the virtues of knighthood they feel would apply to the current situation. **Possible response:** Bravery and keeping one's word would apply. Fairness to enemies, honor, and loyalty to king might also be named.

- Then, **ask** students the Literary Analysis question: In what way do Gawain's actions in lines 359–387 fit the ideals of knighthood? In what way might they depart from those ideals? **Answer:** The ideals are shown in Gawain's baring his neck for the blow and in his promise not to flinch the second time. He departs from them when he winces.

- Explain that it is the inclusion of human emotions that made this poem popular. It presented heroes who possessed chivalric virtues, but who still had human qualities. The author gently mocks the tradition of the flawless hero and still upholds the pursuit of the ideal.

25 **Vocabulary Builder**
Word Root -droit-

- Point out the word *adroitly* in line 384 and its definition. Explain to students that the word root *-droit-* is derived from French and means "right."

- Explain that, in French, *droit* means both direction and legal obligation—just as *right* has both meanings in English.

- Note that one definition of *adroit* is "dexterous." In Latin, *dexter* means "right."

- Relate that the idea of *right* being "good" or "skilled" can be found in most cultures across most of time. Because most people are right-handed, the right hand was equated with strength or usefulness. *Right* came to symbolize honor and power. Among Arabs, the right hand is honorable and the left is unclean. Buddhists and Hindus walking near a sacred object keep it to their right. In the Bible, "the right hand of God" means God's power. We still talk of having a "right-hand man," and the place of honor is to the host's right.

- On the flip side, *left* often has unpleasant connotations: French for *left* is *gauche* and Latin for *left* is *sinister*.

172

Then the grim man in green gathers his strength,
Heaves high the heavy ax to hit him the blow.
355 With all the force in his frame he fetches it aloft,
With a grimace as grim as he would grind him to bits;
Had the blow he bestowed been as big as he threatened,
A good knight and gallant had gone to his grave.
But Gawain at the great ax glanced up aside
360 As down it descended with death-dealing force,
And his shoulders shrank a little from the sharp iron.
Abruptly the brawny man breaks off the stroke,
And then reproved with proud words that prince among knights.
"You are not Gawain the glorious," the green man said,
365 "That never fell back on field in the face of the foe,
And now you flee for fear, and have felt no harm:
Such news of that knight I never heard yet!
I moved not a muscle when you made to strike,
Nor caviled[22] at the cut in King Arthur's house;
370 My head fell to my feet, yet steadfast I stood,
And you, all unharmed, are wholly dismayed—
Wherefore the better man I, by all odds, must be."
    Said Gawain, "Strike once more;
    I shall neither flinch nor flee;
375   But if my head falls to the floor
    There is no mending me!"

"But go on, man, in God's name, and get to the point!
Deliver me my destiny, and do it out of hand,
For I shall stand to the stroke and stir not an inch
380 Till your ax has hit home—on my honor I swear it!"
"Have at thee then!" said the other, and heaves it aloft,
And glares down as grimly as he had gone mad.
He made a mighty feint, but marred not his hide;
Withdrew the ax <u>adroitly</u> before it did damage.
385 Gawain gave no ground, nor glanced up aside,
But stood still as a stone, or else a stout stump
That is held in hard earth by a hundred roots.
Then merrily does he mock him, the man all in green:
"So now you have your nerve again, I needs must strike;
390 Uphold the high knighthood that Arthur bestowed,
And keep your neck-bone clear, if this cut allows!"
Then was Gawain gripped with rage, and grimly he said,
"Why, thrash away, tyrant, I tire of your threats;
You make such a scene, you must frighten yourself."
395 Said the green fellow, "In faith, so fiercely you speak
That I shall finish this affair, nor further grace allow."
    He stands prepared to strike

---

22. caviled raised trivial objections.

Literary Analysis
Medieval Romance In what way do Gawain's actions in lines 359–387 fit the ideals of knighthood? In what way might they depart from those ideals?

Vocabulary Builder
adroitly (ə droit′ lē) *adv.* with physical or mental skill

Enrichment

Illuminated Manuscripts

In the Middle Ages, part of the population was highly educated, but many people were only partially literate. Because producing a single book involved a great deal of work, most books were designed to appeal to both of these groups, with both text and illustrations.

Books were laboriously copied by hand. Most medieval manuscripts were created by monks, who beautifully hand lettered each page before turning them over to illuminators.

An illuminated manuscript did not simply have a few illustrations. It had highly decorative initial letters and ornate borders in all the margins, and it included little paintings called miniatures. All were painted in bright colors and real gold. The works were gorgeously and lavishly decorated. These manuscripts were produced on vellum, which was treated and stretched calfskin. This material was expensive but was beautiful and incredibly long lasting.

Miniature of Gawain leaving Arthur's court and arriving at the White Abbey in search of Lancelot. MS. Douce 199, fol. 151v, Bodleian Library, University of Oxford.

And scowls with both lip and brow;
No marvel if the man mislike
400 Who can hope no rescue now.

He gathered up the grim ax and guided it well:
Let the barb at the blade's end brush the bare throat;
He hammered down hard, yet harmed him no whit
Save a scratch on one side, that severed the skin;
405 The end of the hooked edge entered the flesh,
And a little blood lightly leapt to the earth.
And when the man beheld his own blood bright on the snow,
He sprang a spear's length with feet spread wide,
Seized his high helm, and set it on his head,
410 Shoved before his shoulders the shield at his back,
Bares his trusty blade, and boldly he speaks—
Not since he was a babe born of his mother
Was he once in this world one half so blithe—
"Have done with your hacking—harry me no more!
415 I have borne, as behooved, one blow in this place;
If you make another move I shall meet it midway
And promptly, I promise you, pay back each blow with brand.
    One stroke acquits me here;
    So did our covenant stand
420   In Arthur's court last year—
    Wherefore, sir, hold your hand!"

He lowers the long ax and leans on it there,
Sets his arms on the head, the haft on the earth,
And beholds the bold knight that bides there afoot,

from Sir Gawain and the Green Knight ■ 173

▲ Critical Viewing 27
Compare the scenes in the picture with the text. What episodes are included or omitted? [Compare and Contrast]

Reading Strategy
Summarizing What is the key point of Gawain's speech in lines 414–421?

29 ✓ Reading Check
What happens on the Green Knight's third stroke with the ax?

---

425 How he faces him fearless, fierce in full arms,
And plies him with proud words—it pleases him well.
Then once again gaily to Gawain he calls,
And in a loud voice and lusty, delivers these words:
"Bold fellow, on this field your anger forbear!
430 No man has made demands here in manner uncouth,
Nor done, save as duly determined at court.
I owed you a hit and you have it; be happy therewith!
The rest of my rights here I freely resign.
Had I been a bit busier, a buffet, perhaps,
435 I could have dealt more directly; and done you some harm.
First I flourished with a feint, in frolicsome mood,
And left your hide unhurt—and here I did well
By the fair terms we fixed on the first night;
And fully and faithfully you followed accord:
440 Gave over all your gains as a good man should.
A second feint, sir, I assigned for the morning
30 You kissed my comely wife—each kiss you restored.
For both of these there behooved but two feigned blows by right.
        True men pay what they owe;
445   No danger then in sight.
        You failed at the third throw,
        So take my tap, sir knight.

"For that is my belt about you, that same braided girdle,
My wife it was that wore it; I know well the tale,
450 And the count of your kisses and your conduct too,
And the wooing of my wife—it was all my scheme!
She made trial of a man most faultless by far
Of all that ever walked over the wide earth;
As pearls to white peas, more precious and prized,
455 So is Gawain, in good faith, to other gay knights.
Yet you lacked, sir, a little in loyalty there,
But the cause was not cunning, nor courtship either,
But that you loved your own life; the less, then, to blame."
The other stout knight in a study stood a long while,
460 So gripped with grim rage that his great heart shook.
All the blood of his body burned in his face
As he shrank back in shame from the man's sharp speech.
The first words that fell from the fair knight's lips:
31 "Accursed be a cowardly and covetous heart!
465 In you is villainy and vice, and virtue laid low!"
Then he grasps the green girdle and lets go the knot,
Hands it over in haste, and hotly he says:
"Behold there my falsehood, ill hap betide it!
Your cut taught me cowardice, care for my life,
470 And coveting came after, contrary both
To largesse and loyalty belonging to knights.

174 ■ *From Legend to History (449–1485)*

Enrichment

Redemption

The conclusion of this tale reflects a common theme of Arthurian legends—that of reconciliation and redemption. Throughout the tales, one finds King Arthur's knights battling evil kings or bad knights, then showing them kindness, at which point they realize that virtue and civilization are better than evil and barbarity, vow allegiance to Arthur, and usually join the Round Table.

In some stories, hideous hags are transformed into beautiful maidens by the breaking of spells. In others, individuals are freed from prisons. Throughout these stories, the real quest is how to get the unknown, the threatening, the wild in line with civilized, idealized chivalric society.

While much of this obviously reflects the influence of the church and the Christian ideals of redemption and forgiveness, it also reflects the emergence of society from barbarity. Just as knighthood reflected a change from unrestrained Viking carnage, society as a whole was struggling to move away from brutality and survival toward refinement and civilization.

Now am I faulty and false, that fearful was ever
Of disloyalty and lies, bad luck to them both! and greed.
    I confess, knight, in this place,
475   Most dire is my misdeed;
    Let me gain back your good grace,
    And thereafter I shall take heed."

Then the other laughed aloud, and lightly he said,
"Such harm as I have had, I hold it quite healed.
480 You are so fully confessed, your failings made known,
And bear the plain penance of the point of my blade,
I hold you polished as a pearl, as pure and as bright
As you had lived free of fault since first you were born.
And I give you sir, this girdle that is gold-hemmed
485 And green as my garments, that, Gawain, you may
Be mindful of this meeting when you mingle in throng
With nobles of renown—and known by this token
How it chanced at the Green Chapel, to chivalrous knights.
And you shall in this New Year come yet again
490 And we shall finish out our feast in my fair hall with cheer."

Critical Reading

1. **Respond:** If you were King Arthur, would you have allowed Sir Gawain to accept the Green Knight's challenge? Why?

2. **(a) Recall:** How do Arthur's knights first respond to the Green Knight's challenge? **(b) Analyze:** Why does the Green Knight laugh at their response? **(c) Draw Conclusions:** Judging from Arthur's reaction, how important is honor in Arthur's court?

3. **(a) Recall:** What does Gawain offer to do? **(b) Analyze:** How does he manage to make his offer seem humble, not boastful? **(c) Infer:** Why are the offer and his manner of making it appropriate for a knight?

4. **(a) Interpret:** In lines 464–477, how does Sir Gawain react when he considers his own actions? **(b) Draw Conclusions:** What do you think Sir Gawain has learned from his second encounter with the Green Knight?

5. **Make a Judgment:** In your opinion, has Sir Gawain failed to live up to his knightly ideals? Explain.

6. **Take a Position:** Using the example of Sir Gawain, explain whether you think it is more important to achieve one's goals or to learn from one's mistakes.

from *Sir Gawain and the Green Knight* ■ 175

175

32

About the Selection

No one knows for sure whether King Arthur was real, but his name has popped up since the sixth century, and by the ninth century, he was a folk hero. During the fourteenth and fifteenth centuries, there was a revival of interest in Arthurian legends, mainly due to *Sir Gawain and the Green Knight* and to *Morte d'Arthur*. Unlike the former, written in verse, *Morte d'Arthur* was the first English prose version of King Arthur's life. After reading, students will understand why, with its realistic detail and natural dialogue, it has become a classic.

Literary Analysis
Medieval Romance

▶ **Reteach:** Remind students that medieval romance includes such elements as kings, knights, battles between good and evil, honor, love, and elements of the supernatural.

• **Ask** students what elements of medieval romance they find in the first two paragraphs of this selection.

Possible response: Elements of medieval romance in these paragraphs include a king, knights, squires, yeomen, imagery of a battle against evil, and elements of the supernatural, as the dead Sir Gawain appears to Arthur.

32

from **Morte d'Arthur**

Sir Thomas Malory

This selection begins after King Arthur has traveled to France at the insistence of his nephew, Gawain, to besiege his former friend and knight, Lancelot, for his involvement with Queen Guenevere. However, the king's attempts to punish Lancelot are halfhearted, and he is soon forced to abandon them altogether when he learns that his illegitimate son, Mordred, has seized control of England. Arthur leads his forces back to England, and Mordred attacks them upon their landing. Gawain is killed in the fighting, but before he dies, he manages to send word to Lancelot that Arthur is in need of his assistance.

So upon Trinity Sunday at night King Arthur dreamed a wonderful dream, and in his dream him seemed[1] that he saw upon a chafflet[2] a chair, and the chair was fast to a wheel, and thereupon sat King Arthur in the richest cloth of gold that might be made. And the King thought there was under him, far from him, an hideous deep black water, and therein was all manner of serpents, and worms, and wild beasts, foul and horrible. And suddenly the King thought that the wheel turned upside down, and he fell among the serpents, and every beast took him by a limb. And then the King cried as he lay in his bed, "Help, help!"

And then knights, squires, and yeomen awaked the King, and then he was so amazed that he wist[3] not where he was. And then so he awaked until it was nigh day, and then he fell on slumbering again, not sleeping nor thoroughly waking. So the King seemed[4] verily that

---

1. **him seemed** It seemed to him.
2. **chafflet** platform.
3. **wist** knew.
4. **the King seemed** It seemed to the King.

176 ■ From Legend to History (449–1485)

King Arthur's Round Table and the Holy Grail, Art Resource, NY

▲ **Critical Viewing** Using your knowledge of chivalry, draw conclusions about King Arthur's decision to set his knights at a round table. **[Draw Conclusions]**

there came Sir Gawain unto him with a number of fair ladies with him. So when King Arthur saw him, he said, "Welcome, my sister's son. I weened ye had been dead. And now I see thee on-live, much am I beholden unto Almighty Jesu. Ah, fair nephew and my sister's son, what been these ladies that hither be come with you?"

"Sir," said Sir Gawain, "all these be ladies for whom I have foughten for when I was man living. And all these are those that I did battle for in <u>righteous</u> quarrels, and God hath given them that grace, at their great prayer, because I did battle for them for their right, that they should bring me hither unto you. Thus much hath given me leave God, for to warn you of your death. For and ye fight as tomorn[5] with

Vocabulary Builder
righteous (rī′ chəs) *adj.* acting in a just, upright manner; doing what is right

36 ✓ **Reading Check**
What kind of dreams is Arthur having?

---

5. and . . . tomorn "if you fight tomorrow."

from Morte d'Arthur ■ 177

34 🔴 **Humanities**

King Arthur's Round Table and the Holy Grail

Among the most popular subjects in medieval literature, songs, and art, was the legendary King Arthur. This painting depicts King Arthur's Round Table, around which were seated his knights. The object in the center of the table represents the Holy Grail.

Use these questions for discussion:

1. Does seating knights at a round table really ensure equality? Are some places, for example, those immediately to the left or right of Arthur, more prestigious than others?
   Answer: Being seated next to Arthur would surely have been an honor that elevated a knight above others at the table. In fact, the closer one sits to Arthur, the more elevated he would seem to be.

2. What does this illustration suggest about the status of a knight in Arthur's time?
   Answer: Their dress and sur-roundings suggest nobility.

35 🔴 **Critical Viewing**

Answer: Students should recognize that a round table has no head and no foot. It was designed so all members have equal status.

36 🔴 **Reading Check**

Answer: Arthur is having nightmares—or possibly a prophetic vision.

Reading Strategy
Summarizing
What are three key points
of Sir Gawain's speech in
the dream?

③⑦ Reading Strategy
Summarizing

- Have students review Arthur's dream, looking for the main points.

- **Ask** students the Reading Strategy question: What are three key points of Sir Gawain's speech in the dream?
  Answer: Gawain says that God has sent him to tell Arthur that he will be killed if he fights tomorrow, that he should delay the fight for a month, and that Lancelot will slay Mordred in battle if the fight is delayed.

▶ **Monitor Progress:** Gawain opens with a description of the ladies with him. Why is this not a key point of his speech?
Possible response: It is not part of the message; it is simply in response to Arthur's question.

③⑧ Literary Analysis
Medieval Romance

- Remind students of the Christian influence on the code of chivalry.
  Ask students to name some elements of the dream that reflect this Christian influence.
  Possible responses: Students might mention that the dream takes place on Trinity Sunday, that in the dream Gawain speaks of an afterlife and God's grace, and that Arthur and Gawain extol the name of "Almighty Jesu." Also, students may realize that prophetic dreams appear frequently in the Bible and in Christian tradition.

- Then, **ask** students the Literary Analysis question: What characteristic of medieval romance is illustrated by the dream and Arthur's response to it?
  Answer: The dream suggests that Christian beliefs played a strong role in medieval romance. In addition, both the idea of a prophetic dream and Arthur's immediate willingness to accept the dream as true are characteristic of the supernatural aspects of medieval romance.

---

③⑦ Sir Mordred, as ye both have assigned, doubt ye not ye must be slain, and the most party of your people on both parties. And for the great grace and goodness that Almighty Jesu hath unto you, and for pity of you and many more other good men there shall be slain, God hath sent me to you of his special grace to give you warning that in no wise ye do battle as tomorn, but that ye take a treaty for a month from today. And proffer you largely[6] you so that tomorn ye put in a delay. For within a month shall come Sir Lancelot with all his noble knights and rescue you worshipfully and slay Sir Mordred and all that ever will hold with him."

Then Sir Gawain and all the ladies vanished. And anon the King called upon his knights, squires, and yeomen, and charged them wightly[7] to fetch his noble lords and wise bishops unto him. And when they were come the King told them of his avision,[8] that Sir ③⑧ Gawain had told him and warned him that, and he fought on the morn, he should be slain. Then the King commanded Sir Lucan the Butler and his brother Sir Bedivere the Bold, with two bishops with them, and charged them in any wise to take a treaty for a month from today with Sir Mordred. "And spare not: proffer him lands and goods as much as ye think reasonable."

So then they departed and came to Sir Mordred where he had a grim host of an hundred thousand, and there they <u>entreated</u> Sir Mordred long time. And at the last Sir Mordred was agreed for to have Cornwall and Kent by King Arthur's days, and after that, all England, after the days of King Arthur.

Then were they condescended[9] that King Arthur and Sir Mordred should meet betwixt both their hosts, and each of them should bring fourteen persons. And so they came with this word unto Arthur. Then said he, "I am glad that this is done," and so he went into the field.

And when King Arthur should depart, he warned all his host that, and they see any sword drawn, "Look ye come on fiercely and slay that traitor Sir Mordred, for I in no wise trust him." In like wise Sir Mordred warned his host that "And ye see any manner of sword drawn, look that ye come on fiercely, and so slay all that ever before you standeth, for in no wise I will not trust for this treaty." And in the same wise said Sir Mordred unto his host, "For I know well my father will be avenged upon me."

And so they met as their pointment[10] was and were agreed and accorded thoroughly. And wine was fetched and they drank together. Right so came an adder out of a little heathbush, and it stung a knight in the foot. And so when the knight felt him so stung, he looked down and saw the adder. And anon he drew his sword to slay

---

6. **proffer you largely** make generous offers.
7. **wightly** quickly.
8. **avision** dream.
9. **condescended** agreed.
10. **pointment** arrangement.

178 ■ From Legend to History (449–1485)

Literary Analysis
Medieval Romance What
characteristic of medieval
romance is illustrated by
the dream and Arthur's
response to it?

Vocabulary Builder
entreated (en trēt′ id) *v.*
made an earnest appeal;
pleaded

Enrichment

Armed Forces

In these selections, knights perform the function that the armed forces perform today. Though the "chivalric code" has obviously changed, much of what we expect of a professional military was, in fact, established during the Middle Ages. Loyalty to country, fairness to enemies, protecting the weak, bravery, and skill with weapons are ideals established then that are valued today.

Today, many young people consider one of the armed forces as a career. Over a million men and women now serve in the U.S. Army,

the Air Force, the Navy, the Marine Corps, and the Coast Guard. Each of these services is associated with a four-year academy that provides academic as well as military instruction.

Another military option is the U.S. National Guard, which provides backup for the Army and Air Force. People who join the National Guard are basically civilians with other careers who meet once a month for military training. Under certain conditions, they can be called to active service indefinitely.

the adder, and thought none other harm. And when the host on both parties saw that sword drawn, then they blew beams,[11] trumpets, horns, and shouted grimly. And so both hosts dressed them together. And King Arthur took his horse and said, "Alas, this unhappy day!" and so rode to his party, and Sir Mordred in like wise.

And never since was there never seen a more dolefuller battle in no Christian land, for there was but rushing and riding, lunging and striking; and many a grim word was there spoken of either to other, and many a deadly stroke. But ever King Arthur rode throughout the battle[12] of Sir Mordred many times and did full nobly, as a noble king should do, and at all times he fainted never. And Sir Mordred did his devoir[13] that day and put himself in great <u>peril</u>.

And thus they fought all the long day, and never stinted[14] till the noble knights were laid to the cold earth. And ever they fought still till it was near night, and by then was there an hundred thousand laid dead upon the down. Then was King Arthur wood-wroth[15] out of measure when he saw his people so slain from him. And so he looked about him and could see no more of all his host, and good knights left no more on-live, but two knights: the t'one was Sir Lucan the Butler and the other his brother Sir Bedivere. And yet they were full sore wounded.

"Jesu, mercy," said the King, "where are all my noble knights become? Alas that ever I should see this doleful day! For now," said King Arthur, "I am come to mine end. But would to God," said he, "that I wist now where were that traitor Sir Mordred that has caused all this mischief."

Then King Arthur looked about and was ware where stood Sir Mordred leaning upon his sword among a great heap of dead men.

"Now give me my spear," said King Arthur unto Sir Lucan, "for yonder I have espied the traitor that all this woe hath wrought."

"Sir, let him be," said Sir Lucan, "for he is unhappy. And if ye pass this unhappy day ye shall be right well revenged upon him. And, good lord, remember ye of your night's dream, and what the spirit of Sir Gawain told you tonight, and yet God of his great goodness hath preserved you hitherto. And for God's sake, my lord, leave off by this, for, blessed be God, ye have won the field: for yet we been here three on-live, and with Sir Mordred is not one on-live. And therefore if ye leave off now, this wicked day of destiny is past."

"Now, tide[16] me death, tide me life," said the King, "now I see him yonder alone, he shall never escape mine hands. For at a better avail shall I never have him."

"God speed you well!" said Sir Bedivere.

---

11. **beams** type of trumpet.
12. **battle** battalion.
13. **devoir** (də vwär´) *n.* duty (from the French; obsolete).
14. **stinted** stopped.
15. **wood-wroth** wild with rage.
16. **tide** befall.

Vocabulary Builder
peril (per´ əl) *n.* exposure to harm or injury

Literary Analysis
Medieval Romance and Legend What features of this account seem more typical of legend than of written forms of story telling?

 **Reading Check**
What happens to the truce between Arthur and Mordred?

from Morte d'Arthur ■ 179

Humanities

Detail from The Nine Heroes Tapestries

The Nine Heroes Tapestries, which hang in the Cloisters in New York City, were made in France during the fourteenth century, probably around 1385. This detail was originally part of a set of three large panels, 16 by 21 feet in size. Each panel showed three heroes: One showed three pagans, one showed three Hebrews, and the last showed three Christians. Of the latter, only Arthur remains.

The three crowns shown on Arthur's tunic and banner represent England, Scotland, and Brittany.

Use these questions for discussion:

1. What aspects of Arthur's life are symbolized by what he wears?
   Answer: The crown shows kingship, the armor shows that he is a warrior, his tunic shows association with England, Scotland, and Brittany. Students may also note that it indicates wealth and a high degree of civilization.

2. What does the background convey about Arthur?
   Answer: The cathedral conveys that Arthur is a Christian king.

43 Critical Viewing

Possible response: His regal pose shows that he is a leader; his expression shows that he is serious, focused, and probably strong willed; and his presence in a church shows him to be devout.

44 Reading Strategy
Summarizing

- Have students read pp. 179–180, making note of the main points.

- Then, **ask** the Reading Strategy question: Summarize the events leading to the death of Mordred and the mortal wounding of King Arthur.
  Answer: Everyone on Mordred's side is dead, and Arthur has only two men left. Sir Lucan tries to dissuade Arthur, but the king realizes he will never have a better opportunity, so he attacks Mordred and gives him a mortal wound. As he dies, Mordred strikes King Arthur's head with his sword.

42

43 ⋏ **Critical Viewing** What can you deduce about King Arthur's character from his depiction in this tapestry? [Deduce]

Then the King got his spear in both his hands and ran toward Sir Mordred, crying and saying, "Traitor, now is thy deathday come!"

And when Sir Mordred saw King Arthur he ran until him with his sword drawn in his hand, and there King Arthur smote Sir Mordred under the shield, with a thrust of his spear, throughout the body more than a fathom. And when Sir Mordred felt that he had his death's **44** wound, he thrust himself with the might that he had up to the burr[17] of King Arthur's spear, and right so he smote his father King Arthur with his sword holden in both his hands, upon the side of the head, that the sword pierced the helmet and the casing of the brain. And therewith Sir Mordred dashed down stark dead to the earth.

17. burr hand guard.

180 ■ *From Legend to History (449–1485)*

Reading Strategy
Summarizing Summarize the events leading to the death of Mordred and the mortal wounding of King Arthur.

Enrichment

Tapestries

Technically, a tapestry is a decorative fabric with a design created by the threads from which the material is woven. However, the term has been used to describe almost any heavy material with pictures. For example, the famous *Bayeaux Tapestry,* which depicts the Norman Conquest of England, is not a woven tapestry but a crewel-embroidered hanging.

Wall tapestries added insulation to cold stone walls and they told stories. Popular topics were historical events, legends (such as tales of King Arthur), Bible stories, and even scenes from daily life.

Like the art of stained glass, western European tapestry flourished beginning in the Gothic period in the thirteenth century. By the fourteenth century, the western European tradition of woven tapestry was well established. Tapestries such as this add to our knowledge of the eras in which they were produced.

Though tapestry making is not as important as it once was (so few castles are left to decorate), it remains a popular art form.

And noble King Arthur fell in a swough[18] to the earth, and there he swooned oftentimes, and Sir Lucan and Sir Bedivere ofttimes heaved him up. And so, weakly betwixt them, they led him to a little chapel not far from the seaside, and when the King was there, him thought him reasonably eased. Then heard they people cry in the field. "Now go thou, Sir Lucan," said the King, "and do me to wit[19] what betokens that noise in the field."

So Sir Lucan departed, for he was grievously wounded in many places. And so as he walked he saw and harkened by the moonlight how that pillagers and robbers were come into the field to pill and to rob many a full noble knight of brooches and bracelets and of many a good ring and many a rich jewel. And who that were not dead all out there they slew them for their harness and their riches. When Sir Lucan understood this work, he came to the King as soon as he might and told him all what he had heard and seen. "Therefore by my read,"[20] said Sir Lucan, "it is best that we bring you to some town."

"I would it were so," said the King, "but I may not stand, my head works so. Ah, Sir Lancelot," said King Arthur, "this day have I sore missed thee. And alas that ever I was against thee, for now have I my death, whereof Sir Gawain me warned in my dream."

Then Sir Lucan took up the King the t'one party[21] and Sir Bedivere the other party; and in the lifting up the King swooned and in the lifting Sir Lucan fell in a swoon that part of his guts fell out of his body, and therewith the noble knight's heart burst. And when the King awoke he beheld Sir Lucan how he lay foaming at the mouth and part of his guts lay at his feet.

"Alas," said the King, "this is to me a full heavy sight to see this noble duke so die for my sake, for he would have helped me that had more need of help than I. Alas that he would not complain him for his heart was so set to help me. Now Jesu have mercy upon his soul."

Then Sir Bedivere wept for the death of his brother.

"Now leave this mourning and weeping gentle knight," said the King, "for all this will not avail me. For wit thou well, and might I live myself, the death of Sir Lucan would grieve me evermore. But my time passeth on fast," said the King. "Therefore," said King Arthur unto Sir Bedivere, "take thou here Excalibur my good sword and go with it to yonder water's side; and when thou comest there I charge thee throw my sword in that water and come again and tell me what thou sawest there."

"My lord," said Sir Bedivere, "your commandment shall be done, and I shall lightly[22] bring you word again."

So Sir Bedivere departed. And by the way he beheld that noble sword, that the pommel and the haft[23] was all precious stones. And

---

18. **swough** forcible movement
19. **me to wit** "let me know."
20. **read** advice.
21. **party** side.
22. **lightly** quickly.
23. **pommel . . . haft** hilt and hand guard.

Literary Analysis
Medieval Romance What note of realism does this paragraph strike?

Literary Analysis
Medieval Romance What note of fantasy does this paragraph strike?

 Reading Check
What happens in the combat between Arthur and Mordred?

from *Morte d'Arthur* ■ 181

then he said to himself, "If I throw this rich sword in the water, thereof shall never come good, but harm and loss." And then Sir Bedivere hid Excalibur under a tree. And so, as soon as he might, he came again unto the King and said he had been at the water and had thrown the sword into the water.

"What saw thou there?" said the King.

"Sir," he said, "I saw nothing but waves and winds."

"That is untruly said of thee," said the King. "And therefore go thou lightly again and do my commandment; as thou art to me loved and dear, spare not, but throw it in."

Then Sir Bedivere returned again and took the sword in his hand. And yet him thought sin and shame to throw away that noble sword. And so eft[24] he hid the sword and returned again and told the King that he had been at the water and done his commandment.

"What sawest thou there?" said the King.

"Sir," he said, "I saw nothing but waters wap and waves wan."[25]

"Ah, traitor unto me and untrue," said King Arthur, "now hast thou betrayed me twice. Who would have weened that thou that has been to me so loved and dear, and thou art named a noble knight, and would betray me for the riches of this sword. But now go again lightly, for thy long tarrying putteth me in great jeopardy of my life, for I have taken cold. And but if thou do now as I bid thee, if ever I may see thee I shall slay thee mine own hands, for thou wouldest for my rich sword see me dead."

Then Sir Bedivere departed and went to the sword and lightly took it up, and so he went to the water's side; and there he bound the girdle about the hilts, and threw the sword as far into the water as he might. And there came an arm and an hand above the water and took it and clutched it, and shook it thrice and brandished; and then vanished away the hand with the sword into the water. So Sir Bedivere came again to the King and told him what he saw.

"Alas," said the King, "help me hence, for I dread me I have tarried overlong."

Then Sir Bedivere took the King upon his back and so went with him to that water's side. And when they were at the water's side, even fast[26] by the bank floated a little barge with many fair ladies in it;

---
24. **eft** again.
25. **waters . . . wan** waters lap and waves grow dark.
26. **fast** close.

182 ■ *From Legend to History (449–1485)*

48 ▲ Critical Viewing
Compare the mood of this depiction of Arthur's departure with that of Malory's account.
[Compare and Contrast]

Literary Analysis
Medieval Romance What element does the appearance of the hand add to the tale?

and among them all was a queen; and all they had black hoods, and all they wept and shrieked when they saw King Arthur.

"Now put me into that barge," said the King; and so he did softly. And there received him three ladies with great mourning, and so they set them down. And in one of their laps King Arthur laid his head, and then the queen said, "Ah, my dear brother, why have ye tarried so long from me? Alas, this wound on your head hath caught overmuch cold." And anon they rowed fromward the land, and Sir Bedivere beheld all those ladies go froward him.

Then Sir Bedivere cried and said, "Ah, my lord Arthur, what shall become of me, now ye go from me and leave me here alone among mine enemies?"

"Comfort thyself," said the King, "and do as well as thou mayest, for in me is no trust for to trust in. For I must into the vale of Avilion[27] to heal me of my grievous wound. And if thou hear nevermore of me, pray for my soul."

But ever the queen and ladies wept and shrieked, that it was pity to hear. And as soon as Sir Bedivere had lost sight of the barge he wept and wailed, and so took the forest and went all that night.

And in the morning he was ware, betwixt two bare woods, of a chapel and an hermitage. Then was Sir Bedivere glad, and thither he went, and when he came into the chapel he saw where lay an hermit groveling on all fours, close thereby a tomb was new dug. When the hermit saw Sir Bedivere he knew him well, for he was but little tofore Bishop of Canterbury, that Sir Mordred put to flight.

"Sirs," said Sir Bedivere, "what man is there here <u>interred</u> that you pray so fast for?"

"Fair son," said the hermit. "I wot not verily but by guessing. But this same night, at midnight, here came a number of ladies and brought here a dead corpse and prayed me to inter him. And here they offered an hundred tapers, and gave me a thousand gold coins."

"Alas," said Sir Bedivere, "that was my lord King Arthur, which lieth here buried in this chapel."

Then Sir Bedivere swooned, and when he awoke he prayed the hermit that he might abide with him still, there to live with fasting and prayers:

"For from hence will I never go," said Sir Bedivere, "by my will, but all the days of my life here to pray for my lord Arthur."

"Sir, ye are welcome to me," said the hermit, "for I know you better than ye think that I do: for ye are Sir Bedivere the Bold, and the full noble duke Sir Lucan the Butler was your brother."

Then Sir Bedivere told the hermit all as you have heard tofore, and so he stayed with the hermit that was beforehand Bishop of Canterbury. And there Sir Bedivere put upon him poor clothes, and served the hermit full lowly in fasting and in prayers.

Thus of Arthur I find no more written in books that been authorized, neither more of the very certainty of his death heard I nor read, but

---

27. **Avilion** legendary island where Arthur is said to dwell until his return.

Literary Analysis
Medieval Romance and Legend Does the description of Sir Bedivere's reaction sound more like a description you might find in a folk tale or in a modern short story? Explain.

Vocabulary Builder
interred (in turd´) *v.* buried

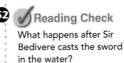
Reading Check
What happens after Sir Bedivere casts the sword in the water?

from Morte d'Arthur ■ 183

50 Literary Analysis
Medieval Romance and Legend

- Have students **identify** the specific elements of Bedivere's reaction to the events, and discuss how they fit into the ideals of chivalry.
Possible response: Specific elements include asking Arthur what he'll do without a king to follow, weeping at Arthur's departure, swooning at news of Arthur's death, and vowing to stay by the grave and pray. Loyalty to king is the foremost element of chivalry here, but Christian piety is also present.

- Point out that Malory says he got the story from the hermit, who had it from Bedivere. This "eyewitness" device is a common one in fiction, still used today to give the appearance of credibility to a far-fetched tale.

- **Ask** students the Literary Analysis question: Does the description of Sir Bedivere's reaction sound more like a folk tale or a modern short story?
Possible response: The response seems to suit a folk tale. It seems unlikely that a warrior would be portrayed as swooning or weeping in a modern story. Also, such devotion to a king seems more legendary than modern.

51 Reading Strategy
Summarizing

- Ask students to notice the evidence that seems to support the theory that Arthur is dead.

- Discuss whether the inscription on the tombstone supports the theory that Arthur is alive or the theory that he is dead.

- Then, **ask** students: According to Malory, what details about the death of Arthur are uncertain?
Answer: According to Malory, no one can verify that the body buried was Arthur's, nor can anyone say he or she witnessed his death.

52 Reading Check
Answer: After Sir Bedivere casts the sword into the water, a hand reaches out and grabs it, then vanishes underwater.

1. Students may respond that they would be willing to throw the sword away if they were bid to do so by the king.

2. (a) Sir Gawain warns Arthur that if he fights tomorrow, he will be killed. (b) Arthur makes a truce with Mordred, but when a knight draws his sword to kill a snake, the truce is voided and war begins. (c) Though Arthur does everything he can to avoid the battle, it still overtakes him, and so it seems fated.

3. (a) Mordred is Arthur's illegitimate son. (b) Arthur feels betrayed because Mordred is both his son and a knight. This betrayal of father and king seems to signal the breakdown of the loyalties that once sustained Camelot.

4. (a) The description of Sir Lucan's death is gruesome, but Arthur's speech is full of noble thoughts and remembrances. (b) The range of medieval tastes in literature is great. They move easily from the physical to the spiritual, from real-istic to idealistic, from battle to poetry.

5 (a) Twice, Bedivere hides the sword and lies to Arthur. The third time, he completes Arthur's instructions. (b) It shows that real loyalty does not question logic or cost.

6. **Possible response:** Leaders such as the Dalai Lama have been forced out of their own countries. The people of the country hope he will return and so remain loyal to him.

7. **Possible response:** While it might be necessary in battle to follow an experienced military leader unquestioningly, in most situations, it is wise to examine a leader's decisions.

---

thus was he led away in a ship wherein were three queens; that one was King Arthur's sister, Queen Morgan le Fay, the other was the Queen of North Galis, and the third was the Queen of the Waste Lands.

Now more of the death of King Arthur could I never find, but that these ladies brought him to his grave, and such one was interred there which the hermit bare witness that was once Bishop of Canterbury. But yet the hermit knew not in certain that he was verily the body of King Arthur; for this tale Sir Bedivere, a knight of the Table Round, made it to be written.

Yet some men say in many parts of England that King Arthur is not dead, but carried by the will of our Lord Jesu into another place; and men say that he shall come again, and he shall win the Holy Cross. Yet I will not say that it shall be so, but rather I would say: here in this world he changed his life. And many men say that there is written upon the tomb this:

HIC IACET ARTHURUS, REX QUONDAM, REXQUE FUTURUS[28]

---

28. HIC . . . FUTURUS Here lies Arthur, who was once king and king will be again.

Critical Reading

1. **Respond:** If Arthur had asked you to throw his sword into the water, would you have hesitated? Why or why not?

2. **(a) Recall:** What warning does King Arthur receive in his dream? **(b) Recall:** How do circumstances frustrate his attempt to heed this warning? **(c) Interpret:** How does this series of events make the ending of the tale seem fated?

3. **(a) Recall:** What is the relationship between Mordred and Arthur? **(b) Interpret:** How does the conflict between them emphasize the theme of betrayal in the tale?

4. **(a) Compare and Contrast:** How does the description of Sir Lucan's death contrast with the speech in which Arthur bemoans his passing? **(b) Draw Conclusions:** What conclusions can you draw about the range of medieval taste in literature?

5. **(a) Recall:** How does Sir Bedivere respond when Arthur asks him to throw Excalibur in the water? **(b) Interpret:** What lesson about loyalty does the tale of Sir Bedivere and the sword suggest?

6. **Generalize:** At the tale's end, rightful authority has been betrayed and may yet return, but it is not here now. What idea of leadership and loyalty in the present does this ending suggest?

7. **Apply:** Do you think leaders are "Arthurs"—those who should receive perfect obedience—or should people sometimes question their leader's decisions? Explain.

Apply the Skills

**from *Sir Gawain and the Green Knight* •
from *Morte d'Arthur***

Literary Analysis

Medieval Romance

1. Identify three characteristics of Sir Gawain that make him an ideal hero for a **medieval romance.** Explain each answer.
2. **(a)** Identify one way in which Sir Gawain falls short of the ideals of chivalry. **(b)** What do his shortcomings suggest about the theme of human weakness in medieval romances?
3. In the excerpt from *Morte d'Arthur,* how do the supernatural events surrounding King Arthur's death link the story to the future?

Comparing Literary Works

4. **(a)** Which of these elements of romance is least emphasized in *Sir Gawain:* chivalry, a far-off setting, the supernatural, adventure, or love? Explain. **(b)** Which is least emphasized in *Morte d'Arthur?*
5. What characteristics of a **legend** do the two selections share?
6. Identify a feature or section of each work that the writer may have added to the original legend. Explain your choices.
7. **(a)** Compare the characterization of Gawain in lines 459–477 of *Sir Gawain* with Malory's description of Bedivere as he reacts to Arthur's imminent death. Use a graphic organizer like the one below. **(b)** Explain which author has done more to add literary elements, such as plot twists, descriptions, and characterization.

	Gawain's Reactions	Bedivere's Reactions
What He Says		
What He Does		
What He Feels		

Reading Strategy

Summarizing

8. If you were retelling *Sir Gawain and the Green Knight* for an audience of fifth graders, which key events would you emphasize?
9. As Sir Bedivere, **summarize** for a curious traveler who is visiting your hermitage the events leading up to King Arthur's death.

Extend Understanding

10. **Contemporary Connection:** Explain why you think the legend of King Arthur has remained popular to this day.

from Sir Gawain and the Green Knight / from *Morte d'Arthur* ■ 185

QuickReview

Medieval romances are narratives featuring adventure, love, the supernatural, and the ideals of chivalry.

A **legend** is a traditional story telling of heroic figures or deeds, which may be based in fact.

To **summarize** a work or passage, identify and restate its main ideas.

Assessment

For: Self-test
Visit: www.PHSchool.com
Web Code: esa-6108

Go Online
Assessment

Students may use the **Self-test** to prepare for **Selection Test A** or **Selection Test B**.

185

Build Language Skills

❶ Vocabulary Lesson

Word Analysis

1. *Maladroit* means "unskilled."
2. *Gauche* means "left."

Spelling Strategy

1. *Finesse* comes from the French word *fin,* which means "fine."
2. *Knight* comes from the Anglo-Saxon *cniht,* which meant "boy, youth," "military follower." It was related to the German *knecht,* a servant, which is only two letters different from the current spelling. (Note that neither French nor Latin had the letter "k.")
3. *Neighbor* comes from the Anglo-Saxon (Old English) *neahgebur: neah* means "near," and *gebur* means "dweller" or "countryman." It is related to the German *nachbar,* which appears to have influenced the final, modern English spelling.

Vocabulary Builder

1. a   4. c   7. a
2. b   5. a   8. c
3. c   6. b   9. c

❷ Grammar and Style Lesson

1. Superlative: most faultless
2. Superlative: weakest, feeblest
3. Superlative: least
4. Comparative: more need
5. Comparative: more

Writing Application

Possible response: Gawain was the humblest of the knights, though he was the greatest. He seems more noble than Bedivere, who wants to keep the sword. Gawain died earlier than Arthur.

---

❶ Vocabulary Lesson

Word Analysis: Root *-droit-*

The word *adroitly,* meaning "with skill," is based on the root *-droit-,* meaning "right." This root meaning reveals a historical bias toward right-handedness.

1. Given that the prefix *mal-* means "bad," what might *maladroit* mean?
2. *Gauche* means "socially maladroit." Which of these two might it also mean: "left" or "right"?

Spelling Strategy

The *-esse* in *largesse* comes from the English adaptation of medieval French spelling patterns. Using a dictionary, explain the influence the origin of the following words has had on their spelling.

1. finesse   2. knight   3. neighbor

Vocabulary Builder: Definitions

For each word from the vocabulary list on page 161, write the letter of its definition.

1. assay: **(a)** test, **(b)** deny, **(c)** ignore
2. adjure: **(a)** reject, **(b)** request, **(c)** withhold
3. feigned: **(a)** asked, **(b)** refused, **(c)** pretended
4. adroitly: **(a)** rightly, **(b)** boldly, **(c)** skillfully
5. largesse: **(a)** nobility, **(b)** insignificance, **(c)** wisdom
6. righteous: **(a)** awkward, **(b)** virtuous, **(c)** dishonorable
7. entreated: **(a)** pleaded, **(b)** requested, **(c)** refused
8. peril: **(a)** safety, **(b)** security, **(c)** danger
9. interred: **(a)** kept, **(b)** delayed, **(c)** buried

❷ Grammar and Style Lesson

Comparative and Superlative Forms

The **comparative form** of a modifier compares one thing with another. It is formed by adding *-er* to short modifiers and by using *more* with most modifiers of two or more syllables.

The **superlative form** compares more than two things. It is formed by adding *-est* to one-syllable modifiers and by using *most* with modifiers of two or more syllables.

> **Comparative Form:** Grow green as the grass, and greener, it seemed. / Then green fused on gold more glorious by far.
>
> **Superlative Form:** . . . thereupon sat King Arthur in the richest cloth of gold that might be made.

Practice Identify the comparative and superlative forms of modifiers in the following passages.

1. She made trial of a man most faultless by far. . . .
2. ". . . I am the weakest, well I know, and of wit feeblest; . . ."
3. "And the loss of my life would be least of any; . . ."
4. ". . . he would have helped me that had more need of help than I."
5. Thus of Arthur I find no more written in books that [have] been authorized, . . .

Writing Application Use comparatives and superlatives to compare characters from the selections.

W̶G *Prentice Hall Writing and Grammar Connection: Chapter 24, Section 1*

Assessment Practice

Signal Words **(For more practice, see *Standardized Test Preparation Workbook,* p. 6.)**

Many tests require students to identify the sequence of events. Have students read pp. 176–179. Help students determine the time between events using signal words. Then, answer the following question:

When do King Arthur and Sir Mordred begin their battle?

A on Trinity Sunday
B a month after Arthur's dream
C on Monday after Trinity Sunday
D cannot tell from the information given

Signal words such as *tomorn* and *morn* help determine time between events. Arthur dreams on Trinity Sunday and the next day is the appointed battle with Sir Mordred. The correct answer is C.

Writing Lesson

Interior Monologue

As Sir Gawain approaches the Green Chapel, he reacts in a monologue. In an **interior monologue,** a character speaks only to himself to reveal thoughts and feelings. Write a monologue in which Gawain reacts to another event in the story. In your monologue, create a distinctive voice as you develop Gawain's situation. Consider having Gawain react to unfolding events, giving your monologue narrative interest.

Prewriting List characteristics of Gawain, and jot down notes on the dramatic situation he is confronting.

Drafting Writing in the first person, have Gawain "discuss" the situation with himself. Make sure that key details explaining the situation emerge early in your draft. Refer to your prewriting notes to ensure that you clearly convey Gawain's character. Have Gawain's reactions help tell the story to readers.

> **Model: Using Reactions to Develop a Situation**
>
> By St. Peter's sail, will no one answer this strange knight's challenge? I would, forsooth, were it not presumptuous-seeming and—what! Arthur himself is answering!
>
> When Gawain interrupts himself to remark on a new disturbance, the reader sees the situation through the character's reactions.

Revising Star sections of your draft in which Gawain's feelings are especially strong. Review these passages, replacing dull phrases with vivid expressions of his personality or reactions.

*W*G *Prentice Hall Writing and Grammar Connection: Chapter 5, Section 2*

Extend Your Learning

Listening and Speaking Write a **proposal for a multimedia presentation** on Arthurian legends. Discuss using materials such as these:

- Clips from movies
- Reproductions of fine art
- Computer games
- Audio excerpts of songs and music
- Graphics, such as maps and charts

Explain which type of media would be most effective in conveying each major idea or theme.

Research and Technology With a group, research and give a brief **oral report** on medieval illuminated manuscripts. Use a variety of strategies for research, such as Internet searches and interviews with experts at a museum. Based on your research, draw conclusions about medieval trade, lifestyles, and values. **[Group Activity]**

For: An additional research activity
Visit: www.PHSchool.com
Web Code: esd-7107

from Sir Gawain and the Green Knight / from *Morte d'Arthur* ■ 187

Assessment Resources

The following resources can be used to assess students' knowledge and skills.

Unit 1 Resources
    Selection Test A, pp. 129–131
    Selection Test B, pp. 132–134

General Resources
    Rubrics for Response to Literature,
      pp. 65–66
    Rubric for Speaking: Presenting a Proposal, p. 91

Go **Online**
—Assessment
Selection Test B.

Students may use the **Self-test** to prepare for **Selection Test A** or

---

❸ Writing Lesson

- Explain that *interior monologue* is basically a literary form of talking to oneself. In literature, the monologue helps readers know what characters are thinking and experiencing.
- Have students consider the kinds of things they process by talking to themselves—disappointment, challenges, worry, anticipation.
- Point out that a written monologue must supply information that the reader does not already have.
- Tell students that listing characteristics of a speaker will help them determine how the speaker would react to things.
- Encourage students to refer to the guidelines in the student book for revising their work.
- To guide students in writing this interior monologue, give them the **Support for Writing Lesson** page (*Unit 1 Resources,* p. 126).
- Use the Response to Literature rubrics, pp. 65–66 in *General Resources,* to evaluate student work.

❹ Listening and Speaking

- Review with students the steps needed to create a multimedia presentation (research, documentation, selection of media, revision, presentation).
- Challenge students to search for other sources of Arthurian legends, besides those in this section.
- Tell students to think about what kind of information is best presented as art, as text, as movies, or as computer games.
- Encourage students to consider as many media as possible in their proposals. Proposals may be made orally.
- The **Support for Extend Your Learning** page (*Unit 1 Resources,* p. 127) provides guided note-taking opportunities to help students complete the Extend Your Learning activities.
- Use the Speaking: Presenting a Proposal rubric, p. 91 in *General Resources,* to evaluate student work.

Go **Online**
—Research
Have students type in the Web Code for another research activity.

187

Meeting Your Standards

Students will

1. **analyze and respond to literary elements.**
   - Literary Analysis: Letter; Folk Ballads

2. **read, comprehend, analyze, and critique nonfiction and poems.**
   - Reading Strategy: Understanding Dialect
   - Reading Check questions
   - Apply the Skills questions
   - Assessment Practice (ATE)

3. **develop vocabulary.**
   - Vocabulary Lesson: Latin Root: *-cert-*

4. **understand and apply written and oral language conventions.**
   - Spelling Strategy
   - Grammar and Style Lesson: Direct Address

5. **develop writing proficiency.**
   - Writing Lesson: Investigative Report

6. **develop appropriate research strategies.**
   - Extend Your Learning: Holidays Chart

7. **understand and apply listening and speaking strategies.**
   - Extend Your Learning: Phone Conversation

Block Scheduling: Use one 90-minute class period to preteach the skills and have students read the selection. Use a second 90-minute class period to assess students' mastery of skills, extend their learning, and monitor their progress.

Homework Suggestions

Following are possibilities for homework assignments:

- Support pages from *Unit 1 Resources:*
  - Literary Analysis
  - Reading Strategy
  - Vocabulary Builder
  - Grammar and Style

- An Extend Your Learning project and the Writing Lesson for this selection may be completed over several days.

Step-by-Step Teaching Guide	Pacing Guide
PRETEACH	
• Administer Vocabulary and Reading Warm-ups as necessary.	5 min.
• Engage students' interest with the motivation activity.	5 min.
• Read and discuss author and background features. **FT**	10 min.
• Introduce the Literary Analysis Skill: Letter; Folk Ballads. **FT**	5 min.
• Introduce the Reading Strategy: Understanding Dialect. **FT**	10 min.
• Prepare students to read by teaching the selection vocabulary. **FT**	
TEACH	
• Informally monitor comprehension while students read independently or in groups. **FT**	30 min.
• Monitor students' comprehension with the Reading Check notes.	as students read
• Reinforce vocabulary with Vocabulary Builder notes.	as students read
• Develop students' understanding of letters and folk ballads with the Literary Analysis annotations. **FT**	5 min.
• Develop students' ability to understand dialect with the Reading Strategy annotations. **FT**	5 min.
ASSESS/EXTEND	
• Assess students' comprehension and mastery of the Literary Analysis and Reading Strategy by having them answer the Apply the Skills questions. **FT**	15 min.
• Have students complete the Vocabulary Lesson and the Grammar and Style Lesson. **FT**	15 min.
• Apply students' ability to revise for logical organization by using the Writing Lesson. **FT**	45 min. or homework
• Apply students' understanding by using one or more of the Extend Your Learning activities.	20–90 min. or homework
• Administer Selection Test A or Selection Test B. **FT**	15 min.

Resources

PRINT

Reader's Notebook [L2]
Reader's Notebook: Adapted Version [L1]
Reader's Notebook: English Learner's Version [EL]

TECHNOLOGY

Listening to Literature Audio CDs [L2, EL]

PRINT

Unit 1 Resources

TECHNOLOGY

Go Online: Research [**L3**]
Go Online: Self-test [**L3**]
ExamView® Test Bank [**L3**]

Choosing Resources for Differentiated Instruction

[**L1**] Special Needs Students
[**L2**] Below-Level Students
[**L3**] All Students
[**L4**] Advanced Students
[**EL**] English Learners

For Vocabulary and Reading Warm-ups and for Selection Tests, A signifies "less challenging" and B "more challenging." For Graphic Organizer Transparencies, A signifies "not filled in" and B "filled in."

FT Fast Track Instruction: To move the lesson more quickly, use the strategies and activities identified with **FT**.

Scaffolding for Less Proficient and Advanced Students

The leveled Critical Thinking questions after selections progress in the levels of thinking required to answer them. To address the needs of your different students, you may use the (a) level questions for your less proficient students and the (b) level questions with your on-level and advanced students. The occasional (c) level questions are appropriate for your advanced students.

PRENTICE HALL
Teacher EXPRESS™ Use this complete
Plan · Teach · Assess   suite of powerful
teaching tools to make lesson planning and testing quicker and easier.

PRENTICE HALL
Student EXPRESS™ Use the interac-
Learn · Study · Succeed   tive textbook
(online and on CD-ROM) to make selections and activities come alive with audio and video support and interactive questions.

Benchmark

After students have completed these selections, administer **Benchmark Test 2** (*Unit 1 Resources*, pp. 159–164). If the Benchmark Test reveals that some students need further work, use the **Interpretation Guide** to determine the appropriate reteaching page in the **Reading Kit** and on **Success Tracker.**

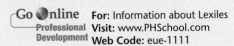

Go Online   **For:** Information about Lexiles
Professional   **Visit:** www.PHSchool.com
Development   **Web Code:** eue-1111

Motivation

To help students get beyond the difficult language and into the plots of the ballads, ask them to name a book, soap opera, or movie in which they've encountered characters or situations like the following:

- a handsome young man is mysteriously killed by an enemy.

- a husband and wife squabble, unaware that they are about to be mugged.

- two characters discuss the situation following a man's death.

- a woman is cruel to a man she loves.

❶ Background
More About the Author

Margaret Mauteby married John Paston when he was 19 and she was between the ages of 12 and 18. An only child of a well-connected family, she brought valuable land to her marriage. Margaret and John had seven children: five boys and two girls.

The Paston letters were collected by William Worcester, servant of Sir John Fastolf, a friend and neighbor of John Paston. Several of the lawsuits for which the letters were needed as evidence involved Fastolf—including the dispute mentioned on p. 192 in the student text.

(Fastolf achieved some degree of immortality when he was transformed by Shakespeare into Sir John Falstaff. However, the real Fastolf, a career soldier who fought with distinction, bore little resemblance to Shakespeare's cowardly clown.)

It is not known how the letters were kept from the fifteenth to the eighteenth century, but they reemerged in 1735. The letters were divided between Oxford's Bodleian Library and the British Museum. The collection, edited and published in six volumes, remains an important source of information about fifteenth-century England.

Build Skills | *Primary Source • Poems*

❶ Letters of Margaret Paston • Four Ballads

Margaret Paston
(1423–1484)

Brokering deals, managing staff, fighting lawsuits—tasks like these challenge today's top executives. Yet, in fifteenth-century England, they fell to Margaret Paston simply because her family owned land.

Margaret Paston, born Margaret Mautby, came to these responsibilities through her marriage to John Paston, a lawyer and son of a well-to-do landowner. The Paston family, having recently emerged from the upper segment of the peasantry, was eager to increase its landholdings and rise in society. Just holding onto their estates, though, proved to be a challenge. The Pastons lived in a time of social turmoil and violence. They were sued, threatened, and bullied over the years by those who wanted their holdings.

Throughout the Pastons' married life, John Paston was frequently called away to London on business for his law practice. As a result, Margaret was left to run the estates, settle rent disputes, and defend their manors against takeovers—which she did admirably.

The Legacy of the Pastons While John was away, he and Margaret exchanged letters frequently. In the letters, the Pastons often discuss the everyday business of running an estate as well as local political matters, providing historians with a detailed insight into the life of the times. Sometimes, the letters read like a medieval soap opera, as when they tell of the secret marriage of one daughter to the family's bailiff and the marriage of another daughter to her father's rival's son.

The letters between the Pastons are part of a collection of more than 1,000 papers. Although they were originally preserved as evidence for impending lawsuits, today they offer us an invaluable, vivid glimpse into fifteenth-century life.

Folk Ballads

Long before most people in Britain could read or write, they listened to ballads. A ballad is a song or poem that tells a story in short verses and simple words. Much like modern country-western songs, medieval ballads tell of the fate of lovers (usually tragic), of sensational crimes, of the dangers of the working life, and of historical disasters.

The Ballad's Origins The first folk ballads in England may have appeared during the twelfth century. Ballads were passed along orally for many centuries. As a result, they were subject to constant variation in both text and tune, as singers' memories altered or as they added ideas.

Most ballads consist of a sixteen-bar melody with two beats to the measure. Consistency among ballads emerged in the fifteenth century as people wrote them down.

Border Ballads The ballads in this grouping originated in the rugged border region between England and Scotland. Their language is a Scots dialect of English. Folk ballads typically thrived in areas such as the Border, where a formal, written literature had yet to develop.

Ballads and Literature Ballads did eventually join the literary tradition. In 1765, ballad enthusiast Bishop Thomas Percy published *Reliques of Ancient English Poetry,* an extensive collection of ballads. People then began to appreciate the ballads for their literary value as well as for the fascinating glimpses they offered into life in the past. Percy's collection even had its own dramatic story. Just as a housemaid was about to light a fire with an old manuscript, Percy intervened, saving a collection of treasures from the past. Later poets, and even contemporary songwriters such as American Bob Dylan, have drawn on this rich tradition.

Preview

Connecting to the Literature

Trouble always moves people to words: asking for advice, calling for assistance, or just seeking the comfort of talk. In her letters, Margaret Paston talks about her troubles—and what she has done about them.

Literary Analysis

Letter and Folk Ballad

A **letter** addresses a specific person or group and is meant to be read within a specific time. The best letters preserve a moment of life. As you read Paston's letters, note what they reveal about medieval times.

A **folk ballad,** is a narrative poem, intended to be sung and without a known author. While some ballads are humorous, many starkly insist on the doom that haunts our loves and lives. Most ballads use these features:

* Four-line stanzas in which the second and fourth lines rhyme
* Repeated key phrases or a regularly repeated section, called a refrain
* Dialogue

As you read the ballads, note the views of life they express.

Comparing Literary Works

In different ways—by recording a local event or by expressing a common attitude—letters and ballads can serve as **primary sources**—documents from the past that report or indicate events or values of the time. Primary sources include letters, inscriptions, legal documents, and songs. Compare the information these selections offer about medieval life.

Reading Strategy

Understanding Dialect

A **dialect** is a form of a language, spoken by people in a particular region or group. To understand the Scottish-English dialect of these ballads, read unfamiliar words aloud. Their sound and context may lead you to the corresponding current English word. Also, consult footnotes for guidance. To help you decode dialect, use a chart like the one here.

Phrase in Dialect	The wind sae cauld blew...
Meaning Suggested	**sound:** cauld = cold **context:** How does the wind blow?
Meaning Given in Footnote	

Vocabulary Builder

aldermen (ôl′ dər mən) *n.* chief officers in a shire, or district (p. 191)

enquiry (en kwir′ ē) *n.* question; investigation (p. 191)

succor (suk′ ər) *v.* help; aid; relieve (p. 191)

certify (surt′ ə fī′) *v.* declare a thing true or accurate; verify; attest (p. 191)

remnant (rem′ nənt) *n.* what is left over; remainder; residue (p. 191)

ransacked (ran′ sakt′) *v.* searched through for plunder; pillaged; robbed (p. 192)

asunder (ə sun′ dər) *adv.* into parts or pieces (p. 192)

assault (ə sôlt′) *v.* violently attack (p. 192)

Letters of Margaret Paston / Four Ballads ■ *189*

❷ Literary Analysis
Letter and Folk Ballad

* Tell students that letters go back just about as far as writing does. Because rhyme and rhythm make memorization easier and oral recitation more entertaining, poetry is actually older than letter writing.

* Relate that ballads, though common entertainment, were also often used as a way of spreading news.

* Have students read the items in the student text about letters, folk ballads, and primary sources.

* Explain that a primary source is any source of information that is first-hand. When someone writes about what he or she has learned second-hand (research, interview), that work is called a secondary source.

❸ Reading Strategy
Understanding Dialect

* Tell students that *dialect* is a regional variation of a language. There are dialect forms of most languages.

* Explain that dialect is not the same as accent. Dialects use different words and grammar from the standard language; an accent does not.

* Provide students with a copy of **Reading Strategy Graphic Organizer A,** p. 29 in *Graphic Organizer Transparencies,* to use as they read the selections.

* Use the **Listening to Literature Audio CD** recording of one or more of the poems in dialect to help students with pronunciation.

* Tell students that words from major English dialects can often be found in modern dictionaries.

Vocabulary Builder

* Pronounce each vocabulary word for students, and read the definitions as a class. Have students identify any words with which they are already familiar.

Learning Modalities
Visual/Spatial Learners Obtain photographs of medieval tools of war and armor and display them for students to help them get a better understanding of what Margaret Paston's world was like. You may also want to display drawings or art that depicts the lifestyle of the times.

❶ About the Selection

Letters are a way of sharing life's news, and, in the case of Margaret Paston, the news is dramatic, detailed, and very directly stated. Letters can also go a long way toward revealing the personality of the writer. In the first pair of letters, Paston tells her husband that one of their homes, Hellesdon, has been attacked, seized, and ransacked by the Duke of Suffolk. As she details the events, her outrage is palpable.

The third letter, written almost two years later, warns her son of yet another impending attack. This letter reveals Paston's keen awareness of political turmoil.

By reading these letters, students will receive firsthand information about life in the Middle Ages. They will also come to appreciate and respect Margaret Paston herself. She was a remarkable woman.

❶ *Letters of Margaret Paston*

Margaret Paston

Background His father, King Henry V, had brought much of France under English rule, but Henry VI's weakness as a ruler plunged England into chaos. Some English nobles took advantage of his weak government, terrorizing the countryside with small armies. Overseas, the French fought to regain their lands, while back in England a power struggle broke out for the throne. The House of York, a noble family, disputed the right of Henry's family, the House of Lancaster, to rule. Eventually, their quarrel plunged the country into the Wars of the Roses. In the midst of this upheaval and uncertainty, many families such as the Pastons were able to rise from poverty by taking properties to which they had a questionable (or at least easily challenged) legal claim.

Hellesdon, one of the Paston manors, was coveted by the Duke of Suffolk. The duke bribed the mayor of Norwich, a town northeast of London, to assist him in launching a campaign of terror to force the Pastons to surrender their property. Although Margaret Paston, along with a garrison of sixty, successfully repelled the first attacks, Hellesdon eventually was seized and plundered by the duke. In the first two letters, Margaret writes to her husband in London with the news.

190   *From Legend to History (449–1485)*

Margaret Paston to John Paston
17 October 1465
Norwich

. . . The Duke came to Norwich on Tuesday at 10 o'clock with some 500 men. And he sent for the mayor and <u>aldermen</u> with the Sheriffs, desiring them in the King's name that they should make <u>enquiry</u> of the constables of every ward in the City as to what men had gone to help or <u>succor</u> your men at any time during these gatherings and, if they could find any, that they should take and arrest and correct them, and <u>certify</u> to him the names by 8 o'clock on Wednesday. Which the Mayor did and will do anything that he may for him and his men. . . .

I am told that the old Lady [the Dowager Duchess] and the Duke are fiercely set against us on the information of Harleston, the bailiff of Costessey . . . and such other false shrews which would have this matter carried through for their own pleasure. . . . And as for Sir John Hevening, Sir John Wingfield and other worshipful men, they are but made their doggebolds [lackeys], which I suppose will cause their disworship hereafter. I spoke with Sir John Hevening and informed him of the truth of the matter and of all our demeaning at Drayton, and he said he would that all things were well, and that he would inform my Lord what I told him, but that Harleston had all the influence with the Duke here, and at this time he was advised by him and Dr. Aleyn.

The lodge and the <u>remnant</u> of your place was beaten down on Tuesday and Wednesday and the Duke rode on Wednesday to Drayton and so forth to Costessey while the lodge at Hellesdon was being beaten down. And this night at midnight Thomas Slyforth . . . and others had a cart and fetched away featherbeds and all our stuff that was left at the parson's and Thomas Waters' house to be kept. . . . I pray you send me word how I shall act—whether you wish that I abide at Caister or come to you at London. . . .

Margaret Paston to John Paston
27 October 1465
Norwich

. . . Please you to know that I was at Hellesdon on Thursday last and saw the place there, and, in good faith, nobody would believe how foul and horrible it appears unless they saw it. There come many people daily to wonder at it, both from Norwich and many other

Vocabulary Builder
aldermen (ôl′ dər mən) *n.* chief officers in a shire, or district

enquiry (en kwir′ ē) *n.* question; investigation

succor (suk′ ər) *v.* help; aid; relieve

certify (sʉrt′ ə fī′) *v.* declare a thing true or accurate; verify; attest

Vocabulary Builder
remnant (rem′ nənt) *n.* what is left over; remainder; residue

◄ **Critical Viewing** The Pastons' manors were often attacked by their enemies. Judging from this photograph of a manor house, how easy would it have been to defend such a manor? Explain. **[Speculate]**

5 ✔ **Reading Check**
What has the Duke done against the Pastons?

Letters of Margaret Paston ■ 191

2 **Literary Analysis**
Letter

- Explain that a manor was more than a grand house. A manor included much land and often a whole village. The lodge mentioned in the letter is probably a caretaker's cottage.

- Point out the dates at the beginning of each letter. Explain to students that many countries, including most European countries, still write the date in this order—day, month, year.

- Students may be unfamiliar with the symbol for the British pound (£), which appears in the second letter. Point it out and explain that it is a monetary unit.

- Have students review the first paragraph and **find** three details that indicate that Paston was an observant correspondent.
Answer: Paston notes the time and day of the events, the number of men, and the precise actions of the duke, including the date and time by which names had to be certified.

3 **Vocabulary Builder**
Latin Root -cert-

- Point out the word *certify* and its definition to students. Explain that the Latin root -cert- means "sure."

- Have students **suggest** words that contain this root, and list the words on the board. Feel free to add to the list if students have difficulty thinking of words.
Possible responses: certain, certainty, certified, certifiable, certification, certitude, ascertain

- Have students look up the words in dictionaries. Ask them how the meaning of *certus* relates to the current meaning.

4 **Critical Viewing**

Possible response: The manor house appears to be solidly built, which would help in its defense. It also appears to be very large, requiring numerous soldiers to defend it.

5 **Reading Check**

Answer: The Duke has asked the mayor to arrest anyone who has helped the Pastons or the Pastons' men.

❻ Literary Analysis
Letter

- Read the Enrichment below, so students know the extent of an estate.

- **Ask** students how the detail about the "high altar" shows the desperation of the situation.

  Possible response: It shows that those who are attacking respect nothing. If they treat the church this way, the damage they are causing elsewhere must be truly "foul and horrible."

❼ Literature in Context
Land Rights

The customs of land rights dated back centuries. Population centers were scattered, and a central government (if it existed) could take weeks to reach. Smaller units of control made civilized existence possible. Each manor was a self-contained economic system.

The decline of this system began in the eleventh century. The growth of cities began to change economic realities. Add to that the upheaval caused by the Wars of the Roses (1455–85), with the English monarchy up for grabs, and it is easy to see how things got tumultuous. Land could now change hands as a reward for faithful service—or by the work of a clever lawyer. However, land could be lost to one of the private armies roaming the countryside.

Connect to the Literature
Encourage students to reread p. 192 before answering the question.
Possible answer: Three reasons why they had to fight were because the land had been willed to them by a non-family member, land was usually kept in the hands of the aristocracy, and women had limited land property rights.

❽ Literary Analysis
Letter and Primary Sources

- Have students describe Margaret Paston's fears and cite reasons why her fears are justifiable.

- Then, **ask** students the Literary Analysis question: What does this letter show about the position of medieval women?

  Answer: It shows that women had little knowledge of fighting and were therefore not respected as leaders by soldiers.

places, and they speak of it with shame. The Duke would have been a £1000 better off if it had not happened, and you have the more good will of the people because it was so foully done. They made your tenants of Hellesdon and Drayton, with others, break down the walls of both the place and the lodge—God knows full much against their wills, but they dare not refuse for fear. I have spoken with your tenants of Hellesdon and Drayton and comforted them as well as I can. The Duke's men <u>ransacked</u> the church and bore away all the goods that were left there, both of ours and of the tenants, and even stood upon the high altar and ransacked the images and took away those that they could find, and put the parson out of the church till they had done, and ransacked every man's house in the town five or six times. . . . As for lead, brass, pewter, iron, doors, gates and other stuff of the house, men from Costessey and Cawston have it, and what they might not carry away they have hewn <u>asunder</u> in the most spiteful manner. . . .

At the reverence of God, if any worshipful and profitable settlement may be made in your matters, do not forsake it, to avoid our trouble and great costs and charges that we may have and that may grow hereafter. . . .

⮕⬥⬅

The following letter was sent to Sir John Paston, Margaret's knighted son. Caister, a castle with many manors and estates, had been willed to the Paston family by Sir John Fastolf, for whom John Paston worked as financial advisor. There followed years of legal wrangles during which the Pastons faced numerous challenges to the will. Because her husband had died the year before, Margaret turned to her son Sir John for help defending Caister. Sir John sent his younger brother, also named John, to protect the castle. John failed, however, surrendering the castle after his protector, King Edward IV, was captured during the Wars of the Roses.

⮕⬥⬅

Margaret Paston to Sir John Paston
11 July 1467
Norwich

. . . Also this day was brought me word from Caister that Rising of Fritton had heard in divers places in Suffolk that Fastolf of Cowhawe gathers all the strength he may and intends to <u>assault</u> Caister and to enter there if he may, insomuch that it is said that he has five score men ready and daily sends spies to know what men guard the place. By whose power or favor or support he will do this I know not, but you know well that I have been afraid there before this time, when I had other comfort

192 ■ *From Legend to History (449–1485)*

Vocabulary Builder
ransacked (ran´ sakt´) v. searched through for plunder; pillaged; robbed

asunder (ə sun´ dər) adv. into parts or pieces

assault (ə sôlt´) v. violently attack

Literature in Context

History Connection
Land Rights

When the Pastons struggled to retain their land, they were fighting history. In the Middle Ages, land ownership was bound up with social privilege, and laws kept large tracts of land in the hands of aristocrats. Even if a nobleman wanted to sell a small part of his land to a lower-class family, he could not: Inheritance laws forbade aristocrats from dividing up their estates. The Pastons were fortunate to live during a time of social turmoil, when the grip of tradition and law had been loosened. At the same time, the chaos of the day threatened their own hold on the lands they had acquired. For women such as Margaret Paston, the situation was especially difficult, since women had only limited rights to property.

Connect to the Literature

Identify three reasons that explain why the Pastons fought so tirelessly to keep their land.

Enrichment

Manors and Tenants

The manor system began at the end of the Roman Empire. Weak governments, civil disorder, and invasions made it difficult for people to operate independently. Farmers and laborers began to trade their land, freedom, or services for the protection of powerful landowners, who could afford to support a military force. This system spread throughout Europe and into Asia.

The landowners, who became lords or kings over time, gained the benefit of laborers to work their lands. The workers gained both protection and permanent access to a plot of land.

Because the land was owned by the lord, no one could take it away from even the poorest farmer. It was not only the lords who enjoyed hereditary rights—these workers, called tenants, also inherited their positions.

The typical manor included a manor house, land for farming and grazing livestock, and the cottages, barns, and gardens of its tenants. These were often gathered into a small village. There might also be a church and shops.

than I had now: I cannot guide nor rule soldiers well and they set not by [do not respect] a woman as they should by a man. Therefore I would that you should send home your brothers or else Daubeney to take control and to bring in such men as are necessary for the safeguard of the place. . . . And I have been about my livelode to set a rule therein, as I have written to you, which is not yet all performed after my desire, and I would not go to Caister till I had done. I do not want to spend more days near thereabouts, if I can avoid it; so make sure that you send someone home to keep the place and when I have finished what I have begun I shall arrange to go there if it will do any good—otherwise I had rather not be there. . . .

. . . I marvel greatly that you send me no word how you do, for your enemies begin to grow right bold and that puts your friends in fear and doubt. Therefore arrange that they may have some comfort, so that they be not discouraged, for if we lose our friends, it will be hard in this troublous world to get them again . . .

Literary Analysis
Letter and Primary Sources What does this letter show about the position of medieval women?

Critical Reading

1. **Respond:** Would you have liked Margaret Paston? Why?

2. **(a) Recall:** What has the Duke done at Hellesdon?
   (b) Draw Conclusions: Explain what Margaret Paston's references to those who aid the Duke and her conversation with Sir Heveningham show about the Pastons' relationship with the Duke.

3. **(a) Infer:** When the Duke forces the tenants to assist him, what effect does Margaret Paston hope his act will have?
   (b) Draw Conclusions: What do Margaret Paston's actions among the tenants show about the relationship she wants to have with the lower classes?

4. **(a) Analyze:** To what extent does Margaret Paston use emotional appeals in her requests for help to her husband and son? To what extent does she use reason? **(b) Draw Conclusions:** What were relations like among the Paston family?

5. **(a) Generalize:** What do the letters suggest to you about life in the Middle Ages? **(b) Evaluate:** What do you think is the most important difference, positive or negative, between life then and life today? Why?

6. **Apply:** What professions today involve tasks comparable to those performed by the Pastons? Explain your answer.

For: More about Margaret Paston
Visit: www.PHSchool.com
Web Code: ese-9105

Letters of Margaret Paston ■ *193*

❾ Twa Corbies

Background

During the Middle Ages, death before the age of thirty-five was the norm. The stark facts of mortality intruded on any medieval picture of life, and it promoted the unsentimentalized outlook of medieval folk ballads. Ballads tell of adventure, love, and disaster with an unflinching attention to the limits of life and the dangerous depths of passion.

As I was walking all alane,
I heard twa corbies[1] making a mane.[2]
The tane unto the tither did say,
"Whar sall we gang and dine the day?"

5 "In behint yon auld fail dyke,[3]
I wot[4] there lies a new-slain knight;
And naebody kens[5] that he lies there
But his hawk, his hound, and his lady fair.

"His hound is to the hunting gane,
10 His hawk to fetch the wild-fowl hame,
His lady's ta'en anither mate,
So we may mak our dinner sweet.

"Ye'll sit on his white hause-bane,[6]
And I'll pike out his bonny blue e'en;[7]
15 Wi' ae lock o' his gowden hair
We'll theek[8] our nest when it grows bare.

"Mony a one for him maks mane,
But nane sall ken whar he is gane.
O'er his white banes, when they are bare,
20 The wind sall blaw for evermair."

1. **twa corbies** two ravens.
2. **mane** moan.
3. **fail dyke** bank of earth.
4. **wot** know.
5. **kens** knows.
6. **hause-bane** neck-bone.
7. **e'en** eyes.
8. **theek** thatch.

Enrichment

Ballads and the Oral Tradition

Ballads are part of the oral tradition. Oral literature forms the basis of almost every literary history in every culture. Often, oral literature consists of myths and tales, and in particular, emphasizes creation myths. This is the case in the Native American and African literary traditions.

Ballads, which tell stories without much character development, resemble many early myths in which the emphasis is on plot and especially outcome, rather than on motivation or any other psychological dimension of human action.

Have students speculate about why literature from the oral tradition reveals so much about the culture from which it sprang.

Lord Randall

O where hae ye been, Lord Randall, my son?
O where hae ye been, my handsome young man?"
"I hae been to the wild wood; mother, make my bed soon,
For I'm weary wi' hunting, and fain[1] wald[2] lie down."

5   "Where gat ye your dinner, Lord Randall, my son?
Where gat ye your dinner, my handsome young man?"
"I dined wi' my true-love; mother, make my bed soon,
For I'm weary wi' hunting, and fain wald lie down."

"What gat ye to your dinner, Lord Randall, my son?
10 What gat ye to your dinner, my handsome young man?"
"I gat eels boil'd in broo;[3] mother, make my bed soon,
For I'm weary wi' hunting, and fain wald lie down."

"What became of your bloodhounds, Lord Randall, my son?
What became of your bloodhounds, my handsome young man?"
15 "O they swell'd and they died; mother, make my bed soon,
For I'm weary wi' hunting, and fain wald lie down."

"O I fear ye are poison'd, Lord Randall, my son!
O I fear ye are poison'd, my handsome young man!"
"O yes! I am poison'd; mother, make my bed soon,
20 For I'm sick at the heart, and I fain wald lie down."

---

1. **fain** gladly.   2. **wald** would.   3. **broo** broth.

Critical Reading

1. **Infer:** In "Twa Corbies," what does the ravens' discussion of the knight's animals and lady suggest about his fate?

2. **Interpret:** What do the images of the knight's hair and the wind across his bones suggest about the effect of death on identity?

3. **(a) Infer:** In "Lord Randall," who has caused Lord Randall to feel sick?
(b) Interpret: What two meanings might line 20 have?

4. **(a) Analyze:** How might love itself be like a poison?
(b) Draw Conclusions: What idea of love does "Lord Randall" express?

5. **Evaluate:** These poems are about extraordinary situations. Are their messages relevant to ordinary life? Explain.

Reading Strategy
Understanding Dialect
Use sound, context, and a footnote to give the modern equivalents of "gat ye to your dinner" and "boil'd in broo."

Lord Randall ■ 195

⓬ Reading Strategy
Understanding Dialect

- Explain that dialects form when populations are separated from others who speak related languages.

- They have the same origins as the standard form of a language but grow in different directions. For example, Latin for *crow* or *raven* is *corvus*. It's not hard to see how *corvus* became *crow*—but it is also possible to see how *corvus* became *corbie* (say both aloud and the similarity is greater).

- Another example is the middle Irish word *bruith,* which means "to boil." It became *broth* in English, and *broo* in the dialect of the ballad's writer.

- **Ask** students the Reading Strategy question: Use sound, context, and a footnote to give the modern equivalents of lines 10–11.
Answer: "Gat ye to your dinner" is "get for your dinner" (so the whole line would be "what did you get for dinner") and "boil'd in broo" is "boiled in broth."

- Tell students that eels are a common seafood item still consumed in many parts of the world, including England.

ASSESS

Answers

1. Their discussion seems to indicate that the lady and animals may have been responsible for the knight's fate.

2. The images suggest that death erases identity.

3. (a) His true-love has caused him to feel sick. (b) He is heartsick because he is dying and heartsick to know he has been betrayed by his true-love.

4. (a) Love might be compared to poison because it can make one "love sick"; once a person is "in your system," he or she can hurt you. (b) Love can bring great hurt.

5. **Possible response:** Love is betrayed even today, and "true loves" become enemies. While it is not common to be poisoned or killed when breaking up, one does still hear tales of such things.

196

⑬ Get Up and Bar the Door

It fell about the Martinmas time,[1]
      And a gay time it was then,
When our goodwife got puddings to make,
      She's boild them in the pan.

5   The wind sae cauld blew south and north.
      And blew into the floor;
Quoth our goodman to our goodwife,
      "Gae out and bar the door."

"My hand is in my hussyfskap,[2]
10   Goodman, as ye may see;
An it should nae be barrd this hundred year,
      It's no be barrd for me."[3]

They made a paction[4] tween them twa.
      They made it firm and sure.
15   That the first word whaeer shoud speak,
      Shoud rise and bar the door.

⑯ Then by there came two gentlemen,
      At twelve o'clock at night,
And they could neither see house nor hall,
20   Nor coal nor candlelight.

"Now whether is this a rich man's house,
      Or whether it is a poor?"
But neer a word wad ane o' them[5] speak,
      For barring of the door.

---

1. **Martinmas time** November 11.
2. **hussyfskap** household duties.
3. **An it should . . . me** "If it has to be barred by me, then it will not be barred in a hundred years."
4. **paction** agreement.
5. **them** the man and his wife.

⑮ **▲ Critical Viewing**
What does this painting tell you about domestic life in medieval times? [Infer]

Literary Analysis
Folk Ballad How does the rhyme scheme of lines 17–20 illustrate the typical ballad stanza?

⑰ Reading Strategy
Understanding Dialect

- Point out that in many of the dialect words, exchanging *a* for *o* can clarify meaning. For example, in the previous ballads, *nane* was *none*, *banes* was *bones*, and *mony* was *many*. In this poem, *aff* is *off*. Similarly, *sae* is *so*, *cauld* is *cold*, and so forth. It does not work every time, but it is useful to try.

- Tell students that they can look for other words in which a letter or two could be changed or added—but they should also take advantage of the footnotes.

- **Ask** students the Reading Strategy question: Restate lines 30–31 in modern English.
  Answer: Here, man, take my knife and cut off the old man's beard.

⑱ Literary Analysis
Folk Ballad

- Have students discuss how this poem differs from the usual folk ballads in terms of subject matter.

- Then, **ask** students the Literary Analysis question: Why might listeners find this ballad both amusing and insightful?
  Answer: It is amusing to see how stubborn the husband and wife are, yet insightful that people would do things that harm themselves rather than admit defeat.

ASSESS

Answers

1. **Possible response:** I like the goodman better because he at least took offense at the intruders' behavior rather than suffer to win a bet.

2. (a) They agree that the first to speak shall get up and bar the door. (b) She is busy, he is lazy, both are stubborn.

3. (a) They must decide which is worse, being burglarized or losing the bet. (b) She wins because the goodman is the first to speak.

4. Stubbornness is often stupid and can be harmful.

5. **Possible response:** The goodwife, because she is so focused on the bet, does not seem to notice her danger.

25 And first they[6] ate the white puddings,
    And then they ate the black:
Tho muckle[7] thought the goodwife to hersel,
    Yet neer a word she spake.

 30 Then said the one unto the other,
    "Here, man, take ye my knife;
Do ye tak aff the auld man's beard,
    And I'll kiss the goodwife."

    "But there's nae water in the house,
    And what shall we do than?"
35 "What ails ye at the pudding broo,[8]
    That boils into[9] the pan?"

O up then started our goodman,
    An angry man was he:
"Will ye kiss my wife before my een,
40   And scad[10] me wi pudding bree?"[11]

 Then up and started our goodwife,
    Gied three skips on the floor:
"Goodman, you've spoken the foremost word;
    Get up and bar the door."

Reading Strategy
Understanding Dialect
Restate lines 30–31 in modern English.

Literary Analysis
Folk Ballad Why might listeners find this ballad both amusing and insightful?

---

6. **they** the strangers.
7. **muckle** much.
8. **What . . . broo** "What's the matter with pudding water?"
9. **into** in.
10. **scad** scald.
11. **bree** broth.

Critical Reading

1. **Respond:** Whom do you like better—the goodman or the goodwife? Explain.

2. **(a) Recall:** What agreement do the goodman and his wife make?
   (b) Analyze: What are their main motives in making this agreement?

3. **(a) Summarize:** What new dilemma do the goodman and his wife face when the strangers arrive? **(b) Interpret:** In what sense does the wife "win"?

4. **Interpret:** What serious point about stubborness does the ballad make?

5. **Evaluate:** Which of the two characters is more foolish? Why?

Get Up and Bar the Door ■ 197

Differentiated Instruction   Solutions for All Learners

Strategy for Special Needs Students
To help students understand the dialect, select one of the ballads to go through line by line. As students determine the meaning of a line, write it on the board, so that a complete "translation" is created. Then ask students to state the ballad's story in their own words.

Background for English Learners
Pick one ballad and write all the words of dialect on the board. Then, write the standard English version of each word next to it. Most of the standard English words are relatively simple once translated (one, have, get), but some may be unfamiliar (thatch, scald, ravens), so help students understand these terms. Have students substitute the standard English words for the dialect in the selected ballad to discover the story being told.

About the Selection

Over time, "Barbara Allan" has had more than a dozen titles and has been spoken in countless local accents. A ballad historian found ninety-two versions in Virginia alone!

In this popular ballad, Barbara Allan uses her last moments with Graeme, on his deathbed, to remind him that he slighted her. Yet, when she returns home, it is only to die tomorrow, because Graeme, her own true love, died today. (Actually, this ballad is still popular, especially among people of Scottish descent. It commonly appears on recordings of Scottish songs.)

20 **Humanities**

Veronica Veronese, 1872, by Dante Gabriel Rossetti

A poet and a painter, Rossetti was a founding member of the Pre-Raphaelite brotherhood, a group of artists who admired and sought to emulate the work of Italian painters who preceded Raphael.

Use these questions for discussion.

1. Does the woman in the painting seem to have the same strength of character as Barbara Allan has in this ballad?
Possible responses: Some may say that this woman seems more feminine and contemplative than Barbara Allan. Others may feel that this seems like the portrait of a woman on the verge of lying down to die because her true love has died.

2. Why do you think this painting was chosen to illustrate this ballad? Do you think it is an apt illustration?
Possible response: The ballad is about a woman making a difficult decision in a very sad situation. Both the sadness and the deeply considered decision are reflected in the painting's subject and mood.

21 **Critical Viewing**

Answer: The colors suggest a dark and vibrant personality; the posture suggests a tired, depressed woman. Barbara Allan must have been vibrant to win Sir John's heart, but her slow movements, sighing, and, ultimately, death reveal her feelings of depression.

198

20

21 ▲ **Critical Viewing** How does the artist's choice of color and the posture of the subject suit the description of the fictional Barbara Allan? [Interpret]

198 ■ *From Legend to History (449–1485)*

Enrichment

Popularizing Ballads

By the seventeenth century, English presses were beginning to pour out ballad texts printed on broadsides. (Broadsides are large sheets of paper printed on one side only.) However, most of these ballad texts disappeared almost as quickly as most of today's pop songs.

Ballad singers hawked the broadsides around country towns and at places for social entertainment, such as fairs and public houses, so a few of the street ballad texts passed into oral circulation. At the same time, a few songs that had previously existed only in oral tradition were learned by the ballad hawkers. Texts were carried to London, printed on broadsides and then carried back to the countryside. Some ballads—such as "Barbara Allan"—owed their widespread and long continued life in the oral tradition to the constant interaction between printed and oral traditions.

⑲

Barbara Allan

It was in and about the Martinmas time,[1]
    When the green leaves were a-fallin';
That Sir John Graeme in the West Country
    Fell in love with Barbara Allan.

⑳

5 He sent his man down through the town
    To the place where she was dwellin':
"O haste and come to my master dear,
    Gin[2] ye be Barbara Allan."

O slowly, slowly rase[3] she up,
10   To the place where he was lyin',
And when she drew the curtain by:
    "Young man, I think you're dyin'."

"O it's I'm sick, and very, very sick,
    And 'tis a' for Barbara Allan."
15 "O the better for me ye sal[4] never be,
    Though your heart's blood were a-spillin'.

"O dinna ye mind,[5] young man," said she,
    "When ye the cups were fillin',
That ye made the healths gae round and round,
20   And slighted Barbara Allan?"

---

1. **Martinmas time** November 11.
2. **Gin** if.
3. **rase** rose.
4. **sal** shall.
5. **dinna ye mind** don't you remember.

Literary Analysis
Folk Ballad What does the phrase "his man" tell you about the society of the time?

㉓  **Reading Check**
How does Barbara Allan react to Sir John's confession of love?

Barbara Allan ■ *199*

㉒ Literary Analysis
Folk Ballad and Primary Sources

• Point out that in the first stanza, we learn that the gentleman who falls in love with Barbara Allan is Sir John Graeme. **Ask** students what his title tells about him.
Answer: The fact that he is called *sir* means that he is probably a knight and a member of the nobility.

• **Ask** students the Literary Analysis question: What does the phrase "his man" tell you about the society of the time?
Possible response: Because we know that Sir John was probably a member of the nobility, this phrase tells us that knights and nobles had servants that they could send to do errands or carry messages.

• Point out that the "man" refers to Sir John as "my master dear." Explain that individuals hired as personal servants often became almost like family members.

• **Ask** students if they think Sir John knew that he had offended Barbara Allan even before she spoke to him of the slight.
Possible response: It seems likely he knew, or he would not have been heartsick. He could just woo her otherwise.

• Point out that in lines 17–20, the slight of which Barbara Allan speaks was a public insult. Even if she wanted to forgive him, honor might not permit her to do so, at least not without a public apology. This would explain why he accepts her comment, rather than arguing.

㉓ Reading Check
Answer: Barbara Allan reminds Sir John of a time when he slighted her.

Differentiated Instruction   Solutions for All Learners

Strategy for Less Proficient Readers
Have students make a flowchart of the actions presented in the ballad. Each stanza should be summarized in one phrase or short sentence. Help students use context clues and the footnote definitions to understand what is happening. When all the summaries are complete, help students put the actions in chronological order.

Enrichment for Advanced Readers
Have students reread the ballad, looking at the order in which the events are presented. Ask students to compare this to the previous ballads. Which are in chronological order and which are not? Is there a difference in how one learns of the actions presented? Discuss the effect of retelling past events out of order.

Folk Ballad

- Remind students that repeated phrases are a common element of folk ballads.

- **Ask** students the Literary Analysis question: What phrase repeated from earlier in the poem appears in lines 25–28?
Answer: The phrase "slowly, slowly" is repeated from line 9.

- **Ask** students what emotion Barbara Allan's leaving slowly reveals.
Answer: It would indicate that she is sad to leave Sir John. Perhaps she had hoped for an apology.

- Point out that in many places, there are words or phrases repeated within the same sentence (slowly, sick, adieu, dead-bell, mother). Discuss the effect the repetitions create.
Possible responses: They add to the sense of mournfulness. They create a rhythm that makes the poem memorable.

ASSESS

Answers

1. **Possible responses:** I find Sir John more sympathetic. He seems to love Barbara Allan. I find Barbara Allan more sympathetic. She loves Sir John, but he will not apologize.

2. (a) He is sick because of Barbara Allan. (b) She acts unconcerned because he slighted her in public. (c) She is controlling her feelings for him.

3. At the end of the poem, Barbara Allan reveals that she loves Sir John, so it is possible that his death inspired her emotions.

4. (a) When she appears not to care about Sir John's health. (b) When she reveals that she loves him.

5. (a) Barbara Allan was too proud to overlook Sir John's slight. If she had, they might have reconciled. (b) **Possible responses:** Life is impossible without the loved one. There is no changing your mind.

6. **Possible response:** The view is too extreme. Death does not solve anything; while there is life, there is hope.

200

He turned his face unto the wall,
    And death with him was dealin':
"Adieu, adieu, my dear friends all,
    And be kind to Barbara Allan."

25 And slowly, slowly rase she up,
    And slowly, slowly left him;
And sighing said she could not stay,
    Since death of life had reft[6] him.

She had not gane a mile but twa,[7]
30   When she heard the dead-bell knellin',
And every jow[8] that the dead-bell ga'ed[9]
    It cried, "Woe to Barbara Allan!"

"O mother, mother, make my bed,
    O make it soft and narrow:
35 Since my love died for me today,
    I'll die for him tomorrow."

---

6. **reft** deprived.
7. **not . . . twa** gone but two miles.
8. **jow** stroke.
9. **ga'ed** made.

Literary Analysis
Folk Ballad What phrase repeated from earlier in the poem appears in lines 25–28?

Critical Reading

1. **Respond:** Which character—Sir John or Barbara Allan—do you find more sympathetic? Why?

2. **(a) Recall:** According to Sir John, why is he "sick, and very, very sick"? **(b) Recall:** What reason does Barbara Allan give for acting unconcerned about his plight? **(c) Interpret:** What is another reason she might put on a show of indifference?

3. **Interpret:** Do you think Barbara Allan was in love with Sir John before her visit, or do you think the knowledge that he is dying for her inspires her with love? Explain.

4. **(a) Analyze:** At what point does the ballad make you critical of Barbara Allan? **(b) Analyze:** At what point does it make you sympathize with her?

5. **(a) Support:** Explain how, in the poem, Barbara Allan's pride is an obstacle to her happiness in love. **(b) Support:** Explain how, in the poem, death is the ultimate expression of love.

6. **Evaluate:** Do you agree with the view of love in the poem, or do you think the view is too extreme? Explain.

Apply the Skills

Letters of Margaret Paston • Four Ballads

Literary Analysis

Letter and Folk Ballad

1. What does the content and style of Margaret Paston's **letters** reveal about the kind of life she led? Support your answer with examples.
2. What does the style of the letters reveal about family life in her time? Explain.
3. Choose two of the **ballads,** and explain how repetition and dialogue add to the drama of each.
4. Compare and contrast the theme of love in each of the folk ballads. Explain which show a lighter side of love and which, a darker side.

Comparing Literary Works

5. **(a)** What do both Paston's letters and the ballads suggest about violence in fifteenth-century society? **(b)** Explain which of these **primary sources** indicates the causes of violence at the time.
6. Use a Venn diagram like the one shown to compare the kinds of historical information you can find in Paston's letters and the ballads.

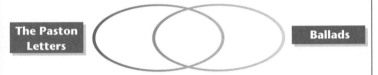

The Paston Letters | Ballads

7. If you were researching the roles of women in medieval times, which of these selections would be most effective as primary sources? Explain

Reading Strategy

Understanding Dialect

8. Identify the standard modern English words whose pronunciation is similar to the italicized **dialect** words: **(a)** And *naebody kens* that he lies there. . . . **(b)** But *neer* a word *wad ane* o' them speak, . . .
9. Find three other dialect words in the ballads, and explain the strategy you used to decode the meaning of each.

Extend Understanding

10. **History Connection:** What primary sources could a future historian use to reconstruct present-day life?

Letters of Margaret Paston / Four Ballads ■ 201

QuickReview

Letters are written for a specific audience on a specific occasion and usually contain a date, greeting, body, and closing.

A **folk ballad** is a traditional narrative poem meant to be sung.

Primary sources are documents, inscriptions, songs, and other records from the past that shed light on the time period when they were created.

Dialect is a distinctive form of a language, spoken by people in a particular region or group.

Go Online
Assessment
For: Self-test
Visit: www.PHSchool.com
Web Code: esa-6109

Answers

Answers continued

Go Online
Assessment Students may use the **Self-test** to prepare for **Selection Test A** or **Selection Test B.**

❶ Vocabulary Lesson

Latin Root -cert-

1. c
2. a
3. b
4. a

Vocabulary Builder

1. c
2. h
3. g
4. d
5. e
6. a
7. f
8. b

Spelling Strategy

1. fault
2. maul
3. haul
4. bawl

❷ Grammar and Style Lesson

1. mother
2. Goodman
3. man
4. young man
5. my dear friends all

Writing Application
Possible response:

"<u>John</u>, I hardly know what to do. We have so little remaining since the Duke plundered Hellesdon. I fear, <u>dear husband</u>, that we will starve in quick time."

"Don't worry, <u>Margaret</u>. We still have the manor at Caister, which offers protection and succor. Hasten to that manor, <u>wife</u>, and see to it that all tenants remain in our camp."

𝒲𝒢 **Writing and Grammar, Diamond Level**

Students will find further instruction and practice on direct address in Chapter 27, Section 2.

Build Language Skills

❶ Vocabulary Lesson

Word Analysis: Latin Root -cert-

Margaret Paston uses the phases "certify to him the names of. . . ." The root of *certify*, *-cert-*, comes from the Latin *certus*, which means "sure." *Certify* means "to make sure," or "to verify offically." Use your knowledge of the root *-cert-* to choose the best definition for the words that follow.

1. ascertain: **(a)** question, **(b)** sort through, **(c)** determine definitely
2. certificate: **(a)** written proof of qualifications, **(b)** bill for receipt of goods, **(c)** application form for a diploma
3. certitude: **(a)** vagueness, **(b)** sureness, **(c)** righteousness
4. certified: **(a)** guaranteed, **(b)** imprisoned, **(c)** doubtful

Vocabulary Builder: Definitions

Match each vocabulary word with its definition.

1. aldermen   **a.** looted
2. enquiry   **b.** attack
3. succor   **c.** officials
4. certify   **d.** guarantee
5. remnant   **e.** remainder
6. ransacked   **f.** into pieces
7. asunder   **g.** assist
8. assault   **h.** investigation

Spelling Strategy

The ô sound in words may be spelled *au*, as in *assault*, *vault*, *cautious*, and *auction*. It is less commonly spelled *aw*, as in *awl* and *shawl*. Choose between these spellings to complete the following words.

1. f__lt   3. h__l
2. m__l   4. b__l

❷ Grammar and Style Lesson

Direct Address

These folk ballads employ **direct address**—the use of a person's name or title or a descriptive phrase referring to the person when the speaker directly addresses someone.

> **Direct Address:** "O where hae ye been, <u>Lord Randall, my son?</u>"

In writing, terms of direct address are set off by commas. Direct address helps readers identify characters and adds drama by mimicking spoken language in which speakers may indicate strong feelings by calling someone by name.

Practice In your notebook, identify each phrase that serves as a term of direct address.

1. ". . . mother, make my bed soon, . . ."
2. "My hand is in my hussyfskap, / Goodman, as ye may see; . . ."
3. "Here, man, take ye my knife; . . ."
4. "O dinna ye mind, young man," said she, . . .
5. "Adieu, adieu, my dear friends all, / And be kind of Barbara Allan. . . ."

Writing Application Write a brief dialogue between Margaret Paston and her husband. Use at least three instances of direct address.

𝒲𝒢 *Prentice Hall Writing and Grammar Connection: Chapter 27, Section 2*

Assessment Practice

Sequential Order   (For more practice, see *Standardized Test Preparation Workbook*, p. 7.)

Many tests require students to identify the sequence of events. Events may be presented out of sequence, as when they appear in dialogue. Have students read pp. 199–200 and answer the following question:

Which of the following series *best* describes the sequence of events?

A Sir John offends Barbara Allan; he becomes sick; he dies of a broken heart.

B Sir John sends for Barbara Allan; he falls in love with her; he dies of a broken heart.

C Sir John sends for Barbara Allan; he offends her; he dies of a broken heart.

D Sir John falls in love with Barbara Allan; she dies for love; he dies of a broken heart.

The correct answer is *A*. Though the poem does not mention the slight until after Sir John is sick, it happened before.

Writing Lesson

Investigative Report

Margaret Paston's letters shed some light on life in fifteenth-century England. Draw three conclusions from her letters about events and life in her time. Then, check your conclusions in secondary sources. Write an investigative report in which you evaluate the accuracy and value of Paston's letters as a primary source.

Prewriting Review the letters, and formulate three historical conclusions based on them. Then, do research to locate resources on the Paston letters and on fifteenth-century England.

Drafting Begin your draft with background on the Paston letters. Introduce the three conclusions you have reached, and then explain what other sources indicated about your hypotheses. Conclude with an evaluation of the letters based on your investigation.

Revising Review your draft, highlighting repetitious or out-of-sequence ideas. Cut or reorder these passages.

> **Model: Revising for Logical Organization**
>
> ~~The Pastons' claims to their land were easily disputed because of the family's lower class origins.~~
>
> The question of whether the Pastons ì really" owned their land is probably a false one. At the time, a claim to land depended on the goodwill of one's neighbors, who could easily argue that a person was a serf and so not entitled to own land. ←
>
> The circled detail belongs in the paragraph introduced by the topic sentence shown.

W̃G Prentice Hall Writing and Grammar Connection: Chapter 13, Section 4

Extend Your Learning

Research and Technology With a group, research the origins of several medieval holidays, such as Martinmas. Make a **holidays chart** that:

- Lists each holiday
- Describes the way in which it was celebrated
- Explains its origins

Incorporate graphics in your chart.
[Group Activity]

Listening and Speaking With a classmate, write and present a **phone conversation** between Margaret and John. Research English accents, and apply what you learn as you speak your parts.

 **For:** An additional research activity
Visit: www.PHSchool.com
Web Code: esd-7108

Assessment Resources

The following resources can be used to assess students' knowledge and skills.

Unit 1 Resources
  Selection Test A, pp. 146–148
  Selection Test B, pp. 149–151
  Benchmark Test 2, pp. 159–164

General Resources
  Rubrics for Research: Research Report, pp. 51–52
  Rubric for Speaking: Delivering a Research Presentation, p. 92.

Go Online — Assessment Students may use the **Self-test** to prepare for **Selection Test A** or **Selection Test B**.

Benchmark
Administer **Benchmark Test 2.** If some students need further work, use the **Interpretation Guide** to determine the appropriate reteaching page in the **Reading Kit** and on **Success Tracker.**

---

❸ Writing Lesson

- Review with students the specifics of the assignment: to draw conclusions about the fifteenth century based on Margaret Paston's letters, to investigate the history of the period to determine the validity of the conclusions, and then to write a report that supports the conclusions with research.

- Suggest that students first review the letters and list everything that reveals some aspect of life and the events of the era. Then, they can pick the elements that seem most promising for research.

- To guide students in writing this investigative report, give them the **Support for Writing Lesson** page (*Unit 1 Resources,* p. 143).

- Use the Research: Research Report rubrics, pp. 51–52 in *General Resources,* to evaluate student work.

❹ Research and Technology

- Have students name several holidays that are celebrated today and predict which would have been celebrated in the fifteenth century.

- Tell students that some ancient holidays that are not celebrated in the United States are still carried on in England and Europe.

- Encourage students to use both print and Internet resources for their research. If students need inspiration, you may suggest that they search for Martinmas and see if other holidays are suggested, and then do searches for Middle Ages, holidays, or medieval holidays.

- The **Support for Extend Your Learning** page (*Unit 1 Resources,* p. 144) provides guided note-taking opportunities to help students complete the Extend Your Learning activities.

- Use the Speaking: Delivering a Research Presentation rubric, p. 92 in *General Resources,* to evaluate students' holiday charts.

Go Online — Research Have students type in the Web Code for another research activity.

Students will

1. learn about the heritage of African Americans.

2. consider the importance of oral tradition in American history.

❶ Connections
American Literature

Students might reread the excerpts from *Beowulf* and note the importance of scops in keeping the story of Beowulf alive. Just as *Beowulf* was preserved through oral tradition, so too is the story of Haley's ancestors. As students read the selection, have them consider the importance of oral tradition, including how it provides connections to the past.

❷ Speaking Memories

• Have students discuss the role of oral tradition in both *Beowulf* and the excerpt from "My Furthest-Back Person." Discuss how storytellers contribute to each work.

• Beowulf's heroic status in British culture is evidence of oral tradition's ability to link the past with the present. Discuss how Alex Haley's story impacts other African Americans. Have students compare and contrast how *Beowulf* and Haley's story help preserve their culture's identity.

❶

CONNECTIONS
American Literature

❷

Speaking Memories

Because few people in early Britain could read or write, important historical events and cultural legends were kept alive and passed from generation to generation by word of mouth. Often, these tales were told by professional storytellers, or *scops*, Anglo-Saxon minstrels who traveled from village to village bearing news and stories from places far away. These valued artists were greeted by entire communities and offered food and lodging as payment for their recitation of favorite heroic epics. In this way, the preservation of *Beowulf* (pages 40–62) and the culture it represented relied for centuries on the talent of scops.

Oral History in America The preservation of American history has also depended upon the oral tradition. Alex Haley's essay "My Furthest-Back Person" is based on his memory of bits of family history passed from old to young through word of mouth. These nuggets of personal history lead him all the way to Africa, where a *griot*, or village oral historian, completes Haley's knowledge by telling him the story of how his African ancestor had been kidnapped into slavery. This selection from "My Furthest-Back Person" demonstrates how the words of oral tradition serve not only as a historical record, but also as a living link that reunited long-lost relatives.

204 ■ From Legend to History (449–1485)

from

MY FURTHEST-BACK PERSON

(the inspiration for ROOTS)

Alex Haley

CONNECTIONS

The old *griot* stepped away from my interpreters and the crowd quickly swarmed around him—all of them buzzing. An interpreter named A.B.C. Salla came to me; he whispered: "Why they stare at you so, they have never seen here a black American." And that hit me: I was symbolizing for them twenty-five millions of us they had never seen. What did they think of me—of us?

Then abruptly the old *griot* was briskly walking toward me. His eyes boring into mine, he spoke in Mandinka, as if instinctively I should understand—and A.B.C. Salla translated:

"Yes . . . we have been told by the forefathers . . . that many of us from this place are in exile . . . in that place called America . . . and in other places."

I suppose I physically wavered, and they thought it was the heat; rustling whispers went through the crowd, and a man brought me a low stool. Now the whispering hushed—the musicians had softly begun playing *kora* and *balafon*, and a canvas sling lawn seat was taken by the *griot*, Kebba Kanga Fofana, aged 73 "rains" (one rainy season each year). He seemed to gather himself into a physical rigidity, and he began speaking the *Kinte* clan's ancestral oral history; it came rolling from his mouth across the next hours . . . 17th- and 18th-century *Kinte* lineage details, predominantly what men took wives; the children they "begot," in the order of their births; those children's mates and children.

Events frequently were dated by some proximate[1] singular physical occurrence. It was as if some ancient scroll were printed indelibly within the *griot's* brain. Each few sentences or so, he would pause for an interpreter's translation to me. I distill here the essence:

The *Kinte* clan began in Old Mali, the men generally blacksmiths ". . . who conquered fire," and the women potters and weavers. One large branch of the clan moved to Mauretania from where one son of the clan,

1. **proximate** (präks′ ə mət) *adj.* near in time.

◀ **Critical Viewing** Which details in this image reflect both modern and traditional lifestyles? **[Analyze]**

❸ Critical Thinking
Infer

Ask students: Why do you think the villagers are so interested in the author?

Possible response: The author looks similar to them but is from a different country—a country in which many exiled Africans now live. They are curious to meet the author.

❹ Critical Thinking
Draw Conclusions

Ask students: How can you tell that the griot is an important member of the clan?

Possible response: The villagers gather around him and rely on him to speak with the author. The griot speaks with confidence and authority.

❺ Critical Viewing

Answer: The people are wearing a mix of modern and traditional clothing. They are carrying their things in a traditional manner and walking on a dirt road.

Differentiated Instruction
Solutions for All Learners

Strategy for Special Needs Students
Have groups of students choose a story, such as a fairy tale or fable, with which they are all familiar. Have them list the most important characters and events of the story, and then present a brief retelling of the story to the class. Have students consider how oral tradition might alter a story over time.

Background for English Learners
Explain that the ancestors of most African Americans in the United States were enslaved and taken by force to this country from Africa. Therefore, few records of their vital statistics exist. Point out that Haley's successful search for his ancestral roots served as an inspiration for African Americans everywhere.

Strategy for Advanced Readers
Tell students that critics have suggested that Haley presented fictional segments of *Roots* as fact. Have students read portions of *Roots*, and then write brief essays explaining whether they think the blurring of fact and fiction detracts from the book's value.

Dance Africa, by Synthia Saint James

This painting was created to promote the 1996 tour of Dance African America, a North Carolina-based company. Each year, founding director Chuck Davis travels with his students to Africa so that they can learn the authentic African rhythms and dances that are the hallmark of the company's electrifying performances. In this painting, Davis, the central male figure, is represented in the role of the griot. Use the following question for discussion:

• How is the portrayal of the male figure symbolic of his role as the griot?
  Possible response: He unites the figures in the painting, just as the griot is the keeper of a clan's shared history.

❼ **Critical Viewing**

Possible response: The people in the painting appear animated and vibrant, as do the people that Haley describes in his piece.

Kairaba Kunta Kinte, a Moslem Marabout holy man, entered Gambia. He lived first in the village of Pakali N'Ding; he moved next to Jiffarong village; ". . . and then he came here, into our own village of Juffure."

In Juffure, Kairaba Kunta Kinte took his first wife, ". . . a Mandinka maiden, whose name was Sireng. By her, he begot two sons, whose names were Janneh and Saloum. Then he got a second wife, Yaisa. By her, he begot a son, Omoro.'"

The three sons became men in Juffure. Janneh and Saloum went off and found a new village, Kinte-Kundah Janneh-Ya. "And then Omoro, the youngest son, when he had 30 rains, took as a wife a maiden, Binta Kebba.

"And by her, he begot four sons—Kunta, Lamin, Suwadu, and Madi . . ."

Sometimes, a "begotten," after his naming, would be accompanied by some later-occurring detail, perhaps as ". . . in time of big water (flood),

❻

❼ ▼ **Critical Viewing**
What details in this image suit Haley's description of the African village he visits? **[Connect]**

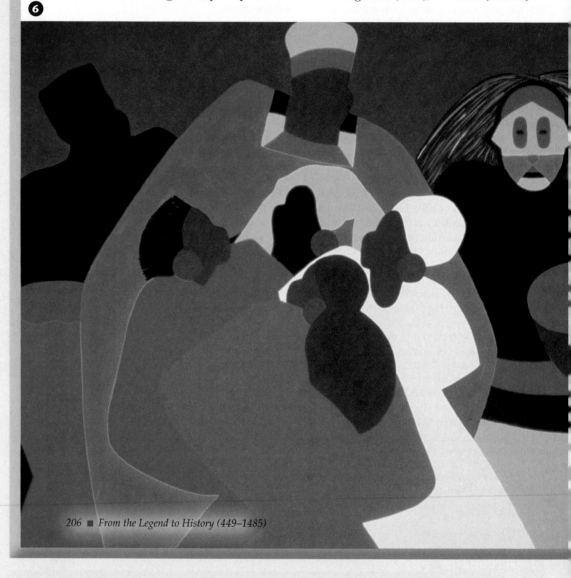

he slew a water buffalo." Having named those four sons, now the griot stated such a detail.

"About the time the king's soldiers came, the eldest of these four sons, Kunta, when he had about 16 rains, went away from his village, to chop wood to make a drum . . . and he was never seen again . . ."

Goose-pimples the size of lemons seemed to pop all over me. In my knapsack were my cumulative notebooks, the first of them including how in my boyhood, my Grandma, Cousin Georgia and the others told of the African "*Kin-tay*" who always said he was kidnapped near his village—while chopping wood to make a drum . . .

I showed the interpreter, he showed and told the *griot,* who excitedly told the people; they grew very agitated. Abruptly then they formed a human ring, encircling me, dancing and chanting. Perhaps a dozen of the women carrying their infant babies rushed in toward me, thrusting the infants into my arms conveying, I would later learn, "the laying on of hands . . . through this flesh which is us, we are you, and you are us." The men hurried me into their mosque, their Arabic praying later being translated outside: "Thanks be to Allah for returning the long lost from among us." Direct descendants of Kunta Kinte's blood brothers were hastened, some of them from nearby villages, for a family portrait to be taken with me, surrounded by actual ancestral sixth cousins. More symbolic acts filled the remaining day.

When they would let me leave, for some reason I wanted to go away over the African land. Dazed, silent in the bumping Land Rover, I heard the cutting staccato of talking drums. Then when we sighted the next village, its people came thronging to meet us. They were all—little naked ones to wizened elders—waving, beaming; amid a cacophony of crying out; and then my ears identified their words: "*Meester Kinte! Meester Kinte!*"

Let me tell you something: I am a man. But I remember the sob surging up from my feet, flinging up my hands before my face and bawling as I had not done since I was a baby . . . the jet-black Africans were jostling,[2] staring . . . I didn't care, with the feelings surging. If you really knew the odyssey of us millions of black Americans, if you really knew how we came in the seeds of our forefathers, captured, driven, beaten, inspected, bought, branded, chained in foul ships, if you really knew, you needed weeping . . .

Back home, I knew that what I must write, really, was our black saga, where any individual's past is the essence of the millions'.

---

2. jostling (jäs´ ling) *v.* bumping and pushing, as in a crowd.

Connecting American Literature

1. Describe Alex Haley's reaction when he hears his personal history retold by the griot.
2. **(a)** How does Haley's visit to the griot in Africa contribute to his personal and cultural identity? **(b)** Besides preserving a sense of history, in what way do scops and griots protect a cultural identity?

Alex Haley
(1921–1992)

Alex Haley grew up in Tennessee and Alabama. As a teenager, he joined the Coast Guard to see more of the world. While aboard ships, he began writing sea adventure stories. After twenty years in the Coast Guard, Haley retired to begin a full-time career as a writer. His best-known work is *Roots: The Saga of an American Family.* "My Furthest-Back Person" explains how he began this book. *Roots,* an immediate bestseller, led to a groundbreaking television mini-series viewed by 140 million people. Together, the book and the mini-series inspired many people to research their own family histories.

from My Furthest-Back Person ■ 207

Meeting Your Standards

Students will

1. analyze literary periods.
2. use writing strategies to generate ideas, plan, organize, evaluate, and revise a composition.

Prewriting

- Have students volunteer the names of characters from the works they have read in this unit. Write the characters' names on the board. Then, select one of the characters and ask students to suggest details they know about the social situation of the character based on what they have read.

- Point out that the character and one or more of the details can be combined to create a thesis statement. For example, if the character is Beowulf and one detail states that he was a warrior, suggest that "Beowulf is an exemplary hero in a warrior culture" is a possible thesis.

- Tell students to be discriminating as they gather details in the text about the culture and social position of a character.

Tips for
Test Taking

A writing prompt on the SAT or ACT test may assess students' ability to analyze a topic, state a point of view regarding the topic, and support the point of view with evidence. When writing under timed circumstances, students will need to quickly clarify a point of view (their thesis statement) and the evidence that supports it. Since they will not be able to refer to a text, their evidence must be based on their own experiences, readings, or observations.

Analyzing Literary Periods

In the Middle Ages, what one's father did for a living, or whom one married, determined one's place in a complex social hierarchy. From peasants to kings, from monks to warriors, characters in romances, ballads, and epics reflect the rigid social structure of their time. Their actions and thoughts are often determined by what is expected of them: A hero responds courageously, and a wife loves devotedly. Write an essay that explains whether or not characters of the Middle Ages ever break the boundaries of their roles and exhibit individuality. Refer to the box at right for the specific details of the assignment.

Prewriting

Find a focus. To respond to the question, think about the medieval characters you have encountered in the unit. Answer the following questions to help you evaluate each of them.

- What is the character's social position?
- What were the expectations for that position during this period?
- How do the character's thoughts, words, and actions reflect his or her social role?
- Do any of the character's thoughts, words, or actions reflect a unique personality? Does the character have an individual difficulty with or question about his or her role?

Review at least four or five characters, writing your notes in a chart like the one shown. Then, choose the three characters that best support your ideas about individuality in the Middle Ages.

Model: Listing to Find a Focus

Character	Social Position	Elements Reflecting Social Position	Elements Reflecting Individuality
Beowulf in *Beowulf*	Warrior/ Hero	He acts heroically. He protects his followers.	As a young man, he boasts. As an older man, he is more humble.

Gather details. After you choose the characters you will discuss, return to the text and gather details about their words, thoughts, and actions. Look for specific passages you may want to quote. Pay special attention to sections in which characters reflect on themselves or in which they act in a defining way.

Write a working thesis. Your thesis summarizes your response to the question. Writing your thesis as you collect details will focus your search. As you think more about a topic, you can modify your thesis.

Assignment: Individuality in Medieval Characters

Are characters in medieval literature solely defined by the role in society, or do they also exhibit signs of individuality? Write an analytical essay in which you explain your response using at least three examples from this unit.

Criteria:
- Include a thesis statement that summarizes your response to the essay question.
- Analyze three characters from different works in this unit.
- Approximate length: 700 words.

Read to Write

As you reread the texts, look for characters that behave in unexpected ways. Are they stepping outside their social roles?

Teaching Resources

The following resources can be used to extend or enrich the instruction for Writing About Literature.

Unit 1 Resources
Writing About Literature, pp. 152–153

General Resources
Rubrics for Response to Literature, pp. 65–66

Graphic Organizer Transparencies
Five-column Chart, p. 276.

Drafting

Organize. A logical organization connects your ideas. It can also strengthen your argument. For example, you could discuss the characters in chronological order, but a thematic order would sharpen your response. Prepare an outline to help you adjust your organization and ensure that you include all of your best ideas in your first draft.

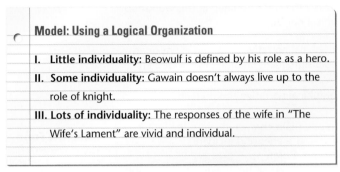

> **Model: Using a Logical Organization**
>
> I. **Little individuality:** Beowulf is defined by his role as a hero.
>
> II. **Some individuality:** Gawain doesn't always live up to the role of knight.
>
> III. **Lots of individuality:** The responses of the wife in "The Wife's Lament" are vivid and individual.

Provide support. As you draft, include quotations from works to support each major point you make. For each quotation, write a clause or sentence showing its relevance to the idea you are illustrating.

Revising and Editing

Review content: Check your analysis for thoroughness. Review your exploration of each character. Make sure that you have included enough insights to offer a complete analysis.

Review style: Use transitions to link ideas. If your sentences sound choppy and disconnected, consider combining some of them.

Choppy	Revised
The wife acts according to her role. She waits patiently. It tortures her. She appears to be the model medieval wife. Her attitude is individual.	The wife acts according to her role, waiting patiently although it tortures her. Though she might appear to be the model medieval wife, her attitude is in fact individual.

Publishing and Presenting

Give a lecture. Develop a brief talk to share the ideas you have developed in your essay. You might prepare a character chart for display to help your audience follow your analysis. Be sure to provide time for your listeners to ask questions.

 Prentice Hall Writing and Grammar Connection: Chapter 14

Writing About Literature ■ 209

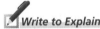 **Write to Learn**

An outline is a guide, not a prison. Your writing may take an unexpected turn as you start drafting. Follow your new ideas. You can review your fresh thoughts for accuracy and relevance when you revise.

Write to Explain

Make sure that you explain why each of your examples supports your thesis.

Drafting

- Explain to students that a logical organization helps them to outline the information they have collected during the prewriting stage.
- Have students choose from their prewriting notes the three characters who best support their thesis statement. Then, have them arrange this information using a logical organization.

Revising and Editing

- If students find that one or more of their characters weaken their thesis, they might consider removing the irrelevant character and replacing it with a more effective one.
- Remind students that when they revise, they should not sacrifice accuracy to improve the transitions or sound of sentences.

Publishing and Presenting

- When conducting their lectures, students should use their charts or displays to reinforce the material they are discussing, rather than reading from them verbatim.

Writing and Grammar, Diamond Level

Students will find further instruction and practice on writing a response to literature in Chapter 14.

Writing and Grammar Interactive CD–ROM

Students can use the following tools as they complete their responses to literature:

- Chart
- Customizable Outliner
- Transition Words

Six Traits Focus

✔	Ideas	Word Choice
✔	Organization	✔ Sentence Fluency
	Voice	Conventions

Assessing the Essay

To evaluate students' essays, use the Rubrics for Response to Literature, pp. 65–66 in *General Resources*.

Students will

1. write an autobiographical narrative.

2. use writing strategies to generate ideas and to plan, organize, evaluate, and revise the composition.

3. apply grammar skills.

 From the Translator's Desk

Burton Raffel

Show students Segment 3 on Burton Raffel on *From the Author's Desk DVD*. Discuss the "creative room" Raffel finds in translating, and suggest that students can find room for creativity in writing autobiographical narratives.

Writing Genres

Using the Form Point out to students that autobiographical narration is often incorporated into other types of writing. Use these examples:

- The letters students write to their friends often contain narratives drawn from life experiences.

- Reflective essays and most journal entries have autobiographical narratives at their core.

- In a personal anecdote, students can turn an autobiographical narrative into an amusing tale or supporting evidence for an argument.

 Online Essay Scorer

A writing prompt for this mode of writing can be found on the **PH Online Essay Scorer** at PHSuccessNet.com.

Writing Workshop

Narration: Autobiographical Narrative

The best stories are often true—they tell us about the real events in a writer's life. From memories of childhood to funny anecdotes to dramatic encounters, true stories touch and inspire us. Such stories are called **autobiographical narratives.** Follow the steps outlined in this workshop to write your own autobiographical narrative.

Assignment Write an autobiographical narrative about an event or an incident in your life that marked a significant change or provided an important insight.

What to Include Your autobiographical narrative should feature the following elements.

- characters, with a focus on one main character—you, the writer
- a setting with specifically located scenes and incidents
- a sequence of events that forms a plot
- conflict or tension between characters or between a character and another force
- insights that you gained from the experience

To preview the criteria on which your autobiographical narrative may be assessed, see the rubric on page 217.

Using the Form
You may use elements of autobiographical narrative in these writing situations:

- letters to friends
- journal entries
- reflective essays
- anecdotes

Reading Writing Connection

To get a feel for autobiographical writing, read ìThe Letters of Margaret Paston" on page 190.

Teaching Resources

The following resources can be used to enrich or extend instruction for the Writing Workshop.

Unit 1 Resources
Writing Workshop: Autobiographical Narrative, pp. 154
Writing Workshop: Eliminate Unnecessary Tense Changes, p. 155

General Resources
Rubrics for Narration: Autobiographical Narrative, pp. 43–44

Graphic Organizer Transparencies
Rubric for Self-Assessment, p. 33
Plot Diagram, p. 280
Three-Column Chart, p. 282

From the Author's Desk DVD
Burton Raffel, Segments 3 and 4

Prewriting

Choosing Your Topic

Choose an event or an experience that made a real difference to you. For example, you might write about the first time you met your best friend or about a significant triumph in your life. To help you choose your topic, use one of the following strategies:

- **Listing** Create a chart with three columns. Label the first column *People,* the second *Places,* and the third *Events.* In each column, list names and descriptions of memorable people, places, and events in your life. Then, review the chart, looking for connections between the various items. When you find a connection, circle the two items and draw an arrow between them. Review the connections for narrative ideas.

- **Using Sentence Starters** Finishing an unfinished sentence can help you generate writing ideas. Complete several sentence starters like the ones shown. Then, choose one as the starting point for your writing.

  - The funniest thing happened when _____.
  - My favorite holiday was _____.
  - My strongest memory from childhood is _____.

Narrowing Your Topic

Once you have a general idea of what you want to write about, make your topic more specific by concentrating on one idea you want to convey. For example, if you decide to write about an experience that you shared with a person who is important to you, be sure that the incident reveals something meaningful about that person.

Gathering Details

Make sure that you gather enough details to cover all important parts of the narrative. To enliven your writing, list concrete details you will include. Sensory images will convey the sights, sounds, and smells of scenes. Details recording characters' acts, movements, thoughts, words, and gestures will add depth and realism. As you collect details, categorize them according to the part of your narrative to which they belong. Approximate how much space and emphasis you will give to elements such as background information, setting, the event itself, and any lessons learned. The plan shown works for many narratives.

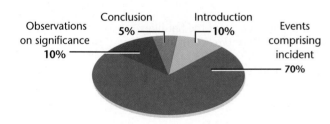

Writing Workshop ■ 211

Tips for
Using Rubrics

- Before students begin work on this assignment, have them preview the **Rubric for Self-Assessment,** p. 217 to know what is expected.

- Review the Assessment criteria in class. Before students use the Rubric for Self-Assessment, work with them to rate the Student Model by applying one or two criteria to it.

- If you wish to assess students' autobiographical narratives with either a 4-point, a 5-point, or a 6-point scoring rubric, see *General Resources,* pp. 43–44.

Prewriting

- Encourage students to read the assignment carefully. Be sure they understand that they are writing about events or experiences that have made a difference and affected their lives in significant ways.

- Use the Three-Column Chart (*Graphic Organizer Transparencies,* p. 282) to model the Listing strategy for students. Ask volunteers to complete the chart on the board. Then, distribute the chart to the class.

- For students using Sentence Starters to generate ideas, suggest these examples: One thing I'll never forget is _____; Everything changed for me when _____; The most important thing I ever learned was _____.

- Point out to students that when they respond to writing prompts on standardized tests, it is important to narrow their topics quickly. Writing topics should be narrow enough so that students have a clear focus for their compositions.

- Encourage students to create their own charts as they gather details. Charts can list sensory details describing a scene, or they can list the chronology that the narrative will follow.

Six Traits Focus

✔	Ideas		Word Choice
✔	Organization		Sentence Fluency
	Voice		Conventions

WG **Writing and Grammar, Diamond Level**

Students will find additional instruction on prewriting for an autobiographical narrative in Chapter 4, Section 2.

Writing and Grammar Interactive Textbook CD-ROM

Students can use the following tools as they complete their autobiographical narratives:

- List Organizer
- Story Map Organizer
- Transition Words Revising Tool

Drafting

- Explain to students that openings are strong only if they are appropriate for the narrative. For example, if the narrative focuses on a relationship, it might be appropriate to start with a character. If the narrative focuses on an event, it might be more appropriate to start with dialogue.

- To help students pace their narratives effectively, use the Plot Diagram (*Graphic Organizer Transparencies,* p. 280). Recommend that students keep expositions short and begin to build towards their climaxes quickly. Point out that in a test-taking situation, getting bogged down in background details will eat up time. (For more on details, see Burton Raffel's comments on the next page.)

- Review the models of dull and vivid conflicts with the class. Explain that to be striking, a conflict needs more than vivid language; it should have significance beyond the superficial or obvious. Students should focus their narratives on conflicts that were important to their lives and that have had a lasting effect on them.

- Ask students to read their closing paragraphs for the class. Discuss what strategy each closing uses. Do the closings offer epilogues, sum up what the characters learned, or answer questions that would otherwise go unanswered? Do the closings add a finishing touch for readers, or would a different ending work better?

Six Traits Focus

✔	Ideas	✔	Word Choice
✔	Organization		Sentence Fluency
✔	Voice		Conventions

Writing and Grammar, Diamond Level

Students will find additional instruction on drafting an autobiographical narrative in Chapter 4, Section 3.

Writing Workshop

Drafting

Shaping Your Writing

Start out strong. Catch your readers' interest with a strong opening. Consider one of these options:

- **Start with a character:** A description or an anecdote about the main character is effective if your narrative centers around a relationship.
- **Start with the setting:** This approach works well if time and place are critical elements of your narrative.
- **Start with dialogue:** Besides intriguing the reader, dialogue can provide quick insight into a situation.

Choose a Starting Point

Character
Bob doesn't say much, no matter what may be going on, but when you see that gleam in his eye, you know mischief is afoot.

Setting
The wind whistled through the cracks in the attic window.

Dialogue
"I said, did anybody leave this package on the counter?"

Pace your writing. Make sure you do not get bogged down in insignificant details. Establish background information quickly and then set your main incident in motion.

Providing Elaboration

Choose a striking conflict. Describe the conflict vividly, showing your readers the reason for the conflict instead of just telling them.

Dull: We just could not agree about our plans for the prom.
Vivid: Day after day, Petra and I traded conflicting ideas about flowers, transportation, and food for prom night. When our dialogue veered toward insults, we knew we needed someone to mediate.

End well. Devise an interesting closing. You might put the finishing touch on your story or leave readers hoping for more. Consider ending with an epilogue about what happened after the incident, a summary of the main character's insights, or an unanswered question related to the conflict.

212 ■ From Legend to History (449–1485)

Tips for Test-Taking

Students may encounter standardized tests that require them to write about personal experiences—in other words, to write autobiographical narratives. Remind students not to waste time agonizing over a topic when faced with such prompts. They should choose topics with an eye toward drafting. Ideal topics for timed writing situations will have striking conflicts that drive the pace, as well as clear climaxes and resolutions. For example, a friend with whom you were once close but from whom you have drifted apart slowly would probably not be an ideal topic. A brief but dramatic experience, such as a sudden loss, would be a more effective topic. Often, the farther back students go in their lives, the clearer the situation will be.

From the Translator's Desk
Burton Raffel on Shaping a Narrative

This is an excerpt from an autobiographical piece I wrote about thirty years ago. It tries to re-create, in adult language, some of those well-rubbed but rarely verbalized feelings that all small children surely have. Children are not simply the "small adults" that our civilization used to think they were. Nor is childhood merely another, though different, route to the same landing place.

Professional Model:

from Out in the Backyard of My Mind

When I think of myself, as a small child, I remember, first, the sensation of offensive clothing—floppy clothing, clothing buttoned and snapped and fastened in places I could not reach and affixed for reasons I knew I would not approve of if I could have understood what they were. I remember shirts strapped to my back, somehow; and I remember ghastly knickers of worn corduroy, hanging baggy at the knees; and floppy coats that had belonged to cousins and uncles unseen, handed down, a little shabbier and floppier each time, until they came to me. I remember the faintly dank smell of cheap wool (mixed with what?), and especially its coarse, hairy feel—and the whistle of corduroy pants, as I walked—and the good, powdery smell and full softness of a big brown automobile lap robe, always and still called "the horse blanket." Skin was no better: if I was ever without clothing, in those days, I do not remember it, nor remember any pleasure from it. And I can remember hiding from my nakedness. Not just the way all little children do, sometimes, but compulsively, fiercely. One summer—I was eight, I think—my mother had a serious operation and I spent two months with a relative. Two summer months, and hot work of it, playing outdoors, but I did not know how to take a bath by myself and I would not let anyone give me a bath; no one unauthorized was to be allowed to see me unclothed.

Burton Raffel

> "*I realized that I was inventing a reality that wasn't real.*"
> —— *Burton Raffel*

These first two sentences are not "laundry lists": their detail is simply what they, and the piece as a whole, are about.

The details of the third sentence introduce a quiet shift in focus, from myself to the exterior world: walking, first, and then cars.

The last sentences move the focus of the piece even further into society.

Writing Workshop ■ 213

- Show students Segment 4 on Burton Raffel on *From the Author's Desk DVD*. Discuss the relationship that Raffel sees between the classic literature he teaches and translates and the daily experiences of contemporary students and readers.

- Point out to students that the subject of this excerpt from the autobiographical *Out in the Backyard of My Mind* is not a character, an event, or a setting, but the childhood experience of wearing clothes. Explain that any important aspect of a writer's life and experiences can be a compelling topic for an autobiographical narrative.

- Call students' attention to Raffel's comments about *Out in the Backyard of My Mind*. Be sure students recognize that the details Raffel uses are central to the narrative. Tell students that they should enrich their own autobiographical narratives with details that are important to their topics.

Differentiated Instruction   Solutions for All Learners

Support for Special Needs Students
Before students read the excerpt, explain that Raffel uses vivid details to express feelings he had as a child. Read the first two sentences with students, making sure they understand that the details deal only with Raffel's feelings. Have them read the next two sentences on their own. Point out that in these sentences, Raffel refers to his relatives, to walking, and to riding in a car. Then, have students read the rest of the excerpt. Guide them to see how Raffel's discomfort with clothes extends to a discomfort with the outside world.

Strategy for Less Proficient Readers
Explain that in the excerpt from *Out in the Backyard of My Mind*, the focus is on the details Raffel includes. Have students reread the excerpt, writing down every sensory detail they find. Review the list with students, and guide them to recognize the points at which Raffel moves outside of his own feelings to his actions, and then to his interactions with other people. Explain that in their own autobiographical narratives, students should give details both of their own feelings and the outside world.

Revising

- Point out that many autobiographical narratives will unfold in more than one time and place. Ask students to list the settings—the times and locations—that appear in their narratives.

- Use the Revising to Clarify Time and Place model to demonstrate the revising strategy for students. Be sure they recognize that shifts in time and place in their own narratives need descriptive words and transitional phrases to be clear.

- Have students work on the revising strategy in pairs. You may wish to have peers review drafts before students star time and location shifts and underline transitional words and phrases. Then, have students conduct peer reviews for clarity after revising the structures of their narratives.

- After students revise the structures of their narratives, have them focus on eliminating unnecessary changes in verb tense. Tell students to look for changes in tense where they have made shifts in place and, especially, time. Passages they have revised for clarity may still have unnecessary shifts in tense.

- Instruct students to pay special attention to the tenses of such verbs as *to be* (*is/are, was/were*) and *to have* (*has/have, had*).

Six Traits Focus

✔	Ideas		Word Choice
	Organization		Sentence Fluency
	Voice		Conventions

 **Writing and Grammar, Diamond Level**

Students will find additional instruction on revising an autobiographical narrative in Chapter 4, Section 4.

Revising

Revising Your Overall Structure

Clarify the time and the place. Make sure that shifts in place and time in your narrative are clearly indicated.

1. Star any places where there is a time or location change.

2. Underline in red the words you have used to indicate the change. Have a partner check to make sure that each shift comes through clearly.

3. Clarify time or place shifts by adding descriptive words or transitional phrases. To highlight the impact of shifts, insert paragraph breaks.

To read the complete student model, see page 216.

Model: Revising to Clarify Time and Place

¶ That day was more than nine years ago. I have lived in America now for nearly ten years.

It was a good experience, to be surprised by the taste of a drink. Today, I struggle to hold on to everything about myself that makes me un-American.

> Mircea added information to show a gap in time.

Peer Review: Share your draft with a classmate. Explain why you made your revision choices, and ask your reader to give you feedback about the time and place shifts you have included.

Revising Your Word Choice

Eliminate unnecessary tense changes. Even though you may be moving back and forth in time in your narrative, do not change tenses unnecessarily. Do not move among tenses without a good reason.

Example: It *was* midnight when the vote tally *is* finally complete.

Corrected: It *was* midnight when the vote tally *was* finally completed.

Strengthen your transitions. Good transitions carry readers through a written work. Both between paragraphs and within them, strong transitions can improve sentence clarity, indicate the passage of time, and signal changes in topic.

Transitions that show contrast: *however, although, despite*

Transitions that indicate passage of time: *since, after, then, before*

Transitions that signal a conclusion: *therefore, consequently, so*

---

214 ■ *From Legend to History (449–1485)*

Tips for
Test-Taking

Students may be expected to revise the compositions they write for standardized tests. However, time constraints of the test-taking situation put strict limits on how much revising students can complete. Suggest to students that the most time-effective revision strategy is planning and, especially, drafting carefully. For example, students should pay close attention to shifts in time or location as they write their initial drafts. They may mark these shifts as they draft, making them easier to review. Rather than rewriting the entire composition, students should make simple changes to clarify setting shifts directly on their drafts. You may wish to have students practice by giving them 15 minutes to plan, write, and revise an opening paragraph for an autobiographical narrative.

Developing Your Style

Vivid Word Choice

Word Choice Choose strong verbs and adjectives that show the characters, events, setting, and conflict of your autobiographical narrative rather than just tell about them. Avoid words that are weak, dull, or vague.

Weak: I drank the soda, and it was delicious.
Strong: I took a sip, and to my joyous surprise, it was sweet and refreshing, and the bubbles tickled the inside of my mouth.

Strong Verbs and Adjectives Instead of settling for general, overused verbs and adjectives, take the time to find precise, vivid examples.

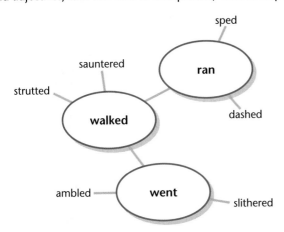

Find It in Your Reading Read or reread the selection from "Letters of Margaret Paston" on pages 190–193.

- Find two sentences that use strong verbs and two that use strong adjectives.
- Choose two words from this selection that you find particularly vivid.

Apply It to Your Writing Review the draft of your autobiographical narrative, focusing on your choice of words. Follow these steps as you read:

- When you come to a word that seems dull, weak, or vague, circle it. Also circle any jargon or clichés you find.
- When you have read through your entire draft, challenge yourself to replace each circled word with a more vivid alternative.
- Use a thesaurus or dictionary, but check to be sure that your new words accurately reflect what you want to say about your characters, setting, or conflict.

W/G *Prentice Hall Writing and Grammar Connection: Chapter 1*

Developing Your Style

- Tell students that their autobiographical narratives will be more compelling if their word choice is as vivid as the characters and events their narratives describe.

- Read the examples of weak and strong passages with the class. Point to the verb *tickled* and the adjectives *joyous, sweet,* and *refreshing* as examples of strong, vivid word choices.

- Explain to students that verbs and adjectives are often the weakest words in any piece of writing. Extensive use of common verbs such as *walked, ran,* and *went,* for example, can make their narratives overly general and dull. Tell students to pay special attention to verbs and adjectives as they revise for style.

- Have students read the strong sentences they find in "Letters of Margaret Paston," pp. 190–193. Write these sentences on the board, underlining the strongest words. Discuss with the class what Paston's vivid word choices add to her letters.

- Tell students to use the Apply It to Your Writing strategy on their narratives. Point out that on standardized writing tests, they will have limited time for revising. In test-taking situations, students can look for weak word choices as they edit for grammar, usage, and mechanics.

W/G **Writing and Grammar, Diamond Level**

Students will find additional instruction on vivid word choice in autobiographical narratives in Chapter 4, Section 4.

Tips for
Improving Word Choice

Give students these suggestions for developing their style by focusing on vivid word choice.

- Prepare a list of strong, vivid words that you might want to include in your autobiographical narrative. Think about your topic, and write down any vivid words that come to mind. Strong verbs and adjectives will be especially useful.

- Look for places in your draft where words—especially verbs and adjectives—are vague, overly general, or repetitive. Mark these words for possible revision, and see whether any words from your list will fit in their places.

- Be careful not to overload your autobiographical narrative with vivid words. Your style should be strong and exciting, but not overblown. Too many vivid words will clutter your narrative, making your plot difficult to follow.

Student Model

- Explain that the Student Model is a sample, and that autobiographical narratives may be longer.

- Point out that Mircea Vlaicu's narrative unfolds in a specific time and place. **Ask** students to identify the setting.
  Answer: The setting is the center aisle of a 747 sitting outside a Chicago airport. The plane will be heading to Los Angeles. Mircea has just come to the United States.

- Be sure students recognize that Mircea uses his description of the many choices of soda available to him to establish his main focus: the conflict of cultures he faces as an immigrant.

- Discuss with the class how Mircea paces his narrative. Be sure students understand that the details about soda are not insignificant; they are essential to the experience he is describing.

- Call students' attention to Mircea's use of sensory details and vivid word choices. Help them recognize how his language enriches and enlivens the narrative.

- Remind students that a strong closing is an important part of an autobiographical narrative. **Ask** them how Mircea closes his narrative.
  Possible response: Mircea connects his experience on the plane with the insight he gained about how things often differ from their appearance.

Writing Genres

Autobiographical Writing on College Applications Explain to students that many college applications will ask them to write about a significant event in their lives and explain how it has shaped them. Ask volunteers to explain why a college might ask an applicant to write this kind of autobiographical narrative. Guide students to recognize that these narratives can reveal a great deal about the writer's character and personal strengths. Point out that a challenge or problem they have faced or a change they have gone through can be an excellent focus for these narratives.

Student Model: **Mircea Vlaicu**
Palm Springs, California

A Toast to the Future

I came to this country on a plane. Just a kid, not even eight years old yet, I sat on the center aisle of a huge 747 in Chicago waiting to fly to Los Angeles. These names—Chicago, Los Angeles—were abstract to me. All I knew was that I was in America, the place where everybody drives a nice car and lives in a great house or apartment and the bad guys always lose. At least, that was what the television back in Romania had shown me.

I was very thirsty, sitting in that center aisle. I kept asking my mom when they were going to bring us drinks. I don't know how much time went by before the cart came around, but it finally arrived.

That moment was my first real encounter with America. There were so many cans to choose from, so many colors. I had no idea which one to take. I chose the blue one since blue was my favorite color. I opened it up and poured it in my clear plastic cup. The soda was also clear, and I was very disappointed. Out of all those different cans I had to chose club soda, a drink I already knew the taste of. But I was wrong. I took a sip, and to my joyous surprise, it was sweet and refreshing and the bubbles tickled the inside of my mouth. It tasted nothing like club soda. It was a good experience, to be surprised by the taste of a drink.

That day was more than nine years ago. I have lived in America now for nearly ten years. I have since passed through feelings of isolation and fears of being different. I have learned to make friends and to lead life as I want to.

Today, I struggle to hold on to everything about myself that makes me un-American. I try not to forget the Romanian language, I try to remember that I was not born in America. I think about Romania every day. I will not forget it, ever. A Romanian flag hangs in my bedroom alongside pictures of American rock stars. The thought of my homeland always makes me feel a certain way. A kind of bittersweet feeling, calm, a glimpse of home, a feeling of happiness. I picture a warm sunny day on which I am walking alone on the little winding street that surrounded our building complex.

When I think of the future, though, I have a simple hope. I hope the future will be like the moment one tastes the first sip of sweet, crisp, bubbly soda, when a second before it looked like just plain old club soda.

> Mircea clearly establishes the setting of his story.

> The narrative centers on the conflict of cultures.

> Mircea devotes several sentences to the choice of sodas, using pacing to focus his reader's attention and build interest.

> Vivid sensory details draw a reader into Mircea's experience. See *Developing Your Style*, p. 215.

> Mircea clearly states the insight he has gained and poetically links it to the incident he narrates.

Differentiated Instruction   Solutions for All Learners

Strategy for English Learners
Students may have had experiences similar to the one Mircea describes in his narrative on this page. Encourage students to focus on their experiences learning a new culture to help them generate a topic for their own autobiographical narrative. For example, they could describe an experience that, while familiar in their original country, differs greatly in the United States—as does Mircea's experience of drinking a soda.

Strategy for Advanced Writers
Encourage these students to pay close attention to Mircea's use of sensory details in his narrative. Discuss the way strong, vivid words enhance the sensory images, helping readers to see the soda can and feel the soda in their mouth. Remind students that these details are connected to Mircea's central focus, the positive experience of a new culture. Point out that sensory details and strong word choice can make students' autobiographical narratives as compelling as Mircea's.

Editing and Proofreading

Carefully read your autobiographical narrative to make sure it is free from errors in grammar, usage, spelling, and punctuation.

Focus on Punctuation: To punctuate direct quotations, place commas or periods inside the final quotation mark, and semicolons or colons outside it. Place question marks or exclamation marks inside the quotation mark only if the end mark is part of the quotation.

Publishing and Presenting

Consider the following activities to share your writing:

Maintain a portfolio. To follow your growth as a writer, keep your autobiographical narrative and other works in a writing portfolio.
Publish a literary magazine. Collect your classmates' narratives for publication in a student magazine. Have writers provide illustrations and introductions for their works. Copy and distribute the magazines.

Reflecting on Your Writing

Writer's Journal Jot down your thoughts on the experience of writing an autobiographical narrative. Begin by answering the following questions:

- What did you learn as you wrote your autobiographical narrative?
- What stage of the writing provided the most surprising learning experience?

$\mathcal{W}_G$ *Prentice Hall Writing and Grammar Connection: Chapter 4*

Rubric for Self-Assessment

Evaluate your autobiographical narrative *using the following criteria and rating scale, or, with your classmates, determine your own reasonable evaluation criteria.*

Criteria	Rating Scale
	not very *very*
Focus: How clearly do you establish yourself as the main character?	1　2　3　4　5
Organization: How effectively do you organize the sequence of events?	1　2　3　4　5
Support/Elaboration: How well do you use details to describe scenes and incidents?	1　2　3　4　5
Style: How well do you use strong verbs and adjectives to establish your characters and setting?	1　2　3　4　5
Conventions: How correct is your grammar, especially your use of punctuation?	1　2　3　4　5

Tips for
Using Technology in Writing

Students may find it helpful to use computers as they plan a storytelling festival. They can use word processing programs to create advertisements, flyers, and schedules. Graphics programs can be used to design posters and maps of the event space. Students may also want to use the Internet to promote their festival. Supervise students who want to create a Web site for the festival or send e-mails promoting it.

Students interested in assembling and publishing a literary magazine will also find a word processor to be useful. Most word processing programs offer features that will help students format a magazine. Students may want to illustrate their magazine with appropriate digital photographs. An appropriately supervised Web site might also be an excellent way to seek and receive submissions for the magazine.

Editing and Proofreading

- Remind students that in timed writing situations, they will need to edit quickly. To do so, students should focus only on grammar, usage, and mechanics.

- Explain that quotations often appear in autobiographical narratives in the form of dialogue. Review the rules for using quotation marks with students.

Six Traits Focus

Ideas		Word Choice	
Organization	✔	Sentence Fluency	
Voice		Conventions	✔

ASSESS

Publishing and Presenting

- Help students reserve the time and space for a storytelling festival. Supervise the selection of participants, possibly bringing in adults from the community. You may also want to help students advertise the festival.

- Point out to students the audience for a student magazine would include their classmates, teachers, and possibly parents. Discuss the interests of these readers with the class.

Reflecting on Your Writing

- Suggest to students that working through the stages of the writing process may have changed how they feel about the people, places, and experiences in their autobiographical narratives.

- Before they begin writing in their journals, encourage students to discuss how their ideas have changed and evolved. Do they see their experiences differently now? How are they different?

$\mathcal{W}_G$ **Writing and Grammar, Diamond Level**

Students will find additional guidance for editing and proofreading, publishing and presenting, and reflecting on an autobiographical narrative in Chapter 4, Sections 5 and 6.

Meeting Your Standards

Students will

1. learn the terms *define, identify,* and *label.*

2. apply knowledge of these terms in standardized-test situations.

Know Your Terms: Recalling Information

Explain that the terms listed under Terms to Learn will be used in standardized-test situations when students are asked to recall information from a reading passage.

Terms to Learn

- Review *define* and *definition,* explaining that a definition is the essential meaning. If they are basing their definitions on a reading passage, tell students to focus on the essential meaning, not on the details.

- Review *identify,* explaining that identification is the process of selecting or pointing out. When a test item says to identify an error in usage, for example, students are being asked to point out a specific error.

- Review *label,* explaining that to label is to put a name on something. To label, for example, the subject and verb in a sentence, students first have to identify those words and then write "subject" beside the subject and "verb" beside the verb.

ASSESS

Answers

Possible response: An epic hero is the brave, virtuous, and larger-than-life main character of an epic poem.

1. A; *receives* should be changed to *receive* because *heroes* is plural.

Answer: The last invaders [subject] in the ninth century <u>were</u> [verb] the Norse and the Danes.

High-Frequency Academic Words

High-frequency academic words are words that appear often in textbooks and on standardized tests. Though you may already know the meaning of many of these words, they usually have a more specific meaning when they are used in textbooks and on tests.

Know Your Terms: Recalling Information

Each of the words listed is a verb that tells you to show that you remember and understand the significance of the information in the text. The words indicate the kind of details and information you should provide in your answer.

Terms to Learn

Define Tell the specific qualities or features that make something what it is.

    Sample test item: *Define* legend.

    Sample test item: What is the *definition* of feudalism?

Identify Name or show that you recognize something.

    Sample test item: In the following sentence, *identify* the error in usage.

Label Attach the correct name to something.

    Sample test item: *Label* the parts of a microscope.

Practice

Directions: *Read the following passage. Then, on a separate piece of paper, define epic hero.*

    An epic hero is a larger-than-life central character in an epic poem. The epic hero is brave and virtuous, though sometimes flawed, and usually proves his heroism on a long, dangerous journey, or quest. In the epic *Beowulf,* a brave warrior named Beowulf aids a Danish king in the fight against Grendel. Beowulf epitomizes the epic hero in his feats of strength, victories in battle, and boastful self-confidence.

Directions: *Identify the usage error in the following sentence.*

    Epic heroes receives help with their quests from supernatural forces.

1. The usage error in the sentence is

  A receives   **C** help

  B their   **D** interested

Directions: *Write the following sentence on a separate piece of paper. Then, label the subject and the verb.*

    The last invaders in the ninth century were the Norse and the Danes.

218 ■ From Legend to History (449–1485)

Tips for Test-Taking

Explain to students that a multiple-choice question asking them to identify or label has only one correct answer.

    If a multiple-choice question asks students to define a concept, however, they may find that more than one of the choices includes elements of the concept's essential meaning. The best choice will most clearly and concisely include the essential elements of the definition.

 Go Online Vocabulary

For: Interactive Crossword Puzzles
Visit: www.PHSchool.com
Web Code: esj-5101

These crossword puzzles contains vocabulary that reflects the concepts in Unit 1. After students have completed Unit 1, give students the Web code and have them complete the crossword puzzles.

Critical Reading:
Sequential Order

In the reading sections of some tests, you are required to read a passage and to answer questions on the sequential order of events. Use these strategies to help you answer such questions.

- To help clarify sequential order, identify the logical relations between causes and effects, or actions and consequences.
- Watch for key sequence words labeling time order: for example, *first, next, then,* and *finally.*
- Do not mistake the order of statements in the passage for the order of events.

Practice

Directions: *Read the passages and then answer the questions that follow.*

Passage A. To wash a car the correct way, start by hosing the car down to remove the surface grime. Next, prepare a bucket of warm, soapy water, and grab two sponges. Starting with the hood, use a soapy sponge on the car's surface. Work your way along each side, and end with the trunk lid. Wash and rinse small sections of the surface as you go. Finish by buffing the car with a chamois cloth.

Passage B. While we were in search of some good water, we came upon a village of the natives about half a league from the place where the ships lay; the inhabitants on discovering us in fear, they abandoned their houses, and took to flight, carrying off their goods to the mountains. I ordered that nothing which they had left should be taken. Presently, we saw several of the natives advancing toward our party, and one of them came up to us, to whom we gave some hawk's bells and glass beads. We asked him, in return, for water.
—Christopher Colombus

Test-Taking Strategies

- As you read, assign sequential numbers to events, indicating which happened first, which happened next, and which happened last.

1. According to Passage A, when should you rinse off the soap?

  A before you wash the car   C after you wash each section

  B after you spray the tires   D before you wash the car's hood

2. According to Passage B, when did the natives abandon their houses?

  A after the travelers received water   C after the natives discovered the travelers

  B before the travelers landed   D after the natives received glass beads

3. In Passage B, when did the travelers ask for water?

  A when they arrived   C before the natives left

  B when they saw the natives   D after they gave the natives gifts

Assessment Workshop ■ *219*

Meeting Your Standards

Students will

1. identify sequential order in a standardized test situation.

2. identify key sequence words while reading the passage.

Critical Reading

- Have students read Passage A. Then, **ask** them to write down the main idea of the passage.
  Answer: The passage explains how to wash a car correctly.

- Next, ask students to reread the passage to identify all the steps necessary for washing a car properly, being careful to arrange them in sequential order.
  Answer: To wash a car, hose the car down; prepare a bucket of warm, soapy water; grab two sponges; start with the hood, using a soapy sponge to clean the car's surface gently; work from front to back, along each side; end with the trunk lid; wash and rinse small sections of the surface; after washing and rinsing, buff the car with a chamois cloth.

- Have students read Passage B and answer the questions.

- The passage mentions that the inhabitants abandoned their houses upon discovering the travelers. Point out that in question 2, A, B, and D are incorrect because they refer to events before or after the natives discovered the travelers.

- Point out in question 3 that D is correct because the travelers asked for water in exchange for gifts they gave the natives.

ASSESS

Answers

1. C
2. D
3. D

Tips for
Test-Taking

Explain to students that rereading can help them identify the order of details in a passage. For example, when answering the sample test item, students should reenter the passage and reread the sentence that tells what steps should be taken first and last. Students can use this tip to answer standardized test questions.

Generate Your Presentation

- Remind students to develop an organization that will be easy for their listeners to follow. Tell them that transitions between paragraphs will help their listeners better understand the progress of their presentation.

- Encourage students to use vivid language in their presentation to enable listeners to visualize the presentation.

- After students complete the Activity on this page, have them respond to classmate feedback. Then, have them incorporate this feedback into their presentations.

Practice Your Presentation

- **Ask** students to name two aspects of a presentation that a speaker might enhance with practice. **Possible response:** A speaker might practice incorporating audiovisual effects and highlighting points of emphasis.

- Help students to understand that making eye contact with listeners helps listeners feel as though they are being addressed directly. Explain that emphasizing points of the speech will enable listeners to focus on the most important passages and ideas.

Assess the Activity

To evaluate students' delivery, use the Peer Assessment: Speech rubric, p. 129 in *General Resources*.

220

Delivering Autobiographical Presentations

In an **autobiographical presentation**, a speaker tells the story of an event, period, or person in his or her life. (To review the characteristics of effective autobiographical narration, see the Writing Workshop, pp. 210–217.) Use the checklist and follow the steps below when preparing an autobiographical presentation.

Generate Your Presentation

Like a written autobiographical incident, an effective oral autobiographical presentation begins with a conversational style and clear organization.

Outline your subject. Before drafting, develop a logical organization. Begin your draft with a clear introduction and end with a conclusion clearly stating the significance of the story.

Grab the audience's attention. As you draft, use style and word choices that capture your audience's attention:

- Figurative language—images, comparisons, and sound devices that enrich descriptions

- Characterization—the vivid portrayal of a character through narration, description, and dialogue

- Dialogue—direct conversation between characters

Choose sound and visual effects. Consider adding visuals and sound effects to enhance—but not clutter—your presentation.

Practice Your Presentation

Once you have drafted and edited your presentation, practice delivering it until you are confident. Follow these tips:

Practice with a classmate. Practice in front of a "live" audience to become comfortable. As you practice, use your draft as a reminder, not as a text to be read word for word. Look up from your draft frequently.

Rehearse with audiovisual effects. Your effects will be a nuisance, not an enhancement, if you do not practice with them. Make sure they are well integrated in your presentation.

Find points of emphasis. Look for places in your presentation to create emphasis with your voice. For instance, slowing your delivery and lowering the pitch of your voice will convey seriousness.

> **Activity** Presentation and Feedback ▶ Rehearse your autobiographical speech until you feel comfortable. Then, present your speech to your classmates. Ask them for feedback on your presentation.

> **Generating Your Presentation**
>
> - Do your ideas follow logical order?
>
> - Did you connect your story to a concluding observation or insight?
>
> - Do you use strategies to grab audience attention?
>
> - Have you carefully reviewed your choices of sound or visual effects?

Differentiated Instruction   Solutions for All Learners

Strategy for Less Proficient Readers
Have students carefully practice their narratives, using sticky notes to identify any difficult or confusing passages. Students can then go back to these passages and rephrase lines that they find long-winded or unclear.

Strategy for English Learners
Encourage students who are intimidated by speaking in front of a group of peers to read their presentations several times before delivering them. Tell them that by practicing repeatedly in front of friends, family members, and even the mirror, and repeating any words that give them difficulty, students will build up their confidence.

Suggestions for Further Reading

Featured Titles:

The Once and Future King

T. H. White *Ace, 1987*

Novel This novel tells a variety of exciting tales about the legendary King Arthur and his Knights of the Round Table. Among these stories are "The Sword and the Stone," the tale of how young Arthur proved himself to be the rightful king of England; "The Queen of Air and Darkness," an account of the enmity between Arthur and Queen Morgause, his half sister; and "The Ill-Made Knight," a narrative about King Arthur's most valiant follower, Sir Lancelot. T. H. White's humorous, imaginative, and suspenseful retellings of these ancient legends will delight today's readers.

The Book of Merlyn

T. H. White *Ace, 1977*

Fiction T. H. White's last book about the legends of King Arthur's court focuses on the figure of Merlyn, or Merlin as it is sometimes spelled. Merlyn is a wizard whose magic and wisdom are behind much of what happens in Arthur's world. In this charming and thought-provoking fantasy, White explores the relationships among Arthur, Merlyn, and various animal teachers, including ants, geese, and a badger. Written during World War II, this story has as one of its main themes, the attempt—in White's words—"to find an antidote to war." It looks forward to a time when Arthur will return, bringing "happiness . . . and chivalry. . . ."

*Many of these titles are available in the **Prentice Hall/Penguin Literature Library.** Consult your teacher before choosing one.*

Works Presented in Unit One:

If sampling a portion of the following texts has built your interest, treat yourself to the full works.

Beowulf: A Verse Translation

Translated by Burton Raffel

Signet Classic, 1963

The Canterbury Tales

Geoffrey Chaucer, translated by Nevill Coghill

Penguin Books, 1977

Sir Gawain and the Green Knight

Translated by Brian Stone

Penguin Books, 1974

Continued

***Sir Gawain and the Green Knight* translated by Brian Stone**

This extended poem contains references to religious figures, detailed descriptions of the killing of animals, and instances of gory violence between knightly combatants.

Lexile: NP

Planning Students' Further Reading

Discussions of literature can raise sensitive and often controversial issues. Before you recommend further reading to your students, consider the values and sensitivities of your community as well as the age, ability, and sophistication of your students. It is also good policy to preview literature before you recommend it to students. The notes below offer some guidance on specific titles.

The Once and Future King by T. H. White

This book describes jousts between knights that result in deaths and injuries. There is also some cruelty to animals. There are no explicit sexual scenes; however, some readers may be offended by sexual relations between unmarried people. Morgause bears Arthur's son Mordred, and Lancelot has an illicit affair with Guenevere, Arthur's wife.

Lexile: 1080L

The Book of Merlyn by T. H. White

The Book of Merlyn includes occasional references to violent acts among people and animals. There is an extensive discussion of war, but it is from a metaphysical point of view and should not be offensive to most readers.

Lexile: Appropriate for high school students

Beowulf translated by Burton Raffel

This book includes scenes of death and violence, as when Grendel's arm is ripped from his body and his mother's head is slashed from her body.

Lexile: Appropriate for high school students

The Canterbury Tales by Geoffrey Chaucer

The tales contain ribald remarks, references to adultery, rape, and other sexual content; crude humor; gender bias; anti-Semitism and other ethnic slurs; clergy who break their vows; and other bad behavior, often for purposes of satire.

Lexile: NP

Students will

1. read selections from the English Renaissance, including the work of William Shakespeare.

2. apply a variety of reading strategies, particularly strategies for reading poetry, appropriate for reading these selections.

3. analyze literary elements.

4. use a variety of strategies to read unfamiliar words and build vocabulary.

5. learn elements of grammar, usage, and style.

6. use a recursive writing process to write in a variety of forms.

7. develop listening and speaking skills.

8. express and support responses to various types of text.

9. prepare, organize, and present literary interpretations.

Unit Instructional Resources

In **Unit 2 Resources,** you will find materials to support students in developing and mastering the unit skills and to help you assess their progress.

▶ **Vocabulary and Reading**

Additional vocabulary and reading support, based on Lexile scores of vocabulary words, is provided for each selection or grouping.

• **Word Lists A and B** and **Practices A and B** provide vocabulary-building activities for students reading two grades or one grade below level, respectively.

• **Reading Warm-ups A and B,** for students reading two grades or one grade below level, respectively, consist of short readings and activities that provide a context and practice for newly learned vocabulary.

▶ **Selection Support**

• Reading Strategy
• Literary Analysis
• Vocabulary Builder
• Grammar and Style
• Support for Writing
• Support for Extend Your Learning
• Enrichment

 You may also access these resources on TeacherExpress.™

Unit 2
Celebrating Humanity
1485–1625

Assessment Resources

Skills Assessment

Unit 2 Resources
  Selection Tests A and B

TeacherExpress™
  ExamView® Test Bank
    Software

Adequate Yearly Progress Assessment

Unit 2 Resources
  Diagnostic Tests 3 and 4
  Benchmark Tests 3 and 4

Standardized Assessment

Standardized Test Preparation Workbook

The English Renaissance Period

" What a piece of work is a man! how noble in reason! how infinite in faculties! in form and moving how express and admirable! in action how like an angel! "

—William Shakespeare,
from *Hamlet*

◁ This painting by Pieter Brueghel illustrates the wedding celebration of a peasant in 1500.

Celebrating Humanity (1485–1625) ■ 223

The literature of Unit 2 emerges from one of the most exciting and dynamic times in British history: the English Renaissance. In the essay below, scholar Frank Kermode paints a vivid picture of daily life in London during the reigns of Queen Elizabeth and James I. Later, in the unit introduction and in the literature, you will discover some of the authors and works that revolutionized writing in Britain.

From the Scholar's Desk
Frank Kermode Talks About the Time Period

Frank Kermode

Introducing Frank Kermode (b. 1919) Kermode is a literary critic whose in-depth analyses range from the Bible to Shakespeare to D. H. Lawrence. He is a former professor of Modern English at University College, London, and was knighted by Queen Elizabeth in 1991.

Life in Elizabethan and Jacobean England

London expanded greatly during the reign of Queen Elizabeth I, becoming one of the largest and wealthiest European capitals. Essentially a medieval city, its southern boundary was the River Thames, which was also its principal thoroughfare. To the north was the old Roman wall, but the city was spreading beyond it. Upstream was Westminster, the historic seat of the court and the national government. And across the river was Southwark, outside the jurisdiction of the City of London and therefore the favored site for enterprises, including theaters, deplored by the virtually autonomous and puritanical City government.

The population was swollen by country people, escaping the restrictions of rural life and famine, and by immigrants from Europe. The narrow, traffic-crowded streets were lined by shops and workshops, by civic mansions and rich halls of the trade guilds, and by the Inns of Court, haunts of lawyers and young gentlemen continuing their studies after leaving Oxford or Cambridge. The class system was strict—clothes were appropriate to rank, whether gentleman, citizen, craftsman, or laborer.

The Challenges of Urban Life London was not clean or healthy. Sanitation was crude—the Thames was a beautiful sewer. Deadly diseases—plague, malaria, smallpox—ensured a high mortality rate. Cheats,

▼ **Critical Viewing**
Which details in this painting support Kermode's description of London? **[Analyze]**

ricksters, and thieves abounded. Men carried weapons—swords or pistols—in the street. Meanwhile, as the fields and woods were built over, access to country air grew more difficult.

Inflation was unchecked but money flowed freely. Among the expensive luxuries of the day were ostentatious clothes and tobacco, a recent import from the New World. London was perpetual bustle, noise and display. Imagine how a young man from the provinces, like Shakespeare, might react to it. Shakespeare's Stratford, though a sturdy community with its own guilds and its good grammar school, hardly offered adequate preparation for London, among other things a great port and the gateway to the larger world. The splendor of the river and the mansions lining its bank won the keen admiration of foreign visitors, who compared its magnificence with that of Paris and other great European cities.

From Stratford to London In Shakespeare's day, the journey from Stratford to London took four days on foot, two on a horse. Shakespeare, new to London, probably took time to settle down. His London was the area around the old St. Paul's cathedral. The theaters were across the river in wicked Southwark. Westminster, site of Whitehall Palace, was a couple of miles to the west. There, in ancient halls, the great affairs of state were decided; there the queen contended with the pope and her other foreign and domestic enemies. Later, James catered to his favorites and dreamed of establishing absolute monarchy and universal peace. However, their majesties both liked plays, so there was hope for an aspiring playwright. There was the prospect of pleasure and success, though there was also risk. Perhaps that's why Shakespeare left his family in Stratford: to take his place in the London theater—and eventually, literary immortality.

Go Online
—Author Link

For: A video clip of
Frank Kermode
Visit: www.PHSchool.com
Web Code: ese-8201

For: More about
Frank Kermode
Visit: www.PHSchool.com
Web Code: ese-9201

Reading the Unit Introduction

Reading for Information and Insight Use the following terms and questions to guide your reading of the unit introduction on pages 228–235.

Names and Terms to Know
Renaissance
Martin Luther
Wars of the Roses
Henry VIII
Elizabeth I
James I
Mary Stuart
Puritans
Elizabethan Age

Focus Questions As you read this introduction, use what you learn to answer these questions:

- What are the characteristics of the spirit of the Renaissance?
- In what ways did religion make an impact on English life in the fifteenth century?
- In what way does literature provide a forum for criticisms of social institutions during this period?

From the Scholar's Desk: Frank Kermode ■ 225

Tell students that the terms and questions listed here are the key points in this introductory material. This information provides a context for the selections in the unit. Students should use the terms and questions as a guide to focus their reading of the unit introduction. When students have completed the unit introduction, they should be able to identify or explain each of these terms and answer or discuss the Focus Questions.

To provide students with additional help in reading the Unit 2 Introduction, give them pages 5 and 6 from *Unit 2 Resources.*

Concept Connector

After students have read the unit introduction, return to the Focus Questions to review the main points. For key points, see p. 235.

Go Online
—Author Link Typing in the Web Codes when prompted will bring students to a video clip and more information on Frank Kermode.

Getting an Overview

Use the Timeline to help students get a quick overview of themes and events of the period. This approach will benefit all students but may be especially helpful for visually oriented students, English learners, and those less proficient in reading. (For strategies in using the Timeline as an overview, see the bottom of this page.)

Thinking Critically

Questions are provided on the facing page. Use these questions to have students review the events, discuss their significance, and examine the *so what* behind the *what happened.*

Connecting to Selections

Have students refer to the Timeline when beginning to read individual selections. By consulting the Timeline regularly, they will gain a better sense of the period's chronology. In addition, they will appreciate the world events that gave rise to these works of literature.

Projects

Students can use the Timeline as a launching pad for projects like these:

- **Customized Timeline** Have students create a period timeline in their notebooks, adding key dates as they read new selections. They can use dates from this Timeline as a starting framework. If they wish, they can create a specialized timeline for political, scientific, or artistic developments.

- **Report on an Illustration** Have students scan the Timeline for a visual that interests them, research the story behind the picture, and report on their findings to the class.

1485   1520   1550

BRITISH EVENTS

- 1485 Henry VII becomes the first Tudor king.
- c. 1500 *Everyman* first performed.
- 1512 First masque performed.
- 1516 **Thomas More** publishes *Utopia.*

- 1534 Henry VIII issues Act of Supremacy. ▲
- 1534 Church of England established.
- 1535 **Thomas More** executed. ◄
- 1541 John Knox leads Calvinist reformation in Scotland.
- 1547 Henry VIII dies.
- 1549 The *Book of Common Prayer* issued.

- 1558 **Elizabeth I** becomes queen. ►
- 1560 Thomas Tallis publishes English cathedral music.
- 1563 More than 20,000 Londoners die in plague.
- 1564 **William Shakespeare** born. ▼

WORLD EVENTS

- 1492 Columbus lands in Western Hemisphere.
- 1497 Africa: Vasco da Gama rounds Cape of Good Hope.
- 1503 Italy: Leonardo da Vinci paints *Mona Lisa.*
- 1509 Italy: Michelangelo paints ceiling of Sistine Chapel.
- 1513 North America: Ponce de León explores Florida.
- 1518 Africa: Algiers and Tunisia founded.

- 1521 Italy: Pope Leo X excommunicates Martin Luther.
- 1532 Peru: Pizarro conquers Incas.
- 1532 France: Rabelais publishes *Gargantua and Pantagruel,* Book 1.
- 1534 Spain: St. Ignatius Loyola founds Jesuit brotherhood.
- 1535 Spain: King Charles I captures Tunis.
- 1540 Poland: Copernicus completes treatise on astronomy.

- 1554 Italy: Cellini completes bronze statue of Perseus.
- 1556 India: Akbar the Great comes to power.
- 1566 Belgium: Bruegel paints *The Wedding Dance.*
- 1567 South America: 2 million Indians die of typhoid.
- 1567 Brazil: Rio de Janeiro founded by Portuguese.

226 ■ *Celebrating Humanity (1485–1625)*

Getting an Overview of the Period

Introduction To give students an overview of the period, indicate the span of dates in the upper left-hand corner. Next, point out that the Timeline is divided into specifically British Events (on the top) and World Events (on the bottom). Have students practice scanning the Timeline across, looking at both the British Events and the World Events. Finally, point out that the events in the Timeline often represent beginnings, turning points, and endings. (For example, 1558 marks the start of Elizabeth I's reign.)

Key Events Have students **identify** key political events.
Answer: In 1534, the Church of England was established; in 1588, the Spanish Armada was defeated.

Then, have students **trace** events that suggest cultural excitement and confidence in humanity.
Possible responses: In 1580, Drake circumnavigated the Earth; in 1599, the Globe theater opened; in 1623, the first patent laws were passed.

570   1600   1610   1625

- **1580** Francis Drake returns from circumnavigating the globe.
- **c. 1582 Sir Philip Sidney** writes *Astrophel and Stella.*
- **1588** English navy defeats Spanish Armada. ▲
- **1590 Edmund Spenser** publishes *The Faerie Queene,* Part I.
- **1594 Shakespeare** writes *Romeo and Juliet.*
- **1599** Globe theater opens.

- **1600** East India Company founded.
- **1603 Elizabeth I** dies; James I becomes king.
- **1606** Guy Fawkes executed for Gunpowder Plot.
- **1606** Royal debt amounts to more than £600,000.
- **1609** *The Faerie Queene* by **Edmund Spenser** is published in its entirety.

- **1611** King James Bible published. ▼
- **1620** Francis Bacon publishes *Novum Organum.*
- **1623** First patent laws passed.
- **1625** James I dies.

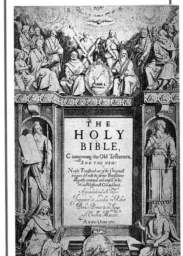

- **1580** France: Montaigne's *Essays* published.
- **1582** Italy: Pope Gregory XIII introduces new calendar. ▼
- **1595** South America: Sir Walter Raleigh explores Orinoco River.

- **1605** Spain: Cervantes publishes Part I of *Don Quixote.*
- **1607** North America: British colony established at Jamestown.
- **1608** North America: French colony of Quebec established.
- **1609** Italy: Galileo builds first telescope. ▶

- **1618** Germany: Kepler proposes laws of planetary motion.
- **1618** Europe: Beginning of the Thirty Years' War, a series of European conflicts fought for various reasons.
- **1620** North America: Pilgrims land at Plymouth Rock.
- **1620** China: Death of the T'ai-Ch'ang emperor after a one-month reign sparks new conflicts.

Introduction ■ 227

Analyzing the Timeline

1. (a) What two important religious works were published during this period? (b) What connections might there be between those publications and the creation of the Church of England (1534)? **[Connect]**
Answer: (a) The *Book of Common Prayer* appeared in 1549; the King James Bible appeared in 1611. (b) These books helped establish the authority of the Church of England following its break with the Pope.

2. (a) Name two seafaring exploits during this period. (b) What do these exploits suggest about seafaring and navigation during this period? **[Hypothesize]**
Answer: (a) Seafaring exploits include the expeditions of Francis Drake (1580) and Vasco da Gama (1497). (b) These exploits indicate that seafaring and navigation had recently reached a new level of proficiency.

3. (a) Name two disasters, one in Britain and one in the world, that occurred in the period 1550–1570. (b) What do these events suggest about medical science? **[Infer]**
Answer: (a) In 1563, more than 20,000 Londoners died in the plague. In 1567, two million Indians died of typhoid in South America. (b) These events suggest that medical science was not very advanced.

4. (a) Name two events that indicate British presence in the New World. (b) What do these events suggest about the importance of overseas trade to Britain? **[Infer]**
Possible responses: (a) Britain's presence in the New World is evident in the establishment of the East India Company in 1600, Raleigh's explorations in South America in 1595, and the establishment of Jamestown in 1607. (b) These events indicate Britain's commercial interest in the New World.

Critical Viewing

1. (a) How does the artist impress upon us Elizabeth I's power? (b) Does the overall impression make her seem inhuman? Explain. **[Interpret]**

Answers continued

Answer: (a) By showing her in rich clothing, her arms held confidently, the artist stresses her power. (b) Her face is distinctive, preserving a sense of her personality.

2. Speculate about the design of the antique telescope (1609). (a) Why is it mounted on a spherical support? (b) Why are there two tubes? **[Speculate]**
Possible response: (a) The "globe" allows the user to track accurately the direction in which the telescope is pointed.

(b) One tube is a finder, showing a greater area under less magnification than the other.

3. What devices do the designers of this edition of the Bible (1611) use to create an effect of seriousness and respect? **[Speculate]**
Answer: The title appears set back in a shrine-like space; the bearded figures convey seriousness; the scribe (lower right) appears to expect inspiration.

Historical Background

The Renaissance, one of the most exciting periods in history, was both a worldly and a religious age. It blossomed first in the Italian city-states (1350–1550), where commerce and a wealthy middle class supported learning and the arts. Slowly, Renaissance ideas spread northward, giving rise to the English Renaissance (1485–1625). During the Renaissance, scholars reacted against what they saw as the "dark ages" of medieval Europe, and they revived the learning of ancient Greece and Rome. They wanted to bring about a rebirth of civilization.

The Age of Exploration The Renaissance thirst for knowledge prompted a great burst of exploration by sea. Navigators ventured far and wide, aided by the development of the compass and by advances in astronomy, which freed them from the need to cling to the shores of the Atlantic. Their explorations reached a high point with Columbus's arrival in the Western Hemisphere in 1492.

England's participation in the Age of Exploration began in 1497, when the Italian-born explorer John Cabot, sailing in the service of an English company, reached Newfoundland (an island off the east coast of what is now Canada) and perhaps also the mainland. Cabot thus laid the basis for future English claims in North America.

Religion Along with the Renaissance spirit, a growing sense of nationalism led many Europeans to question the authority of the Roman Catholic Church. Many people had grievances against the Church. Some felt that Church officials were corrupt; others questioned Church teachings and hierarchy.

The edition of the New Testament by the great Dutch scholar Desiderius Erasmus (1466–1536) raised serious questions about standard interpretations of the Bible. Because of his friendship with such English writers as Thomas More (1478–1535), Erasmus focused attention on issues of morality and religion that continued to be central concerns of the English Renaissance.

Although Erasmus himself remained a Roman Catholic, he helped pave the way for a split in the Church that began in 1517, when a German monk named Martin Luther (1483–1546) nailed a list of dissenting beliefs to the door of a German church. Although this was not his intent, Luther's protest resulted in the division of the Church and a new Christian denomination that became known as Lutheranism. The process that Luther started has come to be called the Protestant Reformation.

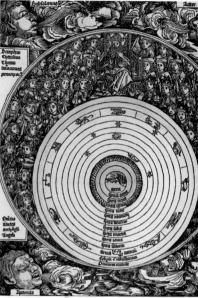

▲ **Critical Viewing**
Ptolemy was a second century A.D. astronomer and mathematician. Renaissance thinkers believed in his Earth-centered model of the universe, shown above. Compare and contrast this view of the universe with our view of the universe today.
[Compare and Contrast]

The Tudors The ending of the Wars of the Roses and the founding of the Tudor dynasty in 1485 opened a new era in English life. Monarchs assured stability by increasing their own power and undercutting the strength of the nobles. At the same time, they dramatically changed England's religious practices and helped transform the country from a small island nation into one of the world's great powers.

The first Tudor monarch, Henry VII, inherited an England that had been depleted and exhausted by years of civil war. By the time he died in 1509, he had rebuilt the nation's treasury and established law and order. In doing so, he restored the prestige of the monarchy and set the stage for his successors.

Henry VII was succeeded by his handsome and athletic son, Henry VIII. Like his father, Henry VIII was a practicing Catholic. He even wrote a book against Martin Luther, for which a grateful Pope granted him the title "Defender of the Faith."

Henry VIII's good relationship with the Pope did not last, however. Because his marriage to Catherine of Aragon had not produced a son, Henry tried to obtain an annulment from the Pope so that he could marry Anne Boleyn. When the Pope refused, Henry remarried anyway. This defiance of papal authority led to an open break with the Roman Catholic Church. Henry seized the Catholic Church's English property and dissolved the powerful monasteries. He even had his former friend and leading advisor, Thomas More, executed because More had refused to renounce his Catholic faith.

Henry married six times. His first two marriages produced two daughters, Mary and Elizabeth. His third wife, Jane Seymour, bore a son, Edward, who was still a child when Henry died in 1547.

Religious Turmoil Henry VIII's son became King Edward VI at the age of nine and died at the age of fifteen. During his brief reign, a series of parliamentary acts dramatically changed the nation's religious practices. English replaced Latin in church ritual, and the Anglican prayer book, the Book of Common Prayer, became required in public worship. By the time of Edward's death in 1553, England was well on its way to becoming a Protestant nation.

Roman Catholicism made a turbulent comeback, however, when Edward's half sister Mary took the throne. Mary I was a Catholic, and she restored Roman practices to the Church of England. She also restored the authority of the Pope over the English Church. Ordering the execution of about 300 Protestants, Queen Mary earned the nickname "Bloody Mary" and strengthened anti-Catholic sentiment in England.

▲ Critical Viewing
The English navy gained supremacy on the sea after defeating the Spanish Armada in 1588. Examine this painting of the battle between the two navies, and infer the types of war tactics used by the English that may have contributed to their success. **[Infer]**

Introduction ■ 229

Fueled by political discontent, the Protestant Reformation swept through much of Europe. It led to frequent wars between European nations whose rulers had opposing religious beliefs. Protestants themselves were divided, and in Germany the followers of Luther (called Lutherans) persecuted the followers of another Protestant Reformer, John Calvin of Geneva. Calvin's ideas (called Calvinism) gained a foothold in Switzerland, England, and Scotland, however, and helped bring about the establishment of the Puritan and Presbyterian sects.

Critical Viewing

Possible response: People who wore such clothes must have attended occasions at which display counted for a great deal—the clothing is not designed for comfort or ease of movement.

The British Tradition
Close-up on Society

- Ask a student to read the box aloud to the class. Refer students to the portraits on the page for examples of the clothing being described.

- Discuss how fashion has changed over the centuries. **Ask** students to name other items that were once at the height of fashion.

Possible responses: Students may suggest flapper dresses, poodle skirts, leg warmers, and corsets.

Elizabeth I When Mary I died after a five-year reign, her half sister, Elizabeth, came to the throne. Strong and clever, Elizabeth I was probably England's ablest monarch since William the Conqueror. She had received a Renaissance education and had read widely in the Greek and Latin classics. Becoming a great patron of the arts, she gathered around her the best writers of her day.

Elizabeth also put an end to the religious turmoil that had existed during Mary I's reign. She reestablished the monarch's supremacy over the Church of England and restored the Book of Common Prayer. Overall, she instituted a policy of religious compromise, enforcing reforms that she felt both moderate Catholics and Protestants could accept.

Elizabeth's one outstanding problem was her Catholic cousin Mary Stuart, queen of Scotland by birth and next in line for the throne of England. Because Catholics did not recognize Henry VIII's marriage to Elizabeth's mother, Anne Boleyn, they considered Mary Stuart the queen of England. Imprisoned by Elizabeth for eighteen years, Mary instigated numerous Catholic plots against her. Following the recommendations of her advisors, Elizabeth stepped up punishment of the Catholics but let her royal cousin live. Finally, Parliament insisted on Mary's execution. She was beheaded in 1587, a Catholic martyr.

The British Tradition   Close-Up on Society

High Fashion in the Elizabethan Age

Noblewomen looked like dolls on display, tightly laced into dresses that resembled giant bells. Noblemen were arrayed like showy peacocks in close-fitting jackets and wide collars that seemed to serve up their heads on plates of lace. High fashion was indeed a statement during Elizabeth's reign. As shown in the accompanying pictures—one of Queen Elizabeth and one of Sir Walter Raleigh—clothing was elaborate and theatrical in an age that loved the drama and dramatized itself.

Two devices that helped create these effects were the ruff and the farthingale, both of which came from the Spanish court. Even after the English navy defeated the Spanish Armada in 1588, Spanish fashions held sway among the English nobility. The ruff was a pleated, starched collar worn by both sexes. It varied in size, but as you can see from the picture of Raleigh, above, it could expand to the size of a very large platter. The farthingale was a linen underskirt stretched over a thick iron wire that supported a skirt or dress and gave it a bell shape.

Toward the end of Elizabeth's reign, fashions became a little less showy. Men began to wear a falling collar more like that of today, and a simpler doublet, or close-fitting jacket. Women changed their bell-shaped gowns for drum-shaped ones, and in the early seventeenth century, the farthingale itself was replaced by padding.

230 ■ *Celebrating Humanity (1485–1625)*

▲ Critical Viewing
These portraits show Queen Elizabeth and Sir Walter Raleigh dressed in elaborate fashions. Speculate about the types of lives led by the people who could afford these clothes. [Speculate]

Enrichment

Renaissance Science
Explain to students that Renaissance science, like much of Renaissance painting, was born of a new thirst for observation. Yet at the same time, the claims of ancient authorities on people's belief were strong.

The bold explorers of the time had already shaken one Ptolemaic theory: They had discovered a new continent in the West. In 1540, the Polish astronomer Nicolaus Copernicus dealt Ptolemy another blow—the Earth, he said, went around the sun. It would take some time before Copernicus's theory gained wide acceptance.

Ask students to speculate about other links they can see between the exploration of the world and the science of the time.

Stuarts and Puritans The English Renaissance continued after Elizabeth died in 1603, although a new dynasty—the Stuarts—came to the throne of England. Determined to avoid a dispute over the throne and a return of civil strife, Elizabeth had named King James VI of Scotland as her successor, making him James I of England. James's claim to the throne of England rested on his descent from King Henry VII of England through his mother, Mary Stuart, Elizabeth's old antagonist. Unlike Mary, however, James was a Protestant.

The years of James I's reign are sometimes described as the Jacobean Era, from *Jacobus*, the Latin word for James. Like his predecessor, James I was a strong supporter of the arts. He also took measures to expand England's position as a world power, sponsoring the establishment of its first successful American colony—Jamestown, Virginia.

During his reign, however, James and Parliament struggled for power, a conflict that would later erupt into war. Guided by the idea of the "divine right of kings," James I often treated Parliament with contempt, and they quarreled over taxes and foreign wars. James I also persecuted the Puritans, who were strongly represented in the House of Commons. Prompted by the king's religious intolerance, a group of Puritans migrated to America and established the Plymouth Colony in 1620.

The British Tradition — Art in the Historical Context

Hans Holbein the Younger, Portraitist of the English Court

During the English Renaissance, the visual arts did not flourish as they had in Italy and other European countries. Perhaps that is why the greatest English painter of this period was a German, Hans Holbein the Younger (1497–1543). Born in south Germany, Holbein traveled to Switzerland and eventually settled in England.

Working at the English court, Holbein painted many of its most prominent figures, including Sir Thomas More. In this portrait, Holbein focuses on the most powerful man in early sixteenth-century England, King Henry VIII.

Holbein's portrait of King Henry VIII is not much larger than 2½ feet by two feet, but some scholars have argued that it makes Henry seem very large indeed.

▶ **Critical Viewing** Considering details such as body language, costume, facial expression, position, and pose, support or refute this analysis of the painting by the art critic H. W. Janson: ". . . the [frontal view] and physical bulk of Henry VIII create an overpowering sensation of the king's ruthless commanding presence." **[Draw Conclusions]**

Introduction ■ 231

---

to the class. Tell students that Holbein did other jobs besides painting while he was Henry VIII's court painter. He created sketches of items, such as bridles and buttons, that were used by the royal household. He also designed state robes for the king. Discuss the advantages and disadvantages of being employed by the king. Then ask the Critical Viewing question.

Critical Viewing

Possible response: Students may agree with Janson's view of Henry VIII as physically imposing and intimidating in his regal costume; others may feel that he looks unfit to lead a nation.

Literature of the Period

• If the Italian Renaissance paved the way for the English Renaissance, the Italian poet Petrarch's use of the sonnet paved the way for the Elizabethan fascination with the form. Students can read the sonnets of Spenser, Sir Philip Sidney, and Shakespeare.

• In reading *Macbeth*, p. 306, students will encounter Shakespeare's flattery of James I.

Historical Background
Comprehension Check

1. (a) Over what did Henry VIII quarrel with the Pope? (b) What did Henry do as a result?
   Answer: (a) They quarreled over the annulment of Henry's marriage to Catherine of Aragon. (b) Henry declared himself, not the Pope, the supreme ruler of the Church of England.

2. (a) How did Elizabeth I address England's religious difficulties? (b) For what is her rule remembered?
   Answer: (a) Elizabeth I returned England to Protestantism, but kept a policy of moderation in religion. (b) She is remembered for her strong, tactful rule and her patronage of literature.

Critical Thinking

1. How does Henry VIII's desire to remarry demonstrate the political significance of a monarch's marriage? **[Analyze]**

Answers continued

Answer: Henry VIII wanted to remarry so that he could have a son, presumably to provide England with a ruler.

2. Mary Stuart, Queen of Scots, plotted against Elizabeth I. Why did Elizabeth I keep her in prison instead of executing her right away? **[Infer]**
   Answer: Elizabeth I probably thought that Mary's execution would inflame Catholics.

1. What type of poetry did Renaissance writers favor?
   Answer: Renaissance writers favored lyric poetry.

2. What poetic form was of particular significance during the period?
   Answer: The sonnet and the sonnet cycle were particularly popular during the time.

3. What is a sonnet cycle?
   Answer: A sonnet cycle is a series of sonnets that fit loosely together to form a story.

Critical Viewing

Possible response: The simple lives of shepherds offered a contrast to the busy intrigues of court.

The Hireling Shepherd, William Holman Hunt © Manchester City Art Galleries

Literature of the Period

The Elizabethan Age produced an explosion of cultural energy. English architects designed and constructed beautiful mansions. Composers turned out new hymns to fit the Anglican service and popularized the English madrigal, a love song performed without musical accompaniment, often by several harmonizing voices. Painters and sculptors were busy, too. Although the Renaissance masters generally were not English, some—like the German artist Hans Holbein the Younger (1497–1543), court painter to Henry VIII—did move to England.

Like painting and sculpture, literature expressed the spirit of the Renaissance. Narratives, poetry, dramas, and comedies reflected the ideas of the times. They also provided a forum for subtle and satirical criticisms of social institutions such as the monarchy and the Church.

Elizabethan Poetry During the reign of Elizabeth I, English literature came of age. The most significant literary developments took place in the area of poetry. Favoring lyric poetry, rather than the narrative poems enjoyed by their medieval predecessors, the Elizabethan poets perfected the sonnet and began experimenting with other poetic forms.

The Sonnet: Sidney, Spenser, and Shakespeare One of the most popular literary forms during the Elizabethan Age was the sonnet cycle, a series of sonnets that fit loosely together to form a story. A sonnet is a fourteen-line poem which in English is usually in iambic pentameter and whose rhyme scheme varies. The first of the great Elizabethan sonnet cycles was *Astrophel*

▲ **Critical Viewing**
This picture dates from the nineteenth century, but it portrays the type of pastoral scene that appealed to many Elizabethan poets. Why do you think the lives of shepherds and shepherdesses like these interested court poets? **[Infer]**

and Stella by Sir Philip Sidney. Sidney also helped adapt classical verse forms to the English language.

Another major Elizabethan poet was Edmund Spenser, who wrote intricate verse filled with rich imagery. His sonnet cycle *Amoretti* is unique in that it was addressed to his wife.

The brilliant lyric poet William Shakespeare, also the era's greatest dramatist, brought the Elizabethan sonnet to new heights. Shakespeare changed the pattern and rhyme scheme of the Petrarchan, or Italian, sonnet, employing a form now known as the English, or Shakespearean, sonnet. The Petrarchan sonnet is divided into an octave, with a rhyme scheme *abbaabba,* and a sestet, with a rhyme scheme *cdecde, cdcdcd,* or a similar pattern, avoiding a closing couplet. The Shakespearean sonnet is divided into four quatrains and a closing couplet, with a rhyme scheme *abab cdcd efef gg.*

Pastoral Poetry: Marlowe and Raleigh Christopher Marlowe (1564–1593) was also a noted playwright and a gifted lyric poet. Marlowe helped popularize pastoral verse, which idealizes the rustic simplicity of rural life, in such poems as "The Passionate Shepherd to His Love."

Marlowe's poem inspired Sir Walter Raleigh (1552?–1618) to write a famous response, "The Nymph's Reply to the Shepherd." Poet, historian, courtier, soldier, and explorer, Raleigh was a typical Renaissance man whose adventurous life mirrored the restless spirit of his day.

Elizabethan Drama During the Elizabethan Age, playwrights turned away from religious subjects and began writing more complex and sophisticated plays. Drawing upon the classical models of ancient Greece and Rome, they reintroduced tragedies and dramas.

Christopher Marlowe as Playwright Besides being a leading poet, Christopher Marlowe became the first major Elizabethan dramatist in the 1580s, writing such plays as *Tamburlaine the Great* and *The Tragical History of Doctor Faustus.* Had Marlowe lived past the age of thirty, he might well have rivaled Shakespeare as England's greatest playwright.

William Shakespeare as Playwright Shakespeare began his involvement with the theater as an actor. By 1592, he was a popular playwright, whose works were performed even at Elizabeth I's court.

After the Globe theater was built in 1599, many of Shakespeare's plays were performed there. Shakespeare wrote thirty-seven plays,

▼ **Critical Viewing**
What could readers learn about Shakespeare's *Romeo and Juliet* from this illustration? **[Infer]**

Romeo and Juliet

Introduction ■ 233

rative poetry. From this fact, what can you deduce about the audience for poetry? **[Deduce]**
Possible responses: Poetry readers had become more sophisticated, and they were interested in nuances of feeling or description rather than in the presentation of action.

2. What evidence can you give that English writers were not just imitating, but were expanding upon Renaissance Italian influences? **[Support]**
Answer: Shakespeare adapted the form of the Italian sonnet by changing its rhyme scheme and stanza structure.

3. Name two major prose works of the period, and explain how each reflects developments of the time. **[Connect]**
Possible responses: The King James Bible reflects the growing concern with matters of religious authority; Sir Francis Bacon's *Novum Organum,* a comprehensive work on knowledge, shows the period's new spirit of enquiry.

Critical Viewing

Possible response: Students may say that the title characters were physically affectionate and quite young.

Activities

1. **Monarchs on the Air** Have several students each assume the identity of a monarch discussed in the Historical Background. Then, have them appear together on a late-night television discussion show. Have each monarch tell about his or her experiences and discuss with other monarchs the challenges and tribulations of ruling.

2. **Letter From the Future** Ask students to select a figure discussed in the Historical Background and write a letter to him or her warning of or applauding the future consequences of his or her acts. Students should make an effort to appeal to the values of the person to whom they are writing.

dramatist of the time?

Answer: Christopher Marlowe was the period's first major playwright.

2. What body of work from the period has had the greatest influence?

Answer: Shakespeare's plays continue to be highly valued.

3. What was the central prose achievement of the period?

Answer: The central prose achievement of the period was the King James translation of the Bible into English.

The British Tradition
A Writer's Voice

• Tell students that many of Shakespeare's works contain "plays-within-plays." *Hamlet, A Midsummer Night's Dream,* and *The Tempest* all use this device to comment on Elizabethan theater or the nature of reality and illusion, in addition to the functions the playlets perform in the plots of the larger plays.

• **Ask** students: In what ways are actors "spirits" that are "melted into air"?

Possible answer: Actors take on the spirits of their characters, which disappear when the play is over.

• **Discuss** with students lines 9–10: "We are such stuff as dreams are made on." To whom is the speaker referring?

Possible answers: He may be referring to actors, who make writers' dreams come alive for an audience. He may be talking about the "spirits" or supernatural beings who Prospero says played the parts, but who do not exist in the everyday world. He may also be referring to all human beings, who are capable of dreaming during "our little life" on earth.

---

among them many of the greatest dramas of all time. He wrote nine tragedies, including *Romeo and Juliet, Hamlet,* and *Macbeth;* several comedies, including *The Merchant of Venice* and *A Midsummer Night's Dream;* ten histories (plays based on historical characters), including *Richard II, Richard III,* and *Henry V;* and a number of plays often classified as "tragic comedies" or "romances," such as *The Tempest.*

Filled with powerful and beautiful language, his works display his deep understanding of human nature. Because of their eloquent language and depth, Shakespeare's plays have retained their popularity through the centuries. Fellow poet and playwright Ben Jonson said of Shakespeare, "He was not of an age, but for all time."

Elizabethan and Jacobean Prose Prose took a back seat to poetry and drama during the English Renaissance. Scholars still preferred to write in Latin, and their English prose had a Latin flavor. Because they used long words and ornate sentences, their work is often difficult to read today.

A Writer's Voice

William Shakespeare's Farewell in *The Tempest*

The Tempest, which may have been Shakespeare's last play, is often regarded as his farewell to the theater. One speech, given by a character named Prospero, seems to embody this farewell. Prospero has just staged an elaborate, magical play-within-a-play in which "spirits" are the actors, but he quickly ends it when he recalls what he still must do to thwart his enemies.

In his speech, the references to the vanishing scenery of the play could also refer to a vanishing world: "The cloud-capped towers, the gorgeous palaces, / The solemn temples, the great globe itself. . . ." This double reference to reality and play is supported by his pun on the word *globe,* which could refer to the Earth or to the Globe theater, where so many of Shakespeare's dramas were staged. In good Elizabethan fashion, Shakespeare equates life with theater, at the same time suggesting the illusory quality of life.

from *The Tempest,* Act IV, Scene i

Our revels° now are ended. These our actors,	°Entertainments
As I foretold you, were all spirits and	
Are melted into air, into thin air;	
And, like the baseless fabric° of this vision,	°Structure without
5 The cloud-capped towers, the gorgeous places,	foundation
The solemn temples, the great globe itself,	
Yea, all which it inherit,° shall dissolve,	°All who inhabit it
And, like this insubstantial pageant faded,	
Leave not a rack° behind. We are such stuff	°A drifting cloud
10 As dreams are made on, and our little life	
Is rounded with a sleep. . . .	

The Prose of Sidney, Nashe, and Raleigh Several Elizabethan poets also contributed major works of prose. Sir Philip Sidney's *Defence of Poesie* (about 1582) is one of the earliest works of English literary criticism. Thomas Nashe's *The Unfortunate Traveler* (1594), a fictional tale, was a forerunner of the novel. *History of the World*, another important work of prose, was written by Sir Walter Raleigh during his imprisonment in the Tower of London.

Sir Francis Bacon Perhaps the leading prose writer of the English Renaissance was Sir Francis Bacon, a high government official under James I. "I have taken all knowledge to be my province," Bacon wrote, and his literary output reflects his scholarship in many fields. *Novum Organum* (1620), his greatest work, made major contributions to natural science and philosophy. Bacon is also known for his formal essays, short prose works focusing on single topics.

The King James Bible The most monumental prose achievement of the entire English Renaissance is undoubtedly the English translation of the Bible commissioned by King James on the advice of Protestant clergymen. Fifty-four scholars labored for seven years to bring this magnificent work to fruition. The King James Bible, or Authorized Version, is among the most widely quoted and influential works in the English language.

The Achievements of the Renaissance The English Renaissance moved England out of its medieval past and into the modern world. No writers since have surpassed the literary achievements of Shakespeare or the majestic language of the King James Bible. They provide the standard against which all English literature has been judged right down to the present time.

▲ **Critical Viewing**
Doctors could do little to stop epidemics of smallpox, measles, influenza, and yellow fever. Study this picture to speculate about the measures taken in epidemics: (a) Why has the door been padlocked? (b) Why is a fire burning before the house? **[Speculate]**

Concept Connector

Have students return to the Focus Questions on p. 225. Ask them to use these questions to orally summarize the main points in the Unit Introduction. Students' summaries should include the following points:

Characteristics of the spirit of the Renaissance:

- A thirst for knowledge was characteristic of the English Renaissance. It spurred exploration of new lands by sea.
- The revitalization in the arts blossomed under the support of the monarchy.

- The restless spirit brought about religious reforms.

Impact of religion on English life:

- Many people became disillusioned with Catholicism. The religious battle that ensued eventually led to the English Reformation.
- Changes in the monarchy affected changes in religious practices. English replaced Latin, and the Book of Common Prayer was instituted.

- Eventually, Elizabeth I created reforms that were acceptable to both Protestants and Catholics.

Literature and criticism of social institutions:

- Many writers expressed the ideas and spirit of the Renaissance in their work. Literature was used to subtly criticize social institutions.
- Writers such as Sir Thomas More used their prose to address social injustices.

Critical Thinking

1. What other factor, besides his innovativeness, might account for the fact that Shakespeare's use of many words was their first appearance in print? [Speculate]
Answer: The people of Shakespeare's day may have used some of these words in their speech, but considered them unfit—too ordinary or vulgar—for writing.

2. Speculate on how the people of Shakespeare's day would have "heard" his style. (Draw evidence from the chart and from the phrases in the Activity.) [Speculate]
Possible response: Some students may speculate that Shakespeare's audience may have found his style difficult to follow because of all the new words he used and his metaphorical style; others may argue that his success proves that his audiences found his style interesting and memorable.

Critical Viewing

1. Use the chart to find two very common words introduced by Shakespeare into writing. [Interpret]
Possible responses: Students may cite *bedroom, useless.*

2. Use the chart to find two words that Shakespeare probably derived from another language. [Interpret]
Possible responses: Students may cite *assassination, exposure.*

Answers to the Activity

1. Neither a borrower nor a lender be
2. All the world's a stage
3. With bated breath
4. Break the ice
5. Come full circle
6. Eaten me out of house and home
7. A foregone conclusion
8. Laugh yourself into stitches
9. Not budge an inch
10. Too much of a good thing

"A Man of Fire-New Words"

BY RICHARD LEDERER

THE AGELESS BARD

Shakespeare's plays, which he wrote in London between approximately 1590 and 1613, have been in almost constant production since their creation. Because the playwright dealt with universal truths and conflicts in human nature, his tragedies, comedies, and history plays continue to draw audiences from all walks of life, just as they did in their own day. Time has proved the truth of what Shakespeare's contemporary, Ben Jonson, said of him: "He was not of an age but for all time."

WORD-MAKER SUPREME

William Shakespeare's words, as well as his works, were not just of an age, but for all time. He was, quite simply, the greatest word maker who ever lived—an often neglected aspect of his genius.

Of the 20,138 different words that Shakespeare employs in his plays, sonnets, and other poems, his is the first known use of more than 1,700 of them. The most verbally innovative of our authors, Shakespeare made up more than 8.5 percent of his written vocabulary. Reading his works is like witnessing the birth of language itself.

"I pitied thee, / Took pains to make thee speak," says Prospero to Caliban in *The Tempest*. "I endow'd thy purposes / With words that made them known." Shakespeare is our Prospero; he dressed our thoughts with words and set our tongue teeming with phrases.

Consider the following list of thirty representative words that, as far as we can tell, Shakespeare was the first to use in writing. So great is his influence on his native tongue that we find it hard to imagine a time when these words did not exist.

aerial	amazement	assassination	auspicious
baseless	bedroom	bump	castigate
countless	courtship	critic	dishearten
dislocate	dwindle	exposure	frugal
generous	gloomy	hurry	impartial
invulnerable	lapse	laughable	lonely
majestic	monumental	perusal	pious
sneak	useless		

The striking compound that Shakespeare fashioned to describe Don Adriano de Armando in *Love's Labour's Lost* is an important label for the playwright himself: "a man of fire-new words." No day goes by that we do not speak and hear, and read and write using his legacy.

Activity

Oscar Wilde once quipped, "Now we sit through Shakespeare in order to recognize the quotations." Unrivaled in his invention of words, William Shakespeare is unequaled as a phrase-maker.

Complete the following expressions, each of which first saw the light in one of his plays:

1. Neither a _____ or a _____ be
2. All the world's a _____
3. With bated _____
4. Break the _____
5. Come full _____
6. Eaten me out of house and _____
7. A foregone _____
8. Laugh yourselves into _____
9. Not _____ an inch
10. Too much of a good _____

Enrichment

The Language of Technology

Shakespeare flooded our language with new coinages, some invented or derived from other languages. Explain to students that, in our own time, science and technology have become a major source of new words.

From the *byte* (a minimal unit of information) to the *fax* (short for *facsimile,* a copy), technospeak has flooded the language. Traces of technology's influence may also be evident in the brisker, more clipped style of new coinages: to *upgrade,* for instance, or *to impact,* used transitively.

Lovers and Their Lines

The Sonnet, William Mulready, Victoria and Albert Museum

Selection Planning Guide

The poems in this section celebrate love—witty love, sincere love, and love for love's sake. Edmund Spenser, in "little love poems," is unique in his choice of romantic subject (his wife) and in that the love was requited and stable. Sir Philip Sidney, unlike Spenser, followed the Petrarchan mode and wrote of his agonized love for a woman who would not or could not return his ardor. Shakespeare's sonnets run the gamut from quiet introspection about the nature of love and marriage to a backhanded celebration of his unlovely love.

In addition to these sonnets is a selection of pastoral poetry that pairs Christopher Marlowe's idealistic poem with Sir Walter Raleigh's tart, commonsense response.

Humanities

The Sonnet by William Mulready

Born in Ireland, William Mulready (1786–1863) is best known as a "genre painter" of rural scenes that told stories. Mulready was trained at the Royal Academy and experienced success at a young age. When he was in his twenties, the style of British painting shifted to incorporate the earth tones and solid figures used by the Dutch painters, and Mulready followed the fashion, as is clearly indicated by the glowing colors and palpable figures of *The Sonnet*. Use these questions for discussion:

1. What is the young woman reading here, and what is the young man doing?
   Possible responses: Students will probably assume that the young woman is reading a sonnet written by the young man, who appears to be watching for her response.

2. What clues does the body language of each figure provide about that person's mood?
   Answer: The young woman holds her hand over her mouth, possibly indicating her excitement or her absorption in what she is reading; the young man bends over to try to read or gauge the woman's reaction to his sonnet.

Monitoring Progress

Before students read the selections in Part 1, administer **Diagnostic Test 3** (*Unit 2 Resources*, pp. 2–4). This test will determine students' level of readiness for the reading and vocabulary skills.

Differentiated Instruction   Solutions for All Learners

Accessibility at a Glance

More Accessible	Average	More Challenging
Sonnet 31 by Sidney	Sonnet 116 by Shakespeare	Sonnet 1 by Spenser
Sonnet 39 by Sidney	Sonnet 130 by Shakespeare	Sonnet 35 by Spenser
The Passionate Shepherd		Sonnet 75 by Spenser
The Nymph's Reply		Sonnet 29 by Shakespeare
		Sonnet 106 by Shakespeare

Meeting Your Standards

Students will

1. **analyze and respond to literary elements.**
   - Literary Analysis: The Sonnet

2. **read, comprehend, analyze, and critique a poem.**
   - Reading Strategy: Paraphrasing
   - Reading Check questions
   - Apply the Skills questions
   - Assessment Practice (ATE)

3. **develop vocabulary.**
   - Vocabulary Lesson: Related Words: Forms of *languished*

4. **understand and apply written and oral language conventions.**
   - Spelling Strategy
   - Grammar and Style Lesson: Capitalization of Proper Nouns

5. **develop writing proficiency.**
   - Writing Lesson: Introduction to a Sonnet Sequence

6. **develop appropriate research strategies.**
   - Extend Your Learning: Biographical Report

7. **understand and apply listening and speaking strategies.**
   - Extend Your Learning: Scene With Dialogue

Block Scheduling: Use one 90-minute class period to preteach the skills and have students read the selection. Use a second 90-minute class period to assess students' mastery of skills, extend their learning, and monitor their progress.

Homework Suggestions
Following are possibilities for homework assignments:

- Support pages from *Unit 2 Resources:*
  - Literary Analysis
  - Reading Strategy
  - Vocabulary Builder
  - Grammar and Style

- An Extend Your Learning project and the Writing Lesson for this selection group may be completed over several days.

Step-by-Step Teaching Guide	Pacing Guide
PRETEACH	
• Administer Vocabulary and Reading Warm-ups as necessary.	5 min.
• Engage students' interest with the motivation activity.	5 min.
• Read and discuss author and background features. **FT**	10 min.
• Introduce the Literary Analysis Skill: The Sonnet. **FT**	5 min.
• Introduce the Reading Strategy: Paraphrasing. **FT**	10 min.
• Prepare students to read by teaching the selection vocabulary. **FT**	
TEACH	
• Informally monitor comprehension while students read independently or in groups. **FT**	30 min.
• Monitor students' comprehension with the Reading Check notes.	as students read
• Reinforce vocabulary with Vocabulary Builder notes.	as students read
• Develop students' understanding of the sonnet with the Literary Analysis annotations. **FT**	5 min.
• Develop students' ability to paraphrase with the Reading Strategy annotations. **FT**	5 min.
ASSESS/EXTEND	
• Assess students' comprehension and mastery of the Literary Analysis and Reading Strategy by having them answer the Apply the Skills questions. **FT**	15 min.
• Have students complete the Vocabulary Lesson and the Grammar and Style Lesson. **FT**	15 min.
• Apply students' knowledge of taking notes for a summary by using the Writing Lesson. **FT**	45 min. or homework
• Apply students' understanding by using one or more of the Extend Your Learning activities.	20–90 min. or homework
• Administer Selection Test A or Selection Test B. **FT**	15 min.

Resources

Choosing Resources for Differentiated Instruction

[L1] Special Needs Students
[L2] Below-Level Students
[L3] All Students
[L4] Advanced Students
[EL] English Learners

For Vocabulary and Reading Warm-ups and for Selection Tests, **A** signifies "less challenging" and **B** "more challenging." For Graphic Organizer transparencies, **A** signifies "not filled in" and **B** "filled in."

FT Fast Track Instruction: To move the lesson more quickly, use the strategies and activities identified with **FT**.

Scaffolding for Less Proficient and Advanced Students

The leveled Critical Thinking questions after selections progress in the levels of thinking required to answer them. To address the needs of your different students, you may use the (a) level questions for your less proficient students and the (b) level questions with your on-level and advanced students. The occasional (c) level questions are appropriate for your advanced students.

PRENTICE HALL
TeacherEXPRESS™ Use this complete
Plan · Teach · Assess   suite of powerful
teaching tools to make lesson planning and testing quicker and easier.

PRENTICE HALL
StudentEXPRESS™ Use the interactive textbook
Learn · Study · Succeed
(online and on CD-ROM) to make selections and activities come alive with audio and video support and interactive questions.

Monitoring Progress

Before students read these selections, administer **Diagnostic Test 3** (*Unit 2 Resources,* pp. 2–4).

 **For:** Information about Lexiles
Visit: www.PHSchool.com
Web Code: eue-1111

Motivation

These sonnets by Spenser and Sidney recount the conflicting emotions inherent in romantic love. To stimulate interest, have the class act together as an advice columnist. What advice would they give to:

• someone who has been rejected by the person he or she loves?

• a person who is too shy to announce his or her love?

Have students discuss these problems. Then tell them that the sonnets they are about to read were written by poets who were in love, one happily, one sadly.

❶ Background
More About the Authors

Edmund Spenser's knowledge of Latin and Greek classics and Italian, French, and English literature provided a foundation for his highly original work. His book *The Shepheardes Calendar,* which was dedicated to Philip Sidney, is considered the first work of the English literary Renaissance. Surrounded by conflict (Protestant v. Catholic, Irish v. English), Spenser saw his poetry as a way to illuminate the human experience, the battle between good and evil, and the importance of virtue.

Sir Philip Sidney was considered the ideal gentleman of his day. He was an excellent horseman, and was among the few Englishmen of his time who were interested in the Americas. His *Defence of Poesie* introduced the critical ideas of Renaissance theorists to England. His travels in Europe made it possible for him to perfect his Latin, French, and Italian, and to gain a knowledge of European politics and ideas.

Build Skills | *Poems* |

❶ *from* Spenser's Sonnets • *from* Sidney's Sonnets

Edmund Spenser
(1552–1599)

Born into a working-class family, Edmund Spenser attended the Merchant Taylors' School on a scholarship and managed to work his way through Cambridge University. During his university years, Spenser published his first poems.

Pay for Poetry Unlike many other poets of the day, Spenser depended on the payments he received for his work. When the queen's treasurer balked at paying him, he sent this verse to the queen: "I was promised on a time / To have reason for my rhime. / From that time unto this season / I have received nor rhime, nor reason." Spenser was paid immediately.

The Faerie Queene In 1580, Spenser took a position as secretary to the Lord Deputy of Ireland. On a visit to Ireland in 1589, Sir Walter Raleigh (see p. 244) read and was impressed with one of Spenser's unfinished poems. He persuaded Spenser to take the first three books of this long poem to London for publication. That poem became Spenser's greatest work, *The Faerie Queene.*

Written in an intentionally archaic style, *The Faerie Queene* recounts the adventures of several knights, each representing a virtue. This allegory of good and evil, dedicated to Queen Elizabeth I (who appears as the Faerie Queene in the poem), brought Spenser a small pension.

A Poet's Poet Spenser was an innovative poet. In *The Farie Queene,* he created a new type of nine-line stanza, which was later named for him. He also created a sonnet form, known as the Spenserian sonnet, containing a unique structure and rhyme scheme. His sonnet sequence *Amoretti* is unique among such works—it is addressed to the poet's own wife, not some inaccessible, idealized beauty.

Sir Philip Sidne
(1554–1586)

Sir Philip Sidney was a courtier, scholar, poet, and soldier—a true "Renaissan man." He attended both Oxford and Cambridge, an furthered his knowledge b traveling extensively through Europe. He became a favorite in the cou of Queen Elizabeth I.

Groomed for Success Nephew of the earl o Leicester and son of the statesman Sir Henry Sidney, Philip Sidney was certainly well connected. Throughout his life, though, he carried himself with remarkable modesty. His schoolmate and, later, biographer Fulke Grevil remarked on his "staidness of mind, [and] lovely and familiar gravity."

A Brave Soldier Around 1580, Sidney fell ou of favor with the queen when he wrote a letter urging her not to marry the duke of Anjou. Eventually, he regained status with her and wa knighted in 1583. In 1586, during a military engagement against the Spanish Catholics in Holland, Sidney was severely wounded. As he lay on the battlefield, he bravely insisted that th water offered to him be given to another wounded soldier. Twenty-six days later he diec to the great grief of his country.

Pioneering Sonneteer Sidney wrote the firs great sonnet sequence in English, *Astrophel and Stella.* Before Sidney, Sir Thomas Wyatt and others had written excellent sonnets, but Sidney's were the first linked by subject matter and theme. Each sonnet addresses an aspect of Astophel's love for Stella. This sonnet sequenc was inspired by Penelope Devereux (Stella), to whom Sir Philip (Astrophel) had been engagec The engagement was later broken, and Penelop married Lord Rich. Yet, for most readers, Stella name will forever be linked with Astrophel's.

Preview

Connecting to the Literature

Expressing your heart is never easy, yet Elizabethan sonneteers like Spenser and Sidney were able to pour their hearts out in just fourteen lines.

Literary Analysis

The Sonnet

A **sonnet** is a fourteen-line lyric poem with a single theme. Each line in a sonnet is usually in iambic pentameter—five groups of two syllables, each with the accent on the second syllable. Sonnets take definite forms.

- The **Petrarchan sonnet** is divided into an eight-line octave, rhyming *abba abba,* followed by a six-line sestet, rhyming *cdecde.* Often, the octave poses a problem that is answered in the sestet.
- The **Spenserian sonnet** rhymes *abab bcbc cdcd ee.* Note the *abab* rhyme scheme in these lines of Spenser's:

> One day I wrote her name upon the <u>strand,</u>
> But came the waves and washèd it <u>away</u>:
> Again I wrote it with a second <u>hand,</u>
> But came the tide, and made my pains his <u>prey.</u>

In a **sonnet sequence,** sonnets are linked by theme or person addressed. As you read these sonnets, identify their form and how they are linked.

Comparing Literary Works

Notable writers of the Elizabethan Age such as Spenser and Sidney made their mark by writing sonnet sequences. To connect one hundred or more poems without growing dull, they used a basic fictional situation:

- The speaker in the sequence is in love—some sonnets may explain the depth of his love, while others may praise his beloved.
- His love is unfulfilled—poems may dramatize his hopes and disappointments or analyze the nature of love.

As you read, compare Spenser's and Sidney's uses of this basic situation.

Reading Strategy

Paraphrasing

To **paraphrase** a poem, read until you find a complete thought. Then, distinguish between essential and non-essential information. Restate the essential information in your own words. Use a chart like this one to help.

Vocabulary Builder

deign (dān) *v.* condescend; lower oneself (p. 240)

assay (a sā´) *v.* try (p. 242)

devise (di vīz´) *v.* work out or create; plan (p. 242)

wan (wän) *adj.* sickly; pale (p. 243)

languished (laŋ´ gwisht) *adj.* weakened; dulled (p. 243)

balm (bäm) *n.* ointment or other thing that heals or soothes (p. 244)

Poet's Lines

"One day I wrote her name upon the strand,/ But came the waves and washed it away:"

↓

Paraphrase

One day the speaker wrote his beloved's name in the sand at the beach, but the waves came and erased his writing.

---

from *Spenser's Sonnets* / from *Sidney's Sonnets* ■ 239

❷ Literary Analysis
The Sonnet

- Tell students that, as they read "Sonnet 1" and "Sonnet 35," they will focus on the rhythmic and thematic elements of sonnets, 14–line lyric poems with a single theme, often written in iambic pentameter.

- Read the instruction about the sonnet together as a class. Call students' attention to the two common rhyme schemes of Petrarchan and Spenserian sonnets.

- Use the instruction for Comparing Literary Works to compare the sonnets in this selection in terms of their basic fictional situations and their roles in a sonnet sequence.

❸ Reading Strategy
Paraphrasing

- Remind students that when you paraphrase, you restate another person's thoughts or ideas using your own words. Explain to students that paraphrasing can help them clarify ideas they don't understand and help them to better comprehend what they read.

- Then, review a passage from the selections with students and ask them to paraphrase aloud what they have read.

- Give students a copy of **Reading Strategy Graphic Organizer A** in *Graphic Organizer Transparencies*, p. 34. Have students use the chart as they read complicated passages from Spenser's sonnets.

Vocabulary Builder

- Pronounce each vocabulary word for students, and read the definitions as a class. Have students identify any words with which they are already familiar.

Differentiated Instruction   Solutions for All Learners

Support for Special Needs Students
Have students complete the **Preview** and **Build Skills** pages for these selections in the *Reader's Notebook: Adapted Version.* These pages provide a selection summary, an abbreviated presentation of the reading and literary skills, and the graphic organizer on the **Build Skills** page in the student book.

Support for Less Proficient Readers
Have students complete the **Preview** and **Build Skills** pages for these selections in the *Reader's Notebook.* These pages provide a selection summary, an abbreviated presentation of the reading and literary skills, and the graphic organizer on the **Build Skills** page in the student book.

Support for English Learners
Have students complete the **Preview** and **Build Skills** pages for these selections in the *Reader's Notebook: English Learner's Version.* These pages provide a selection summary, an abbreviated presentation of the skills, additional contextual vocabulary, and the graphic organizer on the **Build Skills** page in the student book.

❶ About the Selections

The three sonnets by Edmund Spenser in this section come from a longer work—the sonnet sequence *Amoretti,* Italian for "little love poems." The sonnet sequence is unique in that it is addressed to the poet's wife, Elizabeth Boyle, not to some distant, unattainable, or unrequited love.

In Spenser's sonnets, his love inspires the speaker's poetry (Sonnet 1) and becomes the sole subject of her gaze (Sonnet 35). However, the poet's triumph will be to immortalize her in verse (Sonnet 75).

❷ Reading Strategy
Paraphrasing

• Remind students that when you paraphrase, you restate a passage in your own words to better understand the meaning. Tell students that changing the word order may be helpful when paraphrasing.

• Read the bracketed lines out loud, first for the beauty of the verse, then more slowly to accentuate the meter. Point out that the *-ed* at the end of a word was pronounced as a separate syllable whenever it was needed for the poem's meter. So in *derived, blessed,* and *lacked,* there is an extra syllable that we would not normally hear today.

• **Ask** students to paraphrase lines 9–12.
Possible response: My rhymes will be happy when they are seen by and see my beloved, who, like the Muses, inspires poetry.

---

❶ # *Sonnet 1*
Edmund Spenser

Background Elizabethans believed that they lived in an orderly world based on a grand universal design. For example, they imagined that the heavens were so perfectly balanced that the planets and stars created a glorious music, which they called the "music of the spheres." It is hardly surprising that the sonnet, a perfectly designed little poem, became wildly popular. In many sonnets, lovers are idealized and compared to other "perfect" things, such as the sun and stars.

Happy ye leaves when as those lily hands,
Which hold my life in their dead doing[1] might,
Shall handle you and hold in love's soft bands,
Like captives trembling at the victor's sight,
5 And happy lines, on which with starry light,
Those lamping[2] eyes will <u>deign</u> sometimes to look
And read the sorrows of my dying spright,[3]
Written with tears in heart's close[4] bleeding book.
And happy rhymes bathed in the sacred brook
 10 Of Helicon[5] whence she derived is,
When ye behold that angel's blessed look,
My soul's long lacked food, my heaven's bliss.
Leaves, lines, and rhymes, seek her to please alone,
Whom if ye please, I care for other none.

Vocabulary Builder
deign (dān) *v.* condescend; lower oneself

1. **doing** killing.
2. **lamping** flashing.
3. **spright** spirit.
4. **close** secret.
5. **sacred . . . Helicon** In Greek mythology, the Helicon mountains were the home of the Muses, goddesses of the arts, and the site of the Hippocrene, the fountain from which the waters of poetic inspiration flowed.

Differentiated Instruction Solutions for All Learners

Accessibility at a Glance

	Sonnet 1	Sonnet 35	Sonnet 75	Sonnet 31	Sonnet 39
Context	Elizabethan	Elizabethan	Elizabethan	Elizabethan	Elizabethan
Language	Accessible (Footnotes on vocabulary)	Accessible (Footnotes on vocabulary)	Complex syntax	Poetic diction	Poetic diction
Concept Level	Accessible (love)	Accessible (love)	Accessible (love)	Accessible (love)	Accessible (love)
Literary Merit	Classic	Classic	Classic	Classic	Classic
Lexile	NP	NP	NP	NP	NP
Overall Rating	More challenging	More challenging	More challenging	More accessible	More accessible

Sonnet 35

Edmund Spenser

4

My hungry eyes through greedy covetize,[1]
Still[2] to behold the object of their pain,
With no contentment can themselves suffice:
But having pine[3] and having not complain.
5 For lacking it they cannot life sustain,
And having it they gaze on it the more:
In their amazement like Narcissus[4] vain
Whose eyes him starved: so plenty makes me poor.
Yet are mine eyes so fillèd with the store
10 Of that fair sight, that nothing else they brook,
But loathe the things which they did like before,
And can no more endure on them to look.
All this world's glory seemeth vain to me,
And all their shows but shadows, saving she.

---

1. **covetize** *v.* excessive desire.
2. **Still** *adv.* always.
3. **pine** *v.* yearn.
4. **Narcissus** in Greek mythology, a youth who fell in love with his own reflection in a pool, wasted away with yearning, and was changed after his death into the narcissus flower.

❸ ▼ **Critical Viewing**
How does the sight of the distant horizon, as in this photograph, suggest the "desire" eyes may have to see, referred to in Sonnet 35? **[Speculate]**

❺ ✔ **Reading Check**
What does the speaker long for, even though it causes him pain?

Spenser's Sonnet 35 241

Differentiated
Instruction   Solutions for All Learners

Enrichment for Advanced Readers
Suggest that students read additional works by Edmund Spenser. Provide students with copies of *The Faerie Queene, Amoretti, Epithalamion, The Shepheardes Calender, Astrophel and Stella, The Defence of Poesie,* and *Arcadia.* You may also wish to use **Authors In Depth,** *The British Tradition,* which contains the following selections:
• "January" from *The Shepheardes Calender*
• Sonnets 9, 26, 30, 34, and 37 from *Amoretti*
• "The Redcross Knight and the Old Dragon" from *The Faerie Queene*

After students have read additional works by Spenser, have them form discussion groups in which they compare and contrast the selections they have read. Suggest criteria for comparison, such as theme, language, sentiment, style, or ideas. To extend that activity, have volunteers present to the class brief oral reports on their favorite Spenser selections.

❸ **Critical Viewing**
Possible responses: The distant horizon of the photograph suggests the "desire" eyes may have to see because you can't really see what is at the horizon, though you may gaze long and hard.

❹ **Literary Analysis**
The Sonnet

▶ **Reteach** Remind students that a sonnet has 14 lines. Point out that, because this sonnet is by Edmund Spenser, it's a safe guess that it's a Spenserian sonnet. However, have students compare the line endings in this sonnet with the rhyme scheme of a Spenserian sonnet (*abab bcbc cdcdee*) to confirm this pattern.

• Explain that poets often utilize strict forms of poetry because these forms force them to be extremely precise with their word choice and images.

• Have students read the last line of Sonnet 35; then have them turn to Sonnet 75 and look at the last line. What literary technique does Spenser use to make the last line of each sonnet memorable?
Answer: Spenser uses alliteration (the repetition of initial sounds in two or more words used near each other) to make the last line of these two sonnets memorable.

• Explain that poetry was often read aloud as a form of entertainment, so sound techniques, such as alliteration, were useful and added to the musical quality created by the meter.

❺ **Reading Check**
Answer: The speaker longs for the sight of his beloved.

241

1. **Possible response:** Students may find Sonnet 75 the most enjoyable because the dialogue is realistic and fresh.

2. (a) The speaker addresses the leaves (pages of a book), lines, and rhymes. (b) The speaker hopes their combined effect will please the lady who beholds them.

3. (a) The speaker's eyes desire to gaze on his love. (b) Constant desire to behold his beloved produces a state of pain and grief in the speaker.

4. (a) The lady says the speaker's efforts are futile because she will eventually die and be forgotten. (b) The speaker believes that his lines of poetry will forever capture or immortalize his love. (c) The poem claims that verse has the power to make immortal the relationship between the speaker and his beloved.

5. In Sonnet 1, the speaker is in awe of his love; in Sonnet 35, the speaker has become thoroughly in love with the woman and can't bear to gaze upon anyone else; in Sonnet 75, the speaker and the woman are on more equal terms.

6. **Possible responses:** No, the speakers are not overreacting to their situations; they are convinced of the gravity of their feelings for the women they love. Yes, the speakers are overreacting to their situations; they are driven by their emotions and cannot recognize that their feelings are causing them to be irrational.

Go Online
Author Link For additional information about Edmund Spenser, have students type in the Web Code, then select S from the alphabet, and then select Edmund Spenser.

Sonnet 75
Edmund Spenser

One day I wrote her name upon the strand,[1]
But came the waves and washèd it away:
Again I wrote it with a second hand,
But came the tide, and made my pains his prey.
5   "Vain man," said she, "that dost in vain <u>assay</u>,
A mortal thing so to immortalize,
For I myself shall like to this decay,
And eek[2] my name be wipèd out likewise."
"Not so," quod[3] I, "let baser things <u>devise</u>
10 To die in dust, but you shall live by fame:
My verse your virtues rare shall eternize,
And in the heavens write your glorious name.
Where whenas death shall all the world subdue,
Our love shall live, and later life renew."

1. **strand** beach.
2. **eek** also.
3. **quod** said.

Vocabulary Builder
assay (a sā´) v. try
devise (di vīz´) v. work out or create; plan

Critical Reading

1. **Respond:** Which of Spenser's sonnets do you like the best? Why?

2. **(a) Recall:** In Sonnet 1, what are the three things the speaker addresses? **(b) Interpret:** What does the speaker hope their combined effect will be on the lady?

3. **(a) Recall:** In Sonnet 35, what do the speaker's eyes desire? **(b) Interpret:** Describe the state that desire produces in him.

4. **(a) Interpret:** In Sonnet 75, why does the lady say the speaker's efforts are futile? **(b) Summarize:** Summarize the speaker's response. **(c) Draw Conclusions:** What connection does the poem make between immortality and poetry?

5. **Compare and Contrast:** Compare and contrast the relationship between the speaker and his love in each of the sonnets.

6. **Take a Position:** Are these speakers overreacting to their situations? Explain.

Go Online
Author Link
For: More about Edmund Spenser
Visit: www.PHSchool.com
Web Code: ese-9202

Enrichment

Dreams

Throughout history, sleep and dreams have been a source of mystery and debate. Explanations for this human phenomenon have ranged from planetary influences to the actions of spiritual and fanciful creatures. Opinions on the meaning of dreams have also varied greatly.

In the late nineteenth century, the psychoanalyst Sigmund Freud proposed that one's dreams revealed important information about that individual. However, psychologists differ strongly on the issue, some believing that dreams hold meaning, others insisting that they are meaningless.

It has been only recently that sleeping and dreaming have been subjected to controlled, scientific study under laboratory conditions.

$\mathscr{S}$onnet 31

6

Sir Philip Sidney

With how sad steps, O Moon, thou climb'st the skies!
How silently, and with how <u>wan</u> a face!
What, may it be that even in heavenly place
That busy archer[1] his sharp arrows tries?
5　Sure, if that long-with-love-acquainted eyes
Can judge of love, thou feel'st a lover's case.
7 | I read it in thy looks, thy <u>languished</u> grace,
To me, that feel the like, thy state descries.[2]
Then even of fellowship, O Moon, tell me
10　Is constant love deemed there but want of wit?[3]
Are beauties there as proud as here they be?
Do they above love to be loved, and yet
Those lovers scorn whom that love doth possess?
Do they call virtue there ungratefulness?

1. **busy archer** Cupid, the Roman god of love.
2. **descries** reveals.
3. **wit** intelligence.

Vocabulary Builder

wan (wän) *adj.* sickly; pale

languished (laŋ´ gwisht)
adj. weakened; dulled

8 ✓ **Reading Check**

What does the speaker
claim he and the moon
have in common?

▲ **Critical Viewing** Which details of this photograph of the moon convey the
mood of Sonnet 31? **[Evaluate]**

Sidney's Sonnet 31 ■ 243

6 About the Selections

The sonnet cycle from which these sonnets by Sir Philip Sidney come is titled *Astrophel and Stella*. Because it is known that this sequence of one hundred and eight sonnets plus eleven songs deals with Sidney's love for Penelope Devereaux, we know that Astrophel represents Sidney and Stella represents Devereaux.

These sonnets offer reflections on the course of Astrophel's love. In Sonnet 31, a frustrated lover sees his own lovesickness mirrored in the pale moon, and in Sonnet 39, he seeks in sleep a release from his suffering.

7 Vocabulary Builder
Related Words: Forms of *Languished*

- Call students' attention to the word *languished* and its definition. Tell students that *languished* is a past tense of the verb *languish*, which means "to become weak or weary."

- Write *languorous* and *languid* on the board, and ask students if they know the meanings. If they do, have them use the words in sentences.

- If students are not familiar with the words, have them predict meanings, then have them look up the words in a dictionary.

8 Reading Check

Answer: The speaker claims he and the moon are both lovesick.

9 Critical Viewing

Possible responses: Most students will say that the paleness of the moon and calmness of the sea and the serene water effectively convey the quiet, contemplative, sad mood of the poem.

Differentiated
Instruction   Solutions for All Learners

Support for Special Needs Students
Pick a sonnet and write it on the board in sentences, rather than in sonnet format. Then, suggest substitutes for words students might not understand. Write the substitutes above the words they define/replace. Show students where changing word order might help. Discuss the meaning of altered sentences, working as a group on a paraphrase. Once each sentence is understood, reassemble the ideas of the whole sonnet for students, so they understand what is being said.

Enrichment for Gifted/Talented Students
Ask students to think of a love story they've read. Challenge them to write a sonnet about the emotions, dreams, and thoughts of one of the individuals in the story they've selected. Remind students to keep the sonnet to 14 lines, to pick an appropriate rhyme scheme, and to use consistent meter.

Sonnet 39
Sir Philip Sidney

Come sleep! O sleep, the certain knot of peace,
The baiting place[1] of wit, the <u>balm</u> of woe,
The poor man's wealth, the prisoner's release,
The indifferent[2] judge between the high and low;
5   With shield of proof[3] shield me from out the prease[4]
Of those fierce darts Despair at me doth throw:
O make in me those civil wars to cease;
I will good tribute pay, if thou do so.
Take thou of me smooth pillows, sweetest bed,
10   A chamber deaf to noise, and blind to light,
A rose garland, and a weary head:
And if these things, as being thine by right,
Move not thy heavy grace, thou shalt in me,
Livelier than elsewhere, Stella's image see.

---

1. **baiting place** place for refreshment.
2. **indifferent** impartial.
3. **proof** proven strength.
4. **prease** crowd.

Literary Analysis
The Sonnet How does the
rhyme scheme of lines 1–8
make this sonnet differen
from a typical Spenserian
or Petrarchan sonnet?

Critical Reading

1. **Respond:** Do you sympathize with the speakers? Explain.
2. **(a) Recall:** In Sonnet 31, how does the moon appear to the speaker?
   (b) Infer: To what does the speaker attribute the moon's mood?
   (c) Analyze: How does the speaker reveal his own situation by addressing the moon?
3. **(a) Recall:** What benefits does the speaker attribute to sleep in lines 1–4 of Sonnet 39? **(b) Recall:** What "reward" does he promise sleep in lines 13–14? **(c) Interpret:** Judging from this "reward," why does he crave sleep?
4. **Draw Conclusions:** What conclusion can you draw about each speaker's relationship with his lady?
5. **Generalize:** Do you think both sonnets express moods that people in love always experience? Explain.

244 ■ *Celebrating Humanity (1485–1625)*

Go Online
Author Link
For: More about
Sir Philip Sidney
Visit: www.PHSchool.com
Web Code: ese-9203

Go Online
Author Link For additional information about Sir
Philip Sidney, have students type in
the Web Code, then select S from the alphabet, and
then select Sir Philip Sidney.

---

❿ Literary Analysis
The Sonnet

- **Ask** students the Literary Analysis question: How does the rhyme scheme of lines 1–8 make this sonnet different from a typical Spenserian or Petrarchan sonnet?
  Answer: The rhyme scheme Sidney uses is *abab abab,* rather than the Spenserian *abab bcbc* or the Petrarchan *abba abba.*

▶ **Monitor Progress: Ask** students to identify the rhyme scheme of the last six lines. Then, have them identify which of the two forms this sonnet is more like.
  Answer: The rhyme scheme is *cdcdee,* so this sonnet is more like a Spenserian sonnet.

▶ **Reteach:** Remind students that Petrarchan sonnets have a rhyme scheme of *abba abba cdecde,* while Spenserian sonnets have a rhyme scheme of *abab bcbc cdcdee.*

ASSESS
Answers

1. **Possible response:** Students may sympathize because most people have some experience of love's difficulties.

2. (a) The moon appears sad. (b) The speaker thinks that the moon is lovesick. (c) The speaker reveals his own situation by claiming that the moon looks as pale as he feels, prompting his questions—all of which tell something of his own experience.

3. (a) Sleep assures one of peace; it restores the keen mind; it heals sorrows; it is the poor man's wealth; it allows the prisoner to wander far and wide in his dreams; and it treats all people the same. (b) The speaker promises sleep the reward of seeing Stella's image in the speaker's dreams. (c) The speaker craves sleep because he'll dream of Stella.

4. It appears that the object of love is unattainable.

5. **Possible responses:** Students may say the sonnets express timeless emotional reactions that people commonly feel when in love.

244

Apply the Skills

from *Spenser's Sonnets* • from *Sidney's Sonnets*

Literary Analysis

The Sonnet

1. Reread Sidney's Sonnets 31 and 39, and analyze their rhyme schemes. Do these **sonnets** more closely follow the **Spenserian** or the **Petrarchan** form? Explain.

2. Review Spenser's three sonnets. Then, explain what poets can achieve in a **sonnet sequence** that they cannot in individual poems. Consider such factors as shifting moods and developing characters.

3. Using a chart like the one here, compare and contrast one of Sidney's sonnets with one of Spenser's.

Petrarchan/ Spenserian?	Speaker's Situation	Addressed to . . .	Types of Images	Speaker's Conclusion

Comparing Literary Works

4. **(a)** Compare the person or thing addressed in each of the sonnets. **(b)** Explain how the basic **sonnet sequence** situation justifies or motivates each choice of addressee.

5. **(a)** Compare the dominant purpose of each sonnet—to express hope, to persuade, to complain, and so on. **(b)** Explain how the sonnet sequence situation justifies or motivates each purpose.

6. Explain how, in each sonnet, the writer goes beyond the basic sonnet situation to give a general insight into the nature of love or life.

Reading Strategy

Paraphrasing

7. Reread the octave of Sidney's Sonnet 39. **(a)** Write a **paraphrase** of lines 1–4. **(b)** Paraphrase lines 5–8. **(c)** Which detail in Sonnet 39 is nonessential? Why?

8. Reread and then paraphrase the sestet of Sonnet 39. You may break the sestet into smaller sections for paraphrasing.

Extend Understanding

9. **Cultural Connection:** Renaissance poets compared their beloveds to "perfect" things in nature or to timeless figures from mythology. To what "perfect" things do songwriters compare their loves today?

QuickReview

The **sonnet** is a fourteen-line lyric poem with a single theme.

A **sonnet sequence** is a group of sonnets linked by theme, subject, or the person addressed.

The **Spenserian sonnet** has the following rhyme scheme: *abab bcbc cdcd ee.*

The **Petrarchan sonnet** has the following rhyme scheme: *abba abba cdecde.*

The basic **sonnet sequence** situation involves the speaker's unfulfilled love for his beloved.

To **paraphrase**, restate an author's ideas in your own words.

Go Online
Assessment

For: Self-test
Visit: www.PHSchool.com
Web Code: esa-6202

from *Spenser's Sonnets* / from *Sidney's Sonnets* ■ 245

Go Online
Assessment
Students may use the **Self-test** to prepare for **Selection Test A** or **Selection Test B.**

245

❶ Vocabulary Lesson
Related Words

1. languor
2. languid
3. languished

Vocabulary Builder

Possible response: The young woman *languished* because of neglect. She looked *wan* and sighed frequently. She felt that just seeing her beloved would be a *balm* to her spirits, and she began to *devise* all sorts of plans. She would *assay* to see him again. She would not *deign* to call him or e-mail him, preferring for him to contact her.

Spelling Strategy

1. maybe   3. neighbor
2. reindeer   4. payment

❷ Grammar and Style Lesson

1. Elizabeth   4. Despair
2. Narcissus   5. Stella's
3. Moon

Writing Application

Answer: After staring at the moon for a while, Romeo the cat howled as though his heart were broken. The moon dimmed as though she too felt Romeo's pain. Softly, Luna's whispering tones floated down through the night air to Cupid's wounded victim. "Let Morpheus soothe you, and when you awaken, all will be well."

𝒲𝒢 **Writing and Grammar, Diamond Level**

Students will find further instruction and practice on capitalization of proper nouns in Chapter 26.

Build Language Skills

❶ Vocabulary Lesson

Related Words: Forms of *languished*

Languished is the past participle of the verb *languish,* which means "to become weak." Other forms of this word are *languid,* an adjective that means "drooping" or "weak," and the noun *languor,* meaning "weakness." Choose from these related words to complete each sentence below.

1. His __?__ was caused by overexertion.
2. The worker's movements were __?__ at the end of the day.
3. Everyone __?__ in the heat.

Vocabulary Builder: Context

Write a paragraph describing the plight of a longing lover using forms of all the words on the vocabulary list on page 239.

Spelling Strategy

The long *a* sound can be spelled in several different ways. Two examples are *ei* as in *deign* and *ay* as in *assay.* In your notebook, complete the spelling of the long *a* sound in each word.

1. m__be   3. n__ghbor
2. r__ndeer   4. p__ment

❷ Grammar and Style Lesson

Capitalization of Proper Nouns

A **proper noun** is the name of a specific person, place, or thing. It begins with a capital letter. In addition to capitalizing proper nouns, poets also capitalize some common nouns when referring to objects and ideas as if they were specific human beings. Note the following examples from Spenser's Sonnet 1 and Sidney's Sonnet 31.

> **Proper Noun:** And happy rhymes bathed in the sacred brook Of <u>Helicon</u> whence she derived is, . . .
>
> **Direct Address:** With how sad steps, O <u>Moon</u>, thou climb'st the skies!

In the second example, Sidney capitalizes *moon,* ordinarily an uncapitalized common noun, because he is addressing the moon as if it were a person.

𝒲𝒢 *Prentice Hall Writing and Grammar Connection: Chapter 26*

Practice Identify the proper noun in each item.

1. Both poets had met Elizabeth.
2. . . . In their amazement like Narcissus vain . . .
3. Then even of fellowship, O Moon, tell me. . . .
4. . . . Of those fierce darts Despair at me doth throw: . . .
5. . . . thou shalt in me, / Livelier than elsewhere, Stella's image see.

Writing Application Rewrite the following sentences, capitalizing the proper nouns.

After staring at the moon for a while, romeo the cat howled as though his heart were broken. The moon dimmed as though she too felt romeo's pain. Softly, luna's whispering tones floated down through the night air to cupid's wounded victim. "Let morpheus soothe you, and when you awaken, all will be well."

Assessment Practice

Fact and Opinion   (For more practice, see *Standardized Test Preparation Workbook,* p. 8.)

Many tests require students to distinguish between fact and opinion. Use the following sample item to show students how to distinguish fact from opinion.

Which of the following lines from Spenser's Sonnet 75 is a statement of opinion?

  A One day I wrote her name upon the strand.

  B But came the waves and washed it away.

  C My verse your virtues rare shall eternize.

  D For I myself shall like to this decay.

Lead students to recognize that the phrase "virtues rare" is the speaker's personal opinion. Responses A, C, and D are events; therefore, the correct answer is C.

Writing Lesson

Introduction to a Sonnet Sequence

Write an introduction to Spenser's or Sidney's sonnet sequence. In addition to an insight to interest readers, include a summary of two of the poems from the sequence.

Prewriting   Choose one of the authors, and do background research on his sequence. Then, choose two poems from the sequence. Divide each into parts, following the meaning. Jot down a paraphrase of each section.

Model: Taking Notes for a Summary

SECTION	LINES	SUMMARY
Beginning	1–4	The man twice writes his love's name in the sand, but the waves wash it away.
Middle	5–8	
	9–12	
End	13–14	

This chart organizes Spenser's Sonnet 75 into three sections: beginning, middle, and end, with space to summarize each part.

Drafting   Introduce the sonnet sequence, explaining when it was written and the variety of poems it contains. Then, summarize the two sonnets, clearly noting the beginning, middle, and end of each. Indicate connections with transitions such as *as a result* and *however.*

Revising   Review your introduction. Draw a square at points in your draft where ideas shift. Check the square when you have used a transition to indicate the connection between ideas. Otherwise, consider adding transitions to help readers follow the sequence of ideas.

W_G *Prentice Hall Writing and Grammar Connection: Chapter 14, Section 2*

Extend Your Learning

Listening and Speaking With a small group, prepare Sonnet 75 as a **scene with dialogue.**

1. Rewrite the poem as a dialogue.
2. Appoint a director, who should suggest effective ways to deliver lines.
3. Rehearse, choosing ways to memorize until you have command of lines and the director is satisfied.

Present your scene to the class. **[Group Activity]**

Research and Technology Do further research on the lives and works of Spenser and Sidney, and write a **biographical report** comparing the two and their contributions to literature. Include timelines of their lives and important events of their era.

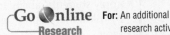
Go Online
Research
For: An additional research activity
Visit: www.PHSchool.com
Web Code: esd-7201

Assessment Resources

The following resources can be used to assess students' knowledge and skills.

Unit 2 Resources
   Selection Test A, pp. 18–20
   Selection Test B, pp. 21–23

General Resources
   Rubrics for Response to Literature, pp. 65–66
   Rubric for Peer Assessment: Dramatic Performance, p. 131

Go Online
Assessment
Students may use the **Self-test** to prepare for **Selection Test A** or **Selection Test B.**

---

❸ Writing Lesson

You may use this Writing Lesson as timed-writing practice, or you may allow students to develop the essay as a writing assignment over several days.

- Review with students their understanding of a sonnet sequence as a group of sonnets linked by theme, subject, or the person addressed. Remind them that sonnets can be divided into octaves and sestets, or quatrains and couplets, and that their arrangement may follow Spenserian or Petrarchan rhythmic conventions.

- Explain to students they should summarize a sonnet according to its beginning, middle, and end.

- Tell students that their introductions to works of literature need to include basic factual information, such as when the work was written, by whom, and what the work contains.

- Give students the **Support for Writing Lesson**, p. 15, in *Unit 2 Resources* to guide them in choosing their author and drafting their introductions and summaries.

- Use the rubrics for Response to Literature, pp. 65–66 in *General Resources.*

❹ Research and Technology

- Have interested students gather biographical and critical materials related to Sidney and Spenser and their work.

- Explain to students that in their biographical report they should compare the poets and their individual contributions to literature.

- Ask students to include timelines of the poets' lives that mark important events of their era.

- The **Support for Extend Your Learning** page (*Unit 2 Resources*, p. 16) provides guided note-taking opportunities to help students complete the Extend Your Learning activities.

- Provide students with the Peer Assessment rubric for Dramatic Performance, p. 131 in *General Resources.*

Go Online
Research
Have students type in the Web Code for another research activity.

Meeting Your Standards

Students will

1. **analyze and respond to literary elements.**
   - Literary Analysis: Pastoral

2. **read, comprehend, analyze, and critique poetry.**
   - Reading Strategy: Identifying with the Speaker of a Poem
   - Reading Check questions
   - Apply the Skills questions

3. **develop vocabulary.**
   - Vocabulary Lesson: Word origins: *wither*

4. **understand and apply written and oral language conventions.**
   - Spelling Strategy
   - Grammar and Style Lesson: Adjective and Adverb Phrases

5. **develop writing proficiency.**
   - Writing Lesson: Compare-and-Contrast Essay

6. **develop appropriate research strategies.**
   - Extend Your Learning: Display Poster

7. **understand and apply listening and speaking strategies.**
   - Extend Your Learning: Oral Interpretation

Block Scheduling: Use one 90-minute class period to preteach the skills and have students read the selection. Use a second 90-minute class period to assess students' mastery of skills, extend their learning, and monitor their progress.

Homework Suggestions

Following are possibilities for homework assignments:

- Support pages from *Unit 2 Resources:*
  - **Literary Analysis**
  - **Reading Strategy**
  - **Vocabulary Builder**
  - **Grammar and Style**

- An Extend Your Learning project and the Writing Lesson for this selection group may be completed over several days.

Step-by-Step Teaching Guide	Pacing Guide
PRETEACH	
• Administer Vocabulary and Reading Warm-ups as necessary.	5 min.
• Engage students' interest with the motivation activity.	5 min.
• Read and discuss author and background features. **FT**	10 min.
• Introduce the Literary Analysis Skill: Pastoral. **FT**	5 min.
• Introduce the Reading Strategy: Identifying With the Speaker of a Poem. **FT**	10 min
• Prepare students to read by teaching the selection vocabulary. **FT**	
TEACH	
• Informally monitor comprehension while students read independently or in groups. **FT**	30 min.
• Monitor students' comprehension with the Reading Check notes.	as students read
• Reinforce vocabulary with Vocabulary Builder notes.	as students read
• Develop students' understanding of pastorals with the Literary Analysis annotations. **FT**	5 min.
• Develop students' ability to identify with the speaker in a poem with the Reading Strategy annotations. **FT**	5 min.
ASSESS/EXTEND	
• Assess students' comprehension and mastery of the Literary Analysis and Reading Strategy by having them answer the Apply the Skills questions. **FT**	15 min.
• Have students complete the Vocabulary Lesson and the Grammar and Style Lesson. **FT**	15 min.
• Apply students' ability to discern writer's viewpoints by using the Writing Lesson. **FT**	45 min. or homework
• Apply students' understanding by using one or more of the Extend Your Learning activities.	20–90 min. or homework
• Administer Selection Test A or Selection Test B. **FT**	15 min.

Resources

Choosing Resources for Differentiated Instruction

[**L1**] Special Needs Students

[**L2**] Below-Level Students

[**L3**] All Students

[**L4**] Advanced Students

[**EL**] English Learners

For Vocabulary and Reading Warm-ups and for Selection Tests, **A** signifies "less challenging" and **B** "more challenging." For Graphic Organizer transparencies, **A** signifies "not filled in" and **B** "filled in."

FT Fast Track Instruction: To move the lesson more quickly, use the strategies and activities identified with **FT**.

Scaffolding for Less Proficient and Advanced Students

The leveled Critical Thinking questions after selections progress in the levels of thinking required to answer them. To address the needs of your different students, you may use the (a) level questions for your less proficient students and the (b) level questions with your on-level and advanced students. The occasional (c) level questions are appropriate for your advanced students.

PRENTICE HALL
TeacherEXPRESS™ Use this complete
Plan · Teach · Assess suite of powerful
teaching tools to make lesson planning and testing quicker and easier.

PRENTICE HALL
StudentEXPRESS™ Use the interac-
Learn · Study · Succeed tive textbook
(online and on CD-ROM) to make selections and activities come alive with audio and video support and interactive questions.

Go Online **For:** Information about Lexiles
Professional **Visit:** www.PHSchool.com
Development **Web Code:** eue-1111

Motivation

These poems by Marlowe and Raleigh are an exchange between a shepherd and his love. To stimulate interest, have students discuss what they would offer to win over the person they love. Tell students that in the poems they are about to read they will see what one speaker offers to win his love. While reading, have them consider if the shepherd's offers would win their love.

❶ Background
More About the Authors

Christopher Marlowe was born in Canterbury in 1564, the same year as William Shakespeare. He received his bachelor's and master's degrees from Corpus Christi College in Cambridge. School records show that his numerous absences nearly prevented him from earning a degree.

Sir Walter Raleigh, an adventurer and sailor, was affiliated with a poetic group called the "School of Night." This group, which included Christopher Marlowe, gained notoriety for being atheists because of their critical interpretation of Scripture. In 1595, Raleigh and Laurence Kemys journeyed to find the city of El Dorado. He published a book on his findings from their excursion called *Discovery of Guiana*.

Build Skills | *Poems*

❶ The Passionate Shepherd to His Love • The Nymph's Reply to the Shepherd

Christopher Marlowe
(1564–1593)

Killed before the age of thirty, Christopher Marlowe nonetheless managed to achieve renown as a brilliant playwright and poet. He spent his college days writing plays and serving as a government agent.

A Pioneer in Drama *Tamburlaine*, Marlowe's first drama, dazzled the public with its dynamic characterization of the tyrant-hero. All of Marlowe's subsequent plays may be seen as variations on a single theme: the larger-than-life hero who "overreaches," seeking to dominate everything around him. The most famous example is the protagonist in *Doctor Faustus*, who thirsts for supreme knowledge and sells his soul to the devil. Marlowe matched the grandeur of his heroes with the grandeur of language, forging blank verse into a powerfully expressive medium for the first time in English drama.

A Life of Intrigue Marlowe has been described as a scoundrel, a ladies' man, and a hothead. By all accounts, his personal magnetism attracted both friends and enemies. When the court of Queen Elizabeth I wrote a letter implying that Marlowe had performed important government services, rumors flew about that he was a spy.

A Violent Death Marlowe was knifed to death in a tavern brawl in 1593. To this day, scholars question whether his death was really caused by his drunken refusal to pay his bill or whether he was murdered because of his undercover activities.

Sir Walter Raleigh
(1554?–1618)

Sir Walter Raleigh is famed for having been a courtier, a navigator, a poet, and a historian.

A Charmed Life The half-brother of a famous sailor and an explorer, Raleigh began to satisfy his taste for adventure early in life, when he volunteered as a teenager for army service in France. A favorite of Queen Elizabeth I, he was given estates and prestigious appointments. In 1584, he set up a colony on Roanoke Island, Virginia.

Disaster When it was discovered that Raleigh had been secretly married to one of the queen's maids of honor, he and his wife were imprisoned in the Tower of London for a time but then released. Following the queen's death in 1603, Raleigh was accused of conspiring against King James I and was imprisoned again in the Tower, where he remained for thirteen years. He was eventually released to seek out gold along the Orinoco River in Venezuela. Despite a royal command not to engage in battle with Spain, Raleigh's fleet entered Spanish territory. In the ensuing fight, Raleigh lost his son and was forced to return to England. There, Raleigh was executed for disobeying the king's orders.

Literary Achievements Raleigh was a friend of some of the leading poets of his age, including Sir Philip Sydney and Edmund Spenser. Like them, he wrote elegant verse, rich in vivid imagery and classical allusions. Among Raleigh's numerous prose works is an ambitious book entitled *The History of the World* (1614), composed while he was in prison.

Preview

Connecting to the Literature

The subjects of nature and love often bring contradictory images to mind. Some people think of roses and happiness, others of ice and heartbreak. These two poems, one inspired by the other, present both perspectives.

Literary Analysis

Pastoral

A **pastoral** work celebrates the pleasures of simple life in the country. In pastoral poems, some of the usual conventions include a shepherd, who addresses or describes a shepherdess with whom he is in love, and an idealized world of nature. Though pastoral poems seem to be about a carefree, country existence, such works are often written by sophisticated artists. Their literature allows urban readers to experience what they imagine to be the free and untroubled life of ordinary people.

- Look for details in "The Passionate Shepherd to His Love" that idealize the natural world.
- Identify details in "The Nymph's Reply to the Shepherd" that comment critically on the idealized landscape in Marlowe's poem.

Comparing Literary Works

In these poems, Marlowe and Raleigh raise a number of **common themes** that occur so often in literature as to have a claim of being universal. One of these themes is the link between love and the delights of youth and nature. Another is the relationship of love to time. From one perspective, time stops for lovers. From another point of view, though, time and change are love's enemy, since youth gives way to age. This sober thought often prompts, in turn, the theme of *carpe diem,* or "seize the day." Note the variations of these common themes as you read each poem.

Reading Strategy

Identifying With the Speaker of a Poem

When you **identify with the speaker of a poem,** you put yourself in the speaker's place to understand his or her feelings and goals. Reconstructing these emotions can help you determine a poem's theme. As you read these poems, fill in a chart like the one shown to help you identify with each speaker.

Vocabulary Builder

melodious (mə lō′ dē əs) *adj.* sweet-sounding; tuneful (p. 250)

madrigals (ma′ dri gəls) *n.* short love poems set to music (p. 250)

move (mo͞ov) *v.* persuade or impel (p. 250)

reckoning (rek′ ən iŋ) *n.* accounting (p. 251)

wither (wi*th*′ ər) *v.* fade or waste away (p. 252)

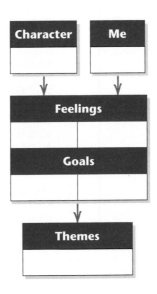

The Passionate Shepherd to His Love / The Nymph's Reply to the Shepherd ■ 249

---

❷ **Literary Analysis**
Pastoral

- As students read the Literary Analysis instruction, emphasize that pastoral poetry—with its farmland or pastureland settings—idealizes nature as gentle and tamed.

- Make sure that students understand that Marlowe's poem embraces pastoral conventions, and Raleigh's poem calls these conventions into question.

- Encourage students to use a Venn diagram or other graphic organizer as they read to compare and contrast Marlowe and Raleigh's attitudes toward the pastoral.

❸ **Reading Strategy**
Identifying With the Speaker of a Poem

- Tell students that in addition to considering a speaker's feelings and goals, a reader must consider the speaker's point of view and attitude toward the subject matter.

- Give students a copy of **Reading Strategy Graphic Organizer A** in *Graphic Organizer Transparencies,* p. 38, to use as they read the poems. Help students understand that they will use the chart to draw parallels between their own feelings and goals and the speaker's.

Vocabulary Builder

- Pronounce each vocabulary word for students, and read the definitions as a class. Have students identify any words with which they are already familiar.

Differentiated Instruction   Solutions for All Learners

Support for Special Needs Students
Have students read the adapted version of these selections in the *Reader's Notebook: Adapted Version.* This version provides basic-level instruction in an interactive format with questions and write-on lines. Completing these pages will prepare students to read the selection in the Student Edition.

Support for Less Proficient Readers
Have students read these selections in the *Reader's Notebook.* This version provides basic-level instruction in an interactive format with questions and write-on lines. After students finish the selection in the *Reader's Notebook,* have them complete the questions and activities in the Student Edition.

Support for English Learners
Have students read these selections in the *Reader's Notebook: English Learner's Version.* This version provides basic-level instruction in an interactive format with questions and write-on lines. Completing these pages will prepare students to read the selection in the Student Edition.

❶ About the Selections

"The Passionate Shepherd to His Love" is perhaps one of the world's best-known examples of pastoral poetry. It has a lyric that celebrates the beauty and pleasures of country life. The poem also makes use of a number of traditional conventions: The speaker is a shepherd addressing a shepherdess with whom he is in love. The world of nature is idealized, and the speaker pleads with the shepherdess to live with him in harmony with nature.

In Raleigh's "The Nymph's Reply to the Shepherd," the nymph (shepherdess) replies to the earnest, idealistic shepherd of Marlowe's poem in a skeptical, clear-eyed fashion, turning down his proposal.

❷ Literary Analysis
Pastoral

- Remind students that pastoral poetry uses imagery to create an idealized portrait of nature. Then, read aloud the second stanza of Marlowe's poem.

- **Ask** students the Literary Analysis question: Which details in this stanza idealize the landscape? **Answer:** The shepherds feeding their flocks, the "shallow rivers," and "melodious" songs of the birds all create an unthreatening, idyllic vision of the landscape.

Go **Online** For additional information about Christopher Marlowe, have students type in the Web Code, then select M from the alphabet, and then select Christopher Marlowe.
—Author Link

The Passionate Shepherd to His Love
CHRISTOPHER MARLOWE

Come live with me, and be my love,
And we will all the pleasures prove[1]
That valleys, groves, hills, and fields,
Woods, or steepy mountain yields.

5 And we will sit upon the rocks,
Seeing the shepherds feed their flocks,
By shallow rivers to whose falls
<u>Melodious</u> birds sing <u>madrigals</u>.

And I will make thee beds of roses,
10 And a thousand fragrant posies,
A cap of flowers, and a kirtle[2]
Embroidered all with leaves of myrtle;

A gown made of the finest wool,
Which from our pretty lambs we pull;
15 Fair lined slippers for the cold,
With buckles of the purest gold;

A belt of straw and ivy buds,
With coral clasps and amber studs;
And if these pleasures may thee <u>move</u>,
20 Come live with me, and be my love.

The shepherds' swains shall dance and sing
For thy delight each May morning;
If these delights thy mind may move,
Then live with me and be my love.

1. **prove** experience.
2. **kirtle** skirt.

Literary Analysis
Pastoral Which details in this stanza idealize the landscape?

Vocabulary Builder
melodious (me lō′dē əs) *adj.* sweet-sounding; tuneful

madrigals (ma′ dri gəls) *n.* short love poems set to music

move (mōōv) *v.* persuade or impel

Reading Strategy
Identifying With the Speaker of a Poem Would you find the speaker's offers enticing? Why or why not?

Differentiated Instruction   Solutions for All Learners

Accessibility at a Glance

	The Passionate Shepherd	The Nymph's Reply
Context	Pastoral poetry	Raleigh's Response to poem
Language	Formal, some inverted sentences	Formal, period vocabulary; some inverted sentences
Concept Level	Accessible (idealized descriptions of nature)	Challenging (realistic view of nature and life)
Literary Merit	Classic	Classic
Lexile	NP	NP
Overall Rating	Average	More challenging

The Nymph's Reply to the Shepherd

SIR WALTER RALEIGH

Background "The Passionate Shepherd to His Love" and "The Nymph's Reply to the Shepherd" are examples of reply poems. Many poets travel in similar social circles, and their association with each other sometimes motivates them to construct poems in response to one another's work. In addition to Sir Walter Raleigh, for example, John Donne also wrote a reply poem, "The Bait," to Marlowe's "The Passionate Shepherd to His Love." Such linkages can be found in many literary epochs and cultures: for example, twentieth-century Chinese poet Shu Ting composed a poem, titled "Also All," in response to Bei Dao's poem "All."

❹
If all the world and love were young
And truth in every shepherd's tongue
These pretty pleasures might me move
To live with thee, and be thy love.

5 Time drives the flocks from field to fold,
When rivers rage and rocks grow cold,
And Philomel[1] becometh dumb,
The rest complains of cares to come.

The flowers do fade, and wanton fields
10 To wayward winter <u>reckoning</u> yields:
A honey tongue, a heart of gall,
Is fancy's spring, but sorrow's fall.

---

1. **Philomel** the nightingale.

Vocabulary Builder
reckoning (rekʹ ən iŋ) *n.* accounting

**Reading Check**
According to stanza 3, what effect does time have on the fields and flowers?

The Nymph's Reply to the Shepherd ■ 251

---

❸ Reading Strategy
Identifying With the Speaker of a Poem

• Have students paraphrase the speaker's offers to the shepherdess.

• Then, **ask** students the Reading Strategy question: Would you find the speaker's offers enticing? Why or why not?
Possible response: The speaker's offers are enticing because they promise a life of harmony.

❹ Reading Check

Answer: Time takes away the beauty and life of fields and flowers.

Differentiated Instruction   Solutions for All Learners

Strategy for Less Proficient Readers
Have students use a Venn diagram to compare these poems. Students should include the following elements in each circle of the diagram: the speaker, the speaker's main point, and the tone. Students should also list in the overlapping portion at least one similarity between the poems.

Vocabulary for English Learners
Students may have difficulty with the words *thee* and *thy*. Explain that these words are archaic, or no longer in general use. Then, explain that *thee* means "you" and *thy* means "your." Encourage students to substitute *you* and *your* for the archaic words as they read both poems.

Enrichment for Advanced Readers
Explain to students that a nymph is a figure in Greek mythology. Certain nymphs represented different natural features. Encourage students to use research the following nymphs: Oceanids, Oreads, Limoniads, Limniads, and Napaea. Have students present their findings to the class.

251

• Remind students that the imagery in Marlowe's poem portrays an idealized natural world in which one can live a carefree life. Raleigh's poem shatters this vision.

• Have students read the bracketed stanza. Then, **ask** the Literary Analysis question: What contrast does the nymph draw between the idealized world and the real world? **Answer:** In the real world, the idyllic elements described in Marlowe's poem fade with time.

ASSESS

Answers

1. Students should explain the reasoning behind their responses.

2. (a) He asks her to come live with him and be his love. (b) The life the speaker envisions is one in harmony with nature.

3. (a) A variation of line 19—"And if these pleasures may thee move"—is used in line 23: "If these delights thy mind may move." The phrase "live with me and be my love" is repeated in lines 20 and 24. (b) The repetition reinforces the speaker's desires.

4. (a) Lines 3 and 4 echo the first stanza. (b) The echoes create a mocking tone.

5. (a) The nightingale can no longer sing. (b) In the nymph's world, time takes its toll and nature is harsh. (c) Words such as "rage," "cold," and "dumb" create these feelings.

6. (a) The nymph might be persuaded if the idyllic world that the shepherd promised really existed. (b) Students should explain the reasoning behind their responses. (c) The nymph recognizes the ephemeral nature of beauty and understands the ravages of time.

7. Students should explain the reasoning behind their responses.

15

Thy gowns, thy shoes, thy beds of roses,
Thy cap, thy kirtle,[2] and thy posies
Soon break, soon wither, soon forgotten,
In folly ripe, in reason rotten.

Thy belt of straw and ivy buds,
Thy coral clasps and amber studs,
All these in me no means can move
20   To come to thee and be thy love.

But could youth last and love still breed,
Has joy no date[3] nor age no need,
Then these delights my mind might move,
To live with thee and be thy love.

---

2. **kirtle** skirt.
3. **date** ending.

Vocabulary Builder
wither (*with′ ər*) *v.* fade or waste away

Literary Analysis
Pastoral and Common Themes What contrast does the nymph draw between the idealized world and the real world?

Critical Reading

1. **Respond:** Do you think the speaker in "The Nymph's Reply to the Shepherd" responds effectively to the shepherd? Why or why not?

2. **(a) Recall:** In "The Passionate Shepherd to His Love," what does the speaker ask his love to do in the first stanza?
(b) Interpret: What kind of future life together does the speaker envision?

3. **(a) Recall:** What examples of repetition occur in the last two stanzas of "The Passionate Shepherd"? **(b) Draw Conclusions:** What is the effect of this repetition?

4. **(a) Recall:** Which lines in the first stanza of "The Nymph's Reply" echo the first stanza of Marlowe's poem? **(b) Infer:** What is the poet's purpose in these echoes?

5. **(a) Recall:** What happens to the nightingale in line 7 of "The Nymph's Reply"? **(b) Compare and Contrast:** According to lines 5 through 8, in what ways is the nymph's world different from that of the shepherd? **(c) Analyze:** Which words in this stanza evoke a feeling of ruin or despair?

6. **(a) Recall:** According to lines 21–22 of "The Nymph's Reply," what might persuade the nymph to live with the shepherd?
(b) Speculate: Do you think these lines would console the shepherd?
(c) Analyze: How does the nymph present a realistic portrayal of time and change in the poem?

7. **Relate:** If you were the shepherd, what counterargument might you make in response to the "The Nymph's Reply"?

Author Link
For: More about Christopher Marlowe and Sir Walter Raleigh
Visit: www.PHSchool.com
Web Code: ese-9204

Go Online
Author Link
For additional information about Sir Walter Raleigh, have students type in the Web Code, then select R from the alphabet, and then select Sir Walter Raleigh.

Apply the Skills

The Passionate Shepherd to His Love • The Nymph's Reply to the Shepherd

Literary Analysis

Pastoral

1. Although both Marlowe and Raleigh's poems reflect the **pastoral** tradition, the speakers present opposing views of rural life. **(a)** Use a chart like the one shown to identify details that signal the shepherd's idealized view and the nymph's more realistic view of country life.

Shepherd's Idealism	Nymph's Realism

   (b) Based on their attitudes toward nature, what conclusions can you draw about the personalities of the shepherd and the nymph?
2. In line 16 of "The Nymph's Reply to the Shepherd," in what way does the speaker use a striking balance of opposites to illustrate the effect of time?

Comparing Literary Works

3. Love is one of the **common themes** in these poems, but the speakers present contrasting views. **(a)** What offerings does the shepherd make to the nymph in "The Passionate Shepherd to His Love"? **(b)** In today's world, what might the shepherd offer to win the nymph's affections? **(c)** Do you think material offerings like the shepherd's are idealistic, or do they have practical purposes? Explain.
4. Renaissance lyric poems often linked the inevitable passage of time with the Latin motto *carpe diem,* meaning "seize the day." **(a)** In what way does this motto apply to this pair of poems? **(b)** In what way is this theme universal to all people?

Reading Strategy

Identifying With the Speaker of a Poem

5. Do you sympathize with the **speaker** in "The Passionate Shepherd to His Love"? Why or why not?
6. **(a)** In "The Nymph's Reply," how does the speaker reveal a skeptical side to her nature? **(b)** How does she reveal a wistful side?
7. **(a)** What experiences might have shaped the nymph's attitudes in "The Nymph's Reply"? **(b)** If you were the nymph, what kind of future might you project for the shepherd? **(c)** If you were the shepherd, what experiences might you wish for the nymph?

Extend Understanding

8. **Cultural Connection:** What modern technologies allow people to write responses to one another? In what ways do these technologies make it challenging to communicate emotions accurately?

The Passionate Shepherd to His Love / The Nymph's Reply to the Shepherd ■ 253

QuickReview

A **pastoral** is a work that celebrates the joys of simple country life.

Common themes are insights or messages that recur regularly in literary works from many different times and places.

When you **identify with a poem's speaker,** you put yourself in the speaker's place to understand his or her feelings, needs, problems, or goals.

Go Online
Assessment

For: Self-test
Visit: www.PHSchool.com
Web Code: esa-6203

Answers Continued

Go Online
Assessment

Students may use the **Self-test** to prepare for Selection Test A or Selection Test B.

253

TIME AND RESOURCE MANAGER

 Meeting Your Standards

Students will

1. **analyze and respond to literary elements.**
   - Literary Analysis: Shakespearean Sonnet
2. **read, comprehend, analyze, and critique a poem.**
   - Reading Strategy: Relating Structure to Theme
   - Reading Check questions
   - Apply the Skills questions
   - Assessment Practice (ATE)
3. **develop vocabulary.**
   - Vocabulary Lesson: Greek Root: *-chron-*
4. **understand and apply written and oral language conventions.**
   - Spelling Strategy
   - Grammar and Style Lesson: Participles as Adjectives
5. **develop writing proficiency.**
   - Writing Lesson: Analysis of a Sonnet's Imagery
6. **develop appropriate research strategies.**
   - Extend Your Learning: Multimedia Report
7. **understand and apply listening and speaking strategies.**
   - Extend Your Learning: Sonnet Recital

Block Scheduling: Use one 90-minute class period to preteach the skills and have students read the selection. Use a second 90-minute class period to assess students' mastery of skills, extend their learning, and monitor their progress.

Homework Suggestions
Following are possibilities for homework assignments:

- Support pages from *Unit 2 Resources:*
  - Literary Analysis
  - Reading Strategy
  - Vocabulary Builder
  - Grammar and Style
- An Extend Your Learning project and the Writing Lesson for this selection group may be completed over several days.

Step-by-Step Teaching Guide	Pacing Guide
PRETEACH	
• Administer Vocabulary and Reading Warm-ups as necessary.	5 min.
• Engage students' interest with the motivation activity.	5 min.
• Read and discuss author and background features. **FT**	10 min.
• Introduce the Literary Analysis Skill: Shakespearean Sonnet. **FT**	5 min.
• Introduce the Reading Strategy: Relating Structure to Theme. **FT**	10 min
• Prepare students to read by teaching the selection vocabulary. **FT**	
TEACH	
• Informally monitor comprehension while students read independently or in groups. **FT**	30 min.
• Monitor students' comprehension with the Reading Check notes.	as students read
• Reinforce vocabulary with Vocabulary Builder notes.	as students read
• Develop students' understanding of Shakespearean sonnets with the Literary Analysis annotations. **FT**	5 min.
• Develop students' ability to relate structure to theme with the Reading Strategy annotations. **FT**	5 min.
ASSESS/EXTEND	
• Assess students' comprehension and mastery of the Literary Analysis and Reading Strategy by having them answer the Apply the Skills questions. **FT**	15 min.
• Have students complete the Vocabulary Lesson and the Grammar and Style Lesson. **FT**	15 min.
• Apply students' ability to gather details by using the Writing Lesson. **FT**	45 min. or homework
• Apply students' understanding by using one or more of the Extend Your Learning activities.	20–90 min. or homework
• Administer Selection Test A or Selection Test B. **FT**	15 min.

Resources

Choosing Resources for Differentiated Instruction

[L1] Special Needs Students

[L2] Below-Level Students

[L3] All Students

[L4] Advanced Students

[EL] English Learners

For Vocabulary and Reading Warm-ups and for Selection Tests, **A** signifies "less challenging" and **B** "more challenging." For Graphic Organizer transparencies, **A** signifies "not filled in" and **B** "filled in."

FT Fast Track Instruction: To move the lesson more quickly, use the strategies and activities identified with **FT**.

Scaffolding for Less Proficient and Advanced Students

The leveled Critical Thinking questions after selections progress in the levels of thinking required to answer them. To address the needs of your different students, you may use the (a) level questions for your less proficient students and the (b) level questions with your on-level and advanced students. The occasional (c) level questions are appropriate for your advanced students.

PRENTICE HALL

Teacher EXPRESS™
Plan · Teach · Assess Use this complete suite of powerful teaching tools to make lesson planning and testing quicker and easier.

PRENTICE HALL

Student EXPRESS™
Learn · Study · Succeed Use the interactive textbook (online and on CD-ROM) to make selections and activities come alive with audio and video support and interactive questions.

Go Online
Professional Development
For: Information about Lexiles
Visit: www.PHSchool.com
Web Code: eue-1111

Motivation

What is love? How long does it truly last? Can the mere thought of a loved one ease pain or take away sorrow? Engage students with questions like these. Then have them respond to the following statements as true or false.

1. A person who has true love is better off than the richest king.

2. People no longer express their love as well as they used to.

3. True love lasts forever; nothing on earth stops it.

4. It is better to be honest about someone's shortcomings than to glorify them.

Allow students to share their responses and discuss reasons for their opinions. Then tell them that Shakespeare addresses each of these issues in these sonnets.

❶ Background
More About the Author

It is clear that Shakespeare made the most of his education. His astonishingly large vocabulary and broad knowledge of history and literature indicate that he read widely, and did so throughout his life.

There is a gap in the record between the birth of his children and Shakespeare's appearance in London theater records. But in 1592, dramatist Robert Greene declared in a pamphlet that an "upstart crow" had appeared on the scene. The insult brought a swift response from many corners, indicating that Shakespeare had already made many influential friends in London.

His life was not without sadness. His only son, Hamnet, died at age 11. But his daughters survived and married.

Probably the most famous comment made about Shakespeare was written by his contemporary, Ben Jonson: "He was not of an age, but for all time!"

Build Skills `Poems`

❶ Sonnet 29 • Sonnet 106 • Sonnet 116 • Sonnet 130

William Shakespeare
(1564–1616)

Shakespeare may be the most admired author of all time. If he were living today, he would be a celebrity, and the facts of his life would be widely available in magazine articles, books, Web pages, and chat rooms. Instead, we know few facts about him, and these few had to be painstakingly traced from legal and church records or deduced from references in his work.

Bare-Bones Biography Shakespeare was born in the country town of Stratford-on-Avon and probably attended the town's free grammar school. When he was eighteen, he married twenty-six-year-old Anne Hathaway. They had a daughter, Susanna, and twins, Hamnet and Judith.

Shakespeare acquired a public reputation as an actor and a playwright. In addition, he was part owner of a London theater called the Globe, where many of his plays were performed. (For more about Shakespeare and his work as a dramatist, see pages 294–299.)

The Sonnet In the years 1592–1594, London's theaters were closed because of an outbreak of the plague. This general misfortune may have had at least one benefit: It may have provided the time that Shakespeare needed to write some of his 154 sonnets.

In writing a long sequence of sonnets, Shakespeare was being fashionable. Elizabethan poets enjoyed the sonnet form, writing fourteen-line lyric poems to both real and imaginary lovers. The great Italian poet Petrarch (1304–1374) began the writing of sonnet sequences, and Henry Howard, Earl of Surrey, developed the English form of the sonnet that Shakespeare used.

Petrarch set the thematic course of the sonnet for generations to come. His sequence charts each pang and longing of the speaker's unfulfilled love for an idealized lady. This poetic device led to endless inventiveness—the beloved's beauty invites extravagant comparisons, and she provides a focus for the poet's ingenuity.

Shakespeare's Sequence Like the sonnet sequences of other poets, Shakespeare's 154 sonnets are numbered. Most of them are addressed to a handsome, talented, young man urging him to marry and have children who can carry on his talents. The speaker also warns the young man about the destructive powers of time, age, and moral weakness. Midway through the sequence, the sonnets focus on a rival poet who has also addressed poems to the young man. Twenty-five of the later sonnets are addressed to a "dark lady" who is romantically involved with both the speaker and the young man. These later sonnets focus on the grief she causes by her betrayal of the speaker.

A Mystery Scholars fiercely debate the identity of the young man (Mr. W. H.), the "dark lady," and the rival poet. Leading candidates for the role of Mr. W. H. are Henry Wriothesley, third earl of Southampton, to whom Shakespeare dedicated his narrative poems, and William Herbert, third earl of Pembroke. Those favoring Southampton claim Mrs. John Davenant was the "dark lady," but the Pembroke side believes she was Mary Fitton, a woman of doubtful reputation. The many nominees for the rival poet include Edmund Spenser, Christopher Marlowe, Ben Jonson, and John Donne—even the name of Chaucer, a poet who had been dead for two hundred years, has been proposed!

Scholarly debates aside, readers treasure Shakespeare's masterful use of the sonnet to bring the fundamental experiences of life—time, death, love, and friendship—into tight focus.

Preview

Connecting to the Literature

Feelings may sink you into gloom or send you floating with joy. If you are a Shakespeare, your strong feelings will erupt in a sonnet!

Literary Analysis

The Shakespearean Sonnet

Shakespeare uses a variation of the sonnet form, a variation that has since been named after him. Like other sonnets, a **Shakespearean sonnet** has fourteen lines, with five iambic feet to the line (an iambic foot is an unstressed syllable followed by a stressed one).

Unlike Petrarchan and Spenserian sonnets, a Shakespearean sonnet follows the rhyme scheme *abab cdcd efef gg*, giving it this structure:

- three **quatrains,** or four-line stanzas
- a rhyming **couplet**—often a dramatic statement that resolves, restates, or redefines the central problem of the sonnet

Notice the artful way in which Shakespeare uses the first twelve lines of each sonnet to present a problem that he resolves or restates in the couplet.

Comparing Literary Works

Though all Shakespearean sonnets have fourteen rhyming lines, there are no rules about the number or type of sentences they contain. Shakespeare uses this freedom of **syntax,** or sentence structure, to create dazzling dramatic effects. By saving his main idea until the end of one long sentence, he makes Sonnet 106 build and build like a lawyer's statement to a jury. Using alternating short clauses, setting up and then delivering punchlines, he turns Sonnet 130 into a miniature comedy routine. As you read, compare the effects Shakespeare achieves with syntax.

Reading Strategy

Relating Structure to Theme

As you read, **relate structure to theme.** Notice how Shakespeare builds on or varies his theme—his main concern—from quatrain to quatrain, using the couplet to deliver a dramatic concluding statement. Use a chart like the one shown to record the main idea of each section of a sonnet.

Vocabulary Builder

scope (skōp) *n.* range of perception or understanding (p. 259)

sullen (sul′ ən) *adj.* gloomy; dismal (p. 259)

chronicle (krän′ i kəl) *n.* historical record of events in chronological order (p. 260)

prefiguring (prē fig′ yər iŋ) *v.* resembling and so suggesting beforehand (p. 260)

impediments (im ped′ ə mənts) *n.* obstacles (p. 261)

alters (ôl′ tərz) *v.* changes (p. 261)

Quatrain 1
Speaker has bad luck, which causes him to feel isolated. He pities himself and bemoans his condition. **Theme:** *bad fortune; self-pity*

$+$

Quatrain 2
Theme:

$=$

Relation of 1 and 2
Change in Theme:

Sonnet 29 / Sonnet 106 / Sonnet 116 / Sonnet 130 ■ 257

❷ Literary Analysis
The Shakespearean Sonnet

- Tell students that in this lesson they will focus on a variation of the sonnet form known as the Shakespearean sonnet.

- Read the instruction about the Shakespearean sonnet together as a class. Call students' attention to the typical characteristics of its composition—such as the three quatrains and rhyming couplet that constitute its 14 lines, a meter of iambic pentameter, and the rhyme scheme *abab cdcd efef gg.*

- Use the instruction for Comparing Literary Works to have students consider the unusual syntax used in Shakespearean sonnets.

❸ Reading Strategy
Relating Structure to Theme

- Remind students that a theme is the subject of a work and structure is the form of a work.

- Then, tell students that a good use of structure in a short literary form like a sonnet can enhance or emphasize the progress of the theme. To illustrate this point, review the chart on the student page.

- Give students a copy of **Reading Strategy Graphic Organizer A** in *Graphic Organizer Transparencies,* p. 42, to record the progress of theme as it connects to structure in these sonnets by Shakespeare.

Vocabulary Builder

- Pronounce each vocabulary word for students, and read the definitions as a class. Have students identify any words with which they are already familiar.

Differentiated Instruction   Solutions for All Learners

Support for Special Needs Students

Have students complete the **Preview** and **Build Skills** pages for these selections in the *Reader's Notebook: Adapted Version.* These pages provide a selection summary, an abbreviated presentation of the reading and literary skills, and the graphic organizer on the **Build Skills** page in the student book.

Support for Less Proficient Readers

Have students complete the **Preview** and **Build Skills** pages for these selections in the *Reader's Notebook.* These pages provide a selection summary, an abbreviated presentation of the reading and literary skills, and the graphic organizer on the **Build Skills** page in the student book.

Support for English Learners

Have students complete the **Preview** and **Build Skills** pages for these selections in the *Reader's Notebook: English Learner's Version.* These pages provide a selection summary, an abbreviated presentation of the skills, additional contextual vocabulary, and the graphic organizer on the **Build Skills** page in the student book.

**Learning Modalities
Musical/Rhythmic Learners**

Much of Shakespeare's poetry has been set to music. Play recordings of musical settings of one or more of the bard's verses to help students hear the rhythm. Alternatively, play the **Listening to Literature Audio CD** of these sonnets, using a tambourine to tap out the meter, so students can clearly hear the rhythm.

❶ About the Selections

In Sonnet 29, when things are going badly and the speaker feels envious of others, he has only to remember a special person's love in order to feel joyous again.

In Sonnet 106, all previous descriptions of handsome men and beautiful women only anticipated the beauty of a special person the poet knows. Ironically, these earlier descriptions are inadequate because they were only "prophecies"; however, those who live today lack the skill to praise this person.

❷ Humanities

Autumn, by Frederick Walker

A contemporary of Walker's said that the painter was very fond of "air, dew, sunshine, and the freshness of the morning among spring leaves and flowers." An architect, illustrator, and painter, Walker is remembered for expressing the sheer poetry of nature.

Use these questions for discussion:

1. **Explain** how the painting matches the mood of the sonnet.
Possible response: The quietness of the scene creates a mood of stillness. The woman's posture and facial expression match the thoughtful, serious mood of the poem.

2. Why do you think a painting of autumn is used to illustrate this sonnet?
Possible response: In literature, autumn is often associated with a quieter time in life. It is a season of change; a time when people tend to look back instead of forward.

❷

❸ ▲ **Critical Viewing** What details suggest that the person in this painting shares the mood of the speaker of Sonnet 29? **[Analyze]**

258 ■ *Celebrating Humanity (1485–1625)*

Differentiated Instruction   Solutions for All Learners

Accessibility at a Glance

	Sonnet 29	**Sonnet 106**	**Sonnet 116**	**Sonnet 130**
Context	Elizabethan	Elizabethan	Elizabethan	Elizabethan
Language	Poetic diction	Poetic diction	Metaphors	Sensory imagery
Concept Level	Accessible (hope)	Accessible (beauty)	Accessible (love)	Accessible (beauty)
Literary Merit	Classic	Classic	Classic	Classic
Lexile	NP	NP	NP	NP
Overall Rating	More challenging	More challenging	Average	Average

❸ Critical Viewing

Answer: Students may suggest that the woman seems contemplative, or wrapped up in serious thoughts, like the speaker of the poem.

❹ Reading Strategy
Relating Structure to Theme

Remind students that, in these sonnets, Shakespeare uses the structure of the sonnet to help him develop his theme.

• After students have read the sonnet, have them **suggest** what the speaker is saying in lines 5–7.
Answer: He envies people who have friends and hope, and he desires the creativity and intelligence that others possess.

• **Ask** students how the third quatrain relates to the previous two.
Answer: It marks the beginning of a change in direction. The first two quatrains show alienation (Q1) and envy (Q2), but this one begins with the transition word "yet," which notes that this is a turning point. He thinks of something other than misery.

• Then, **ask** students how the third quatrain leads into the closing couplet.
Answer: The third quatrain shows the change of thoughts, and the closing couplet shows the change of mood produced by the change of thought.

❺ Reading Check

Answer: The speaker's state of mind at the end of the poem is one of contentment and self-satisfaction.

❶

Sonnet 29
William Shakespeare

❹

When in disgrace with fortune and men's eyes,
I all alone beweep my outcast state,
And trouble deaf heaven with my bootless[1] cries,
And look upon myself and curse my fate,
5   Wishing me like to one more rich in hope,
Featured like him, like him with friends possessed,
Desiring this man's art, and that man's <u>scope</u>,
With what I most enjoy contented least.
Yet in these thoughts myself almost despising,
10 Haply[2] I think on thee, and then my state,
Like to the lark at break of day arising
From <u>sullen</u> earth, sings hymns at heaven's gate;
    For thy sweet love remembered such wealth brings
    That then I scorn to change my state with kings.

1. **bootless** futile.
2. **haply** *adv.* by chance.

Vocabulary Builder

scope (skōp) *n.* range of perception or understanding

sullen (sul′ ən) *adj.* gloomy; dismal

❺ ✔ Reading Check

What is the speaker's state of mind at the end of the poem?

Sonnet 29 ■ 259

260

❻ Vocabulary Builder
Greek Root: -chron-

- Call students' attention to the word *chronicle* and its definition. Tell them that the word *chronicle* contains the root -chron- from the Greek word, *chronos*, meaning "time."

- Have students **suggest** words that contain this root, and list them on the chalkboard.
  Possible responses: *chronic, chronology, chronometer*

- Have students look up any unfamiliar words in a dictionary.

ASSESS
Answers

1. **Possible response:** Students may say that it seems believable; a shift in thoughts often changes one's mood.

2. (a) He is in disgrace with luck and people's opinions. (b) It makes him curse his fate and hate his life.

3. (a) Thoughts of his beloved cause the shift in mood. (b) The first eight lines are somber and dark in mood, while the final six lines are happy and bright. (c) The speaker states that his love makes him wealthier than a king.

4. (a) It is prefiguring the speaker's beloved. (b) The writers of the past did not have enough skill; the writers of the present cannot speak at all. (c) Their failures show that the lady's beauty is inexpressible.

5. **Possible response:** The speaker in Sonnet 29 seems humble and sincere. The speaker in Sonnet 106 seems to be a romantic who may be prone to exaggeration.

6. **Possible response:** Students may say that Sonnet 29 is more convincing, because it is natural to have one's mood lifted by thoughts of a loved one. Sonnet 106 is more abstract in its expression of love.

---

❶ SONNET 106
WILLIAM SHAKESPEARE

❻ | When in the chronicle of wasted time
  I see descriptions of the fairest wights,[1]
  And beauty making beautiful old rhyme,
  In praise of ladies dead and lovely knights,
5 Then in the blazon[2] of sweet beauty's best
  Of hand, of foot, of lip, of eye, of brow,
  I see their antique pen would have express'd
  Even such a beauty as you master now.
10 So all their praises are but prophecies
  Of this our time, all you prefiguring;
  And, for they look'd but with divining eyes,
  They had not skill enough your worth to sing:
      For we, which now behold these present days,
      Have eyes to wonder, but lack tongues to praise.

---

1. **wights** (wīts) *n.* human beings; people.
2. **blazon** *n.* coat of arms; emblem.

Vocabulary Builder
chronicle (krän′ i kəl) *n.* historical record of events in chronological order

prefiguring (prē fig′ yer in) *v.* resembling and so suggesting beforehand

---

Critical Reading

1. In Sonnet 29, did you find the shift in the speaker's mood believable? Explain.

2. **(a) Recall:** With whom is the speaker in Sonnet 29 in "disgrace"? **(b) Analyze:** What overall effect does this disgrace have on the speaker's state of mind?

3. **(a) Recall:** According to line 12 of Sonnet 29, what causes the shift in the speaker's mood? **(b) Analyze:** How would you describe the shifting moods in the sonnet? **(c) Interpret:** How do the last two lines summarize the theme?

4. **(a) Recall:** In Sonnet 106, what is ancient poetry "prefiguring"? **(b) Compare and Contrast:** Compare the ways in which writers past and present fail. **(c) Synthesize:** How are their failures a testament to the lady's beauty?

5. **Evaluate:** Based on what he reveals of himself, assess the character of the speaker in each sonnet.

6. **Make a Judgment:** Which sonnet, if either, presents a more convincing picture of love? Explain your answer.

Go Online
Author Link
For: More about William Shakespeare
Visit: www.PHSchool.com
Web Code: ese-9206

Enrichment

Romantic Love and the Sonnet

Elizabethan poets were neither the first, nor the last, to use the sonnet form to express romantic love. Nearly three hundred years before Shakespeare, the Italian poet Francesco Petrarch was writing love poetry in sonnet form to his beloved Laura. Elizabeth Barrett Browning, whose *Sonnets from the Portuguese* was published in 1850, describes the growth and development of her love for Robert Browning in sonnet form. The title of the book was meant to disguise the personal nature of the poems by suggesting they were a translation; in fact, it was a secret reference to Browning's nickname for Elizabeth Barrett, "The Portuguese." And more than three hundred years after Shakespeare, Chilean poet Pablo Neruda used the sonnet to express his romantic love to a lady. The American poet Robert Lowell also used confessional sonnets in his book *The Dolphin* to examine his growing love for the woman who would become his wife, Lady Caroline Blackwood.

❼

Justa, Bartolome Esteban Murillo

❽ ◄ **Critical Viewing**
Which elements of this portrait seem idealized? Which seem realistic? [Classify]

❾

Sonnet 116
William Shakespeare

Let me not to the marriage of true minds
Admit <u>impediments</u>. Love is not love
Which <u>alters</u> when it alteration finds,
Or bends with the remover to remove.
5   O, no! It is an ever-fixèd mark
That looks on tempests and is never shaken;
It is the star to every wandering bark,[1]
Whose worth's unknown, although his height be taken.[2]
Love's not Time's fool, though rosy lips and cheeks
10 Within his bending sickle's compass[3] come;
Love alters not with his brief hours and weeks,
But bears it out even to the edge of doom.[4]
      If this be error, and upon me proved,
      I never writ, nor no man ever loved.

---

1. **star . . . bark** the star that guides every wandering ship: the North Star.
2. **Whose . . . be taken** whose value is unmeasurable, although navigators measure its height in the sky.
3. **compass** range; scope.
4. **doom** Judgment Day.

Vocabulary Builder

impediments (im ped′ ə mənts) *n.* obstacles

alters (ôl′ tərs) *v.* changes

❿ ✓ Reading Check

According to the speaker, how long does true love last?

Sonnet 116 ■ *261*

Differentiated Instruction   **Solutions for All Learners**

Support for Special Needs Students
Students may experience difficulty identifying the key elements of Sonnet 130 that make it essentially Shakespearean. Have students read Sonnet 130 aloud with teacher guidance. Then, model for students the three quatrains and rhyming couplet, the rhyme scheme of *abab cdcd efef gg,* and the iambic pentameter.

Enrichment for Gifted/Talented Students
Have students compose their own Shakespearean sonnets, borrowing from themes and forms used in the works in this group. Students should write their 14-line sonnets in iambic pentameter, and should structure their poems with three quatrains and a closing couplet. Encourage students to use the form to enhance the themes of their sonnets.

---

❼ Humanities

Justa, by Bartolomé Esteban Murillo

Murillo (1617–1682) was to become Spain's most popular painter by the year 1660. He was known primarily as a colorist, and was famed for his sense of color contrasts. Murillo focused on religious subjects for most of his works, investing them with warmth and humanity. In his later work, Murillo focused on solving problems having to do with light, color, and atmosphere. Use these questions for discussion.

1. Judging from the details in the picture, do you think the woman has the same views about love as the speaker? Explain.
Possible responses: Yes; she seems serious and steady, so she probably agrees with the ideas of the speaker in Sonnet 116; no, she seems to be a dreamer because she is gazing into space and perhaps is longing for adventure or romance.

2. Does the woman in the picture resemble the woman described by Shakespeare in Sonnet 130? Explain.
Possible responses: Yes, she is not exceptionally beautiful, but she seems earthy, warm, and kind; no, she is too conventionally beautiful to be the woman described by the speaker of Sonnet 130.

❽ Critical Viewing

Possible response: The woman's perfectly shaped head and pure complexion may be idealized. The posture and expression of the model seem artificial or posed. Her clothing and hairstyle seem realistic.

❾ About the Selections

In Sonnet 116, Shakespeare praises the constancy and steadfastness of true love.

In Sonnet 130, Shakespeare makes fun of the figures of speech that Petrarchan poets used to describe their ideal but remote mistresses. He shows how those figures of speech do not apply to his mistress, who is no goddess, but still beautiful.

❿ Reading Check

Answer: True love lasts forever, even "to the edge of doom."

- Review with students the rhyme scheme and iambic meter of Shakespearean sonnets.

- Then, **ask** students the Literary Analysis question: Identify the rhyme scheme of the sonnet's first quatrain. Which line does not begin with an iambic foot? **Answer:** The rhyme scheme of the first quatrain is *abab*, and the second line does not begin with an iambic foot.

ASSESS

Answers

1. **Possible response:** The speaker's idea of love in Sonnet 116 is preferable because it retains a bit of romance and mystery.

2. (a) Love is compared to the North Star. (b) True love and the North Star are constant and unchanging. Like the North Star, love is a guide in one's life.

3. (a) **Possible response:** The effects of time include the death of "rosy lips and cheeks" within Time's sickle, and the passing of "brief hours and weeks." (b) Time has little or no effect on love; love outlasts time.

4. (a) Her lips are not red as coral; her cheeks aren't like roses; her breath is not like perfume; her voice is not music. (b) He may mean that she is an earthly being, as opposed to idealized lovers who are compared to angels.

5. (a) He says his love is as delightful as any of those who are praised with false comparisons. (b) That true love is based on reality. (c) It is anti-Petrarchan because it does not idealize the state of love; instead, it shows the speaker's love with all her imperfections.

6. **Possible response:** Sonnet 130 seems more typical of love in our times. In today's world, idealized beauty still battles reality.

262

❾ SONNET 130
WILLIAM SHAKESPEARE

⓫ My mistress' eyes are nothing like the sun,
Coral is far more red than her lips' red;
If snow be white, why then her breasts are dun;
If hairs be wires, black wires grow on her head.
5   I have seen roses damasked,¹ red and white,
But no such roses see I in her cheeks;
And in some perfumes is there more delight
Than in the breath that from my mistress reeks.²
I love to hear her speak. Yet well I know
10   That music hath a far more pleasing sound.
I grant I never saw a goddess go;³
My mistress, when she walks, treads on the ground.
      And yet, by heaven, I think my love as rare
      As any she belied⁴ with false compare.

---

1. **damasked** variegated.
2. **reeks** emanates.
3. **go** walk.
4. **belied** (bē lid´) misrepresented.

Critical Reading

1. **Respond:** Which speaker's idea of love do you prefer? Why?

2. **(a) Recall:** To what is love compared in the second quatrain of Sonnet 116? **(b) Analyze:** Why is love similar to this object?

3. **(a) Recall:** Identify two images in Sonnet 116 that show the effects of time. **(b) Compare and Contrast:** Compare the effects of time on love with the ideal of love in the poem.

4. **(a) Recall:** How are the mistress's eyes, lips, cheeks, breath, and voice inferior, according to Sonnet 130? **(b) Interpret:** Why does the speaker say she "treads on the ground"?

5. **(a) Recall:** In Sonnet 130, what does the final couplet say about the speaker's feelings? **(b) Interpret:** What general truth does the couplet suggest? **(c) Draw Conclusions:** In his sonnets, Petrarch worshiped his mistress. Why has Sonnet 130 been called anti-Petrarchan?

6. **Apply:** In which of these sonnets does the speaker's attitude toward love seem more typical of our times? Explain.

Literary Analysis
The Shakespearean Sonnet Identify the rhyme scheme of the sonnet's first quatrain. Which line does not begin with an iambic foot?

Go Online
Author Link
For: More about William Shakespeare
Visit: www.PHSchool.com
Web Code: ese-9206

Go Online   For additional information about
Author Link   William Shakespeare, have students
type in the Web Code, then select S from the
alphabet, and then select William Shakespeare.

Apply the Skills

Sonnet 29 • Sonnet 106 • Sonnet 116 • Sonnet 130

Literary Analysis

The Shakespearean Sonnet

1. **(a)** Identify the three quatrains and the couplet of the **Shakespearean sonnet,** Sonnet 29. **(b)** Which rhyming words represent the *b's*, *e's*, and *g's* of the rhyme scheme?

2. Using a chart organized like the one below, show how Shakespeare conveys his message in the sonnet form in Sonnet 106.

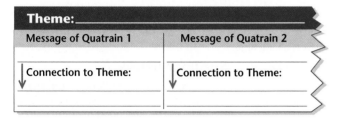

Theme:_____

Message of Quatrain 1	Message of Quatrain 2
Connection to Theme:	Connection to Theme:

3. Explain whether the couplet in Sonnet 116 affirms the rest of the sonnet or represents a sudden shift in attitude.

Comparing Literary Works

4. Explain how Shakespeare uses references to other poetry in Sonnets 106 and 130 to make these sonnets seem more in touch with life.

5. Which two of the sonnets use complex **syntax,** featuring sentences full of phrases and clauses?

6. **(a)** Compare the complex syntax of these two sonnets with the syntax of the other two sonnets. **(b)** Why does Shakespeare use each type of syntax?

Reading Strategy

Relating Structure to Theme

7. **(a)** List the main idea of each section of Sonnets 106 and 116. **(b)** Does each idea correspond to a quatrain or couplet? Explain.

8. If Shakespeare had adapted one of these sonnets to the Petrarchan form (an eight-line octet followed by a six-line sestet), how might the new form have affected the way he presented his message?

Extend Understanding

9. **Cultural Connection:** Which sonnet do you think best expresses modern attitudes? Support your choice with examples.

QuickReview

A **Shakespearean sonnet** consists of three four-line quatrains and a final two-line couplet. Each line is normally written in iambic pentameter—it contains five pairs of syllables, with the first syllable in each pair unstressed and the second stressed. The rhyme scheme is usually *abab cdcd efef gg.*

Syntax is the sentence structure a writer uses.

When you **relate structure to theme,** you note how variations of the theme—the work's central concern—are tied to different parts of the work.

Go Online
Assessment
For: Self-test
Visit: www.PHSchool.com
Web Code: esa-6204

Sonnet 29 / Sonnet 106 / Sonnet 116 / Sonnet 130 ■ 263

Answers continued

9. **Possible response:** Sonnet 130 seems more typical of love in our times. In today's world, idealized beauty is still in conflict with reality.

Go Online   Students may use the
Assessment   **Self-Test** to prepare for
Selection Test A or **Selection Test B.**

263

❶ Vocabulary Lesson
Word Analysis

1. c	4. b
2. d	5. f
3. a	6. e

Vocabulary Builder
Synonyms

1. b	4. c
2. c	5. a
3. a	6. b

Spelling Strategy

1. tentacle
2. barnacle
3. crackle

❷ Grammar and Style Lesson

1. When in the chronicle of *wasted* time/I see descriptions of the fairest wights, . . . (*wasted* modifies *time*)

2. It is the star to every *wandering* bark, . . . (*wandering* modifies *bark*)

3. . . . rosy lips and cheeks/Within his *bending* sickle's compass come; . . . (*bending* modifies *sickle*)

4. It is an ever-*fixèd* mark. . . . (*fixèd* modifies *mark*)

5. Yet well I know/That music hath a far more *pleasing* sound. (*pleasing* modifies *sound*)

Writing Application

Possible answer: Sonnet 116 presents a *compelling* image of love. I think everyone wants to find the kind of *lasting* love described in the poem. An *unaltered* love may seem like an ideal, but it is certainly an *appealing* goal.

W𝒢 Writing and Grammar, Diamond Level

Students will find further instruction and practice on participles as adjectives in Chapter 19, Section 2.

Build Language Skills

❶ Vocabulary Lesson

Word Analysis: Greek Root -chron-

The word *chronicle* contains the Greek root -*chron*-, meaning "time." A chronicle is a record of events arranged in the order in which they occurred. Match the following related words with their definitions.

1. chronic		**a.**	person who records events by date
2. chronology		**b.**	arranged in order of occurrence
3. chronicler		**c.**	lasting over a long time
4. chronological		**d.**	a list of important events by date
5. chronometer		**e.**	keeping the same time
6. synchronized		**f.**	device for measuring time

Vocabulary Builder: Synonyms

Identify the synonym for each word below.

1. scope: **(a)** shovel, **(b)** range, **(c)** exploration
2. sullen: **(a)** strained, **(b)** dull, **(c)** sulky
3. impediments: **(a)** obstacles, **(b)** utensils, **(c)** commands
4. alters: **(a)** argues, **(b)** sacrifices, **(c)** changes
5. chronicle: **(a)** record, **(b)** paper, **(c)** dates
6. prefiguring: **(a)** guessing, **(b)** foreshadowing **(c)** introducing

Spelling Strategy

Many words end in -*le* or -*el*. Usually, when a *k* sound precedes the ending, -*le* is used, as in *chronicle, sparkle,* and *tickle.* In your notebook, use *el* or *le* to complete each of the following words.

1. tentac__ **2.** barnac__ **3.** crack__

❷ Grammar and Style Lesson

Participles as Adjectives

A **participle** is a verb form ending with -*ing* or -*ed*. A participle can act as an **adjective,** a word that modifies a noun or pronoun. For clarity, a participle must always appear near the noun or pronoun that it modifies.

In these examples, the participles are underlined.

For thy sweet love <u>remembered</u> such wealth brings . . . (modifies *love*)

And, for they look'd but with <u>divining</u> eyes, . . . (modifies *eyes*)

Though they function as adjectives, participles remind readers of the associated verbs, and so give a more active tone to a writer's descriptions.

Practice Copy each of the following sentences. Then, underline each participle, and draw an arrow to the noun that it modifies.

1. When in the chronicle of wasted time / I see descriptions of the fairest wights, . . .
2. It is the star to every wandering bark, . . .
3. . . . rosy lips and cheeks / Within his bending sickle's compass come; . . .
4. It is an ever-fixèd mark. . . .
5. Yet well I know / That music hath a far more pleasing sound.

Writing Application Write a brief review of your favorite sonnet. Include three participles.

W𝒢 *Prentice Hall Writing and Grammar Connection: Chapter 19, Section 2*

264 ■ *Celebrating Humanity (1485–1625)*

Assessment Practice

Fact and Opinion   **(For more practice, see** *Standardized Test Preparation Workbook,* **p. 9.)**

Many tests require students to distinguish between fact and opinion. Use the following lines from Sonnet 130 to help students recognize statements that are fact.

Which of these lines from Sonnet 130 are fact?

A Coral is far more red than her lips' red
B Yet well I know that music hath a far more pleasing sound

C I love to hear her speak
D My mistress' eyes are nothing like the sun

Choices *A, B,* and *D* are not facts. They are the author's opinions. *C* is the correct answer.

Writing Lesson

Timed Writing: Analysis of a Sonnet's Imagery

In his sonnets, Shakespeare uses contrasts in imagery—word pictures—to suggest the complexities of love. Analyze the imagery in one of his sonnets, quoting from the poem to support your ideas. *(40 minutes)*

Prewriting
(10 minutes)

Describe the images in a sonnet of your choice. Next to each image, note the idea that it expresses and its relationship to other images in the poem. Use a chart like the one shown here.

Model: Gathering Details

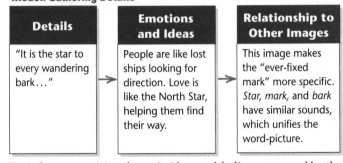

Details	Emotions and Ideas	Relationship to Other Images
"It is the star to every wandering bark…"	People are like lost ships looking for direction. Love is like the North Star, helping them find their way.	This image makes the "ever-fixed mark" more specific. *Star, mark,* and *bark* have similar sounds, which unifies the word-picture.

Drafting
(20 minutes)

Begin by summarizing the main ideas and feelings conveyed by the sonnet's imagery. Then, use the details you have gathered to support your ideas. Note especially relationships of similarity, contrast, and development among images.

Revising
(10 minutes)

Review your analysis. If necessary, refine your main idea to fit the details or add details to support the main idea.

WG Prentice Hall Writing and Grammar Connection: Chapter 14, Section 3

Extend Your Learning

Listening and Speaking Hold a **sonnet recital,** taking turns reciting sonnets with classmates.

- On a copy of the poem you choose, mark words to emphasize and shifts in tone.
- Rehearse using facial expressions and tone of voice to convey emotions.

After the recital, discuss the works. **[Group Activity]**

Research and Technology Use the Internet, CD-ROM encyclopedias, or recordings from your public library to research Elizabethan music. Analyze the distinguishing characteristics of the music. Present your findings in a **multimedia report.**

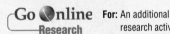

Go Online
Research

For: An additional research activity
Visit: www.PHSchool.com
Web Code: esd-7203

Sonnet 29 / Sonnet 106 / Sonnet 116 / Sonnet 130 ■ 265

---

❸ Writing Lesson

You may use this Writing Lesson as timed-writing practice, or you may allow students to develop the essay as a writing assignment over several days.

- Review with students their understanding of imagery.
- Tell students that in preparing their analyses, they should look for passages which include images that express emotions and ideas.
- Model the Prewriting chart for students to help stimulate their thinking about Shakespeare's use of imagery.
- Give students the Support for Writing Lesson, p. 49, in *Unit 2 Resources* to guide them in developing their essays.
- Use the Rubrics for Response to Literature, pp. 65–66 in *General Resources,* to evaluate students' essays.

❹ Listening and Speaking

- Have students select a sonnet and practice reading it silently to themselves.
- Encourage students to mark words that emphasize shift in tone for their presentation.
- Have students rehearse with a partner the facial expressions and tone of voice they will use.
- The **Support for Extend Your Learning** page (*Unit 2 Resources,* p. 50) provides guided note-taking opportunities to help students complete the Extend Your Learning activities.
- Have students use the Rubric for Peer Assessment: Oral Interpretation, p. 130 in *General Resources,* to evaluate one another's recitals.

Go Online
Research Activity Have students type in the Web Code for another research activity.

Assessment Resources

The following resources can be used to assess students' knowledge and skills.

Unit 2 Resources
  Selection Test A, pp. 52–54
  Selection Test B, pp. 55–57

General Resources
  Rubrics for Response to Literature
    p. 65–66
  Rubric for Peer Assessment:
    Oral Interpretation, p. 130

Go Online
Assessment Students may use the **Self-test** to prepare for **Selection Test A** or **Selection Test B.**

Connections
Literature Around the World

Both Petrarch's and Neruda's sonnets convey universal feelings relating to romantic love, and both incorporate traditional elements of the sonnet. What similarities and differences can students identify in the ways these authors advance the themes of romantic love?

Humanities
Portrait of Laura

This is a portrait of Laura, the woman to whom Petrarch addressed his sonnets. In the sonnets she is extolled for her incredible beauty and grace.

From era to era and culture to culture, people's ideas of beauty differ. For example, paleness of complexion was once admired because it indicated that the person was wealthy or privileged enough to spend his or her days indoors, without needing to work outside; in more recent times, however, suntans are admired because they indicate that the person has leisure time to be outside in the sun. Use this question for discussion: Judging from this picture, what were the standards of beauty in Petrarch's time?

Answer: Students may mention long, fair hair; plucked eyebrows; thin lips; long, straight nose; and average weight.

Critical Viewing

Answer: The expression on the woman's face seems remote and haughty. She does not look warm and friendly.

CONNECTIONS
Literature Around the World

Italy and Chile

Shadows of the Imagination

The years 1350 to 1550 marked a rebirth of interest in the literature of ancient Greece and Rome. It also marked a rebirth of interest in the nature of human experience, including love. The Italian poet Francesco Petrarcha, known by the English as Petrarch (pe´ trärk´), perfected a new type of poem to write about love in a new way.

The Invention of the Modern Sonnet A **sonnet** is a fourteen-line lyric with an elaborate rhyme scheme. In his sequence of 366 sonnets, Petrarch invented many of the attitudes and conventions that would be imitated by all proper poet-lovers, including the poets of the English Renaissance. Armed with this new tool of self-exploration, poets could disclose every aspect of love as they experienced it.

The Immortal Sonnet The sonnet continues to be a thriving form. While Petrarch devoted hundreds of sonnets to an unattainable, idealized woman, the modern Chilean poet Pablo Neruda seems to address an intimate companion in his sonnets.

Portrait of Laura, Biblioteca Laurenziana, Firenze

◄ **Critical Viewing**
Petrarch invented the idea of the "unattainable woman". What details in this portrait reflect such an ideal? **[Analyze]**

Sonnet 18

Francesco Petrarch
Translated by Noti

Ashamed sometimes thy beauties should remain
As yet unsung, sweet lady, in my rhyme;
When first I saw thee I recall the time.
Pleasing as none shall ever please again.
5 But no fit polish can my verse attain,
Not mine is strength to try the task sublime:
My genius, measuring its power to climb,
From such attempt doth prudently refrain.
Full oft I oped my lips to chant thy name;
10 Then in mid-utterance the lay was lost:
But say what muse can dare so bold a flight?
Full oft I strove in measure to indite;
But ah, the pen, the hand, the vein I boast,
At once were vanquish'd by the mighty theme!

Sonnet 28

Francesco Petrarch
Anonymous Translator

Alone, and lost in thought, the desert glade
Measuring I roam with ling'ring steps and slow;
And still a watchful glance around me throw,
Anxious to shun the print of human tread:
5 No other means I find, no surer aid
From the world's prying eye to hide my woe:
So well my wild disorder'd gestures show,
And lovelorn looks, the fire within me bred,
That well I deem each mountain, wood and plain,
10 And river knows, what I from man conceal,
What dreary hues my life's fond prospects dim.
Yet whate'er wild or savage paths I've ta'en,
Where'er I wander, love attends me still,
Soft whisp'ring to my soul, and I to him.

Thematic Connection
What attitudes toward love do Sidney and Spenser share with Petrarch?

Francesco Petrarch (1304–1374)

Along with Dante, Petrarch was among the great Italian poets of the fourteenth century. Born in Arezzo, Italy, he moved to Avignon, France, when he was eight. In 1320, Petrarch returned to Italy to study law but began to write poetry.

He returned to Avignon in 1326, where he first saw the famous Laura, whom he celebrates in his love poetry. Laura died in the Great Plague of 1348.

A Rebirth of Love and Poetry

- Explain to students that, like Shakespeare's sonnets, the sonnets in this section explore timeless themes such as love, despair, and obsession.

- Have students identify ways in which these sonnets deviate from the Shakespearean sonnet.

- As students read Petrarch's and Neruda's sonnets, have them pay attention to the ways in which the speakers express their complaints. Do students think that Petrarch's and Neruda's speakers' expression of romantic desperation is more affecting than that expressed by the speakers of Shakespeare's sonnets?

Thematic Connection

Answer: Sidney and Spenser both wrote sonnets expressing their frustration, loneliness, or disappointment in love, which is consistent with Petrarch's sonnets about an unattainable love.

Sonnet 89

Pablo Neruda

Translated by Stephan Tapscott

When I die, I want your hands on my eyes:
I want the light and wheat of your beloved hands
to pass their freshness over me once more:
I want to feel the softness that changed my destiny.

5 I want you to live while I wait for you, asleep.
I want your ears still to hear the wind, I want you
to sniff the sea's aroma that we loved together,
to continue to walk on the sand we walk on.

I want what I love to continue to live,
10 and you whom I love and sang above everything else
to continue to flourish, full-flowered:

so that you can reach everything my love directs you to,
so that my shadow can travel along in your hair,
so that everything can learn the reason for my song.

Pablo Neruda
(1904–1973)

Pablo Neruda was born in Parral, Chile, the son of a railway worker. He was only twenty when his book Twenty Love Poems and a Desperate Song earned him recognition as one of Chile's best young poets. Much of Neruda's work expresses political sentiments. However, he never lost his sense of poetry's irrational magic. In 1971, he received the Nobel Prize for Literature.

Connecting Literature Around the World

1. Of all the sonnets you read in Part One: Lovers and Their Lines, including Petrarch's and Neruda's, which were your favorites? Why?

2. Compare and contrast the expressions of love in Neruda's Sonnet 89 with those in Spenser's Sonnet 1.

3. Compare and contrast the message in Petrarch's Sonnet 28 with that in Shakespeare's Sonnet 29.

The Influence of the Monarchy

The Influence of the Monarchy   269

Selection Planning Guide

The selections in this section demonstrate the influence of three British monarchs on the literature of the sixteenth and early seventeenth centuries. Thomas More's *Utopia* was written in response to the excesses of Henry VIII. Elizabeth I's "Speech Before Defeating the Spanish Armada" reveals the public persona of this extremely powerful monarch. A committee appointed by Elizabeth's successor, James I, produced one of the most enduring and influential works of English literature, as is evident in the excerpts from the King James Bible.

Humanities

King Henry VIII of England, after Hans Holbein

Elizabeth I of England, unknown artist

James I of England, by John De Critz the Elder

These portraits show three monarchs who made their marks on their times and its literature. The elaborate pattern on Henry's clothing is blackwork embroidery. Elizabeth is resplendent in gold brocade lavishly trimmed with ermine. James wears white satin trimmed at the collar and cuff with *punto-in-aria* lace. Like his predecessors, he is richly jeweled.

Use the following questions for discussion.

1. Why were royal portraits important?
   Answer: They allowed people to see what the monarchs looked like, which was important in the days before photography.

2. Are these portraits completely accurate? What might the artists have changed?
   Answer: Most students will assume that the artists have adjusted cosmetic details to show the monarchs in the best possible light.

Differentiated
Instruction   Solutions for All Learners

Accessibility at a Glance

More Accessible	Average	More Challenging
Speech Before Her Troops	Psalm 23	from Utopia
	from The Sermon on the Mount	
	The Parable of the Prodigal Son	

TIME AND RESOURCE MANAGER

Meeting Your Standards

Students will

1. **analyze and respond to literary elements.**
   - Literary Analysis: The Monarch as Hero

2. **read, comprehend, analyze, and critique fiction and a speech.**
   - Reading Strategy: Summarizing
   - Reading Check questions
   - Apply the Skills questions
   - Assessment Practice (ATE)

3. **develop vocabulary.**
   - Vocabulary Lesson: Latin Root: -*sequent*-

4. **understand and apply written and oral language conventions.**
   - Spelling Strategy
   - Grammar and Style Lesson: Complex Sentences

5. **develop writing proficiency.**
   - Writing Lesson: Letter to an Editor

6. **develop appropriate research strategies.**
   - Extend Your Learning: Illustrated Timeline

7. **understand and apply listening and speaking strategies.**
   - Extend Your Learning: Debate

Block Scheduling: Use one 90-minute class period to preteach the skills and have students read the selection. Use a second 90-minute class period to assess students' mastery of skills, extend their learning, and monitor their progress.

Homework Suggestions

Following are possibilities for homework assignments:

- Support pages from *Unit 2 Resources:*
  - Literary Analysis
  - Reading Strategy
  - Vocabulary Builder
  - Grammar and Style

- An Extend Your Learning project and the Writing Lesson for this selection group may be completed over several days.

Step-by-Step Teaching Guide	Pacing Guide
PRETEACH	
• Administer Vocabulary and Reading Warm-ups as necessary.	5 min.
• Engage students' interest with the motivation activity.	5 min.
• Read and discuss author and background features. **FT**	10 min.
• Introduce the Literary Analysis Skill: The Monarch as Hero. **FT**	5 min.
• Introduce the Reading Strategy: Summarizing. **FT**	10 min.
• Prepare students to read by teaching the selection vocabulary. **FT**	
TEACH	
• Informally monitor comprehension while students read independently or in groups. **FT**	30 min.
• Monitor students' comprehension with the Reading Check notes.	as students read
• Reinforce vocabulary with Vocabulary Builder notes.	as students read
• Develop students' understanding of the monarch as hero with the Literary Analysis annotations. **FT**	5 min.
• Develop students' ability to summarize with the Reading Strategy annotations. **FT**	5 min.
ASSESS/EXTEND	
• Assess students' comprehension and mastery of the Literary Analysis and Reading Strategy by having them answer the Apply the Skills questions. **FT**	15 min.
• Have students complete the Vocabulary Lesson and the Grammar and Style Lesson. **FT**	15 min.
• Apply students' knowledge of using parallelism to create persuasive tone by using the Writing Lesson. **FT**	45 min. or homework
• Apply students' understanding by using one or more of the Extend Your Learning activities.	20–90 min. or homework
• Administer Selection Test A or Selection Test B. **FT**	15 min.

Resources

Choosing Resources for Differentiated Instruction

[**L1**] Special Needs Students

[**L2**] Below-Level Students

[**L3**] All Students

[**L4**] Advanced Students

[**EL**] English Learners

For Vocabulary and Reading Warm-ups and for Selection Tests, **A** signifies "less challenging" and **B** "more challenging." For Graphic Organizer transparencies, **A** signifies "not filled in" and **B** "filled in."

FT Fast Track Instruction: To move the lesson more quickly, use the strategies and activities identified with **FT**.

Scaffolding for Less Proficient and Advanced Students

The leveled Critical Thinking questions after selections progress in the levels of thinking required to answer them. To address the needs of your different students, you may use the (a) level questions for your less proficient students and the (b) level questions with your on-level and advanced students. The occasional (c) level questions are appropriate for your advanced students.

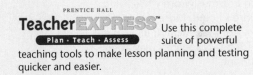

Use this complete suite of powerful teaching tools to make lesson planning and testing quicker and easier.

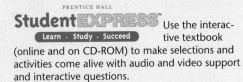

Use the interactive textbook (online and on CD-ROM) to make selections and activities come alive with audio and video support and interactive questions.

 **For:** Information about Lexiles
Visit: www.PHSchool.com
Web Code: eue-1111

Motivation

When students today think of a monarchy, they may think of the royal families of Britain, Thailand, or Spain. Ask students to identify any royalty with which they are familiar. Point out that there is a difference between an institution, such as the monarchy, and the individuals in it. Invite students to consider the monarchy as an institution. Use these questions to focus their thinking:

• What is the role of a good monarch?

• How should that person govern others?

• What qualities should monarchs have?

Explain that the writings they will read directly address these issues.

❶ Background
More About the Authors

Thomas More, who once hoped to be a priest, was a man of immense curiosity and energy. In addition to a full law practice, he read widely and wrote extensively, trying his hand at all literary genres. More's satirical *Utopia* was philosophically related to Erasmus's *The Praise of Folly*, which Erasmus wrote while living at More's home. More also wrote *History of King Richard III*, inspiration for Shakespeare's play about the tyrant.

It is almost impossible to overstate the brilliance and influence of Queen Elizabeth I. She loved learning and set aside large sums of money for public education. A skilled dancer and poet, she enthusiastically supported the arts. Elizabeth's interests extended beyond politics into most fields of learning, and she even experimented with machinery for making coins. She was friend and patron to some of the most famous individuals in English history, including Sir Francis Drake, Sir Walter Raleigh, and William Shakespeare.

❶ *from* Utopia • Speech Before Her Troops

Sir Thomas More
(1477–1535)

Even the king who had him put to death respected him. Sir Thomas More—devoted husband and father, passionate defender of the common citizen, sophisticated legal advisor, and deeply religious man—ultimately came to grief through the very quality that made him admirable: his integrity.

Early Career Trained in Latin, logic, and the law, More pursued a successful legal and political career. He championed the cultural movement know as Humanism, writing poems on behalf of the renewal of scholarship and religion advocated by the Dutch Humanist Desidirius Erasmus (1469–1536).

Opposing the King More entered King Henry VIII's service full-time in 1518 and soon became an important advisor. At times, his opinions made him a friend, and at other times, a bitter enemy of the king.

The final break with the king came when Henry asked Pope Clement VII for a divorce from Catherine of Aragon. She had not born him a male child, and Henry was eager for an heir. The pope denied the request, and in 1534, Henry broke with the Roman Catholic Church, establishing the Church of England, with himself as the head.

A devout Catholic, More opposed the king's divorce, arousing his anger. In 1535, the king had More beheaded for his refusal to swear an oath that violated his beliefs.

An Ideal Kingdom More, however, had a kind of revenge. His book *Utopia*, an account of an ideal kingdom (the title means "not a place"), exposes the injustices of his time. It still stands today as a challenge to leaders to pursue social justice.

Elizabeth I
(1533–1603)

The Elizabethan Age was a period rich in cultural activity and political success. It owes its name to an equally energetic ruler, Queen Elizabeth I. Elizabeth's path to the throne, though, was fraught with peril and sadness, and serious political challenges awaited her once she arrived.

A Tumultuous Childhood Elizabeth grew up surrounded by danger and intrigue. When she was not yet three years old, her mother, Anne Boleyn, was executed by her father, Henry VIII. After her father's death, Elizabeth's brother, Edward VI, inherited the throne. At his death six years later, Elizabeth's half sister, Mary, took the throne. Ever suspicious of Elizabeth, Mary even had her jailed at one point. Finally, in 1558 after Mary's death, Elizabeth was crowned queen of England and Ireland.

A Triumphant Ruler Once on the throne, Elizabeth met problems with decisive action and subtle diplomacy. Reigning as a single woman, she wielded her unmarried status as a political tool, taking suitors from all factions as a way of keeping the peace. During her reign, England won significant victories against its archenemy, Spain. With the destruction of the Spanish Armada (navy), England entered its long term as the world's supreme naval power.

The Elizabethan Age Today, Elizabeth I is regarded as one of the finest English monarchs. Highly intelligent, beloved by her subjects, she governed during a time of artistic achievement, military success, and economic advance. The young girl who grew up in danger left her name on a glorious era: the Elizabethan Age.

Preview

Connecting to the Literature

Picture a crowd wandering around a mall. Now, picture a basketball team racing downcourt, flipping passes back and forth. To turn a crowd into a team, you need unity. With rousing words, Elizabeth I and More try to unify the English people.

Literary Analysis

Theme: The Monarch as Hero

The literature of the English Renaissance (1485–1625) contains many depictions of the **monarch as hero,** the ruler as a perfect or larger-than-life person. Writers created heroic portraits to inspire confidence and loyalty in citizens. Praising, or even flattering, rulers in power could also help a writer establish strong connections with the court.

Look for this **theme** in these selections.

Comparing Literary Works

In *Utopia,* More paints a picture of the heroic monarch with brisk logic, connecting the qualities of a monarch with the effects of his or her actions. By contrast, Elizabeth I needs no arguments—as she gives her speech, she acts out the part of the heroic monarch, from the armor she wears to her offer to join the troops on the front lines. Compare the different **persuasive devices** these writers use to bring their audience to accept their presentation of the heroic monarch. These include the following techniques:

- **Reasoned argument**—the use of one idea to logically support another.
- **Charged language**—words with strong positive or negative connotations used to create a memorable perspective on an issue.

Reading Strategy

Summarizing

To understand a difficult work, **summarize** it by restating the main ideas. As you read these selections, track main ideas with a chart like the one shown.

Vocabulary Builder

confiscation (kän′ fis kā′ shən) *n.* act of seizing private property (p. 273)

sloth (slôth) *n.* laziness; idleness (p. 273)

subsequently (sub′ si kwənt lē) *adv.* at a later time (p. 273)

abrogated (ab′rō gāt′ id) *v.* repealed; annulled (p. 273)

forfeited (fôr′ fit id) *v.* gave up, as a penalty (p. 273)

fraudulent (frô′ jə lənt) *adj.* characterized by deceit or trickery (p. 273)

treachery (trech′ ər ē) *n.* betrayal of trust, faith, or allegiance (p. 275)

stead (sted) *n.* position of a person as filled by a replacement (p. 276)

More's Sentence

Let him curb crime, and by his wise conduct prevent it rather than allow it to increase, only to punish it subsequently.

Main Idea

A good king should try to prevent crime.

from *Utopia / Speech Before Her Troops* ■ 271

- Ask students to explain what the term *heroism* means to them. Tell students that in this lesson they will focus on the theme of the monarch as hero.

- Read the note on the theme of the monarch as hero together as a class. Call students' attention to how heroic portraits of monarchs could inspire patriotism and loyalty in subjects.

- Use the instruction for Comparing Literary Works to consider the persuasive devices used by More and Elizabeth I in their portraits of the heroic monarch. Review with students the difference between reasoned arguments and charged language.

❸ **Reading Strategy**
Summarizing

- Remind students that summarizing is restating the main ideas of a work. Explain that summarizing is one way to help understand a long or difficult work.

- Give students a copy of **Reading Strategy Graphic Organizer A,** p. 46 in *Graphic Organizer Transparencies* to record the progress of ideas in works by Thomas More and Elizabeth I.

Vocabulary Builder

- Pronounce each vocabulary word for students, and read the definitions as a class. Have students identify any words with which they are already familiar.

Differentiated Instruction — Solutions for All Learners

Support for Special Needs Students
Have students read the adapted version of these selections in the *Reader's Notebook: Adapted Version*. This version provides basic-level instruction in an interactive format with questions and write-on lines. Completing these pages will prepare students to read the selections in the Student Edition.

Support for Less Proficient Readers
Have students read these selections in the *Reader's Notebook*. This version provides basic-level instruction in an interactive format with questions and write-on lines. After students finish the selection in the *Reader's Notebook*, have them complete the questions and activities in the Student Edition.

Support for English Learners
Have students read these selections in the *Reader's Notebook: English Learner's Version*. This version provides basic-level instruction in an interactive format with questions and write-on lines. Completing these pages will prepare students to read the selections in the Student Edition.

❶ About the Selection

Though others have written about utopian communities, it was Thomas More's work that gave the world the term that most people use to describe an ideal society. *Utopia* comes from the Greek *ou topos*, which means "no place." This passage will give students a glimpse of one man's version of a political ideal.

❷ Humanities
Gardens at Llanerch, Denbighshire

This picture clearly emphasizes the garden instead of the house, which is set in the background. The careful arrangement of the elements reflects a love of order and proportion.

In Elizabethan times, a garden was viewed as an extension of the house. The garden was placed so that it provided splendid views from the main windows of the house. Most gardens had formal flower beds, often surrounded by walls or hedges. In addition, most gardens had fountains and sculptures.

Use these questions for discussion:

1. What is noteworthy about the trees in this garden?
   Answer: They are laid out in neat rows.

2. Do you think this house and garden are typical? Why?
   Possible response: Most students will notice that other homes in the picture are not as large or ornate.

❸ Critical Viewing

Answer: Everything is neat and beautifully maintained. Plants are in precise rows, there is no litter, and it even seems as if the deer know enough to stay out of the road.

---

❶ *from* Utopia *Sir Thomas More*

Gardens at Llanerch, Denbighshire, c. 1662–72, British School, Yale Center for British Art, New Haven, Connecticut

❷

❸ ▲ Critical Viewing
How does this painting illustrate the orderliness of the well-run kingdom More advocates? [Apply]

Background Running a kingdom is expensive. Waging wars and living in royal style requires money, and raising enough money was often a problem for the kings and queens of England. Henry VIII's father, Henry VII (ruled 1485–1509), approached the problem in several ways. He avoided costly wars, and he encouraged trade, which he then taxed. He also taxed the poor harshly and took advantage of outdated laws that gave monarchs the right to impose fines in certain matters. (More refers to such laws when he speaks of "laws already abrogated by disuse.") As a result, he acquired a large fortune for the Crown. In *Utopia*, More casts a critical eye on some of the ways in which monarchs like Henry VII collected wealth.

❹ Suppose I should maintain that men choose a king not for his sake, but for theirs, that by his care and efforts they may live comfortably and safely. And that therefore a prince ought to take more care of his people's happiness than of his own, as a shepherd ought to take more care of his flock than of himself. Certainly it is wrong to

Reading Strategy
Summarizing Summarize the main ideas in the first two sentences.

272 ■ *Celebrating Humanity (1485–1625)*

think that the poverty of the people is a safeguard of public peace. Who quarrel more than beggars do? Who long for a change more earnestly than the dissatisfied? Or who rushes in to create disorders [with] such desperate boldness as the man who has nothing to lose and everything to gain? If a king is so hated and scorned by his subjects that he can rule them only by insults, ill-usage, <u>confiscation</u>, and impoverishment, it would certainly be better for him to quit his kingdom than to keep the name of authority when he has lost the majesty of kingship through his misrule. It is less befitting the dignity of a king to reign over beggars than over rich and happy subjects. Thus Fabricius, a man of noble and exalted spirit, said he would rather govern rich men than be rich himself. When a ruler enjoys wealth and pleasure while all about him are grieving and groaning, he acts as a jailor rather than as a king. He is a poor physician who cannot cure a disease except by throwing his patient into another. A king who can only rule his people by taking from them the pleasures of life shows that he does not know how to govern free men. He ought to shake off either his <u>sloth</u> or his pride, for the people's hatred and scorn arise from these faults in him. Let him live on his own income without wronging others, and limit his expenses to his revenue. Let him curb crime, and by his wise conduct prevent it rather than allow it to increase, only to punish it <u>subsequently</u>. Let him not rashly revive laws already <u>abrogated</u> by disuse, especially if they have been long forgotten and never wanted. And let him never seize any property on the ground that it is <u>forfeited</u> as a fine, when a judge would regard a subject as wicked and <u>fraudulent</u> for claiming it.

5

Critical Reading

1. **Respond:** Do you think More's ideas would lead to greater fairness?
2. **(a) Recall:** What reason does More give for viewing poverty as a threat to a nation? **(b) Analyze:** How does he connect this idea to the notion that a king should rule for the sake of his people?
3. **(a) Recall:** According to More, what does a king lose when he rules by "insults, ill-usage, confiscation, and impoverishment"? **(b) Infer:** What assumption about monarchs or the monarchy does this point reveal?
4. **Generalize:** Explain how More appeals to the self-interest and even the vanity of kings to strengthen his argument.
5. **(a) Summarize:** What general rule for good leadership does More advocate in this selection? **(b) Apply:** How do More's views of good government resemble modern democratic ideals?

Vocabulary Builder

confiscation (kän′ fis kā′ shən) *n.* act of seizing private property

sloth (slôth) *n.* laziness; idleness

subsequently (sub′ si kwənt lē) *adv.* at a later time

abrogated (ab′rō gāt′ id) *v.* repealed; annulled

forfeited (fôr′ fit id) *v.* gave up, as a penalty

fraudulent (frô′ jə lənt) *adj.* characterized by deceit or trickery

Go Online
Author Link

For: More about Sir Thomas More
Visit: www.PHSchool.com
Web Code: ese-9207

from Utopia ■ 273

④ Reading Strategy
Summarizing

▶ **Reteach:** Remind students that by restating the main ideas of a passage, or summarizing, they can understand a difficult work.

• **Ask** students to follow the Reading Strategy directions on p. 272: Summarize the main ideas in the first two sentences.
Answer: More suggests that people might choose a king for their own comfort and safety. Therefore, a good king should put his subjects' happiness before his own.

⑤ Vocabulary Builder
Latin Root: *-sequent-*

• Call students' attention to the word *subsequently* and its definition. Tell students that the Latin root *-sequent-* means "following in time or order."

• Have students **suggest** words and phrases that contain this root, and list them on the chalkboard.
Possible responses: *consequence; non sequitur; sequel; sequential*

ASSESS

Answers

1. **Possible response:** Students may say that More's ideas of a just ruler would lead to greater fairness and less political corruption.

2. (a) Poverty makes it more likely that people will be quarrelsome, discontented, and disorderly. (b) More shows that ruling for the people safeguards the peace that poverty disrupts.

3. (a) He loses "the majesty of kingship." (b) It reveals that some monarchs use these tactics.

4. More appeals to rulers by showing that they can avoid people's hatred, and even enhance their dignity, by being virtuous.

5. (a) A good monarch should be unselfish and care for his people's happiness. (b) They mirror modern ideals: those who govern should obey the law and should put the needs and welfare of the people above their own desires.

Go Online
Author Link For additional information about Sir Thomas More, have students type in the Web Code, then select M from the alphabet, and then select Sir Thomas More.

Differentiated
Instruction Solutions for All Learners

Support for Less Proficient Readers
If students find the two pieces in this selection challenging, you may want to have them read this selection in the **Reader's Notebook**. A summary and story map of each piece is followed by the full SE text. There are prompts, notes, and additional questions in the margins to help students understand the text and apply strategies.

Strategy for Advanced Readers
Have students address whether or not More's ideas about the qualities of a good leader apply today. Have students work in small groups compiling evidence from More's work about what he thinks a good leader or monarch must do. Then, have students consider the behavior of current world leaders that is consistent with or different from what More suggests. Have students present their findings in an essay or oral report.

Portrait of Queen Elizabeth I,
Anonymous

Many portraits were painted of Elizabeth I, and often, each would emphasize a different aspect of her. This painting, known as the Armada portrait, stresses her victory over Spain.

Use these questions for discussion:

1. What are some of the clues in the painting that the woman portrayed is the queen of an empire?
   Answer: The crown to the right of the queen suggests royalty. Her hand is on the globe of the Earth, suggesting conquest and the idea that the world is under her control. Her jewelry and clothing indicate that she is a person of wealth and importance.

2. What evidence is there in the picture that Spain's famed Armada had met its end?
   Answer: The images of ships in the background allude to the naval battle, and the picture at left of the Armada broken and battered on a stormy sea reflects its defeat.

3. Monarchs were viewed as the embodiment of their nation. What does Elizabeth's appearance tell you about England during this period?
   Answer: On the basis of Elizabeth's appearance, one might guess that England was formal, wealthy, powerful, and in control.

7 **Critical Viewing**

Answer: Elizabeth's elaborate dress and jewelry suggest that she was an important symbol of majesty and empire to her subjects as well as to those who might visit from other countries. Pageantry emphasized the glory and power of both Elizabeth and the country as a whole.

Portrait of Queen Elizabeth I, Anonymous Artist, Private Collection

7 ▲ **Critical Viewing** What does this rendering of Elizabeth indicate about the importance of pageantry—ceremony and theatrical presence—in her court? Explain your reasoning. **[Interpret]**

Enrichment

Rulers

The beliefs people have about their monarchs have varied across time and place. The ancient Egyptian pharaohs, and later some Roman emperors, were considered gods, and their subjects were expected to revere them as such. The Aztec "sun kings" were seen as gods and expected human sacrifice.

The seventeenth-century French king Louis XIV made the famous statement, "I am the State," meaning that he embodied the nation of France. Though monarchs of this era did not believe they were gods, they did believe that they ruled by divine right. Today, several countries still have monarchs. Generally, today's rulers are dedicated to helping their people and strengthening their countries. Good examples of this trend are found in Thailand and Spain.

Speech Before Her Troops
QUEEN ELIZABETH I

❽ About the Selection
Part of a leader's job is rallying support for causes that the government proposes. Queen Elizabeth's speech exemplifies some of the techniques that a persuasive speaker uses, including flattery and rhetorical devices such as repetition and parallel structure.

❾ Literary Analysis
Theme: The Monarch as Hero
• Read aloud the entire speech to students.
• As you read, have students make a list of words that Elizabeth uses that make her appear heroic.
Answer: Students may identify words and phrases such as *we; resolved; live or die amongst you all; my honor; heart of a king; take up arms; be your general, judge, and rewarder;* and *noble and worthy.*

❿ Reading Check
Answer: Elizabeth's advisers have cautioned her about walking among the soldiers, because someone might try to hurt her.

Background In 1587, Protestant Queen Elizabeth agreed to have her Catholic cousin, Mary, Queen of Scots, executed. This act gave Philip II, the Catholic king of Spain and England's archenemy, an excuse to attack England with the Spanish Armada (navy). As nerves grew frayed and soldiers began to grumble about delays in pay, Elizabeth, wearing a white gown and a silver breast-plate, appeared before her land troops to rally them. She delivered the following speech. (At the time, the Armada had already been defeated, but the news had not yet reached Elizabeth and her troops. Invasion seemed imminent.)

As the speech shows, the physical presence of a monarch had a special significance in Elizabeth's day. The touch of a monarch, it was said, could cure certain diseases, and people acknowledged the presence of royalty with gestures such as the removal of hats. In her speech, Queen Elizabeth makes effective use of people's reverence for the monarch's person.

My loving people, we have been persuaded by some, that are careful of our safety, to take heed how we commit ourselves to armed multitudes,[1] for fear of <u>treachery</u>; but I assure you, I do not desire to live to distrust my faithful and loving people. Let tyrants fear; I have always so behaved myself that, under God, I have placed my chiefest strength and safeguard in the loyal hearts and good will of my subjects. And therefore I am come amongst you at this time, not as for my recreation or sport, but being resolved, in the midst and heat of the battle, to live or die amongst you all; to lay down, for my God, and for my kingdom, and for my people, my honor and my blood, even the dust. I know I have but the body of a weak and feeble woman; but I

Vocabulary Builder
treachery (trech´ ər ē) *n.* betrayal of trust, faith, or allegiance

❿ Reading Check
What have Elizabeth's advisers cautioned her about?

---

1. **armed multitudes** troops such as she is addressing.

Speech Before Her Troops ■ 275

Differentiated
Instruction   Solutions for All Learners

Background for Special Needs Students
Explain to students that Elizabeth I was speaking to soldiers. Spain had threatened to invade. Elizabeth is reminding the soldiers of how wonderful England is, and how it is worth defending, as well as how highly she regards the soldiers and their sense of duty. She also states that she is prepared to die with them, if necessary. Listening to this selection on **Listening to Literature Audio CDs** may help students understand better what is being said.

Enrichment for Gifted/Talented Students
Have students make a collage in which they illustrate or excerpt parts of Elizabeth I's speech that suggest the theme of monarch as hero. Encourage students to reread the speech independently, noting words, passages, or persuasive elements that allude to Elizabeth I's heroism. Then, have students work in small groups to make an illustration that conveys the way in which the theme is broached in her speech. Students may want to listen to the speech on **Listening to Literature Audio CDs.**

⓫ **Critical Viewing**

Answer: Most students will hypothesize that those who received the medals were treated with respect.

ASSESS

Answers

1. **Possible response:** Students may say that they would have responded favorably to the speech, which is a rousing call to patriotism and loyalty.

2. (a) Elizabeth's advisors have warned her to avoid close, personal contact with her subjects. (b) Elizabeth trusts her faithful and loving people. (c) This introduction is designed to have her audience feel close to the Queen, who trusts them and wants to be with them.

3. (a) Elizabeth addresses the concerns of invasion and lack of proper payment. (b) Elizabeth says that she scorns the invaders and that she is certain that the soldiers will be victorious. Also, she will herself see that they are rewarded.

4. (a) Elizabeth will take up arms rather than see her country dishonored. (b) She is answering criticism that a woman cannot rule soldiers.

5. (a) **Possible responses:** Elizabeth's presence on the scene underscores her trust of her people and her belief that England is safe in their hands. Her femininity might make soldiers want to protect her. Her regal bearing would make them feel encouraged, awed, and honored that their monarch would mingle with them.

(b) **Possible responses:** It still retains that "star quality" that creates excitement. Today, not everyone is in awe of leaders. Leaders are often surrounded by bodyguards, and not as trusting as Elizabeth.

Go **Online**
—Author Link For additional information about Queen Elizabeth I, have students type in the Web Code, then select E from the alphabet, and then select Queen Elizabeth I.

---

⑨ have the heart of a king, and of a king of England, too; and think foul scorn that Parma[2] or Spain, or any prince of Europe, should dare to invade the borders of my realms: to which, rather than any dishonor should grow by me, I myself will take up arms; I myself will be your general, judge, and rewarder of every one of your virtues in the field. I know already, by your forwardness, that you have deserved rewards and crowns; and we do assure you, on the word of a prince, they shall be duly paid you. In the mean my lieutenant general shall be in my <u>stead</u>, than whom never prince commanded a more noble and worthy subject; not doubting by your obedience to my general, by your concord in the camp, and by your valor in the field, we shall shortly have a famous victory over the enemies of my God, of my kingdom, and of my people.

---

2. **Parma** Alessandro Farnese (1545–1592), duke of the state of Parma and Piacenza in Italy and King Philip of Spain's representative in the Netherlands. Philip had him prepare troops for the invasion of England.

Critical Reading

1. **Respond:** If you were a British soldier at the time, how would you have responded to Elizabeth's speech?

2. **(a) Recall:** What have Elizabeth's advisors warned her not to do? **(b) Recall:** According to her speech, why does she do it anyway? **(c) Interpret:** What effect is this introduction designed to have on her audience?

3. **(a) Recall:** Name two concerns of Elizabeth's audience that she addresses. **(b) Analyze:** How does she put these concerns to rest?

4. **(a) Recall:** What does Elizabeth promise to do rather than permit her country to be dishonored? **(b) Analyze:** Which criticism of her capacity to rule is she answering?

5. **(a) Analyze:** Explain two ways in which Elizabeth's physical "person"—for instance, her presence on the scene or her femininity—plays a role in this speech. **(b) Apply:** Does the physical presence of leaders today count as much as it did in Elizabeth's time? Explain.

276 ■ Celebrating Humanity (1485–1625)

⓫ ◄ **Critical Viewing**
These *Dangers Averted* medals celebrated the defeat of the Spanish Armada. How do you think those who received this medal were treated by average British citizens? [Hypothesize]

Vocabulary Builder
stead (sted) *n.* position of a person as filled by a replacement

—Author Link
For: More about Queen Elizabeth I
Visit: www.PHSchool.com
Web Code: ese-9208

Apply the Skills

from *Utopia* • *Speech Before Her Troops*

Literary Analysis

Theme: The Monarch as Hero

1. **(a)** How idealistic is More's presentation of the **theme of the monarch as hero?** **(b)** How realistic?
2. **(a)** Explain how More paints a picture of a rather unheroic monarch even as he describes an ideal monarch. **(b)** What effect might More have hoped this picture would have?
3. Elizabeth says, "I know I have but the body of a weak and feeble woman; but I have the heart of a king, and of a king of England, too. . . ." Relate this assertion to the idea of a heroic monarch.

Comparing Literary Works

4. **(a)** Identify a **persuasive device** in each work. **(b)** Do these devices appeal to logic, ethics, or feelings? Explain.
5. **(a)** Analyze how Elizabeth's speech turns her appearance among the troops into a persuasive device. Use a chart like the one below, noting under the appropriate heading each reference she makes to the reasons for her appearance. **(b)** Do you think this device is more effective than one of More's arguments? Explain.

6. **(a)** Contrast the role of persuasive arguments in More's work with their role in Elizabeth's speech. **(b)** Which work has stronger arguments? Explain. **(c)** Which is more persuasive? Explain.

Reading Strategy

Summarizing

7. **Summarize** More's *Utopia,* listing each main idea.
8. Summarize Elizabeth's speech.

Extend Understanding

9. **Career Connection:** Motivational speakers inspire audiences to achieve goals. What tips might a speaker learn from these authors?

QuickReview

A **theme** is the central idea, concern, or purpose of a literary work.

In the literature presenting the **theme of the monarch as hero,** a ruler is portrayed as a larger-than-life person with noble qualities.

A **persuasive device** is the use of words to lead an audience to accept a particular position or attitude. Persuasive devices include **reasoned arguments,** ideas supported by their logical connections to other ideas, and **charged language,** words with strong positive or negative connotations.

To **summarize,** restate the main ideas of a work.

Go Online
Assessment

For: Self-test
Visit: www.PHSchool.com
Web Code: esa-6205

from Utopia / Speech Before Her Troops ■ 277

Answers continued

8. Summaries should include the idea that Elizabeth relies on her people and encourages them to rely on her.
9. **Possible answer:** The most important thing is to know your audience and choose your arguments accordingly.

Go Online
Assessment Students may use the **Self-test** to prepare for **Selection Test A** or **Selection Test B.**

Answers

1. (a) **Possible response:** Students may reply that it is idealistic, because people, rulers or otherwise, are more interested in themselves than in others.
   (b) **Possible response:** The observations on how people behave when poor and on the acts of bad rulers are realistic.

2. (a) He defines the ideal primarily in terms of the things a monarch should not do: take pleasures away from people, insult them, seize property, create bad laws. (b) More probably wanted to persuade leaders to rule well.

3. Elizabeth shows that she has escaped normal limitations, which makes her heroic. She reminds people of England's great kings and aligns herself with that heritage, and she flatters her subjects, saying that she is made great by those she rules.

4. (a) More shows how badly things turn out when people are unhappy. Elizabeth both appeals to people's loyalty and offers to take up arms herself. (b) More's appeal is to ethics first, but also to logic. If a monarch doesn't care about people's happiness, at least he should care about the kingdom being in an uproar. Elizabeth's appeal is almost entirely to feelings.

5. (a) *Despite:* warnings that it would be dangerous to mingle; *Because:* she loves her people; *In order to:* show her trust; *In order to:* inspire them and lead them; *Because:* Spain is attacking; *Not for:* sport or recreation; *But for:* laying down her honor and blood. (b) **Possible response:** When people are at war, the personal appearance made by a leader is more effective than More's philosophy.

6. (a) More's arguments are intellectual and are aimed at kings. Elizabeth's persuasion is more emotional, because she is speaking to soldiers going to battle. (b) **Possible response:** Both have arguments that suit the purpose and audience. (c) **Possible response:** Elizabeth's argument would be more persuasive because she delivers it in person.

7. Summaries should include the idea of kings ruling to serve their subjects.

continued

❶ Vocabulary Lesson
Word Analysis
1. b   3. a
2. d   4. c

Spelling Strategy
surfeit, mischievous

Vocabulary Builder
1. confiscation   5. fraudulent
2. subsequently   6. sloth
3. abrogated   7. treachery
4. stead   8. forfeited

❷ Grammar and Style Lesson

1. He is a poor king who rules unfairly.
2. A king should not seize property when a subject would be wrong to do the same.
3. Elizabeth's advisors warned her that appearing before the troops was risky.
4. She knew that the troops were unpaid.
5. Her general, than whom there was no better commander, led the troops.

Writing Application
Possible response: An ideal leader is a person who acts sensibly when all others are acting irrationally. When fellow citizens fear making difficult decisions, the ideal leader acts. When others disagree with his or her decisions, the ideal leader is open to suggestions.

WG **Writing and Grammar, Diamond Level**

Students will find further instruction and practice on complex sentences in Chapter 19, Section 4.

Build Language Skills

❶ Vocabulary Lesson

Word Analysis: Latin Root -sequent-

The word *subsequently*, meaning "at a later time," is derived from the Latin root -*sequent*-, meaning "following in time or order." Use the meaning of -*sequent*- to match each word below with its definition.

1. consequence   a. something that does not follow
2. sequential
3. non sequitur   b. result of an action
4. subsequent   c. at a later time
                      d. coming in order

Spelling Strategy

Either *i, ei,* or *ie* can spell the short *i* sound, as in the words *different, forfeited,* and *omniscient.* Correct the misspellings in the following passage.

A surfiet of unfair laws will yield disloyalty. The people must be considered, no matter how mischeivous they seem.

Vocabulary Builder: Analogies

An analogy compares two relationships to show their basic similarity. For each analogy below, analyze the relationship between the first and second words. Then, in your notebook, write the vocabulary word from page 271 that forms the same relationship with the third word.

1. lending : borrowing :: grant :   ?
2. front : back :: beforehand :   ?
3. built : constructed :: repealed :   ?
4. goal : ambition :: place :   ?
5. honorable : untrustworthy :: authentic :   ?
6. nervousness : calm ::   ?   : energy
7. goodness : virtue :: betrayal :   ?
8. praised : honored :: surrendered   ?

❷ Grammar and Style Lesson

Complex Sentences

Complex sentences contain a main clause and one or more subordinate clauses. The main clause can stand by itself as a sentence. The subordinate clauses modify the main clause.

> SUB. CLAUSE
> **Example:** When a ruler enjoys wealth . . .
> SUB. CLAUSE
> while all about him are grieving, . . .
> MAIN CLAUSE
> he acts as a jailor. . . .

Writers use complex sentences to show the connections between ideas or events.

Practice Copy the sentences below, underlining main clauses once and subordinate clauses twice.

1. He is a poor king who rules unfairly.
2. A king should not seize property when a subject would be wrong to do the same.
3. Elizabeth's advisors warned her that appearing before the troops was risky.
4. She knew that the troops were upaid.
5. Her general, than whom there was no better commander, led the troops.

Writing Application Using three complex sentences, write your own description of an ideal leader.

WG *Prentice Hall Writing and Grammar Connection: Chapter 19, Section 4*

Assessment Practice

Forms of Propaganda (For more practice, see *Standardized Test Preparation Workbook,* p. 10.)

Many tests require students to recognize propaganda. Use this item to reinforce the concept.

My loving people . . . being resolved, in the midst and heat of the battle, to live or die amongst you all; . . . by your valor in the field, we shall . . . have a famous victory over the enemies of my God, of my kingdom, and of my people.

The passage can be characterized as propaganda because

A it was spoken by a political leader
B it contains examples of hyperbole
C it is very dramatic
D its purpose was to persuade the people to support the speaker's cause

Choice *D* is correct, because the purpose of propaganda is to persuade people to support a particular cause.

Writing Lesson

Letter to an Editor

Thomas More and Queen Elizabeth I have definite ideas about the characteristics of a good leader. In a letter to the editor, apply their criteria of good leadership—or the example they set in their lives—to a contemporary leader.

Prewriting   Review the selections and the biographical information on page 270, taking notes on the writers' ideas about and their practice of leadership. Then, research a modern leader, taking notes on his or her leadership skills as shown in news stories.

Drafting   Begin by stating the ideas of leadership you will apply, and then apply these ideas in an analysis of the leader you have chosen.

Revising   Reread your draft, highlighting passages in which you express parallel ideas—ideas that are similar to one another. Consider rewriting marked passages using parallel phrases.

Model: Using Parallelism to Create Persuasive Tone

When a senator suddenly changes his or her mind about

an important issue, he or she begins to look irresponsible.

When a senator makes and then apologizes for hasty,

~~A congressperson who makes and then apologizes for hasty~~

inaccurate statements, he or she starts to look careless.

~~and innaccurate statements seems careless.~~

By rewriting the second sentence to begin with a subordinate clause, the writer uses parallelism to create a persuasive rhythm and to convey confidence.

W̶G̶ Prentice Hall Writing and Grammar Connection: Chapter 7, Section 4

Extend Your Learning

Listening and Speaking Form two groups, and prepare for a **debate** on this question: Do More's ideas apply to today's leaders? Use the following persuasive devices:

- reasoned argument
- effective emotional appeals
- charged language
- vivid images

Hold your debate before the class. **[Group Activity]**

Research and Technology Create a large **illustrated timeline** of the Elizabethan Age, indicating major achievements and events. Use library and Internet references to identify entries. Collect information on notecards, and organize the cards chronologically as you plan the timeline.

 **Go Online Research**   **For:** An additional research activity
Visit: www.PHSchool.com
Web Code: esd-7204

Assessment Resources

The following resources can be used to assess students' knowledge and skills.

Unit 2 Resources
Selection Test A, pp. 69–71
Selection Test B, pp. 72–74

General Resources
Rubrics for Persuasion: Persuasive Essay, pp. 45–46
Rubric for Delivering a Persuasive Speech, p. 89

Go Online Assessment   Students may use the **Self-test** to prepare for **Selection Test A** or **Selection Test B.**

---

❸ Writing Lesson

You may use this Writing Lesson as timed-writing practice, or you may allow students to develop the essay as a writing assignment over several days.

- Review with students what a letter to the editor should include.
- Tell students that they should develop their ideas on leadership based on the perspectives of Thomas More or Queen Elizabeth.
- Have students review current news stories to help them pick a leader to target.
- Give students the **Support for Writing Lesson,** p. 66, in *Unit 2 Resources*, to guide them in developing their letters to the editor. Model for students the technique of parallelism using the example on this page.
- Use the Rubrics for Persuasion: Persuasive Essay, pp. 45–46 in *General Resources*, to evaluate student work.

❹ Listening and Speaking

- Divide the class into two groups. Have each group discuss how More's ideas apply to today's leaders. Then have each group adopt a different position on the relevance of More's ideas.
- Encourage students to use the persuasive speaking techniques listed in their texts.
- Have students practice delivering their response before they present it to the class.
- The **Support for Extend Your Learning** page (*Unit 2 Resources,* p. 67) provides guided note-taking opportunities to help students complete the Extend Your Learning activities.
- Use the **Rubric for Speaking: Delivering a Persuasive Speech,** p. 89 in *General Resources*.

Go Online Research   Have students type in the Web Code for another research activity.

Meeting Your Standards

Students will

1. **analyze and respond to literary elements.**
   - Literary Analysis: Psalm, Sermon, and Parable

2. **read, comprehend, analyze, and critique Scripture.**
   - Reading Strategy: Inferring Meaning
   - Reading Check questions
   - Apply the Skills questions
   - Assessment Practice (ATE)

3. **develop vocabulary.**
   - Vocabulary Lesson: Latin Root: -*stat*-

4. **understand and apply written and oral language conventions.**
   - Spelling Strategy
   - Grammar and Style Lesson: Infinitive Phrases

5. **develop writing proficiency.**
   - Writing Lesson: Parable in King James Style

6. **develop appropriate research strategies.**
   - Extend Your Learning: Evaluative Report

7. **understand and apply listening and speaking strategies.**
   - Extend Your Learning: Retelling

Block Scheduling: Use one 90-minute class period to preteach the skills and have students read the selection. Use a second 90-minute class period to assess students' mastery of skills, extend their learning, and monitor their progress.

Homework Suggestions

Following are possibilities for homework assignments:

- Support pages from *Unit 2 Resources*:
  - Literary Analysis
  - Reading Strategy
  - Vocabulary Builder
  - Grammar and Style

- An Extend Your Learning project and the Writing Lesson for this selection group may be completed over several days.

Step-by-Step Teaching Guide	Pacing Guide
PRETEACH	
• Administer Vocabulary and Reading Warm-ups as necessary.	5 min.
• Engage students' interest with the motivation activity.	5 min.
• Read and discuss background feature. **FT**	10 min.
• Introduce the Literary Analysis Skill: Psalm, Sermon, and Parable. **FT**	5 min.
• Introduce the Reading Strategy: Inferring Meaning. **FT**	10 min.
• Prepare students to read by teaching the selection vocabulary. **FT**	
TEACH	
• Informally monitor comprehension while students read independently or in groups. **FT**	30 min.
• Monitor students' comprehension with the Reading Check notes.	as students read
• Reinforce vocabulary with Vocabulary Builder notes.	as students read
• Develop students' understanding of psalms, sermons, and parables with the Literary Analysis annotations. **FT**	5 min.
• Develop students' ability to infer meaning with the Reading Strategy annotations. **FT**	5 min.
ASSESS/EXTEND	
• Assess students' comprehension and mastery of the Literary Analysis and Reading Strategy by having them answer the Apply the Skills questions. **FT**	15 min.
• Have students complete the Vocabulary Lesson and the Grammar and Style Lesson. **FT**	15 min.
• Apply students' knowledge of creating a consistent style by using the Writing Lesson. **FT**	45 min. or homework
• Apply students' understanding by using one or more of the Extend Your Learning activities.	20–90 min. or homework
• Administer Selection Test A or Selection Test B. **FT**	15 min.

Resources

Choosing Resources for Differentiated Instruction

[**L1**] Special Needs Students

[**L2**] Below-Level Students

[**L3**] All Students

[**L4**] Advanced Students

[**EL**] English Learners

For Vocabulary and Reading Warm-ups and for Selection Tests, **A** signifies "less challenging" and **B** "more challenging." For Graphic Organizer transparencies, **A** signifies "not filled in" and **B** "filled in."

FT Fast Track Instruction: To move the lesson more quickly, use the strategies and activities identified with **FT**.

Scaffolding for Less Proficient and Advanced Students

The leveled Critical Thinking questions after selections progress in the levels of thinking required to answer them. To address the needs of your different students, you may use the (a) level questions for your less proficient students and the (b) level questions with your on-level and advanced students. The occasional (c) level questions are appropriate for your advanced students.

PRENTICE HALL
TeacherEXPRESS™ Use this complete
Plan · Teach · Assess suite of powerful
teaching tools to make lesson planning and testing quicker and easier.

PRENTICE HALL
StudentEXPRESS™ Use the interac-
Learn · Study · Succeed tive textbook
(online and on CD-ROM) to make selections and activities come alive with audio and video support and interactive questions.

Go **Online** **For:** Information about Lexiles
Professional **Visit:** www.PHSchool.com
Development **Web Code:** eue-1111

Motivation

Point out to students that literally hundreds of expressions still in common use come from the King James Bible. Examples include: *Salt of the earth. Like mother, like daughter. By the skin of my teeth. Can a leopard change its spots? The blind leading the blind. Good Samaritan. Out of the mouths of babes. God forbid. Physician, heal thyself.* Show students books with titles based on biblical phrases, such as Robert Heinlein's *Stranger in a Strange Land* or William Barrett's *The Lilies of the Field.*

Explain that before this version existed, only highly educated people could read the Bible, which was available only in Latin. This edition made the work accessible to ordinary people. It used what was then simple English. In addition, the language had a rhythm and beauty that profoundly influenced English literature.

❶ Background
More About the Authors

When translating the Bible, scholars have a greater number of ancient documents from which to work than for any other literature of such age. Its historical record is so accurate that archaeologists in the Middle East have used it to locate lost cities. But more significant is its impact on Western culture. From the Bible, we get ideas as diverse as trial by jury, the right of women to inherit property, and fair wages. Much writing in English contains at least some biblical allusion, from Edgar Allan Poe's "thief in the night" to the song "Turn, Turn, Turn" (Eccl. 3). Though the Bible's inspiration is attributed to God, the words were written down by people across 1,200 years, from Moses and King David in the Old Testament to the disciples of Jesus in the New Testament.

---

❶ *from* The King James Bible

The King James Bible
(completed 1611)

For centuries, the Bible was the cornerstone of European culture—the ultimate reference for rulers and priests, the ultimate authorization for laws and religious practices, a treasury of images and subjects for art. Yet, the book that shaped the lives of Europeans was inaccessible to the majority of them. During the Reformation of the 1500s, a time of religious dispute and division, the need for a closer study of the Bible was widely acknowledged, which led to translations of the work into the vernacular, or common languages. For the first time, this grounding work became widely accessible.

The King James Bible, the authoritative English translation, was created at the command of King James I, who ascended the English throne upon the death of Queen Elizabeth I. In 1604, James commissioned fifty-four scholars and clergymen to compare all known texts of the Bible and prepare the definitive English edition.

Early Bibles To understand the magnitude of King James's project, consider the nature of the work to be translated. The Bible, a collection of books developed over more than 1,200 years, consists of two main parts—the Old Testament, written in Hebrew, and the New Testament, written in Greek. In about A.D. 405, St. Jerome finished translating the Bible into Latin. This translation, the Vulgate, remained the standard Bible of the West for centuries. King James's translators, though, were to review the original sources, as well as translations of the work.

A Systematic Plan The project was carefully organized from the start. The books of the Bible were divided among six groups of scholars in Westminster, Oxford, and Cambridge. A set of fifteen guidelines for the project was drafted, governing everything from the translation of names to the procedure for review.

The groups took four years to produce their initial drafts. Then, two scholars from each region spent nine months in London reviewing and revising the draft. The preface to the first edition acknowledged the importance of rewriting during the project—"Neither did we disdain to revise that which we had done, and to bring back to the anvil that which we had hammered." After laboring for seven years, the group produced one of the great works of English literature. The King James Bible has been called "the only classic ever created by a committee."

Early English Bibles The King James Bible was not the first English translation of the book. The reformer John Wycliffe had translated the Bible into English in the late 1300s. It was William Tyndale's sixteenth-century version, though, that most influenced James's translators.

Tyndale's Legacy Tyndale was a Protestant chaplain and tutor in England. As Protestants across Europe challenged the authority of the Catholic Church, Tyndale decided to translate the Bible. Facing clerical opposition at home, he fled to what is now Germany, where he published his translation of the New Testament. Before he had completed work on the Old Testament, however, he was arrested for heresy and executed near Brussels, Belgium, in 1536.

As England became more Protestant, Tyndale came to be viewed, not as a heretic, but as a hero. King James's committee closely followed the magnificent diction and rhythms of Tyndale's groundbreaking translation.

A Lasting Vision Generations of English-speakers have grown up reading the King James Bible. It has contributed hundreds of phrases to the language—"fat of the land," "out of the mouths of babes," "suffer fools gladly"—and left a lasting mark on English prose style.

Preview

Connecting to the Literature

Not too long ago, the development of the Web opened up a world of information. Yet, that event was small compared to an earlier "information revolution"—the translation of the Bible into modern languages.

Literary Analysis

Psalm, Sermon, and Parable

The Bible conveys themes of faith in a few genres, including these:

- **Psalms**—sacred songs or lyric poems in praise of God. The Old Testament's Book of Psalms contains 150 such pieces.
- **Sermons**—speeches offering religious or moral instruction. Given by Jesus on a mountainside in Galilee, the Sermon on the Mount contains the basic teachings of Christianity.
- **Parables**—simple stories from which a moral or religious lesson can be drawn. The most famous are in the New Testament.

Notice the different impact and features of each genre.

Comparing Literary Works

Psalms, sermons, and parables all convey deep messages about life. Each type of writing communicates messages in a manner suited to its form.

- Psalms are songs. To engage an audience, psalms may feature vivid, memorable **metaphors**—comparisons of unlike things.
- To help listeners understand, sermons may feature **analogies**—explanations comparing abstract relationships to familiar ones.
- Parables are **narratives**—they tell a story illustrating a message.

As you read, compare the methods by which each selection conveys its message and the appeal and effectiveness of each.

Reading Strategy

Inferring Meaning

Some portions of the Bible require you to **make inferences**—to uncover meaning that is implied but not directly stated. To make inferences, identify key details in the text and then examine the relation of one detail to another. Use a chart like the one shown.

Vocabulary Builder

righteousness (rī′ chəs nis) *n.* the characteristic of acting in a just, virtuous manner (p. 283)

stature (stach′ ər) *n.* height; level of achievement (p. 284)

prodigal (präd′ i gəl) *adj.* recklessly wasteful (p. 285)

entreated (en trēt′ id) *v.* begged; pleaded with (p. 287)

transgressed (trans grest′) *v.* overstepped or broke (a law or commandment) (p. 287)

Text

The Lord is my shepherd.

Associations

| A shepherd watches over a flock. | A shepherd protects and leads. |

Inference

The Lord watches over faithful people, protecting them from danger and leading them to the right place.

from *The King James Bible* ■ 281

---

② Literary Analysis
Psalm, Sermon, and Parable

- Tell students that they will focus on three of the genres that appear in the Bible: psalms, sermons, and parables.
- Read the feature on psalms, sermons, and parables together as a class. Call students' attention to the similarities and differences among these three genres.
- Use the instruction for Comparing Literary Works to compare psalms, sermons, and parables. Review with students the definitions for *analogy* and *metaphor*.

③ Reading Strategy
Inferring Meaning

- Remind students that inferring meaning is like detective work—clues in the reading offer partial answers, and other key details can be identified in the text and examined in relation to each other. Explain that inferring meaning is one way of understanding a text that has a message not directly stated.
- Give students a copy of **Reading Strategy Graphic Organizer A**, p. 50 in *Graphic Organizer Transparencies*, to record the way in which the meaning of the Bible can be inferred.

Vocabulary Builder

- Pronounce each vocabulary word for students, and read the definitions as a class. Have students identify any words with which they are already familiar.

Learning Modalities

Interpersonal Learners Encourage students to put themselves into the role of each speaker. Under what circumstances would they say the psalm, give the sermon, or tell the parable? Who would be the audience in each case?

❶ About the Selection

Although the Book of Psalms contains 150 sacred poems, this is undoubtedly the best known. It is recited at funerals, in times of trouble, and when people are in need of comfort. This psalm was written by a young shepherd named David—the same David who killed the giant Goliath and later became King of Israel. In other writings, David relates that wild animals, including lions, often attacked the flocks, so he had faced "the shadow of death."

❷ Humanities

King James Bible, title page, 1611

This frontispiece appeared in the first edition of the English Bible of 1611, which is now known as the King James or Authorized version. It was created by an unknown artist working for the king's printer, Robert Barker (d. 1643). Barker's position gave him exclusive rights to print English Bibles, prayer books, statutes, and proclamations.

Use these questions for discussion:

1. Why do you think the artist dressed the figures this way?
   Answer: The clothes reflect the artist's vision of how people at the time dressed or actual descriptions in the Bible.

2. What is emphasized in the illustration?
   Possible response: The illustration emphasizes the word "Holy" and the wealth of stories in the Bible.

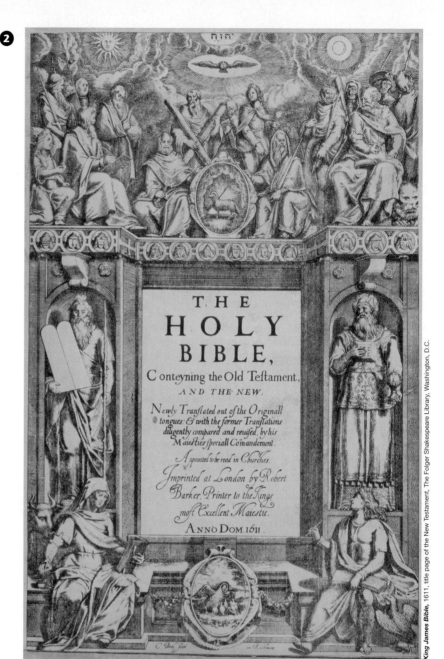

❷

King James Bible, 1611, title page of the New Testament, The Folger Shakespeare Library, Washington, D.C.

❶ ▲ **Critical Viewing** What can you infer about the King James Bible from the style of the art on this title page? **[Infer]**

282 ■ *Celebrating Humanity (1485–1625)*

Differentiated Instruction   Solutions for All Learners

Accessibility at a Glance

	Psalm 23	from Sermon on the Mount	Prodigal Son
Context	Poetic hymn	Biblical sermon	Parable
Language	Elizabethan diction	Rhetorical questions	Storytelling
Concept Level	Accessible (thanks)	Abstract (God's care)	Abstract (redemption)
Literary Merit	Classic	Classic	Classic
Lexile	870L	880L	1350L
Other	Analogies	Analogies	Extended analogy
Overall rating	Average	Average	Average

Psalm 23

from The King James Bible

Background
Up to the middle 1400s, Bibles were painstakingly copied by hand. The resulting manuscripts, though often quite beautiful, were rare and costly. When the German inventor Johann Gutenberg devised a method of printing with movable type, widespread distribution of the Bible began.

1 The Lord is my shepherd; I shall not want.

2 He maketh me to lie down in green pastures: he leadeth me beside the still waters.

3 He restoreth my soul: he leadeth me in the paths of righteousness for his name's sake.

4 Yea, though I walk through the valley of the shadow of death, I will fear no evil: for thou art with me; thy rod and thy staff they comfort me.

5 Thou preparest a table before me in the presence of mine enemies; thou anointest my head with oil; my cup runneth over.

6 Surely goodness and mercy shall follow me all the days of my life: and I will dwell in the house of the Lord forever.

Vocabulary Builder
righteousness (rī′ chəs nis) *n.* the characteristic of acting in a just, virtuous manner

Critical Reading

1. **Respond:** Which phrases in Psalm 23 are familiar to you?
2. **(a) Recall:** What image is developed in the opening verses?
   (b) Infer: Why might this image provide comfort to listeners?
   (c) Draw Conclusions: How does the inclusion of the images of the valley of death and of enemies strengthen the psalm?
3. **Draw Conclusions:** What is the message of the psalm?
4. **Evaluate:** Does the psalm offer comfort, express hope of comfort, or both?
5. **Apply:** What images of comfort and guidance might a modern psalm writer use?

Psalm 23 ■ *283*

Answers continued

3. God guides his children, protects them, and provides all that they need.
4. The psalm offers comfort now: provision, protection, goodness, and mercy; plus hope of comfort: dwelling with God forever.

5. **Possible responses:** Students may suggest an ideal parent, a religious leader, a favorite teacher or counselor, law enforcement officials, or even a movie hero.

---

❸ Critical Viewing
Possible response: The art is elegant yet dynamic, so one can infer that the King James Bible would be, too.

❹ Reading Strategy
Inferring Meaning

▶ **Reteach** Remind students that meaning is sometimes not directly stated. Details, background, and metaphors need to be considered in order to make inferences.

• Discuss with students what the life of a shepherd was like. Point out that a shepherd would live outdoors much of the time (so dwelling in a house would be appealing) and that he would fight wild animals that attacked the sheep (hence the rod and staff). Have students look for other ideas.

• Ask students to **infer** the meaning of the water and pasture.

Answer: God provides the needs of his "sheep," those who follow him.

Background
Language

Some conventions of English have been lost over the years. One is having two versions of the word "you." Students who speak or have studied other languages will be familiar with the idea of two forms—for example, *tu* and *vous* in French. In English, "you" was once the plural and formal term, and "thee" and "thou" were singular and familiar, generally used with family and friends. Another usage that has changed is *man*. This once referred to all humans. For example, in Genesis, the Bible says "God created man, both male and female."

ASSESS
Answers

1. Many students will have heard the phrase "shadow of death." Otherwise, familiarity will depend largely on students' backgrounds.

2. (a) God cares for the speaker, as a shepherd cares for his sheep. (b) It shows God as provider and protector. (c) It shows that things can look bad, but God is still there.

⑤

from The Sermon on the Mount

from The King James Bible Matthew 6: 24-30

24 No man can serve two masters: for either he will hate the one, and love the other; or else he will hold to the one, and despise the other. Ye cannot serve God and mammon.[1]

25 Therefore I say unto you, Take no thought for your life, what ye shall eat, or what ye shall drink; nor yet for your body, what ye shall put on. Is not the life more than meat, and the body than raiment?[2]

26 Behold the fowls of the air: for they sow not, neither do they reap, nor gather into barns; yet your heavenly Father feedeth them. Are ye not much better than they?

⑦|⑥ 27 Which of you by taking thought can add one cubit unto his stature?

28 And why take ye thought for raiment? Consider the lilies of the field, how they grow; they toil not, neither do they spin:

29 And yet I say unto you, That even Solomon[3] in all his glory was not arrayed like one of these.

30 Wherefore, if God so clothe the grass of the field, which to day is, and to morrow is cast into the oven, *shall he* not much more *clothe* you, O ye of little faith?

---

1. **mammon** (mam´ ən) *n.* money, personified as a false god.
2. **raiment** (rā´ mənt) *n.* clothing; wearing apparel.
3. **Solomon** (säl´ ə mən) *n.* tenth-century B.C. king of Israel.

Critical Reading

1. **Respond:** How do you view worries about the future?
2. **(a) Recall:** What human activities do the fowls and lilies of the parable avoid? **(b) Analyze:** How does this "omission" affect their lives? **(c) Interpret:** Describe the attitude towards life that Jesus advocates.
3. **Draw Conclusions:** Does Jesus, the speaker of this sermon, mean that his followers should literally "take no thought for life"? Explain.
4. **Speculate:** Explain what a life lived like the lilies might be like.

284 ■ Celebrating Humanity (1485–1625)

The Parable of the Prodigal Son

from The King James Bible Luke 15: 11–32

11 And he said, A certain man had two sons:

12 And the younger of them said to *his* father, Father, give me the portion of goods that falleth *to me*. And he divided unto them *his* living.

13 And not many days after the younger son gathered all together, and took his journey into a far country, and there wasted his substance with riotous living.

14 And when he had spent all, there arose a mighty famine in that land; and he began to be in want.

15 And he went and joined himself to a citizen of that country; and he sent him into his fields to feed swine.

16 And he would fain[1] have filled his belly with the husks that the swine did eat: and no man gave unto him.

17 And when he came to himself, he said, How many hired servants of my father's have bread enough and to spare, and I perish with hunger!

18 I will arise and go to my father, and will say unto him, Father, I have sinned against heaven, and before thee,

19 And am no more worthy to be called thy son: make me as one of thy hired servants.

20 And he arose, and came to his father. But when he was yet a great way off, his father saw him, and had compassion, and ran, and fell on his neck, and kissed him.

21 And the son said unto him, Father, I have sinned against heaven, and in thy sight, and am no more worthy to be called thy son.

22 But the father said to his servants, Bring forth the best robe, and put *it* on him; and put a ring on his hand, and shoes on *his* feet:

23 And bring hither the fatted calf, and kill *it;* and let us eat, and be merry:

24 For this my son was dead, and is alive again; he was lost, and is found. And they began to be merry.

---

1. **fain** *adv.* gladly.

Vocabulary Builder
prodigal (präd´ i gəl) *adj.*
recklessly wasteful

❾ **Reading Check**
How does the father respond to his prodigal son's return?

The Parable of the Prodigal Son ■ 285

---

❽ About the Selection
Many religions, including Judaism and Zen Buddhism, teach lessons by means of parables. In this parable, a young man demands his inheritance and leaves home. Later, he returns home in disgrace but is welcomed back by his father with open arms. This parable symbolizes God's readiness to forgive those who fall from grace.

❾ Reading Check
Answer: The father welcomes his son back, dresses him, gives him a ring, and throws a party to celebrate his return.

Differentiated Instruction   Solutions for All Learners

Strategy for Special Needs Students
Relate to students the basic ideas and actions of the story. Identify the verses in which key events occur, one event at a time, and have students read those verses. Then discuss how the verses relate to the basic story. Lead students through the ideas that the son ruins his life, comes to his senses, returns to his father, and is welcomed back by that father. Remind students that the story is a parable, intended to show God's forgiveness.

Enrichment for Gifted/Talented Students
Suggest that students create a script for performing the tale of the prodigal son. They could do it as a dramatic reading. They could tell the tale from the different points of view (the prodigal, the father, the older brother). Or they could script the story as is, from the son's asking for his inheritance to his return home. Encourage them to rehearse and present to the class whatever they prepare.

Humanities

The Return of the Prodigal Son, by Lionello Spada

Italian baroque painter Lionello Spada (1576–1622) studied art in his hometown of Bologna, Italy, at the workshop of the Carracci brothers. He later became a follower of Caravaggio, frequently creating dramatic oil renditions of biblical scenes and the lives of saints and martyrs. Spada's style reflects Caravaggio's paintings, which used dramatic effects of light and shadow and realistic portrayals of ordinary people in the roles of biblical figures. Caravaggio's focus on naturalistic portrayals of religious figures was a radical departure from the idealized beauty depicted in earlier Renaissance treatments of similar themes in religious art.

In Spada's interpretation of the parable, the believably tattered and grubby clothing of the son, the warm colors of the father's clothing, and the contrast between the father's lined visage and the youth's expressive face bring to life the characters of forgiving father and prodigal son.

Use these questions for discussion.

1. Which verse of the parable might have inspired Spada's painting?
Possible responses: Some students may say that Spada's painting depicts verse 21, in which the son apologizes. Other students may say that it represents verse 24, in which the father rejoices that his son is alive.

2. How does this painting illustrate the theme of this unit—Celebrating Humanity?
Possible response: Spada's painting dramatizes a scene from the parable in a way that makes clear the human emotions of the participants. The figures in the painting are everyday people, not remote, unapproachable ideals or abstract symbols of sin and forgiveness.

⑪ **Critical Viewing**

Possible response: Verses 21 and 22 are best illustrated. These verses describe the moment when the son, weary from his experiences, returns and is embraced by the father. In the image, the tattered clothes of the son and the father's embrace clearly illustrate these verses.

286 ■ Celebrating Humanity (1485–1625)

25 Now his elder son was in the field: and as he came and drew nigh to the house, he heard music and dancing.

26 And he called one of the servants, and asked what these things meant.

27 And he said unto him, Thy brother is come; and thy father hath killed the fatted calf, because he hath received him safe and sound.

28 And he was angry, and would not go in: therefore came his father out, and entreated him.

29 And he answering said to *his* father, Lo, these many years do I serve thee, neither transgressed I at any time thy commandment: and yet thou never gavest me a kid, that I might make merry with my friends:

30 But as soon as this thy son was come, which hath devoured thy living with harlots, thou hast killed for him the fatted calf.

31 And he said unto him, Son, thou art ever with me, and all that I have is thine.

32 It was meet² that we should make merry, and be glad: for this thy brother was dead, and is alive again; and was lost, and is found.

---

2. meet *adj.* fitting.

Vocabulary Builder
entreated (en trēt′ id) *v.*
begged; pleaded with

transgressed (trans grest′)
v. overstepped or broke
(a law or commandment)

Critical Reading

1. **Respond:** If you were the elder son, how would you have reacted to the father's response at the end? Why?

2. **(a) Recall:** What causes the younger son to return home? **(b) Compare and Contrast:** Contrast the father's and the older son's responses to the younger son's return. Why do they respond differently?

3. **(a) Recall:** How does the younger son express his repentance?
   (b) Deduce: How truly repentant do you think the younger son is?
   (c) Draw Conclusions: What does the parable suggest about the importance of the motives for repentance?

4. **(a) Recall:** What specific complaint does the older son make?
   (b) Assess: How effectively does the father address his concerns?

5. **(a) Interpret:** Why does the father say that the younger son is "alive again"? **(b) Apply:** In what circumstances might the lesson of the parable apply today?

6. **Take a Position:** Do you think mercy and forgiveness are more important than, less important than, or equal in importance to justice? Explain, using examples from the parable.

⑪ ◀ Critical Viewing
Which verses from the selection are best illustrated by this painting? Explain.
[Interpret]

The Parable of the Prodigal Son ■ 287

Apply the Skills

from *The King James Bible*

Literary Analysis

Psalm, Sermon, and Parable

1. **(a)** What is the message of the selection from the Sermon on the Mount? **(b)** Why is the form of a **sermon** suited to this lesson?

2. **(a)** What is the chief moral lesson of the Parable of the Prodigal Son? **(b)** Why is the form of a **parable** suited to this lesson?

Comparing Literary Works

3. **(a)** Contrast the styles of the **psalm,** the sermon, and the parable. **(b)** How is the style of each selection appropriate to its purpose?

4. The **metaphor** of the shepherd in Psalm 23, the **analogy** of the birds in the Sermon on the Mount, and the **narrative** in the Parable of the Prodigal Son are all designed to appeal to their original audience of simple, rural folk. Explain, using a chart like the one below.

Images: Familiar / Unfamiliar?	Simple / Difficult?	Memorable? Why?

5. Of the following, which did you find easiest to understand: the metaphor of the shepherd, the analogy of the lilies, or the lesson of the prodigal son? For each, explain what was clear and what was complex.

Reading Strategy

Inferring Meaning

6. **Make inferences** about the meaning of this quotation from Psalm 23: "I will dwell in the house of the Lord forever."

7. What inference can you make from the fact that this excerpt from the Sermon on the Mount closes with "O ye of little faith?"

8. After reading the Parable of the Prodigal Son, what inference can you make about the value the Bible places on forgiveness?

Extend Understanding

9. **Career Connection:** If you wanted to commission a new translation of the Bible, would you choose a committee of translators or a single translator? Why?

288 ■ Celebrating Humanity (1485–1625)

Go Online
Assessment
Students may use the **Self-test** to prepare for **Selection Test A** or **Selection Test B.**

Build Language Skills

Vocabulary Lesson

Word Analysis: Latin Root -stat-

The word *stature,* meaning "height when standing," comes from the Latin root -*stat*-, sometimes spelled -*stit*-, which means "to stand" or "to set up." Use this meaning to match the following words with their definitions.

1. statue   **a.** to set up a procedure

2. stationary   **b.** standing still; not moving

3. institute   **c.** a figure that stands

Spelling Strategy

Remember that the word-ending -*ious*, found in *precious*, is more common, but that some words, such as *righteous*, end with -*eous*. In your notebook, correct any misspellings among the following words.

1. religeous   2. deliceous   3. bountious

Vocabulary Builder: Synonyms

For each item, choose the letter of the word that is the synonym of (the word closest in meaning to) the word from the vocabulary list on page 281.

1. righteousness: **(a)** justness, **(b)** neatness, **(c)** error

2. stature: **(a)** depth, **(b)** standing, **(c)** interference

3. prodigal: **(a)** brilliant, **(b)** wasteful, **(c)** repugnant

4. entreated: **(a)** agreed, **(b)** financed, **(c)** begged

5. transgressed: **(a)** sinned, **(b)** traveled, **(c)** crossed

Grammar and Style Lesson

Infinitive Phrases

An **infinitive phrase** consists of an infinitive (the base form of the verb preceded by *to*) and its modifiers and complements. It can function as a noun, an adjective, or an adverb.

Noun: The younger son chose <u>to take his inheritance.</u> (*What* did he choose?)

Adjective: Soon, he had no more money <u>to spend.</u> (*What* kind of money?)

Adverb: <u>To avoid starvation,</u> he returned to his home. (*Why* did he return?)

Infinitive phrases are often used to give reasons and explain motives, so they are often found in writing about ethics and conduct.

Practice In your notebook, identify each infinitive phrase in the following sentences and identify its function (noun, adjective, or adverb).

1. He kneeled to seek his father's forgiveness.

2. The father decided to hold a celebration.

3. He made plans to feast his son lavishly.

4. The elder brother did not want to attend the feast.

5. To persuade the elder brother, the father explained his joy.

Writing Application Write a paragraph evaluating the father's decision to welcome the prodigal's return in the Parable of the Prodigal Son. Use at least three infinitive phrases to add variety to your writing.

WG Prentice Hall Writing and Grammar Connection: Chapter 19, Section 2

---

❶ Vocabulary Lesson

Word Analysis

1. c
2. b
3. a

Spelling Strategy

1. religious
2. delicious
3. bounteous

Vocabulary Builder

1. a
2. b
3. b
4. c
5. a

❷ Grammar and Style Lesson

1. *to seek his father's forgiveness* (adverb)

2. *to hold a celebration* (noun)

3. *to feast his son lavishly* (adjective)

4. *to attend the feast* (noun)

5. *to persuade the elder brother* (adverb)

Writing Application

Possible answer: The father's decision to welcome his son is surprising. The younger son did not expect him to accept him back. Still, the father wanted to forgive his son's actions, which is something one would hope for from a parent, if one turned to that parent in desperation.

WG **Writing and Grammar,** Diamond Level

Students will find further instruction and practice on infinitive phrases in Chapter 19, Section 2.

Assessment Practice

Fact and Opinion   **(For more practice, see *Standardized Test Preparation Workbook*, p. 11.)**

Many tests require students to distinguish between fact and opinion. Use the following sample item to show students how certain words can signal a statement of opinion.

Which of the following lines from the Sermon on the Mount is an opinion?

   A Behold the fowls of the air: for they sow not. . .

   B Consider the lilies of the field. . . they toil not. . .

   C That even Solomon. . . was not arrayed like one of these (lilies)

   D . . .the grass of the field. . . is cast into the oven. . .

Lead students to recognize that judgments about what is beautiful or wonderful often signal a statement of opinion. Such statements are difficult to prove, and a fact must be provable. The correct answer is C.

❸ Writing Lesson

You may use this Writing Lesson as timed-writing practice, or you may allow students to develop the essay as a writing assignment over several days.

- Review with students the definition of a parable as a short, simple story from which a religious lesson or moral can be drawn.

- Tell students that they should reread the Parable of the Prodigal Son to help them capture the style, tone, and impact. Encourage students to think about ideals and virtues that are important to them. Suggest that they think of incidents in their lives or stories they know that might illustrate these ideals or virtues.

- Give students the **Support for Writing Lesson**, p. 83, in *Unit 2 Resources,* to guide them in developing their parables.

- Use the **Rubrics for Narration: Short Story**, pp. 57–58 in *General Resources.*

❹ Listening and Speaking

- Explain to students that they will retell the parable to an audience of young children. Ask them to define things their listeners might not understand, incorporate vivid words to keep their audience interested, and use expressions that will help listeners connect to the story.

- Have students practice their retelling of the parable before they present it to an audience.

- The **Support for Extend Your Learning** page (*Unit 2 Resources,* p. 84) provides guided note-taking opportunities to help students complete the Extend Your Learning activities.

- Use the rubric for Peer Assessment: Oral Interpretation, p. 129 in *General Resources.*

Go Online Have students type in
—Research— the Web Code for another research activity.

---

❸ Writing Lesson

Parable in King James Style

Write a parable that supports a moral in which you believe. Study the style of the Parable of the Prodigal Son, and adapt it to your purposes.

Prewriting Choose a moral to teach, and sketch the plot of a story to illustrate it. Then reread the Parable of the Prodigal Son, taking notes on the style in which it is told, noting sentence length, typical sentence beginnings, and word choice.

Drafting Follow your notes as you draft, setting out the events of your story in clear sequence. Emphasize those elements—character traits or events—that will lead the reader to understand your lesson. Be sure to include metaphors in your parable.

Revising Highlight parts of your work that do not fit the general style you have adopted. Rewrite marked passages for consistency.

> **Model: Revising for Consistent Style**
>
> And, lo, the bully descended like a wolf on the
>
> playground. ìO ut of my way, meathead," he said.
>
> ~~laid about him mightily.~~
> And he ~~started wailing on the nearest person.~~

The revision maintains the style: formal, simple, biblical-sounding narration contrasting with the character's slang dialogue.

WG *Prentice Hall Writing and Grammar Connection: Chapter 5, Section 3*

❹ Extend Your Learning

Listening and Speaking Prepare a **retelling** of the Parable of the Prodigal Son for an audience of young children. As you rehearse, choose language appropriate to your audience:

- Speak in language that listeners will readily understand.
- Include vivid words and phrases to hold their interest.
- Use informal expressions to help listeners connect the story to their experiences.

Deliver your version to a suitable audience.

Research and Technology Working in a small group, write an **evaluative report** comparing one of the selections here with two other translations of the same passage. As you review the translations, consider how word choice, tone, and style affect the meaning and impact of the text. Write up the group's impressions in an essay, citing sources accurately. **[Group Activity]**

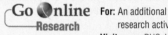

Go Online
—Research—
For: An additional research activity
Visit: www.PHSchool.com
Web Code: esd-7205

Assessment Resources

The following resources can be used to assess students' knowledge and skills.

Unit 2 Resources
   Selection Test A, pp. 86–88
   Selection Test B, pp. 89–91

General Resources
   Rubrics for Narration: Short Story,
      pp. 57–58
   Rubric for Peer Assessment: Oral Interpretation, p. 129

Go Online Students may use the Self-test to
—Assessment— prepare for **Selection Test A** or
Selection Test B.

Focus on Literary Forms: Drama

GLOBE. SOUTHWARK.

Selection Planning Guide

William Shakespeare's *The Tragedy of Macbeth* is one of the greatest dramatic tragedies ever staged. *Macbeth* works on many levels: it is a human tragedy wherein the war hero develops a raging lust for power that leads him to commit murder and lose his humanity. It is also an exciting, gruesome tale of fate, war, the supernatural, greed, and retribution.

Humanities

The Globe Theater, London

This early drawing of the Globe, the theater in which many of Shakespeare's plays were staged, shows not only the building but also some of Southwark, the part of London in which the Globe was located. It also shows a few people lined up to attend a performance.

Ask the following question:

• Judging from the appearance of the Globe and the other details in the drawing, would you say that attending the theater in Elizabethan England was a special event or a commonplace one?
Possible response: Students may say that because the theater stands by itself in a clearing, it looks like a special building. The people lining up may be an indication that going to the theater was a special event for Elizabethans.

Benchmark

After students have completed *The Tragedy of Macbeth,* Act II, administer **Benchmark Test 3** (*Unit 2 Resources* pp. 126–131). If the Benchmark Test reveals that some of the students need further work, use the Interpretation Guide to determine the appropriate reteaching page in the **Reading Kit** and on **Success Tracker.**

Monitoring Progress

Before students read *The Tragedy of Macbeth,* Act III, administer **Diagnostic Test 4** (*Unit 2 Resources,* pp. 132–134). This test will determine students' level of readiness for the reading and vocabulary skills.

Benchmark

After students have completed *The Tragedy of Macbeth,* Act V, administer **Benchmark Test 4** (*Unit 2 Resources,* pp. 191–196). If the Benchmark Test reveals that some students need further work, use the Interpretation Guide to determine the appropriate reteaching page in the **Reading Kit** and on **Success Tracker.**

Differentiated
Instruction   Solutions for All Learners

Accessibility at a Glance

More Challenging
Macbeth, Act I
Macbeth, Act II
Macbeth, Act III
Macbeth, Act IV
Macbeth, Act V

291

❶ Elements of Drama

- Tell students that in Part 3 they will focus on drama. Have a student read p. 292 aloud to the class. Point out that reading a play is very different from reading other genres. Tell students that it is important to look at stage directions and text in brackets to fully understand the action of the play. **Ask** students: What are ways that drama gives instructions to readers?

- Elicit answers that get at the performance of drama—the stage directions that tell readers where to stand, or the asides that give special information to the audience.

- Review the elements of drama. Clarify the information available on these pages. Suggest that students use these pages as a reference as they read *Macbeth*.

Defining Drama

Drama is a form of literature that tells a story through performances by actors in front of an audience. Because a drama, or play, has to hold the interest of a live audience, the usual ingredients of plot—tension, confrontation between characters, and resolution—are heightened. In fact, emotional intensity is so characteristic of drama that we use the adjective "dramatic" to describe anything vivid, striking, or exciting.

❶ **Elements of Drama**

Plays consist of two kinds of writing, each with a different purpose: **Dialogue** tells the story, while **stage directions** help the cast and production staff to bring the text to life.

> ## ᗪRAMA IS LIFE WITH
> ## THE DULL BITS CUT OUT.
> *—Alfred Hitchcock*

Dialogue

Any lines spoken by actors are considered *dialogue*. It is through dialogue and action that the playwright, or author, tells the story. Most dialogue consists of characters speaking to one another. However, playwrights also use these dramatic conventions to communicate with the audience:

- **Soliloquy:** a long speech expressing private thoughts, delivered by a character who is alone onstage

- **Monologue:** a long speech delivered by one character to another or to a group of characters

- **Aside:** a private remark to one character or to the audience that breaks convention because it is understood not to be heard by other characters onstage

- **Chorus:** a single character or a group of characters whose words may connect scenes or convey the collective thoughts or feelings of the community. The chorus is usually limited to classical drama.

Stage Directions

Many playwrights include stage directions, or instructions, about the setting, costumes, lighting, scenery, and props, or objects used onstage. This text may also indicate how and when characters should move and deliver their lines. Stage directions are usually printed in italics and sometimes set in brackets or parentheses.

292 ■ Celebrating Humanity (1485–1625)

Structure of a Play
Plays are usually divided into large units, called *acts*, which are often made up of smaller units, called *scenes*.

Dialogue
MACBETH. [*Aside*] Glamis, and Thane of Cawdor:/The greatest is behind. [*To* ROSS *and* ANGUS] —Act I, Scene iii

Stage Directions
[*Reenter fighting, and* MACBETH *slain. Exit* MACDUFF, *with* MACBETH. *Retreat and flourish.*]

Kinds of Drama

The ancient Greeks developed drama into a sophisticated art form. They created two broad categories of drama: tragedy and comedy.

Tragedy

Tragedies end with the downfall or death of the protagonist, or main character. Shakespeare's *Macbeth* is a clear example of the genre, and it includes many of these key elements of tragedy:

- **Tragic hero:** In ancient Greek and Shakespearean tragedy, the *tragic hero* is the main character—an outstanding person of high rank whose downfall is caused by his own flawed behavior.
- **Tragic flaw:** A *tragic flaw* is a part of the hero's character that leads him to make a fatal mistake. Macbeth, for example, is led astray by his "vaulting ambition, which o'erleaps itself / And falls on th' other—."
- **Comic relief:** To relieve tension, playwrights often include humorous scenes or characters that provide *comic relief*. Shakespeare usually uses characters from the lower ranks of society, such as servants, for comic relief.

Comedy

Comedies show ordinary people in conflict with society. Comedic conflicts typically arise from misunderstandings, deceptions, disapproving authority figures, and mistaken identities, and are always resolved happily. Some comic protagonists are ridiculous; others are sympathetic and likable. There are two basic forms of comedy:

- A **romantic comedy** involves problems among lovers.
- A **comedy of manners** satirizes social customs of society.

Tragedy

- Features noble or outstanding protagonist
- Emphasizes human greatness
- Arouses pity, fear, awe
- Ends unhappily with destruction of hero

Comedy

- Features an ordinary protagonist
- Emphasizes human foibles and weaknesses of society
- Arouses sympathy, amusement
- Ends happily with protagonist making peace with society

Strategies for Reading Drama

Use these strategies as you read a Shakespearean drama.

Reread for Clarification Rereading passages that seem unclear or confusing can help clarify the characters' actions and words. Rereading previous passages can help you follow the action as it progresses.

Paraphrase To better understand complicated Elizabethan verse, read to the end of a sentence. Reorder words or phrases so that they make sense to you. Then, paraphrase the sentence in your own words.

Envision the Drama As you read, imagine how the scenes would look on stage, how the dialogue would sound, and how the characters would move.

Focus on Literary Forms: Drama ■ 293

noting that there can be moments of comedy within a tragic play, and that serious topics may be discussed in a comedy.

- Point out that Shakespeare was adept at writing both comedies and tragedies. Observe that *Macbeth* continues to move audiences to feel disappointment, fear, and grief because his tragic hero is such a fully drawn character.

❸ Strategies for Reading Drama

- Suggest that students write down difficult passages on a piece of paper as they are reading and note what is unclear. If they do not understand the meaning by the end of the scene, they should reread the difficult passage, looking for key words that might point to an answer.
- After students paraphrase difficult passages, have them return to the original language of the play. When students have determined the author's meaning, they can more fully appreciate the complexity and richness of the original text.
- Remind students that drama was meant to be performed, not read. Some passages that seem difficult make sense when they are viewed. Reading text aloud or watching a filmed version of a scene may aid understanding.

Differentiated Instruction   Solutions for All Learners

Strategy for Less Proficient Readers
Help familiarize students with a drama's appearance on the page. First, have students compare a page of prose text with a page of *Macbeth,* and ask students to describe the differences they see. Then, have them analyze a page of *Macbeth,* identifying the elements that help readers and performers, such as the names of the speakers, the stage directions, and the numbering of acts and scenes.

Strategy for Gifted/Talented Students
Challenge students to give a class demonstration of a short scene from *Macbeth.* Then, ask them to explain how they decided where to stand, how to deliver certain lines, and what gestures or facial expressions they used. Ask the performers to explain what parts of the stage directions or dialogue helped them make their decisions, and what parts they felt free to interpret on their own.

Students will

1. understand the architecture of theaters in Elizabethan times.
2. communicate effectively with others in a group situation.

Background
Shakespeare's Globe Theater

Although Shakespeare did not have the advantages of modern theaters to draw on, the theaters of his day must be considered highly sophisticated. The greatest dramas in our language were produced on the sixteenth-century English stage. This fact alone suggests how advanced the theater arts were when Shakespeare was writing his masterpieces.

Most of Shakespeare's plays were performed at the Globe. It was built by Richard and Cuthbert Burbage, sons of James Burbage, who had constructed The Theater, London's first theater. Richard Burbage was multitalented: He was a leading actor in Shakespeare's acting company!

The foundation of the original Globe was discovered in 1990. The excavation revealed clues about the theater itself as well as the actors and the audience. The tiny part of the foundation that was originally uncovered yielded a great number of hazelnuts shells. Hazelnuts were the Elizabethan equivalent of popcorn.

The Elizabethan Theater

English drama came of age during the reign of Elizabeth I, developing into a sophisticated and popular art form. Although playwrights like Shakespeare were mainly responsible for the great theatrical achievements of the time, audiences and theater buildings were equally important.

Before the reign of Elizabeth I, traveling theater companies put on plays wherever they could find an audience, often performing in the open courtyards of inns. Spectators watched from the ground or from balconies or galleries above.

England's First Playhouse

When Shakespeare was twelve years old, an actor named James Burbage built London's first theater, called simply The Theater. Actors—even prominent and well-to-do actors like James Burbage—were frowned upon by the city fathers. Nonetheless, they were wildly popular with the common people and were called on frequently to perform at court. A man like Burbage enjoyed a reputation somewhat like a rock star's today.

The Globe In 1597, the city fathers closed down The Theater. In late 1598, Richard Burbage (James Burbage's son) and his men dismantled it and hauled it in pieces across the Thames to Southwark. It took them six months to rebuild it, and when they did, they renamed it the Globe.

> " *Can this cockpit hold*
> *The vasty fields of France? Or may we cram*
> *Within this wooden O the very casques*
> *That did affright the air at Agincourt?* "
>
> —*Shakespeare, from* Henry V

Scholars disagree about what the Globe actually looked like because there are no surviving drawings from the time or detailed descriptions. Shakespeare refers to the building in *Henry V* as "this wooden O." The building had to have been small enough for the actors to be heard, and we know that performances drew as many as 2,500 to 3,000 people. These truly packed houses must have been uncomfortable —especially when you consider that people of the era didn't bathe or change their clothes very often! Most spectators stood throughout the performance. Some of the audience sat in a gallery behind the performers. Though they saw only the actors' backs and probably could not hear very well, they were content to be seen by the rest of the audience.

294 ■ *Celebrating Humanity (1485–1625)*

The Revival of European Theater

Though ancient Greece and Rome had established a significant tradition of theater as an independent art, theater survived in medieval Western Europe only in diminished forms. Wandering players entertained common folk with mime, juggling, and storytelling. Villagers performed seasonal folk rituals enacting the slaying of winter or the fortunes of the Fool. The Church began to incorporate theatrical elements into its festivities, which evolved into mystery plays staging Biblical scenes and morality plays, allegories of temptation, good, and evil. It was only in the Renaissance, when people turned new attention to the art and learning of the classical world, that drama was renewed as an independent form, with complex stories and individualized characters.

There were no sets or lighting at the Globe. Plays were performed in sunlight, and a playwright's words alone had to create moods like the one in the eerie first scene of *Macbeth*. Holding an audience spellbound was complicated by the fact that most spectators ate and drank throughout the performance.

The first Globe met its demise in 1613, when a cannon fired as part of a performance of *Henry VIII* ignited the theater's thatched roof. Everyone escaped unharmed, but the Globe burned to the ground. Although the theater was rebuilt, the Puritans had it permanently closed in 1642.

The New Globe

Building a replica of Shakespeare's Globe was the American actor Sam Wanamaker's dream. After long years of fund-raising and construction, the theater opened to its first full season on June 8, 1997, with a production of *Henry V*. Like the earlier Globe, this one is made of wood, with a thatched roof and lime plaster covering the walls. The stage and the galleries are covered, but the "bear pit," where the modern-day groundlings stand, is open to the skies.

Perhaps the most striking aspect of seeing Shakespeare's plays performed at the Globe is the immediacy of the action. The performers, as Benedict Nightingale noted in the *London Times*, "are talking to you, asking you questions, involving you in their fears." Is that not what theater is all about?

▲ Critical Viewing
Judging from the photograph of the reconstructed Globe, what part of the theater might the upper-class audience members have occupied? Explain. **[Speculate]**

Activity

Theater Today

Today, most patrons expect a certain level of comfort and technical sophistication when attending a theatrical event—whether a concert, a Broadway show, or a school assembly.

With a group, discuss your experiences while attending live performances. Use these questions to guide your discussion:
• In what ways do modern shows compare with what you have read about Elizabethan theater?
• Do you think live theater is more popular or less popular today than in Shakespeare's day? Explain.
Choose a point person to share your group's ideas with the class.

The Elizabethan Theater ■ 295

The New Globe

London's new Globe theater is located on the Thames. It retains the characteristics of the original—including its circular shape, open center, and thatched roof. Since few details of the original remain, the builders referred to the building contracts that exist for the rival theaters, the Rose and the Fortune, which were built by the same master carpenter who built the Globe.

The new Globe seats 1,000 people. Because the seats curve around the stage, everyone has a different view of the action. The yard, or pit, has room for 450 groundlings. As in Elizabethan times, the audience tends to join in the proceedings, commenting on the action.

Plays are performed as they would have been in Shakespeare's time, with little or no scenery, people moving around in the yard, and vendors circulating to sell refreshments. The experience contrasts with performances in modern theaters, which take place in a darkened, quiet theater with an attentive and respectful audience.

Critical Thinking

What additional understanding of Shakespeare might one gain from attending a production at the new Globe?
Possible response: One might better appreciate the dramatic quality of the plays, since actors had to hold the attention of a large standing crowd.

Critical Viewing

Answer: This photograph suggests that the upper-class audience might have been seated in the balcony and mezzanine seats, since the ground-level occupants had to stand during the entire performance.

Activity

Organize students in small groups. Suggest that they begin by discussing the difference between modern movies and plays presented in an Elizabethan theater. If any students in the group have attended a live theater performance, encourage them to share their experiences. Students may wish to research attendance figures for Broadway and off-Broadway plays, or for local live theater performances, before they discuss the second question.

Background
Sarah Siddons

Sarah Siddons (1755–1831) was a great English actress known for her portrayal of Lady Macbeth. She played this part a number of times over a span of twenty-seven years, and it was in this role that she gave the farewell performance of her acting career (1812).

Siddons portrayed Lady Macbeth as a strong, manlike woman, chilling in her ruthlessness. Her private notes, however, reveal that she saw another side to Lady Macbeth that she was unwilling or unable to communicate in performance. She wrote, for instance, that Lady Macbeth is "fair, feminine, nay, perhaps, even fragile" and "captivating in feminine loveliness."

Critical Viewing

Possible response: Shakespeare's play is universal in its themes of fate, destiny, and the nature of evil. That it can be staged in so many different ways suggests this universality.

Shakespeare on Stage

A play on the page is only half a play. The script is a recipe for a performance—incomplete until it is staged in a theater, in a reader's mind, or on screen. When a play is staged, actors and directors bring the words to life through their interpretations. Decisions about scenery, costumes, timing, and casting, as well as about a character's gestures, expressions, and motivations, can call forth contrasting meanings from even the most familiar play.

> **"** *The script itself is a recipe for a performance— incomplete until it is staged. . . .***"**

For over four hundred years, Shakespeare's plays have demanded brilliant performances and daring reinterpretations. The best interpretations of his plays shed new light by asking imaginative questions that the texts themselves answer.

Character and Motivation

Shakespeare's Lady Macbeth conspires with her husband to murder their king, leading generations of actresses to ask about the source of Lady Macbeth's evil.

Inhuman Monster? Sarah Siddons, who played the role of Lady Macbeth about two hundred years ago, portrayed Lady Macbeth as a driven woman, in whom "the passion of ambition has almost obliterated all the characteristics of human nature. . . ."

Evil Beauty? Vivien Leigh found in Lady Macbeth an evil beauty who gives a good-night kiss to the man she is plotting to murder that same evening.

Weak Woman? At the other end of the spectrum, nineteenth-century actress Ellen Terry played Lady Macbeth as "essentially feminine," noting that she faints after the murder of the king.

▼ ➤ **Critical Viewing**
What does the fact that Shakespeare's *Macbeth* can be staged in such different ways as these suggest about its power? **[Draw Conclusions]**

Enrichment

The Curse of *Macbeth*

Theater buffs say that *Macbeth* is cursed—that all an actor need do is quote from the play in a theater, or just mention its title, and disasters will come flying. Superstitions aside, in three centuries of productions, *Macbeth* has met with some flesh-and-blood difficulties.

When the English theaters reopened in 1660 after years of Puritan rule, Charles II asked William Davenant to produce the play. Davenant liked color—he added dancing, singing, and chanting to the witches' scenes.

This was mere tinkering, though; the serious work began when he enlarged Lady Macduff's role. Scenes in which Lady Macbeth goads on Macbeth alternated with scenes in which Lady Macduff warns her husband against ambition. As if to keep up with the Macbeths and their spirit problems, the new, improved Lady Macduff has a run-in with Duncan's ghost. After years of these outrageous productions, actor David Garrick restored *Macbeth* to something more closely resembling the original.

Setting and Action

Realism? Some directors attempt to keep faith with a playwright's vision by staging the action as realistically as possible. To bring realism to the woodland setting of *A Midsummer Night's Dream,* the director of a 1905 production brought live rabbits onstage! The famous actor Laurence Olivier brought unintentional realism to the part of Macbeth when he injured the actor playing Macduff in their staged sword fight. On another occasion, Olivier fought so vigorously that his sword broke and flew into the audience.

Relevance? Orson Welles also struck a note of realism in his 1936 version of *Macbeth,* but he did so by radically departing from Shakespeare's text: He set the play in Haiti instead of Scotland! By using an all-black cast and modeling Macbeth after a famous Haitian dictator, Welles found a new application for Shakespeare's message about power.

Activity

Staging Shakespeare

Directors often stage Shakespeare in a contemporary cultural setting, rather than a traditional Elizabethan setting, to allow an audience to connect to the play in ways a traditional setting might not foster.

Watch scenes from any film version of a Shakespeare play. Then, discuss the scenes with a group, using the following questions to guide your discussion:

• What is the purpose of a film director? Which details in the scenes might the director have influenced or controlled?
• What culture or historical era influenced the directorial choices in these scenes? Support your response with evidence from the scenes.
• Choose four adjectives that describe the perspective of the director—for example, were the scenes bright, bleak, intense, or dream-like?

Choose a point person to share your group's ideas with the class.

Shakespeare on Stage ■ 297

Ellen Terry (1847–1928) tried to express "the feminine" quality of Lady Macbeth in her interpretation of the role. She wrote the following note to herself: "Play with his [Macbeth's] hands and *charm* him." In a letter to the critic William Winter she was clear about wanting to break away from Sarah Siddons's portrayal of Lady Macbeth as a monster:

"Everyone seems to think that Mrs. McB is a *Monstrousness* & I can only see that she's a *woman*—a mistaken woman—& weak—not a Dove—of course not—but *first of all* **a wife**—I don't think she's *at all clever* ("Lead Macbeth" *indeed!*—she's not even clever enough to *sleep!*)."

Critical Thinking

1. What conclusions can you draw about the character of Lady Macbeth from the variety of interpretations she has received? **Possible responses:** Students may note that they indicate the complexity of the character, or that Shakespeare has given only the outline of a character, which directors must fill in. Others may argue that some of the actresses cited were simply wrong in their interpretations.

2. What is the minimum a director needs to do to keep faith with a play by Shakespeare? Explain. **Possible responses:** The director should not change the ending; the director should include Shakespeare's original language. Students may note that, if an element is changed, then it is as if the director has created a new play.

Activity

If possible, show a scene from *West Side Story, 10 Things I Hate About You,* or another modern adaptation of a Shakespeare play. Challenge student groups to select a play by Shakespeare and a modern setting, and then to describe how they would update that play. As an alternative, challenge each group to create a different way to modernize the same play.

Students will

1. become familiar with various filmed versions of Shakespeare's plays.
2. listen and discuss casting choices with others.

Background
The Changing Face of Movies

Moviemakers today are often torn between the desire to appeal to the broadest possible tastes—and sell the most tickets—and the desire to make, or to appear to be making, artistic statements. From the 1920s through the 1940s, the Hollywood studio system turned out profitable movies that often met high artistic standards. Under the system, a few competing companies contracted for long-term relations with actors and directors and owned chains of theaters. Though profits were still the bottom line, the studio system nurtured individual talent, supporting the vision of gifted, even idiosyncratic directors and screenwriters such as Ernst Lubitsch, Howard Hawks, and Orson Welles.

Those who ran the studio system were interested in respectability, even an appearance of culture. Early versions of Shakespeare on film reflect this ambition and help explain why a studio would have spent millions on George Cukor's reconstruction of Verona for *Romeo and Juliet* in 1936.

At the end of the studio era, moviemaking began to split up between the creation of popular movies with little pretension to sophistication and "highbrow" films. With the development of the category of the "art film," attempts to commit Shakespeare to celluloid became painstaking labors of authenticity or artistic innovation. It is only more recently that growing intellectual comfort with popular culture has enabled productions like the 1996 *Romeo and Juliet*.

A Closer Look

Shakespeare on Film

William Shakespeare wrote for the same audience that moviemakers write for today. Rich and poor, smart and not-so-smart, sentimentalists, action-lovers, and comedy fans—all crowded into the Globe theater to watch Shakespeare's plays. A similarly diverse audience exists today for movies. Not surprisingly, film versions of many Shakespearean plays are readily available.

> " *Critics have hailed Kurosawa's* Macbeth *as a masterpiece for its dramatic visual effects and editing.* "

Filmmakers have taken varied approaches to Shakespeare's plays, reflecting popular tastes and interests as well as the plays themselves. The timeless themes, powerful characters, and resonant language form a treasure trove, from which a creative filmmaker can borrow materials for his or her own work.

Romeo and Juliet Shakespeare's *Romeo and Juliet* has been filmed more often than any other play in history.

- In 1908, the first movie version, a ten-minute silent short, was created. Lines from the play were displayed on title cards while the actors mimed the action.
- In 1936, Hollywood director George Cukor produced a full-length feature film of the play. The movie cost $2 million—at the time, the most MGM had ever paid for a film.
- In 1996, Australian filmmaker Baz Luhrmann created an "updated" version of *Romeo and Juliet* starring Leonardo DiCaprio. Characters wear designer clothes and carry automatic weapons—not swords—while a television newscast provides narration.
- The 1998 film *Shakespeare in Love*, cowritten by Marc Norman and Tom Stoppard, imagines what led Shakespeare to write *Romeo and Juliet*. In the movie, lines from the play weave together Shakespeare's life with the play he is writing.

Enrichment

Film

The first movie camera was invented in Thomas Edison's laboratories in 1888. Early films were short features, generally of exotic scenes, displayed through devices that accommodated one viewer at a time. Later, filmmakers such as Georges Méliès in France began to tell stories on film. His "Voyage to the Moon" (1902), a spoof of Jules Verne's science fiction, was internationally distributed. For decades, silent feature films were an important form of popular entertainment. D.W. Griffith's *The Birth of a Nation* (1915) is one of the monumental works of the era. Hollywood became the seat of the movie-making industry. In the 1920s, sound was introduced into film, and in 1926, major Hollywood studios began to incorporate sound into their movies.

Hamlet Like *Romeo and Juliet*, Shakespeare's tragedy *Hamlet* also had its film debut during the silent film era.

- The most famous *Hamlet* on film is the 1948 version starring Laurence Olivier as Hamlet. Olivier's performance as the melancholic prince is considered a high point of dramatic art.
- In 1990, director Franco Zeffirelli filmed *Hamlet* with Mel Gibson in the title role. Zeffirelli shot the play on location and encouraged actors to deliver lines as prose rather than as poetry.
- Six years later, actor director Kenneth Branagh filmed the play nearly whole, editing out few lines, a project never before attempted. The result runs 242 minutes long.

Macbeth

- One of the best-known film versions of *Macbeth* was created by David Bradley for a mere $5,000. Costumes and props were bought at rummage sales and at junk stores, helmets were fashioned from papiermâché, swords were cut from wood, and Bradley's mother catered for the cast and crew.
- In 1971, director Roman Polanski filmed *Macbeth* during the winter: The bleak weather, he felt, suited the grim atmosphere. To keep his cast from falling ill, Polanski insisted that they take daily dosages of vitamin C.
- Perhaps the most successful adaptation of *Macbeth* is Japanese director Akira Kurosawa's *Throne of Blood*. The dialogue and setting of the film is Japanese, but Kurosawa carefully builds his drama directly from Shakespeare's story. Critics have hailed the film as a masterpiece for its dramatic visual effects and editing.

◄ ▼**Critical Viewing**
What effect does the work of popular actors—such as Claire Danes, Gwyneth Paltrow, and Mel Gibson—have on Shakespeare's accessibility? Explain. **[Hypothesize]**

Activity

Casting Call

Popular actors like Leonardo DiCaprio, Clare Danes, Gwyneth Paltrow, and Mel Gibson have brought Shakespeare's work to life on film.

Suppose you were casting a new film version of *Macbeth*. With a group, choose three popular actors who can perform the title role from the play, a single character with the following qualities:

- a soldier, husband, swordsman, and murderer
- a man with a conscience who doubts himself at nearly every turn

Identify three actresses whom you might cast as Macbeth's wife, the strong and scheming Lady Macbeth. Choose a point person to share your ideas with the class. Then, when you have finished reading the play, decide whether you might change your casting choices.

Possible responses: Students should support their choices with reference to a value such as entertainment value, artistry, depth of insight into Shakespeare, or their own preferences among the plays.

2. Which do you think would make a more valid film version of *Macbeth*: a complete presentation of the text using period costumes, Scottish settings, and unobtrusive camera techniques, or an innovative production that freely used special effects, original costume designs, and contemporary settings?
Possible responses: The conservative production would have the advantage of allowing the audience to concentrate directly on Shakespeare's language; the "conceptual" version might convey the drama and conflict in a truly cinematic way, making it a better movie.

3. What conclusions can you draw from the fact that film versions of Shakespeare's plays continue to be made?
Possible responses: The continued production of films of the plays shows their power over the imagination, the universality of their message, their power as reference points in our culture, and their dramatic integrity (they can be adapted in innumerable ways).

Critical Viewing

Answer: Famous actors and actresses like Danes, Paltrow, and Gibson will attract viewers who might not be inclined to see a film based on Shakespeare's plays.

Activity

Organize students in groups and allow time for them to brainstorm. As the representatives from each group name their cast, list them on the board. To stimulate further discussion, ask students to imagine distinctive actors such as John Wayne and Glenn Close playing Macbeth and Lady Macbeth. How would these casting choices affect a production of the play?

Differentiated Instruction   Solutions for All Learners

Enrichment for Less Proficient Readers
Have students read Shakespeare on Film. As they read *Macbeth,* have them note scenes for which they can readily picture a movie treatment. Have them write brief descriptions or storyboards of these scenes.

Enrichment for Gifted/ Talented Students
Have students read Shakespeare on Film. As they read *Macbeth,* have them create a treatment for a film version of the play, including decisions about modernizing the setting, dominant colors in the scene, use of close-ups, and so on. Have them share their treatments with the class.

Enrichment for Advanced Readers
Have students read Shakespeare on Film. Have them view at least two film versions of *Macbeth* and write essays comparing these versions and evaluating performances, cinematography, and the interpretation each makes of the play.

Meeting Your Standards

Students will

1. **analyze and respond to literary elements.**
   - Literary Analysis: Elizabethan Drama

2. **read, comprehend, analyze, and critique a drama.**
   - Reading Strategy: Using Text Aids
   - Reading Check questions
   - Apply the Skills questions
   - Assessment Practice (ATE)

3. **develop vocabulary.**
   - Vocabulary Lesson: Power Words

4. **understand and apply written and oral language conventions.**
   - Spelling Strategy
   - Grammar and Style Lesson: Action Verbs and Linking Verbs

5. **develop writing proficiency.**
   - Writing Lesson: Response to Criticism (follows Act V)

6. **develop appropriate research strategies.**
   - Extend Your Learning: Oral Report

7. **develop writing strategies.**
   - Extend Your Learning: Speech of Welcome

Block Scheduling: Use one 90-minute class period to preteach the skills and have students read the selection. Use a second 90-minute class period to assess students' mastery of skills, extend their learning, and monitor their progress.

Homework Suggestions

Following are possibilities for homework assignments.

- Support pages from *Unit 2 Resources:*
  - Literary Analysis
  - Reading Strategy
  - Vocabulary Builder
  - Grammar and Style

- An Extend Your Learning project and the Writing Lesson for this selection may be completed over several days.

Step-by-Step Teaching Guide	Pacing Guide
PRETEACH	
• Administer Vocabulary and Reading Warm-ups as necessary.	5 min.
• Engage students' interest with the motivation activity.	5 min.
• Read and discuss author, background, and From the Scholar's Desk features. **FT**	10 min.
• Introduce the Literary Analysis Skill: Elizabethan Drama. **FT**	5 min.
• Introduce the Reading Strategy: Using Text Aids. **FT**	10 min
• Prepare students to read by teaching the selection vocabulary. **FT**	
TEACH	
• Informally monitor comprehension while students read independently or in groups. **FT**	30 min.
• Monitor students' comprehension with the Reading Check notes.	as students read
• Reinforce vocabulary with Vocabulary Builder notes.	as students read
• Develop students' understanding of Elizabethan drama with the Literary Analysis annotations. **FT**	5 min.
• Develop students' ability to use text aids with the Reading Strategy annotations. **FT**	5 min.
ASSESS/EXTEND	
• Assess students' comprehension and mastery of the Literary Analysis and Reading Strategy by having them answer the Apply the Skills questions. **FT**	15 min.
• Have students complete the Vocabulary Lesson and the Grammar and Style Lesson. **FT**	15 min.
• Apply students' understanding by using one or more of the Extend Your Learning activities.	20–90 min. or homework
• Administer Selection Test A or Selection Test B. **FT**	15 min.

Resources

Choosing Resources for Differentiated Instruction

[**L1**] Special Needs Students

[**L2**] Below-Level Students

[**L3**] All Students

[**L4**] Advanced Students

[**EL**] English Learners

For Vocabulary and Reading Warm-ups and for Selection Tests, **A** signifies "less challenging" and **B** "more challenging." For Graphic Organizer transparencies, **A** signifies "not filled in" and **B** "filled in."

FT Fast Track Instruction: To move the lesson more quickly, use the strategies and activities identified with **FT**.

Scaffolding for Less Proficient and Advanced Students

The leveled Critical Thinking questions after selections progress in the levels of thinking required to answer them. To address the needs of your different students, you may use the (a) level questions for your less proficient students and the (b) level questions with your on-level and advanced students. The occasional (c) level questions are appropriate for your advanced students.

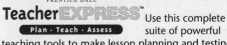

Use this complete suite of powerful teaching tools to make lesson planning and testing quicker and easier.

Use the interactive textbook (online and on CD-ROM) to make selections and activities come alive with audio and video support and interactive questions.

For: Information about Lexiles
Visit: www.PHSchool.com
Web Code: eue-1111

Frank Kermode

- Tell students that Frank Kermode has written and taught extensively about Shakespeare as a professor at Cambridge University and as the author of books such as *Shakespeare's Language.* He finds that the job of a literary critic is to "help make available the great works to non-specialists." Shakespeare's *A Winter's Tale* may be his favorite play, he says, but "Hamlet is always in one's head."

- Show Segment 2 on Kermode on the *From the Author's Desk DVD* to provide insight into the work of a literary critic. After students have watched the segments, **ask:** How can reading books about Shakespeare's plays help readers better understand the text?
Answer: Reading books can help readers see the text's nuances and complexities. It can also show the successes and failures of the text.

Macbeth's Dramatic History

- Have students read Kermode's comments about the play's revelations of Macbeth's thoughts.
Ask: What does Macbeth's speech reveal about his feelings regarding the murder he is about to perform?
Answer: Macbeth is conflicted because he knows that murdering Duncan will violate the laws of kinship and hospitality. He recognizes that he is driven by ambition.

- Kermode says that Macbeth's soliloquy is famous because it provides a "vivid expression to an acute crisis of conscience."
Ask students why they think a soliloquy might be a good format for exploring a "crisis of conscience."
Possible response: Students may say that a soliloquy provides an opportunity to think out loud. The performance of a soliloquy may appear more spontaneous than an essay or other written format in which a character examines a decision.

- Ask students to look for other instances of references to religious or ethical thoughts as they read *Macbeth.* Discuss how the weight of religious defiance affects Macbeth's conscience and actions.

FRANK KERMODE INTRODUCES
Macbeth by William Shakespeare

Macbeth's Dramatic History

   Macbeth, first performed in 1606, is a play about the murder of a good king of Scotland, its cruel consequences for his country, and the final overthrow of the murderous usurper. Shakespeare takes many liberties with history, for King Duncan was not really a saintly character and Macbeth not a particularly evil one. Banquo is presented in a favorable light because he was held to be the ancestor of King James, the Scottish king who inherited Elizabeth's throne in 1603. Shakespeare's company was called The King's Men; as servants of the king, they had good reason to praise his ancestry and his virtues. Considering the period background, the play is remarkable for the allusions it makes to events in the early years of James's reign.

Portraying The Tumult of Mind and Conscience Yet these allusions are matters of secondary interest to the modern reader. *Macbeth* is a work of the author's full maturity. He had already written the tragedies *Hamlet, Othello,* and *King Lear* and had learned how to represent not merely outward actions but the tumults of the mind and conscience. In the passage shown from Act I, Macbeth is at the moment of decision, the interim between desire and action, debating within himself whether to go ahead with the plot he devised with his wife to murder the king, their guest. He is weighing the benefits that act would bring him against the powerful reasons for not doing it. He knows that time won't stand still when Duncan is dead. The killing will start a train of events calling for further action.

   He is willing to risk judgment after death but knows it will happen in this life. In the here and now. And he gives ordinary social, human reasons for not committing the crime: He is Duncan's kinsman and his host. Moreover, for a subject to kill an innocent monarch is an offense so horrible that his imagination foretells the dreadful disturbances and great sorrows that must ensue. And he admits he has no motive except overweening ambition.

The Actions of a Common Man The reason why Macbeth's soliloquy is so famous is not that it concerns the early history of Scotland, and the foundation of the Stuart dynasty, but that it gives incomparably vivid expression to an acute crisis of conscience. For a moment, Macbeth is every man or woman, who must, in the course of his or her life, be faced by the need to decide which of two choices is the right one.

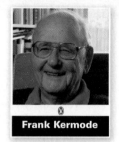

Frank Kermode

Literary critic Frank Kermode wrote the award-winning *Shakespeare's Language* in 2000. Other works by Kermode include *The Uses of Errors* (1991) and *An Appetite for Poetry* (1989).

▼ **Critical Viewing**
What general traits might be worthy of note in a tribute to a young king, like James I pictured here? **[Speculate]**

Teaching Resources

The following resources can be used to enrich or extend the instruction for From the Scholar's Desk.

Unit 2 Resources
   From the Scholar's Desk:
      Frank Kermode, p. 92
      Viewing and Listening, p. 93
From the Author's Desk DVD
   Frank Kermode, Segment 2

The language of this soliloquy is sometimes unusual and full of feverish excitement. But, at first, do not bother too much about the details; just allow yourself to be swept along by the movement of passionate thought.

This soliloquy indicates the extraordinary range and flexibility of the play's language, incomparably greater than English could have provided even fifty or sixty years before. This new fluency owes something to sixteenth-century Bible translations.

Religious and Ethical Thought As this soliloquy also reflects, *Macbeth* is notable for complying with native ethical traditions. Shakespeare is not often explicitly religious, but Macbeth speaks as one aware of the Christian religion—he understands the danger to his soul, yet gives his "eternal jewel" to "the common enemy of man" (3.1.68–69). Behind such remarks there is a great weight of religious and ethical thought.

> "He's here in double trust:
> First, as I am his kinsman and his subject,
> Strong both against the deed; then, as his host,
> Who should against his murderer shut the door,
> Not bear the knife myself. Besides, this Duncan
> Hath borne his faculties so meek, hath been
> So clear in his great office, that his virtues
> Will plead like angels, trumpet-tongue'd, against
> The deep damnation of his taking-off. . .
>   I have no spur
> To prick the sides of my intent, but only
> Vaulting ambition, which o'erleaps itself
> And falls on th'other."
> — *Macbeth*, Act I, Scene vii

Thinking About the Commentary

1. (a) Recall: What English king did Shakespeare intend to honor by writing *Macbeth*? **(b) Speculate:** What benefits might a company of actors and playwrights reap by presenting their king in a favorable light?

2. (a) Recall: According to Kermode, what reason does Macbeth provide for wanting to kill King Duncan? **(b) Speculate:** If, in the course of the play, Macbeth is punished for killing the king, what message might this send to the audience in Shakespeare's day?

As You Read Macbeth . . .

3. Note moments in which Banquo and most kings in the play are presented in a positive light as a way to honor James I of England.

4. Look for evidence that supports Kermode's characterization of Macbeth as "every man or woman . . . faced by the need to decide which of two choices is the right one."

From the Scholar's Desk: Frank Kermode ■ 301

ASSESS

Answers

1. (a) Shakespeare intended to honor King James, the Scottish king, by writing *Macbeth*. (b) Actors who presented their king in a favorable light might be invited to perform for the king. Royal performances might receive more publicity and increase their company's attendance.

2. (a) Macbeth is ambitious and wants to kill Duncan so he can advance himself. (b) Macbeth's punishment might send the message not to challenge the king's authority.

Background
More About the Author

The known facts regarding Shakespeare's life tell us little about him as a person. Born in April 1564 in Stratford-on-Avon, Shakespeare probably attended grammar school there. The principal subject of Elizabethan grammar school was Latin, so Shakespeare no doubt read the works of Cicero, Ovid, and Virgil. Frequent allusions are made to such classics in his works. In 1582, he married Anne Hathaway. They had three children. Although best known as a playwright, Shakespeare also wrote 154 sonnets and 2 narrative poems, "Venus and Adonis," (1593) and "The Rape of Lucrece" (1594), as well as another long poem, "The Phoenix and the Turtle."

Like Chaucer before him, Shakespeare was a gifted storyteller. Most of the stories portrayed in his dramas had already been told by others. In Shakespeare's hands, however, these stories took on a dramatic new life. His ability to use just the right word or phrase is evident in the many familiar expressions first penned by the Bard of Avon: "Now is the winter of our discontent . . ." (*Richard III*), ". . . parting is such sweet sorrow . . ." (*Romeo and Juliet*), ". . . it was Greek to me" (*Julius Caesar*), "All the world's a stage . . ." (*As You Like It*). Shakespeare died in Stratford-on-Avon in 1616 and was buried near the altar in the church. His wife died seven years later.

Build Skills Drama

Macbeth

William Shakespeare
(1564–1616)
Because of his deep understanding of human nature, his compassion for all types of people, and the power and beauty of his language, William Shakespeare is regarded as the greatest writer in English. Nearly four hundred years after his death, Shakespeare's plays continue to be read widely and produced throughout the world. They have the same powerful impact on today's audiences as they had when they were first staged.

Timeline of Praise No other writer in English has won such universal and enthusiastic praise from critics and fellow writers. Here are just a few samples of that praise, shown on a timeline from Shakespeare's day to our own:

The Playwright in His Own Time It is a myth that we know absolutely nothing about Shakespeare's life. As critic Irving Ribner attests, "we know more about him than we do about virtually any other of his contemporary dramatists, with the exception of Ben Jonson." Shakespeare was born on April 23, 1564, in Stratford-on-Avon, which is northwest of London. (The date is based on a record of his baptism on April 26.) Stratford, with a population of about two thousand in Shakespeare's day, was the market town for a fertile agricultural region.

Shakespeare's father, John, was a successful glove maker and businessman who held a number of positions in the town's government. His mother, whose maiden name was Mary Arden, was the daughter of John's landlord. Their marriage, therefore, boosted the Shakespeare family's holdings. Nevertheless, there is evidence that in the late 1570s, John Shakespeare began to suffer financial reverses.

Shakespeare's Education No written evidence of Shakespeare's boyhood exists—not even a name on a school attendance list.

Timeline of Praise

Ben Jonson (1572–1637)
"He was not of an age, but for all time!"

Samuel Johnson (1709–1784)
"Shakespeare is, above all writers, at least above all modern writers, the poet of nature: the poet that holds up to his readers a faithful mirror of manners and life."

A.C. Bradley (1851–1935)
"Where his power of art is fully exerted, it really does resemble that of nature."

| 1600 | 1700 | 1800 | 1900 |

John Dryden (1631–1700)
"He was the man who of all modern, and perhaps ancient, poets had the largest and most comprehensive soul."

Samuel Taylor Coleridge (1772–1834)
"The Englishman, who, without reverence, a proud and affectionate reverence, can utter the name of William Shakespeare, stands disqualified for the office of critic."

T.S. Eliot (1888–1965)
"About any one so great as Shakespeare, it is probable that we can never be right . . ."

Enrichment

The Shakespeare Question

There is a persistent argument in some circles that Shakespeare did not actually write the plays attributed to him. People cite as evidence everything from the talent of others to their belief that Shakespeare was too busy. They overlook the fact that everyone who knew Shakespeare acknowledged him as the author. Ben Jonson, a contemporary and one of Shakespeare's more vocal critics, wrote that Shakespeare was a naturally gifted writer who lacked discipline—but never questioned his authorship. Approximately 50 people wrote during his lifetime that Shakespeare wrote the plays. In an era when gossip was a national pastime, it seems unlikely that Jonson and Shakespeare's many theatrical associates could have or would have kept such a secret quiet. Those who suggest that Shakespeare was not sufficiently educated fail to explain how he could have circulated among the age's literary greats without something as obvious as illiteracy being noticed. Despite the ongoing controversy, Shakespeare is still considered to be the most likely writer of the plays.

However, given his father's status, it is highly probable that he attended the Stratford Grammar School, where he acquired a knowledge of Latin.

Although Shakespeare did not go on to study at a university, his attendance at the grammar school from ages seven to sixteen would have provided him with a good education. Discipline at such a school was strict, and the school day lasted from 6:00 A.M. in the summer (7:00 in the winter) until 5:00 P.M. From 11:00 to 1:00, students were dismissed to eat lunch with their families. At 3:00, they were allowed to play for a quarter of an hour!

Shakespeare's Marriage and Family

Shakespeare's name enters the official records again in November 1582, when he received a license to marry Anne Hathaway. The couple had a daughter, Susanna, in 1583, and twins, Judith and Hamnet, in 1585. Beyond names and years in which his children were born, we know little about his family life. Some writers have made much of the fact that Shakespeare left his wife and children behind when he went to London not long after his twins were born. However, he visited his family in Stratford regularly during his years as a playwright, and they may have lived with him for a time in London.

His Career as Actor and Playwright

It is uncertain how Shakespeare became connected with the theater in the late 1580s and early 1590s. By 1594, however, he had become a part owner and the principal playwright of the Lord Chamberlain's Men, one of the most successful theater companies in London.

In 1599, the company built the famous Globe theater on the south bank of the Thames River, in Southwark. This is where most of Shakespeare's plays were performed. When James I became king in 1603, after the death of Elizabeth I, James took control of the Lord Chamberlain's Men and renamed the company the King's Men.

Retirement In about 1610, Shakespeare retired to Stratford, where he continued to write plays. He was a prosperous middle-class man, who profited from his share in a successful theater company. Six years later, on April 23, 1616, he died and was buried in Holy Trinity Church in Stratford. Because it was a common practice to move bodies after burial to make room for others, Shakespeare wrote the following as his epitaph:

Blest be the man that spares these stones,
And curst be he that moves my bones.

His Literary Record Shakespeare did not think of himself as a man of letters. He wrote his plays to be performed and did not bring out editions of them for the reading public. The first published edition of his work, called the First Folio, was issued in 1623 by two members of his theater company, John Heminges and Henry Condell. It contained thirty-six of the thirty-seven plays now attributed to him.

Shakespeare's varied output includes romantic comedies, like *A Midsummer Night's Dream* and *As You Like It*; history plays, like *Henry IV*, Parts 1 and 2; tragedies, like *Romeo and Juliet, Hamlet, Othello, King Lear,* and *Macbeth*; and later romances, like *The Tempest*. In addition to his plays, he wrote 154 sonnets and three longer poems.

Speaking Shakespeare

You may not realize the extent to which you already "speak" Shakespeare. For example, have you ever used or heard any of these common phrases?

He's full of *the milk of human kindness.* (I, v, 17)
Don't worry about it, *what's done is done!* (III, ii, 12)
That will last until *the crack of doom.* (IV, i, 117)
She finished the jobs in *one fell swoop.* (IV, iii, 219)

Shakespeare invented each of these now common phrases, which were unknown in English before their appearance in *Macbeth*. Look for them as you read and discover if their meanings have changed since Shakespeare's time.

Macbeth ■ 303

Background
James I and Witchcraft

While some Elizabethans believed in witches, others were skeptical. Among the skeptics was Reginald Scot, who wrote *Discovery of Witchcraft* (1584) to demonstrate "that the compacts and contracts of witches with all Devils and all Infernal Spirits or familiars are but erroneous novelties and imaginary conceptions."

The king, when he was still King James VI of Scotland, objected to Scot's "damnable opinions" about witches and wrote a book entitled *Daemonology* (1597) to state his case. King James's strong opinions on this matter came from a personal experience. A group of Scottish witches had been accused of plotting against his life. One of the suspects, Agnes Sampson, made such wild statements that James was convinced the whole affair was absurd. At that point, Agnes Sampson spoke to the king in private and "declared unto him the very words which passed between the King's Majesty and his Queen at Upslo in Norway the first night of their marriage; whereat the king wondered greatly and swore by the living God that he believed that all the devils in Hell could not have discovered the same." Sampson's skill, clairvoyance, or lucky guess made the king a firm believer in the power of witchcraft.

The sensational news from this trial was fully covered in England, and it is tempting to imagine Shakespeare reading this account and storing it up for future use.

Tell students that they should not be critical of the king and his beliefs. Today, with science and technology far more advanced than anything that Shakespeare or King James could have ever imagined, there is widespread interest in witchcraft.

Motivation

Write *Fate* on the board and ask students to define the word. Then lead students into a discussion of the role, if any, fate plays in our lives. Explain that in Macbeth, they will encounter a man who has brilliantly served in battle, has the favor of the king of Scotland, and has an extremely promising future. When three "weird sisters"—the witches—reveal his fate, his life begins to change irrevocably.

❶ Background
More About Macbeth

The following is Holinshed's version of Macbeth's encounter with the three witches:

Shortly after happened a strange and uncouth wonder, which afterward was the case of much trouble in the realm of Scotland, as ye shall after hear. It fortuned as Macbeth and Banquo journeyed toward Forres, where the king then lay, they went sporting by the way together without other company, save only themselves, passing through the woods and fields, when suddenly in the midst of a laund [lawn, open place] there met them three women in strange and wild apparel, resembling creatures of elder world, whom when they attentively beheld, wondering much at the sight, the first of them spake and said: "All hail, Macbeth, Thane of Glammis!" (for he had lately entered into that dignity and office by the death of his father Sinell). The second of them said: "Hail Macbeth, Thane of Cawdor!" But the third said: "All hail, Macbeth, that hereafter shalt be King of Scotland!"

Build Skills   *Drama*

❶ Macbeth

Shakespeare's Sources

Fact and Legend By Shakespeare's time, the story of the eleventh-century Scottish king Macbeth was a mixture of fact and legend. Shakespeare and his contemporaries, however, probably regarded the account of Macbeth in Raphael Holinshed's *Chronicles of England, Scotland, and Ireland* as completely factual. The playwright drew on the *Chronicles* as a source for the play, yet, as you will see, he freely adapted the material for his own purposes.

Holinshed's *Chronicles* Holinshed's account contains a description of a meeting between Macbeth and the witches. His account also tells how Macbeth and his friends, angry at the naming of King Duncan's son Malcolm as Prince of Cumberland, ambush and slay Duncan. However, the historical Macbeth's claim to the throne has some basis. (See page 388 for an explanation of the ancient Scottish custom of choosing kings.) Finally, Holinshed indicates that Banquo is Macbeth's accomplice in the assassination. Lady Macbeth, prominent in Shakespeare's play, does not play a significant role in Holinshed.

Shakespeare's *Macbeth* Shakespeare took what he needed from the *Chronicles* and shaped it into a tragic plot. Seeing the theatrical possibilities of the meeting with the witches, Shakespeare staged such an encounter in Act I, Scene iii. However, he changed Holinshed's account in order to make King Duncan an innocent victim: Shakespeare's Macbeth does not have a legitimate claim to the throne. Further, Shakespeare used another story in the *Chronicles*—one in which a wife urges her husband to kill a friend and guest—as the basis for the character Lady Macbeth. She becomes Macbeth's co-conspirator, replacing Banquo. Read on to discover Shakespeare's political motives for holding Banquo innocent.

A Tribute to the King

A Dangerous Plot *Macbeth* is set in eleventh-century Scotland. However, Shakespeare wrote the play with an eye on seventeenth-century events in England. In November 1605, a group of Catholics seeking revenge for the increasing oppression of Catholics plotted to blow up the king and Parliament. With the help of Guy Fawkes, a soldier of fortune, they rented a cellar directly below the House of Lords, in which to stockpile barrels of gunpowder. Incredibly, the conspirators succeeded in storing thirty-six barrels of gunpowder there. To appreciate the magnitude of the threat, imagine modern terrorists smuggling tons of explosives into the Capitol building in Washington, D.C.

The Plot Revealed The plot was revealed when a lord, who happened to be a brother-in-law of one of the conspirators, was anonymously warned by letter not to attend the opening of Parliament. This warning helped the authorities break the case, and they arrested Guy Fawkes as he entered the cellar. Fawkes and some of the other chief conspirators were executed. Although their numbers were few, their plan was so frightening that it led, for a time, to increased persecution of all English Catholics. In England, Guy Fawkes Day is still commemorated on November 5 each year with fireworks, bonfires, and the burning of effigies representing Guy Fawkes.

Sympathy for the King In *Macbeth*, Shakespeare capitalized on the sympathy generated for the king by this incident. He chose the Scottish setting for his play, knowing that James's family, the Stuarts, first came to the Scottish throne in the eleventh century. One of the most virtuous characters in the play, Banquo, was thought to be the father of the first of the Stuart kings. Knowing that James I had written a book on witches, Shakespeare included the three hags in the play.

Preview

Connecting to the Literature

If you have ever been elbowed aside by a team member eager for glory, you have experienced the effects of fierce ambition. In *Macbeth,* ambition causes a brave soldier to become an evil plotter.

Literary Analysis

Elizabethan Drama

During the late sixteenth century, **Elizabethan drama** came into full bloom. Playwrights turned away from religious subjects and began writing more sophisticated plays. Drawing on models from ancient Greece and Rome, writers reintroduced **tragedies**—plays in which disaster befalls a hero or heroine. Dramatists also began writing their plays in carefully crafted unrhymed verse, using rich language and vivid imagery.

Because the Globe, like other Elizabethan theaters, had no lighting, plays were performed in broad daylight. There were also no sets, so the words of the play had to create the illusion of time and place for the audience.

Connecting Literary Elements

In a play, a **soliloquy** is a long speech, usually made by a character who is alone (*soliloquy* comes from the Latin *solus,* meaning "alone") and thus reveals private thoughts and feelings to the audience, but not to other characters. In Shakespeare's tragedies, the greatest works of Elizabethan drama, tragic characters reveal secret desires or troubling fears through their soliloquies. For example, as you read the following soliloquies in this act, use a chart like the one shown here to note the inner struggles each reveals.

- Lady Macbeth's soliloquy, Act I, Scene v
- Macbeth's soliloquy, Act I, Scene vii

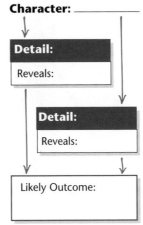

Reading Strategy

Using Text Aids

Like many dramas, Shakespeare's plays were meant to be performed, not read. Playwrights and editors, however, provide **text aids,** explanatory features that help you interpret the plays. These aids include stage directions in brackets and notes on the side of the text. Use these aids when you read.

Vocabulary Builder

valor (val´ ər) *n.* marked courage or bravery (p. 308)

treasons (trē´ zənz) *n.* betrayals of one's country or oath of loyalty (p. 314)

imperial (im pir´ ē əl) *adj.* of an empire; having supreme authority (p. 314)

liege (lēj) *n.* lord or king (p. 315)

sovereign (säv´ rən) *adj.* supreme in power, rank, or authority (p. 320)

Macbeth ■ 305

❷ Literary Analysis
Elizabethan Drama

- Tell students that, as they read *Macbeth,* they should focus on the elements that make it typical of Elizabethan drama, such as unrhymed verse, rich language, and vivid imagery.
- Have students read the description of Elizabethan drama.
- Use Connecting Literary Elements to explain the important function of the soliloquy in Elizabethan drama. Give students a copy of **Literary Analysis Graphic Organizer A,** p. 54 in *Graphic Organizer Transparencies,* to use as they read *Macbeth,* Act I.

❸ Reading Strategy
Using Text Aids

- Point out to students that there are two types of text aids in a Shakespearean drama—those supplied by the playwright, so actors and directors know what to do, and those later supplied by editors to explain words and phrases that are no longer in use.
- Have students turn to the play and find an example of each type of text aid. Discuss how this information can help them better understand both the action and ideas of the play.

Vocabulary Builder

- Pronounce each vocabulary word for students, and read the definitions as a class. Have students identify any words with which they are already familiar.

Differentiated
Instruction — Solutions for All Learners

Support for Special Needs Students
Have students use the support pages for *The Tragedy of Macbeth* in the *Reader's Notebooks.* Completing these pages will prepare students to read the selection in the Student Edition.

Support for Less Proficient Readers
Have students use the support pages for *The Tragedy of Macbeth* in the *Reader's Notebooks.* After students finish the selection in the *Reader's Notebooks,* have them complete the questions and activities in the Student Edition.

Support for English Learners
Have students use the support pages for *The Tragedy of Macbeth* in the *Reader's Notebooks: English Learner's Version.* Completing these pages will prepare students to read the selection in the Student Edition.

Learning Modalities
Visual/Spatial Learners

Throughout the reading of *Macbeth,* have students refer to the photograph of the reconstructed Globe theater on p. 295. Suggest that they envision the action as it would take place in the acting areas.

❶ About the Selection

In *The Tragedy of Macbeth,* Act I, the war hero Macbeth returns home and, on the way, encounters three witches who prophesy that he will one day be king of Scotland. Seized by ruthless ambition and spurred on by his wife, Macbeth plans to murder King Duncan, thus setting in motion a series of events that will lead to his eventual downfall.

❷ Background
Reading Shakespeare

Many students will find Shakespeare's language a challenge. He uses words and structures not familiar to the modern ear. This situation is less of a problem in a theater, where actors communicate meaning through their interpretation, but it does pose a problem for readers. (Underscore that the richness of the language and insights into human nature make Shakespeare worth the work.)

It may help students to see a performance. Encourage them to watch one of the recent film versions of Shakespeare's plays, to hear how the language sounds in performance. You may also wish to listen in class to the **Listening to Literature Audio CDs.**

Because some words are no longer in common use or have evolved different meanings, encourage students to refer often to the margin notes. Also, Shakespeare plays with standard English word order. Suggest that students look for the subject and verb and then determine how other sentence parts fit.

As with poetry, students should read in sentences, rather than in lines. A sentence may extend over a number of lines, so encourage students to be guided by the punctuation.

THE TRAGEDY OF
Macbeth
William Shakespeare

❶

❷ **Background** The Elizabethans viewed the universe, in its ideal state, as both orderly and interconnected. They believed that a great chain linked all beings, from God on high to the lowest beasts and plants. They also believed that universal order was based on parallels between different realms. Just as the sun ruled in the heavens, for example, the king ruled in the state and the father in the family. Because everything was linked, a disturbance in one area would cause a disturbance in others. In keeping with this concept of order, a Shakespearean tragedy shows how a tragic hero's bad choices can disturb the whole universe. As *Macbeth* gets underway, notice the parallel disorders in the mind of the hero, the weather, and the kingdom.

306 ■ *Celebrating Humanity (1485–1625)*

Differentiated
Instruction   Solutions for All Learners

Accessibility at a glance

	Macbeth
Context	11th Century Scotland; ruling classes
Language	Difficult vocabulary and syntax
Concept Level	Accessible (ambition)

Literary Merit	Shakespearean Tragedy
Lexile	NP
Overall Rating	More challenging

CHARACTERS

DUNCAN, King of Scotland
MALCOLM } his sons
DONALBAIN
MACBETH
BANQUO
MACDUFF
LENNOX   noblemen
ROSS   of Scotland
MENTEITH
ANGUS
CAITHNESS
FLEANCE, son to Banquo
SIWARD, Earl of Northumberland,
        general of the English forces
YOUNG SIWARD, his son

SEYTON, an officer attending on Macbeth
SON TO MACDUFF
AN ENGLISH DOCTOR
A SCOTTISH DOCTOR
A PORTER
AN OLD MAN
THREE MURDERERS
LADY MACBETH
LADY MACDUFF
A GENTLEWOMAN attending
    on Lady Macbeth
HECATE
WITCHES
APPARITIONS
LORDS, OFFICERS, SOLDIERS, ATTENDANTS,
    AND MESSENGERS

Setting: Scotland; England

Act I

Scene i. An open place.

[*Thunder and lightning. Enter* THREE WITCHES.]

FIRST WITCH. When shall we three meet again?
   In thunder, lightning, or in rain?

SECOND WITCH. When the hurlyburly's done,
   When the battle's lost and won.

5 **THIRD WITCH.** That will be ere the set of sun.

FIRST WITCH. Where the place?

SECOND WITCH.   Upon the heath.

THIRD WITCH. There to meet with Macbeth.

❸ FIRST WITCH. I come, Graymalkin.[1]

SECOND WITCH. Paddock[2] calls.

THIRD WITCH.   Anon![3]

10 **ALL.** Fair is foul, and foul is fair.
   Hover through the fog and filthy air.   [*Exit.*]

Scene ii. A camp near Forres, a town in northeast Scotland.

[*Alarum within.*[1] *Enter* KING DUNCAN, MALCOLM, DONALBAIN, LENNOX,
with ATTENDANTS, *meeting a bleeding* CAPTAIN.]

Reading Strategy

Using Text Aids Who or what are Graymalkin and Paddock in lines 8 and 9? How do you know?

1. **Graymalkin** first witch's helper, a gray cat.

2. **Paddock** second witch's helper, a toad.

3. **Anon** at once.

1. **Alarum within** trumpet call offstage.

❺ 🔖 Reading Check
Where, when, and with whom will the witches next meet?

Macbeth, Act I, Scene ii ■ 307

---

❸ Reading Strategy
Using Text Aids

• Read aloud the bracketed passage.

• **Ask** students the Reading Strategy question: Who or what are Graymalkin and Paddock? How do you know?
Answer: Graymalkin is the first witch's helper, a gray cat, and Paddock is the second witch's helper, a toad. The margin notes explain this.

• Discuss with students resources that could contribute more insight or information than the included text aids do. (Ideas might include illustrated books, videos of the play, or Internet sites that are related to Shakespeare, theater, or the concept of witches during the era.)

❹ Critical Thinking
Analyze

• Point out to the class that Shakespeare often used rhyming couplets to end scenes.

• Have students read lines 10–11.

• Then, **ask** students why Shakespeare might have chosen to end the first scene with these lines.
Possible responses: The couplet sums up the mood of the scene; the use of alliteration and the rhyme make the couplet memorable; it makes it clear that the scene is over.

❺ Reading Check

Answer: The witches will meet with Macbeth upon the heath, when the hurlyburly's done and when the battle's lost and won.

❻ Humanities

The Three Witches, 1783, by Henry Fuseli

Henry Fuseli (1741–1825), a Swiss-born English artist, began as a writer, but with the encouragement of Sir Joshua Reynolds, the head of the Royal Academy of Art, he began to paint. His formal art education consisted of an eight-year residence in Rome, where he studied the art of the Italian master Michelangelo. His style is a combination of romanticism, fantasy, and the grotesque. Throughout his life, Fuseli was influenced by literature, especially the works of William Shakespeare.

The strong composition is enhanced by the rhythm of the three outstretched arms ending in talon-like hands.

Use these questions for discussion:

1. Read Banquo's description of the witches in lines 40–47 of Scene iii. Is Fuseli's painting faithful to this description?
Possible response: The witches appear to be withered, with choppy fingers and skinny lips, as described by Banquo.

2. Does this painting give you a better understanding of the fright felt by the characters upon encountering the witches?
Possible responses: Yes, they certainly seem strange; no, they are merely old women, nothing to be afraid of.

❼ Critical Viewing

Answer: Fuseli's shrouding of the witches in darkness and having them perform the same mysterious gesture captures the eerie mood of their presence in Act I, Scene i.

❻

The Three Witches, 1783, Henry Fuseli, Kunsthaus Zurich
Kunsthaus Zurich. All rights reserved

❼ ▲ **Critical Viewing** Examine Fuseli's rendering of the witches. Does the mood he creates correspond to the mood in Act I, Scene i? Why or why not? **[Connect]**

KING. What bloody man is that? He can report,
As seemeth by his plight, of the revolt
The newest state.

MALCOLM.   This is the sergeant[2]
Who like a good and hardy soldier fought
5 'Gainst my captivity. Hail, brave friend!
Say to the king the knowledge of the broil[3]
As thou didst leave it.

CAPTAIN.   Doubtful it stood,
As two spent swimmers, that do cling together
And choke their art.[4] The merciless Macdonwald—
10 Worthy to be a rebel for to that
The multiplying villainies of nature
Do swarm upon him—from the Western Isles[5]
Of kerns and gallowglasses[6] is supplied;
And fortune, on his damnéd quarrel[7] smiling,
15 Showed like a rebel's whore:[8] but all's too weak:
For brave Macbeth—well he deserves that name—
Disdaining fortune, with his brandished steel,
Which smoked with bloody execution,
Like valor's minion[9] carved out his passage

2. **sergeant** officer.

3. **broil** battle.

4. **choke their art** prevent each other from swimming.

5. **Western Isles** the Hebrides, off Scotland.

6. **Of kerns and gallow-glasses** with lightly armed Irish foot soldiers and heavily armed soldiers.

7. **damned quarrel** accursed cause.

8. **Showed . . . whore** falsely appeared to favor Macdonwald.

9. **minion** favorite.

Vocabulary Builder
valor (val′ ər) *n.* marked courage or bravery

308 ■ Celebrating Humanity (1485–1625)

Enrichment

Witchcraft in the English Renaissance

Scholars believe that one reason Shakespeare included witches in *Macbeth* is the fact that the king, James I, had openly expressed his belief in witches. Witchcraft was a topic of controversy in seventeenth-century Europe and America. The attitude toward witches and witchcraft varied widely.

Some regarded the existence of witches to be nothing more than a harmless superstition. Others felt witches to be real and a source of evil that had to be wiped out.

As a result, waves of hysteria over witches and their supposed links to the devil sometimes swept over the land. Between the fifteenth and eighteenth centuries, thousands of people were convicted of being witches and executed. The most famous trials in America occurred in 1692 in Salem, Massachusetts, where nineteen people were convicted of being witches and hanged.

Till he faced the slave;
Which nev'r shook hands, nor bade farewell to him,
Till he unseamed him from the nave to th' chops,[10]
And fixed his head upon our battlements.

KING. O valiant cousin! Worthy gentleman!

25 **CAPTAIN.** As whence the sun 'gins his reflection[11]
Shipwracking storms and direful thunders break,
So from that spring whence comfort seemed to come
Discomfort swells. Mark, King of Scotland, mark:
No sooner justice had, with valor armed,
30 Compelled these skipping kerns to trust their heels
But the Norweyan lord,[12] surveying vantage,[13]
With furbished arms and new supplies of men,
Began a fresh assault.

KING. Dismayed not this
Our captains, Macbeth and Banquo?

CAPTAIN. Yes;
35 As sparrows eagles, or the hare the lion.
If I say sooth,[14] I must report they were
As cannons overcharged with double cracks;[15]
So they doubly redoubled strokes upon the foe.
Except[16] they meant to bathe in reeking wounds,
40 Or memorize another Golgotha,[17]
I cannot tell—
But I am faint; my gashes cry for help.

KING. So well thy words become thee as thy wounds;
They smack of honor both. Go get him surgeons.

[*Exit* CAPTAIN, *attended.*]

[*Enter* ROSS *and* ANGUS.]

Who comes here?

45 **MALCOLM.** The worthy Thane[18] of Ross.

⑨ LENNOX. What a haste looks through his eyes! So should he look
That seems to[19] speak things strange.

ROSS. God save the king!

KING. Whence cam'st thou, worthy Thane?

ROSS. From Fife, great King;
Where the Norweyan banners flout the sky
50 And fan our people cold.
Norway[20] himself, with terrible numbers,
Assisted by that most disloyal traitor
The Thane of Cawdor, began a dismal[21] conflict;
Till that Bellona's bridegroom, lapped in proof,[22]

Literary Analysis
Elizabethan Drama What offstage scene does the captain describe in this speech (lines 7–23)?

10. unseamed . . . chops split him open from the navel to the jaws.

11. 'gins his reflection rises.

12. Norweyan lord king of Norway.

13. surveying vantage seeing an opportunity.

14. sooth truth.

15. cracks explosives.

16. except unless.

17. memorize . . . Golgotha (gŏl′ gə thə) make the place as memorable for slaughter as Golgotha, the place where Christ was crucified.

18. Thane Scottish title of nobility.

19. seems to seems about to.

20. Norway king of Norway.

21. dismal threatening.

22. Bellona's . . . proof Macbeth is called the mate of Bellona, the goddess of war, clad in tested armor.

Literary Analysis
Elizabethan Drama How do Lennox's words here (lines 46–47) supply a clue for the actor playing Ross?

⑩ ✔ Reading Check
What role has Macbeth played in the battle?

Macbeth, Act I, Scene ii ■ 309

---

❽ Literary Analysis
Elizabethan Drama

- Have students read the captain's speech in lines 7–23.

- **Ask** students the first Literary Analysis question: What offstage scene does the captain describe in this speech?
  Answer: The captain describes a battle between Macdonwald and Macbeth in which Macbeth was victorious.

▶ **Monitor Progress:** Knowing what they do about the Elizabethan stage, have students **consider** why Shakespeare might have chosen to have a character relate this scene rather than have it performed.
Answer: The battle would have been difficult to represent and much easier to discuss.

- Discuss with the class the events related in the speech, to make certain students understand that Macbeth is the hero, battling incredible odds.

❾ Literary Analysis
Elizabethan Drama

- Read aloud Lennox's words in lines 46–47.

- Then, **ask** students the second Literary Analysis question: How do Lennox's words here supply a clue for the actor playing Ross?
  Possible responses: The comment that haste looks through Ross's eyes and that he looks like he's going to speak strange things would be clues to the actor playing Ross that there is a sense of urgency in his behavior. He should probably look excited, as if he were eager to share what he knew. It might also suggest that he would enter quickly, because he has important news.

❿ Reading Check
Answer: Macbeth was the hero of the day, killing Macdonwald in hand-to-hand combat, then helping to defeat the Norwegians.

Differentiated Instruction **Solutions for All Learners**

Support for Special Needs Students
To help students understand the role of soliloquys in *Macbeth,* show them **Literary Analysis Graphic Organizer B** (*Graphic Organizer Transparencies,* p. 55). This completed sample will model how to interpret the details of a soliloquy to understand a character. They can use the completed graphic organizer as a model for making further interpretations.

Enrichment for Gifted/Talented Students
Students may enjoy exploring aspects of early Scottish society. Encourage them to research one of the many colorful, often highly visual symbols associated with Scotland, such as tartans, clan emblems, flags, highland dress, Scottish landscapes, bagpipes, weapons, or military dances (for example, the sword dance). Have them prepare displays, collages, or demonstrations to share with the class what they discover. (If you need resources, many cities have Scottish societies that would assist you or students with this effort.)

- Point out the text aid that opens Scene iii.

- Then, **ask** students the Reading Strategy question: What information about the setting for Scene iii do you learn from the italicized stage directions?
Answer: The stage directions state that the scene takes place on a heath near Forres; thunder sounds, and the three witches enter.

- Explain that a heath is an open wasteland with heather or low bushes growing on it, but few or no trees. It is similar to what the English call a moor.

- **Ask** students how standing in an open wasteland enhances the eeriness of the scene.
Answer: The characters are exposed and unprotected from the lightning and thunder. Also, it makes the appearance of the witches more surprising.

12 **Critical Thinking**
Draw Conclusions

- Have students read line 10 to themselves.

- **Ask** students what they think the first witch means by "I'll do, I'll do, and I'll do."
Possible responses: She'll seek to injure the sailor to get revenge on the sailor's wife.

- **Ask** students what is being established about the witches in Scene iii.
Answer: That they are evil, murderous, and destructive.

---

55   Confronted him with self-comparisons,[23]
    Point against point, rebellious arm 'gainst arm,
    Curbing his lavish[24] spirit: and, to conclude,
    The victory fell on us.

KING.   Great happiness!

ROSS.   That now
    Sweno, the Norways' king, craves composition;[25]
60   Nor would we deign him burial of his men
    Till he disbursed, at Saint Colme's Inch,[26]
    Ten thousand dollars to our general use.

KING. No more that Thane of Cawdor shall deceive
    Our bosom interest:[27] go pronounce his present[28] death,
65   And with his former title greet Macbeth.

ROSS. I'll see it done.

KING. What he hath lost, noble Macbeth hath won.

                                          [*Exit.*]

11   *Scene iii. A heath near Forres.*

[*Thunder. Enter the* THREE WITCHES.]

FIRST WITCH. Where hast thou been, sister?

SECOND WITCH. Killing swine.[1]

THIRD WITCH. Sister, where thou?

FIRST WITCH. A sailor's wife had chestnuts in her lap,
    And mounched, and mounched, and mounched.
5   "Give me," quoth I.
    "Aroint thee,[2] witch!" the rump-fed ronyon[3] cries.
    Her husband's to Aleppo[4] gone, master o' th' Tiger:
    But in a sieve[5] I'll thither sail,
    And, like a rat without a tail,[6]
12 10   I'll do, I'll do, and I'll do.

SECOND WITCH. I'll give thee a wind.

FIRST WITCH. Th' art kind.

THIRD WITCH. And I another.

FIRST WITCH. I myself have all the other;
15   And the very ports they blow,[7]
    All the quarters that they know
    I' th' shipman's card.[8]
    I'll drain him dry as hay:
    Sleep shall neither night nor day
20   Hang upon his penthouse lid;[9]
    He shall live a man forbid:[10]

310 ■ *Celebrating Humanity (1485–1625)*

---

23. self-comparisons counter movements.

24. lavish insolent.

25. composition terms of peace.

26. St. Colme's Inch island near Edinburgh, Scotland.

27. our bosom interest my heart's trust.

28. present immediate.

Reading Strategy
Using Text Aids What information about the setting for Scene iii do you learn from the italicized stage directions?

1. Killing swine It was commonly believed that witches killed domestic animals.

2. Aroint thee Be off.

3. rump-fed ronyon fat-rumped, scabby creature.

4. Aleppo trading center in Syria.

5. sieve It was commonly believed that witches often sailed in sieves.

6. rat . . . tail According to popular belief, witches could assume the form of any animal, but the tail would always be missing.

7. they blow to which the winds blow.

8. card compass.

9. penthouse lid eyelid.

10. forbid cursed.

Enrichment

Scotland

After centuries of bitter hostility, Scotland and England were joined in 1707 to form Great Britain, a single kingdom. However, the Scots have retained a distinct culture that is deeply embedded in their history and the rugged terrain of the countryside. For example, the steep mountains forced Scottish highlanders to live in small groups called *clans.* Most clans consisted of people with the same surname, such as MacDonald, MacKinnon, and MacLeod. They each developed their own fabric pattern or tartan and displayed it on kilts—short skirts that made it easy to climb hills—and other clothing.

If students have seen the movie *Braveheart*, you may wish to discuss with them the images they have of Scotland, the clans, and the hostile relations with England. Point out that the events in *Macbeth* take place in 1040, and *Braveheart* is set 250 years later, but much of life in the highlands remained the same.

Weary sev'nights[11] nine times nine
Shall he dwindle, peak,[12] and pine:
Though his bark cannot be lost,
25   Yet it shall be tempest-tossed.
Look what I have.

SECOND WITCH. Show me, show me.

FIRST WITCH. Here I have a pilot's thumb,
Wracked as homeward he did come.

[Drum within.]

30   **THIRD WITCH.** A drum, a drum!
Macbeth doth come.

ALL. The weird[13] sisters, hand in hand,
Posters[14] of the sea and land,
Thus do go about, about:
35   Thrice to thine, and thrice to mine,
And thrice again, to make up nine.
Peace! The charm's wound up.

[Enter MACBETH and BANQUO.]

MACBETH. So foul and fair a day I have not seen.

BANQUO. How far is 't called to Forres? What are these
40   So withered, and so wild in their attire,
That look not like th' inhabitants o' th' earth,
And yet are on 't? Live you, or are you aught
That man may question? You seem to understand me,
By each at once her choppy[15] finger laying
45   Upon her skinny lips. You should be women,
And yet your beards forbid me to interpret
That you are so.

MACBETH.   Speak, if you can: what are you?

FIRST WITCH. All hail, Macbeth! Hail to thee, Thane of Glamis!

SECOND WITCH. All hail, Macbeth! Hail to thee, Thane of Cawdor!

50   **THIRD WITCH.** All hail, Macbeth, that shalt be King hereafter!

BANQUO. Good sir, why do you start, and seem to fear
Things that do sound so fair? I' th' name of truth,
Are you fantastical,[16] or that indeed
Which outwardly ye show? My noble partner
55   You greet with present grace[17] and great prediction
Of noble having[18] and of royal hope,
That he seems rapt withal:[19] to me you speak not.
If you can look into the seeds of time,
And say which grain will grow and which will not,

---

11. sev'nights weeks.

12. peak waste away.

13. weird destiny-serving.

14. Posters swift travelers.

**Literary Analysis
Elizabethan Drama** What descriptive details does Banquo use in his speech about the witches (lines 39–47)?

15. choppy chapped.

16. fantastical imaginary.

17. grace honor.

18. having possession.

19. rapt withal entranced by it.

✓ **Reading Check**
What has Macbeth earned through his exploits?

Macbeth, Act I, Scene iii ■ 311

**⑬ Literary Analysis
Elizabethan Drama**

• Have students read lines 39–47.

• **Ask** students the Literary Analysis question: What descriptive details does Banquo use in his speech about the witches?
Answer: Banquo describes the witches as withered, wild in their dress, not human, perhaps ghostly ("Live you?"), with dry hands and skinny lips, womanish in appearance, but having beards.

• **Discuss** with students what Banquo's reactions might be like in this passage. For example, he begins with a simple question to Macbeth, then suddenly catches sight of the witches. You may wish to have students act out the reactions.
Possible responses: Students will probably realize that there would be a considerable amount of surprise and even revulsion expressed in Banquo's body language.

⑭ Reading Check

Answer: Macbeth has earned a new title, Thane of Cawdor, for his exploits.

Macbeth and the Witches, by Clarkson Stanfield

Clarkson Stanfield (1793–1867) did not start out as a painter. He was a sailor who passed time on board ship by painting, drawing marine scenes and making scenery for the sailors' plays. Upon leaving the navy, Stanfield took a job as a scene painter in a London theater. There, he gained an outstanding reputation for his painted scenery. This water-color, *Macbeth and the Witches,* was done for a production of *Macbeth* at one of the theaters in which Stanfield worked. It was painted between 1813 and 1829. This skillfully exe-cuted design serves to explain the popularity Stanfield enjoyed in the-ater circles.

Use the following questions for discussion:

1. In what ways does this sketch help you to visualize the impact of this scene on a theater audience?
Possible response: The dim light and deep shadows transmit the sense of possible danger and foreboding that the play's scene also produces.

2. Does the setting in this picture match the one you envision for this scene? Why or why not?
Possible response: No; this setting is more majestic, with a mountain and low-lying clouds.

16 **Critical Viewing**

Answer: The soldier on the right seems taller and appears to be more nobly attired, suggesting that this soldier is Macbeth.

16 ▲ **Critical Viewing** Which of the two soldiers on the right do you think is Macbeth? Explain your reasoning. **[Deduce]** **15**

60	Speak then to me, who neither beg nor fear Your favors nor your hate.
	FIRST WITCH. Hail!
	SECOND WITCH. Hail!
	THIRD WITCH. Hail!
17 65	**FIRST WITCH.** Lesser than Macbeth, and greater.
	SECOND WITCH. Not so happy,[20] yet much happier.
	THIRD WITCH. Thou shalt get kings, though thou be none. So all hail, Macbeth and Banquo!
	FIRST WITCH. Banquo and Macbeth, all hail!
70	**MACBETH.** Stay, you imperfect[21] speakers, tell me more: By Sinel's[22] death I know I am Thane of Glamis; But how of Cawdor? The Thane of Cawdor lives, A prosperous gentleman; and to be King Stands not within the prospect of belief,
75	No more than to be Cawdor. Say from whence You owe[23] this strange intelligence?[24] Or why

Literary Analysis
Elizabethan Drama How could Elizabethan actors have made this scene with the witches mysterious without help from special lighting effects?

20. **happy** fortunate.

21. **imperfect** incomplete.
22. **Sinel's** (sī´ nəlz) Macbeth's father's.

23. **owe** own.
24. **intelligence** information.

Enrichment

The Fates
In Greek mythology, a person's fate was deter-mined by three women, sometimes called the "weird sisters." They were usually pictured spinning or weaving the fabric of a person's life, which was then arbitrarily cut. In fact, the Middle English word *werde* meant "fate."

In *Macbeth,* three witches (also known as the three weird sisters) appear throughout the play to foretell Macbeth's future—and deter-mine his fate.

Upon this blasted heath you stop our way
With such prophetic greeting? Speak, I charge you.

[WITCHES *vanish.*]

80 **BANQUO.** The earth hath bubbles as the water has,
And these are of them. Whither are they vanished?

MACBETH. Into the air, and what seemed corporal[25] melted
As breath into the wind. Would they had stayed!

18 **BANQUO.** Were such things here as we do speak about?
Or have we eaten on the insane root[26]
85 That takes the reason prisoner?

MACBETH. Your children shall be kings.

BANQUO. You shall be King.

MACBETH. And Thane of Cawdor too. Went it not so?

BANQUO. To th' selfsame tune and words. Who's here?

[*Enter* ROSS *and* ANGUS.]

ROSS. The King hath happily received, Macbeth,
90 The news of thy success; and when he reads[27]
Thy personal venture in the rebels' fight,
His wonders and his praises do contend
Which should be thine or his.[28] Silenced with that,
In viewing o'er the rest o' th' selfsame day,
95 He finds thee in the stout Norweyan ranks,
Nothing afeard of what thyself didst make,
Strange images of death.[29] As thick as tale
Came post with post,[30] and every one did bear
Thy praises in his kingdom's great defense,
And poured them down before him.

100 **ANGUS.** We are sent
To give thee, from our royal master, thanks;
Only to herald thee into his sight,
Not pay thee.

ROSS. And for an earnest[31] of a greater honor,
105 He bade me, from him, call thee Thane of Cawdor;
In which addition,[32] hail, most worthy Thane!
For it is thine.

BANQUO. [*Aside*] What, can the devil speak true?

MACBETH. The Thane of Cawdor lives: why do you dress me
In borrowed robes?

ANGUS. Who was the thane lives yet,
110 But under heavy judgment bears that life
Which he deserves to lose. Whether he was combined[33]

---

25. **corporal** real.

26. **insane root** henbane or hemlock, believed to cause insanity.

Reading Strategy
Using Text Aids What does Banquo mean by the "insane root" (line 84)?

27. **reads** considers.

28. **His wonders . . . his** His admiration contends with his desire to praise you.

29. **Nothing . . . death** killing, but not being afraid of being killed.

30. **As thick . . . post** as fast as could be counted came messenger after messenger.

31. **earnest** pledge.

32. **In which addition** with this new title.

33. **combined** allied.

19 Reading Check

What do the witches promise Macbeth and Banquo?

Macbeth, Act I, Scene iii ■ 313

---

17 **Literary Analysis**
Elizabethan Drama
• After students have read the scene with the witches, **ask** them what Banquo and Macbeth have learned. **Answer:** They have learned that the witches predict that Macbeth will become Thane of Cawdor and king, while Banquo will have descendants that become kings.

• **Ask** students the Literary Analysis question: How could Elizabethan actors have made this scene with the witches mysterious without help from special lighting effects? **Possible responses:** Actors would make this scene mysterious with actions and voices. The witches would act threatening and otherworldly. Macbeth and Banquo would be shaken, horrified, disbelieving. They would show shock at the entrance and disappearance of the witches.

• Point out that Macbeth learns almost immediately that the witches' prediction is true—he is Thane of Cawdor by line 105. Macbeth compares the title to robes that aren't his. You may want to tell students that this image has its parallel in a famous line in Act V, Scene ii: "Now does he feel his title hang loose about him, like a giant's robe upon a dwarfish thief."

18 **Reading Strategy**
Using Text Aids
• Have students read lines 83–84.
• **Ask** students the Reading Strategy question: What does Banquo mean by the "insane root"? **Answer:** Banquo means henbane or hemlock, a plant believed to cause insanity.

▶ **Monitor Progress: Ask** students what clue in the text helped them come to this conclusion. **Answer:** The text annotation in the margin explains what the "insane root" means.

19 **Reading Check**

Answer: The witches promise Macbeth that he will be Thane of Cawdor and king. They promise Banquo that his descendants shall be kings.

313

With those of Norway, or did line[34] the rebel
With hidden help and vantage,[35] or that with both
He labored in his country's wrack,[36] I know not;

115   But <u>treasons</u> capital, confessed and proved,
Have overthrown him.

    MACBETH.   [*Aside*] Glamis, and Thane of Cawdor:
The greatest is behind.[37] [*To* ROSS *and* ANGUS]
Thanks for your pains.
[*Aside to* BANQUO] Do you not hope your children shall be kings,
When those that gave the Thane of Cawdor to me
Promised no less to them?

120   **BANQUO.** [*Aside to* MACBETH] That, trusted home,[38]
Might yet enkindle you unto[39] the crown,
Besides the Thane of Cawdor. But 'tis strange:
And oftentimes, to win us to our harm,
The instruments of darkness tell us truths,
125   Win us with honest trifles, to betray 's
In deepest consequence.
Cousins,[40] a word, I pray you.

    MACBETH.   [*Aside*] Two truths are told,
As happy prologues to the swelling act
Of the <u>imperial</u> theme.[41]—I thank you, gentlemen.—
130   [*Aside*] This supernatural soliciting
Cannot be ill, cannot be good. If ill,
Why hath it given me earnest of success,
Commencing in a truth? I am Thane of Cawdor:
If good, why do I yield to that suggestion[42]
135   Whose horrid image doth unfix my hair
And make my seated[43] heart knock at my ribs,
Against the use of nature?[44] Present fears

22 ◀ **Critical Viewing** In what way does the design of this crown reflect the belief that kings were divinely appointed? [**Analyze**]

314 ■ Celebrating Humanity (1485–1625)

Are less than horrible imaginings.
My thought, whose murder yet is but fantastical
140 Shakes so my single[45] state of man that function
Is smothered in surmise, and nothing is
But what is not.

BANQUO. Look, how our partner's rapt.

MACBETH. [*Aside*] If chance will have me King, why,
chance may crown me,
Without my stir.

BANQUO. New honors come upon him,
145 Like our strange[46] garments, cleave not to their mold
But with the aid of use.

MACBETH. [*Aside*] Come what come may,
Time and the hour runs through the roughest day.

BANQUO. Worthy Macbeth, we stay upon your leisure.[47]

MACBETH. Give me your favor.[48] My dull brain was wrought
150 With things forgotten. Kind gentlemen, your pains
Are registered where every day I turn
The leaf to read them. Let us toward the King.
㉓ [*Aside to* BANQUO] Think upon what hath chanced,
and at more time,
The interim having weighed it,[49] let us speak
Our free hearts[50] each to other.

155 **BANQUO.** Very gladly.

MACBETH. Till then, enough. Come, friends. [*Exit.*]

Scene iv. Forres. The palace.

[*Flourish.*[1] *Enter* KING DUNCAN, LENNOX, MALCOLM, DONALBAIN,
and ATTENDANTS.]

KING. Is execution done on Cawdor? Are not
Those in commission[2] yet returned?

MALCOLM. My liege,
They are not yet come back. But I have spoke
With one that saw him die, who did report
㉔ 5 That very frankly he confessed his treasons,
Implored your Highness' pardon and set forth
A deep repentance: nothing in his life
Became him like the leaving it. He died
As one that had been studied[3] in his death,
10 To throw away the dearest thing he owed[4]
As 'twere a careless[5] trifle.

Reading Strategy
Using Text Aids What
does the stage direction
for line 153 indicate to the
actor playing Macbeth?

45. single unaided, weak.

46. strange new.

47. stay upon your leisure
await your convenience.

48. favor pardon.

49. The interim . . . it when
we have had time to think
about it.

50. Our free hearts our
minds freely.

1. Flourish trumpet fanfare.

2. in commission commissioned to oversee the
execution.

Vocabulary Builder
liege (lēj) *n.* lord or king

3. studied rehearsed

4. owed owned.

5. careless worthless.

 Reading Check
As Macbeth thinks about
what the witches have
promised, what "horrid
image" frightens him?

Macbeth, Act I, Scene iv ■ 315

㉓ Reading Strategy
Using Text Aids

- Direct students' attention to the
stage direction in line 153 and tell
them to think about how it would
affect delivery of the line.

- Then, **ask** the Reading Strategy
question: What does this stage
direction indicate to the actor playing Macbeth?
Answer: It indicates that the actor
playing Macbeth should turn to
Banquo or speak only to him.

- Point out the stage directions in
lines 143 and 146. **Ask** how they
differ from the one in line 153.
Answer: They don't specify to
whom Macbeth speaks.

- Explain that Shakespeare often has
characters speak directly to the
audience in "asides," to let the
audience know what characters are
thinking.

㉔ Critical Thinking
Interpret

- Have students read Malcolm's
speech in lines 3–11.

- **Ask** students to describe Cawdor's
death.
Possible responses: He confessed
his treasons, repented, and begged
the king's forgiveness. He was more
noble in dying than in living.

- Remind students that "dying well"
was seen as a virtue that showed
nobility and strength and that
could be admired even in an
enemy.

- **Ask** students how Macbeth finishes
his internal debate in lines 143–145.
Answer: If chance (fate) wants
him as king, then chance may
make it happen, without his doing
anything.

- Point out to students that the
rhyming couplet for this scene is in
lines 146–147. **Ask** why they think
it comes at this point.
Possible response: The serious
ideas and plot elements of the
scene end at this point. The rest of
the scene is just "let's get on the
road."

㉕ Reading Check
Answer: Macbeth is frightened by
the horrible image of his murdering
Duncan to achieve the events the
witches foretold.

Differentiated
Instruction   Solutions for All Learners

Strategy for Special Needs Students
Before moving on, review the events on these
pages. Macbeth has seen one prophecy come
true. Ask students which prophecy (he is now
Thane of Cawdor). If necessary, take them back
to the place in the text where the witches predicted this (line 49). Emphasize that Macbeth is
already having his first thoughts of what might
need to happen to make the next prophecy
come true—King Duncan would have
to die.

Strategy for English Learners
Discuss the events that have occurred thus far
in the play, so that students do not lose the
thread of the story. Then take time to make
certain that students understand the definitions
given in the side notes. For example, the definition of *treason* includes the words "betrayal"
and "loyalty," both of which might be new
to English learners.

KING.   There's no art

28 To find the mind's construction[6] in the face:
He was a gentleman on whom I built
An absolute trust.

[*Enter* MACBETH, BANQUO, ROSS, *and* ANGUS.]

                              O worthiest cousin!
15   The sin of my ingratitude even now
     Was heavy on me: thou art so far before,
     That swiftest wing of recompense is slow
     To overtake thee. Would thou hadst less deserved,
     That the proportion both of thanks and payment
20   Might have been mine![7] Only I have left to say,
     More is thy due than more than all can pay.

MACBETH.   The service and the loyalty I owe,
     In doing it, pays itself.[8] Your Highness' part
     Is to receive our duties: and our duties
25   Are to your throne and state children and servants;
     Which do but what they should, by doing every thing
     Safe toward[9] your love and honor.

KING.   Welcome hither.
     I have begun to plant thee, and will labor
     To make thee full of growing. Noble Banquo,
30   That hast no less deserved, nor must be known

6. mind's construction person's character.

7. Would . . . mine If you had been less worthy, my thanks and payment could have exceeded the rewards you deserve.

8. pays itself is its own reward.

9. Safe toward with sure regard for.

27 ▼ Critical Viewing How does this Scottish castle reflect the mood of the play? [Connect]

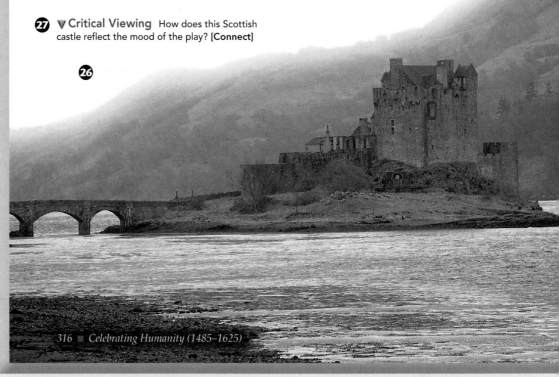

316 ■ *Celebrating Humanity (1485–1625)*

316

No less to have done so, let me enfold thee
And hold thee to my heart.

BANQUO.   There if I grow,
The harvest is your own.

KING.   My plenteous joys,
Wanton[10] in fullness, seek to hide themselves
35 In drops of sorrow. Sons, kinsmen, thanes,
And you whose places are the nearest, know,
We will establish our estate upon
Our eldest, Malcolm,[11] whom we name hereafter
The Prince of Cumberland: which honor must
40 Not unaccompanied invest him only,
But signs of nobleness, like stars, shall shine
On all deservers. From hence to Inverness,[12]
And bind us further to you.

MACBETH. The rest is labor, which is not used for you.[13]
45 I'll be myself the harbinger,[14] and make joyful
The hearing of my wife with your approach;
So, humbly take my leave.

KING.   My worthy Cawdor!

MACBETH. [*Aside*] The Prince of Cumberland! That is a step
On which I must fall down, or else o'erleap,
50 For in my way it lies. Stars, hide your fires;
Let not light see my black and deep desires:
The eye wink at the hand;[15] yet let that be
Which the eye fears, when it is done, to see.   [*Exit.*]

KING. True, worthy Banquo; he is full so valiant,
55 And in his commendations I am fed;
It is a banquet to me. Let's after him,
Whose care is gone before to bid us welcome.
It is a peerless kinsman.   [*Flourish. Exit.*]

Scene v. Inverness. Macbeth's castle.

[*Enter* MACBETH'S WIFE, *alone, with a letter.*]

LADY MACBETH. [*Reads*] "They met me in the day of
success; and I have learned by the perfect'st report
they have more in them than mortal knowledge.
When I burned in desire to question them further,
5 they made themselves air, into which they vanished.
Whiles I stood rapt in the wonder of it, came
missives[1] from the King, who all-hailed me 'Thane
of Cawdor'; by which title, before, these weird sisters
saluted me, and referred me to the coming on
10 of time, with 'Hail, King that shalt be!' This have I

Literary Analysis
Elizabethan Drama
From what area of human
activity do King Duncan
and Banquo draw the
imagery in this passage
(lines 28–33)?

10. Wanton unrestrained.

11. establish . . . Malcolm
make Malcolm the heir to my
throne.

12. Inverness Macbeth's
castle.

13. The rest . . . you
anything not done for you
is laborious.

14. harbinger advance representative of the army or
royal party who makes
arrangements for a visit.

15. wink at the hand be
blind to the hand's deed.

Reading Strategy
Using Text Aids What do
the stage directions with
line 48 tell you about how
Macbeth is to deliver this
speech?

1. missives messengers.

Reading Check
What action of Duncan's
upsets Macbeth?

Macbeth, Act I, Scene v ■ 317

㉙ Literary Analysis
Elizabethan Drama
- Have students read lines 28–33.
- Encourage students to focus on the imagery in Banquo's and King Duncan's dialogue.
- Then, **ask** students the Literary Analysis question: From what area of human activity do King Duncan and Banquo draw their imagery? **Answer:** King Duncan and Banquo draw on imagery from agriculture or farming.

㉚ Reading Strategy
Using Text Aids
- Direct students' attention to line 48, and the stage direction there.
- **Ask** students the Reading Strategy question: What do the stage directions with line 48 tell you about how Macbeth is to deliver this speech? **Answer:** Macbeth is to deliver his comment as an aside, speaking to the audience, as if speaking to himself. He should turn away from the king toward the audience.
- Point out that it is common in productions for the actor to put his hand to the side of his mouth, as if to prevent the other characters from hearing, and to signal to the audience "this is just between you and me."

㉛ Reading Check
Answer: Duncan names his son, Malcolm, as heir to his throne and Prince of Cumberland.

Differentiated Instruction   Solutions for All Learners

Strategy for Less Proficient Readers
Have students compare the way Macbeth addresses the king in lines 22–27 and 44–47 with the thoughts he expresses in his aside to the audience in lines 48–53. Do students think Macbeth is being honest with the king? Make sure students know that, by making his eldest son heir to the throne, the king has put a barrier in Macbeth's way. Discuss what Macbeth wants hidden, what deed he wants the eye to "wink at."

Strategy for Gifted/Talented Students
Have students pick a speech from Act I and prepare it for a dramatic reading. Remind students to look at text aids for clues (are they on a battlefield, is this an aside), but explain that it is primarily from the emotions and ideas expressed that they will gain an understanding of how to deliver the speech. Encourage them to think about how a person would speak and act when coming from a battle or plotting a murder, for example.

317

▶ **Reteach:** Remind students that a soliloquy is a long speech, usually made by a character who is alone. Soliloquies were important elements of Elizabethan drama.

• Point out that lines 1–14 are Macbeth's recounting to Lady Macbeth the meeting with the witches and the fulfilling of the first promise. What do lines 11–14 tell us about Macbeth's feelings for his wife?
Answer: He loves her, sees her as an equal, and knows that she, too, is ambitious.

• **Ask** the Literary Analysis question: What does Lady Macbeth's soliloquy in lines 15–30 reveal about her ambitions and plans?
Answer: Lady Macbeth decides that the witches' prophecy will come true, and she states that she plans to persuade Macbeth to fulfill his destiny.

• **Discuss** how, in lines 18–25, Lady Macbeth thinks Macbeth would approach the situation.
Answer: She sees Macbeth as not being sufficiently wicked to accomplish his ambitions. She says he'd rather do it "holily" (in a holy manner) and would rather not play false and win dishonestly. But she also says that she thinks that he'd be willing to accept the results of foul play, even if he didn't consider them his first choice.

33 **Critical Thinking**
Compare and Contrast

• **Ask** students how Lady Macbeth's reaction to the situation (lines 38–53) contrasts with Macbeth's.
Answer: While Macbeth is reluctant to consider murder, Lady Macbeth embraces the idea immediately and calls on the forces of evil to help her.

• **Ask** students to reread lines 50–54. With which earlier comments of Macbeth's does Lady Macbeth's desire for concealment compare?
Answer: In Scene iv, lines 48–54, Macbeth asks that the stars hide and that his eyes not see what his hand does, which is very similar to Lady Macbeth's request that thick night hide their evil deeds.

---

thought good to deliver thee,[2] my dearest partner of greatness, that thou mightst not lose the dues of rejoicing, by being ignorant of what greatness is promised thee. Lay it to thy heart, and farewell."

15   Glamis thou art, and Cawdor, and shalt be
     What thou art promised. Yet do I fear thy nature;
     It is too full o' th' milk of human kindness
     To catch the nearest[3] way. Thou wouldst be great,
     Art not without ambition, but without
20   The illness[4] should attend it. What thou wouldst highly,
     That wouldst thou holily; wouldst not play false,
     And yet wouldst wrongly win. Thou'dst have, great Glamis,
     That which cries "Thus thou must do" if thou have it;
     And that which rather thou dost fear to do
25   Than wishest should be undone.[5] Hie thee hither,
     That I may pour my spirits in thine ear,
     And chastise with the valor of my tongue
     All that impedes thee from the golden round[6]
     Which fate and metaphysical aid doth seem
     To have thee crowned withal.

[*Enter* MESSENGER.]

30   What is your tidings?

MESSENGER. The King comes here tonight.

LADY MACBETH.   Thou'rt mad to say it!
     Is not thy master with him, who, were't so,
     Would have informed for preparation?

MESSENGER. So please you, it is true. Our thane is coming.
35   One of my fellows had the speed of him,[7]
     Who, almost dead for breath, had scarcely more
     Than would make up his message.

LADY MACBETH.   Give him tending;
     He brings great news.   [*Exit* MESSENGER.]
                       The raven himself is hoarse
     That croaks the fatal entrance of Duncan
40   Under my battlements. Come, you spirits
     That tend on mortal[8] thoughts, unsex me here,
     And fill me, from the crown to the toe, top-full
     Of direst cruelty! Make thick my blood,
     Stop up th' access and passage to remorse,[9]
45   That no compunctious visitings of nature[10]
     Shake my fell[11] purpose, nor keep peace between
     Th' effect[12] and it! Come to my woman's breasts,
     And take my milk for gall,[13] you murd'ring ministers,[14]
     Wherever in your sightless[15] substances
50   You wait on[16] nature's mischief! Come, thick night,

318 ■ *Celebrating Humanity (1485–1625)*

---

2. deliver thee report to you.

Literary Analysis
Elizabethan Drama and
Soliloquy What does Lady Macbeth's soliloquy in lines 15–30 reveal about her ambitions and plans?

3. nearest quickest.

4. illness wickedness.

5. that which . . . undone
What you are afraid of doing you would not wish undone once you have done it.

6. round crown.

7. had . . . him overtook him.

8. mortal deadly.
9. remorse compassion.
10. compunctious . . .
nature natural feelings of pity.
11. fell savage.
12. effect fulfillment.
13. milk for gall kindness in exchange for bitterness.
14. ministers agents.
15. sightless invisible.
16. wait on assist.

Enrichment

A Writer Responds
William Hazlitt (1778–1830), one of the most outspoken critics in the Romantic era, made the following observation in *Characters of Shakespeare's Plays* about the scope of Shakespeare's work:

 Macbeth and *Lear, Othello* and *Hamlet,* are usually reckoned Shakespeare's four principal tragedies. . . . If the force of genius shown in each of these works is astonishing, their variety is not less so. They are like different creations of the same mind, not one of which has the slightest reference to the

rest. This distinctness and originality is indeed the necessary consequence of truth and nature. Shakespeare's genius alone appeared to possess the resources of nature. He is "your only tragedy maker." His plays have the force of things upon the mind. What he represents is brought home to the bosom as a part of our experience, implanted in the memory as if we had known the places, persons, and things of which he treats.

◀ **Critical Viewing**
This is an artist's rendering of nineteenth-century actress Ellen Terry playing Lady Macbeth. Judging by the picture, how do you think Terry would have spoken lines 38–53 in Act I, Scene v? **[Deduce]**

And pall¹⁷ thee in the dunnest¹⁸ smoke of hell,
That my keen knife see not the wound it makes,
Nor heaven peep through the blanket of the dark,
To cry "Hold, hold!"

[*Enter* MACBETH.]

        Great Glamis! Worthy Cawdor!
55 Greater than both, by the all-hail hereafter!
Thy letters have transported me beyond
This ignorant¹⁹ present, and I feel now
The future in the instant.²⁰

MACBETH.   My dearest love,
Duncan comes here tonight.

LADY MACBETH.   And when goes hence?

MACBETH. Tomorrow, as he purposes.

17. **pall** enshroud.
18. **dunnest** darkest.

19. **ignorant** unknowing.
20. **instant** present.

✓ **Reading Check**
What does Lady Macbeth feel is Macbeth's weakness?

Macbeth, Act I, Scene v ■ 319

Humanities

Ellen Terry as Lady Macbeth, 1889, by John Singer Sargent

Sargent (1856–1925) was born in Italy of American parents. He began his training as a painter at the Paris studio of Carolus-Duran. He eventually settled in London and became one of the most highly sought-after portrait painters of his day.

Ellen Terry was a brilliant actress and one of the most socially prominent people of the time. Her pose is theatrical and impressive. The drapery of the costume is painted in many tones and textures to convey the richness of nobility. The crown was added for dramatic effect. The painting reveals more of the actress than of the character she represents.

Use these questions for discussion:

1. What has the costume designer tried to communicate with the outfit made for Ellen Terry?
Possible response: The costume is very dramatic. It reflects a vaguely medieval image, with the flowing sleeves and multiple belts. The richness of the colors and all the gold accentuate nobility and power.

2. Sargent was best known as a portrait painter. How is his skill as a portraitist reflected in this painting? How might Henry Fuseli have rendered this scene?
Answer: This painting is static, realistic, and somewhat posed. Fuseli has a more dynamic quality and is less concerned with realism than with evoking emotions from those who view his work.

Critical Viewing
Answer: The actress's pose and regal bearing indicate that she would have spoken these lines with confidence and strength.

Reading Check
Answer: Lady Macbeth feels Macbeth's kindness is his weakness.

• Point out the use of the word *sovereign* in line 70, and its definition.

• Tell students that, like many other words, *sovereign* came into English through the French-speaking Normans. The French word is *souverain*. *Royal* also came from the French. The French word for king is *roi*, kingship is *royauté*, and kingly is *royal*. Ultimately, the first part of both the English and French relate back to the Latin word *super*, which means *over*.

• You may wish to have students look up other words, such as *govern* and *reign*, to learn the etymologies of these power words.

• Point out that *sovereign* can be used as a noun or as an adjective. In this case, it modifies *sway*. Explain that *sway* here means *influence, control*. **Ask** students what Lady Macbeth is saying that their deeds will give them.
Answer: They will have the influence of supreme authority; they will be masters.

38 **Literary Analysis**
Elizabethan Drama

• Have students read Banquo's speech, lines 3–10.

• Have students focus on the descriptive content of the images in the passage.

• Have students look up *delicate*, or tell them that one meaning, the one intended here, is "pleasing to the senses."

• Then, **ask** students to answer the first Literary Analysis question on the facing page: What details does Banquo use in Scene vi, lines 3–10, to paint a word picture of Macbeth's castle?
Answer: Banquo notes that martins, birds usually drawn to churches, are plentiful here. Every projection and vantage point has a nest (pendent bed—martins' nests hang down), where chicks hatch. He says that he has noticed that the air is pleasing to the senses in places where martins nest.

60 LADY MACBETH.   O, never
Shall sun that morrow see!
Your face, my Thane, is as a book where men
May read strange matters. To beguile the time,[21]
Look like the time; bear welcome in your eye,
65 Your hand, your tongue: look like th' innocent flower,
But be the serpent under 't. He that's coming
Must be provided for: and you shall put
This night's great business into my dispatch;[22]
Which shall to all our nights and days to come
37 **70** Give solely <u>sovereign</u> sway and masterdom.

MACBETH. We will speak further.

LADY MACBETH.   Only look up clear.[23]
To alter favor ever is to fear.[24]
Leave all the rest to me.   [*Exit.*]

Scene vi. Before Macbeth's castle.

[*Hautboys.*[1] *Torches. Enter* KING DUNCAN, MALCOLM, DONALBAIN, BANQUO, LENNOX, MACDUFF, ROSS, ANGUS, *and* ATTENDANTS.]

KING. This castle hath a pleasant seat;[2] the air
Nimbly and sweetly recommends itself
Unto our gentle[3] senses.

BANQUO.   This guest of summer,
The temple-haunting martlet,[4] does approve[5]
5 By his loved mansionry[6] that the heaven's breath
Smells wooingly here. No jutty,[7] frieze,
Buttress, nor coign of vantage,[8] but this bird
Hath made his pendent bed and procreant cradle.[9]
Where they most breed and haunt,[10] I have observed
The air is delicate.

[*Enter* LADY MACBETH.]

10 KING.   See, see, our honored hostess!
The love that follows us sometime is our trouble,
Which still we thank as love. Herein I teach you
How you shall bid God 'ield us for your pains
And thank us for your trouble.[11]

LADY MACBETH.   All our service
15 In every point twice done, and then done double,
Were poor and single business[12] to contend
Against those honors deep and broad wherewith
Your Majesty loads our house: for those of old,
And the late dignities heaped up to them,
We rest your hermits.[13]

320 ■ *Celebrating Humanity (1485–1625)*

21. beguile the time deceive the people tonight.

22. dispatch management.

23. look up clear appear innocent.

Vocabulary Builder
sovereign (säv´ rən) *adj.* supreme in power, rank, or authority

24. To alter . . . fear to show a disturbed face will arouse suspicion.

1. Hautboys oboes announcing the arrival of royalty.

2. seat location.

3. gentle soothed.

4. temple-haunting martlet martin, a bird that usually nests in churches. In Shakespeare's time, *martin* was a slang term for a person who is easily deceived.

5. approve show.

6. mansionry nests.

7. jutty projection.

8. coign of vantage advantageous corner.

9. procreant (prō´ krē ənt) **cradle** nest where the young are hatched.

10. haunt visit.

11. The love . . . trouble Though my visit inconveniences you, you should ask God to reward me for coming, because it was my love for you that prompted my visit.

12. single business feeble service.

13. rest your hermits remain your dependents bound to pray for you. Hermits were often paid to pray for another person's sou

20 **KING.** Where's the Thane of Cawdor?
We coursed[14] him at the heels, and had a purpose
To be his purveyor:[15] but he rides well,
And his great love, sharp as his spur, hath holp[16] him
To his home before us. Fair and noble hostess,
We are your guest tonight.

25 **LADY MACBETH.** Your servants ever
Have theirs, themselves, and what is theirs, in compt,[17]
To make their audit at your Highness' pleasure,
Still[18] to return your own.

KING. Give me your hand.
Conduct me to mine host: we love him highly,
30 And shall continue our graces towards him.
By your leave, hostess. [*Exit.*]

Scene vii. Macbeth's castle.

[*Hautboys. Torches. Enter a* SEWER,[1] *and diverse* SERVANTS *with dishes and service over the stage. Then enter* MACBETH.]

MACBETH. If it were done[2] when 'tis done, then 'twere well
It were done quickly. If th' assassination
Could trammel up the consequence, and catch,
With his surcease, success;[3] that but this blow
5 Might be the be-all and the end-all—here,
But here, upon this bank and shoal of time,
We'd jump the life to come.[4] But in these cases
We still have judgment here; that we but teach
Bloody instructions, which, being taught, return
10 To plague th' inventor: this even-handed[5] justice
Commends[6] th' ingredients of our poisoned chalice[7]
To our own lips. He's here in double trust:
First, as I am his kinsman and his subject,
Strong both against the deed; then, as his host,
15 Who should against his murderer shut the door,
Not bear the knife myself. Besides, this Duncan
Hath borne his faculties[8] so meek, hath been
So clear[9] in his great office, that his virtues
Will plead like angels trumpet-tongued against
20 The deep damnation of his taking-off;
And pity, like a naked newborn babe,
Striding the blast, or heaven's cherubin[10] horsed
Upon the sightless couriers[11] of the air,
Shall blow the horrid deed in every eye,
25 That tears shall drown the wind. I have no spur
To prick the sides of my intent, but only
Vaulting ambition, which o'erleaps itself
And falls on th' other—

14. **coursed** chased.

15. **purveyor** advance supply officer.

16. **holp** helped.

17. **compt** trust.

18. **Still** always.

Literary Analysis
Elizabethan Drama What details does Banquo use in Scene vi, lines 3–10 to paint a word picture of Macbeth's castle?

1. **sewer** chief butler.

2. **done** over and done with.

3. **If . . . success** if the assassination could be done successfully and without consequence.

4. **We'd . . . come** I would risk life in the world to come.

5. **even-handed** impartial.

6. **commends** offers.

7. **chalice** cup.

8. **faculties** powers.

9. **clear** blameless.

10. **cherubin** angels.

11. **sightless couriers** unseen messengers (the wind).

Literary Analysis
Elizabethan Drama and Soliloquy What doubts does Macbeth reveal in his soliloquy (lines 1–28)?

40 ✓**Reading Check**
What deed does Lady Macbeth urge her husband to perform?

Macbeth, Act I, Scene vii ■ 321

39 Literary Analysis
Elizabethan Drama and Soliloquy

• Have students read Macbeth's soliloquy, lines 1–28.

• Then, **ask** students to answer the second Literary Analysis question: What doubts does Macbeth reveal in his soliloquy?
Answer: Macbeth has doubts about the consequences of his deed in this world—his plans may go awry. He also expresses doubts about the deed due both to his obligations as kinsman, subject, and host of Duncan and to Duncan's own virtues.

40 Reading Check

Answer: Lady Macbeth urges her husband to look innocent and leave the murder plot to her.

Differentiated
Instruction Solutions for All Learners

Support for Special Needs Students
Summarize the events and thoughts on these pages. Then focus on Macbeth's soliloquy, lines 1–28. Go over the speech one sentence at a time, so that students can discuss the ideas in more manageable amounts. Once students understand what is being said, have them discuss what the images reveal about Macbeth.

Strategy for Less Proficient Readers
Have students discuss these scenes in small groups. Ask them to consider what the king and Banquo perceive, what Lady Macbeth wants them to think, and what the reality is. Then, have students discuss Macbeth's soliloquy. Do they think that Macbeth knows what he is doing is wrong?

Vocabulary for English Learners
Briefly explain what Macbeth is saying in lines 1–28. With guidance from the teacher or more fluent students, have students go through the speech slowly, stopping to determine meanings for unfamiliar words. Any pictures you can supply to illustrate such images as a chalice or trumpet-tongued angels would aid comprehension.

- Direct students' attention to line 42.

▶ **Monitor Progress: Ask** students the Reading Strategy question: In line 42, what does Lady Macbeth mean by the "ornament of life"? **Answer:** The "ornament of life" to which Lady Macbeth refers is the crown.

- Point out that the sentence in which this expression appears is easier to understand in context. In the previous sentence, Lady Macbeth states that Macbeth is afraid to be the same in action as he is in desire. The sentence that follows notes that Macbeth wishes but will not act. Explain that *would* here means *desire* or *wish*. Then, have students **paraphrase** the sentence that includes "ornament of life."
Possible response: Do you want to have the crown, and yet continue to be a coward about it?

- Remind students that Shakespeare is not only a great storyteller, but also a great wordsmith. He plays words off of each other at every opportunity. An example is seen in lines 41 and 42, where *esteem'st* means value highly and *esteem* refers to Macbeth's attitude toward himself—the two uses again connect Macbeth with the crown.

- Encourage students to look for uses of words such as this, where Macbeth ties ideas together in a speech, or people together from one scene to another, with similar words used in slightly different ways.

42 Critical Thinking
Interpret

- Have students read Lady Macbeth's speech, lines 47–59.

- Then, **ask** students what arguments Lady Macbeth uses to convince Macbeth to carry out the murder.
Answer: Lady Macbeth asks Macbeth if his hopes have all died out. She implies that her love is directly linked to his ambitions. She also accuses him of being cowardly.

322

[*Enter* LADY MACBETH.]

                        How now! What news?

LADY MACBETH. He has almost supped. Why have you
    left the chamber?

MACBETH. Hath he asked for me?

30 LADY MACBETH.   Know you not he has?

MACBETH. We will proceed no further in this business:
    He hath honored me of late, and I have bought[12]
    Golden opinions from all sorts of people,
    Which would be worn now in their newest gloss,
    Not cast aside so soon.

35 LADY MACBETH.   Was the hope drunk
    Wherein you dressed yourself? Hath it slept since?
    And wakes it now, to look so green and pale
    At what it did so freely? From this time
    Such I account thy love. Art thou afeard
40 To be the same in thine own act and valor
    As thou art in desire? Wouldst thou have that
    Which thou esteem'st the ornament of life,[13]
    And live a coward in thine own esteem,
    Letting "I dare not" wait upon[14] "I would,"
    Like the poor cat i' th' adage?[15]

45 MACBETH.   Prithee, peace!
    I dare do all that may become a man;
    Who dares do more is none.

LADY MACBETH.   What beast was 't then
    That made you break[16] this enterprise to me?
    When you durst do it, then you were a man;
50 And to be more than what you were, you would
    Be so much more the man. Nor time nor place
    Did then adhere,[17] and yet you would make both.
    They have made themselves, and that their[18] fitness now
    Does unmake you. I have given suck, and know
55 How tender 'tis to love the babe that milks me:
    I would, while it was smiling in my face,
    Have plucked my nipple from his boneless gums,
    And dashed the brains out, had I so sworn as you
    Have done to this.

MACBETH.   If we should fail?

LADY MACBETH.   We fail?
60 But[19] screw your courage to the sticking-place[20]
    And we'll not fail. When Duncan is asleep—
    Whereto the rather shall his day's hard journey
    Soundly invite him—his two chamberlains

---

12. bought acquired.

Reading Strategy
Using Text Aids In line 42, what does Lady Macbeth mean by the "ornament of life"?

13. ornament of life the crown.

14. wait upon follow.

15. poor . . . adage from an old proverb about a cat who wants to eat fish but is afraid of getting its paws wet.

16. break reveal.

17. Did then adhere was then suitable (for the assassination).

18. that their their very.

19. But only.

20. sticking-place the notch that holds the bowstring of a taut crossbow.

Assessment Practice

Fact and Opinion   **(For more practice, see** *Standardized Test Preparation Workbook,* **p. 12.)**
Many tests require students to distinguish between fact and opinion. Have students read Act I, scene ii, lines 7–23. Use the following sample item to teach students to extract facts from statements that contain both fact and opinion. Which of the following statements is a fact from the Captain's report?

  A Fortune favored Macdonwald.
  B Macbeth killed Macdonwald.

  C Macbeth and Banquo fought like lions.
  D Macdonwald is a slave.

Help students identify literary devices in the Captain's report, such as personification (choice A), simile (choice C), and metaphor (choice D). Point out that literary devices are usually indications of opinion. The correct answer is *B*.

Will I with wine and wassail[21] so convince,[22]

65 That memory, the warder of the brain,
    Shall be a fume, and the receipt of reason
    A limbeck only:[23] when in swinish sleep
    Their drenchèd natures lies as in a death,
    What cannot you and I perform upon

70 Th' unguarded Duncan, what not put upon
    His spongy[24] officers, who shall bear the guilt
    Of our great quell?[25]

MACBETH.   Bring forth men-children only;
    For thy undaunted mettle[26] should compose
    Nothing but males. Will it not be received,

75 When we have marked with blood those sleepy two
    Of his own chamber, and used their very daggers,
    That they have done 't?

LADY MACBETH.   Who dares receive it other,[27]
    As we shall make our griefs and clamor roar
    Upon his death?

MACBETH.   I am settled, and bend up

80 Each corporal agent to this terrible feat.
    Away, and mock the time[28] with fairest show:
    False face must hide what the false heart doth know.   [Exit.]

21. wassail carousing.

22. convince overpower.

23. That . . . only that memory, the guardian of the brain, will be confused by the fumes of the drink, and the reason become like a still, distilling confused thoughts.

24. spongy sodden.

25. quell murder.

26. mettle spirit.

27. other otherwise.

28. mock the time mislead the world.

Critical Reading

1. **Respond:** What mood did Act I evoke in you? Explain.

2. **(a) Recall:** What statements do the witches and Macbeth make about "foul and fair"? **(b) Interpret:** What meaning (or meanings) does each remark have?

3. **(a) Recall:** Describe Banquo's and Macbeth's reactions to the witches. **(b) Compare and Contrast:** Compare and contrast their reactions to the witches.

4. **(a) Recall:** In his soliloquy at the beginning of Scene vii, what arguments against killing Duncan does Macbeth express? **(b) Analyze Cause and Effect:** Which of these arguments seems to influence him the most? Explain.

5. **(a) Recall:** What is Lady Macbeth's opinion of her husband's character? **(b) Analyze:** How does she use her knowledge of his character to convince him to kill Duncan?

6. **Speculate:** Does the meeting with the witches suggest that evil is something people choose or a force that seeks out people? Explain.

Go Online
Author Link

For: More about
William Shakespeare
Visit: www.PHSchool.com
Web Code: ese-9209

Macbeth, Act I, Scene vii ■ 323

Go Online
Author Link For additional information about William Shakespeare, have students type in the Web Code, then select S from the alphabet, and then select the author's name.

ASSESS

Answers

1. **Possible response:** Students may feel a sense of foreboding or dread for what will happen to Duncan or Macbeth and his wife.

2. (a) The witches say "fair is foul, and foul is fair," and Macbeth says "so foul and fair a day I have not seen." (b) The witches may mean that the fair promise of a crown will be fulfilled, but only through foul treachery, or that Macbeth, who appears so fair, is really foul, and that Macbeth decides that foul play is fair play. Macbeth appears to be referring to the awful weather and the great victory.

3. (a) Banquo questions their presence, and whether or not they are human. Macbeth asks them to speak. (b) Ambition surges through Macbeth, filling his mind with the possibilities of wearing the crown. Banquo wonders if the instruments of darkness aren't tempting them with promises only to bring them harm in the end.

4. (a) Macbeth reveals his concerns for the chain of events his deed may set in motion, his fears that what he does to Duncan will be done to him, his worry that Duncan is a relative, a guest in his home, and his ruler—three facts that make his betrayal worse—and that Duncan is much beloved by his people, and they will be outraged by the act of murder. (b) The fact that Duncan is a guest in his home, and the murder would violate the code of hospitality, seems to bother Macbeth the most. He says that as host he should be protecting Duncan against murder, not carrying it out himself.

5. (a) Lady Macbeth thinks her husband is too kind. (b) Lady Macbeth says that it would be manly and brave, that her love is tied to his ambition, that he can't let her down now that he's suggested it.

6. **Possible response:** The meeting with the witches suggests that evil is something people choose *and* a force that seeks people out. Unlike Macbeth, who chooses to follow evil, Banquo—to whom the witches also appeared—does not choose evil.

323

Answers

1. (a) In Elizabethan drama, costumes would be used to identify characters and their positions in society, and borrowing robes would be taking another's part. (b) It shows that Macbeth is uneasy with taking on a title that is not his.

2. Meeting witches would be ominous by itself, and if their predictions are to come true, people must die.

3. I, i, 10–11: fair is foul, foul is fair, fog and filthy air; modern sets: fog from fog machine; austere stage and backdrop. I, vi, 3–10: sweet air, birds nesting; modern sets: bright stage, bird sounds playing, attractive picture of castle as backdrop.

   Another sample answer can be found on **Literary Analysis Graphic Organizer B**, p. 57 in *Graphic Organizer Transparencies*.

4. (a) Lady Macbeth reveals that she is ready to do whatever it takes but worries that her husband is too kind. She resolves to talk him into killing the king. (b) Macbeth thinks he should get it over with. However, his concern over consequences and his dislike for injuring a guest make him hesitate.

5. **Possible response:** The soliloquies reveal more, because Macbeth is more open in talking to himself than to another.

6. Their soliloquies add to the sense that they are moving toward disaster, because they show that they are talking themselves into committing horrible acts.

7. (a) The witches enter an open place; there is thunder and lightning. They speak of things and refer to their helpers, a cat and a toad, and depart. (b) Lady Macbeth is alone inside Inverness; she reads a letter. A messenger enters.

8. (a) *Anon* means "at once." (b) *Thane* was a Scottish title of nobility. (c) *Cousins* was a term of courtesy used between fellow noblemen.

9. **Possible responses:** Julius Caesar was similar to Macbeth in that he was a military figure who had great ambition and killed others in his quest for power.

324

Apply the Skills

Macbeth, Act I

Literary Analysis

Elizabethan Drama

1. **(a)** What vivid image, typical of **Elizabethan drama,** does Shakespeare create when Macbeth says to Ross, "why do you dress me / In borrowed robes?" (Act I, Scene iii, lines 108–109)? **(b)** What uneasiness in Macbeth does this word picture reveal?

2. How does Macbeth's encounter with the witches show that the play will probably be a **tragedy**?

3. Using a chart like this one, analyze the details of setting in the lines shown. Then, indicate how modern sets and lighting might produce such a setting.

Shakespeare's Words		Modern Sets and Lighting
I, i, 10–11	→	
I, vi, 3–10		

Connecting Literary Elements

4. What do each of the following **soliloquies** reveal about their speaker's thoughts and plans: **(a)** Lady Macbeth, Act I, Scene v, lines 1–30 and **(b)** Macbeth, Act I, Scene vii, lines 1–28?

5. In Act I, which type of speech directed to the audience is more effective in revealing Macbeth's thoughts: asides or a soliloquy? Explain.

6. Do Lady Macbeth's and Macbeth's soliloquies add to the sense that the characters are moving toward disaster? Why or why not?

Reading Strategy

Using Text Aids

7. Use **text aids** such as stage directions and side notes to describe the action in these scenes: **(a)** Act I, Scene i, **(b)** beginning of Act I, Scene v.

8. Use the side notes to describe the following terms: **(a)** anon, **(b)** Thane, **(c)** cousins.

Extend Understanding

9. **Social Studies Connection:** Identify a person in history who is similar to a character in *Macbeth*. Then, explain your choice.

324 ■ Celebrating Humanity (1485–1625)

QuickReview

Elizabethan drama is written in unrhymed verse, contains rich language and vivid imagery, and depends on words to set a scene. Many Elizabethan dramas are **tragedies,** in which disaster befalls a hero or heroine.

A **soliloquy** is a long speech in which a character who is alone reveals his or her thoughts to the audience.

By **using text aids** such as stage directions and notes, readers can supplement their reading of a drama.

Go Online
Assessment

For: Self-test
Visit: www.PHSchool.com
Web Code: esa-6207

Build Language Skills

Vocabulary Lesson

Concept Development: Power Words

Liege refers to the role of the king as chief lord in a feudal system. *Sovereign* contains a form of the Latin root *super*, meaning "above" and can be used as a noun or an adjective.

1. Why might "my *liege*" be an appropriate phrase to use when addressing a king?
2. Name a modern-day *sovereign*.

Spelling Strategy

When *i* and *e* spell the long *e* sound, they usually appear as *ie*, as in *liege*. In your notebook, complete the spelling of these words with *ie* or *ei*.

1. rel___f   2. caff___ne   3. ach___ve

Grammar and Style Lesson

Action Verbs and Linking Verbs

Action verbs depict physical or mental actions. **Linking verbs**—like *seem* and forms of the verb *to be*—connect the subject of a sentence with a word that renames or describes it.

Action Verb: The Thane of Cawdor <u>lives</u>.

Linking Verb: You <u>shall be</u> King.

Practice Identify each verb in these sentences from *Macbeth* as an action or a linking verb.

1. Fair is foul, and foul is fair. (I, i, 10)

Vocabulary Builder: Antonyms

In your notebook, write the letter of the word that is the antonym (opposite in meaning) of the first word.

1. valor: (a) courage, (b) bravery, (c) cowardice
2. treason: (a) loyalty, (b) betrayal, (c) treachery
3. imperial: (a) royal, (b) submissive, (c) powerful
4. liege: (a) authority, (b) king, (c) peasant
5. sovereign: (a) insignificant, (b) supreme, (c) solid

2. But I am faint; my gashes cry for help. (I, ii, 42)
3. Speak then to me, . . . (I, iii, 60)
4. Stars, hide your fires; . . . (I, iv, 50)
5. It is too full o' th' milk of human kindness. . . . (I, v, 17)

Writing Application Write a brief paragraph predicting what will happen in Act II. Base your predictions on the events of Act I, and use at least two linking verbs and two action verbs.

WG Prentice Hall Writing and Grammar Connection: Chapter 17, Section 2

Extend Your Learning

Writing Write the **speech of welcome** that Macbeth might have addressed to Duncan as Duncan entered Macbeth's castle. Use prose or blank verse, and include vivid images designed to make Duncan feel at home.

3 Research and Technology With a group, view different film versions of *Macbeth*. Present an **oral report** on the ways each actress portrayed Lady Macbeth in Act I. Judge the aesthetic strengths and weaknesses in the films. **[Group Activity]**

Macbeth, Act I ■ 325

Assessment Resources

The following resources can be used to assess students' knowledge and skills.

Unit 2 Resources:
Selection Test A, pp. 104–106
Selection Test B, pp. 107–109

Go Online Students may use the **Self-test** to **Assessment** prepare for **Selection Test A** or **Selection Test B**.

---

❶ Vocabulary Lesson
Power Words

1. It acknowledges the king's role as chief lord in a feudal society.
2. **Possible response:** Queen Elizabeth of England.

Spelling Strategy
1. relief   3. achieve
2. caffeine

Antonyms
1. c   3. b   5. a
2. a   4. c

❷ Grammar and Style Lesson

1. *is,* linking; *is,* linking
2. *am,* linking; *cry,* action
3. *speak,* action
4. *hide,* action
5. *is,* linking

Writing Application

Possible response: In Act I, Macbeth is eager for the throne. In Act II, Macbeth and his wife will kill Duncan. Duncan is a beloved king. Duncan's kinsmen will seek revenge.

❸ Research and Technology

- You may wish to research available versions and make recommendations. Several films exist, as well as excellent BBC video productions. Be advised that Roman Polanski's 1971 version is quite gory.
- Encourage students to compare all aspects of the portrayals of Lady Macbeth including delivery, mannerisms, and actions. Have them consider what each reveals.
- The **Support for Extend Your Learning** page (*Unit 2 Resources,* p. 102) provides guided note-taking opportunities to help students complete the Extend Your Learning activities.

Writing and Grammar, Diamond Level

WG Students will find further instruction and practice on action verbs and linking verbs in Chapter 17, Section 2.

325

Meeting Your Standards

Students will

1. **analyze and respond to literary elements.**
   - Literary Analysis: Blank Verse

2. **read, comprehend, analyze, and critique a drama.**
   - Reading Strategy: Reading Verse for Meaning
   - Reading Check questions
   - Apply the Skills questions
   - Assessment Practice (ATE)

3. **develop vocabulary.**
   - Vocabulary Lesson: Latin Root: *-voc-*

4. **understand and apply written and oral language conventions.**
   - Spelling Strategy
   - Grammar and Style Lesson: Commonly Confused Words: *Lie* and *Lay*

5. **develop writing proficiency.**
   - Writing Lesson: Response to Criticism (follows Act V)

6. **develop writing strategies.**
   - Extend Your Learning: Investigational Journal

7. **understand and apply listening and speaking strategies.**
   - Extend Your Learning: Debate

Block Scheduling: Use one 90-minute class period to preteach the skills and have students read the selection. Use a second 90-minute class period to assess students' mastery of skills, extend their learning, and monitor their progress.

Homework Suggestions

Following are possibilities for homework assignments.

- Support pages from *Unit 2 Resources:*
  Literary Analysis
  Reading Strategy
  Vocabulary Builder
  Grammar and Style

- An Extend Your Learning project and the Writing Lesson for this selection group may be completed over several days.

Step-by-Step Teaching Guide	Pacing Guide
PRETEACH	
• Administer Vocabulary and Reading Warm-ups as necessary.	5 min.
• Engage students' interest with the motivation activity.	5 min.
• Introduce the Literary Analysis Skill: Blank Verse. **FT**	5 min.
• Introduce the Reading Strategy: Reading Verse for Meaning. **FT**	10 min.
• Prepare students to read by teaching the selection vocabulary. **FT**	
TEACH	
• Informally monitor comprehension while students read independently or in groups. **FT**	30 min.
• Monitor students' comprehension with the Reading Check notes.	as students read
• Reinforce vocabulary with Vocabulary Builder notes.	as students read
• Develop students' understanding of blank verse with the Literary Analysis annotations. **FT**	5 min.
• Develop students' ability to read verse for meaning with the Reading Strategy annotations. **FT**	5 min.
ASSESS/EXTEND	
• Assess students' comprehension and mastery of the Literary Analysis and Reading Strategy by having them answer the Apply the Skills questions. **FT**	15 min.
• Have students complete the Vocabulary Lesson and the Grammar and Style Lesson. **FT**	15 min.
• Apply students' understanding by using one or more of the Extend Your Learning activities.	20–90 min. or homework
• Administer Selection Test A or Selection Test B. **FT**	15 min.

Resources

Choosing Resources for Differentiated Instruction

[L1] Special Needs Students

[L2] Below-Level Students

[L3] All Students

[L4] Advanced Students

[EL] English Learners

For Vocabulary and Reading Warm-ups and for Selection Tests, **A** signifies "less challenging" and **B** "more challenging." For Graphic Organizer transparencies, **A** signifies "not filled in" and **B** "filled in."

FT Fast Track Instruction: To move the lesson more quickly, use the strategies and activities identified with **FT**.

Scaffolding for Less Proficient and Advanced Students

The leveled Critical Thinking questions after selections progress in the levels of thinking required to answer them. To address the needs of your different students, you may use the (a) level questions for your less proficient students and the (b) level questions with your on-level and advanced students. The occasional (c) level questions are appropriate for your advanced students.

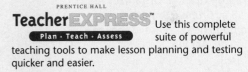

Use this complete suite of powerful teaching tools to make lesson planning and testing quicker and easier.

Use the interactive textbook (online and on CD-ROM) to make selections and activities come alive with audio and video support and interactive questions.

Benchmark

After students have completed this selection, administer **Benchmark Test 3** (*Unit 2 Resources*, pp. 126–131). If the Benchmark Test reveals that some students need further work, use the Interpretation Guide to determine the appropriate reteaching page in the **Reading Kit** and on **Success Tracker.**

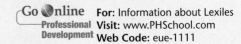 **For:** Information about Lexiles **Visit:** www.PHSchool.com **Web Code:** eue-1111

Macbeth, Act II

Motivation

Review the plan Macbeth and Lady Macbeth have made for "the perfect crime." Ask students whether there are any flaws in the plan. Ask them to anticipate how Duncan's sons might react and how Macbeth and Lady Macbeth might deal with them.

❶ Literary Analysis
Blank Verse

- Tell students that as they read Act II of *Macbeth*, they should be aware of the play's use of blank verse.

- Explain that blank verse is unrhymed iambic pentameter. Have students read the definition of iambic pentameter. Then, read a few lines aloud.

- Review **Connecting Literary Elements**, explaining that blank verse is usually used by noble characters. Also, tell students that comic relief is common in plays of this era.

❷ Reading Strategy
Reading Verse for Meaning

- Explain that it is important to read by sentences, rather than by lines. Give students a copy of **Reading Strategy Graphic Organizer A**, p. 58 in *Graphic Organizer Transparencies*, to use as they read *Macbeth*, Act II.

Vocabulary Builder

- Pronounce each vocabulary word for students, and read the definitions as a class. Have students identify any words with which they are already familiar.

❶ Literary Analysis
Blank Verse

Blank verse—unrhymed iambic pentameter—was invented during the English Renaissance to reflect natural speech. An **iamb** consists of an unstressed syllable followed by a stressed syllable (˘ ′). In iambic pentameter, there are five such feet (units) to the line. *Macbeth* is written mainly in blank verse:

> Methought I heard a voice cry, "Sleep no more!" (II, ii, 34)

For interest, Shakespeare varies his meter, as when he begins this line with a **trochaic foot** (′ ˘): "List'ning their fear, I could not say 'Amen'" (II, ii, 28). Another variation is the **anapestic foot** (˘ ˘ ′). As you read, listen for the rhythm as well as the meaning of the dialogue.

Connecting Literary Elements

Shakespeare interrupts his blank verse with **prose,** which is writing that is not divided into poetic lines and lacks a definite rhythm. In his tragedies, lower-ranking characters often speak in prose to provide **comic relief,** a humorous break from a tense mood. Notice this effect as you read the porter's speech at the start of Act II, Scene iii.

❷ Reading Strategy
Reading Verse for Meaning

To **read blank verse for meaning,** follow sentences past line endings. For instance, you must follow this sentence past the end of the line to learn what the owl does:

> "It was the owl that shrieked, the fatal bellman,
> Which gives the stern'st good-night. . . ." (II, ii, 3–4).

Use a chart like this one to distinguish between lines and sentences.

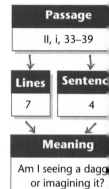

Passage
II, i, 33–39

Lines	Sentence
7	4

Meaning
Am I seeing a dagg or imagining it?

Vocabulary Builder

augment (ôg ment′) *v.* make greater; enlarge (p. 328)

palpable (pal′ pə bəl) *adj.* capable of being touched or felt (p. 328)

stealthy (stel′ thē) *adj.* sly (p. 328)

multitudinous (mul′ tə tōōd′ ′n əs) *adj.* existing in great numbers (p. 332)

equivocate (ē kwiv′ ə kāt′) *v.* to use terms that have two or more meanings to mislead purposely or deceive (p. 332)

predominance (prē däm′ ə nəns) *n.* superiority (p. 338)

326 ■ Celebrating Humanity (1485–1625)

Review and Anticipate

In Act I, we learn that Macbeth has distinguished himself in battle. Returning from the battlefield, he and Banquo meet three witches who predict that Macbeth will not only be rewarded by King Duncan, but that he will become king himself. However, the witches also greet Banquo as a father of kings. Motivated by the witches' prophecies, Macbeth considers killing Duncan. The assassination becomes more likely when the king decides to visit Macbeth's castle. Lady Macbeth, on hearing about the witches' predictions and the king's visit, resolves that she and her husband will kill Duncan. When Macbeth hesitates, she urges him on. As Act II begins, they are about to perform this evil deed.

 ▼ Critical Viewing
What sort of person would be worthy of wearing a crown such as this one? [Generalize]

 Act II

Scene i. Inverness. Court of Macbeth's castle.

[*Enter* BANQUO, *and* FLEANCE, *with a torch before him.*]

BANQUO. How goes the night, boy?

FLEANCE. The moon is down; I have not heard the clock.

BANQUO. And she goes down at twelve.

FLEANCE.   I take't, 'tis later, sir.

BANQUO. Hold, take my sword. There's husbandry[1] in heaven.
5   Their candles are all out. Take thee that[2] too.
    A heavy summons[3] lies like lead upon me,
    And yet I would not sleep. Merciful powers,
    Restrain in me the cursèd thoughts that nature
    Gives way to in repose!

[*Enter* MACBETH, *and a* SERVANT *with a torch.*]

                    Give me my sword!
10   Who's there?

MACBETH. A friend.

BANQUO. What, sir, not yet at rest? The King's a-bed:
    He hath been in unusual pleasure, and
    Sent forth great largess to your offices:[4]
15   This diamond he greets your wife withal,
    By the name of most kind hostess; and shut up[5]
    In measureless content.

MACBETH.   Being unprepared,
    Our will became the servant to defect,
    Which else should free have wrought.[6]

Reading Strategy
Reading Verse for Meaning Which line endings in lines 12–17 do not require a pause?

1. **husbandry** thrift.

2. **that** probably his sword belt.

3. **summons** weariness.

4. **largess . . . offices** gifts to your servants' quarters.

5. **shut up** retired.

6. **Being . . . wrought** Because we did not have enough time to prepare, we were unable to entertain as lavishly as we wanted to.

⑤ ✔ Reading Check
Where and when do Macbeth and Banquo meet?

Macbeth, Act II, Scene i ■ 327

❶ About the Selection

In this act, thoughts become deeds. It appears that Macbeth and Lady Macbeth have committed the perfect crime. In fact, it may have been more successful than they had hoped—the attendants are slain and unable to defend themselves, and Duncan's sons flee, casting suspicion on themselves. However, their plot begins to unravel and hints of tragedy begin to appear. One of the play's major themes—the fatal flaw of excessive ambition—begins to be developed as Macbeth becomes tortured by guilt.

❷ Critical Viewing

Possible response: Someone honorable and noble would be worthy.

❸ Critical Thinking
Infer

• Direct students' attention to lines 1–3.

• **Ask** students how Shakespeare uses the opening dialogue to inform the audience of the time of the action.
Answer: Banquo and Fleance discuss the moon and the hour, letting the audience know that it is past midnight.

❹ Reading Strategy
Reading Verse for Meaning

• Remind students that reading blank verse for meaning often requires following sentences past their line endings.

• Have students look at lines 12–17.

• Then, **ask** them the Reading Strategy question: Which line endings in lines 12–17 do not require a pause?
Answer: Lines 13 and 16 do not require a pause.

• **Ask** students what this passage reveals about the king and how it heightens the impact of his impending death.
Answer: The king is generous and kind, and he has gone to bed happy. These facts make his undeserved death more pitiable.

❺ Reading Check

Answer: Macbeth and Banquo meet after midnight in a court of Inverness.

BANQUO.   All's well.
20 I dreamt last night of the three weird sisters:
To you they have showed some truth.

MACBETH.   I think not of them.
Yet, when we can entreat an hour to serve,
We would spend it in some words upon that business,
If you would grant the time.

BANQUO.   At your kind'st leisure.

25 **MACBETH.** If you shall cleave to my consent, when 'tis,[7]
It shall make honor for you.

BANQUO.   So[8] I lose none
In seeking to augment it, but still keep
My bosom franchised[9] and allegiance clear,
I shall be counseled.

MACBETH.   Good repose the while!

30 **BANQUO.** Thanks, sir. The like to you!

                          [*Exit* BANQUO *with* FLEANCE.]

MACBETH. Go bid thy mistress, when my drink is ready,
She strike upon the bell. Get thee to bed.

                          [*Exit* SERVANT.]

Is this a dagger which I see before me,
The handle toward my hand? Come, let me clutch thee.
35 I have thee not, and yet I see thee still.
Art thou not, fatal vision, sensible[10]
To feeling as to sight, or art thou but
A dagger of the mind, a false creation,
Proceeding from the heat-oppressèd brain?
40 I see thee yet, in form as palpable
As this which now I draw.
Thou marshal'st[11] me the way that I was going;
And such an instrument I was to use.
Mine eyes are made the fools o' th' other senses,
45 Or else worth all the rest. I see thee still;
And on thy blade and dudgeon[12] gouts[13] of blood,
Which was not so before. There's no such thing.
It is the bloody business which informs[14]
Thus to mine eyes. Now o'er the one half-world
50 Nature seems dead, and wicked dreams abuse[15]
The curtained sleep; witchcraft celebrates
Pale Hecate's offerings;[16] and withered murder,
Alarumed by his sentinel, the wolf,
Whose howl's his watch, thus with his stealthy pace,
55 With Tarquin's[17] ravishing strides, towards his design
Moves like a ghost. Thou sure and firm-set earth,

328 ■ *Celebrating Humanity (1485–1625)*

7. **cleave . . . 'tis** Join my cause when the time comes.

8. **So** provided that.

Vocabulary Builder
augment (ôg ment´) *v.* make greater; enlarge

9. **bosom franchised** heart free (from guilt)

10. **sensible** able to be felt.

Vocabulary Builder
palpable (pal´ pə bəl) *adj.* capable of being touched or felt

11. **marshal'st** leads.

12. **dudgeon** wooden hilt.

13. **gouts** large drops.

14. **informs** takes shape.

15. **abuse** deceive.

16. **Hecate's** (hek´ə tēz) **offerings** offerings to Hecate, the Greek goddess of witchcraft.

Vocabulary Builder
stealthy (stel´ thē) *adj.* sly

17. **Tarquin's** of Tarquin, a Roman tyrant.

Hear not my steps, which way they walk, for fear
Thy very stones prate of my whereabout,
And take the present horror from the time,
60   Which now suits with it.[18] Whiles I threat, he lives:
Words to the heat of deeds too cold breath gives.

[*A bell rings.*]

I go, and it is done: the bell invites me.
Hear it not, Duncan, for it is a knell
That summons thee to heaven, or to hell.   [*Exit.*]

Scene ii. *Macbeth's castle*

[*Enter* LADY MACBETH.]

LADY MACBETH. That which hath made them drunk hath made
            me bold;
        What hath quenched them hath given me fire. Hark! Peace!
        It was the owl that shrieked, the fatal bellman,
        Which gives the stern'st good-night.[1] He is about it.
5   The doors are open, and the surfeited grooms[2]
        Do mock their charge with snores. I have drugged their possets,[3]
        That death and nature do contend about them,
        Whether they live or die.

MACBETH.   [*Within*] Who's there? What, ho?

LADY MACBETH. Alack, I am afraid they have awaked
10   And 'tis not done! Th' attempt and not the deed
        Confounds[4] us. Hark! I laid their daggers ready;
        He could not miss 'em. Had he not resembled
        My father as he slept, I had done 't.

[*Enter* MACBETH.]

                        My husband!

MACBETH. I have done the deed. Didst thou not hear a noise?

15 LADY MACBETH. I heard the owl scream and the crickets cry.
        Did not you speak?

MACBETH.   When?

LADY MACBETH.   Now.

MACBETH.   As I descended?

LADY MACBETH. Ay.

MACBETH. Hark!
        Who lies i' th' second chamber?

LADY MACBETH.   Donalbain.

20 MACBETH. This is a sorry[5] sight.

18. take . . . it remove the horrible silence which suits this moment.

1. bellman . . . good-night It was customary for a bell to be rung at midnight outside a condemned person's cell on the night before an execution.

2. surfeited grooms overfed servants.

3. possets warm bedtime drinks.

4. Confounds ruins.

Literary Analysis
Blank Verse Notice that the iambic pentameter of line 16 is shared in dialogue between Macbeth and Lady Macbeth. Why might the playwright have chosen this artistry?

5. sorry miserable.

⑩ ✓ **Reading Check**
What deed have Macbeth and Lady Macbeth performed?

Macbeth, Act II, Scene ii ■ 329

❽ Critical Thinking
Analyze

- Have students review Lady Macbeth's comments in lines 1–13. **Ask** students what it is that she has contributed to the murder plot.
  Answer: She has drugged the king's servants and has placed their daggers where they can easily be found.

- **Ask** students what comments indicate that Lady Macbeth is not as hard and cold as she'd like to think.
  Answer: In line 2, she is jumpy, spooked by the owl. In lines 12–13, she admits that she could not have murdered Duncan herself, because he looked like her father while he slept.

❾ Literary Analysis
Blank Verse

- **Ask** students what mood or atmosphere the series of short lines of dialogue, lines 14–19, creates.
  Answer: These lines suggest an atmosphere of tension, as if the characters are jumping at the sound of each other's voice.

- Point out that, though it looks at first as if Shakespeare has abandoned writing in verse, the iambic pentameter is actually continued across these lines of dialogue, starting in line 16. **Ask** students the Literary Analysis question: Why might the playwright have chosen this artistry?
  Possible response: The choppy speech contributes to the mood. Also, having Macbeth and Lady Macbeth finishing each other's lines adds to the sense of their complicity in the murder.

❿ Reading Check
Answer: They have murdered Duncan.

329

- **Ask** students why Macbeth would have listened with such care to what was being said by the two wakened sleepers.
  Answer: He would want to know if they heard him, if he was about to be discovered.

- **Ask** students what significance they draw from the fact that Macbeth is unable to respond to the blessing with "Amen."
  Possible responses: Macbeth's inability to engage in prayer suggests that he feels a strong sense of guilt and of divine disapproval of his act; he has descended so far into evil that he can no longer do anything that would be viewed as good or holy.

⓬ **Critical Thinking**
Analysis

- Have students **analyze** lines 34–38 and list at least three qualities that Macbeth ascribes to sleep.
  Possible responses: Sleep is innocent. Sleep helps untangle the worrisome issues of life. Sleep helps one's body heal from the day's work and one's mind heal from the day's problems. Sleep is nourishing—it builds one up and gives strength.

- **Ask** students what Macbeth means when he says that he has murdered sleep.
  Possible response: As is stated in line 42, "Macbeth shall sleep no more;" by murdering sleep, Macbeth has lost the vital gifts bestowed by sleep.

- In the lines that follow, how does Lady Macbeth react to Macbeth's guilt and worry?
  Answer: She chides him for losing his nerve and mocks him for being childlike in his fear.

- Have students review lines 43–62.
  Ask how Macbeth's reaction to the blood on his hands compares with Lady Macbeth's.
  Answer: She sees the blood as evidence that must be washed off. He sees it as the symbol of his crime and the guilt he'll never escape.

LADY MACBETH. A foolish thought, to say a sorry sight.

MACBETH. There's one did laugh in 's sleep, and one cried "Murder!"
That they did wake each other. I stood and heard them.
But they did say their prayers, and addressed them
Again to sleep.

25 **LADY MACBETH.** There are two[6] lodged together.

MACBETH. One cried "God bless us!" and "Amen" the other,
As they had seen me with these hangman's hands:
List'ning their fear, I could not say "Amen,"
When they did say "God bless us!"

LADY MACBETH.   Consider it not so deeply.

30 **MACBETH.** But wherefore could not I pronounce "Amen"?
I had most need of blessing, and "Amen"
Stuck in my throat.

LADY MACBETH.   These deeds must not be thought
After these ways; so, it will make us mad.

MACBETH. Methought I heard a voice cry "Sleep no more!
35 Macbeth does murder sleep"—the innocent sleep,
Sleep that knits up the raveled sleave[7] of care,
The death of each day's life, sore labor's bath,
Balm of hurt minds, great nature's second course,[8]
Chief nourisher in life's feast—

LADY MACBETH.   What do you mean?

40 **MACBETH.** Still it cried "Sleep no more!" to all the house:
"Glamis hath murdered sleep, and therefore Cawdor
Shall sleep no more: Macbeth shall sleep no more."

LADY MACBETH. Who was it that thus cried? Why, worthy Thane,
You do unbend[9] your noble strength, to think
45 So brainsickly of things. Go get some water,
And wash this filthy witness[10] from your hand.
Why did you bring these daggers from the place?
They must lie there: go carry them, and smear
The sleepy grooms with blood.

MACBETH.   I'll go no more.
50 I am afraid to think what I have done;
Look on 't again I dare not.

LADY MACBETH.   Infirm of purpose!
Give me the daggers. The sleeping and the dead
Are but as pictures. 'Tis the eye of childhood
That fears a painted devil. If he do bleed,
55 I'll gild[11] the faces of the grooms withal,
For it must seem their guilt.   [*Exit. Knock within.*]

330 ■ *Celebrating Humanity (1485–1625)*

6. **two** Malcolm and Donalbain, Duncan's sons.

7. **knits . . . sleave** straightens out the tangled threads.

8. **second course** main course; sleep.

9. **unbend** relax.

10. **witness** evidence.

11. **gild** paint.

Enrichment

Psychology

Psychologists have devoted considerable research to the subject of guilt and its effect on an individual who has committed a crime. Certain patterns of behavior have been noted in research and have been used to identify suspects and to further our understanding of human behavior.

The effect of profound guilt on individuals is also an important theme in literature. One of the best known examples is Hawthorne's *The*

Scarlet Letter, which explores the effects of concealed guilt and confessed guilt. Shakespeare's *Macbeth* is, to a large degree, also a study of the effects of guilt. In Act II, the guilt Macbeth feels after he murders Duncan is manifest in several ways: He is unable to answer a blessing with "Amen," and he thinks he hears a voice saying "Sleep no more!" The effects of guilt are manifested even more dramatically in later acts.

⓮ ▲ **Critical Viewing** How do these images from a poster advertising a production of *Macbeth* capture the suspense created in Act II? **[Connect]**

Macbeth, Act II, Scene ii ■ 331

⓭ **Humanities**
Poster for Orson Welles's film of *Macbeth*

Orson Welles, famous for the film *Citizen Kane* and the radio broadcast *War of the Worlds,* adapted Shakespeare's *Macbeth* for the screen and then directed and starred in the production. This 1948 version also featured Jeanette Nolan and Roddy McDowall. The production is notable for its papier-mâché sets and brooding atmosphere.

The shadowy poster for Welles's 1948 version of *Macbeth* emphasizes the darkness of the play's content. Orson Welles's face, made up as Macbeth at various points during the drama, conveys to viewers that the play is about a tortured individual.

Use these questions for discussion:

1. What emotion is portrayed by each of the expressions in Welles's face in this poster?
   Possible responses: Welles's face conjures up images of cold-blooded determination, fear, hate, helplessness, remorse, and resignation.

2. Do you find that the poster captures the essence of *The Tragedy of Macbeth*?
   Possible responses: Yes, the various expressions of Macbeth show that it is ultimately a human tragedy; no, the poster focuses too much on the Macbeth character and not enough on the others.

⓮ **Critical Viewing**

Answer: The sinister shadows reflect the treachery that is hatched in Act II. The eyes of Macbeth reflect a sense of shock at the horrible nature of the crime. Lady Macbeth's posture and facial expression suggest cold, almost mechanical determination.

Differentiated
Instruction   Solutions for All Learners

Strategy for Special Needs Students
Have students use the *Reader's Notebook: Adapted Version* to help them get involved in the story. The summary and simplified version of the first scene may give them just the start they need to discover the story "buried" in the language. Then, as students continue reading Act II in the Student Edition, summarize each scene, so they don't lose the thread of the story. Read important speeches aloud, so that the students can begin to get a feel for the language without getting lost in it.

Enrichment for Gifted/Talented Students
Suggest that students create their own "movie posters" for this play, using color, images, and words to "hook" potential audiences into coming to see *Macbeth*. Encourage them to think about the characters, actions, emotions, and images of the play as they plan their posters. When their posters are done, have students describe what message they were trying to get across, and what elements they chose to highlight. Hang their posters in the classroom.

▶ **Reteach:** Remind students that Shakespeare sometimes interrupts his blank verse with prose. Prose is usually reserved for low-ranking characters. Also, only low-ranking characters were bawdy or vulgar. Their often humorous speeches helped break up the dramatic narrative. This device is called comic relief and is common in Elizabethan drama.

• Then, **ask** students the Literary Analysis question: How do the shift from verse to prose in Scene iii and the porter's remarks affect the mood?
Answer: The mood shifts from one of great tension to one of light-hearted humor; this scene offers the audience some relief from the tension.

• **Discuss** how and why the porter's reaction to the knocking is different from the reactions of Macbeth and Lady Macbeth in the previous scene.
Possible responses: For the porter, it is a job; for Macbeth and Lady Macbeth, it is a warning that people approach. Macbeth is appalled, certain that the knocking is related to his guilt; Lady Macbeth views it as a signal to get moving, so they don't get caught; the porter is annoyed at being awakened.

16 **Vocabulary Builder**
The Latin Root -voc-

• Call students' attention to the word *equivocate* and its definition. Tell students that the Latin word root -*voc*- means "voice" or "calling."

• Tell students that this root is sometimes spelled -*vok*-, and it is the root of a large number of words.

• Ask students to suggest any words they can think of that contain this word. Supplement their suggestions as necessary, writing the words on the board. Possibilities include *advocate, avocation, convocation, equivocal, evoke, invocation, irrevocable, provocation, provocative, revoke, vocabulary, vocal, vocation, vociferous.*

• Have students look up the meanings of unfamiliar words in the dictionary.

MACBETH.   Whence is that knocking?
How is 't with me, when every noise appalls me?
What hands are here? Ha! They pluck out mine eyes!
Will all great Neptune's ocean wash this blood
60   Clean from my hand? No; this my hand will rather
The <u>multitudinous</u> seas incarnadine,[12]
Making the green one red.

[*Enter* LADY MACBETH.]

LADY MACBETH. My hands are of your color, but I shame
To wear a heart so white. [*Knock.*] I hear a knocking
65   At the south entry. Retire we to our chamber.
A little water clears us of this deed:
How easy is it then! Your constancy
Hath left you unattended.[13] [*Knock.*] Hark! more knocking.
Get on your nightgown, lest occasion call us
70   And show us to be watchers.[14] Be not lost
So poorly in your thoughts.

MACBETH. To know my deed, 'twere best not know myself. [*Knock.*]
Wake Duncan with thy knocking! I would thou couldst!

[*Exit.*]

Scene iii. *Macbeth's castle.*

[*Enter a* PORTER.[1] *Knocking within.*]

PORTER. Here's a knocking indeed! If a man were porter
of hell gate, he should have old[2] turning the key.
[*Knock.*] Knock, knock, knock! Who's there, i' th'
name of Beelzebub?[3] Here's a farmer, that
5   hanged himself on th' expectation of plenty.[4] Come
in time! Have napkins enow[5] about you; here you'll
sweat for 't. [*Knock.*] Knock, knock! Who's there, in
th' other devil's name? Faith, here's an equivocator,
that could swear in both the scales against
10   either scale;[6] who committed treason enough for
God's sake, yet could not <u>equivocate</u> to heaven. O,
come in, equivocator. [*Knock.*] Knock, knock, knock!
Who's there? Faith, here's an English tailor come
hither for stealing out of a French hose:[7]
15   come in, tailor. Here you may roast your goose.[8]
[*Knock.*] Knock, knock; never at quiet! What are you?
But this place is too cold for hell. I'll devil-porter it no
further. I had thought to have let in some of all
professions that go the primrose way to th'
20   everlasting bonfire. [*Knock.*] Anon, anon!
[*Opens an entrance.*] I pray you, remember the porter.

Vocabulary Builder
multitudinous (mul′ tə tōōd′ 'n əs) *adj.* existing in great numbers

12. incarnadine (in kär′ nə din) redden.

13. Your constancy . . . unattended Your firmness of purpose has left you.

14. watchers up late.

Literary Analysis
Blank Verse, Prose, and Comic Relief How do the shift from verse to prose in Scene iii and the porter's remarks affect the mood?

1. porter doorkeeper.

2. should have old would have plenty of.

3. Beelzebub (bē el′ zə bub′) the chief devil.

4. A farmer . . . plenty a farmer who hoarded grain, hoping that the prices would come up after a bad harvest.

5. enow enough.

Vocabulary Builder
equivocate (ē kwiv′ ə kāt′) *v.* to use terms that have two or more meanings to mislead purposely or deceive

6. an equivocator . . . scale a liar who could make two contradictory statements and swear that both were true.

7. stealing . . . hose stealing some cloth from the hose while making them.

8. goose pressing iron.

Enrichment

The Porter's Scene

This excerpt is from Thomas De Quincey's (1785–1859) essay "On the Knocking at the Gate in *Macbeth*":

> The knocking at the gate which succeeds to the murder of Duncan produced to my feelings an effect for which I never could account. The effect was that it reflected back upon the murderer a peculiar awfulness and a depth of solemnity.
> . . . All action in any direction is best expounded, measured, and made apprehensible by reaction.

Now apply this to the case in *Macbeth*. Here, as I have said, the retiring of the human heart and the entrance of the fiendish heart was to be expressed and made sensible. Another world has stepped in . . . Hence it is that, when the deed is done, when the work of darkness is perfect, then the world of darkness passes away like a pageantry in the cloud: the knocking at the gate is heard, and it makes known audibly that the reaction has commenced.

[Enter MACDUFF and LENNOX.]

MACDUFF. Was it so late, friend, ere you went to bed,
  That you do lie so late?

25 **PORTER.** Faith, sir, we were carousing till the second
  cock:[9] and drink, sir, is a great provoker of three
  things.

MACDUFF. What three things does drink especially
  provoke?

30 **PORTER.** Marry, sir, nose-painting, sleep, and urine.
  Lechery, sir, it provokes and unprovokes; it provokes
  the desire, but it takes away the performance: therefore much drink may be said to be an equivocator
  with lechery: it makes him and it mars him; it
35   sets him on and it takes him off; it persuades him
  and disheartens him; makes him stand to and not
  stand to; in conclusion equivocates him in a sleep,
  and giving him the lie, leaves him.

MACDUFF. I believe drink gave thee the lie[10] last night.

40 **PORTER.** That it did, sir, i' the very throat on me: but I
  requited him for his lie, and, I think, being too strong
  for him, though he took up my legs sometime, yet I
  make a shift to cast[11] him.

MACDUFF. Is thy master stirring?

[Enter MACBETH.]

  Our knocking has awaked him; here he comes.

LENNOX. Good morrow, noble sir.

45 **MACBETH.**   Good morrow, both.

MACDUFF. Is the king stirring, worthy Thane?

MACBETH.   Not yet.

MACDUFF. He did command me to call timely[12] on him:
  I have almost slipped the hour.

MACBETH.   I'll bring you to him.

MACDUFF. I know this is a joyful trouble to you;
50   But yet 'tis one.

MACBETH. The labor we delight in physics pain.[13]
  This is the door.

MACDUFF.   I'll make so bold to call,
  For 'tis my limited service.[14]   [Exit MACDUFF.]

LENNOX. Goes the king hence today?

---

9. **second cock** 3:00 A.M.

10. **gave thee the lie** laid you out.

11. **cast** vomit.

Literary Analysis
Blank Verse Why is it appropriate for the dialogue in lines 43–44 to change back from prose to blank verse?

12. **timely** early.

13. **labor . . . pain** Labor that we enjoy cures discomfort.

14. **limited service** assigned duty.

19 ✓ **Reading Check**
To what gate does the porter compare the gate of Macbeth's castle?

Macbeth, Act II, Scene iii ■ 333

---

17 **Critical Thinking**
Interpret

- Explain that, while the porter's speech does not really further the plot, his slowness does.
- Point out that the ideas the porter raises, though apparently off the point, still are tied to the ideas of the play: References to the diabolical reflect the character of Macbeth and references to drink reflect the condition of the king's servants.
- Note that the porter uses two versions of the same word several times. **Ask** students to identify it and determine how it reflects on the play. (Hint: One form is a vocabulary word.)
Answer: *equivocator* (lines 8, 12, 32) and *equivocate* (lines 11, 36). They reflect on what is about to happen—intentional misleading and deception.

18 **Literary Analysis**
Blank Verse

- Direct students' attention to lines 43–44.
- ▶ **Monitor Progress:** Then, **ask** students to answer the Literary Analysis question: Why is it appropriate for the dialogue in lines 43–44 to change back from prose to blank verse?
Answer: It is appropriate for the dialogue to change back from prose to blank verse because the comic relief provided by the porter has ended, and serious matters are about to begin. Also, prose is used for low-ranking characters, such as the porter, so blank verse is appropriate for the high-ranking Macduff and Lennox.

19 **Reading Check**
Answer: The porter compares the gate of Macbeth's castle to the gate of hell.

Differentiated
Instruction   Solutions for All Learners

Strategy for Less Proficient Readers
Explain that the porter's speeches are comic interruptions. Other than the delay in opening the door, there is no plot development. "Knock, knock! Who's there" in line 7 adds only humor. Discuss whether the lines are funny, or if the porter's behavior adds the most humor.

Background for English Learners
Explain that low-ranking characters are often vulgar in Shakespeare. Hence, this humorous passage uses images that students may be surprised to see in "serious" literature. Ask them to think of what they know of drunkenness, for example, as they read lines 29–37. Their knowledge may help them understand the images.

Strategy for Advanced Readers
Ask students to review the definitions of prose and comic relief on p. 326. Have students discuss the comic impact of the porter's speech. Then, have them research the use of comic relief in drama. You may wish to have them share their findings with the class.

- Have students read lines 55–62.

- **Ask** them the first Reading Strategy question: How many sentences are there in these lines? **Answer:** There are three sentences in lines 55–62.

- Have students **describe** the night Lennox has experienced. **Answer:** The wind was wild and blew down the chimney. There were a lot of ominous sounds. An owl screeched all night. Some reported an earthquake.

21 **Reading Strategy**
Reading Verse for Meaning

- Have students read the bracketed passage on this page and the next page.

- Then **ask** them the second Reading Strategy question: Where should you not pause at the ends of lines? **Answer:** You should *not* pause at the ends of lines 77, 78, and 80.

- **Ask** what comparison Macduff makes between sleep and death. **Answer:** He says that sleep is a counterfeit, or "fake" death.

22 **Literature in Context**

Elizabethan Concepts of Monarchy The idea that the monarch was appointed by God fit into the whole Elizabethan idea of an ordered universe. Remind students of the idea of a universal order, where everything is connected. Point out that this connection is reflected in Lennox's speech in lines 55–62; because the king has been killed, the order of nature itself responds with howling and shaking. But the idea of a monarch being appointed by God is not an Elizabethan invention. The idea goes back thousands of years.

Connect to the Literature Point out the religious imagery Macduff uses in lines 68–69. Then **ask** the Connect to the Literature question: How does Macduff's line 68 reflect this concept of monarchy? **Answer:** Macduff refers to the king's body as the "Lord's anointed temple" and calls the murder "sacrilegious."

MACBETH. He does: he did appoint so.

55 **LENNOX.** The night has been unruly. Where we lay,
Our chimneys were blown down, and, as they say,
Lamentings heard i' th' air, strange screams of death,
And prophesying with accents terrible
Of dire combustion[15] and confused events
60 New hatched to th' woeful time: the obscure bird[16]
Clamored the livelong night. Some say, the earth
Was feverous and did shake.

MACBETH. 'Twas a rough night.

LENNOX. My young remembrance cannot parallel
A fellow to it.

[*Enter* MACDUFF.]

65 **MACDUFF.** O horror, horror, horror! Tongue nor heart
Cannot conceive nor name thee.

MACBETH AND LENNOX. What's the matter?

MACDUFF. Confusion[17] now hath made his masterpiece.
Most sacrilegious murder hath broke ope
The Lord's anointed temple,[18] and stole thence
The life o' th' building.♦

70 **MACBETH.** What is 't you say? The life?

LENNOX. Mean you his Majesty?

MACDUFF. Approach the chamber, and destroy your sight
With a new Gorgon:[19] do not bid me speak;
See, and then speak yourselves. Awake, awake!

[*Exit* MACBETH *and* LENNOX.]

75 Ring the alarum bell. Murder and Treason!
Banquo and Donalbain! Malcolm! Awake!
Shake off this downy sleep, death's counterfeit,

15. **combustion** confusion.

16. **obscure bird** bird of darkness, the owl.

17. **Confusion** destruction.

18. **The Lord's anointed temple** the King's body.

19. **Gorgon** Medusa, a mythological monster whose appearance was so ghastly that those who looked at it turned to stone.

Literature in Context

Cultural Connection

♦ *Elizabethan Concepts of Monarchy*
For the Elizabethans, the monarch was God's representative on Earth. For this reason, the expression "the Lord's anointed" is used to describe the head of state. Killing the ruler, therefore, was not just an act of political assassination; it was also a horrifying desecration of religious values.

Connect to the Literature

How does Macduff's line 68 reflect this concept of monarchy?

334 ■ *Celebrating Humanity (1485–1625)*

Enrichment

Forensics

In Shakespeare's time, little was known of blood types, fingerprints, and similar modern evidence-gathering methods. As is seen in Act II, conclusions about the manner in which a crime was committed and the guilt or innocence of a suspect were made largely on the basis of appearances and unsubstantiated theories.

Today, crime scenes are preserved and investigated in depth. Blood samples and fingerprints are collected. Weapons are scientifically examined, and witnesses, victims, and suspects are questioned. Of course, even modern forensic methods might not have prevailed in this case. The weapons used belonged to the accused; the blood on them was the victim's blood. Even today, some crimes are solved because the criminals "crack" from fear or guilt—or they brag about their deeds.

And look on death itself! Up, up, and see
The great doom's image![20] Malcolm! Banquo!
80 As from your graves rise up, and walk like sprites,[21]
To countenance[22] this horror. Ring the bell.

[*Bell rings. Enter* LADY MACBETH.]

LADY MACBETH. What's the business,
That such a hideous trumpet calls to parley[23]
The sleepers of the house? Speak, speak!

MACDUFF.   O gentle lady,
85 'Tis not for you to hear what I can speak:
The repetition, in a woman's ear,
Would murder as it fell.

[*Enter* BANQUO.]

                            O Banquo, Banquo!
Our royal master's murdered.

LADY MACBETH.   Woe, alas!
What, in our house?

BANQUO.   Too cruel anywhere.
90 Dear Duff, I prithee, contradict thyself,
And say it is not so.

[*Enter* MACBETH, LENNOX, *and* ROSS.]

MACBETH. Had I but died an hour before this chance,
I had lived a blessèd time; for from this instant
There's nothing serious in mortality:[24]
95 All is but toys.[25] Renown and grace is dead,
The wine of life is drawn, and the mere lees[26]
Is left this vault[27] to brag of.

[*Enter* MALCOLM *and* DONALBAIN.]

DONALBAIN. What is amiss?

MACBETH.   You are, and do not know 't.
The spring, the head, the fountain of your blood
100 Is stopped; the very source of it is stopped.

MACDUFF. Your royal father's murdered.

MALCOLM.   O, by whom?

LENNOX. Those of his chamber, as it seemed, had done 't:
Their hands and faces were all badged[28] with blood;
So were their daggers, which unwiped we found
105 Upon their pillows. They stared, and were distracted.
No man's life was to be trusted with them.

MACBETH. O, yet I do repent me of my fury,
That I did kill them.

---

20. great doom's image
likeness of Judgment Day.

21. sprites spirits.

22. countenance be in
keeping with.

23. parley war conference.

24. serious in mortality
worthwhile in mortal life.

25. toys trifles.

26. lees dregs.

27. vault world.

Literary Analysis
Blank Verse Where is
there a pause in line 100?
How does it reinforce the
meaning?

28. badged marked.

✓**Reading Check**

According to Lennox,
what evidence proves that
the guards killed Duncan?

Macbeth, Act II, Scene iii ■ *335*

㉓ Critical Thinking
Analyze

• Point out that each of Macbeth's
speeches on this page are designed
to make him look loyal and loving
toward the king.

• **Ask** students to paraphrase
Macbeth's words in lines 92–97.
Possible response: He says that,
if he had died without hearing this
bad news, he would have had a
happy life. From now on, there's
nothing worthwhile in his life.

• Have students **compare** Macbeth's
"act" with that of Lady Macbeth.
Does it seem, since the previous
night, that the control and passion
have shifted from one to the other?
Possible response: Lady Macbeth
seems to be at a loss, now. All she
can say is, "What, in our house?"
Suddenly, Macbeth is the one in
control. He has the passion, the
speeches, the action—and he
springs pretty easily into committing the next murder.

㉔ Literary Analysis
Blank Verse

• Direct students' attention to
line 100.

• **Ask** students the Literary Analysis
question: Where is there a pause in
line 100? How does it reinforce the
meaning?
Answer: The pause occurs after
the phrase, "Is stopped," at the
semicolon. The pause underscores
the emotion, as if the dreadful
words are catching in his throat or
he is choking back tears.

• **Ask** students what Macbeth's
words in lines 98–100 mean.
Answer: Malcolm and Donalbain
are Duncan's sons, so Duncan was
the "source" of their blood. They
don't know it yet, but their father is
dead.

㉕ Reading Check

Answer: According to Macbeth, he
killed the grooms because he was
unable to be calm and rational after
having seen Duncan's body. He
claims his emotions got the better
of him.

26 Humanities

Lady Macbeth Seizing the Daggers,
1812 by Henry Fuseli

This painting by Henry Fuseli
(1741–1825) depicts the scene
immediately after the murder of
Duncan. It shows the horror Macbeth
feels for what he has done and the
unshaken control Lady Macbeth has
over him. Like most of Fuseli's work,
it has a surrealistic, nightmarish quality that reflects the disordered minds
of the characters. He created this
painting from a sketch he made in
1760 after seeing David Garrick and
Mrs. Pritchard in a performance of
Macbeth. Use these questions for discussion:

1. How does the lack of color contribute to the mood of this scene?
   Answer: The lack of color creates
   a dream-like scene, as if the characters were ghosts, or from
   another world. It also makes the
   blood on the daggers stand out.

2. How does the artist's depiction of
   these two characters compare
   with your conception of them?
   Possible responses: Some students will be surprised by the
   cowardly, submissive appearance
   of Macbeth. Lady Macbeth's
   aggressive posturing and determined look may be more in keeping with students' mental picture
   of the character.

27 Critical Viewing

Answer: Lady Macbeth's face and
body suggest a determined and
aggressive personality. She seems to
dominate her shrinking, horrified
husband.

28 Critical Thinking
Interpret

• Direct students' attention to lines
  119–120.

• **Ask** students if they think Lady
  Macbeth has actually fainted, or if
  she is merely pretending to faint to
  deflect suspicion.
  Possible responses: A case can
  be made for either position.
  However, most students will probably think that Lady Macbeth has
  shown herself to be a treacherous,
  plotting villain, and her actions are
  as false as Macbeth's protests of
  love and loyalty.

26

27 ▲ **Critical Viewing** This painting depicts the moment when Macbeth comes from
murdering Duncan (II, ii, 14). However, it also captures the nature of the relationship
between Macbeth and Lady Macbeth in the first part of the play. What do their facial
expressions and body language suggest about that relationship? **[Interpret]**

MACDUFF.	Wherefore did you so?

MACBETH. Who can be wise, amazed, temp'rate and furious,
110   Loyal and neutral, in a moment? No man.
The expedition[29] of my violent love
Outrun the pauser, reason. Here lay Duncan,
His silver skin laced with his golden blood,
And his gashed stabs looked like a breach in nature
115   For ruin's wasteful entrance: there, the murderers,
Steeped in the colors of their trade, their daggers
Unmannerly breeched with gore.[30] Who could refrain,

29. expedition haste.

30. breeched with gore
covered with blood.

336 ■ Celebrating Humanity (1485–1625)

That had a heart to love, and in that heart
Courage to make 's love known?

LADY MACBETH.   Help me hence, ho!

MACDUFF. Look to the lady.

120 **MALCOLM.** [*Aside to* DONALBAIN] Why do we hold our tongues,
That most may claim this argument for ours?[31]

DONALBAIN. [*Aside to* MALCOLM] What should be spoken here,
Where our fate, hid in an auger-hole,[32]
May rush, and seize us? Let's away:
Our tears are not yet brewed.

125 **MALCOLM.** [*Aside to* DONALBAIN] Nor our strong sorrow
Upon the foot of motion.[33]

BANQUO.   Look to the lady.

[LADY MACBETH *is carried out.*]

And when we have our naked frailties hid,[34]
That suffer in exposure, let us meet
And question[35] this most bloody piece of work,
130 To know it further. Fears and scruples[36] shake us.
In the great hand of God I stand, and thence
Against the undivulged pretense[37] I fight
Of treasonous malice.

MACDUFF.   And so do I.

ALL.   So all.

MACBETH. Let's briefly[38] put on manly readiness,
And meet i' th' hall together.

135 **ALL.**   Well contented.

[*Exit all but* MALCOLM *and* DONALBAIN.]

MALCOLM. What will you do? Let's not consort with them.
To show an unfelt sorrow is an office[39]
Which the false man does easy. I'll to England.

DONALBAIN. To Ireland, I; our separated fortune
140 Shall keep us both the safer. Where we are
There's daggers in men's smiles; the near in blood,
The nearer bloody.[40]

MALCOLM.   This murderous shaft that's shot
Hath not yet lighted,[41] and our safest way
Is to avoid the aim. Therefore to horse;
145 And let us not be dainty of leave-taking,
But shift away. There's warrant[42] in that theft
Which steals itself[43] when there's no mercy left.

[*Exit.*]

---

31. That most . . . ours who are the most concerned with this topic.

32. auger-hole tiny hole, an unsuspected place because of its size.

33. Our tears . . . motion We have not yet had time for tears nor to turn our sorrow into action.

34. when . . . hid when we have put on our clothes.

35. question investigate.

36. scruples doubts.

37. undivulged pretense hidden purpose.

38. briefly quickly.

Reading Strategy
Reading Verse for Meaning How do the brief sentences in lines 136–138 reinforce the meaning?

39. office function.

40. the near . . . bloody The closer we are in blood relationship to Duncan, the greater our chance of being murdered.

41. lighted reached its target.

42. warrant justification.

43. that theft . . . itself stealing away.

32 ✔ **Reading Check**
What do Malcolm and Donalbain decide to do?

Macbeth, Act II, Scene iii ■ 337

---

29 Critical Thinking
Analyze

• Duncan's sons are quick to assess their danger. Have students read the exchanges between the brothers (lines 120–126 and 136–147), then **ask** what their biggest concern is.
Answer: They are concerned that whoever is behind the murder will want to murder them, too.

• What does this tell us about their thoughts regarding the dead servants?
Answer: They believe that the two servants are either innocent or in the employ of someone else. Otherwise, they would feel safe.

• Why do they decide to go in different directions?
Answer: They feel that if they are separate, the chances of one of them surviving is greater.

30 Critical Thinking
Infer

• **Ask** students what is significant about Banquo's words.
Answer: Banquo feels that things are not as they appear and warrant further investigation.

• **Ask** students what two recent events might make Banquo think that someone would have a reason for killing the king.
Answer: Banquo heard the witches promise Macbeth the crown; Malcolm was just named heir to the thrown.

31 Reading Strategy
Reading Verse for Meaning

• Have students **explain** what Malcolm is saying in lines 136–138.
Answer: He asks Donalbain what he's going to do. He suggests that they not talk with the others. He states that those who are lying can easily make a show of their sorrow. He says he's heading for England.

▶ **Monitor Progress:** Then, **ask** students the Reading Strategy question: How do the brief sentences in lines 136–138 reinforce the meaning?
Answer: The brief sentences lend a sense of urgency to the conversation.

32 Reading Check

Answer: Malcolm and Donalbain decide to flee the scene.

Differentiated Instruction — Solutions for All Learners

Strategy for Special Needs Students
Have students consider the painting by Henry Fuseli on the facing page. Read aloud Act II, scene ii, in which Lady Macbeth and Macbeth carry out the murder of Duncan. Discuss in class how the image contributes to an understanding of the events.

Enrichment for Gifted/Talented Students
Have students work in small groups to act out the dialogue between Malcolm and Donalbain in Act II, scene iii. Remind students that they should capture in their performances the feelings of people who are suspicious of the people around them.

Enrichment for Advanced Readers
Have students consider the dialogue between Malcolm and Donalbain in Act II, scene iii. Then, have students work in pairs gathering "evidence" that either supports or refutes the following thesis: **Duncan's sons should never have left Inverness.** Students may wish to read ahead in the play to bolster their arguments.

- Have students read line 23 aloud, listening for the meter.

- Encourage students to look at metric patterns listed under Meter in the Literary Terms Handbook at the back of their texts.

- Then, **ask** students to answer the Literary Analysis question: What rhythmic variation in the blank verse do you find at the beginning of line 23?
  Answer: The line begins with two stressed syllables creating a spondee: **Those** / that / Mac/ beth / hath/ **slain.**

34 **Critical Thinking**
Analyze

- Point out that, in lines 8–9, Ross notes that it is dark out, when it should be light. **Ask** students what this fact signifies.
  Answer: It is, like the wild night, a sign that the natural order is disrupted by Duncan's murder.

- Explain to students that the old man's comment that the darkness is unnatural, like the deed that is done, is the first indication that Duncan's sons are suspect. The child's loyalty to a parent was seen as being as much a part of the natural order as a subject's loyalty to the king.

- Have students look at lines 22–30. **Ask** them what is now believed to have been the plot behind the murder. Why?
  Answer: It is believed that Duncan's sons paid the servants to commit the murder. This is believed because the servants would have nothing to gain from the murder without someone paying them, and Duncan's sons have fled the scene of the crime.

- Remind students that one of the reasons Macbeth hesitated to kill Duncan is that they were related. What does that explain in this scene?
  Answer: It explains why the crown would come next to Macbeth. A member of the royal family would inherit the throne.

Scene iv. Outside Macbeth's castle.

[*Enter* ROSS *with an* OLD MAN.]

OLD MAN. Threescore and ten I can remember well:
  Within the volume of which time I have seen
  Hours dreadful and things strange, but this sore[1] night
  Hath trifled former knowings.

ROSS.   Ha, good father,
5 Thou seest the heavens, as troubled with man's act,
  Threatens his bloody stage. By th' clock 'tis day,
  And yet dark night strangles the traveling lamp:[2]
  Is 't night's <u>predominance</u>, or the day's shame,
  That darkness does the face of earth entomb,
  When living light should kiss it?

10 **OLD MAN.**   'Tis unnatural,
  Even like the deed that's done. On Tuesday last
  A falcon, tow'ring in her pride of place,[3]
  Was by a mousing owl hawked at and killed.

ROSS. And Duncan's horses—a thing most strange
      and certain—
15 Beauteous and swift, the minions of their race,
  Turned wild in nature, broke their stalls, flung out,
  Contending 'gainst obedience, as they would make
  War with mankind.

OLD MAN.   'Tis said they eat[4] each other.

ROSS. They did so, to th' amazement of mine eyes,
  That looked upon 't.

[*Enter* MACDUFF.]

20   Here comes the good Macduff.
  How goes the world, sir, now?

MACDUFF.   Why, see you not?

ROSS. Is 't known who did this more than bloody deed?

33 **MACDUFF.** Those that Macbeth hath slain.

ROSS.   Alas, the day!
  What good could they pretend?[5]

34 **MACDUFF.**   They were suborned:[6]
25 Malcolm and Donalbain, the king's two sons,
  Are stol'n away and fled, which puts upon them
  Suspicion of the deed.

ROSS.   'Gainst nature still.
  Thriftless ambition, that will ravin up[7]
  Thine own life's means! Then 'tis most like

338 ■ Celebrating Humanity (1485–1625)

---

1. **sore** grievous.

2. **traveling lamp** the sun.

Vocabulary Builder
predominance (prē däm′ ə nəns) *n.* superiority

3. **tow'ring . . . place** soaring at its summit.

4. **eat** ate.

Literary Analysis
Blank Verse What rhythmic variation in the blank verse do you find at the beginning of line 23?

5. **pretend** hope for.

6. **suborned** bribed.

7. **ravin up** devour greedily.

Assessment Practice

Forms of Propaganda (**For more practice,** see *Standardized Test Preparation Workbook,* p. 13.)

Many tests require students to recognize a persuasive speech. Use the following to teach students how to recognize the purpose of a speech.

  Macbeth. . . . The expedition of my violent love
Outrun the pauser, reason. Here lay Duncan,
His silver skin laced with his golden blood,
  . . . .there, the murderers,
Steeped in the colors of their trade, their daggers . . .

Macbeth speaks these lines in the presence of the other characters *primarily* to—

A explain why he killed the grooms

B persuade them that the grooms were guilty and that he was loyal to Duncan

C describe the appearance of the grooms

D convince them that he lost control and that he killed the grooms out of revenge.

Choices *A, C,* and *D* are true but are not the primary purposes of the speech. The correct answer is *B.*

30   The sovereignty will fall upon Macbeth.

MACDUFF. He is already named, and gone to Scone[8]
          To be invested.

ROSS.   Where is Duncan's body?

MACDUFF. Carried to Colmekill,
          The sacred storehouse of his predecessors
          And guardian of their bones.

35 **ROSS.**   Will you to Scone?

MACDUFF. No, cousin, I'll to Fife.[9]

ROSS.   Well, I will thither.

MACDUFF. Well, may you see things well done there.
          Adieu,
          Lest our old robes sit easier than our new!

ROSS. Farewell, father.

40 **OLD MAN.** God's benison[10] go with you, and with those
          That would make good of bad, and friends of foes!

                                        [*Exit.*]

8. **Scone** (skoōn) where Scottish kings were crowned.

9. **Fife** where Macduff's castle is located.

10. **benison** blessing.

Critical Reading

1. **Respond:** Whom do you blame more for the murder of King Duncan—Macbeth or Lady Macbeth? Explain.

2. **(a) Recall:** Describe Macbeth's and Lady Macbeth's reactions to the murder just after it is committed. **(b) Compare and Contrast:** Compare and contrast their reactions to the deed.

3. **(a) Recall:** What kind of gate does the porter imagine he is tending? **(b) Interpret:** In what way is the porter's playful fantasy a comment on Macbeth's situation?

4. **(a) Recall:** What two strange occurrences are reported in this act? **(b) Interpret:** Why would Shakespeare include reports of such occurrences at this point in the play? **(c) Connect:** In what way do these strange occurrences relate to the Elizabethan notion of an orderly and interconnected universe?

5. **(a) Analyze:** What question does Ross ask that indicates he doubts that the grooms committed the murder? Explain. **(b) Infer:** Is Ross satisfied by the answer? Explain.

6. **Speculate:** Do you think a political assassination like the one Macbeth commits is ever justifiable? Why or why not?

Go Online
Author Link
For: More about
         William Shakespeare
Visit: www.PHSchool.com
Web Code: ese-9209

Macbeth, Act II, Scene iv ■ *339*

Go Online
Author Link For additional information about William Shakespeare, have students type in the Web Code, then select S from the alphabet, and then select the author's name.

Apply the Skills

Macbeth, Act II

Literary Analysis

Blank Verse

1. To analyze Shakespeare's use of **blank verse,** complete a chart like this one by identifying the rhythm of each of the lines indicated.

Line	Iambic Feet	Trochaic or Anapestic Feet
"It is the bloody business which informs. . . ."		
"'Macbeth does murder sleep' —the innocent sleep, . . . "		

2. Mark stressed and unstressed syllables in Act II, Scene ii, lines 59–62.

3. Identify three metrical variations in Act II, Scene ii, lines 59–62.

Connecting Literary Elements

4. **(a)** Contrast the porter's speech (Act II, Scene iii, lines 1–21) with the two speeches at the end of II, ii, to show that the porter's speech is written in **prose** form. **(b)** Why might prose be suitable for a "low" character? **(c)** How does the speech offer **comic relief**?

5. The nineteenth-century English writer Thomas De Quincey argued that the scene with the porter reinforces the shock of the king's murder by a striking contrast: ". . . the re-establishment of the goings-on of the world in which we live, first makes us profoundly sensible of the awful [episode] that had suspended them." Do you agree or disagree? Explain.

Reading Strategy

Reading Verse for Meaning

6. **(a)** How many sentences are there in Act II, Scene i, lines 62–64? **(b)** In **reading these lines for meaning,** would you pause at any of the line ends? Explain.

7. In your own words, express the meaning of the sentences in Act II, Scene i, lines 62–64.

Extend Understanding

8. **Psychology Connection:** Macbeth has a strong imagination. In what way does this trait both prompt him to commit a crime and make it hard for him to commit it?

QuickReview

Blank verse is unrhymed iambic pentameter—an iamb is an unstressed syllable followed by a stressed syllable. In **iambic pentameter,** there are five such feet to the line.

The following variations in blank verse break the regular iambic rhythm: **trochaic feet** (stressed, unstressed) and **anapestic feet** (unstressed, unstressed, stressed).

Prose is writing presented in sentences and paragraphs without a predictable rhythm.

Comic relief provides a humorous break in an otherwise tense mood.

To **read verse for meaning,** focus on sentences, not lines.

Go Online
Assessment

For: Self-test
Visit: www.PHSchool.com
Web Code: esa-6208

Build Language Skills

Vocabulary Lesson

Word Analysis: Latin Root -voc-

The Latin root -voc- means "voice" or "calling." *Equivocate* means "to speak in two equal voices," or "to mislead." Knowing this root, define each of the words below.

1. vocalist   2. vocal   3. invocation

Spelling Strategy

Many words end in an unstressed syllable spelled with a consonant + *le*. To add *-ly*, drop the *le*: *palpable* becomes *palpably*. To add other endings, drop the final *e*, except when it helps to spell a separate syllable, as in *trickled*. In your notebook, add the suffixes indicated.

1. capable + *ly*   2. nestle + *ing*   3. dazzle + *ment*

Grammar and Style Lesson

Commonly Confused Words: *Lie* and *Lay*

Do not confuse *lie* with *lay*. *Lie* (past: *lay*; past participle: *lain*) means "to lie down or on," and *lay* (past and past participle: *laid*) means "to place."

Examples: He <u>lies</u> silently in wait.
She <u>lays</u> the knives on the table.

Practice   Choose the correct form of *lie* or *lay* for each item.

1. Macbeth kills Duncan as the king __?__ in bed.

W/G   *Prentice Hall Writing and Grammar Connection: Chapter 25, Section 2*

Extend Your Learning

Listening and Speaking   In a group, present a **debate** on this proposition: Ross is a self-seeking flatterer, not a loyal Scot. **[Group Activity]**

Writing   As a detective, create an **investigational journal** of Duncan's murder. Record clues at the scene and each person's testimony.

Vocabulary Builder: Synonyms

In your notebook, write the letter of the word that is the synonym of the first word.

1. augment: **(a)** add, **(b)** reduce, **(c)** move
2. palpable: **(a)** imperceptible, **(b)** touchable, **(c)** obvious
3. stealthy: **(a)** reputable, **(b)** sneaky, **(c)** open
4. multitudinous: **(a)** scarce, **(b)** agitated, **(c)** many
5. equivocate: **(a)** mislead, **(b)** declare, **(c)** ruin
6. predominance: **(a)** equality, **(b)** superiority **(c)** inferiority

2. Lady Macbeth thought the daggers should __?__ beside King Duncan.
3. Lady Macbeth went to __?__ the daggers beside King Duncan.
4. Macbeth intended to __?__ down.
5. After the murder, Duncan's dead body was __?__ to rest.

Writing Application   Write a speech in prose in which the porter tells a friend about the murder of Duncan. Use *lie* and *lay* correctly.

Macbeth, Act II ■ 341

Assessment Resources

The following resources can be used to assess students' knowledge and skills.

Unit 2 Resources
   Selection Test A, pp. 120–122
   Selection Test B, pp. 123–125
   Benchmark Test 3, pp. 126–131

General Resources
   Rubric for Speaking: Delivering a
   Persuasive Speech, p. 89

Go **Online** Students may use the **Self-test**
—Assessment— to prepare for **Selection Test A** or
Selection Test B.

Benchmark
Administer **Benchmark Test 3.** If some students need further work, use the Interpretation Guide to determine the appropriate reteaching page in the **Reading Kit** and on **Success Tracker.**

❶ Vocabulary Lesson

Word Analysis

1. *Vocalist* – someone who uses his or her voice
2. *Vocal* – having to do with the voice
3. *Invocation* – the act of calling for something

Spelling Strategy

1. capably   3. dazzlement
2. nestling

Synonyms

1. a   3. b   5. a
2. b   4. c   6. b

❷ Grammar and Style Lesson

1. lies   3. lay   5. laid
2. lay   4. lie

Writing Application

Possible response: They tell me the king went to lie down, and the next thing you know he's dead. It's almost as if his servants wanted to get caught: They laid their daggers on the ground nearby.

❸ Listening and Speaking

- Divide the class into groups. Have each group skim Act II for Ross's lines.
- Ask students to make a list of things Ross says that seem selfish and a list of things that make him seem like a loyal Scot.
- Have some students argue for Ross's loyalty and others argue for his selfishness.
- The **Support for Extend Your Learning** page (*Unit 2 Resources*, p. 118) provides guided note-taking opportunities to help students complete the Extend Your Learning activities.
- Have students use the Rubric for presenting Pros and Cons, p. 92 in *General Resources.*

W/G   **Writing and Grammar, Diamond Level**

Students will find further instruction and practice on commonly confused words *lie* and *lay* in Chapter 25, Section 2.

341

✓ Meeting Your Standards

Students will

1. **analyze and respond to literary elements.**
   - Literary Analysis: Conflict

2. **read, comprehend, analyze, and critique a drama.**
   - Reading Strategy: Reading Between the Lines
   - Reading Check questions
   - Apply the Skills questions
   - Assessment Practice (ATE)

3. **develop vocabulary.**
   - Vocabulary Lesson: Latin Prefix: *mal-*

4. **understand and apply written and oral language conventions**
   - Spelling Strategy
   - Grammar and Style Lesson: Subject and Verb Agreement

5. **develop writing proficiency.**
   - Writing Lesson: Response to Criticism (follows Act V)

6. **develop appropriate research strategies.**
   - Extend Your Learning: Annotated Bibliography

7. **develop writing strategies.**
   - Extend Your Learning: Diary Entry

Block Scheduling: Use one 90-minute class period to preteach the skills and have students read the selection. Use a second 90-minute class period to assess students' mastery of skills, extend their learning, and monitor their progress.

Homework Suggestions

Following are possibilities for homework assignments.

- Support pages from *Unit 2 Resources:*
  - Literary Analysis
  - Reading Strategy
  - Vocabulary Builder
  - Grammar and Style

- An Extend Your Learning project and the Writing Lesson for this selection may be completed over several days.

Step-by-Step Teaching Guide	Pacing Guide
PRETEACH	
• Administer Vocabulary and Reading Warm-ups as necessary.	5 min.
• Engage students' interest with the motivation activity.	5 min.
• Introduce the Literary Analysis Skill: Conflict. **FT**	5 min.
• Introduce the Reading Strategy: Reading Between the Lines. **FT**	10 min.
• Prepare students to read by teaching the selection vocabulary. **FT**	
TEACH	
• Informally monitor comprehension while students read independently or in groups. **FT**	30 min.
• Monitor students' comprehension with the Reading Check notes.	as students read
• Reinforce vocabulary with Vocabulary Builder notes.	as students read
• Develop students' understanding of conflict with the Literary Analysis annotations. **FT**	5 min.
• Develop students' ability to read between the lines with the Reading Strategy annotations. **FT**	5 min.
ASSESS/EXTEND	
• Assess students' comprehension and mastery of the Literary Analysis and Reading Strategy by having them answer the Apply the Skills questions. **FT**	15 min.
• Have students complete the Vocabulary Lesson and the Grammar and Style Lesson. **FT**	15 min.
• Apply students' understanding by using one or more of the Extend Your Learning activities.	20–90 min. or homework
• Administer Selection Test A or Selection Test B. **FT**	15 min.

Resources

Choosing Resources for Differentiated Instruction

[**L1**] Special Needs Students

[**L2**] Below-Level Students

[**L3**] All Students

[**L4**] Advanced Students

[**EL**] English Learners

For Vocabulary and Reading Warm-ups and for Selection Tests, **A** signifies "less challenging" and **B** "more challenging." For Graphic Organizer transparencies, **A** signifies "not filled in" and **B** "filled in."

FT Fast Track Instruction: To move the lesson more quickly, use the strategies and activities identified with **FT**.

Scaffolding for Less Proficient and Advanced Students

The leveled Critical Thinking questions after selections progress in the levels of thinking required to answer them. To address the needs of your different students, you may use the (a) level questions for your less proficient students and the (b) level questions with your on-level and advanced students. The occasional (c) level questions are appropriate for your advanced students.

PRENTICE HALL

TeacherEXPRESS™ Use this complete
Plan · Teach · Assess   suite of powerful
teaching tools to make lesson planning and testing quicker and easier.

PRENTICE HALL

StudentEXPRESS™ Use the interac-
Learn · Study · Succeed   tive textbook
(online and on CD-ROM) to make selections and activities come alive with audio and video support and interactive questions.

Monitoring Progress

Before students read Act III, administer **Diagnostic Test 4** (*Unit 2 Resources,* pp. 132–134).

Go **Online**
Professional Development
For: Information about Lexiles
Visit: www.PHSchool.com
Web Code: eue-1111

Macbeth, Act III

Motivation

Motivation

Write on the board: "To be thus [king] is nothing, but to be safely thus" (III, i, 48). Ask students: What might Macbeth mean by this statement? Students should realize that Macbeth has achieved his desire, but he is not satisfied. Have students discuss ways in which Macbeth might try to ensure the safety of his position. Who might pose a threat? Based on this quotation, have students predict the course of action in Act III.

❶ Literary Analysis
Conflict

Conflict—the struggle between two forces—is what creates drama.

* An **external conflict** is a struggle between two characters or groups.
* An **internal conflict** is a struggle within a character.

The **climax** of a play is the point at which the internal and external conflicts are greatest. The action rises to the climax—the moment of highest tension—and then falls as the conflicts are resolved.

In Act III of *Macbeth,* notice how the rising action leads the new king to a state dinner and the sight of a guest—a guest who should not be there!

Connecting Literary Elements

Macbeth makes this critical remark to Banquo at Act III, Scene i, line 27: "Fail not our feast."

This invitation is an example of dramatic irony, a device that playwrights use to heighten conflict. **Dramatic irony** occurs when the words or actions of a character take on a meaning for the audience or readers different from the one the character intends. Observe how Macbeth's remark takes on dramatic irony as events unfold, and becomes a different kind of invitation, answered by a different kind of guest.

❷ Reading Strategy
Reading Between the Lines

By connecting a character's remark to later events, you are **reading between the lines**—linking different parts of the play and finding their deeper meanings. Reading line by line tells you *what* happens, but reading between the lines tells you *why*. Fill in a chart like this one to help you read between the lines of Act III.

Vocabulary Builder

indissoluble (in´ di säl´ yōō bəl) *adj.* not able to be dissolved or undone (p. 343)

dauntless (dônt´ lis) *adj.* fearless; cannot be intimidated (p. 344)

jocund (jäk´ ənd) *adj.* cheerful; jovial (p. 348)

infirmity (in fur´ mə tē) *n.* physical or mental defect; illness (p. 353)

malevolence (mə lev´ ə ləns) *n.* ill will; spitefulness (p. 357)

❶ Literary Analysis
Conflict

* Tell students that, as they read Act III of *Macbeth,* they should focus on the way in which conflict creates drama.

* Read the definition of conflict together as a class. Discuss examples of internal and external conflicts.

* Read Connecting Literary Elements and discuss the use of dramatic irony to heighten conflict.

❷ Reading Strategy
Reading Between the Lines

* Remind students that what characters say often reveals information about their future behavior.

* Explain that connecting what is said with what has already happened can give clues to what may happen in the future.

* Give students a copy of **Reading Strategy Graphic Organizer A,** p. 62 in *Graphic Organizer Transparencies* to use as they read *Macbeth,* Act III.

Link to I, iii, 65

Witches prophesy that Banquo would f[...] kings. Macbeth may [...] Fleance, Banquo's s[...] as a threat.

Macbeth's Lines, III, i, 3[...]

Banquo is going for a ride. Macbet[...] asks, "Goes Fleanc[...] with you?"

Link to Future Actio[...]

Is Macbeth plann[...] the murder of Ba[...] and Fleance?

❶ Review and Anticipate In Act II, Lady Macbeth drugs
Duncan's guards, enabling Macbeth to kill the king. Macbeth then kills the
guards, too, so that he can more easily blame them for the king's murder.
Duncan's sons, Malcolm and Donalbain, flee, afraid that they will be assas-
sinated by a kinsman eager to claim the throne. Because they run away,
some suspect them of killing their father. As the act closes, it seems that
Macbeth will be named king.

Act III begins with Macbeth on the throne—as the witches had predicted.
All seems to be going well for him, but he feels threatened by Banquo.

Scene i. Forres. The palace.

[*Enter* BANQUO.]

    BANQUO. Thou hast it now: King, Cawdor, Glamis, all,
      As the weird women promised, and I fear
      Thou play'dst most foully for 't. Yet it was said
      It should not stand[1] in thy posterity,
5   But that myself should be the root and father
      Of many kings. If there come truth from them—
      As upon thee, Macbeth, their speeches shine—
      Why, by the verities on thee made good,
      May they not be my oracles as well
10   And set me up in hope? But hush, no more!

[*Sennet*[2] *sounded. Enter* MACBETH *as King,* LADY MACBETH,
LENNOX, ROSS, LORDS, *and* ATTENDANTS.]

    MACBETH. Here's our chief guest.

    LADY MACBETH.   If he had been forgotten,
      It had been as a gap in our great feast,
      And all-thing[3] unbecoming.

    MACBETH. Tonight we hold a solemn[4] supper, sir,
      And I'll request your presence.

15 **BANQUO.**   Let your Highness
      Command upon me, to the which my duties
      Are with a most <u>indissoluble</u> tie
      For ever knit.

    MACBETH. Ride you this afternoon?

    BANQUO.   Ay, my good lord.

20 **MACBETH.** We should have else desired your good advice
      (Which still hath been both grave and prosperous[5])

Macbeth, Act III, Scene i ■ 343

❷ ◀ Critical Viewing
After wielding a dagger
like this against Duncan,
can Macbeth expect to
rule in peace? Explain.
[Predict]

1. **stand** continue.

2. **Sennet** trumpet call.

3. **all-thing** altogether.

4. **solemn** ceremonious.

5. **grave and prosperous**
weighty and profitable.

Vocabulary Builder
indissoluble (in´ di säl´ yo͞o
bəl) *adj.* not able to be
dissolved or undone

❹ ✓ Reading Check
What does Banquo
suspect about Macbeth?

---

❶ About the Selection
Act III marks a turning point in the
action. Up until now, things have
gone very much the way Macbeth
had planned. However, his sense of
insecurity leads him to fear Banquo
and his offspring. When his plan to
murder Banquo and his son is only
partially successful, a series of events
is set in motion, leading to Macbeth's
downfall.

❷ Critical Viewing
Possible response: Macbeth has
begun his reign in blood and violence; he cannot expect to rule in
peace.

❸ Reading Strategy
Reading Between the Lines
• Direct students' attention to
lines 1–10. **Ask** them to consider
Banquo's speech and to discuss
what threat Banquo poses to
Macbeth. Why might Banquo have
kept the information about the
witches to himself?
Possible responses: Banquo
poses a threat because if he tells
what he knows, he might cast suspicion on Macbeth. He may have
kept the information to himself to
use to his advantage, or he may
have been afraid that telling others
might implicate him in the murder.
After all, he was promised that his
descendants would be kings.

• In the lines that follow, Macbeth
is cordial and invites Banquo to a
feast. Banquo, in turn, pledges loyalty. **Ask** students if they think
either is sincere.

• In lines 18 and following, Macbeth
questions Banquo about his afternoon ride, when and where he is
going. **Ask** students why they
think Macbeth might want to know
this.
Answer: Macbeth is worried about
Banquo and wants to keep an eye
on him. Some students may even
suspect additional foul play.

❹ Reading Check
Answer: Banquo suspects that
Macbeth was involved in foul play
to bring about what the witches
prophesied.

343

- Have students look at lines 29–32.

- Remind students that the term *cousin* in the Elizabethan period meant kinsman, not necessarily an actual cousin.

- Then, **ask** them who are the "bloody cousins" referred to by Macbeth. What do we learn about these "cousins"?
  Answer: Duncan's sons are the "bloody cousins," because they are rumored to have plotted their father's murder. We learn that they have reached England and Ireland and are telling "lies"—which, coming from the actual murderer, Macbeth, means they are probably telling the truth.

❻ Critical Thinking
Analyze

- **Review** what the witches promised Macbeth and Banquo when they visited them in Act I.

  Answer: They promised that Macbeth would be king, and that Banquo's heirs will be kings.

- Have students **divide** the soliloquy into two parts and describe the topics of each of the two parts.

  Answer: The first part of the soliloquy runs from lines 48 to 57. It reveals that Macbeth fears Banquo. The second part runs from the middle of line 57 through line 72. In this part, Macbeth reveals his resentment of the prophecy that Banquo's descendants, not his own, will sit on the throne in the future.

In this day's council; but we'll take tomorrow.
Is't far you ride?

BANQUO. As far, my lord, as will fill up the time
25 'Twixt this and supper. Go not my horse the better,[6]
I must become a borrower of the night
For a dark hour or twain.

MACBETH. Fail not our feast.

BANQUO. My lord, I will not.

MACBETH. We hear our bloody cousins are bestowed
30 In England and in Ireland, not confessing
Their cruel parricide, filling their hearers
With strange invention.[7] But of that tomorrow,
When therewithal we shall have cause of state
Craving us jointly.[8] Hie you to horse. Adieu,
35 Till you return at night. Goes Fleance with you?

BANQUO. Ay, my good lord: our time does call upon 's.

MACBETH. I wish your horses swift and sure of foot,
And so I do commend you to their backs.
Farewell.   [*Exit* BANQUO.]
40 Let every man be master of his time
Till seven at night. To make society
The sweeter welcome, we will keep ourself
Till suppertime alone. While[9] then, God be with you!

          [*Exit* LORDS *and all but* MACBETH *and a* SERVANT.]

Sirrah,[10] a word with you: attend those men
45 Our pleasure?

ATTENDANT. They are, my lord, without the palace gate.

MACBETH. Bring them before us.   [*Exit* SERVANT.]
To be thus[11] is nothing, but[12] to be safely thus—
Our fears in Banquo stick deep,
50 And in his royalty of nature reigns that
Which would be feared. 'Tis much he dares;
And, to[13] that <u>dauntless</u> temper of his mind,
He hath a wisdom that doth guide his valor
To act in safety. There is none but he
55 Whose being I do fear: and under him
My genius is rebuked,[14] as it is said
Mark Antony's was by Caesar. He chid[15] the sisters,
When first they put the name of King upon me,
And bade them speak to him; then prophetlike
60 They hailed him father to a line of kings.
Upon my head they placed a fruitless crown
And put a barren scepter in my gripe,[16]

344 ■ Celebrating Humanity (1485–1625)

6. Go not . . . better unless my horse goes faster than I expect.

7. invention lies.

8. cause . . . jointly matters of state demanding our joint attention.

9. While until.

10. Sirrah common address to an inferior.

11. thus king.

12. but unless.

Vocabulary Builder
dauntless (dônt' lis) *adj.*
fearless; cannot be intimidated

13. to added to.

14. genius is rebuked guardian spirit is cowed.

15. chid scolded.

16. gripe grip.

Enrichment

Plutarch

Though he was also a mathematician, philosopher, world traveler, politician, educator, and priest of the Delphic oracle, the reputation of the Greek essayist and biographer Plutarch (A.D. 46–c. 119) rested on his writing. Of all his works, the most important is *Parallel Lives*. This collection contains biographies of every important soldier, leader, and orator of ancient Rome and Greece.

Plutarch's *Lives* was translated into English in the 16th century. It became the story source for Shakespeare's Roman history plays but also influenced the development of his concept of the tragic hero.

While the mention of Mark Antony and Caesar in Scene i, line 57, clearly connects with Plutarch's reports of their lives, there are other elements that Plutarch contributed to *Macbeth*. In his *Life of Caesar,* he reports of strange phenomena at Caesar's death (such as "noises heard in the night"), prophecies and omens, and Caesar's ghost appearing to his murderers (which also occurs in Shakespeare's *Julius Caesar*).

Thence to be wrenched with an unlineal hand,
No son of mine succeeding. If 't be so,
65 For Banquo's issue have I filed[17] my mind;
For them the gracious Duncan have I murdered;
Put rancors in the vessel of my peace
Only for them, and mine eternal jewel[18]
Given to the common enemy of man,[19]
70 To make them kings, the seeds of Banquo kings!
Rather than so, come, fate, into the list,
And champion me to th' utterance![20] Who's there?

[*Enter* SERVANT *and* TWO MURDERERS.]

Now go to the door, and stay there till we call.

[*Exit* SERVANT.]

Was it not yesterday we spoke together?

MURDERERS. It was, so please your Highness.

75 **MACBETH.**   Well then, now
Have you considered of my speeches? Know
That it was he in the times past, which held you
So under fortune,[21] which you thought had been
Our innocent self: this I made good to you
80 In our last conference; passed in probation[22] with you,
How you were born in hand,[23] how crossed, the instruments,
Who wrought with them, and all things else that might
To half a soul[24] and to a notion[25] crazed
Say "Thus did Banquo."

FIRST MURDERER.   You made it known to us.

85 **MACBETH.** I did so; and went further, which is now
Our point of second meeting. Do you find
Your patience so predominant in your nature,
That you can let this go? Are you so gospeled,[26]
To pray for this good man and for his issue,
90 Whose heavy hand hath bowed you to the grave
And beggared yours for ever?

FIRST MURDERER.   We are men, my liege.

MACBETH. Ay, in the catalogue ye go for[27] men;
As hounds and greyhounds, mongrels, spaniels, curs,
Shoughs, water-rugs[28] and demi-wolves, are clept[29]
95 All by the name of dogs: the valued file[30]
Distinguishes the swift, the slow, the subtle,
The housekeeper, the hunter, every one
According to the gift which bounteous nature
Hath in him closed,[31] whereby he does receive
100 Particular addition,[32] from the bill

---

17. **filed** defiled.

18. **eternal jewel** soul.

19. **common . . . man** the Devil.

20. **champion me to th' utterance** Fight against me to the death.

21. **held . . . fortune** kept you from good fortune.

22. **passed in probation** reviewed the proofs.

23. **born in hand** deceived.

24. **half a soul** halfwit.

25. **notion** mind.

26. **gospeled** ready to forgive.

27. **go for** pass as.

28. **Shoughs** (shuks), **water-rugs** shaggy dogs, long-haired dogs.

29. **clept** called.

Reading Strategy

Reading Between the Lines What does the first murderer mean in line 91 when he answers Macbeth, "We are men"?

30. **valued file** classification by valuable traits.

31. **closed** enclosed.

32. **addition** distinction (to set it apart from other dogs).

9 ✓ **Reading Check**

Why does Macbeth fear Banquo?

Macbeth, Act III, Scene i ■ 345

---

7 **Critical Thinking**
Infer

- Direct students' attention to Macbeth's speech in lines 75–84.
- **Ask** students what they can infer about what Macbeth has told these men.
  Answer: He appears to have told them that whatever miseries they have suffered can be blamed on Banquo.
- **Ask** students why he might have told them this.
  Answer: He wanted to give them a reason to murder Banquo, to motivate them in a way that would make them feel that they would be solving a problem of their own.

8 **Reading Strategy**
Reading Between the Lines

- Ask students to think about the comment made by the first murderer in line 91.
- Have students reread Lady Macbeth's views on manhood in Act I, Scene vii, lines 49–54 (p. 322).
- Then, **ask** students the Reading Strategy question: What does the first murderer mean in line 91 when he answers Macbeth, "We are men"?
  Answer: The murderer means that they, as men, would not let such an outrage go unpunished, which echoes Lady Macbeth's earlier views that it is manly to kill someone who stands in your way.

9 **Reading Check**

Answer: Macbeth fears Banquo because Banquo knows about the prophecies and might be suspicious. Also, if Banquo's descendants will be kings, Macbeth will have no heir on the throne. Both things are a threat to Macbeth.

Differentiated
Instruction   Solutions for All Learners

Support for Less Proficient Readers
Help students "read between the lines." Read Banquo's speech as a group. Ask students how much Banquo knows about what Macbeth has done. Also, discuss Banquo's reasons for imagining himself the father of kings. When you finish, analyze one of Macbeth's speeches on page 344 or 345.

Vocabulary for English Learners
Make certain students understand the definitions given in the side notes. For example, on the facing page, the definition of *dauntless* includes the words *fearless* and *intimidated*, both of which might be new to English learners. Pronounce the words, and make certain students understand them in the story's context.

Strategy for Advanced Readers
Allow students to read Act III independently. Have them note lines or speeches that are clues about what is going to happen. Then, have them note where in the play their suspicions are confirmed. Suggest that they also note events that remind them of clues they didn't previously write down, even from other acts.

▶ **Reteach:** Review with students their understanding of internal and external conflicts. Reread the definition of conflict on p. 342. Explain to students that a conflict can have both internal and external dimensions at the same time.

▶ **Monitor Progress: Ask** students the Literary Analysis question: What conflict does Macbeth express in lines 116–126?
Answer: The external conflicts are between Macbeth and Banquo and between Macbeth and public opinion. An internal conflict, though not directly stated, may be identified as existing between Macbeth and his fear.

• **Ask** students if they believe the reasons Macbeth gives for not killing Banquo himself. What reasons might he really have for not wanting to kill Banquo himself?
Possible responses: Macbeth's reasons are partially true, because he would lose friends and allies. However, his having the power is doubtful, because none of the things Macbeth has said about Banquo are true. His real reason is that he wants to look innocent of the murder. He also may be concerned about getting injured if he attacks Banquo alone.

⑪ **Critical Thinking**
Analyze

• Direct students' attention to lines 134–139.

• Point out that in this passage, Macbeth refers to Banquo's son, Fleance, almost as if he were an afterthought. **Ask** students how important Fleance's death is to Macbeth and why.
Answer: Fleance's death is very important. The witches said that Banquo would father kings. While Banquo's death is necessary to make Macbeth feel safe, Fleance's death is necessary if Macbeth wants to have his own sons inherit the throne.

• **Ask** students in which speech Macbeth expressed his reasons for wishing to end Banquo's line.
Answer: lines 57–72 of this scene.

346

That writes them all alike: and so of men.
Now if you have a station in the file,[33]
Not i' th' worst rank of manhood, say 't,
And I will put that business in your bosoms
105 Whose execution takes your enemy off,
Grapples you to the heart and love of us,
Who wear our health but sickly in his life,[34]
Which in his death were perfect.

SECOND MURDERER.   I am one, my liege,
Whom the vile blows and buffets of the world
110 Hath so incensed that I am reckless what
I do to spite the world.

FIRST MURDERER.   And I another
So weary with disasters, tugged with fortune,
That I would set[35] my life on any chance,
To mend it or be rid on 't.

MACBETH.   Both of you
Know Banquo was your enemy.

115 **BOTH MURDERERS.**   True, my lord.

MACBETH. So is he mine, and in such bloody distance[36]
That every minute of his being thrusts
Against my near'st of life:[37] and though I could
With barefaced power sweep him from my sight
120 And bid my will avouch[38] it, yet I must not,
For certain friends that are both his and mine,
Whose loves I may not drop, but wail his fall[39]
Who I myself struck down: and thence it is
That I to your assistance do make love,
125 Masking the business from the common eye
For sundry weighty reasons.

SECOND MURDERER.   We shall, my lord,
Perform what you command us.

FIRST MURDERER.   Though our lives—

MACBETH. Your spirits shine through you. Within this hour at most
I will advise you where to plant yourselves,
130 Acquaint you with the perfect spy o' th' time,
The moment on 't;[40] for 't must be done tonight,
And something[41] from the palace; always thought[42]
That I require a clearness:[43] and with him—
To leave no rubs[44] nor botches in the work—
135 Fleance his son, that keeps him company,
Whose absence is no less material to me
Than is his father's, must embrace the fate

346 ■ *Celebrating Humanity (1485–1625)*

---

33. file ranks.

34. wear . . . life are sick as long as he lives.

35. set risk.

36. distance disagreement.

37. near'st of life most vital parts.

38. avouch justify.

39. wail his fall (I must) bewail his death.

Literary Analysis
Conflict What conflict does Macbeth express in lines 116–126?

40. the perfect . . . on't exact information of the exact time.

41. something some distance.

42. thought remembered.

43. clearness freedom from suspicion.

44. rubs flaws.

Of that dark hour. Resolve yourselves apart:[45]
I'll come to you anon.

MURDERERS.   We are resolved, my lord.

140 **MACBETH.** I'll call upon you straight.[46] Abide within.
It is concluded: Banquo, thy soul's flight,
If it find heaven, must find it out tonight.   [*Exit.*]

Scene ii. The palace.

[*Enter* MACBETH'S LADY *and a* SERVANT.]

LADY MACBETH. Is Banquo gone from court?

SERVANT. Ay, madam, but returns again tonight.

LADY MACBETH. Say to the King, I would attend his leisure
For a few words.

SERVANT.   Madam, I will.   [*Exit.*]

LADY MACBETH.   Nought's had, all's spent,
5   Where our desire is got without content:
'Tis safer to be that which we destroy
Than by destruction dwell in doubtful joy.

[*Enter* MACBETH.]

How now, my lord! Why do you keep alone,
Of sorriest fancies your companions making,
10 Using those thoughts which should indeed have died
With them they think on? Things without all remedy
Should be without regard: what's done is done.

MACBETH. We have scotched[1] the snake, not killed it:
She'll close[2] and be herself, whilst our poor malice
15 Remains in danger of her former tooth.[3]
But let the frame of things disjoint,[4] both the worlds[5] suffer,
Ere we will eat our meal in fear, and sleep
In the affliction of these terrible dreams
That shake us nightly: better be with the dead,
20 Whom we, to gain our peace, have sent to peace,
Than on the torture of the mind to lie
In restless ecstasy.[6] Duncan is in his grave;
After life's fitful fever he sleeps well.
Treason has done his worst: nor steel, nor poison,
25 Malice domestic, foreign levy,[7] nothing,
Can touch him further.

LADY MACBETH.   Come on.
Gentle my lord, sleek o'er your rugged looks;
Be bright and jovial among your guests tonight.

MACBETH. So shall I, love; and so, I pray, be you:

---

45. Resolve yourselves apart Make your own decision.

46. straight immediately.

Reading Strategy
Reading Between the Lines In Scene ii, lines 4–7, what has Lady Macbeth realized about her actions?

1. scotched wounded.

2. close heal.

3. in . . . tooth in as much danger as before.

4. frame of things disjoint universe collapse.

5. both the worlds heaven and earth.

6. ecstasy frenzy.

7. Malice . . . levy civil and foreign war.

Reading Check
What does Macbeth ask the murderers to do?

Macbeth, Act III, Scene ii ■ 347

⓬ Reading Strategy
Reading Between the Lines

- **Ask** students the Reading Strategy question: In Scene ii, lines 4–7, what has Lady Macbeth realized about her actions?
  Answer: Lady Macbeth is realizing that she and Macbeth have paid a very high price for desires that have left them discontented and worried.

- Point out that her feelings reflect something of the uncertainty that Macbeth is feeling, but with a difference. She is beginning to sound doubtful about their actions.

- **Discuss** with students why they think her four lines might be rhymed, when rhyme is normally saved for the end of a scene.
  Possible response: They might reflect a turning point for Lady Macbeth.

- Explain that, in showing uncertainty, she has now changed places with Macbeth. He was doubtful before Duncan's murder, now she is. We already know more than Lady Macbeth does—that Macbeth has ordered the murder of Banquo and Fleance. We see in the speeches that make up the rest of the scene that Macbeth is now the one in charge and determined to work evilly.

⓭ Critical Thinking
Analyze

- Direct students' attention to lines 13–26.

- Point out that Shakespeare often makes use of the comparison between sleep and death. It was a relatively common comparison of biblical origin. However, Shakespeare uses it masterfully as a thread in the play. Remind students of the speech in Act II, Scene ii, when Macbeth says "Sleep no more! Macbeth does murder sleep."

- **Ask** students who Macbeth feels is sleeping better than he is in this passage.
  Answer: He says that murdered Duncan sleeps better than he does.

⓮ Reading Check

Answer: Macbeth asks the murderers to kill Banquo and his son, Fleance.

Differentiated Instruction   Solutions for All Learners

Strategy for Special Needs Students
To help students visualize the building conflict in the play, list the main characters on the board. Then discuss the conflicts. You may wish to create an additional conflict chart on the board, adding to it as Macbeth runs afoul of additional characters. Discuss the nature of each conflict. Point out how Macbeth's solutions always create both more internal conflict for himself and additional external conflicts.

Strategy for Gifted/Talented Students
Ask students to create a "one-man show," in which the story thus far is told from Macbeth's viewpoint. Have them note his thoughts about the witches, about his wife's speeches, about the murder, about Banquo. They may lift speeches from the play, but encourage them to add their own material. Tell students that they need to prepare only a page or two. Ask them to do a dramatic reading of their creations.

⓯ Humanities

Mrs. Siddons as Lady Macbeth
by G. H. Harlow

The actress depicted in this painting is Sarah Siddons (1755–1831), one of the greatest English actresses of her time. She came from a family of traveling actors and began acting as a child. She played the part of Lady Macbeth early in her career and performed the role at London's Drury Lane theater for the first time in 1785, terrifying audiences with her vivid portrayal of the famous character.

Use these questions for discussion:

1. How does Harlow portray Sarah Siddons as Lady Macbeth?
   Answer: Harlow portrays Lady Macbeth in a timid posture. She is surrounded by darkness. She looks more fearful and demure than sinister. Her white robe gives her an angelic, or perhaps ghostly, appearance.

2. Ask students how this portrait of Lady Macbeth compares with the ones on pp. 319 and 336.
   Possible responses: Most students will say that this portrait portrays Lady Macbeth as quieter, meeker, and more dainty than the other portraits, in which she's depicted as larger than life, vibrant, and wild.

⓰ Critical Viewing

Answer: The clasped hands and sad expression suggest the insecurity and unhappiness in lines 4–7 of Scene ii.

⓱ Literary Analysis
Conflict and Irony

- Remind students that **dramatic irony** occurs when the words or actions of a character take on a meaning different from the one the character intends.

- Have students **discuss** and answer the Literary Analysis question: What is ironic about Macbeth's idea about disguising the couple's real conflict with Banquo?
  Answer: It is ironic that Macbeth is telling Lady Macbeth that they need to disguise their feelings, because he is in the process of having Banquo murdered.

⓯

Mrs. Siddons as Lady Macbeth, G. H. Harlow, Garrick Club, London

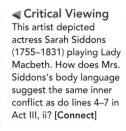

⓰ ◀ **Critical Viewing**
This artist depicted actress Sarah Siddons (1755–1831) playing Lady Macbeth. How does Mrs. Siddons's body language suggest the same inner conflict as do lines 4–7 in Act III, ii? **[Connect]**

Literary Analysis
Conflict and Irony What is ironic about Macbeth's idea about disguising the couple's real conflict with Banquo (Scene ii, lines 30–35)?

8. Present him eminence Honor him.

9. Unsafe . . . lave We are unsafe as long as we have to wash.

10. vizards (viz′ ərdz) masks

11. nature's . . . eterne Nature's lease is not eternal.

Vocabulary Builder
jocund (jäk′ ənd) *adj.* cheerful; jovial

12. shard-borne borne on scaly wings.

---

30   Let your remembrance apply to Banquo;
Present him eminence,[8] both with eye and tongue:
⓱ Unsafe the while, that we must lave[9]
Our honors in these flattering streams
And make our faces vizards[10] to our hearts,
Disguising what they are.

35 **LADY MACBETH.**   You must leave this.

  MACBETH. O, full of scorpions is my mind, dear wife!
    Thou know'st that Banquo, and his Fleance, lives.

  LADY MACBETH. But in them nature's copy's not eterne.[11]

  MACBETH. There's comfort yet; they are assailable.
40   Then be thou jocund. Ere the bat hath flown
    His cloistered flight, ere to black Hecate's summons
    The shard-borne[12] beetle with his drowsy hums

Hath rung night's yawning peal, there shall be done
A deed of dreadful note.

LADY MACBETH. What 's to be done?

45 **MACBETH.** Be innocent of the knowledge, dearest chuck,[13]
Till thou applaud the deed. Come, seeling[14] night,
Scarf up[15] the tender eye of pitiful day,
And with thy bloody and invisible hand
Cancel and tear to pieces that great bond[16]
50 Which keeps me pale! Light thickens, and the crow
Makes wing to th' rooky[17] wood.
Good things of day begin to droop and drowse,
Whiles night's black agents to their preys do rouse.
Thou marvel'st at my words: but hold thee still;
55 Things bad begun make strong themselves by ill:
So, prithee, go with me. [*Exit.*]

Scene iii. Near the palace.

[*Enter* THREE MURDERERS.]

FIRST MURDERER. But who did bid thee join with us?

THIRD MURDERER. Macbeth.

SECOND MURDERER. He needs not our mistrust; since he delivers
Our offices[1] and what we have to do
To the direction just.[2]

FIRST MURDERER. Then stand with us.
5 The west yet glimmers with some streaks of day.
Now spurs the lated traveler apace
To gain the timely inn, and near approaches
The subject of our watch.

THIRD MURDERER. Hark! I hear horses.

BANQUO. [*Within*] Give us a light there, ho!

SECOND MURDERER. Then 'tis he. The rest
10 That are within the note of expectation[3]
Already are i' th' court.

FIRST MURDERER. His horses go about.[4]

THIRD MURDERER. Almost a mile: but he does usually—
So all men do—from hence to th' palace gate
Make it their walk.

[*Enter* BANQUO *and* FLEANCE, *with a torch*]

SECOND MURDERER. A light, a light!

THIRD MURDERER. 'Tis he.

---

13. chuck term of endearment.

14. seeling eye-closing. Falconers sometimes sewed a hawk's eyes closed in order to train it.

15. Scarf up blindfold.

16. great bond between Banquo and fate.

17. rooky full of rooks, or crows.

Reading Strategy
Reading Between the Lines To what specific action do you think Macbeth is indirectly referring in lines 45–56?

1. offices duties.
2. direction just exact detail.

3. within . . . expectation on the list of expected guests.

4. His . . . about His horses have been taken to the stable.

Reading Check
What does Macbeth tell Lady Macbeth and what does he hold back from her?

Macbeth, Act III, Scene iii ■ 349

349

- **Ask** students to **provide** a review of the events of scene iii.
  Answer: A mystery murderer has joined the two hired to kill Banquo. Banquo and his son approach on horseback but dismount and walk the rest of the way to the castle. The three murderers set on them. Fleance escapes and Banquo is killed.

- Remind students that Banquo is a great warrior, and it is likely that his son, who is probably a teenager, is also skilled in battle. So, it is likely that Fleance could escape the fight.

- **Ask** students why Fleance's escape creates an external conflict for Macbeth.
  Answer: Macbeth had hoped to cheat fate. He had hoped that, though the witches' predictions came true about him, he could keep them from coming true about Banquo and the promised line of kings to come from Banquo.

- Tell students that many scholars consider the climax of the play to occur with the stage directions "Exit Fleance." **Ask** students why Fleance's escape is important to the drama.
  Answer: The escape is important because it means that Macbeth still has an enemy to reckon with and the witches' prophecy about Banquo's heirs can still come true. It is the first time that one of Macbeth's plans has gone wrong. It also means someone has lived to tell of an attempted murder, which might lead people to doubt the original story about Duncan's murder—especially because Banquo had probably told Fleance about the prophecies and his concerns.

- Tell students that, though some scholars feel that Fleance's exit is the climax, others believe the climax is in line 21, when Macbeth learns that Fleance has escaped. You may wish to have students discuss in class which event they feel is more climactic.

350

---

15 **FIRST MURDERER.**   Stand to 't

BANQUO. It will be rain tonight.

FIRST MURDERER.   Let it come down.

[*They set upon* BANQUO.]

BANQUO. O, treachery! Fly, good Fleance, fly, fly, fly!

                              [*Exit* FLEANCE.]

                    Thou mayst revenge. O slave! [*Dies.*]

21

THIRD MURDERER. Who did strike out the light?

FIRST MURDERER.   Was't not the way?[5]   **5. way** thing to do.

20 **THIRD MURDERER.** There's but one down; the son is fled.

SECOND MURDERER. We have lost best half of our affair.

FIRST MURDERER. Well, let 's away and say how much is done.

                              [*Exit.*]

Scene iv. The palace.

[*Banquet prepared. Enter* MACBETH, LADY MACBETH, ROSS, LENNOX, LORDS, *and* ATTENDANTS.]

MACBETH. You know your own degrees;[1] sit down: **1. degrees** ranks. At state
    At first and last, the hearty welcome.   banquets guests were seated
                                                          according to rank.

LORDS. Thanks to your Majesty.

MACBETH. Ourself will mingle with society[2]   **2. society** company.
5   And play the humble host.
    Our hostess keeps her state,[3] but in best time   **3. keeps her state** remains
    We will require[4] her welcome.   seated on her throne.

                                                          4. require request.
LADY MACBETH. Pronounce it for me, sir, to all our friends,
    For my heart speaks they are welcome.

[*Enter* FIRST MURDERER.]

10 **MACBETH.** See, they encounter thee with their hearts' thanks.
    Both sides are even: here I'll sit i' th' midst:
    Be large in mirth; anon we'll drink a measure[5]   **5. measure** toast.
    The table round. [*Goes to* MURDERER] There's blood upon thy face.

MURDERER. 'Tis Banquo's then.

15 **MACBETH.** 'Tis better thee without than he within.[6]   **6. thee . . . within** you
    Is he dispatched?   outside than he inside.

MURDERER. My lord, his throat is cut; that I did for him.

MACBETH. Thou art the best o' th' cutthroats.
    Yet he's good that did the like for Fleance;
20   If thou didst it, thou art the nonpareil.[7]   **7. nonpareil** without equal.

350 ■ Celebrating Humanity (1485–1625)

Enrichment

Ghosts

When Shakespeare included ghosts in his plays, he knew that many people believed in restless spirits who returned to Earth. Some people in Western culture believe that the ghosts of murdered people appear to seek retribution (an idea at least 1,600 years old at the time Shakespeare picked it up).

Though the idea of ghosts or restless spirits is fairly universal, different groups have different views. Some groups of Native Americans and Pacific Islanders believe that ghosts return to Earth for both good and evil purposes. Some members of these cultures perform ceremonies to call forth the ghosts and ask for their help in earthly matters.

In Australia, traditional Aboriginal groups would leave a campsite when someone died, to avoid the person's spirits. In Asia, some people honor the spirits of dead ancestors, which are believed to bring good fortune to families who show proper respect.

In Western cultures, some people are afraid of ghosts, while others are fascinated by them.

MURDERER. Most royal sir, Fleance is 'scaped.

MACBETH. [*Aside*] Then comes my fit again: I had else been perfect,
　　Whole as the marble, founded as the rock,
　　As broad and general as the casing[8] air:
25　But now I am cabined, cribbed, confined, bound in
　　To saucy[9] doubts and fears.—But Banquo's safe?

MURDERER. Ay, my good lord: safe in a ditch he bides,
　　With twenty trenchèd[10] gashes on his head,
　　The least a death to nature.[11]

MACBETH.　　　　　　　　　　Thanks for that.
30　[*Aside*] There the grown serpent lies; the worm that's fled
　　Hath nature that in time will venom breed,
　　No teeth for th' present. Get thee gone. Tomorrow
　　We'll hear ourselves[12] again.　　　　　　[*Exit* MURDERER.]

LADY MACBETH.　　　　　　My royal lord,
　　You do not give the cheer.[13] The feast is sold
35　That is not often vouched, while 'tis a-making,
　　'Tis given with welcome.[14] To feed were best at home;
　　From thence, the sauce to meat is ceremony;[15]
　　Meeting were bare without it.

[*Enter the* GHOST *of* BANQUO *and sits in* MACBETH'S *place.*]

MACBETH.　　　　　　　　Sweet remembrancer!
　　Now good digestion wait on appetite,
　　And health on both!

40　**LENNOX.**　　　　　　May't please your Highness sit.

MACBETH. Here had we now our country's honor roofed,[16]
　　Were the graced person of our Banquo present—

8. **as . . . casing** as unrestrained as the surrounding.

9. **saucy** insolent.

10. **trenchèd** trenchlike.

11. **nature** natural life.

12. **hear ourselves** talk it over.

13. **give the cheer** make the guests feel welcome.

14. **The feast . . . welcome** The feast at which the host fails to make the guests feel welcome while the food is being prepared is no more than a bought dinner.

15. **From . . . ceremony** Ceremony adds a pleasant flavor to the food.

16. **our . . . roofed** the most honorable men in the country under one roof.

 Reading Check

What do the murderers fail to do?

Literature in Context

Cultural Connection

Stagecraft at the Globe

　　It took some sophisticated Elizabethan theatrics to manage entrances and exits such as those of Banquo's ghost. (Macbeth reacts to the ghost in this picture.) In the farthest reaches of the Globe theater's stage was a small area called the rear stage, which was open to the audience but enclosed by a wall at the back and cloth hangings on the sides. A trapdoor in the floor of the rear stage was the means by which Banquo's ghost made an entrance. The trapdoor operated silently, and it was not completely visible to the audience.

Connect to the Literature

What other characters in *Macbeth* might have used a trapdoor for exits or entrances?

Macbeth, Act III, Scene iv ■ *351*

22 Literary Analysis
Dramatic Irony

- Explain that this scene contains asides within asides. Macbeth is obviously off to the side talking to the blood-soaked murderers, because no one else sees them (their appearance would certainly have raised questions). Within this side conversation, Macbeth directs asides to the audience.

- Tell students that the word *worm* in line 30 had a different meaning in Shakespeare's day. Then, it was often used as another word for snake. **Ask** students if lines 30–33 remind them of anything else Macbeth has said recently about snakes.
Answer: In Scene ii, lines 13–15, Macbeth speaks of danger in general as being a snake and says that killing Duncan has wounded the snake but not killed it. Killing Banquo and Fleance was a way to remove that danger.

- **Ask** students to identify the dramatic irony in Macbeth's speech as he converses with his guests.
Answer: In lines 41–42, Macbeth says that everything would be perfect if Banquo were there. In reality, he has done everything possible to ensure that Banquo will not be there—he has had Banquo murdered.

23 Literature in Context

Cultural Connection *Macbeth* is not the only play that needed a trapdoor for a ghost. Another famous apparition was "Great Caesar's ghost" in Shakespeare's *Julius Caesar*. In fact, astonishing entrances were included in most writers' works—special effects have always been popular.

Connect to the Literature Ask students what other supernatural characters appear in Macbeth. Then, **ask** the Connect to the Literature question: What other characters in *Macbeth* might have used a trapdoor for exits or entrances?
Answer: The three witches might have used a trapdoor.

24 Reading Check

Answer: The murderers fail to kill Fleance.

Differentiated
Instruction　　Solutions for All Learners

Enrichment for Gifted/Talented Students
Explain that Shakespeare's plays have provided inspiration to many artists over the centuries. Some of the best-known works inspired by *Macbeth* are included in the Student Edition. Have students review these paintings. Students may also wish to find other images by looking at other versions of this play. Then, encourage students to choose a setting, character, or event from *Macbeth* and capture it artistically.

Enrichment for Advanced Readers
Tell students that, quite obviously, special effects have changed a lot over the centuries. Movies depend on computers and other technologies to create effects. However, though theater effects are now more sophisticated, they still depend on trapdoors for surprise entries. Have students study the current state of the art in special effects, either for theaters or for movies. Alternatively, they may wish to compare how the same effect would be created on film versus stage. Have students share their discoveries with the class.

25 Reading Strategy
Reading Between the Lines

- After students have read scene iv, **ask** them how it is consistent with the play thus far.
Answer: Macbeth has seen floating daggers, and Duncan's death was accompanied by strange events, so a ghost fits right in.

- Macbeth is very agitated. Note that, in lines 22–26, after learning of Fleance's escape, he says "Then comes my fit again" and goes on to describe how he is again the prisoner of his fears.

- **Ask** the Reading Strategy question: How might you connect Macbeth's agitation with his knowledge that Fleance has escaped?
Answer: Macbeth is concerned about the power the witches predicted for Fleance and is upset that his latest murder plot was not successful and might, therefore, be discovered.

- Remind students of the scene in which Macbeth saw the "air-drawn dagger" of which Lady Macbeth speaks (Act II, scene i, lines 33–47).

- **Ask** students what Macbeth's comments in lines 76–84 indicate about his view of murder.
Answer: Macbeth seems to view murder as not human or civilized, but not particularly evil. His comments indicate that he is more unnerved by seeing ghosts than he is concerned about the immorality of his actions.

26 Literary Analysis
Conflict

▶ **Reteach:** Remind students that an **external conflict** is a struggle between two characters or groups and an **internal conflict** is a struggle within a character.

▶ **Monitor Progress: Ask** the Literary Analysis question: How does the incident with Banquo's ghost convey Macbeth's inner conflict?
Answer: The ghost appears when Macbeth mentions Banquo, indicating that he may be feeling guilty about Banquo's death, or at least worried and fearful of consequences. Macbeth's shock at the sight of the ghost reveals his agitation—both about the actions he has taken and the course of future events.

Who may I rather challenge for unkindness
Than pity for mischance![17]

ROSS.   His absence, sir,
45 Lays blame upon his promise. Please 't your Highness
To grace us with your royal company?

MACBETH. The table's full.

LENNOX. Here is a place reserved, sir.

MACBETH. Where?

LENNOX. Here, my good lord. What is 't that moves your Highness?

MACBETH. Which of you have done this?

50 **LORDS.**   What, my good lord?

MACBETH. Thou canst not say I did it. Never shake
Thy gory locks at me.

ROSS. Gentlemen, rise, his Highness is not well.

LADY MACBETH. Sit, worthy friends. My lord is often thus,
55 And hath been from his youth. Pray you, keep seat.
The fit is momentary; upon a thought[18]
He will again be well. If much you note him,
You shall offend him and extend his passion.[19]
Feed, and regard him not.—Are you a man?

60 **MACBETH.** Ay, and a bold one, that dare look on that
Which might appall the devil.

LADY MACBETH.   O proper stuff!
This is the very painting of your fear.
This is the air-drawn dagger which, you said,
Led you to Duncan. O, these flaws[20] and starts,
65 Impostors to true fear, would well become
A woman's story at a winter's fire,
Authorized[21] by her grandam. Shame itself!
Why do you make such faces? When all's done,
You look but on a stool.

MACBETH.   Prithee, see there!
70 Behold! Look! Lo! How say you?
Why, what care I? If thou canst nod, speak too.
If charnel houses[22] and our graves must send
Those that we bury back, our monuments
Shall be the maws of kites.[23]   [*Exit* GHOST.]

75 **LADY MACBETH.**   What, quite unmanned in folly?

MACBETH. If I stand here, I saw him.

LADY MACBETH.   Fie, for shame!

17. Who . . . mischance whom I hope I may reproach for being absent due to discourtesy rather than pity because he has had an accident.

Reading Strategy
Reading Between the Lines How might you connect Macbeth's agitation with his knowledge that Fleance has escaped?

Literary Analysis
Conflict How does the incident with Banquo's ghost convey Macbeth's inner conflict?

18. upon a thought in a moment.

19. passion suffering.

20. flaws gusts of wind; outbursts of emotion.

21. Authorized vouched for.

22. charnel houses vaults containing human bones dug up in making new graves.

23. our . . . kites Our tombs shall be the bellies of birds of prey.

27

28 ◄ **Critical Viewing**
In what ways does the artist's use of light and shadow suggest the conflict in Act III, Scene iv? **[Interpret]**

Scene from Macbeth, Cattermole, The Folger Shakespeare Library, Washington, D.C.

MACBETH. Blood hath been shed ere now, i' th' olden time,
Ere humane statute purged the gentle weal;[24]
Ay, and since too, murders have been performed
Too terrible for the ear. The times has been
80 That, when the brains were out, the man would die,
And there an end; but now they rise again,
With twenty mortal murders on their crowns,[25]
And push us from our stools. This is more strange
Than such a murder is.

LADY MACBETH.   My worthy lord,
Your noble friends do lack you.

85 **MACBETH.**   I do forget.
Do not muse at me, my most worthy friends;
I have a strange infirmity, which is nothing
To those that know me. Come, love and health to all!
Then I'll sit down. Give me some wine, fill full.

[*Enter* GHOST.]

90 I drink to th' general joy o' th' whole table,
And to our dear friend Banquo, whom we miss;
Would he were here! To all and him we thirst,[26]
And all to all.

LORDS.   Our duties, and the pledge.

MACBETH. Avaunt![27] and quit my sight! Let the earth hide thee!
95 Thy bones are marrowless, thy blood is cold;

24. Ere . . . weal before humane laws civilized the state and made it gentle.

25. mortal . . . crowns deadly wounds on their heads.

Vocabulary Builder
infirmity (in fur′ me tē) *n.* physical or mental defect; illness

26. thirst drink.

27. Avaunt Be gone!

29 ✓ **Reading Check**
Why is Macbeth startled at the feast?

Macbeth, Act III, Scene iv ■ *353*

27 Humanities

***Scene from Macbeth*, by George Cattermole**

George Cattermole (1800–1868) was born in Norfolk, England. Trained as an architectural draftsman, he later turned to illustrating historical events, particularly scenes of battles and duels. He is best known for his illustrations and watercolors. Cattermole was good friends with Charles Dickens, whose writings he illustrated. He also created romantic illustrations for works of Lord Byron and Sir Walter Scott. His sense of history drove him to always pay careful attention to such details as the backgrounds and costumes the characters wore.

Use these questions for discussion:

1. Does Macbeth's body language suggest anything about his state of mind?
   Answer: Though Macbeth is depicted as a large, powerful man, his body language suggests that he is fearful and taken aback.

2. What might the bright light in the center of the painting represent?
   Possible response: Some students may say the bright light in the center of the painting represents Macbeth's fear that the truth about his plot will surface. It also highlights the line of kings who will descend from Banquo—the good that will survive Macbeth's evil.

28 Critical Viewing

Possible reponse: The artist's use of shadow may symbolize Macbeth's emotional state: He attempts to stay in the light, acting the jovial host, but the shadows, Banquo's ghost, and Macbeth's guilty conscience keep intruding.

29 Reading Check

Answer: Macbeth is startled at the feast because he sees the ghost of Banquo.

30 Reading Strategy
Reading Between the Lines

• **Ask** students to consider how they would react if they were at a dinner party where the host began to act as Macbeth does.
Possible response: Students will probably say that they would be concerned or afraid that the host was hallucinating, insane, or unwell.

• Have students consider Lady Macbeth's comments in this scene. Then, **ask** them the Reading Strategy question: Do Lady Macbeth's remarks in this scene suggest that she, too, sees the ghost? Why or why not?
Possible response: It seems unlikely that Lady Macbeth sees the ghost, because she is too calm in making excuses, and she is too annoyed with Macbeth's reactions, which she would understand if she saw the ghost. Also, she was not involved in Banquo's murder and doesn't know about it yet, so it is likely that she would react pretty strongly to the gore-soaked image of a butchered Banquo. However, some students may feel that she must see the ghost, because of her own guilt.

• **Ask** students why they think Lady Macbeth is covering up for Macbeth.
Answer: Though it seems likely that she is worried only about Duncan's murder, having not yet been told about Banquo, Lady Macbeth knows that her own security rests on Macbeth's crime remaining a secret. She was an aide in the crime, and would therefore be condemned. Even if Macbeth fell and she escaped punishment, she would no longer be queen, and her ambition is also behind Duncan's murder.

Thou hast no speculation[28] in those eyes
Which thou dost glare with.

LADY MACBETH.   Think of this, good peers,
But as a thing of custom, 'tis no other.
Only it spoils the pleasure of the time.

100 **MACBETH.** What man dare, I dare.
Approach thou like the rugged Russian bear,
The armed rhinoceros, or th' Hyrcan[29] tiger;
Take any shape but that,[30] and my firm nerves
105 Shall never tremble. Or be alive again,
And dare me to the desert[31] with thy sword.
If trembling I inhabit[32] then, protest me
The baby of a girl. Hence, horrible shadow!
Unreal mock'ry, hence!   [*Exit* GHOST.]
                          Why, so: being gone,
I am a man again. Pray you, sit still.

30

LADY MACBETH. You have displaced the mirth, broke the
110 good meeting,
With most admired[33] disorder.

MACBETH.   Can such things be,
And overcome us[34] like a summer's cloud,
Without our special wonder? You make me strange
Even to the disposition that I owe,[35]
115 When now I think you can behold such sights,
And keep the natural ruby of your cheeks,
When mine is blanched with fear.

ROSS.   What sights, my lord?

LADY MACBETH. I pray you, speak not: He grows worse and worse;
Question enrages him: at once, good night.
120 Stand not upon the order of your going,[36]
But go at once.

LENNOX.   Good night; and better health
Attend his Majesty!

LADY MACBETH.   A kind good night to all!
                          [*Exit* LORDS.]

MACBETH. It will have blood, they say: blood will have blood.
Stones have been known to move and trees to speak;
125 Augures and understood relations[37] have
By maggot-pies and choughs[38] and rooks brought forth
The secret'st man of blood.[39] What is the night?

LADY MACBETH. Almost at odds[40] with morning, which is which.

MACBETH. How say'st thou, that Macduff denies his person
At our great bidding?

354 ■ Celebrating Humanity (1485–1625)

28. **speculation** sight.

29. **Hyrcan** (hər′ kən) from Hyrcania, a province of the ancient Persian and Macedonian empires south of the Caspian Sea.

30. **that** Banquo's shape.

31. **desert** place where neither of us could escape.

32. **inhabit** remain indoors.

33. **admired** amazing.

34. **overcome us** come over us.

35. **disposition. . .owe** my own nature.

Reading Strategy
Reading Between the Lines Do Lady Macbeth's remarks in this scene suggest that she, too, sees the ghost? Why or why not?

36. **Stand . . . going** Do not wait to depart in order of rank.

37. **Augures and understood relations** omens and the relationship between the omens and what they represent.

38. **maggot-pies and choughs** (chufs) magpies and crows.

39. **man of blood** murderer.

40. **at odds** disputing.

Enrichment

Hecate and Scene v

Hecate (pronounced *hekaty*—so it would almost rhyme with *angerly* in line 1) was a goddess accepted at an early date into Greek religion. However, she was probably derived from an early people in southwest Asia Minor. The name in Greek means "she who works her will." Hecate was the chief goddess of magic and spells. Because of associations between magic and the moon, she was often identified with the moon-goddess Diana. However, Hecate was considered the infernal aspect of the moon.

Interestingly, it is possible that Shakespeare didn't create this appearance of Hecate in the play. Most scholars believe that this scene was written by someone else. They think it was added because Elizabethan audiences enjoyed the witches so thoroughly. Some attribute the passage to playwright Thomas Middleton (1580–1627), a contemporary of Shakespeare who was known for his social satires. The scene is clever, but contributes nothing to the action of the play.

130 **LADY MACBETH.**   Did you send to him, sir?

   MACBETH. I hear it by the way, but I will send:
        There's not a one of them but in his house
        I keep a servant fee'd.[41] I will tomorrow,
        And betimes[42] I will, to the weird sisters:
135   More shall they speak, for now I am bent[43] to know
        By the worst means the worst. For mine own good

31 All causes shall give way. I am in blood
        Stepped in so far that, should I wade no more,
        Returning were as tedious as go o'er.
140   Strange things I have in head that will to hand,
        Which must be acted ere they may be scanned.[44]

   LADY MACBETH. You lack the season of all natures,[45] sleep.

   MACBETH. Come, we'll to sleep. My strange and self-abuse[46]
        Is the initiate fear that wants hard use.[47]
145   We are yet but young in deed.   [*Exit.*]

Scene v. A witches' haunt.

[*Thunder. Enter the* THREE WITCHES, *meeting* HECATE.]

   FIRST WITCH. Why, how now, Hecate! you look angerly.

   HECATE. Have I not reason, beldams[1] as you are,
        Saucy and overbold? How did you dare
        To trade and traffic with Macbeth
5   In riddles and affairs of death;
        And I, the mistress of your charms,
        The close contriver[2] of all harms,
        Was never called to bear my part,
        Or show the glory of our art?
10   And, which is worse, all you have done
        Hath been but for a wayward son,
        Spiteful and wrathful; who, as others do,
        Loves for his own ends, not for you.
        But make amends now: get you gone,
15   And at the pit of Acheron[3]
        Meet me i' th' morning: thither he
        Will come to know his destiny.
        Your vessels and your spells provide,
        Your charms and everything beside.
20   I am for th' air; this night I'll spend
        Unto a dismal and a fatal end:
        Great business must be wrought ere noon.
        Upon the corner of the moon
        There hangs a vap'rous drop profound;
25   I'll catch it ere it come to ground:
        And that distilled by magic sleights[4]

Side notes:

41. **fee'd** paid to spy.

42. **betimes** quickly.

43. **bent** determined.

Literary Analysis
Conflict How do lines 136–139 in Scene iv mark a turning point in Macbeth's inner conflict?

44. **scanned** examined.

45. **season . . . natures** preservative of all living creatures.

46. **My . . . self-abuse** my strange delusion.

47. **initiate . . . use** beginner's fear that will harden with experience.

1. **beldams** hags.

2. **close contriver** secret inventor.

3. **Acheron** (ak´ ər än´) hell; in Greek mythology the river of Hades.

4. **sleights** devices.

Reading Check
Why will Macbeth visit "the weird sisters" again?

Macbeth, Act III, Scene v ■ 355

31 Literary Analysis
Conflict

• Have students read Macbeth's comments in lines 131–141 and 143–145 carefully.

• Have students **identify** the comment that lets them know that Macbeth already doesn't trust anyone.
Answer: In lines 132–133, he says he is paying servants in everyone's households to spy for him.

• **Ask** students the Literary Analysis question: How do lines 136–139 in Scene iv mark a turning point in Macbeth's inner conflict?
Answer: Macbeth has come to the point where he feels that he will do anything to protect his position, without his previous doubts. He has reached what he himself views as the point of no return, where he has gone so far that it's as far forward as it is back.

• **Ask** students what they think these lines, along with the comment in line 145, tell the audience about what events they can expect in the future.
Answer: It indicates that Macbeth will visit the witches, but it also indicates that a lot more people will be murdered. "We are yet but young in deed" indicates that the killing has only just begun.

▶ **Reteach:** Remind students that the climax of a play is the point at which the conflict reaches its highest point, and after that the action falls as the conflicts are resolved. **Ask** students how they feel Macbeth's attitude at this point reflects the beginning of the resolution of conflicts.
Possible response: Macbeth's inner conflict appears to have been resolved; he no longer seems to be slowed up by any sense of guilt or fear of consequences. The decision to resolve the external conflict has been made, as Macbeth spies on and plans to kill his enemies.

32 Reading Check

Answer: Macbeth decides to visit the weird sisters again to demand that they tell him more about his future, now that he has done so much.

- As students read Scene vi, tell them to look for subtle comments that would let the audience know that Lennox and the other lord are not as fond of Macbeth as they might at first seem. In fact, you may wish to tell them to read it with the idea in mind that they hate Macbeth.

- Have students look at lines 18–19. **Ask** them what Lennox says that lets us know that he believes that Duncan's sons are innocent. **Answer:** His comment that, if it pleases heaven, Duncan's sons will never be in Macbeth's power, shows that he feels that they should not be punished.

- Have students **identify** the word (lines 22–26) that both men use that tells us their true feelings about Macbeth. **Answer:** Both use the word *tyrant*, which implies injustice and a usurped throne.

- **Ask** students how the second lord's description of England's Edward lets us know that this lord feels that Duncan's son is innocent. **Answer:** He calls him pious and holy, which implies that he would be on the side of right and goodness. Therefore, if he has received Duncan's son, the son must be innocent.

- Have students **discuss** what coming action and events they can anticipate from the information supplied in lines 24–39. **Answer:** Macbeth will probably try to kill Macduff. Macbeth will soon face an English army, as well as unhappy Scots, in battle.

Shall raise such artificial sprites[5]
As by the strength of their illusion
Shall draw him on to his confusion.[6]

30 He shall spurn fate, scorn death, and bear
His hopes 'bove wisdom, grace, and fear:
And you all know security[7]
Is mortals' chiefest enemy.

[*Music and a song.*]

Hark! I am called; my little spirit, see,
35 Sits in a foggy cloud and stays for me.   [*Exit.*]

[*Sing within,* "Come away, come away," *etc.*]

FIRST WITCH. Come, let's make haste; she'll soon be
back again.   [*Exit.*]

Scene vi. The palace.

[*Enter* LENNOX *and another* LORD.]

LENNOX. My former speeches have but hit[1] your thoughts,
Which can interpret farther.[2] Only I say
Things have been strangely borne.[3] The gracious Duncan
Was pitied of Macbeth: marry, he was dead.
5 And the right-valiant Banquo walked too late;
Whom, you may say, if 't please you, Fleance killed,
For Fleance fled. Men must not walk too late.
Who cannot want the thought,[4] how monstrous
It was for Malcolm and for Donalbain
10 To kill their gracious father? Damnèd fact![5]
How it did grieve Macbeth! Did he not straight,
In pious rage, the two delinquents tear,
That were the slaves of drink and thralls[6] of sleep?
Was not that nobly done? Ay, and wisely too;
15 For 'twould have angered any heart alive
To hear the men deny 't. So that I say
He has borne all things well: and I do think
That, had he Duncan's sons under his key—
As, an 't[7] please heaven, he shall not—they should find
20 What 'twere to kill a father. So should Fleance.
But, peace! for from broad[8] words, and 'cause he failed
His presence at the tyrant's feast, I hear,
Macduff lives in disgrace. Sir, can you tell
Where he bestows himself?

LORD.   The son of Duncan,
25 From whom this tyrant holds the due of birth,[9]
Lives in the English court, and is received
Of the most pious Edward[10] with such grace

5. **artificial sprites** spirits created by magic.

6. **confusion** ruin.

7. **security** overconfidence.

1. **hit** coincided with.

2. **Which . . . farther** from which you can draw your own conclusions.

3. **borne** managed.

4. **cannot . . . thought** can fail to think.

5. **fact** deed.

6. **thralls** slaves.

7. **an 't** if it.

8. **broad** unguarded.

9. **due of birth** birthright; claim to the throne.

10. **Edward** Edward the Confessor, king of England 1042–1066.

Assessment Practice

Forms of Propaganda

Many tests require students to recognize persuasive devices. Use this item to show that sometimes rhetorical questions are a persuasive device.

Macbeth. . . . Do you find
Your patience so predominant in your nature,
That you can let this go? Are you so gospeled,
To pray for this good man and for his issue,
Whose heavy hand hath bowed you to the grave

(For more practice, see *Standardized Test Preparation Workbook*, p. 14.)

And beggared yours forever?
Macbeth asks the murderers these questions because he wants them to—
  A answer him truthfully
  B be patient and forgiving
  C know what Banquo has done to them
  D agree to kill Banquo
Macbeth is persuading the murderers to kill Banquo. The correct answer is *D*.

356

34 That the <u>malevolence</u> of fortune nothing
30 Takes from his high respect.[11] Thither Macduff
Is gone to pray the holy King, upon his aid[12]
To wake Northumberland and warlike Siward;[13]
That by the help of these, with Him above
To ratify the work, we may again
Give to our tables meat, sleep to our nights,
35 Free from our feasts and banquets bloody knives,
Do faithful homage and receive free honors:[14]
All which we pine for now. And this report
Hath so exasperate the King that he
Prepares for some attempt of war.

LENNOX.   Sent he to Macduff?

40 **LORD.** He did: and with an absolute "Sir, not I,"
The cloudy[15] messenger turns me his back,
And hums, as who should say "You'll rue the time
That clogs[16] me with this answer."

LENNOX.   And that well might
Advise him to a caution, t' hold what distance
45 His wisdom can provide. Some holy angel
Fly to the court of England and unfold
His message ere he come, that a swift blessing
May soon return to this our suffering country
Under a hand accursed!

LORD.   I'll send my prayers with him.   [*Exit.*]

Critical Reading

1. **(a) Recall:** In the banquet scene, what complaint does Macbeth make about murdered men? **(b) Analyze:** Is there anything humorous or even ridiculous in this complaint? Why or why not? **(c) Connect:** Does Shakespeare use humor for comic relief in this scene, as he does in the earlier scene with the porter? Explain.

2. **(a) Recall:** What does Macbeth think as he anticipates the murder of Banquo? **(b) Compare and Contrast:** Compare and contrast Macbeth's thoughts about Banquo's murder with his thoughts before the murder of Duncan.

3. **Synthesize:** Has the relationship between Macbeth and Lady Macbeth changed? Explain.

4. **Generalize:** What does this act suggest about the effects of evil on evildoers? Explain.

Vocabulary Builder

malevolence (mə lev´ə ləns)
n. ill will; spitefulness

11. **with . . . respect** does not diminish the high respect he is given.

12. **upon his aid** to aid Malcolm.

13. **To . . . Siward** to call to arms the commander of the English forces, the Earl of Northumberland, and his son Siward.

14. **free honors** honors given to freemen.

15. **cloudy** disturbed.

16. **clogs** burdens.

Go Online
Author Link
For: More about
William Shakespeare
Visit: www.PHSchool.com
Web Code: ese-9209

Macbeth, Act III, Scene vi ■ 357

Go Online For additional information about
Author Link William Shakespeare, have students
type in the Web Code, then select S from the alphabet, and then select the author's name.

357

Answers

1. (a) Macbeth is involved in this external conflict because the witches predicted that Banquo would father a line of kings. (b) He fails to have Banquo's son murdered.

2. **Action:** murder of Banquo; Fleance escapes. **Internal Conflict:** Macbeth struggles with fear, first because Fleance is alive, posing a threat, then because of the appearance of Banquo's ghost. **Proposed Actions:** Macbeth says he'll visit the witches; he also says the killing will escalate.

3. (a) The fact that Macbeth argues with the ghost, which represents his conscience, is a sign of the internal conflict. (b) Macbeth turns his thoughts to Macduff's absence and to his future plans.

4. **Possible responses:** Some may say Duncan's son, Malcolm, because he is rightful heir to the throne.

5. (a) Macbeth tells Banquo that he'll ask his advice tomorrow, asks him to not miss the feast, and wishes Banquo a safe journey. (b) Tension is heightened because the audience does not know what to believe.

6. Macbeth's ironic comment about Banquo's absence creates tension because, even without expecting a ghost, one still expects someone to confront him and reveal his guilt.

7. Other remarks occur earlier in this act, when Macbeth urges the murderers to kill Banquo, and in Act I, when Lady Macbeth tells Macbeth to be manly and kill Duncan.

8. Manhood is defined as ruthless action and not letting anything stand in the way of one's ambitions.

9. **Possible answer:** It seems unlikely, because Macbeth wouldn't have been surprised to learn of Fleance's escape.

10. **Possible response:** Students may suggest a moving camera, to take in the reactions of the guests to Macbeth's outbursts, combined with close-ups of Macbeth, to show his reactions.

Apply the Skills

Macbeth, Act III

Literary Analysis

Conflict

1. **(a)** Why is Macbeth involved in an **external conflict** with Banquo? **(b)** In what way does Macbeth fail to resolve this conflict?

2. Complete a chart like the one below to show the intensification of **conflict** and the movement toward a climax in Act III.

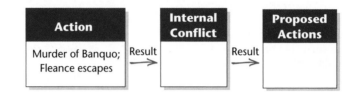

3. **(a)** How is Macbeth's behavior at the banquet a sign of an **internal conflict**? **(b)** How does he temporarily resolve this conflict?

4. Macbeth is personifying evil. Who do you think will lead the forces of good in a campaign against him? How do you know?

Connecting Literary Elements

5. **(a)** Identify three examples of **dramatic irony** in Macbeth's speeches to Banquo in Act III, Scene i, lines 20–38. **(b)** In what way do these examples heighten the tension?

6. How does the dramatic irony in Act III, Scene iv, lines 41–44 create an expectation of a tense encounter?

Reading Strategy

Reading Between the Lines

7. "What man dares, I dare," proclaims Macbeth (III, iv, 100). **Read between the lines** by identifying another remark on manhood earlier in the play.

8. Using Macbeth's and Lady Macbeth's remarks, define their idea of manhood.

9. Some critics suggest that the third murderer is Macbeth himself. By reading between the lines, support or refute this interpretation.

Extend Understanding

10. **Media Connection:** What camera shots would you use to film the banquet scene for a movie version of *Macbeth*? Explain.

358 ■ *Celebrating Humanity (1485–1625)*

QuickReview

Conflict, the struggle between two forces, can be **external,** a struggle between individuals or groups, or **internal,** a struggle within an individual. Both types of conflict rise to a **climax,** the point of greatest tension.

Dramatic irony occurs when a character's words or actions take on a meaning different from the one the character intends.

To **read between the lines,** look for suggested meanings and connect earlier passages with later ones.

For: Self-test
Visit: www.PHSchool.com
Web Code: esa-6209

Build Language Skills

Vocabulary Lesson

Word Analysis: Latin Prefix *mal-*

The Latin prefix *mal-* means "bad or badly, poorly, or wrong." For example, *malevolence* means "ill will." Define the words below. Then, use a dictionary to verify your definitions.

1. maladjusted
2. malformed
3. malcontent
4. malady

Grammar and Style Lesson

Subject and Verb Agreement

Verbs **agree with their subjects in number**—singular subjects must have singular verbs and plural subjects must have plural verbs.

> **Singular:** "After life's fitful fever he sleeps well."
>
> **Plural:** "Our fears in Banquo stick deep, . . ."

Practice Choose the correct form of the verb. Do not be misled by words that come between the subject and the verb.

1. Macbeth, of all the Scottish kings, (is, are) most evil.

Vocabulary Builder: Context

Use all the words from the vocabulary list on page 342 to write a brief profile of Macbeth.

Spelling Strategy

Nouns ending in *-ence* usually end in *-ent* and *-ently* in their adjectival and adverbial forms: the noun *malevolence* becomes *malevolent* (adjective) and *malevolently* (adverb). In your notebook, write the adjectival and adverbial forms for these nouns:

1. permanence   2. diligence   3. intelligence

2. Scotland, country of stark contrasts, (is, are) the setting of *Macbeth.*
3. Malcolm, despite his worries, (does, do) what must be done.
4. Lady Macbeth, expressing some concerns, (begin, begins) to doubt what she has done.
5. Not everyone in this country of ghosts (support, supports) Macbeth.

Writing Application As a Scottish lord, write a note to Malcolm at the English court reporting on conditions in Scotland. Be sure that subjects and verbs agree—even when they are separated by phrases.

W̲G *Prentice Hall Writing and Grammar Connection: Chapter 23, Section 1*

Extend Your Learning

Writing As a lord returning from Macbeth's banquet, write a **diary entry** about the strange events you have just witnessed. Use fresh and vivid language to convey a tone of shock, outrage, bewilderment, or some combination of these.

❸ **Research and Technology** Scan critical works for comments on the banquet scene in *Macbeth.* To record your findings, compile an **annotated bibliography,** a list of your sources together with a summary of what each says about the scene.

Macbeth, Act III ■ *359*

Assessment Resources

The following resources can be used to assess students' knowledge and skills.

Unit 2 Resources
   Selection Test A, pp. 145–147
   Selection Test B, pp. 148–150

Go **O**nline
Assessment
Selection Test B.

Students may use the **Self-test** to prepare for **Selection Test A** or

---

❶ Vocabulary Lesson

Word Analysis

1. *Maladjusted* means poorly adjusted or integrated.
2. *Malformed* means deformed.
3. *Malcontent* means one who is irritable or perpetually at odds.
4. A *malady* is an illness.

Vocabulary Builder

Possible response: Before he killed Duncan, Macbeth was **jocund,** and a **dauntless** warrior. Then, fear triggered **malevolence.** Soon, his fear became an **infirmity.** Macbeth's ties to evil seem **indissoluble.**

Spelling Strategy

1. permanent; permanently
2. diligent; diligently
3. intelligent; intelligently

❷ Grammar and Style Lesson

1. is   3. does   5. supports
2. is   4. begins

Writing Application

Possible response: The conditions here are bad. Banquo is dead; his son, Fleance, escaped. There is suspicion of foul play. Macbeth seems to be losing his mind.

❸ Research and Technology

- Have students use library and Internet resources to search for comments on the banquet scene.
- Have each student present orally one summary from his or her bibliography.
- The **Support for Extend Your Learning** page (*Unit 2 Resources,* p. 143) provides guided note-taking opportunities to help students complete the Extend Your Learning activities.

W̲G **Writing and Grammar, Diamond Level**

Students will find further instruction and practice on subject and verb agreement in Chapter 23, Section 1.

Meeting Your Standards

Students will

1. **analyze and respond to literary elements.**
   - Literary Analysis: Imagery

2. **read, comprehend, analyze, and critique a drama.**
   - Reading Strategy: Using Your Senses
   - Reading Check questions
   - Apply the Skills questions
   - Assessment Practice (ATE)

3. **develop vocabulary.**
   - Vocabulary Lesson: Latin Root: -cred-

4. **understand and apply written and oral language conventions.**
   - Spelling Strategy
   - Grammar and Style Lesson: Possessive Forms

5. **develop writing proficiency.**
   - Writing Lesson: Response to Criticism (follows Act V)

6. **develop appropriate writing strategies.**
   - Extend Your Learning: Motivational Flyer

7. **understand and apply listening and speaking strategies.**
   - Extend Your Learning: Interview

Block Scheduling: Use one 90-minute class period to preteach the skills and have students read the selection. Use a second 90-minute class period to assess students' mastery of skills, extend their learning, and monitor their progress.

Homework Suggestions
Following are possibilities for homework assignments.

- Support pages from *Unit 2 Resources:*
    Literary Analysis
    Reading Strategy
    Vocabulary Builder
    Grammar and Style
- An Extend Your Learning project and the Writing Lesson for this selection may be completed over several days.

Step-by-Step Teaching Guide	Pacing Guide
PRETEACH	
• Administer Vocabulary and Reading Warm-ups as necessary.	5 min.
• Engage students' interest with the motivation activity.	5 min.
• Introduce the Literary Analysis Skill: Imagery. **FT**	5 min.
• Introduce the Reading Strategy: Using Your Senses. **FT**	10 min.
• Prepare students to read by teaching the selection vocabulary. **FT**	
TEACH	
• Informally monitor comprehension while students read independently or in groups. **FT**	30 min.
• Monitor students' comprehension with the Reading Check notes.	as students read
• Reinforce vocabulary with Vocabulary Builder notes.	as students read
• Develop students' understanding of imagery with the Literary Analysis annotations. **FT**	5 min.
• Develop students' ability to use their senses with the Reading Strategy annotations. **FT**	5 min.
ASSESS/EXTEND	
• Assess students' comprehension and mastery of the Literary Analysis and Reading Strategy by having them answer the Apply the Skills questions. **FT**	15 min.
• Have students complete the Vocabulary Lesson and the Grammar and Style Lesson. **FT**	15 min.
• Apply students' understanding by using one or more of the Extend Your Learning activities.	20–90 min. or homework
• Administer Selection Test A or Selection Test B. **FT**	15 min.

Resources

Choosing Resources for Differentiated Instruction

[**L1**] Special Needs Students

[**L2**] Below-Level Students

[**L3**] All Students

[**L4**] Advanced Students

[**EL**] English Learners

For Vocabulary and Reading Warm-ups and for Selection Tests, **A** signifies "less challenging" and **B** "more challenging." For Graphic Organizer transparencies, **A** signifies "not filled in" and **B** "filled in."

FT Fast Track Instruction: To move the lesson more quickly, use the strategies and activities identified with **FT.**

Scaffolding for Less Proficient and Advanced Students

The leveled Critical Thinking questions after selections progress in the levels of thinking required to answer them. To address the needs of your different students, you may use the (a) level questions for your less proficient students and the (b) level questions with your on-level and advanced students. The occasional (c) level questions are appropriate for your advanced students.

PRENTICE HALL

Teacher**EXPRESS**™ Use this complete
Plan · Teach · Assess   suite of powerful
teaching tools to make lesson planning and testing quicker and easier.

PRENTICE HALL

Student**EXPRESS**™ Use the interac-
Learn · Study · Succeed   tive textbook
(online and on CD-ROM) to make selections and activities come alive with audio and video support and interactive questions.

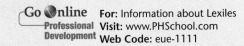

Go **O**nline   **For:** Information about Lexiles
Professional   **Visit:** www.PHSchool.com
Development   **Web Code:** eue-1111

Motivation

Call attention to line 123 in Scene i of Act IV: ". . . the blood-boltered Banquo smiles upon me." Point out that *Macbeth* contains so much blood that it has caused comment. Critic Mark Van Doren claimed, "Never in a play has there been so much of this substance, and never has it been so sickening. . . . We see, feel, and smell it on everything." Ask students to recall images of blood they have encountered so far in the play and to say if they agree with Van Doren's statement. Ask them to think about Shakespeare's reason(s) for making this drama so bloody.

❶ Literary Analysis
Imagery

- Tell students that, as they read Act IV of Macbeth, they should focus on Shakespeare's imagery, the language used to recreate sensory experiences.

- Use the instruction for Connecting Literary Elements to show that Shakespeare's use of archetypal images helps explain the universal appeal of these plays.

❷ Reading Strategy
Using Your Senses

- Ask students to name the five senses, and encourage them to be aware of the senses to which images appeal. Point out the examples in the chart.

- Give students a copy of **Reading Strategy Graphic Organizer A,** p. 66 in *Graphic Organizer Transparencies,* to use as they read *Macbeth,* Act IV.

Build Skills   `Drama`

Macbeth, Act IV

❶ Literary Analysis

Imagery

Imagery is the language that writers use to re-create sensory experiences and stir emotions. It is what helps you see, hear, feel, smell, and taste, rather than just read or listen to words. Shakespeare uses imagery to pack sensory experiences and strong emotions into almost every line. Further, he creates these patterns of images that run through the whole play:

- Blood
- Ill-fitting clothes
- Babies and children, sometimes killed by Macbeth and sometimes threatening him

These images reinforce important themes in the play. The last group of images suggests that Macbeth is in some way warring against the future, which babies and children represent. As you read, link patterns of images to the play's central ideas.

Connecting Literary Elements

Some images are powerful because they are **archetypal**—they relate to ideas and emotions expressed by people in many cultures. In Act IV, for example, **images of a fallen world**—shrieking, groaning, and bleeding—indicate that Macbeth's Scotland resembles an underworld region where the dead are punished. Look for such archetypal images as you read.

❷ Reading Strategy

Using Your Senses

You will enjoy a literary work more if you **use your senses** to experience the imagery it contains. Fill out an imagery chart like this one to ensure that you read with your senses. The chart analyzes the passage in Act IV, Scene i, lines 52–55.

Line	Images Senses
IV, i, 52 "untie the winds"	hearing; touch
IV, i, 53 "yesty waves"	sight

Vocabulary Builder

pernicious (pər nish′ əs) *adj.* fatal; deadly (p. 366)

judicious (jōō dish′ əs) *adj.* showing good judgment (p. 367)

sundry (sun′ drē) *adj.* various; miscellaneous (p. 371)

intemperance (in tem′ pər əns) *n.* lack of restraint (p. 372)

avarice (av′ ə ris) *n.* greed (p. 372)

credulous (krej′ ōō ləs) *adj.* tending to believe too readily (p. 373)

360 ■ Celebrating Humanity (1485–1625)

Review and Anticipate

Macbeth hires murderers to kill Banquo and Banquo's son, Fleance. The murderers botch the job, killing Banquo but allowing Fleance to escape. Then, at a state banquet, Macbeth is shocked to see the ghost of Banquo sitting in the king's chair. Macbeth decides to visit the witches again, determined to know "the worst." At the end of Act III, we learn that Malcolm is in England preparing to invade Scotland and that Macduff has gone to join him.

Act IV will be a turning point in the play. Macbeth seeks help from the witches to secure his power. The forces of good, however, are beginning to gather against him.

Act IV

Scene i. A witches' haunt.

[*Thunder. Enter the* THREE WITCHES.]

FIRST WITCH. Thrice the brinded[1] cat hath mewed.

SECOND WITCH. Thrice and once the hedge-pig[2] whined.

THIRD WITCH. Harpier[3] cries. 'Tis time, 'tis time.

FIRST WITCH. Round about the caldron go:
5   In the poisoned entrails throw.
    Toad, that under cold stone
    Days and nights has thirty-one
    Swelt'red venom sleeping got,[4]
    Boil thou first i' th' charmèd pot.

10 **ALL.** Double, double, toil and trouble;
    Fire burn and caldron bubble.

SECOND WITCH. Fillet of a fenny snake,
    In the caldron boil and bake;
    Eye of newt and toe of frog,
15   Wool of bat and tongue of dog,
    Adder's fork[5] and blindworm's[6] sting,
    Lizard's leg and howlet's[7] wing,
    For a charm of pow'rful trouble,
    Like a hell-broth boil and bubble.

20 **ALL.** Double, double, toil and trouble;
    Fire burn and caldron bubble.

THIRD WITCH. Scale of dragon, tooth of wolf,
    Witch's mummy, maw and gulf[8]
    Of the ravined[9] salt-sea shark,

 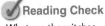

❸ ▲ Critical Viewing
What is the significance of a burning cauldron—like this one—to the play? [Connect]

1. **brinded** striped.

2. **hedge-pig** hedgehog.

3. **Harpier** one of the spirits attending the witches.

4. **Swelt'red . . . got** venom sweated out while sleeping.

5. **fork** forked tongue.

6. **blindworm's** small, limbless lizard's.

7. **howlet's** small owl's.

8. **maw and gulf** stomach and gullet.

9. **ravined** ravenous.

❹ ☑ Reading Check
What are the witches doing as the act begins?

Macbeth, Act IV, Scene i ■ 361

Poster for Macbeth, by
Edmund Dulac

Edmund Dulac (1882–1953) was
born in France and settled in England
in 1904. He is most widely known as
a book illustrator of fairy tales and
legends, but he also was
a caricaturist and a portrait painter.
He did a lot of work for the British
stage, such as this poster for
Macbeth. In 1953, he was commissioned to produce a stamp com-
memorating the coronation of
Queen Elizabeth II.

Use these questions for discussion:

1. Why is it ironic that Macbeth
   should be standing above the
   witches with his arms crossed?
   Answer: Despite the fact that
   Macbeth is commanding the
   three witches, he is actually at
   their mercy.

2. How does this depiction of the
   witches compare to the one
   on p. 308?
   Possible responses: Students
   may say that the picture on
   p. 308 shows three old women
   who look strange and gnarled,
   but the picture on this page
   depicts the witches as more obviously demonic or evil, and even
   shows one witch as being fairly
   young.

❻ Critical Viewing

Possible responses: Students may
say that the gloomy colors and the
ragged appearance of the witches do
seem appropriate. They also might
say the artist has successfully
depicted the witches' brew as a
powerful, supernatural force that
is capable of bringing forth the
apparitions.

❻ ▲ **Critical Viewing** Has this artist captured the spirit of the
witches as it is portrayed in IV, i? Explain. **[Evaluate]**

Enrichment

Shakespeare, The Entertainer

Many students approach Shakespeare as
"Literature" and cannot get beyond the difficult
language. Remind students that Shakespeare's
first and foremost purpose in writing plays was
not to create great literature, but to entertain
his audience.

Encourage students to think about a scary
movie they have seen. Point out that, even
though the movie may have depicted something really horrible, they enjoyed that experience at some level. Point out that this first

scene in Act IV had the same effect on
Shakespeare's audiences, many of whom
believed in witches and the occult—and still
delights audiences today, who appreciate the
archetypal images of evil and ambition.

The first 47 lines show the witches chanting
as they cast their evil spell. The witches are evil,
and their intent is to deceive Macbeth and pull
him into further evil. Tell students to keep in
mind the horror-movie aspects of *Macbeth* as
they read lines 1–47.

Root of hemlock digged i' th' dark,
Liver of blaspheming Jew,
Gall of goat, and slips of yew
Slivered in the moon's eclipse,
Nose of Turk and Tartar's lips,[10]
30 Finger of birth-strangled babe
Ditch-delivered by a drab,
Make the gruel thick and slab:[11]
Add thereto a tiger's chaudron,[12]
For th' ingredience of our caldron.

35 **ALL.** Double, double, toil and trouble;
Fire burn and caldron bubble.

SECOND WITCH. Cool it with a baboon's blood,
Then the charm is firm and good.

[*Enter* HECATE *and the other* THREE WITCHES.]

HECATE. O, well done! I commend your pains;
40 And every one shall share i' th' gains:
And now about the caldron sing,
Like elves and fairies in a ring,
Enchanting all that you put in.

[*Music and a song:* "Black Spirits," *etc. Exit* HECATE *and the other* THREE WITCHES.]

SECOND WITCH. By the pricking of my thumbs,
45 Something wicked this way comes:
Open, locks,
Whoever knocks!

[*Enter* MACBETH.]

MACBETH. How now, you secret, black, and midnight hags!
What is 't you do?

ALL.   A deed without a name.

50 **MACBETH.** I conjure you, by that which you profess,
Howe'er you come to know it, answer me:
Though you untie the winds and let them fight
Against the churches; though the yesty[13] waves
Confound[14] and swallow navigation up;
55 Though bladed corn be lodged[15] and trees blown down;
Though castles topple on their warders' heads;
Though palaces and pyramids do slope[16]
Their heads to their foundations; though the treasure
Of nature's germens[17] tumble all together,
60 Even till destruction sicken, answer me
To what I ask you.

FIRST WITCH.   Speak.

---

10. blaspheming Jew . . . Tartar's lips For many in Shakespeare's audience, the words "Jew," "Turk," and "Tartar" evoked stereotypical enemies of Christianity.

11. slab sticky.

12. chaudron (shô´ drən) entrails.

Reading Strategy
Using Your Senses
How do you picture the strange world described in Scene i ?

---

13. yesty foamy.

14. Confound destroy.

15. lodged beaten down.

16. slope bend.

17. nature's germens seeds of all life.

❾ **Reading Check**
What does Macbeth demand of the witches?

Macbeth, Act IV, Scene i ■ *363*

---

❼ Reading Strategy
Using Your Senses

• Tell students that one of the senses to which this passage appeals is the sense of hearing. Read the witches' dialogue aloud or play the *Listening to Literature Audio CD,* so that the music of the spell weaving can be heard.

• **Ask** students the Reading Strategy question: How do you picture the strange world described in Scene i? **Possible response:** The scene is dark and chaotic, with wind and thunder. The only light is the fire under the witches' cauldron. It is eerie and frightening.

• Have students imagine that they are watching the witches work. Have them **describe** their reactions to the ingredients, as well as what the brew looks and smells like. **Possible response:** Everything is disgusting, but the body parts are the worst. The brew looks kind of green and glowing with brown lumps. The smell is like wet dog and burning hair.

• Point out that, as in Act III, the entrance here of Hecate may have been written and inserted by someone else.

❽ Literary Analysis
Imagery

• In Macbeth's speech, note the use of the word *conjure.* It can mean "earnestly ask," but Shakespeare likely chose it because of the strong and more common connection to magic spells.

• **Ask** students which images in lines 50–61 parallel things the witches have related in their several appearances. **Possible response:** The witches have, particularly in Act I, described themselves as controlling the winds and sinking ships ("swallowing navigation"). Mayhem is implied in all they say. The comments about toppling castles may refer to the overthrow of governments, of which Macbeth is a participant.

❾ Reading Check

Answer: Macbeth demands that the witches answer whatever he asks.

Differentiated
Instruction   Solutions for All Learners

Strategy for Less Proficient Readers
Point out that imagery goes beyond literature. For example, saying "It's as cold as ice in here" is imagery—it relates a sensory experience. Writers use imagery in a similar way. Review the list of images in the play, and encourage students to look for these as they read.

Support for English Learners
Explain that imagery in literature is in some ways similar to imagery in paintings. Have students look at the painting on the facing page and describe what they see. Explain that the words they use to describe a visual image are, in effect, imagery. They are translating a visual experience into words.

Strategy for Advanced Readers
Explain that many of Shakespeare's images are archetypal, relating to universal ideas and emotions. Have students record images that they encounter that they feel are archetypal. Tell them that a good gauge would be if the images seem valid today. If the images survive time, they are likely archetypal.

363

- Explain that an "armed head" would be a head wearing a war helmet. "Armed" refers to armor.

- **Ask** students the Literary Analysis question: How do the apparitions that Macbeth sees in Scene i, lines 68, 75, and 86 connect with the patterns of imagery in the play? **Possible response:** The first apparition connects with the images of war, which open the play and seem to signal how the play will end. The second combines the images of blood—which symbolizes revenge, murder, or guilt—and a child, which represents the future. The third apparition has a child but adds a crown, another recurring image, especially in Macbeth's dreams of being king.

- **Ask** students if, after reading the prophecy of the third apparition, they know why the child holds a tree.
  Answer: It probably relates to the prophecy about Birnam Wood.

- Remind students that an important theme in *Macbeth* has been things not always being what they seem. In light of this, **ask** students what they predict about the prophecies.
  Answer: At least some of the prophecies are not as positive as Macbeth believes they are. He is not completely safe.

11 **Critical Thinking**
Analyze

- Direct students' attention to line 77.

- Point out that the apparition speaks Macbeth's name three times. Macbeth replies with a comment about three ears. **Ask** students to recall other occurrences of the number three or things occurring in threes.
  Possible response: There are three witches. In Act I, they hail Macbeth three times. Macbeth heard three prophecies during his first encounter with the witches; during this encounter, he meets their "masters," three apparitions, who will deliver three more prophecies.

364

SECOND WITCH.   Demand.

THIRD WITCH.   We'll answer.

FIRST WITCH. Say, if th' hadst rather hear it from our mouths,
  Or from our masters?

  MACBETH.   Call 'em, let me see 'em.

  FIRST WITCH. Pour in sow's blood, that hath eaten
65   Her nine farrow;[18] grease that's sweaten
   From the murderer's gibbet[19] throw
   Into the flame.

  ALL.   Come, high or low,
   Thyself and office[20] deftly show!

10 | [*Thunder.* FIRST APPARITION: *an Armed Head.*[21]]

  MACBETH. Tell me, thou unknown power—

  FIRST WITCH.   He knows thy thought:
70   Hear his speech, but say thou nought.

  FIRST APPARITION. Macbeth! Macbeth! Macbeth! Beware Macduff!
   Beware the Thane of Fife. Dismiss me: enough.

                         [*He descends.*]

  MACBETH. Whate'er thou art, for thy good caution thanks:
   Thou hast harped[22] my fear aright. But one word more—

75 **FIRST WITCH.** He will not be commanded. Here's another,
   More potent than the first.

10 | [*Thunder.* SECOND APPARITION: *a Bloody Child.*[23]]

  11 | **SECOND APPARITION.** Macbeth! Macbeth! Macbeth!

  MACBETH. Had I three ears, I'd hear thee.

  SECOND APPARITION. Be bloody, bold, and resolute! Laugh to scorn
80   The pow'r of man, for none of woman born
   Shall harm Macbeth.   [*Descends.*]

  MACBETH. Then live, Macduff: what need I fear of thee?
   But yet I'll make assurance double sure,
   And take a bond of fate.[24] Thou shalt not live;
85   That I may tell pale-hearted fear it lies,
   And sleep in spite of thunder.

10 | [*Thunder.* THIRD APPARITION: *a Child Crowned, with a tree in his hand.*[25]]

                         What is this,
   That rises like the issue of a king,
   And wears upon his baby-brow the round
   And top of sovereignty?[26]

  ALL.   Listen, but speak not to 't.

364 ■ *Celebrating Humanity (1485–1625)*

---

18. **farrow** young pigs.
19. **gibbet** (jib′ it) gallows.

20. **office** function.

21. *an Armed Head* symbol of Macduff.

22. **harped** hit upon.

23. *a Bloody Child* symbol of Macduff at birth.

24. **take . . . fate** get a guarantee from fate (by killing Macduff).

25. *a Child . . . hand* symbol of Malcolm.

26. **top of sovereignty** crown.

Enrichment

The Weird Sisters

Scholars have long debated whether Macbeth's tragedy results from the inexorable pressures of fate or from his own free choice of evil. This debate tends to focus on the role of the witches. The great Shakespearean scholar George Lyman Kittredge argued that these weird sisters were not just run-of-the-mill crones, but arbiters of human destiny. He identified them with the Norns, Scandinavian goddesses of fate, who shaped men's lives, setting the course at birth.

Irving Ribner, among other scholars, argued against this position. He felt that Shakespeare was writing from a Christian rather than a pagan perspective. While Christians acknowledge the reality of evil, they believe that God gave humans the power to choose evil or good. Though he is presented with temptation to do wrong, Macbeth chooses his own course. An argument for Macbeth's free will is that Banquo, subject to the same temptation, remains virtuous.

90　**THIRD APPARITION.**　Be lion-mettled, proud, and take no care
　　　　Who chafes, who frets, or where conspirers are:
　　　　Macbeth shall never vanquished be until
　　　　Great Birnam Wood to high Dunsinane Hill
　　　　Shall come against him.　　　　　　　　　　[Descends.]

　　MACBETH.　　　　　　　　That will never be.
95　　　Who can impress[27] the forest, bid the tree
　　　　Unfix his earth-bound root? Sweet bodements,[28] good!
　　　　Rebellious dead, rise never, till the Wood
　　　　Of Birnam rise, and our high-placed Macbeth
　　　　Shall live the lease of nature,[29] pay his breath
100　　To time and mortal custom.[30] Yet my heart
　　　　Throbs to know one thing. Tell me, if your art
　　　　Can tell so much: shall Banquo's issue ever
　　　　Reign in this kingdom?

　　ALL.　　　　　　　　Seek to know no more.

　　MACBETH.　I will be satisfied. Deny me this,
105　　And an eternal curse fall on you! Let me know.
　　　　Why sinks that caldron? And what noise is this?

[Hautboys.]

　　FIRST WITCH.　Show!

　　SECOND WITCH.　Show!

　　THIRD WITCH.　Show!

110　**ALL.**　Show his eyes, and grieve his heart;
　　　　Come like shadows, so depart!

[A show of eight KINGS and BANQUO, last KING with a glass[31] in his hand.]

　　MACBETH.　Thou art too like the spirit of Banquo. Down!
　　　　Thy crown does sear mine eyelids. And thy hair,
　　　　Thou other gold-bound brow, is like the first.
115　　A third is like the former. Filthy hags!
　　　　Why do you show me this? A fourth! Start, eyes!
　　　　What, will the line stretch out to th' crack of doom?
　　　　Another yet! A seventh! I'll see no more.
　　　　And yet the eighth appears, who bears a glass
120　　Which shows me many more: and some I see
　　　　That twofold balls and treble scepters[32] carry:
　　　　Horrible sight! Now I see 'tis true;
　　　　For the blood-boltered[33] Banquo smiles upon me,
　　　　And points at them for his.[34] What, is this so?

125　**FIRST WITCH.**　Ay, sir, all this is so. But why
　　　　Stands Macbeth thus amazedly?
　　　　Come, sisters, cheer we up his sprites,
　　　　And show the best of our delights:

---

27. impress force into service.

28. bodements prophecies.

29. lease of nature natural lifespan.

30. mortal custom natural death.

31. glass mirror.

Literary Analysis
Imagery What does Macbeth learn from the images of the eight kings?

32. twofold . . . scepters coronation emblems and insignia of the kingdoms of England, Scotland, and Ireland, united in 1603 when James VI of Scotland became James I of England.

33. blood-boltered with his hair matted with blood.

34. his his descendants.

⓮ ✔ Reading Check
What do the three apparitions tell Macbeth, and what further vision does he see?

Macbeth, Act IV, Scene i ■ *365*

⓬ Critical Thinking
Draw Conclusions

- **Ask** students what, in lines 100–103, is still bothering Macbeth.
  Answer: That Banquo's descendants might be kings worries Macbeth.

- **Ask** students why they think the witches don't want to give him this information.
  Possible responses: Perhaps they want to leave Macbeth feeling happy and overconfident. This motive seems to be confirmed by line 110. Perhaps they think it will change Macbeth's plans.

- Point out to students that the *Hautboys* mentioned after line 106 are wooden, pipelike wind instruments, used here to signal the appearance of the kings.

⓭ Literary Analysis
Imagery

▶ **Reteach:** Remind students that, in addition to re-creating sensory experiences, imagery is also used to relate information and stir the emotions.

- **Ask** students the Literary Analysis question: What does Macbeth learn from the images of the eight kings?

  Answer: He learns that Banquo's descendants will reign. He also sees that the last one has a mirror (glass) that shows that there will be more than eight kings. He sees images (balls and scepters) that let him know that more than one country will be ruled by these kings (as explained in the margin note).

- Point out that, though Macbeth threatened the witches so that he could find out about Banquo, he now asks in line 116 why they showed him this. **Ask** students to explain the change.
  Possible response: When he asked, he had received nothing but good prophecies (or so he believes). Now he feels he has been betrayed because he has received bad news.

⓮ Reading Check

Answer: They tell Macbeth to beware Macduff, that no one born of woman will harm him, that he will not be conquered until Birnam Wood comes to Dunsinane Hill. Macbeth sees a line of eight kings and Banquo.

365

Compare and Contrast

- Have students read lines 144–156.

- Tell students to think about what Macbeth felt before he murdered Duncan.

- Then, **ask** students to compare Macbeth's attitude toward murdering Macduff and his family with his attitude about murdering Duncan.

Possible response: Students should point out that Macbeth has lost all semblance of humanity and is coldbloodedly planning the execution of an entire family. When he was planning to kill Duncan, he was filled with doubt and guilt.

- **Ask** students how Macbeth has interpreted the prophecies made by the apparitions, and then have them consider how his interpretation makes the murders he is now planning seem even worse than the others.

Answer: Macbeth has interpreted the prophecies as meaning he cannot be touched. Therefore, the murders he is currently planning seem much worse because they are completely unnecessary. They gain him nothing and are against people who are not a threat.

---

130   I'll charm the air to give a sound,
      While you perform your antic round,[35]
      That this great king may kindly say
      Our duties did his welcome pay.

[*Music.* THE WITCHES *dance, and vanish.*]

MACBETH. Where are they? Gone? Let this <u>pernicious</u> hour
      Stand aye accursèd in the calendar!
      Come in, without there!

[*Enter* LENNOX.]

135 **LENNOX.**   What's your Grace's will?

MACBETH. Saw you the weird sisters?

LENNOX.   No, my lord.

MACBETH. Came they not by you?

LENNOX.   No indeed, my lord.

MACBETH. Infected be the air whereon they ride,
      And damned all those that trust them! I did hear
140   The galloping of horse. Who was 't came by?

LENNOX. 'Tis two or three, my lord, that bring you word
      Macduff is fled to England.

MACBETH.   Fled to England?

LENNOX. Ay, my good lord.

MACBETH. [*Aside*] Time, thou anticipat'st[36] my dread exploits.
145   The flighty purpose never is o'ertook
      Unless the deed go with it.[37] From this moment
      The very firstlings of my heart[38] shall be
      The firstlings of my hand. And even now,
      To crown my thoughts with acts be it thought and done:
150   The castle of Macduff I will surprise;
      Seize upon Fife; give to th' edge o' th' sword
      His wife, his babes, and all unfortunate souls
      That trace[39] him in his line. No boasting like a fool;
      This deed I'll do before this purpose cool:
155   But no more sights!—Where are these gentlemen?
      Come, bring me where they are.

                                    [*Exit.*]

Scene ii. Macduff's castle.

[*Enter* MACDUFF'S WIFE, *her* SON, *and* ROSS.]

LADY MACDUFF. What had he done, to make him fly the land?

ROSS. You must have patience, madam.

---

35. antic round grotesque circular dance.

Vocabulary Builder
pernicious (pər nish′ əs) *adj.* fatal; deadly

36. anticipat'st foretold.

37. The flighty . . . it The fleeting plan is never fulfilled unless it is carried out at once.

38. firstlings . . . heart first thoughts, impulses.

39. trace succeed.

---

366 ■ Celebrating Humanity (1485–1625)

Enrichment

Castles

When Macbeth lived, the idea of Scotland as a country was new. In fact, the idea of England as a united country was fairly new. These countries had long been made up of clans, tribes, and ethnic groups who were frequently at war, either with outside invaders (fairly common) or with each other (even more common). Hence, the head of any group, whether a chieftain, thane, or king, usually lived in a castle.

Castles were designed for defense. They were built in places that gave them a clear view of approaching enemies or that protected them from that approach, such as on cliffs or islands. They would have heavy doors, thick walls, and lots of places from which weapons could be shot, thrown, or dropped.

While only the ruler had a castle as a primary residence, all castles were designed so that everyone from the surrounding villages and farms (along with their animals) could be safe within the castle during times of attack.

LADY MACDUFF. He had none:
His flight was madness. When our actions do not,
Our fears do make us traitors.

ROSS. You know not
Whether it was his wisdom or his fear.

LADY MACDUFF. Wisdom! To leave his wife, to leave his babes,
His mansion and his titles,[1] in a place
From whence himself does fly? He loves us not;
He wants the natural touch:[2] for the poor wren,
The most diminutive of birds, will fight,
Her young ones in her nest, against the owl.
All is the fear and nothing is the love;
As little is the wisdom, where the flight
So runs against all reason.

ROSS. My dearest coz,[3]
I pray you, school[4] yourself. But, for your husband,
He is noble, wise, judicious, and best knows
The fits o' th' seasons,[5] I dare not speak much further:
But cruel are the times, when we are traitors
And do not know ourselves;[6] when we hold rumor
From what we fear,[7] yet know not what we fear,
But float upon a wild and violent sea
Each way and move. I take my leave of you.
Shall not be long but I'll be here again.
Things at the worst will cease, or else climb upward
To what they were before. My pretty cousin,
Blessing upon you!

LADY MACDUFF. Fathered he is, and yet he's fatherless.

ROSS. I am so much a fool, should I stay longer,
It would be my disgrace and your discomfort.[8]
I take my leave at once. [*Exit* ROSS.]

LADY MACDUFF. Sirrah, your father's dead;
And what will you do now? How will you live?

SON. As birds do, mother.

LADY MACDUFF. What, with worms and flies?

SON. With what I get, I mean; and so do they.

LADY MACDUFF. Poor bird! thou'dst never fear the net nor lime,[9]
The pitfall nor the gin.[10]

SON. Why should I, mother? Poor birds they are not set for.
My father is not dead, for all your saying.

LADY MACDUFF. Yes, he is dead: how wilt thou do for a father?

SON. Nay, how will you do for a husband?

Literary Analysis
Imagery What image is suggested by Lady Macduff's use of the words "fly" and "flight" in lines 8 and 13?

1. **titles** possessions.

2. **wants . . . touch** lacks natural affection.

3. **coz** cousin.

4. **school** control.

Vocabulary Builder
judicious (jo͞o dish′ əs) *adj.* showing good judgment

5. **fits o' th' season** disorders of the time.

6. **when . . . ourselves** when we are treated as traitors but do not know of any treason.

7. **when . . . fear** believe rumors based on our fears.

8. **It . . . discomfort:** I would disgrace myself and embarrass you by weeping.

Literary Analysis
Imagery What does the imagery in Scene ii, 34–35 suggest about what might happen?

9. **lime** birdlime, a sticky substance smeared on branches to catch birds.

10. **gin** trap.

18 **Reading Check**
Where has Macduff gone, and how will Macbeth revenge himself against Macduff?

16 Literary Analysis
Imagery

- Tell students to look out for repeated words, ideas, and images throughout this scene. For example, the words *traitor* and *fears* appear frequently, as do *fly* and *flight*.
- **Ask** the first Literary Analysis question: What image is suggested by Lady Macduff's use of the words "fly" and "flight"?
  Answer: The words "fly" and "flight" suggest images of birds and support the extended metaphor of the Macduffs as birds used by both Lady Macduff and her son.
- Further discuss the bird imagery used by Lady Macduff in lines 6–14. **Ask** students how the imagery shows both her nobility and her helplessness.
  Answer: She compares herself to the wren, which she identifies as the smallest of birds. This smallness makes her seem vulnerable. However, she also points out that her love would, like the instincts of the wren, cause her to fight the owl, a bird of prey, to protect her children.
- Point out the wordplay in lines 13–14. Shakespeare writes that flight *runs*. Remind students to keep an eye out for the ways in which Shakespeare plays with the language.
- You may also want to point out to students that, in the speech that follows, Ross reiterates the idea of fear of traitors. He also, in contrast to Macbeth, shows that he does not have any idea what the future holds.

17 Literary Analysis
Imagery

- Read aloud lines 34–35.
- Then, have students use the text aids to define *lime* and *gin*.
- **Ask** students the second Literary Analysis question: What does the imagery in Scene ii, lines 34–35, suggest about what might happen?
  Answer: These images suggest that Lady Macduff and her son will be trapped by the murderers.

18 Reading Check

Answer: Macduff has fled to England, and Macbeth will revenge himself against Macduff by killing his wife and children.

Differentiated Instruction
Solutions for All Learners

Strategy for Special Needs Students
Shakespeare's reliance on imagery to get ideas across may confuse some students. Show illustrations of as many images as possible, for example, from a heavily illustrated version of *Macbeth* or, in the case of the wren and owl, from a bird book. Have students read along while listening to this scene on ***Listening to Literature Audio CDs,*** stopping frequently to discuss what is happening and what the images are telling the audience/reader.

Support for English Learners
Illustrations may help students better understand the images. Drawings or photos of birds (wren and owl), crowns, an "armed head" (helmets), or more detailed illustrations in another version of *Macbeth* may help clarify meanings. Discuss and define any unfamiliar words that are not listed in the side notes. Then, listen to this scene on ***Listening to Literature Audio CDs.*** This will help students hear both the pronunciation and the rhythm of the language.

⓳ Critical Thinking
Analyze

• Have students read the first bracketed passage.

• Explain to students that unlikely characters are often clever in Shakespeare's plays.

• Then, **ask** students why it is significant that Macduff's son makes this observation about liars and swearers, when just eight lines earlier he has to ask what a traitor is.
Possible response: Shakespeare seems to be juxtaposing childlike innocence with a more mature, unadulterated truth. Shakespeare may be implying that children are wiser than the adults around them.

⓴ Reading Strategy
Using Your Senses

▶ **Reteach:** Remind students that imagery can appeal to any of the five senses. Point out, too, that because this is a play and is intended to be visual, there are also often hints about what the people look like or how they behave.

• **Ask** students how they think the messenger appears, and what the delivery of his lines would be like.
Possible response: He would probably have been in a hurry, and his lines would probably be delivered in a rushed, somewhat breathless manner.

▶ **Monitor Progress: Ask** students the Reading Strategy question: What do the content of the messenger's speech and the context suggest about his dress, appearance, and manner?
Answer: He is probably in a hurry, so he may be abrupt. The fact that he observes that he has frightened Lady Macduff (line 68) confirms that he has probably rushed in and just blurted out his warning. He may also be a little disheveled, because of his rush. He says he is "homely," which means simple, not part of the nobility. Hence, he is probably dressed in the clothing of a worker or farmer.

• You may wish to point out that, because the messenger speaks in blank verse, we know that, even if he is simple, he is not a servant or someone who can be ignored.

40 **LADY MACDUFF.** Why, I can buy me twenty at any market.

SON. Then you'll buy 'em to sell[11] again.

LADY MACDUFF. Thou speak'st with all thy wit, and yet i' faith, With wit enough for thee.[12]

SON. Was my father a traitor, mother?

45 **LADY MACDUFF.** Ay, that he was.

SON. What is a traitor?

LADY MACDUFF. Why, one that swears and lies.[13]

SON. And be all traitors that do so?

LADY MACDUFF. Every one that does so is a traitor, and must be hanged.

50 **SON.** And must they all be hanged that swear and lie?

LADY MACDUFF. Every one.

SON. Who must hang them?

LADY MACDUFF. Why, the honest men.

⓳ 55 **SON.** Then the liars and swearers are fools; for there are liars and swearers enow[14] to beat the honest men and hang up them.

LADY MACDUFF. Now, God help thee, poor monkey! But how wilt thou do for a father?

SON. If he were dead, you'd weep for him. If you would not, it were 60 a good sign that I should quickly have a new father.

LADY MACDUFF. Poor prattler, how thou talk'st!

[*Enter a* MESSENGER.]

MESSENGER. Bless you, fair dame! I am not to you known, Though in your state of honor I am perfect.[15]
65 I doubt[16] some danger does approach you nearly:
⓴ If you will take a homely[17] man's advice,
Be not found here; hence, with your little ones.
To fright you thus, methinks I am too savage;
To do worse to you were fell[18] cruelty,
70 Which is too nigh your person. Heaven preserve you!
I dare abide no longer.   [*Exit* MESSENGER.]

LADY MACDUFF.   Whither should I fly?
I have done no harm. But I remember now
I am in this earthly world, where to do harm
Is often laudable, to do good sometime
75 Accounted dangerous folly. Why then, alas,
Do I put up that womanly defense,
To say I have done no harm?—What are these faces?

368 ■ *Celebrating Humanity (1485–1625)*

11. sell betray.

12. for thee for a child.

13. swears and lies takes an oath and breaks it.

14. enow enough.

15. in . . . perfect I am fully informed of your honorable rank.

16. doubt fear.

17. homely simple.

18. fell fierce.

Reading Strategy
Using Your Senses What do the content of the messenger's speech and the context suggest about his dress, appearance, and manner?

Enrichment

The Rules of Hospitality

When Macbeth murdered Duncan, he broke two tenets of his society: he killed his king, and at the same time, he killed a guest under his roof.

According to the rules of hospitality in most cultures, guests are to be treated with a deliberate respect and kindness. Though there were sometimes different ideas about who received hospitality, once visitors were your guests, they were to be protected.

In ancient Greek culture, Zeus was the god of hospitality. People treated all guests well, lavishing attention and gifts on them, lest they dis-

cover that the poor traveler they had treated badly was actually Zeus in disguise, testing them. Hospitality was also an important part of Middle Eastern culture, and is reflected in ancient Jewish and Christian literature; the Bible commands that its followers show hospitality.

Even today, in many areas of Latin America, Africa, and Asia, any traveler, whether an acquaintance or a complete stranger, can expect to receive a warm welcome. "My house is your house" is taken literally in many cultures.

[*Enter* MURDERERS.]

MURDERER. Where is your husband?

LADY MACDUFF. I hope, in no place so unsanctified
Where such as thou mayst find him.

80 **MURDERER.**   He's a traitor.

SON. Thou li'st, thou shag-eared[19] villain!

MURDERER.   What, you egg!

                              [*Stabbing him.*]
Young fry[20] of treachery!

SON.   He has killed me, mother:
Run away, I pray you!   [*Dies.*]

          [*Exit* LADY MACDUFF *crying "Murder!" followed by* MURDERERS.]

Macbeth, Act IV, Scene ii ■ 369

19. **shag-eared** hairy-eared.

20. **fry** offspring.

22 ✔ Reading Check

Whom do Macbeth's men kill?

23 ▼ Critical Viewing

This engraving shows the murderers menacing Macduff's family. In what way does the artist capture the defiance reflected in Act IV, Scene ii, line 81? [Interpret]

24 Literary Analysis
Imagery

- **Ask** students the Literary Analysis question: How do the images in Scene iii, lines 1–4 help establish a contrast between Malcolm and Macduff?
  Answer: Malcolm is showing a sentimental, emotional side; Macduff is displaying no weakness and remains warrior-like.

- **Ask** students to what they might attribute the differences between the two men.
  Possible response: Malcolm is young. He has just seen his father murdered and his kingdom lost, so he is already in an emotional state. Macduff is an experienced soldier.

25 Critical Thinking
Analyze

- **Ask** students how Malcolm's comment in line 14 is ironic.
  Answer: Malcolm states Macduff has not yet suffered personal loss at the hands of Macbeth. Neither of them knows that Macduff's entire family has just been murdered at Macbeth's order.

- Though he is young, Malcolm is not a fool. **Ask** students what Malcolm is saying in lines 15–24.
  Answer: Malcolm is saying that Macduff would have much to gain by turning him over to Macbeth. Even if Macduff is virtuous, he might do it because it was commanded by the king. Also, even angels have fallen.

26 Literature in Context

Shifting Meanings Language changes over time. However, old and new definitions are usually related. For example, both definitions of *mortal* include the idea of death—and anyone who knows the phrases "mortal combat" and "mortal enemy" is familiar with Shakespeare's use of *mortal* to mean "deadly."

Connect to the Literature
Discuss with students the meanings they know for the word *recoil*. Mention the action of springs if students do not do so. Then, **ask** the Connect to the Literature question: What possible meanings might the word *recoil* have in line 19?
Answer: The usual meaning of *recoil* is "to shrink back"; in line 19, it means "to give way."

Scene iii. England. Before the King's palace.

[*Enter* MALCOLM *and* MACDUFF.]

MALCOLM. Let us seek out some desolate shade, and there
　Weep our sad bosoms empty.

MACDUFF. 　　　　　　　　　Let us rather
　Hold fast the mortal◆ sword, and like good men
　Bestride our down-fall'n birthdom.¹ Each new morn
5　New widows howl, new orphans cry, new sorrows
　Strike heaven on the face, that it resounds
　As if it felt with Scotland and yelled out
　Like syllable of dolor.²

MALCOLM. 　　　　　　　What I believe, I'll wail;
　What know, believe; and what I can redress,
10　As I shall find the time to friend,◆ I will.
　What you have spoke, it may be so perchance.
　This tyrant, whose sole◆ name blisters our tongues,
　Was once thought honest:◆ you have loved him well;
　He hath not touched you yet. I am young; but something
15　You may deserve of him through me;³ and wisdom⁴
　To offer up a weak, poor, innocent lamb
　T' appease an angry god.

MACDUFF. I am not treacherous.

26 Literature in Context

Vocabulary Connection

◆ *Shifting Meanings*
　Because language is always changing, some words used by Shakespeare have shifted in meaning.

Mortal (IV, iii, 3) means "deadly," which is somewhat unlike its current meaning, "subject to death or decay."

Friend (IV, iii, 10), which today is a noun, is used as a verb meaning "to be friendly."

Sole (IV, iii, 12), which now means "single" or "one and only," is used as an intensifier meaning "very."

Honest (IV, iii, 13) has the broad sense of "good."

　As you read, be alert to shifts in meaning like these, and use the context of a word or phrase as well as the side notes to help you determine Shakespeare's meaning.

Connect to the Literature

What possible meanings might the word *recoil* have in line 19?

Literary Analysis
Imagery How do the images in Scene iii, lines 1–4 help establish a contrast between Malcolm and Macduff?

1. **Bestride . . . birthdom** Protectively stand over our native land.

2. **Like . . . dolor** similar cry of anguish.

3. **deserve . . . me** earn by betraying me to Macbeth.

4. **wisdom** It is wise.

370 ■ *Celebrating Humanity (1485–1625)*

MALCOLM.   But Macbeth is.
A good and virtuous nature may recoil
In an imperial charge. But I shall crave your pardon;
That which you are, my thoughts cannot transpose:
Angels are bright still, though the brightest[5] fell:
Though all things foul would wear[6] the brows of grace,
Yet grace must still look so.[7]

MACDUFF.   I have lost my hopes.

MALCOLM. Perchance even there where I did find my doubts.
Why in that rawness[8] left you wife and child,
Those precious motives, those strong knots of love,
Without leave-taking? I pray you,
Let not my jealousies be your dishonors.
But mine own safeties.[9] You may be rightly just
Whatever I shall think.

MACDUFF.   Bleed, bleed, poor country:
Great tyranny, lay thou thy basis sure,
For goodness dare not check thee: wear thou thy wrongs:
The title is affeered.[10] Fare thee well, lord:
I would not be the villain that thou think'st
For the whole space that's in the tyrant's grasp
And the rich East to boot.

MALCOLM.   Be not offended:
I speak not as in absolute fear of you.
I think our country sinks beneath the yoke;
It weeps, it bleeds, and each new day a gash
Is added to her wounds. I think withal
There would be hands uplifted in my right;[11]
And here from gracious England[12] have I offer
Of goodly thousands: but, for all this,
When I shall tread upon the tyrant's head,
Or wear it on my sword, yet my poor country
Shall have more vices than it had before,
More suffer, and more <u>sundry</u> ways than ever,
By him that shall succeed.

MACDUFF.   What should he be?

MALCOLM. It is myself I mean, in whom I know
All the particulars of vice so grafted[13]
That, when they shall be opened,[14] black Macbeth
Will seem as pure as snow, and the poor state
Esteem him as a lamb, being compared
With my confineless harms.[15]

MACDUFF.   Not in the legions
Of horrid hell can come a devil more damned
In evils to top Macbeth.

---

5. **the brightest** Lucifer.

6. **would wear** desire to wear.

7. **so** like itself.

8. **rawness** unprotected state or condition.

9. **safeties** protections.

10. **affeered** legally confirmed.

Literary Analysis
Imagery Why are the images Malcolm uses to describe Scotland in lines 39–41 more effective than a simple statement that the country is in trouble and getting worse?

11. **in my right** on behalf of my claim.

12. **England** king of England.

Vocabulary Builder
sundry (sun′ drē) *adj.* various; miscellaneous

13. **grafted** implanted.

14. **opened** in bloom.

15. **confineless harms** unbounded evils.

Reading Check
How does Malcolm describe himself to Macduff?

Macbeth, Act IV, Scene iii ■ 371

㉗ Literary Analysis
Imagery

- **Ask** students to list some of the images Malcolm uses to describe Scotland.

- Students may not be familiar with the image of a yoke. Explain that, while some yokes were used to connect working animals to plows or wagons, the yoke referred to here is a wooden frame that a person would put across his or her shoulders to help with carrying a heavy load, with half of the load on each side of the yoke.

- Then, **ask** the Literary Analysis question: Why are the images Malcolm uses to describe Scotland in lines 39–41 more effective than a simple statement that the country is in trouble and getting worse?
Answer: The imagery used helps the reader or audience "feel" the badness of what is happening to Scotland by creating sensory images of a crushing burden (sinks beneath the yoke), sorrow (it weeps), and terrible pain (bleeding wounds).

▶ **Monitor Progress: Ask** students to **consider** in what way this imagery connects to some of the repeated images in *Macbeth*.
Answer: The image of Scotland wounded and bloody is consistent with the repeated images of bloodshed in the play.

㉘ Reading Check
Answer: Malcolm describes himself as having so many vices that Macbeth will seem "pure as snow."

Differentiated Instruction   Solutions for All Learners

Strategy for Special Needs Students
Explain to students that this entire scene with Malcolm and Macduff is one of testing Macduff's loyalty. Malcolm believes, quite reasonably, that if Macduff were really worried about Macbeth, he wouldn't have left his wife and children in Scotland (lines 25–29). Emphasize that Malcolm's description of his own evil is part of his effort to test Macduff, primarily to make sure that his life is safe in Macduff's hands. Macbeth once appeared to be loyal, so Malcolm must be careful.

Vocabulary for English Learners
Students may be concerned about the Literature in Context note, which might make Shakespeare's language look inaccessible. Emphasize that most of Shakespeare's words are still in use. Explain that understanding Shakespeare can actually help them build a better, larger vocabulary, because the difficulty most students have is not that Shakespeare's words are old, but simply that his vocabulary was so much larger than is common today. Remind them that, even though some of the words are unfamiliar, the themes are universal.

29 Critical Thinking

Analyze

- Point out that, as the dialogue between Malcolm and Macduff progresses, Malcolm stops talking about his worries and his safety and begins talking about how awful he is.

- **Ask** students if the things Malcolm is saying about himself sound believable.
  Possible response: Students may respond that they do not sound reasonable. First, if he were that bad, he wouldn't tell anyone; he'd be secretive, like Macbeth. Second, it is unlikely that he could be that bad and not have anyone at all notice before now.

- **Ask** students if they can imagine a reason Malcolm would talk this way about himself.
  Possible responses: Perhaps he is still worried about Macduff and is trying to drive him away. Perhaps he is testing Macduff.

- Have students **consider** Macduff's response in lines 84–90. How does he feel about Malcolm's claim of avarice? How does he reply to Malcolm's confession?
  Answer: Macduff considers avarice to be worse than the previously confessed lust. However, Macduff says that Scotland can afford to satisfy Malcolm's greed.

30 Literary Analysis

Imagery

- **Discuss** with students what Malcolm is saying he will do in line 98.
  Answer: He says that he will destroy the harmony (concord) of life in Scotland.

- **Ask** students the Literary Analysis question: How does the image in Act IV, Scene iii, line 98 echo those in Act I, Scene v, lines 17 and 47–48?
  Answer: In all three passages, milk represents something good—kindness, concord—and it is shown as the thing that stands between good acts and evil. Hence, Lady Macbeth says Macbeth has too much "milk of human kindness" to kill, she asks to have her milk exchanged for the bitterness of gall, and Malcolm threatens to pour this same milk into hell, implying that nothing will stop him then from evil.

372

MALCOLM.   I grant him bloody,
Luxurious,[16] avaricious, false, deceitful,
Sudden,[17] malicious, smacking of every sin
60   That has a name: but there's no bottom, none,
In my voluptuousness: your wives, your daughters,
Your matrons and your maids, could not fill up
The cistern of my lust, and my desire
All continent impediments[18] would o'erbear,
65   That did oppose my will. Better Macbeth
Than such an one to reign.

MACDUFF.   Boundless <u>intemperance</u>
In nature[19] is a tyranny; it hath been
Th' untimely emptying of the happy throne,
And fall of many kings. But fear not yet
70   To take upon you what is yours: you may
Convey[20] your pleasures in a spacious plenty,
And yet seem cold, the time you may so hoodwink.
We have willing dames enough. There cannot be
That vulture in you, to devour so many
75   As will to greatness dedicate themselves,
Finding it so inclined.

MALCOLM.   With this there grows
In my most ill-composed affection[21] such
A stanchless[22] <u>avarice</u> that, were I King,
I should cut off the nobles for their lands,
80   Desire his jewels and this other's house:
And my more-having would be as a sauce
To make me hunger more, that I should forge
Quarrels unjust against the good and loyal,
Destroying them for wealth.

MACDUFF.   This avarice
85   Sticks deeper, grows with more pernicious root
Than summer-seeming[23] lust, and it hath been
The sword of[24] our slain kings. Yet do not fear.
Scotland hath foisons[25] to fill up your will
Of your mere own.[26] All these are portable,[27]
90   With other graces weighed.

MALCOLM. But I have none: the king-becoming graces,
As justice, verity, temp'rance, stableness,
Bounty, perseverance, mercy, lowliness,
Devotion, patience, courage, fortitude,
95   I have no relish of them, but abound
In the division of each several crime,[28]
Acting it many ways. Nay, had I pow'r, I should
Pour the sweet milk of concord into hell,
Uproar the universal peace, confound[29]

16. luxurious lecherous.

17. Sudden violent.

18. continent impediments restraints.

Vocabulary Builder
intemperance (in tem′ pər əns) *n.* lack of restraint

19. nature man's nature.

20. Convey secretly manage.

21. affection character.

Vocabulary Builder
avarice (av′ ə ris) *n.* greed

22. stanchless never-ending.

23. summer-seeming summerlike.

24. of that killed.

25. foisons (foi′ zənz) plenty.

26. mere own own property.

27. portable bearable.

28. division . . . crime variations of each kind of crime.

29. confound destroy.

Enrichment

The Number Three

Three appears often in Macbeth. Three is significant in an astonishing range of connections. The more one looks, the more "threes" one sees. In art, there are three primary colors, from which all others are created. In math, three is the fewest number of points needed to create a closed figure (a triangle). For this reason, three has come to symbolize that which is real, solid, and complete.

Celtic art and literature (and the Scots were largely Celts) was preoccupied with the number three. One often sees objects repeated three times or with three faces.

The Greeks used the number three a lot. The infernal goddess Hecate is always shown as one of three. There were three fates, three graces, and three furies.

In the Bible, three is important, from the Holy Trinity to the three denials of Peter. Blessings, questions, and judgments are often repeated three times. It is often a symbol of things being completed, either in judgment or in redemption.

All unity on earth.

100 **MACDUFF.**   O Scotland, Scotland!

MALCOLM. If such a one be fit to govern, speak:
I am as I have spoken.

MACDUFF.   Fit to govern!
No, not to live. O nation miserable!
With an untitled[30] tyrant bloody-sceptered,
105 When shalt thou see thy wholesome days again,
Since that the truest issue of thy throne[31]
By his own interdiction[32] stands accursed,
And does blaspheme his breed?[33] Thy royal father
Was a most sainted king: the queen that bore thee,
110 Oft'ner upon her knees than on her feet,
Died[34] every day she lived. Fare thee well!
These evils thou repeat'st upon thyself
Hath banished me from Scotland. O my breast,
Thy hope ends here!

MALCOLM.   Macduff, this noble passion,
115 Child of integrity, hath from my soul
Wiped the black scruples, reconciled my thoughts
To thy good truth and honor. Devilish Macbeth
By many of these trains[35] hath sought to win me
Into his power; and modest wisdom[36] plucks me
120 From over-credulous haste: but God above
Deal between thee and me! For even now
I put myself to thy direction, and
Unspeak mine own detraction,[37] here abjure
The taints and blames I laid upon myself,
125 For[38] strangers to my nature. I am yet
Unknown to woman, never was forsworn,
Scarcely have coveted what was mine own,
At no time broke my faith, would not betray
The devil to his fellow, and delight
130 No less in truth than life. My first false speaking
Was this upon myself. What I am truly,
Is thine and my poor country's to command:
Whither indeed, before thy here-approach,
Old Siward, with ten thousand warlike men,
135 Already at a point,[39] was setting forth.
Now we'll together, and the chance of goodness
Be like our warranted quarrel![40] Why are you silent?

MACDUFF. Such welcome and unwelcome things at once
'Tis hard to reconcile.

[*Enter a* DOCTOR.]

140 **MALCOLM.** Well, more anon. Comes the King forth, I pray you?

Literary Analysis
Imagery How does the image in Act IV, Scene iii, line 98 echo those in Act I, Scene v, line 17 and Act I, Scene v, lines 47–48?

30. untitled having no right to the throne.

31. truest . . . throne child of the true king.

32. interdiction exclusion.

33. blaspheme his breed slander his ancestry.

34. Died prepared for heaven.

35. trains enticements.

36. modest wisdom prudence.

Vocabulary Builder
credulous (krej´ o͞o ləs) *adj.* tending to believe too readily

37. detraction slander.

38. For as.

39. at a point prepared.

40. the chance . . . quarrel May our chance of success equal the justice of our cause.

Reading Check
What response by Macduff convinces Malcolm that Macduff is being honest?

Macbeth, Act IV, Scene iii ■ 373

---

continued from right column

33 Reading Check

Answer: Macduff laments that Malcolm is not fit to govern or to live, that he cannot compare to his father Duncan, and he banishes himself from Scotland because he despairs of its ever righting itself with Malcolm in power. This response convinces Malcolm that Macduff is being honest.

---

31 Literary Analysis
Imagery

• **Ask** students to notice how many of the recurring themes or ideas of this play are found in lines 102–117.
Answer: Possibilities include tyrant, blood, child, black, and devilish.

• Point out that this exchange marks a departure from what has come before. For the first time, a man is exactly what he appears to be. Both Malcolm and Macduff are honest men, who speak without hiding secrets.

• **Ask** students how Duncan and Macbeth are contrasted in these lines.
Answer: Duncan was sainted and Macbeth is devilish—so they are total opposites.

• Point out that, though she isn't mentioned, there is an implied contrast with Lady Macbeth. The saintliness and tender care of Duncan's queen contrast with Lady Macbeth's evil, particularly her comment about her being willing to dash her child's brains out.

• **Ask** students if Macduff's comment in line 138 reminds them of anything they read earlier in the play.
Possible response: The line is similar to several lines in which things were opposites, such as Macbeth's comment in Act I, Scene iii, "So foul and fair a day I have not seen."

32 Vocabulary Builder
The Latin Word Root -cred-

• Call students' attention to the word *credulous* and its definition. Tell students that the Latin word root -*cred*- means "belief."

• Have students suggest words and phrases that contain this root, and list them on the chalkboard. Feel free to add to students' suggestions.
Possible responses: *incredible, incredulous, credibility, incredulity, credence, credential, credit, creed, credo*

• Next, have students look up these words in a dictionary.

continued

- Point out that Macduff and Ross both use a type of figurative language called personification. That is, they give human qualities to Scotland, which stands, is afraid, is conscious (knows), is a mother, and can feel pain and die.

- **Ask** students to **identify** the senses to which Ross appeals in this description of Scotland in lines 164–173. You may wish to have them make a chart that shows which images appeal to which senses.
Possible responses: Hearing: sighs, groans, shrieks, ringing bell (knell); Sight: most of the additional images, including country, mother, grave, smile, men, flower, cap. Students may also suggest smell because of the flower. They may also suggest that violent death implies the sense of touch.

- **Ask** students the Reading Strategy question: How does the description in lines 164–173 help you envision the condition of Scotland?
Answer: This description gives an impression of a country in chaos, where death and sorrow are so common no one even comments. The country is so helpless and sad that it is in danger of becoming numb to its own suffering.

- You may wish to explain to students that the "dead man's knell" mentioned in line 170 refers to the old tradition of ringing the church bell when someone in a town died. (Explain that both *knell* and *toll* are other ways of saying *ring*, though both imply the deeper sound of a large bell.) It was a common practice and appears in many works. Among the most famous appearances are in John Donne's "Meditation 17," which begins "Perchance he for whom this bell tolls may be so ill, as that he knows not it tolls for him," and Ernest Hemingway's novel *For Whom the Bell Tolls*.

DOCTOR. Ay, sir. There are a crew of wretched souls
That stay[41] his cure: their malady convinces
The great assay of art;[42] but at his touch,
Such sanctity hath heaven given his hand,
They presently amend.[43]

145 **MALCOLM.**   I thank you, doctor.

                                   [*Exit* DOCTOR.]

MACDUFF. What's the disease he means?

MALCOLM.   'Tis called the evil:[44]
A most miraculous work in this good King,
Which often since my here-remain in England
I have seen him do. How he solicits heaven,
150 Himself best knows: but strangely-visited people,
All swoll'n and ulcerous, pitiful to the eye,
The mere[45] despair of surgery, he cures,
Hanging a golden stamp[46] about their necks,
Put on with holy prayers: and 'tis spoken,
155 To the succeeding royalty he leaves
The healing benediction. With this strange virtue
He hath a heavenly gift of prophecy,
And sundry blessings hang about his throne
That speak him full of grace.

[*Enter* ROSS.]

MACDUFF.   See, who comes here?

160 **MALCOLM.** My countryman; but yet I know him not.

MACDUFF. My ever gentle[47] cousin, welcome hither.

MALCOLM. I know him now: good God, betimes[48] remove
The means that makes us strangers!

ROSS.   Sir, amen.

MACDUFF. Stands Scotland where it did?

ROSS.   Alas, poor country!
165 Almost afraid to know itself! It cannot
Be called our mother but our grave, where nothing[49]
But who knows nothing is once seen to smile;
Where sighs and groans, and shrieks that rent the air,
Are made, not marked, where violent sorrow seems
170 A modern ecstasy.[50] The dead man's knell
Is there scarce asked for who,[51] and good men's lives
Expire before the flowers in their caps,
Dying or ere they sicken.

MACDUFF.   O, relation
Too nice,[52] and yet too true!

374 ■ Celebrating Humanity (1485–1625)

41. stay wait for.

42. convinces . . . art defies the efforts of medical science.

43. presently amend immediately recover.

44. evil scrofula (skräf´ yə lə), skin disease called "the king's evil" because it was believed that it could be cured by the king's touch.

45. mere utter.

46. stamp coin.

47. gentle noble.

48. betimes quickly.

Reading Strategy
Using Your Senses How does the description in lines 164–173 help you envision the condition of Scotland?

49. nothing no one.

50. modern ecstasy ordinary emotion.

51. The dead . . . who People can no longer keep track of Macbeth's victims.

52. nice exact.

Enrichment

Facts versus Entertainment

Macbeth was probably performed for King James I during the summer of 1606. Scholars believe that Shakespeare wanted to flatter the king, so he made the characters of Banquo and Fleance more noble than they appeared in Holinshed's account. But flattery was only a small part of Shakespeare's motivation.

Shakespeare's audiences knew Holinshed well. These histories were far from accurate but were widely accepted. However, people didn't expect facts from a play. They expected to be entertained—and no one did that better than Shakespeare. He invented wonderfully, but he gladly borrowed any good plot devices he found. For example, Holinshed related that, a century before Macbeth lived, there was a Scot named Donwald whose wife nagged him into killing King Duff. Shakespeare adapted this scenario for *Macbeth*.

MALCOLM.   What's the newest grief?

175 **ROSS.** That of an hour's age doth hiss the speaker;[53]
Each minute teems[54] a new one.

MACDUFF.   How does my wife?

ROSS. Why, well.

MACDUFF.   And all my children?

ROSS.   Well too.

MACDUFF. The tyrant has not battered at their peace?

ROSS. No; they were well at peace when I did leave 'em.

180 **MACDUFF.** Be not a niggard of your speech: how goes 't?

ROSS. When I came hither to transport the tidings,
Which I have heavily borne, there ran a rumor
Of many worthy fellows that were out;[55]
Which was to my belief witnessed[56] the rather,
185 For that I saw the tyrant's power[57] afoot.
Now is the time of help. Your eye in Scotland
Would create soldiers, make our women fight,
To doff[58] their dire distresses.

MALCOLM.   Be 't their comfort
We are coming thither. Gracious England hath
190 Lent us good Siward and ten thousand men;
An older and a better soldier none
That Christendom gives out.

ROSS.   Would I could answer
This comfort with the like! But I have words

53. That . . . speaker Report of the grief of an hour ago is hissed as stale news.

54. teems gives birth to.

Literary Analysis
Imagery Why do you think Ross uses such an exaggerated image in lines 186–188?

55. out in rebellion.

56. witnessed confirmed.

57. power army.

58. doff put off.

36 ✓Reading Check
What report from Scotland does Ross bring?

37 ▼ Critical Viewing
How does this castle compare with your image of Inverness? [Connect]

Macbeth, Act IV, Scene iii ▪ 375

---

35 Literary Analysis
Imagery

- **Ask** the Literary Analysis question: Why do you think Ross uses such an exaggerated image in lines 186–188?
  Possible responses: Ross uses such an exaggerated image because he wants to convince Malcolm how much his presence would inspire people to fight against Macbeth.

- **Ask** students what real opinion of Malcolm Ross's speech reflects.
  Answer: Ross has a high opinion of Malcolm. He believes people will be inspired by someone who is honorable.

- Point out that, in the lines preceding this speech, Macduff asks why Ross suddenly has so little to say. (Explain that *niggard* means *stingy*.)
  Ask students why Ross might be reluctant to tell Macduff about his family. Also, in what way might saying "they are at peace" be viewed by Ross as kind of a truth?
  Possible responses: Ross is reluctant to speak because no one likes telling someone about a loved one's death. As for what he says about their being "at peace," it is fairly common to say that someone who is dead is at peace, and tombstones often read "Rest in Peace."

36 Reading Check

Answer: Ross brings a report from Scotland that the country suffers greatly.

37 Critical Viewing

Possible responses: This castle is strongly fortified, and looks imposing and regal, as Inverness would. Some students might think that this castle is much more modern than Inverness would be, and much larger. They might also observe that the large number of windows would make it harder to defend, so it doesn't seem to be the kind of castle one would expect in a war-like era, such as that of the play.

Differentiated Instruction   Solutions for All Learners

Strategy for Less Proficient Readers
Review with students the events in this scene and the information gained: Malcolm tests Macduff, Ross arrives, Scotland's distress is described, an army is growing, and news of Macduff's family is received. Discuss how this scene fits into the plot. (It shows that opposition to Macbeth is growing.) To help students connect words with emotions, have them listen to this scene on the *Listening to Literature Audio CDs*. Discuss how the images, events, and emotions build on or contribute to each other.

Enrichment for Gifted/Talented Students
Emotions run high in this scene. Malcolm is nervous. Ross mourns Scotland's distress. There are two anguished outbursts from Macduff—when he thinks hope for Scotland is lost and then when he learns of the death of his family. Have students pick a speech from this scene, or work with partners and pick a passage of dialogue, and prepare it for presentation. Encourage them to think about how they would feel under the circumstances and to bring these emotions to their performances.

38 Literary Analysis
Imagery

38 Literary Analysis
Imagery

- **Ask** students what Ross means by "To relate the manner, were. . . to add the death of you."
Answer: He means that it was so ghastly that, if Macduff heard the whole story, he'd die, too.

- **Ask** students the Literary Analysis question: How does the imagery in line 206 emphasize the ghastly fate of Macduff's family?
Answer: By comparing them to deer and a heap of game after a hunt, it emphasizes that they were innocent and that they were treated inhumanly.

39 Critical Thinking
Deduce

- **Ask** students whom Malcolm is addressing. What is his advice?
Answer: Malcolm addresses Macduff; he tells him not to hold in his grief.

- **Ask** students how Macduff's disbelief and then sorrow are reflected in the dialogue that follows.
Answer: He keeps asking who was killed, as if it isn't sinking in, it's too horrible to believe. He then swings from disbelief to sorrow and to fury.

- **Ask** what Macduff means in line 216 when he says, "He has no children."
Answer: He is saying that, because Malcolm has no children, he can't understand what Macduff is feeling.

40 Literary Analysis
Imagery

- Point out that, as the act ends, a lot of the imagery used thus far appears in the closing speeches.

- **Ask** students what image used by Lady Macduff to her son in scene ii is echoed in lines 217–218.
Answer: Both use bird imagery.

- Note that manhood is discussed in line 219 and following. How do these images differ from previous ones?
Answer: Here, a more traditional image of manhood—loving husband and father, protector, upholder of what is right—contrasts with previous images of manhood as being murderous.

- Point out that the closing line echoes the recurring theme of light and dark.

That would be howled out in the desert air,
Where hearing should not latch[59] them.

195 **MACDUFF.** What concern they?
The general cause or is it a fee-grief[60]
Due to some single breast?

ROSS. No mind that's honest
But in it shares some woe, though the main part
Pertains to you alone.

MACDUFF. If it be mine,
200 Keep it not from me, quickly let me have it.

ROSS. Let not your ears despise my tongue for ever,
Which shall possess them with the heaviest sound
That ever yet they heard.

MACDUFF. Humh! I guess at it.

ROSS. Your castle is surprised; your wife and babes
205 Savagely slaughtered. To relate the manner,
38 ┃ Were, on the quarry[61] of these murdered deer,
To add the death of you.

MALCOLM. Merciful heaven!
What, man! Ne'er pull your hat upon your brows;
Give sorrow words. The grief that does not speak
210 Whispers the o'er-fraught[62] heart and bids it break.

MACDUFF. My children too?

ROSS. Wife, children, servants, all
That could be found.

MACDUFF. And I must be from thence!
My wife killed too?

ROSS. I have said.

MALCOLM. Be comforted.
Let's make us med'cines of our great revenge,
215 To cure this deadly grief.

MACDUFF. He has no children. All my pretty ones?
Did you say all? O hell-kite![63] All?
What, all my pretty chickens and their dam
At one fell swoop?

40 **MALCOLM.** Dispute it[64] like a man.

220 **MACDUFF.** I shall do so;
But I must also feel it as a man.
I cannot but remember such things were,
That were most precious to me. Did heaven look on,
And would not take their part? Sinful Macduff,

376 ■ *Celebrating Humanity (1485–1625)*

59. **latch** catch.

60. **fee-grief** personal grief.

Literary Analysis
Imagery How does the image in line 206 emphasize the ghastly fate of Macduff's family?

61. **quarry** heap of game slain in a hunt.

62. **o'er-fraught** over-burdened.

63. **hell-kite** hellish bird of prey.

64. **Dispute it** Counter your grief.

Assessment Practice

Fact and Opinion **(For more practice, see** *Standardized Test Preparation Workbook*, p. 15.**)**

Many tests ask students to distinguish between fact and opinion. Use this sample item to give students practice.

    Ross When I came hither to transport the tidings,
Which I have heavily borne, there ran a rumor
Of many worthy fellows that were out. . .
Your eye in Scotland
Would create soldiers, make our women fight.

Which of the following is an opinion from this speech?
    A Ross brought news.
    B Ross was sad about the news.
    C There was a rumor in Scotland.
    D Malcolm's return would create soldiers.
    Malcolm's return is in the future, so Ross is simply stating what he believes. The correct answer is *D*.

225 They were all struck for thee! Naught[65] that I am,
Not for their own demerits but for mine
Fell slaughter on their souls. Heaven rest them now!

MALCOLM. Be this the whetstone of your sword. Let grief
Convert to anger; blunt not the heart, enrage it.

230 **MACDUFF.** O, I could play the woman with mine eyes,
And braggart with my tongue! But, gentle heavens,
Cut short all intermission; front to front[66]
Bring thou this fiend of Scotland and myself;
Within my sword's length set him. If he 'scape,
235 Heaven forgive him too!

MALCOLM.   This time goes manly.
Come, go we to the King. Our power is ready;
Our lack is nothing but our leave.[67] Macbeth
Is ripe for shaking, and the pow'rs above
Put on their instruments.[68] Receive what cheer you may.
240 The night is long that never finds the day.   [*Exit.*]

65. Naught wicked.

66. front to front face to face.

67. Our . . . leave We need only to take our leave.

68. Put . . . instruments urge us onward as their agents.

Critical Reading

1. **Respond:** Do you blame Macduff for abandoning his family? Why or why not?

2. **(a) Recall:** What are the predictions made by the second and third apparitions? **(b) Analyze:** Why does Macbeth readily accept these predictions?

3. **(a) Recall:** What happens to Macduff's family? **(b) Infer:** What does the fate of Macduff's family suggest about Macbeth's state of mind?

4. **(a) Recall:** How does Malcolm test Macduff? **(b) Analyze:** What does this test reveal about both Malcolm and Macduff? Explain.

5. **(a) Recall:** How does Macduff respond when asked to take the news about his family "like a man"? **(b) Interpret:** How would you characterize Macduff, based on his reaction to the murder of his wife and son? **(c) Compare and Contrast:** Compare and contrast Macduff's understanding of manhood with definitions of it earlier in the play.

6. **(a) Hypothesize:** If Shakespeare were alive today, would he argue that evildoers are primarily influenced by genetics, upbringing, or their own free choice? Base your answer on evidence from Act IV.
(b) Evaluate: Would you agree with his position? Explain.

Go Online
Author Link
For: More about William Shakespeare
Visit: www.PHSchool.com
Web Code: ese-9209

Macbeth, Act IV, Scene iii ■ 377

Go Online   For additional information about
Author Link   William Shakespeare, have students
type in the Web Code, then select S from the
alphabet, and then select the author's name.

1. **Possible responses:** Yes. He could have secured his castle with guards or taken his family with him to England. No. He couldn't have foreseen the extent of Macbeth's wrath and evil.

2. (a) The second apparition says that none of woman born shall harm Macbeth. The third apparition tells Macbeth he won't be vanquished until Birnam Wood comes to Dunsinane. (b) Macbeth accepts the predictions because they appear favorable. Also, the witches' other prophecies came true.

3. (a) Macduff's wife and children are murdered. (b) Macbeth has degenerated into complete, unbridled evil.

4. (a) Malcolm tests Macduff by claiming to be worse than Macbeth. (b) Malcolm is a cautious man, testing Macduff. He is no fool and shows signs of being a great leader. Macduff is an honorable, honest man who is loyal to his country and the vows he has taken.

5. (a) He says that he must feel his grief as a man does. (b) Macduff reacts as a deeply loving man who is staggered by the news of his family's death. (c) Macduff's idea of manhood includes tenderness, love, and honor; earlier definitions do not. However, Macduff and Macbeth both speak of making wrongs right as manly, though Macduff's motives are honorable and Macbeth's aren't.

6. (a) **Possible response:** Shakespeare would argue that everyone has free choice.
(b) **Possible response:** Macbeth chooses evil—he even says that no one should trust the witches; he says that whatever he thinks he will do, which shows that he knows what he is doing. Malcolm believes that Macduff, who has a similar background to Macbeth, might have chosen evil, but he has not. Macduff, who knows the goodness of Duncan and his queen, cannot believe that Malcolm has chosen evil.

Answers

1. **Possible response:** Students may choose imagery from Lady Macduff's speech in scene ii, lines 6–14:"poor wren, / The most diminutive of birds," expresses helplessness and innocence; "the owl" expresses being ravenous and deadly.

2. (a) In Act IV, scene i, the second and third apparition—a bloody child, and a child crowned— threaten Macbeth. In Act IV, scene ii, the murder of Macduff's children is an image of children in danger from Macbeth. (b) Macbeth is at war with the future because the future holds the chance of failure, death, and loss of the crown. Macbeth tries to change the predicted future by killing Banquo, and guarantee his own future by killing everyone else.

3. (a) Scene iii, lines 140–159 and scene iii, lines 168–174 contain imagery of sickness and disease. (b) Macbeth is the disease, and Malcolm is the cure.

4. In scene iii, lines 39–41, Malcolm describes Scotland: "It weeps, it bleeds, and each new day a gash is added to her wounds." In scene iii, lines 168–170, Ross adds that Scotland sighs, groans, and shrieks, and that violence and death are common.

5. These images combined with references to hell, demons, and Lucifer (the fallen angel Malcolm mentions) indicate that Macbeth has chosen evil (the fall) and has turned Scotland into a place of torment.

6. "Bleeding" and "carrying a yoke" appeal to sight; "sinking beneath the burden" and "gashes" appeal to touch; "weeping" appeals to hearing.

7. Reading with the senses, one has a sense of the pain and horror Scotland is enduring. It makes Macduff's agony over thinking there is no hope more poignant.

8. **Possible response:** Students may say that it makes it more effective as a drama, just as all the other altered facts do.

Apply the Skills

Macbeth, Act IV

Literary Analysis

Imagery

1. Identify a passage in Act IV that has vivid **imagery.** Using a chart like the one shown, indicate the emotions that the images express.

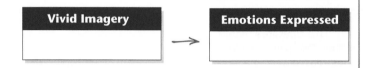

Vivid Imagery		Emotions Expressed

2. **(a)** In Act IV, Scene i and Act IV, Scene ii, find images that show children and babies are in danger from Macbeth and also threaten him. **(b)** Why is Macbeth at war with the future, which babies and children represent?

3. **(a)** Find two passages in Act IV, Scene iii with images of sickness. **(b)** Explain how these images relate to the conflict between Macbeth and Malcolm.

Connecting Literary Elements

4. In Act IV, Scene iii, identify two **archetypal images of a fallen world** that describe Scotland in terms of weeping, bleeding, or both.

5. What do the images of a fallen world and the references to the Christian underworld indicate about Macbeth's rule over Scotland? Explain.

Reading Strategy

Using Your Senses

6. Indicate how Malcolm's description of Scotland in Act IV, Scene iii, lines 39–41 appeals to the **senses** of touch, sight, and sound.

7. Why does reading this description of Scotland with your senses give a greater urgency to the dialogue between Macduff and Malcolm in Act IV, Scene iii?

Extend Understanding

8. **Social Studies Connection:** To flatter James I, Shakespeare transformed Banquo from a co-conspirator to an innocent victim. Did Shakespeare's politically motivated decision make *Macbeth* less effective as a drama? Why or why not?

378 ■ *Celebrating Humanity (1485–1625)*

QuickReview

Imagery is the language that writers use to re-create sensory experiences and stir emotions.

An **archetypal image** is one that has a powerful appeal in many different cultures. One such image is that of a **fallen world** where, according to the beliefs of many, the dead are confined.

By **using your senses,** you can experience the imagery in a literary text.

Go Online
Assessment
For: Self-test
Visit: www.PHSchool.com
Web Code: esa-6210

Build Language Skills

Vocabulary Lesson

Word Analysis: Latin Root -cred-

The root -cred- means "belief." To be credulous is "to believe something too readily." Use the word parts shown below to build five -cred- words. Then, write the meanings of these words, and verify your definitions by referring to a dictionary.

in-   -ulous   -ible   -ulity

Spelling Strategy

The letter c combines with the i of the suffix -ious to spell the sh sound, as in pernicious and judicious. In your notebook, correctly spell the following words with ci or sh.

1. suspi__ous   2. avari__ous 3. __oemaker

Grammar and Style Lesson

Possessive Forms

To form the **possessive forms** of most singular nouns and plural nouns not ending in s, add an apostrophe and s. For plural nouns ending in s, just add an apostrophe, but do not use an apostrophe to make a word plural. Shakespeare uses both singular and plural possessives in this act:

Singular: adder's traitor's baboon's

Plural: witches' warders' men's

WG *Prentice Hall Writing and Grammar Connection: Chapter 27, Section 6*

Vocabulary Builder: Context

In your notebook, answer each question.

1. Whose influence in this play is the most *pernicious*? Why?
2. Which character do you think is the most *judicious*? Why?
3. If you were staging IV, i, what *sundry* items might you use as props?
4. Does *intemperance*, rather than *ambition*, cause Macbeth's downfall? Explain.
5. Is ambition a kind of *avarice*? Why or why not?
6. How would you refute someone's claim that Malcolm is too *credulous* to rule Scotland?

Practice In your notebook, write the possessive for the following nouns.

1. the Macbeths   3. Ross   5. the women
2. the nobles   4. Fleance   6. Lennox

Writing Application Using the possessive forms of these characters' names or designations, briefly explain what role they play in the drama: Banquo, Lady Macbeth, and the witches.

Extend Your Learning

Writing Write a **motivational flier** that will inspire young, working-class Englishmen to join the army that will be invading Scotland. Use repetition and parallelism, the expression of similar ideas in similar grammatical structures.

Listening and Speaking With a small group, role-play an **interview** between Malcolm's staff and a young Englishman who wants to join their cause. Have the staff test the young man's motivation and abilities. **[Group Activity]**

Macbeth, Act IV ■ 379

Assessment Resources

The following resources can be used to assess students' knowledge and skills.

Unit 2 Resources
   Selection Test A, pp. 161–163
   Selection Test B, pp. 164–166

Go **Online**
Assessment

Students may use the **Self-test** to prepare for **Selection Test A** or **Selection Test B.**

---

❶ Vocabulary Lesson
Word Analysis

1. *Incredible* means *unbelievable.*
2. *Incredulous* means *disbelieving.*
3. *Credible* means *believable.*
4. *Credulity* means *too great readiness to believe.*

Spelling Strategy

1. suspicious   3. shoemaker
2. avaricious

Vocabulary Builder

Possible responses:

1. Macbeth's influence is *pernicious;* he is evil and destructive.
2. Malcolm is the most *judicious;* he is cautious and wise.
3. *Sundry* items include the eye of newt, toe of frog, and so on.
4. *Intemperance* causes Macbeth's downfall. His behavior is excessive.
5. Ambition is *avarice* for success or power.
6. Malcolm, though young, is not *credulous.*

❷ Grammar and Style Lesson

1. the Macbeths'   4. Fleance's
2. the nobles'   5. the women's
3. Ross's   6. Lennox's

Writing Application

Possible answer: Banquo's role is to serve as a symbol of the future that is denied to Macbeth. Lady Macbeth's role is to urge Macbeth to kill Duncan. The witches' role is to reveal the future.

❸ Listening and Speaking

- Have students work in groups to devise both interview questions and answers.
- The **Support for Extend Your Learning** page (*Unit 2 Resources,* p. 159) provides guided note-taking opportunities to help students complete the Extend Your Learning activities.

WG **Writing and Grammar, Diamond Level**

Students will find further instruction and practice on possessive forms in Chapter 27, Section 6.

Meeting Your Standards

Students will

1. **analyze and respond to literary elements.**
   - Literary Analysis: Shakespearean Tragedy

2. **read, comprehend, analyze, and critique a drama.**
   - Reading Strategy: Inferring Beliefs of the Period
   - Reading Check questions
   - Apply the Skills questions
   - Assessment Practice (ATE)

3. **develop vocabulary.**
   - Vocabulary Lesson: Latin Root: -*turb*-

4. **understand and apply written and oral language conventions.**
   - Spelling Strategy
   - Grammar and Style Lesson: Pronouns and Antecedents

5. **develop writing proficiency.**
   - Writing Lesson: Response to Criticism

6. **develop appropriate research strategies.**
   - Extend Your Learning: Annotated Bibliography

7. **understand and apply listening and speaking strategies.**
   - Extend Your Learning: Battlefield Report

Block Scheduling: Use one 90-minute class period to preteach the skills and have students read the selection. Use a second 90-minute class period to assess students' mastery of skills, extend their learning, and monitor their progress.

Homework Suggestions
Following are possibilities for homework assignments.

- Support pages from *Unit 2 Resources:*
   - Literary Analysis
   - Reading Strategy
   - Vocabulary Builder
   - Grammar and Style
- An Extend Your Learning project and the Writing Lesson for this selection may be completed over several days.

Step-by-Step Teaching Guide	Pacing Guide
PRETEACH	
• Administer Vocabulary and Reading Warm-ups as necessary.	5 min.
• Engage students' interest with the motivation activity.	5 min.
• Introduce the Literary Analysis Skill: Shakespearean Tragedy. **FT**	5 min.
• Introduce the Reading Strategy: Inferring Beliefs of the Period. **FT**	10 min.
• Prepare students to read by teaching the selection vocabulary. **FT**	
TEACH	
• Informally monitor comprehension while students read independently or in groups. **FT**	30 min.
• Monitor students' comprehension with the Reading Check notes.	as students read
• Reinforce vocabulary with Vocabulary Builder notes.	as students read
• Develop students' understanding of Shakespearean tragedy with the Literary Analysis annotations. **FT**	5 min.
• Develop students' ability to infer beliefs of the period with the Reading Strategy annotations. **FT**	5 min.
ASSESS/EXTEND	
• Assess students' comprehension and mastery of the Literary Analysis and Reading Strategy by having them answer the Apply the Skills questions. **FT**	15 min.
• Have students complete the Vocabulary Lesson and the Grammar and Style Lesson. **FT**	15 min.
• Apply students' ability to include references and citations by using the Writing Lesson. **FT**	45 min. or homework
• Apply students' understanding by using one or more of the Extend Your Learning activities.	20–90 min. or homework
• Administer Selection Test A or Selection Test B. **FT**	15 min.

Resources

Choosing Resources for Differentiated Instruction

[**L1**] Special Needs Students

[**L2**] Below-Level Students

[**L3**] All Students

[**L4**] Advanced Students

[**EL**] English Learners

For Vocabulary and Reading Warm-ups and for Selection Tests, **A** signifies "less challenging" and **B** "more challenging." For Graphic Organizer transparencies, **A** signifies "not filled in" and **B** "filled in."

FT Fast Track Instruction: To move the lesson more quickly, use the strategies and activities identified with **FT**.

Scaffolding for Less Proficient and Advanced Students

The leveled Critical Thinking questions after selections progress in the levels of thinking required to answer them. To address the needs of your different students, you may use the (a) level questions for your less proficient students and the (b) level questions with your on-level and advanced students. The occasional (c) level questions are appropriate for your advanced students.

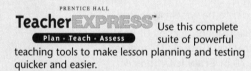

Use this complete suite of powerful teaching tools to make lesson planning and testing quicker and easier.

Use the interactive textbook (online and on CD-ROM) to make selections and activities come alive with audio and video support and interactive questions.

Benchmark

After students have completed Act V, administer **Benchmark Test 4** (*Unit 2 Resources*, pp. 191–196). If the Benchmark Test reveals that some of the students need further work, use the Interpretation Guide to determine the appropriate reteaching page in the **Reading Kit** and on **Success Tracker**.

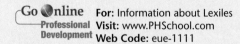

Go **Online**
Professional
Development

For: Information about Lexiles
Visit: www.PHSchool.com
Web Code: eue-1111

Motivation

Review the last three predictions made by the apparitions in Act IV: Macbeth should beware Macduff; No man born of woman shall ever harm Macbeth; Macbeth will never be vanquished until Birnam Wood comes to Dunsinane. Solicit ideas from the class about how these predictions may or may not come true. Also ask students to predict what will become of Lady Macbeth.

❶ Literary Analysis
Shakespearean Tragedy

- Read aloud the four elements of Shakespearean tragedy. Have students give examples from previous acts that support these elements.

- Use the instruction for Connecting Literary Elements to connect Macbeth's tragic impulse to the elements of Shakespearean tragedy.

❷ Reading Strategy
Inferring Beliefs of the Period

- Explain that, while all works of literature reflect beliefs to a certain degree, popular works, such as Shakespeare's plays, must reflect a higher degree of an era's beliefs in order to be widely accepted.

- Give students a copy of **Reading Strategy Graphic Organizer A,** p. 70 in *Graphic Organizer Transparencies,* to use as they read *Macbeth,* Act V.

Build Skills Drama

Macbeth, Act V

❶ Literary Analysis
Shakespearean Tragedy

Shakespearean tragedy usually contains these elements:

- A central character of high rank and personal quality, yet with a **tragic flaw** or weakness
- Causally related events that lead this character to disaster, at least partly through his or her flaw
- Lively action that creates a vivid spectacle
- The use of comic scenes to temper and offset the mood of sadness

In viewing the destruction of the central character, members of the audience experience a mixture of pity, fear, and awe that lifts them out of their everyday lives.

As you read, look for the elements of Shakespearean tragedy in this act and recall their appearance in previous acts.

Connecting Literary Elements

Viewing a Shakespearean tragedy is often an uplifting experience despite the disasters that befall the hero. The source of this positive experience is the **tragic impulse,** which shows the tragic hero confronting his or her limits in a noble way. Notice, for instance, how Shakespeare gives Macbeth a streak of reckless bravery in Act V.

❷ Reading Strategy
Inferring Beliefs of the Period

As products of a certain era, great plays reflect the **beliefs** of their period. Infer those beliefs by looking carefully at the ideas the characters express and comparing them to modern ideas on the same subject.

In Act V, Scene i, for example, you have the opportunity to watch a doctor in action. Listen carefully to what he says about a case of mental disturbance. Then, use a chart like the one shown to compare his ideas with those that a modern psychiatrist might express.

Vocabulary Builder

perturbation (pʉr′ tər bā′ shən) *n.* disturbance (p. 381)

pristine (pris′ tēn′) *adj.* original; unspoiled (p. 387)

clamorous (klam′ ər əs) *adj.* noisy (p. 390)

harbingers (här′ bin jərz) *n.* forerunners (p. 390)

Comparison of Beliefs

Doctor in *Macbeth*

↓

Modern Psychiatrist

Review and Anticipate

In Act IV, Macbeth learns from the witches that he must "Beware Macduff!" but that he need not fear any man "of woman born." He also learns that he will never be vanquished until the forest itself marches against him. However, he sees a vision indicating that Banquo will indeed father a long line of kings.

Armed with his new knowledge, Macbeth orders the murder of Macduff's wife and son. Macduff himself is in England to join forces with Malcolm and is overcome when he hears the news. Nevertheless, he and Malcolm will lead an army against Macbeth.

Act V will determine the outcome as Macbeth, grown reckless in evil, battles against Malcolm and his men.

Act V

Scene i. Dunsinane. In the castle.

[*Enter a* DOCTOR OF PHYSIC *and a* WAITING-GENTLEWOMAN.]

DOCTOR. I have two nights watched with you, but can perceive no truth in your report. When was it she last walked?

GENTLEWOMAN. Since his Majesty went into the field.[1] I have seen
5   her rise from her bed, throw her nightgown upon her, unlock her closet,[2] take forth paper, fold it, write upon 't, read it, afterwards seal it, and again return to bed; yet all this while in a most fast sleep.

DOCTOR. A great <u>perturbation</u> in nature, to receive at
10   once the benefit of sleep and do the effects of watching![3] In this slumb'ry agitation, besides her walking, and other actual performances, what, at any time, have you heard her say?

15 **GENTLEWOMAN.** That, sir, which I will not report after her.

DOCTOR. You may to me, and 'tis most meet[4] you should.

GENTLEWOMAN. Neither to you nor anyone, having no witness to confirm my speech.

[*Enter* LADY MACBETH, *with a* taper.]

Lo you, here she comes! This is her very guise,[5] and, upon my
20   life, fast asleep! Observe her; stand close.[6]

DOCTOR. How came she by that light?

GENTLEWOMAN. Why, it stood by her. She has light by her continually. 'Tis her command.

25 **DOCTOR.** You see, her eyes are open.

▲ **Critical Viewing** ❸
Who will slay Macbeth with a sword like this one? [Predict]

1. **field** battlefield.

2. **closet** chest.

Vocabulary Builder
perturbation (pʉr′ tər bā′ shən) *n.* disturbance

3. **effects of watching** deeds of one awake.

4. **meet** suitable.

5. **guise** custom.

6. **close** hidden.

❹ ✓ **Reading Check**
Why has the gentlewoman summoned the doctor?

Macbeth, Act V, Scene i ■ *381*

TEACH

❶ About the Selection

This act shows with great poignancy the final effects of Macbeth's actions on himself, his wife, and the kingdom of Scotland. As the act begins, Macbeth has fortified himself behind the stone walls of Dunsinane, armed with the prophecy of the apparitions. Lady Macbeth has suffered a mental and emotional breakdown. As the army of angry Scots who are determined to overthrow Macbeth approaches, Lady Macbeth kills herself. What's left of Macbeth's former glory will not allow him to die without a fight.

The final speech by Macbeth is meant to lift the mood of the audience. However, this play's main message is a dark one: Even the noblest and most heroic humans can fall into the depths of depravity and ruin.

❷ Vocabulary Builder
The Latin Word Root -*turb*-

- Call students' attention to the word *perturbation* and its definition. Tell students that the Latin word root -*turb*- means "to disturb."

- Write on the board the following words that include this root: *disturbing, disturbance, turbulence, turbulent, turbid, imperturbable.*

- Explain that this root is related to the Latin words *turba*, which means turmoil, *turbare*, which means to confuse, and *turbinem*, which is a whirling object. It is this last Latin word from which we get *turbine* and *turbo*.

- Have students look up the meaning of these words in a dictionary.

❸ Critical Viewing

Possible response: Students may predict that Macduff will slay Macbeth with such a sword, because Macbeth has been warned to beware of Macduff.

❹ Reading Check

Answer: The gentlewoman has summoned the doctor because she has seen Lady Macbeth sleepwalking and she wants another witness.

381

➎ Humanities

Lady Macbeth Sleepwalking, by Henry Fuseli

Fuseli was considered one of the early Romantics. Like other Romantics, he had an interest in dreams, nightmares, and waking visions. In fact, the first painting to make him famous was titled *The Nightmare.* His interest in the deeply psychological made him a natural for illustrating *Macbeth.* Fuseli loved Shakespeare, and illustrated many of his works. Fuseli's pictorial fantasies later influenced the work of William Blake.

This painting captures the nightmarish quality of Lady Macbeth's sleepwalking scene. Painted in 1784, this oil painting on canvas now hangs in the Louvre in Paris.

Use these questions for discussion:

1. How well does this painting capture the feel of the sleepwalking scene? How does your own mental image of the scene compare with the one in the painting? **Possible responses:** Students may say that the painting captures the agitation suffered by Lady Macbeth. Students may say that this painting differs from their own mental image, because Lady Macbeth seems stronger and more vibrant than the character they pictured.

2. In what ways do the colors used in the painting capture the mood of the sleepwalking scene? **Answer:** The yellow color of Lady Macbeth's gown and her vivid red hair make her the focal point of the painting. The shadowy dark colors used in the background emphasize that this is a nightmarish scene.

➏ Critical Viewing

Possible responses: Details of the scene that students might identify include the presence of the female servant (gentlewoman); the presence of the doctor, who appears to be prepared to take notes; Lady Macbeth holding a candle (taper), with her eyes open and looking as if she is suffering "slumb'ry agitation."

Lady Macbeth Sleepwalking, Henry Fuseli, Louvre, Paris

➏ ▲ **Critical Viewing** Identify four details from the sleepwalking scene (V, i) that the artist illustrates in this picture. **[Connect]**

382 ■ *Celebrating Humanity (1485–1625)*

Enrichment

Shakespeare's Universal Appeal

All the world is truly Shakespeare's stage. His plays have been performed continually since they first appeared. Though the plays seem to be about specific places and times, they are actually about universal themes that speak across time and borders. Ambition, honor, love, death, deceit, humor, guilt, pain, joy— Shakespeare's themes—are simply the human condition distilled into powerful theater.

In addition, specific ideas or elements may find favor in different places or situations. For example, the Japanese are particularly fond of Shakespeare's wise fools, and the plays in which tyrants are killed have been popular among those who feel downtrodden.

Because Shakespeare is also about a good story, directors often give his work new looks and new settings, to share their own vision or to reach new audiences. In recent years, movies have been made of *Hamlet, A Midsummer Night's Dream, Much Ado About Nothing, Romeo and Juliet,* and *Henry V.*

GENTLEWOMAN. Ay, but their sense[7] are shut.

DOCTOR. What is it she does now? Look, how she rubs her hands.

30 **GENTLEWOMAN.** It is an accustomed action with her, to seem thus washing her hands: I have known her continue in this a quarter of an hour.

LADY MACBETH. Yet here's a spot.

35 **DOCTOR.** Hark! She speaks. I will set down what comes from her, to satisfy[8] my remembrance the more strongly.

LADY MACBETH. Out, damned spot! Out, I say! One: two: why, then 'tis time to do 't. Hell is murky. Fie, my lord, fie! A soldier, and afeard? What need we fear who knows it, when none can call our pow'r to
40 accompt?[9] Yet who would have thought the old man to have had so much blood in him?

DOCTOR. Do you mark that?

LADY MACBETH. The Thane of Fife had a wife. Where is she now? What, will these hands ne'er be clean? No
45 more o' that, my lord, no more o' that! You mar all with this starting.

DOCTOR. Go to, go to! You have known what you should not.

GENTLEWOMAN. She has spoke what she should not, I am
50 sure of that. Heaven knows what she has known.

LADY MACBETH. Here's the smell of the blood still. All the perfumes of Arabia will not sweeten this little hand. Oh, oh, oh!

55 **DOCTOR.** What a sigh is there! The heart is sorely charged.[10]

GENTLEWOMAN. I would not have such a heart in my bosom for the dignity[11] of the whole body.

DOCTOR. Well, well, well—

GENTLEWOMAN. Pray God it be, sir.

60 **DOCTOR.** This disease is beyond my practice. Yet I have known those which have walked in their sleep who have died holily in their beds.

LADY MACBETH. Wash your hands; put on your nightgown; look not so pale! I tell you yet again, Banquo's
65 buried. He cannot come out on 's[12] grave.

DOCTOR. Even so?

LADY MACBETH. To bed, to bed! There's knocking at the gate. Come, come, come, come, give me your hand!

Macbeth, Act V, Scene i ■ 383

Side notes:

7. **sense** powers of sight.

8. **satisfy** support.

9. **to accompt** into account.

Literary Analysis
Shakespearean Tragedy
Does the sleepwalking scene suggest that Lady Macbeth is a tragic heroine? Explain.

10. **charged** burdened.

11. **dignity** worth.

12. **on 's** of his

❾ ✓ **Reading Check**
What does Lady Macbeth do and say as she sleepwalks?

---

❼ Critical Thinking
Analyze

- After students have read the sleepwalking scene, ask them why it is ironic that Lady Macbeth is so concerned about washing her hands.
  Answer: She was so matter-of-fact about Macbeth's washing his hands after the murder.

- **Ask** students to think of a speech of Macbeth's about sleep and one about hand washing in Act II, Scene ii that are echoed in this scene.
  Answer: Act II, Scene ii, lines 34–41, "Macbeth does murder sleep," and lines 57–61, "Will all great Neptune's ocean wash this blood/Clean from my hand?"

- Point out that Lady Macbeth switches back and forth from past to present, as she "washes" her hands and then relives the night of Duncan's murder and ensuing events. (Explain that the Thane of Fife, line 43, is Macduff, so Lady Macbeth knows of his wife's murder.)

- Discuss in class what mental state has brought on this sleepwalking.
  Possible response: Students may feel that it is guilt, fear, or both. They may observe that she is not as tough and ruthless as she thought she was. Her conscience is torturing her.

❽ Literary Analysis
Shakespearean Tragedy

- Review with students the four central aspects of Shakespearean tragedy listed on p. 380.

- Then, **ask** the Literary Analysis question: Does the sleepwalking scene suggest that Lady Macbeth is a tragic heroine? Explain.
  Answer: Lady Macbeth is a tragic figure because her flaw, unbridled ambition, has led her to this tragic point, where her conscience has caught up with her and she is suffering for her actions.

❾ Reading Check

Answer: As she sleepwalks, Lady Macbeth rubs her hands, as if to wash them, and speaks of blood, the deaths for which she and Macbeth are responsible, and such elements of previous events as the knocking at the gate.

- Remind students that the play is set in Scotland in the 11th century, but that it was written and performed in the 17th century.

- **Ask** students the Reading Strategy question: What can you infer about medicine during this time from the doctor's words in lines 72–80?
Answer: Students should note that the doctor recognizes that Lady Macbeth's illness stems not from physical suffering, but from emotional suffering. Realizing the depth of her emotional suffering, he admits that while he is unable to help her, perhaps God could. Students should remark that the doctor's willingness to call on divine aid represents a blending of religion and medicine that was characteristic of the time.

⓫ **Literary Analysis**
Shakespearean Tragedy

- Have students read the speech in lines 12–16 to themselves.

- Ask them to think about madness, or insanity, and Macbeth's murderous acts.

- Then, **ask** students the Literary Analysis question: Do you agree with those whom Caithness quotes in line 13? Is Macbeth "mad"? Why or why not?
Possible responses: Students who agree that Macbeth is mad should support their answers by pointing out that the theme of evil runs throughout the play, and that Macbeth has become evil and cannot redeem himself. His lack of restraint or human caring at this point might indicate madness. Those who say he is not mad might state that he is simply a man who has allowed his selfish ambition to rule his judgment, and is suffering for the actions that resulted from his wrong decisions. They might say that it is a weakness of character, not madness, which drives his actions.

70   What's done cannot be undone. To bed, to bed, to bed!

[*Exit* LADY MACBETH.]

DOCTOR. Will she go now to bed?

GENTLEWOMAN. Directly.

DOCTOR. Foul whisp'rings are abroad. Unnatural deeds
Do breed unnatural troubles. Infected minds
To their deaf pillows will discharge their secrets.
75   More needs she the divine than the physician.
God, God forgive us all! Look after her;
Remove from her the means of all annoyance,[13]
And still keep eyes upon her. So good night.
My mind she has mated[14] and amazed my sight:
80   I think, but dare not speak.

GENTLEWOMAN.   Good night, good doctor.

[*Exit.*]

Scene ii. The country near Dunsinane.

[*Drum and colors. Enter* MENTEITH, CAITHNESS, ANGUS, LENNOX, SOLDIERS.]

MENTEITH. The English pow'r[1] is near, led on by Malcolm,
His uncle Siward and the good Macduff.
Revenges burn in them; for their dear causes
Would to the bleeding and the grim alarm
Excite the mortified man.[2]

5   **ANGUS.**   Near Birnam Wood
Shall we well meet them; that way are they coming.

CAITHNESS. Who knows if Donalbain be with his brother?

LENNOX. For certain, sir, he is not. I have a file[3]
Of all the gentry: there is Siward's son,
10   And many unrough[4] youths that even now
Protest[5] their first of manhood.

MENTEITH.   What does the tyrant?

CAITHNESS. Great Dunsinane he strongly fortifies.
Some say he's mad; others, that lesser hate him,
Do call it valiant fury: but, for certain,
15   He cannot buckle his distempered cause
Within the belt of rule.[6]

ANGUS.   Now does he feel
His secret murders sticking on his hands;
Now minutely revolts upbraid his faith-breach.[7]
Those he commands move only in command,
20   Nothing in love. Now does he feel his title

Reading Strategy
Inferring Beliefs of the Period What can you infer about medicine during this time from the doctor's words in lines 72–80?

13. **annoyance** injury.

14. **mated** baffled.

1. **pow'r** army.

2. **Would . . . man** would incite a dead man to join the bloody, grim call to arms.

3. **file** list.

4. **unrough** beardless.

5. **Protest** assert.

Literary Analysis
Shakespearean Tragedy Do you agree with those whom Caithness quotes in Scene ii, line 13? Is Macbeth "mad"? Why or why not?

6. **rule** self-control.

7. **minutely . . . faith-breach** Every minute revolts rebuke his disloyalty.

Enrichment

Malcolm's Reign

As the play closes, Duncan's son Malcolm takes the throne of Scotland. In reality, Malcolm Canmore did become king in 1057, seventeen years after Duncan's death. He reigned as Malcolm III for thirty-five years.

Malcolm had been protected during exile by Edward the Confessor and was later able to return the favor to England. After England was defeated in the Battle of Hastings in 1066 by William of Normandy, the grandchildren of Edmund Ironside, half-brother to Edward the Confessor, fled in exile to Scotland to be protected by Malcolm. The names of the grandchildren were Edgar and Margaret. Malcolm and Margaret eventually married.

After the brief reign of Malcolm's brother, Donalbain, three of Malcolm and Margaret's sons ruled in succession. It was from the last of these sons, David I, that all future kings of Scotland, including the Stuarts, descended. Queen Elizabeth II is the twenty-eighth generation of this line.

Hang loose about him, like a giant's robe
Upon a dwarfish thief.

MENTEITH. Who then shall blame
His pestered[8] senses to recoil and start,
When all that is within him does condemn
Itself for being there?

25 **CAITHNESS.** Well, march we on,
To give obedience where 'tis truly owed.
Meet we the med'cine of the sickly weal,[9]
And with him pour we, in our country's purge,
Each drop of us.[10]

LENNOX. Or so much as it needs
30 To dew the sovereign flower and drown the weeds.[11]
Make we our march towards Birnam.

[*Exit, marching.*]

Scene iii. Dunsinane. In the castle.

[*Enter* MACBETH, DOCTOR, *and* ATTENDANTS.]

MACBETH. Bring me no more reports; let them fly all![1]
Till Birnam Wood remove to Dunsinane
I cannot taint[2] with fear. What's the boy Malcolm?
Was he not born of woman? The spirits that know
5 All mortal consequences[3] have pronounced me thus:
"Fear not, Macbeth; no man that's born of woman
Shall e'er have power upon thee." Then fly, false thanes,
And mingle with the English epicures.[4]
The mind I sway[5] by and the heart I bear
10 Shall never sag with doubt nor shake with fear.

[*Enter* SERVANT.]

The devil damn thee black, thou cream-faced loon.[6]
Where got'st thou that goose look?

SERVANT. There is ten thousand—

MACBETH. Geese, villain?

SERVANT. Soldiers, sir.

MACBETH. Go prick thy face and over-red thy fear.
15 Thou lily-livered boy. What soldiers, patch?[7]
Death of thy soul! Those linen[8] cheeks of thine
Are counselors to fear. What soldiers, whey-face?

SERVANT. The English force, so please you.

MACBETH. Take thy face hence. [*Exit* SERVANT.]
Seyton!—I am sick at heart.

---

8. **pestered** tormented.

9. **med'cine . . . weal**
Malcolm and his supporters
are "the medicine" that will
heal "the sickly" common-
wealth.

10. **Each . . . us** every last
drop of our blood.

11. **dew . . . weeds** water
the royal flower (Malcolm) and
drown the weeds (Macbeth).

1. **let . . . all** let them all
desert me!

2. **taint** become infected.

3. **mortal consequences**
future human events.

4. **epicures** gluttons.

5. **sway** move.

6. **loon** fool.

7. **patch** fool.

8. **linen** pale as linen.

14 **Reading Check**

Why is Macbeth unafraid
even though Malcolm's
army is marching
against him?

Macbeth, Act V, Scene iii ■ 385

---

12 **Literary Analysis**
Shakespearean Tragedy

- Macbeth is now experiencing the consequences of his actions. His "tragic flaw" is public knowledge, and Scottish nobles discuss its root even as they desert him for Malcolm's army.

- Point out how the recurring themes of the play are once again woven into the dialogue. Explain that this recurrence of themes not only helps tie the play together but also makes it easier for an audience to recognize important elements. Examples in Scene ii include guilty hands (line 17), clothing (lines 15–16 and 21), sickness and medicine (lines 27–28), and blood (lines 28–29).

- Tell students that England as a garden (line 30) is a metaphor that is found in many of Shakespeare's plays.

- Point out that Menteith in Scene ii prepares us for the reappearance of Macbeth in Scene iii by noting that he is tormented, and that he is jumpy (recoils and starts).

- **Ask** students what comments Menteith and Angus make that show that Macbeth is suffering because of his guilt.
Answer: Lines 16–17, "Now does he feel his secret murders sticking on his hands," and lines 24–25, "all that is within him does condemn itself for being there."

13 **Critical Thinking**
Analyze

- Point out that this is Macbeth's first appearance since his meeting with the witches in Act IV.

- **Ask** students what Macbeth's state of mind seems to be in Scene iii, lines 1–10.
Possible response: He seems almost defensive in his overconfidence; "let them fly all"—is like a child's defensive "who needs you anyway?" One can imagine him pacing, raging, repeating out loud the prophecies (except the one about Macduff), as if to reassure himself.

14 **Reading Check**

Answer: Macbeth believes that Malcolm was born of a woman, and the apparitions told him that he need not fear harm from any man born of woman.

⓯ Literary Analysis
Shakespearean Tragedy

- **Ask** students the Literary Analysis question: Do lines 20–28 evoke sympathy for Macbeth? Explain.
  Answer: Shakespeare seems to be trying to evoke sympathy for Macbeth at this point. As the possibility of death approaches, Macbeth experiences a moment of truth when the consequences of his actions become clear to him. He knows that life could bring no joy to him now and, in weariness, he makes his peace with the thought of dying.

- **Discuss** why Shakespeare would want to make Macbeth sympathetic at this point.
  Answer: A tragic hero is, by definition, someone who has nobility and personal quality, but whose tragic flaw brings about destruction. Macbeth would not be a tragic hero if there were not some positive qualities, and it would not be a tragedy if we did not care about his death, if we did not wonder what might have happened if he had made better choices.

⓰ Reading Strategy
Inferring Beliefs of the Period

- **Explain** to students that medicine, like most sciences, was in its infancy in Shakespeare's time, though it was gaining ground rapidly. Major side effects of the Reformation were a belief in the rational, the invention of the scientific method, and an explosion of experimentation and research.

- **Point out** that today, we are rediscovering the close connection between mind and body, and the influence of the emotions on health.

- **Ask** students the Reading Strategy question: Would a modern psychiatrist answer as the doctor does in lines 45–46? Why or why not?
  Possible response: Students may respond that, yes, a modern psychiatrist would recognize that Lady Macbeth's distress was caused by mental anguish, not physical illness. Even modern psychoanalysis is largely concerned with leading patients into healing themselves.

20　When I behold—Seyton, I say!—This push[9]
　Will cheer me ever, or disseat[10] me now.
　I have lived long enough. My way of life
　Is fall'n into the sear,[11] the yellow leaf,
　And that which should accompany old age,
25　As honor, love, obedience, troops of friends,
　I must not look to have; but, in their stead,
　Curses not loud but deep, mouth-honor, breath,
　Which the poor heart would fain deny, and dare not.
　Seyton!

[*Enter* SEYTON.]

SEYTON. What's your gracious pleasure?

30　MACBETH.　　　　　　　　　　　What news more?

SEYTON. All is confirmed, my lord, which was reported.

MACBETH. I'll fight, till from my bones my flesh be hacked.
　Give me my armor.

SEYTON.　　　　　　　'Tis not needed yet.

MACBETH. I'll put it on.
35　Send out moe[12] horses, skirr[13] the country round.
　Hang those that talk of fear. Give me mine armor.
　How does your patient, doctor?

DOCTOR.　　　　　　　　　　Not so sick, my lord,
　As she is troubled with thick-coming fancies
　That keep her from her rest.

MACBETH.　　　　　　　　　Cure her of that.
40　Canst thou not minister to a mind diseased,
　Pluck from the memory a rooted sorrow,
　Raze out[14] the written troubles of the brain,
　And with some sweet oblivious antidote
　Cleanse the stuffed bosom of that perilous stuff
　Which weighs upon the heart?

9. **push** effort.

10. **disseat** unthrone.

11. **the sear** withered state.

Literary Analysis
Shakespearean Tragedy
Do lines 20–28 evoke sympathy for Macbeth? Explain.

12. **moe** more.

13. **skirr** scour.

Reading Strategy
Inferring Beliefs of the Period Would a modern psychiatrist answer as the doctor does in lines 45–46? Why or why not?

14. **Raze out** erase.

386　Celebrating Humanity (1485–1625)

45   **DOCTOR.**   Therein the patient
  Must minister to himself.

  MACBETH. Throw physic[15] to the dogs, I'll none of it.
  Come, put mine armor on. Give me my staff.
  Seyton, send out.—Doctor, the thanes fly from me.—
50   Come, sir, dispatch. If thou couldst, doctor, cast
  The water[16] of my land, find her disease
  And purge it to a sound and <u>pristine</u> health,
  I would applaud thee to the very echo,
  That should applaud again.—Pull 't off,[17] I say.—
55   What rhubarb, senna, or what purgative drug,
  Would scour these English hence? Hear'st thou of them?

  DOCTOR. Ay, my good lord; your royal preparation
  Makes us hear something.

  MACBETH.   Bring it[18] after me.
  I will not be afraid of death and bane[19]
60   Till Birnam Forest come to Dunsinane.

  DOCTOR. [*Aside*] Were I from Dunsinane away and clear,
  Profit again should hardly draw me here.   [*Exit.*]

Scene iv. Country near Birnam Wood.

[*Drum and colors. Enter* MALCOLM, SIWARD, MACDUFF, SIWARD'S SON,
MENTEITH, CAITHNESS, ANGUS, *and* SOLDIERS, *marching.*]

  MALCOLM. Cousins, I hope the days are near at hand
  That chambers will be safe.[1]

  MENTEITH.   We doubt it nothing.

  SIWARD. What wood is this before us?

  MENTEITH.   The Wood of Birnam.

  MALCOLM. Let every soldier hew him down a bough
5   And bear 't before him. Thereby shall we shadow[2]
  The numbers of our host, and make discovery[3]
  Err in report of us.

  SOLDIERS.   It shall be done.

  SIWARD. We learn no other but the confident tyrant
  Keeps still in Dunsinane, and will endure
  Our setting down before 't.[4]

10   **MALCOLM.**   'Tis his main hope,
  For where there is advantage to be given
  Both more and less[5] have given him the revolt,
  And none serve with him but constrained things
  Whose hearts are absent too.

---

15. physic medicine.

16. cast the water diagnose the illness.

Vocabulary Builder
pristine (pris tēn') *adj.*
original; unspoiled

17. Pull 't off Pull off a piece of armor, which has been put on incorrectly in Macbeth's haste.

18. it his armor.

19. bane destruction.

Literary Analysis
Shakespearean Tragedy
How does Malcolm's order in Scene iv, lines 4–7 increase the sense of tension surrounding the play's outcome and Macbeth's fate?

1. That . . . safe that people will be safe in their own homes.

2. shadow conceal.

3. discovery those who see us.

4. setting down before 't laying siege to it.

5. more and less people of high and low rank.

 **Reading Check**
How will Malcolm's men disguise themselves?

Macbeth, Act V, Scene iv ■ *387*

---

⑰ Critical Thinking
Analyze
- Point out that Macbeth is talking to more than one person at a time. In performance, he would likely be turning, or at least facing, in different directions as he talks to Seyton, then the doctor, then turns back to donning his armor.
- **Ask** students to describe Macbeth's mental state as he speaks lines 47–56.
  Possible response: Students will probably say that Macbeth is very emotional, weighed down by his wife's illness and the approaching battle. This mood is shown in his outbursts and in his increasing impatience.
- Point out that the idea of the sick country reemerges in this passage, with Macbeth asking the doctor how he can cure Scotland of her illness and purge it of the English. Explain that rhubarb and senna were (and still are) commonly used as laxatives (purgatives).

⑱ Literary Analysis
Shakespearean Tragedy
- Have students **explain** why Malcolm has suggested the strategy found in lines 4–7.
  Answer: Carrying branches would disguise the number of soldiers. Malcolm may hope to approach the castle without having Macbeth consider escaping.
- **Ask** students to recall the prophecy made in Act IV by the apparition of the child holding a tree.
  Answer: The apparition said that Macbeth should be brave, because he would not be vanquished until Birnam Wood came to Dunsinane.
- **Ask** the Literary Analysis question: How does Malcolm's order in lines 4–7 increase the tension surrounding the play's outcome and Macbeth's fate?
  Possible response: The soldiers carrying boughs would look like moving trees. Macbeth, seeing them, would begin to fear that he was misled by the prophecy.

⑲ Reading Check
Answer: Malcolm's men will disguise themselves with branches of trees from the Wood of Birnam.

387

20

Background

Sieges

Macbeth's attitude in scene v, lines 1–7 was not bravado—he had reason to believe Dunsinane might withstand attack. Battles were as hard on attackers as on the attacked. It was easier to fight from the castle than to approach unprotected. Poor hygiene, inadequate supplies, and exposure to the elements often seriously diminished the ranks of the besiegers. Also, normally hostile groups that joined together for battle, such as the English and Scottish, sometimes fell to fighting among themselves.

21 Literature in Context

The Real Macbeth Macbeth's claim to the crown was probably stronger than Duncan's. Macbeth was the grandson of Scottish king Kenneth II, and Lady Macbeth (Gruoch) was the granddaughter of Kenneth III.

Duncan's grandfather, Malcolm II, became king after he killed Kenneth III. He wanted to make sure that Duncan became king, so he tried to kill rival claimants. However, Macbeth survived.

Duncan may be the only Scottish king of the era who became king without killing for it, but he soon found himself fighting—the battles at the beginning of *Macbeth* reflect the tenor of Duncan's reign.

Many other references in the play are loosely connected to real people, places, and events. Macbeth vanquished a rebel army near Birnam Wood. Siward, Earl of Northumbria, unsuccessfully attempted to dethrone Macbeth in favor of Malcolm in 1046. Macbeth was eventually killed in battle against Malcolm, who was aided by the English.

Connect to the Literature Remind students that Shakespeare often departed from historical fact to heighten the drama of his plays. Then, **ask** the Connect to the Literature question: Use this history of the real Macbeth to predict the end of the play.

Answer: Students may predict that Macbeth will die in battle, killed by Malcolm or by Macduff, as the witches warned.

MACDUFF. Let our just censures
15 Attend the true event,[6] and put we on
Industrious soldiership.

SIWARD. The time approaches,
That will with due decision make us know
What we shall say we have and what we owe.[7]
Thoughts speculative their unsure hopes relate,
20 But certain issue strokes must arbitrate:[8]
Towards which advance the war.[9] *[Exit, marching.]*

Scene v. Dunsinane. Within the castle.

[Enter MACBETH, SEYTON, *and* SOLDIERS, *with drum and colors.]*

MACBETH. Hang out our banners on the outward walls.
The cry is still "They come!" Our castle's strength
Will laugh a siege to scorn. Here let them lie
Till famine and the ague[1] eat them up.
5 Were they not forced[2] with those that should be ours,
We might have met them dareful,[3] beard to beard,
And beat them backward home.

[A cry within of women.]
What is that noise?

SEYTON. It is the cry of women, my good lord. *[Exit.]*

MACBETH. I have almost forgot the taste of fears:
10 The time has been, my senses would have cooled
To hear a night-shriek, and my fell[4] of hair

6. **our . . . event** True judgment awaits the actual outcome.

7. **owe** own.

8. **strokes . . . arbitrate** Fighting must decide.

9. **war** army.

1. **ague** fever.

2. **forced** reinforced.

3. **dareful** boldly.

4. **fell** scalp.

21

Literature in Context

History Connection

The Real Macbeth

The real Macbeth, who ruled Scotland from 1040 to 1057, did, in fact, become king by killing King Duncan. However, Macbeth's claim to the throne was legitimate due to the ancient Scottish custom of tanistry.

According to this system, the ablest, oldest male in an extended royal family could declare war on his competitors for the crown. The real Macbeth declared war on King Duncan, and killed him fairly in battle. Eventually, Duncan's son Malcolm led a Northumbrian invasion force into Scotland. In 1057, he killed Macbeth.

Connect to the Literature

Use this history of the real Macbeth to predict the end of the play.

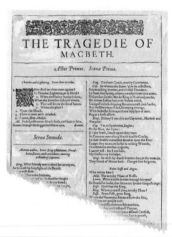

Enrichment

Quotable Shakespeare

Only the Bible has been the source of more titles, quotes, and allusions than Shakespeare.

Shakespeare has given us such familiar lines as "Neither a borrower nor a lender be," "To thine own self be true," "Dead as a doornail," "The dogs of war," and "All that glitters is not gold." From *Macbeth,* we get "The milk of human kindness," "One fell swoop," "A charmed life," and "The crack of doom."

Titles have been lifted from the text throughout the play, such as Steinbeck's *The Moon is Down* (II, i), but the famous speech in Act V, scene v, lines 17–28 has been the richest source of titles, from Robert Frost's poem "Out, Out—" to William Faulkner's novel *The Sound and the Fury.* In fact, almost every line of this speech has been used at least once for the title of some work: *Tomorrow and Tomorrow and Tomorrow, This Petty Pace, All Our Yesterdays, The Way to Dusty Death, Brief Candle, Walking Shadow, A Poor Player.*

Would at a dismal treatise[5] rouse and stir
As life were in 't. I have supped full with horrors.
Direness, familiar to my slaughterous thoughts,
Cannot once start[6] me.

[*Enter* SEYTON.]

15   Wherefore was that cry?

SEYTON. The queen, my lord, is dead.

MACBETH. She should[7] have died hereafter;
There would have been a time for such a word.[8]
Tomorrow, and tomorrow, and tomorrow
20   Creeps in this petty pace from day to day,
To the last syllable of recorded time;
And all our yesterdays have lighted fools
The way to dusty death. Out, out, brief candle!
Life's but a walking shadow, a poor player
25   That struts and frets his hour upon the stage
And then is heard no more. It is a tale
Told by an idiot, full of sound and fury
Signifying nothing.

[*Enter a* MESSENGER.]

     Thou com'st to use thy tongue; thy story quickly!

30   MESSENGER. Gracious my lord,
I should report that which I say I saw,
But know not how to do 't.

MACBETH.   Well, say, sir.

MESSENGER. As I did stand my watch upon the hill,
I looked toward Birnam, and anon, methought,
The wood began to move.

35   MACBETH.   Liar and slave!

MESSENGER. Let me endure your wrath, if 't be not so.
Within this three mile may you see it coming;
I say a moving grove.

MACBETH.   If thou speak'st false,
Upon the next tree shalt thou hang alive,
40   Till famine cling[9] thee. If thy speech be sooth,[10]
I care not if thou dost for me as much.
I pull in resolution, and begin
To doubt th' equivocation of the fiend
That lies like truth: "Fear not, till Birnam Wood
45   Do come to Dunsinane!" And now a wood
Comes toward Dunsinane. Arm, arm, and out!
If this which he avouches[11] does appear,

---

5. **treatise** story.

6. **start** startle.

7. **should** inevitably would.

8. **word** message.

Literary Analysis
Shakespearean Tragedy and the Tragic Impulse
This speech in lines 17–28 is a powerful expression of life's futility. Is Macbeth's story really "a tale/Told by an idiot, full of sound and fury / Signifying nothing"? Why or why not?

Literary Analysis
Shakespearean Tragedy
In lines 42–50, how does Macbeth's allusion to the witches' prophecies disclose a growing awareness of his own doom?

9. **cling** wither.

10. **sooth** truth.

11. **avouches** asserts.

  **Reading Check**
To what two things does Macbeth compare life when he hears that Lady Macbeth is dead?

Macbeth, Act V, Scene v ■ 389

---

22 **Literary Analysis**
Shakespearean Tragedy and the Tragic Impulse

- Explain that the speech in lines 17–28 is one of the most famous in all of Shakespeare's work.

- Remind students that the tragic impulse shows a tragic hero confronting his or her limits in a noble way.

▶ **Monitor Progress: Ask** students the first Literary Analysis question: Is Macbeth's story really "a tale/Told by an idiot, full of sound and fury/Signifying nothing"? Why or why not?
  Possible responses: Students who agree may note that Macbeth said in Scene iii that he lacked most things worth having, and now he has lost his wife. His life has come to nothing. Those who disagree may say that Macbeth's life gains meaning by serving as a warning to others.

- Point out that lines 24–26 reflect a common Shakespearean metaphor that "all the world's a stage."

- Explain that lines 26–27 show Shakespeare's familiarity with the Bible, and his assumption that his audience knows it, too. It refers to Psalm 90, which states that "we spend our years as a tale that is told." The psalm speaks of how, because life is brief, we must "apply our hearts to wisdom" to avoid evil and judgment that might make it shorter—sentiments that suit this speech.

23 **Literary Analysis**
Shakespearean Tragedy

- Tell students that *equivocation* in line 43 refers to the ambiguous language of the prophecy.

- Then, **ask** them the second Literary Analysis question: In lines 42–50, how does Macbeth's allusion to the witches' prophecies disclose a growing awareness of his own doom?
  Answer: Macbeth realizes that the promise of the third apparition has misled him. Now Birnam Wood is moving, which means Macbeth might be vulnerable.

24 **Reading Check**

Answer: Macbeth compares life to an actor and a senseless story.

㉕ Critical Viewing

Possible response: It appears that this is Macbeth killing Young Siward. The fallen man looks younger than the man with the upraised sword. Plus, the man with the sword looks weary, as one would expect of Macbeth, rather than eager for battle.

㉖ Reading Strategy

Inferring Beliefs of the Period

- Explain to students that the action in the final three scenes (vi, vii, viii) is continuous, focusing in turn on different groups of soldiers and different parts of the battlefield.

- Tell students that, unlike in modern warfare, it was common through most of Europe's history for kings and nobles to lead their soldiers into war. If students have read *Beowulf,* you may wish to remind them that the warrior-king is an archetype that was a reality for centuries.

- **Ask** students what belief about battle is reflected in Siward's comments in lines 7–8.
  Answer: It reflects the belief that fighting in a just cause is worthwhile even if one loses.

㉕ ◄ Critical Viewing
Do you think this picture portrays the fight between Macbeth and Young Siward (V, vii, 10–11) or that between Macbeth and Macduff (V, viii, 34–35)? Explain.
[Make a Judgment]

> There is nor flying hence nor tarrying here.
> I 'gin to be aweary of the sun,
> 50   And wish th' estate o' th' world were now undone.
> Ring the alarum bell! Blow wind, come wrack!
> At least we'll die with harness[12] on our back.   [*Exit.*]

12. **harness** armor.

Scene vi. Dunsinane. Before the castle.

[*Drum and colors. Enter* MALCOLM, SIWARD, MACDUFF, *and their army, with boughs.*]

> **MALCOLM.** Now near enough. Your leavy[1] screens throw down,
> And show like those you are. You, worthy uncle,
> Shall, with my cousin, your right noble son,
> Lead our first battle.[2] Worthy Macduff and we
> 5   Shall take upon 's what else remains to do,
> According to our order.[3]

1. **leavy** leafy.

2. **battle** battalion.

3. **order** plan.

> **SIWARD.**   Fare you well.
> Do we find the tyrant's power[4] tonight,
> Let us be beaten, if we cannot fight.

4. **power** forces.

> **MACDUFF.** Make all our trumpets speak; give them all breath.
> 10   Those <u>clamorous</u> <u>harbingers</u> of blood and death.

> [*Exit. Alarums continued.*]

Vocabulary Builder
clamorous (klam´ ər əs)
adj. noisy

harbingers (här´ bin jərs)
n. forerunners

390 ■ Celebrating Humanity (1485–1625)

Enrichment

Bearbaiting

In Scene vii, lines 1–2, Macbeth compares himself to a bear tied to a stake. This metaphor refers to bearbaiting, a form of entertainment popular from the 12th to the 19th century. Bull-baiting was also popular. In these "sports," a bear or bull was chained to a stake by the neck or a leg. The animal was then attacked by specially trained dogs. In fact, the breed of dog we call the bulldog was developed especially for bull-baiting.

Large groups of bears were often kept just for bearbaiting. For example, records reveal

that 13 bears were provided for an entertainment attended by Queen Elizabeth I in 1575.

Bearbaiting and bull-baiting were outlawed in England by the Puritans during the Commonwealth (1642–60). Though they were reinstituted with the return of the monarchy, they declined in popularity after this and were permanently outlawed in 1835.

The metaphor shows that Macbeth, for all his bravery, realizes he has little chance of surviving.

Scene vii. Another part of the field.

[*Enter* MACBETH.]

    MACBETH. They have tied me to a stake; I cannot fly,
       But bearlike I must fight the course.[1] What's he
       That was not born of woman? Such a one
       Am I to fear, or none.

[*Enter* YOUNG SIWARD.]

    YOUNG SIWARD. What is thy name?

5 **MACBETH.**   Thou'lt be afraid to hear it.

    YOUNG SIWARD. No; though thou call'st thyself a hotter name
       Than any is in hell.

    MACBETH.   My name's Macbeth.

    YOUNG SIWARD. The devil himself could not pronounce a title
       More hateful to mine ear.

    MACBETH.   No, nor more fearful.

10 **YOUNG SIWARD.** Thou liest, abhorrèd tyrant; with my sword
       I'll prove the lie thou speak'st.

            [*Fight, and* YOUNG SIWARD *slain.*]

    MACBETH.   Thou wast born of woman.
       But swords I smile at, weapons laugh to scorn,
       Brandished by man that's of a woman born.   [*Exit.*]

[*Alarums. Enter* MACDUFF.]

    MACDUFF. That way the noise is. Tyrant, show thy face!
15   If thou be'st slain and with no stroke of mine,
       My wife and children's ghosts will haunt me still.
       I cannot strike at wretched kerns, whose arms
       Are hired to bear their staves.[2] Either thou, Macbeth,
       Or else my sword, with an unbattered edge,
20   I sheathe again undeeded.[3] There thou shouldst be;
       By this great clatter, one of greatest note
       Seems bruited.[4] Let me find him, Fortune!
       And more I beg not.   [*Exit. Alarums.*]

[*Enter* MALCOLM *and* SIWARD.]

    SIWARD. This way, my lord. The castle's gently rend'red:[5]
25   The tyrant's people on both sides do fight;
       The noble thanes do bravely in the war;
       The day almost itself professes yours,
       And little is to do.

    MALCOLM.   We have met with foes
       That strike beside us.[6]

---

1. bearlike . . . .course Like a bear chained to a stake being attacked by dogs, I must fight until the end.

Literary Analysis
Shakespearean Tragedy
In Scene vii, does Macbeth show signs of bravery or is he just overconfident because of what the witches said? Explain.

2. staves spears.

3. undeeded unused.

4. bruited reported.

5. gently rend'red easily surrendered.

6. strike . . . us deliberately miss us.

29 **Reading Check**
What is the outcome of the hand-to-hand combat between Macbeth and Young Siward?

Macbeth, Act V, Scene vii ■ 391

---

27 Literary Analysis
Shakespearean Tragedy

- Remind students that the prophecy of the second apparition was that no man born of woman can harm Macbeth.

- Then, **ask** the Literary Analysis question: In Scene vii, does Macbeth show signs of bravery or is he just overconfident because of what the witches said?
Possible responses: Students who say Macbeth is showing bravery should note the fact that Shakespeare has left him some of the admirable traits he had in the beginning in order to evoke pity in the audience. Students who say he is simply overconfident should explain that he is overcompensating for the fact that he already knows the truth: he was misled by the prophecies, and there is really no hope left for him.

- Explain that *kerns,* mentioned in line 17, were hired Irish foot soldiers. The fact that Macbeth's troops are hired underscores the fact that Macbeth is alone.

28 Critical Thinking
Make a Judgment

- **Ask** if students find it surprising that Macbeth so easily defeats Young Siward. Why or why not?
Possible responses: Students may cite the battles at the beginning of the play as proof of Macbeth's skill as a fighter and proof that he was brave even before he heard from the witches. They may say that, now, with almost nothing left to lose, he would be a deadly opponent.

- **Ask** students why Macbeth still seems to be clinging to the last remaining hope of the witches' promises (lines 11–13).
Possible responses: It may be all he has left to hold onto. He may see his victory over Young Siward as a confirmation of it. He may not really believe it, but may just say it out of habit. It may simply be a plot device, to prepare us for a surprise at the end.

29 Reading Check
Answer: Macbeth kills Young Siward.

Interpret

• Point out that, when Macduff first heard of his family's death, he called Macbeth a hell-kite (hellish bird of prey), and now in line 3, he calls him a hell-hound (hounds were used for hunting). Both reflect the evil and bloody image created for Macbeth in this play.

• **Ask** students why they believe Macbeth has been avoiding Macduff.
Possible responses: Some may say that it is because of the warning of the first apparition: "Beware Macduff." Others may note that Macbeth says it is because he feels he has shed too much Macduff blood already.

• You may want to **discuss** whether Macbeth's comments about being "too much charged with blood" shows sorrow or fear.
Possible responses: Some may cite Macbeth's new awareness of the shortness of life and sorrow over the death of his own wife as reasons he would be sad. Others may say that he worries about Macduff's vengeful rage.

• **Ask** students to explain the significance of Macduff's comments in lines 13–16.
Answer: Macbeth's last hope is destroyed by this revelation. Because Macduff's mother died, he was delivered by the equivalent of a caesarean section. Hence, faith in an apparition's promise has again misled Macbeth.

31 Literary Analysis

Shakespearean Tragedy

• **Ask** students what Macbeth is admitting in lines 19–21, and how these lines increase the tragic feeling of this scene.
Possible response: Macbeth is admitting that he should never have trusted the prophecies of the fiends. It heightens the sense of tragedy because Macbeth realizes that his tragic flaw, ambition, has driven him to believe what he wanted to hear, rather than to do what he knew to be right.

• Point out that, when he loses his courage (line 18), we are reminded that he did have good qualities—also part of tragedy.

392

SIWARD.   Enter, sir, the castle.

                        [*Exit. Alarum.*]

Scene viii. Another part of the field.

[*Enter* MACBETH.]

MACBETH. Why should I play the Roman fool, and die
     On mine own sword?[1] Whiles I see lives,[2] the gashes
     Do better upon them.

[*Enter* MACDUFF.]

MACDUFF.   Turn, hell-hound, turn!

MACBETH. Of all men else I have avoided thee.
5   But get thee back! My soul is too much charged
     With blood of thine already.

MACDUFF.   I have no words:
     My voice is in my sword, thou bloodier villain
     Than terms can give thee out![3]

            [*Fight. Alarum.*]

MACBETH.   Thou losest labor:
     As easy mayst thou the intrenchant[4] air
10   With thy keen sword impress[5] as make me bleed:
     Let fall thy blade on vulnerable crests;
     I bear a charmèd life, which must not yield
     To one of woman born.

MACDUFF.   Despair thy charm,
     And let the angel[6] whom thou still hast served
15   Tell thee, Macduff was from his mother's womb
     Untimely ripped.[7]

MACBETH. Accursèd be that tongue that tells me so,
     For it hath cowed my better part of man![8]
     And be these juggling fiends no more believed,
20   That palter[9] with us in a double sense;
     That keep the word of promise to our ear,
     And break it to our hope. I'll not fight with thee.

MACDUFF. Then yield thee, coward,
     And live to be the show and gaze o' th' time:[10]
25   We'll have thee, as our rarer monsters[11] are,
     Painted upon a pole,[12] and underwrit,
     "Here may you see the tyrant."

MACBETH.   I will not yield,
     To kiss the ground before young Malcolm's feet,
     And to be baited with the rabble's curse.
30   Though Birnam Wood be come to Dunsinane,

392 ■ Celebrating Humanity (1485–1625)

1. play . . . sword die like Brutus or Cassius, who killed themselves with their own swords in the moment of defeat.

2. While . . . lives so long as I see living men.

3. terms . . . out words can describe you.

4. intrenchant incapable of being cut.

5. impress make a dent in.

6. angel fallen angel; fiend.

7. his . . . ripped Macduff's mother died before giving birth to him.

8. better. . . man courage.

9. palter juggle.

10. gaze o' th' time spectacle of the age.

11. monsters freaks.

12. Painted . . . pole pictured on a banner stuck on a pole by a showman's booth.

Enrichment

Sword-play on the Elizabethan Stage

Macbeth ends with a flurry of sword-play. In furious succession, the villainous king stabs Young Siward and then is outdueled by the virtuous Macduff.

Londoners of Shakespeare's time were connoisseurs of the art of fencing and would have been disappointed to see a half-hearted duel.

Some Elizabethan actors became so skillful at fencing that they won awards for it. Richard Tarleton, for example, a theater star of the 1580s, was made Master of Fence. As the highest degree offered by fencing schools, this designation was akin to today's black belt in karate.

Elizabethan audiences, however, wanted blood as well as skill. As a result, Elizabethan actors would wear bladders of animal blood, such as a sheep's, which would burst open the instant they were "stabbed." The chances are that Elizabethan theater-goers watched Macbeth die after a dazzling exhibit of sword-play and a copious spilling of blood.

And thou opposed, being of no woman born,
Yet I will try the last. Before my body
I throw my warlike shield. Lay on, Macduff;
And damned be him that first cries "Hold, enough!"

[*Exit, fighting. Alarums.*]

[*Re-enter fighting, and* MACBETH *slain. Exit* MACDUFF, *with* MACBETH. *Retreat and flourish.*[13] *Enter, with drum and colors,*
MALCOLM, SIWARD, ROSS, THANES, *and* SOLDIERS.]

35 **MALCOLM.** I would the friends we miss were safe arrived.

SIWARD. Some must go off;[14] and yet, by these I see,
So great a day as this is cheaply bought.

MALCOLM. Macduff is missing, and your noble son.

ROSS. Your son, my lord, has paid a soldier's debt:
40 He only lived but till he was a man;
The which no sooner had his prowess confirmed
In the unshrinking station[15] where he fought,
But like a man he died.

SIWARD.   Then he is dead?

ROSS. Ay, and brought off the field. Your cause of sorrow
45 Must not be measured by his worth, for then
It hath no end.

SIWARD.   Had he his hurts before?

ROSS. Ay, on the front.

SIWARD.   Why then, God's soldier be he!
Had I as many sons as I have hairs,
I would not wish them to a fairer death:
And so his knell is knolled.

50 **MALCOLM.**   He's worth more sorrow,
And that I'll spend for him.

SIWARD.   He's worth no more:
They say he parted well and paid his score:
And so God be with him! Here comes newer comfort.

[*Enter* MACDUFF, *with* MACBETH'S *head.*]

MACDUFF. Hail, King! for so thou art: behold, where stands
55 Th' usurper's cursèd head. The time is free.[16]
I see thee compassed with thy kingdom's pearl,[17]
That speak my salutation in their minds,
Whose voices I desire aloud with mine:
Hail, King of Scotland!

ALL.   Hail, King of Scotland!
[*Flourish.*]

---

13. Retreat and flourish
trumpet call to withdraw and
fanfare.

14. go off die.

15. unshrinking station
place where he stood firmly.

16. The ... free Our country
is liberated.

17. compassed ... pearl
surrounded by the noblest
people in the kingdom.

 **Reading Check**

Who finally slays Macbeth?

Macbeth, Act V, Scene viii ■ 393

---

1. **Possible responses:** There is a sense of pity and fear—pity because Macbeth had many good qualities and might have been a great man, and a lot of good people have died; fear, because one realizes that bad decisions have consequences.

2. (a) The doctor sees Lady Macbeth acting like she's washing her hands and muttering about blood and ill deeds. The doctor speculates that she has been involved in evil, "unnatural" deeds. (b) At first, Macbeth is aghast at the thought of murder, yet by the end he is wiping out entire families; Lady Macbeth pushed the idea of killing Duncan, yet in the end, she cannot live with the guilt.

3. (a) Macbeth says "She should have died hereafter." (b) **Possible response:** His reaction shows that he knew that, if she was not cured of her madness, death was inevitable. His reflection on the briefness of life shows sadness, but it seems likely that their relationship, like everything else in Macbeth's life, was unraveling.

4. (a) He says that their words were ambiguous and intentionally misleading. (b) He realizes that he may be vulnerable, after all. (c) He is angry over having been misled, and in despair, because he knows he will die.

5. (a) Malcolm and Siward learn of the deaths of Young Siward and Macbeth. Malcolm is hailed as king. Malcolm thanks everyone. (b) **Possible response:** The story ends with Macbeth's death, but for a play in particular, one expects a final comment on what has happened and what it means or brings about.

6. **Possible response:** Because ordinary people possess noble qualities, a tragedy could certainly be written about someone living today. The terrible consequences of bad choices are still tragic and can still leave one wondering how the person would have turned out if he or she had made the right choices.

---

60 **MALCOLM.** We shall not spend a large expense of time
  Before we reckon with your several loves,[18]
  And make us even with you.[19] My thanes and kinsmen,
  Henceforth be earls, the first that ever Scotland
  In such an honor named. What's more to do,
65 Which would be planted newly with the time[20]—
  As calling home our exiled friends abroad
  That fled the snares of watchful tyranny,
  Producing forth the cruel ministers
  Of this dead butcher and his fiendlike queen,
70 Who, as 'tis thought, by self and violent hands
  Took off her life—this, and what needful else
  That calls upon us, by the grace of Grace
  We will perform in measure, time, and place:[21]
  So thanks to all at once and to each one,
75 Whom we invite to see us crowned at Scone.

            [Flourish. Exit all.]

18. **reckon . . . loves** reward each of you for your devotion.

19. **make . . . you** pay what we owe you.

20. **What's . . . time** what remains to be done at the beginning of this new age.

21. **in measure . . . place** fittingly at the appropriate time and place.

Critical Reading

1. **Respond:** Does the ending of the play inspire in you feelings of pity and an almost wondrous sense of fear? Why or why not?

2. **(a) Recall:** What does the doctor see in the sleepwalking scene, and what does he speculate about the causes for what he sees?
   (b) Analyze: How have Macbeth and Lady Macbeth reversed roles by the end of the play?

3. **(a) Recall:** What does Macbeth say when he hears of Lady Macbeth's death? **(b) Draw Conclusions:** What does his reaction to her death reveal about their relationship and his state of mind?

4. **(a) Recall:** What does Macbeth say about the witches when he learns that Birnam Wood is apparently moving and that Macduff "was from his mother's womb / Untimely ripped"? **(b) Infer:** What growing realization do these statements about the witches seem to reflect?
   (c) Draw Conclusions: What is Macbeth's state of mind in his final battle with Macduff? Explain.

5. **(a) Recall:** What occurs in Act V, Scene viii, lines 35–75?
   (b) Evaluate: Would the play be complete if it ended with Macbeth's death but omitted these lines? Why or why not?

6. **Speculate:** Do you think that a tragedy could be written about an ordinary person living today? Why or why not?

For: More about William Shakespeare
Visit: www.PHSchool.com
Web Code: ese-9209

Go Online — Author Link — For additional information about William Shakespeare, have students type in the Web Code, then select S from the alphabet, and then select the author's name.

Apply the Skills

Macbeth, Act V

Literary Analysis

Shakespearean Tragedy

1. Identify all the elements of **Shakespearean tragedy** in *Macbeth*, citing examples from the play.

2. Use a chart like this one to show how Banquo's response to the witches emphasizes Macbeth's **tragic flaw.**

3. What role does Lady Macbeth play in Macbeth's choice of evil?

4. **(a)** How does Macbeth's tragic flaw lead him to disaster? **(b)** Once Macbeth kills Duncan, can he turn back? Why or why not?

5. Find three passages that show how the intensity of Macbeth's imagination adds to the tragedy. Support your choices.

Connecting Literary Elements

6. **(a)** What positive qualities does Macbeth display in Act V? Explain. **(b)** How do Macbeth's positive qualities contribute to the **tragic impulse** revealed in the play?

7. How does the tragic impulse involve a conflict between limitations and the ability to go beyond limitations? Support your answer with references to the play.

Reading Strategy

Inferring Beliefs of the Period

8. What do the doctor's remarks lead you to **infer** about Elizabethan concepts of and treatments for mental illness?

9. Compare and contrast Elizabethan concepts of mental illness with those of today.

Extend Understanding

10. **Philosophy Connection:** Is tragedy an inescapable part of life at any time, or is it a perspective on life that makes sense only in certain eras? Explain.

QuickReview

In **Shakespearean tragedy,** a central character possessing both nobility and a **tragic flaw** or weakness is caught up in events that lead to his or her downfall.

The **tragic impulse** celebrates the way in which the tragic hero confronts his or her limitations in a noble way.

To **infer the beliefs** of the period, compare the ideas expressed by the characters with modern ideas on the same subject.

Go Online
Assessment

For: Self-test
Visit: www.PHSchool.com
Web Code: esa-6211

Macbeth, Act V ■ *395*

---

continued from right column

9. We are relearning that the mind affects the body, so many would accept the doctor's diagnosis. Current doctors might offer sedatives and therapy.

10. **Possible response:** Tragedy, if defined as a personal flaw leading to destruction, is not inevitable. But it is common, because many people make bad choices.

Answers

1. **Possible response:** *Macbeth* has a central character of high rank and personal quality, with a tragic flaw (ambition). Events triggered by Macbeth's ambition lead to disaster. The play has lively action (murders, sword fights). The play includes comic scenes (with the porter).

2. **Predictions:** Macbeth will be king; Banquo's heirs will be kings; Banquo's response: mistrust, may be a lure to evil; Macbeth's response: total belief, kills everyone.

   Another sample answer can be found on **Literary Analysis Graphic Organizer B**, p. 73 in *Graphic Organizer Transparencies.*

3. Lady Macbeth is a catalyst. Macbeth has considered murder, but she fuels the fire.

4. (a) He allows his ambition to start him down a road that could only lead to more evil. (b) There might have been a kind of moral turning back in confession and surrender, but there would have been no going back to the way things were before.

5. **Possible response:** Act I, he imagines killing Duncan. Act II, phantom dagger, hands that will never be clean. Act III, Banquo's ghost. His imagination adds to the tragedy because it drives him to do more evil.

6. (a) He shows pride and courage. He will not bend, even when faced with certain death. (b) His realization that life is short and witches cannot be trusted, combined with his bravery, remind us that things could have turned out better had he made different choices.

7. Facing his limits—knowing that all is lost, the witches lied, and he will die—Macbeth moves beyond them, falling back on the pride and courage that sustained him in better times.

8. **Possible response:** We can infer that they understood the mind/wellness connection. His advice (watch her, remove things she could use to injure herself) sounds fairly modern.

continued

Build Language Skills

❶ Vocabulary Lesson

❶ Vocabulary Lesson

Word Analysis

1. *Turbulence*: "commotion, tumult"
2. *Turbulent*: "stormy, unruly, violent"
3. *Perturbation*: "disturbance"
4. *Perturbed*: "made uneasy or troubled"
5. *Turbid*: "muddy or disordered"

Vocabulary Builder

1. *clamorous*
2. *harbingers*
3. *pristine*
4. *perturbation*

Spelling Strategy

1. treasonous   3. nervous
2. glamorous

❷ Grammar and Style Lesson

1. *Donalbain* (m., sing., third)
2. *tyrant* (m., sing., third)
3. *trumpets* (n., pl., third)
4. *kerns* (m., pl., third)
5. *sons* (m., pl., third)

Writing Application

Students' paragraphs should reflect proper use of pronouns and antecedents.

₩G Writing and Grammar, Diamond Level

Students will find further instruction and practice on pronouns and antecedents in Chapter 23, Section 2.

Word Analysis: Latin Root -*turb*-

The root -*turb*- means "to disturb." To experience *perturbation* is to experience "a great disturbance." Knowing the meaning of the root -*turb*-, define the italicized words below. Then, verify your definitions with a dictionary.

1. Macbeth encounters *turbulence* in battle.
2. The eleventh century was a *turbulent* time in Scotland.
3. Elizabethans believed that a *perturbation* in the heavens meant disorder in society.
4. Macbeth was very *perturbed* by Fleance's escape.
5. After being stirred, the witches' potion was *turbid*.

❷ Grammar and Style Lesson

Pronouns and Antecedents

Pronouns, which take the place of nouns, agree with their **antecedents,** the nouns that they replace, in these ways:

• in gender (male, female, or neuter)
• number (singular or plural)
• person (first person, second person, or third person)

In this example of pronoun-antecedent agreement from Act V, the pronoun is set in boldface and the antecedent is underlined.

> **Example:** The English pow'r is near, led on by <u>Malcolm,</u> **his** uncle Siward and the good Macduff. (*Malcolm,* singular and masculine takes *his,* a singular masculine pronoun.)

Vocabulary Builder: Sentence Completion

Fill in each blank with a word from the vocabulary list on page 380.

1. The movement of Birnam Wood began with a __?__ rustling of trees.
2. The first trees that approached Dunsinane were __?__ of the army.
3. Farmers were shocked to see the untouched, __?__ wood suddenly move.
4. These farmers confessed to feeling a __?__ in their hearts.

Spelling Strategy

Add -*ous* to some nouns to make adjectives: *famous* from *fame* (dropping the final *e*). In your notebook, turn each noun into an adjective.

1. treason   2. glamor   3. nerve

Practice Identify the antecedents and the gender, number, and person of the italicized pronouns.

1. "Who knows if Donalbain be with *his* brother?"
2. "What does the tyrant? / Great Dunsinane *he* strongly fortifies."
3. "Make all our trumpets speak; give *them* all breath."
4. "I cannot strike at wretched kerns, whose arms / Are hired to bear *their* staves."
5. "Had I as many sons as I have hairs, / I would not wish *them* to a fairer death: . . ."

Writing Application Write a lead paragraph for a news story about Malcolm's victory. Be sure that pronouns agree with their antecedents.

₩G *Prentice Hall Writing and Grammar Connection: Chapter 23, Section 2*

Assessment Practice

Fact and Opinion **(For more practice, see *Standardized Test Preparation Workbook*, p. 16.)**

Many tests require students to distinguish between fact and opinion. Use the following to show students that statements of fact are often simple and reflect what the speaker can actually know.

Which of the following lines is a statement of fact?

  A Now he does feel/His secret murders sticking on his hands.

  B Those he commands move only in command,/Nothing in love.

  C Make we our march towards Birnam.

  D He cannot buckle his distempered cause/Within the belt of rule.

Lead students to recognize that, when people talk about what someone else must be feeling, it often signals an opinion. Students should determine that choice C is correct.

Writing Lesson

Timed Writing: Response to Criticism

A. C. Bradley wrote about *Macbeth*: "darkness, we may even say blackness, broods over this tragedy. . . . all the scenes which at once recur to memory take place either at night or in some dark spot." In an essay, evaluate this statement, supporting your response with specific references to the play. *(40 minutes)*

Prewriting
(10 minutes)
List the play's memorable scenes, circling those that fit Bradley's description. Based on this list, decide whether you agree with the criticism. Then, determine the effect of the connection between darkness and the play's theme.

Drafting
(20 minutes)
Introduce the drama and the quotation. Then, choose two or three key scenes to analyze. As you draft, refer to specific characters, settings, or events to make your argument.

Model: Including References and Citations

The play begins in the darkness of a thunderstorm—the stage is lit only by the flash of lightning. Three witches appear, chanting. ì When shall we three meet again?/In thunder, lightning, or in rain?" (I, i, 1-2) As the witches plan, they choose only dark weather, a perfect beginning for a play that examines the darkness of the human heart.

> A direct reference to dialogue strengthens the analysis. Parenthetical citations indicate act, scene, and line numbers.

Revising
(10 minutes)
Review your draft to ensure you have developed an analysis of each scene. If necessary, revise your conclusion to clearly address the effectiveness of darkness in the play.

W︠G Prentice Hall Writing and Grammar Connection: Chapter 14, Section 2

Extend Your Learning

Listening and Speaking With a group, cover the battle described in Act V for radio in a **battlefield report.**

- Use vivid images and figurative language.
- Include battlefield interviews.

After agreeing on a sequence of battlefield descriptions and interviews, perform your coverage for the class. **[Group Activity]**

Research and Technology Research some of the many books on Shakespearean tragedy, and produce an **annotated bibliography.** Next to each entry, briefly describe the source and evaluate its reliability.

 **Go Online Research**

For: An additional research activity
Visit: www.PHSchool.com
Web Code: esd-7209

Macbeth ■ 397

Assessment Resources

The following resources can be used to assess students' knowledge and skills.

Unit 2 Resources
> **Selection Test A,** pp. 178–180
> **Selection Test B,** pp. 181–183
> **Benchmark Test 4,** pp. 191–196

General Resources
> **Rubrics for Response to Literature,** pp. 65–66

Go Online Assessment Students may use the **Self-test** to prepare for **Selection Test A** or **Selection Test B.**

Benchmark
Administer **Benchmark Test 4.** If some students need further work, use the Interpretation Guide to determine the appropriate reteaching page in the **Reading Kit** and on **Success Tracker.**

---

❸ Writing Lesson

You may use this Writing Lesson as timed-writing practice, or you may allow students to develop the essay as a writing assignment over several days.

- Encourage students to scan the play and brainstorm for memorable scenes or comments about darkness and/or light in *Macbeth*. Remind them to include references to day or night, or any other elements related to dark and light, as well.

- Emphasize that students need to develop a clear thesis and back it up with evidence from the play.

- To guide students in writing this response to criticism, give them the **Support for Writing Lesson** page (*Unit 2 Resources*, p. 175).

- Use the Rubrics for Response to Literature, pp. 65–66 in *General Resources,* to evaluate students' work.

❹ Listening and Speaking

- You may wish to show video clips of news reports of current battles, or pass out copies of newspaper reports on either recent or famous battles.

- Divide the class into groups, and have students review the events of Act V.

- Tell students that they are not limited to the words in the play. They are to imagine that they are reporters giving their own version of what is happening.

- Encourage students to use imagery and figurative language, and to include "interviews" of people on both sides.

- The **Support for Extend Your Learning** page (*Unit 2 Resources*, p. 176) provides guided note-taking opportunities to help students complete the Extend Your Learning activities.

Go Online Research Have students type in the Web Code for another research activity.

See Teacher Express™/Lesson View for a detailed lesson plan for Reading Informational Materials.

About Newspaper Articles

- Have students read A bout Newspaper Articles."

- Explain to students that newspapers generally tell about events that happened during the past day or week, for example, city meetings or government events. Tell students that reporters gather information and try to make their articles both factual and interesting.

- Show students examples of different types of newspapers from the school library.

- Ask students to give examples of different types of newspaper articles they have read at school or at home. Have students discuss their reasons for reading newspapers and the particular types of information they can get from newspapers.

Reading Strategy
Evaluating Information

- Review with students the chart for evaluating newspaper information.

- Explain that stories written for newspapers must answer basic questions about the event described. Have students look closely at the second, fourth, and fifth paragraphs of the article. Tell them that many articles are written with the most important information at the top of the article in case readers do not read all the way to the end.

- Have students look at other news articles and identify the *who, what, when, where,* and *how* described in the story.

Newspaper Articles

About Newspaper Articles

Newspaper articles are concise, factual summaries of current events. Sometimes they provide in-depth descriptive or analytical information about a person, place, or thing. Other times they simply report the facts by answering the questions *who, what, when, where,* and *why.*

Newspaper articles often include direct quotations from the people whom the reporter interviewed. They may also provide statistics, names, dates, and firsthand information about the article's topic. Newspaper articles are written with a specific audience in mind. Although many newspapers claim readership around the world, most newspapers typically present information of interest to the local community that the newspaper serves.

Reading Strategy

Evaluating Information

Newspapers have an obligation to make sure that their articles provide in-depth, factual, and unbiased information in a concise format that is easy to read and understand. To **evaluate information** in a newspaper article, identify the facts and details that are provided about the topic, the key people, and the events. Then, determine whether the information provided is enough to form a complete picture of the subject.

As you read the newspaper article from the *Salisbury Post,* complete a chart like the one shown, to evaluate the information in the article.

Title and Subject of the Article	Key Events	Key People	Missing Information
"Shakespearean expert brings skills to Rowan County;" a Shakespearean training program for students	What? When? Where?	Who?	What else would you like to know?

Conclusion: *Do you think this article was clear, concise, and complete? Explain.*

Reading Newspaper Articles

- Tell students that this is an article that they might find in the features section of a newspaper.

- Have students read "Shakespearean Expert Brings Skills to Rowan County."

- **Ask** students to identify the features of the article that they notice on this page.
  Answer: The features seen on this page are the headline and the opening paragraph.

- **Ask** students who would be interested in reading this article.
  Answer: People who live in Rowan County, parents of children in Rowan County schools, and perhaps people who enjoy Shakespeares plays would be interested.

continued on p. 400

This head identifies the section of the newspaper and helps readers anticipate the kind of article they will read.

The opening paragraphs of this article provide the who?, where?, and what? of the subject matter.

November 4, 2001

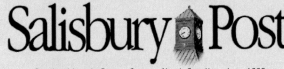

Salisbury Post

Serving historic Rowan County, North Carolina since 1905.

Though the story is a local one, the article mentions the program's international component.

Shakespearean expert brings skills to Rowan County

By Cortney L. Hill

"Hey, Lady Macbeth! Don't stand that way, and uncross your legs," shouted Bob Moyer.

The director of theater arts from the North Carolina School of the Arts was speaking to Salisbury High tenth grader Heather Clayton.

Constantly spewing "Stop," "Do it again," "Louder next time," and "Ugh, I keep forgetting that line," students and teachers responded throughout the morning Saturday.

They filled the Teaching Auditorium at Rowan-Cabarrus County Community College for a dress rehearsal for the Shakespeare Festival performance of "The Tragedy of Macbeth."

Training teachers to breathe life back into the classic works of Shakespeare, Saturday's event was Salisbury's third year hosting the Shakespeare Festival's "Shakespeare Lives!" program.

The program is a collaboration among the International Shakespeare Globe Center in London, the North Carolina School of the Arts, and the Kenan Institute for the Arts, with support from the Robertson Family Foundation of Rowan County.

This year, students and a total of 12 teachers from South Rowan High, Salisbury High, West Rowan High and other high schools and middle schools from Forsyth and Cabarrus counties brought their rendition of the play to the stage by dividing and performing different acts and scenes.

For preparation, students spent three weeks memorizing lines, learning to pronounce the Shakespearean words and understanding the plot of "Macbeth."

The teachers had been preparing for the performance since last spring, including spending two weeks at the International Globe Theater in London in July. They received direction from Patrick Spottiswoode, director of the Globe Theater program, Fiona Banks, assistant director of the Globe Theater, and Gerald Freedman, a Tony Award-winning director of Shakespeare in New York.

"To actually get a feel for Shakespeare's words and meanings, the teachers got to perform scenes from the plays on stage at the Globe Theater in London," Moyer said while sporting a blue and green Bankside London England hat and a Shakespeare face pendant on his shirt.

"Their (teachers') purpose for being there was for them to learn different ways to teach Shakespeare and become energized about it.... That way the students can grasp it and become energized too."

Impressed by the talents of these young student actors (many of them having no acting experience), Moyer sat intensely at the edge of his seat, examining the students' every move and every word. He gasped in relief if their practice went well or shook his head in dissatisfaction if it did not.

Reading Informational Materials: Newspaper Articles ■ 399

Differentiated Instruction   Solutions for All Learners

Strategy for Less Proficient Readers
To make sure students can identify the speakers in a newspaper article, have them practice identifying quotations. Ask students to highlight the quotations in the newspaper article and underline the name of each speaker. Have students note when speakers change and how the speakers are identified on the second reference.

Vocabulary for English Learners
English learners may need help with slang and idiomatic expressions such as "ugh," "twist your tongue," and "morphed." Work with English learners to restate unfamiliar phrases using more familiar vocabulary. In addition, explain any unfamiliar references such as "Globe Theater," "West Side Story," and "Martin Lawrence."

- Draw students' attention to the extensive use of quotations in the article. Indicate the difference between the author's paraphrase of sources' information and the quotes that restate the sources' exact words. **Ask** students why a writer might choose to quote a source directly rather than para-phrase.
Answer: The writer might use a quotation when the source says something particularly interesting, important, or colorful.

- **Ask** students why the background information about the students was important to the story.
Answer: Some of the students have learning difficulties, and their participation in the Shakespeare program indicates how much they have learned.

"Next time be bigger, make me believe you," Moyer told one student.

Scott Bosch, a Salisbury High English teacher, sat quietly in the front row of the auditorium while he watched his students perform.

> *The sources for the quotations are identified by their profession or their role in the event.*

"All of my students are tenth graders, and they all volunteered to be a part of this play. It comes from a great interest in theater." Bosch said.

Unlike most of the other students, Kevin Felder and Nicky Blakeley, two of Bosch's students, have a background in theater arts.

> *Background information about the people involved gives the article depth.*

"I'm a little nervous today because Shakespeare tends to twist your tongue so," said Felder, who has been in theater arts since the fifth grade. For this performance, Felder played the character "Banquo," whom he described as an envied character who people try to have killed.

"In preparation for this character, I try to think back on other characters I have played and look at it as being no bigger than what I've done before." said Felder, who in the past acted as "Baby John" in a school presentation of "West Side Story."

Felder hopes to someday be as good an actor and as universally known as Martin Lawrence or Eddie Murphy, whom he said he mimics constantly and looks up to.

Nicky Blakeley, who played Macbeth, has been acting since she was in the second grade and was eager to get on stage and perform.

> *Quotation marks call out direct quotations from people interviewed.*

"I am just so excited to be playing the main character," Blakeley said, "and Macbeth, a character normally played by a guy, is just totally awesome to me.... What a challenge!"

Next week, the honors theater student will be performing in a folk tale play at

Salisbury High called "Jack Tales", and for the next five weekends she will be starring in other plays

"The most challenging thing for me to do is memorize lines," Blakeley said. "For Macbeth's character, I have to be aggressive. But with much practice and script cramming, I should be fine."

South Rowan English teacher Gerrie Blackwelder sat in tears through her students' practice run through their part of the tragedy. Moyer credits Blackwelder with being a big part of the entire event.

"I am very nervous about today," Blackwelder said. "It's just so emotional and overwhelming to see children do Shakespeare and look as if they are enjoying it.... It's like they've actually morphed themselves into their characters. This is truly wonderful."

As the final groups ran through one last practice before showtime on Saturday, teachers gave pep talks and paced around as if they were trying to memorize their students' lines.

Ingrid Madlock, assistant principal of the Learning Enrichment Acceleration Program (LEAP) Academy in Winston-Salem, is eager to see her students perform because they have never had any exposure to Shakespeare and had a hard time grasping the whole concept.

"I won't be shocked if I'm not in tears by the end of their performance," Madlock said. "When they came to the LEAP Academy, it was to catch up on their academics, but these kids are being challenged doing this.

"I chose the students who I felt needed some help with their self-esteem, because I want them to know that they can do this and that Shakespeare can somehow be a part of their everyday life. I think when this is over, they'll realize that."

Assessment Practice

Reading: Evaluating Information

Directions: *Choose the letter of the best answer to each question about the newspaper article.*

1. Based only on the article's title, which of the following best describes the information the article should cover?
   A A group of amateur actors are participating in a Shakespearean festival.
   B Teachers from South Rowan High sponsor an annual Shakespearean festival.
   C A Shakespearean expert has brought his or her skills to the Rowan County area.
   D The Globe Theater in London hosts training sessions for theater teachers.

2. Which of the following suggests the general popularity of the program?
   A "[Participants] filled the Teaching Auditorium at Rowan-Cabarrus County Community College. . . ."
   B "This year, students and a total of 12 teachers . . . brought their rendition of the play. . . ."
   C "The teachers had been preparing for the performance since last spring. . . ."
   D "For preparation, students spent three weeks memorizing lines. . . ."

3. Which of the following questions is not answered in the article?
   A Which student is playing the lead role of Macbeth?
   B What is the performance time and ticket cost of the festival?
   C Which theater professionals helped train the students and teachers?
   D What schools are involved in the festival?

Reading: Comprehension

Directions: *Write your answers on a separate sheet of paper.*

4. Describe the program that is featured in the article.

5. What are the emotions of the two students who are quoted in the article? Why do they feel that way?

6. Why is Ingrid Madlock eager to see her students perform?

Timed Writing: Explanation

Explain the reasons why you think this program will or will not interest high-school students in the works of William Shakespeare. Use information from the article to support your opinion. *(20 minutes)*

Reading Informational Materials: Newspaper Articles ■ 401

Reading: Evaluating Information

1. C
2. A
3. B

Reading: Comprehension

4. The Shakespeare Lives! Program is a program in which theater professionals, including those from the International Shakespeare Globe Center, work with high school and middle school teachers from Rowan, Forsyth, and Cabarrus counties. The teachers and theater professionals work with students, who perform different acts and scenes from Shakespeare's plays.

5. Student Kevin Felder is nervous because he finds Shakespeare's dialogue difficult. Student Nicky Blakeley is excited by the challenge of playing a character as important as Macbeth.

6. She is eager to see her students perform because some of them have been challenged academically. This program has given them a chance to achieve and do well.

Timed Writing

- Suggest that student review the quotations from students involved in the program, evaluating their responses and reactions.

- Suggest that students plan their time to give 5 minutes to planning, 10 minutes to writing, and 5 minutes to reviewing and revising.

Extend the Lesson

Comparison

To give students further practice with newspaper articles, have students evaluate the information in a variety of newspaper departments. Have students work in pairs to find newspapers in the school library and locate an international news story, a sports story, and a feature story in each. Ask students to identify the headlines, quotations, and background information in each story. Then ask each pair to summarize the articles and draw conclusions about whether the articles are clear and complete.

Students will

1. understand the connection between fictional and nonfictional accounts that describe preparations for war.

2. recognize similar and differing emotions about war in different eras and places.

Connections
American Literature

Students might reread Act V, scenes iv and v, and note Macduff's preparation for attacking Macbeth's castle and Macbeth's preparation for a siege. Just as Macduff and Macbeth prepare for war, so Major Anderson meets with Colonel Chesnut, negotiating to see if war can be avoided. Have students identify similarities between Macbeth's position in Dunsinane Castle and Major Anderson's position in the harbor at Fort Sumter.

Whispers of War

• Have students discuss the role of war in both *Macbeth* and Mary Chesnut's diary. Does either of the authors indicate that war could or should be avoided?

• Mary Chesnut's anticipation of war is filled with the excitement of colorful uniforms and thrilling dinner-table discussions. In what way is Macbeth's preparation for war more or less realistic than the real-life account?

CONNECTIONS
American Literature

Whispers of War

Like the final act of William Shakespeare's *Macbeth* (pages 306–394), Mary Chesnut's *Civil War* is an account of a fort under siege. Just as Shakespeare did, American writer Mary Chesnut describes the mounting tension of a battle brewing between friends, relatives, and countrymen. Though Shakespeare's is a fictionalized drama about Macbeth's stand in Dunsinane Castle for the Scottish crown, Chesnut's account conveys some of the real-life suspenseful buildup to the American Civil War.

Similarities Crossing Time and Geography Both Chesnut's diary excerpt and the final scene of *Macbeth* contain an overwhelming sense of the inevitability of war. As you read Mary Chesnut's work, look for other points of comparison with *Macbeth*.

from Mary Chesnut's
CIVIL WAR
Mary Chesnut

April 7, 1861. Today things seem to have settled down a little.

One can but hope still. Lincoln or Seward[1] have made such silly advances and then far sillier drawings back. There may be a chance for peace, after all.

Things are happening so fast.

My husband has been made an aide-de-camp[2] of General Beauregard.

Three hours ago we were quietly packing to go home. The convention has adjourned.

---

1. **Seward** William Henry Seward (1801–1872), U.S. Secretary of State from 1861 through 1869.
2. **aide-de-camp** (ād′ də kamp′) *n.* officer serving as assistant and confidential secretary to a superior.

Now he tells me the attack upon Fort Sumter[3] may begin tonight. Depends upon Anderson and the fleet outside. The *Herald* says that this show of war outside of the bar is intended for Texas.

John Manning came in with his sword and red sash. Pleased as a boy to be on Beauregard's staff while the row goes on. He has gone with Wigfall to Captain Hartstene with instructions.

Mr. Chesnut is finishing a report he had to make to the convention.

Mrs. Hayne called. She had, she said, "but one feeling, pity for those who are not here."

Jack Preston, Willie Alston—"the take-life-easys," as they are called—with John Green, "the big brave," have gone down to the island—volunteered as privates.

Seven hundred men were sent over. Ammunition wagons rumbling along the streets all night. Anderson burning blue lights—signs and signals for the fleet outside, I suppose.

Today at dinner there was no allusion to things as they stand in Charleston Harbor. There was an undercurrent of intense excitement. There could not have been a more brilliant circle. In addition to our usual quartet (Judge Withers, Langdon Cheves, and Trescot) our two governors dined with us, Means and Manning.

These men all talked so delightfully. For once in my life I listened.

That over, business began. In earnest, Governor Means rummaged a sword and red sash from somewhere and brought it for Colonel Chesnut, who has gone to demand the surrender of Fort Sumter.

And now, patience—we must wait.

Why did that green goose Anderson go into Fort Sumter? Then everything began to go wrong.

Now they have intercepted a letter from him, urging them[4] to let him surrender. He paints the horrors likely to ensue if they will not.

He ought to have thought of all that before he put his head in the hole.

---

3. **Fort Sumter** fort in Charleston Harbor, South Carolina. At the time, the fort was occupied by Union troops commanded by Major Robert Anderson.
4. Here, Chesnut refers to Anderson's superiors in the federal government, namely, President Lincoln and his administration.

Connecting American Literature

1. Compare and contrast the emotional state of Shakespeare's Lady Macbeth in Act V of *Macbeth* to that of Mary Chesnut.
2. Compare and contrast Macbeth's situation to Major Anderson's.
3. **(a)** What advantages does Chesnut's journal have over Shakespeare's play in conveying information and mood? **(b)** What advantages does Shakespeare's drama have over Chesnut's diary entry?

Mary Boykin Chesnut (1823–1886)

Because her father was a cotton plantation owner and a United States senator, Mary Boykin was raised in an aristocratic family in Charleston, South Carolina. At the age of seventeen, she married James Chesnut, Jr., a wealthy lawyer and future senator.

Although no one was hurt when the opening shots of the Civil War were fired on Fort Sumter on April 12, 1860, Chesnut seems to have sensed the carnage to come. She conveyed her fears in her journal, now hailed as an invaluable primary document of the times. With a bird's-eye view from the rooftop of her house, along with inside information through her husband, Mary Chesnut gave generations of readers an insightful record of what people saw and felt during the opening days of the Civil War.

from Mary Chesnut's Civil War ■ 403

1. Lady Macbeth is disturbed as she remembers her involvement in Duncan's murder. Mary Chesnut is excited as she hears more news about the conflict at Fort Sumter.

2. Macbeth has murdered Duncan and Macduff's family. He is in his castle waiting for Macduff's forces to attack. Major Anderson is guarding a U.S. government fort in South Carolina, a state that has seceded from the Union. Major Anderson is waiting for Confederate forces to attack his post.

3. **(a)** Chesnut's journal does not have to convey emotions through dialogue. She can use prose to explain why people feel nervous or excited. **(b)** Shakespeare's drama can describe actions and give stage directions about what characters should move in particular directions.

Writing About Literature

Meeting Your Standards

Students will

1. write an essay that compares and contrasts two texts from the British Renaissance.

2. use writing strategies to generate ideas and to plan, organize, evaluate, and revise writing.

Compare and Contrast Literary Trends

In literature of the Renaissance, writing often celebrated formal techniques. Readers found beauty and satisfaction in a well-crafted poem with wittily presented sentiments. Although the simplest way to share an idea or feeling is to state it directly, the popular writing styles of the Renaissance featured indirect, ornate statements. They relied on conventions: standard forms, subjects, comparisons, and references. How well did Renaissance writers express experience within these constraints? Write an essay on this topic, completing the assignment described in the yellow box, reviewing and analyzing the selections in this unit.

Prewriting

Find a focus. First, you need to select the two works you will compare and contrast. You can use charts like the pair shown here to take notes on works or passages you have read. Use these questions to help you categorize the writing:

- What formal conventions or styles is the writer following?
- What ideas or thoughts does the writer want to express?
- What is the main goal of the writing: formal beauty and wit or direct communication? How can you tell?

Model: Categorizing to Select Works to Compare

Writing That Emphasizes Form and Style	Writing That Emphasizes Direct Communication
Sidney, Sonnet 31 Creates clever lyrical images within the sonnet form	**Shakespeare, Sonnet 130** Uses direct language and challenges conventional compliments
Spenser, Sonnet 1 Uses complex language and rigid form	**The Parable of the Prodigal Son** Uses direct language to tell a moral story

Gather details. After you select two works, read them together to find the most important similarities and differences. You might use a Venn diagram to collect your ideas. Use the criteria in the assignment—the contrast between crafted writing and direct statements—to guide you.

Test your ideas. Once you have selected and reviewed two works, test your ideas about them. Look for details in each that would permit you to categorize them differently.

Write a working thesis. Your thesis should connect the works you have chosen with the contrast in the assignment. Writing your thesis statement early will help you focus on key distinctions between works.

Assignment: Craft or Content?

Write an essay in which you compare and contrast two works from the Renaissance: one that emphasizes formal conventions and the writer's craft and one that emphasizes the writer's direct statement of a thought or feeling.

Criteria:
- Include a thesis statement that introduces the primary distinction between the two works you choose.
- Discuss the similarities and differences between the two works.
- Approximate length: 700 words.

**Read to Write**

Think about the writer's motivation as you reread the texts. Did the writer want to dazzle an audience with gorgeous language or express a personal or moral idea?

Prewriting

- To give students guidance in developing this assignment, give them the **Writing About Literature** support pages in *Unit 2 Resources.*

- Have a class discussion on ways in which the writers represented in this unit express their ideas cleverly, indirectly, or through a well-known literary form. The discussion should focus on writers' reasons for concealing their main ideas, and should help students find ideas for topics.

- Suggest that students use a graphic organizer such as a Venn diagram or the organizer pictured on this page. They can record information in the organizers as they read.

- Students should make sure that their thesis clearly states the comparison and contrast that they are making.

Tips for Test Taking

The SAT scores essays holistically, basing an essay's score on a final impression. A clearly organized essay will make a good impression on the people evaluating students' work. An essay that has an introduction, supporting paragraphs, and a conclusion presents ideas in a format that is easy for readers to understand. Students should use at least two body paragraphs to develop and support their ideas.

Teaching Resources

The following resources can be used to extend or enrich the instruction for Writing About Literature.

Unit 2 Resources
Writing About Literature, pp. 184–185

General Resources
Rubrics for Exposition: Comparison-and-Contrast Essay, pp. 69–70

Graphic Organizer Transparencies
Venn Diagram, p. 286

Drafting

Prepare an outline. Preparing a detailed outline can help you organize your comments and guide your first draft. Each subsection of your outline can become a single, focused paragraph.

> **Model: Making a Detailed Outline**
>
> C. Shakespeare's "Sonnet 130" uses conventional form, but turns conventional compliments upside down to create a direct statement.
> 1. follows rigid sonnet form
> 2. but uses simple, direct language
>   a. "the breath that from my mistress reeks"
>   b. "black wires grow on her head"

Cite specific examples. Your essay will be more effective if you use quotations from the works you are comparing. Choose examples that make the contrast between the two works clear. Read your quotations aloud to make sure they support your analysis.

Revising and Editing

Review content: Test logical connections. Make sure that your ideas flow logically within each sentence and each paragraph, and within the essay as a whole. Check the connections in your comparison to be sure that every link in your analysis is sensible.

Illogical connection: In this sonnet, Shakespeare pokes fun at poetic conventions, but he concludes with a direct expression of love.

Logical connection: In this sonnet, Shakespeare pokes fun at poetic conventions, but he then shows the true power of poetry by concluding with a poetic yet believable, direct expression of love.

Review style: Vary sentence length. Using a variety of sentence lengths builds interest and flow. You might look for paragraphs that include only long sentences. In such cases, add a short, emphatic sentence to grab your readers' attention.

Publishing and Presenting

Prepare a dramatic presentation. Rehearse readings of the two works you chose to compare. Direct performers to emphasize the qualities you discuss in your essay. After the presentation, share your analysis.

Prentice Hall Writing and Grammar Connection: Chapter 14

✏ Write to Learn

Explaining quotations can deepen your analysis. For example, you might find fine craft in a poem that you use as an example of direct communication.

✏ Write to Explain

Remember to explain your reason for including each quotation—do not just quote a line and expect your readers to understand why you included it.

Drafting

Make sure that students know they will need specific examples from literary works to support each of their points. Their essay will make an argument about similarities and differences, but it must be based on particular passages, not just on general statements.

Revising and Editing

Students may want to have peers check their analysis for logic. Another student can make sure that comparisons and connections support the points that the essay is trying to make.

Publishing and Presenting

You may want to pair students to prepare to read their essays aloud. Have students work together to determine how to emphasize the elements in the selections that they want to compare or contrast.

Writing and Grammar, Diamond Level

Students will find additional instruction on writing a comparison-and-contrast essay in Chapter 9.

Writing and Grammar Interactive Textbook CD-ROM

Students can use the following tools as they complete their comparison-and-contrast essays:

- Topic Bank
- Compare and Contrast

Six Traits Focus

✔ Ideas		Word Choice
✔ Organization		Sentence Fluency
	Voice	✔ Conventions

Assessing the Essay

To evaluate students' essays, use the **Rubrics for Exposition: Comparison-and-Contrast Essay**, pp. 69–70 in *General Resources*.

Differentiated Instruction — Solutions for All Learners

Vocabulary for Less Proficient Writers
Work with these students to identify vocabulary that may be unfamiliar because of its historical context. Encourage them to reorder words in a more familiar pattern and to restate vocabulary in their own words.

Background for English Learners
Provide the cultural background these students may need to understand Renaissance poems and prose. Point out the conventions of Renaissance writing and the importance to writers of expressing themselves within that form.

Strategy for Advanced Writers
Encourage students to work closely with the quotations they have selected to support their ideas. Tell students to look beyond the obvious, literal meanings to find the nuance or allusions that writers may have intended.

Meeting Your Standards

Students will

1. write a persuasive essay.
2. use writing strategies to generate ideas, organize, evaluate, and revise the persuasive essay.
3. apply grammar skills.

 From the Scholar's Desk

Frank Kermode

Show students Segment 3 on Frank Kermode on *From the Author's Desk DVD*. Discuss Kermode's approach to lectures. Ask students how his lectures are a form of persuasive speech.

Writing Genres

Using the Form Point out to students that persuasive writing is often incorporated into other types of writing. Provide these examples:

- Letters to the editor are primarily persuasive essays.
- E-mail messages and other business correspondence often include elements of persuasive writing.
- Speeches are often written to persuade the audience to believe something or buy something.

Persuasion: Persuasive Essay

English Renaissance writers such as Sir Thomas Moore and Queen Elizabeth I argued vigorously for their humanistic ideals and objectives in **persuasive essays.** A persuasive essay is a prose work that presents a case for or against a position using supporting evidence and clear, convincing language. Follow the steps outlined in this workshop to write your own persuasive essay.

Assignment Write a persuasive essay focusing on an issue of concern or importance to you.

What to Include To succeed, your persuasive essay must feature the following elements:

- a clear thesis statement that identifies your position and the action you want readers to take
- details, facts, reasons, examples, and descriptions that support your position
- an understanding of the knowledge, experience, needs, and concerns of your intended audience
- language and arguments that are fair but convincing

To preview the criteria on which your persuasive essay may be judged, see the rubric on page 413.

Using the Form
You may use elements of a persuasive essay in these writing situations:
- speeches
- letters to the editor
- advertisements
- cover letters
- newspaper articles

 *Reading* **Writing** *Connection*

To get a feel for persuasive writing, read from *Utopia* by Sir Thomas More, page 272.

406 ■ *Celebrating Humanity (1485–1625)*

Teaching Resources

The following resources can be used to enrich or extend the instruction for the Writing Workshop.

Unit 2 Resources
  Writing Workshop: Persuasion: Persuasive Writing, pp. 186–187
  Writing Workshop: Use Vivid, Specific Language, p. 187

General Resources
  Rubrics for Persuasion: Persuasive Essay, pp. 45–46

Graphic Organizer Transparencies
  Three-Column Chart, p. 280

From the Author's Desk DVD
  Frank Kermode, Segments 3 and 4

Prewriting

Choosing Your Topic

Select a topic that provokes your own strong opinion. Be sure that you can support your position with several convincing reasons, facts, and examples. To help find a topic, use one of the following strategies:

- **Conduct a news scan.** Read newspapers or listen to news broadcasters to learn about current, controversial issues. Political controversies as well as decisions affecting school life are potential topic sources. Avoid issues on which your only opinion is "I like _____" or "I dislike _____." Instead, consider a topic that allows you to take a clearly articulated stand.

| **Weak:** | I dislike the proposed changes to update the mall. |
| **Strong:** | Rather than piecemeal projects, our community needs a coherent revitalization plan. |

- **Hold a discussion group.** Tap into school or community issues by holding a discussion with students, neighbors, or local residents. Find out what key issues and concerns really get people talking. Note topics that generate the most controversy or disagreement. You may find that one topic is particularly interesting to you. If so, choose that as the topic for your persuasive essay.

Narrowing Your Topic

Once you have a general idea for a topic, focus on a specific aspect that you can fully and completely support. For example, if you choose to write about health care, narrow your focus to one element, such as preventive care. Consider the needs of your intended audience as you make notes about your topic.

Gathering Details

Gather facts and arguments to support your position. Use libraries, the Internet, personal interviews, or other resources. Make note also of any facts that contradict your opinion, so you can prepare counterarguments. You might begin by filling out a chart like the one shown.

Focusing on Purpose and Audience		
Specific Purpose	**Audience**	**Arguments to Convince This Audience**
To persuade seniors to apply early to college	Seniors at my school	• Choosing early admissions may improve your chances of acceptance. • Applications will just hang over your head if you delay.

Writing Workshop ■ 407

Tips for Using Rubrics

- Before students begin work on this assignment, have them preview the Rubric for Self-Assessment (p. 413) to know what is expected.
- Review the Self-Assessment criteria in class. Before students use the Rubric for Self-Assessment, work with them to rate the student model by applying one or two criteria to it.

- If you wish to assess students' persuasive essays with either a 4-point or a 6-point scoring rubric, see *General Resources*, pp. 45–46, **Persuasion: Persuasive Essay.**

TEACH

Prewriting

- Have volunteers share topic ideas from their news scan. Write the ideas on the board. Then, select one of the topics and ask students to share facts that they already know about it. This will help students gauge how much more research they will need to conduct.
- Tell students to plan ahead for a discussion group by listing subjects that will stimulate conversation. Ask them to prepare general questions for discussion, such as the following: What environmental issues are of the greatest concern to you? Do you think our community is doing all it can to provide public transportation?
- As students gather information on their topics, advise them to keep in mind what their audience may or may not know about their topic. Also remind them that they do not need to include every fact they gather. They will need to choose those that support their thesis statements.
- Remind students that all Internet sites are not equally reliable. Discuss how they can decide to trust information from individual sites and how to verify information.

Six Traits Focus

✔	Ideas		Word Choice
✔	Organization		Sentence Fluency
	Voice		Conventions

Writing and Grammar, Diamond Level

Students will find additional instruction on prewriting for a persuasive essay in Chapter 8, Section 2.

Writing and Grammar Interactive Textbook CD-ROM

Students can use the following tools as they complete their persuasive essays:

- Audience Profile Organizer
- Descriptive Word Bin
- Vague Adjectives Revising Tool

Drafting

- Explain to students that a strong opening paragraph provides an important "boost" to their position. Encourage them to craft opening paragraphs that lead to direct statements of their viewpoints. Tell students that using clear, concise sentences will help solidify their position and prepare the reader for their argument.

- Review with students how to use inductive and deductive reasoning as they articulate their positions.

- Guide a discussion of logical, ethical, and emotional appeals. Invite students to talk about which they may want to use and why it would be effective for their essay.

Six Traits Focus

✔	Ideas	✔	Word Choice
✔	Organization		Sentence Fluency
	Voice		Conventions

Writing and Grammar, Diamond Level

Students will find additional instruction on drafting a persuasive essay in Chapter 8, Section 3.

Drafting

Shaping Your Writing

Showcase your thesis statement. Present your position on the issue in your first paragraph. You might want to build up to your viewpoint by stating it in the final sentence of the first paragraph. The chart shown explains some patterns you can use in your introduction.

Create a call for action. Use the body of your writing to defend your ideas. Then, conclude your essay with a restatement of your thesis idea and a clear call for action—a statement of what you want done.

Providing Elaboration

Elaborate with strong appeals and arguments. Use these types of arguments to build a strong case.

- **Inductive reasoning:** Specific facts used to lead to a general truth.

  Example: Exercise helps you to get in shape. Exercise can help you to lose weight. Exercise makes you feel good. Therefore, exercise is good.

- **Deductive reasoning:** A general truth applied to a particular case.

  Example: All exercise can help you to get in shape. Weightlifting is a form of exercise. If I lift weights, I'll be in better shape.

  Use inductive or deductive reasoning to make the following kinds of appeals:

- **Logical appeals:** If one thing happens, something else will follow.
- **Ethical appeals:** If a thing has a certain characteristic, and all things with that characteristic are good, then that thing is good.
- **Emotional appeals:** If a thing has a certain characteristic, and all things with that characteristic are horrible, then you should reject that thing.

Use a chart like the one shown to develop a list of appeals for your topic position.

Developing Opening Paragraphs

Pattern 1

- Example
- Example → Thesis statement

Pattern 2

- Fact
- Fact → Thesis statement

Pattern 3

- Brief anecdote → Thesis statement

The Importance of Preventive Health Care	
Logical Appeal	If you take good care of yourself, then you reduce your chances of being inconvenienced by a cold or flu.
Ethical Appeal	The responsible course of action is, whenever possible, to prevent yourself and others from catching a cold.
Emotional Appeal	No one enjoys the fever, the chills, or the sore throat that comes with a cold or flu.

408 ■ Celebrating Humanity (1485–1625)

Tips for
Using Technology in Writing

If students are using computers, encourage them to consider creating separate files of details for each audience that they hope to persuade. Students can list the types of persuasion that they feel would be effective for each audience. Key points directed at each audience can also be put into the files. This will make information for specific audiences easily accessible.

From the Scholar's Desk
Frank Kermode on Persuasion

This passage is excerpted from my essay in *DAEDALUS, The Journal of the American Academy of Arts and Sciences.* It briefly considers the notion of the common reader from the eighteenth century up to the present day. To Dr. Samuel Johnson, the common reader of the eighteenth century was identified as a member of the leisured class. Now, it is argued, the term applies to people who have benefited by a college education.

Frank Kermode

"A society containing subtle readers is at least a more interesting, perhaps a richer, society. ..."

———— *Frank Kermode*

Professional Model:

from *"The Common Reader"*

I have assumed that the modern Common Reader passes through a college or university. The number of people now teaching literature in such institutions is probably greater than the total of critics who formerly existed throughout history, and they must have some effect on the millions of readers who frequent their classes. Does good come of this? The eminent American critic Richard Poirier says he sees "no reason in the world" why common readers should care to read the classics or serious contemporary fiction and poetry; "I don't think it makes them better people, better citizens, better anything." By some criteria he must be right. Indeed, it is immodest to propose that by making people read these things we are improving them, ethically or civically. All we dare claim is that we are making them better readers. We might or might not go on to claim that bad reading has often had disastrous consequences; or that a society containing subtle readers is at least a more interesting, perhaps a richer, society than one that does not; or that good readers are likely to be more resistant to the exploitative forces of "the ruling system." But we should not say we are improving them, except as readers.

← The arts of reading are now entrusted to college and university teachers. Should we assume that this is a wholly good thing?

← Richard Poirier, an eminent teacher, denies that enhanced reading skills confer ethical benefits on the student.

← Even if his argument is persuasive, it could be maintained that skillful reading has other socially beneficial effects.

Frank Kermode

- Show students Segment 4 on Frank Kermode on *From the Author's Desk DVD.* Discuss Kermode's opinions on the impact of literary criticism on society.

- **Ask** students why Kermode asks "Does good come of this?" **Answer:** The question engages readers with the text by challenging them to agree or disagree.

- Point out that Kermode is using an "expert witness" when he quotes Richard Poirier. Readers might regard this technique as an authoritative reinforcement of their point of view or as a further challenge to them to argue their own opinions.

- Explain that in refuting Poirier, Kermode is using a logical appeal. He treats Poirier's opinion respectfully and acknowledges that he may be right. Kermode then builds his own claim logically by pointing out other benefits of reading.

Differentiated Instruction   Solutions for All Learners

Strategies for Special Needs Students
Many special needs students can articulate their ideas very clearly but may have trouble organizing them and putting them on paper. Suggest that these students work in pairs. Using a tape recorder, have students tell each other about their topics. The listener should question the speaker about issues that are not clear or raise additional points. The taped conversation can form a starting point for the written draft.

Strategies for English Learners
English learners may have difficulty understanding the vocabulary and complex structures of Frank Kermode's essay. Before asking them to read it, provide a quick summary of the piece, and review some of the more difficult vocabulary and concepts, such as the following:

leisured class	common reader
eminent	classics
contemporary fiction	immodest
propose	ethically
civically	consequences
exploitative forces	ruling system

Revising

- Have students exchange drafts with a partner. Readers should then mark sentences or paragraphs that need transitions to make the relationships among ideas clearer.

- Ask students to give definitions and examples of figurative language, parallelism, and repetition. Explain that these devices create strong visual images and sound effects that appeal to readers. Advise students to not overly use these devices in their essays; otherwise they will weaken their arguments instead of strengthening them.

- Make sure students understand that good organization can make an argument easier to follow. The careful placement of ideas positions key points where they will have the greatest impact.

- Ask a student to read the example of vague language aloud to the class. Then, ask another student to read the vivid image. **Ask** students what makes the second sentence so powerful and vivid.

  Answer: It expresses the idea as a simile, allowing the reader to visualize the idea.

Six Traits Focus

Ideas	✔	Word Choice
✔ Organization	✔	Sentence Fluency
✔ Voice	✔	Conventions

Writing and Grammar,
Diamond Level

Students will find additional instruction on revising a persuasive essay in Chapter 8, Section 4.

Revising

Revising Your Overall Structure

Arrange arguments in a logical order. Review your writing to make sure that your evidence is arranged logically and sequenced so that it will have the strongest impact on your audience. Follow these steps to organize your evidence logically:

1. Use transition words that show cause and effect, chronological sequence, or comparison and contrast.
2. Consider using figurative language, parallelism, or repetition to strengthen your appeals to readers.
3. Experiment with arranging your arguments in order of importance, either from least important to most important, or vice versa.

Reading / Writing / Connection

To read the complete student model, see page 412.

Student Model: Use Transition Words

In order to play a sport,

^You are required to pass your classes, which of cource

motivates athletes to make good grades.

The transition words in order to indicate cause and effect.

Revising Your Word Choice

Replace weak language with powerful words or images. Examine your writing for its powerful, emotional impact. To strengthen your arguments by improving the way your words state ideas, circle passages that are vague or lack force. For each one, brainstorm for charged words, vivid images, and dramatic analogies to help you make your points.

Vague: Getting into a good college can be tough.

Vivid Image: Like a thousand cattle trying to pass through the same gate, vast numbers of people across the nation apply each year for a limited number of places at colleges.

Dull: Suddenly, you get nervous and apprehensive about choosing a college.

Vivid: Suddenly, a feeling bubbles up from the pit of your stomach, an achy, acidic feeling of panic. "Which college is the right college?"

Peer Review: Share your draft with a partner. Discuss your ideas for replacing dull language with images or analogies. Together, choose the most vivid words or phrases. Repeat the process if necessary to develop the strongest possible argument.

Tips for
Using Transitions

Remind students that transitions show the relationship among ideas. Moreover, different relationships are shown with different kinds of transitions. Write these examples on the board, and challenge students to suggest additional transitions for each category.

Cause-and-Effect Transitions

because	although	therefore
as a result	so that	consequently

Chronological Transitions

after	before	since
first	next	then

Comparison-and-Contrast Transitions

like	but	neither . . . nor
instead	however	compared to

Encourage students to keep a list of these transitions to use while revising their essays.

Developing Your Style

Persuasive Evidence

Fact vs. Opinion Writers use both facts and opinions in persuasive essays. A fact is a statement that can be verified or proved true by records, experimentation, or personal observation. An opinion is a belief or judgment that cannot be proved true. Before an opinion can be accepted, it must be supported or validated by satisfactory sources or facts.

> **Opinion:** I like the new carpeting in the school hallways.
>
> **Fact in Support of Opinion:** The new carpeting in the hallways reduces noise as students pass from one room to another, eliminating distractions while students are learning.

Logical Fallacies Be alert for logical fallacies, which occur when the rules of logic do not work. There are three types of logical fallacies:

A **hasty generalization** is based on only a few facts or samples.

> *Example:* I tasted only one apple from the basket, and it tasted sweet. Therefore, all of the apples in the basket must be sweet.

A **non sequitur** (Latin for "it does not follow") draws a conclusion that does not follow from the evidence given.

> *Example:* Members of Congress are elected by the people and make the laws. The President knows what is best for the people.

A **false analogy** ignores obvious and important differences between the things being compared.

> *Example:* Children are like little adults. Just as adults can be trusted to make sound financial decisions, so can children.

Find It in Your Reading Read or review "Speech Before Her Troops" by Queen Elizabeth I on page 275.

1. Find two facts that Elizabeth includes in her speech.

2. Identify two opinions, and explain how these opinions contribute to the total effect of the speech.

Apply It to Your Writing Review the draft of your persuasive essay. For each paragraph in your draft, follow these steps:

1. Underline the facts or statistics you have used to support your position. Check to see that your facts come from current, reputable sources and that you have cited them accurately.

2. Circle the opinions you have used to support your arguments. Verify that the opinions can be validated by facts, expert opinions, or logical arguments.

3. Evaluate the appeals you have made and revise any faulty logic.

𝑊𝐺 *Prentice Hall Writing and Grammar, Chapter 7*

Developing Your Style

- Have students **identify** the following statements as facts or opinions.

  1. *People do not trust the information they get from newspapers as they once did.*

  2. *Readership of our newspaper has decreased by 12 percent in ten years.*

  3. *We don't need more schools!*
     Answers: 1. opinion; 2. fact; 3. opinion

- Provide these examples of logical fallacies, and have students identify their type.

  1. *Our neighbor's dog barks all the time. Dogs are nuisances and shouldn't be allowed in apartments.*

  2. *School is just like a job. Students should be paid for attending.*
     Answers: 1. non sequitur; 2. false analogy

- Discuss students' responses to the Find It in Your Reading questions.
  Possible answers:

  1. Two facts are that Elizabeth is sending a lieutenant general in her stead during the battle and that her advisors cautioned her not to walk amongst the people.

  2. Two opinions that heighten her appeal are her feebleness as a woman and her heart of a king. These opinions strengthen her argument by showing the people how great a ruler she is.

  3. She says that they will shortly have a victory in battle because of the obedience and courage of the soldiers. This is not logical because it is a hasty generalization. The English will not be victorious just because they are brave and loyal.

- Encourage students to exchange copies of their essays with partners. Have students highlight opinions with one color marker and highlight facts with another color. Have them jot notes in the margin about opinions they think are unsupported or any instances of faulty logic.

𝑊𝐺 **Writing and Grammar, Diamond Level**

Students will find additional instruction on facts and opinions and modes of reasoning in Chapter 30, Section 2.

Differentiated Instruction Solutions for All Learners

Background for Special Needs Students
Emphasize to students that information from a book or from any other source is not automatically factual or reliable. Students should answer these questions before taking the information as authoritative:

- Is the source an expert on the topic?
- Is it possible that the speaker or writer is biased?
- Is the information a fact or an opinion?
- If it is an opinion, are there any facts to support it?

Support for Less Proficient Readers
Give students copies of an editorial from a newspaper and then read the editorial aloud. Pause whenever a fact or opinion is expressed. Have students analyze it and decide whether it is a fact or an opinion. If it is an opinion, have them search the editorial for facts that may support it. Discuss the opinions and why they may or may not strengthen the thesis of the editorial.

Student Model

- Explain that the student model is a sample and that essays may be longer.

- Discuss the opening paragraph, pointing out that Kristen raises an interesting issue in the first line. Then she builds on the idea with supporting details and finishes the paragraph with a strong thesis statement.

- Point out that each paragraph in the body of the essay begins with a clearly stated main idea. The sentences that follow give reasons and facts to support that main idea. **Ask** students to identify the main idea of the second paragraph. **Answer:** The main idea is "One of the main priorities for teenagers is preparing for the 'real world.'"

- Emphasize that Kristen does not include extraneous information in the essay.

- Point out that Kristen uses inductive reasoning to build her arguments. For example, in paragraph three she first describes how student athletes are required to make good grades. She then states a general truth by telling how this skill gives them more scholarship opportunities.

- Direct students' attention to the final paragraph and point out that Kristen finishes her essay with a call for action.

Writing Genres

Persuasive Writing in the Workplace

Tell students that persuasive writing is useful in many jobs. Professional writers are hired to write speeches for politicians, copy for advertisers, and editorials for newspapers. In addition, many jobs require that people who are not professional writers write persuasively to get people to take action. Discuss work situations in which persuasive writing would be appropriate, such as a manager writing a memo to employees explaining a new policy, or an employee writing a memo asking for changes in benefits.

Student Model: Kristen Metcalf
Black Mountain, North Carolina

Why It Is Important To Be a Student Athlete

You may believe that being a student athlete is a big waste of time. If so, you probably think about having to spend most of your free time at practice or competitions, or about having to stay up late at night doing homework that most students do right after school. You might fear not being able to go to that big party this weekend because of the example you are supposed to be. While it's true that being a student athlete is a huge commitment that calls for a lot of sacrifices and takes a lot of time, it is more than worth it. Every teenager with the opportunity to play a sport should take advantage of it.

One of the main priorities for teenagers is preparing for the "real world." When teenagers go off on their own, there are many things they need to be able to do to make it in the world. They need to be able to take on responsibilities, make smart decisions, set and work for goals, and manage their time well. All of these things are also required by student athletes in order to be successful. So, athletes actually have practice in these important skills outside of the sport itself that lead them to find success as adults.

Most teenagers today want to go to college, and—let's face it—unless you have good grades, you're probably not going to be able to get in. For student athletes, making good grades is a pressing need all the way through school. In order to play a sport, you are required to pass your classes, which of course motivates athletes to make good grades. Along with making good grades comes more scholarship opportunities for student athletes.

Maintaining good health is important to everyone. Research shows that healthy habits begun young dramatically improve good health throughout life. When you are a student athlete, you are physically fit from running, lifting weights, or whatever it is your sport requires of you to be prepared. Healthy eating is another component to good health, and the diets that your coaches put you on take care of that. Student athletes learn how to take care of their bodies, making them healthier than most other people.

Take advantage of the opportunities and great outcomes that being a student athlete can bring. If you decide to participate in school athletics, you will find that your life will improve all around.

Kristen ends her introduction with a clear thesis statement that she defends in the body of the essay.

Kristen lists examples and facts—she identifies the many benefits of school athletics. (See *Developing Your Style,* p. 411.)

With this paragraph, Kristen addresses the needs of the audience beyond school.

Editing and Proofreading

Review your essay to make sure your work is free from errors in grammar, punctuation, capitalization, and spelling.

Focus on commonly confused words. Look for words that are commonly mistaken for one another: for example, *adapt* and *adopt, accept* and *except,* or *affect* and *effect.* If necessary, consult a dictionary or handbook to make sure you are using the correct word.

Publishing and Presenting

Consider one of the following ways to share your writing.

Deliver a speech. Use your persuasive essay as the basis for a speech to your classmates or to another audience. While making your presentation, make frequent eye contact with your audience, and use hand gestures and a strong voice to emphasize your key points. Incorporate visuals, such as tables, maps, or graphs, to persuade your audience. If possible, videotape your delivery so that you can evaluate your own presentation. **Submit a letter to the editor.** Condense your persuasive essay and reformat it as a letter to the editor of your school or community newspaper.

Reflecting on Your Writing

Writer's Journal Jot down your thoughts on the experience of writing a persuasive essay. Begin by answering these questions:

- What have you learned about the effect of logical, ethical, and emotional appeals on your audience?
- What new information did you discover while researching your essay?

Prentice Hall Writing and Grammar Connection: Chapter 7.

Rubric for Self-Assessment

Evaluate your persuasive essay *using the following criteria and rating scale, or, with your classmates, determine your own reasonable evaluation criteria.*

Criteria	Rating Scale				
	not very				*very*
Focus: How clear is your thesis statement?	1	2	3	4	5
Organization: How effectively do you organize your arguments?	1	2	3	4	5
Support/Elaboration: How well do you use evidence, including facts and examples, to support your position?	1	2	3	4	5
Style: How well do you use convincing language?	1	2	3	4	5
Conventions: How correct is your grammar, especially your use of commonly confused words?	1	2	3	4	5

Editing and Proofreading

- Tell students that it is impossible to do a thorough job of proofreading by reading the draft once. Advise students to concentrate on one type of error each time.
- You may wish to review a list of commonly confused words with students. Encourage them to make their own personal list of words they sometimes confuse.

Six Traits Focus

Ideas		✔	Word Choice
Organization	✔		Sentence Fluency
Voice		✔	Conventions

ASSESS

Publishing and Presenting

- If students are delivering their essay as a speech, tell students to practice their oral presentations. Encourage them to record their practice session and use the recording to critique themselves.
- Before students reformat their essays as letters to the editor, advise them to check the newspaper's guidelines for letters.
- Point out that many city newspapers encourage submission of letters to the editor over the Internet.

Reflecting on Your Writing

- After students respond to the questions in their Writer's Journals, have them discuss their answers in class.
- Encourage students to talk about these additional questions: What part of the writing process remains the most challenging? What parts of the process are getting easier for you?

Writing and Grammar, Diamond Level

Students will find additional instruction on editing and proofreading, publishing and presenting, and reflecting on a persuasive essay in Chapter 8, Sections 5 and 6.

Tips for Test Taking

When taking a test that includes a persuasive writing prompt, students should be careful to allow enough time for each step of the process. Though it is likely that a topic will be given, prewriting is still important because this is the stage at which students gather support and determine a position on the topic. Suggest that students use an Audience Profile chart like the one on p. 407 to jot down what they know about their audience. If students are asked to choose between two topics, this exercise may also be used to help them identify the topic with which they are more comfortable.

Students will

1. learn the terms *recall*, *predict*, and *summarize*.

2. apply knowledge of these terms in standardized-test situations.

Know Your Terms: Recalling Information and Understanding Meaning

Explain that students will use the words listed under Terms to Learn when they are asked to recall information from a reading passage in standardized-test situations.

Terms to Learn

- Review *recall*. Tell students that they will be asked to know important details in the passage.

- Review *predict*. Emphasize that predicting is a process of noticing actions that can cause changes. For example, students can ask themselves, "What might Lady Macbeth's past actions lead her to do?"

- Review *summarize*. Remind students that summarizing involves identifying main ideas and stating them concisely.

 Go Online
Vocabulary

For: An Interactive Crossword Puzzle
Visit: www. PHSchool.com
Web Code: esj-5201

ASSESS

Answers

1. She should protect herself from crowds.

2. She is willing to fight beside them.

3. She may say that that her people's loyalty has triumphed.

SAT PREP ACT   **Vocabulary Workshop**

High-Frequency Academic Words

High-frequency academic words are words that appear often in textbooks and on standardized tests. Though you may already know the meaning of many of these words, they usually have a more specific meaning when they are used in textbooks and on tests.

Know Your Terms: Recalling Information and Understanding Meaning

The words listed are verbs that guide you to demonstrate that you remember and understand the significance of the information in the text. The words indicate the kind of details and information you should provide.

Terms to Learn

Recall Tell the details as you remember them.

> Sample test item: *Recall* More's argument in *Utopia*.

Predict Tell what you think will happen based on details in the text.

> Sample test item: Considering the evidence in Act I, what do you *predict* Macbeth will do when King Duncan visits his castle?

Summarize Briefly state the most important information and ideas in the text.

> Sample test item: *Summarize* Marlowe's appeal to the shepherdess in "The Passionate Shepherd."

Practice

Directions: Read the passage from "Speech Before Her Troops" by Queen Elizabeth I. Then, on a separate piece of paper, answer the questions.

My loving people, we have been persuaded by some, that are careful of our safety, to take heed how we commit ourselves to armed multitudes, for fear of treachery; but I assure you, I do not desire to live to distrust my dear and loving people. Let tyrants fear; I have always so behaved myself that, under God, I have placed my chiefest strength and safeguard in the loyal hearts and good will of my subjects. And therefore I am . . . resolved, in the midst and heat of the battle, to live or die amongst you all; to lay down, for my God, and for my kingdom, and for my people, my honor and my blood, even the dust. I know I have but the body of a weak and feeble woman; but I have the heart of a king, and of a king of England, too . . . . I myself will take up arms; I myself will be your general, judge, and rewarder of your virtues in the field . . .

1. *Recall* Elizabeth's opening words. What have some of her councilors advised her to do?

2. *Summarize* Elizabeth's attitude towards her people in this passage.

3. What do you *predict* Elizabeth will say when her troops are victorious?

Tips for Test Taking

- Remind students that when they are answering multiple-choice questions, the correct answer is always given. Tell them that finding the incorrect answers may be easier than finding the correct answer. By eliminating the incorrect answers, they improve their chances of finding the correct answer.

- Students may be asked to summarize a passage or give its main idea. Remind them that paragraphs often have a topic sentence. Tell students to underline topic sentences as they read, since they may be questioned about those ideas later.

Assessment Workshop

Critical Reading:
Forms of Propaganda

On certain tests, you are required to recognize forms of propaganda and to distinguish between fact and opinion. Use the following strategies to help you answer questions testing these skills.

- As you read, remember that propaganda distorts or conceals facts and manipulates emotions to advance a particular cause.
- Realize that charged language, exaggeration, and name-calling are tactics often used in propaganda to manipulate opinion.

Practice

Directions: Read the passages, and then answer the questions.

Passage A (1) More than 5,000 people voted last week in favor of building a new shopping center, but the opposition won out. (2) The margin of victory is irrelevant. (3) Those radical voters who opposed the center are obviously self-serving elitists who do not care about anyone but themselves. (4) This month's unemployment figures for Braden are 12 percent, which represents an increase of some 3 percent over the figures for last year. (5) These figures mean that unemployment in Braden is worsening. (6) But the people who voted against the mall probably do not care about creating new jobs.

Passage B (1) The first new Tiger automobiles rolled off the assembly line at the Dearborn assembly plant on Monday. (2) The cars, which feature such luxury appointments as programmable destination mapping, retail at $48,000 each. (3) Nothing compares with the Tiger's luxury. (4) Tigers are available in 17 colors, ranging from Dark Midnight to Dazzle Red. (5) And they offer 37 percent better gas mileage over last year's model. (6) When you are behind the wheel of a Tiger, you are the envy of every driver on the road.

1. In Passage A, which of the statements can be labeled as propaganda?

A Statements 1, 2, and 6

B Statements 2 and 5

C Statements 2, 3, and 6

D Statements 2 and 4

2. In Passage B, which statements might be considered propaganda?

A Statement 1

B Statements 4 and 5

C Statements 2 and 4

D Statements 3 and 6

3. What is the purpose of Statement 5 in Passage B?

A to state a fact

B to conceal a fact

C to inspire desire

D to state an opinion

Test-Taking Strategies

- Recall the claims made in a passage, and then question their significance and validity.

- Look for symbols—highly positive or negative images—used to influence your opinion.

Critical Reading

- Remind students that propaganda is meant to be persuasive. Give students examples of advertisements or editorials, and have them identify what the advertiser wants readers to buy or what the writer wants readers to believe or to do.

- Have students list the ways that propaganda may influence them. Have them identify tactics that writers use to make an opinion seem convincing.

- After students have read the Practice passages and answered the questions, point out that in question 1, statements 1, 4, and 5 in Passage A offer data that can be checked. The other statements use words to attack opponents.

- Point out that in Question 2, statements 1, 2, 4, and 5 contain facts or figures that can be verified. Statements 3 and 6 offer opinions to appeal to the buyer's vanity.

- Discuss the possible implications of statement 5 in Passage B. It appears to state that the car offers improved gas mileage, but it compares the new Tiger to last year's model, not to other cars. The Tiger has improved its gas mileage, but its gas mileage may not be better than comparable cars from other manufacturers.

Tips for
Test Taking

Remind students of the importance of reading an answer completely. In sample Question 1, point out the similarities between the correct answer, C, and answer A, which includes two of the three correct statements. Also point out that in Question 3, the correct answer, B, has words in common with answer A ("a fact"). Tell students that marking through incorrect answers can help eliminate confusion and keep them from accidentally marking incorrect answers.

ASSESS

Answers

1. C   2. D   3. B

415

Taking an Advertisement Apart

- Focus students' attention on an advertisement or advertising campaign that is currently running in the media. As an alternative, you may wish to show the class one of several collections of award-winning commercials that are available on video.

- Review the key elements of an advertisement listed on this page. Work with the class to develop an extended list of charged language, adding such words as *new, clean, powerful,* and *free.*

- Tell students that often a key element of an advertisement is information that is *not* present: details about cost, side effects, or complexity that the advertiser deliberately omits.

Interpreting Its Meaning

- Review the questions. Ask students if they can think of other questions that might be added to the list. For example: What important information is missing from the advertisement?

- You may wish to do the activity as a class, using the chart shown to analyze two or more commercials. If you have a number of commercials available on video, analyze two or three as a class and have students work independently on the rest.

Assess the Activity

To evaluate students' analyses, use the Exposition: Comparison-and-Contrast Essay Rubrics, pp 69–70 in *General Resources.*

Analyzing Advertising

A commercial is a kind of **advertisement**, a persuasive message in print or in broadcast form, sponsored by an individual or a group to achieve a goal, such as selling a product or persuading people to adopt an opinion. To **analyze an advertisement**, identify the key persuasive elements it contains, following the steps outlined here.

Taking an Advertisement Apart

To analyze an advertisement, identify the following key elements:

- **Concept**—central theme of the ad; for instance, that a specific toothpaste will improve the user's popularity
- **Hook**—a memorable or catchy jingle or slogan
- **Charged language**—words that imply a certain view of the product; for instance, *efficient, cool, fabulous*
- **Characterization**—the creation of memorable characters
- **Special effects**—visual and sound effects used to grab viewer attention
- **Information**—facts versus opinions, accuracy, ambiguities, or inconsistencies

Interpreting Its Meaning

To understand how these elements are intended to work in the advertisement, ask yourself the following questions. For each response, identify the elements—concept, hook, language, characters, or effects—that support your answer.

- Who is the targeted audience of this advertisement?
- What is the message of this ad?
- What is the overall mood of the commercial? Is it exciting, scary, or funny?
- Is the viewer expected to identify or sympathize with the speakers or to reject or condemn their general character?
- What cultural values (generosity, sharing, winning) are illustrated in the ad?

Generate additional questions, then sum up your analysis by answering these questions: How does the ad use persuasive elements to send its message? What impact does the ad make on its intended audience?

Activity ▶ *View and Analyze* ▶ Compare and contrast two commercials using the questions listed above. Use a chart like the one shown to guide your analysis.

Evidence	
Target Audience:	
Message:	
Mood:	
Attitude Towards Characters:	
Values:	

Suggestions for Further Reading

Featured Titles:

Hamlet
William Shakespeare
Pearson Prentice Hall, 2000

Drama Shakespeare's most celebrated play is a story of murder and revenge. It begins with the ghost of Hamlet's father haunting the castle of Elsinore on a dark and cold night. Young Hamlet soon confronts the apparition and learns that his suspicions are true: His uncle murdered his father to seize the crown. Urged on to vengeance by the ghost, Hamlet swears that he will kill his uncle but also expresses his dismay: "The time is out of joint. O cursed spite / That ever I was born to set it right." As time passes, Hamlet mysteriously delays his revenge, until events themselves speed to a bloody conclusion.

The Tempest
William Shakespeare
Pearson Prentice Hall, 2000

Drama Shakespeare's last play is also his most enchanting work. It is set on a remote island inhabited by the magician Prospero and his daughter. They were stranded there after Prospero's evil brother stole his kingdom from him and set father and daughter adrift on a boat. Among the strange beings who share the island with them are Ariel, the spirit who performs Prospero's magic, and Caliban, the surly creature who does all the hard labor. When a tempest shipwrecks the evil brother on the same island, Prospero has the opportunity for revenge, reconciliation, or both—if only his magic powers do not fail him.

A Midsummer Night's Dream
William Shakespeare
Pearson Prentice Hall, 2000

Drama This high-spirited comedy is about the confusions, mishaps, and joys of young love. Though Shakespeare's characters live in ancient Greece and their enchanted night takes place in a forest near Athens, they are not unlike American teenagers: Hermia loves Lysander, but her father wants her to marry Demetrius, and Helena loves Demetrius, who is interested in Hermia. It all gets hilariously more complicated before true love prevails!

Works Presented in Unit Two:

If sampling a portion of the following texts has built your interest, treat yourself to the full works.

The Sonnets
William Shakespeare
Signet Classic, 1999

Utopia
Thomas More, translated by Paul Turner
Penguin Books, 2003

Many of these titles are available in the **Prentice Hall/Penguin Literature Library.** *Consult your teacher before choosing one.*

The Sonnets by William Shakespeare Sonnets 1-126 center on a "young man" for whom the poet professes love. You may wish to remind your students that little is known about the circumstances of the creation and publication of the sonnets or about Shakespeare's private life. The speaker of the poem may or may not be expressing the feelings of the poet himself. You may also wish to remind students that in sixteenth-century England, it was common for men to express affection and admiration for one another in a manner that is uncommon today.
Lexile: NP

Utopia by Thomas More This book contains passages that satirize certain aspects of systems of government as well as religious observance.
Lexile: 1260L

Planning Students' Further Reading

Discussions of literature can raise sensitive and often controversial issues. Before you recommend further reading to your students, consider the values and sensitivities of your community as well as the age, ability, and sophistication of your students. It is also good policy to preview literature before you recommend it to students. The notes below offer some guidance on specific titles.

Hamlet by William Shakespeare
The play focuses on murder and revenge. It features ghosts and other supernatural elements; the implied suicide of Ophelia and contemplation of suicide by Hamlet; a dated view of mental illness; passing reference to drink; crude references to pregnancy and Ophelia's virginity; a widow's hasty remarriage to her brother-in-law and husband's killer; and a pre-occupation on Hamlet's part with his mother's sexual relations with Claudius, which some view as an Oedipal jealousy.

Lexile: NP

The Tempest by William Shakespeare
As with much of Shakespearean drama, this play contains sexual references and bawdy jokes, most of which may not be initially evident to students. The play presents the use of magic to control human events and some students may find the magician/sprite structure offensive. The shipwreck and tempest are powerful scenes and may trouble students who have experienced traumatic life events.

Lexile: NP

A Midsummer Night's Dream by William Shakespeare
The play contains some oblique references to sexual activities, especially in the remarks of Oberon and Titania. In addition, some students may be offended by the "doormat" behavior of female characters—Helena in particular—or by the stereotyping of the working-class tradesmen as poorly educated buffoons.

Lexile: NP

417

Students will

1. read selections from seventeenth- and eighteenth-century English literature.

2. apply a variety of reading strategies, particularly strategies for constructing meaning, appropriate for reading these selections.

3. analyze literary elements.

4. use a variety of strategies to read unfamiliar words and to build vocabulary.

5. learn elements of grammar, usage, and style.

6. use recursive writing processes to write in a variety of forms.

7. develop listening and speaking skills.

8. express and support responses to various types of texts.

9. evaluate and critique oral presentations and performances.

Unit Instructional Resources

▶ **Vocabulary and Reading**

Additional vocabulary and reading support, based on Lexile scores of vocabulary words, is provided for each selection or grouping.

• **Word Lists A and B** and **Practices A and B** provide vocabulary-building activities for students reading two grades or one grade below level, respectively.

• **Reading Warm-ups A and B,** for students reading two grades or one grade below level, respectively, consist of short readings and activities that provide a context and practice for newly learned vocabulary.

▶ **Selection Support**

• Reading Strategy
• Literary Analysis
• Vocabulary Builder
• Grammar and Style
• Support for Writing
• Support for Extend Your Learning
• Enrichment

Unit
3

A Turbulent Time
1625–1798

Assessment Resources

Skills Assessment

Unit 3 Resources
   Selection Tests A and B

TeacherExpress™
   ExamView® Test Bank Software

Adequate Yearly Progress Assessment

Unit 3 Resources
   Diagnostic Tests 5 and 6
   Benchmark Tests 5 and 6

Standardized Assessment

Standardized Test Preparation Workbook

The Seventeenth and Eighteenth Centuries

" Methinks I see in my mind a noble . . . nation rousing herself like a strong man after sleep, and shaking her invincible locks.

—John Milton,
from *Areopagitica*

◁ This painting, *King Charles I After the Battle of Naseby*, depicts one of the closing events in Charles I's turbulent reign.

A Turbulent Time (1625–1798) ■ *419*

419

Introduce Richard Rodriguez

- Richard Rodriguez introduces the unit and provides insights into the role of a spectator in London. A selection from his work *Days of Obligation:* "In Athens Once," and his commentary about it appear later in the unit on pages 604–611.

- Have students read the introductory paragraph about Richard Rodriguez. Tell them that he is an editor at Pacific News Service and a contributing editor and writer for many highly respected publications. His *NewsHour Essays on American Life* won him the 1997 George Foster Peabody Award. His work contains his observations on life.

- Use the *From the Author's Desk DVD* to introduce Richard Rodriguez. Show Segment 1 to provide insight into his writing career. After students have watched the segment, **discuss** what observations on life Rodriguez chooses to write about.
  Answer: He chooses to comment on society and cultural differences.

- **Ask** students what issues they would write about.
  Possible response: Students may suggest issues in their school.

From Small Towns to Big Cities

- Have students read Rodriguez's commentary on Joseph Addison. Point out Rodriguez's mention of loneliness among journalists.
  Ask: Why do you think that journalists have to choose solitude?
  Possible answer: In order to comment on society, one must be able to step back and observe. Close interaction within society creates a biased perspective.

- Tell students that they will also read an excerpt *from Days of Obligation:* "In Athens Once" by Richard Rodriguez in Part 4 of this unit. Rodriguez will also explain his writing of that piece.

Critical Viewing

Possible answer: He might wish to read about the lives and behavior of other people in his own social class.

Setting the Scene

The literature in Unit 3 covers a tumultuous time in English history. The period begins with the beheading of a king, and it ends with a revolution just beyond the English Channel. In this introductory essay, author Richard Rodriguez discusses the role of a spectator in London at this time in history, and how two journalists watched and commented on the turbulent events unfolding before them. Later, the unit introduction and the literature examine change as it affects individuals and the world around them.

Richard Rodriguez

From the Author's Desk
Richard Rodriguez Talks About the Time Period

Introducing Richard Rodriguez (b. 1944) The focus of Rodriguez's work, both journalistic and literary, is often on issues of affirmative action and bilingualism. His two autobiographical works, *Hunger of Memory: The Education of Richard Rodriguez* (1982) and *Days of Obligation: An Argument with My Mexican Father* (1992) explore those very themes.

From Small Towns to Big Cities
In high school, whenever teachers assigned texts of British literature, I responded most to the idea of London. I lived in Sacramento, at that time, more a town than a city. By senior year, because my body and mind were growing, I began to feel the need of a city—a place of contest and ambition. I left home, as so many seekers of fortune in English novels leave home, for the city.

London, Market for Commodities and Ideas London at the beginning of the eighteenth century was becoming the center of the world. Most of the world's commodities and many of the world's ideas passed through London. A city of so much invested interest was interested. People required news: of ships, of trade, of exploration. To get the news, people required newspapers. Londoners also wanted to read about themselves, about plays and books, about fashions and personalities.

Birth of the *Spectator* In 1711, an ex-soldier and ex-scholar named Richard Steele published a journal called the *Spectator*. The *Spectator*'s innovation was to notice and to comment upon the social and moral life of London. Steele enlisted a young writer named Joseph Addison to contribute to the paper. Addison developed the persona of the *Spectator*:

> I am frequently seen in most public places . . . (But) I live rather as a spectator of mankind than as one of the species . . .

Addison's essays are fictional observations of real places and real habits. They remain among the best records we have of

> ▼ **Critical Viewing**
> What might a fashionable young man, like the one pictured here, wish to read about in the *Spectator*? **[Speculate]**

Teaching Resources

The following resources can be used to enrich or extend the instruction for the Unit 3 Introduction.

From the Author's Desk DVD
　　Richard Rodriguez, Segment 1

Unit 3 Resources
　　Names and Terms to Know, p. 5
　　Focus Questions, p. 6
　　Listening and Viewing, p. 198

...ow several classes of men and women behaved and thought and spoke in London in the eighteenth century.

Joining "the conversation of cities" It was my ambition, when I left my schoolbooks behind, to join the conversation of cities. I became a journalist. My fate, as Addison might have foretold: In order to write, one must seek solitude. To create a public voice, one must choose loneliness.

Addison benefited from his solitude as a spectator; he was thrilled to have found readers in the male clubs and coffee houses of London. And he also wanted women readers.

When I was in high school and teachers instructed me to compose an essay, I never wondered about my reader. My reader was the teacher—her ear a pair of spectacles, her voice a fluent red ink.

What one never learns in high school about writing is just how large the world is and how a writer in the world must find an audience—must seduce, amuse, or infuriate a stranger's attention.

The Beginning and End of Print The reading audience of eighteenth-century London was avid, middle-class, growing as the city was growing—whereas we live near the end of a long age of print. Now, fewer people read for their news; fewer still for their pleasure. Today's blogger, tossing words into the void of the Web, must sense this. I sense it, writing for newspapers. Yet one is confident that one is, somehow, recorded. One lives in the age of mass media, after all.

But writing, although lonely, cannot be completed alone. In order to write, in order to continue writing, the writer needs to find, as Addison found, a reader—"you"—someone willing to complete the meaning of this sentence by the act of reading.

Go Online
—Author Link

For: A video clip of Richard Rodriguez
Visit: www.PHSchool.com
Web Code: ese-8301

For: More about Richard Rodriguez
Visit: www.PHSchool.com
Web Code: ese-9301

Reading the Unit Introduction

Reading for Information and Insight Use the following terms and questions to guide your reading of the unit introduction on pages 424–431.

Names and Terms to Know
Charles I
Parliament
Oliver Cromwell
English Commonwealth
Puritans
Restoration
Glorious Revolution
Enlightenment
Age of Reason

Focus Questions As you read this introduction, use what you learn to answer these questions:
- What was the result of the civil war between the royalists and the forces of Parliament?
- In what ways was the court of Charles II different from the government of the Puritan leaders?
- How does the literature of this period reflect its political and social realities?

From the Author's Desk: Richard Rodriguez ■ 421

Getting an Overview

Use the Timeline to help students get a quick overview of themes and events of the period. This approach will benefit all students but may be especially helpful for visually oriented students, English learners, and those less proficient in reading. (For strategies in using the Timeline as an overview, see the bottom of this page.)

Thinking Critically

Questions are provided on the facing page. Use these questions to have students review the events, discuss their significance, and examine the *so what* behind the *what happened*.

Connecting to Selections

Have students refer to the Timeline when beginning to read individual selections. By consulting the Timeline regularly, they will gain a better sense of the period's chronology. In addition, they will appreciate the world events that gave rise to these works of literature.

Projects

Students can use the Timeline as a launching pad for projects like these:

- **The Beginnings of Modernity** Have students look for events in the Timeline that helped make the world look more as it does today. Ask them to create a customized timeline charting the beginnings of the modern world, adding dates of related events and themes as they read new selections.

- **Report on a Painting** Have students scan the Timeline for a painting that interests them, research the topic and its significance, then report on their findings to the class.

British and World Events

1625   1640   1655

BRITISH EVENTS

- 1627 Sir Francis Bacon publishes *The New Atlantis.* ▼

- 1628 William Harvey explains blood circulation.
- 1633 **John Donne's** *Songs and Sonnets* published.
- 1635 Public mail service established.
- 1638 **John Milton** publishes *Lycidas.*

- 1640 Charles I summons Long Parliament.
- 1642 English Civil War begins.
- 1642 Puritans close theaters.
- 1646 **John Suckling** publishes *Fragmenta Aurea.*
- 1647 George Fox founds Society of Friends (Quakers).
- 1648 **Robert Herrick** publishes *Hesperides.*
- 1649 Charles I beheaded.
- 1649 **Richard Lovelace** publishes *Lucasta.*
- c. 1650 Early newspaper ads appear.
- c. 1650 Full-bottomed wigs come into fashion.
- 1653 Oliver Cromwell becomes Lord Protector.

- 1658 Oliver Cromwell dies.
- 1658 Puritan government collapses.
- 1660 Monarchy restored.
- 1660 Theaters reopened.
- 1660 **Samuel Pepys** begins *Diary.*
- 1662 Royal Society chartered.
- 1663 Drury Lane Theater opens.
- 1666 Great Fire of London.
- 1667 **John Milton's** *Paradise Lost* published. ▲
- 1668 John Dryden publishes *An Essay of Dramatic Poesy.*

WORLD EVENTS

- c. 1600 Japan: Kabuki theater developed. ▼

- 1614 North America: Dutch found New Amsterdam.

- 1640 India: English settlement established at Madras.
- 1640 North America: *Bay Psalm Book* published in Massachusetts.
- 1642 Holland: Rembrandt paints *The Nightwatch.*
- 1643 France: Louis XIV becomes king.
- 1644 China: Ming Dynasty ends.
- 1650 North America: Anne Bradstreet's collection of poems *The Tenth Muse Lately Sprung Up in America* published.
- 1651 North America: William Bradford finishes *Of Plymouth Plantation.*

- 1662 France: Louis XIV begins building palace at Versailles. ▼

- 1664 North America: Britain seizes New Netherlands.
- 1664 France: Molière's *Tartuffe* first produced.
- 1666 Italy: Stradivari labels first violin.

422 ■ *A Turbulent Time (1625–1798)*

Getting an Overview of the Period

Introduction To give students an overview of the period, indicate the span of dates in the upper left-hand corner. Next point out that the Timeline is divided into specifically British Events (on the top) and World Events (on the bottom). Have students practice scanning the Timeline across, looking both at the British Events and the World Events. Finally, point out that the events in the Timeline often represent beginnings, turning points, and endings. (The restoration of the monarchy in 1660 is an example.)

Key Events Have students identify key political events.
Answer: In 1642, the Civil War begins; in 1649, the king is executed.
Then, have students find evidence of cultural trends running parallel to these political developments.
Possible responses: In 1642, the year the Puritans take over, the theaters are closed; they reopen when the monarchy is restored, in 1660. In 1688, the Glorious Revolution occurs; in 1702, daily newspapers appear.

- 1685 James II becomes king.
- 1687 Sir Isaac Newton publishes his *Principia*.
- 1688 Glorious Revolution.
- 1689 Bill of Rights becomes law.
- 1690 John Locke publishes his *Two Treatises of Government*. ▼

- 1702 First daily newspaper begins publication.
- 1707 Great Britain created by Act of Union.

- 1712 **Alexander Pope** publishes *The Rape of the Lock*.
- 1714 George I becomes king.
- 1719 First organized cricket match takes place. ▲
- 1719 **Daniel Defoe** publishes *Robinson Crusoe*.
- 1726 **Jonathan Swift** publishes *Gulliver's Travels*.
- 1735 William Hogarth paints *The Rake's Progress*.
- 1745 Last Jacobite rebellion in Scotland.
- 1749 Henry Fielding publishes *Tom Jones*.
- 1751 **Thomas Gray** publishes "Elegy in a Country Churchyard."

- 1755 **Samuel Johnson** publishes *Dictionary of the English Language*.
- 1756 Britain enters Seven Years' War.
- 1775 Actress Sarah Siddons debuts at Drury Lane Theater. ▼

- 1791 **James Boswell** publishes *The Life of Samuel Johnson*.
- 1793 England goes to war with France.

- 1680 Dodo becomes extinct.
- 1682 North America: La Salle claims Louisiana for France.
- 1684 China: All ports open to foreign trade.
- 1685 France: Louis XIV revokes Edict of Nantes, provoking persecution of Protestants.
- 1690 India: Calcutta founded by British.
- 1703 Russia: Peter the Great begins building St. Petersburg.

- 1715 France: Louis XV succeeds to throne.
- 1721 Germany: Bach composes *Brandenburg Concertos*. ▶
- 1727 Brazil: First coffee planted.
- 1740 Prussia: Frederick the Great succeeds to the throne.
- 1748 France: Montesquieu publishes *The Spirit of the Laws*.
- 1752 North America: Benjamin Franklin invents lightning rod.

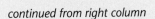

- 1759 Canada: British troops capture Quebec.
- 1773 North America: Boston Tea Party.
- 1775 North America: American Revolution begins.
- 1784 France: First school for the blind established.
- 1789 France: Revolution begins with storming of the Bastille.

Introduction ■ 423

continued from right column

(1666); the Glorious Revolution took place (1688) (b) After going through a period of instability characterized by the conflicts of Charles I with Parliament, government became more centralized—with Cromwell and then Charles II. However, Parliament also seemed to be asserting its power and limiting that of the monarch.

tural, or technological achievements in this period. (b) What do these achievements suggest about the kind of observations made by scientists of this period? [Hypothesize]
Possible responses: (a) Harvey explained the circulation of the blood in 1628; the first coffee was planted in Brazil in 1727 (b) Their observations were probably "hands-on." Also, scientists were just beginning to discover things that we take for granted today.

2. (a) What dramatic change marked English political life between 1649 and 1660? (b) What later world events might this period have influenced? Explain. [Speculate]
Answer: (a) During this time, England was not ruled by a monarch. (b) **Possible response:** The American Revolution, begun in 1775, may have owed some inspiration to the prior English experience of government without a king.

3. (a) What trend in publishing characterizes this period? (b) What does this trend suggest about society of the time? [Hypothesize]
Answer: (a) Newspapers and magazines were popular (see c. 1650 and 1702). (b) **Possible responses:** More people at this time could read; people took an active interest in the general affairs of the day.

4. (a) Name two events before 1710 showing Britain's expanding power. (b) What connection might there be between these events and events after 1750? [Connect]
Answer: (a) Madras (1640) and New Netherlands (1664) become British territories. (b) British colonial expansion led to rivalry with other European nations, reflected in the Seven Years' War (1756) and its taking of Quebec (1759).

5. (a) Name two events suggesting the chaos and unrest that mark this period. (b) What do these events indicate about the direction in which the government was moving? [Speculate] **Possible responses:** (a) England fought a civil war (1642); the king was beheaded (1649); the Puritan government collapsed (1658); London was ravaged by fire

Historical Background

In 1649, the English shocked the world by beheading their king and abolishing the monarchy. In the decades before civil wars tore England apart, revolutions in science and religion had already unsettled people's worldview. The new astronomy had exiled the Earth from the center of the universe to the vastness of infinite space. New religious creeds had altered or abolished the traditions of centuries. John Donne wrote, with his newfound insecurity, "Tis all in pieces, all coherence gone." By the 1700s, though, a monarch was back on the throne, and a new, competitive society had sprung up, with a looser social structure and greater freedom in religion and politics.

▲ **Critical Viewing**
(a) Describe the style in which Charles's execution is rendered in this picture. (b) How would the mood of the picture and your sense of the event be different if the picture were more realistic? **[Interpret]**

Charles I and Parliament Charles I, crowned in 1625, frequently clashed with Parliament over money. King Charles needed money for his wars, and Parliament refused to fund them. The king then extorted loans from his wealthy subjects and pressed the poor into service as soldiers and sailors. Parliament tried to prevent such abuses of power, so Charles eventually dissolved Parliament and would not call it into session for eleven years.

Charles I also turned up the flame under a simmering religious controversy. He insisted that clergymen "conform," or observe all the ceremonies of the Anglican Church. Puritans—Calvinists who wished to purify the Church of its Catholic traditions—were enraged by some of these requirements. Radical Puritans believed that each group of worshipers, moved by the members' divinely granted consciences, had the right to choose its own minister—an idea dangerously close to democracy. For these and other ideas, "dissenters" were persecuted and tortured as criminals.

The Civil War Charles's problems grew worse after he was forced to fight Scottish rebels outraged by his insistence on religious conformity. Desperate for money, he summoned a hostile Parliament, which passed wave upon wave of reforms. Angered when Charles tried to outmaneuver the reformers, Parliament condemned him as a tyrant in 1642. Civil war broke out. In 1645, Parliament's forces, led by Oliver Cromwell, defeated the royalist army and, in 1647, took Charles as a prisoner. Radical Puritans, who by then dominated Parliament, tried the king and convicted him of treason. Charles I was beheaded on January 30, 1649.

Cromwell led the new government, called the English Commonwealth. Facing discontent at home and wars abroad, he dissolved Parliament in 1653 and named himself Lord Protector. Until his death in 1658, he ruled as a virtual dictator.

424 ■ *A Turbulent Time (1625–1798)*

Civil war had not led to the free society that many who had fought against the king expected. Their hopes, coupled with economic hardships, brought unrest. The Commonwealth also fueled discontent by outlawing gambling, horse racing, newspapers, fancy clothes, public dancing, and the theater.

The Restoration By the time of Cromwell's death, England had had enough of taxation, violence, and disorder. Two chaotic years later, Parliament offered the crown to the exiled son of Charles I, who became Charles II in 1660. The monarchy was restored.

In sharp contrast to the drab Puritan leaders, Charles II and his court copied the plush fashions of Paris. An avid patron of the arts and sciences, Charles invited Italian composers and Dutch painters to live and work in London.

A Glorious Revolution Religious differences resurfaced with Charles II's successor, James II, a devout Catholic. Parliament eventually invited Mary, the Protestant daughter of James II, to rule England jointly with her husband, William of Orange. Rather than fight, James escaped to France. The people of

The British Tradition   **Point/Counterpoint**

Royal Victim or Devious King?

Was Charles I at least partly a victim of circumstances, or was he a schemer whose plotting backfired and led to his own downfall? Two scholars disagree about this question.

Royal Victim

ì We may perhaps set aside the personal appeal which the royal martyr and sainted cavalier has always made, but we should not forget that all along he had had a large share of legality, if not of equity, honesty, and intelligence, on his side. And the king lacked not only revenue but a national civil service, a solid framework of royal authority . . . we cannot . . . idealize the Long Parliament as an assembly of political Galahads, and the behavior of the victorious army . . . was scarcely in accord with the doctrine of the supremacy of law for which they had fought."

—**Douglas Bush,** *English Literature in the Earlier Seventeenth Century*

Devious King

"Cromwell and his associates negotiated seriously with the king to preserve the monarchy and the changes that had been accomplished. Charles invariably eluded them, reaching a peak of deviousness when he agreed to accept a presbyterian church and so launched the Scots against the English in the second Civil War in 1648. Cromwell . . . finally came to believe that it was necessary to get rid of Charles Stuart . . . and Charles was seized and brought to trial . . . He was convicted on the charge of high treason against the state and executed on January 30, 1649."

—**R. K. Webb,** "Elizabethans and Puritans," *The Columbia History of the World*

remains a contested political issue today. Then, ask the following questions.

1. Why are the two viewpoints so different?
   Answer: The historians believe that Charles was either a vulnerable victim or the deserving culprit.

2. Is it possible that both historians are correct? Explain.
   Answer: Answers should include the concept that any historical figure or event can be analyzed from any number of viewpoints.

3. Who are some figures in contemporary culture whom future historians might view in positive or negative terms?
   Possible responses: Answers might include world leaders, politicians, philosophers, or charismatic religious figures.

Differentiated Instruction   Solutions for All Learners

Strategy for Less Proficient Readers
Explain to these students that, during this time, people were shaken up by the major changes in their lives and their basic beliefs. Ask students to look for two of these major changes as they read.

Strategy for English Learners
Have these students look over the illustrations throughout this section and for each of three pictures, create a question they would like answered. Ask them to see if they can find the answers to their question in "A Turbulent Time."

Strategy for Advanced Readers
Challenge more advanced students to use the illustrations in this selection and the text to examine how changes in institutions, symbols, ideas, and work through this period changed the ties that bound people together in society.

When Charles II's brother James II inherited the throne of England in 1685, he made no secret of his Catholic faith. Riding roughshod over Parliamentary laws that he did not like, he appointed a number of Catholics to high offices. Parliament resented his lack of respect for their power. Fears spread among the people that James II, like Bloody Mary before him, would restore the Catholic Church to England.

Rather than risk returning to the kingless days of Cromwell's rule, Parliamentary leaders took an innovative step. They asked James's Protestant daughter, Mary, and her husband, William III of Orange, to become rulers of England.

Critical Viewing

Answer: Both Locke and Hobbes believe that government arises from people's original surrender of their full liberty. Locke feels that the purpose of government is to protect people's rights to life, liberty, and property. Hobbes feels a government should ensure order by suppressing rebellion.

European Political Thinkers

Thinker	Major Ideas	Quotation
Thomas Hobbes *Leviathan* (1651) 	People are driven by selfishness and greed. To avoid chaos, they give up their freedom to a government that will ensure order. Such a government must be strong and able to suppress rebellion.	"The condition of man [in the state of nature] . . . is a condition of war of everyone against everyone."
John Locke *Two Treatises of Government* (1690) 	People have a natural right to life, liberty, and property. Rulers have a responsibility to protect those rights. People have the right to change a government that fails to do so.	"Men being . . . by nature all free, equal, and independent, no one can be put out of this estate and subjected to the political power of another without his own consent."
Baron de Montesquieu *The Spirit of the Laws* (1748) 	The powers of government should be separated into executive, legislative, and judicial branches, to prevent any one group from gaining too much power.	"In order to have . . . liberty, it is necessary that government be set up so that one man need not be afraid of another."

◀ **Critical Viewing** Compare Locke's and Hobbes's notions of the purpose of government. **[Read a Chart]**

England hailed the event as the "Glorious Revolution of 1688" because not a drop of blood had been shed.

In 1689, William and Mary agreed to respect a Bill of Rights passed by Parliament. This bill guaranteed Parliament the right to approve all taxes and forbade the monarch to suspend the law. England thus attained a limited, or constitutional, monarchy. In ensuing decades, two political factions crystallized in Parliament: the conservative, aristocratic Tories and the Whigs, drawn largely from Britain's growing merchant class. A cabinet of ministers drawn from Parliament, and eventually unified under the leadership of a prime minister, began to rule the country.

An Agricultural Revolution By the late 1600s, new farm tools made it possible for farms to produce much more food. With more food available, the population surged upward. Because fewer farmhands were needed, many people left the countryside. In the growing towns, they became the factory

Enrichment

The Early Industrial Revolution

Emphasize for students that the Industrial Revolution began with agriculture. In the 1700s, new technologies increased food production. Jethro Tull, for instance, invented a seed drill, a plow with a hopper that deposited seeds in straight lines. Seeds were no longer scattered and lost.

The next advance was the discovery of steam power, much more efficient than wind or water power. In a steam engine, water is heated by burning fuel, such as coal; the resulting steam enters an enclosed cylinder, where it pushes against a piston. James Watt's clever 1769 design improved fuel efficiency by three fourths.

hands who ran the machines of the early Industrial Revolution.

The Industrial Age British inventions after 1750 made the spinning and weaving of cloth much more efficient. The steam engine was perfected and adapted to run a power loom. Factories were built to produce vast quantities of cotton cloth. Merchants sold the goods all over the world, adding more gold to the nation's coffers. As late as the 1790s, the majority of British people still earned their living as farmers. Yet, the economic revolution of the 1700s increased Britain's wealth enormously.

The Enlightenment The scientific revolution that made industry possible stemmed from a larger development in thought known as the Enlightenment. Enlightenment thinkers in all fields believed that, through reason and observation of nature, human beings could discover the order underlying all things. In 1687, Sir Isaac Newton published one of the touchstone works of the Enlightenment, a monumental study of gravity.

By 1750, Britain was rapidly industrializing and the social theories of the Enlightenment were eclipsed. Mills and factories belched smoke into the country air. Men, women, and children toiled at machines for twelve to fourteen hours a day. Poor people crowded into the towns and cities, unable to find regular work and barely able to survive. By the late 1700s, "progress" seemed to mean misery for millions. Writers and intellectuals began to lose faith in the ability of human reason to solve every problem.

Literature of the Period

The Schools of Jonson and Donne In his writing, Ben Jonson (1572–1637) strove for the perfection and harmony he found in his beloved classical authors, turning away from the ornate style of Elizabethan times to create his own modern, strong voice. He wrote poems, plays, and masques (court entertainments). His critical opinion exercised a powerful influence on other poets of the time. Among the best-known "Sons of Ben" were Robert Herrick (1591–1674), Sir John Suckling (1609–1642), and Richard Lovelace (1618–1657).

John Donne (1572–1631) pioneered a new, witty, cerebral style later known as metaphysical poetry. Metaphysical poetry is characterized by an unusual degree of intellectualism. Even Donne's love poems are frequently structured like ingenuous, subtle arguments that raid the worlds of science, law, and philosophy for surprising but strangely accurate comparisons. In "A Valediction: Forbidding Mourning," for example, he compares parted lovers to the two legs of a drawing compass. In "A Valediction: Of Weeping," he compares his tears, which reflect his lover's face, to coins that are stamped with her image.

The most notable followers of John Donne were George Herbert (1593–1633) and Andrew Marvell (1621–1678). Herbert's mother was a friend of Donne's, and in many ways the life of Herbert parallels Donne's. He keenly felt the tension between wordly ambition and religious devotion.

Introduction ■ 427

the poet. He believed, in fact, that no other profession could compare to it. Poets, he wrote, encourage "young men to all good disciplines, inflame grown men to all great virtues, [and] keep old men in their best and supreme state." A person could not be "the good poet without first being a good man," he asserted.

Literature of the Period

Samuel Pepys's *Diary*, p. 504, and Defoe's *A Journal of the Plague Year*, p. 511, can introduce students to seventeenth- and eighteenth-century England from the "inside."

Historical Background
Comprehension Check

1. Over what did Parliament and King Charles I clash?
   Answer: Parliament and the king clashed over money—Parliament refused to give him any for his wars.

2. Describe Charles I's policies regarding religion.
   Answer: The king insisted that clergymen use the ceremonies of the Church of England. He persecuted religious dissenters, such as Puritans.

3. (a) What actions did Parliament finally take against Charles I? (b) Who led England after him?
   Answer: (a) Parliament named him traitor, raised an army against him, captured him, and, eventually, executed him. (b) Oliver Cromwell led England after Charles I.

4. How was the monarchy restored to England?
   Answer: Parliament invited Charles's son, Charles II, back to rule.

Enrichment

Technology and Society

Emphasize for students that efficiency in agriculture and industry had deep social consequences. In the 1700s, rich landowners pushed ahead with enclosure, by which they took over and fenced off the common land formerly shared by peasant villagers. Enclosures enabled them to consolidate small strips of farmland into more efficient fields.

As millions of acres were enclosed, farm output rose. Profits also rose because large fields needed fewer people to work them. Small farmers were forced off their land because they could not compete with large landholders. The jobless or landless farm workers who migrated to towns and cities formed the growing labor force crucial to the success of the factories of the future.

the poem to students. Tell students that the poem reflects Herbert's concern with speech. Note the precision of the language.

- **Ask** students to provide examples of the conversational style of the poem.
  Possible answer: "Love took my hand, and smiling did reply,/'Who made the eyes but I?'"(Lines 11-12)

- Herbert's poetry often contains characteristics of metaphysical poetry. Have students review the definition of metaphysical poetry on p. 427. Discuss how "Love (III)" is a metaphysical poem.

Critical Thinking

1. What political consequences did some Puritan ideas have? **[Infer]**
   Answer: Some believed that groups of worshipers, guided by their inner light, were competent to pick their own ministers. This belief challenged the idea that the Church (led by the king) had special authority over worshipers.

2. (a) Into what classes could Britain be divided at the beginning of the period? (b) What political trends demonstrate the rise of new classes after the Glorious Revolution? **[Analyze]**
   Answers: (a) The king's quarrels with Parliament show a society divided into royalty, the wealthy, and the poor. (b) Political parties formed, one representing a new merchant class, different from traditional aristocrats.

Tempted for a time by the sparkling life at the court of James I, he later became an Anglican deacon. Herbert's best poems are the religious lyrics collected in *The Temple*. Marvell's best lyrics blend the brilliance of Donne and the classical finish of Jonson. They offer observations on nature, love, and God that, at first, seem urbane and perhaps conventional, but on closer inspection, prove profound. His best-known poem, "To His Coy Mistress," is one of the best lyrics in English literature.

The British Tradition — A Living Tradition

The Poet Laureate of Brooklyn Invokes George Herbert

Recently, D. Nurkse, the poet laureate of Brooklyn, New York, and author of *Voices Over Water* and *Leaving Xaia*, wrote a response to George Herbert's dialogue with God in *The Temple*, quoting from Herbert's poem "Love (III)":

"At the end of the twentieth century, George Herbert's voice carries intimately from the seventeenth, pitched just above a breath, often strangely uncertain. He describes his poetry to a friend as "a picture of the many spiritual conflicts" between the soul and God. . . . Always the voice persists, hushed in fear of its own unpredictability ("Love bade me welcome: yet my soul drew back"), its strangely powerful freedom. [To] this conversation with the unknown . . . the reader is invited as a guest. . . ."

Love (III) by George Herbert

Love bade me welcome: yet my soul drew back,
    Guilty of dust and sin.
But quick-eyed Love, observing me grow slack
    From my first entrance in,
5 Drew nearer to me, sweetly questioning,
    If I lacked any thing.

"A guest," I answered, "worthy to be here":
    Love said, "You shall be he."
"I the'unkind, ungrateful? Ah my dear
10   I cannot look on thee."
Love took my hand, and smiling did reply,
    "Who made the eyes but I?"

"Truth Lord, but I have marred° them: let my shame   °spoiled
    Go where it doth deserve."
15 "And know you not," says Love, "who bore the blame?"
    "My dear, then I will serve."
"You must sit down," says Love, "and taste my meat":
    So I did sit and eat.

Enrichment

The Paintings of Hogarth

William Hogarth (1697–1764) was one of the first English-born artists to gain recognition abroad. Committed to a realistic, popular, satirical art, he compared his paintings to a stage on which the characters silently acted their parts. His idea of beauty was "a composed intricacy of form" that "leads the eye a kind of chase"—a justification for the humorous exaggeration and dynamic quality of his paintings and engravings. Many of Hogarth's works reveal an easy familiarity with the tumult of ordinary life. Often, they have morals, and a few take the form of full-blown narratives. The eight paintings that make up "A Rake's Progress," for instance, tell the tale of a young man who falls prey to the temptations and follies of the world. To a large extent, this naturalism of Hogarth's put him at odds with the neoclassical ideals of his day, though he shared a taste for satire with Dryden, Pope, and Swift.

Marriage à la Mode: The Marriage Contract,
1743, William Hogarth. Reproduced by
courtesy of the Trustees, National Gallery
of Art, London.

▲ Critical Viewing
In William Hogarth's
satirical *Signing the
Marriage Contract,* the
fathers of the bride and
groom (both seated)
discuss the property the
bride will give her new
husband. What
conclusions can you draw
about the characters'
attitudes and Hogarth's
opinion of them?
[Draw Conclusions]

The Puritan Writers Perhaps the greatest poet of the seventeenth century was a Puritan, not a Cavalier: John Milton. The Puritan movement also produced the best-selling prose writer of the century, John Bunyan. Only the Bible sold more copies than Bunyan's religious narrative, *The Pilgrim's Progress.*

John Milton Like Ben Jonson, John Milton (1608–1674) was a learned disciple of the classical Greek and Latin authors. However, unlike the Elizabethan humanists and Cavalier poets, he was also a profound Calvinist and studied the Old Testament in Hebrew.

Milton was born in London to a prosperous middle-class family. He received a good basic education, studied at Cambridge, and spent the next six years reading and studying on his own. In the 1640s, as the battle between Charles I and Parliament grew hotter, Milton began writing political pamphlets for the Puritan cause. One of his greatest contributions to the "pamphlet wars" was *Areopagitica,* a ringing call for freedom of the press.

Milton supported the Commonwealth and Protectorate and even defended the execution of Charles I. As Cromwell's rule turned to a dictatorship, however, Milton lost hope in the possibility of forming a just society on Earth. Having gone completely blind by 1652 as a result of his labors for the Commonwealth, he set about composing an epic that would explain why God allows suffering in this world. That epic, *Paradise Lost,* reflects Milton's humanistic love of poetry and his Puritan devotion to God.

John Bunyan A tinker by trade, John Bunyan (1628–1688) had little education beyond reading the Bible. Like many others of his time, he wandered

Introduction ■ 429

Comprehension Check

1. Name two influential authors of the early seventeenth century.
   Answer: Ben Jonson and John Donne were the early seventeenth century's key authors.

2. What two influences combined in John Milton's poetry?
   Answer: Milton combined a humanist's appreciation of the Greek and Latin classics with a Calvinist's devotion to God.

3. Name two literary genres that came into prominence after the Restoration of Charles II.
   Answer: The popularity of drama burgeoned when Charles reopened the theaters. The first novel, *Robinson Crusoe,* and the first essayistic periodicals appeared later in the period.

4. (a) Define neoclassical style.
   (b) Name two exponents of this style.
   Answer: (a) Neoclassical writers modeled their style after classical writers, emphasizing harmony, restraint, and clarity. (b) John Dryden and Alexander Pope are two important practitioners of this style.

5. What new class of readers began to influence literature in the eighteenth century?
   Answer: The growing middle classes were the audience for the novels and periodical essays of the day.

6. Aside from his writing, how did Samuel Johnson contribute to literature?
   Answer: Johnson befriended and encouraged young talents.

Critical Viewing

Possible response: The fathers of the bride and groom look as if they are involved in a business deal. The father with his hand on his breast looks as if he is making a self-consciously dramatic point.

Activities

1. **Role Play** Have students choose a person mentioned in "A Turbulent Time." Then, speaking as that person, they can comment on a contemporary issue that would interest him or her. For example, Oliver Cromwell might have a great deal to say about censorship

continued

Continued from right column

and Charles I might comment on the troubles of today's royal family.

2. **Fathers and Sons** Have students write an entry from Charles II's journal in which he reflects on his father's policies, virtues, shortcomings, and eventual fate. They should explore the ways in which exile and his father's fate have shaped Charles II's outlook.

429

duce? [Infer]
Answer: They gave poetry a new, mature voice and exploited new sources of imagery.

2. (a) Contrast Milton's use of poetry of the past with the neoclassicists' use. (b) Relate your contrast to the times in which each lived. [Compare and Contrast]
Answer: (a) Milton used an old poetic form (the epic) to give grandeur to *Paradise Lost*—he was trying to equal the past. (b) The neoclassicists took the past as a source of standards for taste and sense.

3. The Restoration enjoyed satire—literature that pokes fun at people's ways. Speculate about a society that nurtures satire. (a) Is it large or small? (b) Are roles rigidly defined, or is there social mobility? Explain. [Speculate]
Possible responses: (a) It is probably large, with many institutions to satirize. (b) It may be rigid and pretentious because those qualities suggest more targets for satirists.

Critical Viewing

Possible responses: Students may say that these new theaters separated the dramatic experience from the audience but were more realistic in their use of women to play women's roles and special effects and props to add artistic touches to performances.

---

from town to town in rural England, preaching wherever people would listen. After the restoration of Charles II, Bunyan was imprisoned, and it was there that he wrote *The Pilgrim's Progress*. This allegory, in which events have a hidden meaning, relates how a man flees sin to lead a holy life.

Literature of the Age of Reason Enlightenment writers discovered the qualities they admired most—harmony, restraint, and clarity—among the writers of ancient Greece and Rome, such as Homer, Virgil, and Horace. Neoclassical writers—English writers who imitated the styles of classical writers—often referred to the myths, gods, and heroes of ancient times. They favored generalities rather than the viewpoint of the individual, displayed a fondness for satires that poked fun at society's follies, and often expressed their thoughts in aphorisms—short, quotable sentences—such as, "The proper study of mankind is man."

John Dryden From 1660 to 1700, a period known as the Restoration, John Dryden (1631–1700) dominated literature. Named poet laureate, England's official poet for life, by Charles II, he wrote plays, satirical poems, and celebratory poems that hailed the achievements of humanity. His essays about drama and his other prose compositions represent the first modern prose.

Restoration Theater The Restoration was also noted for its plays, especially its comedies. When Charles II became king, he reopened the London theaters. The Restoration theaters, fancier and more costly than those of Shakespeare's time, did a thriving business.

Alexander Pope The poetry of Alexander Pope (1688–1744), written in the early 1700s, is a shining example of neoclassical style, exhibiting wit, elegance, and moderation. All these qualities show forth in his most famous work, *The Rape of the Lock,* a satire on the war between the sexes. Pope also had enormous influence as a critic.

Jonathan Swift A close friend of Pope's, Jonathan Swift (1667–1745) was a scornful critic of England's rising merchant class, whom he viewed as shameless money-grubbers. In his great satires, *Gulliver's Travels* and *A Modest Proposal,* he presents human nature

▼ **Critical Viewing**
Unlike Elizabethan theaters, Restoration theaters had a proscenium arch separating the stage from the audience, real changes of scenery, lighting, and female actors. How do you think these changes affected the way that theater goers experienced plays? [Speculate]

as deeply flawed, suggesting that moral progress must begin with a recognition of our intellectual and moral limitations.

Daniel Defoe The first English novel, *Robinson Crusoe* by Daniel Defoe (1660–1731), appeared in this period. This new form of fiction would, in the 1800s, become the favorite reading matter of the growing middle classes.

Addison and Steele England's first literary periodicals, *The Tatler* and *The Spectator,* also appeared in the early 1700s. Written by Joseph Addison (1672–1719) and Richard Steele (1672–1729), these one-page papers included crisply written, reflective essays and news addressed to the middle classes.

The Age of Johnson Samuel Johnson (1709–1784) dominated his age not only with his writings but also with his conversation and acquaintanceships. A brilliant and inexhaustible talker, he befriended most of the writers, painters, and actors of his time. His wise advice helped nurture the careers of many younger talents. *The Dictionary of the English Language,* published in 1755, is his most important work. It is the first dictionary to be considered a standard and authoritative reference work on English.

The Eclipse of the Enlightenment By the late 1700s, the "progress" that had once been celebrated by Enlightenment thinkers seemed to be causing millions to suffer. As they lost faith in the power of human reason, writers turned away from the standards of neoclassicism. Writing in the language of everyday life, writers such as Thomas Gray charged their poems with fresh new emotion. The Age of Reason was coming to an end. Emerging voices would make the 1800s a new literary age.

▲ **Critical Viewing**
The landscape paintings of Richard Wilson (1714–1782) influenced the work of nineteenth-century Romantic painters such as John Constable and J.W.M. Turner. What feelings do Wilson's use of light and his choice of a vantage point inspire in you? **[Respond]**

Introduction ■ 431

Concept Connector

Have students return to the Focus Questions on p. 421. Ask them to use these questions to orally summarize the main points in the Unit Introduction. Students' summaries should include the following points:

Results of the civil war between the royalists and Parliament:
- Oliver Cromwell led Parliament's forces to victory over the royalists. Charles I was convicted of treason and beheaded.
- A new government, the English Commonwealth, was instituted and Parliament was dissolved. Cromwell named himself Lord Protector.

Differences between Charles II and Puritan leaders:
- Charles II was a patron of the sciences and arts. He invited painters and composers to live in London.
- Unlike the dull Puritan leaders, Charles II and his court copied the fashions of Paris.

Political and social realities reflected in the literature:
- John Milton aided the Puritan cause by writing political pamphlets. His views on the politics of the time are reflected in *Paradise Lost.*
- Enlightenment writers, such as Alexander Pope and Jonathan Swift, produced satires to comment on society.

Critical Thinking

1. Speculate about the state of spelling in English in the days before dictionaries. [Speculate] **Possible responses:** There may have been more than one way to spell a word; people may have improvised spellings more.

2. Why might Johnson's illustrative quotations have been valuable to historians of the language? [Hypothesize] **Answer:** By gathering together earlier usages, Johnson allowed later readers to chart changes in the meaning of words.

Critical Viewing

1. What three items found in modern dictionaries are missing from the entries in this depiction of a page of Johnson's dictionary? [Interpret Layout] **Answer:** The part of speech, pronunciation, and derivation of each word are missing.

2. Judging from this mock-up of a page from the *Dictionary*, how reliable is Johnson's capitalization? [Analyze] **Answer:** It is not faultless: Tory, a proper noun, is capitalized, while Whig, another proper noun, is not.

Answers to Activities

1. Johnson's opinionated definitions contrast sharply with the neutral definitions we expect from contemporary dictionaries. His solemn definition of Tory and abbreviated definition of *whig* show him to be a Tory. His definition of *excise* demonstrates he was violently opposed to excise taxes.

2. Encourage students to be opinionated and biased, as Johnson is.

3. Have students look for definitions that are clearly influenced by Johnson's opinions and prejudices or reflect ideas that seem unusual to us today.

4. Encourage students to research how modern dictionaries are made, using encyclopedias and the Internet, visiting Web sites like www.refdesk.com to find out more about dictionaries.

No Harmless Drudge, He

BY RICHARD LEDERER

On April 15, 1755, Dr. Samuel Johnson—blind in one eye, impoverished, and incompletely educated—produced the first modern *Dictionary of the English Language*. "Languages are the pedigrees of nations," he proclaimed, and, in compiling his wordbook, Johoson conferred a pedigree on the English-speaking nations. In garnering the rich, exuberant vocabulary of eighteenth-century England, the *Dictionary of the English Language* marks a turning point in the history of our tongue.

JOHNSON'S FIRSTS

Johnson set himself the task of making a different kind of dictionary, one of the first that would include all the words in the English language, not just the difficult ones. In addition, he would show how to divide words into syllables and where words came from. He would establish a consistent system of defining words and draw from his own gigantic learning to provide, for the first time in any dictionary, illustrative quotations from famous writers. Johnson's lexicon, like its modern descendants, is a report on the way writers actually used the English language.

Underfunded and working almost alone in a Fleet Street garret room, Johnson defined some 43,000 words and illuminated their meanings with more than 114,000 supporting quotations drawn from every area of literature. Laboring for almost nine years, he captured the majesty of the English language and gave it a dignity that was long overdue.

Johnson defined a lexicographer as "a writer of dictionaries, a harmless drudge that busies himself in tracing the original and detailing the signification of words." However, he was obviously far more than a harmless drudge, and his two-volume dictionary was by far the most comprehensive and readable that had appeared. The reputation of the *Dictionary of the English Language* was so great that it dominated the field until the turn of this century.

From Johnson's *Dictionary*

dedication. A servile address to a patron
excise. A hateful tax levied upon commodities, and adjudged not by the common judges of property, but wretches hired by those to whom excise is paid.
gambler. (A cant word, I suppose, for game, or gamster.) A knave whose practice it is to invite the unwary to game and cheat them.
opera. An exotic and irrational entertainment.
parasite. One that frequents rich tables, and earns his welcome by flattery.
patron. One who supports with insolence, and is paid with flattery.
pensioner. A slave of state hired by a stipend to obey his master. In England it is generally understood to mean pay given to a state hireling for treason to his country.
Tory. One who adheres to the ancient constitution of the state, and the apostolical hierarchy of the church of England, opposed to a whig.
whig. The name of a faction.

1. How do the definitions in the box at left differ from those you would find in current dictionaries? For example, what can you tell about Johnson's political loyalties from his definition of Tory and Whig? What can you tell about Johnson's political opinions from his definition of *excise*?

2. Reviewing Johnson's definitions, write three definitions in his style.

3. Secure a copy from your school or local library of *Johnson's Dictionary: A Modern Selection*, edited by E. L. McAdam, Jr., and George Milne (Pantheon Books). Browse through it and report any interesting and unusual definitions to the class.

4. Research the techniques of modern dictionary makers. Then, compare and contrast their techniques with Johnson's.

Enrichment

Dictionaries and Their Makers

Explain to students that while we take dictionaries very much for granted, Johnson's dictionary actually had a great deal of influence in shaping the language we use today.

Early dictionary makers made, for instance, some useful decisions that have become rules for English users since: after Johnson, for instance, *flower* always means a growing thing, *flour* an ingredient of bread.

The American Noah Webster (1758–1843) was famous for his attempt to standardize spelling. For better or worse, his insistence in a 1788 spelling guide that *tough* was better spelled *tuf* and *group* spelled *groop* never caught on. His support, though, of *theater* instead of *theatre* and *aluminum* instead of *aluminium* (among others) helped establish the differences between American and British spelling.

432

The War Against Time

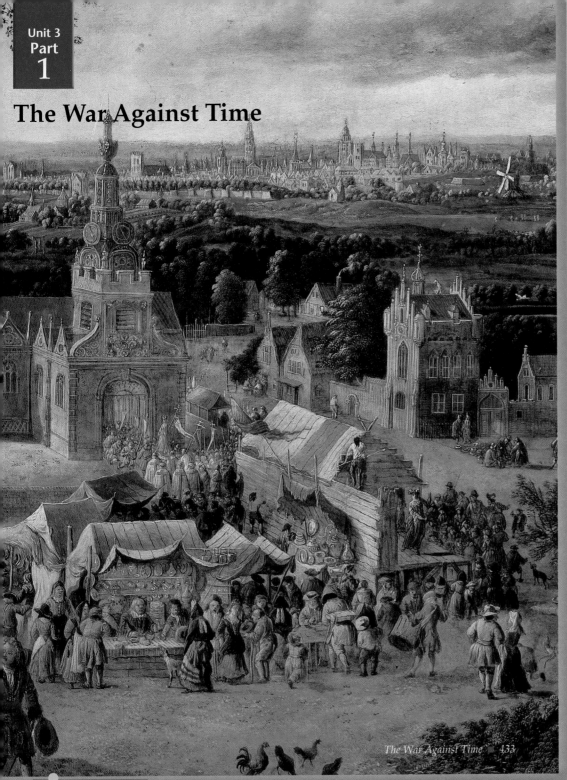

The War Against Time 433

Selection Planning Guide

The selections in this section present the great writers of seventeenth-century England. The section opens with four works by John Donne, Meditation 17, "Song," "A Valediction: Forbidding Mourning," and Holy Sonnet 10, works that capture the essence of the metaphysical writings that characterized his era and that captivated the twentieth century as well. Three pieces by Ben Jonson make up the next grouping: "On My First Son," "To Celia," and "Still to Be Neat." Three love poems with the theme of *carpe diem* follow in the next grouping, "To His Coy Mistress" by Andrew Marvell, "To the Virgins, to Make Much of Time," by Robert Herrick, and "Song," by Sir John Suckling.

Humanities

Outskirts of London, England, by Jan Griffier

Jan Griffier the Elder (1652–1718) was a Dutch landscape, portrait, and marine painter. He did much of his work in England and eventually died there. This painting shows a festival day, just outside of London, with groups of people and multiple events. This work demonstrates the degree of detail he often incorporated into his works. Have students examine the work for details of the time period. Then, **ask** them to describe the mood of this scene, and tell what details help create the mood.
Possible response: The scene projects a positive, festive mood: People are mingling, conversing, and participating in a church pageant. They appear to be taking pleasure in their various activities on what seems to be a special day.

Monitoring Progress

Before students read the works by John Donne, administer **Diagnostic Test 5** (*Unit 3 Resources*, pp. 2–4). This test will determine students' level of readiness for the reading and vocabulary skills.

Differentiated
Instruction   Solutions for All Learners

Accessibility at a Glance

Average
A Valediction: Forbidding Mourning
Meditation 17
On My First Son
Still to Be Neat
Song: To Celia
Song by Suckling

More Challenging
Song
Holy Sonnet 10
To His Coy Mistress
To the Virgins, to Make Much of Time

TIME AND RESOURCE MANAGER

Meeting Your Standards

Students will

1. **analyze and respond to literary elements.**
   - Literary Analysis: Metaphysical Poetry

2. **read, comprehend, analyze, and critique nonfiction and poems.**
   - Reading Strategy: Recognizing the Speaker's Situation and Motivation
   - Reading Check questions
   - Apply the Skills questions
   - Assessment Practice (ATE)

3. **develop vocabulary.**
   - Vocabulary Lesson: Latin Prefix: *inter-*

4. **understand and apply written and oral language conventions.**
   - Spelling Strategy
   - Grammar and Style Lesson: Active and Passive Voice

5. **develop writing proficiency.**
   - Writing Lesson: Persuasive Speech

6. **develop appropriate research strategies.**
   - Extend Your Learning: Science Report

7. **understand and apply listening and speaking strategies.**
   - Extend Your Learning: Dramatic Reading

Block Scheduling: Use one 90-minute class period to preteach the skills and have students read the selection. Use a second 90-minute class period to assess students' mastery of skills, extend their learning, and monitor their progress.

Homework Suggestions

Following are possibilities for homework assignments:

- Support pages from *Unit 3 Resources:*
  - Literary Analysis
  - Reading Strategy
  - Vocabulary Builder
  - Grammar and Style

- An Extend Your Learning project and the Writing Lesson for this selection group may be completed over several days.

Step-by-Step Teaching Guide	Pacing Guide
PRETEACH	
• Administer Vocabulary and Reading Warm-ups as necessary.	5 min.
• Engage students' interest with the motivation activity.	5 min.
• Read and discuss author and background features. **FT**	10 min.
• Introduce the Literary Analysis Skill: Metaphysical Poetry. **FT**	5 min.
• Introduce the Reading Strategy: Recognizing the Speaker's Situation and Motivation. **FT**	10 min.
• Prepare students to read by teaching the selection vocabulary. **FT**	
TEACH	
• Informally monitor comprehension while students read independently or in groups. **FT**	30 min.
• Monitor students' comprehension with the Reading Check notes.	as students read
• Reinforce vocabulary with Vocabulary Builder notes.	as students read
• Develop students' understanding of metaphysical poetry with the Literary Analysis annotations. **FT**	5 min.
• Develop students' ability to recognize speaker's situation and motivation with the Reading Strategy annotations. **FT**	5 min.
ASSESS/EXTEND	
• Assess students' comprehension and mastery of the Literary Analysis and Reading Strategy by having them answer the Apply the Skills questions. **FT**	15 min.
• Have students complete the Vocabulary Development Lesson and the Grammar and Style Lesson. **FT**	15 min.
• Apply students' knowledge of unity by using the Writing Lesson. **FT**	45 min. or homework
• Apply students' understanding by using one or more of the Extend Your Learning activities.	20–90 min. or homework
• Administer Selection Test A or Selection Test B. **FT**	15 min.

Resources

Choosing Resources for Differentiated Instruction

[**L1**] Special Needs Students

[**L2**] Below-Level Students

[**L3**] All Students

[**L4**] Advanced Students

[**EL**] English Learners

For Vocabulary and Reading Warm-ups and for Selection Tests, **A** signifies "less challenging" and **B** "more challenging." For Graphic Organizer transparencies, **A** signifies "not filled in" and **B** "filled in."

FT Fast Track Instruction: To move the lesson more quickly, use the strategies and activities identified with **FT**.

Scaffolding for Less Proficient and Advanced Students

The leveled Critical Thinking questions after selections progress in the levels of thinking required to answer them. To address the needs of your different students, you may use the (a) level questions for your less proficient students and the (b) level questions with your on-level and advanced students. The occasional (c) level questions are appropriate for your advanced students.

 Use this complete suite of powerful teaching tools to make lesson planning and testing quicker and easier.

 Use the interactive textbook (online and on CD-ROM) to make selections and activities come alive with audio and video support and interactive questions.

Monitoring Progress

Before students read these selections, administer **Diagnostic Test 5** (*Unit 3 Resources*, pp. 2–4). This test will determine students' level of readiness for the reading and vocabulary skills.

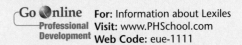 **For:** Information about Lexiles **Visit:** www.PHSchool.com **Web Code:** eue-1111

Motivation

Ask students to think of people they know who have a dramatic flair. Perhaps there is a student who would qualify for the title "Most Dramatic" in their school yearbook. Without naming students, have students consider the qualities they would use to describe that person—for example, lively, outspoken, personable. Tell students that John Donne was such a person, but that he also had a quiet, meditative aspect to his personality. Suggest as they read his poetry that students look for these two sides to Donne's personality—the dramatic and the meditative—along with any other surprising facets they may note.

❶ Background
More About the Author

Fired and briefly imprisoned for eloping with the seventeen-year-old Anne, Donne reportedly wrote his briefest and, some would say, most accessible poem: "John Donne, Anne Donne, Undone." From this simple beginning, Donne's marriage would inspire some of the most profound love poems in the English language.

The marriage also produced children. The Donnes had twelve, of whom seven were still living when Anne died in childbirth in 1617.

Build Skills *Poems • Meditation*

❶ Works of John Donne

John Donne
(1572?–1631)

Donne's life and poetry seem to fall neatly into two contradictory parts. Wild, young Jack Donne wrote clever love poems read by sophisticated aristocrats. In later life, sober Dr. John Donne, Dean of St. Paul's and the most popular preacher in England, published widely read meditations and sermons. Contradiction and conflict were the stuff of Donne's life; they are also at the heart of his poetic style. As Jack or as John, Donne the writer excelled at dramatizing—and wittily resolving—the contradictions of life.

Religious Conflict A distant relative of Sir Thomas More, Donne was raised a Catholic. In the England of Queen Elizabeth I, Catholics faced prejudice and restrictive laws. Although Donne studied at Oxford and Cambridge, he never obtained his degree, probably because of his refusal to compromise his Catholicism by swearing an oath acknowledging the supremacy of the king over the church. Later, he abandoned Catholicism and joined the official Church of England. To this day, scholars debate whether Donne experienced a genuine conversion or made a shrewd move to gain advancement in court society.

A Secret Marriage After taking part in two naval expeditions against the Spanish, Donne served as private secretary to one of the queen's highest-ranking officials, Sir Thomas Egerton. Bright, clever, and charming, Donne secretly wed Anne More, his employer's niece, in 1601. Again, scholars throw doubt on Donne's motives. Some hold that he married for love; others maintain that he hoped his marriage to the daughter of an influential family would promote his career. If Donne counted on this possibility, though, he was sadly mistaken. Anne's father disapproved of the union, and so Donne's marriage temporarily ruined his chances for social advancement.

For many years, the devoted couple lived plagued by poverty and illness, in the midst of which Donne still managed to write influential poetry. He eked out a living writing religious tracts and serving as temporary secretary to several aristocrats. Donne finally attained a secure position in 1615 when, at the insistence of King James, he entered the clergy.

Success After serving as a royal chaplain, Donne became dean of St. Paul's Cathedral in London in 1621, a post he held until his death. He became one of the most popular preachers of his day. No longer the writer of sly or witty passionate verses, he published widely read sermons and religious meditations. Jack Donne's days were over, and John Donne's fame was spreading.

A Modern Individual Even after his death, John Donne's reputation has been subject to dramatic changes. His writings, popular during his lifetime, soon went out of favor. At the beginning of the twentieth century, however, interest in Donne's poetry rekindled. Earlier critics had faulted Donne for overworking his ideas. The noted modern poet T. S. Eliot, though, found in Donne's work a valuable unification of intellect and feeling.

Renewed interest in Donne might stem from a kind of self-recognition by modern readers. The conflicts Donne faced have a distinctively contemporary flavor. His family's faith and his secret marriage pitted the private man against the demands of the world. Society in his time, as in ours, was no longer ready with clear answers to the question, Where do I fit in? Donne, in his contradictory life and complex poetry, had to invent his own answers.

Preview

Connecting to the Literature

In a dark and lonely place, a person may whistle a tune to keep his or her spirits up. Donne is perhaps our greatest whistler in the dark. In his poems, he confronts the uncertainties of parting and death, filling the silence with extravagant improvisations.

Literary Analysis

Metaphysical Poetry

Donne and his followers wrote **metaphysical poetry**—poetry characterized by intellectual displays and concern with metaphysical, or philosophical, issues. It uses the following poetic devices:

- **Conceits** are extended comparisons that link objects or ideas not commonly associated, often mixing abstract ideas and emotional matters. In one of his poems, for example, Donne compares two lovers to the two legs of a drawing compass.
- **Paradoxes** are images or descriptions that appear self-contradictory but that reveal a deeper truth. Donne uses a paradox in Holy Sonnet 10 when he writes, "Death, thou shalt die."

Interpret the conceits and paradoxes you find in Donne's work.

Comparing Literary Works

Donne's work falls into two distinctive periods—the youthful phase in which he wrote love poems such as "Song," and a later phase in which he wrote religious works such as Holy Sonnet 10. His appointment as a clergyman in 1621 is a key cause of this shift. The works in this section are arranged in rough chronological order. As you read, compare the influence of Donne's changing life on his subject matter and attitude toward life. Also, note the features of his style that do not change.

Reading Strategy

Recognizing the Speaker's Situation and Motivation

To understand these poems, imagine the **speaker's situation** and figure out his **motivation** for addressing another person, often his beloved. Use a chart like the one here to help you as you read.

Vocabulary Builder

profanation (präf´ ə nā´ shən) *n.* action showing disrespect for something sacred (p. 438)

laity (lā´ i tē) *n.* those not initiated into a priesthood (p. 438)

trepidation (trep´ ə dā´ shən) *n.* trembling (p. 438)

breach (brēch) *n.* a break (p. 439)

contention (kən ten´ shən) *n.* dispute; argument (p. 443)

piety (pī´ ə tē) *n.* devotion to sacred duties (p. 443)

intermit (in´ tər mit´) *v.* stop for a time (p. 443)

covetousness (kuv´ ət əs nis) *n.* greediness (p. 444)

Speaker's Words
ìS weetest love, I do not go, For weariness of thee, . . ."

Situation
He has to leave his beloved.

Motivation
He is reassuring her that he is not leaving because he is tired of her.

Works of John Donne ■ 435

❷ Literary Analysis
Metaphysical Poetry

- Tell students that Dr. Samuel Johnson was first to use "metaphysical" to describe the philosophical preoccupations of poets like Donne. Johnson and others were critical of the intellectual rigor and oddness of ideas characteristic of metaphysical poets—and their apparent carelessness regarding rhyme and meter.

- Read the definitions of conceits and paradoxes together with the class. Point out that the metaphysical conceit is distinguished by the bold linking of unlikely elements. For example, Donne once used a flea to symbolize a love relationship.

❸ Reading Strategy
Recognizing the Speaker's Situation and Motivation

- Remind students that much can be learned by paying attention to a speaker's situation and how this situation motivates his or her actions.

- Give students a copy of **Reading Strategy Graphic Organizer A,** p. 75 in *Graphic Organizer Transparencies*, to use as they read the poems.

Vocabulary Builder

- Pronounce each vocabulary word for students, and read the definitions as a class. Have students identify any words with which they are already familiar.

Differentiated Instruction — Solutions for All Learners

Support for Special Needs Students
Have students use the support pages for these selections in the *Reader's Notebook: Adapted Version.* Completing these pages will prepare students to read the selections in the Student Edition.

Support for Less Proficient Readers
Have students use the support pages for these selections in the *Reader's Notebook.* After students finish the pages in the Reader's Notebook, have them complete the questions and activities in the Student Edition.

Support for English Learners
Have students use the support pages for these selections in the *Reader's Notebook: English Learner's Version.* Completing these pages will prepare students to read the selections in the Student Edition.

Fair Is My Love, Edwin A. Abbey. The Harris Museum and Art Gallery, Preston

TEACH

Learning Modalities
Musical/Rhythmic Learners Help students appreciate the music of the words as well as the content by pointing out the *ababcddc* rhyme scheme.

❶ About the Selection

This poem expresses what it feels like to be separated from the person one loves. Donne's argument is artfully presented through a conceit that compares a temporary absence to the permanent absence of death.

❷ Humanities

Fair Is My Love, by Edwin A. Abbey

Although Abbey (1852–1911) was an American painter, muralist, and illustrator, he lived in England.

Use the following question to stimulate discussion:

• Do you think this piece of art is a good or poor choice for an illustration of this poem? Why?
Answer: Some students may find it too romantic and not cerebral enough; others may think it is a good choice because it shows such strong emotions.

❸ Critical Viewing

Answer: Students might comment on the fact that the man in the painting seems deeply moved or fascinated by the woman's song, where the speaker in the poem hopes his "song" will change how the woman feels.

❹ Reading Strategy
Recognizing the Speaker's Situation and Motivation

• **Ask** students what hypothesis can be drawn from the first line.
Answer: The speaker is about to depart from his beloved.

• **Ask** the students: What does the speaker's situation tell you about his motive for comparing his departure to a death?
Answer: Students may infer that parting from his beloved is a fearful, painful event.

❶

SONG
JOHN DONNE

Sweetest love, I do not go,
    For weariness of thee,
Nor in hope the world can show
    A fitter love for me;
        But since that I
5   Must die at last, 'tis best
To use[1] myself in jest,
        Thus by feigned[2] deaths to die.

Yesternight the sun went hence,
10   And yet is here today;
He hath no desire nor sense,
    Nor half so short a way;
        Then fear not me,
But believe that I shall make
15 Speedier journeys, since I take
    More wings and spurs than he.

❹

❸ ⚠ Critical Viewing

How does the relationship of the man and woman in this painting compare with the relationship described in the poem? **[Compare and Contrast]**

1. **use** condition.
2. **feigned** (fānd) *adj.* imagined.

436 ■ *A Turbulent Time (1625–1798)*

Differentiated Instruction   Solutions for All Learners

Accessibility at a Glance

	Song	Valediction	Holy Sonnet 10	Meditation 17
Context	Metaphysical	Metaphysical	Metaphysical	Metaphysical
Language	Poetic diction	Footnotes for vocabulary	Formal language	Long sentences
Concept Level	Moderate (love, death)	Accessible (love)	Challenging (death)	Moderate (mortality)
Literary Merit	Classic	Classic	Classic	Classic
Lexile	NP	NP	NP	1130L
Overall Rating	More challenging	Average	More challenging	Average

O how feeble is man's power,
    That if good fortune fall,
Cannot add another hour,
20   Nor a lost hour recall!
        But come bad chance,
And we join to it our strength,
And we teach it art and length,
    Itself o'er us to advance.

25 When thou sigh'st, thou sigh'st not wind,
    But sigh'st my soul away;
When thou weep'st, unkindly kind,
    My life's blood doth decay.
        It cannot be
30 That thou lovest me as thou say'st,
    If in thine my life thou waste,
    That art the best of me.

Let not thy divining heart
    Forethink me any ill,
35 Destiny may take thy part,
    And may thy fears fulfill;
        But think that we
Are but turned aside to sleep.
They who one another keep
40   Alive, ne'r parted be.

The British Tradition

❺ Mind and Feeling

The twentieth-century poet T. S. Eliot celebrated Donne as one of the best—and last—poets to integrate mind and heart: "A thought to Donne was an experience; it modified his sensibility [feeling and perception]." Eliot praised Donne's "direct sensuous apprehension of thought" and his "recreation of thought into feeling."

Eliot claimed that later poets did not "feel their thought as immediately as the odor of a rose" and that "[in] the seventeenth century a dissociation of sensibility set in, from which we have never recovered."

Connect to the Literature

In what ways are lines 27–28 an integration of mind and heart?

Critical Reading

1. **Respond:** Do you agree with the speaker when, in lines 17–24, he says that we add to our own misfortunes? Why?

2. **(a) Recall:** What does the speaker say his reason is for leaving?
   (b) Infer: To what remark of his beloved might he be responding in this poem?

3. **(a) Analyze:** How would you outline the speaker's argument?
   (b) Speculate: What might the argument's effect on the beloved be?

4. **Draw Conclusions:** Imagine that the speaker's beloved is in tears as he is leaving. Why might the speaker have chosen to present his feelings in the form of witty arguments?

5. **Generalize:** The speaker uses exaggeration to persuade his beloved. Do you think exaggeration is a useful or a valid persuasive tool?

Go Online
Author Link

For: More about John Donne
Visit: www.PHSchool.com
Web Code: ese-9302

Song ■ 437

❺ The British Tradition

Mind and Feeling Poet, playwright, and literary critic T. S. Eliot was among the first modern writers to rediscover Donne. His literary analyses of the metaphysical poets played an important role in rescuing their work from centuries of neglect.

Connect to the Literature
Encourage students to support their answers with evidence from the poem.
Possible response: The thought of leaving his beloved evokes images of weeping and bleeding.

ASSESS

Answers

1. Some students may believe that bad luck just happens; others will recall misfortunes that resulted from mistakes or bad choices.

2. (a) He says that his departure is a preparation for their ultimate separation in death. (b) Students may infer that his beloved had asked if he was leaving because he no longer cared for her.

3. (a) The speaker denies that he would ever leave his beloved because he had tired of her or had found a better love; he exaggerates a worse separation, his eventual death; he reminds her that like the sun he will return; he tells her not to make it worse by crying; he begs her not to think ill of him lest she tempt fate and he truly die; and he tells her she should think of them as turned aside in sleep since remembering their devoted love keeps them ever together. (b) Students may speculate that the speaker's argument will convince her of his love.

4. He needs to soothe her fears about separation and to distract her attention with cleverness.

5. Students may respond that although exaggeration can undermine credibility, it can also make arguments more vivid, persuasive, and powerful.

Go Online
Author Link   For additional information about John Donne, have students type in the Web Code, then select D from the alphabet, and then select the author's name.

❻ A VALEDICTION:[1]
FORBIDDING MOURNING

JOHN DONNE

As virtuous men pass mildly away,
    And whisper to their souls to go,
Whilst some of their sad friends do say
    The breath goes now, and some say, No;

5 So let us melt, and make no noise,
    No tear-floods, nor sigh-tempests move,
'Twere profanation of our joys
    To tell the laity our love.

Moving of th'earth brings harms and fears,
10   Men reckon what it did and meant;
But trepidation of the spheres,[2]
    Though greater far, is innocent.

Dull sublunary[3] lovers' love
    (Whose soul is sense) cannot admit
15 Absence, because it doth remove
    Those things which elemented it.[4]

But we by a love, so much refined,
    That our selves know not what it is,
Inter-assurèd of the mind,[5]
20   Care less, eyes, lips, and hands to miss.

Our two souls therefore, which are one,
    Though I must go, endure not yet

1. **valediction** farewell speech.
2. **trepidation of the spheres** movements of the stars and planets that are inconsistent with a perfect circular orbit.
3. **sublunary** (sub´ l⊙⊙ nər´ ē) referring to the region below the moon, considered in early astronomy to be the domain of changeable and perishable things.
4. **Those things . . . elemented it** the basic materials or parts of their love.
5. **Inter-assurèd of the mind** mutually confident of each other's thoughts.

Enrichment

"A Valediction"

According to Donne biographer Sir Izaak Walton, "A Valediction: Forbidding Mourning" has a specific and tragic biographical context. Anne Donne was in the late stages of a problematic pregnancy when Donne was assigned to a diplomatic mission in France. Filled with foreboding, Anne urged Donne not to go. Donne responded by writing "A Valediction" to ease the pain of their parting.

Shortly after arriving in Paris, Donne had a vision of Anne walking across his room carrying a dead child in her arms. He later learned that on that very day, after an agonizing labor, Anne "had been delivered of a dead child."

A <u>breach</u>, but an expansion,
    Like gold to airy thinness beat.

25 If they be two, they are two so
    As stiff twin compasses[6] are two;
    Thy soul the fixed foot, makes no show
      To move, but doth, if th'other do.

And though it in the center sit,
30   Yet when the other far doth roam,
It leans, and hearkens after it,
    And grows erect, as that comes home.

Such wilt thou be to me, who must
    Like th'other foot, obliquely[7] run;
35 Thy firmness makes my circle just,[8]
    And makes me end where I begun.

6. twin compasses the two legs of a drawing compass.
7. obliquely at an angle; not straight.
8. just true; perfect.

❾ ◄ Critical Viewing
Why is a comparison of lovers to a compass such as this one unexpected? **[Connect]**

Vocabulary Builder
breach (brēch) *n.* a break

Critical Reading

1. **Respond:** If you were the woman addressed by the speaker, how persuasive would you find his reassurances? Explain.

2. **(a) Recall:** According to the speaker, how should he and his beloved part? **(b) Infer:** What does he think that this manner of parting shows about their love? **(c) Interpret:** Describe two other claims the speaker makes to show how special their love is.

3. **Draw Conclusions:** The poem compares the lovers to the legs of a compass—she is fixed in place while he moves. What does the comparison indicate about their relationship?

4. **Support:** The speaker links love with the order and stability of the world. Support this insight with details from the poem.

5. **Apply:** Do you, like the speaker, see love as a union of two souls, or do you think that lovers should be independent? Explain.

Go Online
Author Link

For: More about John Donne
Visit: www.PHSchool.com
Web Code: ese-9302

A Valediction: Forbidding Mourning ■ 439

❾ Critical Viewing
Answer: Students may cite the unlikeliness of a mechanical device expressing a truth about human love.

❿ Literary Analysis
Metaphysical Poetry

• **Ask** students to identify elements of metaphysical poetry in the last three verses.
  Possible responses: Students' responses may include the conceit comparing the lovers to a compass; the interest in science; the seeming paradox in the last line.

• **Ask** students how the fixed leg of the compass responds when its "lover" returns home.
  Answer: The fixed leg rises as the lover comes home.

ASSESS

Answers

1. **Possible response:** Students might be persuaded by the description of a love so deeply felt that two souls are one.

2. (a) He suggests they part "mildly." (b) It shows unity and their confidence in their love. (c) Students may respond that their love is "refined" and needs no physical reassurance. Their souls won't be separated but will expand like beaten gold to cover the distance between them.

3. The comparison shows that he relies on the beloved's stable center; his life revolves around her.

4. The image asserts an unbreakable bond—the lovers are a single entity like the feet of a compass.

5. Some students may reply that they agree with this statement, while others may feel that lovers should be independent.

Go Online For additional infor-
Author Link mation about John Donne, have students type in the Web Code, then select D from the alphabet, and then select the author's name.

⓫ About the Selection

This is one of the best-known poems about death and how it was viewed by Donne and his contemporaries. Donne addresses death directly, as if death were a personal adversary whom the speaker no longer fears. Donne explains why he does not fear death, and his argument is relatively easy to follow.

⓬ Humanities

Sir Thomas Aston at the Deathbed of His Wife, by John Souch

John Souch was a British portrait painter who did most of his work between 1617 and 1636. This, one of his few surviving portraits, was probably commissioned by Thomas Aston, high sheriff of Cheshire, as a memorial to his first wife, Magdalene. Use these questions to stimulate discussion:

1. In what ways does this painting reflect the ideas of the sonnet?
   Answer: It shows that death is not final; memory can overcome it; it reflects the idea that death lives with sickness.

2. Why is the wife, Magdalene, shown twice, do you think?
   Answer: It shows her in her life as well as in her death; perhaps it indicates the continuum between life and death.

3. What can you infer about the man from this picture?
   Possible responses: Students may respond that his clothes show he is wealthy and in mourning. His hand on the skull may indicate that he has accepted death.

⓭ Critical Viewing

Answer: Both the painting and the poem show a form of life everlasting and a refusal to shrink from death.

⓫

HOLY SONNET 10

JOHN DONNE

Sir Thomas Aston at the Deathbed of His Wife, John Souch, Manchester City Art Galleries

⓭ ▲ **Critical Viewing** The painting shows Lady Aston both when she is alive and when she is dead. Compare the relationship between death and life implied by the painting with that developed in Holy Sonnet 10. [**Compare and Contrast**]

Enrichment

Death

Though some modern viewers may find it morbid, Souch's painting encapsulates a very typical seventeenth-century attitude toward death, one shared by Donne and other metaphysical poets. This attitude included a candid recognition of the reality of death; a constant awareness (as T. S. Eliot wrote) of the "skull beneath the skin"; a refusal to flinch from or evade mortality.

Images of death can appear in unlikely places in the seventeenth century. Souch incorporates them in his family portrait of the Astons. Andrew Marvell casually employs gruesome images to romance his "coy mistress" (see p. 461). Donne brazenly scolds death in Holy Sonnet 10. Near the end of his life, Donne was not afraid to pose in his own death shroud. A statue of the result stands in St. Paul's Cathedral in London, an enduring monument to his era's attitude toward death.

Background

Background Writers in Donne's day often depended on the support of patrons, wealthy supporters of the arts. The young Donne did not publish his poems (most were printed only after his death). Instead, they were circulated among a select literary audience that included patrons such as the Countess of Bedford. After Donne was dismissed from his position with Sir Thomas Egerton, he and his family depended in part on patrons for financial support. When he became a clergyman, Donne no longer needed to capture the interest of patrons. He continued, though, to write impassioned, witty verse such as the Holy Sonnets.

Death be not proud, though some have called thee
Mighty and dreadful, for thou art not so;
For those whom thou think'st thou dost overthrow,
Die not, poor death, nor yet canst thou kill me.
5 From rest and sleep, which but thy pictures[1] be,
Much pleasure; then from thee much more must flow,
And soonest our best men with thee do go,
Rest of their bones, and soul's delivery.[2]
Thou art slave to fate, chance, kings, and desperate men,
10 And dost with poison, war, and sickness dwell,
And poppy,[3] or charms can make us sleep as well
And better than thy stroke; why swell'st[4] thou then?
One short sleep past, we wake eternally,
And death shall be no more; Death, thou shalt die.

1. **pictures** images.
2. **And . . . delivery** Our best men go with you to rest their bones and find freedom for their souls.
3. **poppy** opium.
4. **swell'st** swell with pride.

Literary Analysis
Metaphysical Poetry
What paradox does the speaker use to end his argument with Death?

Critical Reading

1. **Respond:** Do you picture death as arrogant? Explain.

2. **(a) Recall:** What "pictures" of death does the speaker mention?
   (b) Infer: What positive lesson about death does the speaker draw from this resemblance?

3. **(a) Interpret:** In what sense is death a slave (line 9)? **(b) Connect:** How does this point justify the opening line?

4. **(a) Interpret:** What does the statement "Death, thou shalt die" mean? **(b) Draw Conclusions:** Why might the speaker react to death by challenging its "strength" and "pride"?

5. **Evaluate:** Does the speaker sound like a man talking himself out of fear or like one who has triumphed over fear? Explain.

Go Online
Author Link
For: More about John Donne
Visit: www.PHSchool.com
Web Code: ese-9302

Holy Sonnet 10 ■ 441

---

15 About the Selection

In "Meditation 17," the author faces his own mortality when he listens to a bell toll for someone else's death. Donne used memorable comparisons or "conceits" to express the idea that all people are connected to each other and to God.

16 Critical Viewing

Answer: Students may suggest other major life events, such as marriage, the birth of a child, or a religious or national holiday.

15 MEDITATION 17

JOHN DONNE

16 ▲ Critical Viewing The bells in this tower might ring on the occasion of someone's death, as Donne notes. On what other occasions might they ring? **[Deduce]**

442 ■ *A Turbulent Time (1625–1798)*

Enrichment

Ernest Hemingway

When Ernest Hemingway used a phrase from this work as the title for his novel *For whom the Bell Tolls* and included some of the text in the book, he sparked so much interest that publishers rushed to reissue "Meditation 17." The concept that "No man is an island" was used to stir interest in a conflict (the Spanish Civil War) half a world away.

Nunc lento sonitu dicunt, Morieris.
(Now, this bell tolling softly for another,
says to me, Thou must die.)

Perchance he for whom this bell tolls may be so ill as that he knows not it tolls for him; and perchance I may think myself so much better than I am as that they who are about me and see my state may have caused it to toll for me, and I know not that. The church is catholic,[1] universal, so are all her actions; all that she does belongs to all. When she baptizes a child, that action concerns me; for that child is thereby connected to that head which is my head too, and ingrafted into that body[2] whereof I am a member. And when she buries a man, that action concerns me: all mankind is of one author and is one volume; when one man dies, one chapter is not torn out of the book, but translated into a better language; and every chapter must be so translated. God employs several translators; some pieces are translated by age, some by sickness, some by war, some by justice; but God's hand is in every translation, and his hand shall bind up all our scattered leaves again for that library where every book shall lie open to one another. As therefore the bell that rings to a sermon calls not upon the preacher only, but upon the congregation to come, so this bell calls us all; but how much more me, who am brought so near the door by this sickness. There was a <u>contention</u> as far as a suit[3] (in which both <u>piety</u> and dignity, religion and estimation,[4] were mingled) which of the religious orders should ring to prayers first in the morning; and it was determined that they should ring first that rose earliest. If we understand aright the dignity of this bell that tolls for our evening prayer, we would be glad to make it ours by rising early, in that application, that it might be ours as well as his whose indeed it is. The bell doth toll for him that thinks it doth; and though it <u>intermit</u> again, yet from that minute that that occasion wrought upon him, he is united to God. Who casts not up his eye to the sun when it rises? but who takes off his eye from a comet when that breaks out? Who bends not his ear to any bell which upon any occasion rings? but who can remove it from that bell which is passing a piece of himself out of this world? No man is an island, entire of itself; every man is a piece of the continent, a part of the main.[5] If a clod be washed away by the sea, Europe is the less, as well as if a promontory were, as well as if a manor of thy friend's or of thine own were. Any man's death diminishes me because I am involved in mankind, and therefore never send to know for whom the bell tolls; it tolls for thee. Neither can we call this a begging of misery or a borrowing of misery,

---

1. **catholic** applying to humanity generally.
2. **head . . . body** In the Bible, St. Paul calls Jesus the head (spiritual leader) of all men (1 Corinthians 11:3) and a body in which the faithful are unified (1 Corinthians 12:12).
3. **suit** lawsuit.
4. **estimation** self-esteem.
5. **main** mainland.

Literary Analysis
Metaphysical Poetry In this passage, to what does Donne compare mankind?

Vocabulary Builder
contention (kən ten′ shən) *n.* dispute; argument

piety (pī′ ə tē) *n.* devotion to sacred duties

intermit (in′ tər mit′) *v.* stop for a time

19 **Literary Analysis**
Metaphysical Poetry
What extended metaphor does Donne use here to show a single individual's relationship to all of mankind?

20 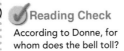 Reading Check
According to Donne, for whom does the bell toll?

Meditation 17 ■ *443*

---

17 **Literary Analysis**
Metaphysical Poetry

- Remind students that *metaphysical conceits* are extended comparisons that link objects or ideas not commonly associated.

- **Ask** students the first Literary Analysis question: In this passage, to what does Donne compare mankind?
  Answer: He compares mankind to a volume in a library.

- Have students **analyze** the conceit that compares mankind to a volume.
  Answer: Mankind is the volume; God is the author; each individual is a chapter; death is not destruction of that chapter but a kind of translation. Sickness, war, and justice are translators, and all show God's work. That library is everyone's final end.

18 **Vocabulary Builder**
Latin Prefix: *inter-*

- Point out that the word *intermit* contains the prefix *inter-*, meaning "between." It is related to the more familiar word *intermissions*.

- Then, **ask** students how *intermit* and *intermission* are alike.
  Answer: Both words describe a pause. One is a verb and the other is a noun.

19 **Literary Analysis**
Metaphysical Poetry

- **Ask** students the second Literary Analysis question: What extended metaphor does Donne use here to show a single individual's relationship to all mankind?
  Answer: He asserts that man is not set apart from mankind as an island is from the mainland, but is rather a part of a continent, and thereby joined together with the rest of mankind.

20 **Reading Check**

Answer: It tolls for every individual member of the human race; "It tolls for thee."

1. Some students may recoil at the idea, but others may observe how they or others have grown as a result of overcoming hardships.

2. (a) The bell tolls for a person's death. (b) People share a common humanity; the death of one person affects another.

3. (a) Donne says, "Any man's death diminishes me" because he is "involved in mankind." (b) Individuals are connected—no one is isolated or so alone that he or she doesn't need other human beings, or is not affected by them. (c) The continent comparison emphasizes that humanity is a single entity that is diminished by one loss.

4. (a) The "treasure of affliction" turns into "current money" when people wisely use hardships to grow and transcend them, moving closer to heaven by doing so. (b) Donne finds affliction valuable because people are "matured and ripened by it, and made fit for God" by it. (c) The "tolling bell" tells us of others' afflictions and warns us of our own vulnerabilities.

5. Donne may be implying that attachment to worldly things is a distraction from spiritual priorities.

6. Students may respond "No man is an island" applies even more in today's world than it did in Donne's time, as the world has gotten smaller, through developments in communication, transportation, and political alliances.

Go Online
Author Link   For additional information about John Donne, have students type in the Web Code, then select D from the alphabet, and then select the author's name.

as though we were not miserable enough of ourselves but must fetch in more from the next house, in taking upon us the misery of our neighbors. Truly it were an excusable <u>covetousness</u> if we did; for affliction is a treasure, and scarce any man hath enough of it. No man hath affliction enough that is not matured and ripened by it, and made fit for God by that affliction. If a man carry treasure in bullion, or in a wedge of gold, and have none coined into current money,[6] his treasure will not defray him as he travels. Tribulation is treasure in the nature of it, but it is not current money in the use of it, except we get nearer and nearer our home, heaven, by it. Another man may be sick too, and sick to death, and this affliction may lie in his bowels as gold in a mine and be of no use to him; but this bell that tells me of his affliction digs out and applies that gold to me, if by this consideration of another's danger, I take mine own into contemplation and so secure myself by making my recourse to my God, who is our only security.

---

6. current money currency; wealth in spendable form.

Vocabulary Builder
covetousness (kuv′ ət əs nis) *n.* greediness

Critical Reading

1. **Respond:** Do you think suffering is ever a good thing? Explain.

2. **(a) Recall:** What event does the tolling bell announce? **(b) Analyze:** Why does Donne say the tolling bell applies to him as well as to others?

3. **(a) Recall:** What reason does Donne give for saying, "Any man's death diminishes me"? **(b) Interpret:** What does Donne mean by "No man is an island, entire of itself; every man is a piece of the continent"? **(c) Analyze:** How does the comparison of humanity to a continent support the idea that one death affects all people?

4. **(a) Analyze:** In Donne's metaphor, when does the "treasure" of affliction turn into "current [spendable] money"? **(b) Interpret:** Why does Donne find affliction valuable? **(c) Connect:** In what sense does the tolling bell "apply" one person's affliction to another?

5. **Draw Conclusions:** Donne says that, once one takes the bell as tolling for oneself, one is "united to God." In urging people to think about their own deaths, what might he be implying about people's attachment to worldly things such as money, success, and popularity?

6. **Apply:** Do you think the statement "No man is an island" applies more, less, or about the same in today's world, compared to how it applied in Donne's time? Explain.

Go Online
Author Link

For: More about John Donne
Visit: www.PHSchool.com
Web Code: ese-9302

Apply the Skills

Works of John Donne

Literary Analysis

Metaphysical Poetry

1. Identify and interpret a **conceit** that the speaker in "Song" uses to reassure his beloved. Explain what things are being compared.
2. **(a)** What **paradox** does the speaker use in the fourth stanza of "Song"? **(b)** Explain the truth underlying this contradiction.
3. **(a)** Identify a conceit in Holy Sonnet 10. **(b)** Explain the speaker's point in making the comparison.
4. In Meditation 17, Donne uses a conceit comparing suffering and treasure. **(a)** Use a chart like the one shown to analyze the forms of treasure he discusses. **(b)** Explain how each relates to suffering.

Main Idea: There are two forms of suffering, just as there are two forms of treasure.		
First Form of Treasure: _____	Second Form of Treasure: _____	Relationship Between Forms of Treasure: _____

Comparing Literary Works

5. **(a)** What important differences distinguish "Song" and "Valediction" from Holy Sonnet 10? **(b)** Identify an element of metaphysical poetry that all three share, giving examples from each.
6. In the poems, the speaker uses conceits and paradoxes to move from uncertainty (his own or his listener's) to certainty. In Meditation 17, he uses these devices to inspire uncertainty in his listener. Explain, using examples from each work.

Reading Strategy

Recognizing the Speaker's Situation and Motivation

7. **(a)** In each of Donne's works, who is the speaker and what is the **speaker's situation**? **(b)** What is each speaker's **motivation**?
8. Choose a line from each work, and describe how knowledge of the speaker's situation and motivation helps you understand the text.

Extend Understanding

9. **World Events Connection:** During World War II, the British used the phrase "No man is an island" to justify joining the fight against Nazi Germany. Would Donne approve? Explain.

QuickReview

Metaphysical poetry is characterized by the use of conceits and paradoxes.

A **conceit** is an extended comparison linking objects or ideas that are not commonly associated.

A **paradox** is an image or a description that appears to contradict itself but really reveals a deeper truth.

An **analogy** compares the relationship between one pair of things with the relationship between another pair.

To **recognize a speaker's situation and motivation,** picture the speaker's circumstances and determine his or her reasons for speaking or acting.

Go Online
Assessment

For: Self-test
Visit: www.PHSchool.com
Web Code: esa-6302

Works of John Donne ■ 445

Answers continued

9. Students may say that he would agree that our common fate requires us to help others.

Go Online
Assessment Students may use the **Self-test** to prepare for **Selection Test A** or **Selection Test B**.

Answers

1. The speaker compares himself to the sun, which departs and returns every day, with far less motivation than he, as her lover, has to return to her.
2. **(a)** The paradox is "unkindly kind." **(b)** Grief can undermine the confidence of the beloved.
3. **(a)** The conceit is death as a proud person. **(b)** His intent is to make death seem less powerful.
4. **First Form:** affliction; **Second Form:** current money; **Relationship:** Affliction becomes "current money" when used to make one more fit for God.
5. **(a)** In "Song" and "Valediction," the speaker addresses his true love. In Holy Sonnet 10, the speaker addresses death. **(b)** All three works have paradoxes. In "Song" the paradox is "unkindly kind"; in "Valediction" it is "Two souls are one"; and in Holy Sonnet 10, it is "Death, thou shalt die."
6. **Sample response:** "Valediction": The speaker answers his beloved's uncertainties with the conceit of the compass; he argues that their souls are as firmly bound together as the two feet of a compass and that even as he travels, his life revolves around her; if she accepts the conceit, she will be certain that their love cannot be harmed. **Holy Sonnet 10:** The speaker confronts human uncertainty in the face of death with the paradox that death will die; this paradoxical belief moves those who accept it to certainty about their triumph over death. **Meditation 17:** The conceit of the tolling bell is intended to shake loose readers' certainties about life.
7. **Sample response:** "Song": **Speaker:** devout lover; **Situation:** impending separation; **Motivation:** to reassure beloved.
8. **Sample responses:** "Valediction" *Motive:* to reassure his beloved; *Situation:* The speaker is departing; *lines 21 to 24:* He says their separation will not part their souls but will expand them, reassuring her of his love. **Holy Sonnet 10** *Motive:* to reassure himself; *Situation:* He confronts fears of death; *line 9:* He says that death is a "slave to fate"; by insulting death, he keeps up his own courage.

445

❶ Vocabulary Lesson

Word Analysis

1. interstate: existing between or connecting two or more states

2. international: of, relating to, or involving two or more nations

3. interdependent: mutually dependent

4. intermediary: existing or occurring between

Spelling Strategy

1. facility   3. agility

2. society

Vocabulary Builder

1. c   5. a
2. c   6. a
3. b   7. b
4. a   8. c

❷ Grammar and Style Lesson

1. Separation expands their love.

2. Her sighs sigh away his soul.

3. Her weeping weakens his life's blood.

4. Someone has said that death is mighty.

5. Death does not conquer life.

Writing Application

Sample sentences:

Many years ago, it was decided that John Donne's employment with Sir Egerton would be terminated. Since that time, Donne and his family have been subject to a life of penury.

✍️ Writing and Grammar, Diamond Level

Students will find further instruction and practice on active and passive voice in Chapter 21, Section 4.

Build Language Skills

❶ Vocabulary Lesson

Word Analysis: Latin Prefix *inter-*

The Latin prefix *inter-* means "between" or "among." It appears in the word *intermit,* meaning "to put a space between" or "to pause." The prefix also appears in many words that describe relationships in society. Use the meaning of the prefix to help you define the following words:

1. interstate   3. interdependent
2. international   4. intermediary

Spelling Strategy

In English, the suffix *-ity,* used in the word *laity,* is more common than the suffix *-ety.* Often, *-ety* is used to avoid two *i*'s in a row when a word stem ends in an *i,* as in the word *anxiety.*

Complete the following words with *-ity* or *-ety.*

1. facil___   2. soci___   3. agil___

Vocabulary Builder: Synonyms

Choose the letter of the word or phrase closest in meaning to each vocabulary word.

1. contention: **(a)** gathering, **(b)** campsite, **(c)** dispute

2. piety: **(a)** roundness, **(b)** partiality, **(c)** devotion

3. intermit: **(a)** interfere, **(b)** pause, **(c)** deny

4. covetousness: **(a)** greed, **(b)** agreement, **(c)** sloth

5. profanation: **(a)** violation, **(b)** arson, **(c)** prediction

6. laity: **(a)** the uninitiated, **(b)** those who stand, **(c)** professionals

7. trepidation: **(a)** hunger, **(b)** trembling, **(c)** calm

8. breach: **(a)** birth, **(b)** pants, **(c)** break

❷ Grammar and Style Lesson

Active and Passive Voice

In the **active voice,** a verb expresses an action performed by its subject. In the **passive voice,** the subject receives the action of the verb. The passive voice uses a form of *to be* with the past participle (the form usually ending in *-ed*) of the main verb.

> **Active Voice:** Donne <u>compares</u> death to sleep. (Subject, *Donne,* performs action.)
>
> **Passive Voice:** Sleep <u>is compared</u> to death by Donne. (Subject, *Sleep,* receives action.)

In many cases, writers prefer the active voice because it creates a more forceful impression.

Practice   In your notebook, rewrite the following sentences in the active voice.

1. Their love is expanded by separation.

2. His soul is sighed away by her sighs.

3. His life's blood is weakened by her weeping.

4. It has been said that death is mighty.

5. Life is not conquered by death.

Writing Application   The passive voice helps hide who did what to whom, so it is often used in press releases. Using the passive voice, write a brief press release explaining Donne's loss of his job with Anne More's uncle. (See the biography on p. 434 for details.) For instance, you might begin "It was decided that . . .".

✍️ *Prentice Hall Writing and Grammar Connection: Chapter 21, Section 4*

Assessment Practice

Writer's Point of View   **(For more practice, see *Standardized Test Preparation Workbook,* p. 17.)**

Many tests require students to identify the writer's point of view. Use the following sample item to show the importance of careful attention to a writer's wording.

. . . No man hath affliction enough that is not matured and ripened by it, and made fit for God by that affliction . . .

Based on the passage, Donne views suffering—

A with pleasure   **C** with compassion

B with distaste   **D** with approval

Lead students to recognize that the correct answer is *D*; choice *A, B,* and *C* are not supported by anything in the passage.

Writing Lesson

Persuasive Speech Based on Donne's Work

Many of Donne's works are written as speeches. Adapt one of them to a contemporary situation, writing the speech Donne's speaker might make today.

Prewriting Review the selection of your choice to identify the speaker's situation, audience, and persuasive purpose. Outline Donne's arguments, and then list images and comparisons from contemporary experience that could be used in their place.

Drafting Begin with an emphatic statement or vivid image. Develop the images and arguments supporting your point in language suited to a contemporary audience.

Revising Review your draft to evaluate its unity. If you find parts that do not clearly connect to your theme and to one another, consider eliminating or rewriting them. You might make a post-draft outline of the ideas in your draft to aid you.

Model: Making a Post-Draft Outline to Revise for Unity

Paragraph A: Topic _____

   1. Connection to purpose: _____

   2. Connection to next paragraph: _____

Paragraph B: Topic _____

Using a format like this one, a writer can analyze the unity of a draft.

 *Prentice Hall Writing and Grammar Connection: Chapter 7, Section 4*

Extend Your Learning

Listening and Speaking With a partner, prepare a **dramatic reading** of two of Donne's poems. Use these tips:

1. Determine the appropriate tone of voice, whether comforting, cajoling, or challenging.
2. Analyze the text to find appropriate points at which to add dramatic gestures.
3. Help each other find places to add emphasis.

Perform your readings for the class.

Research and Technology What Donne called "trepidations of the spheres" are known as "perturbations" in modern astronomy. Compile a **science report** about these movements. Include maps and tables, incorporating them into your word-processor file.

Go Online
Research
For: An additional research activity
Visit: www.PHSchool.com
Web Code: esd-7301

Works of John Donne ■ 447

---

❸ Writing Lesson

You may use this Writing Lesson as timed-writing practice, or you may allow students to develop the essay as a writing assignment over several days.

- To guide students in writing this persuasive speech, give them the **Support for Writing Lesson** page (*Unit 3 Resources,* p. 15).
- Tell students a persuasive speech is a spoken statement that presents a position and tries to convince an audience to accept that position or to take action.
- Tell students that a good speech, like most writing, has an introduction with a strong statement of the theme, a body, and a conclusion. Each part of an effective speech— one that can move or please an audience—is connected to the others in clear ways.
- Use the Persuasive Essay rubrics in *General Resources,* pp. 45–46, to evaluate students' work.

❹ Listening and Speaking

- Have pairs select two poems. Students should familiarize themselves with the content of each poem.
- Have students follow the tips to determine the appropriate tone of voice to use and to identify places in the poems that would benefit from dramatic gestures.
- Have students practice their dramatic readings with partners before presenting them to the class.
- The **Support for Extend Your Learning** page (*Unit 3 Resources,* p. 16) provides guided note-taking opportunities to help students complete the Extend Your Learning activities.

Go Online
Research
Have students type in the Web Code for another research activity.

Assessment Resources

The following resources can be used to assess students' knowledge and skills.

Unit 3 Resources
  Selection Test A, pp. 18–20
  Selection Test B, pp. 21–23

General Resources
  Rubrics for Persuasive Essay, pp. 45–46

Go Online
Assessment
Students may use the **Self-test** to prepare for **Selection Test A** or **Selection Test B.**

TIME AND RESOURCE MANAGER

Meeting Your Standards

Students will

1. **analyze and respond to literary elements**
   - Literary Analysis: Epigrams

2. **read, comprehend, analyze, and critique a poem**
   - Reading Strategy: Hypothesizing
   - Reading Check questions
   - Apply the Skills questions
   - Assessment Practice (ATE)

3. **develop vocabulary**
   - Vocabulary Lesson: Archaic Words

4. **understand and apply written and oral language conventions**
   - Spelling Strategy
   - Grammar and Style Lesson: Placement of *only*

5. **develop writing proficiency**
   - Writing Lesson: Critical Response

6. **develop appropriate research strategies**
   - Extend Your Learning: Biographical Report

7. **understand and apply listening and speaking strategies**
   - Extend Your Learning: Debate

Block Scheduling: Use one 90-minute class period to preteach the skills and have students read the selection. Use a second 90-minute class period to assess students' mastery of skills, extend their learning, and monitor their progress.

Homework Suggestions

Following are possibilities for homework assignments:

- Support pages from *Unit 3 Resources:*
  - Literary Analysis
  - Reading Strategy
  - Vocabulary Builder
  - Grammar and Style

- An Extend Your Learning project and the Writing Lesson for this selection group may be completed over several days.

Step-by-Step Teaching Guide	Pacing Guide
PRETEACH	
• Administer Vocabulary and Reading Warm-ups as necessary.	5 min.
• Engage students' interest with the motivation activity.	5 min.
• Read and discuss author and background features. **FT**	10 min.
• Introduce the Literary Analysis skill: Epigrams. **FT**	5 min.
• Introduce the Reading Strategy: Hypothesizing. **FT**	10 min.
• Prepare students to read by teaching the selection vocabulary. **FT**	
TEACH	
• Informally monitor comprehension while students read independently or in groups. **FT**	30 min.
• Monitor students' comprehension with the Reading Check notes.	as students read
• Reinforce vocabulary with Vocabulary Builder notes.	as students read
• Develop students' understanding of epigrams with the Literary Analysis annotations. **FT**	5 min.
• Develop students' ability to hypothesize with the Reading Strategy annotations. **FT**	5 min.
ASSESS/EXTEND	
• Assess students' comprehension and mastery of the Literary Analysis and Reading Strategy by having them answer the Apply the Skills questions. **FT**	15 min.
• Have students complete the Vocabulary Development Lesson and the Grammar and Style Lesson. **FT**	15 min.
• Apply students' skill at connecting the general to the specific by using the Writing Lesson. **FT**	45 min. or homework
• Apply students' understanding by using one or both of the Extend Your Learning activities.	20–90 min. or homework
• Administer Selection Test A or Selection Test B. **FT**	15 min.

Resources

Choosing Resources for Differentiated Instruction

[L1] Special Needs Students

[L2] Below-Level Students

[L3] All Students

[L4] Advanced Students

[EL] English Learners

For Vocabulary and Reading Warm-ups and for Selection Tests, **A** signifies "less challenging" and **B** "more challenging." For Graphic Organizer transparencies, **A** signifies "not filled in" and **B** "filled in."

FT Fast Track Instruction: To move the lesson more quickly, use the strategies and activities identified with **FT**.

Scaffolding for Less Proficient and Advanced Students

The leveled Critical Thinking questions after selections progress in the levels of thinking required to answer them. To address the needs of your different students, you may use the (a) level questions for your less proficient students and the (b) level questions with your on-level and advanced students. The occasional (c) level questions are appropriate for your advanced students.

PRENTICE HALL
TeacherEXPRESS™ Use this complete
Plan · Teach · Assess suite of powerful teaching tools to make lesson planning and testing quicker and easier.

PRENTICE HALL
StudentEXPRESS™ Use the interactive
Learn · Study · Succeed tive textbook (online and on CD-ROM) to make selections and activities come alive with audio and video support and interactive questions.

 For: Information about Lexiles
Professional **Visit:** www.PHSchool.com
Development **Web Code:** eue-1111

Motivation

Ask students what makes them remember a line of poetry or a quotation from a speech. Ask them to cite a few memorable quotations and explain why they are memorable. Then, tell them that Ben Jonson's writing was designed to produce quotable lines and phrases.

❶ Background
More About the Author

Historic accounts help us picture Jonson at the Mermaid Tavern, surrounded by admirers and engaged in duels of wit with Shakespeare. Jonson's emphasis on graceful, balanced expression in verse shaped a generation of young poets, offering an alternative to Donne's "rough" lines. Critic Douglas Bush writes, "Jonson demanded, and unceasingly strove for, the ageless classical virtues of clarity, unity, symmetry, and proportion." Jonson was the first English poet with a "school"; he was also the first to insist that poetry was in itself an important vocation. Shakespeare, who did not publish his plays, regarded himself as a working dramatist, a tradesman in words. Jonson, however, risked controversy by publishing his verse in the form of a "Collected Works"—a format previously reserved for theological or historical works.

❶ On My First Son • Still to Be Neat • Song: To Celia

Ben Jonson
(1572–1637)

Ben Jonson lived a nearly mythic life. Even in his physical stature, he seemed a little larger than life—he was a big man with boundless energy and enormous courage. Brilliant in his poetry and dangerous in a duel, a classical scholar and a veteran soldier, an astute critic and a brassy talker, Jonson had a colorful, sometimes violent career that culminated in his reputation as an esteemed judge of literature. The friend as well as the chief rival of Shakespeare and Donne, he set literary tastes for a generation of poets. From bricklayer to poet laureate, his life story is a true "rags to riches" tale.

A Poet at War Adopted in infancy, Jonson worked for his stepfather, a bricklayer, while attending the equivalent of high school under a private tutor. Too poor to study at a university, Jonson joined the army and fought in the wars for Dutch independence from Spain. The brawny Jonson at one point met an enemy champion in single combat before the massed armies of Holland and Spain. Jonson won.

Scandal and Success After returning to England, Jonson became an actor. Despite his turbulent life—jailed for his part in a "slanderous" play, almost hanged for killing a fellow actor in a duel, and even suspected of plotting against the king—Jonson became a major dramatist. Some say William Shakespeare acted in his first play, and the chief acting companies of the day, including Shakespeare's company, performed his later dramas.

Jonson was so successful that he was granted a handsome pension by King James I and treated as if he were poet laureate of England. Over the years, he wrote masques—elaborate entertainments—for the royal court, where he was a favorite writer.

Dictator of Taste Jonson became extremely influential in literary affairs of the day, functioning as a virtual dictator of taste. Historic accounts help us picture him at the Mermaid Tavern, surrounded by admirers and engaged in duels of wit with Shakespeare. His followers, including Robert Herrick and Sir John Suckling, took to calling themselves the "Sons of Ben" or "Tribe of Ben."

The Importance of a Poet Jonson's own opinion of his work and status may be judged by the fact that when he published his collected works in 1616, he entitled the volume *The Works of Benjamin Jonson*—a style of title used largely with celebrated ancient authors. With this gesture, Jonson may have become the first English-language poet to claim true professional dignity for himself. The esteem in which the occupation of poet is held in later times owes something to Jonson's self-confidence.

Varied Styles Jonson's experiences ranged from tavern brawls to elegant entertainments, and his poetic styles are equally varied. He favored satire in his dramas, poking fun at contemporary character types in plays such as *Volpone* and *The Alchemist*. In contrast, his masques provided the king's court with lavish pageants, often based on Greek and Roman myths and topped off with flattering references to the king and queen—far from the satirical bite of his stage plays.

Jonson wrote many of his poems in an impersonal style, one suited to inscriptions on monuments. Others are filled with nasty wit. As diverse as his styles are, though, one of his consistent strengths is the clear, direct expression of ideas.

A Lasting Influence In his varied experiences and diverse literary output, Jonson might seem to sum up the age in which he lived. Yet his importance does not end with the seventeenth century. Jonson's influence on writers is still felt today, and his plays continue to be produced. What Jonson said of Shakespeare can also be said of him: "He was not of an age, but for all time."

Preview

Connecting to the Literature

Mottos emblazoned on T-shirts or inscribed on mugs reflect the same urge that brought Ben Jonson to write—the desire to pass on memorable sayings.

Literary Analysis

Epigrams

An **epigram** (from the Greek for "inscription") is a short poem in which the writer strives for brevity, clarity, and permanence. Ben Jonson's famous lines have the qualities of an epigram: "Drink to me only with thine eyes,/ And I will pledge with mine." Epigrams include these features:

- Short lines with bouncy rhythms
- Paradoxical twists, as in the lines quoted above
- Parallel phrases or clauses, as in the line "Still to be neat, still to be dressed, . . ."

As you read, analyze the elements that make Jonson's lines memorable.

Comparing Literary Works

Jonson writes epigrammatic poems on a variety of subjects. You may be impressed by his range of feeling in them. "On My First Son" is a sharp testament to a personal grief. By contrast, you may find "Song: To Celia" quite generalized—as if it might have been written by anyone to anyone. Compare the sentiment—personal or generalized—of each poem.

Reading Strategy

Hypothesizing

To read actively, **hypothesize** by making informed guesses about the people, events, or ideas in the work. Reading further, check your hypothesis against new information, using a chart like the one shown.

Vocabulary Builder

In his poems, Johnson uses **archaic words,** words that are no longer in general use. Familiarize yourself with the following words before you read.

thou you (second-person singular; used instead of *you* with family and friends)

thy your (second-person singular; used with family and friends)

thine yours or, before a word beginning with a vowel, your (second-person singular; used with family and friends)

wast were (used with *thou*)

wert were (used with *thou*)

hast have (used with *thou*)

hath has (used with *he, she, it*)

dost do (used with *thou,* usually as a helping verb)

doth does (used with *he, she, it,* usually as a helping verb)

Hypothesis	
Line 1: Speaker is a father whose son has gone away or died.	

Proved	Disproved
Lines 3–7: Boy lived 7 years and ìsc aped world's, and flesh's rage."	

On My First Son / Still to Be Neat / Song: To Celia ■ 449

❶ About the Selection

Whereas Donne's work argues that death does not matter because it leads to eternal life, Jonson's poem "On My First Son" shows that death sorely wounds those grieving people left behind.

❷ Vocabulary Builder

Archaic Words

- **Ask** students to "translate" the words *thou, thee, thou wert, thee,* and *thy* in the first four lines.
  Answer: They translate as "you," "you," you were," "you," and "your."

- Explain to students that these are examples of archaic words—words that are not in general use any longer.

- Have students provide examples of other archaic words with which they are familiar.

❸ Reading Strategy

Hypothesizing

- **Ask** students what they can hypothesize from the first line of the poem.
  Answer: Students may hypothesize that the speaker is a father.

- Tell students to **formulate** a hypothesis about the situation and the speaker's relationship with his son using only lines 1–4.
  Answer: Students may hypothesize that the first four lines refer to a beloved child who has died.

- Then, **ask** students whether lines 5–8 require them to modify their hypotheses.
  Answer: No, they underscore the torment of loss and grief.

▶ **Monitor Progress: Ask** students what final hypothesis can be drawn about the speaker's feelings for his son.
  Answer: Students may respond that the speaker is inconsolable.

❶ On My First Son

Ben Jonson

Differentiated Instruction Solutions for All Learners

Accessibility at a Glance

	On My First Son	Still to Be Neat	Song: To Celia
Context	Metaphysical	Metaphysical	Metaphysical
Language	archaic words	archaic words	archaic words
Concept Level	Accessible (love for child)	Accessible (natural beauty)	Accessible (love)
Literary Merit	Classic	Classic	Classic
Lexile	NP	NP	NP
Overall Rating	Average	Average	Average

Background

Ben Jonson was indebted to ancient Greek and Roman poets, whose work shaped his taste for clear, brief expression. Like ancient poets, Jonson composed poetry with a definite social function. Jonson's poems praising other writers appeared at the beginning of their books. Poems such as "On My First Son" marked the occasion of a death. Songs such as "Still to Be Neat" were written by Jonson for his masques (royal entertainments).

Farewell, thou child of my right hand,[1] and joy;
    My sin was too much hope of thee, loved boy,
Seven years thou wert lent to me, and I thee pay,
    Exacted by thy fate, on the just[2] day.
5 O, could I lose all father,[3] now. For why
    Will man lament the state he should envy?
To have so soon scaped world's, and flesh's rage,
    And, if no other misery, yet age?
Rest in soft peace, and, asked, say here doth lie
10   Ben Jonson his best piece of poetry.
For whose sake, henceforth, all his vows be such,
    As what he loves may never like[4] too much.

1. **child . . . hand** literal translation of the Hebrew name Benjamin, the name of Jonson's son. Jonson's son was born in 1596 and died in 1603.
2. **just** exact.
3. **lose . . . father** shed an identity as a father.
4. **like** possibly meant in the old sense of "please."

Literary Analysis

Epigrams Do you think this poem was written to create a sense of permanence? Explain.

Critical Reading

1. **Respond:** Do you think the speaker in "On My First Son" is wise in not wanting to love anything so strongly again? Explain.

2. **(a) Recall:** What is the sin the speaker refers to in line 2?
   (b) Interpret: Why does the speaker call this feeling a sin?

3. **(a) Interpret:** Why does the speaker wish to "lose all father, now"?
   (b) Interpret: What does he vow in lines 11–12?
   (c) Draw Conclusions: Why would grief lead to these reactions?

4. **(a) Interpret:** Does the speaker ever present his feelings of grief directly? Explain. **(b) Evaluate:** Why might this manner of presenting grief strengthen the impression made on the reader?

5. **(a) Apply:** Contrast the ideas in lines 5–8 with contemporary attitudes.
   (b) Evaluate: Which makes more sense to you?

Go Online
Author Link

For: More about Ben Jonson
Visit: www.PHSchool.com
Web Code: ese-9303

On My First Son ■ 451

Enrichment

Jonson's Vision of His Son

According to an anecdote related by William Drummond, Jonson experienced a premonition about his son Benjamin. Jonson was visiting at the country home of Sir Robert Cotton when he had a dream in which his eldest son appeared, fully grown but "with the mark of a bloody cross on his forehead, as if it had been cutted with a sword." Amazed and distressed, Jonson related his vision to a friend, who assured him that it was only a dream. Soon after, Jonson received letters from his wife bearing news of seven-year-old Benjamin's death of plague.

People who were able to do so spent the summer "plague seasons" in the countryside, away from the infections of London. It is not known whether Jonson felt regret for having been away while his family remained at risk in the city.

451

❺

Portrait of Mrs. Richard Brinsley Sheridan, Thomas Gainsborough, National Gallery of Art, Washington, D.C.

❻ ▲ Critical Viewing Given his sentiments in the poem, of what details of this woman's appearance would Jonson approve? Explain. **[Connect]**

Still to Be Neat

Ben Jonson

8

Still[1] to be neat, still to be dressed,
As you were going to a feast;
Still to be powdered, still perfumed;
Lady, it is to be presumed,
5 Though art's hid causes[2] are not found,
All is not sweet, all is not sound.

Give me a look, give me a face,
That makes simplicity a grace;
Robes loosely flowing, hair as free;
10 Such sweet neglect more taketh me
                Than all th'adulteries[3] of art.

9 They strike mine eyes, but not my heart.

---

1. **Still** always.
2. **causes** reasons.
3. **adulteries** adulterations; corruptions.

Reading Strategy
Hypothesize What response might the lady have made to the message in this poem?

Critical Reading

1. **Respond:** Do you agree with the speaker about the attractiveness of a spontaneous look? Why or why not?

2. **(a) Recall:** To what style of dress and grooming is the speaker reacting in the first stanza? **(b) Interpret:** What are the "hid causes" that he suspects lie behind this style? **(c) Infer:** Why does he prefer the style of "sweet neglect"?

3. **(a) Analyze:** How does Jonson use repetition to support his meaning? **(b) Evaluate:** How might Jonson's ideas about fashion apply to his own poem?

4. **Relate:** Which trends in modern advertising can you connect with the ideas in the poem?

Go Online
Author Link

For: More about Ben Jonson
Visit: www.PHSchool.com
Web Code: ese-9303

Still to Be Neat ■ 453

---

8 Reading Strategy
Hypothesize

- Review the definition of *hypothesize*. To hypothesize is to make informed guesses about the people, events or ideas in the work.

- Read the first six lines of the poem and **ask** students to hypothesize what the speaker's attitude is toward fancy dress and perfumes. **Answer:** Students may detect a note of disapproval.

- **Ask** students the Reading Strategy Question: What response might the lady have made to the message in this poem? **Possible response:** The lady might respond that she dresses up to please herself, not others.

9 Vocabulary Builder
Archaic Words

- Ask students what the word *mine* means in this context. **Answer:** It means my.

- Have students use the dictionary to discover archaic meanings of familiar words, such as *just* and *late*.

ASSESS

Answers

1. Some students may agree that a natural look is appealing.

2. (a) The speaker is reacting to an overdone appearance. (b) The speaker suspects that flaws are masked by perfume and powder. (c) He prefers the style of sweet neglect because it touches his heart as well as his eyes.

3. (a) The repetition of "still to be" indicates the speaker's displeasure of the lady's appearance. The repetition of "give me" is softer and reflects the simplicity he prefers. (b) He writes clean, simple verse.

4. Cosmetic advertisements spotlight natural beauty—even though cosmetics are perfect examples of artifice.

Go Online
Author Link For additional information about Ben Jonson, have students type in the Web Code, then select J from the alphabet, and then select the author's name.

Song: To Celia

Ben Jonson

Drink to me only with thine eyes,
And I will pledge with mine:
Or leave a kiss but in the cup,
And I'll not look for wine.
5   The thirst that from the soul doth rise,
Doth ask a drink divine:
But might I of Jove's[1] nectar sup,
I would not change for thine.

I sent thee late[2] a rosy wreath,
10   Not so much honoring thee,
As giving it a hope, that there
It could not withered be.
But thou thereon did'st only breathe,
And sent'st it back to me;
15   Since when it grows and smells, I swear,
Not of itself, but thee.

---

1. **Jove's** Jupiter's. In Roman mythology, Jupiter is the ruler of the gods.
2. **late** recently.

Critical Reading

1. **(a) Recall:** For what does the soul thirst in lines 5–6 of "Song: To Celia"? **(b) Interpret:** Explain how this idea of the soul's thirst extends the image in lines 1–2.

2. **(a) Analyze:** Which images suggest sensory experiences? **(b) Analyze:** Which words or images suggest emotional states? **(c) Generalize:** What do these two categories of image suggest about the process of falling in love?

3. **(a) Assess:** How much do you know about the speaker of "Song: To Celia" or his beloved? **(b) Make a Judgment:** How would more information affect your appreciation of the poem?

4. **Evaluate:** Does Jonson's poem seem artificial or false by today's standards, or does it capture true sentiment? Explain.

Apply the Skills

On My First Son • Still to Be Neat • Song: To Celia

Literary Analysis

Epigrams

1. Would any lines from "On My First Son" be suitable for engraving on the subject's tombstone? Explain.

2. Identify three pairs of parallel phrases or clauses in "Still to Be Neat."

3. Explain how the phrase "sweet neglect" in "Still to Be Neat" appears self-contradictory but makes memorable sense.

4. Use a chart like the one shown to identify and characterize lines that give "Song: To Celia" the style of an **epigram.**

"Bouncy" Rhythms	Parallelism	Witty Wordings	Paradoxes
Lines:	Lines:	Lines:	Lines:

Comparing Literary Works

5. (a) Identify two details in "On My First Son" that make it a sincere, personal statement of grief. Explain your choices. (b) Identify two details in "Song" that give it a formal, impersonal quality. Explain your choices. (c) Are both types of poem valuable? Explain.

6. (a) Which details in "Still to Be Neat" give it a generalized quality? (b) Which details make it seem heartfelt? (c) Compare the sentiment in this poem with the sentiment of the other two.

Reading Strategy

Hypothesizing

7. (a) Using only lines 1–4 of "On My First Son," make a **hypothesis** about the speaker's feelings for his son. (b) Do lines 5–8 of the poem support your hypothesis? Explain.

8. Basing your answer on lines 11–12 of "On My First Son," what final hypothesis can you make about the speaker's reaction to his son's death?

Extend Understanding

9. **Career Connection:** In what modern occupations might Jonson's witty, epigrammatic style be effective? Why?

QuickReview

An **epigram** is a short poem in which the poet strives for brevity, clarity, and memorability.

To **hypothesize**, stop and make informed guesses and predictions based on the information you have read to that point.

Go Online
Assessment

For: Self-test
Visit: www.PHSchool.com
Web Code: esa-6306

On My First Son / Still to Be Neat / Song: To Celia ■ 455

 Students may use the **Self-test** to prepare for **Selection Test A** or **Selection Test B**.

455

❶ Vocabulary Lesson

Word Analysis

1. Thy
2. wert
3. hath

Spelling Strategy

1. enviable
2. miseries
3. replying

Vocabulary Builder

For, if I thought my judgment were of years/I should commit you surely with your peers/And tell, how far you did our Lyly outshine,/Or sporting Kyd, or Marlowe's mighty line./And though you had little Latin, and less Greek,/From that time to honor you, I would not seek./For names; but call forth thundering Aeschylus . . .

❷ Grammar and Style Lesson

1. Drink only to me with thine eyes.
2. Drink to me with only thine eyes.
3. Give me only a look.
4. Only they strike mine eyes.
5. They strike only mine eyes.

Writing Application

Sample sentences:

Jonson was too poor to study at a university, and had only a high school education. It was only Jonson's energy, courage and talents that brought him to the attention of King James I himself.

𝒲𝒢 Writing and Grammar, Diamond Level

Students will find further instruction and practice on modifiers in Chapter 20, Section 5.

Build Language Skills

❶ Vocabulary Lesson

Word Analysis: Archaic Words

Ben Jonson's poetry and many other works of English literature contain **archaic words**—words that are no longer in general use. Choose the correct archaic word to complete each sentence.

1. (Thy / Thine) looks are like the nectar of the gods.
2. Thou (wert / doth) too dear to me.
3. She (hast / hath) dressed neatly once again.

Spelling Strategy

When a word ends in a consonant and *y*, change the *y* to *i* before adding most suffixes, as when Jonson adds *-es* to *adultery* to form *adulteries*. When adding the suffixes *-ing* and *-ish*, however, keep the final *y*. Write the words formed by each of the following combinations.

1. *envy + -able* 2. *misery + -es* 3. *reply + -ing*

Vocabulary Builder: Archaic Words

"Translate" the following passage from Jonson's "To the Memory of My Beloved Master, William Shakespeare" into modern English.

> For, if I thought my judgment were
>   of years,
> I should commit thee surely with
>   thy peers,
> And tell, how far thou didst our Lyly
>   outshine,
> Or sporting Kyd, or Marlowe's mighty
>   line.
> And though thou hadst small Latin, and
>   less Greek,
> From thence to honor thee, I would not
>   seek
> For names; but call forth thund'ring
>   Aeschylus. . . .

❷ Grammar and Style Lesson

Modifiers: Placement of *only*

Modifiers should always be placed as close as possible to the words they modify. Changing the placement of a modifier such as *only* can change the meaning of a sentence.

> **Example:** Drink to me <u>only</u> with thine eyes. (Drink only with your eyes, not with anything else.)
>
> <u>Only</u> drink to me with thine eyes. (Only gaze at the speaker; don't do anything else.)

Poets such as Jonson face a complex task. They must place modifiers close to the words they modify while at the same time creating the right rhythm.

Practice Add the word *only* to the following sentences to convey the meanings in parentheses.

1. Drink to me with thine eyes. (just to me, no one else)
2. Drink to me with thine eyes. (use your eyes, no one else's)
3. Give me a look. (just a look, nothing else)
4. They strike mine eyes. (they, and no others)
5. They strike mine eyes. (only my eyes, not my heart)

Writing Application Write a paragraph about Ben Jonson, using information from page 448. Use the modifier *only* at least twice.

𝒲𝒢 *Prentice Hall Writing and Grammar Connection: Chapter 20, Section 5*

456 ■ *A Turbulent Time (1625–1798)*

Assessment Practice

Writer's Purpose (For more practice, see *Standardized Test Preparation Workbook*, p. 18.)

Use the following passage from "Still to be Neat" to teach students how to identify a writer's main purpose.

> . . . Give me a look, give me a face, That makes simplicity a grace; Robes loosely flowing, hair as free; Such sweet neglect more taketh me
> Than all th'adulteries of art,
> They strike mine eyes, but not my heart

Jonson wrote this passage *primarily* to

A ridicule the lady

B inform the lady that he finds natural beauty more attractive than artificial beauty

C tell the lady that he knows she uses "art" to appear more beautiful

D express his love for the lady

Based on the last three lines, students should determine that the correct answer is *B*.

Writing Lesson

Timed Writing: Critical Response

Critic Douglas Bush defends what some have called the dullness of Jonson's style: "... Jonson demanded ... the ageless classical virtues of clarity, unity, symmetry, and proportion. ... His poems are wholes, not erratic displays of verbal fireworks." Drawing on details from the selections, write a response to this idea. *(40 minutes)*

Prewriting
(10 minutes)
Using parts of the quotation above as heads (for example, "Clarity"), categorize examples from Jonson's poems that illustrate or contradict Bush's defense. Then, write a brief summary of your own reaction to Jonson's style.

Drafting
(20 minutes)
Begin with a summary of Bush's point and of your position. As you draft, support generalizations with quotations from Jonson.

Revising
(10 minutes)
Highlight generalizations in your draft and check off supporting details for each. At points where there are few or no checkmarks, consider adding support.

Model: Adding Support by Connecting General to Specific

For instance, the lines "But might I of Jove's nectar sup / I would not change for thine" unify the images of drinking. The reference to Jove, though, is artificial.

Jonson may achieve unity, but in some cases it is at the expense of spontaneous feeling. What is the virtue of formal unity if the poem seems lifeless?

Added details from the poem strengthen support for the generalization.

W̶G̶ Prentice Hall Writing and Grammar Connection: Chapter 14, Section 4

Extend Your Learning

Listening and Speaking Hold a **debate** between supporters of "natural" styles (grunge, long hair) and supporters of "artificial" styles (black-colored clothes, dyed hair). Each side should prepare

- A generalization that sums up its position
- A deductive argument—an argument applying a general truth to a specific case
- Visual images that illustrate and support its arguments

Hold your debate for the class. **[Group Activity]**

Research and Technology Research and write a **biographical report** on Ben Jonson's life. Begin by writing a list of questions about him. Then, check various sources, including writings from the time and modern commentaries, to answer your questions. Include a list of sources, annotated with your comments, at the end of your report.

Go Online
Research
For: An additional research activity
Visit: www.PHSchool.com
Web Code: esd-7302

On My First Son / Still to Be Neat / Song: To Celia ■ 457

---

❸ Writing Lesson

You may use this Writing Lesson as timed-writing practice, or you may allow students to develop the essay as a writing assignment over several days.

- To guide students in writing this critical response, give them the **Support for Writing Lesson** page (*Unit 3 Resources*, p. 32).

- Tell students a critical response is a piece of nonfiction writing that presents a reaction to, or an analysis of, a literary work.

- You may wish to use the Response to Literature rubrics in *General Resources* pp. 65–66, to evaluate students' critical responses.

❹ Listening and Speaking

- Divide the class into two groups.

- Assign hair and clothing styles to each group, and tell the students to follow the steps outlined on this page to organize their tasks.

- Ask the students to seek out possible symbolic and cultural meanings associated with the varying hair and clothing styles. Have them conduct research on the Internet, or ask people they know, or ask hair stylists in order to find supporting evidence for their arguments.

- The **Support for Extend Your Learning** page (*Unit 3 Resources*, p. 33) provides guided note-taking opportunities to help students complete the Extend Your Learning activities.

Go Online
Research
Have students type in the Web Code for another research activity.

Assessment Resources

The following resources can be used to assess students' knowledge and skills.

Unit 3 Resources
  Selection Test A, pp. 35–37
  Selection Test B, pp. 38–40

Go Online
Assessment
Students may use the Self-test to prepare for Selection Test A or Selection Test B.

General Resources
  Rubrics for Response to Literature, pp. 65–66

Meeting Your Standards

Students will

1. **analyze and respond to literary elements**
   - Literary Analysis: *Carpe Diem* Theme

2. **read, comprehend, analyze, and critique a poem**
   - Reading Strategy: Inferring the Speaker's Attitude
   - Reading Check questions
   - Apply the Skills questions
   - Assessment Practice (ATE)

3. **develop vocabulary**
   - Vocabulary Lesson: Related Forms of *prime*

4. **understand and apply written and oral language conventions**
   - Spelling Strategy
   - Grammar and Style Lesson: Irregular Forms of Adjectives

5. **develop writing proficiency**
   - Writing Lesson: Witty Poem

6. **develop appropriate research strategies**
   - Extend Your Learning: Comparative Biographical Essay

7. **understand and apply listening and speaking strategies**
   - Extend Your Learning: Phone Skit

Block Scheduling: Use one 90-minute class period to preteach the skills and have students read the selection. Use a second 90-minute class period to assess students' mastery of skills, extend their learning, and monitor their progress.

Homework Suggestions

Following are possibilities for homework assignments:

- Support pages from *Unit 3 Resources:*
  - Literary Analysis
  - Reading Strategy
  - Vocabulary Builder
  - Grammar and Style

- An Extend Your Learning project and the Writing Lesson for this selection group may be completed over several days.

Step-by-Step Teaching Guide	Pacing Guide
PRETEACH	
• Administer Vocabulary and Reading Warm-ups as necessary.	5 min.
• Engage students' interest with the motivation activity.	5 min.
• Read and discuss author and background features. **FT**	10 min.
• Introduce the Literary Analysis Skill: *Carpe Diem* Theme. **FT**	5 min.
• Introduce the Reading Strategy: Inferring the Speaker's Attitude. **FT**	10 min.
• Prepare students to read by teaching the selection vocabulary. **FT**	
TEACH	
• Informally monitor comprehension while students read independently or in groups. **FT**	30 min.
• Monitor students' comprehension with the Reading Check notes.	as students read
• Reinforce vocabulary with Vocabulary Builder notes.	as students read
• Develop students' understanding of the *carpe diem* theme with the Literary Analysis annotations. **FT**	5 min.
• Develop students' ability to infer the speaker's attitude with the Reading Strategy annotations. **FT**	5 min.
ASSESS/EXTEND	
• Assess students' comprehension and mastery of the Literary Analysis and Reading Strategy by having them answer the Apply the Skills questions. **FT**	15 min.
• Have students complete the Vocabulary Development Lesson and the Grammar and Style Lesson. **FT**	15 min.
• Apply students' knowledge of persuasive tone by using the Writing Lesson. **FT**	45 min. or homework
• Apply students' understanding by using one or more of the Extend Your Learning activities.	20–90 min. or homework
• Administer Selection Test A or Selection Test B. **FT**	15 min.

Resources

PRINT

Unit 3 Resources

TRANSPARENCY

Graphic Organizer Transparencies

PRINT

Reader's Notebook [L2]
Reader's Notebook: Adapted Version [L1]
Reader's Notebook: English Learner's Version [EL]

Unit 3 Resources

TECHNOLOGY

Listening to Literature Audio CDs [L2, EL]

PRINT

Unit 3 Resources

General Resources

TECHNOLOGY

Go Online: Research [L3]
Go Online: Self-test [L3]
ExamView® **Test Bank [L3]**

Choosing Resources for Differentiated Instruction

[**L1**] Special Needs Students

[**L2**] Below-Level Students

[**L3**] All Students

[**L4**] Advanced Students

[**EL**] English Learners

For Vocabulary and Reading Warm-ups and for Selection Tests, **A** signifies "less challenging" and **B** "more challenging." For Graphic Organizer transparencies, **A** signifies "not filled in" and **B** "filled in."

FT Fast Track Instruction: To move the lesson more quickly, use the strategies and activities identified with **FT**.

Scaffolding for Less Proficient and Advanced Students

The leveled Critical Thinking questions after selections progress in the levels of thinking required to answer them. To address the needs of your different students, you may use the (a) level questions for your less proficient students and the (b) level questions with your on-level and advanced students. The occasional (c) level questions are appropriate for your advanced students.

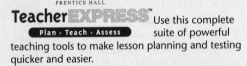

PRENTICE HALL
TeacherEXPRESS™ Use this complete
Plan · Teach · Assess suite of powerful
teaching tools to make lesson planning and testing
quicker and easier.

PRENTICE HALL
StudentEXPRESS™ Use the interac-
Learn · Study · Succeed tive textbook
(online and on CD-ROM) to make selections and
activities come alive with audio and video support
and interactive questions.

Go **Online** **For:** Information about Lexiles
Professional **Visit:** www.PHSchool.com
Development **Web Code:** eue-1111

458b

Motivation

Ask students which statement below best reflects modern attitudes of young people.

> Life is short. Do it now.

> Look before you leap.

Briefly discuss different factors that might be behind the two opposing pieces of advice. Then, point out that the "Do it now" school of thought actually goes back many centuries. An ancient Roman poet, Virgil, first said, "Time flies." One of his contemporaries coined the phrase "Seize the day; put no trust in tomorrow." The writers whom the students will read next also subscribed to this idea.

❶ Background
More About the Authors

Though their poems here betray no hint of political turbulence, the lives of all three poets were deeply affected by the Revolution, Puritan Commonwealth, and Restoration. A remote country parish could not insulate Herrick from the winds of change, and Suckling's Royalist involvements led him to a sad end in exile. Only Marvell was able to keep his balance as England whipsawed from monarchy to Commonwealth and back to monarchy. His political adroitness was as important to English literature as his poetic gifts, for when the monarchy was restored in 1660, Marvell was able to intercede on behalf of John Milton, saving his former mentor from imprisonment or worse.

Build Skills | Poems |

❶ To His Coy Mistress • To the Virgins, to Make Much of Time • Song

Andrew Marvell
(1621–1678)

Marvell showed an extraordinary adaptability in a turbulent time. Although he was the son of a Puritan minister and frowned on the abuses of the monarchy, he enjoyed close friendships with supporters of Charles I in the king's dispute with Parliament. He also opposed the government of Oliver Cromwell, leader of the Puritan rebellion and then ruler of England.

Beginning in 1651, however, Marvell worked for Lord Fairfax, the commanding general of the Parliamentary army. Still later, he tutored Cromwell's ward. Marvell gained the sponsorship of the Puritan and great English poet John Milton, whose assistant he became.

Marvell wrote masterful poetry in various veins—some works share the metaphysical qualities of Donne's verse, while others have the classical qualities recommended by Jonson. Thought of chiefly as a satirist until the nineteenth century, much of his work has become classic.

Robert Herrick
(1591–1674)

Born into a family of London goldsmiths, Herrick went to Cambridge when he was twenty-two and graduated at the age of twenty-nine. After graduation, he served as a military chaplain. As a reward for his services, he was assigned to a parish in rural England. Here, he performed his churchly duties and wrote religious verse and musical love poems.

Although not politically active, Herrick was evicted from his parish by the Puritans and allowed back only with the Restoration of Charles II. While barred from his church, Herrick returned to his native and beloved London, where he published his poetry in *Noble Numbers* and *Hesperides* (the title comes from an ancient Greek name for a mythical garden at the edge of the world).

Published during a turbulent time and largely ignored by his contemporaries, these verses are highly regarded today.

Sir John Suckling
(1609–1642)

In some ways, Sir John Suckling lived a life more romantic than Marvell's or Herrick's. A privileged young courtier, Suckling inherited his vast estates when he was only eighteen. He later served as a gentleman in the privy chamber of Charles I. Praised as the cleverest of conversationalists, Suckling was said to be able to compose a poem at a moment's notice. He incorporated some of his best lyrics, including the poem "Song," into plays that he lavishly produced at his own expense.

Suckling's military exploits proved less successful than his poems, however. The cavalry troop he raised and lavishly uniformed for the king was defeated in Scotland, and Suckling was mocked for caring more about his men's uniforms than about their military abilities. After joining a failed Royalist plot to rescue a royal minister from prison, he fled to France, where he died in despair at the age of thirty-three. His poems, though, preserve the dash and spirit of his younger days.

Preview

Connecting to the Literature

It is easy for students to feel that life is one big, totally booked schedule. It is just as easy to figure out how the authors of these selections would respond: Make room for some enjoyment, before it is too late!

Literary Analysis

Carpe Diem Theme

Each poem in this grouping expresses a version of the *carpe diem* theme (kär´ pē dē´ em). *Carpe diem* is Latin for "seize the day." The theme might be summed up, "Time is fleeting, so act decisively to enjoy life." Marvell expresses this theme in an extended fashion. First, he playfully describes to his beloved the centuries he would spend wooing her, if they had all of time. Then, he dryly reminds her that life does in fact come to an end, so she must act. Look for the various treatments of this theme in these selections.

Comparing Literary Works

Marvell approaches the *carpe diem* theme with a mix of whimsical fancy and passionate urgency. Herrick delivers a more traditional version of the theme, using familiar imagery to remind his readers of the seasons of life. Suckling gives the theme a new twist—his speaker advises a friend to abandon, not act on, love. As you read, compare the ways in which the poets address the same basic theme.

Reading Strategy

Inferring the Speaker's Attitude

To recognize the tone of a poem, you must **infer the speaker's attitude** toward the subject or audience.

- First, focus on the connotations (positive and negative associations) of the words and images the speaker uses.
- Then, determine what attitude would lead a speaker to choose these words and images.

You may find that the speaker's attitude shifts from one stanza to another, affecting the overall tone of the work. As you read, use a chart like the one shown here to note details that convey the speaker's attitude.

Vocabulary Builder

coyness (koi´ nis) *n.* shyness; aloofness, often as part of a flirtation (p. 461)

amorous (am´ ə res) *adj.* full of love or desire (p. 462)

languish (laŋ´ gwish) *v.* to become weak; droop (p. 462)

prime (prīm) *n.* best stage of a thing or process (p. 463)

wan (wän) *adj.* sickly pale; faint or weak (p. 465)

Passage

"If of herself she will not love, / Nothing can make her: / The devil take her!"

↓

Word Connotations

"Nothing" (negative)

↓

Image Connotations

"The devil" (negative)

↓

Speaker's Attitude

Impatience, but also kindness—he is hoping his words will help his friend

---

To His Coy Mistress / To the Virgins, to Make Much of Time / Song ■ 459

❷ Literary Analysis
Carpe Diem Theme

- Tell students that each poem in this grouping expresses a version of the *carpe diem* theme.

- Explain that this theme expresses the idea that since time is fleeting one should best act decisively to make the most of life.

❸ Reading Strategy
Inferring the Speaker's Attitude

- Explain to students that a poem's speaker may or may not be the poet. Point out that the speaker usually expresses a certain attitude toward the subject or toward the person he or she is addressing.

- Present the following lines from "Song":

  If of herself she will not love,

  Nothing can make her:

  The devil take her!

- Ask students to infer the speaker's attitude, focusing on words, images, and rhythms the speaker uses. Point out how the clipped rhythms of the last two lines suggest the speaker's exasperation.

- Give students a copy of **Reading Strategy Graphic Organizer A** p. 83 in *Graphic Organizer Transparencies*, to note details that convey the speaker's attitude.

Vocabulary Builder

Pronounce each vocabulary word for students, and read the definitions as a class. Have students identify any words with which they are already familiar.

Learning Modalities
Musical/Rhythmic Learners

Help students appreciate the music of the words as well as the content by pointing out the rhythm of the paired couplets.

❶ About the Selection

Marvell's work has been called "the most major minor verse in English," and this poem in particular shows why so many readers enjoy Marvell. Rich in sensory images and flattery, "To His Coy Mistress" is designed to appeal to feelings as well as to the intellect. Its exaggerated emotion and its persuasive tone are humorous to readers who recognize the speaker's goal.

❷ Humanities

The Interrupted Sleep, by François Boucher

The legacy of François Boucher (1703–1770) includes some of the finest examples of Louis XV rococo art. Boucher's style includes excellent draftsmanship, fine brush work, and an eye for drama and decoration.

Use these questions for discussion:

1. How does the artist focus attention on the center of the painting?
   Answer: The converging tree limbs, the red scarf, and the sunlight on the girl all draw attention to the center.

2. Is the girl in the painting asleep, or is she being "coy"?
   Possible response: Though her eyes are closed, the girl seems to be coyly aware of what the youth is doing.

❸ Critical Viewing

Answer: Students might comment that both the painting and the poem show men in active pursuit and women being demure in their response. Students may question whether these traditional rules apply to modern courtship.

The Interrupted Sleep, François Boucher. The Metropolitan Museum of Art

▲ **Critical Viewing** In what way do both the painting and the poem illustrate ❸ the traditional roles of men and women in courtship? [**Compare and Contrast**]

460 ■ *A Turbulent Time (1625–1798)*

Differentiated Instruction   Solutions for All Learners

Accessibility at a Glance

	To His Coy Mistress	To the Virgins	Song
Context	Metaphysical	Metaphysical	Metaphysical
Language	Poetic diction	Archaic words	Informal
Concept Level	Moderate (*carpe diem*)	Moderate (*carpe diem*)	Accessible (unrequited love)
Literary Merit	Classic	Classic	Classic
Lexile	NP	NP	NP
Other			humorous
Overall Rating	More challenging	More challenging	Average

To His Coy Mistress

Andrew Marvell

Background

By the seventeenth century, the English language had become a fluid combination of Anglo-Saxon, Gaelic, Latin, and French. It was more than a tool for basic communication. Through it, one could express philosophical ideas, convey abstract theories, and indulge in humorous wordplay. These poems show the range of this language, from witty puns to fanciful imagery.

Had we but world enough, and time,
This <u>coyness</u> lady were no crime.
We would sit down, and think which way
To walk, and pass our long love's day.

5   Thou by the Indian Ganges' side
Should'st rubies find; I by the tide
Of Humber[1] would complain. I would
Love you ten years before the Flood,
And you should if you please refuse

10 Till the conversion of the Jews.[2]
My vegetable love should grow
Vaster than empires, and more slow;
An hundred years should go to praise
Thine eyes, and on thy forehead gaze;

15 Two hundred to adore each breast,
But thirty thousand to the rest;
An age at least to every part,
And the last age should show your heart.
For, lady, you deserve this state,[3]

20 Nor would I love at lower rate.
     But at my back I always hear
Time's wingèd chariot hurrying near:
And yonder all before us lie
Deserts of vast eternity.

25 Thy beauty shall no more be found,
Nor, in thy marble vault, shall sound

Vocabulary Builder
coyness (koi´ nis) *n.* shyness; aloofness, often as part of a flirtation

1. **Humber** river flowing through Hull, Marvell's home town.
2. **conversion of the Jews** according to Christian tradition, the Jews were to be converted immediately before the Last Judgment.
3. **state** dignity.

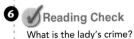

Reading Check

What is the lady's crime?

---

❹ Literary Analysis
Carpe Diem Theme

- Remind students that *carpe diem*—Latin for "seize the day"—permeates world literature and has come to mean "time is fleeting, so enjoy life."
- Read aloud the first two lines. **Ask** students how these lines express the theme of *carpe diem*. **Answer:** The speaker urges the lady to enjoy love now, while they are still in their youthful prime.

❺ Reading Strategy
Inferring the Speaker's Attitude

- Have students read the poem. Then, **ask** what the speaker's feelings for the woman are. **Answer:** Students may say that the fierce images suggest both passion and playfulness.
- **Ask** the students what the speaker's frame of mind is. **Answer:** The speaker seems impatient and persistent.

❻ Reading Check

Answer: From the point of view of the speaker, her crime consists of forestalling his amorous advances.

Differentiated Instruction   Solutions for All Learners

Strategy for Less Proficient Readers
Have students recast Suckling's "Song" as an advice column answer. Ask them to respond to this situation: "I like a girl, but she doesn't seem to know I exist. What should I do?"

Enrichment for Gifted/Talented Students
Have students set Herrick's "To the Virgins, to Make Much of Time" to music, either by finding an existing melody or by writing their own. Encourage them to prepare for a classroom performance of the song.

Strategy for Advanced Readers
Ask students to compare and contrast "Song" with "To His Coy Mistress." Have them cite specific examples from the poems, discussing theme, rhythm, imagery, and speakers' attitudes in a comparison-and-contrast essay.

Carpe Diem Theme

- Call students' attention to the last six lines of the poem. Ask them to rephrase them in their own words.

- Then, **ask** them the Literary Analysis question: What new twist does the speaker apply in order to "solve" the problem of fleeting time?

  Answer: Since the sun (time) cannot be stopped, the speaker proposes to tear through life at such a pace as to force the sun to keep up.

ASSESS

Answers

1. **Possible responses:** Students may say they would advise him to cool down because his passion is clearly intense and the woman may not be interested.

2. (a) The speaker would love his mistress ten years before the flood; his mistress should, if she pleased, refuse till the conversion of the Jews; the speaker would praise his mistress's eyes and gaze at her forehead for a hundred years. (b) These things go very slowly, an appropriate pace if only there were "world enough, and time."

3. (a) Students may infer that the speaker feels his mistress is worth the wait. (b) This willingness shows the sincerity of his feelings for his mistress.

4. (a) The speaker foresees death and an end to loving. (b) The images in the first part of the poem disintegrate.

5. The speaker saves urgent requests for the end in order to close the poem emphatically.

6. (a) In the beginning, the lovers have an eternity. In the middle, time is presented as being limited. In the end, the speaker proposes to outrace time itself. (b) Students may respond that Marvell's awareness of fleeting time and human mortality is realistic; his hope that love might make the sun "run" may seem idealistic.

Go Online
Author Link   For additional information about Andrew Marvell, have students type in the Web Code, then select M from the alphabet, and then select the author's name.

462

My echoing songs; then worms shall try
That long-preserved virginity,
And your quaint honor turn to dust,
30 And into ashes all my lust:
The grave's a fine and private place,
But none I think do there embrace.
        Now therefore, while the youthful hue
Sits on thy skin like morning dew,
35 And while thy willing soul transpires[4]
At every pore with instant fires,
Now let us sport us while we may,
And now, like <u>amorous</u> birds of prey,
Rather at once our time devour
40 Than <u>languish</u> in his slow-chapped[5] power.
Let us roll all our strength, and all
Our sweetness, up into one ball,
And tear our pleasures with rough strife
Thorough[6] the iron gates of life:
45 Thus, though we cannot make our sun
Stand still, yet we will make him run.

4. **transpires** breathes out.
5. **slow-chapped** slow-jawed.
6. **thorough** through.

Critical Reading

1. **Respond:** If you were the lady, how would you respond to the speaker? Why?

2. **(a) Recall:** Name three things the speaker and his mistress would do and the time each would take if time were not an issue. **(b) Connect:** How do these images relate to the charge the speaker makes against his lady in lines 1–2?

3. **(a) Infer:** Why would the speaker be willing to spend so much time waiting for his mistress? **(b) Interpret:** How does this willingness take the sting out of his complaint?

4. **(a) Analyze:** What future does the speaker foresee for himself and his love in lines 25–30? **(b) Connect:** How do the images in lines 21–30 answer the images in the first part of the poem?

5. **Draw Conclusions:** Why does the speaker save the urgent requests in lines 33–46 for the end?

6. **(a) Compare and Contrast:** Compare the attitudes toward time at the beginning, middle, and end. **(b) Evaluate:** Is Marvell's idea of love realistic or idealistic? Explain.

Vocabulary Builder
amorous (am′ ə rəs) *adj.* full of love or desire

languish (laŋ′ gwish) *v.* to become weak; droop

Literary Analysis
Carpe Diem Theme What new twist does the speaker apply in order to "solve" the problem of fleeting time?

Go Online
Author Link
For: More about Andrew Marvell
Visit: www.PHSchool.com
Web Code: ese-9304

Enrichment

The *Carpe Diem* Theme

The *carpe diem* theme is not confined to seventeenth-century England. It can be found among the writings of different cultures and different times. For example, in 2400 B.C., the Egyptian Ptahhotep wrote, "The wasting of time is an abomination to the spirit." The Persian poet Omar Khayyam noted the passage of time in *The Rubáiyát*. There, he wrote, "The Moving Finger Writes; and having writ, / Moves on."

Invite students to explore the concept in other cultures. Encourage students to look for quotations about time or attitudes about it, which might be expressed in a culture's literature, religion, or philosophy.

❽ *To the Virgins, to Make Much of Time*

Robert Herrick

❾

Gather ye rosebuds while ye may,
    Old time is still a-flying;
And this same flower that smiles today
    Tomorrow will be dying.

5 The glorious lamp of heaven, the sun,
    The higher he's a-getting,
The sooner will his race be run,
    And nearer he's to setting.

That age is best which is the first,
10   When youth and blood are warmer;
But being spent, the worse, and worst
    Times still succeed the former.

Then be not coy, but use your time,
    And, while ye may, go marry;
15 For, having lost but once your <u>prime</u>,
    You may forever tarry.[1]

---

1. tarry (tar′ ē) *v.* delay.

Critical Reading

1. **Respond:** How did you respond to Herrick's images?
2. **(a) Recall:** What advice does the speaker give women in lines 1–4?
   (b) Interpret: What does the advice mean? **(c) Analyze:** How do the images he uses convey the idea of passing time?
3. **(a) Interpret:** What does the poem suggest about passing time?
   (b) Connect: How does the last stanza answer these concerns?
4. **Hypothesize:** What response could an opponent offer Herrick?

To the Virgins, to Make Much of Time ■ 463

Literary Analysis
Carpe Diem **Theme**
Which images in lines 5–8 capture the *carpe diem* theme?

Vocabulary Builder
prime (prīm) *n.* best stage of a thing or process

Go Online
Author Link
For: More about Robert Herrick
Visit: www.PHSchool.com
Web Code: ese-9305

Go Online
Author Link For additional information about Robert Herrick, have students type in the Web Code, then select H from the alphabet, and then select the author's name.

463

About the Selection

Although his poem is about love, Suckling takes a humorous, mocking tone that may draw attention away from the poem's careful construction.

⓫ **Humanities**

Young Man Writing, by Joos van Craesbeeck

Flemish artist Joos van Craesbeeck probably met his future teacher—painter Adriaen Brouwer—in an Antwerp prison. Brouwer was imprisoned for tax debts around 1633, at which time Craesbeeck was working as a prison baker. Craesbeeck often painted peasants and tavern scenes but later moved on to depict the middle classes. Use the following question for discussion:

• How does the young man's expression compare or contrast with the speaker's attitude in the poem?
Possible response: The young man in the painting seems serious and thoughtful, like the speaker in the beginning of the poem. The speaker later becomes sharp and impatient, which does not seem to be reflected in the young man's expression.

⓬ **Critical Viewing**

Answer: The speaker tells of a young lover who tries to move his lost love by speaking well of her and making her love him. This young lover may be writing poems to her or sketching her image.

⓫

⓬ ▲ **Critical Viewing** Consider the speaker's words in "Song." What might the young lover pictured here be writing? Explain. **[Speculate]**

⑩ Song

Sir John Suckling

Why so pale and <u>wan</u>, fond lover?
    Prithee, why so pale?
Will, when looking well can't move her,
    Looking ill prevail?
5   Prithee, why so pale?

Why so dull and mute, young sinner?
    Prithee, why so mute?
Will, when speaking well can't win her,
    Saying nothing do't?
10   Prithee, why so mute?

Quit, quit, for shame; this will not move,
    This cannot take her.
If of herself she will not love,
    Nothing can make her:
15   The devil take her!

⑬

Vocabulary Builder

wan (wän) *adj.* sickly pale; faint or weak

Reading Strategy

Inferring the Speaker's Attitude What is the difference between the speaker's attitude toward his listener in lines 6–10 and his attitude in lines 11–15?

Critical Reading

1. **Respond:** Do you think "Song" would make a good popular song? Why?

2. **(a) Recall:** How does the young lover look and act according to the first ten lines of "Song"? **(b) Analyze:** Explain why the speaker treats the friend's behavior as if it were an attempt to achieve a goal.

3. **(a) Interpret:** In the final stanza, what helpful shift in perspective does the speaker encourage? **(b) Draw Conclusions:** What attitude toward love does the last stanza reflect?

4. **(a) Analyze:** What features of the poem make it suitable as song lyrics? **(b) Hypothesize:** Which would be a good audience for such a song: uneducated farmers, young aristocrats, or both? Explain, using details from the poem.

5. **Apply:** How effective would Suckling's advice be for a modern lover? Explain.

Go Online **Author Link**

For: More about Sir John Suckling
Visit: www.PHSchool.com
Web Code: ese-9306

Song ■ *465*

Answers

1. **(a)** Lines 33–46 most clearly state the *carpe diem* theme. **(b)** In lines 21–32, the speaker reminds the coy mistress that they are mortals with limited time. **(c)** Marvell's images of fragile beauty and grim death reinforce the urgency of seizing the moment.

2. **(a)** Herrick relates images from nature to human life: rosebuds, which "tomorrow will be dying" and the sun, racing to set. **(b)** The implication adds authority to his advice by providing evidence from nature.

3. The speaker in "Song" advises his listener to move on and not waste time on someone who doesn't care.

4. Students may say that "To the Virgins, to Make Much of Time" is more persuasive because it is simpler and more direct in its argument.

5. **To His Coy Mistress:** *Carpe Diem* Image: Time's winged chariot; Qualities: Fanciful; Statement of Plea: Let us sport us while we may; Passionate; **To the Virgins:** *Carpe Diem* Image: Old time is flying; Qualities: Simple; Statement of Plea: Gather rosebuds; Reasonable; **Song:** *Carpe Diem* Image: Pale, mute lover; Qualities: Simple; Statement of Plea: Quit; Reasonable.

   Another sample answer can be found on **Literary Analysis Graphic Organizer B**, p. 86 in *Graphic Organizer Transparencies*.

6. **(a)** Students may respond that there is a gentle mockery in the speaker's description of an eternal courtship. **(b)** In lines 21–32 the speaker shifts from the hypothetical to grimly real by offering graphic images of their human mortality.

7. **(a)** The speaker moves from a questioning mode to an impatiently demanding mode in the last stanza. **(b)** In "Song," the speaker's attitude toward love is practical, while in "To the Virgins," the speaker's attitude is benevolent and warm.

8. All three poets lived through the Puritan revolution and its aftermath; sudden change and loss are consistent with the "seize the day" theme of the poems.

Apply the Skills

To His Coy Mistress • To the Virgins, to Make Much of Time • Song

Literary Analysis

Carpe Diem Theme

1. **(a)** Identify the part of "To His Coy Mistress" that most clearly states the *carpe diem* theme. **(b)** Contrast the images in these lines with the conventional images of time and death in lines 21–32. **(c)** How does Marvell's *carpe diem* imagery add power to his plea?

2. **(a)** Explain how Herrick's images imply that the course of human life—including marriage—is part of the natural order. **(b)** Does this implication add authority to his advice? Explain.

3. In what sense does the speaker in Suckling's "Song" advise his listener to "seize the day"?

Comparing Literary Works

4. Of "To His Coy Mistress" and "To the Virgins," which do you find expresses the *carpe diem* message most persuasively? Why?

5. Contrast the treatment of the theme in the three poems, using a chart like the following.

Carpe Diem Images	Qualities: Fanciful? Simple?	Statement of Plea	Humorous? Passionate? Reasonable?

Reading Strategy

Inferring the Speaker's Attitude

6. **(a)** Judging from the exaggerated images he uses, **infer the speaker's attitude** toward his beloved in lines 1–20 of "To His Coy Mistress." **(b)** How does the speaker's attitude shift in lines 21–32?

7. **(a)** Explain where and in what way the speaker's attitude in Suckling's "Song" undergoes a change. **(b)** Compare his attitude toward love with the speaker's attitude in "To the Virgins."

Extend Understanding

8. **World Events Connection:** Review the biographies of these authors (p. 458), and explain how the message of these poems is suited to the turbulent times in which they were written.

QuickReview

The theme of *carpe diem*, or "seize the day," appears when a work warns that time is fleeting, so people should enjoy or make the most of life while they can.

The **speaker** of a poem is the character or imaginary voice in which a poet presents the poem. To **infer the speaker's attitude**, you must examine the connotations (associations) of the words and images the speaker uses.

Go Online
—Assessment

For: Self-test
Visit: www.PHSchool.com
Web Code: esa-6304

Go Online
—Assessment
Students may use the **Self-test** to prepare for **Selection Test A** or **Selection Test B**.

Build Language Skills

Vocabulary Lesson

Word Analysis: Related Forms of *prime*

When Herrick refers to a person's "prime," he means both the first part of adulthood and the best years of a person's life. *Prime* comes from a Latin word meaning "first in importance" or "first in time." Using this information, define the italicized forms of the word *prime* below.

1. The party will hold a *primary*.
2. What is his *primary* reason for going to college?
3. Who is the *prime minister* of Great Britain?
4. Every television actor wants a *prime-time* show.
5. This *primer* will help you start learning computer programming.
6. Babbage's difference engine was a *primitive* form of computer.
7. These trees are survivors of the *primeval* forest once covering the land.

Vocabulary Builder: Apply Word Meaning

Identify each statement as true or false.

1. Flushed with rage, his cheeks were <u>wan</u>.
2. The <u>Prime</u> of Miss Jean Brodie is probably about a woman on her deathbed.
3. A plant without water may <u>languish</u>.
4. An <u>amorous</u> couple is affectionate.
5. <u>Coyness</u> indicates commitment.

Spelling Strategy

The letters *ui* can represent several different sounds: long *i* (*guide*), short *i* (*biscuit*), *oo* (*fruit*), or *wi* (*languish*). For each of the following, give a word spelled with *ui* that matches the definition.

1. a path that returns to its beginning (circ___)
2. a set of formal clothes (s___)
3. to tell apart (disting___)
4. to conceal the identity of (disg___)

Grammar and Style Lesson

Irregular Forms of Adjectives

Herrick's poem contains comparative and superlative forms of the adjectives *good* and *bad*. These forms are **irregular.** Instead of adding *-er* to *good* for the comparative form and *-est* for the superlative, the comparative and superlative forms of *good* and *bad* are as follows:

Regular: good, bad

Comparative: better, worse

Superlative: best, worst

Practice Identify the forms used to compare *good* and *bad* in the following lines. Label each form as comparative or superlative.

> That age is best which is the first,
> When youth and blood are warmer;
> But being spent, the worse, and worst
> Times still succeed the former.

Writing Application Write a paragraph comparing three different periods in your life. Use correct comparative and superlative forms of *good* and *bad* in your writing.

*W*G *Prentice Hall Writing and Grammar Connection: Chapter 24, Section 1*

To His Coy Mistress / To the Virgins, to Make Much of Time / Song ■ 467

❶ Vocabulary Lesson
Word Analysis

1. a preliminary election to nominate candidates for office
2. most important; principal
3. chief minister; premier
4. relating to evening hours with the greatest numbers of television viewers
5. beginner's book
6. first of the kind
7. ancient; having to do with the earliest times

Vocabulary Builder

1. false	4. true
2. false	5. false
3. true	

Spelling Strategy

1. circuit	3. distinguish
2. suit	4. disguise

❷ Grammar and Style Lesson

best; superlative

worse; comparative

worst; superlative

Writing Application
Sample sentences:

When I was four years old, I felt that my oldest sister was worse than my other siblings. Now, older and hopefully wiser, I realize that she was the best sister a girl could ever have had.

*W*G **Writing and Grammar, Diamond Level**

Students will find further instruction and practice on irregular forms of adjectives in Chapter 24, Section 1.

Assessment Practice

Writer's Point of View (For more practice, see *Standardized Test Preparation Workbook,* p. 19.)

Many tests require students to identify the writer's point of view. Use the following sample item to show students that a writer's opinion is often revealed through diction.

> Had we but world enough, and time,
> This coyness lady were no crime...
>
> But at my back I always hear
> Time's wingèd chariot hurrying near...
> The grave's a fine and private place,
> But none I think do there embrace.

The speaker views his lady's hesitation as—

A ignorant but harmless
B inappropriate but excusable
C foolish but charming
D spiteful but virtuous

Marvell exaggerates when he uses the word *crime* to describe his lady's coyness, and he ironically calls the grave a "fine and private place." By keeping in mind Marvell's playful diction, students should determine that *C* is the best answer.

❸ Writing Lesson

You may use this Writing Lesson as timed-writing practice, or you may allow students to develop the essay as a writing assignment over several days.

- To guide students in writing this poem, give them the **Support for Writing Lesson** page (*Unit 3 Resources,* p. 49).

- Tell the students to create a persuasive tone by doing the following: sounding confident about their arguments; using words that create a sense of urgency; and choosing details that will capture the imagination of their audience.

- Ask student volunteers to read their final versions to the class.

❹ Listening and Speaking

- Have students work with partners.

- Tell each pair of students to determine roles and to follow the numbered steps to organize their tasks.

- Follow up with a discussion in which each pair discusses the material they performed. The other pairs should ask questions and respond to the descriptions.

- The **Support for Extend Your Learning** page (*Unit 3 Resources,* p. 50) provides guided note-taking opportunities to help students complete the Extend Your Learning activities.

Go Online
Research
Have students type in the Web Code for another research activity.

---

❸ Writing Lesson

Witty Poem

The speakers in these poems spin clever arguments and witty phrases to persuade their listeners to "seize the day." Write a poem in which you use humor and wordplay to win an argument.

Prewriting   Identify the speaker of your poem, the speaker's purpose, and the audience. Decide on the type of humor and argument that will work with this audience.

Drafting   To give your poem a persuasive tone, be confident in your argument. Use fresh, natural, vivid words and images, and build a sense of urgency by issuing playful commands to your audience. Include puns or other forms of wordplay.

Revising   Review your draft, bracketing "dead spots"—phrases or ideas that lack urgency or vividness or that are too familiar to sound fresh. Revise these sections to give them the punchy, persuasive tone you need.

> **Model: Revising to Achieve a Persuasive Tone**
>
> I can't believe you're
> [You spend your time just] sitting there, E-mailing your
>   he-male's
> life away. / Come on and take your boyfriend's dare. [Let's
> *Get up! Let's go! It's May!*
> have some fun] this May.

The new wording of the first and last lines has a much more urgent tone than the wording in the first draft. The wordplay "he-male" should win a smile from the listener.

WG *Prentice Hall Writing and Grammar Connection: Chapter 6, Connected Assignment*

Extend Your Learning

❹ **Listening and Speaking** With a partner, present a **phone skit** based on "Song."

1. Choose roles: a lovelorn friend or an exasperated giver of advice.
2. "Translate" the poem into advice you might give a lovelorn friend today. Then, work out the friend's reply to each stanza.
3. Rehearse your role play by sitting back to back and speaking into phones.

Perform your skit for your class. **[Group Activity]**

Research and Technology The lives of each of these poets was affected by the English Civil War. Do research on their lives and on the war. Write a **comparative biographical essay** comparing the impact of the war on each of their lives. Incorporate timelines and other graphics to illustrate your comparisons.

Go Online
Research
For: An additional research activity
Visit: www.PHSchool.com
Web Code: esd-7303

Assessment Resources

The following resources can be used to assess students' knowledge and skills.

Unit 3 Resources
   Selection Test A, pp. 52–54
   Selection Test B, pp. 55–57

General Resources
   Rubrics for Rhyming Poem, pp. 73–74

Go Online
Assessment
Students may use the **Self-test** to prepare for **Selection Test A** or **Selection Test B**.

A Nation Divided

Selection Planning Guide

The selections in this section highlight the conflicts that existed in seventeenth-century England. "Sonnet VII" and "Sonnet XIX" deal with problems of a personal nature, whereas the excerpt from *Paradise Lost* deals with the epic conflict between God and Satan. The excerpt from *Eve's Apology in Defense of Women* addresses the long-standing conflict between men and women. "To Lucasta, on Going to the Wars" touches on both the battle for control of England and the conflict between a soldier and a woman who doesn't want him to leave. "To Althea, from Prison" reflects the conflict between Cavaliers and Puritans.

Humanities

Whitehall, January 30, 1649
(Execution of Charles I)

by Ernest Crofts

This painting depicts the moment before King Charles was beheaded for treason in 1649. The execution took place outside the banqueting hall at Whitehall. The king, standing at the far left of the scaffold, faced his death bravely, insisting that he was a "martyr for the people."

  Ask students the following question:

• Why do you think the artist has chosen to present a "long shot" that includes the crowd, rather than a close-up of the king?
  Answer: The artist seems to want to focus on the historic, rather than the personal, aspects of the execution, thereby suggesting the event's significance for the nation.

Differentiated
Instruction   Solutions for All Learners

Accessibility at a Glance

More Accessible	Average	More Challenging
To Lucasta, on Going to the Wars	*from* Eve's Apology in Defense of Women	Sonnet VII
	To Althea, from Prison	Sonnet XIX
		from Paradise Lost

Students will

1. understand some of Milton's motivations for writing *Paradise Lost*.

2. discuss how literature helps people better understand and heal from a historical crisis.

Background
The English Civil War

• Explain to students that John Milton's poetic concerns were shaped in part by the English Civil War (1642–1649). The king of England at the time, Charles I, relied on royal privilege rather than diplomacy, ruling for eleven years without calling Parliament into session once. His wars with Spain and France, however, had drained his resources. Charles called a Parliament to ask for funds, but the body refused to grant his request unless he gave over some of his power. Charles refused, and in 1642 the English Parliament declared war on its own king.

• Note that the Civil War was not simply a quarrel between Parliament and king. Widespread radical religious ideas such as Puritanism invited individuals to see their own conscience, not the king's church, as the ultimate religious authority.

Use the following question for discussion:

Why might the Civil War have left a symbolic void in English culture?

Possible response: A reigning king or queen embodies the rightful authority in the society. Without a king or queen, the nation had no visible figure toward which it could express its allegiance to the social order.

Critical Viewing

Possible response: Adam appears distraught; Eve's clenched hands suggest worry.

Making "Darkness Visible": Milton's Epic Ambition

People tell stories for different reasons. Some tell stories to keep their hopes up. Some tell stories to mark what they have left behind. In the 1650s, the aged John Milton decided to retell the Biblical story of the creation, fall, and redemption of humanity in two epics, *Paradise Lost* and *Paradise Regained*. With these works, Milton reaffirmed Britain's core values after a decade of war.

Storytelling and Adversity Milton had compelling reasons for telling this story. By 1652, Milton was completely blind. Unable to write, he dictated the poem to his daughters, who copied down each word. As he worked, the world crumbled around him. The monarchy he had opposed was restored to England, and he went to jail for a time. Blind, disgraced, and disillusioned, Milton nevertheless persevered. Over perhaps ten years, he dictated nearly 11,000 lines of poetry. The result, critics agree, is the greatest epic in the English language, *Paradise Lost*.

An Overview Like many epics, *Paradise Lost* begins in the middle. Milton introduces Satan who, with his angel allies, has done the unthinkable— rebelled against God. Expelled from Heaven, they have plummeted into Hell, a place devoid of light, life, and even form: "one great furnace flamed, yet from those flames / No light, but rather darkness visible / Served only to discern sights of woe."

▼ **Critical Viewing**
What feeling does this portrayal of Adam and Eve convey? **[Interpret]**

> " *Milton's* Paradise Lost *fed imaginations of generations to come.* "

Satan's war with Heaven is Milton's invention. The remainder of the story is the familiar one of Christian tradition. God has forbidden Adam and Eve to eat of the fruit of the Tree of the Knowledge of Good and Evil. Bent on revenge, Satan tempts Eve into eating of the apple. She then persuades Adam to partake. This event, the Fall of Adam and Eve, leads to their (and so humanity's) expulsion from the Garden of Eden. They leave Paradise with a sense of hope: "The World was all before them, where to choose / Their place of rest, and Providence their guide. . . ."

A Cosmic Commentary Apart from telling this grand story, large portions of *Paradise Lost* are dedicated to another grand project—"justifying the ways of God to man." In the story, God sends the angel Raphael to Paradise to warn Adam of the necessity of obedience. In their conversation, Milton is able to speak on a few issues that were controversial in his day.

• **Reason and Free Will** Humanity can see the difference between right and wrong. With that ability comes the freedom to choose between the two.

Enrichment

The Reformation

In the 1500s, the traditional authority of the Catholic Church in Europe was extensively challenged. In Germany, Martin Luther (1483–1546) interpreted scripture to show that the faith of the individual, not his or her fulfillment of Church practices, was the source of salvation. In Switzerland, John Calvin (1509–1564) argued that salvation was predestined by God for his elect. Europe was plunged into turmoil as sect after sect broke away from the Catholic Church.

In 1534, Henry VIII of England founded his own church, largely for political reasons. The Puritans of Milton's day, influenced by Calvin and others, challenged corruption in Henry's church and sought to restore authority to the individual's conscience.

- **Free Will and Predestination** God knows everything that is, was, and will be. Yet God's foreknowledge does not mean that people's choices are determined in advance by God. People have free will.

By affirming free will, Milton broke with some of the sternest Puritans of his day, who held that men and women were predestined to salvation or damnation. Milton's epic story finds individuals responsible for their own actions and fate and so grants them dignity.

Words in the Void In a sense, *Paradise Lost* is Milton's answer to the great historical crisis through which Britain had just passed. Puritans, including Milton, had challenged the official Church of England. They demanded a return to what they saw as the original principles of the Christian religion. At the same time, religious controversy led to the Civil War (1642–1649) in which Parliament eventually put its own king, Charles I, to death.

These upheavals shattered the symbolic centers of English life and culture, Church and King. With *Paradise Lost,* Milton helped the nation find its bearings again by retelling the central story of its culture. In the figure of Satan, he commemorated the destructive forces that had recently torn through the nation. At the same time, the fall of Satan symbolically puts rebellious urges into their proper place—the netherworld of Hell. It was these tasks, perhaps, that drove the blind Milton to rise above adversity and deliver this epic to his country.

Milton's Legacy Over the centuries Milton's story of the Fall has become as well known as the biblical version. It has influenced writers as diverse as the poets William Blake, the visionary, and John Keats, the introspective dreamer, as well as the novelist George Eliot, a formidable social critic. By the nineteenth century, study of Milton's epic was considered an essential part of a respectable education, and even relatively uneducated people could be expected to have two books in their homes—the King James Bible and *Paradise Lost.* In telling a story to heal his own time, Milton fed the imaginations of generations to come.

Activity

The Healing Power of Literature

Since the time of Milton, many writers have attempted to heal the wounds of collective trauma through works of literature.

With a group, discuss your thoughts about the ways in which literature can bring understanding or closure to people after a period of historical crisis. Use these questions to guide your discussion:

- What examples can you cite where literature, including drama, deals with a real historical crisis?
- Do you think such literature can have meaning for people who have not lived through the crisis in question? If so, how?

Choose a point person to share your ideas with the class.

Making "Darkness Visible": Milton's Epic Ambition ■ 471

Much of Milton's preparation for a life of letters involved the study of Latin. He wrote much of his poetry in Latin. It is not surprising to discover, then, that even in English, his syntax (sentence structure) borrows something from Latin. Because the person, case, and number of words are clearly marked in the language, word order is much freer than in English. The reader will know which adjective belongs with which noun because of their endings. Milton's syntax is Latinate, in that he allows himself greater freedom in word placement than is usual in English. Milton's syntax contributes to the majesty of the poetry, giving it a weight that might remind one of scripture.

Critical Thinking

1. What parallels exist between Satan's fall and the Civil War?
   Possible responses: Like Satan, the English had rebelled against their traditional ruler; like Satan, the English king had demonstrated excessive pride.

2. In what way does the idea in *Paradise Lost* of humanity's fate differ from Puritanism?
   Possible response: Milton emphasizes the dignity and loneliness of human freedom, rejecting ideas of predestination.

3. In what sense does *Paradise Lost* symbolically restore unity to English culture?
   Possible response: The epic retells a story central to English culture and so affirms the nation's common values.

Activity

Organize students in small groups for discussion. Suggest that each group discuss the books, movies, plays, and songs related to a different national or global crisis, such as the Vietnam War, Watergate, the September 11 attacks, or the war in Iraq. Use the groups' reports to stimulate whole-class discussion.

Differentiated Instruction   Solutions for All Learners

Strategy for Less Proficient Readers
Have students read Making "Darkness Visible." As they read the excerpt from *Paradise Lost*, have them identify instances of Milton's difficult and distinctive language. In a group discussion, have students share passages and discuss why Milton's language is suited to retelling a story so central to Milton's culture.

Strategy for Gifted/Talented Students
Have students read Making "Darkness Visible." As they read the excerpt from *Paradise Lost*, have them identify descriptions that create a sense of grand scale. Have students illustrate these passages, and then hold a class discussion reviewing illustrations and exploring how these scenes reflect Milton's ambitions.

Strategy for Advanced Readers
Have students read Making "Darkness Visible." As they read the excerpt from *Paradise Lost*, have them analyze the character of Satan. Hold a discussion in which they evaluate whether the characterization is equal to Milton's poetic ambitions.

TIME AND RESOURCE MANAGER

Meeting Your Standards

Students will

1. **analyze and respond to literary elements**
   - Literary Analysis: The Italian Sonnet; Epic Poetry

2. **read, comprehend, analyze, and critique a poem**
   - Reading Strategy: Breaking Down Sentences
   - Reading Check questions
   - Apply the Skills questions
   - Assessment Practice (ATE)

3. **develop vocabulary**
   - Vocabulary Lesson: Latin Word Root: -*lum*-

4. **understand and apply written and oral language conventions**
   - Spelling Strategy
   - Grammar and Style Lesson: Usage: *Who* and *Whom*

5. **develop writing proficiency**
   - Writing Lesson: Critical Analysis

6. **develop appropriate research strategies**
   - Extend Your Learning: Documentary

7. **understand and apply listening and speaking strategies**
   - Extend Your Learning: Speech

Block Scheduling: Use one 90-minute class period to preteach the skills and have students read the selection. Use a second 90-minute class period to assess students' mastery of skills, extend their learning, and monitor their progress.

Homework Suggestions

Following are possibilities for homework assignments:

- Support pages from *Unit 3 Resources:*
  Literary Analysis
  Reading Strategy
  Vocabulary Builder
  Grammar and Style

- An Extend Your Learning project and the Writing Lesson for this selection group may be completed over several days.

Step-by-Step Teaching Guide	Pacing Guide
PRETEACH	
• Administer Vocabulary and Reading Warm-ups as necessary.	5 min.
• Engage students' interest with the motivation activity.	5 min.
• Read and discuss author and background features. **FT**	10 min.
• Introduce the Literary Analysis skill: The Italian Sonnet; Epic Poetry. **FT**	5 min.
• Introduce the Reading Strategy: Breaking Down Sentences. **FT**	10 min.
• Prepare students to read by teaching the selection vocabulary. **FT**	
TEACH	
• Informally monitor comprehension while students read independently or in groups. **FT**	30 min.
• Monitor students' comprehension with the Reading Check notes.	as students read
• Reinforce vocabulary with Vocabulary Builder notes.	as students read
• Develop students' understanding of the Italian sonnet and epic poetry with the Literary Analysis annotations. **FT**	5 min.
• Develop students' ability to break down sentences with the Reading Strategy annotations. **FT**	5 min.
ASSESS/EXTEND	
• Assess students' comprehension and mastery of the Literary Analysis and Reading Strategy by having them answer the Apply the Skills questions. **FT**	15 min.
• Have students complete the Vocabulary Development Lesson and the Grammar and Style Lesson. **FT**	15 min.
• Apply students' knowledge of using a thought shot to elaborate by using the Writing Lesson. **FT**	45 min. or homework
• Apply students' understanding by using one or both of the Extend Your Learning activities.	20–90 min. or homework
• Administer Selection Test A or Selection Test B. **FT**	15 min.

Resources

Choosing Resources for Differentiated Instruction

[**L1**] Special Needs Students

[**L2**] Below-Level Students

[**L3**] All Students

[**L4**] Advanced Students

[**EL**] English Learners

For Vocabulary and Reading Warm-ups and for Selection Tests, **A** signifies "less challenging" and **B** "more challenging." For Graphic Organizer transparencies, **A** signifies "not filled in" and **B** "filled in."

FT Fast Track Instruction: To move the lesson more quickly, use the strategies and activities identified with **FT**.

Scaffolding for Less Proficient and Advanced Students

The leveled Critical Thinking questions after selections progress in the levels of thinking required to answer them. To address the needs of your different students, you may use the (a) level questions for your less proficient students and the (b) level questions with your on-level and advanced students. The occasional (c) level questions are appropriate for your advanced students.

Use this complete suite of powerful teaching tools to make lesson planning and testing quicker and easier.

Use the interactive textbook (online and on CD-ROM) to make selections and activities come alive with audio and video support and interactive questions.

 For: Information about Lexiles
Visit: www.PHSchool.com
Web Code: eue-1111

Motivation

Ask students to consider this question: In a hundred years, what would you like to be remembered for?

Invite answers and encourage discussion. Then point out that many people have a desire to leave a mark on the world. John Milton was no exception. Near the end of his life, poor, blind, and politically out of favor, he retired from public view to write, hoping, he said, to "leave something to aftertimes as they should not willingly let die." The result was *Paradise Lost,* which many critics have called the greatest epic ever written in English.

❶ Background
More About the Author

Paradise Lost was written as the dust was settling after years of war and turmoil. From 1642–1660, England went from being a monarchy (Charles I) to a commonwealth (Oliver Cromwell) to a protectorate (Lord Protector Cromwell) to a restored monarchy (Charles II). No matter which side of the civil war you were on or how you regarded Cromwell and his politics, at some point during this two-decade period, you experienced both defeat and triumph.

Perhaps Milton wrote *Paradise Lost* because he sensed that the nation needed an anchor, a work of literature that would once again help define and unite a culture. In his epic, Milton seems to have the nation's strife in mind as he offers a poetic explanation for God's allowing suffering and unhappiness in the world. He also seems to have recent conflicts in mind when he describes the fierce open "civil war" in heaven between God and Lucifer.

Build Skills | Poems

❶ Poetry of John Milton

John Milton
(1608–1674)

John Milton is regarded as one of the greatest poets of the English language, yet he owes this regard to comparatively few poems. Much of his work is in Latin, not English, and during the fifteen years he spent writing political pamphlets and other prose works, he wrote little poetry. Although other poets have surpassed him in quantity, Milton's masterpiece, the epic *Paradise Lost,* is enough to establish him as the equal of Chaucer and Shakespeare. Milton himself never lacked self-confidence, setting his sights on poetic greatness at the start of his career.

A Privileged Childhood Milton was born in London to a middle-class family and grew up in a highly cultured environment. His father, a professional scribe who drew up contracts and lent money, was also a composer and musician of considerable ability. Deeply religious, Milton's father was devoted to the Protestant cause. At the age of thirteen, Milton started his formal education, the equivalent of high school. He was also tutored at home. He mastered Greek, Latin, and Hebrew, as well as several modern European languages. After this thorough education, Milton went on to college.

God's Poet When Milton entered Christ's College at Cambridge University, he had already decided to prepare himself for a career as a great poet ("God's poet" was how he described himself). It appears that for a time he also considered entering the ministry. The religious and political situation at the time, though, was quite uncertain, so Milton devoted himself to a life of study. After earning his degrees from Cambridge, he withdrew to his father's house, first at Hammersmith, then at Horton in Buckinghamshire, for nearly six years, where, it is said, he read everything that was written in the ancient and modern languages at his command. It was during this long period of study that he wrote one of his best-known poems, "Lycidas." That work, together with the poems "L'Allegro" and "Il Penseroso," written during his student days, marked the young Milton as a gifted poet destined for fame.

A Man of Ideals Following his studies, Milton went to continental Europe for a planned two-year Grand Tour, during which he called on the astronomer Galileo (1564–1642). While he was away, Parliament rebelled against King Charles I, eventually replacing the monarchy with a government led by Oliver Cromwell. Learning of the revolt, Milton cut short his trip and returned to England. He began writing pamphlets for the Puritan cause, criticizing the control of the bishops over the English church.

Public Service, Private Loss In 1649, when the Puritans decided to execute Charles I, Milton wrote a treatise defending this act. Impressed by Milton's brilliantly presented opinions, Cromwell made him Secretary of State for Foreign Tongues. This position required Milton to translate official documents into Latin and to write in defense of the new government against Royalist attacks. It was while serving in this position that he lost his eyesight.

In 1660, Milton's fortunes took a turn for the worse. The monarchy was restored, and Milton was imprisoned for a time. (His friend, the poet Andrew Marvell, may have been instrumental in gaining his release.) Blind and stripped of most of his property, Milton withdrew once again into words—he wrote *Paradise Lost* (1667), the greatest epic of the English language.

Preview

Connecting to the Literature

At the pauses in life, you may ask, How far have I come? How far yet to go? In these poems, the speaker pauses to reflect on his journey.

Literary Analysis

The Italian Sonnet; Epic Poetry

An **Italian,** or **Petrarchan, sonnet** is a fourteen-line lyric poem. The first eight lines, called the octave, rhyme *abbaabba* and present a problem. A six-line sestet with a variable rhyme scheme responds to the octave. Note how, in Milton's Italian sonnets, one part flows into the next.

An **epic** is a long narrative poem about a hero. For seventeenth-century English writers, ancient epic poets such as Homer—the blind, half-mythical author of the *Iliad* and the *Odyssey*—set the standard for literary greatness. Notice how Milton uses the following features of Homeric epics in *Paradise Lost:*

- A story that begins in the middle of the action (*in medias res*)
- An opening invocation in which the poet calls for divine aid in telling his story
- Extended similes, comparisions using *like* or *as*

Comparing Literary Works

Writing an epic is an ambitious task—the writer of a successful epic is the spokesperson for an entire culture. In his poems, Milton reflects on his own ambitions for poetic greatness, addressing his insecurities about them and the setbacks he faces. Compare the ways in which Milton addresses the theme of poetic ambition, both in reflections on his own life and in his character Satan's angry desires.

Reading Strategy

Breaking Down Sentences

Break down sentences into smaller elements to clarify the meaning. Identify main clauses, which can stand by themselves, and supporting clauses, which cannot. Use a chart like the one shown as you read.

Vocabulary Builder

semblance (sem′ bləns) *n.* appearance; image (p. 475)

illumine (i l\=oo′ mən) *v.* light up (p. 480)

transgress (trans gres′) *v.* violate a law or command (p. 480)

guile (gīl) *n.* artful trickery (p. 480)

obdurate (äb′ d\=oor it) *adj.* stubborn (p. 480)

tempestuous (tem pes′ ch\=oo əs) *adj.* turbulent; stormy (p. 481)

transcendent (tran sen′ dənt) *adj.* exceeding beyond all limits (p. 481)

suppliant (sup′ lē ənt) *adj.* imploring (p. 482)

ignominy (ig′ nə min′ ē) *n.* humiliation; dishonor (p. 482)

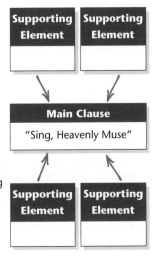

Poetry of John Milton ■ 473

❷ Literary Analysis
The Italian Sonnet; Epic Poetry

- Tell students that they will be reading examples of both Milton's Italian sonnets and his epic poetry. Then, explain the characteristics of each type of poetry as described in the feature.

- The Italian, or Petrarchan, sonnet is a fourteen-line lyric poem divided into an eight-line section, known as an octave, with a rhyming scheme of *abbaabba,* that presents a problem and a six-line sestet, with a variable rhyming scheme, that responds to the octave.

- An epic is a long narrative poem that tells the story of a hero and reflects the values of a culture. For seventeenth-century English writers, ancient Greek and Roman poets such as Homer set the standard for literary greatness.

- Explain to students that Milton was following Homer's epic style in his *Paradise Lost* when he began his epic in the middle of the action (*in medias res*) and used an opening invocation to the Muse calling for divine aid in the telling of his story.

❸ Reading Strategy
Breaking Down Sentences

- Explain the difference between main and supporting clauses. Main clauses are those that stand by themselves. Supporting clauses cannot stand by themselves.

- Tell the students that when they encounter complex sentences like those in *Paradise Lost,* they should break them down to find the main clause.

- Explain to the students how to identify the main clause using the chart on this page. Give them a copy of **Reading Strategy Graphic Organizer A,** p. 87 in *Graphic Organizer Transparencies.* Encourage them to use the chart as they read Milton's poems.

Vocabulary Builder

- Pronounce each vocabulary word for students and read the definitions as a class. Have students identify any words with which they are already familiar.

473

Visual/Spatial Learners Have students read lines 1–8 of Sonnet VII and identify phrases that create visual images. Such phrases "the subtle thief," "stolen on his wing," and "my late spring no bud or blossom showeth."

❶ About the Selection
Readers who know Milton as a literary giant may be surprised to discover that he was not always sure of himself, his abilities, or his future. While Milton expresses his faith in Sonnet VII, he also voices his dissatisfaction.

❷ Literary Analysis
The Italian Sonnet

• Review the definition of an Italian sonnet. The Italian sonnet is a fourteen-line lyric poem divided into an eight-line section and a six-line section. The eight-line section, known as an octave, follows the rhyme scheme *abbaabba*. It presents a problem that is answered in the six-line sestet, which has a variable rhyming scheme.

• Have the students read the octave. **Ask** them what problem it presents. **Answer:** Milton's concern is that at this stage in his life, he has not more worthy work to show.

• Have the students read the sestet, and remind them that the sestet offers a response to the octave. Then **ask** them what response is expressed in the sestet. **Answer:** His progress will be in accordance with the measure which God as the taskmaster deems appropriate.

❶ # Sonnet VII
("How soon hath Time")
John Milton

Background While sonnet writers of the Elizabethan Age, such as Spenser, Sidney, and Shakespeare, had mustered all the force of wit and words to chart the experiences of romantic love, Milton found other topics for his sonnets. The form proved strong enough to accommodate a variety of subjects, as Milton shows in these reflections on the limitations placed on human life.

474 ■ *A Turbulent Time (1625–1798)*

Differentiated Instruction Solutions for All Learners

Accessibility at a Glance

	Sonnet VII	Sonnet XIX	*from* Paradise Lost
Context	Italian sonnet	Italian sonnet	Epic poem
Language	Archaic language	Archaic language	Inverted syntax
Concept Level	Moderate (aging)	Challenging (blindness)	Challenging (the fall of man)
Literary Merit	Classic	Classic	Classic
Lexile	NP	NP	NP
Overall Rating	More challenging	More challenging	More challenging

How soon hath Time, the subtle thief of youth,
　　Stolen on his wing my three and twentieth year!
　　My hasting days fly on with full career,[1]
　　But my late spring no bud or blossom showeth.
5　Perhaps my <u>semblance</u> might deceive[2] the truth,
　　That I to manhood am arrived so near,
　　And inward ripeness doth much less appear,
　　That some more timely-happy spirits[3] endueth.[4]
　　Yet be it less or more, or soon or slow,
10　　It shall be still[5] in strictest measure even
　　To that same lot,[6] however mean or high,
　　Toward which Time leads me, and the will of Heaven;
　　All is, if I have grace to use it so,
　　As ever in my great Taskmaster's eye.

---

1. **career** speed.
2. **deceive** prove false.
3. **timely-happy spirits** others who seem to be more accomplished poets at the age of twenty-four.
4. **endueth** endows.
5. **still** always.
6. **lot** fate.

Vocabulary Builder
semblance (sem′ bləns) *n.*
appearance; image

Critical Reading

1. **Respond:** Do you usually judge people by how much they have accomplished by a certain age? Why or why not?

2. **(a) Recall:** What occasion leads Milton to the thoughts in the poem? **(b) Infer:** Judging from the image in lines 1–2, how does Milton view this occasion?

3. **(a) Recall:** To what season does Milton compare his time of life? **(b) Infer:** Why does he say that this season "no bud or blossom showeth"? **(c) Interpret:** What is his feeling about this situation?

4. **(a) Interpret:** What is the connection between the "bud or blossom" of line 4 and the "semblance" of line 5? **(b) Interpret:** How does the contrast between outward appearance and inward state in lines 5–8 apply to Milton's career as a poet?

5. **(a) Infer:** To what does Milton trust himself and his life in lines 9–14? **(b) Interpret:** In what way does this act of trust answer his worries in the first part of the poem? **(c) Evaluate:** Do you think this "answer" is a valid and effective response to concern about one's progress in life? Explain.

For: More about John Milton
Visit: www.PHSchool.com
Web Code: ese-9307

Sonnet VII ("How soon hath Time") ■ 475

❸ Reading Strategy
Breaking Down Sentences

- **Ask** students to identify the subject and verb in line 5.
  Answer: The subject is "my semblance." The verb is "might deceive."

- Next, **ask** them how the clause in line 6 connects to line 5.
  Answer: It specifies which truth is referred to in line 5.

- Then, **ask** them how line 7 connects with the rest of the sentence.
  Possible answer: Line 7 is an independent clause connected with the previous clause with the conjunction *and*.

- Next, **ask** them: With which part of the sentence does line 8 connect most closely?
  Answer: It modifies "inward ripeness" in line 7; it tells "which" or "what kind" of ripeness.

- Finally, **ask** them to paraphrase the meaning of lines 5–8.
  Possible answer: My appearance might give the false impression that I am not yet an adult, and my inward readiness for accomplishment appears to be much less than the readiness of people who achieve in a timely way.

ASSESS

Answers

1. Students should give reasons for their responses.

2. (a) He is reflecting upon his twenty-third birthday. (b) He is concerned that he has not accomplished more by this point.

3. (a) He compares it to late spring. (b) He is referring to the fact that he has not yet created a greater body of work. (c) Milton is concerned.

4. (a) Like a plant that has not budded or blossomed, Milton has yet to realize his potential. (b) He has yet to write great poems.

5. (a) He puts his trust in God. (b) His trust in God allays his worries that he is personally responsible for his lack of accomplishment. (c) Students may respond that this is a realistic solution.

Go Online
Author Link For additional information about John Milton, have students type in the Web Code, then select M from the alphabet, and then select the author's name.

About the Selection

In this poem, Milton muses on his blindness, which he thought that he had caused by his voracious reading. Although he bemoans his loss of sight, he recognizes that he has to accept it as God's will.

❺ **Humanities**

John Milton, 1878, by Mihaly von Munkacsy.

This oil painting shows Milton as an old, blind man dressed in Puritan garb. The Puritans showed their lack of interest in fashionable whimsy by deliberately choosing to dress in unfashionable, plain clothes. Men and women alike wore dark colors, plain collars and cuffs, and none of the fancy trimmings that distinguished the trendy folk. Because the men wore their hair cut short, they were called "Roundheads," which distinguished them from the Cavaliers, who wore elaborate curls. You may choose to use these questions for discussion:

1. How do simple clothes make a statement about what is important to a spiritual or religious person?
   Answer: They show that the person is not interested in worldly appearance.

2. Do you think that this portrait is a good or poor choice to illustrate this poem? Why?
   Answer: Many students will think it is a good choice, because it suggests the poet's blindness.

❻ **Critical Viewing**

Answer: Students may point out that the poet looks downcast or blind in this picture.

John Milton, 1878, Mihaly von Munkacsy

❻ ⓐ **Critical Viewing** How does Milton's pose in this portrait reflect the theme of the poem? **[Speculate]**

Sonnet XIX

("When I consider how my light is spent")

John Milton

When I consider how my light is spent
    Ere half my days, in this dark world and wide,
    And that one talent[1] which is death to hide,
    Lodged with me useless, though my soul more bent
5 To serve therewith my Maker, and present
    My true account, lest he returning chide;
    "Doth God exact day labor, light denied?"
    I fondly[2] ask; but Patience to prevent
That murmur, soon replies, "God doth not need
10 Either man's work or his own gifts; who best
    Bear his mild yoke, they serve him best. His state
Is kingly. Thousands[3] at his bidding speed
    And post[4] o'er land and ocean without rest:
    They also serve who only stand and wait."

---

1. **talent** allusion to the parable of the talents (Matthew 25: 14–30). The servant who earns interest for his master on five talents (a large unit of money) is commended. The servant who hides and then returns a talent is condemned to "outer darkness."
2. **fondly** foolishly.
3. **Thousands** thousands of angels.
4. **post** travel.

Critical Reading

1. **(a) Recall:** According to the poem, at what point in his life did the speaker's eyesight fail? **(b) Infer:** In line 2, how does his way of identifying this point in his life emphasize the despair he feels?

2. **(a) Recall:** What has happened to the speaker's "one talent"? **(b) Infer:** Why does blindness have this effect on his talent?

3. **(a) Connect:** In lines 3–6, what connection does the speaker make between the use of one's talent and service to God? **(b) Interpret:** What dilemma does this connection create for him? **(c) Interpret:** What does his complaint in line 7 mean?

4. **(a) Infer:** What answers the speaker? **(b) Interpret:** How does this new speaker interpret the idea of service to God?

5. **Apply:** Do you think that this poem could inspire a contemporary person who is facing a physical challenge? Explain.

Literary Analysis
The Italian Sonnet and Poetic Ambition What setback to his poetic ambition does Milton describe in this sonnet?

For: More about John Milton
Visit: www.PHSchool.com
Web Code: ese-9307

Sonnet XIX ("When I consider how my light is spent") ■ 477

❽ About the Selection

In these opening lines to *Paradise Lost,* Milton tells of Satan's rebellion against God, and describes how the fallen archangel and his followers, defeated, are cast into a fiery pit. In creating a Satan that is unrepentant, proud, and in his own way heroic, Milton makes a powerful statement about the alluring nature of evil. It would be easy to avoid evil if it were completely repugnant; evil that has admirable qualities is far more insidious and dangerous.

❾ Humanities

Paradise Lost, 1688, by Jacob Tonson

Jacob Tonson (1656–1736), a London printer and the secretary of a local literature club, the Kit-Cat Club, bought the rights to publish *Paradise Lost.* It turned out to be a highly profitable endeavor. He then produced this engraving as an illustration for a large-sized 1688 edition of the work. The engraving reflects the art style that was then current, the baroque style, which features fantastic, elaborate, and highly decorative images. The images are designed to be dramatic and to engage the viewer with their energy. Like *Paradise Lost,* the image is grotesque and nightmarish.

Use these questions for discussion:

1. **Ask** students whether they think the style is in keeping with Milton's literary style. Why?
   Answer: Most students will think it is, since Milton includes many details.

2. **Ask** students which details of the picture they find to be most striking?
   Answer: Students may mention the figure of Satan, the writhing snakes, the black hole, or some other detail.

❿ Critical Viewing

Answer: Students may comment on the lack of flames or a furnace or darkness. There are no whirlwinds of tempestuous fire, for instance. However, the mood is similar.

from
❽ PARADISE LOST

John Milton

❾

Paradise Lost, 1688, From the British Library

❿ ▲ **Critical Viewing** Is this illustration an accurate visual representation of Milton's Hell? Explain. **[Evaluate]**

478 ■ *A Turbulent Time (1625–1798)*

Enrichment

Views of Paradise

Curiously, the description of Paradise differs little among various cultures. Throughout the ages, it is seen as a beautiful garden free from violence or pain.

An early account of Paradise appears on tablets produced by the Sumer tribe in southern Mesopotamia around the year 5000 B.C. The plain of Babylon, called "Edinn," is described as an innocent, clear, and sun-filled land, where gods are forever young, healthy, and amiable. At the command of the water god Enki, the sun god Utu brings water to Paradise and creates a lush garden bursting with fruit.

In Greek mythology, Paradise is the garden of the Hesperides, the home of the daughters of Atlas, the evening star. Assisted by a dragon, the inhabitants guard the tree that gives the golden apples.

In African tales, Paradise is a beautiful garden with ample food and leisure. There is no death or disease. Humans live in harmony with animals.

Background *Paradise Lost* was written as the dust was settling after years of war and turmoil. From 1642 to 1660, the government of England went from a monarchy to a commonwealth (rule by Parliament) to a protectorate (rule by one man, Oliver Cromwell) to a monarchy. During this two-decade period, no matter which side a person was on, he or she experienced both defeat and triumph.

Perhaps Milton wrote *Paradise Lost* because he sensed that the nation needed an anchor, a literary work that would once again help define and unite a culture. His explanation of God's reason for allowing suffering in the world, and the dark, proud figure of the rebel Satan pitted against God in civil war, must have led readers to reflect on England's own civil war.

> Of man's first disobedience, and the fruit
> Of that forbidden tree, whose mortal[1] taste
> Brought death into the world, and all our woe,
> With loss of Eden, till one greater Man[2]
> 5 Restore us, and regain the blissful seat,
> Sing Heavenly Muse,[3] that on the secret top
> Of Oreb, or of Sinai,[4] didst inspire
> That shepherd, who first taught the chosen seed,
> In the beginning how the Heavens and Earth
> 10 Rose out of Chaos: or if Sion hill[5]
> Delight thee more, and Siloa's brook[6] that flowed
> Fast[7] by the oracle of God, I thence
> Invoke thy aid to my adventurous song,
> That with no middle flight intends to soar
> 15 Above the Aonian mount,[8] while it pursues
> Things unattempted yet in prose or rhyme.
> And chiefly thou O Spirit,[9] that dost prefer
> Before all temples the upright heart and pure,
> Instruct me, for thou know'st; thou from the first

1. **mortal** deadly.
2. **one . . . Man** Christ.
3. **Heavenly Muse** Urania, the muse of astronomy and sacred poetry in Greek mythology. Here, Milton associates Urania with the holy spirit that inspired Moses ("That shepherd") to receive and interpret the word of God for the Jews ("the chosen seed"). To convey the message of God to his people, Moses wrote the first five books of the Bible, including Genesis, the book on which *Paradise Lost* is based.
4. **Oreb** (ôr´ eb) . . . **Sinai** (sī´ nī´) alternate names for the mountain where God communicated the laws to Moses.
5. **Sion** (sī´ ən) **hill** hill near Jerusalem on which the temple ("the oracle of God") stood.
6. **Siloa's** (sī lō´ əz) **brook** stream near Sion hill.
7. **Fast** close.
8. **Aonian** (ā ō´ nē ən) **mount** Mount Helicon in Greek mythology, home of the Muses. Milton is drawing a comparison between the epic he is now presenting and the epics written by the classical poets, Homer and Virgil.
9. **Spirit** the Holy Spirit, the voice that provided inspiration for the Hebrew prophets.

Literary Analysis
Epic Poetry What epic convention does Milton follow in his opening sentence?

 **Reading Check**
Whom does Milton call to help him tell his story?

from *Paradise Lost* ■ 479

- Have students **identify** the speaker's purpose.
  Answer: In line 26, the speaker says that he will justify the ways of God to men.

- Remind students that *Paradise Lost* was written in the aftermath of English Civil War (you will find information about this in the Background, More About the Author note on p. 472). Then **ask** students why this purpose is particularly significant, given the work's historical context.
  Answer: *Paradise Lost* can be seen as both an explanation for the suffering that occurs in the world and also a way of giving that suffering meaning.

15 **Literary Analysis**
Epic Poetry

- Students will find Milton's syntax complex. Point out that he was deliberately writing in what was known as the "high style" —a dignified style that used sentence forms modeled on Latin grammar.

- **Ask** students why this is appropriate for an epic.
  Answer: An epic is supposed to be lofty.

- **Ask** students the Literary Analysis question: What does the story Milton has chosen to retell reveal about his poetic ambition?
  Answer: Milton's choice of the grand biblical theme recounting the Fall from the Garden of Eden is extremely ambitious.

---

20   Wast present, and with mighty wings outspread
     Dovelike sat'st brooding on the vast abyss
     And mad'st it pregnant: what in me is dark
     Illumine, what is low raise and support;
     That to the height of this great argument[10]
25   I may assert Eternal Providence,
     And justify the ways of God to men.

       Say first, for Heaven hides nothing from thy view
     Nor the deep tract of Hell, say first what cause
     Moved our grand[11] parents in that happy state,
30   Favored of Heaven so highly, to fall off
     From their Creator, and transgress his will
     For[12] one restraint,[13] lords of the world besides?[14]
     Who first seduced them to that foul revolt?
     The infernal Serpent; he it was, whose guile
35   Stirred up with envy and revenge, deceived
     The mother of mankind, what time his pride
     Had cast him out from Heaven, with all his host
     Of rebel angels, by whose aid aspiring
     To set himself in glory above his peers,
40   He trusted to have equaled the Most High,
     If he opposed; and with ambitious aim
     Against the throne and monarchy of God
     Raised impious war in Heaven and battle proud,
     With vain attempt. Him the Almighty Power
45   Hurled headlong flaming from the ethereal sky
     With hideous ruin and combustion down
     To bottomless perdition, there to dwell
     In adamantine[15] chains and penal fire,
     Who durst defy the Omnipotent to arms.
50   Nine times the space that measures day and night
     To mortal men, he with his horrid crew
     Lay vanquished, rolling in the fiery gulf,
     Confounded though immortal. But his doom
     Reserved him to more wrath; for now the thought
55   Both of lost happiness and lasting pain
     Torments him; round he throws his baleful eyes
     That witnessed[16] huge affliction and dismay,
     Mixed with obdurate pride and steadfast hate.
     At once as far as angels' ken,[17] he views

---

10. argument theme.
11. grand first in importance and in time.
12. For because of.
13. one restraint commandment that Adam and Eve should not eat of the fruit of the tree of knowledge.
14. besides in every other respect.
15. adamantine (ad´ ə man´ tēn) *adj.* unbreakable.
16. witnessed gave evidence of.
17. ken view; scope of knowledge.

480 ■ *A Turbulent Time (1625–1798)*

Vocabulary Builder
illumine (i lōō´ mən) *v.* light up

transgress (trans gres´) *v.* violate a law or command

guile (gīl) *n.* artful trickery

Literary Analysis
Epic Poetry and Poetic Ambition What does the story Milton has chosen to retell reveal about his poetic ambition?

Vocabulary Builder
obdurate (äb´ door it) *adj.* stubborn

Enrichment

Angels

Milton's poem had a profound influence on the way Christians viewed angels. The term "angel" comes from the Greek word *angelos,* which means messenger. However, angels are not unique to the related religions of Judaism, Christianity, and Islam. Many cultures have benevolent or mischievous spirits that act as messengers between humans and a deity.

Encourage students to look for similarities and differences among cultures in regard to angels. They may also be interested to know

how the Christian view of angels has changed over time. Angels were not always thought of as looking like humans with a single pair of bird wings, and the notion of the souls of the dead becoming angels appears to have arisen quite recently, during Victorian times.

Besides having them research written information, have students look at depictions of angels in illustrations and other works of art.

60 The dismal situation waste and wild:
    A dungeon horrible, on all sides round,
    As one great furnace flamed, yet from those flames
    No light, but rather darkness visible
    Served only to discover sights of woe,
65 Regions of sorrow, doleful shades, where peace
    And rest can never dwell, hope never comes
    That comes to all; but torture without end
    Still urges,[18] and a fiery deluge, fed
    With ever-burning sulfur unconsumed:
70 Such place eternal justice had prepared
    For these rebellious, here their prison ordained
    In utter darkness, and their portion set
    As far removed from God and light of Heaven
    As from the center thrice to the utmost pole.[19]
75 O how unlike the place from whence they fell!
    There the companions of his fall, o'erwhelmed
    With floods and whirlwinds of <u>tempestuous</u> fire,
    He soon discerns, and weltering by his side
    One next himself in power, and next in crime,
80 Long after known in Palestine, and named
    Beelzebub.[20] To whom the archenemy,
    And thence in Heaven called Satan, with bold words
    Breaking the horrid silence thus began:
       "If thou beest he; but O how fallen! how changed
85 From him, who in the happy realms of light
    Clothed with <u>transcendent</u> brightness didst outshine
    Myriads though bright: if he whom mutual league,
    United thoughts and counsels, equal hope
    And hazard in the glorious enterprise,
90 Joined with me once, now misery hath joined
    In equal ruin: into what pit thou seest
    From what height fallen, so much the stronger proved
    He with his thunder:[21] and till then who knew
    The force of those dire arms? Yet not for those,
95 Nor what the potent Victor in his rage
    Can else inflict, do I repent or change,
    Though changed in outward luster, that fixed mind
    And high disdain, from sense of injured merit,
    That with the Mightiest raised me to contend,
100 And to the fierce contention brought along
    Innumerable force of spirits armed

---

18. **urges** afflicts.
19. **center . . . . pole** three times the distance from the center of the universe (Earth) to the outermost sphere of the universe.
20. **Beelzebub** (bē el′ zə bub′) traditionally, the chief devil, or Satan. In this poem, Satan's chief lieutenant among the fallen angels.
21. **He . . . thunder** God.

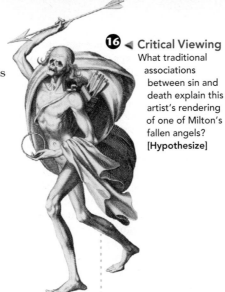

❶❻ ◀ Critical Viewing
What traditional associations between sin and death explain this artist's rendering of one of Milton's fallen angels? **[Hypothesize]**

Vocabulary Builder
tempestuous (tem pes′ chōō əs) *adj.* turbulent; stormy

transcendent (tran sen′ dənt) *adj.* exceeding beyond all limits

Literary Analysis
Epic Poetry What details in these lines might suggest to some readers that Satan is the hero of Milton's epic?

❶❽ ✓ Reading Check
Whom does Satan discover lying next to him?

from *Paradise Lost* ■ 481

⑲ Literary Analysis
Epic Poetry

- Have students read lines 102–124 and have them describe the opposition between God and Satan.

- **Ask** students the Literary Analysis question: In what way does Milton's vision of the opposition between Satan and God fit the expectation that epics tell of famous battles?
  Answer: Milton envisions this opposition as a grand battle, not unlike the battles fought by epic heroes.

⑳ Reading Strategy
Breaking Down Sentences

- Explain the difference between main and supporting clauses. Main clauses are those that stand by themselves. Supporting clauses cannot stand by themselves.

- Tell the students to read lines 134–142 and to distinguish between main and supporting clauses. Then **ask** students the Reading Strategy question: Rewrite lines 134–142 in your own words, putting the ideas in the main clause first.
  Possible responses: Students' rewriting of the lines should be something similar to the following: I rue this sad outcome that has lost us Heaven, and I rue that this mighty host has been laid as low as gods and heavenly essences can perish. I rue these circumstances because the mind and spirit remains invincible although their glory is extinct and their former happiness is swallowed up in endless misery.

That durst dislike his reign, and me preferring,
His utmost power with adverse power opposed
In dubious battle on the plains of Heaven,
105 And shook his throne. What though the field be lost?
All is not lost; the unconquerable will,
And study[22] of revenge, immortal hate,
And courage never to submit or yield:
And what is else not to be overcome?
110 That glory never shall his wrath or might
Extort from me. To bow and sue for grace
With <u>suppliant</u> knee, and deify his power
Who from the terror of this arm so late
Doubted[23] his empire, that were low indeed,
115 That were an <u>ignominy</u> and shame beneath
This downfall; since by fate the strength of gods
And this empyreal substance[24] cannot fail,
Since through experience of this great event,
In arms not worse, in foresight much advanced,
120 We may with more successful hope resolve
To wage by force or guile eternal war
Irreconcilable, to our grand Foe,
Who now triumphs, and in the excess of joy
Sole reigning holds the tyranny of Heaven."
125　　So spake the apostate angel, though in pain,
Vaunting aloud, but racked with deep despair;
And him thus answered soon his bold compeer.[25]
　　"O prince, O chief of many thronèd Powers,
That led the embattled Seraphim[26] to war
130 Under thy conduct, and in dreadful deeds
Fearless, endangered Heaven's perpetual King,
And put to proof his high supremacy,
Whether upheld by strength, or chance, or fate!
Too well I see and rue the dire event[27]
135 That with sad overthrow and foul defeat
Hath lost us Heaven, and all this mighty host
In horrible destruction laid thus low,
As far as gods and heavenly essences
Can perish: for the mind and spirit remains
140 Invincible, and vigor soon returns,
Though all our glory extinct, and happy state
Here swallowed up in endless misery.

---

22. study pursuit.
23. Doubted feared for.
24. empyreal (em pir′ ē əl) **substance** the indestructible substance of which Heaven, or the empyrean, is composed.
25. compeer comrade; equal.
26. Seraphim (ser′ ə fim′) the highest order of angels.
27. event outcome.

Literary Analysis
Epic Poetry In what way does Milton's vision of the opposition between Satan and God fit the expectation that epics tell of famous battles?

Vocabulary Builder
suppliant (sup′ lē ənt) *adj.* imploring

ignominy (ig′ nə min′ ē) *n.* humiliation; dishonor

Reading Strategy
Breaking Down Sentences Rewrite lines 134–142 in your own words, putting the ideas in the main clause first.

Enrichment

Lucifer
Students may be interested to learn that *Lucifer*, which means "light-bearer" in Greek, is, according to Christian theology, Satan's name when he was the Angel of Light, before he rebelled against God. You might want to have students evaluate the appropriateness of Satan's punishment given this information. Students will probably find it appropriate that the former angel of light is punished by being cast into darkness.

But what if he our conqueror (whom I now
Of force[28] believe almighty, since no less
145 Than such could have o'erpowered such force as ours)
Have left us this our spirit and strength entire
Strongly to suffer and support our pains,
That we may so suffice[29] his vengeful ire,
Or do him mightier service as his thralls
150 By right of war, whate'er his business be
Here in the heart of Hell to work in fire,
Or do his errands in the gloomy deep?
What can it then avail though yet we feel
Strength undiminished, or eternal being
155 To undergo eternal punishment?"
Whereto with speedy words the Archfiend replied:
    "Fallen cherub, to be weak is miserable,
Doing or suffering:[30] but of this be sure,
To do aught[31] good never will be our task,
160 But ever to do ill our sole delight,
As being the contrary to his high will
Whom we resist. If then his providence
Out of our evil seek to bring forth good,
Our labor must be to pervert that end,
165 And out of good still[32] to find means of evil;
Which oft times may succeed, so as perhaps
Shall grieve him, if I fail not,[33] and disturb
His inmost counsels from their destined aim.
But see the angry Victor[34] hath recalled
170 His ministers of vengeance and pursuit
Back to the gates of Heaven: the sulfurous hail
Shot after us in storm, o'erblown hath laid
The fiery surge, that from the precipice
Of Heaven received us falling, and the thunder,
175 Winged with red lightning and impetuous rage,
Perhaps hath spent his shafts, and ceases now
To bellow through the vast and boundless deep.
Let us not slip[35] the occasion, whether scorn,
Or satiate[36] fury yield it from our Foe.
180 Seest thou yon dreary plain, forlorn and wild,
The seat of desolation, void of light,
Save what the glimmering of these livid flames

---

28. **Of force** necessarily.
29. **suffice** satisfy.
30. **doing or suffering** whether one is active or passive.
31. **aught** anything.
32. **still** always.
33. **if . . . not** unless I am mistaken.
34. **angry Victor** God.
35. **slip** fail to take advantage of.
36. **satiate** (sā′ shē āt′) satisfied.

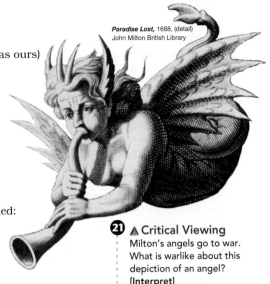

Paradise Lost, 1688, (detail)
John Milton British Library

21 ⚠ **Critical Viewing**
Milton's angels go to war.
What is warlike about this
depiction of an angel?
[Interpret]

Literary Analysis
Epic Poetry What assumptions about the epic struggle between good and evil does Milton make in lines 159–168?

23 ✓ **Reading Check**
What does Satan tell
Beelzebub their sole
purpose will be?

from *Paradise Lost* ■ 483

483

② The British Tradition
Renewing the Literary Tradition

By now students should be quite familiar with reworkings of past literary heritages. Have them review the selections they have read thus far and examine the ways in which the author has reworked the British literary tradition in his or her unique way.

Connect to the Literature Remind students of the characteristics of an epic. Then **ask** students the Connect to the Literature question: In what way does Milton create in Satan a character of epic proportions?

Possible response: Like many epic heroes, Satan is a character with supernatural or divine powers who is brought down by a tragic flaw.

Casts pale and dreadful? Thither let us tend
From off the tossing of these fiery waves,
185 There rest, if any rest can harbor there,
And reassembling our afflicted powers,[37]
Consult how we may henceforth most offend
Our Enemy, our own loss how repair,
How overcome this dire calamity,
190 What reinforcement we may gain from hope,
If not what resolution from despair."
      Thus Satan talking to his nearest mate,
With head uplift above the wave, and eyes
That sparkling blazed; his other parts besides
195 Prone on the flood, extended long and large,
Lay floating many a rood,[38] in bulk as huge
As whom the fables name of monstrous size,
Titanian, or Earthborn, that warred on Jove,
Briareos or Typhon,[39] whom the den
200 By ancient Tarsus[40] held, or that sea beast
Leviathan,[41] which God of all his works
Created hugest that swim the ocean stream:
Him haply slumbering on the Norway foam
The pilot of some small night-foundered skiff,
205 Deeming some island, oft, as seamen tell,
With fixed anchor in his scaly rind
Moors by his side under the lee, while night
Invests[42] the sea, and wished morn delays:
So stretched out huge in length the Archfiend lay
210 Chained on the burning lake, nor ever thence
Had risen or heaved his head, but that the will
And high permission of all-ruling Heaven
Left him at large to his own dark designs,
That with reiterated crimes he might
215 Heap on himself damnation, while he sought
Evil to others, and enraged might see
How all his malice served but to bring forth
Infinite goodness, grace and mercy shown
On man by him seduced, but on himself
220 Treble confusion, wrath and vengeance poured.

---

37. afflicted powers overthrown armies.
38. rood old unit of measure equal to seven or eight yards.
39. Titanian (tī tā′ nē ən) . . . **Earthborn . . . Briareos** (brī ar′ ē əs) . . . **Typhon** (tī′ fən) In classical mythology, both the Titans, led by Briareos, who had a hundred hands, and the Giants (Earthborn), led by Typhon, a hundred-headed serpent monster, fought with Jove. As punishment for their rebellion, both Briareos and Typhon were thrown into the underworld.
40. Tarsus (tär′ səs) capital of Cilicia (sə lish′ə). Typhon is said to have lived in Cilicia near Tarsus.
41. Leviathan (lə vī′ ə thən) in the Bible, a great sea monster.
42. Invests covers.

484 ■ *A Turbulent Time (1625–1798)*

We value a poet like Milton for his originality, but like many poets, he creates what is original by returning to a tradition—a developing body of work widely read and respected by a culture. By going back to past works, Milton is able to define his own poetic tasks and tools in unique ways. To create *Paradise Lost*, he borrowed the form of the epic from ancient Greek and Roman writers and drew on the Bible for the story of Adam and Eve. The result, though, is a new, disenchanted vision of the human condition with all its stark limitations.

Like Milton, modern poets also consciously return to a tradition. When Irish poet Seamus Heaney retranslates the Anglo-Saxon epic *Beowulf*, he explores his own poetic vision by reworking his literary heritage.

Connect to the Literature

In what way does Milton create in Satan a character of epic proportions?

Enrichment

Milton's Gaffe

You may wish to point out to students that even a great poet like Milton could make mistakes. His reference to Briareos and Typhon in line 199 shows that he believed that both of these mythological figures were sent to the underworld by Zeus. The original source for this myth goes back to the ancient Greek poet Hesiod. In his epic poem, the *Theogony,*

Briareos was *not* an enemy of Zeus but was rather his ally in the war against the Titans. Moreover, although Zeus did send the Titans to the underworld once the battle had been won, Briareos, his ally, was not among them. Instead, Zeus stationed Briareos as a guard over the Titans, including Typhon, who were henceforth imprisoned in the underworld.

Forthwith upright he rears from off the pool
His mighty stature; on each hand the flames
Driven backward, slope their pointing spires, and rolled
In billows leave in the midst a horrid vale.
225 Then with expanded wings he steers his flight
Aloft, incumbent[43] on the dusky air
That felt unusual weight, till on dry land
He lights, if it were land that ever burned
With solid, as the lake with liquid fire;
230 And such appeared in hue, as when the force
Of subterranean wind transports a hill
Torn from Pelorus, or the shattered side
Of thundering Etna,[44] whose combustible
And fueled entrails thence conceiving fire,
235 Sublimed[45] with mineral fury, aid the winds,
And leave a singèd bottom all involved[46]
With stench and smoke: such resting found the sole
Of unblessed feet. Him followed his next mate,
Both glorying to have scaped the Stygian[47] flood
240 As gods, and by their own recovered strength,
Not by the sufferance[48] of supernal[49] power.
    "Is this the region, this the soil, the clime,"
Said then the lost Archangel, "this the seat
That we must change[50] for Heaven, this mournful gloom
245 For that celestial light? Be it so, since he
Who now is sovereign can dispose and bid
What shall be right: farthest from him is best,
Whom reason hath equaled, force hath made supreme
Above his equals. Farewell happy fields,
250 Where joy forever dwells. Hail horrors! Hail
Infernal world! and thou, profoundest Hell
Receive thy new possessor, one who brings
A mind not to be changed by place or time.
The mind is its own place, and in itself
255 Can make a Heaven of Hell, a Hell of Heaven.
What matter where, if I be still the same,
And what I should be, all but less than he
Whom thunder hath made greater? Here at least
We shall be free; the Almighty hath not built
260 Here for his envy, will not drive us hence:

---

43. **incumbent** lying.
44. **Pelorus** (pə lôr′ əs) . . . **Etna** volcanic mountains in Sicily.
45. **Sublimed** vaporized.
46. **involved** enveloped.
47. **Stygian** (stij′ ē ən) of the river Styx, which, in Greek mythology, encircled Hades (hā′ dēz′), the home of the dead.
48. **sufferance** permission.
49. **supernal** (sə purn′ əl) heavenly.
50. **change** exchange.

Reading Strategy
Breaking Down Sentences Put the ideas in lines 221–222 in a more natural order. Then, explain how Milton's wording makes the description more dramatic.

Literary Analysis
Epic Poetry and Poetic Ambition In what way is the attitude expressed in lines 250–258 fitting both for a hero and a poet?

27 Reading Check
In what manner do Satan and Beelzebub travel to land?

from *Paradise Lost* ■ 485

---

1. You may suggest that readers compare and contrast Milton's description of Hell with other portrayals they have read or seen.

2. (a) Milton writes that Satan deceived Eve out of revenge on God for casting him out of Heaven. (b) Adam and Eve, like Satan, question God's sovereignty.

3. (a) Milton's Hell is dark, eternally burning, and filled with tortured souls who have no hope of relief. (b) Satan reacts to his fall into Hell with a sense of injury.

4. (a) Satan is determined to regain Heaven at any cost. (b) Satan's motives for war are revenge, a determination that God shall not extort his, Satan's, glory. (c) Failing to regain Heaven for himself, Satan brings about the downfall of Adam and Eve.

5. (a) Satan's attitude, that the mind is its own place, and in itself can make a Heaven of Hell, proves that adversity will not change his mind. (b) Attitude and outlook, not only the judgments and values of others, help to determine an individual's experience of one's situation and place.

6. (a) Satan implies that the following three things are more important than the fact he is in Hell: (1) Satan and the fallen angels will be free; (2) they can stay, they will not be exiled; and (3) they will reign. He says it is better to reign in Hell than serve in Heaven. (b) Satan is rebellious and stubborn, but he is also courageous in refusing to be conquered. (c) Students may say that Satan's determination to make the best of what he has and his desire for freedom at all costs are heroic.

7. (a) Milton means that he intends to make God's decisions, especially those that have determined the human situation, understandable to people. (b) Students may respond to lines 209–221 and give a reasonable explanation for why God allows evil in the world.

Go Online
Author Link   For additional information about John Milton, have students type in the Web Code, then select M from the alphabet, and then select the author's name.

486

Here we may reign secure, and in my choice
To reign is worth ambition though in Hell:
Better to reign in Hell than serve in Heaven.
But wherefore[51] let we then our faithful friends,
265 The associates and copartners of our loss
Lie thus astonished[52] on the oblivious[53] pool,
And call them not to share with us their part
In this unhappy mansion, or once more
With rallied arms to try what may be yet
Regained in Heaven, or what more lost in Hell?"

---

51. wherefore why.
52. astonished stunned.
53. oblivious causing forgetfulness.

Critical Reading

1. **Respond:** What part of Milton's description of Hell do you find the most vivid? Explain.

2. **(a) Recall:** Summarize the story of Adam and Eve as Milton tells it in lines 28–36. **(b) Connect:** How is the fall of Adam and Eve connected to the fall of Satan and his cohorts?

3. **(a) Recall:** Lines 59–74 describe Hell. What does Milton describe as its main features? **(b) Interpret:** Explain Satan's reaction in lines 94–99 to his fall into Hell.

4. **(a) Infer:** In lines 116–124, what kind of war does Satan propose to wage against Heaven? **(b) Interpret:** Judging from lines 105–116, what is his motive for such a war? **(c) Hypothesize:** How will this war lead to the fall of Adam and Eve?

5. **(a) Interpret:** Explain how Satan's attitude toward Hell in lines 250–252 proves that he is "one who brings / A mind not to be changed by place or time" (lines 252–253). **(b) Draw Conclusions:** Explain how the mind "Can make a Heaven of Hell, a Hell of Heaven" (line 255).

6. **(a) Analyze:** In lines 256–263, what three things does Satan imply are infinitely more important than the place in which he happens to be? **(b) Summarize:** Characterize Satan, supporting your description with quotations. **(c) Evaluate:** To what extent does Satan seem admirable? To what extent despairing? Explain.

7. **(a) Interpret:** What does Milton mean when he says he wants to "justify the ways of God to men" (line 26)? **(b) Assess:** How good a start has Milton made toward this goal?

Go Online
Author Link

For: More about John Milton
Visit: www.PHSchool.com
Web Code: ese-9307

Apply the Skills

Poetry of John Milton

Literary Analysis

The Italian Sonnet; Epic Poetry

1. **(a)** Which **Italian sonnet** has the more regular pattern of rhymes in the sestet? **(b)** Does this regularity strengthen the "solution" the sestet gives to the problem set out in the octave? Explain.
2. **(a)** In Sonnet XIX, how does sentence structure break with the pattern of octave and sestet? **(b)** What effect is achieved?
3. **(a)** What major event has occurred before the beginning of Milton's epic? **(b)** How does picking up the story after this event follow the conventions of epic form?
4. A traditional epic character has a powerful personality. How does Milton make Satan a suitable epic character?

Comparing Literary Works

5. In Sonnets VII and XIX, Milton reflects on setbacks to his poetic ambition. Use a chart like the one shown to compare the two poems.

Speaker's Situation	Effect on Ambition	Solution	How Solution Helps

6. **(a)** Explain how, by writing *Paradise Lost,* Milton aspires to the literary greatness of Homer and the Bible. Provide lines from the poem in support. **(b)** Compare Milton's ambition with the moral of Sonnet XIX: "They also serve who only stand and wait."
7. **(a)** What ideas about the power of a poet might lines 254–255 of *Paradise Lost* suggest? **(b)** What parallel can you draw between the situation of Satan and the ambition of a poet?

Reading Strategy

Breaking Down Sentences

8. **(a)** Identify the main clause in lines 1–8 of Sonnet XIX.
   (b) Explain what each supporting clause adds to its meaning.

Extend Understanding

9. **Art Connection:** With what artistic depictions of Hell are you familiar? Share your recollections with the class.

QuickReview

An **Italian sonnet** is a fourteen-line poem with an eight-line octave and a six-line sestet. The rhyme scheme of the octave is *abbaabba,* and the rhyme scheme of the sestet varies.

An **epic** is a long narrative poem featuring a larger-than-life hero, and reflecting the values of the society in which it was created.

When you **break down sentences,** you identify the main clause and then determine what the other, supporting, phrases and clauses add to the meaning of the sentence.

Go Online
Assessment

For: Self-test
Visit: www.PHSchool.com
Web Code: esa-6305

Poetry of John Milton ■ 487

Answers continued

Answers

1. **(a)** The sestet in Sonnet XIX has a more regular pattern. **(b)** The regularity does strengthen the "solution" as it gives a strong feeling of resolution.
2. **(a)** Milton changes the pattern by using run-on rhymes. **(b)** This links the problem and solution even more closely.
3. **(a)** Satan and the fallen angels have been expelled from Heaven. **(b)** The epic begins *in media res* (in the middle of things).
4. Milton depicts Satan as a figure who is courageous in the face of calamity.
5. **Possible response:** In Sonnet VII, the speaker answers his own concerns about his lack of accomplishment by drawing on his conviction that whatever he achieves is the will of Heaven. In Sonnet XIX, Milton confronts the obstacle that his loss of sight presents in his career; he comforts himself with his conviction that submission to God's will is all that God requires of him.
6. **(a)** Milton aspires to the greatness of Homer by invoking the assistance of the Muse; he aspires to the greatness of the Bible in his retelling of the tale of Satan. **(b)** Rather than succumbing to his handicap, Milton went on to create his great epic.
7. **(a)** Certainly Milton made his own "place" in his mind. **(b)** In *Paradise Lost,* Satan declares he will make a new Heaven out of Hell. The poet Milton also makes a heaven out of his hell—blindness—when he goes on to create the sublime epic.
8. **(a)** The main clause is "I fondly ask." **(b)** The clause "'Doth God exact day labor, light denied?'" is the direct object of the verb *ask.* "When I consider how my light is spent ere half my days, in this dark world and wide" makes it clear Milton's concern is with his own blindness. "And that one talent which is death to hide/lodged with me useless though my soul more bent/to serve therewith my Maker . . ." makes the reader understand that Milton feels there is nothing worse than losing his "one talent"—poetry—because using that talent is the only way he knows to serve God.

continued

Answers continued

9. Students may mention Hieronymus Bosch (*Garden of Earthly Delights, Haywain, The Last Judgment,* or *Paradise and Hell*).

Go Online Students may use the **Assessment** **Self-test** to prepare for **Selection Test A** or **Selection Test B.**

❶ Vocabulary Lesson

Word Analysis: Latin Root -lum-

1. c
2. e
3. a
4. b
5. d

Spelling Strategy

1. ine
2. ine
3. en

Vocabulary Builder

1. f   6. b
2. i   7. a
3. e   8. d
4. g   9. h
5. c

❷ Grammar and Style Lesson

1. whom
2. who
3. whom
4. who
5. whom

Writing Application

Sample sentences:

Who hasn't stumbled over the proper choice of *who* versus *whom?* On whom can we place the blame for these awkward English usages?

𝒲G Writing and Grammar, Diamond Level

Students will find further instruction and practice on usage in Chapter 22, Section 2.

Build Language Skills

❶ Vocabulary Lesson

Word Analysis: Latin Root -*lum*-

The Latin root -*lum*-, found in *illumine*, means "light" or "lamp." It is the base of many scientific words about light. Use this fact to match each word with its definition.

1. illumine
2. luminous
3. lumen
4. luminescence
5. illuminant

a. a unit of light
b. emission of light with little heat
c. light up
d. something that gives off light
e. giving off light

Spelling Strategy

The sound *in* at the end of words may be spelled *ine*, as in *illumine*, or *en*, as in *darken*. For each item below, fill in the blanks to spell the *in* sound correctly.

1. determ___   2. fam___   3. sull___

Vocabulary Builder: Synonyms

Synonyms are words that have the same or nearly the same meaning as each other. Review the vocabulary list on page 473. Then, for each numbered vocabulary word from the selections, identify its synonym and write its letter in your notebook.

1. transcendent   a. appearance
2. ignominy   b. stubborn
3. tempestuous   c. violate
4. supplicant   d. trickery
5. transgress   e. stormy
6. obdurate   f. surpassing
7. semblance   g. pleading
8. guile   h. light
9. illumine   i. disgrace

❷ Grammar and Style Lesson

Usage: *who* and *whom*

Who is used as the subject of a verb. *Whom* is used as the object of a verb or of a preposition.

Subject: Poets <u>who</u> become great do not always publish early. [*Who* is the subject of the verb *become*.]

Object of a Verb: Fame comes to those <u>whom</u> fate chooses. [*Whom* is the direct object of *chooses*.]

Object of a Preposition: Fame may not come to the poet to <u>whom</u> it matters most. [*Whom* is the object of the preposition *to*.]

Practice Choose *who* or *whom* to complete each sentence correctly.

1. With __?__ did the serpent quarrel?
2. __?__ lay chained on the burning lake?
3. To __?__ did Eve offer the apple?
4. __?__ condemned the pair to eternal punishment?
5. __?__ did Adam and Eve blame for their fate?

Writing Application Describe a setback you have experienced. In your writing, use *who* and *whom* at least once each.

𝒲G *Prentice Hall Writing and Grammar Connection: Chapter 22, Section 2*

Assessment Practice

Writer's Purpose   (For more practice, see *Standardized Test Preparation Workbook*, p. 20.)

Use the following passage to remind students that writers may directly state their purpose.

Sing heavenly Muse . . .
. . . what in me is dark
Illumine, what is low raise and support;
That to the height of this great argument
I may assert Eternal Providence
And justify the ways of God to men . . .

Milton's main purpose is to—

A convert people to Christianity
B retell the story of Adam and Eve
C be compared with Homer, who composed the *Iliad*
D justify God's actions to humankind

Students should determine that the correct answer is *D*.

Writing Lesson

Timed Writing: Critical Analysis of a Literary Theme

Eighteenth-century poet William Blake said that Milton "wrote in fetters when he wrote of Angels & God, and at liberty when of Devils & Hell." In an essay, explain why villains such as Milton's Satan engage the imagination. *(40 minutes)*

Prewriting
(10 minutes)
Review the excerpt from Milton's epic. Take notes on the character of Satan, and write two sentences explaining his appeal. Then, jot down notes on other villains with whom you are familiar.

Drafting
(20 minutes)
Begin with an analysis of Satan's appeal, and relate your observations about other villains to this analysis. Draw a conclusion about why villains can be fascinating.

Revising
(10 minutes)
Circle key words in your draft—terms that you use to identify central themes or character features. For each key word, write a "thought shot"—a list of associated terms. Review each list for ideas that will help you elaborate on your insights.

Model: Using Thought Shots to Elaborate

defiance
disobedience
tantrums rebellion
hopeless rebellion

He is not a spoiled child throwing a tantrum, though; he

knows exactly how hopeless his situation is. By setting him so

completely against his circumstances, his

Satan is defiant. His defiance makes him seem noble.

The added images and ideas clarify and deepen the writer's insight.

WG *Prentice Hall Writing and Grammar Connection: Chapter 14, Section 4*

Extend Your Learning

Listening and Speaking Douglas Bush writes of *Paradise Lost*, "Its characterization of Satan is one of the supreme achievements of world literature." Prepare a **speech** defending or opposing Bush's opinion. Include the following:

1. Arguments evaluating the characterization of Satan against a standard you define
2. Emotional appeals based on your own response to the character of Satan
3. Supporting details from the poem

Deliver your speech to the class.

Research and Technology Milton's blindness did not prevent him from writing *Paradise Lost*. With a group, produce a **documentary** on the achievements of community members with disabilities. Divide the following tasks: conducting interviews, videotaping, researching, and writing a script. Present your documentary to the class. **[Group Activity]**

Go Online
Research
For: An additional research activity
Visit: www.PHSchool.com
Web Code: esd-7304

Poetry of John Milton ■ 489

Assessment Resources

The following resources can be used to assess student's knowledge and skills.

Unit 3 Resources
Selection Test A, pp. 69–71
Selection Test B, pp. 72–74

General Resources
Rubrics for Response to Literature,
pp. 65–66

Go Online
Assessment Students may use the **Self-test** to prepare for **Selection Test A** or **Selection Test B.**

---

❸ Writing Lesson

You may use this Writing Lesson as timed-writing practice, or you may allow students to develop the essay as a writing assignment over several days.

- To guide students in writing this critical analysis, give them the **Support for Writing Lesson** page (*Unit 3 Resources,* p. 66).

- Tell students that writing can be done from a few different points of view. Point out to the students that Milton himself, for example, writes from an omniscient point of view that enables him to tell the reader the thoughts of any character.

- Some students might prefer, however, to use first person and write as though they themselves were Satan.

- Others may prefer third-person limited, in which someone outside the events tells the story knowing only the thoughts of a single character.

- Tell them that whichever option they choose, they need to keep a consistent point of view so that readers do not become confused.

- Model an essay segment for the students by modifying a passage from *Paradise Lost.*

❹ Research and Technology

- Divide the class into three groups.

- Assign the interviews to one group, the production of the video to another, and the research and writing to the third.

- Tell the students to follow the steps outlined in the textbook to organize their tasks.

- After the students present the documentary to the class, follow up with a discussion in which each group makes a presentation on their part of the assignment.

- The **Support for Extend Your Learning** page (*Unit 3 Resources,* p. 67) provides guided note-taking opportunities to help students complete the Extend Your Learning activities.

Go Online
Research Have students type in the Web Code for another research activity.

Meeting Your Standards

Students will

1. **analyze and respond to literary elements.**
   - Literary Analysis: Tradition and Reform

2. **read, comprehend, analyze, and critique a poem.**
   - Reading Strategy: Using Historical Context
   - Reading Check questions
   - Apply the Skills questions
   - Assessment Practice (ATE)

3. **develop vocabulary.**
   - Vocabulary Lesson: Terms With *breach*

4. **understand and apply written and oral language conventions.**
   - Spelling Strategy
   - Grammar and Style Lesson: Correlative Conjunctions

5. **develop writing proficiency.**
   - Writing Lesson: Essay Connecting Literature With Experience

6. **develop appropriate research strategies.**
   - Extend Your Learning: Report With Spreadsheets

7. **understand and apply listening and speaking strategies.**
   - Extend Your Learning: Ballad

Block Scheduling: Use one 90-minute class period to preteach the skills and have students read the selection. Use a second 90-minute class period to assess students' mastery of skills, extend their learning, and monitor their progress.

Homework Suggestions

Following are possibilities for homework assignments:

- Support pages from *Unit 3 Resources:*
  - Literary Analysis
  - Reading Strategy
  - Vocabulary Builder
  - Grammar and Style

- An Extend Your Learning project and the Writing Lesson for this selection group may be completed over several days.

Step-by-Step Teaching Guide	Pacing Guide
PRETEACH	
• Administer Vocabulary and Reading Warm-ups as necessary.	5 min.
• Engage students' interest with the motivation activity.	5 min.
• Read and discuss author and background features. **FT**	10 min.
• Introduce the Literary Analysis skill: Tradition and Reform. **FT**	5 min.
• Introduce the Reading Strategy: Using Historical Context. **FT**	10 min
• Prepare students to read by teaching the selection vocabulary. **FT**	
TEACH	
• Informally monitor comprehension while students read independently or in groups. **FT**	30 min.
• Monitor students' comprehension with the Reading Check notes.	as students read
• Reinforce vocabulary with Vocabulary Builder notes.	as students read
• Develop students' understanding of tradition and reform with the Literary Analysis annotations. **FT**	5 min.
• Develop students' ability to use historical context with the Reading Strategy annotations. **FT**	5 min.
ASSESS/EXTEND	
• Assess students' comprehension and mastery of the Literary Analysis and Reading Strategy by having them answer the Apply the Skills questions. **FT**	15 min.
• Have students complete the Vocabulary Development Lesson and the Grammar and Style Lesson. **FT**	15 min.
• Apply students' knowledge of relating broad themes to personal experience by using the Writing Lesson. **FT**	45 min. or homework
• Apply students' understanding by using one or more of the Extend Your Learning activities.	20–90 min. or homework
• Administer Selection Test A or Selection Test B. **FT**	15 min.

Resources

Choosing Resources for Differentiated Instruction

[**L1**] Special Needs Students

[**L2**] Below-Level Students

[**L3**] All Students

[**L4**] Advanced Students

[**EL**] English Learners

For Vocabulary and Reading Warm-ups and for Selection Tests, **A** signifies "less challenging" and **B** "more challenging." For Graphic Organizer transparencies, **A** signifies "not filled in" and **B** "filled in."

FT Fast Track Instruction: To move the lesson more quickly, use the strategies and activities identified with **FT**.

Scaffolding for Less Proficient and Advanced Students

The leveled Critical Thinking questions after selections progress in the levels of thinking required to answer them. To address the needs of your different students, you may use the (a) level questions for your less proficient students and the (b) level questions with your on-level and advanced students. The occasional (c) level questions are appropriate for your advanced students.

PRENTICE HALL

Use this complete suite of powerful teaching tools to make lesson planning and testing quicker and easier.

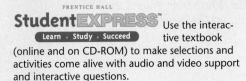

PRENTICE HALL

Use the interactive textbook (online and on CD-ROM) to make selections and activities come alive with audio and video support and interactive questions.

For: Information about Lexiles
Visit: www.PHSchool.com
Web Code: eue-1111

Motivation

Write "The pen is mightier than the sword" on the chalkboard. Ask students what it means. Discuss examples, including editorials, pamphlets, and other works that have changed public sentiment.

Explain that the poets featured in this grouping were people who disagreed with each other in matters of politics but were united in their belief that people should be outspoken supporters of ideas, even if those ideas were unpopular.

❶ Background
More About the Authors

Amelia Lanier was unusual for a woman of her time. Her contention in "Eve's Apology in Defense of Women" that Eve was less responsible than Adam for the fall of humanity was considered radical in the male dominated era in which men held hierarchical positions in both the church and at home. Lanier's use of the church as the focus of her feminist writing was significant for two reasons: the church was an integral part of Renaissance life for both nobility and peasantry, and women were already reevaluating their roles in religion.

Richard Lovelace, a Royalist, was imprisoned twice during these turbulent years. During his incarceration, he wrote some of his finest poetry, including "To Althea, From Prison" and "To Lucasta, on Going to the Wars."

Build Skills   *Poems*

from Eve's Apology in Defense of Women • To Lucasta, on Going to the Wars • To Althea, from Prison

Amelia Lanier
(1569–1645)

Amelia Lanier (also spelled "Lanyer") saw the need for women's rights three hundred years before the women's movement for equality. Daring to question her society's vision of women and the limited roles it allowed them, she anticipated future ideas of justice for women.

From Court Life to Working Woman
Lanier had ties to the royal court, where her father, Baptista Bassano, was a musician to Queen Elizabeth I. Lanier's husband, Alphonso, and her son, Henry, were also court musicians. Despite her court connections, however, Lanier and her husband were not wealthy. When her husband died in 1613, Lanier sought to make a living by opening a school outside London.

A Radical Work   In 1611, Lanier published a volume of poetry called *Salve Deus Rex Judaeorum (Hail, God, King of the Jews)*. In this groundbreaking work, of which "Eve's Apology in Defense of Women" is a section, Lanier questioned the privileges of the upper class and called for women's social and religious equality with men.

Although a woman sat on the throne of England during much of Lanier's lifetime, few women in her day published poetry. The poems in *Salve Deus Rex Judaeoroum* reflect her sense that women were underrepresented in the culture of the time. Sections of the work praise her female patrons, while others re-evaluate the role of women in stories from the Bible.

"Dark Lady" or Visionary?   In later times, Lanier was perhaps more famous as a possibility for Shakespeare's "dark lady" (the mysterious woman to whom he addresses some of his sonnets) than for her poetry. As scholars have explored the political undercurrents of past literature, though, interest in Lanier has revived. Today, Lanier is considered a visionary feminist who spoke out against injustice.

❶

Richard Lovelace
(1618–1657)

Richard Lovelace, son of a wealthy family and firm supporter of his king, had the misfortune to live at a time when the English monarchy was under violent assault. The Civil War that culminated in the execution of the king plunged the privileged Lovelace into prison and poverty.

Looks and Talent   Before England's Civil War, Lovelace profited by his association with royalty. It is said that, charmed by this winning young man, the king and queen ordered Oxford to grant him a degree before he had completed his studies! Lovelace did not, however, lack talent. While at Oxford, he wrote a play, painted, and played music.

The Price of Loyalty   Lovelace was about twenty-six when Parliament challenged the king's authority and civil war broke out. Perhaps because of his personal charm, Lovelace was chosen to demand that Parliament restore the king's authority. Parliament was not impressed, though, and Lovelace was immediately arrested.

A Daring Life   While imprisoned, Lovelace wrote "To Althea, From Prison," a moving affirmation of the value of personal integrity, even if it meant imprisonment. When released, he rejoined Charles's forces and spent his fortune equipping the king's army. Upon Charles's defeat in 1645, Lovelace joined the wars against Spain.

An Untimely End   Returning to England years later, Lovelace was again imprisoned by the Puritans. During this time, he prepared for publication the volume that included "To Lucasta, on Going to the Wars." No one knows for certain how Lovelace's life ended, but it is believed that the charming young man who had won the heart of his king and queen died in discouragement and poverty at the age of thirty-nine.

Preview

Connecting to the Literature

If you don't like the way things are, you can always speak up, but sometimes speaking up means paying a price. Unpopularity and punishment can be the costs of speaking out on controversial issues. Both Lanier and Lovelace had the courage to take such risks, speaking their minds in the face of opposition.

Literary Analysis

Tradition and Reform

Although they may seem to be opposites, tradition and reform go hand in hand.

- **Tradition** consists of a society's approved values, beliefs, roles, and practices.
- **Reform** attempts to change traditional practices and ideas.

Lanier is a clear reformer, fighting against stereotypes of women, while Lovelace fights for tradition, going to war and to prison for his king and his honor. As you read, note the appearance of themes of tradition and reform in their works.

Comparing Literary Works

Even when reformers' proposals are radical, they are often based on traditional beliefs. Lanier, for example, turns to the Bible, a traditional text, to support her new ideas about the equality between men and women. Lovelace, a supporter of the traditional power of his king, finds a new kind of freedom in love and integrity.

Both use a key strategy for interpreters of a tradition: They explore the multiple meanings of value terms such as *strength, honor,* and *freedom.* By redefining such terms, they find new ways to apply traditional ideas. As you read, compare the ways in which literary and political traditions and the spirit of reform weave their way through these works.

Reading Strategy

Using Historical Context

As you read a work, place it in its **historical context** by identifying ideas and assumptions that are typical of its era. Consider also which ideas may be responses to events of the period. To place Lanier's and Lovelace's poems in their context, complete a chart like the one shown for each work.

Vocabulary Builder

breach (brēch) *n.* breaking or being broken; failure to observe the terms of an agreement (p. 493)

discretion (di skresh′ ən) *n.* care in what one does and says (p. 493)

inconstancy (in kän′ stən sē) *n.* fickleness; changeableness (p. 494)

Poem
"Eve's Apology"
Historical Context
Seventeenth-century women's rights were restricted; story of Eve was used to justify these restrictions
Connection

from Eve's Apology in Defense of Women / To Lucasta, on Going to the Wars / To Althea, from Prison ■ 491

❷ Literary Analysis
Tradition and Reform

- Tell students that in these selections they will be encountering the issues of tradition and reform.

- Explain to students how the relationship between tradition and reform figures in the works that follow.

  Tradition: While Lovelace finds a new kind of freedom in love and integrity, he is nonetheless a supporter of the traditional power of his king.

  Reform: Lanier is a clear reformer who turns to the Bible, a traditional text, however, to support her new ideas about the equality between men and women.

❸ Reading Strategy
Using Historical Context

- Explain to students how to use the chart on this page. Give students a copy of **Reading Strategy Graphic Organizer A,** p. 91 in *Graphic Organizer Transparencies.* Have students use the chart to help them place each work in its historical context.

Vocabulary Development

Pronounce each vocabulary word for students, and read the definitions as a class. Have students identify any words with which they are already familiar.

Differentiated Instruction   Solutions for All Learners

Support for Special Needs Students
Have students complete the **Preview** and **Build Skills** pages for these selections in the *Reader's Notebook: Adapted Version.* These pages provide a selection summary, an abbreviated presentation of the reading and literary skills, and the graphic organizer on the **Build Skills** page in the student book.

Support for Less Proficient Readers
Have students complete the **Preview** and **Build Skills** pages for these selections in the *Reader's Notebook.* These pages provide a selection summary, an abbreviated presentation of the reading and literary skills, and the graphic organizer on the **Build Skills** page in the student book.

Support for English Learners
Have students complete the **Preview** and **Build Skills** pages for these selections in the *Reader's Notebook: English Learner's Version.* These pages provide a selection summary, an abbreviated presentation of the skills, additional contextual vocabulary, and the graphic organizer on the **Build Skills** page in the student book.

❶ About the Selection

Lanier would have made a wonderful lawyer. The book from which this passage is taken argues that women should have full equality with men both socially and in religion. Such ideas were considered quite radical in Lanier's day, and some people might find them so today.

❷ Background
Cultural Background

The political overtones of this and the following selections will evoke different reactions in readers. Ask students how a seventeenth-century minister—a man—would feel about the ideas in "Eve's Apology."

❸ Literary Analysis
Tradition and Reform

• Have students summarize the speaker's arguments.
Possible responses: Adam was created first and had more authority than Eve, so he was more to blame than she was.

• **Ask** students whether they think this argument is reasonable and why.
Possible responses: Some students may say the argument makes sense. Others may think that Eve is still not excused for eating the fruit in the first place.

• **Ask** students the Literary Analysis question: On what tradition does Lanier draw in these lines?
Answer: The biblical tradition of Genesis.

❶ from *Eve's Apology in Defense of Women*

AMELIA LANIER

❷ Background During the late sixteenth and early seventeenth centuries, a war of words raged, known as the *querelle des femmes*—"the debate about women." Each side fired off pamphlets and poems against the other. The issue: Were women by nature idle, vain, and immoral, or were they by nature good? Most of the debaters, pro or con, turned to the biblical story of Eve to support their points. Eve, their assumption went, was the first woman and the image of all women after her, so all women share her nature. Lanier's poem, making the same assumption, joins the controversy with powerful pro-woman arguments.

❸

But surely Adam cannot be excused,
Her fault though great, yet he was most to blame;
What weakness offered, strength might have refused,
Being Lord of all, the greater was his shame:
5 Although the serpent's craft had her abused,
God's holy word ought all his actions frame,
    For he was Lord and King of all the earth,
    Before poor Eve had either life or breath.

Who being framed by God's eternal hand,
10 The perfectest man that ever breathed on earth;

Literary Analysis
Tradition and Reform On what tradition does Lanier draw in these lines?

492 ■ *A Turbulent Time (1625–1798)*

Differentiated
Instruction   Solutions for All Learners

Accessibility at a Glance

	from Eve's Apology	To Lucasta	To Althea
Context	17th century England	17th century England	17th century England
Language	Poetic argument	Some inverted syntax	Archaic language
Concept Level	Accessible (equality)	Accessible (love, honor)	Accessible (love, honor)
Literary Merit	Period piece	Classic	Classic
Lexile	NP	NP	NP
Overall Rating	Average	More accessible	Average

And from God's mouth received that strait command,
The <u>breach</u> whereof he knew was present death;
Yea, having power to rule both sea and land,
Yet with one apple won to lose that breath
15   Which God had breathéd in his beauteous face,
    Bringing us all in danger and disgrace;

And then to lay the fault on patience's back,
That we (poor women) must endure it all;
We know right well he did <u>discretion</u> lack,
20 Being not persuaded thereunto at all.
If Eve did err, it was for knowledge sake;
The fruit being fair persuaded him to fall.
    No subtle serpent's falsehood did betray him;
    If he would eat it, who had power to stay him?

25 Not Eve, whose fault was only too much love,
Which made her give this present to her dear,
That what she tasted he likewise might prove,
Whereby his knowledge might become more clear;
He never sought her weakness to reprove
30 With those sharp words which he of God did hear;
    Yet men will boast of knowledge, which he took
    From Eve's fair hand, as from a learned book.

Critical Reading

1. **(a) Recall:** Who does Lanier blame more for the Fall—Adam or Eve?
(b) Connect: How does the second stanza connect Adam's "superiority" to Eve with his blameworthiness?

2. **(a) Recall:** According to Lanier, what motive did Eve have for tasting of the Tree of Knowledge? **(b) Recall:** According to Lanier, why did Eve offer Adam a taste of the apple? **(c) Summarize:** Describe Eve's character according to Lanier.

3. **(a) Recall:** According to the last stanza, what should Adam have done?
(b) Infer: What view of Adam is suggested by Lanier's description of him?

4. **Interpret:** According to the poem, in what way do men apply a double standard to the story of the Fall?

5. **Generalize:** Explain why the interpretation of this story was so important in seventeenth-century arguments about the nature of women.

6. **Take a Position:** Do you think Lanier's argument is convincing? Why or why not?

For: More about
Amelia Lanier
Visit: www.PHSchool.com
Web Code: ese-9308

from Eve's Apology in Defense of Women ■ 493

Vocabulary Builder

breach (brēch) *n.* breaking or being broken; failure to observe the terms of an agreement

discretion (di skresh′ ən) *n.* care in what one does and says

❹ Reading Strategy
Using Historical Context

- **Ask** students to infer from the poem the common attitude at the time toward the actions of Adam and Eve.
Answer: Eve was blamed for the fall, and Adam was seen as the victim.

- **Ask** how this belief might have affected people's attitudes toward women in general.
Answer: People may have perceived women as weak and the source of humanity's troubles.

ASSESS

Answers

1. (a) Lanier blames Adam more for the Fall. (b) Adam's privileged position—having been made the "perfectest man" and instructed directly by God—makes him more responsible for bringing danger and disgrace to "us all."

2. (a) Eve's motive was to gain knowledge. (b) Eve wanted to give Adam the apple in order that he too would have clearer knowledge. (c) Eve is loving and thoughtful.

3. (a) He should have reproved her by quoting what God had told him directly. (b) Adam lacks discretion; he took the fruit for no other reason than it was "fair."

4. Men blame Eve for being banished from the Garden of Eden, but they boast about the knowledge they gained from Eve's hand.

5. The story of Adam and Eve was used to validate seventeenth-century stereotypes of women and their role in society.

6. Students may respond that Lanier's argument is convincing; she gives realistic insight into Eve's character and gives Adam blame in proportion to his greater responsibilities.

Go Online
Author Link   For additional information about Amelia Lanier, have students type in the Web Code, then select L from the alphabet, and then select the author's name.

❺ To Lucasta, on Going to the Wars

Richard Lovelace

Background Tensions between the Church of England and the Puritans who wished to reform it had risen to a dangerous level. Foreign wars had led to a money shortage. Charles I made the situation worse by mishandling Parliament, by pressuring nobles for money, and by forcing commoners to serve in his armies. In 1642, England's Parliament went to war against England's king. Lovelace, a loyal supporter of Charles, was twice imprisoned by the king's opponents.

Tell me not, Sweet, I am unkind,
    That from the nunnery
Of thy chaste breast, and quiet mind,
    To war and arms I fly.

5 True, a new mistress now I chase,
    The first foe in the field;
And with a stronger faith embrace
    A sword, a horse, a shield.

Yet this <u>inconstancy</u> is such,
10   As you too shall adore;
❻ I could not love thee, Dear, so much,
    Loved I not honor more.

Vocabulary Builder
inconstancy (in kän′ stən sē) *n.* fickleness; changeableness

Going to the Battle, Edward Burn-Jones, Fitzwilliam Museum, Cambridge

△ **Critical Viewing** Like the speaker in "To Lucasta," the knight in the background of this image is going to war. Do the knight and the poem's speaker seem to be leaving in the same spirit? Explain. [**Compare and Contrast**]

Going to the Battle, 1858, by Sir Edward Burne-Jones

Sir Edward Burne-Jones (1833–1898) called his paintings "romantic dreams," and they were. He loved to include images from mythology, legends, and medieval times in his work.

During the nineteenth century, Burne-Jones was an important figure in the English Arts and Crafts Movement. His elegant designs influenced members of the Art Nouveau movement, especially Aubrey Beardsley.

Use these questions for discussion:

1. In what way is this painting stylized?
   Answer: The patterns, the drapery, and the poses are stylized.

2. What aspects of the poem are reflected in the drawing?
   Answer: Aspects of the poem reflected in the drawing include the man leaving for war, the women staying behind, and the romantic tone of the piece.

❽ **Critical Viewing**

Possible response: The knight appears to be leaving in a more subdued, regretful spirit, than the speaker of the poem.

• Have students analyze the movement in the poem from specific to general.
Possible Response: Students may respond that the first stanza is about love of one woman; the second about love of friends; the third about love of king and, therefore, country; and finally, the fourth is about freedom in general.

• **Ask** students if they think this poem is primarily a love poem or an expression of support for the king. Have them give reasons for their answers.
Possible Response: Students may respond that it could be a love poem, since it begins and ends with verses about love; however, it could be political because the writer is content to be in jail and sing the praises of the king.

⁵'To Althea, from Prison

Richard Lovelace

> When love with unconfined wings
>   Hovers within my gates,
> And my divine Althea brings
>   To whisper at the grates;
> 5 When I lie tangled in her hair
>   And fettered to her eye,
> The gods[1] that wanton[2] in the air
>   Know no such liberty.
>
> When flowing cups run swiftly round,
> 10   With no allaying Thames,[3]
> Our careless heads with roses bound,
>   Our hearts with loyal flames;
> When thirsty grief in wine we steep,
>   When healths[4] and drafts[5] go free,
> 15 Fishes that tipple in the deep,
>   Know no such liberty.

❾

---

1. **gods** The word *gods* is replaced by *birds* in some versions of this poem.
2. **wanton** play.
3. **cups . . . Thames** (temz) wine that has not been diluted by water (from the river Thames).
4. **healths** toasts.
5. **drafts** drinks.

When, like committed linnets,[6] I
    With shriller throat shall sing
The sweetness, mercy, majesty,
20   And glories of my King;
When I shall voice aloud how good
    He is, how great should be,
      Enlarged[7] winds that curl the flood,
    Know no such liberty.

25 Stone walls do not a prison make,
     Nor iron bars a cage;
Minds innocent and quiet take
     That for an hermitage;[8]
If I have freedom in my love,
30   And in my soul am free,
Angels alone that soar above,
     Enjoy such liberty.

❿

---

6. **committed linnets** caged finches.
7. **Enlarged** released.
8. **hermitage** (hur´ mi tij) a place of religious seclusion.

Literary Analysis
Tradition and Reform
In lines 25–28, how does Lovelace use the multiple associations of *walls* to shift from the idea of a prison to the idea of a place of religious seclusion?

Critical Reading

1. **Respond:** If you were Lucasta or Althea, would you be persuaded by Lovelace's arguments? Why or why not?

2. **(a) Recall:** In lines 1–4 of "To Lucasta," where is the speaker going?
(b) Infer: How does he expect Lucasta to respond?

3. **(a) Recall:** What does the speaker "now . . . chase" in line 5?
(b) Interpret: In what sense does the speaker admit to having two loves? **(c) Draw Conclusions:** In the final two lines, why does the strength of the speaker's love for Lucasta depend on the strength of his other love?

4. **(a) Recall:** In "To Althea," what are three things the poet does in prison? **(b) Interpret:** Explain the kind of "liberty" expressed in each of these activities.

5. **(a) Recall:** In the fourth stanza of "To Althea," which two freedoms does the poet say are most important? **(b) Interpret:** What is the meaning of lines 25–26? **(c) Evaluate:** Do you agree with Lovelace's views on freedom? Explain.

For: More about
   Richard Lovelace
Visit: www.PHSchool.com
Web Code: ese-9309

To Althea, from Prison ■ 497

Differentiated Instruction   Solutions for All Learners

Strategy for Less Proficient Readers
Point out to students that each stanza of "To Althea" is one separate sentence about a particular kind of pleasure. Tell them to first read the stanza through and then reread it looking for the main idea.

Strategy for Advanced Readers
Ask students to compare and contrast "To Lucasta, on Going to the Wars" with John Donne's "Song," which is also an argument designed to persuade a beloved to accept a leave-taking. Have them present their findings in an essay.

---

❿ Literary Analysis
Tradition and Reform

- Tell students that poetry often accomplishes its effects by the use of multiple meanings, or abrupt shifts in meaning. Then, have students read the last stanza of the poem.

- **Ask** students to answer the Literary Analysis question: In lines 25–28, how does Lovelace use the multiple associations of *walls* to shift from the idea of a prison to the idea of a place of religious seclusion? **Answer:** Through an act of spiritual transcendence, Lovelace turns the prison walls into a sanctuary that protects the speaker from the distractions of daily life.

ASSESS

Answers

1. Have the class discuss how they would feel if they received such arguments, and how they might respond to the speaker.

2. (a) The speaker is going to war. (b) He expects Lucasta to respond that he is unkind.

3. (a) He chases a new mistress— "the first foe in the field"—war. (b) His mistresses are Lucasta and honor. (c) **Possible response:** Students may say that the speaker cannot love himself if he is not honorable; and if he does not love himself, then he cannot love Lucasta.

4. (a) He dreams about Althea, toasts his friendships, and sings the praises of his king. (b) When he has freedom in his love and loyalties, his soul is free and cannot be caged by iron bars.

5. (a) The poet says freedom in love and freedom in one's soul are important. (b) Stone walls and iron bars cannot imprison the soul. (c) Have the class discuss Lovelace's views on freedom, and explain whether they agree with him or not.

Go Online For additional informa-
—**Author Link** tion about Richard Lovelace, have students type in the Web Code, then select L from the alphabet, and then select the author's name.

497

1. (a) Lanier attempts to reform the notion that women are weak and troublesome. (b) Lanier uses the biblical story of Adam and Eve to make her point. (c) She explains Eve's motives for giving the apple to Adam and assigns him the greater blame for the Fall.

2. The Bible story provides a common point of reference.

3. (a) Lovelace defends the traditions of freedom of thought and political choice. (b) Both Martin Luther King, Jr., and Gandhi were imprisoned for, but never abandoned, their beliefs in political freedom.

4. **Possible response:** (a) "To Althea, From Prison" best represents tradition because it supports the traditional value of loyalty to one's king. The speaker holds that value higher than physical freedom. (b) "Eve's Apology" best represents reform because it argues for a reevaluation of traditional ideas of woman's nature.

5. (a) Adam's greater power and authority give him a greater responsibility for the Fall. (b) Lanier says "What weakness offered, strength might have refused," referring to Eve's moral weakness in offering the apple, on the one hand, and to the moral strength with which Adam is credited by Lanier's opponents, on the other. Lanier goes on to say "If he would eat it, who had power to stay him?" meaning if Adam chose to eat the apple, Eve was too weak—physically and in terms of authority—to stop him. (c) Students' charts should compare the shift in meaning of the given words.

6. Entrenched ideas are hardest to revise, and one powerful way of doing so is by obliging readers to reexamine their understanding of common words.

7. Women in Lanier's time lacked educational opportunities. She notes that Adam took knowledge from Eve's hand yet, later, men boast as if it were their own achievement.

8. Imprisoned for his steadfast support of the king, Lovelace defies

continued

Apply the Skills

from *Eve's Apology in Defense of Women* • To Lucasta, on Going to the Wars • To Althea, from Prison

Literary Analysis

Tradition and Reform

1. **(a)** In "Eve's Apology," what traditional assumptions is Lanier trying to **reform**? **(b)** What **tradition** does she use to aid her? **(c)** How does she reinterpret this tradition to make her point?

2. How does Lanier's use of a Bible story make it easier for her to communicate with readers, even if they disagree with her arguments?

3. **(a)** In "To Althea, From Prison," what tradition does Lovelace defend? **(b)** Compare the spirit of lines 29–32 with the principles of a reformer such as Gandhi or Martin Luther King, Jr.

Comparing Literary Works

4. **(a)** Which poem in this grouping best represents tradition? Explain. **(b)** Which poem best represents reform? Explain.

5. **(a)** In "Eve's Apology," lines 1–8, what conclusion about the Fall does Lanier draw from Adam's strength? **(b)** Explain how she shifts between meanings of the word *weakness*—meaning both "moral weakness" and "powerlessness to influence"—to make her point. **(c)** Using a chart like the one below, compare this shift to a similar shift in the meaning of *freedom* in "To Althea."

Meaning 1	Meaning 2	Reasoning Behind Shift	Valid?

6. Explain why redefining key traditional terms like *weakness* might be important to a poet trying to reform a tradition.

Reading Strategy

Using Historical Context

7. Explain the historical facts about education that help you understand lines 31–32 of "Eve's Apology."

8. Explain how **historical context** helps you interpret the third stanza of "To Althea."

Extend Understanding

9. **World Events Connection:** Name an example of a reform movement of today, and compare its message with Lanier's or Lovelace's.

Tradition consists of a society's approved values, beliefs, roles, and practices. **Reform** refers to attempts to change traditional practices.

To **use historical context** to help you understand a work, consider the common assumptions and important events of the era in which the work was written and decide to what extent the piece reflects them.

Assessment

For: Self-test
Visit: www.PHSchool.com
Web Code: esa-6303

Answers continued

his captors and asserts that, like a caged bird, he will sing the king's praises even more effectively.

9. Students may cite both national and international reform movements.

Go Online
Assessment — Students may use the **Self-Test** to prepare for **Selection Test A** or **Selection Test B**.

Build Language Skills

Vocabulary Lesson

Fluency: Terms With *breach*

Use your knowledge of the word *breach*, meaning "a breaking or state of being broken," to write a definition of the italicized terms below.

1. The woman sued her fiancé for *breach of promise.*
2. The policewoman arrested the girls for a *breach of the peace.*
3. After his *breach of etiquette,* he was never invited back.
4. Selling the land to someone else would be a *breach of contract.*
5. From the shore, he watched the *breach* of the whale.
6. Unwilling to commit a *breach of honor,* he accepted the challenge.

Vocabulary Builder: Synonyms

For each word, choose the letter of its synonym.

1. discretion: **(a)** prudence, **(b)** falseness, **(c)** speed
2. inconstancy: **(a)** faithlessness, **(b)** doubt, **(c)** anger
3. breach: **(a)** promise, **(b)** help, **(c)** violation

Spelling Strategy

The endings *-ant* and *-ent* are both used to form adjectives. To spell the related noun, match the vowel in the ending of the adjective. For example, *constant* becomes *constancy,* while *insistent* becomes *insistence.*

Correctly spell each word below. If a word is spelled correctly, write *correct.*

1. eloquence   2. competance   3. dominence

Grammar and Style Lesson

Correlative Conjunctions

Correlative conjunctions are paired conjunctions that connect two words or groups of words of equal significance. Correlative conjunctions include *either . . . or; both . . . and; neither . . . nor; whether . . . or;* and *not only . . . but also.*

> **Example:** For he was lord and king of all the earth,
>
> Before poor Eve had <u>either</u> life <u>or</u> breath, ...

Practice   Rewrite each item, using correlative conjunctions to combine the sentences.

1. Lanier did not put man before God. She did not put woman before God, either.

2. When in prison, Lovelace was able to feel free. When spending time with friends, he was also able to feel free.
3. Lanier believed that men had to take responsibility for sin. She believed that women also had to take responsibility.
4. Richard Lovelace fought for the king. He also fought for honor.
5. Lanier was traditional in her poem. Lanier was radical in her poem.

Writing Application   Write a brief paragraph defining your idea of freedom and explaining how it compares to Lovelace's views in "To Althea, from Prison." Use at least two pairs of correlative conjunctions in your paragraph.

W̵G̵ Prentice Hall Writing and Grammar Connection: Chapter 17, Section 4

from *Eve's Apology in Defense of Women / To Lucasta, on Going to the Wars / To Althea, from Prison* ■ 499

---

❶ Vocabulary Lesson
Fluency

1. failure to fulfill a promise, especially a promise to marry
2. disruption; public disturbance
3. lapse in good manners
4. violation of a binding agreement
5. leap above the surface of the water
6. an act contrary to principle; violation of integrity

Vocabulary Builder

1. a   2. a   3. c

Spelling Strategy

1. correct   3. dominance
2. competence

❷ Grammar and Style Lesson

1. Lanier put neither man nor woman before God.
2. Both when he was in prison and when he was with friends, Lovelace was able to feel free.
3. Lanier believed that both men and women had to take responsibility for sin.
4. Richard Lovelace fought not only for the king but also for honor.
5. Lanier was both traditional and radical in her poem.

Writing Application

Sample sentences:
Freedom has both advantages and disadvantages. It entails not only life-enriching privileges but also considerable responsibility.

W̵G̵ **Writing and Grammar, Diamond Level**

Students will find further instruction and practice on correlative conjunctions in Chapter 17, Section 4.

Assessment Practice

Writer's Purpose   **(For more practice, see *Standardized Test Preparation Workbook*, p.21.)**

Use the following to show students how to determine a writer's purpose.

> But surely Adam cannot be excused;
> Her fault though great, yet he was most to blame.
> What weakness offered, strength might have refused . . .
> And then to lay the fault on patience's back
> That we (poor women) must endure it all . . .

Lanier uses the word *poor* to—

A evoke anger
B make an ironic point
C evoke sympathy for women
D emphasize that women could not own property

Choices *B* and *D* do not fit the meaning of the passage, and A is not consistent with the tone. *C* is the correct answer.

499

❸ Writing Lesson

You may use this Writing Lesson as timed-writing practice, or you may allow students to develop the essay as a writing assignment over several days.

- To guide students in writing this essay, give them the **Support for Writing Lesson** page (*Unit 3 Resources*, p. 83).

- Briefly review with students Lovelace's statements about freedom and honor.

- Use the Writing for Assessment rubrics in *General Resources*, pp. 67–68, to evaluate students' timed essays.

❹ Listening and Speaking

- As a class select a worthy cause as the topic of a "reform ballad."

- Divide the class into three groups. Tell all the groups to select the cause they will write about. Tell the first group to develop the questions and answers. Tell the second group to develop the images. Have the third group develop the refrain.

- Follow up with a discussion in which each group discusses the material they produced. The other groups should ask questions and respond to the description.

- To evaluate students' ballads, use the rubrics for Rhyming Poem in *General Resources*, pp. 73–74.

- The **Support for Extend Your Learning** page (*Unit 3 Resources*, p. 84) provides guided note-taking opportunities to help students complete the Extend Your Learning activities.

Go Online
Research
Have students type in the Web Code for another research activity.

---

❸ Writing Lesson

Timed Writing: Essay Connecting Literature With Experience

Lovelace strengthens his poetry by linking broad themes—freedom and honor—to his own experiences. Write an essay in which you draw general conclusions from personal experience about one of these themes. Compare your experiences and conclusions with Lovelace's. **(40 minutes)**

Prewriting
(10 minutes)
Jot down notes on experiences that have shaped your views of freedom or honor. Then, write a summary of Lovelace's view of the topic and the experiences that led him to that view.

Drafting
(20 minutes)
Begin your draft with a summary comparing your experiences to Lovelace's. Support your comparison by linking specific incidents and quotations from Lovelace with your broader point.

> **Model: Relating Broad Themes to Personal Experience**
>
> - **Broad Theme:** Lovelace says freedom is a state of mind.
>
> - **Personal Experience:** I hated taking piano lessons because I was made to. When my friend asked me to teach her "Chopsticks," I saw music in a new light and began practicing devotedly.
>
> - **Link experience to theme:** Being "made to" practice piano was only a constraint when I did not embrace it.

This organization allows the writer to explore the experience fully before analyzing its larger meaning.

Revising
(10 minutes)
Review your draft, strengthening connections between incidents, quotations, and general points.

WG Prentice Hall Writing and Grammar Connection: Chapter 4, Section 2

Extend Your Learning

❹ **Listening and Speaking** Write and perform a rhymed **ballad** about a reform you support.

1. Use a question-and-answer dialogue format. Question why the cause is worthy of support, and provide answers.
2. Use strong images to dramatize the cause.
3. Repeat a catchy phrase as your refrain.

After rehearsing, perform your ballad in class.

Research and Technology Research and write a **report with spreadsheets** on the English Civil War. Include in your report a spreadsheet documenting an aspect of the subject, such as the regional distribution of Royalists and Puritans.

Go Online
Research
For: An additional research activity
Visit: www.PHSchool.com
Web Code: esd-7305

Assessment Resources

The following resources can be used to assess students' knowledge and skills.

Unit 3 Resources
  Selection Test A, pp. 86–88
  Selection Test B, pp. 89–91

General Resources
  Rubrics for Writing for Assessment, pp. 67–68
  Rubrics for Rhyming Poem, pp. 73–74

Go Online
Assessment
Students may use the **Self-test** to prepare for **Selection Test A** or **Selection Test B.**

The Ties That Bind

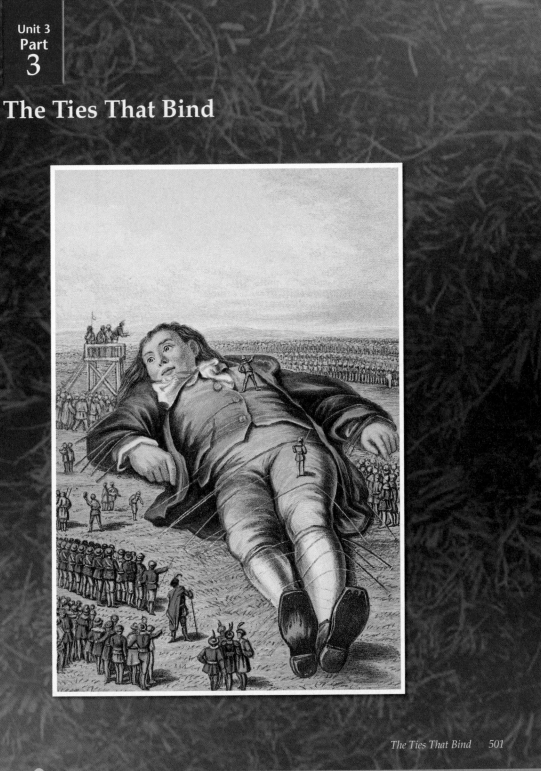

The Ties That Bind   501

Selection Planning Guide

The selections in this section all reveal or comment on the ties that bind together a family, community, or nation. Samuel Pepys's *Diary* provides a firsthand glimpse of how citizens of London pulled together as they dealt with two terrible disasters that struck in the mid-1600s: the bubonic plague and the Great Fire.

Although Defoe's *A Journal of the Plague Year* is a work of fiction, it contains profound and heartbreaking insights into the effects the plague had on families and communities.

Jonathan Swift also, through his satiric *Gulliver's Travels,* reveals how, for better or worse, religious and national identities inform the actions and thoughts of congregations and citizenry.

Humanities

Illustration from *Gulliver's Travels*

Explain to students that this illustration depicts Lemuel Gulliver in Lilliput. He is surrounded by people of small stature and is tethered to the ground with ropes and stakes. **Ask:**

1. In what way is Gulliver literally bound? In what other ways might he be bound?
   Answer: Gulliver is literally tied down with ropes. He may be figuratively bound in that he could possibly escape from the situation but chooses not to.

2. What idea does the image of a large man bound by many small people suggest to you?
   Possible response: It suggests the idea of a tyrant being brought down by the united force of less powerful people.

Benchmark

After students have completed the excerpt from *A Journal of the Plague Year,* administer **Benchmark Test 5.** If the Benchmark Test reveals that some students need further work, use the **Interpretation Guide** to determine the appropriate reteaching page in the **Reading Kit** and on **Success Tracker.**

Monitoring Progress

Before students read *Gulliver's Travels: Chapter 1,* administer **Diagnostic Test 6.** This test will determine students' level of readiness for the reading and vocabulary skills.

Differentiated Instruction   Solutions for All Learners

Accessibility at a Glance

More Accessible	Average	More Challenging
from A Dictionary of the English Language	*from* The Diary *from* A Journal of the Plague Year *from* Gulliver's Travels *from* the Life of Samuel Johnson	*from* An Essay on Man *from* The Rape of the Lock Elegy Written in a Country Churchyard A Nocturnal Reverie

501

Meeting Your Standards

Students will

1. analyze and respond to literary elements.
   - Literary Analysis: Diaries and Journals

2. read, comprehend, analyze, and critique nonfiction and fiction.
   - Reading Strategy: Drawing Conclusions
   - Reading Check questions
   - Apply the Skills questions
   - Assessment Practice (ATE)

3. develop vocabulary.
   - Vocabulary Lesson: Latin Prefix: *dis-*

4. understand and apply written and oral language conventions.
   - Spelling Strategy
   - Grammar and Style Lesson: Gerunds

5. develop writing proficiency.
   - Writing Lesson: Response to Criticism

6. develop appropriate research strategies.
   - Extend Your Learning: Fact-Check Report

7. understand and apply listening and speaking strategies.
   - Extend Your Learning: Performance as a Town Crier

Block Scheduling: Use one 90-minute class period to preteach the skills and have students read the selection. Use a second 90-minute class period to assess students' mastery of skills, extend their learning, and monitor their progress.

Homework Suggestions

Following are possibilities for homework assignments.

- Support pages from *Unit 3 Resources:*
    - Literary Analysis
    - Reading Strategy
    - Vocabulary Builder
    - Grammar and Style

- An Extend Your Learning project and the Writing Lesson for this selection may be completed over several days.

Step-by-Step Teaching Guide	Pacing Guide
PRETEACH	
• Administer Vocabulary and Reading Warm-ups as necessary.	5 min.
• Engage students' interest with the motivation activity.	5 min.
• Read and discuss author and background features. **FT**	10 min.
• Introduce the Literary Analysis Skill: Diaries and Journals. **FT**	5 min.
• Introduce the Reading Strategy: Drawing Conclusions. **FT**	10 min.
• Prepare students to read by teaching the selection vocabulary. **FT**	
TEACH	
• Informally monitor comprehension while students read independently or in groups. **FT**	30 min.
• Monitor students' comprehension with the Reading Check notes.	as students read
• Reinforce vocabulary with Vocabulary Builder notes.	as students read
• Develop students' understanding of diaries and journals with the Literary Analysis annotations. **FT**	5 min.
• Develop students' ability to draw conclusions with the Reading Strategy annotations. **FT**	5 min.
ASSESS/EXTEND	
• Assess students' comprehension and mastery of the Literary Analysis and Reading Strategy by having them answer the Apply the Skills questions. **FT**	15 min.
• Have students complete the Vocabulary Development Lesson and the Grammar and Style Lesson. **FT**	15 min.
• Apply students' ability to check for accuracy by using the Writing Lesson. **FT**	45 min. or homework
• Apply students' understanding by using one or more of the Extend Your Learning activities.	20–90 min. or homework
• Administer Selection Test A or Selection Test B. **FT**	15 min.

Liter...

Diarie...
A di...
reaction...
misadve...
provide...

• Pe...
  ev...
• D...
  st...
  po...
In re...
events.

Comp...
In jo...
experie...
help bri...
intimac...
How...
for othe...
qualitie...

Read...

Draw...
As...
each w...
draw fr...

Vocal...

appreh...
n. fears...

abated

lament...
distressi...

combu...
capable...
flamma...

malicio...
harmful...

Resources

PRINT

Unit 3 Resources

Vocabulary Warm-up Word Lists [L1, L2, EL]	p. 92
Vocabulary Warm-up Practice [L1, L2, EL]	p. 93
Reading Warm-up A [L1, L2, EL]	p. 94
Reading Warm-up B [L1, L2, L3]	p. 95

TRANSPARENCY

Graphic Organizer Transparencies

Literary Analysis Graphic Organizer A [L3]	p. 97
Literary Analysis Graphic Organizer B [L1, L2, EL]	p. 98
Reading Strategy Graphic Organizer A [L3]	p. 95
Reading Strategy Graphic Organizer B [L1, L2, EL]	p. 96

PRINT

Reader's Notebook [L2]
Reader's Notebook: Adapted Version [L1]
Reader's Notebook: English Learner's Version [EL]
Unit 3 Resources

Literary Analysis [L3]	p. 96
Reading Strategy [L3]	p. 97
Vocabulary Builder [L3]	p. 98

TECHNOLOGY

Listening to Literature Audio CDs [L2, EL]
Reader's Notebook: Adapted Version Audio CD [L1, L2]

PRINT

Unit 3 Resources

Grammar and Style [L3]	p. 99
Support for Writing Lesson [L3]	p. 100
Support for Extend Your Learning [L3]	p. 101
Enrichment [L4]	p. 102
Selection Test A [L1, L2, EL]	pp. 103–105
Selection Test B [L3, L4]	pp. 106–108

General Resources

Rubrics for Response to Literature [L3]	pp. 65–66

TECHNOLOGY

Go Online: Research [L3]
Go Online: Self-test [L3]
ExamView® **Test Bank [L3]**

Choosing Resources for Differentiated Instruction

[L1] Special Needs Students

[L2] Below-Level Students

[L3] All Students

[L4] Advanced Students

[EL] English Learners

For Vocabulary and Reading Warm-ups and for Selection Tests, **A** signifies "less challenging" and **B** "more challenging." For Graphic Organizer transparencies, **A** signifies "not filled in" and **B** "filled in."

FT Fast Track Instruction: To move the lesson more quickly, use the strategies and activities identified with **FT**.

Scaffolding for Less Proficient and Advanced Students

The leveled Critical Thinking questions after selections progress in the levels of thinking required to answer them. To address the needs of your different students, you may use the (a) level questions for your less proficient students and the (b) level questions with your on-level and advanced students. The occasional (c) level questions are appropriate for your advanced students.

PRENTICE HALL
Teacher EXPRESS™ Use this complete
Plan · Teach · Assess suite of powerful
teaching tools to make lesson planning and testing quicker and easier.

PRENTICE HALL
Student EXPRESS™ Use the interac-
Learn · Study · Succeed tive textbook
(online and on CD-ROM) to make selections and activities come alive with audio and video support and interactive questions.

Benchmark

After students have completed these selections, administer **Benchmark Test 5** (*Unit 3 Resources*, pp. 109–114). If the Benchmark Test reveals that some students need further work, use the **Interpretation Guide** to determine the appropriate reteaching page in the **Reading Kit** and on **Success Tracker**.

Go Online
Professional
Development
For: Information about Lexiles
Visit: www.PHSchool.com
Web Code: eue-1111

502b

Mot...

Ask st...
they h...
ter mo...
could...
wreck...
group...
time. ...
the de...
great...
years...
unforg...

❶ B...

More...

Samu...

Samu...
His ca...
devoti...
He re...
Royal...
and sa...
Great...
anyon...
tions i...
prison...
cued...
diplor...
one o...
his da...
includ...
Isaac...
almos...

Dani...

Danie...
cated...
minis...
instea...
"belo...
invest...
he re...
years...
pily n...
politi...
wrote...
which...
dang...
to jou...
that h...
of the...

Learning Modalities

Interpersonal Learners Suggest that students imagine how they would have reacted had they lived during the plague or the fire. Remind them that medicine was helpless in the face of the plague, and firefighting techniques were almost nonexistent. As they read, encourage students to use their insights about the human condition to understand the experiences of Pepys and the narrator of *A Journal of the Plague Year.*

❶ About the Selection

Samuel Pepys wrote his diary in code, believing that it would not be read by anyone else. The diary has remained popular because it shows an extraordinarily honest and detailed picture of one person's real life, as well as the historical events that he witnessed or took part in. Today, readers who want to learn about seventeenth-century London still turn to Pepys's diary.

❷ Humanities

Last page of Samuel Pepys's *Diary,* 31 May 1669

Pepys wrote this diary using a particular system of shorthand devised by Thomas Shelton. However, because some passages contained sensitive information, Pepys added further safeguards, using a cipher that he had created as well as foreign words. The contents remained secret until 1825, when the diary was finally decoded.

Use these questions for discussion:

1. What kinds of details would a person such as Pepys want to keep private?
   Possible responses: Because he worked for the Navy, any military knowledge would be guarded. Also, due to political turmoil, criticisms or opinions might be dangerous.

2. What value does a diary such as this one have for the person who keeps it?
   Answer: It helps the person remember events; writing it may help the person see events in a new light.

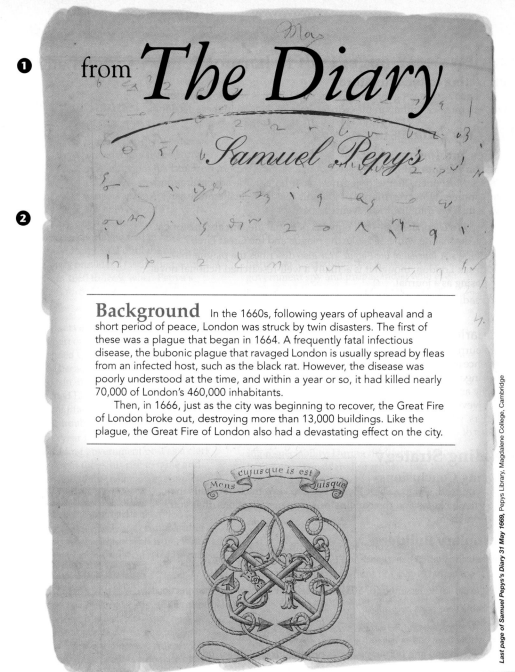

❶ ❷ from *The Diary*

Samuel Pepys

Background In the 1660s, following years of upheaval and a short period of peace, London was struck by twin disasters. The first of these was a plague that began in 1664. A frequently fatal infectious disease, the bubonic plague that ravaged London is usually spread by fleas from an infected host, such as the black rat. However, the disease was poorly understood at the time, and within a year or so, it had killed nearly 70,000 of London's 460,000 inhabitants.

Then, in 1666, just as the city was beginning to recover, the Great Fire of London broke out, destroying more than 13,000 buildings. Like the plague, the Great Fire of London also had a devastating effect on the city.

Mens cujusque is est Quisque

Last page of Samuel Pepys's Diary 31 May 1669, Pepys Library, Magdalene College, Cambridge

❸ ▲ **Critical Viewing** What evidence on this page of *The Diary* suggests that Pepys never meant to share his writing with the world? **[Infer]**

504 ■ *A Turbulent Time (1625–1798)*

The Plague

Sept. 3, 1665. (Lord's Day.) Church being done, my Lord Bruncker, Sir J. Minnes, and I up to the vestry[1] at the desire of the Justices of the Peace, Sir Theo. Biddulph and Sir W. Boreman and Alderman Hooker, in order to the doing something for the keeping of the plague from growing; but Lord! to consider the madness of the people of the town, who will (because they are forbid) come in crowds along with the dead corps[2] to see them buried; but we agreed on some orders for the prevention thereof.[3] Among other stories, one was very passionate, methought of a complaint brought against a man in the town for taking a child from London from an infected house. Alderman Hooker told us it was the child of a very able citizen in Gracious Street, a saddler,[4] who had buried all the rest of his children of the plague, and himself and wife now being shut up and in despair of escaping, did desire only to save the life of this little child; and so prevailed to have it received stark-naked into the arms of a friend, who brought it (having put it into new fresh clothes) to Greenwich; where upon hearing the story, we did agree it should be permitted to be received and kept in the town. Thence with my Lord Bruncker to Captain Cocke's, where we mighty merry and supped, and very late I by water to Woolwich, in great <u>apprehensions</u> of an ague. . . .

Sept. 14, 1665. When I come home I spent some thoughts upon the occurrences of this day, giving matter for as much content on one hand and melancholy on another, as any day in all my life. For the first; the finding of my money and plate,[5] and all safe at London, and speeding in my business of money this day. The hearing of this good news to such excess, after so great a despair of my Lord's doing anything this year; adding to that, the decrease of 500 and more, which is the first decrease we have yet had in the sickness since it begun: and great hopes that the next week it will be greater. Then, on the other side, my finding that though the bill[6] in general is <u>abated</u>, yet the city within the walls is increased, and likely to continue so, and is close to our house there. My meeting dead corpses of the plague, carried to be buried close to me at noonday through the city in Fanchurch Street. To see a person sick of the sores, carried close by me by Grace church in a hackney coach.[7] My finding the Angell Tavern at the lower end of Tower Hill, shut up, and more than that, the alehouse at the Tower Stairs, and more than that, the person was then dying of the plague when I was last there, a little while ago, at night, to write a short letter there, and I overheard the mistress of the

---

1. **vestry** (ves' trē) *n.* church meeting-room.
2. **corps** corpses.
3. **but we . . . thereof** Funeral processions were forbidden in London during the plague. However, the law was often ignored.
4. **saddler** *n.* person who makes, sells, and repairs saddles.
5. **plate** valuable serving dishes and flatware.
6. **bill** weekly list of burials.
7. **hackney coach** carriage for hire.

Reading Strategy
Drawing Conclusions
What conclusions can you draw about Pepys from the entry for "Sept. 3, 1665"? Explain.

Vocabulary Builder
apprehensions (ap' rē hen' shenz) *n.* fears; concerns

Vocabulary Builder
abated (ə bāt' id) *v.* lessened

 Reading Check
What gives Pepys "much content" and what makes him "melancholy"?

from The Diary ■ 505

Differentiated Instruction   Solutions for All Learners

Enrichment for Gifted/Talented Students
Have students create an illustration for a scene described in *The Diary*. Encourage students to incorporate as much of the imagery of either the plague or the Great Fire into their illustrations as possible. Students may want to do additional research on the plague or the Great Fire, or they may want to consider the examples of fine art related to these subjects throughout this lesson. As an alternative to drawing or painting the illustration, students could consider a collage, or even a multimedia presentation of images that support the selection.

Strategy for Advanced Readers
Tell students that one of the reasons these two works have maintained their popularity is the level of detail each writer includes in his work. Have students focus on the level of detail and think about how it contributes to a reader's ability to draw conclusions about the era being described. Suggest that students make a mental note each time a writer answers one of the questions journalists are trained to ask: *who? what? when? where?* and *why?*

---

③ Critical Viewing
Possible response: The use of a code, instead of a recognizable alphabet, shows that Pepys was not writing for others.

④ Reading Strategy
Drawing Conclusions
- Ask students what details or interesting observations they note in the passage. Write their responses on the chalkboard.
- Then, **ask** the Reading Strategy question: What conclusions can you draw about Pepys from the entry for Sept. 3, 1665?
Possible responses: Pepys is a Christian who attends church; he is an important member of society who makes decisions and rules; he is compassionate; he is concerned for his own health.

▶ **Monitor Progress: Ask** students why the child was stripped of its clothes.
Answer: People feared that the clothes might spread the plague.

⑤ Background
Science History
The belief expressed in Pepys's diary that clothes were involved in spreading the plague was not as odd as it seems. Smallpox was another major killer then and was spread by contact with clothing, or anything else, that had come into contact with an infected person—even as much as two years after the contact.

Bubonic plague was spread by fleas and by the coughing or sneezing of an infected person. In Pepys's day, though, little was known about the transmission of the disease. Removing clothes that had been in contact with those who had died in the house was intended as an effort to stop the spread of the disease. If plague-bearing fleas were destroyed along with the clothing, this method might have been partially effective.

⑥ Reading Check
Answer: Pepys is content because his money and plate are safe in London, his business is going well, and there has been a decrease in the disease. He is melancholy because he has encountered many sick and dying people, and various establishments are closed.

505

The Great Fire of London, 1666

At the time of the fire, photography did not exist, so artists were relied on to create visual records of events of the time. These artists often worked outdoors in the midst of the events they recorded. We do not know who created this painting, which hangs in the Museum of London, England. However, he or she left a vivid record of the disaster. The accuracy of the image is confirmed by the ease with which one can identify important landmarks, such as the Tower of London on the right and London Bridge to the left.

Use these questions for discussion:

1. How might such an event be visually recorded and shared today?
Possible response: Photographs and videos are likely ways that it would be recorded, and the information might be shared in newspapers, magazines, on the Internet, or on television.

2. Why do people like to keep visual records of such events?
Possible response: Most people like to have some way of remembering major events, or even of proving that something was as bad as they remember when they relate the stories years later.

❽ Critical Viewing

Possible response: The line "and there I did see the houses at that end of the bridge all on fire, and an infinite great fire on this and the other side of the bridge . . ." would be an appropriate caption.

❾ Literary Analysis
Diaries and Journals

- **Ask** students the Literary Analysis question: What does the abbreviated language in the entry for "Sept. 14" suggest about the audience for whom Pepys was writing? Explain.
Answer: His use of incomplete sentences throughout this passage indicates that Pepys was writing for himself and did not expect anyone else to read the diary.

- Remind students that, in addition to being private, the diary was written in code, which may also have contributed to the choppiness of the writing.

❼ *The Great Fire of London,* 1666

house sadly saying to her husband somebody was very ill, but did not think it was of the plague. To hear that poor Payne, my waiter, hath buried a child, and is dying himself. To hear that a laborer I sent but the other day to Dagenhams, to know how they did there, is dead of the plague; and that one of my own watermen, that carried me daily, fell sick as soon as he had landed me on Friday morning last, when I had been all night upon the water (and I believe he did get his infection that day at Brainford), and is now dead of the plague. To hear that Captain Lambert and Cuttle are killed in the taking these ships; and that Mr. Sidney Montague is sick of a desperate fever at my Lady Carteret's, at Scott's Hall. To hear that Mr. Lewes hath another daughter sick. And, lastly, that both my servants, W. Hewer and Tom Edwards, have lost their fathers, both in St. Sepulcher's parish, of the plague this week, do put me into great apprehensions of melancholy, and with good reason. But I put off the thoughts of sadness as much as I can, and the rather to keep my wife in good heart and family also. After supper (having eat nothing all this day) upon a fine tench[8] of Mr. Shelden's taking, we to bed.

The Fire of London

Sept. 2, 1666. (Lord's day.) Some of our maids sitting up late last night to get things ready against our feast today, Jane called us up about three in the morning, to tell us of a great fire they saw in the

---

8. tench *n.* type of fish.

❽ ⚠ **Critical Viewing**
What line from Pepys's account of the fire would be an appropriate caption for this painting? Why? **[Connect]**

Literary Analysis
Diaries and Journals
What does the abbreviated language in the entry for "Sept. 14" suggest about the audience for whom Pepys was writing? Explain.

Enrichment

Bubonic Plague

The plague reported in these selections was not the worst one to hit Europe. In the fourteenth century, an outbreak started in China, then swept across Russia and into Europe. By the time it ended, one third of the population of Europe was dead.

International trade helped spread the disease. Major trading ports were always the most endangered, because the rats from ships could bring the plague to shore at any time.

The disease is called bubonic plague when it is spread by the bite of fleas. When it is spread from person to person, it becomes pneumonic plague, and attacks the lungs. Outbreaks still occur. The last urban plague in the U.S. was in 1924–25 in Los Angeles, but there was an outbreak in India in 1994. Today, about 1,000–3,000 cases are reported worldwide each year, with about 10–15 occurring in the U.S. To learn more about this and other diseases, visit the Web site of the Centers for Disease Control at http://www.cdc.gov.

city. So I rose and slipped on my night-gown, and went to her window, and thought it to be on the back side of Mark Lane at the farthest; but, being unused to such fires as followed, I thought it far enough off; and so went to bed again and to sleep. About seven rose again to dress myself, and there looked out at the window, and saw the fire not so much as it was and farther off. So to my closet to set things to rights after yesterday's cleaning. By and by Jane comes and tells me that she hears that above 300 houses have been burned down tonight by the fire we saw, and that it is now burning down all Fish Street, by London Bridge. So I made myself ready presently, and walked to the Tower,[9] and there got up upon one of the high places, Sir J. Robinson's little son going up with me; and there I did see the houses at that end of the bridge all on fire, and an infinite great fire on this and the other side the end of the bridge; which, among other people, did trouble me for poor little Michell and our Sarah on the bridge. So down, with my heart full of trouble, to the Lieutenant of the Tower, who tells me that it begun this morning in the King's baker's house in Pudding Lane, and that it hath burned St. Magnus's Church and most part of Fish Street already. So I down to the waterside, and there got a boat and through bridge, and there saw a <u>lamentable</u> fire. Poor Michell's house, as far as the Old Swan, already burned that way, and the fire running farther, that in a very little time it got as far as the steel yard, while I was there. Everybody endeavoring to remove their goods, and flinging into the river or bringing them into lighters that lay off; poor people staying in their houses as long as till the very fire touched them, and then running into boats, or clambering from one pair of stairs by the waterside to another. And among other things, the poor pigeons, I perceive, were loth to leave their houses, but hovered about the windows and balconies till they were, some of them burned, their wings, and fell down. Having stayed, and in an hour's time seen the fire rage every way, and nobody, to my sight, endeavoring to quench it, but to remove their goods, and leave all to the fire, and having seen it get as far as the steel yard, and the wind mighty high and driving it into the city; and everything, after so long a drought, proving <u>combustible</u>, even the very stones of churches, and among other things the poor steeple by which pretty Mrs.— lives, and whereof my old schoolfellow Elborough is parson, taken fire in the very top, and there burned till it fell down. I to Whitehall (with a gentleman with me who desired to go off from the Tower, to see the fire, in my boat), and there up to the King's closet in the chapel, where people come about me, and I did give them an account dismayed them all, and word was carried in to the King. So I was called for, and did tell the King and Duke of York what I saw, and that unless his Majesty did command houses to be pulled down nothing could stop the fire. They seemed much troubled, and the King commanded me to go to my Lord Mayor from him, and

9. **Tower** Tower of London.

Vocabulary Builder
lamentable (lam′ ən tə bəl)
adj. distressing

Vocabulary Builder
combustible (kəm bus′ tə bəl) *adj.* capable of igniting and burning; flammable

 Reading Check

What does Pepys learn about the fire from his visit to the Tower?

from The Diary ■ 507

❿ Background
Language
Point out to students that, when Pepys writes that Jane "called us up," he is not referring to a phone. This is a British expression for "woke us up by calling to us." One hears in Britain, even today, the expression *knock me up,* which means "knock on the door to wake me up."

⓫ Critical Thinking
Infer
• **Ask** students to paraphrase this passage.
  Answer: Worried and saddened, I visited the Lieutenant of the Tower, who told me that the fire had begun this morning in the King's baker's house in Pudding Lane, and that it already had spread to St. Magnus's Church and most of Fish Street.

• Then, **ask** why the fire might have started in a bakery. What would cause the fire to spread?
  Answer: The ovens were heated by actual fires; fires were easily spread because the buildings were constructed of wood, were built close together, and had no sprinkler systems or fire extinguishers.

⓬ Critical Thinking
Analyze
• Have students identify things that contributed to making the fire worse.
  Answer: There had been a drought, so everything was very dry, and there were high winds.

• **Ask** students how people are reacting to the fire.
  Answer: They are making no effort to stop the fire but are simply trying to save their valuables and then get away.

• You may wish to discuss why people would behave this way.
  Possible response: They must have felt completely helpless. They were certain that there was nothing they could do, so they just tried to escape with their lives and a few belongings.

⓭ Reading Check
Answer: Pepys learns that the fire started at the King's baker's house, burned down St. Magnus's Church, and spread to most of Fish Street.

507

Reading Strategy
Drawing Conclusions

14 Reading Strategy
Drawing Conclusions

- Point out that Pepys was called for by the King of England and Duke of York. **Ask** students what conclusion can be drawn about Pepys's position in society.
  Possible response: Pepys must be well known and respected, with an important role in society.

- Explain that, in suggesting that houses be torn down, Pepys is recommending the creation of a fire break. Ask if students have ever seen news reports about modern firefighters battling blazes. Creating a fire break—that is, destroying flammable materials in the path of the fire in order to stop the fire's spreading—is still often used as a final measure in such situations.

- **Ask** students what conclusions can be drawn from Pepys's suggestion and from the fact that the king immediately acted on his suggestion.
  Possible response: The suggestion shows Pepys's practical intelligence in recognizing what needed to be done. The king's response shows either that he recognized the suggestion as a good one, or that he trusted Pepys's judgment.

15 Reading Strategy
Drawing Conclusions

- Discuss in class the strategy people in London used to protect their belongings as well as what is implied by the fact that people could keep moving their goods from house to house.
  Possible responses: Students may be surprised that people simply moved their valuables from one house to another. The fact that people could keep moving their goods might indicate that people knew and trusted their neighbors.

- You might want to ask students what they think they would carry out of their homes if a disaster struck today.

- Then, **ask** the Reading Strategy question: What conclusion about the fire can you draw from the fact that goods were removed "from one burned house to another"?
  Possible responses: The fire kept spreading to houses that were at first assumed to be safe.

---

14 command him to spare no houses, but to pull down before the fire every way. The Duke of York bid me tell him that if he would have any more soldiers he shall; and so did my Lord Arlington afterwards, as a great secret. Here meeting with Captain Cocke, I in his coach, which he lent me, and Creed with me to Paul's,[10] and there walked along Watling Street, as well as I could, every creature coming away loaden with goods to save, and here and there sick people carried away in beds. Extraordinary good goods carried in carts and on backs. At last met my Lord Mayor in Canning Street, like a man spent, with a handkerchief about his neck. To the King's message he cried, like a fainting woman, "Lord! what can I do? I am spent: people will not obey me. I have been pulling down houses; but the fire overtakes us faster than we can do it." That he needed no more soldiers; and that, for himself, he must go and refresh himself, having been up all night. So he left me, and I him, and walked home, seeing people all almost distracted, and no manner of means used to quench the fire. The houses, too, so very thick thereabouts, and full of matter for burning, as pitch and tar, in Thames Street; and warehouses of oil, and wines, and brandy, and other things. Here I saw Mr. Isaake Houblon, the handsome man, prettily dressed and dirty, at his door at Dowgate, receiving some of his brothers' things, whose houses were on fire; and, as he says, have been removed twice already; and he doubts (as it soon proved) that they must be in a little time removed from his house also, which was a sad consideration. And to see the churches all filling with goods by people who themselves should have been quietly there at this time. By this time it was about twelve o'clock; and so home. Soon as dined, and walked through the city, the streets full of nothing but people and horses and carts loaden with goods, ready to run over one another, and removing goods from **15** one burned house to another. They now removing out of Canning Street (which received goods in the morning) into Lumbard Street, and farther; and among others I now saw my little goldsmith, Stokes, receiving some friend's goods, whose house itself was burned the day after. I to Paul's Wharf, where I had appointed a boat to attend me, and took in Mr. Carcasse and his brother, whom I met in the street, and carried them below and above bridge to and again to see the fire, which was now got farther, both below and above, and no likelihood of stopping it. Met with the King and Duke of York in their barge, and with them to Queenhithe, and there called Sir Richard Browne to them. Their order was only to pull down houses apace, and so below bridge at the waterside; but little was or could be done, the fire coming upon them so fast. Good hopes there was of stopping it at the Three Cranes above, and at Buttolph's Wharf below bridge, if care be used; but the wind carries it into the city, so as we know not by the waterside what it do there. River full of lighters and boats taking in goods, and good goods swimming in the water, and only I

---

10. Paul's St. Paul's Cathedral.

508 ■ *A Turbulent Time (1625–1798)*

Reading Strategy
Drawing Conclusions
What conclusion about the fire can you draw from the fact that goods were removed "from one burned house to another"?

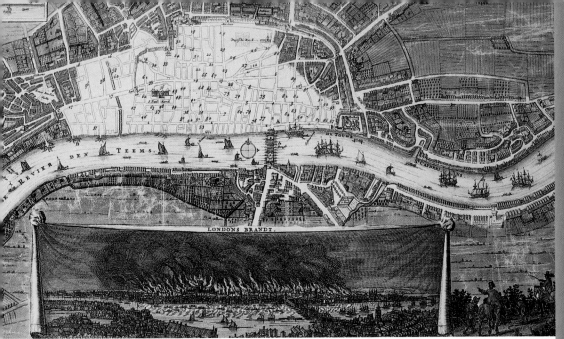

The Great Fire, 1666, Marcus Willemsz Doornik, Guildhall Library, Corporation of London

16

observed that hardly one lighter or boat in three that had the goods of a house in, but there was a pair of virginals[11] in it. Having seen as much as I could now, I away to Whitehall by appointment, and there walked to St. James's Park, and there met my wife and Creed and Wood and his wife, and walked to my boat; and there upon the water again, and to the fire up and down, it still increasing, and the wind great. So near the fire as we could for smoke; and all over the Thames, with one's face in the wind, you were almost burned with a shower of firedrops. This is very true; so as houses were burned by these drops and flakes of fire, three or four, nay, five or six houses, one from another. When we could endure no more upon the water, we to a little alehouse on the Bankside, over against the Three Cranes, and there stayed till it was dark almost, and saw the fire grow; and, as it grew darker, appeared more and more, and in corners and upon steeples, and between churches and houses, as far as we could see up the hill of the city, in a most horrid <u>malicious</u> bloody flame, not like the fine flame of an ordinary fire. Barbary and her husband away before us. We stayed till, it being darkish, we saw the fire as only one entire arch of fire from this to the other side the bridge, and in a bow up the hill for an arch of above a mile long: it made me weep to see it. The churches, houses, and all on fire and flaming at once; and a horrid noise the flames made, and the cracking of houses at their ruin.

---

11. **virginals** *n.* small, legless harpsichords.

17 ⚠ **Critical Viewing**
This map of London includes an inset depicting the area destroyed by the Great Fire. Does this image enhance Pepys's eyewitness description? Explain. **[Make a Judgment]**

Vocabulary Builder
malicious (mə lish′ əs) *adj.* deliberately harmful; destructive

19 ✓ **Reading Check**
According to Pepys's observations, what are people doing to save their goods?

from *The Diary* ■ 509

1. **Possible response:** Yes, the many details and first-person commentary vividly bring to life the plague and the fire.

2. (a) A saddler and his wife, who had lost all but one of their children to the plague and feared for their own lives, asked a friend to take the sole surviving child to safety. Pepys and his peers agreed that the child should be allowed to stay where it had been taken. (b) The entry for September 3, 1665, reveals that Pepys is a compassionate man. He bent the rules and allowed a saddler to send his only remaining child to Greenwich for safety.

3. (a) Pepys recommended that houses be torn down to stop the advance of the fire. (b) **Possible responses:** Pepys's recommendation was good, because it might prevent the fire's spread. Pepys's recommendation was good, but it didn't stop the fire, because it was spreading too quickly.

4. (a) Pepys helps his fellow citizens during both the plague and the fire. During the fire, Pepys offers suggestions to the king on how to slow the fire's spread, he worries about his friends, and he protects their belongings. He also secures his own belongings from the fire. (b) **Possible response:** Pepys is *curious* about the fire, and he climbs the Tower to get a better view of it. He is *observant,* which we know from the details he includes in his diary. He is *helpful* in suggesting ways to prevent the fire's spread, and he is *competent* in managing his own affairs so that his belongings are spared.

5. (a) **Possible response:** The plague was the greater disaster because tens of thousands of people died. (b) **Possible responses:** the Great Chicago Fire, floods in Bangladesh or China, AIDS in Africa

Go Online For additional informa-
—**Author Link** tion about Samuel
Pepys, have students type in the Web Code, then select *P* from the alphabet, and then select the author's name.

So home with a sad heart, and there find everybody <u>discoursing</u> and lamenting the fire; and poor Tom Hater come with some of his few goods saved out of his house, which is burned upon Fish Street Hill. I invited him to lie at my house, and did receive his goods, but was deceived in his lying there, the news coming every moment of the growth of the fire; so as we were forced to begin to pack up our own goods, and prepare for their removal; and did by moonshine (it being brave dry, and moonshine, and warm weather) carry much of my goods into the garden, and Mr. Hater and I did remove my money and iron chests into my cellar, as thinking that the safest place. And got my bags of gold into my office, ready to carry away, and my chief papers of accounts also there, and my tallies into a box by themselves. So great was our fear, as Sir W. Batten hath carts come out of the country to fetch away his goods this night. We did put Mr. Haters, poor man, to bed a little; but he got but very little rest, so much noise being in my house, taking down of goods.

3rd. About four o'clock in the morning, my Lady Batten sent me a cart to carry away all my money, and plate, and best things, to Sir W. Rider's at Bednall Green. Which I did, riding myself in my nightgown in the cart; and, Lord! to see how the streets and the highways are crowded with people running and riding, and getting of carts at any rate to fetch away things. I find Sir W. Rider tired with being called up all night, and receiving things from several friends. His house full of goods, and much of Sir W. Batten's and Sir W. Pen's. I am eased at my heart to have my treasure so well secured. Then home, with much ado to find a way, nor any sleep all this night to me nor my poor wife.

Vocabulary Builder
discoursing (dis' kôrs' iŋ) *v.* talking about; discussing

Critical Reading

1. **Recall:** Does Pepys's *Diary* make the plague and fire seem real to you? Why or why not?

2. **(a) Recall:** According to the entry for September 3, 1665, what happened to the saddler's family? **(b) Infer:** What does Pepys's reaction to these events tell you about his personality?

3. **(a) Recall:** What does Pepys recommend to the King and the Duke of York during the fire? **(b) Evaluate:** Was the recommendation a good one? Why or why not?

4. **(a) Classify:** Briefly describe the main types of things Pepys does during the plague and the fire. **(b) Draw Conclusions:** Explain why each of the following adjectives does or does not apply to him: *curious, observant, helpful,* and *competent.*

5. **(a) Compare and Contrast:** Which do you think was a greater disaster— the plague or the Great Fire? Why? **(b) Relate:** What modern disasters compare with these events? Explain.

Go Online
—**Author Link**
For: More about Samuel Pepys
Visit: www.PHSchool.com
Web Code: ese-9310

510 ■ *A Turbulent Time (1625–1798)*

Enrichment

Firefighting

The modern city grew rapidly from its medieval roots. Urban growth brought advances in education, opportunity, and affluence, but it also brought problems. Sanitation-related disease was a big issue, but that was controlled sooner than fire, which continues to be a problem.

Pulling down buildings to stop the fire was the only strategy that had been devised by the time of London's Great Fire in 1666. After the Great Fire, the first fire brigades were created by London's insurance companies (the government didn't get involved until 1865). The first fire hose was invented in the Netherlands in 1672. Benjamin Franklin helped create the first fire department in the 1700s, but it wasn't until 1830 that the first modern standards for a fire department were introduced, in Edinburgh, Scotland.

from A Journal of the Plague Year

Daniel Defoe

The face of London was now indeed strangely altered, I mean the whole mass of buildings, city, liberties, suburbs, Westminster, Southwark, and altogether; for as to the particular part called the city, or within the walls, that was not yet much infected. But in the whole the face of things, I say, was much altered; sorrow and sadness sat upon every face; and though some parts were not yet overwhelmed, yet all looked deeply concerned; and as we saw it apparently coming on, so everyone looked on himself and his family as in the utmost danger. Were it possible to represent those times exactly to those that did not see them, and give the reader due ideas of the horror that everywhere presented itself, it must make just impressions upon their minds and fill them with surprise. London might well be said to be all in tears; the mourners did not go about the streets indeed, for nobody put on black or made a formal dress of mourning for their nearest friends; but the voice of mourning was truly heard in the streets. The shrieks of women and children at the windows and doors of their houses, where their dearest relations were perhaps dying, or just dead, were so frequent to be heard as we passed the streets, that it was enough to pierce the stoutest heart in the world to hear them. Tears and lamentations were seen almost in every house, especially in the first part of the visitation; for toward the latter end men's hearts were hardened, and death was so always before their eyes, that they did not so much concern themselves for the loss of their friends, expecting that themselves should be summoned the next hour. . . .

I went all the first part of the time freely about the streets, though not so freely as to run myself into apparent danger, except when they dug the great pit in the churchyard of our parish of Aldgate. A terrible pit it was, and I could not resist my curiosity to go and see it. As near as I may judge, it was about forty feet in length, and about fifteen or sixteen feet broad, and, at the time I first looked at it, about nine feet deep; but it was said they dug it near twenty feet deep afterwards in one part of it, till they could go no deeper for the water; for they had, it seems, dug several large pits before this. For though the plague was long a-coming to our parish, yet, when it did come, there was no parish in or about London where it raged with such violence as in the two parishes of Aldgate and Whitechapel.

Literary Analysis
Diaries and Journals
Where in the first paragraph does the narrator indicate that he is providing a personal account intended to be read by others? Explain.

Reading Check
In what ways was the "face of London . . . strangely altered"?

---

⑳ About the Selection
Daniel Defoe combined his journalism skills with his creative energy and developed an unusual hybrid: a fictional narrative in the form of a journal. Although this "true history" was narrated by a fictional inhabitant of London identified only as H.F., the book contained a great deal of historical accuracy. Defoe, who was born just four years before the plague epidemic, perhaps had vague memories of it personally. Certainly he had access to people who remembered it vividly, as well as to official documents. Defoe's groundbreaking work of fiction set English literature on a new path.

㉑ Literary Analysis
Diaries and Journals

- Point out that Defoe's style is considerably different from Pepys's. **Ask** students to identify the major difference between the two works, with regard to writing style. **Answer:** While Pepys's work is in fragments and bursts of thought, Defoe's work uses complete sentences and reads more like literature.

- **Ask** the Literary Analysis question: Where in the first paragraph does the narrator indicate that he is providing a personal account intended to be read by others? Explain. **Answer:** The narrator's use of the pronouns *I* and *my* are evidence that this is a personal account. When the narrator says that he is representing the plague times to "give the reader due ideas of the horror that everywhere presented itself," he suggests that this is a work intended for others.

㉒ Reading Check

Answer: The face of London was strangely altered in the sense that so many of its citizens were in perpetual mourning for the loss of loved ones.

The Dead Cart, The British Library

24 ▲ Critical Viewing The cart in this picture carries the bodies of people killed by the plague. What can you infer about the plague's impact on daily life from the number of people on the street and from the gestures of the men in conversation? **[Infer]**

512 ■ *A Turbulent Time (1625–1798)*

I saw they had dug several pits in another ground, when the distemper began to spread in our parish, and especially when the dead carts began to go about, which was not, in our parish, till the beginning of August. Into these pits they had put perhaps fifty or sixty bodies each; then they made larger holes, wherein they buried all that the cart brought in a week, which, by the middle to the end of August, came to from 200 to 400 a week; and they could not well dig them larger, because of the order of the magistrates confining them to leave no bodies within six feet of the surface; and the water coming on at about seventeen or eighteen feet, they could not well, I say, put more in one pit. But now, at the beginning of September, the plague raging in a dreadful manner, and the number of burials in our parish increasing to more than was ever buried in any parish about London of no larger extent, they ordered this dreadful gulf to be dug, for such it was rather than a pit.

They had supposed this pit would have supplied them for a month or more when they dug it, and some blamed the churchwardens for suffering[1] such a frightful thing, telling them they were making preparations to bury the whole parish, and the like; but time made it appear the churchwardens knew the condition of the parish better than they did, for the pit being finished the 4th of September, I think, they began to bury in it the 6th, and by the 20th, which was just two weeks, they had thrown into it 1114 bodies, when they were obliged to fill it up, the bodies being then come to lie within six feet of the surface. I doubt not but there may be some ancient persons alive in the parish who can justify the fact of this, and are able to show even in what place of the churchyard the pit lay better than I can. The mark of it also was many years to be seen in the churchyard on the surface, lying in length parallel with the passage which goes by the west wall of the churchyard out of Houndsditch, and turns east again into Whitechapel, coming out near the Three Nuns' Inn.

It was about the 10th of September that my curiosity led, or rather drove, me to go and see this pit again, when there had been near 400 people buried in it; and I was not content to see it in the daytime, as I had done before, for then there would have been nothing to have been seen but the loose earth; for all the bodies that were thrown in were immediately covered with earth by those they called the buriers, which at other times were called bearers; but I resolved to go in the night and see some of them thrown in.

There was a strict order to prevent people coming to those pits, and that was only to prevent infection. But after some time that order was more necessary, for people that were infected and near their end, and delirious also, would run to those pits, wrapped in blankets or rugs, and throw themselves in, and, as they said, bury themselves. I cannot say that the officers suffered any willingly to lie there; but I have heard that in a great pit in Finsbury, in the parish of

---

1. **suffering** allowing.

Vocabulary Builder
distemper (dis tem′ pər) *n.* infectious disease such as the plague

Reading Strategy
Drawing Conclusions
From the information in the paragraph beginning, "It was . . . ," what do you conclude about the narrator's motives? Explain.

 Reading Check
What provisions does the parish make for disposing of the bodies of plague victims?

from A Journal of the Plague Year ■ 513

25 Vocabulary Builder
Latin Prefix *dis-*
- Call students' attention to the word *distemper* and its definition. Tell students that the Latin prefix *dis-* means "the opposite of." It can also mean "apart," "not," and "cause to be the opposite of."
- Have students suggest other words that contain this prefix, and list them on the chalkboard.
  Possible Responses: *disarray, discomfort, disentangle, disrespect, dishonest, disappoint, dislike*
- Have students look up any unfamiliar words. You may wish to have them discuss which meaning of *dis-* is being used in each word.

26 Reading Strategy
Drawing Conclusions
- **Ask** the Reading Strategy question: From the information in the paragraph beginning "It was . . . ," what do you conclude about the narrator's motives?
  Answer: The narrator says that he was curious, and he was probably both attracted to and repelled by the horror of the scene.
- Point out that, in the paragraph that follows, Defoe explains why there was a ban on visiting the pit. Discuss the emotions, thoughts, or motivations revealed by what was happening.
  Possible responses: People must have felt totally hopeless or desperate. They may have felt that they were keeping the disease from their families by throwing themselves in the pit. It may have been the delirium caused by the disease, or it may have been the fact that they were in so much pain they wished they were dead.

27 Reading Check
Answer: The parish digs an enormous pit for the corpses, about 40 feet in length and 15 or 16 feet wide and 9 to 25 feet deep.

A sexton is a person who is charged with keeping the church and parish building prepared for meetings. (And a parish is a district that has its own church and clergy.) The sexton's duties would include caring for church equipment, and might also involve other minor duties, such as ringing the church bell, arranging for burials, and sometimes (depending on the era or country), actually digging the graves.

29 **Literary Analysis**
Diaries, Journals, and First-Person Narrators

- **Ask** students what effect the sexton's arguments against visiting the pit might have on them, if they were in the narrator's position.
Possible responses: Some students will say that it would give them the creeps and they'd leave. Some may say that it wouldn't bother them, and they'd still go in.

- **Remind** students that, by this time, there were more than 1,000 bodies in the pit, though most of them would be covered with a thin layer of dirt.

- **Ask** students the Literary Analysis question: In the paragraph beginning, "His discourse . . . ," which details make Defoe's fictional narrator seem like a real person? Why?
Possible response: The fact that he is torn between leaving and going in makes the narrator seem real. He is horrified by what he hears and wavers, but the approach of the dead cart renews his curiosity. Other details that make the narrator seem real include his saying he couldn't see anything at first, and the sympathy he felt for both the "desperate creatures" and the mourner by the grave's edge.

- **Remind** students that, though the narrator is fictional, the events in the story are all real. The horrible deaths, mass burials, body collecting, and people throwing themselves into the pit all happened. You may want to **ask** students how they think people's lives and focus change in such situations.
Possible response: Students might mention that people would give up ordinary pursuits and try to do things that meant the most to them.

514

Cripplegate, it lying open then to the fields, for it was not then walled about, [some] came and threw themselves in, and expired there, before they threw any earth upon them; and that when they came to bury others, and found them there, they were quite dead, though not cold.

This may serve a little to describe the dreadful condition of that day, though it is impossible to say anything that is able to give a true idea of it to those who did not see it, other than this, that it was indeed very, very, very dreadful, and such as no tongue can express.

28 I got admittance into the churchyard by being acquainted with the sexton who attended, who, though he did not refuse me at all, yet earnestly persuaded me not to go, telling me very seriously, for he was a good, religious, and sensible man, that it was indeed their business and duty to venture, and to run all hazards, and that in it they might hope to be preserved; but that I had no apparent call to it but my own curiosity, which, he said, he believed I would not pretend was sufficient to justify my running that hazard. I told him I had been pressed in my mind to go, and that perhaps it might be an instructing sight, that might not be without its uses. "Nay," says the good man, "if you will venture upon that score, name of God go in; for, depend upon it, 't will be a sermon to you, it may be, the best that ever you heard in your life. 'T is a speaking sight," says he, "and has a voice with it, and a loud one, to call us all to repentance"; and with that he opened the door and said, "Go, if you will."

His discourse had shocked my resolution a little, and I stood wavering for a good while, but just at that interval I saw two links[2] come over from the end of the Minories, and heard the bellman, and then appeared a dead cart, as they called it, coming over the streets; so I could no longer resist my desire of seeing it, and went in. There was nobody, as I could perceive at first, in the churchyard, or going into it, but the buriers and **29** the fellow that drove the cart, or rather led the horse and cart; but when they came up to the pit they saw a man go to and again,[3] muffled up in a brown cloak, and making motions with his hands under his cloak, as if he was in a great agony, and the buriers immediately gathered about him, supposing he was one of those poor delirious or desperate creatures that used to pretend, as I have said, to bury themselves. He said nothing as he walked about, but two or three times groaned very deeply and loud, and sighed as he would break his heart.

When the buriers came up to him they soon found he was neither a person infected and desperate, as I have observed above, or a person distempered in mind, but one oppressed with a dreadful weight of grief indeed, having his wife and several of his children all in the cart that was just come in with him, and he followed in an agony and excess of sorrow. He mourned heartily, as it was easy to see, but with a kind of masculine grief that could not give itself vent by tears; and

---

2. **links** torches.
3. **to and again** to and fro.

Literary Analysis
Diaries, Journals, and First-Person Narrators In the paragraph beginning, "His discourse . . . ," which details make Defoe's fictional narrator seem like a real person? Why?

Enrichment

Graveyard Scenes

The famous scene in Daniel Defoe's *A Journal of the Plague Year,* in which a father who has lost his wife and family visits the churchyard in which they are to be buried, is memorable and evokes sympathy from readers. Many of Defoe's readers would have been familiar with other iconic graveyard scenes from such works as Shakespeare's *Hamlet,* in which Hamlet discovers the skull of "poor Yorick" in a tomb and ponders his own mortality. Another memorable graveyard scene is the one in *The Tragedy of Romeo and Juliet,* in which the star-crossed lovers die surrounded by the dead in the Capulet tomb. Charles Dickens used a graveyard as the backdrop for scenes of intrigue and danger in *Great Expectations.* In the eighteenth century, the term "graveyard poets" was used to describe poets who wrote melancholy, reflective works, often set in graveyards, on the theme of human mortality. Gray's "Elegy Written in a Country Churchyard" is the best known of these poems.

calmly defying the buriers to let him alone, said he would only see the bodies thrown in and go away, so they left <u>importuning</u> him. But no sooner was the cart turned round and the bodies shot into the pit promiscuously,[4] which was a surprise to him, for he at least expected they would have been decently laid in, though indeed he was afterwards convinced that was impracticable; I say, no sooner did he see the sight but he cried out aloud, unable to contain himself. I could not hear what he said, but he went backward two or three steps and fell down in a swoon. The buriers ran to him and took him up, and

___

4. **promiscuously** mixed together without care or thought.

Vocabulary Builder
importuning (im′ pôr tōōn′ iŋ) v. pleading with

✓ **Reading Check**
What touching scene does the narrator observe in the churchyard?

③①

▼ **Critical Viewing** Explain how the *Journal* helps you make sense of details in this picture. **[Connect]**

from *A Journal of the Plague Year* ■ 515

③⓪ Reading Check
Answer: The narrator observes a grieving man faint in the churchyard when the bodies of his loved ones are unceremoniously dumped into the mass grave.

③① Humanities
This illustration is a woodcut. Its rough style shows that it was intended for distribution, rather than as fine art. The advantage of a woodcut over painting was that, once the image was carved into a wood block, it could be used over and over to print as many images as needed.

Although the English used is modern English, it still shows the influences of languages that contributed to English, such as the "u" in "haue," which would reflect the influence of Latin, which does not have a "v."

Use the following questions for discussion:

1. What might be the reason for the confrontation shown at the far right?
Possible response: People who didn't know what caused the plague would be reluctant to allow anyone from an infected area to come into their towns, because they would fear getting the disease themselves.

2. How does the overall emotional impact of the image compare with that of the *Journal*?
Possible response: The figure of death, obviously on the attack with those arrows in its fists, is frightening; the many dead people, including women and children, is sad; the people trying to flee seem hopeless; the plea of "Lord, have mercy" is desperate. All these emotions are reflected in the *Journal*.

③② Critical Viewing
Possible responses: The *Journal* relates that there are so many people dying that there is no time to build coffins. This seems to be reflected in the image. The people fleeing seem in keeping with the panic revealed in the account.

1. Students should provide reasons for choosing particular passages.

2. (a) The pit served as a communal grave for plague victims. (b) The narrator is trying to convey the horrible realities of the plague.

3. (a) The narrator is curious. (b) The sexton warns the narrator that he will be reminded of his own mortality and will be moved to repent his sins.

4. (a) The man in the brown cloak was mourning the deaths of his wife and several of his children and had come to see his family buried. When he saw their bodies being dumped into the pit with hundreds of others, he cried out in anguish and fainted. (b) After several paragraphs of statistics about massive numbers of deaths and bodies being dumped by the cartload, this incident confronts the reader with the personal suffering the plague brought, with the grief and loss of the individual. It returns it to being a story about humans, not numbers.

5. (a) Defoe is much more descriptive about his narrator's experience during the plague. His fictionalized journal dramatizes the mass burials. Pepys downplays the mass burials, choosing not to focus on them. (b) **Possible responses:** Defoe's account is more effective because it shows the true horrors of the plague. Pepys's account is more effective because it has the breathless quality of a firsthand observer writing even as the drama unfolds.

6. Have students defend their views with examples from the texts. Arguments may focus on whether or not the reader is informed of the mixing.

7. **Possible response:** Like a reporter Defoe includes many visual details, gets the "human interest" angle into his narrative, and talks about cause and effects. However, he includes a little more of his own reactions than a reporter would.

---

in a little while he came to himself, and they led him away to the Pie Tavern over against the end of Houndsditch, where, it seems, the man was known, and where they took care of him. He looked into the pit again as he went away, but the buriers had covered the bodies so immediately with throwing in earth, that though there was light enough, for there were lanterns, and candles in them, placed all night round the sides of the pit, upon heaps of earth, seven or eight, or perhaps more, yet nothing could be seen.

This was a mournful scene indeed, and affected me almost as much as the rest; but the other was awful and full of terror. The cart had in it sixteen or seventeen bodies: some were wrapped up in linen sheets, some in rags, some little other than naked, or so loose that what covering they had fell from them in the shooting out of the cart, and they fell quite naked among the rest; but the matter was not much to them, or the indecency much to anyone else, seeing they were all dead, and were to be huddled together into the common grave of mankind, as we may call it, for here was no difference made, but poor and rich went together; there was no other way of burials, neither was it possible there should, for coffins were not to be had for the <u>prodigious</u> numbers that fell in such a calamity as this.

Vocabulary Builder
prodigious (prō′ dij′ əs)
adj. enormous; huge

Critical Reading

1. **Recall:** Which passages in *A Journal of the Plague Year* seem especially vivid to you? Why?

2. **(a) Recall:** What was the purpose of the great pit dug in Aldgate? **(b) Infer:** Why do you think the narrator describes the pit in such detail?

3. **(a) Recall:** What prompts the narrator to visit the pit? **(b) Interpret:** What does the Sexton mean when he says that visiting the pit will "be a sermon" to the narrator?

4. **(a) Summarize:** Retell the incident concerning the man in the brown cloak. **(b) Draw Conclusions:** In what way does this incident add a new dimension of meaning to the previous general descriptions of the plague? Explain.

5. **(a) Compare and Contrast:** Compare and contrast Pepys's true account of the plague with Defoe's fictional account of it. **(b) Assess:** Which description do you find more effective? Why?

6. **Generalize:** Do you think that literary works should avoid mixing fiction and nonfiction? Why or why not?

7. **Apply:** Compare Defoe's approach to that of a television reporter reporting from a news scene.

Go Online
Author Link
For: More about Daniel Defoe
Visit: www.PHSchool.com
Web Code: ese-9311

Go Online For additional informa-
Author Link tion about Daniel
Defoe, have students type in the Web Code, then select *D* from the alphabet, and then select the author's name.

Apply the Skills

from *The Diary* • from *A Journal of the Plague Year*

Literary Analysis

Diaries and Journals

1. Using specific references, show how the texts by Pepys and Defoe are good examples of **diaries** or **journals.**

2. Find a passage in each work that reflects the immediacy of real life and one that teaches you about history. Explain your choices.

3. **(a)** Use a chart like this one to determine which of the questions in the left column can be answered by reading Pepys's *Diary.* **(b)** What do your results suggest about diaries as sources of historical information? Explain.

Questions About the Great Fire	Answer in *Diary*? Yes/No	Pepys's Answer
What parts of the city were most damaged?		
How many houses were destroyed?		
What was the total monetary damage?		

Comparing Literary Works

4. What clues in Pepys's *Diary* and Defoe's *Journal* indicate that both these works are told by **first-person narrators**? Explain.

5. Which of these works would be more changed if it were written by a third-person narrator who did not participate in the action? Explain.

6. For which of these works would it be easier to capture the first-person narrative in a film version? Why?

Reading Strategy

Drawing Conclusions

7. Referring to the entry dated "Sept. 14, 1665," in Pepys's *Diary,* **draw a conclusion** about Pepys's position in society.

8. **(a)** Which narrator—Pepys or Defoe's fictional narrator—seems more observant to you? **(b)** On what details do you base your conclusion?

Extend Understanding

9. **Science Connection:** What do the selections reveal about medical knowledge in the late seventeenth century?

QuickReview

Diaries and **journals** are a daily account of a writer's experiences and reactions.

First-person narrators describe their own experiences and are identified by the pronoun *I.*

Using details in a text, you can **draw conclusions**, or make generalizations, about the author or subject.

For: Self-test
Visit: www.PHSchool.com
Web Code: esa-6307

Answers continued

9. They reveal that people did not yet know what caused the disease, and they had no means of treating serious infections.

Go Online
Assessment   Students may use the **Self-test** to prepare for **Selection Test A** or **Selection Test B.**

---

❶ Vocabulary Lesson
Word Analysis: Latin Prefix *dis-*

1. *Disable* means "to stop something from functioning or being able to work."

2. *Dismiss* means "to send away."

3. *Disobey* means "the opposite of obey."

4. *Dissatisfied* means "the opposite of satisfied."

Spelling Strategy

1. machine-washable
2. forgettable
3. suggestible
4. flexible

Vocabulary Builder: Words in Context

1. malicious	6. discoursing
2. combustible	7. distemper
3. importuning	8. apprehensions
4. prodigious	9. lamentable
5. abated	

❷ Grammar and Style Lesson

1. mourning	4. dying
2. Suffering	5. none
3. none	

Writing Application

Possible response: When we learned that they were going to tear down the old theater, waiting was the hardest part. We hated to lose the old place, but complaining was all we could do, because we couldn't stop it from happening. Preparing for the demolition took a long time, but destruction of the old building went quickly. Building on the site began almost immediately.

Build Language Skills

❶ Vocabulary Lesson

Word Analysis: Latin Prefix *dis-*

The prefix *dis-* can mean "apart," "not," "cause to be the opposite of," or "the opposite of." In *distemper, dis-* makes "the opposite of" *temper* or "balance"—in other words, that state of imbalance called "disease."

Use your knowledge of *dis-* to define each of the following words.

1. disable   3. disobey
2. dismiss   4. dissatisfied

Spelling Strategy

In the words *combustible* and *lamentable*, the related suffixes *-ible* and *-able* mean "capable of" or "worthy of." New words, such as *skiable*, always use the suffix *-able*.

On your paper, add *-ible or -able* to each word.

1. machine-wash   3. suggest
2. forget   4. flex

Vocabulary Builder: Context

Identify the word from the vocabulary list on page 503 that best completes each sentence.

1. The flames of the fire seemed ___?___, as if they wanted to devour the city.
2. The wooden buildings were ___?___.
3. People fleeing the flames began ___?___ boatmen to take them aboard.
4. The fire did a ___?___ amount of damage.
5. When the fire at last ___?___, 13,000 buildings had been destroyed.
6. Worried people were ___?___ about raising money to rebuild their homes.
7. They also worried about quelling the spread of ___?___.
8. Many Londoners had ___?___ about another fire.
9. Others just wished to forget the ___?___ episode.

❷ Grammar and Style Lesson

Gerunds

Both Pepys and Defoe use **gerunds,** verb forms that end in *-ing* and function as nouns. Do not mistake gerunds for participles, which also end in *-ing* but serve as verbs and adjectives.

> **Gerund:** In the dark, the <u>wailing</u> continued.
>
> **Present Participle as Verb:** Those whose loved ones had died were <u>wailing</u>.
>
> **Present Participle as Adjective:** The <u>wailing</u> mourner bowed his head in sorrow.

Practice In your notebook, identify the gerund in the sentence or write *none* if there is no gerund.

1. The plague was a time for deep mourning.
2. Suffering was everywhere in evidence.
3. Lamenting people were fleeing London.
4. The ranks of the dead and dying were swelling daily.
5. Still shuddering, London had just finished burying its dead when the fire broke out.

Writing Application Write a paragraph describing a dramatic event. Use at least four gerunds in your description.

W̸G   *Prentice Hall Writing and Grammar Connection: Chapter 19, Section 2*

518 ■ *A Turbulent Time (1625–1798)*

Assessment Practice

Writer's Point of View (For more practice, see *Standardized Test Preparation Workbook*, p. 22.)

Many tests require students to identify a writer's point of view. Use this sample test item.

> *Sept. 3, 1665. . . . but Lord! To consider the madness of the people of the town, who will (because they are forbid) come in crowds along with the dead corps[es] to see them buried . . .*

Sept. 2, 1666. [I had] seen the fire rage every way, and nobody, to my sight, endeavoring to quench it, but to remove their goods. . . . [I] walked home, seeing people all almost distracted.

Pepys would probably agree that _____.

A people do not act in their best interests during a crisis

B people are by nature selfish and self-serving

C force is required to deal with the masses

D most people are lazy

The facts Pepys records and his use of the word *madness* show that the correct answer is *A*.

Writing Lesson

Timed Writing: Response to Criticism

Critic Brian Fitzgerald says Defoe "used literature to express his views on social and other questions and only secondarily as a craftsman and artist." In an essay, support or refute Fitzgerald's comment. *(40 minutes)*

Prewriting
(10 minutes)
Note details from Defoe's *A Journal of the Plague Year* that show him expressing views on social conditions. Then, gather examples that show him to be a craftsman, such as vivid images, figures of speech, and passages creating a mood.

Drafting
(20 minutes)
Write a thesis statement supporting or refuting Fitzgerald's remark. Referring to your prewriting notes, back up your thesis statement with details from Defoe's writing.

Revising
(10 minutes)
Check your essay for accuracy by highlighting statements that can be proved true or false. Then, verify these statements using Defoe's *Journal* or a reference source.

Model: Checking for Accuracy

 In this excerpt from *A Journal*, Defoe uses statistics or measurements ten times to describe accurately the conditions of plague-ridden London. However, his literary artistry is just as evident as his precision.

> The author has highlighted a fact that must be checked by reviewing the excerpt from Defoe's *Journal*.

WG Prentice Hall Writing and Grammar Connection: Chapter 14, Section 3

Extend Your Learning

Listening and Speaking Many seventeenth-century Londoners heard their news from a town crier. Plan a **performance as a town crier,** calling out news at the time of the plague or fire.

- Research how town criers performed their jobs.
- Apply what you learn to devise effective gestures and vocal styles for the job.

After your performance, share your insights into this early news format.

Research and Technology With a group, write a **fact-check report** on Pepys's account of the fire or Defoe's account of the plague. Identify facts presented in the selection, and divide them among group members, who should check them in online technical documents and other reference sources. Assemble your findings in a report. **[Group Activity]**

 **For:** An additional research activity
Visit: www.PHSchool.com
Web Code: esd-7306

from The Diary / from A Journal of the Plague Year ■ 519

Assessment Resources

The following resources can be used to assess students' knowledge and skills.

Unit 3 Resources
Selection Test A, pp. 103–105
Selection Test B, pp. 106–108
Benchmark Test 5, pp. 109–114

General Resources
Rubrics for Response to Literature, pp. 65–66

Go Online — Assessment Students may use the **Self-test** to prepare for **Selection Test A** or **Selection Test B.**

Benchmark
Administer **Benchmark Test 5.** If some students need further work, use the **Interpretation Guide** to determine the appropriate reteaching page in the **Reading Kit** and on **Success Tracker.**

---

❸ Writing Lesson

You may use this Writing Lesson as timed-writing practice, or you may allow students to develop the essay as a writing assignment over several days.

- To guide students in writing this critical response, give them the **Support for Writing Lesson** page (*Unit 3 Resources,* p. 100).
- Review with students the difference between fact and opinion. Be sure they understand that both facts and opinions can be used to express one's views.
- Point out that figures of speech and sensory images can emphasize a point a writer is making. These can be evidence of Defoe's craft and of his desire to make a point.
- Use the Writing Lesson to guide students in developing their responses.
- Use the rubrics for Response to Literature in *General Resources* pp. 65–66, to evaluate students' critical responses.

❹ Listening and Speaking

- Explain to students that one way of broadcasting news reports in seventeenth-century London was through town criers, who literally stood on street corners and called out the summarized events of the day.
- Direct students to choose an event from Pepys's *Diary* or Defoe's *Journal* to announce as a "town crier."
- Encourage interested students to research how town criers performed their jobs and to come up with an "original" bit of news to announce.
- Have students practice speaking loudly and clearly, using gestures and inflections to emphasize the news.
- The **Support for Extend Your Learning** page (*Unit 3 Resources,* p. 101) provides guided note-taking opportunities to help students complete the Extend Your Learning activities.

Go Online — Research Have students type in the Web Code for another research activity.

TIME AND RESOURCE MANAGER

 Meeting Your Standards

Students will

1. **analyze and respond to literary elements.**
   - Literary Analysis: Satire

2. **read, comprehend, analyze, and critique fiction.**
   - Reading Strategy: Interpreting
   - Reading Check questions
   - Apply the Skills questions
   - Assessment Practice (ATE)

3. **develop vocabulary.**
   - Vocabulary Lesson: Latin Word Root: *-jec-*

4. **understand and apply written and oral language conventions.**
   - Spelling Strategy
   - Grammar and Style Lesson: Usage: *between* and *among*

5. **develop writing proficiency.**
   - Writing Lesson: Descriptive Satire

6. **develop appropriate research strategies.**
   - Extend Your Learning: Research Report

7. **understand and apply listening and speaking strategies.**
   - Extend Your Learning: Special-effects Plan

Block Scheduling: Use one 90-minute class period to preteach the skills and have students read the selection. Use a second 90-minute class period to assess students' mastery of skills, extend their learning, and monitor their progress.

Homework Suggestions

Following are possibilities for homework assignments.

- Support pages from *Unit 3 Resources:*
  Literary Analysis
  Reading Strategy
  Vocabulary Builder
  Grammar and Style

- An Extend Your Learning project and the Writing Lesson for this selection may be completed over several days.

Step-by-Step Teaching Guide	Pacing Guide
PRETEACH	
• Administer Vocabulary and Reading Warm-ups as necessary.	5 min.
• Engage students' interest with the motivation activity.	5 min.
• Read and discuss author and background features. **FT**	10 min.
• Introduce the Literary Analysis skill: Satire. **FT**	5 min.
• Introduce the Reading Strategy: Interpreting. **FT**	10 min.
• Prepare students to read by teaching the selection vocabulary. **FT**	
TEACH	
• Informally monitor comprehension while students read independently or in groups. **FT**	30 min.
• Monitor students' comprehension with the Reading Check notes.	as students read
• Reinforce vocabulary with Vocabulary Builder notes.	as students read
• Develop students' understanding of satire with the Literary Analysis annotations. **FT**	5 min.
• Develop students' ability to interpret with the Reading Strategy annotations. **FT**	5 min.
ASSESS/EXTEND	
• Assess students' comprehension and mastery of the Literary Analysis and Reading Strategy by having them answer the Apply the Skills questions. **FT**	15 min.
• Have students complete the Vocabulary Development Lesson and the Grammar and Style Lesson. **FT**	15 min.
• Apply students' knowledge of satire by using the Writing Lesson. **FT**	45 min. or homework
• Apply students' understanding by using one or more of the Extend Your Learning activities.	20–90 min. or homework
• Administer Selection Test A or Selection Test B. **FT**	15 min.

Resources

Choosing Resources for Differentiated Instruction

[**L1**] Special Needs Students

[**L2**] Below-Level Students

[**L3**] All Students

[**L4**] Advanced Students

[**EL**] English Learners

For Vocabulary and Reading Warm-ups and for Selection Tests, **A** signifies "less challenging" and **B** "more challenging." For Graphic Organizer transparencies, **A** signifies "not filled in" and **B** "filled in."

FT Fast Track Instruction: To move the lesson more quickly, use the strategies and activities identified with **FT**.

Scaffolding for Less Proficient and Advanced Students

The leveled Critical Thinking questions after selections progress in the levels of thinking required to answer them. To address the needs of your different students, you may use the (a) level questions for your less proficient students and the (b) level questions with your on-level and advanced students. The occasional (c) level questions are appropriate for your advanced students.

PRENTICE HALL
Teacher EXPRESS™ Use this complete
Plan · Teach · Assess   suite of powerful
teaching tools to make lesson planning and testing quicker and easier.

PRENTICE HALL
Student EXPRESS™ Use the interac-
Learn · Study · Succeed   tive textbook
(online and on CD-ROM) to make selections and activities come alive with audio and video support and interactive questions.

Monitoring Progress

Before students read these excerpts from *Gulliver's Travels*, administer **Diagnostic Test 6** (*Unit 3 Resources*, pp. 115–117). This test will determine students' level of readiness for the reading and vocabulary skills.

Go **Online**   **For:** Information about Lexiles
Professional **Visit:** www.PHSchool.com
Development **Web Code:** eue-1111

520b

List the following on the chalkboard and ask students to make connections among the entries. (Students should recognize that all of these mock or satirize something.)

- *Doonesbury*
- *Saturday Night Live* skits
- Weird Al Yankovic songs

Explain that during the time Jonathan Swift wrote, openly mocking or criticizing religious and political leaders was too dangerous, so instead he wrote satires in which he camouflaged, exaggerated, and then skewered the objects of his scorn. If a religious figure or member of the king's court had recognized himself in the story, it would have been as good as saying, "If the shoe fits, wear it!"

❶ Background
More About the Author

Swift began his writing career at Moor Park, the home of Sir William Temple. Temple, a distant relative of Swift's mother, encouraged learning, giving Swift access to his rich library and assisting him in getting his M.A. at Oxford.

Swift was skilled in any form of writing he attempted, including poetry, but became best known for his prose satires. For the sake of safety, Swift published most of his work under the pseudonym Isaac Bickerstaff.

After the death of Queen Anne (1714), the Tory party was in ruins, and Swift's career in England was over. He returned to Ireland, where he began to pour out satires and poetry. Dating to this "exile" are both of his most famous works, *Gulliver's Travels* and *A Modest Proposal.* The biting satire of the latter still has the power to shake up readers: the narrator suggests that both hunger and overpopulation can be halted by selling the children of the Irish as food.

Swift is considered the greatest prose satirist in the English language.

❶ *from* Gulliver's Travels

Jonathan Swift
(1667–1745)

While Swift was writing *Gulliver's Travels,* he had already started to suffer from the inner ear disease that eventually disabled him. "I always expect tomorrow to be worse," he wrote in a letter, "but I enjoy today as well as I can." The result of the author's determination to keep up his spirits was that rarest of books, a literary masterpiece that is loved by children and adults alike.

Finding His Way Swift was born in Dublin, Ireland, to English parents, although his father died before he was born. With the assistance of relatives, he received a good education and then obtained an appointment in the household of Sir William Temple, a wealthy diplomat who lived on an estate in Surrey, England. Swift hoped for a career in politics, but receiving no support from Sir William, he decided on a career in the church. After Temple's death in 1699, he was given a small parish near London.

The satirical writing Swift had done while in the Temple household was out of character for a clergyman, but its brilliance was widely acknowledged in 1704 when he published his satires as two separate books: *A Tale of a Tub,* which satirizes excesses in religion and learning, and *The Battle of the Books,* which describes a comic encounter between ancient and modern literature.

Ambition and Achievement In Swift's day, religion was interwoven with politics. When the authorship of Swift's religious satires became known, Swift lost favor in the eyes of many church officials and also lost opportunities for advancement. Although he failed to achieve his goal of becoming a bishop in the Church of England, Swift remained a staunch defender of the Anglican faith. His political allegiance, however, shifted completely in 1710 when he left the Whig party to join the Tory party favored by Queen Anne. He benefited immediately from this move. As the leading party writer for the government, he wrote many pamphlets and wielded considerable political influence. He also continued to write anonymous satires, ridiculing the English policy in Ireland in works such as *Drapier's Letters* (1724).

The Story Behind *Gulliver's Travels* Swift's most famous book, the novel *Gulliver's Travels,* began as a humorous assignment from the Scriblerus Club, a group of Swift's sharp-witted literary friends. These writers, who delighted in making fun of literary pretensions, gave Swift the project of writing a series of amusing, imaginary journeys because they knew he enjoyed reading travel books. The result was *Gulliver's Travels* (1726), which was an instant triumph. Ten thousand copies were sold in the first three weeks following its publication.

Later Years Although embittered by his failure to be named a bishop, Swift served for more than thirty years as dean of St. Patrick's Cathedral in Dublin. His caustic wit did not flag, as shown in the savage satire *A Modest Proposal* (1729), on starvation in Ireland.

In his later years, Swift suffered from a disease of the inner ear that affected both his memory and his sense of balance. His death in 1745 deprived the world of a generous and learned man who despised the fanaticism, selfishness, and pride to which humanity is often prey, but who admired certain individuals.

Swift's Epitaph Swift wrote his own epitaph, which still hangs in St. Patrick's Cathedral as a reminder of his memorable career: "The body of Jonathan Swift, Doctor of Sacred Theology, dean of this cathedral church, is buried here, where fierce indignation can no more lacerate his heart. Go, traveler, and imitate, if you can, one who strove with all his strength to champion liberty."

Preview

Connecting to the Literature

Jonathan Swift's strange distortions of humanity seem to be the products of pure fantasy—until you realize that you are seeing your own failings and foibles in his funhouse mirror.

Literary Analysis

Satire

Satire is writing that uses humor to expose and ridicule human vice and folly. This type of writing can be good-humored or bitter in its attack on what is evil, harmful, or just plain foolish. Satire can appear in many genres—from stories and novels to poems and songs.

Although satirists like to unmask evils, they also mask their targets in order to avoid the dangers involved in naming real people, places, or beliefs. Swift uses masks such as these:

- Imaginary lands, like Lilliput and Brobdingnag
- Made-up characters, like the King of Brobdingnag
- Fictional conflicts of belief, like that between Big-Endians and Little-Endians

Swift expects you to pull off these fictional masks as you read so that you can identify the real targets of his satire.

Connecting Literary Elements

Swift uses masks in another way, too. He disguises his true meanings by attacking vice and folly indirectly through **irony,** a contradiction between reality and appearance or between the actual and intended meaning of words. Use a chart like this one to decode his irony.

Reading Strategy

Interpreting

Satirists cannot expose folly if you, the reader, fail to interpret the fictional and ironic masks they use to disguise their true targets. To **interpret,** or figure out, a satire, follow these tips:

- Use background and footnotes to identify historical references.
- Recognize and figure out ironic meanings.

Vocabulary Builder

conjecture (kən jek´ chər) *v.* guess (p. 523)

expostulate (eks päs´ chə lāt´) *v.* reason earnestly with (p. 525)

schism (siz´ əm) *n.* division of a group into factions (p. 525)

expedient (ek spē´ dē ənt) *n.* device used in an emergency (p. 526)

habituate (hə bich´ ōō āt´) *v.* make used to (p. 529)

odious (ō´ dē əs) *adj.* hateful; disgusting (p. 530)

Statement or Situation

ìM any . . . volumes have been published" about the best way to break an egg.

↓

Ironic Contradiction

Appearance vs. Reality

(Serious   (Silly
Debate)   Topic)

↓

Interpretation

Swift shows how crazy people get about silly issues. See footnotes for the historical link.

---

from *Gulliver's Travels* ■ 521

Learning Modalities
Interpersonal Learners To explore character and to better understand satire, invite students to create personality profiles on Gulliver and one other character of their choosing. Encourage them to identify a wide variety of details. These might include straightforward "facts," such as occupation, but might also include personality traits, biases, opinions, and other things that can be found or inferred from the tale.

❶ **About the Selection**

Swift sends Gulliver to Lilliput to do a job he probably could never have done so well at home: make fun of the religious conflicts of his day. By exposing the conflict between the Big-Endians and the Little-Endians over which end of the egg to break, Swift, through Gulliver, comments with wry wit on the religious and political absurdities over which people do serious battle.

In "A Voyage to Brobdingnag," Swift satirizes English attitudes and modern warfare. To do so, he sends Gulliver to Brobdingnag, a place in which the people are twelve times as tall as Gulliver. There, Gulliver is treated almost as a pet by the royal family, who express their amazement and horror at his tales of his life in his native land.

❶

from Gulliver's TRAVELS

Jonathan Swift

Background Swift's era was marked by religious and political strife. Reacting against the intolerance displayed in these conflicts, he ridiculed those whose pride overcame their reason. His novel *Gulliver's Travels* satirizes such intolerance by means of four imaginary voyages of Lemuel Gulliver, the narrator, a well-educated but unimaginative ship's surgeon. In "A Voyage to Lilliput," for example, Swift focuses on disputes between the established Church of England and Roman Catholicism, calling the followers of each Little-Endians and Big-Endians, respectively. He also satirizes the religious wars between Protestant England and Catholic France, disguising them as a conflict between Lilliput and Blefuscu. In "A Voyage to Brobdingnag," he suggests that the politicians leading England are guilty of "ignorance, idleness, and vice."

522 ■ *A Turbulent Time (1625–1798)*

Differentiated Instruction   Solutions for All Learners

Accessibility at a Glance

	Gulliver's Travels
Context	Satire
Language	Long sentences
Concept Level	Moderate (religious disputes; royalty)
Literary Merit	Classic
Lexile	1500 L
Other	Explain historical context
Overall Rating	Average

from A Voyage to Lilliput

*After being shipwrecked, Gulliver swims to shore and drifts off to
sleep. When he awakens, he finds that he has been tied down by the
Lilliputians (lil' ə pyoo' shənz), a race of people who are only six
inches tall. Though he is held captive and his sword and pistols are
taken from him, Gulliver gradually begins to win the Lilliputians' favor
because of his mild disposition, and he is eventually granted his freedom.
Through Gulliver's exposure to Lilliputian politics and court life, the reader
becomes increasingly aware of the remarkable similarities between the
English and Lilliputian affairs of state. The following excerpt begins
during a discussion between the Lilliputian Principal Secretary of Private
Affairs and Gulliver concerning the affairs of the Lilliputian empire.*

We are threatened with an invasion from the island of Blefuscu,[1]
which is the other great empire of the universe, almost as large and
powerful as this of his Majesty. For as to what we have heard you
affirm, that there are other kingdoms and states in the world, inhabited
by human creatures as large as yourself, our philosophers are in much
doubt, and would rather <u>conjecture</u> that you dropped from the moon,
or one of the stars; because it is certain, that an hundred mortals of
your bulk would, in a short time, destroy all the fruits and cattle of his
Majesty's dominions. Besides, our histories of six thousand moons
make no mention of any other regions, than the two great empires of
Lilliput and Blefuscu. Which two mighty powers have, as I was going
to tell you, been engaged in a most obstinate war for six and thirty
moons past. It began upon the following occasion. It is allowed on all
hands, that the primitive way of breaking eggs before we eat them, was
upon the larger end; but his present Majesty's grandfather, while he
was a boy, going to eat an egg, and breaking it according to the ancient
practice, happened to cut one of his fingers. Whereupon the Emperor,
his father, published an edict, commanding all his subjects, upon great
penalties, to break the smaller end of their eggs. The people so highly
resented this law that our histories tell us there have been six rebellions
raised on that account; wherein one emperor lost his life, and another
his crown.[2] These civil commotions were constantly fomented by the
monarchs of Blefuscu; and when they were quelled, the exiles always
fled for refuge to that empire. It is computed that eleven thousand
persons have, at several times, suffered death rather than submit to
break their eggs at the smaller end. Many hundred large volumes have
been published upon this controversy; but the books of the Big-Endians
have been long forbidden, and the whole party rendered incapable by

---

1. **Blefuscu** represents France.
2. **It is allowed . . . crown** Here, Swift satirizes the dispute in England between the
   Catholics (Big-Endians) and Protestants (Little-Endians). King Henry VIII who "broke"
   with the Catholic church, King Charles I, who "lost his life," and King James, who lost
   his "crown," are each referred to in the passage.

Vocabulary Builder

conjecture (kən jek' chər) *v.*
guess

Literary Analysis

Satire Why do you think
Swift chooses the correct
way to break eggs as the
cause of conflict between
Lilliput and Blefuscu?

 **Reading Check**

What sparked the war
between Lilliput and
Blefuscu?

from Gulliver's Travels ■ 523

❷ Vocabulary Builder
Latin Root -*jec*-

- Call students' attention to the word
  conjecture and its definition. Tell
  students that the word is derived
  from the Latin root *-jec-*, which
  means "throw." To conjecture is
  "to guess by throwing facts or
  inferences together."

- Have students suggest other words
  that contain this word root, and list
  them on the chalkboard.
  Possible responses: *project, rejection, injection, projectile, projector,
  interject, interjection, abject*

- Add to the list of words to show
  that there are many words with this
  word root. Have students look up
  the meanings of unfamiliar words.

❸ Literary Analysis
Satire

- Review with students their understanding of satire as writing that
  uses humor to expose and ridicule
  human vice and folly.

- **Ask** students to name some of the
  "masks" Swift uses to conceal real
  people, places, or beliefs.
  Answer: Swift uses imaginary lands,
  made-up characters, and fictional
  conflicts of belief to conceal the
  identities of real people and issues.

- Point out the amusing and satirical
  nature of the secretary's comments
  that Gulliver's land and people cannot exist. Note that Swift is satirizing those who, even faced with
  evidence, are not convinced.
  Explain that it is often difficult for
  people to accept new evidence
  because they would have to question everything else they believe if
  one thing were proved wrong.

▶ **Monitor Progress: Ask** the
  Literary Analysis question: Why do
  you think Swift chooses the correct
  way to break eggs as the cause of
  conflict between Lilliput and
  Blefuscu?
  Possible responses: Students
  might think that Swift is suggesting
  that all wars are, at root, absurd, or
  that people ought to be more
  accepting about differences in
  habits or preferences.

❹ Reading Check

Answer: The war between Lilliput
and Blefuscu began when an
emperor issued an edict commanding
all of his subjects to crack their eggs
on the smaller end of the shell.

523

❺ Humanities

This illustration from a nineteenth-century edition of *Gulliver's Travels* shows a large, wide-eyed, and somewhat cherubic looking Gulliver in the typical English dress of his day. Pink-cheeked and serene, Gulliver seems undisturbed by the extraordinary situation in which he finds himself—tied down to a vast plain and surrounded by endless regiments of Lilliputians.

Use these questions for discussion:

1. Why do you think the artist shows Gulliver looking so relaxed?
Possible responses: Gulliver is not worried about these little people. He may realize that the cords cannot hold him. Perhaps Gulliver is amused by what he sees. Perhaps Gulliver looks relaxed because he is actually in a state of shock.

2. Why are there so many Lilliputians in this picture? Why are they arranged in regiments, or what seem to be military groupings?
Answer: The number of Lilliputians makes it clear that Gulliver has found himself among an entire race of people who are just six inches tall. The Lilliputians may be shown in "formations" to make them appear just as organized and serious as "big" people: they are an organized, legitimate society, capable of doing the things full-sized people do.

❻ Critical Viewing

Possible responses: The entire conversation with the secretary shows that they trust Gulliver as well as the fact that Gulliver is allowed to make suggestions. The emperor trusts him to leave in pursuit of the Blefuscu ships.

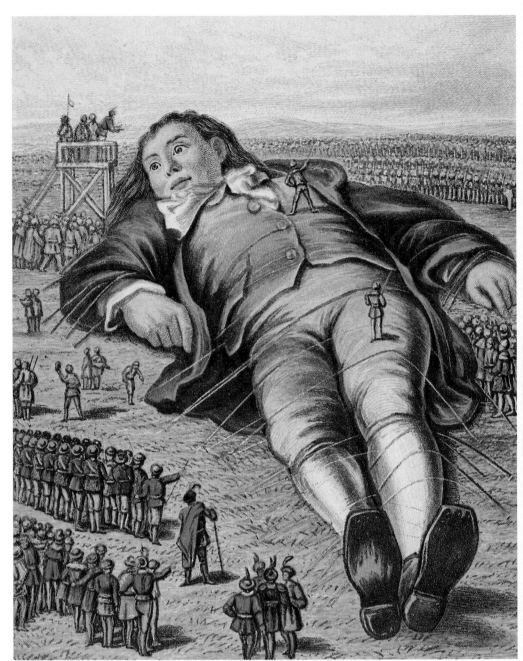

❻ ▲ **Critical Viewing** What passages in the text reveal that Lilliputians now trust Gulliver more than they did in the episode depicted here? **[Infer]**

524 ■ *A Turbulent Time (1625–1798)*

Enrichment

Swift's Beliefs

Though Swift mocks belief in his tales, it was his own deeply-held beliefs that directed his career. With his intellect deeply rooted in seventeenth-century rationalism (with its emphasis on reason and distrust of emotion), he was convinced that it was everyone else's beliefs that caused problems.

For Swift, religion meant rational Anglicanism, so both Catholics and Nonconformists were seen as a threat. (Nonconformists, or Dissenters, were English Protestants who did not conform to the doctrines of the Church of England. The main conflict was that Dissenters viewed God, rather than the King of England, as head of the church.)

Swift's reason for leaving the Whigs, with whom he agreed on most points of politics, was that they were tolerant of Nonconformists. He remained passionately devoted to the Anglican church, even as he wrote pamphlets in Ireland deriding the English government.

law of holding employments.[3] During the course of these troubles, the emperors of Blefuscu did frequently <u>expostulate</u> by their ambassadors, accusing us of making a <u>schism</u> in religion, by offending against a fundamental doctrine of our great prophet Lustrog, in the fifty-fourth chapter of the *Brundecral* (which is their Alcoran).[4] This, however, is thought to be a mere strain upon the text, for the words are these: That all true believers shall break their eggs at the convenient end; and which is the convenient end, seems, in my humble opinion, to be left to every man's conscience, or at least in the power of the chief magistrate[5] to determine. Now the Big-Endian exiles have found so much credit in the Emperor of Blefuscu's court, and so much private assistance and encouragement from their party here at home, that a bloody war hath been carried on between the two empires for six and thirty moons with various success; during which time we have lost forty capital ships, and a much greater number of smaller vessels, together with thirty thousand of our best seamen and soldiers; and the damage received by the enemy is reckoned to be somewhat greater than ours. However, they have now equipped a numerous fleet, and are just preparing to make a descent upon us; and his Imperial Majesty, placing great confidence in your valor and strength, hath commanded me to lay this account of his affairs before you.

I desired the Secretary to present my humble duty to the Emperor, and to let him know, that I thought it would not become me, who was a foreigner, to interfere with parties; but I was ready, with the hazard of my life, to defend his person and state against all invaders.

The empire of Blefuscu is an island situated to the north-northeast side of Lilliput, from whence it is parted only by a channel of eight hundred yards wide. I had not yet seen it, and upon this notice of an intended invasion, I avoided appearing on that side of the coast, for fear of being discovered by some of the enemy's ships, who had received no intelligence of me, all intercourse between the two empires having been strictly forbidden during the war, upon pain of death, and an embargo laid by our Emperor upon all vessels whatsoever. I communicated to his Majesty a project I had formed of seizing the enemy's whole fleet; which, as our scouts assured us, lay at anchor in the harbor ready to sail with the first fair wind. I consulted the most experienced seamen upon the depth of the channel, which they had often plumbed, who told me, that in the middle at high water

---

3. **the whole party . . . employments** The Test Act (1673) prevented Catholics from holding office.
4. **Alcoran** Koran, the sacred book of Muslims.
5. **chief magistrate** ruler.

Vocabulary Builder

expostulate (eks päs′ chə lāt′) *v.* reason earnestly with

schism (siz′ əm) *n.* division of a group into factions

Literature in Context

❼ Vocabulary Connection

The Vocabulary of Religious Conflict

The word *schism*, which Swift uses in describing the conflict between Big-Endians and Little-Endians, is an important term in the history of religious conflict. This term comes from the Greek word *schizein*, meaning "divide," and it can mean simply "to cleave or cut." Traditionally, it has been applied to a split in an organized group (especially a church), the act of trying to cause such a split, or a sect formed by the split. By using this word in describing the controversy between Big-Endians and Little-Endians, Swift signals readers that his fiction refers to a significant religious conflict.

Connect to the Literature

What further divisions have come as a result of Lilliput's schism in religion?

❽ **Reading Check**

How does Gulliver plan to defend the Lilliputians against invasion?

from *Gulliver's Travels* ■ 525

---

❼ Literature in Context

The Vocabulary of Religious Conflict The word *schism* was originally used to describe groups that broke away from the church because of disagreements over something other than church doctrine. The word did not at first imply heresy, but that changed over time. (*Heresy* is religious doctrine or opinion rejected by the authorities of a church. Hence, schism once meant being different but not wrong. Eventually, it meant both.)

The world was still reeling at the time of Swift's writing from the Reformation, when Protestants split from the Roman Catholic church. Not long after the initial split, England's King Henry VIII declared that he was the head of the English Church, rather than the Pope.

During the Restoration of the English monarchy, the Act of Uniformity was passed (1662), which meant that Nonconformists were virtually outlaws. For the "crime" of believing that God, not the King, was head of the church, almost 2,000 ministers were ejected from their positions, and a period of persecution began. The Conventicle Act of 1664 mandated that anyone over the age of 16 years would be punished for attending a religious meeting that did not conform to the Anglican *Book of Common Prayer*.

In 1685, Charles II's Roman Catholic brother, James II, became king. He was tolerated for a while, but the fear of a return to Catholic tyranny temporarily united Anglicans and Nonconformists. During the "Glorious Revolution" (1688) James was deposed and William and Mary became joint rulers of England

Connect to the Literature Explain to students that the English turmoil of schism after schism created Jonathan Swift's horror of religious disagreement. Then, **ask** the Connect to the Literature question: What further divisions have come as a result of Lilliput's schism in religion?
Answer: The religious difference has led to war, rebellion, exile, and discrimination in employment.

❽ Reading Check

Answer: Gulliver plans to defend the Lilliputians against invasion by seizing the enemy's whole fleet.

- Point out to students that Swift goes back and forth between obvious parallels and hidden or ironic parallels. The narrow channel between the two countries clearly reflects the English Channel. Water depth is measured in units that are approximately six feet, as they are in English (the fathom). However, the country that represents France in the tale (Blefuscu) is an island, while Lilliput, which represents the island of Britain, is not. However, as was true for both countries, it was sea power that determined one's strength.

- **Ask** students why Gulliver decides to put on his glasses (spectacles). **Answer:** to protect himself from Blefuscudian arrows

▶ **Reteach:** Remind students that the irony that Swift uses creates a contradiction between reality and appearances.

- **Ask** students the Literary Analysis question: What is ironic about Gulliver using spectacles as a shield in a military operation? **Possible responses:** Being made of glass, the spectacles seem to be a fragile shield, yet they successfully protect Gulliver's eyes, as the arrows bounce off them. Spectacles are generally used for such quiet, civilian pursuits as reading and writing, and one removes them before fights, rather than putting them on.

- You may wish to discuss, in light of Swift's rationalism, the way in which Gulliver, with his reading glasses protecting him from arrows, might represent the man of reason and learning triumphing over brute force.

it was seventy *glumgluffs* deep (which is about six feet of European measure), and the rest of it fifty *glumgluffs* at most. I walked to the northeast coast over against Blefuscu, where, lying down behind a hillock, I took out my small pocket perspective-glass, and viewed the enemy's fleet at anchor, consisting of about fifty men of war, and a great number of transports. I then came back to my house and gave order (for which I had a warrant) for a great quantity of the strongest cable and bars of iron. The cable was about as thick as packthread, and the bars of the length and size of a knitting-needle. I trebled the cable to make it stronger, and for the same reason I twisted three of the iron bars together, bending the extremities into a hook. Having thus fixed fifty hooks to as many cables, I went back to the northeast coast and, putting off my coat, shoes, and stockings, walked into the sea in my leathern jerkin, about half an hour before high water. I waded with what haste I could, and swam in the middle about thirty yards until I felt ground; I arrived at the fleet in less than half an hour. The enemy was so frightened when they saw me, that they leaped out of their ships, and swam to shore, where there could not be fewer than thirty thousand souls. I then took my tackling, and, fastening a hook to the hole at the prow of each, I tied all the cords together at the end. While I was thus employed, the enemy discharged several thousand arrows, many of which struck in my hands and face and, besides the excessive smart, gave me much disturbance in my work. My greatest apprehension was for my eyes, which I should have infallibly lost, if I had not suddenly thought of an <u>expedient</u>. I kept among other little necessaries a pair of spectacles in a private pocket, which, as I observed before,

❾ had escaped the Emperor's searchers. These I took out and fastened as strongly as I could upon my nose and thus armed went on boldly with my work in spite of the enemy's arrows, many of which struck against the glasses of my spectacles, but without any other effect further than a little to discompose them. I had now fastened all the hooks and, taking the knot in my hand, began to pull, but not a ship would stir, for they were all too fast held by their anchors, so that the boldest part of my enterprise remained. I therefore let go the cord, and, leaving the hooks fixed to the ships, I resolutely cut with my knife the cables that fastened the anchors, receiving above two hundred shots in my face and hands; then I took up the knotted end of the cables to which my hooks were tied and, with great ease, drew fifty of the enemy's largest men-of-war after me.

The Blefuscudians, who had not the least imagination of what I intended, were at first confounded with astonishment. They had seen me cut the cables and thought my design was only to let the ships run adrift or fall foul on each other; but when they perceived the whole fleet, moving in order, and saw me pulling at the end, they set up such a scream of grief and despair that it is almost impossible to describe or conceive. When I had got out of danger, I stopped a while to pick out the arrows that stuck in my hands and face, and rubbed on some of the same ointment that was given me at my first arrival, as I have

Vocabulary Builder
expedient (ek spē′ dē ənt) *n.* device used in an emergency

Literary Analysis
Satire and Irony What is ironic about Gulliver using spectacles as a shield in a military operation?

Enrichment

Stuart and Hanovers

The "Glorious Revolution" replaced the unpopular James II with James's Protestant daughter, Mary, and her husband William.

Mary died in 1694. At William's death in 1702, Mary's younger sister, Anne, became queen. While Anne was the first monarch to rule over Great Britain (England and Scotland were fully united in 1707), she was the last sovereign to veto an act of Parliament. She was also the last monarch in the Stuart line.

When Anne died in 1714, George I, from the House of Hanover, became king. George's mother was James I's of England's granddaughter, but George had been born and raised in Germany. George was unpopular, because he favored Germany over England and was often away. Because he spoke no English, he relied heavily on Robert Walpole. Walpole founded the modern cabinet government and became England's first Prime Minister.

A Voyage to Lilliput, Illustration from a nineteenth-century edition of *Gulliver's Travels*

11 ◄ Critical Viewing
What specific details from the text does this picture illustrate? [Connect]

formerly mentioned. I then took off my spectacles, and, waiting about an hour until the tide was a little fallen, I waded through the middle with my cargo and arrived safe at the royal port of Lilliput.

The Emperor and his whole court stood on the shore expecting the issue of this great adventure. They saw the ships move forward in a large half-moon but could not discern me, who was up to my breast in water. When I advanced to the middle of the channel, they were yet

12 ✓ **Reading Check**
Summarize the action Gulliver takes against the fleet of Blefuscu.

from *Gulliver's Travels* ■ 527

10 Humanities

A Voyage to Lilliput: Illustration from a nineteenth-century edition of *Gulliver's Travels*

Here Gulliver indulgently helps the Lilliputians and averts violence by stealing the fleet of their enemies, the Blefuscudians. In the illustration, Gulliver seems intent only on his task, while the Lilliputians cheer their new hero and celebrate such an easy victory over their enemy.

Use these questions for discussion:

1. Why are the Lilliputians pictured in full military dress?
   Possible response: The Lilliputians could not be sure how Gulliver's efforts would turn out. They are ready for attack by the Blefuscudians.

2. Why doesn't Gulliver smile and wave in light of the fact that the crowd is delighted by his efforts on their behalf?
   Possible response: Gulliver has done what he felt needed to be done. He actually has no personal stake in the outcome or any reason to feel particularly proud: His accomplishment was simply a result of being bigger than his opponents.

11 Critical Viewing

Answer: The illustration shows Gulliver returning with the Blefuscudian fleet, while the emperor and his court stand on the shore awaiting him. Gulliver is holding the end of the cable by which the fleet is fastened. It also shows that Gulliver is wearing spectacles (glasses) to protect his eyes.

12 Reading Check

Answer: Gulliver goes to Blefuscu armed with cables and bars. He swims to the fleet, where he fastens hooks to the ships and ties all the cords together at the end. He puts on his glasses to protect his eyes from the enemy's arrows, then cuts the anchors away from the ships and drags them across the channel back to the Lilliputians after the tide goes down.

⓭ Reading Strategy
Interpreting

- **Ask** students why, given his previous assistance, Gulliver refuses to help the Lilliputians take over Blefuscu.
  Answer: Gulliver does not believe that such an action is right. He helped the Lilliputians not in order to further their political ends, but to end the threat of invasion and the resulting loss of life.

- **Ask** students to describe the reactions of the Lilliputians.
  Answer: They were angry that Gulliver would not help them overwhelm Blefuscu, and they turned against him, as if he had never done them any good.

- **Tell** students to think about Swift's own experiences in politics. To what might he relate Gulliver's predicament?
  Possible response: When Queen Anne died, Swift's career in politics was over. Swift may feel that, like the Lilliputians, the government turned against him, though he considered himself to have done some good.

⓮ Literary Analysis
Satire

- **Ask** the Literary Analysis question: Which satirical details in the first paragraph of "A Voyage to Brobdingnag" relate to England and which relate to humanity in general? Explain.
  Answer: References to the king and queen, Whig and Tory, and "the scourge of France" point specifically to England. Details that refer to humanity in general include references to trade, wars by sea and land, religious schisms, political parties, and the entire sentence about "those creatures" and their houses, cities, vanity ("make a figure in dress"), emotions, and shortcomings ("fight," "cheat," "betray").

- **Ask** students to identify the irony in Swift's having Gulliver speak of England as "my own beloved country."
  Answer: Swift's career in England was over, he was living in Ireland, and he was writing pamphlets and stories (including this story) that criticized the English.

more in pain, because I was under water to my neck. The Emperor concluded me to be drowned, and that the enemy's fleet was approaching in a hostile manner; but he was soon eased of his fears; for, the channel growing shallower every step I made, I came in a short time within hearing, and holding up the end of the cable by which the fleet was fastened, I cried in a loud voice, Long live the most puissant[6] Emperor of Lilliput! This great prince received me at my landing with all possible encomiums and created me a *Nardac* upon the spot, which is the highest title of honor among them.

His Majesty desired I would take some other opportunity of bringing all the rest of his enemy's ships into his ports. And so unmeasurable is the ambition of princes, that he seemed to think of nothing less than reducing the whole empire of Blefuscu into a province and governing it by a viceroy; of destroying the Big-Endian exiles and compelling that people to break the smaller end of their eggs, by which he would remain sole monarch of the whole world. But I endeavored to divert him from this design by many arguments drawn from the topics of policy as well as justice, and I plainly protested that I would never be an instrument of bringing a free and brave people into slavery. And when the matter was debated in council, the wisest part of the ministry were of my opinion.

This open bold declaration of mine was so opposite to the schemes and politics of his Imperial Majesty that he could never forgive me; he mentioned it in a very artful manner at council, where I was told that some of the wisest appeared, at least, by their silence, to be of my opinion; but others, who were my secret enemies, could not forbear some expressions, which by a sidewind reflected on me. And from this time began an intrigue between his Majesty and a junta of ministers maliciously bent against me, which broke out in less than two months and had like to have ended in my utter destruction. Of so little weight are the greatest services to princes when put into the balance with a refusal to gratify their passions.

from A Voyage to Brobdingnag

Gulliver's second voyage leads him to Brobdingnag (bräb′ diŋ nag′), *an island located near Alaska that is inhabited by giants twelve times as tall as Gulliver. After being sold to the Queen of Brobdingnag, Gulliver describes the English social and political institutions to the King, who reacts to his description with contempt and disgust.*

It is the custom that every Wednesday (which, as I have before observed, was their Sabbath) the King and Queen, with the royal issue of both sexes, dine together in the apartment of his Majesty, to whom I was now become a favorite; and at these times my little chair

---

6. **puissant** (pyo̅o̅′ i sənt) powerful.

Literary Analysis
Satire Which satirical details in the first paragraph of "A Voyage to Brobdingnag" relate to England and which relate to humanity in general? Explain.

Enrichment

Whigs and Tories

Having the Whigs and the Tories facing off was more than politics as usual. This was, in fact, the first time in political history that there were two clearly defined, opposing parties. The Tory party wanted to maintain the prerogatives of the crown and the authority of the Church of England. It was they who were responsible for the passing of laws against the Dissenters. The Whigs, on the other hand, favored reform, the rights of the people, Parliamentary power, and tolerance of Dissenters.

Whig is short for *Whiggamore*, originally the name of a Scottish group that opposed Charles I of England. *Tory* comes from the Irish for *robber*, and was first applied as an insult by the party's opponents.

Queen Anne hated partisan politics and did all she could to frustrate party leaders—sometimes successfully. With the succession of the House of Hanover at Anne's death, the Whigs became stronger, but the two-party system was now solidly established.

and table were placed at his left hand before one of the saltcellars. This prince took a pleasure in conversing with me, inquiring into the manners, religion, laws, government, and learning of Europe, wherein I gave him the best account I was able. His apprehension was so clear, and his judgment so exact, that he made very wise reflections and observations upon all I said. But I confess, that after I had been a little too copious in talking of my own beloved country, of our trade, and wars by sea and land, of our schisms in religion, and parties in the state, the prejudices of his education prevailed so far, that he could not forbear taking me up in his right hand, and stroking me gently with the other, after an hearty fit of laughing, asked me whether I were a Whig or a Tory.[7] Then turning to his first minister, who waited behind him with a white staff, near as tall as the mainmast of the *Royal Sovereign*,[8] he observed how contemptible a thing was human grandeur, which could be mimicked by such diminutive insects as I. And yet, said he, I dare engage, those creatures have their titles and distinctions of honor, they contrive little nests and burrows, that they call houses and cities; they make a figure in dress and equipage;[9] they love, they fight, they dispute, they cheat, they betray. And thus he continued on, while my color came and went several times, with indignation to hear our noble country, the mistress of arts and arms, the scourge of France, the arbitress of Europe, the seat of virtue, piety, honor and truth, the pride and envy of the world, so contemptuously treated. . . .

He laughed at my odd kind of arithmetic (as he was pleased to call it) in reckoning the numbers of our people by a computation drawn from the several sects among us in religion and politics. He said he knew no reason why those who entertain opinions prejudicial to the public should be obliged to change or should not be obliged to conceal them. And, as it was tyranny in any government to require the first, so it was weakness not to enforce the second; for, a man may be allowed to keep poisons in his closets, but not to vend them about as cordials.

He observed, that among the diversions of our nobility and gentry[10] I had mentioned gaming.[11] He desired to know at what age this entertainment was usually taken up, and when it was laid down. How much of their time it employed; whether it ever went so high as to affect their fortunes. Whether mean vicious people by their dexterity in that art might not arrive at great riches, and sometimes keep our very nobles in dependence, as well as <u>habituate</u> them to vile companions, wholly take them from the improvement of their minds, and force them, by the losses they received, to learn and practice that infamous dexterity upon others.

---

7. **Whig . . . Tory** British political parties.
8. *Royal Sovereign* one of the largest ships in the British Navy.
9. **equipage** (ek′ wi pij′) horses and carriages.
10. **gentry** the class of landowning people ranking just below the nobility.
11. **gaming** gambling.

Reading Strategy

Interpreting What does the King's laughing question about whether Gulliver is "a Whig or a Tory" suggest about Swift's attitude towards disputes between these parties?

Vocabulary Builder
habituate (hə bich′ ōō āt′)
v. make used to

Reading Check

What does the King of Brobdingnag say in response to Gulliver's account of European customs and history?

from *Gulliver's Travels* ■ 529

---

15 Reading Strategy
Interpreting

- Explain to students that, to interpret satire, they must recognize irony and remove the fictional masks that disguise the true targets of humor. Remind them that footnotes help identify historical references.

- Then, **ask** the Reading Strategy question: What does the King's laughing question about whether Gulliver is "a Whig or a Tory" suggest about Swift's attitude toward disputes between these parties? **Answer:** The king's laughter suggests that Swift feels the disputes between these parties are ridiculous in the grand scheme of things.

16 Literary Analysis
Satire

- **Ask** students to identify the device Swift uses to counter Gulliver's enthusiasm and provide the satire in this conversation. **Answer:** Swift uses the king's comments and questions to ridicule the weaknesses and evils of Gulliver's world.

- **Ask** students to explain how Swift satirizes gambling (gaming). **Answer:** The king's questions suggest that the unscrupulous could use gambling to take advantage of others; that the foolish (including the nobility) might get hooked on gambling, which keeps them in bad company and diverts them from useful occupations; and that, to cover their losses, those who lose at gambling would be forced to draw others into it.

- You may also want to discuss in class to what degree students agree with Swift's appraisal of gambling, and how this satire might apply to today's culture.

17 Reading Check

Answer: The king says that human grandeur is a contemptible thing if it can be imitated by "insects" such as Gulliver. He goes on to belittle Gulliver's race.

Differentiated Instruction Solutions for All Learners

Strategy for Less Proficient Readers
To help students get the most out of these tales, discuss in class the differences between Gulliver's encounters in Lilliput and in Brobdingnag. Lead students to notice that, while Gulliver seems more noble than the Lilliputians, he seems more petty than the King of Brobdingnag. Ask students to identify the aspects of British society that appear in each tale. You may want to list this information on the board and discuss how, together, the tales offer a more complete picture of Swift's ideas.

Enrichment for Advanced Readers
Gulliver's Travels suggests a wealth of possible study topics. Students might research the rise of Whigs and Tories, what they believed, and how their rise affected English politics. They may want to learn more about the Dissenters, or about the royals of the era. They might even be interested in tangentially related topics, such as geography (where on the globe did Swift place these countries; what is really there) or physics (could people really be so small or so large?).

18 Literary Analysis
Satire and Irony

18 Literary Analysis
Satire and Irony

- Point out Gulliver's claim that an "extreme love of truth" is why he relates all the nasty things the King of Brobdingnag has said.

- **Ask** students to keep in mind both Swift's purposes for writing and Gulliver's comments farther along in the paragraph, and then ask why this claim is doubly ironic.
  Answer: Rather than being reluctant about saying nasty things, Swift has it as his main purpose. Later in the paragraph, Gulliver speaks of his cleverness in bending the truth—so much for his extreme love.

- Then, **ask** the Literary Analysis question: In Gulliver's remark that he "artfully eluded" the King's questions, what is the difference between the intended meaning and the actual meaning?
  Answer: The intended meaning of Gulliver's remark is that he cleverly avoided the more difficult questions, but the actual meaning is that he lied when he thought the answer would show England in a bad light.

19 Background
History

Point out the description on the next page of the "certain powder" that Gulliver describes. What he is describing, of course, is gunpowder. An early black powder form of gunpowder was invented in the tenth century by the Chinese, who used it largely for fireworks and signals. It is possible that the Arabs invented a type of gunpowder at about the same time. The Arabs may have produced the first gun in the early 1300s, using black powder and a bamboo tube reinforced with iron. Black powder was adopted for use in firearms in Europe by the fourteenth century and was being used for peaceful purposes (mining and road building) by the seventeenth century.

Gunpowder was initially viewed as a way of saving lives, because it would reduce the need for hand-to-hand combat. However, it reduced losses only on the side with the best guns.

Students might be interested in further researching some of the projectiles Gulliver describes.

He was perfectly astonished with the historical account I gave him of our affairs during the last century, protesting it was only an heap of conspiracies, rebellions, murders, massacres, revolutions, banishments, the very worst effects that avarice, faction, hypocrisy, perfidiousness, cruelty, rage, madness, hatred, envy, lust, malice, and ambition could produce.

His Majesty in another audience was at the pains to recapitulate the sum of all I had spoken; compared the questions he made with the answers I had given; then taking me into his hands, and stroking me gently, delivered himself in these words, which I shall never forget, nor the manner he spoke them in. "My little friend Grildrig, you have made a most admirable panegyric upon your country. You have clearly proved that ignorance, idleness, and vice are the proper ingredients for qualifying a legislator. That laws are best explained, interpreted, and applied by those whose interest and abilities lie in perverting, confounding, and eluding them. I observe among you some lines of an institution, which in its original might have been tolerable, but these half erased, and the rest wholly blurred and blotted by corruptions. It doth not appear from all you have said how any one perfection is required toward the procurement of any one station among you, much less that men are ennobled on account of their virtue, that priests are advanced for their piety or learning, soldiers for their conduct or valor, judges for their integrity, senators for the love of their country, or counselors for their wisdom. As for yourself," continued the King, "who have spent the greatest part of your life in traveling, I am well disposed to hope you may hitherto have escaped many vices of your country. But, by what I have gathered from your own relation, and the answers I have with much pains wringed and extorted from you, I cannot but conclude the bulk of your natives to be the most pernicious race of little <u>odious</u> vermin that nature ever suffered to crawl upon the surface of the earth."

Nothing but an extreme love of truth could have hindered me from concealing this part of my story. It was in vain to discover my resentments, which were always turned into ridicule; and I was forced to rest with patience while my noble and most beloved country was so injuriously treated. I am heartily sorry as any of my readers can possibly be that such an occasion was given, but this prince happened to be so curious and inquisitive upon every particular that it could not consist either with gratitude or good manners to refuse giving him what satisfaction I was able. Yet thus much I may be allowed to say in my own vindication that I artfully eluded many of his questions and gave to every point a more favorable turn by many degrees than the strictness of truth would allow. For I have always borne that laudable partiality to my own country, which Dionysius Halicarnassensis[12] with so much justice recommends to an historian. I would hide the

---

12. **Dionysius** (dī′ ə nīsh′ əs) **Halicarnassensis** (hal′ ə kär na sen′ sis) Greek writer who lived in Rome and attempted to persuade the Greeks to submit to their Roman conquerors.

Vocabulary Builder
odious (ō′ dē əs) *adj.* hateful; disgusting

Literary Analysis
Satire and Irony In Gulliver's remark that he "artfully eluded" the King's questions, what is the difference between the intended meaning and the actual meaning?

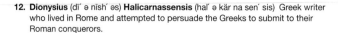

Enrichment

Gulliver's Further Travels

Lilliput and Brobdingnag appear in Books I and II of *Gulliver's Travels*. In Book III, Gulliver visits the floating island of Laputa, where the inhabitants are so lost in thought that they constantly run into each other. Then, in Luggnagg, he meets the Struldbruggs, who are completely senile, but immortal.

Book IV lands Gulliver on the island of the Houyhnhnms; Houyhnhnms are horses; however, they are grave, rational, and virtuous and have created a perfect society. The other race on the island is the Yahoos. These vicious, disgusting creatures are, in fact, humans. The Houyhnhnms tolerate the Yahoos but use them only for menial services. Though Gulliver finds perfect happiness among the wise and noble Houyhnhnms, they cannot view him as anything more than an advanced Yahoo, and they reject him. He returns to England unable to tolerate human society.

frailties and deformities of my political mother and place her virtues and beauties in the most advantageous light. This was my sincere endeavor in those many discourses I had with that mighty monarch, although it unfortunately failed of success.

But great allowances should be given to a king who lives wholly secluded from the rest of the world, and must therefore be altogether unacquainted with the manners and customs that most prevail in other nations: the want of which knowledge will ever produce many prejudices, and a certain narrowness of thinking, from which we and the politer countries of Europe are wholly exempted. And it would be hard indeed, if so remote a prince's notions of virtue and vice were to be offered as a standard for all mankind.

To confirm what I have now said, and further to show the miserable effects of a confined education, I shall here insert a passage which will hardly obtain belief. In hopes to ingratiate myself farther into his Majesty's favor, I told him of an invention discovered between three and four hundred years ago, to make a certain powder, into an heap of which the smallest spark of fire falling, would kindle the whole in a moment, although it were as big as a mountain, and make it all fly up in the air together, with a noise and agitation greater than thunder. That a proper quantity of this powder rammed into an hollow tube of brass or iron, according to its bigness, would drive a ball of iron or lead with such violence and speed as nothing was able to sustain its force. That the largest balls, thus discharged, would not only destroy whole ranks of an army at once, but batter the strongest walls to the ground, sink down ships, with a thousand men in each, to the bottom of the sea; and when linked together by a chain, would cut through masts and rigging, divide hundreds of bodies in the middle, and lay all waste before them. That we often put this powder into large hollow balls of iron, and discharged them by an engine into some city we were besieging, which would rip up the pavement, tear the houses to pieces, burst and throw splinters on every side, dashing out the brains of all who came near. That I knew the ingredients very well, which were cheap, and common; I understood the manner of compounding them, and could direct his workmen how to make those tubes of a size proportionable to all other things in his Majesty's kingdom, and the largest need not be above two hundred foot long; twenty or thirty of which

A Voyage to Brobdingnag, Illustration from a nineteenth-century edition of *Gulliver's Travels*

21 ▲ **Critical Viewing**
Compare the relationship between Gulliver and the King of Brobdingnag as portrayed by the artist with that portrayed in the text. **[Compare and Contrast]**

22 ✔ **Reading Check**
What is the King's opinion of most of Gulliver's countrymen?

from *Gulliver's Travels* ■ 531

20 **Humanities**
A Voyage to Brobdingnag

In this illustration, the King of Brobdingnag carefully listens as Gulliver talks. Like a European king, he wears a golden and jeweled crown, and his dress bespeaks splendor. Gulliver seems perfectly at ease in the royal presence.

Use these questions for discussion:

1. What does the look on the king's face convey?
Possible responses: The king is sadly amused by what he hears. He may feel compassion for Gulliver, who appears to come from such an ignoble world. Some may think the look is one of reluctance to believe what he is hearing.

2. Gulliver's pose is relaxed. Why do you think the artist chose to represent him in such a relaxed manner?
Possible responses: The artist seems to suggest that the king is listening without undue criticism; he is creating an atmosphere in which it is easy for Gulliver to say whatever comes to mind. Also, as is seen in the novel, Gulliver is unaware of the impact of his stories on the king; what seems normal and civilized to Gulliver seems barbaric to the king.

21 **Critical Viewing**

Answer: In the text, Gulliver sits at a small table at the king's left hand, in front of one of the saltcellars. In this illustration, he sits, with no table or saltcellar in sight, at the king's right hand. In the text, the king is described as making wise reflections on what Gulliver has to say. The artist has captured the look of wise conjecture in this illustration, which shows the king in an attitude of concentrated attention and thoughtfulness.

22 **Reading Check**

Answer: The king thinks that most of Gulliver's countrymen are ignorant and barbaric.

1. **Possible responses:** Traveling with Gulliver would be interesting and adventure-filled. Traveling with Gulliver would be too dangerous to enjoy.

2. **(a)** When the emperor of the Lilliputians ordered his subjects to break the small end of their eggs, the Blefuscudians supported the Lilliputian rebels who wanted to continue breaking their eggs at the large end. **(b)** They take their dispute very seriously. It is rooted in their system of beliefs. **(c)** The fact that he picked something as silly as breaking eggs shows that Swift doesn't think the reader should take the dispute seriously.

3. **(a)** The king of Brobdingnag pets Gulliver like a small pet. He speaks disparagingly of English history and culture. **(b) Possible response:** Gulliver recognizes the utility of gunpowder, but the king views gunpowder as destructive and inhuman.

4. **(a)** The Lilliputians are tiny and the Brobdingnagians are enormous. **(b)** Gulliver sees the Lilliputians as smaller in character and the Brobdingnagians as greater. **(c) Possible response:** Gulliver sees himself as superior to Lilliputians, and distances himself from their human follies. In Brobdingnag, he identifies with and defends that folly.

5. **(a)** Swift uses the King's horror to express his hope that people will eventually turn away from war. **(b) Possible response:** Given the subsequent history of the world, it does not appear that the hopes were valid.

6. **Possible responses:** Satires might change behavior if readers recognized their flaws and wished to change.

Go Online For additional information about Jonathan Swift, have students type in the Web Code, then select *S* from the alphabet, and then select the author's name.
Author Link

---

tubes, charged with the proper quantity of powder and balls, would batter down the walls of the strongest town in his dominions in a few hours, or destroy the whole metropolis, if ever it should pretend to dispute his absolute commands. This I humbly offered to his Majesty as a small tribute of acknowledgment in return of so many marks that I had received of his royal favor and protection.

The King was struck with horror at the description I had given of those terrible engines and the proposal I had made. He was amazed how so impotent and groveling an insect as I (these were his expressions) could entertain such inhuman ideas, and in so familiar a manner as to appear wholly unmoved at all the scenes of blood and desolation which I had painted as the common effects of those destructive machines; whereof he said some evil genius, enemy to mankind, must have been the first contriver. As for himself, he protested that although few things delighted him so much as new discoveries in art or in nature, yet he would rather lose half his kingdom than be privy to such a secret, which he commanded me, as I valued my life, never to mention any more.

Critical Reading

1. **Respond:** Would you like to travel with Gulliver? Explain.

2. **(a) Recall:** Describe the conflict between Big-Endians and Little-Endians over the breaking of eggs. **(b) Infer:** Do these two groups take their dispute seriously? Why or why not? **(c) Analyze:** What evidence is there that Swift does not want you to take the dispute seriously? Explain.

3. **(a) Recall:** Citing the text, give one example of how the King of Brobdingnag shows affection toward Gulliver and one example of how he shows distaste for Gulliver's ideas. **(b) Interpret:** Show how the final disagreement between Gulliver and the King reflects a difference between ingenuity and wisdom.

4. **(a) Recall:** What is the most important physical difference between Lilliputians and Brobdingnagians? **(b) Interpret:** How does this physical difference suggest other important ways in which they differ? Explain. **(c) Synthesize:** How do Lilliputians and Brobdingnagians each represent a different way of viewing humanity?

5. **(a) Support:** In the final paragraph of "A Voyage to Brobdingnag," how does Swift use the King's reactions to express his own hopes for humankind? **(b) Assess:** Do you think these hopes are valid? Why or why not?

6. **Take a Position:** Do you think that satires like Swift's can ever change people's behavior? Why or why not?

Author Link
For: More about Jonathan Swift
Visit: www.PHSchool.com
Web Code: ese-9312

Apply the Skills

from *Gulliver's Travels*

Literary Analysis

Satire

1. Use a chart like the one shown to indicate three targets of Swift's **satire**.

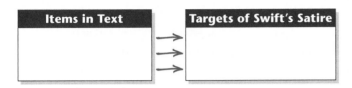

Items in Text		Targets of Swift's Satire
	→	
	→	
	→	

2. **(a)** Compare and contrast Gulliver's impression of the Lilliputians with the King of Brobdingnag's impression of Europeans. **(b)** How does the comparison add to the satire?

3. Summarize the universal and timeless points Swift wants to make with his satire.

Connecting Literary Elements

4. **(a)** Find an example of **irony** that depends on a difference between appearance and reality. **(b)** Explain your choice.

5. **(a)** Find an example of irony in which the real meaning of a passage is the opposite of the expressed meaning. **(b)** Explain your choice.

6. Why might a satirist offer ironic, rather than direct, criticisms of institutions like church and state?

Reading Strategy

Interpreting

7. To **interpret** Gulliver's remark that many have "suffered death rather than submit to break their eggs at the smaller end," what historical facts should you know? Why?

8. In interpreting Gulliver's reference to the King of Brobdingnag's "narrowness of thinking," can you assume that Swift supports his central character's remark? Explain.

9. Why is it necessary to interpret a satirical work like *Gulliver's Travels*?

Extend Understanding

10. **Social Studies Connection:** If Swift were alive today, what recent events might he satirize? Why?

QuickReview

Satire is writing that uses humor to expose and ridicule human vice and folly.

Irony is a difference or contradiction between reality and appearance or between what is meant and what is said.

Interpreting is using clues to determine the meaning of a passage.

Go Online
Assessment

For: Self-test
Visit: www.PHSchool.com
Web Code: esa-6308

from *Gulliver's Travels* ■ 533

Answers

1. **Possible responses:** Items in the Text: Gulliver's description of gunpowder; Lilliput; Blefuscu. Targets of Swift's Satire: People's enthuisiasm for conflict; England; France.

   Another sample answer can be found on **Literary Analysis Graphic Organizer B**, p. 102 in *Graphic Organizer Transparencies.*

2. (a) Gulliver's perceptions of the Lilliputians as silly and barbaric is mirrored in the king's view of Europeans. (b) It adds to the satire by showing that people think their own views are correct.

3. **Possible response:** People are often petty, combative, and self-important.

4. (a) **Possible response:** Swift writes of the Big-Endians and the Little-Endians going to war over how to break an egg. (b) This situation involves an ironic contradiction between reality (trivial egg-breaking) and appearance (an issue serious enough to lead to war).

5. (a) **Possible response:** When the King of Brobdingnag says to Gulliver: "You have made a most admirable panegyric upon your country," he means this ironically. (b) The King's real meaning is found in the next line, where the King says, "You have clearly proved that ignorance, idleness, and vice are the proper ingredients for qualifying a legislator."

6. He might fear retribution from the institutions he criticizes.

7. You should know that conflicts between the Catholics and Protestants had led to many wars and deaths. Knowing this fact explains Swift's satire.

8. **Possible response:** Swift probably does not think so. The qualities he gives the king are humane and civilized.

9. **Possible response:** Folly is not exposed and lessons are not learned if satire is not interpreted.

10. Students may refer to recent political scandals or international conflicts. Reasons should relate to a definition of satire.

Go Online
Assessment Students may use the **Self-test** to prepare for **Selection Test A** or **Selection Test B**.

533

❶ Vocabulary Lesson
Word Analysis: Latin Root -jec

1. b	5. d
2. c	6. h
3. a	7. f
4. e	8. g

Spelling Strategy

1. exchange
2. ex-ambassador
3. extension

Vocabulary Builder: Antonyms

1. c	2. f	3. a
4. b	5. e	6. d

❷ Grammar and Style Lesson

1. between	4. between
2. Among	5. among
3. among	

Writing Application

Possible response: The difference in height between Gulliver and the Lilliputians was remarkable. He could stride among them and crush them with his weight. The contrast between Gulliver and the Brobdingnagians was just as striking. Gulliver was practically invisible when he traveled among the Brobdingnagians.

𝒲𝒢 Writing and Grammar, Diamond Level

Students will find further instruction and practice on usage in Chapter 25, Section 2.

Build Language Skills

❶ Vocabulary Lesson

Word Analysis: Latin Root -jec-

The Latin root *-jec-* means "throw." This root is found in many scientific words, such as *conjecture,* which means "to guess by 'throwing' facts or inferences together."

Choose the letter of the best definition for each word below.

1. inject	a. to "throw" forward
2. eject	b. to "throw" into
3. project	c. to "throw" out of
4. trajectory	d. object designed to be "thrown" or shot
5. projectile	e. path along which an object is "thrown"
6. reject	f. "thrown" away; hopeless
7. abject	g. state of being "thrown" down; depression
8. deject	h. "throw" back at

Vocabulary Builder: Antonyms

For each numbered vocabulary word, identify the letter of the term that is the best antonym (opposite in meaning).

1. conjecture	a. fusion
2. expostulate	b. unworkable device
3. schism	c. certainty
4. expedient	d. pleasant
5. habituate	e. alienate
6. odious	f. keep silent

Spelling Strategy

When adding *ex-* to words, you usually do not include a hyphen, as in *expedient.* You do add a hyphen when *ex-* means "former," as in *ex-president.* On your paper, add *ex-* to these words.

1. change
2. ambassador
3. tension

❷ Grammar and Style Lesson

Usage: *between* and *among*

Use the preposition *between* when referring to only two things or people or groups. Use the preposition *among* when referring to more than two.

> The channel was <u>between</u> Lilliput and Blefuscu.
>
> Gulliver stood <u>among</u> the boats of the fleet.

Practice In your notebook, fill in each blank with the correct preposition: *between* or *among.*

1. A channel eight hundred yards wide lies __?__ the two countries.

2. __?__ the Lilliputians, a Big-Endian faction refused to accept the Emperor's edict.

3. Wednesday is the Sabbath __?__ the Brobdingnagians.

4. The difference in size __?__ Gulliver and the Lilliputians was remarkable.

5. The King notices that gambling is __?__ the pastimes Gulliver mentions.

Writing Application Write four sentences comparing Gulliver with the people he meets on his journeys. Use *between* and *among* twice each.

𝒲𝒢 *Prentice Hall Writing and Grammar Connection: Chapter 25, Section 2*

Assessment Practice

Writer's Purpose (For more practice, see *Standardized Test Preparation Workbook*, p. 23.)

Many tests require students to identify a writer's purpose. Use this sample test item.

It is computed that eleven thousand persons have, at several times, suffered death rather than submit to break their eggs at the smaller end.

Why did Swift include this sentence?

A to quantify the losses of the Big-Endians

B to emphasize the ridiculous extremes to which people will go in support of a cause

C to support his argument with a specific fact

D to show how unjust the Little-Endians are

Remind students that almost every sentence in *Gulliver's Travels* contains a criticism of humankind or of Swift's society. Therefore, the correct answer is *B.*

Writing Lesson

Descriptive Satire

Writers satirize their targets to prompt change, usually for the good of society. Choose a popular institution, condition, or product. Write a descriptive satire that focuses on the shortcomings or vices of your subject.

Prewriting   Focus your satire by choosing a specific target to attack. Then, list characteristics of that subject that you can exaggerate in your writing. Use a chart like the one below to organize your ideas.

Satirical Target: _____

Characteristics	Exaggeration

Drafting   Choose the most obvious characteristics of your subject, and exaggerate them as you re-create and then present your subject. Echo the same language or presentation style that your subject might use in public documents or advertisements. Be sure to reveal your subject's foolish or problematic nature.

Revising   Review your writing to be sure you have caught your readers' attention with vivid language and specific descriptive details.

Prentice Hall Writing and Grammar Connection: Chapter 16, Section 4

Extend Your Learning

Listening and Speaking   With a small group, devise a **special-effects plan** for a filmed version of the voyages to Lilliput and Brobdingnag.

- Review the story. Then, brainstorm for visual, musical, sound, and graphic effects to enhance the narrative.
- Decide where in the story they would be most effective.

Compose an oral summary of your plan that one or more group members can present to the class. **[Group Activity]**

Research and Technology   Write a **research report** on the seventeenth-century religious disputes between Catholics and Protestants that Swift satirizes as a conflict between Big-Endians and Little-Endians. Explain in detail the references Swift makes in his novel, and enhance your report with graphics, timelines, statistical charts, and diagrams.

 **For:** An additional research activity
Visit: www.PHSchool.com
Web Code: esd-7307

from *Gulliver's Travels* ■ 535

Assessment Resources

The following resources can be used to assess students' knowledge and skills.

Unit 3 Resources
    Selection Test A, pp. 129–131
    Selection Test B, pp. 132–134

General Resources
    Rubrics for Descriptive Essay, pp. 63–64

Go **Online** Students may use the
—Assessment **Self-test** to prepare for
Selection Test A or **Selection Test B**.

Meeting Your Standards

Students will

1. **analyze and respond to literary elements.**
   • Literary Analysis: Mock Epic

2. **read, comprehend, analyze, and critique a poem.**
   • Reading Strategy: Recognizing Author's Purpose
   • Reading Check questions
   • Apply the Skills questions
   • Assessment Practice (ATE)

3. **develop vocabulary.**
   • Vocabulary Lesson: Words From Political Science

4. **understand and apply written and oral language conventions.**
   • Spelling Strategy
   • Grammar and Style Lesson: Inverted Word Order

5. **develop writing proficiency.**
   • Writing Lesson: Imitating an Author's Style

6. **develop appropriate research strategies.**
   • Extend Your Learning: Glossary of Literary Terms

7. **understand and apply listening and speaking strategies.**
   • Extend Your Learning: Graduation Speech

Block Scheduling: Use one 90-minute class period to preteach the skills and have students read the selection. Use a second 90-minute class period to assess students' mastery of skills, extend their learning, and monitor their progress.

Homework Suggestions

Following are possibilities for homework assignments.

• Support pages from *Unit 3 Resources:*
   Literary Analysis
   Reading Strategy
   Vocabulary Builder
   Grammar and Style

• An Extend Your Learning project and the Writing Lesson for this selection group may be completed over several days.

Step-by-Step Teaching Guide	Pacing Guide
PRETEACH	
• Administer Vocabulary and Reading Warm-ups as necessary.	5 min.
• Engage students' interest with the motivation activity.	5 min.
• Read and discuss author and background features. **FT**	10 min.
• Introduce the Literary Analysis Skill: Mock Epic. **FT**	5 min.
• Introduce the Reading Strategy: Recognizing Author's Purpose. **FT**	10 min.
• Prepare students to read by teaching the selection vocabulary. **FT**	
TEACH	
• Informally monitor comprehension while students read independently or in groups. **FT**	30 min.
• Monitor students' comprehension with the Reading Check notes.	as students read
• Reinforce vocabulary with Vocabulary Builder notes.	as students read
• Develop students' understanding of mock epic with the Literary Analysis annotations. **FT**	5 min.
• Develop students' ability to recognize author's purpose with the Reading Strategy annotations. **FT**	5 min.
ASSESS/EXTEND	
• Assess students' comprehension and mastery of the Literary Analysis and Reading Strategy by having them answer the Apply the Skills questions. **FT**	15 min.
• Have students complete the Vocabulary Development Lesson and the Grammar and Style lesson. **FT**	15 min.
• Apply students' knowledge of parallelism and antithesis by using the Writing Lesson. **FT**	45 min. or homework
• Apply students' understanding by using one or more of the Extend Your Learning activities.	20–90 min. or homework
• Administer Selection Test A or Selection Test B. **FT**	15 min.

Resources

Choosing Resources for Differentiated Instruction

[**L1**] Special Needs Students

[**L2**] Below-Level Students

[**L3**] All Students

[**L4**] Advanced Students

[**EL**] English Learners

For Vocabulary and Reading Warm-ups and for Selection Tests, **A** signifies "less challenging" and **B** "more challenging." For Graphic Organizer transparencies, **A** signifies "not filled in" and **B** "filled in."

FT Fast Track Instruction: To move the lesson more quickly, use the strategies and activities identified with **FT**.

Scaffolding for Less Proficient and Advanced Students

The leveled Critical Thinking questions after selections progress in the levels of thinking required to answer them. To address the needs of your different students, you may use the (a) level questions for your less proficient students and the (b) level questions with your on-level and advanced students. The occasional (c) level questions are appropriate for your advanced students.

Use this complete suite of powerful teaching tools to make lesson planning and testing quicker and easier.

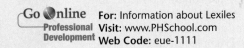

Use the interactive textbook (online and on CD-ROM) to make selections and activities come alive with audio and video support and interactive questions.

Go **Online**
Professional Development

For: Information about Lexiles
Visit: www.PHSchool.com
Web Code: eue-1111

Motivation

Ask students to imagine that someone stole the laces from someone else's sneakers during gym class. Now tell them that their job is to write 794 rhyming lines about that event! With the class, brainstorm a list of things they might include to lead up to the event and to tell about its consequences. For example, students might construct an elaborate story about revenge, love, or spite; they might also, along the way, expose cliques or other social groups in the school, as well as comment on school fads and fashions. Once students have developed a list of ideas, explain that they can read to find out how Pope used a similarly trivial event to generate 794 rhyming lines.

❶ Background
More About the Author

Alexander Pope, who was largely self-educated, was a precocious boy, eagerly reading Latin, Greek, French, and Italian, which he taught himself. Despite his curved spine, he could ride a horse and delighted in travel. However, reading and writing remained his main pursuits. Pope's extremely successful translation of Homer's *Iliad*, which he wrote in heroic couplets and published in 1720, was admired by Pope's peers and later poets. Samuel Taylor Coleridge called it "an astonishing product of matchless talent and ingenuity." Pope followed it with a translation of the *Odyssey*. These translations brought him financial independence.

Pope is among the most quotable writers in the English language. Some of the epigrams from his *Essay on Criticism* are better known than the author. Examples include "To err is human, to forgive, divine," "Fools rush in where angels fear to tread," and "A little learning is a dangerous thing."

❶ *from* An Essay on Man • *from* The Rape of the Lock

Alexander Pope
(1688–1744)

Despite a crippling childhood disease and persistent ill health, Alexander Pope was determined at a young age to become a great poet. He triumphantly achieved his boyhood ambition by the time he was in his twenties, capturing the attention of the leading literary figures of England with *An Essay on Criticism* (1711) and *The Rape of the Lock* (1712–1714). A brilliant satirist in verse, Pope gave his name to the literary era in which he wrote, which is now called the Age of Pope and Swift.

A Struggle Against Prejudice Born into the Roman Catholic family of a London linen merchant, Pope was a member of a persecuted religious minority. After the expulsion of King James II in 1688, English Catholics could not legally vote, hold office, attend a university, or live within ten miles of London. Probably to comply with the rule of residency, his family moved first to the village of Hammersmith and then to Binfield, near Windsor Forest. In this rural setting, Pope spent his formative years writing poetry, studying the classics, and educating himself.

"[T]his long Disease, my Life" In addition to facing religious prejudice, Pope had severe physical problems. Deformed by tuberculosis of the bone, or Pott's disease, Pope stood only about four and a half feet tall—"that little Alexander the women laugh at," he said about himself. Pope also suffered from nervousness and excruciating headaches throughout his life. In a line from his poem *Epistle to Dr. Arbuthnot* (1735), he refers jokingly but also with sadness to "this long Disease, my Life."

Around 1719, two years after his father's death, Pope moved to Twickenham (traditionally pronounced twit′ nəm), a village on the Thames, where he lived for the remainder of his life.

Literary Friendships Although Pope is more often remembered for his wasplike sting in quarrels than for his cordiality—he was called "the Wasp of Twickenham"—he befriended many literary figures of his day. For example, in the coffeehouses of London, he associated with Richard Steele and Joseph Addison, essayists and founders of two prominent periodicals of the time.

Satiric Scribblers Pope also associated with a group that included writers Jonathan Swift and John Gay. Pope joined with these men and others in forming the Scriblerus Club, whose purpose was to ridicule what its members regarded as "false tastes in learning."

Meeting regularly, the members wined, dined, and joked with one another. For example, when Pope read aloud to the group his revised version of *The Rape of the Lock,* one member, Thomas Parnell, humorously objected that Pope had stolen a passage from an old manuscript. Parnell even pretended to produce this manuscript, which was really his own translation of Pope's English into bad Latin.

Although the club did not continue for long, its emphasis on fun and satire probably inspired Swift's masterwork *Gulliver's Travels;* Gay's *Beggar's Opera,* the most successful play of the century; and Pope's *The Dunciad,* which is an assault on his literary enemies.

A Turn to Philosophy In the 1730s, Pope's writing moved out of the satirical mode to become increasingly philosophical. Leaving humor behind, he embarked on a massive work concerning morality and government but completed only *An Essay on Man and Moral Essays.* Nevertheless, the entire body of his work is so noteworthy that critics and fellow writers alike frequently accord him exceptionally high praise. The twentieth-century poet Edith Sitwell, for example, called Pope "perhaps the most flawless artist our race has yet produced."

Preview

Connecting to the Literature

Violating social rules may cause some people to disapprove of you. In the upper-class society of Pope's time, the unwritten rules were so elaborate that Pope made fun of them in *The Rape of the Lock*.

Literary Analysis

Mock Epic

A **mock epic** is a long, humorous narrative poem that treats a trivial subject in the grand style of a true epic like Homer's *Iliad* or Milton's *Paradise Lost*. For example, in *The Rape of the Lock*, Pope applies to the theft of a lady's lock of hair such epic elements as these:

- Boasting speeches of heroes and heroines
- Elaborate descriptions of warriors and their weapons
- Involvement of gods and goddesses in the action
- **Epic similes,** or elaborate comparisons in the style of Homer that sometimes use the words *like, as,* or *so*

As you read, look for the epic elements that convey Pope's affectionate mockery.

Comparing Literary Works

One of these works is a mock epic that pokes fun; the other is a serious look at human nature. In both works, Pope uses a figure of speech from **rhetoric,** or public speaking, called **antithesis**—placing side by side, and in similar grammatical structures, strongly contrasting words, clauses, sentences, or ideas. Using a chart like this one to identify examples of antithesis in both poems, note how the contrast in each example is between what is lofty and what is low or trivial. Also, observe how Pope uses this device to satirize behavior in *The Rape of the Lock* and to define the human condition in *An Essay on Man*.

Reading Strategy

Recognizing Author's Purpose

As you read *The Rape of the Lock*, find evidence of Pope's **purpose,** or reason for writing—to ridicule and to entertain.

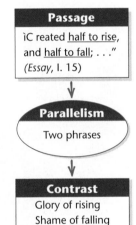

| **Passage** |
| "Created <u>half to rise</u>, and <u>half to fall</u>; . . ." *(Essay,* l. 15) |

↓

| **Parallelism** |
| Two phrases |

↓

| **Contrast** |
| Glory of rising |
| Shame of falling |

Vocabulary Builder

stoic (stō´ ik) *n.* person indifferent to joy, grief, pleasure, or pain (p. 539)

disabused (dis´ ə byoozd´) *adj.* freed from false ideas (p. 539)

obliquely (ə blēk´ lē) *adv.* at a slant; indirectly (p. 542)

plebeian (plē bē´ ən) *adj.* common; not aristocratic (p. 543)

destitute (des´ tə toot´) *adj.* lacking (p. 544)

assignations (as´ ig nā´ shənz) *n.* appointments to meet (p. 546)

from *An Essay on Man* / from *The Rape of the Lock* ■ 537

❷ Literary Analysis
Mock Epic

- Tell students that in this lesson they will focus on the mock epic, a long, humorous narrative poem that treats a trivial subject in the grand style of an epic.
- Call students' attention to the traditional epic elements, listed in the text, that they can expect to find in *The Rape of the Lock*.
- Use the instruction for Comparing Literary Works to familiarize students with the definition of antithesis: strongly contrasting ideas or words placed side by side.
- Give students a copy of **Literary Analysis Graphic Organizer A,** p. 103 in *Graphic Organizer Transparencies*.

❸ Reading Strategy
Recognizing Author's Purpose

- Remind students that an author's purpose is his or her reason for writing.
- Explain to students that an author usually writes to express an opinion, to entertain, to explain, or to persuade readers to do or believe something. Pope's purposes differ in two selections in the text.
- Use the Author's Purpose chart on p. 274 of *Graphic Organizer Transparencies* to model some of the ways in which Pope carries out his purposes.

Vocabulary Builder

- Pronounce each vocabulary word for students, and read the definitions as a class. Have students identify any words with which they are already familiar.

Differentiated Instruction Solutions for All Learners

Support for Special Needs Students
Have students complete the **Preview** and **Build Skills** pages for these selections in the *Reader's Notebook: Adapted Version*. These pages provide a selection summary, an abbreviated presentation of the reading and literary skills, and the graphic organizer on the **Build Skills** page in the student book.

Support for Less Proficient Readers
Have students complete the **Preview** and **Build Skills** pages for these selections in the *Reader's Notebook*. These pages provide a selection summary, an abbreviated presentation of the reading and literary skills, and the graphic organizer on the **Build Skills** page in the student book.

Support for English Learners
Have students complete the **Preview** and **Build Skills** pages for these selections in the *Reader's Notebook: English Learner's Version*. These pages provide a selection summary, a presentation of the skills, contextual vocabulary, and the graphic organizer on the **Build Skills** page in the student book.

537

❶ About the Selection

Pope's heroic couplets are the perfect vehicle to balance the contrary attributes of humankind. The passage asks: What is man? Its answer is: Man is a creature in the middle—more than a beast, less than a god, unsure about whether to trust his mind or body more. Both the glory and the jest of the world, man is, above all, a riddle.

❷ Humanities

The Thinker

by Auguste René Rodin, 1880

Refused admittance to the art school of his choice, Rodin became the foremost sculptor of the nineteenth and early twentieth centuries. Working in bronze and marble, Rodin created two general styles of sculptures. One style, for which he is better known, is characterized by a deliberate roughness of form. The second produces delicate forms with highly polished surfaces. *The Thinker,* cast in bronze, is executed in Rodin's more characteristic style.

Use these questions for discussion:

1. Rodin's *Thinker* is muscular and looks powerful. Is this your idea of a thinker? Explain.
   Possible response: Thinking is hard work and uses the brain's "muscles." This sculpture may be a sort of metaphor.

2. In your opinion, is this sculpture a good choice for illustrating this selection?
   Possible response: Yes; this thinker occupies a middle state, combining physicality and thought.

❸ Critical Viewing

Possible response: Rodin's image is a contemplative one. Pope's descriptions of doubt, thought, and reason compare well with this image. However, the sculpture reflects calmness, which contrasts with the "chaos of thought" in Pope's work.

❶ from

An Essay on Man

❷

Alexander Pope

❸ ▲ **Critical Viewing** Compare and contrast the perspective on humanity indicated by this Rodin sculpture with Pope's perspective in *An Essay on Man*. **[Compare and Contrast]**

538 ■ *A Turbulent Time (1625–1798)*

Differentiated Instruction   Solutions for All Learners

Accessibility at a Glance

	An Essay on Man	The Rape of the Lock
Context	Mock epic	Mock epic
Language	poetic diction	archaic language
Concept Level	Challenging (human nature)	Challenging (social manners)
Literary Merit	Classic	Classic
Lexile	NP	NP
Overall Rating	More Challenging	More Challenging

An Essay on Man is an examination of human nature, society, and morals. In the following passage, Pope cautions against intellectual pride by vividly describing the uncertain "middle state" in which humans have been placed.

Know then thyself, presume not God to scan;
The proper study of mankind is man.
Placed on this isthmus of a middle state,
A being darkly wise, and rudely great:
5 With too much knowledge for the skeptic side,
With too much weakness for the <u>stoic</u>'s pride,
He hangs between; in doubt to act, or rest;
In doubt to deem himself a god, or beast;
In doubt his mind or body to prefer;
10 Born but to die, and reasoning but to err;
Alike in ignorance, his reason such,
Whether he thinks too little, or too much:
Chaos of thought and passion, all confused;
Still by himself abused, or <u>disabused</u>;
15 Created half to rise, and half to fall;
Great lord of all things, yet a prey to all;
Sole judge of truth, in endless error hurled:
The glory, jest, and riddle of the world!

Vocabulary Builder

stoic (stō′ ik) *n.* person indifferent to joy, grief, pleasure, or pain

disabused (dis′ ə byo͞ozd′) *adj.* freed from false ideas

Critical Reading

1. **Respond:** Do you react negatively or positively to Pope's picture of human nature? Explain.

2. **(a) Recall:** What does Pope say should be the object of man's study? **(b) Speculate:** Why do you think Pope says, "presume not God to scan"?

3. **(a) Recall:** According to Pope, what prevents man from being a skeptic or a stoic? **(b) Analyze Cause and Effect:** What is the result of man's being neither skeptic nor stoic? Explain.

4. **(a) Recall:** What does each "half" of man do? **(b) Interpret:** In your own words, express how man can be both a "lord of all things" and "a prey to all."

5. **Connect:** What twentieth-century events suggest that humans are any or all of the following: "The glory, jest, and riddle of the world!" Explain.

Go Online
Author Link

For: More about Alexander Pope
Visit: www.PHSchool.com
Web Code: ese-9313

from An Essay on Man ■ *539*

4 Literary Analysis
Antithesis

- Tell students that, in Pope's time (and, indeed, until very recently), the word *man* meant human being.

- Pope uses antithesis extensively in this poem. **Ask** students to identify the opposites in the passage, then discuss with them how each half of a pair of ideas contributes to the picture Pope is creating.
Possible responses: reasoning/err: only humans use logic, but we also make mistakes; rise/fall: people create great good and great evil.

- **Ask** students what they think Pope's message is in this passage.
Possible response: Humans possess both good and bad traits; reason and passion are often in conflict, as are mind and body.

ASSESS

Answers

1. **Possible responses:** Positively; Pope's picture of human nature suggests that man is a bundle of contradictions but has great potential. Negatively; Pope's view of human nature emphasizes man's worst impulses.

2. (a) The proper study of mankind is man. (b) Pope thinks man should understand himself, not question God.

3. (a) Too much knowledge keeps a person from becoming a skeptic, and too much weakness keeps a person from becoming a stoic. (b) Man lives in doubt, never certain what to do or think.

4. (a) Half of man rises and half falls. (b) **Possible response:** Man's intelligence makes him "lord of all things," but his frailty makes him "a prey to all."

5. (a) **Possible response:** Glorious things range from landing a man on the moon to the kindness of Mother Teresa. However, the horrible things—war, terrorism—show that humans are still a "riddle."

Go Online
Author Link For additional information about Alexander Pope, have students type in the Web Code, then select *P* from the alphabet, and then select the author's name.

Differentiated Instruction   Solutions for All Learners

Support for Special Needs Students
Have students read along as they listen to this excerpt from *An Essay on Man* on the **Listening to Literature Audio CD.** In small groups, have students work to find the opposite elements in Pope's work. Help them discover how each of these opposites helps illustrate Pope's ideas.

Enrichment for Gifted/Talented Students
Ask students to think of something they could describe in the style of Pope, using opposite pairs in the description. Have them identify the topic and list two or three possible comparisons they might make. If students wish, they may try using Pope's rhyming-couplet form.

Enrichment for Advanced Readers
Students might be interested in reading more of Pope's commentary on life and people. They may choose the humorous *Dunciad,* the *Essay on Criticism,* from which we get so many common sayings, or *An Essay on Man.* Have students share any passages that they particularly enjoy.

❺

from *The Rape of the Lock*

Alexander Pope

Background *The Rape of the Lock* is based on an actual incident. Two families, the Petres and the Fermors, became involved in a dispute when Robert Petre flirtatiously cut a lock of hair from the head of lovely Arabella Fermor.

The first of the poem's five cantos opens with a formal statement of theme and an invocation to the Muse for poetic inspiration. Then, Belinda, the poem's heroine, receives a warning from the sylph Ariel that a dreadful event will take place in her immediate future. In Canto II, during a boat ride on the Thames, an adventurous baron admires Belinda's hair and is determined to cut two bright locks from her head and keep them as a prize. Aware of the baron's desires, Ariel urges the spirits to protect Belinda.

Canto III

Close by those meads, forever crowned with flowers,
Where Thames with pride surveys his rising towers,
There stands a structure of majestic frame,[1]
Which from the neighboring Hampton takes its name.
5   Here Britain's statesmen oft the fall foredoom
Of foreign tyrants, and of nymphs at home;
Here thou, great Anna![2] whom three realms obey,
Dost sometimes counsel take—and sometimes tea.
  Hither the heroes and the nymphs resort,
10   To taste awhile the pleasures of a court;

---

1. **structure . . . frame** Hampton Court, a royal palace near London.
2. **Anna** Queen Anne, who ruled England, Ireland, and Scotland from 1702 through 1714.

The Barge, 1895–96 Aubrey Beardsley

▲ **Critical Viewing** Does the artist's portrayal of Belinda, who is shown here, correspond to Pope's portrayal of her in Canto III? Explain. **[Connect]**

from *The Rape of the Lock* ■ 541

6 Humanities

The Barge

by Aubrey Beardsley, 1895

The British illustrator Aubrey Beardsley (1872–1898) achieved in his six productive years a strange and wonderful style. His only formal art training was one year of lessons at the Westminster School of Art in London. His lifelong illness, tuberculosis, did not leave him the strength to explore any form of artistic expression other than the pen-and-ink drawing for which he is remembered. He received his first illustration commission by chance through a bookseller he frequented. This commission led to many others and to fame as an illustrator. His career ended abruptly with his death at the age of twenty-six.

In executing this drawing, Beardsley introduced a technique of using dots to give texture and variety to his usually severe lines.

Use these questions for discussion:

1. What deductions can you make about the people with whom Belinda, the woman in the center, interacts?
   Answer: She moves among the rich and privileged. These people may be quite stiff and formal. On the other hand, they may be so bored as to take risks when speaking or acting. They may also be as silly and as vain as Belinda seems to be.

2. How would you describe the detail in this illustration?
   Answer: There is a huge amount of detail, which, to the modern eye, seems overdone. Nevertheless, this elaborate detailing, though slightly overdone, to match the satirical tone of the poem, still reproduces the style of the rich of this period fairly accurately.

7 Critical Viewing

Possible response: Yes; she is beautifully coifed and dressed, and she holds a fan in an elaborate setting, suggesting a restful afternoon with high-society friends.

Differentiated Instruction   Solutions for All Learners

Strategy for Less Proficient Readers
Review the important information included in *Background.* Emphasize that Belinda is the main character, and that the baron is determined to cut her hair. You may wish to explain that *lock* here means a ringlet of hair. Also be sure students understand that there are spirits present in the poem.

Strategy for English Learners
Both unfamiliar words and Pope's use of inverted word order may cause difficulty. Review with students the general story, to give them a context. Help them find the subjects and verbs in sentences, so they can clarify the meanings of sentences. Also, assist students in pronouncing and defining unfamiliar words.

Enrichment for Advanced Readers
Students may wish to find out more about the era and setting of this poem. Encourage students to select some aspect of life mentioned in the poem (Hampton Court, banking, royalty, or issues of the day) and research it further, finding two or three interesting details to share with the class.

541

8 **Humanities**

The Rape of the Lock

by Aubrey Beardsley, 1895–1896

This drawing is one of the nine produced by Aubrey Beardsley for an 1896 edition of this poem. The satiric nature of the poem appealed to Beardsley's sense of the burlesque. He depicts the incident of the cutting of the hair with a mocking humor comparable to Pope's. The artist's appreciation of the poet's wit and humor adds an extra element to these drawings.

Use these questions for discussion:

1. Who might the central figure in the foreground be?
   Possible response: It is possible that this is Ariel, a male spirit who intercedes on behalf of Belinda. Although he is dressed like others in the drawing room, he is half their size, and he has an entirely different kind of expression on his face.

2. Why do you think the illustrator does not show Belinda's face?
   Possible response: Belinda does not know what is happening. What is important in this illustration is both the act of cutting and the milieu in which the cutting takes place, both of which the artist captures.

9 **Critical Viewing**

Possible answer: Pope makes the fact of the jurymen's needing to dine seem important—sufficiently important that "wretches hang," so that they can eat. In much the same way, the artist captures the trivial goings-on so that they seem the focus.

8

The Rape of the Lock, 1895–96, Aubrey Beardsley

9 ◀ **Critical Viewing**
Where in the poem does Pope make a trivial occasion seem important, as the artist does here? Explain. **[Connect]**

> In various talk th' instructive hours they passed,
> Who gave the ball, or paid the visit last;
> One speaks the glory of the British Queen,
> And one describes a charming Indian screen;
> 15 A third interprets motions, looks, and eyes;
> At every word a reputation dies.
> Snuff, or the fan,[3] supply each pause of chat,
> With singing, laughing, ogling, and all that.
>   Meanwhile, declining from the noon of day,
> 20 The sun <u>obliquely</u> shoots his burning ray;
> The hungry judges soon the sentence sign,

Vocabulary Builder
obliquely (ə blēk' lē) *adv.* at a slant; indirectly

3. **snuff . . . fan** At the time, gentlemen commonly took snuff and ladies usually carried a fan.

Enrichment

Fashion of the Times

The obsession with fashion satirized by Alexander Pope was a phenomenon of the upper classes in the 1700s. Fashions of the European upper class were just as elaborate as hair styles. Women's dresses were made of luxurious fabrics and decorated lavishly with lace and ribbons. High fashion also dictated that women wear hooped skirts and boned corsets that cinched their waists.

Wealthier American colonists bought the fashionable clothes imported from England, but that trade stopped abruptly with the outbreak of the Revolutionary War.

The Industrial Revolution brought dramatic cultural change for both England and the United States. Mass production of goods made stylish clothes available to the middle class.

And wretches hang that jurymen may dine;
The merchant from th' Exchange[4] returns in peace,
And the long labors of the toilet[5] cease.

25 Belinda now, whom thirst of fame invites,
Burns to encounter two adventurous knights,
At omber[6] singly to decide their doom;
And swells her breast with conquests yet to come.
Straight the three bands prepare in arms to join,
30 Each band the number of the sacred nine.[7]
Soon as she spreads her hand, th' aerial guard
Descend, and sit on each important card:
First Ariel perched upon a Matadore,[8]
Then each, according to the rank they bore;
35 For sylphs, yet mindful of their ancient race,
Are, as when women, wondrous fond of place.
      Behold, four kings in majesty revered,
With hoary whiskers and a forky beard;
And four fair queens whose hands sustain a flower,
40 Th' expressive emblem of their softer power;
Four knaves in garbs succinct,[9] a trusty band,
Caps on their heads, and halberts[10] in their hand;
And particolored troops, a shining train,
Draw forth to combat on the velvet plain.
45   The skillful nymph reviews her force with care:
Let spades be trumps! she said, and trumps they were.
      Now move to war her sable Matadores,
In show like leaders of the swarthy Moors.
Spadillio[11] first, unconquerable Lord!
50 Led off two captive trumps, and swept the board.
As many more Manillio[12] forced to yield,
And marched a victor from the verdant field.[13]
Him Basto[14] followed, but his fate more hard
Gained but one trump and one <u>plebeian</u> card.
55 With his broad saber next, a chief in years,
The hoary majesty of spades appears,
Puts forth one manly leg, to sight revealed,
The rest, his many-colored robe concealed.

---

4. **Exchange** London financial center where merchants, bankers, and brokers conducted business.
5. **toilet** dressing tables.
6. **omber** popular card game.
7. **sacred nine** reference to the nine Muses of Greek mythology.
8. **Matadore** powerful card that could take a trick.
9. **succinct** (sək siŋkt′) belted.
10. **halberts** long-handled weapons.
11. **Spadillio** ace of spades.
12. **Manillio** two of spades.
13. **verdant field** the card table, covered with a green cloth.
14. **Basto** ace of clubs.

Reading Strategy
Recognizing Author's Purpose How do the remarks in lines 33–36 serve both to satirize and to entertain?

Vocabulary Builder
plebian (plē bē′ ən) *adj.* common; not aristocratic

13 ✓ **Reading Check**
In what way do Belinda and her friends pass the time?

from *The Rape of the Lock* ■ 543

Differentiated Instruction — Solutions for All Learners

Support for Special Needs Students
Students may find the elaborate description of the game of omber confusing. Have students read this portion of the poem with your help, and use graphics where possible to help students understand the progress of the game. Refer students to the footnotes that explain some of the specialized terms for the card names and suits.

Strategy for English Learners
Students may find the description of the game of omber confusing. Help students read this portion of the poem. Then have students work in small groups to make a set of picture cards with words to aid them in recognizing the names of cards. Students should use the explanatory footnotes that refer to specialized terms for the cards and their suits in preparing their cards.

---

10 **Critical Thinking**
Interpret

• Remind students that Pope often used antithesis—placing side by side strongly contrasting words or ideas—to make his point.

• Then, **ask** students to interpret lines 21–22.
Answer: Jurymen, or those deciding the fate of someone convicted of a crime, quickly deliver a verdict of guilty so that their deliberation won't postpone their dinner.

11 **Reading Strategy**
Recognizing Author's Purpose

• Point out that a reader would have an entirely different reaction to this poem if he or she thought it was serious. That is why it is important to understand the author's purpose. In some cases, the author's purpose is hidden, but Pope's purposes of satire and entertainment are clear.

• Then, **ask** the Reading Strategy question: How do the remarks in lines 33–36 serve both to satirize and to entertain?
Answer: By comparing the status-conscious sylphs to women, Pope satirizes the status-conscious women of the poem and era. He entertains his readers by making the satire light-hearted, charming and humorous.

12 **Vocabulary Builder**
Words From Political Science

• Call students' attention to the word *plebian* and its definition. Explain that it is the adjectival form of *plebs,* a word not simply derived from Latin, but actually used in ancient Rome, where it referred to lower-class citizens.

• Explain that *plebian* is usually used to describe things that are a bit too common or somewhat vulgar.

• Other, related words are *plebe* and *plebiscite*. A *plebe* is the lowest class at a military or naval academy. A *plebiscite* is a direct vote by the qualified voters of a country, state, or community on an important issue. (You may wish to discuss how each of these two terms are related to the meaning of *plebs*.)

13 **Reading Check**
Answer: They play omber, a popular card game of the time.

⓮ Background
The Card Game

Pope describes the card game as if the kings and queens on the cards were actually doing battle. Point out the mock epic elements of this game, but assure students that they need not follow every play to know what is happening. The detail adds to the humorous, mock-heroic tone but does not affect the outcome of the story.

You may wish to explain, however, that Belinda is being aided by the sylphs and so wins the first four "tricks." Then, in lines 66–74, the baron trumps Belinda's king of clubs (the club's black tyrant) with his queen of spades (warlike Amazon, imperial consort of the crown of spades). By line 85, he has taken Belinda's queen of hearts with his jack of diamonds. She grows pale at the thought of defeat. However, in lines 95–98, we learn that she triumphs, as her king of hearts "springs to vengeance" in fond memory of his captured queen. The sylphs who have been aiding Belinda rejoice at this victory.

⓯ Literary Analysis
Mock Epic and Antithesis

- Review with students the definition of mock epic and the rhetorical device of antithesis used by Pope.

- Then, **ask** the Literary Analysis question: Why are lines 97–98 an example of antithesis?
Answer: The antithesis is the contrast between his "springing" and his "falling," motions expressed using a similar grammatical structure (present tense verbs followed by prepositional phrases).

▶ **Monitor Progress: Ask** students: What elements of the mock epic does Pope employ by comparing the card game to a battle in lines 60–75?
Answer: The mock epic takes a trivial subject—a mere card game—and treats it on a grand scale. Also, it makes playing the card game seem as if it were a heroic act.

The rebel knave, who dares his prince engage,
60 Proves the just victim of his royal rage.
Even mighty Pam,[15] that kings and queens o'erthrew
And mowed down armies in the fights of loo,
Sad chance of war! now <u>destitute</u> of aid,
Falls undistinguished by the victor spade!
65   Thus far both armies to Belinda yield;
Now to the baron fate inclines the field.
His warlike Amazon her host invades,
Th' imperial consort of the crown of spades.
The club's black tyrant first her victim died,
70 Spite of his haughty mien, and barbarous pride.
What boots[16] the regal circle on his head,
His giant limbs, in state unwieldy spread;
That long behind he trails his pompous robe,
And, of all monarchs, only grasps the globe?
75   The baron now his diamonds pours apace;
Th' embroidered king who shows but half his face,
And his refulgent queen, with powers combined
Of broken troops an easy conquest find.
Clubs, diamonds, hearts, in wild disorder seen,
80 With throngs promiscuous strew the level green.
Thus when dispersed a routed army runs,
Of Asia's troops, and Afric's sable sons,
    With like confusion different nations fly,
Of various habit, and of various dye,
85 The pierced battalions disunited fall,
In heaps on heaps; one fate o'erwhelms them all.
    The knave of diamonds tries his wily arts,
And wins (oh shameful chance!) the queen of hearts.
At this, the blood the virgin's cheek forsook,
90 A livid paleness spreads o'er all her look;
She sees, and trembles at th' approaching ill,
Just in the jaws of ruin, and codille.[17]
And now (as oft in some distempered state)
On one nice trick depends the general fate.
95 An ace of hearts steps forth; the king unseen
Lurked in her hand, and mourned his captive queen.
He springs to vengeance with an eager pace,
And falls like thunder on the prostrate ace.
The nymph exulting fills with shouts the sky;
100 The walls, the woods, and long canals reply.
    Oh thoughtless mortals! ever blind to fate,
Too soon dejected, and too soon elate.

---

15. Pam knave of clubs, the highest card in the game called "loo."
16. What boots of what benefit is.
17. codille term meaning the defeat of a hand of cards.

544 ■ A Turbulent Time (1625–1798)

Vocabulary Builder
destitute (des′ tə to͞ot) *adj.*
lacking

Literary Analysis
Mock Epic and Antithesis
Why are lines 97–98 an example of antithesis?

Enrichment

Orientalism

In eighteenth-century Europe, decorative items from the Orient, such as porcelain and lacquerware, were in vogue. Such items did not replace characteristic English items but were often used in combination with them. In lines 107–110 of the poem, we read of Japanese lacquer tables and Chinese cups, though the setting is British.

The rise of interest in all things Asian was known as Orientalism. Public interest in the Orient was stimulated by the translation into English in 1705–1708 of the *Arabian Nights*. The popularity of the "Oriental novel" further fueled the desire for exotic objects.

Orientalism encompassed interest in all parts of Asia—the Far East, India, and the Middle East (especially Persia). One sees another hint of this interest in the illustration on p. 547, where one figure is wearing a turban.

Sudden, these honors shall be snatched away,
And cursed forever this victorious day.

105   For lo! the board with cups and spoons is crowned,
The berries crackle, and the mill turns round;[18]
On shining altars of Japan[19] they raise
The silver lamp; the fiery spirits blaze;
From silver spouts the grateful liquors glide,
110 While China's earth[20] receives the smoking tide.
At once they gratify their scent and taste,
And frequent cups prolong the rich repast.
Straight hover round the fair her airy band;
some, as she sipped, the fuming liquor fanned,
115 Some o'er her lap their careful plumes displayed,
Trembling, and conscious of the rich brocade.
Coffee (which makes the politician wise,
And see through all things with his half-shut eyes)
Sent up in vapors to the baron's brain
120 New stratagems, the radiant lock to gain.
Ah cease, rash youth! desist ere 'tis too late,
Fear the just gods, and think of Scylla's fate![21]
Changed to a bird, and sent to flit in air,
She dearly pays for Nisus' injured hair!

125   But when to mischief mortals bend their will,
How soon they find fit instruments of ill!
Just then, Clarissa drew with tempting grace
A two-edged weapon from her shining case:
So ladies in romance assist their knight,
130 Present the spear, and arm him for the fight.
He takes the gift with reverence, and extends
The little engine[22] on his fingers' ends;
This just behind Belinda's neck he spread,
As o'er the fragrant steams she bends her head.
135 Swift to the lock a thousand sprites repair,
A thousand wings, by turns, blow back the hair;
And thrice they twitched the diamond in her ear;
Thrice she looked back, and thrice the foe drew near.
Just in that instant, anxious Ariel sought
140 The close recesses of the virgin's thought;
As on the nosegay in her breast reclined,
He watched th' ideas rising in her mind,
Sudden he viewed, in spite of all her art,

---

18. **The berries . . . round** Coffee beans are ground in a hand mill at the table.
19. **altars of Japan** small imported lacquer tables.
20. **China's earth** earthenware cups imported from China.
21. **Scylla's** (sil′ əz) **fate** Scylla, the daughter of King Nisus, was turned into a sea bird because she cut off the lock of her father's hair on which his safety depended and sent it to his enemy.
22. **engine** instrument.

The British Tradition

Neoclassical Style and The Heroic Couplet

Lines 105–106 or any of the rhyming lines in the poem demonstrate Pope's use of the closed heroic couplet, a rhyming pair of iambic pentameter lines that are "closed" because they express a complete thought. This type of couplet is typical of the Neoclassical style of the eighteenth century, which had these characteristics: a reliance on Greek and Roman models, a stress on human limitations, and a concept of the poet as a kind of public speaker addressing society as a whole.

In keeping with the Neoclassical outlook, the closed heroic couplet allows Pope to indicate human follies and frailties with devices from public speaking like antithesis.

Connect to the Literature

In what ways do lines 125 and 126 fit the Neoclassical style and outlook?

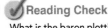 **Reading Check**

What is the baron plotting to do?

from *The Rape of the Lock* ■ 545

⓰ Literary Analysis
Mock Epic and Antithesis

• **Ask** students what Pope is saying in lines 101–104.
Answer: Belinda was too soon dejected by the thought of losing at cards; she actually won. Belinda is also too soon "elate," or happy; she will "lose" later when the baron cuts her lock of hair.

• **Ask** students what antithesis is found in line 104.
Answer: the cursed/victorious day.

• **Ask** how this antithesis parallels a traditional epic, and why it contributes to the mockery here.
Possible response: The parallel is a situation where, for example, someone won a battle but lost valued warriors. Here, it contributes to the mockery because the "battle" was a card game and the loss is a lock of hair.

⓱ The British Tradition

Neoclassical Style and the Heroic Couplet While the literature of many European countries used rhyming couplets in some form, the heroic couplet belonged only to England. Its first use in English poetry is not known, but Chaucer was the first to use it extensively, in *The Canterbury Tales*. By the mid-seventeenth century, heroic couplets became the principal meter used in drama.

Connect to the Literature
Remind students of the elements of Neoclassical style. Then, **ask** the Connect to the Literature question: In what ways do lines 125 and 126 fit the Neoclassical style and outlook?
Answer: The lines refer to the mischief of mortals, a common theme in classical literature; making mischief is a human failing; and the poet addresses the audience, society at large, with this warning.

⓲ Literary Analysis
Mock Epic

• Have students identify elements of the mock epic in lines 125–138.
Possible responses: The image of the trivial scissors elevated to that of a knight's weapon; the intervention of the sylphs.

⓳ Reading Check

Answer: The baron is plotting to cut a lock of Belinda's hair.

545

- Have students identify some of the satirically (and hilariously) exaggerated elements found in lines 145–160.
  Possible responses: fatal engine (scissors), sacred hair, forever and forever, living lightning from her eye.

- Point out that, while most of this is exaggerated, the fact that there had actually been a feud over the cutting of a lock of hair indicates that Belinda's reaction may not be as exaggerated as other elements of this passage.

- **Ask** students to what tragedies Pope compares Belinda's sorrow, and if these things appear to be of equal value.
  Answer: He compares her shrieks to those of someone whose husband has died, whose dog has died, or who has broken a piece of China. These things are not of equal value—not equal to the cutting of the hair or to each other.

- Then, **ask** the Reading Strategy question: Why does the author describe the scene in lines 145–160 in such an elevated manner?
  Answer: Pope's purpose is both to ridicule and to entertain. Both are accomplished by writing in this elevated manner, because it makes the incident very funny while also pointing out the silliness of the reaction to the lost lock of hair.

An earthly lover lurking at her heart.[23]
145   Amazed, confused, he found his power expired,
  Resigned to fate, and with a sigh retired.
     The peer now spreads the glittering forfex[24] wide,
  T' enclose the lock; now joins it, to divide.
  Even then, before the fatal engine closed,
150   A wretched sylph too fondly interposed;
  Fate urged the shears, and cut the sylph in twain,
  (But airy substance soon unites again).
  The meeting points the sacred hair dissever
  From the fair head, forever, and forever!
155   Then flashed the living lightning from her eyes,
  And screams of horror rend th' affrighted skies.
  Not louder shrieks to pitying heaven are cast,
  When husbands, or when lap dogs breathe their last;
  Or when rich China vessels fallen from high,
160   In glittering dust, and painted fragments lie!
     "Let wreaths of triumph now my temples twine,"
  The victor cried, "the glorious prize is mine!"
  While fish in streams, or birds delight in air,
  Or in a coach and six the British Fair,
165   As long as *Atalantis*[25] shall be read
  Or the small pillow grace a lady's bed,
  While visits shall be paid on solemn days,
  When numerous wax lights in bright order blaze,
  While nymphs take treats, or <u>assignations</u> give,
170   So long my honor, name, and praise shall live!
  What time would spare, from steel receives its date,[26]
  And monuments, like men, submit to fate!
  Steel could the labor of the gods destroy,
  And strike to dust th' imperial towers of Troy;
175   Steel could the works of mortal pride confound,
  And hew triumphal arches to the ground.
  What wonder then, fair nymph! thy hairs should feel,
  The conquering force of unresisted steel?

from **Canto V**

   In Canto IV, after Umbriel, "a dusky, melancholy sprite," empties a bag filled with "the force of female lungs, sighs, sobs, and passions, and the war of tongues" onto Belinda's head, the lady erupts over the loss of her lock. Then she "bids her beau," Sir Plume, to "demand the precious hairs," but Plume is unable to persuade the baron to return the hair.

---

23. **earthly lover . . . heart** If in her heart Belinda wants the baron to succeed, they cannot protect her.
24. **forfex** scissors.
25. *Atalantis* popular book of scandalous gossip.
26. **receives its date** is destroyed.

546 ■ *A Turbulent Time (1625–1798)*

Vocabulary Builder
assignations (as´ ig nā´ shənz) *n.* appointments to meet

Enrichment

Wit in Lit
In *An Essay on Criticism* (1711), Pope discussed the role of wit in literature and memorably defined "True Wit" as "Nature to advantage dress'd/What oft was thought but ne'er so well express'd." This impressive poetic essay, written when Pope was just twenty-two, appeared at a crucial time in literary history. Earlier, the term *wit* had been associated with poetic inspiration and highly imaginative conceits of metaphysical poets like Donne. Dryden had, more recently, defined wit as "a propriety of thoughts and words," stressing decorum.

"True Wit," for Pope, related more to the balance of the whole work than to the sputtering of fireworks in particular lines or images. Similarly, "What oft was thought . . ." referred not to platitudes but to widely applicable truths.

Pope believed that the works of ancient authors like Homer were superlative embodiments of "True Wit." These works had stood the test of time because they spoke to all humanity.

The Battle of the Beaux and Belles Aubrey Beardsley

▲ **Critical Viewing** In what ways is the elaborate decorative style of the drawing similar to the language of the poem? **[Evaluate]**

from *The Rape of the Lock* ■ 547

㉑ Humanities

The Battle of the Beaux and the Belles

by Aubrey Beardsley, 1895–1896

This is another of the nine pen-and-ink drawings created by Beardsley for the 1896 edition of *The Rape of the Lock.* This rococo scene is executed with the skill and mocking wit for which Beardsley is noted. The abundance of ruffles and flounces and the extravagance of embroidery and pattern serve to emphasize the silliness of the situation depicted. Beardsley's satiric style appropriately illustrates this social parody by Pope.

Use the following questions for discussion:

1. In what ways are the characters sympathetically portrayed?
   Possible response: The characters are attractive, and seem quite human despite the exaggeration. Though the continued mourning is silly, the initial reaction seems more reasonable when one sees how carefully done Belinda's hair is.

2. Which character seems to communicate the mocking tone of the picture?
   Possible response: The turbaned figure in the middle seems to be the only one not focused on Belinda, and appears to have a posture and facial expression that indicate mockery.

㉒ Critical Viewing

Possible response: The elaborate decorative style of the drawing seems to parallel the elaborate description of everything in the poem. For example, having a cup of coffee lasts for 16 lines, and the drink itself is "grateful liquor," "smoking tide," and "fuming liquor." Everything gets decorated and embroidered, just as it does in the picture.

In the beginning of Canto V, Clarissa, a level-headed nymph, tries to bring an end to the commotion, but rather than being greeted with applause, her sssspeech is followed by a battle cry.

> "To arms, to arms!" the fierce virago[27] cries,
> And swift as lightning to the combat flies.
> All side in parties, and begin th' attack;
> Fans clap, silks rustle, and tough whalebones crack;
> 5 Heroes' and heroines' shouts confusedly rise,
> And bass and treble voices strike the skies.
> No common weapons in their hands are found,
> Like gods they fight, nor dread a mortal wound.
>   So when bold Homer makes the gods engage,
> 10 And heavenly breasts with human passions rage;
> 'Gainst Pallas, Mars, Latona, Hermes[28] arms;
> And all Olympus[29] rings with loud alarms:
> Jove's[30] thunder roars, heaven trembles all around,
> Blue Neptune[31] storms, the bellowing deeps resound;
> 15 Earth shakes her nodding towers, the ground gives way,
> And the pale ghosts start at the flash of day!
>   Triumphant Umbriel on a sconce's height[32]
> Clapped his glad wings, and sat to view the fight;
> Propped on their bodkin spears,[33] the sprites survey
> 20 The growing combat, or assist the fray.
>   While through the press enraged Thalestris[34] flies,
> And scatters death around from both her eyes,
> A beau and witling[35] perished in the throng,
> One died in metaphor, and one in song.
> 25 "O cruel nymph! a living death I bear,"
> Cried Dapperwit, and sunk beside his chair.
> A mournful glance Sir Fopling[36] upwards cast,
> "Those eyes are made so killing"—was his last.
> Thus on Maeander's[37] flowery margin lies
> 30 Th' expiring swan, and as he sings he dies.
>   When bold Sir Plume had drawn Clarissa down,

---

27. **virago** (vi rā' gō) scolding woman.
28. **Pallas . . . Hermes** gods who directed the Trojan War. Pallas and Hermes supported the Greeks, while Mars and Latona sided with the Trojans.
29. **Olympus** mountain which was supposed to be the home of the Greek gods.
30. **Jove's** referring to Jupiter, the ruler of the Gods in Roman mythology: identified with Zeus in Greek mythology.
31. **Neptune** Roman god of the sea; identified with Poseidon in Greek mythology.
32. **sconce's height** candleholder attached to the wall.
33. **bodkin spears** large needles.
34. **Thalestris** (the lēs' tris) an Amazon (a race of female warriors supposed to have lived in Scythia) who played a role in the medieval tales of Alexander the Great.
35. **witling** person who fancies himself or herself a wit.
36. **Dapperwit . . . Sir Fopling** names of amusing characters in comedies of the time.
37. **Maeander's** referring to a river in Asia.

548 ▪ A Turbulent Time (1625–1798)

Literature in Context

24 History Connection

Fashions of the Times

Pope's focus on Belinda's hair indicates the importance that women's hairstyles played in the upper-class obsession with fashion at this time. During the eighteenth century, the world's first fashion magazine was launched by the French, suggesting that nation's leadership in setting styles. Leonard, hairdresser to the French queen Marie Antoinette (1755–1793), whose picture appears below, established a fashion in which women's hairdos rose as high as four feet. These "hair statues" were augmented with horsehair pads and decorated with gauze and feathers. English hairdressers quickly took up the challenge, decorating women's heads with horse-drawn carriages, zoos of miniature lions and tigers, and, if accounts can be believed, a lit stove complete with pots and pans!

Connect to the Literature

Explain how Belinda and other women of her class might reflect their status in their hairstyles.

Chloe[38] stepped in, and killed him with a frown;
She smiled to see the doughty hero slain,
But, at her smile, the beau revived again.
35   Now Jove suspends his golden scales in air,
Weighs the men's wits against the lady's hair;
The doubtful beam long nods from side to side;
At length the wits mount up, the hairs subside.
    See, fierce Belinda on the baron flies,
40 With more than usual lightning in her eyes;
Nor feared the chief th' unequal fight to try,
Who sought no more than on his foe to die.
But this bold lord with manly strength endued,
She with one finger and a thumb subdued:
45 Just where the breath of life his nostrils drew,
A charge of snuff the wily virgin threw;
The gnomes direct, to every atom just,
The pungent grains of titillating dust.
Sudden with starting tears each eye o'erflows,
50 And the high dome re-echoes to his nose.
    "Now meet thy fate," incensed Belinda cried,
And drew a deadly bodkin[39] from her side . . .
    "Boast not my fall," he cried, "insulting foe!
Thou by some other shalt be laid as low.
55 Nor think, to die dejects my lofty mind;
All that I dread is leaving you behind!
Rather than so, ah let me still survive,
And burn in Cupid's flames—but burn alive."
    "Restore the lock!" she cries; and all around
60 "Restore the lock!" the vaulted roofs rebound.
Not fierce Othello in so loud a strain
Roared for the handkerchief that caused his pain.[40]
But see how oft ambitious aims are crossed,
And chiefs contend till all the prize is lost!
65 The lock, obtained with guilt, and kept with pain,
In every place is sought, but sought in vain.
With such a prize no mortal must be blessed,
So Heaven decrees! with Heaven who can contest?
    Some thought it mounted to the lunar sphere,
70 Since all things lost on earth are treasured there.
There heroes' wits are kept in ponderous vases,
And beaux' in snuffboxes and tweezer cases.
There broken vows and deathbed alms are found,

---

38. **Chloe** (klō' ē) heroine of the ancient Greek pastoral romance, *Daphnis and Chloe*.
39. **bodkin** ornamental pin shaped like a dagger.
40. **Not . . . pain** In Shakespeare's *Othello*, the hero is convinced that his wife is being unfaithful to him when she cannot find the handkerchief that he had given her. Actually, the handkerchief had been taken by the villain, Iago, who uses it as part of his evil plot.

Literary Analysis
Mock Epic How are Belinda's words and action in lines 51–52 appropriate for a mock epic?

 Reading Check
For what prize are Belinda and her friends fighting?

from *The Rape of the Lock* ■ 549

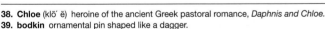
549

1. **Possible response:** They are a combination. They behave ridiculously but are charming. The baron's love despite Belinda's anger makes him sympathetic.

2. (a) Belinda is ahead, then it looks like the baron might win. Belinda wins the game. (b) Belinda went into the game expecting to win. Both are competitive, but one gets the feeling that Belinda would be a sore loser.

3. (a) Clarissa aids the baron in his attempt to cut Belinda's lock of hair, providing the scissors. A battle for possession of the lock results. (b) **Possible response:** Both are described as great battles, and deadly serious. In the first, Belinda becomes pale at the thought of losing; in the second, she becomes enraged. (c) The only thing at stake is relationships—will love survive the day's events?

4. (a) The lock of hair ascends into heaven. (b) Pope's claim that the lock of hair will be more famous than any other and will add glory to the stars is ridiculous, but it is also true in the sense that his poem has immortalized Belinda's lock of hair.

5. (a) **Possible response:** Pope thinks the rituals of the society he parodies are extravagant and silly. (b) **Possible response:** Pope's description of coffee being served and sipped is positive: "The berries crackle, and the mill turns round/. . . At once they gratify their scent and taste,/And frequent cups prolong the rich repast."

6. Answers will vary, but might range from someone at school who breaks up with a beau for a trivial reason to someone famous who thinks that he or she lives by different rules.

7. Students may say that elaborate social rituals seem ridiculous to people outside of that particular culture. Others may say that elaborate social rituals can sometimes seem solemn and serious, like funeral rites.

And lovers' hearts with ends of riband bound . . .
75   But trust the Muse—she saw it upward rise,
        Though marked by none but quick, poetic eyes . . .
        A sudden star, it shot through liquid[41] air
        And drew behind a radiant trail of hair . . .[42] air
            Then cease, bright Nymph! to mourn thy ravished hair,
80   Which adds new glory to the shining sphere!
        Not all the tresses that fair head can boast,
        Shall draw such envy as the lock you lost.
        For, after all the murders of your eye,[43]
        When, after millions slain, yourself shall die;
85   When those fair suns shall set, as set they must,
        And all those tresses shall be laid in dust,
        This lock, the Muse shall consecrate to fame,
        And midst the stars inscribe Belinda's name.

41. **liquid** clear.
42. **trail of hair** The word comet comes from a Greek word meaning long-haired.
43. **murders . . . eye** lovers struck down by her glances.

Critical Reading

1. **Respond:** Are the characters in this poem ridiculous, strange, attractive, heroic, or some combination of these? Explain.

2. **(a) Recall:** What happens during the game of cards? **(b) Infer:** What does the way in which Belinda and the baron play reveal about them?

3. **(a) Recall:** What does Clarissa help the baron do to Belinda, and what struggle results from it? **(b) Compare and Contrast:** Compare and contrast the card game with the final conflict in the poem. **(c) Synthesize:** What is really at stake in all of the poem's conflicts?

4. **(a) Recall:** What happens to the lock of hair in lines 79–88 of Canto V? **(b) Analyze:** In what way is the claim that Pope makes in these lines ridiculous? In what way is it true? Explain.

5. **(a) Interpret:** What do you think is Pope's basic criticism of the rituals he describes in the poem? Explain. **(b) Support:** Which passage or passages indicate that Pope has some positive feelings about the rituals he criticizes? Explain.

6. **Apply:** Pope based this poem on an actual incident. What contemporary incident might inspire a mock epic? Explain.

7. **Take a Position:** Are elaborate social rituals, like the ones Pope mocks, always ridiculous? Why or why not?

For: More about Alexander Pope
Visit: www.PHSchool.com
Web Code: ese-9313

Go Online For additional information about Alexander
Author Link Pope, have students type in the Web Code, then select *P* from the alphabet, and then select the author's name.

Apply the Skills

from *An Essay on Man* • from *The Rape of the Lock*

Literary Analysis

Mock Epic

1. Use a chart like the one shown to identify epic elements and the trivial activities to which they apply in *The Rape of the Lock,* Pope's **mock epic.**

Epic Element	Lines in Poem	Activity
Hero's boasts		
Gods and goddesses		
Description of warriors		

2. **(a)** Why are lines 8–16 in Canto V an **epic simile**? **(b)** How does this simile add to the absurdity of the action Pope is describing?

3. Which of the epic elements Pope uses adds most to his criticism of upper-class courtship rituals? Explain.

4. Referring to a specific passage, show that Pope's criticism of upper-class rituals is affectionate rather than stern.

Comparing Literary Works

5. Explain how line 12 of *An Essay on Man* and Canto III, lines 13–14 of *The Rape of the Lock* are examples of **antithesis.**

6. In what way does antithesis help Pope describe the human condition in *An Essay* and mock upper-class pretensions in *The Rape of the Lock*?

7. Is antithesis a device that is equally essential in both poems? Why or why not?

Reading Strategy

Recognizing Author's Purpose

8. Show how in Canto III, 105–120, Pope's **purpose** is both to poke fun at a social ritual and to entertain readers.

9. How does Pope's use of little spirits like Ariel in Canto III, 135–154 help him fulfill his purpose of poking affectionate fun at upper-class society?

Extend Understanding

10. **Social Studies Connection:** What do you think causes social rituals to become as elaborate as those Pope satirizes?

QuickReview

A **mock epic** is a humorous narrative poem that treats a trivial subject in the elevated style of a true epic. One element of that style is the **epic simile**, an elaborate comparison in the manner of Homer that uses the words *like, as,* or *so.*

Antithesis is a figure of speech from **rhetoric**, or public speaking, that involves placing strongly contrasting words, phrases, clauses, or ideas side by side.

An **author's purpose** is his or her reason for writing.

Go Online
Assessment
For: Self-test
Visit: www.PHSchool.com
Web Code: esa-6309

Answers

1. **Possible response:** Lines in Poem: Canto V, 9–16; Activity: fight to retrieve lock of hair; Lines in Poem: Canto V, 21–34, Activity: "battle," women against men; Lines in Poem: Canto V, 53–56; Activity: the baron's defiance of Belinda.

   Another sample answer can be found on **Literary Analysis Graphic Organizer B,** p. 104 in *Graphic Organizer Transparencies.*

2. (a) These lines offer an elaborate comparison in the style of an epic. (b) By comparing the lovers' quarrel to an epic battle between gods and goddesses, Pope makes the absurdity of the dispute glaringly obvious.

3. **Possible response:** Comparing a card game to an epic battle shows that the courtship rituals are taken too seriously.

4. **Possible response:** During the "battle" in Canto V, lines 21–58, Pope shows that, though the rituals may be silly, the love behind them is real.

5. Both passages place contrasting elements side by side, with similar grammatical structure—the line in *Essay* contrasts thinking too little and thinking too much; those in *Rape* contrast the significant (the monarchy) with the insignificant (furniture).

6. In *An Essay on Man,* antithesis enables Pope to show that the human condition is full of contradictions and opposites. In *The Rape of the Lock,* antithesis helps Pope mock the folly of taking oneself too seriously.

7. **Possible response:** Antithesis reflects the theme of *An Essay on Man,* which takes as its main observation that man is caught between two extremes. *The Rape of the Lock* uses antithesis to achieve humorous effects.

8. Pope pokes fun by describing the preparation and consumption of coffee as a profound and moving ritual. He entertains by describing the effects coffee has on the baron's brain and the sylphs' frantic efforts to keep the coffee from spilling.

9. By making the sprites as concerned about trivia as the humans are, he underscores the fact that too much attention is being paid to trivial things.

10. **Possible response:** People like to feel that what they do is important, so they elaborate. Also, in relationships, social ritual can help people get to know each other in an emotionally safe setting.

Go Online
Assessment

Students may use the **Self-test** to prepare for **Selection Test A** or **Selection Test B.**

❶ Vocabulary Lesson
Word Analysis

1. Belinda is the patrician, because she is of the upper class; her maid, the plebeian, because she is a servant.

2. The coachman, a servant, is the plebeian; the baron, a noble, is the patrician.

3. A four of hearts would be the plebeian or low card, and Basto, the ace of clubs, would be the high or patrician card.

Vocabulary Builder: Synonyms

1. f	3. e	5. a
2. d	4. b	6. c

Spelling Strategy

1. merrily	3. easily
2. wilier	

❷ Grammar and Style Lesson

1. statesmen (s); foredoom (v); the fall (c); Here Britain's statesmen oft foredoom the fall.

2. her host (s); invades (v); Amazon (c); Her host invades his warlike Amazon.

3. baron (s); pours (v); his diamonds (c); The baron now pours apace his diamonds.

4. liquors (s); glide (v); The grateful liquors glide from silver spouts.

5. lightning (s); flashed (v); The living lightning flashed from her eyes.

Looking at Style

1. emphasizes *foredoom*

2. emphasizes *the Amazon her host invades*

3. the inversion maintains the rhythm of the iambic pentameter

4. emphasizes *the silver*

5. emphasizes *flashed*

Build Language Skills

❶ Vocabulary Lesson

Word Analysis: Words From Political Science

Many English words concerning social or political divisions have Latin origins. *Plebeian,* meaning "ordinary or common," comes from the Latin word *plebs,* meaning "the common people." The opposite of *plebeian* is *patrician,* meaning "noble."

Patrician comes from the Latin *pater* ("father"). Roman senators were known as *patres,* or "fathers," of Rome. Other words derived from *pater* include *paternal* and *patron.*

For each pair below, explain who would act the plebeian and who the patrician.

1. Belinda and her maid

2. a coachman and the baron

3. in ombre, Basto and a four of hearts

❷ Grammar and Style Lesson

Inverted Word Order

A sentence with **inverted word order** is one that does not follow the normal word order of subject-verb-complement (s-v-c), as in this example from *The Rape of the Lock:*

> S   C   V
> The hungry judges soon the sentence sign,
> (Canto III, 21)

More typical of poetry than prose, inverted order can emphasize words or ideas by placing them at the beginning or end of a sentence. It can also create a more regular rhythm or intensify sound effects, which can be critical in poetry. You should use this device in prose, however, only in rare cases.

Vocabulary Builder: Synonyms

Choose the letter of the synonym of each numbered word.

1. plebeian	a. lacking
2. obliquely	b. person indifferent to pleasure and pain
3. assignations	c. undeceived
4. stoic	d. indirectly
5. destitute	e. meetings
6. disabused	f. common

Spelling Strategy

To add suffixes to words ending with a consonant and *y,* you usually change the *y* to *i* before adding the suffix: *haughty* becomes *haughtier.* Correctly spell the combinations below.

1. merry +-*ly*   2. wily +-*er*   3. easy +-*ly*

Practice For each item, identify the subject, verb, and any complement. Rewrite each in standard order.

1. Here Britain's statesmen oft the fall foredoom . . . (III, 5)

2. His warlike Amazon her host invades, . . . (III, 67)

3. The baron now his diamonds pours apace; . . . (III, 75)

4. From silver spouts the grateful liquors glide, . . . (III, 109)

5. Then flashed the living lightning from her eyes, . . . (III, 155)

Looking at Style For each item above, explain the emphasis or the rhythm that the order creates.

WG Prentice Hall Writing and Grammar Connection: Chapter 18, Section 2

Assessment Practice

Writer's Point of View (For more practice, see *Standardized Test Preparation Workbook,* p. 24.)

Many tests require students to identify a writer's point of view. Use this sample test item.

> . . . A being [man] darkly wise, and rudely great: With too much knowledge for the skeptic side, With too much weakness for the stoic's pride, He hangs between; in doubt to act, or rest; In doubt to deem himself a god, or beast; In doubt his mind or body to prefer; Born but to die, and reasoning but to err . . .

With which statement would Pope **not** agree?

A Humans are a plague on the face of the earth.

B To err is human.

C Humans are full of contradictions.

D People should recognize their limitations.

Choices *B* and *D* are almost restatements of lines of the poem. The passage points out contradictions in human nature, eliminating *C*. The correct answer is *A*.

Writing Lesson

Imitating an Author's Style

Pope's amusing rhymes and serious treatment of trivial matters make for a distinctive style. Imitate that style as you write a mock-heroic scene or episode.

Prewriting Choose a trivial conflict that you can treat in a mock-heroic way—for example, a dispute over fashions or sports. Then, jot down ideas for applying epic elements—like warriors' boasts and the interventions of gods and goddesses—to this petty struggle.

Drafting As you write your poem, apply stylistic devices like repetition of key words, antithesis, inversion, and parallel grammatical structures.

Model: Using Parallelism and Antithesis
Here the heroes and their girlfriends resort
To taste the pleasures of the basketball court;
In various talk the after-school hours they passed,
Who <u>dribbled best</u> or <u>slam-dunked the baddest</u>.
One worries about low grades from all his teachers,
While another praises high-flying basketball sneakers.

By adapting a passage from Pope (Canto III, 9–14), the writer includes one example of parallelism (underlined) and one of antithesis (highlighted).

Revising Read your poem aloud to a few classmates. If some parts sound uninteresting, add examples of antithesis or parallelism, and be sure you have used epic elements to describe petty events.

Prentice Hall Writing and Grammar Connection: Chapter 20, Section 6

Extend Your Learning

Listening and Speaking Let *An Essay on Man* inspire you to write a **graduation speech.** Summarize Pope's concept of human nature, and link it to the choices graduates must make. Use appeals like these:

- *ethical*—explain what values to apply
- *logical*—show how actions lead to results
- *emotional*—use words that create good feelings

Practice the speech, adding gestures that will stress your ideas. Then, present it to the class.

Research and Technology Help readers of Pope's mock epic by creating a **glossary** of literary terms in the poem. First, note terms you will explain and where in the poem each appears. Then, use reference books to write brief explanations. Alphabetize the annotated terms, including the line reference with each.

Go Online
Research
For: An additional research activity
Visit: www.PHSchool.com
Web Code: esd-7308

Assessment Resources

The following resources can be used to assess students' knowledge and skills.

Unit 3 Resources
Selection Test A, pp. 146–148
Selection Test B, pp. 149–151

General Resources
Rubrics for Poem (Rhyming), pp. 73–74

Go Online
Assessment Students may use the **Self-test** to prepare for **Selection Test A** or **Selection Test B.**

---

❸ Writing Lesson

You may use this Writing Lesson as timed-writing practice, or you may allow students to develop the essay as a writing assignment over several days.

- To guide students in writing this poem, give them the **Support for Writing Lesson** page (*Unit 3 Resources,* p. 143).

- Review with students the elements Pope uses to create his style—elaborate descriptions, heroic elements, alliteration, antithesis, and similes.

- Tell students that they need to supply only a scene or episode (for example, in the poem, a scene might be the card game or serving coffee or the final battle).

- Encourage students to use as many of the elements from Pope's work as they can, and to be as humorous as possible. Remind them that Pope's satire is affectionate, not bitter or hurtful.

- Use the Writing Lesson to guide students in developing their mock-epic scenes.

- Use the Poem (Rhyming) rubrics on *General Resources,* pp. 73–74, to evaluate students' poems.

❹ Listening and Speaking

- Have students review the passage from *An Essay on Man* to get a feel for the tone of the work.

- Point out that students are not being asked to follow either the form or the message, but simply to adopt a similar emotional tone. The ideas should be those of the student; the format should be that of a speech.

- Remind students that a graduation speech should impart wisdom and express ideas clearly and in a way that is easy for a listener to understand.

- Have students rehearse, speaking loudly and clearly.

- The **Support for Extend Your Learning** page (*Unit 3 Resources,* p. 144) provides guided note-taking opportunities to help students complete the Extend Your Learning activities.

Go Online
Research Have students type in the Web Code for another research activity.

TIME AND RESOURCE MANAGER

 Meeting Your Standards

Students will

1. **analyze and respond to literary elements.**
   - Literary Analysis: Dictionary; Biography

2. **read, comprehend, analyze, and critique nonfiction.**
   - Reading Strategy: Establishing a Purpose
   - Reading Check questions
   - Apply the Skills questions
   - Assessment Practice (ATE)

3. **develop vocabulary.**
   - Vocabulary Lesson: Latin Word Root: -*dict*-

4. **understand and apply written and oral language conventions.**
   - Spelling Strategy
   - Grammar and Style Lesson: Parenthetical Expressions

5. **develop writing proficiency.**
   - Writing Lesson: Comparative Analysis of Dictionaries

6. **develop appropriate research strategies.**
   - Extend Your Learning: Biographical Sketch

7. **understand and apply listening and speaking strategies.**
   - Extend Your Learning: Reenactment

Block Scheduling: Use one 90-minute class period to preteach the skills and have students read the selection. Use a second 90-minute class period to assess students' mastery of skills, extend their learning, and monitor their progress.

Homework Suggestions

Following are possibilities for homework assignments.

- Support pages from *Unit 3 Resources:*
  - Literary Analysis
  - Reading Strategy
  - Vocabulary Builder
  - Grammar and Style

- An Extend Your Learning project and the Writing Lesson for this selection group may be completed over several days.

Step-by-Step Teaching Guide	Pacing Guide
PRETEACH	
• Administer Vocabulary and Reading Warm-ups as necessary.	5 min.
• Engage students' interest with the motivation activity.	5 min.
• Read and discuss author and background features. **FT**	10 min.
• Introduce the Literary Analysis skill: Dictionary; Biography **FT**	5 min.
• Introduce the Reading Strategy: Establishing a Purpose **FT**	10 min.
• Prepare students to read by teaching the selection vocabulary. **FT**	
TEACH	
• Informally monitor comprehension while students read independently or in groups. **FT**	30 min.
• Monitor students' comprehension with the Reading Check notes.	as students read
• Reinforce vocabulary with Vocabulary Builder notes.	as students read
• Develop students' understanding of dictionaries and biographies with the Literary Analysis annotations. **FT**	5 min.
• Develop students' ability to establish a purpose with the Reading Strategy annotations. **FT**	5 min.
ASSESS/EXTEND	
• Assess students' comprehension and mastery of the Literary Analysis and Reading Strategy by having them answer the Apply the Skills questions. **FT**	15 min.
• Have students complete the Vocabulary Development Lesson and the Grammar and Style Lesson. **FT**	15 min.
• Apply students' knowledge of comparison by using the Writing Lesson. **FT**	45 min. or homework
• Apply students' understanding by using one or more of the Extend Your Learning activities.	20–90 min. or homework
• Administer Selection Test A or Selection Test B. **FT**	15 min.

Resources

Choosing Resources for Differentiated Instruction

[**L1**] Special Needs Students

[**L2**] Below-Level Students

[**L3**] All Students

[**L4**] Advanced Students

[**EL**] English Learners

For Vocabulary and Reading Warm-ups and for Selection Tests, **A** signifies "less challenging" and **B** "more challenging." For Graphic Organizer transparencies, **A** signifies "not filled in" and **B** "filled in."

FT Fast Track Instruction: To move the lesson more quickly, use the strategies and activities identified with **FT**.

Scaffolding for Less Proficient and Advanced Students

The leveled Critical Thinking questions after selections progress in the levels of thinking required to answer them. To address the needs of your different students, you may use the (a) level questions for your less proficient students and the (b) level questions with your on-level and advanced students. The occasional (c) level questions are appropriate for your advanced students.

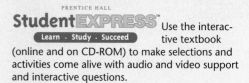

PRENTICE HALL
TeacherEXPRESS™ Use this complete
Plan · Teach · Assess suite of powerful
teaching tools to make lesson planning and testing quicker and easier.

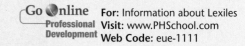

PRENTICE HALL
StudentEXPRESS™ Use the interac-
Learn · Study · Succeed tive textbook
(online and on CD-ROM) to make selections and activities come alive with audio and video support and interactive questions.

Go Online **For:** Information about Lexiles
Professional **Visit:** www.PHSchool.com
Development **Web Code:** eue-1111

Motivation

What does it take to write a diction-ary? You can give students the tiniest taste of the difficulty and complexity of the task by asking them to work in pairs to write an entry for only one word. Suggest a multiple-meaning word such as *try* or *wonder.* Ask students to include some of the things modern dictionaries include: pronunciation, meanings for different parts of speech, idioms, guidance on usage or usage labels, as well as, per-haps, cross references or synonyms. When students are finished, invite them to look up the word in a class-room dictionary and see how well they did. Students might then esti-mate how long they spent writing their entry, add to it the time they might spend to revise it or to make it publishable, and then multiply that time by the number of entries in a college dictionary, which is roughly 100,000 to 160,000 words.

❶ Background

More About the Authors

Samuel Johnson and James Boswell will forever be linked by virtue of Boswell's authoritative biography of Johnson. Johnson's marvelous wit—captured by Boswell so admirably in the *Life of Samuel Johnson*—was sufficiently revered during his lifetime and by generations that followed that the Enlightenment period in which he lived is known today as the Age of Johnson.

Build Skills *Nonfiction*

❶ *from* A Dictionary of the English Language • *from the* Life of Samuel Johnson

Samuel Johnson
(1709–1784)

With his fine mind and dazzling conversation, Samuel Johnson was at the center of a circle that included most of Britain's leading art-ists and intellectuals. So great was his influ-ence on English literature that the second half of the eighteenth century is often called the Age of Johnson.

A Life of Hardship Samuel Johnson overcame severe physical and economic hardships. The son of a bookseller in Lichfield, England, he suffered a series of childhood illnesses that left him weak and disfigured. Bright enough to read Shakespeare as a young boy, he was too poor to attend the schools of the aristocracy and pursued his education largely by reading books in his father's shop. Although he was able to enter Oxford in 1728, lack of funds forced him to leave early.

A Great Work In 1737, Johnson moved to London to try to earn his living as a writer; in 1746, he began work on his *Dictionary of the English Language.* This landmark effort took nine years to complete—difficult years during which his wife died and he continued to be dogged by poverty. When at last the *Dictionary* was published, however, it ensured Johnson's place in literary history. Still, it was not until 1762, when he received a pension from the king, that he did not have to rely on writing for a living. In 1775, he received an honorary degree from Oxford, the school he had been forced to leave.

James Boswell
(1740–1795)

James Boswell is per-haps the greatest biog-rapher in English letters. In his *Life of Samuel Johnson,* he writes with vigor about his fascinating subject, training his eye on the picturesque and the grotesque.

Celebrity Chaser Born into an aristocratic family in Edinburgh, Scotland, Boswell was educated at several universities. Although he received his degree in law and was admitted to the bar in both Scotland and England, his true passion was literature. His father, a prominent judge, was angered by what he saw as his son's "shallow" values. The extremely sensitive Boswell interpreted this dissatisfaction as rejection. In an effort to overcome his low self-esteem and also find a suitable father figure, he became a celebrity chaser.

In Samuel Johnson, he found not only a friendly celebrity but also the father figure he apparently sought. Deciding to become Johnson's biographer, he devoted many years to compiling detailed records of Johnson's life.

Twentieth-Century Author Boswell's *Life of Samuel Johnson* (1791) was an acclaimed book from its first appearance. Then, in the 1920s, scholars discovered Boswell's private papers, long thought to have been destroyed. In 1950, they began publishing the journals they found among these papers—the first volume was *Boswell's London Journal* (1762–1763)—and the great biographer was reborn as a twentieth-century author!

Preview

Connecting to the Literature

Think of the new words constantly entering the language. Johnson's *Dictionary* was one man's heroic attempt to master a changing language.

Literary Analysis

Dictionary; Biography

A **dictionary** defines words and may provide information about their pronunciation, history, and usage. Samuel Johnson compiled the first standard dictionary of the English language. As you read, look for features he initiated that are still in use today.

A **biography** is the account of someone's life written by another person. Just as Johnson's *Dictionary* was a landmark, so was Boswell's *Life of Samuel Johnson*. In reading it, note how Boswell uses many details from his own personal knowledge to reveal Johnson's character.

Comparing Literary Works

Both these selections were natural products of the Enlightenment, the eighteenth-century intellectual movement that stressed the setting down of knowledge. As you read these key works, note one of the qualities of this time period—an elevated language that revealed respect for knowledge. Compare the **diction**, or word choice, of these two works, and notice the attitude—or **tone**—that the language reveals.

Reading Strategy

Establishing a Purpose

To ensure the efficiency of your reading, **establish a purpose**, or goal, before you begin. For example, you might want to learn about Johnson's writing style, to understand the process of compiling a dictionary, or to analyze Johnson's attitudes. As you read, complete a chart like the one shown with details related to your purpose.

Vocabulary Builder

recompense (rek′ əm pens′) *n.* reward; payment (p. 556)

caprices (kə prēs′ iz) *n.* whims (p. 556)

adulterations (ə dul′ tər ā′ shənz) *n.* impurities; added ingredients that are improper or inferior (p. 557)

propagators (präp′ ə gāt′ ərz) *n.* those who cause something to happen or to spread (p. 558)

risible (riz′ ə bəl) *adj.* prompting laughter (p. 558)

abasement (ə bās′ mənt) *n.* condition of being put down or humbled (p. 563)

credulity (krə doo′ lə tē) *n.* tendency to believe too readily (p. 566)

malignity (mə lig′ nə tē) *n.* strong desire to harm others (p. 566)

pernicious (pər nish′ əs) *adj.* causing serious injury; deadly (p. 568)

inculcated (in kul′ kāt′ id) *v.* impressed upon the mind by repetition (p. 568)

from *A Dictionary of the English Language* / from the *Life of Samuel Johnson* ■ 555

---

❷ Literary Analysis
Dictionary; Biography

- Tell students that in this lesson they will focus on the dictionary, a reference source that defines words and provides information about their pronunciation, history, and usage. Students will also focus on the biography, an account of someone's life written by another person.

- Read aloud the notes about dictionary and biography. Call students' attention to the elements of dictionary and biography they can expect to find in Johnson's *A Dictionary of the English Language* and Boswell's *Life of Samuel Johnson*.

- Use the instruction for Comparing Literary Works to review with students the concept of diction, or word choice. Explain that diction often reveals something about the author's attitude toward the subject addressed.

❸ Reading Strategy
Establishing a Purpose

- Explain to students that before they read they should establish a purpose, or goal, for what they want to gain from their reading.

- Give students a copy of **Reading Strategy Graphic Organizer A,** p. 107 in *Graphic Organizer Transparencies,* to help them practice this skill.

Vocabulary Builder

Pronounce each vocabulary word for students, and read the definitions as a class. Have students identify any words with which they are already familiar.

Differentiated Instruction   Solutions for All Learners

Support for Special Needs Students
Have students complete the **Preview** and **Build Skills** pages for these selections in the *Reader's Notebook: Adapted Version.* These pages provide a selection summary, an abbreviated presentation of the reading and literary skills, and the graphic organizer on the **Build Skills** page in the student book.

Support for Less Proficient Readers
Have students complete the **Preview** and **Build Skills** pages for these selections in the *Reader's Notebook.* These pages provide a selection summary, an abbreviated presentation of the reading and literary skills, and the graphic organizer on the **Build Skills** page in the student book.

Support for English Learners
Have students complete the **Preview** and **Build Skills** pages for these selections in the *Reader's Notebook: English Learner's Version.* These pages provide a selection summary, an abbreviated presentation of the skills, additional contextual vocabulary, and the graphic organizer on the **Build Skills** page in the student book.

❶ *from* A Dictionary *of the* English Language

SAMUEL JOHNSON

Background Eighteenth-century thinkers sensed that their era had made great advances in knowledge, and they set down in writing the scientific, philosophical, and historic facts and ideas that were part of this new understanding. Among the intellectual pioneers of this period were Samuel Johnson and James Boswell, whose dictionary and biography, respectively, set the standard for nonfiction works of their type. The eighteenth century also saw the birth of the first *Encyclopedia Britannica* (1768–1771) as well as Adam Smith's *Wealth of Nations* (1776), which revolutionized the study of economics. As you read the following selections, notice how just as Johnson captures in his dictionary the changing English language, Boswell captures in his biography the changeable personality of Johnson.

from The Preface

It is the fate of those who toil at the lower employments of life, to be rather driven by the fear of evil, than attracted by the prospect of good; to be exposed to censure, without hope of praise; to be disgraced by miscarriage, or punished for neglect, where success would have been without applause, and diligence without reward.

Among these unhappy mortals is the writer of dictionaries; whom mankind have considered, not as the pupil, but the slave of science, the pioneer of literature, doomed only to remove rubbish and clear obstructions from the paths through which learning and genius press forward to conquest and glory, without bestowing a smile on the humble drudge that facilitates their progress. Every other author may aspire to praise; the lexicographer can only hope to escape reproach, and even this negative <u>recompense</u> has been yet granted to very few.

I have, notwithstanding this discouragement, attempted a dictionary of the English language, which, while it was employed in the cultivation of every species of literature, has itself been hitherto neglected; suffered to spread under the direction of chance, into wild exuberance; resigned to the tyranny of time and fashion: and exposed to the corruptions of ignorance and <u>caprices</u> of innovation.

When I took the first survey of my undertaking, I found our speech copious without order and energetic without rule: wherever I turned

Vocabulary Builder
recompense (rek´ əm pens´) *n.* reward; payment

caprices (kə prēs´ iz) *n.* whims

A

DICTIONARY

OF THE

ENGLISH LANGUAGE:

IN WHICH

The WORDS are deduced from their ORIGINALS,

AND

ILLUSTRATED in their DIFFERENT SIGNIFICATIONS

BY

EXAMPLES from the beſt WRITERS.

TO WHICH ARE PREFIXED,

A HISTORY of the LANGUAGE,

AND

An ENGLISH GRAMMAR.

By SAMUEL JOHNSON, A. M.

IN TWO VOLUMES

VOL. I.

Cum tabulis animum cenſoris ſumet honeſti;
Audebit quæcunque parum ſplendoris habebant,
Et ſine pondere erunt, et honore indigna ferentur,
Verba movere loco; quamvis invita recedant,
Et verſentur adhuc intra penetralia Veſtæ:
Obſcurata diu populo bonus eruet, atque
Proferet in lucem ſpecioſa vocabula rerum,
Quæ priſcis memorata Catonibus atque Cethegis,
Nunc ſitus informis premit et deſerta vetuſtas. HOR.

LONDON.

Printed by W. STRAHAN,

For J. and P. KNAPTON; T. and T. LONGMAN; C. HITCH and L. HAWES;
A. MILLAR; and R. and J. DODSLEY.

MDCCLV.

3 ◄ **Critical Viewing**
What does this title page of Johnson's *Dictionary* tell you about the contents? [Infer]

my view, there was perplexity to be disentangled and confusion to be regulated; choice was to be made out of boundless variety, without any established principle of selection; <u>adulterations</u> were to be detected, without a settled test of purity; and modes of expression to be rejected or received, without the suffrages of any writers of classical reputation or acknowledged authority.

Having therefore no assistance but from general grammar, I applied myself to the perusal of our writers; and noting whatever might be of use to ascertain or illustrate any word or phrase, accumulated in time the materials of a dictionary, which, by degrees, I reduced to method,

Vocabulary Builder
adulterations (ə dul′ tər ā′ shənz) *n.* impurities; added ingredients that are improper or inferior

4 ✓ **Reading Check**

In what condition did Johnson find the English language when he began work?

from *A Dictionary of the English Language* ■ 557

② Humanities

This title page of Johnson's *Dictionary* tells a bit about the history of printing conventions. Students may notice that almost the entire page is set in capital letters, as if the title page were a matter of the utmost importance. Use these questions for discussion:

1. Do you think Johnson would have been proud of this title page?
Possible responses: It is quite likely he would have been proud of this title page. Not only does it tell readers that a dictionary lies within these covers and announce a history of language and English grammar, but it credits Johnson.

2. Why do you think Samuel Johnson's name appears in relatively small letters?
Answer: Johnson gained fame through his dictionary; he was not famous before its publication. It is also possible that the conventions of the day called more attention to the titles of works than to their authors.

③ Critical Viewing

Answer: The title page gives a great deal of information. It explains that many of the words are accompanied by examples of their use, and that these examples come from "the best writers." It says that information on both the history of the language and on grammar is contained in the dictionary. It says that the work consists of two volumes. Because of its claims, in addition to the quotation from Horace, the reader can infer that this is a scholarly work based on research.

④ Reading Check

Answer: When Johnson began work, he found the English language "copious without order and energetic without rule."

Differentiated
Instruction   Solutions for All Learners

Support for English Learners	**Enrichment for Gifted/Talented Students**
Students may find reading *A Dictionary of the English Language* especially difficult because it is a reference to a language with which they may not be entirely comfortable. Have students read the Preface along with you. Then, have students listen to this selection on **Listening to Literature Audio CDs.** Encourage students to practice repeating words or phrases that are especially difficult.	Have students read Johnson's Preface independently, then assign them partners. One person assumes the role of Johnson, and the other is an interviewer. Have students write scripts in which the interviewer asks Johnson about his experiences writing his dictionary, or about any other relevant life experiences. Students may want to read ahead in Boswell's *Life of Johnson* to enrich their questions and answers. Have students present their interview to the class.

- Review with students Johnson's description of his task. **Ask** students to name some of the difficulties he encountered.
Answer: Johnson found language disordered and confused; he had to identify adulterations in the language; he had to reject or accept "modes of expression," using only grammar and the works of other writers as his guide.

- Then, **ask** the Literary Analysis question: What do the first five paragraphs reveal about how Johnson's task differed from that of dictionary makers today?
Answer: Because Johnson was creating the first dictionary, he had almost no one else's work on which to build, as dictionary makers do today. He had no experts with whom to confer and no computerized databases of word citations; his word-processing equipment consisted of pen and ink.

⑤ establishing to myself, in the progress of the work, such rules as experience and analogy suggested to me; experience, which practice and observation were continually increasing; and analogy, which, though in some other words obscure, was evident in others. . . .

In hope of giving longevity to that which its own nature forbids to be immortal, I have devoted this book, the labor of years, to the honor of my country, that we may no longer yield the palm of philology, without a contest to the nations of the continent. The chief glory of every people arises from its authors. Whether I shall add anything by my own writings to the reputation of English literature, must be left to time. Much of my life has been lost under the pressures of disease; much has been trifled away; and much has always been spent in provision for the day that was passing over me; but I shall not think my employment useless or ignoble, if by my assistance foreign nations and distant ages gain access to the <u>propagators</u> of knowledge, and understand the teachers of truth; if my labors afford light to the repositories of science, and add celebrity to Bacon, to Hooker, to Milton, and to Boyle.[1]

When I am animated by this wish, I look with pleasure on my book, however defective, and deliver it to the world with the spirit of a man that has endeavored well. That it will immediately become popular, I have not promised to myself. A few wild blunders, and <u>risible</u> absurdities, from which no work of such multiplicity was ever free, may for a time furnish folly with laughter, and harden ignorance into contempt; but useful diligence will at last prevail, and there never can be wanting some who distinguish desert; who will consider that no dictionary of a living tongue ever can be perfect, since, while it is hastening to publication, some words are budding, and some falling away; that a whole life cannot be spent upon syntax and etymology, and that even a whole life would not be sufficient; that he, whose design includes whatever language can ⑥ express, must often speak of what he does not understand; that a writer will sometimes be hurried by eagerness to the end, and sometimes faint with weariness under a task which Scaliger[2] compares to the labors of the anvil and the mine; that what is obvious is not always known, and what is known is not always present; that sudden fits of inadvertency will surprise vigilance, slight avocations[3] will seduce attention, and casual eclipses of the mind will darken learning; and that the writer shall often in vain trace his memory at the moment of need, for that which yesterday he knew with intuitive readiness, and which will come uncalled into his thoughts tomorrow.

In this work, when it shall be found that much is omitted, let it not be forgotten that much likewise is performed; and though no book was ever spared out of tenderness to the author, and the world is

---

1. **Bacon . . . Boyle** writers quoted by Johnson in the *Dictionary*.
2. **Scaliger** Joseph Justus Scaliger (1540–1609), a scholar who suggested that criminals should be condemned to writing dictionaries.
3. **avocations** things that call one away or distract one from something.

Vocabulary Builder
propagators (präp´ ə gāt´ ərz) *n.* those who cause something to happen or to spread

Vocabulary Builder
risible (riz´ ə bəl) *adj.* prompting laughter

Enrichment

Dictionaries and Academies
Johnson worked alone, but in many European countries, preserving language was the task of an academy (named after the grove of Academe, in which the ancient Greek philosopher Plato taught).

After Plato's time, academies were established to consolidate and purify the language of a nation. One of the earliest of them, the Accademia della Crusca, was founded during the Renaissance to preserve and purify the Italian language. Similar academies were launched in France, Spain, Sweden, Switzerland, and the Netherlands.

None of the academies, however, has been able to prevent the change of any language. Most modern dictionaries and grammar handbooks, therefore, are less concerned with dictating standards than with recording current usage.

little solicitous to know whence proceed the faults of that which it condemns; yet it may gratify curiosity to inform it, that the *English Dictionary* was written with little assistance of the learned, and without any patronage of the great; not in the soft obscurities of retirement, or under the shelter of academic bowers, but amidst inconvenience and distraction, in sickness and in sorrow. It may repress the triumph of malignant criticism to observe that if our language is not here fully displayed, I have only failed in an attempt which no human powers have hitherto completed. If the lexicons of ancient tongues, now immutably fixed and comprised in a few volumes, be yet, after the toil of successive ages, inadequate and delusive; if the aggregated knowledge and cooperating diligence of the Italian academicians did not secure them from the censure of Beni;[4] if the embodied critics of France, when fifty years had been spent upon their work, were obliged to change its economy[5] and give their second edition another form, I may surely be contented without the praise of perfection, which, if I could obtain, in this gloom of solitude, what would it avail me? I have protracted my work till most of those whom I wished to please have sunk into the grave,[6] and success and miscarriage are empty sounds: I therefore dismiss it with frigid tranquility, having little to fear or hope from censure or from praise.

Selected Entries from *A Dictionary*

athle′ tick. Strong of body; vigorous; lusty; robust.
> Science distinguishes a man of honor from one of those *athletick* brutes, whom undeservedly we call heroes. Dryden.

bang. A blow; a thump; a stroke: a low word.
> I am a bachelor. That's to say, they are fools that marry; you'll bear me a *bang* for that. Shakespeare, *Julius Caesar*.

to ba′rbecue. A term used in the West Indies for dressing a hog whole; which, being split to the backbone, is laid flat upon a large gridiron, raised about two foot above a charcoal fire, with which it is surrounded.
> Oldfield, with more than harpy throat endu'd,
> Cries, send me, gods, a whole hog *barbecu'd*. Pope.

bu′ffleheaded. A man with a large head, like a buffalo; dull; stupid; foolish.

cream. The unctuous or oily part of milk, which, when it is cold, floats on the top, and is changed by the agitation of the churn into butter; the flower of milk.

---

4. **Beni** Paolo Beni severely criticized the first Italian dictionary.
5. **economy** organization.
6. **sunk . . . grave** Johnson's wife had died three years earlier.

from *A Dictionary of the English Language* ■ 559

Reading Strategy

Establishing a Purpose If your purpose were to find out more about Samuel Johnson's feelings about writing his dictionary, what information in the last two paragraphs would be helpful?

❼ ✓ **Reading Check**

Why, according to Johnson, can "no dictionary of a living tongue ever . . . be perfect"?

---

❻ Reading Strategy
Establishing a Purpose

• Remind students that by establishing a purpose before reading a text, they can answer questions about the material. Tell them they should focus on Johnson's feelings about writing his dictionary.

• Have volunteers take turns reading aloud the bracketed passage.

• Then, **ask** the Reading Strategy question: If your purpose were to find out more about Samuel Johnson's feelings about writing his dictionary, what information in the last two paragraphs would be helpful?
Answer: Johnson is proud of his accomplishment. Even though he apologizes for the "much" that may have been omitted, he asserts that "much likewise [was] performed." Johnson is also proud that he did this job on his own—without a rich patron, the help of the learned, or the shelter of a university job.

❼ Reading Check

Answer: According to Johnson, no dictionary can be perfect because while it is on its way to publication, new words are "budding, and some falling away."

Differentiated Instruction Solutions for All Learners

Support for Special Needs Students
Students may have difficulty evaluating how Johnson's dictionary differed from contemporary ones. Show students a modern dictionary and explain each element of an entry, including pronunciation, etymology, and definition. Then, refer students to an example from Johnson's *Dictionary*. Use the **Literary Analysis Graphic Organizer B** transparency on p. 110 of *Graphic Organizer Transparencies* to guide your instruction.

Strategy for Advanced Readers
Have students read Johnson's preface independently. Then, have them consider some of Johnson's dictionary entries. Have partners use modern dictionaries to look up five of the words in Johnson's *Dictionary*. Finally, have students give oral presentations of their research—including any differences in pronunciation, etymology, and definition they have uncovered.

- Review with students their under-standing of diction, or word choice, and how it may reflect an author's attitude.

- You may wish to tell students about Johnson's dealings with Lord Chesterfield, who at one point had expressed interest in supporting the dictionary project. The prom-ised help never came close to meeting Johnson's needs or expectations. When he learned that Chesterfield wished to be regarded as the patron of the now-completed work, Johnson wrote one of the most scathing letters in English literature. "Seven years, my Lord, have now passed, since I waited in your outward rooms, or was repulsed from your door; during which time I have been pushing on my work . . . without one act of assistance, one word of encouragement, or one smile of favor. Such treatment I did not expect, for I never had a patron before. . . . Is not a patron, my Lord, one who looks with uncon-cern on a man struggling for life in the water, and, when he has reached ground, encumbers him with help?"

- Then, **ask** the Literary Analysis question: What effect does Johnson's word choice have on his definition of *patron*?
Answer: Johnson's diction sug-gests his contempt for patrons and for those who receive patronage. In his introduction, he indicated that he compiled the dictionary without any patronage or financial assis-tance.

electri′city. A property in some bodies, whereby, when rubbed so as to grow warm, they draw little bits of paper, or such like substances, to them. Quincy.

Such was the account given a few years ago of electricity; but the industry of the present age, first excited by the experiments of Gray, has discovered in electricity a multitude of philosophical wonders. Bodies electrified by a sphere of glass, turned nimbly round, not only emit flame, but may be fitted with such a quantity of the electrical vapor as, if discharged at once upon a human body, would endanger life. The force of this vapor has hitherto appeared instantaneous, persons at both ends of a long chain seeming to be struck at once. The philosophers are now endeavoring to intercept the strokes of lightning.

to fu′rnace. To throw out as sparks from a furnace. A bad word.
He *furnaces*
The thick sighs from him. Shakespeare's *Cymbeline.*

gang. A number herding together; a troop; a company; a tribe; a herd. It is seldom used but in contempt or abhorrence.

ha′tchet-face. An ugly face; such, I suppose, as might be hewn out of a block by a hatchet.
An ape his own dear image will embrace;
An ugly beau adores a *hatchet-face.* Dryden.

lifegua′rd. The guard of a king's person.

mo′dern. In Shakespeare, vulgar; mean; common.
We have our philosophical persons to make *modern* and familiar things supernatural and causeless. Shakespeare.

❽ pa′tron. One who countenances, supports or protects. Commonly a wretch who supports with insolence, and is paid with flattery.

pi′ckle. Condition; state. A word of contempt and ridicule.
How cam'st though in this *pickle*? Shakespeare.

plu′mper. Something worn in the mouth to swell out the cheeks.
She dex'trously her *plumpers* draws, That serve to fill her hollow jaws. Swift's *Miscellanies.*

shill-I-shall-I. A corrupt reduplication of *shall I?* The question of a man hesitating. To stand *shill-I-shall-I,* is to continue hesitating and procrastinating.
I am somewhat dainty in making a resolution, because

Enrichment

The First Dictionaries
The earliest preserved dictionary is an Akkadian word list from central Mesopotamia. It dates from approximately 600 B.C. Greek philosophers were developing the first Western-style dictionaries at approximately the same time. Pamphilus of Alexandria is credited with the creation of a lengthy Greek dictionary in the first century; after that, the Greeks seem to have created many dictionaries—and many revisions of their dictionaries.

when I make it, I keep it; I don't stand shill-I-shall-I then; if I say't, I'll do't. Congreve's *Way of the World.*

to sneeze. To emit wind audibly by the nose.

wi'llow. A tree worn by forlorn lovers.

to wipe. To cheat; to defraud.
The next bordering lords commonly encroach one upon another, as one is stronger, or lie still in wait to wipe them out of their lands. Spenser, *On Ireland.*

you'ngster, you'nker. A young person.
In contempt.

youth. The part of life succeeding to childhood and adolescence; the time from fourteen to twenty-eight.

Critical Reading

1. **Respond:** Are Johnson's definitions fair? funny? prejudiced? Explain.
2. **(a) Recall:** Among what class of workers does Johnson place writers of dictionaries? **(b) Infer:** What does this ranking suggest about his experience in compiling his *Dictionary*?
3. **(a) Recall:** What did the English language lack when Johnson undertook his work? **(b) Infer:** What do you think Johnson hoped his *Dictionary* would make available to English speakers and writers?
4. **(a) Recall:** What is Johnson's definition of *modern*?
   (b) Compare and Contrast: Compare and contrast Johnson's definition of this word with our definition of it today. Explain what different values each represents. **(c) Draw Conclusions:** What does your comparison indicate about the nature of language?
5. **(a) Analyze:** Which definitions are most revealing of Johnson's character and situation? **(b) Draw Conclusions:** What do these definitions reveal about Johnson?
6. **(a) Speculate:** Why do you think *electricity* receives such a long definition? **(b) Connect:** In what ways is Johnson similar to the scientists whose work he eagerly discusses in this entry?
7. **Apply:** What does Johnson's use of quotations suggest about the role of authors in shaping meanings?
8. **Take a Position:** Do you find Johnson's definitions more or less useful than those in modern dictionaries? Explain.

For: More about
Samuel Johnson
Visit: www.PHSchool.com
Web Code: ese-9314

from A Dictionary of the English Language ■ 561

❾ *from the* Life of Samuel Johnson

James Boswell

Boswell Meets Johnson
1763

❿ This is to me a memorable year; for in it I had the happiness to obtain the acquaintance of that extraordinary man whose memoirs I am now writing; an acquaintance which I shall ever esteem as one of the most fortunate circumstances in my life. Though then but two-and-twenty, I had for several years read his works with delight and instruction, and had the highest reverence for their author, which had grown up in my fancy into a kind of mysterious veneration, by figuring to myself a state of solemn elevated abstraction, in which I supposed him to live in the immense metropolis of London. . . .

Mr. Thomas Davies[1] the actor, who then kept a bookseller's shop in Russel Street, Covent Garden, told me that Johnson was very much his friend, and came frequently to his house, where he more than once invited me to meet him; but by some unlucky accident or other he was prevented from coming to us.

At last, on Monday the 16th day of May, when I was sitting in Mr. Davies's back parlor, after having drunk tea with him and Mrs. Davies, Johnson unexpectedly came into the shop; and Mr. Davies having perceived him through the glass door in the room in which

---

1. **Thomas Davies** English bookseller and unsuccessful actor (1712–1785).

Enrichment

Biographies

The first biographies were probably elaborate inscriptions on the tombs of ancient rulers of Assyria and Babylonia. The accuracy of these glorious accounts is dubious. Plutarch's classic *Parallel Lives* contained the first biographies that sought objectivity. The insights and intimacy of Boswell's famous biography of Johnson influenced many later writers. Only since the nineteenth century, however, have biographers in general striven to give a complete picture of their subjects, showing both favorable and unfavorable aspects of their character.

we were sitting, advancing towards us—he announced his aweful[2] approach to me, somewhat in the manner of an actor in the part of Horatio, when he addresses Hamlet on the appearance of his father's ghost, "Look, my Lord, it comes,"[3] I found that I had a very perfect idea of Johnson's figure, from the portrait of him painted by Sir Joshua Reynolds[4] soon after he had published his *Dictionary*, in the attitude of sitting in his easy chair in deep meditation, which was the first picture his friend did for him, which Sir Joshua very kindly presented to me, and from which an engraving has been made for this work. Mr. Davies mentioned my name, and respectfully introduced me to him. I was much agitated; and recollecting his prejudice against the Scotch, of which I had heard much, I said to Davies, "Don't tell where I come from." "From Scotland," cried Davies roguishly. "Mr. Johnson," said I, "I do indeed come from Scotland, but I cannot help it." I am willing to flatter myself that I meant this as light pleasantry to soothe and conciliate him, and not as an humiliating <u>abasement</u> at the expense of my country. But however that might be, this speech was somewhat unlucky; for with that quickness of wit for which he was so remarkable, he seized the expression "come from Scotland," which I used in the sense of being of that country; and, as if I had said that I had come away from it, or left, retorted, "That, Sir, I find, is what a very great many of your countrymen cannot help." This stroke stunned me a good deal; and when we had sat down, I felt myself not a little embarrassed, and apprehensive of what might come next. He then addressed himself to Davies: "What do you think of Garrick?[5] He has refused me an order for the play for Miss Williams, because he knows the house will be full, and that an order would be worth three shillings." Eager to take any opening to get into conversation with him, I ventured to say, "O, Sir, I cannot think Mr. Garrick would grudge such a trifle to you." "Sir," said he, with a stern look, "I have known David Garrick longer than you have done: and I know no right you have to talk to me on the subject." Perhaps I deserved this check; for it was rather presumptuous in me, an entire stranger, to express any doubt of the justice of his animadversion upon his old acquaintance and pupil. I now felt myself much mortified, and began to think that the hope which I had long indulged of obtaining his acquaintance was blasted. And, in truth, had not my ardor been uncommonly strong, and my resolution uncommonly persevering, so rough a reception might have deterred me forever from making any further attempts. Fortunately, however, I remained upon the field not wholly discomfited; and was soon rewarded by hearing some of his conversation, of which I preserved the following short

---

2. **aweful** awe-inspiring.
3. **Horatio ". . . it comes"** from Shakespeare's *Hamlet* (Act I, Scene iv).
4. **Sir Joshua Reynolds** celebrated portrait painter at the time (1723–1792).
5. **Garrick** David Garrick (1717–1779), a famous actor who had been educated by Johnson. Garrick was also one of the managing partners of the Drury Lane Theatre in London.

Reading Strategy
Establishing a Purpose
If your purpose were to find out more about eighteenth-century English theater, on what details of the third paragraph would you focus?

Vocabulary Builder
abasement (ə bās′ mənt) *n.* condition of being put down or humbled

Reading Check
Why is 1763 "a memorable year" for Boswell?

from the *Life of Samuel Johnson* ■ 563

⓫ Reading Strategy
Establishing a Purpose

- Have partners read the bracketed passage, taking turns reading several sentences at a time.
- Tell students to focus on what is suggested in this passage about eighteenth-century English theater.
- Then, **ask** the Reading Strategy question: If your purpose were to find out more about eighteenth-century English theater, on what details of the third paragraph would you focus?
Answer: Readers would focus on the details about the actor David Garrick.

⓬ Critical Thinking
Draw Conclusions

- Explain to students that on the basis of what Boswell reveals about Johnson, they should be able to make assessments about his personality.
- Then, **ask** if thus far Boswell's picture of Johnson is a flattering one.
Answer: No, for the most part it is not flattering. Johnson is prejudiced against Scots, and while he is quick-witted, he is also quick to criticize someone who offers an opinion contrary to his own.

⓭ Reading Check
Answer: The year 1763 is a memorable one for Boswell because it is when he meets Johnson.

Differentiated Instruction Solutions for All Learners

Strategy for Special Needs Students
Remind students that a biography is a work about someone's life written by another person. Ask them to identify the author of the *Life of Samuel Johnson*. Have them use the Character wheel transparency on p. 276 of *Graphic Organizer Transparencies* to record what they learn about Johnson's character.

Strategy for English Learners
Have pairs of students work together to identify the speaker in each paragraph in the first section of the *Life*. Explain that although paragraphs are enclosed in quotation marks, the speaker does not necessarily change from paragraph to paragraph. Students may also be reminded that while Boswell does insert himself into the biography, his purpose here is to reveal the workings of Johnson's mind.

- Review with students that a biography is a story of someone's life written by another person.

- Have students indicate who is the biographer and who is the subject of biography in this selection.
  Answer: James Boswell is the biographer; Samuel Johnson's life is the subject of his biography.

- Have students read the bracketed passage, noting any details that Boswell uses in describing Johnson's "extraordinary vigor."

▶ **Monitor Progress: Ask** the Literary Analysis question: Has Boswell sufficiently supported his statement about the "extraordinary vigor" of Johnson's conversation? Why or why not?
Answer: Boswell has supported his statement. Johnson seems very quick-witted and extremely articulate. He shows that he is informed about the manners of his day. He uses a Latin term in conversation; he is witty about both the matter of ducking and the butcher; and he produces a pun on the spot about "outrunning [a] character" and the character catching up.

---

minute,[6] without marking the questions and observations by which it was produced.

"People," he remarked, "may be taken in once, who imagine that an author is greater in private life than other men. Uncommon parts require uncommon opportunities for their exertion."

"In barbarous society, superiority of parts is of real consequence. Great strength or great wisdom is of much value to an individual. But in more polished times there are people to do everything for money; and then there are a number of other superiorities, such as those of birth and fortune, and rank, that dissipate men's attention, and leave no extraordinary share of respect for personal and intellectual superiority. This is wisely ordered by Providence, to preserve some equality among mankind."

"Sir, this book (*The Elements of Criticism*,[7] which he had taken up) is a pretty essay, and deserves to be held in some estimation, though much of it is chimerical."

Speaking of one[8] who with more than ordinary boldness attacked public measures and the royal family, he said, "I think he is safe from the law, but he is an abusive scoundrel; and instead of applying to my Lord Chief Justice to punish him, I would send half a dozen footmen and have him well ducked."[9]

"The notion of liberty amuses the people of England, and helps to keep off the *taedium vitae*.[10] When a butcher tells you that his heart bleeds for his country, he has, in fact, no uneasy feeling."

"Sheridan[11] will not succeed at Bath with his oratory. Ridicule has gone down before him, and, I doubt,[12] Derrick[13] is his enemy."

"Derrick may do very well, as long as he can outrun his character; but the moment his character gets up with him, it is all over."

It is, however, but just to record, that some years afterwards, when I reminded him of this sarcasm, he said, "Well, but Derrick has now got a character that he need not run away from."

I was highly pleased with the extraordinary vigor of his conversation, and regretted that I was drawn away from it by an engagement at another place. I had, for a part of the evening, been left alone with him, and had ventured to make an observation now and then, which he received very civilly; so that I was satisfied that though there was a roughness in his manner, there was no ill nature in his disposition. Davies followed me to the door, and when I complained to him a little of the hard blows which the great man had given me he kindly took

---

6. **minute** note.
7. *The Elements of Criticism* one of the works of Scottish philosophical writer Henry Home (1696–1782).
8. **one** John Wilkes (1727–1797), an English political agitator.
9. **ducked** tied to a chair at the end of a plank and plunged into water.
10. *taedium vitae* (tē′ dē əm vī′ tē) boredom.
11. **Sheridan** Thomas Sheridan (1719–1788), an Irish actor and author. At the time, Sheridan was reading lectures at the Oratory at Bath.
12. **doubt** fear.
13. **Derrick** the Master of Ceremonies of the Oratory at Bath.

Literary Analysis
Biography Has Boswell sufficiently supported his statement about the "extraordinary vigor" of Johnson's conversation? Why or why not?

16

◄ **Critical Viewing**
This engraving shows the ghost of Samuel Johnson haunting Boswell. In what ways does the relationship between the men that it portrays reflect the relationship suggested by Boswell's *Life*? **[Interpret]**

Johnson and Boswell, The Trustees of the British Museum

upon him to console me by saying, "Don't be uneasy. I can see he likes you very well."

Johnson's Character

The character of Samuel Johnson has, I trust, been so developed in the course of this work, that they who have honored it with a perusal, may be considered as well acquainted with him. As, however, it may be expected that I should collect into one view the capital and distinguishing features of this extraordinary man, I shall endeavor to acquit myself of that part of my biographical undertaking, however difficult it may be to do that which many of my readers will do better for themselves.

His figure was large and well formed, and his countenance of the cast of an ancient statue; yet his appearance was rendered strange and somewhat uncouth by convulsive cramps, by the scars of that distemper[14] which it was once imagined the royal touch could cure,[15]

17 **Reading Check**
What quality of Johnson's conversation pleased Boswell?

14. **distemper** scrofula, a type of tuberculosis that causes swelling and scarring of the neck.
15. **royal touch . . . cure** it was at one time believed that the touch of an English monarch had the power to heal. As a child Johnson was taken to Queen Anne to receive her touch in the hope that it would cure him.

from the *Life of Samuel Johnson* ■ 565

565

18 Critical Thinking
Make Judgments

- Have students read the bracketed passage. Ask them to focus on Boswell's physical description of Johnson.

- Then, **ask** if they think this physical description of Johnson is objective. Why or why not?
Answer: It appears to be objective. Johnson wasn't, evidently, very pleasing to look at, and Boswell doesn't hesitate to tell the reader so. In addition, he says that Johnson walked strangely and cut a rather ludicrous figure on his horse when he rode. Because it is clear that Boswell keenly admired Johnson, the reader can infer that these details are here simply because they are part of the overall portrait of the man.

19 Critical Thinking
Analyze

- Have volunteers take turns reading aloud the bracketed passage.

- Then, **ask** students what negative aspects of Johnson's character are contained in this description.
Answer: Johnson's prejudices, his sternness, his tendency to be easily offended, his irritability, his moodiness, and his ability to say nasty things even about his friends

18 and by a slovenly mode of dress. He had the use only of one eye; yet so much does mind govern and even supply the deficiency of organs, that his visual perceptions, as far as they extended, were uncommonly quick and accurate. So morbid was his temperament, that he never knew the natural joy of a free and vigorous use of his limbs: when he walked, it was like the struggling gait of one in fetters; when he rode, he had no command or direction of his horse, but was carried as if in a balloon. That with his constitution and habits of life he should have lived seventy-five years, is a proof that an inherent *vivida vis*[16] is a powerful preservative of the human frame.

Man is, in general, made up of contradictory qualities; and these will ever show themselves in strange succession, where a consistency in appearance at least, if not in reality, has not been attained by long habits of philosophical discipline. In proportion to the native vigor of the mind, the contradictory qualities will be the more prominent, and more difficult to be adjusted; and, therefore, we are not to wonder that Johnson exhibited an eminent example of this remark which I have made upon human nature. At different times, he seemed a different man, in some respects; not, however, in any great or essential article, upon which he had fully employed his mind, and settled certain principles of duty, but only in his manners and in the display of argument and fancy in his talk. He was prone to superstition, but not to <u>credulity</u>. Though his imagination might incline him to a belief of the marvelous and the mysterious, his vigorous reason examined the evidence with jealousy.[17] He was a sincere and zealous Christian, of high Church of England and monarchical principles, which he would not tamely suffer to be questioned; and had, perhaps, at an early period, narrowed his mind somewhat too much, both as to religion and politics. His being impressed with the danger of extreme latitude in either, though he was of a very independent spirit, occasioned his appearing somewhat unfavorable to the prevalence of that noble freedom of sentiment which is the best possession of man. Nor can it be denied, that he had many prejudices; which, however, frequently suggested many of his pointed sayings that rather show a playfulness of fancy than any settled <u>malignity</u>. He was steady and inflexible in maintaining the obligations of religion and morality; both from a regard for the order of society, and from a veneration for the Great Source of **19** all order; correct, nay, stern in his taste; hard to please, and easily offended; impetuous and irritable in his temper, but of a most humane and benevolent heart, which showed itself not only in a most liberal charity, as far as his circumstances would allow, but in a thousand instances of active benevolence. He was afflicted with a bodily disease, which made him often restless and fretful; and with a constitutional melancholy, the clouds of which darkened the brightness of his fancy, and gave a gloomy cast to his whole course of thinking: we, therefore,

---

16. *vivida vis* lively force.
17. *jealousy* suspicion.

Vocabulary Builder
credulity (krə dōō′ lə tē) *n.* tendency to believe too readily

Vocabulary Builder
malignity (mə lig′ nə tē) *n.* strong desire to harm others

Enrichment

Boswell's Journals
Though Boswell is famous for his monumental *Life of Samuel Johnson,* he wrote an even larger opus on another life—his own. For more than thirty-three years, until shortly before his death, Boswell kept detailed journals, more than eight thousand pages in all. As in his biography of Johnson, Boswell presents a fully rounded, warts-and-all portrait of himself and his times. His mania for recording the minutiae of his life has given posterity a personal, even intimate look at an eighteenth-century world; and his journals have made an essential contribution to literature. Most critics agree that his biography of Johnson becomes vividly exceptional only after Boswell meets Johnson and can begin to mine the rich vein of anecdotal lore reposing in his own journals.

ought not to wonder at his sallies of impatience and passion at any time; especially when provoked by obtrusive ignorance, or presuming petulance; and allowance must be made for his uttering hasty and satirical sallies even against his best friends. And, surely, when it is considered, that, "amidst sickness and sorrow," he exerted his faculties in so many works for the benefit of mankind, and particularly that he achieved the great and admirable Dictionary of our language, we must be astonished at his resolution. The solemn text, "of him to whom much is given, much will be required," seems to have been ever present to his mind, in a rigorous sense, and to have made him dissatisfied with his labors and acts of goodness, however comparatively great; so that the unavoidable consciousness of his superiority was, in that respect, a cause of disquiet. He suffered so much from this, and from the gloom which perpetually haunted him and made solitude frightful, that it may be said of him, "If in this life only he had hope, he was of all men most miserable."[18] He loved praise, when it was brought to him; but was too proud to seek for it. He was somewhat susceptible of flattery. As he was general and unconfined in his studies, he cannot be considered as master of any one particular science; but he had accumulated a vast and various collection of learning and knowledge, which was so arranged in his mind, as to be ever in readiness to be brought forth. But his superiority over other learned men consisted chiefly in what may be called the art of thinking, the art of using his mind; a certain continual power of seizing the useful substance of all that he knew and exhibiting it in a clear and forcible manner; so that knowledge, which we often see to be no better than lumber[19] in men of dull understanding, was, in him, true, evident, and actual wisdom. His moral precepts are practical; for they are drawn from an intimate acquaintance with human nature. His maxims carry conviction; for they are founded on the basis of common sense, and a very attentive and minute survey of real life. His mind was so full of imagery, that he might have been perpetually a poet; yet it is remarkable, that, however rich his prose is in this respect, his poetical pieces, in general, have not much of that splendor, but are rather distinguished by strong sentiment and acute observation, conveyed in harmonious and energetic verse, particularly in heroic couplets. Though usually grave, and even aweful, in his deportment, he possessed uncommon and peculiar powers of wit and humor; he frequently indulged himself in colloquial pleasantry; and the heartiest merriment was often enjoyed in his company; with this great advantage, that as it was entirely free from any poisonous tincture of vice or impiety, it was salutary to those who shared in it. He had accustomed himself to such accuracy in his common conversation, that he at all times expressed his thoughts with great force, and an elegant choice of language, the effect of which was aided by his having a loud voice, and a slow deliberate

---

18. **"If . . . miserable"** from I Corinthians 15:19.
19. **lumber** rubbish.

Literary Analysis

Biography In what part of his biography—the beginning, middle, or end—would it be appropriate for Boswell to present this analysis of Johnson's character? Why?

Reading Check

What are some of Johnson's "contradictory qualities"?

from the *Life of Samuel Johnson* ■ 567

TIME AND RESOURCE MANAGER

 Meeting Your Standards

Students will

1. **analyze and respond to literary elements.**
   - Literary Analysis: Pre-Romantic Poetry

2. **read, comprehend, analyze, and critique a poem.**
   - Reading Strategy: Paraphrasing
   - Reading Check questions
   - Apply the Skills questions
   - Assessment Practice (ATE)

3. **develop vocabulary.**
   - Vocabulary Lesson: Latin Prefix: *circum-*

4. **understand and apply written and oral language conventions.**
   - Spelling Strategy
   - Grammar and Style Lesson: Pronoun-Antecedent Agreement

5. **develop writing proficiency.**
   - Writing Lesson: Reflective Essay

6. **develop appropriate research strategies.**
   - Extend Your Learning: Daydream Report

7. **understand and apply listening and speaking strategies.**
   - Extend Your Learning: Group Reading

Block Scheduling: Use one 90-minute class period to preteach the skills and have students read the selection. Use a second 90-minute class period to assess students' mastery of skills, extend their learning, and monitor their progress.

Homework Suggestions

Following are possibilities for homework assignments.

- Support pages from *Unit 3 Resources:*
    Literary Analysis
    Reading Strategy
    Vocabulary Builder
    Grammar and Style

- An Extend Your Learning project and the Writing Lesson for this selection group may be completed over several days.

Step-by-Step Teaching Guide	Pacing Guide
PRETEACH	
• Administer Vocabulary and Reading Warm-ups as necessary.	5 min.
• Engage students' interest with the motivation activity.	5 min.
• Read and discuss author and background features. **FT**	10 min.
• Introduce the Literary Analysis Skill: Pre-Romantic Poetry **FT**	5 min.
• Introduce the Reading Strategy: Paraphrasing. **FT**	10 min.
• Prepare students to read by teaching the selection vocabulary. **FT**	
TEACH	
• Informally monitor comprehension while students read independently or in groups. **FT**	30 min.
• Monitor students' comprehension with the Reading Check notes.	as students read
• Reinforce vocabulary with Vocabulary Builder notes.	as students read
• Develop students' understanding of pre-Romantic poetry with the Literary Analysis annotations. **FT**	5 min.
• Develop students' ability to paraphrase with the Reading Strategy annotations. **FT**	5 min.
ASSESS/EXTEND	
• Assess students' comprehension and mastery of the Literary Analysis and Reading Strategy by having them answer the Apply the Skills questions. **FT**	15 min.
• Have students complete the Vocabulary Lesson and the Grammar and Style Lesson. **FT**	15 min.
• Apply students' knowledge of elaborating to make writing personal by using the Writing Lesson. **FT**	45 min. or homework
• Apply students' understanding by using one or more of the Extend Your Learning activities.	20–90 min. or homework
• Administer Selection Test A or Selection Test B. **FT**	15 min.

Resources

Choosing Resources for Differentiated Instruction

[**L1**] Special Needs Students

[**L2**] Below-Level Students

[**L3**] All Students

[**L4**] Advanced Students

[**EL**] English Learners

For Vocabulary and Reading Warm-ups and for Selection Tests, **A** signifies "less challenging" and **B** "more challenging." For Graphic Organizer transparencies, **A** signifies "not filled in" and **B** "filled in."

FT Fast Track Instruction: To move the lesson more quickly, use the strategies and activities identified with **FT**.

Scaffolding for Less Proficient and Advanced Students

The leveled Critical Thinking questions after selections progress in the levels of thinking required to answer them. To address the needs of your different students, you may use the (a) level questions for your less proficient students and the (b) level questions with your on-level and advanced students. The occasional (c) level questions are appropriate for your advanced students.

PRENTICE HALL

TeacherEXPRESS™ Use this complete
Plan · Teach · Assess suite of powerful
teaching tools to make lesson planning and testing quicker and easier.

PRENTICE HALL

StudentEXPRESS™ Use the interac-
Learn · Study · Succeed tive textbook
(online and on CD-ROM) to make selections and activities come alive with audio and video support and interactive questions.

Go **Online** **For:** Information about Lexiles
Professional **Visit:** www.PHSchool.com
Development **Web Code:** eue-1111

Motivation

Ask students: What are the best times and places for reflection? Poll students to determine where and at what time of day they are most likely to reflect on topics such as these:

- the meaning of life
- destiny or fate in life
- relationships
- death

Tell students that the elegy by Thomas Gray is a reflection about such subjects. Have them look for clues that indicate the time and place of the reflection and discuss the appropriateness to its subject.

❶ Background
More About the Authors
Thomas Gray

Thomas Gray's thorough education at Eton College and Cambridge University clearly shows in his erudite poetry, which was highly respected in his day. In 1754, Gray finished a Pindaric ode entitled *The Progress of Poesy.* This was followed by a second Pindaric ode, *The Bard.* Both of these ambitious works marked a shift away from the polished precision of Neoclassical verse toward the sublime and the obscure. Gray's "Elegy Written in a Country Churchyard" remained extremely popular and the work for which he was best known. In 1757, he was offered the title of poet laureate of England, which he declined.

Anne Finch, Countess of Winchilsea

In 1715, Anne Finch became severely ill. She had battled depression for years and was now in failing health. Increasingly, her poetry reflected her religious beliefs and concerns. One of her last poems, "A Contemplation," speaks movingly about her life and beliefs. She died in London on August 5, 1720, and, in accordance with her wishes, was taken to Eastwell to be buried.

❶ Elegy Written in a Country Churchyard •
A Nocturnal Reverie

Thomas Gray
(1716–1771)

The uncertainty of life was something that Thomas Gray understood all too well. The only one of twelve Gray children to survive infancy, he suffered from convulsions as a child. On at least one occasion, his mother was forced to open a vein to relieve the pressure on his brain.

Lavishing affection on her sickly son, Gray's mother saved money from the shop she kept in London and sent Gray to Eton and Cambridge.

A Quiet Life After making the Grand Tour of Europe with his friend the author Horace Walpole, Gray lived with his mother and aunts in the sleepy village of Stoke Poges. There, in the summer of 1742, he wrote his first important poems. The church and graveyard at Stoke Poges probably inspired his best-known poem, "Elegy Written in a Country Churchyard."

A Near Mishap This beloved poem nearly went astray. Gray sent a copy to Walpole, and it fell into the hands of a dishonest editor. It was retrieved only after a struggle. In the end, the poem came to belong to its readers: It contains some of the best-remembered lines in English poetry.

A Lonely Romantic After age thirty, Gray returned to Cambridge, where he studied classical literature and Celtic and Norse mythology. He died after an attack of gout. His literary output was small—he wrote slowly, striving for perfection—but his poems are counted among the finest in the English language. In them, he expresses new, Romantic yearnings in the formal style of his times. The poet Matthew Arnold suggested that if Gray had lived in another era, his accomplishments might have been even greater.

Anne Finch, Countess of Winchilsea
(1661–1720)

Anne Kingsmill Finch, Countess of Winchilsea, lived in an era that rejected women intellectuals. Even her friend Alexander Pope poked fun at her, satirizing her as the character Phoebe Clinket in the play *Three Hours After Marriage.* Despite this mockery, Finch pursued her interest in poetry, publishing a volume of verse in 1713, during an era when publication by women was rare.

An Uncertain Childhood Anne Kingsmill's father died when she was only five months old, and three years later her mother died as well. For eight years, she and her sister, Bridget, lived with their grandmother, while their brother, William, lived with an uncle. The children were reunited under their uncle's care in 1672. By the standards of the day, the girls' education was quite progressive. Anne studied classic Greek and Roman literature, the Bible, French, Italian, history, poetry, and drama.

A Poet and Countess In 1682, Anne Kingsmill left home to become a maid of honor to the wife of the duke of York, later James II. In the duke's household, she met her husband, Heneage Finch.

When James II was driven from power in 1688, the Finches endured a period of poverty until Heneage Finch inherited the title Earl of Winchilsea and an estate at Eastwell in Kent. Many of Anne Finch's poems celebrate the rural pleasures of Eastwell.

Though she was not the most famous of poets, her work had an impact on later writers. In 1801, Romantic poet William Wordsworth praised her in the Preface to the *Lyrical Ballads.*

Preview

Connecting to the Literature

When the bustle of the day has died down, your thoughts may turn inward. Gray and Finch share feelings gathered at the end of the day from contemplative walks.

Literary Analysis

Pre-Romantic Poetry

Eighteenth-century **Pre-Romantic poetry** shares characteristics of two different styles. Like earlier, Neoclassical poetry, Pre-Romantic poetry is characterized by these features:

- The polished expression of ideas
- The use of balanced phrases and sophisticated vocabulary

At the same time, Pre-Romantic poetry anticipates the Romantics. It introduces these new elements:

- A new focus on nature and the life of common folk
- The expression of heightened, sometimes nameless feelings

Look for these characteristics as you read the following poems.

Comparing Literary Works

Like the Romantics who come after them, Gray and Finch express heightened feelings in their poetry. In these poems, each discovers a feeling about life as a whole. Gray's stroll through a country churchyard lets him feel the tragedy of life and discover its true value. Finch's stroll allows her to feel the mind's deep connection with nature. As you read, compare the feelings and lessons the poets discover.

Reading Strategy

Paraphrasing

To aid your understanding, **paraphrase** passages in the poems that follow by identifying key ideas and expressing them in your own words. Use a chart like the one shown.

Vocabulary Builder

penury (pen′ yoo̅ rē) *n.* poverty (p. 577)

circumscribed (sur′ kəm skrībd′) *v.* limited; confined (p. 577)

ingenuous (in jen′ yoo̅ əs) *adj.* naive; simple (p. 577)

ignoble (ig nō′ bəl) *adj.* not noble; common (p. 577)

nocturnal (näk tur′ nəl) *adj.* occurring at night (p. 581)

temperate (tem′ pər it) *adj.* mild (p. 581)

venerable (ven′ ər ə bəl) *adj.* commanding respect because of age, character, or social rank (p. 581)

forage (fôr′ ij) *n.* food grazed for by animals (p. 581)

Original
"Now fades the glimmering landscape on the sight, . . ."

↓

Paraphrase
Nightfall is making it difficult to see the landscape.

Elegy Written in a Country Churchyard / A Nocturnal Reverie ■ 573

❷ Literary Analysis
Pre-Romantic Poetry

- Tell students that in this lesson they will focus on Pre-Romantic poetry—eighteenth-century writing that shares characteristics with Neoclassical poetry of an earlier era and Romantic poetry of a later era.

- Call students' attention to characteristics similar to Neoclassical poetry, such as a polished expression of ideas, balanced phrases, and sophisticated vocabulary.

- Then, call students' attention to characteristics of Romantic poetry, such as an emphasis on nature and common people and heightened emotion.

❸ Reading Strategy
Paraphrasing

- Explain to students that when they paraphrase an idea, they express it in their own words in order to better understand it.

- Use the graphic organizer to model paraphrasing with students.

- Give students a copy of **Reading Strategy Graphic Organizer A**, p. 111 in *Graphic Organizer Transparencies*, to help students practice the skill of paraphrasing.

Vocabulary Builder

- Pronounce each vocabulary word for students, and read the definitions as a class. Have students identify any words with which they are already familiar.

Differentiated Instruction — Solutions for All Learners

Support for Special Needs Students
Have students complete the **Preview** and **Build Skills** pages for these selections in the *Reader's Notebook: Adapted Version*. These pages provide a selection summary, an abbreviated presentation of the reading and literary skills, and the graphic organizer on the **Build Skills** page in the student book.

Support for Less Proficient Readers
Have students complete the **Preview** and **Build Skills** pages for these selections in the *Reader's Notebook*. These pages provide a selection summary, an abbreviated presentation of the reading and literary skills, and the graphic organizer on the **Build Skills** page in the student book.

Support for English Learners
Have students complete the **Preview** and **Build Skills** pages for these selections in the *Reader's Notebook: English Learner's Version*. These pages provide a selection summary, an abbreviated presentation of the skills, additional contextual vocabulary, and the graphic organizer on the **Build Skills** page in the student book.

Learning Modalities
Musical/Rhythmic Learners Both poems can be described as musical: their rhythm is predictable and even; they maintain a steady beat. Ask students to decide which type of music would best capture the mood and message of both of these poems.

❶ About the Selection

This famous poem uses the melancholy setting of a graveyard at twilight to meditate on the lives of the ordinary people interred there. In soulful song, Gray laments not one particular death, but the obscurity into which death may plunge us all.

❷ Humanities

British Isles, Church with Tombstones
by Leonore Weber

This photograph evokes a strong sense of the passage of time. As the roiling clouds suggest the ever-changing yet cyclical patterns in weather, so the graveyard suggests the eternal cycles of life and death. Use these questions for discussion:

1. How do the clouds in the photograph help create a mood and express a theme similar to the mood and theme expressed by the poem?
   Possible responses: Students may say that the clouds suggest a storm to come, just as the poet describes death, which will come to everyone.

2. What deductions might you make about this churchyard and its occupants?
   Possible responses: The church is old and crumbling; moss has begun to grow on it. The surrounding community and those buried in the churchyard are probably poor and obscure.

❸ Critical Viewing

Answer: Students may say that the photograph reflects the loneliness and neglect suggested by Gray's poem.

❸ ▲ **Critical Viewing** The churchyard in this photograph looks untended and forgotten. How does the photograph reflect the meaning of Gray's poem? **[Deduce]**

574 ■ *A Turbulent Time (1625–1798)*

Differentiated
Instruction   Solutions for All Learners

Accessibility at a Glance

	Elegy in a Churchyard	Nocturnal Reverie
Context	Pre-Romantic	Pre-Romantic
Language	Difficult words	Long sentences
Concept Level	Challenging (death, immortality)	Challenging (nature, emotion)
Literary Merit	Classic	Classic
Lexile	NP	NP
Overall Rating	More Challenging	More Challenging

Elegy Written in a Country Churchyard

Thomas Gray

Background
In the eighteenth century, many writers championed reason, clarity, and logic. These values led to the articulate, eloquent couplets of Alexander Pope. They also led to the major scientific discoveries of Sir Isaac Newton, of whom Pope wrote: "God said, Let Newton be! And there was light!" These values might be thought of as belonging to daylight. In contrast, the poems in this grouping are set at twilight or at night. They stress emotion—the not-always-reasonable reaction to circumstances—and mystery—those longings and intuitions of human experience that are not clearly communicable or analyzable. By stressing these "nighttime" qualities, these poets anticipate the artistic movement called Romanticism.

④

> The curfew tolls the knell of parting day,
>   The lowing herd winds slowly o'er the lea,[1]
> The plowman homeward plods his weary way,
>   And leaves the world to darkness and to me.
>
> 5 Now fades the glimmering landscape on the sight,
>   And all the air a solemn stillness holds,
> Save where the beetle wheels his droning flight,
>   And drowsy tinklings lull the distant folds;
>
> Save that from yonder ivy-mantled tower,
> 10   The moping owl does to the moon complain
> Of such as, wandering near her secret bower,
>   Molest her ancient solitary reign.
>
> Beneath those rugged elms, that yew tree's shade,
>   Where heaves the turf in many a moldering heap,
> 15 Each in his narrow cell forever laid,
>   The rude[2] forefathers of the hamlet sleep.

1. **lea** meadow.
2. **rude** uneducated.

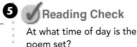

⑤ **Reading Check**
At what time of day is the poem set?

- Have students write paraphrases of the first stanza. When they are finished, ask them to check their paraphrases to be sure they have included time of day and the setting.
Sample response: The speaker hears the curfew bell that calls workers home at sunset; he waits alone in the gathering darkness.

- Encourage students to paraphrase any subsequent stanzas that they have difficulty understanding. They may find the short-stanza format of the poem helpful in paraphrasing. Tell students that Gray himself wanted the poem published without stanza breaks, noting that there are points (in lines 61–72, for example), where a thought continues through a stanza break.

- Point out that the speaker's focus on the graveyard and its inhabitants begins at line 13. You might explain that "heaves" refers to the mounds of earth and that *moldering* means "decaying."

⑤ Reading Check

Answer: The poem is set at dusk.

Differentiated Instruction   Solutions for All Learners

Support for Special Needs Students	Support for Less Proficient Readers	Enrichment for Gifted/Talented Students
Have students read a section from "Elegy Written in a Country Churchyard" with teacher guidance. Then, ask students to visualize each line as they reread this section to themselves. To stimulate student interest, consider playing the poem on **Listening to Literature Audio CDs**.	Students may have difficulty reading "Elegy Written in a Country Churchyard" because it describes an unfamiliar setting and uses unfamiliar vocabulary and poetic syntax. Have students read from the poem silently as they listen to **Listening to Literature Audio CDs**.	Have students work in pairs to write sample tombstone epitaphs for deceased members of the community buried in the cemetery described by Gray in "Elegy Written in a Country Churchyard." Have students reread what Gray says about the people buried in the graveyard and their interests, abilities, goals, and lives.

575

- Ask students to identify the main idea of lines 17–20.

- Have students answer the Reading Strategy question: **Restate** the main ideas in lines 17–20 in your own words.

  Answer: Morning breezes, chirping swallows, rooster's crowing, and hunter's horn will not awaken the dead.

7 Literary Analysis
Pre-Romantic Poetry

- Review with students the characteristics of Pre-Romantic poetry, including the polished expression of ideas, balanced phrases, and sophisticated vocabulary.

- Then, **ask** students the Literary Analysis question: What images and phrasings in lines 33–36 show formal polish?

  Answer: Students may cite the parallel structure of lines 33–34; the alliteration of consonants in "pomp of power," and vowels in "Awaits alike"; the elaborate, periodic sentence structure that withholds meaning until line 35; and the use of abstract nouns such as "power," "beauty," "wealth," and "glory."

6

The breezy call of incense-breathing morn,
    The swallow twittering from the straw-built shed,
The cock's shrill clarion, or the echoing horn,[3]
20   No more shall rouse them from their lowly bed.

For them no more the blazing hearth shall burn,
    Or busy housewife ply her evening care;
No children run to lisp their sire's return,
    Or climb his knees the envied kiss to share.

25 Oft did the harvest to their sickle yield,
    Their furrow oft the stubborn glebe[4] has broke;
How jocund[5] did they drive their team afield!
    How bowed the woods beneath their sturdy stroke!

Let not Ambition mock their useful toil,
30   Their homely joys, and destiny obscure;
Nor Grandeur hear with a disdainful smile
    The short and simple annals of the poor.

7

The boast of heraldry,[6] the pomp of power,
    And all that beauty, all that wealth e'er gave,
35 Awaits alike the inevitable hour.
    The paths of glory lead but to the grave.

Nor you, ye proud, impute to these the fault,
    If memory o'er their tomb no trophies[7] raise,
Where through the long-drawn aisle and fretted vault[8]
40   The pealing anthem swells the note of praise.

Can storied urn,[9] or animated[10] bust,
    Back to its mansion call the fleeting breath?
Can honor's voice provoke[11] the silent dust,
    Or Flattery soothe the dull cold ear of Death?

45 Perhaps in this neglected spot is laid
    Some heart once pregnant with celestial fire;
Hands, that the rod of empire might have swayed,
    Or waked to ecstasy the living lyre.

---

3. **clarion . . . horn** A clarion is a trumpet. The horn is a hunter's horn.
4. **glebe** soil.
5. **jocund** cheerful.
6. **heraldry** noble descent.
7. **trophies** symbolic figures or pictures depicting the achievements of the dead man.
8. **fretted vault** church ceiling decorated with intersecting lines.
9. **storied urn** funeral urn with an epitaph inscribed on it.
10. **animated** lifelike.
11. **provoke** call forth.

Reading Strategy
Paraphrasing Restate the main ideas in lines 17–20 in your own words.

Literary Analysis
Pre-Romantic Poetry
What images and phrasings in lines 33–36 show formal polish?

Enrichment

Gravestones

Students might be interested to know that gravestones are among the earliest examples of sculpture in the United States, dating back to colonial times. New England gravestones are decorated with elaborate symbolic figures and objects. For example, a skeleton represents death and is often shown snuffing out the candle of life; grapes represent eternal life. Epitaphs written on gravestones are often equally memorable, and even humorous, such as this one:

"Here lies as silent as clay Miss Arabella Young/ Who on the 21st of May began to hold her tongue."

But Knowledge to their eyes her ample page
50   Rich with the spoils of time did ne'er unroll;
Chill <u>Penury</u> repressed their noble rage,
    And froze the genial current of the soul.

Full many a gem of purest ray serene
    The dark unfathomed caves of ocean bear:
55 Full many a flower is born to blush unseen,
    And waste its sweetness on the desert air.

Some village Hampden,[12] that, with dauntless breast,
    The little tyrant of his fields withstood,
Some mute inglorious Milton[13] here may rest,
60   Some Cromwell[14] guiltless of his country's blood.

The applause of listening senates to command,
    The threats of pain and ruin to despise,
To scatter plenty o'er a smiling land,
    And read their history in a nation's eyes,

65 Their lot forbade: nor <u>circumscribed</u> alone
    Their growing virtues, but their crimes confined
Forbade to wade through slaughter to a throne,
    And shut the gates of mercy on mankind,

The struggling pangs of conscious truth to hide,
70   To quench the blushes of <u>ingenuous</u> shame,
Or heap the shrine of Luxury and Pride
    With incense kindled at the Muse's flame.

Far from the madding[15] crowd's <u>ignoble</u> strife,
    Their sober wishes never learned to stray;
75 Along the cool sequestered vale of life
    They kept the noiseless tenor[16] of their way.

Yet even these bones from insult to protect
    Some frail memorial still erected nigh,
With uncouth rhymes and shapeless sculpture decked,[17]
80   Implores the passing tribute of a sigh.

---

12. Hampden John Hampden (1594–1643), an English statesman who defied King Charles I, resisting the king's efforts to circumvent Parliament.

13. Milton English poet, John Milton (1608–1674).

14. Cromwell Oliver Cromwell (1599–1658), English revolutionary leader who defeated King Charles I and ruled England as Lord Protector of the Commonwealth from 1653 to 1658.

15. madding frenzied.

16. tenor general tendency or course.

17. Some . . . decked contrasts with "the storied urn[s] or animated bust[s]" (line 41) inside the church.

Vocabulary Builder
penury (pen′ yōō rē) *n.* poverty

Literary Analysis
Pre-Romantic Poetry
How do the images in lines 53–56 give the reader a powerful sense of what is unknown or lost?

Vocabulary Builder
circumscribed (sur′ kəm skrībd) *v.* limited; confined

ingenuous (in jen′ yōō əs) *adj.* naive; simple

ignoble (ig nō′ bəl) *adj.* not noble; common

Reading Check
About whom is the speaker speculating?

---

❽ Literary Analysis
Pre-Romantic Poetry

- Review with students the characteristics of Pre-Romantic poetry: a polished expression of ideas, balanced phrases, sophisticated vocabulary, attention to nature and common people, heightened voices, and nameless feelings given new expression.

- Have students answer the Literary Analysis question: How do the images in lines 53–56 give the reader a powerful sense of what is unknown or lost?
Answer: Students should note the emotional poignancy of these lines. On a factual level, beautiful gems and sweet flowers exist unseen in underwater caves and deserts; the emotional poignancy of the lines arises from the thought of the beauty of human lives wasting unappreciated by anyone.

❾ Vocabulary Builder
Latin Prefix: -circum-

- Call students' attention to the word *circumscribed* and its definition. Show students that the word is derived from the Latin prefix *circum-*, which means "around."

- Have students suggest other words and phrases that contain this prefix, and list them on the chalkboard.
Possible responses: Students may cite *circumspect, circumference, circumstance,* and *circumnavigate.*

- Have students look up any unfamiliar words on the list in a dictionary.

❿ Reading Check
Answer: The speaker is speculating about the people buried in the churchyard cemetery.

Differentiated Instruction   Solutions for All Learners

Support for Special Needs Students
Some students may have difficulty reading "Elegy Written in a Country Churchyard" critically because of its complex vocabulary and poetic use of language. You may want to direct students to **Fine Art Transparency 14, Volume 1,** or illustrations in the text to guide them in their consideration of the key ideas that Gray's poem expresses.

Strategy for Less Proficient Readers
Have students work in pairs to draw the images of the graveyard that Gray evokes in the poem. Students should use their imagination and draw a picture of the melancholy but tranquil environment that Gray describes.

Vocabulary for English Learners
As students read "Elegy Written in a Country Churchyard," have them practice saying aloud any portions of the text or words whose definitions they don't know. Encourage students to use the vocabulary notes and footnotes to better understand any details from the poem.

577

⓫ Reading Strategy

Paraphrasing

- Remind students that paraphrasing a passage can aid their understanding of it.
- After students read lines 85–88, ask them to identify a main idea in the passage.
- Have students answer the Reading Strategy question: **Express** the key idea of lines 85–88 in your own words.
  Possible response: No one passes away without regretting leaving the world behind.

⓬ Literary Analysis

Pre-Romantic Poetry

- Have students read lines 89–92, and then **ask** them what characteristics of Pre-Romantic poetry this passage expresses.
  Possible response: These lines express an attention to nature, a heightened voice, and nameless feelings given new expression.
- Then, **ask** students the Literary Analysis question: What intense, perhaps irrational feelings are expressed in lines 89–92?
  Answer: Humans need to be cared about and remembered, a yearning that survives the tomb and burns "even in our ashes."

Their name, their years, spelt by the unlettered Muse,[18]
　　The place of fame and elegy supply:
And many a holy text around she strews,
　　That teach the rustic moralist to die.

⓫
85　For who, to dumb Forgetfulness a prey,
　　This pleasing anxious being e'er resigned,
Left the warm precincts of the cheerful day,
　　Nor cast one longing lingering look behind?

⓬
90　On some fond breast the parting soul relies,
　　Some pious drops[19] the closing eye requires;
Even from the tomb the voice of Nature cries,
　　Even in our ashes live their wonted fires.

For thee,[20] who, mindful of the unhonored dead,
　　Dost in these lines their artless tale relate;
95　If chance, by lonely contemplation led,
　　Some kindred spirit shall enquire thy fate,

Haply[21] some hoary-headed swain[22] may say,
　　"Oft have we seen him at the peep of dawn
Brushing with hasty steps the dews away,
100　　To meet the sun upon the upland lawn.

"There at the foot of yonder nodding beech,
　　That wreathes its old fantastic roots so high,
His listless length at noontide would he stretch,
　　And pore upon the brook that babbles by.

105　"Hard by yon wood, now smiling as in scorn,
　　Muttering his wayward fancies he would rove;
Now drooping, woeful wan, like one forlorn,
　　Or crazed with care, or crossed in hopeless love.

"One morn I missed him on the customed hill,
110　　Along the heath, and near his favorite tree;
Another came; nor yet beside the rill,[23]
　　Nor up the lawn, nor at the wood was he;

18. **the unlettered Muse** In Greek mythology, the Muses were goddesses who inspired artists and writers. *Unlettered* means "uneducated."
19. **drops** tears.
20. **thee** Gray himself.
21. **haply** perhaps.
22. **hoary-headed swain** white-haired country laborer.
23. **rill** brook.

Reading Strategy

Paraphrasing Express the key idea of lines 85–88 in your own words.

Literary Analysis

Pre-Romantic Poetry What intense, perhaps irrational feelings are expressed in lines 89–92?

Enrichment

"Churchyard" Allusions

Gray's "Elegy Written in a Country Churchyard" has carved a significant niche in English literature; lines and phrases from the poem continue to resonate through literature and media to the present day. Abraham Lincoln, when asked to provide material for a campaign biography, tersely summarized his own impoverished childhood by quoting Gray: "the short and simple annals of the poor." English novelist Thomas Hardy used "Far from the madding crowd" as the title of one of his best-known novels, set in an isolated landscape of rural England. John Schlesinger later directed a film version of *Far From the Madding Crowd* (1967). Stanley Kubrick underlined the mindless futility of World War I combat in his breakthrough film by adopting from Gray the title *Paths of Glory* (1957).

"The next, with dirges due in sad array
        Slow through the churchway path we saw him borne.
115 Approach and read (for thou canst read) the lay
        Graved on the stone beneath yon aged thorn."[24]

The Epitaph

Here rests his head upon the lap of Earth
        A youth, to Fortune and to Fame unknown.
Fair Science[25] frowned not on his humble birth,
120   And melancholy marked him for her own.

Large was his bounty, and his soul sincere,
        Heaven did a recompense as largely send:
He gave to misery (all he had) a tear,
        He gained from Heaven ('twas all he wished) a friend.

125 No farther seek his merits to disclose,
        Or draw his frailties from their dread abode
(There they alike in trembling hope repose),
        The bosom of his Father and his God.

---

24. **thorn** hawthorn tree.
25. **Science** learning.

Critical Reading

1. **Respond:** Which lines do you find memorable? Why?

2. **(a) Recall:** Who are the forefathers to whom the speaker refers in line 16? **(b) Interpret:** In line 35, what is the "inevitable hour" that the rich and ambitious share with their forefathers?

3. **(a) Recall:** According to lines 45–48, what types of people might lie among the forefathers? **(b) Infer:** Why did the forefathers not fulfill their potential? **(c) Interpret:** In what way do the images of the gem and the flower in lines 53–56 express the idea of unfulfilled potential?

4. **(a) Summarize:** What mark have the forefathers left on history? **(b) Connect:** According to lines 77–84, how is their memory preserved? **(c) Interpret:** What do lines 85–92 suggest about the need to be remembered after death?

5. **(a) Summarize:** By what standards is the life of the speaker measured in "The Epitaph"? **(b) Draw Conclusions:** What insight into life does the speaker reach?

6. **Evaluate:** Do you find the feelings in the poem artificial or moving? Explain.

Go Online
Author Link

For: More about Thomas Gray
Visit: www.PHSchool.com
Web Code: ese-9316

Elegy Written in a Country Churchyard ■ 579

Differentiated Instruction — Solutions for All Learners

Support for Special Needs Students
Have students read the final stanzas of the poem with teacher guidance. Review with them the central characteristics of Pre-Romantic poetry using **Literary Analysis Graphic Organizer B** on p. 114 in *Graphic Organizer Transparencies.*

Strategy for Less Proficient Readers
Have students read the final stanzas of the poem in small groups. For students who have difficulty assessing aspects of "Elegy Written in a Country Churchyard" that qualify it as a Pre-Romantic poem, review with them the central characteristics of Pre-Romantic poetry.

Strategy for Advanced Readers
Have students write essays in which they assess whether Thomas Gray's "Elegy Written in a Country Churchyard" is more Neoclassical or more Romantic in its imagery and poetics.

⓭ # A Nocturnal Reverie

⓮

Anne Finch, Countess of Winchilsea

⓯ ▲ **Critical Viewing** What visual elements in this picture help create a mood like that of the poem? **[Analyze]**

580 ■ *A Turbulent Time (1625–1798)*

In such a night, when every louder wind
Is to its distant cavern safe confined;
And only gentle Zephyr[1] fans his wings,
And lonely Philomel,[2] still waking, sings;
5 Or from some tree, famed for the owl's delight,
She, hollowing clear, directs the wanderer right:
In such a night, when passing clouds give place,
Or thinly veil the heavens' mysterious face;
When in some river, overhung with green,
10 The waving moon and trembling leaves are seen;
When freshened grass now bears itself upright,
And makes cool banks to pleasing rest invite,
Whence springs the woodbind, and the bramble-rose,
And where the sleepy cowslip sheltered grows;
15 Whilst now a paler hue the foxglove takes,
Yet checkers still with red the dusky brakes:[3]
When scattered glow-worms, but in twilight fine,
Show trivial beauties watch their hour to shine;
Whilst Salisbury[4] stands the test of every light,
20 In perfect charms, and perfect virtue bright:
When odors, which declined repelling day,
Through temperate air uninterrupted stray;
When darkened groves their softest shadows wear,
And falling waters we distinctly hear;
25 When through the gloom more venerable shows
Some ancient fabric,[5] awful in repose,
While sunburnt hills their swarthy looks conceal,
And swelling haycocks thicken up the vale:
When the loosed horse now, as his pasture leads,
30 Comes slowly grazing through the adjoining meads,[6]
Whose stealing pace, and lengthened shade we fear,
Till torn-up forage in his teeth we hear:

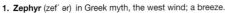

1. **Zephyr** (zef′ ər) in Greek myth, the west wind; a breeze.
2. **Philomel** (fil′ ō mel′) in Greek myth, nightingale.
3. **brakes** overgrown areas; thickets.
4. **Salisbury** This may refer to a Lady Salisbury, daughter of a friend, not to the town of Salisbury.
5. **ancient fabric** edifice or large, imposing building.
6. **meads** archaic term for meadows.

16

Vocabulary Builder
nocturnal (näk tur′ nəl) *adj.* occurring at night

Vocabulary Builder
temperate (tem′ pər it) *adj.* mild

venerable (ven′ ər ə bəl) *adj.* commanding respect because of age, character, or social rank

forage (fôr′ ij) *n.* food grazed for by animals

 Reading Check
Name three sights to which the speaker refers.

A Nocturnal Reverie ■ 581

16 Literary Analysis
Pre-Romantic Poetry

- Call students' attention to lines 1–4. **Ask** students what aspects of these lines are formal.
  Answer: Students may cite the regular rhythm and rhymes and the use of names from classical mythology.

▶ **Monitor Progress:** Then, **ask** students what characterizes these lines as Pre-Romantic.
  Answer: Seeds of feeling are planted in these lines with the words *only* and *lonely,* providing the reader with an anticipatory sense of mystery and emotion.

- **Ask** students what mood Finch develops in lines 1–12.
  Answer: Students may describe the mood as calm, peaceful, and mysterious. The images are positive and pleasant.

17 Reading Check

Possible responses: The speaker describes moonlight and trees reflected in a river; flowers and bushes; glow-worms; an ancient building; a grazing horse.

Differentiated Instruction   Solutions for All Learners

Strategy for English Learners
Students may find the reverie described in "A Nocturnal Reverie" more compelling if they think of it in terms of reveries of their own. Explain to students that a reverie is a fanciful imagining or reflection. Then, have them reread "A Nocturnal Reverie" and think about a moment they experienced that made them feel fanciful or dreamlike. Have them describe the place and the moment using words that appeal to the emotions.

Enrichment for Gifted/Talented Students
Have students work in small groups to write a song or create musical accompaniment as background music to a reading of an excerpt from "A Nocturnal Reverie." Students should listen to the music several times and find places where rhythm and melody might enhance and emphasize the words and mood of the poem. Remind students that their goal is to blend music with language.

1. **Possible responses:** Students may share Finch's appreciation of a time of calm after a hectic day.

2. (a) The setting is a quiet twilight in the country. The foxglove takes "a paler hue" (line 15); the "darkened groves their softest shadows wear" (line 23). (b) These images create a mood of restfulness and serenity.

3. (a) In silent dimness, the speaker's mind begins to seek "something" beyond words; her soul is freed from the distractions of the day; she discovers joy in her natural world. (b) The natural world charms the speaker to "composedness" because it is still and solemn, and "the elements of rage [are] disarmed."

4. (a) People are seeking pleasures that usually elude them. (b) Nature brings about a repose that is in direct contrast to the pursuit of pleasure that goes on in daily life.

5. Students may say that it would be difficult to find a rich rural setting untouched by modern development.

6. **Possible response:** Students may say that the speaker's attitude toward the morning—that it is a time for renewed confusion and strife—is not true of the early hours. Other students may suggest that mornings represent freshness and renewed hope.

Go **Online** For additional informa-
—**Author Link** tion about Anne Finch,
have students type in the Web Code, then select *F* from the alphabet, and then select the author's name.

When nibbling sheep at large pursue their food,
And unmolested kine[7] rechew the cud;
35 When curlews cry beneath the village walls,
And to her straggling brood the partridge calls;
Their shortlived jubilee the creatures keep,
Which but endures, whilst tyrant man does sleep;
When a sedate content the spirit feels,
40 And no fierce light disturbs, whilst it reveals;
But silent musings urge the mind to seek
Something, too high for syllables to speak;
Till the free soul to a composedness charmed,
Finding the elements of rage disarmed,
45 O'er all below a solemn quiet grown,
Joys in the inferior world, and thinks it like her own:
In such a night let me abroad remain,
Till morning breaks, and all's confused again;
Our cares, our toils, our clamors are renewed,
50 Or pleasures, seldom reached, again pursued.

---

7. **kine** archaic plural of *cow*; cattle.

Critical Reading

1. **Respond:** Could you share the speaker's mood? Explain.

2. **(a) Recall:** Describe the setting of the poem, listing specific images from lines 1–24. **(b) Analyze:** What mood do these images create?

3. **(a) Analyze:** Outline the steps that lead from the speaker's "sedate content" to her joy (lines 39–46). **(b) Interpret:** How does the natural world charm the speaker to "composedness"?

4. **(a) Infer:** What is the relation between people and their "pleasures" in line 50? **(b) Compare and Contrast:** What is the main difference between the pursuit of pleasures and the "composedness" caused by nature?

5. **Hypothesize:** If the speaker were taking a nocturnal walk in modern times, do you think her reactions to nature would be the same? Explain.

6. **Evaluate:** Do you think the speaker's attitude toward the morning is justified? Explain.

Go **Online**
—**Author Link**
For: More about Anne Finch
Visit: www.PHSchool.com
Web Code: ese-9317

Apply the Skills

Elegy Written in a Country Churchyard • A Nocturnal Reverie

Literary Analysis

Pre-Romantic Poetry

1. **(a)** What kinds of people does Gray celebrate in his "Elegy"?
   (b) What emotions does he convey about their lives and deaths?

2. **(a)** What is similar about Gray's concern for the unknown dead of a village graveyard and Finch's loving attention to humble "creatures"? **(b)** What is **Pre-Romantic** about this type of subject?

3. Explain how lines 39–50 of "A Nocturnal Reverie" affirm mystery and emotion over achievement and striving.

4. Both poets choose a nighttime setting. How is this choice a reflection of Pre-Romantic ideals?

Comparing Literary Works

5. **(a)** Reread lines 89–92 of Gray's "Elegy." What feelings do they convey? **(b)** Compare these feelings to the feelings in lines 39–46 of "A Nocturnal Reverie," using a chart like the one shown.

Lines	Stated Ideas	Feelings Expressed	Message About Life

6. On her walk, Finch discovers that nature can charm the mind to "composedness." In her poem, what does this feeling imply about humanity's place in the world?

7. Contrast this idea of humanity's place with that expressed in line 36 of Gray's "Elegy."

Reading Strategy

Paraphrasing

8. **Paraphrase** the key ideas in lines 29–32 of Gray's "Elegy."

9. Paraphrase the wish in lines 47–50 of "A Nocturnal Reverie."

10. Compare your paraphrases to the originals. What is lost?

Extend Understanding

11. **World Events Connection:** How do Gray's thoughts on the common man anticipate the democratic ideals of the American Revolution, some thirty years later?

QuickReview

Pre-Romantic poetry has the polish and formality of eighteenth-century poetry, but it anticipates the Romantic emphasis on mystery, emotion, and individual expression.

To **paraphrase**, identify the key ideas in a passage and express them in your own words.

Go Online
Assessment

For: Self-test
Visit: www.PHSchool.com
Web Code: esa-6311

Answers

1. (a) Gray celebrates simple, anonymous people buried in a country churchyard. (b) Gray conveys admiration for their lives and regret for their deaths.

2. (a) Both poets imply that value and dignity lie in the simple beauties of life, not in ambitious pursuits. (b) It deals with common people and things and the mysteries of life; it emphasizes emotions rather than reason.

3. In these lines, Finch contrasts the joys of peaceful reverie with a jarring return to the clamor of human endeavors.

4. Nighttime represents emotion; daytime represents reason.

5. (a) **Possible response:** Lines 89–92 suggest that everyone yearns to be remembered after their death.
   (b) Lines: 89–92 Gray's "Elegy"; Stated Ideas: Humans need to be remembered; nature is part of mankind; Feelings Expressed: wistfulness. Message About Life: Nature is essential to humans in life and death. Lines: 39–46 "Nocturnal Reverie"; Stated Ideas: Nature makes the human spirit content and inspires human beings by its beauty; Feelings Expressed: ecstasy in sublime; Message About Life: Nature gives human beings solace.

6. Finch's poem implies that humans can belong to the world of nature.

7. Line 36 of Gray's "Elegy" lacks Finch's consolation. Human glory ends in death.

8. We should not belittle people who lived simple, obscure lives.

9. When it is so peaceful, the speaker wishes to remain outside all night.

10. **Possible response:** Students may say that the poetic quality of the lines is lost, as well as emotional evocations.

11. **Possible responses:** Gray's thoughts support the assertion that "all men are created equal"; in his view, the common man has the same potential as a Milton or a Cromwell, just a different set of opportunities.

Go Online
Assessment Students may use the **Self-test** to prepare for **Selection Test A** or **Selection Test B**.

❶ Vocabulary Lesson
Word Analysis: Latin Prefix *circum-*
1. sailing or flying around the globe.
2. avoided or bypassed.
3. circular, or digressive forms of argument or conversation.
4. watchful and prudent.
5. the outer boundary or perimeter of a circular area.

Spelling Strategy
1. reasonably　　3. terribly
2. amply

Vocabulary Builder: Synonyms and Antonyms
1. antonyms　　5. antonyms
2. antonyms　　6. synonyms
3. antonyms　　7. synonyms
4. synonyms　　8. synonyms

❷ Grammar and Style Lesson
1. correct
2. Both Finch and Gray set their poems at nighttime.
3. correct
4. In Finch's poem, either the nightingale or the owl sang its song.
5. The woodbine and the bramble-rose wafted their scent into the nighttime air.

Writing Application
Sample response: The herd winds its way over the meadow. The plowman plods on his way home, and the forefathers of the village sleep in their tombs. As the speaker contemplates these scenes, he reflects on his own epitaph.

Build Language Skills

❶ Vocabulary Lesson
Word Analysis: Latin Prefix *circum-*
The Latin prefix *circum-* means "around." The word *circumscribed* literally means "having a line around" and thus means "limited." Use the meaning of *circum-* to define each word below.

1. circumnavigating　　4. circumspect
2. circumvented　　5. circumference
3. circumlocutions

Spelling Strategy
When adding *-ly* to form an adverb from an adjective ending in *-le*, drop the *-le:* for example, venerable + *-ly* = venerably. Write the adverb form of each word below.

1. reasonable　　2. ample　　3. terrible

Vocabulary Builder: Synonyms and Antonyms
In your notebook, indicate whether each pair of words below is composed of synonyms—words sharing nearly the same meaning—or antonyms—words that have opposite meanings.

1. penury, wealth
2. circumscribed, infinite
3. ingenuous, sophisticated
4. ignoble, lowly
5. nocturnal, daytime
6. temperate, moderate
7. venerable, respected
8. forage, fodder

❷ Grammar and Style Lesson
Pronoun-Antecedent Agreement
Pronouns **agree** with their **antecedents**—the words to which they refer—in number and gender.

Singular:	The <u>plowman</u> homeward plods **his** weary way, . . . (singular, masculine)
Plural:	<u>No children</u> run to lisp **their** sire's return, . . . (plural)

There are a few special cases of agreement. For two singular antecedents joined by *and*, the pronoun is plural. For two singular antecedents joined by *or* or *nor*, the pronoun is singular. When a plural and a singular antecedent are joined by *or*, use a plural pronoun. When the antecedent is a singular indefinite pronoun such as *each, every,* or *none*, use a singular pronoun.

Practice Correct errors in pronoun-antecedent agreement in each item, indicating those that are correct already.

1. Finch wrote her poems at a rural estate.
2. Both Finch and Gray set his poems at nighttime.
3. Did Gray or Finch base his or her work on personal experience?
4. In Finch's poem, either the nightingale or the owl sang their song.
5. The woodbine and the bramble-rose wafted its scent into the nighttime air.

Writing Application Write a paragraph on Gray's churchyard, using four pronouns. Be sure that your pronouns agree with their antecedents.

W͛G Prentice Hall Writing and Grammar Connection: Chapter 23, Section 2

Assessment Practice
Writer's Point of View (For more practice, see *Standardized Test Preparation Workbook*, p. 26.)

Use the following sample test item to give students practice in identifying a writer's opinion.

. . . The boast of heraldry, the pomp of power,/And all that beauty, all that wealth e'er gave,/Awaits alike the inevitable hour./The paths of glory lead but to the grave. . . .
. . . Far from the madding crowd's ignoble strife,/Their sober wishes never learned to stray . . .

Based on this passage, the poet believes that _____.

A a person's worth can be measured by his or her contributions to literature
B people who live in the country are more religious than those who live in the city
C one should seize the day
D people should live their lives simply because we are all equal in death

D is the correct answer.

Writing Lesson

Timed Writing: Reflective Essay

Both Gray and Finch draw on specific experiences to reflect on a theme significant to many people. Think of a time and place that inspired you, and write a reflective essay about the general meaning of your experience. *(40 minutes)*

Prewriting
(10 minutes)
Jot down the sensory details of the setting that inspired you. Then, take notes on whatever occurs to you about the place.

Drafting
(20 minutes)
As you draft, refer to the details you have gathered. Clearly link the details of your experience to your general reflections and feelings.

Revising
(10 minutes)
Analyze your essay, drawing arrows to show connections between specific details and general feelings and thoughts. Review your marked-up draft, noting details or general ideas not connected by arrows. Add details or transitions to clarify the connections of these passages to the rest of your draft.

Model: Revising to Connect the Personal and the General

The wind, whipping through my hair, scattered the heaps of leaves spilling out under the autumn sun.

No one would listen to me, so I jumped on my bike. Before my ride was over, I had forgotten about my anger and learned that  sometimes, getting away is the best answer.

The added sentence gives details supporting the circled general point (which has no arrow attached).

Prentice Hall Writing and Grammar Connection: Chapter 6, Section 2

Extend Your Learning

Listening and Speaking Perform a **group reading** of Gray's poem.

- Divide the poem into sections, following the theme, and assign sections to readers.
- Determine where to shift the speed, pitch, or volume. The opening rural descriptions might benefit from a slow reading at a low volume and pitch. A higher, faster reading might suit later stanzas.

Rehearse your reading, and perform it for your class. **[Group Activity]**

Research and Technology In her poem, Finch re-creates a reverie, or daydream, she experienced. Write a **daydream report,** using magazines and the Internet to research the latest findings on the brain activity involved in dreams and daydreams. If possible, integrate spreadsheet charts and graphics into your word-processing draft.

Go Online Research
For: An additional research activity
Visit: www.PHSchool.com
Web Code: esd-7310

Elegy Written in a Country Churchyard / A Nocturnal Reverie ■ 585

❸ Writing Lesson

You may use this Writing Lesson as timed-writing practice, or you may allow students to develop the essay as a writing assignment over several days.

- To guide students in writing this reflective essay, give them the **Support for Writing Lesson** page (*Unit 3 Resources*, p. 177).
- Review with students how Gray and Finch reflect on time and place in their poems.
- Then, explain to students that they will write reflective essays that draw on specific experiences that inspired them in some way.
- Use the Writing Lesson to guide students in developing their reflective essays. Remind them that sensory details make a reflective essay vivid.
- Use the Reflective Essay rubric in *General Resources,* pp. 47–48, to evaluate students reflective essays.

❹ Listening and Speaking

- Have students read the portion of Gray's poem that they've been assigned. Students may want to practice their portion of the poem with a partner.
- Encourage students to determine whether their passages require changes in speed, pitch, or volume.
- The **Support for Extend Your Learning** page (*Unit 3 Resources,* p. 178) provides guided note-taking opportunities to help students complete the Extend Your Learning activities.

Go Online Research Have students type in the Web Code for another research activity.

Assessment Resources

The following resources can be used to assess students' knowledge and skills.

Unit 3 Resources
   Selection Test A, pp. 180–182
   Selection Test B, pp. 183–185

General Resources
   Rubrics for Reflective Essay, pp. 47–48

Go Online Assessment Students may use the **Self-test** to prepare for **Selection Test A** or **Selection Test B.**

Meeting Your Standards

Students will

1. understand the connection between the works that bind members of a community together.

2. identify beliefs expressed in documents that bind communities together and to recognize their unifying effect.

Connections
Literature Around the World

In Pepys's *Diary* and Defoe's *Journal of the Plague Year,* the shared experiences of a community are expressed so vividly that future generations experience them as if they were their own. In *The Analects* by Confucius and the Declaration of Independence by Thomas Jefferson, universal values are expressed in ways that have made these documents timeless. How do these excerpts differ from the works by Pepys and Defoe?

CONNECTIONS
Literature Around the World

China and the United States

The Ties That Bind

Constant Experiences The experiences that bind people together in a community are various. As Pepys and Defoe show, a disaster—a fire or plague—can bring people together, showing them that they share a common destiny. Yet, the deepest ties that bind people together are constant experiences, not isolated incidents. Johnson affirms one important source of national identity when he compiles his Dictionary. With the publication of the Dictionary, the English language, which connects all who speak it, became touchable and portable.

Touchstone Works Like Johnson's Dictionary, the collected sayings of the Chinese philosopher Confucius, *The Analects,* and Thomas Jefferson's Declaration of Independence affirm the links among a people. *The Analects* states the beliefs of Confucianism, which for centuries was the dominant political and ethical philosophy of China. Jefferson's Declaration delineates the bond that united Americans in their struggle to become a nation. Both works define fundamental sources of unity among people. At the same time, the reverence shown to each helps define a national identity.

586 ■ *A Turbulent Time (1625–1798)*

Enrichment

The Zhou Dynasty

Explain to students that Confucius' ideas of order emerged from a time of disorder and upheaval. Though he often speaks as one who wants to restore traditions, Confucius himself became a source of a new tradition in the centuries after his death.

During the Zhou dynasty in China (1122–255 B.C.), the old feudal regions, each of which was ruled from a walled city, grew into big states. While the old feudal nobility had kept power through family ties and traditional loyalties, the rulers of the new big states governed through administrative bureaucracies staffed by bright young men, like Confucius himself, who might travel far to find a post. Peasant farmers, formerly tied to the land, came to own their own plots. Traditional ways of life were eroding as individuals came to depend more and more on their own efforts for success. War became more frequent during this time as rulers struggled for power.

from The Analects

Confucius

Translated by Arthur Waley

The Master said, He who rules by moral force is like the pole-star, which remains in its place while all the lesser stars do homage[1] to it.

The Master said, Govern the people by regulations, keep order among them by chastisements,[2] and they will flee from you, and lose all self-respect. Govern them by moral force, keep order among them by ritual, and they will keep their self-respect and come to you of their own accord.

The Master said, High office filled by men of narrow views, ritual performed without reverence,[3] the forms of mourning observed without grief—these are things I cannot bear to see!

Chi K'ang-tzu asked Master K'ung about government, saying, Suppose I were to slay those who have not the Way in order to help on those who have the Way, what would you think of it? Master K'ung replied saying, You are there to rule, not to slay.

If you desire what is good, the people will at once be good. The essence of the gentleman is that of wind; the essence of small people is that of grass. And when a wind passes over the grass, it cannot choose but bend.

Tzu-kung asked about government. The Master said, sufficient food, sufficient weapons, and the confidence of the common people. Tzu-kung said, Suppose you had no choice but to dispense with one of these three, which would you forgo? The Master said, Weapons. Tzu-kung said, Suppose you were forced to dispense with one of the two that were left, which would you forgo? The Master said, Food. For from of old death has been the lot of all men; but a people that no longer trusts its rulers is lost indeed.

Master Yu said, Those who in private life behave well towards their parents and elder brothers, in public life seldom show a disposition to resist the authority of their superiors. And as for such men starting a revolution, no instance of it has ever occurred. It is upon the trunk that a gentleman works. When that is firmly set up, the Way grows. And surely proper behavior towards parents and elder brothers is the trunk of Goodness?

1. **homage** (häm´ ij) *n.* anything given or done to show honor or respect.
2. **chastisements** (chas tīz´ mənts) *n.* acts of scolding or condemning.
3. **reverence** (rev´ ər əns) *n.* feeling or attitude of deep respect, love, and awe.

Confucius (551–479 B.C.)

Confucius was a Chinese philosopher and reformer who taught respect for tradition during a time of conflict and corruption. In this dark period of Chinese history, he wandered the land and instructed any young men who appeared to have a talent for learning. In the end, the man who sought to revive tradition founded a new tradition of his own. As set out in *The Analects* and developed in centuries of commentary, Confucian beliefs formed the official state doctrine of China until the overthrow of the imperial system in 1911. Confucian thinking still exerts a strong underground influence in China.

Connections: from The Analects ■ 587

Meeting Your Standards

Students will

1. recognize and appreciate formal and informal essays and their purposes.
2. apply strategies for reading essays.

❶ Defining the Essay

- Tell students that in Part 4, they will focus on the essay. Tell students that the essay is a relatively modern form of writing. Ask students where they most often see and read essays.

  Answer: Essays are often found in newspapers (particularly op-ed pages) and magazines. They are also collected in volumes of books and often appear in textbooks.

- Review with students the two main categories of essays—formal and informal.

- Tell students that the essays of Samuel Johnson and Virginia Woolf were formal, while those of Joseph Addison were generally informal.

❷ Purposes of Essay Writing

- Remind students that an author's purpose is his or her reason for writing. Essay writers may want to give information, tell a story, share an observation, or persuade readers. Authors will write the type of essay that best suits their purposes.

- Review the four purposes for writing essays. Challenge students to think of examples of essays they have read that match the purposes listed here. For example, an op-ed piece from the newspaper would likely have been written for the purpose of persuasion. Suggest that students use this page as a reference as they read Part 4 and as they read essays in other units and outside of class.

❶ Defining the Essay

An essay is a short work of nonfiction that explores a specific topic. In 1580, French philosopher Montaigne published a new form of short prose discussions called *Essais*. Four hundred years later, Montaigne is still credited with creating the modern essay.

Most essays fall into one of two main categories:

- **Formal essays** use a serious tone and dignified language, and often analyze public issues or important events.
- **Informal essays**, also called personal essays, use a more casual tone and explore everyday topics, in a relaxed, conversational style.

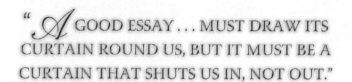

" *A* GOOD ESSAY . . . MUST DRAW ITS CURTAIN ROUND US, BUT IT MUST BE A CURTAIN THAT SHUTS US IN, NOT OUT."

— *Virginia Woolf*

❷ Purposes of Essay Writing

Within the two broad categories, essays can be further classified in a variety of ways. One way to classify an essay is according to the author's purpose.

- A **narrative essay** tells a true story about real people or events.
- *Example: Introduction to* Frankenstein by Mary Shelley, page 692
- A **persuasive essay**, also called an **argumentative essay**, tries to convince the reader to accept the writer's opinion about something or to take a course of action.
  Example: A Modest Proposal by Jonathan Swift, page 614
- A **descriptive essay**, sometimes called an **observational essay**, uses sensory details to create a portrait of a person, a place, or an object.
  Example: from *Days of Obligation* by Richard Rodriguez, page 607
- An **expository essay** presents information, discusses an idea, or explains a process.
  Example: "On Spring" by Samuel Johnson, page 594

A good essayist often combines different elements of essay writing to accomplish his or her broader purpose. Thus, a narrative essay might include descriptive passages, whereas a persuasive essay might contain expository passages or narrative anecdotes.

590 ■ *A Turbulent Time (1625–1798)*

"On Spring"

by Samuel Johnson

- formal essay
- serious and instructive tone
- ornate style

"The mind should be kept open to the access of every new idea. . . ."

"The Aims of *The Spectator*"

by Joseph Addison

- informal essay
- down-to-earth tone
- connects to readers on a personal level

"I . . . recommend these my speculations to all well-regulated families that set apart an hour in every morning for tea and bread and butter. . . ."

Differentiated
Instruction   Solutions for All Learners

Strategy for Special Needs Students
Students may benefit from turning the information on p. 590 into a chart for future reference. Suggest that students create a four-column chart, with the headings *Narrative, Persuasive, Descriptive,* and *Expository.* Under each heading, students should jot down the characteristics of each type of essay. Then, they may add the titles mentioned on the p. 590. Later, as they read the essays in Part 4, invite students to write the titles of the essays in the appropriate columns.

Strategy for Advanced Readers
Ask students to think of essays they have read for school or on their own. Challenge them to label the essays according to their category (formal or informal), purpose, and type. Ask each student to name an essay; identify its category, purpose, and type; and support these judgments with details from the essay. Remind students that an essay may demonstrate more than one purpose or have characteristics of more than one type.

Types of Essay

Essays may be classified by topic or by the writer's approach to the topic.

Type	Definition	Example
Autobiographical essay	Presents the writer's perspective on events from his or her life	"A Child's Christmas in Wales" by Dylan Thomas
Analytical essay	Explores a topic by breaking it down into parts	"Politics and the English Language" by George Orwell
Critical essay	Analyzes and evaluates the merits and faults of a subject, such as a literary or an artistic work	*The Defense of Poesy* by Sir Philip Sydney
Reflective essay	Expresses the writer's thoughts and feelings on a topic that is personally significant	*A Room of One's Own* by Virginia Woolf
Humorous essay	Presents a topic in an amusing way	"An Outline of Shakespeare" by P. G. Wodehouse
Satirical essay	Ridicules, mocks, or questions actions, attitudes, or social institutions	*A Modest Proposal* by Jonathan Swift

For many essays, these categories may overlap. For example, an essay may be both autobiographical and humorous. A persuasive essay might also be satirical if it uses irony to try to change the reader's ideas.

Strategies for Reading an Essay

Use these strategies as you read essays.

Recognize Author's Purpose   As you read an essay, look for evidence of the writer's purpose, or reason for writing. Understanding what the author is trying to do helps you interpret what you read.

Use Historical and Cultural Context   Place an essay in its historical and cultural context by identifying beliefs and ideas common to the era and the culture in which it was written. Compare the essay's historical and cultural contexts with those of today to recognize those aspects of the text that remain relevant.

Break Down Sentences   Break down long sentences into the main clause and its related parts. Then, identify details that answer the *who, what, where, when,* or *why* about these actions.

writer chooses is often determined by his or her purpose. For example, if the author's purpose is to tell a story about real people or events, then he or she may write an auto-biographical essay or a reflective one. If the author's purpose is to explain something, then he or she may write a critical or analytical essay.

- If students are familiar with the titles listed in the chart on p. 591, then take a moment to talk about why those essays are good examples of particular types of essay.

- Suggest that students refer to this chart as they read the essays in Part 4. Challenge students to assign each of the essays to one of the types mentioned in this chart.

❹ Strategies for Reading an Essay

- Tell students that reading essays often requires more concentration than reading fiction.

- Suggest that students ask the following questions as they read essays:

  Why did the author write this essay?

  When did the author write the essay?

  Which of the author's ideas are out of date and which still apply?

- In addition to asking questions, students may benefit from para-phrasing the essays they read, focusing in particular on the paragraphs that use long sentences and complicated language.

Meeting Your Standards

Students will

1. **analyze and respond to literary elements**
   - Literary Analysis: Essay

2. **read, comprehend, analyze, and critique nonfiction**
   - Reading Strategy: Drawing Inferences
   - Reading Check questions
   - Apply the Skills questions
   - Assessment Practice (ATE)

3. **develop vocabulary**
   - Vocabulary Lesson: Latin Word Root: *-spec-*

4. **understand and apply written and oral language conventions**
   - Spelling Strategy
   - Grammar and Style Lesson: Adjective Clauses

5. **develop writing proficiency**
   - Writing Lesson: Essay on Human Behavior

6. **develop appropriate research strategies**
   - Extend Your Learning: Audience Analysis

7. **understand and apply listening and speaking strategies**
   - Extend Your Learning: Monologue

Block Scheduling: Use one 90-minute class period to preteach the skills and have students read the selection. Use a second 90-minute class period to assess students' mastery of skills, extend their learning, and monitor their progress.

Homework Suggestions

Following are possibilities for homework assignments:

- Support pages from *Unit 3 Resources:*
  - Literary Analysis
  - Reading Strategy
  - Vocabulary Builder
  - Grammar and Style
- An Extend Your Learning project and the Writing Lesson for this selection group may be completed over several days.

Step-by-Step Teaching Guide	Pacing Guide
PRETEACH	
• Administer Vocabulary and Reading Warm-ups as necessary.	5 min.
• Engage students' interest with the motivation activity.	5 min.
• Read and discuss author and background features. **FT**	10 min.
• Introduce the Literary Analysis Skill: Essay. **FT**	5 min.
• Introduce the Reading Strategy: Drawing Inferences. **FT**	10 min.
• Prepare students to read by teaching the selection vocabulary. **FT**	
TEACH	
• Informally monitor comprehension while students read independently or in groups. **FT**	30 min.
• Monitor students' comprehension with the Reading Check notes.	as students read
• Reinforce vocabulary with Vocabulary Builder notes.	as students read
• Develop students' understanding of essay with the Literary Analysis annotations. **FT**	5 minutes
• Develop students' ability to draw inferences with the Reading Strategy annotations. **FT**	5 minutes
ASSESS/EXTEND	
• Assess students' comprehension and mastery of the Literary Analysis and Reading Strategy by having them answer the Apply the Skills questions. **FT**	15 min.
• Have students complete the Vocabulary Development Lesson and the Grammar and Style Lesson. **FT**	15 min.
• Apply students' knowledge of balancing the general and the specific by using the Writing Lesson. **FT**	45 min. or homework
• Apply students' understanding by using one or more of the Extend Your Learning activities.	20–90 min. or homework
• Administer Selection Test A or Selection Test B. **FT**	15 min.

Resources

Choosing Resources for Differentiated Instruction

[**L1**] Special Needs Students
[**L2**] Below-Level Students
[**L3**] All Students
[**L4**] Advanced Students
[**EL**] English Learners

For Vocabulary and Reading Warm-ups and for Selection Tests, **A** signifies "less challenging" and **B** "more challenging." For Graphic Organizer transparencies, **A** signifies "not filled in" and **B** "filled in."

FT Fast Track Instruction: To move the lesson more quickly, use the strategies and activities identified with **FT**.

Scaffolding for Less Proficient and Advanced Students

The leveled Critical Thinking questions after selections progress in the levels of thinking required to answer them. To address the needs of your different students, you may use the (a) level questions for your less proficient students and the (b) level questions with your on-level and advanced students. The occasional
(c) level questions are appropriate for your advanced students.

PRENTICE HALL
Teacher EXPRESS Use this complete
Plan · Teach · Assess   suite of powerful
teaching tools to make lesson planning and testing quicker and easier.

PRENTICE HALL
Student EXPRESS Use the interac-
Learn · Study · Succeed   tive textbook
(online and on CD-ROM) to make selections and activities come alive with audio and video support and interactive questions.

Go Online **For:** Information about Lexiles
Professional **Visit:** www.PHSchool.com
Development **Web Code:** eue-1111

Motivation

As a homework assignment, ask students to bring in copies of their favorite magazines and display them in the classroom. Have students discuss why they like their magazines. Then, explain that today's magazine articles owe much of their informative, informal, amusing style to the work of the authors in this selection.

❶ Background

More About the Authors
Samuel Johnson

Samuel Johnson's involvement in *The Gentleman's Magazine* was an important development in the history of the magazine. Johnson avoided the official ban on parliamentary reporting by pretending his reports were from "Lilliput." His regular contributions to the magazine helped to keep it a lively source of news, essays, anecdotes, and information.

Joseph Addison

Joseph Addison's contributions to British periodicals raised the English essay to a degree of technical perfection rarely before achieved. In a prose style marked by simplicity, order, and precision, he sought to engage men's thoughts toward reason, moderation, and a harmonious life. His works also include an opera libretto, *Rosamund* (1707); a prose comedy, *The Drummer* (1716); and a neoclassical tragedy, *Cato* (1713).

❶ On Spring • The Aims of *The Spectator*

Samuel Johnson
(1709–1784)

Samuel Johnson was determined to make his living as a writer. After a few unsuccessful projects, he finally moved to London in 1737. There, he got the break he needed.

Success in the City When Johnson arrived in London, he turned to *The Gentleman's Magazine,* the most successful magazine of the day, and bombarded its editors with ideas. He became an influential contributor. Then, from 1750 to 1752, Johnson published his own magazine, *The Rambler,* a popular biweekly collection of essays and moral tales.

A Man of Leisure In 1762, Johnson was awarded an annual pension of 300 pounds, which made him something of a man of leisure. The next year, he and twenty-two-year-old James Boswell met for the first time. From that fateful meeting sprang a lasting relationship that eventually resulted in Boswell's biography, *The Life of Samuel Johnson.*

Late Works In 1765, Johnson published an acclaimed edition of Shakespeare. His last important work, *The Lives of the Poets,* appeared in ten volumes between 1779 and 1781. This work, a group of fifty-two critical biographies, covers about two hundred years of English literary history.

Classics and Commerce Johnson's style is meticulously balanced, yet he wrote much of his work to meet the needs of the moment. Even the classic essays in *Lives of the Poets* were written for the market—a publisher commissioned them to dress up a new edition of English poetry. Late in life, Johnson won a more permanent kind of recognition, receiving honorary degrees from Oxford and from Trinity College, Dublin. He is buried in Westminster Abbey. (For more on Johnson's life and his *Dictionary,* see p. 554.)

Joseph Addison
(1672–1719)

Born in a village in Wiltshire, England, Joseph Addison was educated at the Charterhouse School in London, where he became a friend of classmate Richard Steele. Both young men went on to Oxford, but, after their school days, their paths diverged. The impetuous Steele immersed himself in London life, editing an early newspaper and managing the Drury Lane Theatre, while the more cautious Addison pursued prestigious political positions. Their paths, though, were to cross again.

Scholar, Poet, and Bureaucrat A Fellow of Magdalen College, Oxford, Addison was invited by John Dryden to do translations of Virgil. After four years of European study and travel, he produced an epic, *The Campaign,* celebrating a notable English victory. In 1706, Addison was named undersecretary of state and later went on to other important posts.

A Reunion In 1709, the story is told, Addison happened to read an article in *The Tatler,* a new literary magazine that had become all the rage in London coffeehouses. The article was signed "Isaac Bickerstaff," but Addison immediately recognized the style of his old school friend Richard Steele. Addison soon became a contributor to *The Tatler.* When publication of *The Tatler* ended, the two founded another journal, *The Spectator.*

A Lifetime Partnership As a team, Addison and Steele became the most celebrated journalists in England. Their essays in *The Tatler* and *The Spectator* earned them a permanent place in English literature. Almost every magazine you can buy today uses an informal, popular style derived from the one they originated.

Preview

Connecting to the Literature

As a small child, you probably bubbled over with questions about the world. As you grew older, though, you probably began to ask questions about yourself. Writing essays is a way to explore such questions.

Literary Analysis

Essay

An **essay** is a short prose piece that explores a topic as if the author were letting you overhear his or her thoughts. Meaning an "attempt" or a "test," the word *essay* was first applied to writing by the French essayist Michel Montaigne (1533–1592).

Johnson's and Addison's essays can be seen as "tests," or experiments, to discover connections between experiences and so learn about the self. As you read, notice how the writers link their observations and anecdotes to form ideas and arguments.

Comparing Literary Works

The essay flourished during a time of social change, and Johnson and Addison wrote essays that help their readers ask and answer questions about themselves—what should I do? Who am I?

In the eighteenth century, England's middle class—lawyers, shopkeepers, merchants—was growing. Neither aristocrats nor laborers, this new class needed a self-definition, and essayists provided one. From Johnson's moral instruction to Addison's humorous observations, the essay set new ideals for—or exposed new follies in—the rising middle classes. As you read, compare the way each essay helps readers ask and answer the question, Who am I?

Reading Strategy

Drawing Inferences

To appreciate a writer's attitudes, you need to **draw inferences**—reach logical conclusions about what the writer leaves unstated. Use a chart like the one shown to make inferences as you read the essays.

Vocabulary Builder

procured (prō kyoord´) *v.* got; obtained through some effort (p. 595)

divert (də vʉrt´) *v.* amuse; entertain; distract (p. 596)

speculation (spek´ yoō lā´ shən) *n.* train of thought on a subject using hypotheses (p. 597)

transient (tran´ shənt) *adj.* temporary; passing (p. 598)

affluence (af´ loō əns) *n.* abundant wealth (p. 599)

contentious (kən ten´ shəs) *adj.* quarrelsome (p. 599)

trifles (trī´ fəlz) *n.* things of little value or importance (p. 600)

embellishments (em bel´ ish məntz) *n.* decorative touches; ornamentation (p. 600)

"On Spring"

Topic
People's hopes for future happiness

↓

Details
Everyone is "in quest of future happiness," but the expected "blessing" of the future does not come. Still, we "press forward again with equal eagerness"— we never learn!

↓

Inference: Author's Attitude
Disapproving but also understanding; mildy amused

On Spring / The Aims of The Spectator ■ 593

❷ **Literary Analysis**
Essay

- Tell students that in this lesson they will focus on the *essay,* a short prose piece that explores a topic in a conversational manner.

- Read the instruction about the essay together as a class. Call students attention to the description of an essay as a "test" or "experiment" that discovers connections between experiences and expresses something novel about the self.

❸ **Reading Strategy**
Drawing Inferences

- Explain to students that to understand an author's attitude, they must draw inferences, or reach conclusions, about what the author leaves unsaid.

- Remind students that they can sometimes draw inferences from background information or knowledge they have about the author or the era in which he or she wrote.

- Use the graphic organizer on this page to model drawing inferences with students.

- Give students a copy of **Reading Strategy Graphic Organizer A,** p. 115 in *Graphic Organizer Transparencies,* to use in practicing the skill of making inferences.

Vocabulary Development

- Pronounce each vocabulary word for students, and read the definitions as a class. Have students identify any words with which they are already familiar.

Differentiated
Instruction   Solutions for All Learners

Support for Special Needs Students	Support for Less Proficient Readers	Support for English Learners
Have students use the support pages for these selections in the *Reader's Notebook: Adapted Version.* Completing these pages will prepare students to read the selections in the Student Edition.	Have students use the support pages for these selections in the *Reader's Notebook.* After students finish the pages in the *Reader's Notebooks,* have them complete the questions and activities in the Student Edition.	Have students use the support pages for these selections in the *Reader's Notebook: English Learner's Version.* Completing these pages will prepare students to read the selections in the Student Edition.

Learning Modalities
Verbal/Linguistic Learners Much of eighteenth-century literature can be characterized by a language that is precise, is sober, and exhibits a sense of control or "decorum." Ask students to choose a passage from their favorite contemporary essay or short story and render it in eighteenth-century language. Then, have them present their paragraphs to the class.

❶ About the Selection

This essay is more than just a tribute to the beauty of spring; it is also a reflection on how people can adjust their attitudes and appreciate their surroundings in order to lead happier, more fulfilling lives.

❷ Humanities
Photography: Crocuses

This photograph captures one of the quintessential spring flowers, the crocus, in full and beautiful bloom. The bright colors and satiny texture of the flowers form a pleasing contrast with the sharp leaves. Use the following for discussion:

What would Johnson say about a person who could behold a sight like this one in nature and pass by it unmoved or unaffected?

Answer: Johnson might regard that person as guilty of wasting what nature has to offer and of wasting his or her life. Such a person would have a "blighted spring," and the only thing that could follow such a spring is a "barren year."

❸ Critical Viewing

Answer: The flowers are open, as people must be open to the experience of spring and to the experience of life. For Johnson, the flowers might also constitute one of the "productions of nature" in which people can find "an inexhaustible stock of materials upon which [to] employ [themselves]."

❶ On Spring ❷

Samuel Johnson

Background The first daily newspapers began appearing in England in 1702. As the nation's middle classes grew, the market for words and information grew more sophisticated. Through the magazines they founded and edited, Johnson, Addison, and Steele helped develop a new, popular taste for sophisticated writing about books, ideas, and fashions.

TUESDAY, APRIL 3, 1750

Et nunc omnis ager, nunc omnis parturit arbos,
Nunc frondent silvae, nunc formosissimus annus.

Now ev'ry field, now ev'ry tree is green;
Now genial nature's fairest face is seen.

VIRGIL, *Eclogues III*, v. 56; TRANSLATOR, ELPHINSTON

Every man is sufficiently discontented with some circumstances of his present state, to suffer his imagination to range more or less in quest of future happiness, and to fix upon some point of time, in which, by the removal of the inconvenience which now perplexes him, or acquisition of the advantage which he at present wants, he shall find the condition of his life very much improved.

When this time, which is too often expected with great impatience, at last arrives, it generally comes without the blessing for which it was desired; but we solace ourselves with some new prospect,[1] and press forward again with equal eagerness.

It is lucky for a man, in whom this temper prevails, when he turns his hopes upon things wholly out of his own power; since he forbears then to precipitate his affairs,[2] for the sake of the great event that is to complete his felicity, and waits for the blissful hour, with less neglect of the measures necessary to be taken in the meantime.

---

1. **solace ourselves with some new prospect** comfort ourselves with something new to look forward to.
2. **forbears then to precipitate his affairs** refrains from rushing his affairs.

594 ■ A Turbulent Time (1625–1798)

❸ ▲ Critical Viewing
Relate the qualities of the flowers in the photograph to Johnson's description of spring. **[Connect]**

Differentiated Instruction   Solutions for All Learners

Accessibility at a Glance

	On Spring	**Aims of *The Spectator***
Context	18th century essay	18th century essay
Language	long sentences	some difficult language
Concept Level	Accessible (nature)	Accessible (news)
Literary Merit	Classic	Historic
Lexile	1530L	1470L
Other		Introduces new magazine
Overall Rating	Average	Average

I have long known a person of this temper, who indulged his dream of happiness with less hurt to himself than such chimerical[3] wishes commonly produce, and adjusted his scheme with such address, that his hopes were in full bloom three parts of the year, and in the other part never wholly blasted. Many, perhaps, would be desirous of learning by what means he <u>procured</u> to himself such a cheap and lasting satisfaction. It was gained by a constant practice of referring the removal of all his uneasiness to the coming of the next spring; if his health was impaired, the spring would restore it; if what he wanted was at a high price, it would fall in value in the spring.

The spring, indeed, did often come without any of these effects, but he was always certain that the next would be more propitious; nor was ever convinced that the present spring would fail him before the middle of summer; for he always talked of the spring as coming till it was past, and when it was once past, everyone agreed with him that it was coming.

By long converse with this man, I am, perhaps, brought to feel immoderate pleasure in the contemplation of this delightful season; but I have the satisfaction of finding many, whom it can be no shame to resemble, infected with the same enthusiasm; for there is, I believe, scarce any poet of eminence, who has not left some testimony of his fondness for the flowers, the zephyrs, and the warblers of the spring. Nor has the most luxuriant imagination been able to describe the serenity and happiness of the golden age,[4] otherwise than by giving a perpetual spring, as the highest reward of uncorrupted innocence.

There is, indeed, something inexpressibly pleasing, in the annual renovation of the world, and the new display of the treasures of nature. The cold and darkness of winter, with the naked deformity of every object on which we turn our eyes, make us rejoice at the succeeding season, as well for what we have escaped, as for what we may enjoy; and every budding flower, which a warm situation brings early to our view, is considered by us as a messenger to notify the approach of more joyous days.

The spring affords to a mind, so free from the disturbance of cares or passions as to be vacant to calm amusements, almost every thing that our present state makes us capable of enjoying. The variegated verdure[5] of the fields and woods, the succession of grateful odors, the voice of pleasure pouring out its notes on every side, with the gladness apparently conceived by every animal, from the growth of his food, and the clemency of the weather, throw over the whole earth an air of gaiety, significantly expressed by the smile of nature.

Yet there are men to whom these scenes are able to give no delight, and who hurry away from all the varieties of rural beauty, to lose

---

3. **chimerical** unrealistic; fantastic.
4. **golden age** in mythology, the time in the past when the world was free from suffering and evil.
5. **variegated verdure** varied greenery, striped or spotted with different colors.

Vocabulary Builder
procured (prō kyoord´) *v.*
got; obtained through
some effort

Literary Analysis
Essay Johnson tests the
value of his feelings of
pleasure in spring. What
test does he use?

⑤ ✔ Reading Check
What does Johnson's
friend perpetually look
forward to enjoying?

On Spring ■ 595

---

❹ Literary Analysis
Essay

- Remind students that essays often cite specific examples to prove or test ideas.

- Ask students to read the paragraph that begins "By long converse with this man. . . ." Have students clarify what Johnson means when he says ". . . I have the satisfaction of finding many, whom it can be no shame to resemble, infected with the same enthusiasm."
Answer: Johnson is saying that he feels his pleasure in spring is justifiable because many people worthy of respect share the pleasure.

- Then, **ask** students the Literary Analysis question: Johnson tests the value of his feelings of pleasure in spring. What test does he use?
Answer: Johnson finds that the best poets have all stated their fondness for spring and used spring as an image for humanity's Golden Age. Johnson's "test" of his feelings is the authority of literature.

❺ Reading Check

Answer: Johnson's friend perpetually looks forward to the arrival of spring.

Essay

- Have students summarize this paragraph in their own words.
Possible response: Diversions are appropriate for those who are troubled, since they are already unable to enjoy contemplation. People who engage in diversions merely to keep themselves from worrying would be better off finding ways of preventing what they fear.

- **Ask** students the first Literary Analysis question: What duties does Johnson propose for his readers in this paragraph?
Possible response: Johnson proposes that readers take responsibility for their preoccupations and find remedies for their fears.

❼ Literary Analysis

Essay

- Have students reread the paragraph that begins "There are animals that borrow . . ."

- Then, **ask** students to describe Johnson's comparison of animal behavior to suggested human behavior.
Answer: Johnson says human beings ought to adapt to their environments and derive their reflections from the objects around them, just as certain animals change color to adapt to their environment.

▶ **Monitor Progress: Ask** students the second Literary Analysis question: What new idea of a person's present state of mind does Johnson try out here?
Answer: Johnson argues that a person's mind should be kept open to the access of every "new idea."

---

their hours, and <u>divert</u> their thoughts by cards, or assemblies, a tavern dinner, or the prattle of the day.

It may be laid down as a position which will seldom deceive, that when a man cannot bear his own company there is something wrong. He must fly from himself, either because he feels a tediousness in life from the equipoise[6] of an empty mind, which, having no tendency to one motion more than another but as it is impelled by some external power, must always have recourse to foreign objects; or he must be afraid of the intrusion of some unpleasing ideas, and, perhaps, is struggling to escape from the remembrance of a loss, the fear of a calamity, or some other thought of greater horror.

❻ Those whom sorrow incapacitates to enjoy the pleasures of contemplation, may properly apply to such diversions, provided they are innocent, as lay strong hold on the attention; and those, whom fear of any future affliction chains down to misery, must endeavor to obviate the danger.

My considerations shall, on this occasion, be turned on such as are burthensome to themselves merely because they want subjects for reflection, and to whom the volume of nature is thrown open, without affording them pleasure or instruction, because they never learned to read the characters.[7]

A French author has advanced this seeming paradox, that *very few men know how to take a walk*; and, indeed, it is true, that few know how to take a walk with a prospect of any other pleasure, than the same company would have afforded them at home.

❼ There are animals that borrow their color from the neighboring body, and, consequently, vary their hue as they happen to change their place. In like manner it ought to be the endeavor of every man to derive his reflections from the objects about him; for it is to no purpose that he alters his position, if his attention continues fixed to the same point. The mind should be kept open to the access of every new idea, and so far disengaged[8] from the predominance of particular thoughts, as easily to accommodate itself to occasional entertainment.

A man that has formed this habit of turning every new object to his entertainment, finds in the productions of nature an inexhaustible stock of materials upon which he can employ himself, without any temptations to envy or malevolence; faults, perhaps, seldom totally avoided by those, whose judgment is much exercised upon the works of art. He has always a certain prospect of discovering new reasons for adoring the sovereign author of the universe, and probable hopes of making some discovery of benefit to others, or of profit to himself. There is no doubt but many vegetables and animals have qualities that might be of great use, to the knowledge of which there is not required much force of penetration, or fatigue of study,

---

6. **equipoise** balanced state.
7. **the characters** nature's signs.
8. **disengaged** free.

Vocabulary Builder
divert (də vʉrt´) v. amuse; entertain; distract

Literary Analysis
Essay What duties does Johnson propose for his readers in this paragraph?

Literary Analysis
Essay What new idea of a person's present state of mind does Johnson try out here?

Enrichment

Art and Life

History has shown that during turbulent times, people can often be soothed by art and literature. When many of the world's nations were divided during World War I, a painter such as Henri Matisse could unite the people of the world with his harmonious, balanced, and serenely colorful paintings. Matisse's ambition was to create art that appeased and soothed; or, in his own words: "Something like a good armchair in which to rest from physical fatigue."

but only frequent experiments, and close attention. What is said by the chemists of their darling mercury, is, perhaps, true of everybody through the whole creation, that if a thousand lives should be spent upon it, all its properties would not be found out.

Mankind must necessarily be diversified by various tastes, since life affords and requires such multiplicity of employments, and a nation of naturalists is neither to be hoped, or desired; but it is surely not improper to point out a fresh amusement to those who languish in health, and repine in plenty, for want of some source of diversion that may be less easily exhausted, and to inform the multitudes of both sexes, who are burthened with every new day, that there are many shows which they have not seen.

He that enlarges his curiosity after the works of nature, demonstrably multiplies the inlets to happiness; and, therefore, the younger part of my readers, to whom I dedicate this vernal[9] <u>speculation</u>, must excuse me for calling upon them, to make use at once of the spring of the year, and the spring of life; to acquire, while their minds may be yet impressed with new images, a love of innocent pleasures, and an ardor for useful knowledge; and to remember, that a blighted spring makes a barren year, and that the vernal flowers, however beautiful and gay, are only intended by nature as preparatives to autumnal fruits.

8 |

Vocabulary Builder
speculation (spek′ yōo lā′ shən) *n.* train of thought on a subject using hypotheses

---

9. **vernal** concerning spring.

Critical Reading

1. **(a) Recall:** According to Johnson, to what feelings and thoughts does a person's "present state" usually lead? **(b) Analyze:** What problem does he find with this habit of thought and feeling?

2. **(a) Recall:** What is unique about the way in which Johnson's friend looks forward to spring? **(b) Connect:** How is his friend's habit a humorous solution to the problem Johnson has identified?

3. **(a) Analyze:** According to Johnson's descriptions, how does spring give us joy in relation to the past, the present and the future? **(b) Draw Conclusions:** What relationship does Johnson find between happiness and the way we experience time?

4. **Compare and Contrast:** In what way are those who "cannot bear their own company" like those who expect future happiness?

5. **(a) Interpret:** How would you sum up Johnson's idea of happiness? **(b) Evaluate:** Do you think Johnson's ideas offer a practical prescription for happiness? Explain.

Go Online
Author Link

For: More about Samuel Johnson
Visit: www.PHSchool.com
Web Code: ese-9320

On Spring ■ 597

⑧ Vocabulary Builder
Latin Roots: *-spec-*

- Call students' attention to the word *speculation* and its definition.

- Explain to students that the word is derived from the Latin root *-spec-*, which means "look."

- Have students suggest other words and phrases that contain this root, and list them on the chalkboard. **Possible responses:** Students may cite *inspection; spectator; respect; spectacle.*

ASSESS
Answers

1. (a) A person's "present state" usually leads him or her to thoughts about some future happiness. (b) This kind of thinking usually results in a cycle of disappointment.

2. (a) Johnson's friend talks of spring coming till it passes and then talks of its coming again. (b) Johnson's friend avoids disappointment because even if spring does not bring what he expects, he is certain that the next will be more successful.

3. (a) Spring makes us rejoice at its arrival. We reflect on the season that has ended, and every budding flower causes us to consider the approach of more joyous days. (b) Johnson sees happiness as a habit of mind in the present, not as a possible future result.

4. Those who cannot bear their own company and those who seek future happiness are both looking for relief beyond themselves and beyond the present.

5. (a) Johnson's idea of happiness involves enlarging one's curiosity about the works of nature. (b) **Possible responses:** Students may feel that the joy that can be derived from a contemplation of spring can be applied equally well to other kinds of natural enjoyments.

Go Online For additional informa-
Author Link tion about Samuel Johnson, have students type in the Web Code, then select J from the alphabet, and then select the author's name.

Differentiated
Instruction   Solutions for All Learners

Support for Special Needs Students
Have students read aloud the passage in which Johnson makes an analogy between animal and human behavior. Then, ask them to go back and reread the passage slowly to themselves until they understand Johnson's argument. Students may have difficulty seeing how Johnson uses the example of animals that change color to suggest a modified behavior for human beings. Explain to students that one way to understand a writer's attitude toward a subject is to draw inferences based on what the writer says. Model this skill for students using the **Reading Strategy Graphic Organizer B**, p. 116 in *Graphic Organizer Transparencies.*

597

The Aims of *The Spectator*

Joseph Addison

**The Spectator, No. 10,
Monday, March 12, 1711**

It is with much satisfaction that I hear this great city inquiring day by day after these my papers, and receiving my morning lectures with a becoming seriousness and attention. My publisher tells me that there are already three thousand of them distributed every day. So that if I allow twenty readers to every paper, which I look upon as a modest computation, I may reckon about three-score thousand[1] disciples in London and Westminster, who I hope will take care to distinguish themselves from the thoughtless herd of their ignorant and unattentive brethren. Since I have raised to myself so great an audience, I shall spare no pains to make their instruction agreeable, and their diversion useful. For which reasons I shall endeavor to enliven morality with wit, and to temper wit with morality, that my readers may, if possible, both ways find their account in the speculation of the day. And to the end that their virtue and discretion may not be short, <u>transient</u>, intermitting[2] starts of thought, I have resolved to refresh their memories from day to day, till I have recovered them out of that desperate state of vice and folly into which the age is fallen. The mind that lies fallow[3] but a single day sprouts up in follies that are only to be killed by a constant and assiduous culture. It was said of Socrates[4] that he brought philosophy down from heaven, to inhabit among men; and I shall be ambitious to have it said of me that I have brought philosophy out of closets and libraries, schools and colleges, to dwell in clubs and assemblies, at tea tables and in coffeehouses.

I would therefore in a very particular manner recommend these my speculations to all well-regulated families that set apart an hour in every morning for tea and bread and butter; and would earnestly advise them for their good to order this paper to be punctually served up, and to be looked upon as part of the tea equipage. . . .

In the next place, I would recommend this paper to the daily perusal of those gentlemen whom I cannot but consider as my good brothers

---

1. **three-score thousand** sixty thousand.
2. **intermitting** pausing at times; not constant.
3. **fallow** unused; unproductive.
4. **Socrates** ancient Greek philosopher (470?–399 B.C.), immortalized as a character in Plato's dialogues, who cross-examined ancient Athenians about their lives and values.

598 ■ *A Turbulent Time (1625–1798)*

and allies, I mean the fraternity of spectators, who live in the world without having anything to do in it; and either by the <u>affluence</u> of their fortunes or laziness of their dispositions have no other business with the rest of mankind but to look upon them. Under this class of men are comprehended all contemplative tradesmen, titular physicians, fellows of the Royal Society, Templars[5] that are not given to be <u>contentious</u>, and statesmen that are out of business; in short, everyone that considers the world as a theater, and desires to form a right judgment of those who are the actors on it.

There is another set of men that I must likewise lay a claim to, whom I have lately called the blanks of society, as being altogether unfurnished with ideas, till the business and conversation of the day has supplied them. I have often considered these poor souls with an eye of great commiseration, when I have heard them asking the first man they have met with, whether there was any news stirring? and by that means gathering together materials for thinking. These needy persons do not know what to talk of till about twelve o'clock in the morning; for by that time they are pretty good judges of the weather, know which way the wind sits, and whether the Dutch mail[6] be come in. As they lie at the mercy of the first man they meet, and are grave or impertinent all the day long, according to the notions which they have imbibed in the morning, I would earnestly entreat them not to stir out of their chambers till they have read this paper, and do promise them that I will daily instil into them such sound and wholesome sentiments as shall have a good effect on their conversation for the ensuing twelve hours.

But there are none to whom this paper will be more useful than to the female world. I have often thought there has not been sufficient pains taken in finding out proper employments and diversions for the fair ones. Their amusements seem contrived for them, rather as they are women, than as they are reasonable creatures; and are more adapted to the sex than to the species. The toilet[7] is their great sense of business, and the right adjusting of their hair the principal employment of their lives. The sorting of a suit of ribbons is reckoned a very good morning's work; and if they make

---

5. **titular physicians, fellows of the Royal Society, Templars** physicians in title only; members of a group dedicated to scientific research; lawyers or law students with offices in the Inner or Middle Temple.
6. **Dutch mail** mail from Europe bearing news of the war.
7. **toilet** act of dressing and grooming oneself.

Literature in Context

World Events
Rise of the Middle Class

In this essay, Addison addresses members of a new and rising social group, the British middle classes. By the mid-1700s, England enjoyed growing prosperity and a high rate of literacy. The careers available in law, medicine, teaching, banking, and government service expanded. As a result, more and more English citizens had the leisure, education, and money needed to enjoy such cultural pursuits as music, art, and reading.

Addison knows his audience, quickly tapping their interests in this essay. He refers, for instance, to the coffeehouses that provided their middle-class patrons with newspapers, gossip, and political debate as well as refreshments. He has great fun with the new custom of the shopping trip. Tongue half in cheek, Addison informs his audience of his intentions: to improve and amuse them.

Connect to the Literature

What benefit does *The Spectator* provide for the men Addison calls "the blanks of society"?

Vocabulary Builder
affluence (af´ loo əns) *n.* abundant wealth

contentious (kən ten´ shəs) *adj.* quarrelsome

✓ Reading Check

To what four groups does Addison recommend his paper?

The Aims of The Spectator ■ 599

---

⑫ Reading Strategy
Drawing Inferences

- Remind students that the title of Addison's new magazine is *The Spectator*.
- After students reread the passage, **ask** them what inferences they can make about Addison's attitude toward his "good brothers and allies."

Answer: Addison is poking fun at "spectators" who do no practical work in the world and content themselves with watching and critiquing those who do. Despite this gentle criticism of spectators, Addison allies himself with them and, of course, names his magazine *The Spectator*.

⑬ Literature in Context
Rise of the Middle Class
Addison's appeal to a new class of readers shows him to be a savvy businessman as well as a journalist. The prosperity enjoyed by many prospective readers of *The Spectator* enabled many people to be able to afford—for some, for the first time—literary entertainment as a regular expense. Addison's description of his aims to both edify and entertain would have satisfied many of his readers.

Connect to the Literature Suggest that students review Addison's aims for *The Spectator* and remember his audience as they answer the question.
Answer: Addison says that *The Spectator* will furnish "the blanks of society," who are lacking ideas of their own, with ideas for their conversations.

⑭ Reading Check

Answer: Addison recommends his paper to families, spectators, "the blanks," and women.

Differentiated Instruction
Solutions for All Learners

Strategy for English Learners
Some students may have difficulty with Addison's language. Have students read the essay in pairs or in small groups, pausing at the end of each paragraph to identify words that they do not understand and passages that are unclear to them. Have them look up the definitions of the words in their dictionaries. Circulate through the class to check on the progress of the groups or pairs and clarify any misinterpretations.

Strategy for Less Proficient Readers
Before students begin reading "The Aims of *The Spectator*," engage them in a discussion about who reads magazines and whether or not certain magazines are targeted at specific groups of people. Point out that magazines exist for a wide variety of people—the elderly, new mothers, poets, sailboat enthusiasts, computer users, sports enthusiasts, and so on. Remind students that in Addison's day, this was not the case. He had to make *The Spectator* seem appealing to everyone.

1. (a) Rodriguez feels that good journalists should be completely transparent in their writing, so readers can see straight through to reality. (b) **Possible response:** Many print journalists (as opposed to opinion columnists) do still strive for this transparency. Many television journalists, however, seem to blur the line between journalistic transparency and subjective opining.

2. (a) Rodriguez sees parallels in the two cities' contradictions—between the large, beautiful homes of the wealthy and the noise, crowds, and chaos of everyone else. (b) As a journalist, Rodriguez must be as accurate as he can, and he must present the city in all of its complexities, without simplification. (c) **Possible response:** Students may say that Rodriguez is not likely to remain objective, because it will be all but impossible to keep himself removed from and uninvolved with the city.

3. (a) Rodriguez sees himself as both Mexican and American, and he sees Tijuana as a city torn between American and Mexican definitions. (b) **Possible response:** Rodriguez wants to convey the reality and facts about his subject as a journalist would, but he also wants to describe his own subjective experience, as a literary artist might.

4. **Possible response:** Students may list such specific words and lines as *from prehistory, la capital* and *in the nineteenth century* as examples of journalistic style; *a Dickensian city with palm trees, with bad skin or bad teeth,* and *paperweights upon a map* are examples of literary language. Students may say that the more journalistic passages give facts and history, while the literary sections paint a picture that brings the city to life. Students are likely to find literary words and phrases in passages dealing with the author's subjective and internal experiences.

The pieces I write for newspapers are usually published on an opinion page; they intend to persuade. My television essays are reserved for the last part of a news program; they are clearly identified as "commentary." They circle a point of view, but cannot express a point of view. The only journalistic pride I own is the fact that I have been called by some readers "left" and by other readers "right." The journalist in me does not want to be slotted among one band of partisans in an argument.

But the writing I prefer attempts a marriage: journalism wedded to literature.

The journalist Richard Rodriguez writes as fairly as possible of the world around him. The writer Richard Rodriguez finds himself caught up in the world he is watching. He may be morally outraged. Or he may simply be made petulant by the heat. He shows his hand, at any rate.

Thinking About the Commentary

1. (a) **Recall:** According to Rodriguez, in what way do good journalists perform a "disappearing act"?
   (b) **Make a Judgment:** Do you think his ideas apply to today's television and print journalists? Explain.

2. (a) **Recall:** What connections does Rodriguez draw between Addison's London and modern-day Tijuana? (b) **Recall:** As a journalist, in what way must Rodriguez present the border town of Tijuana? (c) **Speculate:** Because of the parallels Rodriguez notes between himself and Tijuana, do you think he can be objective in his presentation of the city? Why or why not?

3. (a) **Infer:** In what ways might the connection Rodriguez feels make him the perfect person to write about Tijuana?
   (b) **Interpret:** In your own words, explain what Rodriguez means by "journalism wedded to literature."

As You Read *from* Days of Obligation . . .

4. Note words and phrases that make this a piece of journalism, and words and phrases that make it literature. Explain the differences you note, using what you read in Rodriguez's essay.

5. Consider whether Rodriguez remains a spectator throughout his essay. Identify any moments when you think he becomes a participant rather than an observer.

Answers continued

5. **Possible response:** Students will likely describe the section toward the end of the essay during which Rodriguez is in the museum in Tijuana as the moment when the author becomes a participant in the world he is observing. Here, Rodriguez uses *we* to describe himself and the janitor following him.

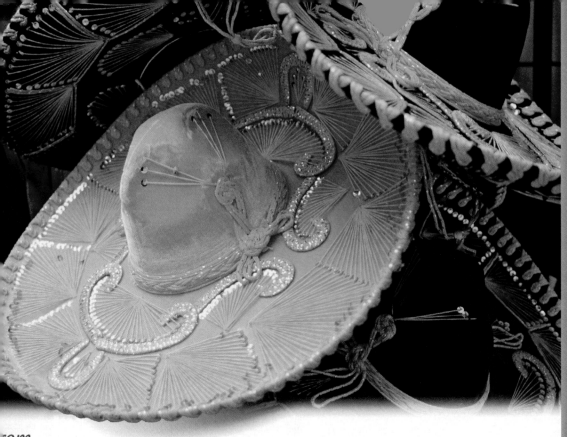

from

Days of Obligation

Richard Rodriguez
from *In Athens Once*

Consider Tijuana from Mexico's point of view. Tijuana is farther away from Mexico City than any other city in Mexico. Tijuana is where Mexico comes to an end.

In Mexico City you will waste an afternoon if you go to bookstores looking for books about Tijuana. The clerk will scarcely conceal his amusement. (And what would be in a book about Tijuana?) People in Mexico City will tell you, if they have anything at all to say about Tijuana, that Tijuana is a city without history, a city without architecture, an American city. San Diego may worry about Mexican hordes

from *Days of Obligation* ■ 607

---

❶ About the Selection

In *Days of Obligation*, Richard Rodriguez writes of Tijuana, Mexico, a city of contradictions. Rodriguez writes that the city reminds him of his own contradictions—torn between the cultures of Mexico and the United States. His comments are acerbic yet humorous, mocking yet introspective.

❷ Critical Thinking
Analyze

• Have students locate Tijuana and Mexico City on a map of Mexico. Then, **ask** students to explain the two meanings of the sentence, "Tijuana is farther away from Mexico City than any other city in Mexico."
Answer: Tijuana may indeed be the farthest city in miles from Mexico. Figuratively, Tijuana is miles away from the culture of Mexico City.

• **Ask** students what effect this word-play has on the tone of the essay.
Answer: Students may describe the effect as humorous or light-hearted.

• **Ask** students what Rodriguez means when he says that Tijuana is "where Mexico comes to an end."
Answer: Tijuana is a border town and, like many border towns, is a mix of cultures.

❸ Critical Viewing

Possible response: It may suggest an essay addressing stereotypical Spanish or Mexican culture, celebratory in nature, colorful and light.

❸ ⚠ Critical Viewing
What does this image suggest about the contents and tone of the essay to come? [Predict]

Differentiated
Instruction   Solutions for All Learners

Support for Special Needs Students
Lead a quick tour of the essay before the students read Rodriguez's essay. Have students focus on the title, questions in the side margin, photographs, footnotes, and reading check question. Ask students to predict what the essay will be about and its tone. Talk about the location of Tijuana and its proximity to the United States. Ask students whether they have heard anything about it or other border towns. Explain that border towns usually have a mix of two cultures, with no strong identity of its own.

Enrichment for Gifted/Talented Students
Rodriguez provides commentary on both Tijuana and San Diego. Ask students to develop a much more objective view of either city by designing and writing a travel brochure or a multimedia virtual tour. Ask students to research the museums, parks, local customs and celebrations, and other attractions of the city using the Internet or other references. Ask them to share their brochures or multimedia tours with the rest of the class.

crawling over the border. Mexico City worries about a cultural spill from the United States.

From prehistory, the North has been the problem. Mexico City (la capital) has been the platform from which all provincialism[1] is gauged. From the North came marauding[2] tribes, iconoclasts,[3] destroyers of high Indian civilization. During the Spanish colonial era, the North was settled, even garrisoned, but scarcely civilized. In the nineteenth century, Mexico's northernmost territories were too far from the center to be defended against America's westward expansion. In after-decades, the North spawned revolutionaries and bandits, or these fled into the North and the North hid them well.

---

1. **provincialism** narrowness of outlook.
2. **marauding** plundering, raiding.
3. **iconoclasts** those who seek to destroy widely accepted beliefs or ideas.

4 ▼ Critical Viewing
In what ways does this photograph depict the contradictory worlds Rodriguez describes? **[Connect]**

Enrichment

A Brief History of Mexico

Indians from the north were the first people who lived in what is now Mexico. They settled there about 8000 B.C., hunting large animals until the climate changed. The herds gradually died off, and the Indians turned to farming. At about the same time, people began living in villages. By 2000 B.C. classes developed among the people, including priests, pottery makers, and weavers. By 1000 B.C., the villages grew into religious centers.

Great Indian civilizations thrived between 259 and 900 A.D. The Indians built great pyra-mids to the sun and the moon. The climate became drier after 900 A.D., and the people began warring with neighboring tribes for more land.

The last great Indian empire was the Aztec during the mid-1400s. The Spanish, conquered the Aztecs in the early 1500s.

Beyond all the ribbon-cutting palaver[4] about good neighbors, there remains an awesome distance of time. Tijuana and San Diego are not in the same historical time zone. Tijuana is poised at the beginning of an industrial age, a Dickensian[5] city with palm trees. San Diego is a postindustrial city of high-impact plastic and despair diets. And palm trees. San Diego faces west, looks resolutely out to sea. Tijuana stares north, as toward the future. San Diego is the future—secular, soulless. San Diego is the past, guarding its quality of life. Tijuana is the future.

On the Mexican side there is flux, a vast migration, a camp of siege. On the Mexican side is youth, with bad skin or bad teeth, but with a naïve optimism appropriate to youth.

On the American side are petitions to declare English the official language of the United States; the Ku Klux Klan; nativists posing as environmentalists, blaming illegal immigration for freeway congestion. And late at night, on the radio call-in shows, hysterical, reasonable American voices say they have had enough. Of this or that. Of trampled flower beds. Of waiting in line or crowded buses, of real or imagined rudeness, of welfare.

In San Diego people speak of "the border" as meaning a clean break, the end of *us*, the beginning of *them*. In Mexican Spanish, the legality takes on distance, even pathos, as *la frontera*, meaning something less fixed, something more akin to the American "frontier." Whereas San Diego remains provincial and retiring, the intrusion of the United States has galvanized Tijuana to cosmopolitanism.[6] There are seven newspapers in Tijuana; there is American television—everything we see they see. Central American refugees and southern California *turistas* cross paths in Tijuana. There are new ideas. Most worrisome to Mexico City has been the emergence of a right-wing idea, a pro-American politics to challenge the one-party system that has governed Mexico for most of this century.

Because the United States is the richer country, the more powerful broadcaster, Mexicans know more about us than we care to know about them. Mexicans speak of America as "the other side," saying they are going to *el otro lado* when they cross for work, legal or illegal. The border is real enough; it is guarded by men with guns. But Mexicans incline to view the border without reverence, referring to the American side as *el otro cachete,* the other buttock.

Traditionally, Mexican cities are centered by a town square or *zócalo,* on either side of which stand city hall and cathedral, counterweights to balance the secular[7] with the eternal. Tijuana never had a

---

4. **palaver** conference or discussion.
5. **Dickensian** having the characteristics of a nineteenth century English novel written by Charles Dickens (1812–1870). Dickensian characteristics would include obscure London streets inhabited by scoundrels and villains, wide-eyed innocents, and eccentric characters.
6. **cosmopolitanism** worldly sophistication.
7. **secular** related to worldly, rather than religious, things.

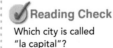 **6** **Reading Check**
Which city is called "la capital"?

from *Days of Obligation* ■ 609

⑦ Critical Viewing

Possible answer: The postcard is clearly meant for non-native tourists. It is written in English, and it has to identify Tijuana as a part of Mexico, as though Tijuana's location or cultural center were in question.

⑧ Critical Thinking
Analyze

• Have students review Rodriguez's journey through Tijuana. If necessary, draw or download a map of the commercial district to trace his steps.

• **Ask** students what impression Rodriguez has of Tijuana's Cultural Center.
Answer: He calls it very clean but very empty, an orange concrete *bomba*.

• **Ask** students to paraphrase the phrase on p. 611, "the umbilical approach narrows to gossamer." Allow students to use a dictionary to define any difficult vocabulary.
Possible response: The connection grew thin and insubstantial.

• **Ask** why the exhibit of Tijuana's history is so small.
Answer: Its history is recent. The city became a municipality in 1917.

zócalo. And, like other California cities, Tijuana is receding from its old downtown.

The new commercial district of Tijuana, three miles east of downtown, is called the Zona del Río. For several blocks within the Zona del Río, on grass islands in the middle of the Paseo de los Héroes, stand monuments to various of Mexico's heroes. There is one American (Abraham Lincoln) in a line that otherwise connects the good Aztec, Cuauhtémoc[8], to the victorious Mexican general, Zaragoza[9]. With Kremlin-like dullness, these monuments were set down upon the city, paperweights upon a map. They are gifts from the capital, meant as reminders.

Prominent along the Paseo de los Héroes is Tijuana's Cultural Center, Mexico City's most insistent token of troth.[10] Tijuana might better have done with sewers or streetlights, but in 1982 the Mexican government built Tijuana a cultural center, an orange concrete bomba[11] in the brutal architectural idioms[12] of the 1970s. The main building is a museum, very clean and empty during my visit, except for

⑦ ▲ **Critical Viewing**
Which details in this postcard support the author's message that Tijuana lacks a clear identity as a city?
[Connect]

---

8. **Cuauhtémoc** the 11th and last Aztec emperor. When captured in battle, Cuauhtémoc refused to reveal the location of Aztec riches, earning him legendary status among Mexico's leaders.
9. **Zaragoza** General Zaragoza and his militia defeated an invading French army on May 5, 1862. Cinco de Mayo is celebrated each year to commemorate the victory.
10. **troth** loyalty.
11. **bomba** bomb
12. **idioms** style of expression.

a janitor who trails me with a vacuum cleaner. Together we tread a ramp past fairly uninteresting displays of Mayan pottery, past folk crafts, past reproductions of political documents and portraits of Mexico's military heroes. The lesson to Tijuana is clear: she belongs to Mexico.

As the exhibits travel in time, south to north, the umbilical approach narrows to gossamer. We reach a display devoted to Tijuana's own history. We find a collection of picture postcards from the twenties, emblazoned in English with "Greetings from Old Mexico."

One sympathizes with the curator's dilemma. How does one depict the history of so unmonumental a city, a city occasioned by defeat and submission to the enemy's will?

The treaty ending the Mexican-American War ruled a longitudinal line between the Gulf of Mexico and the Pacific Ocean. For decades thereafter, Tijuana remained vacant land at the edge of the sea, an arid little clause dangling from Mexico's disgraced nineteenth century.

No one in Tijuana is able to fix for me the derivation of the name of the place. Some say it is an Indian name. Some think the town was named for a woman who lived in a shack at the turn of the century, a Mexican Ma Kettle known in the region as Tía Juana.

Mexico City tried to dispose of the name in 1925. By an act of Mexico's congress, Tijuana was proclaimed to be Ciudad Zaragoza. A good name. A patriot's name. The resolution languished in a statute book on a shelf in Mexico City, two thousand miles away.

Critical Reading

1. **Respond:** Do you think Rodriguez's essay qualifies as a work of objective journalism? Why or why not?

2. **(a) Recall:** According to the residents of Mexico City, what two things does Tijuana lack? **(b) Interpret:** In what way does geography play a part in this reputation? **(c) Speculate:** What effects might a city that lacks a specific urban plan or a sense of identity have on the community and people who live there?

3. **(a) Recall:** According to the essay, which city is actively moving toward its own future? **(b) Hypothesize:** What challenges might arise when a city progresses and grows very quickly? Cite examples from the essay to support your response.

4. **(a) Recall:** Instead of a cultural center, which other improvement might have benefited Tijuana? **(b) Compare and Contrast:** In what ways is Tijuana more American than Mexican in its culture? **(c) Analyze Cause and Effect:** What effect might Rodriguez's American background have on his perception of Tijuana's cultural identity?

5. **Evaluate:** Which characteristics of Tijuana are likely to appear in a positive light in a tourism advertisement? Are these characteristics truly assets to the city? Explain.

from *Days of Obligation* ■ 611

TIME AND RESOURCE MANAGER

Meeting Your Standards

Students will

1. **analyze and respond to literary elements.**
   - Literary Analysis: Satirical Essay

2. **read, comprehend, analyze, and critique a satirical essay.**
   - Reading Strategy: Recognizing Author's Purpose
   - Reading Check questions
   - Apply the Skills questions

3. **develop vocabulary.**
   - Vocabulary Lesson: Word Parts: Prefix: *en-*

4. **understand and apply written and oral language conventions.**
   - Spelling Strategy
   - Grammar and Style Lesson: Vary Sentence Beginnings

5. **develop writing proficiency.**
   - Writing Lesson: Satirical Essay

6. **develop appropriate research strategies.**
   - Extend Your Learning: Timeline

7. **understand and apply listening and speaking strategies.**
   - Extend Your Learning: Interview

Block Scheduling: Use one 90-minute class period to preteach the skills and have students read the selection. Use a second 90-minute class period to assess students' mastery of skills, extend their learning, and monitor their progress.

Homework Suggestions

Following are possibilities for homework assignments:

- Support pages from *Unit 3 Resources:*
  - Literary Analysis
  - Reading Strategy
  - Vocabulary Builder
  - Grammar and Style

- An Extend Your Learning project and the Writing Lesson for this selection may be completed over several days.

Step-by-Step Teaching Guide	Pacing Guide
PRETEACH	
• Administer Vocabulary and Reading Warm-ups as necessary.	5 min.
• Engage students' interest with the motivation activity.	5 min.
• Read and discuss author and background features. **FT**	10 min.
• Introduce the Literary Analysis skill: Satirical Essay **FT**	5 min.
• Introduce the Reading Strategy: Recognizing Author's Purpose **FT**	10 min.
• Prepare students to read by teaching the selection vocabulary. **FT**	
TEACH	
• Informally monitor comprehension while students read independently or in groups. **FT**	30 min.
• Monitor students' comprehension with the Reading Check notes.	as students read
• Reinforce vocabulary with Vocabulary Builder notes.	as students read
• Develop students' understanding of satirical essays with the Literary Analysis annotations. **FT**	5 minutes
• Develop students' ability to recognize author's purpose with the Reading Strategy annotations. **FT**	5 minutes
ASSESS/EXTEND	
• Assess students' comprehension and mastery of the Literary Analysis and Reading Strategy by having them answer the Apply the Skills questions. **FT**	15 min.
• Have students complete the Vocabulary Lesson and the Grammar and Style Lesson. **FT**	15 min.
• Apply students' ability to use irony by using the Writing Lesson. **FT**	45 min. or homework
• Apply students' understanding by using one or more of the Extend Your Learning activities.	20–90 min. or homework
• Administer Selection Test A or Selection Test B. **FT**	15 min.

Resources

PRINT
Unit 3 Resources

TRANSPARENCY
Graphic Organizer Transparencies

PRINT
Reader's Notebook [**L2**]
Reader's Notebook: Adapted Version [**L1**]
Reader's Notebook: English Learner's Version [**EL**]
Unit 3 Resources

TECHNOLOGY
Listening to Literature Audio CDs [**L2, EL**]

PRINT
Unit 3 Resources

General Resources

TECHNOLOGY
Go Online: Research [**L3**]
Go Online: Self-test [**L3**]
ExamView® Test Bank [**L3**]

Choosing Resources for Differentiated Instruction

[**L1**] Special Needs Students
[**L2**] Below-Level Students
[**L3**] All Students
[**L4**] Advanced Students
[**EL**] English Learners

For Vocabulary and Reading Warm-ups and for Selection Tests, **A** signifies "less challenging" and **B** "more challenging." For Graphic Organizer transparencies, **A** signifies "not filled in" and **B** "filled in."

FT Fast Track Instruction: To move the lesson more quickly, use the strategies and activities identified with **FT**.

Scaffolding for Less Proficient and Advanced Students

The leveled Critical Thinking questions after selections progress in the levels of thinking required to answer them. To address the needs of your different students, you may use the (a) level questions for your less proficient students and the (b) level questions with your on-level and advanced students. The occasional (c) level questions are appropriate for your advanced students.

PRENTICE HALL
Teacher EXPRESS™
Plan · Teach · Assess Use this complete suite of powerful teaching tools to make lesson planning and testing quicker and easier.

PRENTICE HALL
Student EXPRESS™
Learn · Study · Succeed Use the interactive textbook (online and on CD-ROM) to make selections and activities come alive with audio and video support and interactive questions.

Benchmark

After students have completed this selection, administer **Benchmark Test 6** (*Unit 3 Resources,* pp. 229–234). If the Benchmark Test reveals that some students need further work, use the **Interpretation Guide** to determine the appropriate reteaching page in the **Reading Kit** and on **Success Tracker.**

Go Online
Professional Development
For: Information about Lexiles
Visit: www.PHSchool.com
Web Code: eue-1111

Motivation

Ask students what they might do to get people to pay attention to a serious problem. Students probably will mention the most obvious and direct methods. If no one mentions humor, exaggeration, or satire, ask them why television shows like *Saturday Night Live* are funny. Guide students to explaining on their own the humor and significance of satire. Then, tell students that satirical works poke fun at the flaws and shortcomings of human beings and institutions. Read aloud the first line of "A Modest Proposal," and have students brainstorm for ways a writer might approach the problem of poverty and hunger among children. Ask students how humor might have more of an impact on readers than a serious tone would.

❶ Background
More About the Author

Despite his high position in the Church of Ireland, Jonathan Swift was involved in a curious love triangle between two Esthers: Esther Johnson, or "Stella" of his *Journal to Stella,* and Esther Vanhomrigh, or "Vanessa" of his poem *Cadenus and Vanessa.* Swift cared for Vanessa but failed to return her affections fully. Vanessa felt slighted and attempted to compromise Swift's relationship with Stella by revealing her own role in his life. Vanessa died in June 1723. It is possible that Swift married Stella, but no one knows for sure. She died in 1728.

Swift suffered from a disease called Meniere's Disease. This sickness of the inner ear causes nausea and vertigo. Unfortunately, not much was known about the disease in Swift's lifetime. The disease became more acute as Swift aged and his memory also began to deteriorate. Senility gripped him and he experienced a paralytic stroke.

❶ ## A Modest Proposal

Jonathan Swift
(1667–1745)

Born in Dublin, Ireland, to English parents, Jonathan Swift was educated in England. As a young man, he hoped for political advancement through the patronage of a relative, Sir William Temple. However, when these hopes were disappointed, Swift turned to a clerical career and was ordained a priest in the Church of Ireland. Eventually, he obtained an appointment as Dean of St. Patrick's Cathedral in Dublin, where he served for more than thirty years.

Ties to Ireland Swift's feelings about Ireland were sharply divided. Though he fulfilled his religious duties in Ireland, the hope for a more prestigious position in bustling England drew him frequently to London. There he enjoyed the company of such cultivated friends as the poet Alexander Pope and the powerful politician Henry Bolingbroke. Despite his attraction to England, Swift cared for the Irish people. He was moved to action by the brutal treatment of the Irish by their English overlords. He spent  one-third of his income on charitable causes in Dublin, and he earmarked another third for the founding there of St. Patrick's Hospital, an institution for the mentally handicapped. In addition, Swift wrote numerous pamphlets during a long, prolific career focusing on the cruel treatment of the Irish. Among those pamphlets were "A Proposal for the Universal Use of Irish Manufacture" (1720) and "A Short View of the State of Ireland" (1728).

Desperate Measures Unfortunately, none of the reasonable propositions in those pamphlets were put to use. Frustrated by the lack of public response to the longstanding Irish plight, Swift presented an ironic and monstrous plan in "A Modest Proposal." He wanted not only to call attention to Ireland's needs but also to shine an embarrassing light on the powerful individuals who refused to take any action.

A Modest Proposition Swift was especially concerned with Ireland's poverty because the dire financial situation of the Irish triggered numerous other problems, including starvation and homelessness. English absentee landlords, or landowners who lived far from the properties they leased, demanded exorbitant rents, and siphoned off most of Ireland's resources.

Periodic famines and food shortages sometimes led to horrifying misery, as Swift describes in the opening paragraph of "A Modest Proposal." Swift saw the English upper class as the only group possessing enough wealth and social influence to right the wrongs of Ireland. At the same time, members of the English aristocracy were among the chief offenders. The upper class reduced Ireland to a state of continual penury and squalor while increasing its own wealth at the expense of the poor Irish. The English government turned a deaf ear to previous reform proposals, and Swift decided that he needed to press satirical exaggeration to the limit. The result was one of the most memorable essays in English literature, "A Modest Proposal."

Swift published his scathing essay in Ireland in 1729. Sadly, his words failed to outrage his readership to the extent he had hoped. Though he never lost interest in this or other Irish causes, "A Modest Proposal" was the last essay he wrote to call attention to the plight of the Irish. Swift continued to write poetry until his death in 1745.

Preview

Connecting to the Literature

An old aphorism says that desperate times call for desperate measures. The desperate measures in this essay, however, are unthinkable acts meant only to raise social awareness.

Literary Analysis

Satirical Essay

A **satirical essay** is a brief prose work that pokes fun at the flaws and shortcomings of human beings and institutions. Writers of satirical essays want to persuade their readers that reform or corrective action is urgently necessary. To achieve this purpose, satirical essays use specific tools for deliberate effect.

- *Understatement:* "I can think of no one objection, that will possibly be raised against this proposal. . . ."
- *Exaggeration or Hyperbole:* "There only remain an hundred and twenty thousand children of poor parents annually born. . . ."
- *Sarcasm:* "I shall now therefore humbly propose my own thoughts. . . ."

As you read "A Modest Proposal," note the way Jonathan Swift pushes these tools to the limit in order to emphasize his message of reform.

Connecting Literary Elements

Style is an author's distinctive way of writing. Many elements contribute to a writer's unique style: for example, word choice, tone, imagery, sentence structure, and figurative language. Jonathan Swift himself once famously defined style as "proper words in proper places." In "A Modest Proposal," Swift gives his essay a unique flavor by combining tools of satire and his own elements of style. Look for these ingredients of style as you read Swift's essay.

Reading Strategy

Recognizing Author's Purpose

An **author's purpose** is his or her reason for writing. In "A Modest Proposal," Swift begins to hint at his purpose in the essay's title. His "proposal," however, is anything but modest: the outrageous solution Swift proposes to end poverty and hunger can only be a mechanism for drawing attention to the social horrors in Ireland. Use a chart like the one shown to find details within Swift's proposal that reveal this deeper purpose.

Vocabulary Builder

sustenance (sus´ tə nəns) *n.* food or money to support life (p. 615)

commodity (kə mäd´ ə tē) *n.* product that is bought or sold (p. 616)

collateral (kə lat´ ər əl) *adj.* parallel; related (p. 617)

deference (def´ ər əns) *n.* courteous regard or respect (p. 618)

censure (sen´ shər) *v.* strongly disapprove; condemn (p. 618)

encumbrance (en kum´ brəns) *n.* burden (p. 619)

contrive (kən trīv´) *v.* think up; devise; scheme (p. 619)

incur (in kʉr´) *v.* acquire or bring upon oneself (p. 621)

Detail:

"There only remain an hundred and twenty thousand children of poor parents annually born. . . ."

↓

Meaning:

There are 120,000 children suitable for Swift's proposal.

↓

Author's Purpose:

Starving children in Ireland are not getting the help they need.

A Modest Proposal ■ 613

---

❷ Literary Analysis
Satirical Essay

- Read aloud the Literary Analysis instruction as students follow along silently. Draw their attention to the three bulleted tools of satire.

- Have students provide everyday examples of understatement, exaggeration, and sarcasm. Guide students to statements such as these: After a big meal, one might make the understatement, "I'm feeling just a bit full" when in fact the person is very full. Conversely, an exaggeration might be the statement "I feel so full that I'll never eat again." Then, remind students that when they use the expression "Yeah, right" they mean the opposite of what they say and are, therefore, using sarcasm.

- Encourage students to keep these definitions and examples in mind as they read the selection.

❸ Reading Strategy
Recognizing Author's Purpose

- Ask a volunteer to read aloud the Reading Strategy instruction. Answer any questions that students may have.

- Tell students that not only statements within the selection reveal an author's purpose, but so do the selection's tone, diction, and point of view.

- Make sure students understand that Swift's proposal is anything but modest and that his purpose is to call attention to a serious situation; his solution to the situation is not to be taken literally.

- Give students a copy of **Reading Strategy Graphic Organizer A** in *Graphic Organizer Transparencies,* p. 119, to use as they read the selection.

Vocabulary Builder

- Pronounce each vocabulary word for students, and read the definitions as a class. Have students identify any words with which they are already familiar.

613

❶ About the Selection

In this satire, Swift mocks the upper class and their insatiable appetites by posing an extreme solution to the problem of Ireland's increasing poverty.

❷ Humanities

The Midday Meal, oil on canvas by Jakob Emmanuel Gaisser (1825–1899)

The intricate details in the painting serve as a perfect representation of the wealthy class Swift chooses to mock. The painting depicts the group shortly after finishing what was most likely a heavy meal. The expressions and body language of the figures on the right-hand side indicate satiation. Details such as the lavish clothing and jewelry, the food and china on the table, and the well-fed children, and the servant in the background, support Swift's view of the rich's insatiable appetites for all things luxurious. The gloves tossed on the stool suggest the leisurely and worry-free attitude of the family. Use this question for discussion:

• **Ask** students how pictures and illustrations can enhance a writer's purpose or argument.
Possible response: Students may suggest that illustrations strengthen the writer's purpose by providing visual support for his or her ideas.

❸ Critical Viewing

Possible response: The extravagant clothing, ornate room, and after-dinner torpor show the pursuit of luxury that Swift addresses.

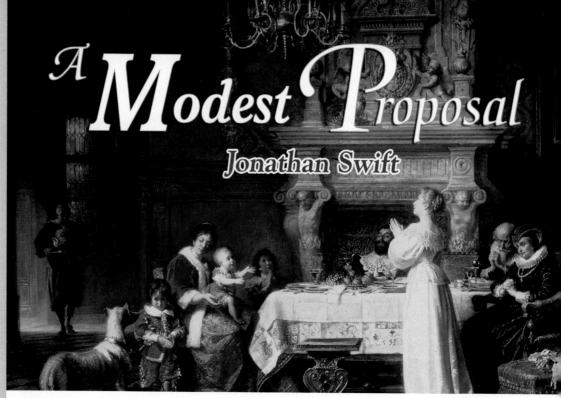

A Modest Proposal
Jonathan Swift

❶ ❷

❸ ▲ Critical Viewing
In what way does this painting embody the "relentless pursuit of luxury" that Swift addresses through his essay? [Interpret]

Background Swift recognized that the best audience for "A Modest Proposal" was the upper class—a group of people who had the ability to make changes for the better in Ireland. On a satirical level, however, Swift's essay mocks this very group of people. He suggests that their relentless pursuit of luxury has developed in them a taste for almost unimaginable delicacies. In this way, they become the perfect target for his modest proposal.

FOR PREVENTING THE CHILDREN OF POOR PEOPLE FROM BEING A BURDEN TO THEIR PARENTS OR COUNTRY, AND FOR MAKING THEM BENEFICIAL TO THE PUBLIC.

It is a melancholy object to those, who walk through this great town,[1] or travel in the country, when they see the streets, the roads, and cabin-doors, crowded with beggars of the female sex, followed by three, four, or six children, all in rags, and importuning every passenger for an alms.[2] These mothers instead of being able to work for their

---
1. **this great town** Dublin.
2. **importuning. . . alms** begging passersby for charity.

Differentiated Instruction Solutions for All Learners

Accessibility at a Glance

	A Modest Proposal
Context	Early eighteenth century
Language	Complicated syntax, formal diction
Concept Level	Challenging (scathing satirical social commentary)
Literary Merit	Classic
Lexile	1490L
Other	Not to be taken literally
Overall rating	Average

honest livelihood, are forced to employ all their time in strolling, to beg <u>sustenance</u> for their helpless infants, who, as they grow up, either turn thieves for want of work, or leave their dear native country to fight for the Pretender in Spain,[3] or sell themselves to the Barbadoes.[4]

I think it is agreed by all parties, that this prodigious number of children, in the arms, or on the backs, or at the heels of their mothers, and frequently of their fathers, is in the present deplorable state of the kingdom, a very great additional grievance; and therefore whoever could find out a fair, cheap and easy method of making these children sound useful members of the commonwealth would deserve so well of the public, as to have his statue set up for a preserver of the nation.

But my intention is very far from being confined to provide only for the children of professed beggars, it is of a much greater extent, and shall take in the whole number of infants at a certain age, who are born of parents in effect as little able to support them, as those who demand our charity in the streets.

As to my own part, having turned my thoughts, for many years, upon this important subject, and maturely weighed the several schemes of other projectors, I have always found them grossly mistaken in their computation. It is true a child, just dropped from its dam[5] may be supported by her milk for a solar year with little other nourishment, at most not above the value of two shillings, which the mother may certainly get, or the value in scraps, by her lawful occupation of begging, and it is exactly at one year old that I propose to provide for them, in such a manner, as, instead of being a charge upon their parents, or the parish, or wanting food and raiment[6] for the rest of their lives, they shall, on the contrary, contribute to the feeding and partly to the clothing of many thousands.

There is likewise another great advantage in my scheme, that it will prevent those voluntary abortions, and that horrid practice of women murdering their bastard children, alas, too frequent among us, sacrificing the poor innocent babes, I doubt, more to avoid the expense, than the shame, which would move tears and pity in the most savage and inhuman breast.

The number of souls in this kingdom being usually reckoned one million and a half,[7] of these I calculate there may be about two hundred thousand couple whose wives are breeders, from which number I subtract thirty thousand couples, who are able to maintain their own children, although I apprehend there cannot be so many under the present distresses of the kingdom, but this being granted, there will remain an hundred and seventy thousand breeders. I again subtract

---

3. **Pretender in Spain** James Edward Stewart (1688–1766), a Catholic, was a claimant (or "Pretender") to the English throne despite being barred against succession.
4. **sell. . . Barbadoes** commit themselves as indentured servants on Barbadian plantations.
5. **dam** female parent, usually an animal.
6. **raiment** clothing.
7. **souls. . . half** censuses from the year 1699 put Ireland's population at approximately 1.2 million.

Vocabulary Builder
sustenance (sus′ tə nəns) *n.* food or money to support life

Reading Strategy
Recognizing Author's Purpose What does Swift suggest about the essay's purpose in this paragraph?

Literary Analysis
Satirical Essay and Style Does Swift's use of the word *dam* affect the impression you have of the poor in Ireland? Explain.

 Reading Check
What contribution to society will infants make if Swift's proposal is accepted?

A Modest Proposal ■ 615

---

❹ Reading Strategy
Recognizing Author's Purpose

- Remind students that they can determine an author's purpose by examining a selection's details.

- Then, read aloud the bracketed passage. **Ask** students the Reading Strategy question: What does Swift suggest about the essay's purpose in this paragraph?
  Answer: Swift suggests that the purpose of the essay is to propose a "fair, cheap and easy" way to solve the problem of the growing population of the poor.

❺ Literary Analysis
Satirical Essay and Style

- Read aloud the bracketed passage while students follow along. Have a volunteer read aloud the definition of *dam* in the footnotes.

- Ask students to describe the speaker's attitude toward the poor. Remind students that essays are like poems in that the speaker or narrator is not to be confused with the author.

- Then, **ask** students the Literary Analysis question: Does Swift's use of the word *dam* affect the impression you have of the poor in Ireland? Explain.
  Possible response: The word *dam* dehumanizes the poor and makes them seem like animals.

❻ Reading Check
Possible response: They will be used as food and clothing for society.

Differentiated Instruction
Solutions for All Learners

Background for Less Proficient Readers
Remind students that Swift uses irony in "A Modest Proposal." Explain that verbal irony is a discrepancy between what is said and what is meant. As students read the selection, help them understand that Swift writes one thing but means something else entirely. Tell them that verbal irony is sarcasm.

Vocabulary for English Learners
Students may be most familiar with the word *modest* as meaning "humble." Explain that *modest* can also mean "free from extravagance," "decent," or "moderate." In this satire, however, Swift uses *modest* ironically to mean the opposite: extravagant, indecent, and extreme.

Enrichment for Advanced Readers
Ask students to use the Internet or other resources to find out how satire differs from parody. Encourage students to find examples of each type of work and share their findings with the class.

615

❼ **Humanities**

A famished boy and girl turning up the ground to seek for a potato to appease their hunger, from *Illustrated London News*

The *Illustrated London News* was founded by Herbert Ingram in 1842. The publication recorded important historical events. Ingram believed he could aid social reform through his publication. He published his liberal views on child labor, factory conditions, and the poor to educate the public. In fact, he was so popular that he was elected as a member of Parliament for Boston, Lincolnshire. Use this question for discussion:

- **Ask** students to explain whether they think Ingram would have published Swift's essay in his paper.
Possible response: Some students may think that because Ingram had the courage to start his own publication and air his views he would probably have published "A Modest Proposal." Others may think that Ingram might not have published so provocative a piece that might have alienated readers.

❽ **Critical Viewing**

Possible response: Students may suggest that the lack of color and rigid lines convey the hardship of poverty.

❾ **Reading Strategy**
Recognizing Author's Purpose

- Read aloud the bracketed passage, and ask students to summarize Swift's proposal.
- **Ask** students the Reading Strategy question: In what two ways would Swift's horrifying proposal satisfy the purpose of this essay—to diminish starvation in Ireland?
Answer: It would provide food for the population while decreasing the number of hungry individuals.

❼

fifty thousand for those women who miscarry, or whose children die by accident, or disease within the year. There only remain an hundred and twenty thousand children of poor parents annually born: The question therefore is, how this number shall be reared, and provided for, which, as I have already said, under the present situation of affairs, is utterly impossible by all the methods hitherto proposed, for we can neither employ them in handicraft, or agriculture; we neither build houses, (I mean in the country) nor cultivate land: they can very seldom pick up a livelihood by stealing till they arrive at six years old, except where they are of towardly parts,[8] although, I confess they learn the rudiments much earlier, during which time, they can however be properly looked upon only as probationers, as I have been informed by a principal gentleman in the County of Cavan, who protested to me, that he never knew above one or two instances under the age of six, even in a part of the kingdom so renowned for the quickest proficiency in that art.

I am assured by our merchants, that a boy or a girl, before twelve years old, is no saleable <u>commodity</u>, and even when they come to this age, they will not yield above three pounds, or three pounds and half-a-crown at most on the Exchange, which cannot turn to account[9] either to the parents or the kingdom, the charge of nutriment and rags having been at least four times that value.

I shall now therefore humbly propose my own thoughts, which I hope will not be liable to the least objection.

❾ I have been assured by a very knowing American of my acquaintance in London, that a young healthy child well nursed is at a year old a most delicious, nourishing, and wholesome food, whether stewed, roasted, baked, or boiled, and I make no doubt that it will equally serve in a fricassee, or a ragout.[10]

❿ I do therefore humbly offer it to public consideration, that of the hundred and twenty thousand children, already computed, twenty thousand may be reserved for breed, whereof only one fourth part to be males, which is more than we allow to sheep, black-cattle, or swine,

---

8. **of towardly parts** highly talented or able.
9. **turn to account** bring a profit.
10. **fricassee** (frik ə sē´)... **ragout** (ra gōō´) meat stews.

616 ■ *A Turbulent Time (1625–1798)*

❽ ▲ **Critical Viewing**
Do you think the technique used in this etching best conveys the hardship of poverty? Explain. **[Criticize]**

Vocabulary Builder
commodity (kə mäd´ ə tē)
n. product that is bought or sold

Reading Strategy
Recognizing Author's Purpose In what two ways would Swift's horrifying proposal satisfy the purpose of this essay—to diminish starvation in Ireland?

and my reason is that these children are seldom the fruits of marriage, a circumstance not much regarded by our savages, therefore one male will be sufficient to serve four females. That the remaining hundred thousand may at a year old be offered in sale to the persons of quality, and fortune, through the kingdom, always advising the mother to let them suck plentifully in the last month, so as to render them plump, and fat for a good table. A child will make two dishes at an entertainment for friends, and when the family dines alone, the fore or hind quarter will make a reasonable dish, and seasoned with a little pepper or salt will be very good boiled on the fourth day, especially in winter.

I have reckoned upon a medium,[11] that a child just born will weigh 12 pounds, and in a solar year if tolerably nursed increases to 28 pounds.

I grant this food will be somewhat dear,[12] and therefore very proper for landlords, who, as they have already devoured[13] most of the parents, seem to have the best title to the children.

Infants' flesh will be in season throughout the year, but more plentiful in March, and a little before and after, for we are told by a grave author an eminent French physician,[14] that fish being a prolific diet, there are more children born in Roman Catholic countries about nine months after Lent, than at any other season; therefore reckoning a year after Lent, the markets will be more glutted than usual, because the number of popish[15] infants, is at least three to one in this kingdom, and therefore it will have one other <u>collateral</u> advantage by lessening the number of Papists[16] among us.

I have already computed the charge of nursing a beggar's child (in which list I reckon all cottagers, laborers, and four-fifths of the farmers) to be about two shillings per annum, rags included, and I believe no gentleman would repine[17] to give ten shillings for the carcass of a good fat child, which, as I have said will make four dishes of excellent nutritive meat, when he has only some particular friend, or his own family to dine with him. Thus the Squire will learn to be a good landlord, and grow popular among his tenants, the mother will have eight shillings net profit, and be fit for work till she produces another child.

Those who are more thrifty (as I must confess the times require) may flay the carcass; the skin of which, artificially dressed, will make admirable gloves for ladies, and summer boots for fine gentlemen.

As to our city of Dublin, shambles[18] may be appointed for this purpose, in the most convenient parts of it, and butchers we may be assured will not be wanting, although I rather recommend buying the

---

11. **reckoned upon a medium** estimated as an average.
12. **dear** costly.
13. **devoured** financially destroyed.
14. **grave. . . physician** François Rabelais, a renown humorist and satirist.
15. **popish** Catholic (derogatory).
16. **Papists** Roman Catholics (derogatory).
17. **repine** (ri pīn´) v. complain.
18. **shambles** slaughterhouses.

Literary Analysis
Satirical Essay and Style
What effect do words like *breed* and *savages* have on the tone in this paragraph?

Literary Analysis
Satirical Essay In what way does Swift's sarcasm sharpen his satirical attack on landlords?

Vocabulary Builder
collateral (kə lat´ ər əl) *adj.*
parallel; related

Reading Strategy
Recognizing Author's Purpose In what way would manufacturing and selling fine goods serve a deeper purpose than the grisly one Swift proposes?

13 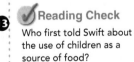 **Reading Check**
Who first told Swift about the use of children as a source of food?

A Modest Proposal ■ 617

---

10 Literary Analysis
Satirical Essay and Style
- Ask a student to read the bracketed passage aloud to the class. Draw students' attention to the words *breed* and *savages*.
- Then, **ask** the first Literary Analysis question: What effect do words like *breed* and *savages* have on the tone in this paragraph?
Answer: The words create a harsh, unsympathetic tone.

11 Literary Analysis
Satirical Essay
- Remind students that satire pokes fun at the flaws and shortcomings of human beings.
- Read aloud the bracketed passage. Then, **ask** students the second Literary Analysis question: In what way does Swift's sarcasm sharpen his satirical attack on landlords?
Answer: Swift's sarcasm suggests that because landlords figuratively "devour" tenants, it would not be difficult for them to devour individuals literally.

12 Reading Strategy
Recognizing Author's Purpose
- Read aloud the bracketed passage.
- **Ask** students the Reading Strategy question: In what way would manufacturing and selling fine goods serve a deeper purpose than the grisly one Swift proposes?
Answer: It would stimulate the economy by providing jobs for those in need.

13 Reading Check
Possible response: An American first told Swift about using children as a source of food.

The Irish Troubles

During colonial times, many Scotch-Irish immigrants came to America to escape religious turmoil and poor economic conditions. Many of these immigrants were skilled workers who quickly assimilated to life in America. They settled mainly in Pennsylvania and other middle colonies.

A large number of Irish-Catholics immigrated to America after the 1845 Potato Blight. Starvation and poor living conditions prompted their move. In the 1840s, Irish immigrants made up almost half of the immigrant population in America. Many of these immigrants were entire families that left Ireland.

Connect to the Literature
Encourage students to reread the selection before answering the question.
Possible response: Swift might be condemning the number of children born to impoverished Irish Catholics.

15 Vocabulary Builder
Prefix en-

- Draw students' attention to the word *encumbrance.* Tell students that *encumbrance* contains the prefix *en-,* which means "in" or "into." It acts as an intensifier before a noun or a verb.

- In *encumbrance,* the prefix *en-* combines with the noun *cumbrance,* which means "burden" or "obstacle."

- **Ask** students to list other words that contain the prefix *en-,* and write them on the board. Then, have students use dictionaries to find each listed word's definition.
Possible responses: Some words are *envision, encourage, encounter,* and *enrage.*

---

children alive, and dressing them hot from the knife, as we do roasting pigs.

A very worthy person, a true lover of his country, and whose virtues I highly esteem, was lately pleased, in discoursing on this matter, to offer a refinement upon my scheme. He said, that many gentlemen of this kingdom, having of late destroyed their deer, he conceived that the want of venison might be well supplied by the bodies of young lads and maidens, not exceeding fourteen years of age, nor under twelve, so great a number of both sexes in every country being now ready to starve, for want of work and service: and these to be disposed of by their parents if alive, or otherwise by their nearest relations. But with due <u>deference</u> to so excellent a friend, and so deserving a patriot, I cannot be altogether in his sentiments; for as to the males, my American acquaintance assured me from frequent experience, that their flesh was generally tough and lean, like that of our schoolboys, by continual exercise, and their taste disagreeable, and to fatten them would not answer the charge. Then as to the females, it would, I think with humble submission, be a loss to the public, because they soon would become breeders themselves: And besides, it is not improbable that some scrupulous people might be apt to <u>censure</u> such a practice, (although indeed very unjustly) as a little bordering upon cruelty, which, I confess, has always been with me the strongest objection against any project, however so well intended.

But in order to justify my friend, he confessed that this expedient was put into his head by the famous Psalmanazar,[19] a native of the island Formosa, who came from thence to London, above twenty years ago, and in conversation told my friend, that in his country when any young person happened to be put to death, the executioner sold the carcass to persons of quality, as a prime dainty, and that, in his time, the body of a plump girl of fifteen, who was crucified for an attempt to poison the emperor, was sold to his Imperial Majesty's Prime Minister of State, and other great Mandarins of the Court, in joints from the gibbet, at four hundred crowns. Neither indeed can I deny, that if the same use were made of several plump young girls in this town, who, without one single groat[20] to their fortunes, cannot stir abroad without a chair, and appear at the playhouse, and assemblies in foreign fineries, which they never will pay for, the kingdom would not be the worse.

 Some persons of a desponding spirit are in great concern about that vast number of poor people, who are aged, diseased, or maimed, and I have been desired to employ my thoughts what course may be

---

19. **Psalmanazar** Here, Swift refers to a fictitious account of cannibalism in Formosa as made by impostor George Psalmanazar.
20. **groat** coin, of trivial amount.

Literature in Context

14 History

The Irish Troubles

In the later seventeenth century, just as Swift was growing up, England encouraged Scottish Protestants to emigrate to Northern Ireland and confiscate land owned by Catholics. Political power in Ireland became concentrated exclusively in the hands of the Protestant upper class, which comprised only about ten per cent of the population. Catholics were the targets of relentless discrimination. For example, they were not allowed to reside in towns, but had to content themselves with living in rural settings. England's exploitative economic policies combined with crop failures in the 1720s to trigger a crisis; many farmers found it impossible to pay rent to their English landlords, and the streets teemed with beggars. This desolate situation was the background for "A Modest Proposal."

Connect to the Literature

In his essay, Swift appears to condemn the Irish Catholics in the same way as the social class he mocks. What possible motives might Swift have for using such a strategy?

Vocabulary Builder
deference (def′ ər əns) *n.* courteous regard or respect

censure (sen′ shər) *v.* strongly disapprove; condemn

Enrichment

Isaac Bickerstaff

"A Modest Proposal" is not Swift's only satirical writing. In 1708, a cobbler-turned-astrologer named John Partridge published an almanac of predictions. Jonathan Swift wrote a scathing parody of the almanac using the pseudonym Isaac Bickerstaff. The parody—titled *Prediction For the Ensuing Year By Isaac Bickerstaff*—included a prediction of Partridge's death to take place in March of 1708. On the date of the predicted death, Swift insisted that Partridge had died even though Partridge himself protested.

In 1709, Swift's friend and contemporary Richard Steele adopted the pseudonym Isaac Bickerstaff when he established his periodical the *Tattler.*

taken to ease the nation of so grievous an <u>encumbrance</u>. But I am not in the least pain upon that matter, because it is very well known, that they are every day dying, and rotting, by cold, and famine, and filth, and vermin, as fast as can be reasonably expected. And as to the younger laborers they are now in almost as hopeful a condition. They cannot get work, and consequently pine away for want of nourishment, to a degree, that if at any time they are accidentally hired to common labor, they have not strength to perform it; and thus the country and themselves are happily delivered from the evils to come.

I have too long digressed, and therefore shall return to my subject. I think the advantages by the proposal which I have made are obvious and many, as well as of the highest importance.

For first, as I have already observed, it would greatly lessen the number of Papists, with whom we are yearly over-run, being the principal breeders of the nation, as well as our most dangerous enemies, and who stay at home on purpose with a design to deliver the kingdom to the Pretender, hoping to take their advantage by the absence of so many good Protestants, who have chosen rather to leave their country, than stay at home, and pay tithes against their conscience, to an Episcopal curate.[21]

Secondly, the poorer tenants will have something valuable of their own, which by law may be made liable to distress,[22] and help to pay their landlord's rent, their corn and cattle being already seized, and money a thing unknown.

Thirdly, whereas the maintenance of an hundred thousand children, from two years old, and upwards, cannot be computed at less than ten shillings a piece per annum, the nation's stock will be thereby increased fifty thousand pounds per annum, besides the profit of a new dish, introduced to the tables of all gentlemen of fortune in the kingdom, who have any refinement in taste, and the money will circulate among ourselves, the goods being entirely of our own growth and manufacture.

Fourthly, the constant breeders, besides the gain of eight shillings sterling per annum, by the sale of their children, will be rid of the charge of maintaining them after the first year.

Fifthly, this food would likewise bring great custom to taverns, where the vintners will certainly be so prudent as to procure the best receipts for dressing it to perfection, and consequently have their houses frequented by all the fine gentlemen, who justly value themselves upon their knowledge in good eating; and a skillful cook, who understands how to oblige his guests will <u>contrive</u> to make it as expensive as they please.

Sixthly, this would be a great inducement to marriage, which all wise nations have either encouraged by rewards, or enforced by laws and penalties. It would increase the care and tenderness of mothers toward their children, when they were sure of a settlement for life, to

---

21. **tithes. . . curate** taxes, paid to the Catholic Church, which Protestants paid against their conscience.
22. **liable to distress** available for seizure by landlords as payment for debts.

Vocabulary Builder
encumbrance (en kum´ brəns) *n.* burden

Reading Strategy
Recognizing Author's Purpose In what way does Swift's example of the younger laborers relate to the deeper purpose of his essay?

Literary Analysis
Satirical Essay What realistic solution to Ireland's problems is suggested in Swift's second argument?

Reading Strategy
Recognizing the Author's Purpose In what way does Swift's fifth argument mock the upper classes? Explain.

Vocabulary Builder
contrive (kən trīv´) *v.* think up; devise; scheme

✓**Reading Check**
According to Swift's third argument, what benefit will his plan bring to Ireland?

A Modest Proposal ■ 619

---

16 Reading Strategy
Recognizing Author's Purpose
- Read aloud the bracketed passage.
- **Ask** students the first Reading Strategy question: In what way does Swift's example of the younger laborers relate to the deeper purpose of his essay? **Answer:** By describing the dire conditions of the Irish poor, Swift emphasizes the need for change.

17 Literary Analysis
Satirical Essay
- Briefly review the economic situation that Swift has described.
- **Ask** the first Literary Analysis question: What realistic solution to Ireland's problems is suggested in Swift's second argument? **Possible answer:** The landlords should not deprive their tenants of all they possess in order to pay rent.

18 Reading Strategy
Recognizing the Author's Purpose
- Remind students that satire pokes fun at or mocks the flaws and shortcomings of human beings and institutions. Draw attention to Swift's fifth argument, and ask a volunteer to read it aloud.
- Then, **ask** students the second Reading Strategy question: In what way does Swift's fifth argument mock the upper classes? Explain. **Answer:** It mocks the upper class's decadent desire for expensive things.

19 Reading Check
Possible response: Swift suggests that the nation's stock will increase. People will be proud that they produced the new delicacy themselves, in their own country.

Differentiated Instruction Solutions for All Learners

Strategy for Less Proficient Readers
The long sentences in this essay may cause difficulty for less proficient readers. Work with these students as they get to the list of benefits that Swift offers. The first benefit is seven lines long. Model breaking down one extended sentence into several sentences. One way to divide this sentence is to begin with the first word and go through *Papists*. Model changing the verb and syntax in the next clause, "with whom we are overrun" so that it becomes a complete sentence. Have students work with partners and continue the process on their own until they finish with the sixth reason. Help partners paraphrase, as necessary. As students offer their summaries, record them on the board. Address any questions the students may have.

⓴ Literary Analysis
Satirical Essay

- Review with students the Literary Analysis instruction on p. 613. Make sure they understand that exaggeration is a satirical tool.

- Ask students to read the bracketed passage independently. Then, have students **respond** to the Literary Analysis item: Explain Swift's use of exaggeration in this passage. **Possible answer:** He uses exaggeration to say that the poor Irish women are breeders whose husbands care little for them. By raising children for market, wives could earn money, and husbands would appreciate them in pregnancy and care for them (as they do their pregnant animals) rather than mistreat them.

㉑ Reading Strategy
Recognizing Author's Purpose

- Ask a volunteer to read aloud the italicized text. Point out to students that this text appears in italics to set it apart from the rest of the essay.

- **Ask** students the Reading Strategy question: In what ways do the proposals in italics contrast with Swift's "modest proposal" in the body of the essay? **Answer:** The proposals in italics are realistic solutions.

㉒ Critical Viewing

Possible response: Employment and housing would provide more long-term relief for Ireland because people would not have to worry about homelessness and would provide steady incomes. A flat sum of shillings might not be spent wisely and thus be of little lasting help.

620

---

the poor babes, provided in some sort by the public to their annual profit instead of expense. We should see an honest emulation[23] among the married women, which of them could bring the fattest child to the market, men would become as fond of their wives, during the time of their pregnancy, as they are now of their mares in foal, their cows in calf, or sows when they are ready to farrow, nor offer to beat or kick them (as it is too frequent a practice) for fear of a miscarriage.

Many other advantages might be enumerated: For instance, the addition of some thousand carcasses in our exportation of barrelled beef; the propagation of swine's flesh, and improvement in the art of making good bacon, so much wanted among us by the great destruction of pigs, too frequent at our tables, which are no way comparable in taste, or magnificence to a well-grown, fat yearling child, which roasted whole will make a considerable figure at a Lord Mayor's feast, or any other public entertainment. But this, and many others I omit being studious of brevity.

Supposing that one thousand families in this city, would be constant customers for infants' flesh, besides others who might have it at merry-meetings, particularly weddings and christenings, I compute that Dublin would take off annually about twenty thousand carcasses, and the rest of the kingdom (where probably they will be sold somewhat cheaper) the remaining eighty thousand.

I can think of no one objection, that will possibly be raised against this proposal, unless it should be urged that the number of people will be thereby much lessened in the kingdom. This I freely own, and was indeed one principal design in offering it to the world. I desire the reader will observe, that I calculate my remedy *for this one individual Kingdom of Ireland, and for no other that ever was, is, or, I think, ever can be upon earth. Therefore let no man talk to me of other expedients:[24] Of taxing our absentees at five shillings a pound: Of using neither clothes, nor household furniture, except what is of our own growth and manufacture: Of utterly rejecting the materials and instruments that promote foreign luxury: Of curing the expensiveness of pride, vanity, idleness, and gaming in our women: Of introducing a vein of parsimony, prudence and temperance: Of learning to love our Country, wherein we differ even from Laplanders, and the inhabitants of Topinamboo:[25] Of quitting our animosities and factions, nor act any longer like the Jews, who were murdering one another at the very moment their city was taken:[26] Of being a little cautious not to sell our country and consciences for nothing: Of teaching landlords to have at least one degree of mercy*

---

23. **emulation** competition.
24. **expedients** Prior to publication, Swift proposed each of the following reasonable mean by which Ireland might find relief, but the government ignored his suggestions. Swift used italics in editions printed during his lifetime to indicate that these proposals were, in fact, serious ones.
25. **Laplanders and. . . Topinamboo** Swift refers to natives of inhospitable lands as examples for the Irish.
26. **city. . . taken** Jerusalem, which was taken by Rome in AD 70 while its Jewish inhabitants were occupied with infighting.

620 ■ A Turbulent Time (1625–1798)

Literary Analysis
Satirical Essay Explain Swift's use of exaggeration in this passage.

Reading Strategy
Recognizing Author's Purpose In what ways do the proposals in italics contrast with Swift's "modest proposal" in the body of the essay?

㉒ ▶ **Critical Viewing** In what way might employment and housing provide more relief to Ireland than a flat sum of shillings and half-crowns, like those pictured here? [Speculate]

Enrichment

Swift's Epitaph

Swift composed an epitaph for himself before his death on October 19, 1745. The epitaph was written in Latin and came with instructions that it should be deeply cut with large letters and strongly guilded. William Butler Yeats, another Irish poet, is quoted as saying, "Swift sleeps under the greatest epitaph in history." Yeats wrote a loose translation of the epitaph in the following poem:

Swift has sailed into his rest;
Savage indignation there

Cannot lacerate his breast.
Imitate him if you dare,
World-besotted traveler; he
Served human liberty.

toward their tenants. Lastly of putting a spirit of honesty, industry and skill into our shopkeepers, who, if a resolution could now be taken to buy only our native goods, would immediately unite to cheat and exact upon us in the price, the measure, and the goodness, nor could ever yet be brought to make one fair proposal of just dealing, though often and earnestly invited to it.

Therefore I repeat, let no man talk to me of these and the like expedients, till he hath at least some glimpse of hope, that there will ever be some hearty and sincere attempt to put them in practice.

But as to myself, having been wearied out for many years with offering vain, idle, visionary thoughts, and at length utterly despairing of success, I fortunately fell upon this proposal, which as it is wholly new, so it hath something solid and real, of no expense and little trouble, full in our own power, and whereby we can <u>incur</u> no danger in disobliging[27] England. For this kind of commodity will not bear exportation, the flesh being of too tender a consistence, to admit a long continuance in salt, although perhaps I could name a country,[28] which would be glad to eat up our whole nation without it.

After all I am not so violently bent upon my own opinion, as to reject any offer, proposed by wise men, which shall be found equally innocent, cheap, easy and effectual. But before something of that kind shall be advanced in contradiction to my scheme, and offering a better, I desire the author, or authors will be pleased maturely to consider two points. First, as things now stand, how they will be able to find food and raiment for an hundred thousand useless mouths and backs. And secondly, there being a round million of creatures in human figure, throughout this kingdom, whose whole subsistence put into a common stock, would leave them in debt two millions of pounds sterling adding those, who are beggars by profession, to the bulk of farmers, cottagers and laborers with their wives and children, who are beggars in effect. I desire those politicians, who dislike my overture, and may perhaps be so bold to attempt an answer, that they will first ask the parents of these mortals, whether they would not at this day think it a great happiness

---

27. **disobliging** offending.
28. **country** England.

Vocabulary Builder
incur (in kʉr´) *v.* acquire or bring upon oneself

Literary Analysis
Satirical Essay What understatement does Swift use in the first sentence of this paragraph?

✓ **Reading Check**
For which countries has Swift developed this plan?

A Modest Proposal ■ 621

- Remind students that word choice contributes to the style of a literary work.

- Read aloud the final paragraph of Swift's essay as students follow along.

- **Ask** students the Literary Analysis question: Why do you think Swift uses the phrases "sincerity of my heart" and "not the least personal interest" in the final paragraph? **Answer:** The sarcasm of the phrases help bring a perfect end to the satire.

ASSESS

Answers

1. Students may suggest that Swift's satire was effective because it drew attention to the plight of the poor. Others may suggest that his solution, even in a satire, was offensive and therefore would not motivate anyone to take steps to remedy the situation.

2. (a) The agreement is that the children of Ireland's poor have become a burden and that a solution is required. (b) Recognizing a general agreement about the problem suggests a general agreement about the solution.

3. (a) They can serve as nourishing and tasty meals. (b) The details suggest that the practice is accepted and even elevated to "fine dining."

4. (a) The children have monetary value. (b) The landlords are already cannibals in a figurative sense.

5. (a) The poor will have something valuable—their children—and the children can be used as payment. (b) Students may suggest crops or farm animals.

6. (a) Swift uses economic terms such as *computed, stock,* and *profit.* (b) The word choice imposes order and economic advantage on a barbaric proposal.

7. (a) The number of people in Ireland will decrease. (b) The plan is cruel, barbaric, and ridiculous.

8. Students should recognize that modern satires use sarcasm, exaggeration, and understatement.

to have been sold for food at a year old, in the manner I prescribe, and thereby have avoided such a perpetual scene of misfortunes, as they have since gone through, by the oppression of landlords, the impossibility of paying rent without money or trade, the want of common sustenance, with neither house nor clothes to cover them from the inclemencies of the weather, and the most inevitable prospect of entailing[29] the like, or greater miseries upon their breed for ever.

25 I profess in the sincerity of my heart that I have not the least personal interest in endeavouring to promote this necessary work, having no other motive than the public good of my country, by advancing our trade, providing for infants, relieving the poor, and giving some pleasure to the rich. I have no children, by which I can propose to get a single penny; the youngest being nine years old, and my wife past child-bearing.

29. **entailing** passing to a later generation.

Literary Analysis
Satirical Essay and Style
Why do you think Swift uses the phrases "sincerity of my heart" and "not the least personal interest" in the final paragraph?

Critical Reading

1. **Respond:** Do you think Swift went too far with his satire in this essay? Why or why not?

2. **(a) Recall:** What agreement "by all parties" does Swift seek to establish in the second paragraph of the essay? **(b) Analyze:** Why is this agreement necessary for setting the groundwork for the satire?

3. **(a) Recall:** According to Swift's American acquaintance in London, what purpose can be served by well-nursed children who are a year old? **(b) Interpret:** In what ways does Swift's use of cooking details in the revelation of his "proposal" make the plan even more shocking?

4. **(a) Recall:** According to Swift, why will children be a very proper food for landlords? **(b) Draw Conclusions:** What satirical point is Swift making in his reference to landlords?

5. **(a) Recall:** In Swift's list of six advantages beginning on page 619, what is the second benefit he mentions for his plan?
   (b) Hypothesize: What saleable products, other than children, might the Irish use for fair trade if the government allowed?

6. **(a) Recall:** Identify three uses of economic language or jargon in the discussion of the third advantage (page 619). **(b) Interpret:** What does this word choice by Swift contribute to the satire?

7. **(a) Recall:** According to Swift, what single objection might be raised against his proposal? **(b) Criticize:** What objections to the proposal might be raised if this plan were misinterpreted as a real suggestion?

8. **Relate:** In what ways do modern satires, including political cartoons, use many of the same techniques Swift used in "A Modest Proposal"?

Go Online
Author Link
For: More about Jonathan Swift
Visit: www.PHSchool.com
Web Code: ese-9322

Go Online For additional informa-
Author Link tion about Jonathan Swift, have students type in the Web Code, then select S from the alphabet, and then select Jonathan Swift.

Apply the Skills

A Modest Proposal

Literary Analysis

Satirical Essay

1. **(a)** What is Swift's chief **satirical** target in "A Modest Proposal"? **(b)** What changes in this target might Swift hope to produce?
2. **(a)** Why do you think Swift only gradually reveals the real nature of his "proposal" in the essay? **(b)** What is ironic, or even misleading, in the author's use of the word *modest* to describe his proposal?
3. In the italicized passage toward the end of the essay, Swift lists a number of "other expedients" for dealing with Ireland's woes. Why do you think he abruptly dismisses all these suggestions in favor of his "modest proposal"?

Connecting Literary Elements

4. Use a chart like the one shown to list four examples of Swift's **style**—such as word choice, imagery, figurative language, or tone. Then, indicate the way these examples contribute to the satire.

Examples	Contribution to the Satire
Word choice: Imagery: Figurative language: Tone:	

5. Why do you think Swift uses economic and mathematical terms such as *calculate, commodity, subtract,* and *computed* with such frequency?
6. At the end of his essay, Swift excludes both himself and his wife from participating in his own proposal. **(a)** How does this strategy add to the satire? **(b)** Did you find this ending humorous? Why or why not?

Reading Strategy

Recognizing Author's Purpose

7. **(a)** Summarize Swift's modest proposal. **(b)** For what serious **purpose** does this proposal serve? **(c)** What details serve this deeper purpose?
8. Does the inclusion of realistic alternatives, printed in italics, help or hinder Swift's purpose, in your opinion? Explain your response.

Extend Understanding

9. **Cultural Connection:** Where, and for what purposes, are satires used today? Do you think they are an effective means of prompting change? Why or why not?

QuickReview

A **satirical essay** mocks an individual, group, or institution with the purpose of provoking reform.

Style is an author's distinctive, characteristic way of writing.

When you **recognize the author's purpose,** you identify his or her reason for writing.

For: Self-test
Visit: www.PHSchool.com
Web Code: esa-6314

A Modest Proposal ■ 623

Answers

1. (a) The rich are Swift's target. (b) Swift may hope to impel them into finding a solution to Ireland's social problems.
2. (a) Swift reveals his proposal gradually in order to establish its "logic" and to avoid shocking readers. (b) The title is ironic because Swift's proposal is far from modest; it is outrageous.
3. (a) Swift sarcastically dismisses the feasible suggestions to intensify his satirical message.
4. **Sample answer—Word choice:** *modest,* **Contribution to the Satire:** sets ironic tone for the proposal; **Imagery:** landlords as cannibals, **Contribution to the Satire:** emphasizes the landlords' figurative cannibalism of their tenants; **Figurative Language:** use of the word *dam,* **Contribution to the Satire:** equates the poor with animals; **Tone:** mock serious, **Contribution to the Satire:** makes it sound more authoritative and believable, thus strengthening the satire.

   Another sample answer can be found on **Literary Analysis Graphic Organizer B** in *Graphic Organizer Transparencies,* p. 122.
5. These words suggest that Swift has arrived at his proposal logically.
6. (a) Swift is willing to see others' children sacrificed but not his own. This strategy reinforces the absurdity of the entire proposal. (b) Students should explain the reasoning behind their responses.
7. (a) Swift proposes that children of the poor be sold and eaten by the wealthy in order to lessen the burden on poor parents and the government of Ireland. (b) The proposal calls attention to the dire living conditions of many in Ireland at the time. (c) **Possible answer:** Details in the first two paragraphs describe these dire conditions.
8. **Possible answer:** The inclusion of realistic alternatives aids Swift's purpose by demonstrating that feasible solutions exist.
9. Students may suggest that satires are used as political or social commentaries. Television programs, political cartoons, and comedy acts are satiric. Some students

---

Answers continued

may find them effective because their messages are strong and because satiric humor gets attention. Others may find satire tasteless and offensive and ineffective.

Go Online
Assessment
Students may use the **Self-test** to prepare for **Selection Test A** or **Selection Test B.**

623

❶ Vocabulary Lesson

Word Parts

1. to impart knowledge
2. to make into law
3. to establish a camp
4. to carry out
5. to convert into code
6. to catch

Vocabulary Builder

1. c, 2. e, 3. f, 4. a, 5. b, 6. d, 7. h, 8. g

Spelling Strategy

1. reality, 2. intensity, 3. variety

❷ Grammar and Style Lesson

1. <u>In the 1700s,</u> Jonathan Swift wrote numerous pamphlets.
2. <u>Interestingly,</u> Swift observed first-hand the miseries of the Irish.
3. <u>Because he sympathized with the plight of the poor,</u> Swift donated a third of his income to charity.
4. <u>Recognizing the power of irony,</u> Swift used extreme exaggeration in his satirical essay.
5. <u>During his day,</u> Swift's satirical prose was unsurpassed.

Writing Application

Students' paragraphs should use at least three varied sentence beginnings.

ᴡ Writing and Grammar, ɢ Ruby Level

Students will find further instruction and practice on varying sentence beginnings in Chapter 20, Section 3.

Build Language Skills

❶ Vocabulary Lesson

Word Parts: Prefix *en-*

The prefix *en-*, meaning *in* or *into*, acts as an intensifier before a noun or verb. For example, you can add the prefix *en-* to the noun *danger* to form the verb *endanger*, meaning "to bring into danger." In the word *encumbrance*, the prefix *en-* combines with the noun *cumbrance*, which means "burden" or "obstacle."

Write a definition for each word below.

1. enlighten
2. enact
3. encamp
4. enforce
5. encode
6. ensnare

Spelling Strategy

The noun *commodity* includes the suffix *-ity*. Sometimes this suffix is spelled *-ety* to avoid a double *i* when the base word part already ends in *i*, as in *society*. In your notebook, add *-ity* or *-ety* to complete these words.

1. real___   2. intens___   3. vari___

Vocabulary Builder: Matching

Review the vocabulary words on page 613. Then, choose the letter of the best definition for each word below.

1. censure
2. commodity
3. collateral
4. incur
5. encumbrance
6. deference
7. sustenance
8. contrive

a. acquire or bring upon oneself
b. burden
c. disapprove; condemn
d. courteous regard or respect
e. a product that is bought or sold
f. parallel; related
g. think up; devise; scheme
h. food or money to support life

❷ Grammar and Style Lesson

Vary Sentence Beginnings

A writer avoids monotony by **varying sentence beginnings**—starting sentences with different parts of speech or sentence elements.

> **Subject:** *Swift* presents both satirical and serious solutions in his essay. . . .
>
> **Adverb:** *Finally,* the poorer tenants will have something valuable of their own. . . .
>
> **Prepositional Phrase:** *For the people of Ireland,* Swift proposed a few drastic measures. . . .
>
> **Participial Phrase:** *Having looked aside,* the English landlord contributed nothing. . . .
>
> **Subordinate Clause:** *When the children are born,* provisions will be made for them. . . .

Practice   In your notebook, revise each sentence by adding the sentence beginning suggested in parentheses. Add new words whenever necessary.

1. Jonathan Swift wrote numerous pamphlets. (*prepositional phrase*)
2. Swift observed firsthand the miseries of the Irish. (*adverb*)
3. Swift donated a third of his income to charity. (*subordinate clause*)
4. Swift used extreme exaggeration in his satirical essay. (*participial phrase*)
5. Swift's satirical prose was unsurpassed. (*prepositional phrase*)

Writing Application   Write a paragraph responding to Swift's outrageous proposal. Use at least three of the sentence beginnings identified here.

ᴡɢ *Prentice Hall Writing and Grammar Connection: Chapter 20, Section 3*

Writing Lesson

Satirical Essay

In his essay, Swift uses sarcasm and exaggeration to ridicule human vices and follies. Write your own satirical essay that targets and mocks a foolish behavior or trend in today's world.

Prewriting   Target your satire by choosing a particular behavior, trend, or attitude to attack. Then, list some of the arguments its supporters use so you can ridicule them in your essay.

Drafting   Refer to your prewriting notes, and select the most outrageous arguments for the behavior, trend, or attitude you are satirizing. Include them in a punchy, ironic lead that pretends to support what you are attacking. Continue by offering further support in a way that seems positive but is actually ridiculous.

Revising   Read your satire aloud to a classmate. If there are passages that fall flat, look for ways to enhance your satire with irony.

> **Model: Revising to Add Irony**
>
> ~~I think the president should~~   *a*
> ~~When adults, who should know better, ride~~these
> *on his way up to give the State of the Union address.*
> little scooters, they look like overgrown kids
>
> The author adds irony to the satire by pretending to advocate something that is actually ridiculous.

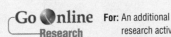 *Prentice Hall Writing and Grammar Connection: Chapter 11, Section 2*

Extend Your Learning

Listening and Speaking   Conduct an **interview** with a classmate to discover his or her reaction to "A Modest Proposal." Be sure to include the following questions during your interview.

- What was your response to the essay?
- In what ways did Swift's research into Ireland's poverty contribute to the effectiveness of the essay?
- Do you think the essay prompted the changes Swift intended? Explain.

Paraphrase your partner's responses, and share your findings with the class. **[Group Activity]**

Research and Technology   Using online resources and databases, research Swift's life and writings. Compose a **timeline** identifying the key political and social experiences that may have motivated Swift to propose his scheme in "A Modest Proposal." Finally, include the dates of any reform that may have affected Ireland as a result of Swift's essay. Present your timeline to the class.

Go Online
Research
For: An additional research activity
Visit: www.PHSchool.com
Web Code: esd-7313

---

❸ Writing Lesson

- To guide students in writing this satirical essay, give them the Support for Writing Lesson page, p. 213 in *Unit 3 Resources*.
- Read aloud the Writing Lesson instruction as students read along silently. Answer any questions that students may have.
- Draw students' attention to the Prewriting chart. Encourage them to cite specific lines from each poem as they complete the chart.
- Remind students that a thesis should state the main idea of the essay. Students should provide details and examples to support this main idea.
- Use the Generic Writing rubrics in *General Resources*, pp. 81–82, to evaluate students' essays.

❹ Research and Technology

- You may allow students to conduct their research during one or more class periods. Encourage them to take detailed notes and to cite each source they use.
- Students may find it beneficial to record each experience and date on a note card. This strategy will allow them to arrange events in chronological order quickly and easily.
- The **Support for Extend Your Learning** page (*Unit 3 Resources*, p. 214) provides guided note-taking opportunities to help students complete the Extend Your Learning activities.

Go Online
Research   Have students type in the Web Code for another research activity.

Assessment Resources

The following resources can be used to assess students' knowledge and skills.

Unit 3 Resources
Selection Test A, pp. 216–218
Selection Test B, pp. 219–221
Benchmark Test 6, pp. 229–234

General Resources
Rubrics for Generic Writing,
    pp. 81–82

Go Online
Assessment   Students may use the **Self-test** to prepare for **Selection Test A** or **Selection Test B.**

Benchmark
Administer **Benchmark Test 6**. If some students need further work, use the **Interpretation Guide** to determine the appropriate reteaching page in the **Reading Kit** and on **Success Tracker.**

Meeting Your Standards

Students will

1. understand the connection between the essays on different subjects.

2. recognize the way in which an essay is a "trial" of an idea.

Connections
American Literature

Essayists like Addison and Samuel Johnson were able to articulate their views memorably in the literary form of the essay.

In her essay, "Homeless," Anna Quindlen sets out the condition of a homeless person in America. Why is the essay an appropriate form for works on subjects as different as those by Addison, Johnson, and Quindlen?

The Essay

- Remind students that the word *essay* originates from the French verb, *essayer*, which means "to attempt," or "to try."

- Encourage them as they read this selection by Anna Quindlen to remember the ways in which Johnson and Addison presented their views in their essays and consider in what ways Quindlen's work differs from and is similar to those works.

- Encourage students to pay attention to the way in which the essay functions as a vehicle for Quindlen's ideas.

CONNECTIONS
American Literature

The Essay

Testing It Out The sixteenth-century French writer Montaigne (män tän´) first applied the word *essay*, meaning "an attempt or a trial," to a form of writing. In his essays, Montaigne explored ideas, "testing" them out. In the eighteenth century, the essay found a home in periodicals created by men like Addison and Steele. There, essays such as Johnson's "On Spring" and Addison's "Aims of *The Spectator*" entertained and informed a wide readership.

Seeing It Afresh Anna Quindlen's essay "Homeless" is a direct descendant of these periodical essays. It also appeared in a periodical, *The New York Times*. Quindlen's column is briefer and more politically oriented than those earlier essays, but, like them, it speaks directly to readers about their world. She helps readers to see a problem that is everywhere around them and to see it differently—not as "the homeless," but as people without homes.

626 ■ *A Turbulent Time (1625–1798)*

Homeless

Anna Quindlen

Thematic Connection
Answer: Quindlen opens her essay with less formality than either Johnson, who begins with a Latin quotation and a general statement, or Addison, who opens his work with a response to the public interest in his paper.

Reading Check
Answer: She shows the author a photograph of her home.

Her name was Ann, and we met in the Port Authority Bus Terminal[1] several Januarys ago. I was doing a story on homeless people. She said I was wasting my time talking to her; she was just passing through, although she'd been passing through for more than two weeks. To prove to me that this was true, she rummaged through a tote bag and a manila envelope and finally unfolded a sheet of typing paper and brought out her photographs.

They were not pictures of family, or friends, or even a dog or cat, its eyes brown-red in the flashbulb's light. They were pictures of a house. It was like a thousand houses in a hundred towns, not suburb, not city, but somewhere in between, with aluminum siding and a chain-link fence, a narrow driveway running up to a one-car garage and a patch of backyard. The house was yellow. I looked on the back for a date or a name, but neither was there. There was no need for discussion. I knew what she was trying to tell me, for it was something I had often felt. She was not adrift, alone, anonymous, although her bags and her raincoat with the grime shadowing its creases had made me believe she was. She had a house, or at least once upon a time had had one. Inside were curtains, a couch, a stove, potholders. You are where you live. She was somebody.

I've never been very good at looking at the big picture, taking the global view, and I've always been a person with an overactive sense of place, the legacy of an Irish grandfather. So it is natural that the thing that seems most wrong with the world to me right now is that there are so many people with no homes. I'm not simply talking about shelter

Thematic Connection
Compare and contrast the opening of Quindlen's essay with the opening of Johnson's or Addison's.

☑ **Reading Check**
What does Ann show the author?

---

1. **Port Authority Bus Terminal** major bus terminal located in New York City.

Connections: Homeless ■ 627

▲ **Critical Viewing** Contrast details in this photograph with the details Quindlen uses to define *home*. **[Connect]**

from the elements, or three square meals a day or a mailing address to which the welfare people can send the check—although I know that all these are important for survival. I'm talking about a home, about precisely those kinds of feelings that have wound up in cross-stitch and French knots on samplers over the years.

Home is where the heart is. There's no place like it. I love my home with a ferocity totally out of proportion to its appearance or location. I love dumb things about it: the hot-water heater, the plastic rack you drain dishes in, the roof over my head, which occasionally leaks. And yet it is precisely those dumb things that make it what it is—a place of certainty, stability, predictability, privacy, for me and for my family. It is where I live. What more can you say about a place than that? That is everything.

Yet it is something that we have been edging away from gradually during my lifetime and the lifetimes of my parents and grandparents. There was a time when where you lived often was where you worked and where you grew the food you ate and even where you were buried. When that era passed, where you lived at least was where your parents

Thematic Connection
Analyze the way Quindlen tests her own concept of home.

had lived and where you would live with your children when you became enfeebled. Then, suddenly, where you lived was where you lived for three years, until you could move on to something else and something else again.

And so we have come to something else again, to children who do not understand what it means to go to their rooms because they have never had a room, to men and women whose fantasy is a wall they can paint a color of their own choosing, to old people reduced to sitting on molded plastic chairs, their skin blue-white in the lights of a bus station, who pull pictures of houses out of their bags. Homes have stopped being homes. Now they are real estate.

People find it curious that those without homes would rather sleep sitting up on benches or huddled in doorways than go to shelters. Certainly some prefer to do so because they are emotionally ill, because they have been locked in before and they are [darned] if they will be locked in again. Others are afraid of the violence and trouble they may find there. But some seem to want something that is not available in shelters, and they will not compromise, not for a cot, or oatmeal, or a shower with special soap that kills the bugs. "One room," a woman with a baby who was sleeping on her sister's floor, once told me, "painted blue." That was the crux of it; not size or location, but pride of ownership. Painted blue.

This is a difficult problem, and some wise and compassionate people are working hard at it. But in the main I think we work around it, just as we walk around it when it is lying on the sidewalk or sitting in the bus terminal—the problem, that is. It has been customary to take people's pain and lessen our own participation in it by turning it into an issue, not a collection of human beings. We turn an adjective into a noun: the poor, not poor people; the homeless, not Ann or the man who lives in the box or the woman who sleeps on the subway grate.

Sometimes I think we would be better off if we forgot about the broad strokes and concentrated on the details. Here is a woman without a bureau. There is a man with no mirror, no wall to hang it on. They are not the homeless. They are people who have no homes. No drawer that holds the spoons. No window to look out upon the world. My [word]. That is everything.

Thematic Connection
In what way is Quindlen's commentary in this passage like Addison's commentary in "The Aims of *The Spectator*"?

**Anna Quindlen
(b. 1953)**
Anna Quindlen is currently a best-selling novelist. However, she first won recognition as a columnist for *The New York Times*. She provided a fresh voice in the editorial pages of that paper, addressing controversial issues like homelessness in a sensitive and caring way. Her commentary won her the highest award in journalism, the Pulitzer Prize.

Connecting American Literature

1. In what ways does Quindlen test our perceptions of the homeless?
2. In what way do both Johnson and Quindlen use their essays to explore core human experiences?
3. Compare and contrast Quindlen—as a narrator—to Swift in "A Modest Proposal."
4. In what ways are the writing styles of contemporary essayists, like Quindlen and Rodriguez, different from the styles of eighteenth-century writers like Johnson and Addison?

Connections: Homeless ■ 629

Thematic Connection

Answer: Quindlen is critiquing her society's lack of appreciation for a stable home, much in the way that Addison critiques the various readers of his newspaper in his essay.

ASSESS

Answers

1. Quindlen tests our perceptions of the homeless by forcing us to consider that these people want homes, not the temporary solutions offered to them by our society.
2. Both Johnson and Quindlen use a conversational, discursive style in their essays to explore core human experiences. Both also draw on their own personal experiences in their essays.
3. **Possible response:** Quindlen, like Swift, is sympathetic to her subject. In contrast, however, Quindlen is more direct in her treatment of the issue, while Swift addresses his subject indirectly though humor and satire.
4. **Possible response:** Contemporary essayists tend to focus more on their own emotions and internal monologue than eighteenth-century writers did, and they are more straightforward in addressing issues. The sentences of contemporary writers, for the most part, are shorter. In general, contemporary writers use a style intended to appeal to a general readership, whereas the writing of Swift and Addison was meant for middle-class, educated readers.

Meeting Your Standards

Students will

1. understand how to use a search engine to locate appropriate online sources.

2. evaluate the appropriateness of online search results.

See Teacher Express™/Lesson View for a detailed lesson plan for Reading Informational Materials.

About Online Search Engines

- Have students read "About Online Search Engines."

- Discuss with students any online searches they have performed. Have them describe the process they used and the success or difficulty they encountered.

- Explain to students that they may have to perform several searches using different key words before they find useful information. As a class, discuss strategies for choosing the best keywords.

Reading Strategy
Evaluating the Appropriateness of a Search Result

- Remind students that an online search may result in many "hits" or potential sources, but it is their job to evaluate the sources. Point out that students must use their evaluation skills to decide which sources are appropriate.

- As a class, review the chart on this page. Explain that the second column, "Search Keywords," is the most critical. Remind students that it helps to try several combinations of keywords.

- Review the fourth column, "Information to Avoid." Remind students that not every online source is reliable. Just as students would not use unreliable printed resources, they should avoid unreliable online sources. Tell students that they should always determine who prepared or sponsored an online source and when it was last updated.

630

Reading Informational Materials

Online Search Engines

About Online Search Engines

An **online search engine** is a tool for finding information on the World Wide Web. Some search engines track and locate information on the entire Web. Others are site-specific—they search only the data and documents within a given Web site.

Most of the major search engines conduct searches using keywords. Providing general keywords results in many pages to search through, but using specific keywords identifies only a few. For example, if you are looking for information on Britain's Cavalier poets, the search term *poetry* calls up many pages, or hits, about all kinds of poetry. A search using the keywords *Cavalier poets* locates information on only those poets in that category. In addition to articles, most search engines provide other media, such as video, audio, and image files, as well as case studies, additional Web sites, and more.

Reading Strategy
Evaluating the Appropriateness of a Search Result

Certain research topics lend themselves to specific types of information. For example, if you are writing a research paper on Cavalier poets, articles yield more useful information than case studies or testimonials.

To **evaluate the appropriateness of a search result,** consider your research topic and the kind of information you need. A chart like the one shown will help you organize your search.

Research Topic	Search Keywords	Types of Information	Information to Avoid
• British Cavalier poets	• Cavalier poets • Poetry (1600–1690) • British poets	• Articles • Videos • Web sites	• Poets prior to 1600 • Poetry other than British • Nonacademic sites

For a focused search, avoid Web sites that do not reflect the topic or the type of information you need. In addition, skip sites lacking credibility—those that are not recognized by experts or sponsored by noteworthy institutions. You may need to modify your keywords to broaden or narrow the focus of your search.

Compare the chart shown to the search engine results from the *Encyclopedia Britannica* Web site to determine which of the search results are appropriate for the research topic British Cavalier poets.

630 ■ A Turbulent Time (1625–1798)

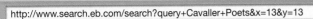

http://www.search.eb.com/search?query+Cavaller+Poets&x=13&y=13

Britannica Online

| Home | New | Workspace | Browse | Help | Guided Tour |

By clicking on active links, images, or text in the navigation bar, users can walk through the Web site, find new information, and get help.

Search Again | All Britiannica Online | Cavalier Poets | Go

Encyclopedia Britannica

Results 1-5 of 5654

▸ Cavalier poet
any of a group of English gentlemen poets, called Cavaliers because of their loyalty to Charles I (1625–49) during the English Civil Wars, as opposed to Roundheads, who supported Parliament. They ...

▸ Jonson and the Cavalier poets
from the English literature article
By contrast, the Jonsonian tradition was, broadly, that of social verse, written with a classical clarity and weight and deeply informed by ideals of civilized reasonableness, ceremonious respect, ...

▸ vers de société
(French: "society verse"), light poetry written with particular wit and polish and intended for a limited, sophisticated audience. It has flourished in cultured societies, particularly in court ...

▸ Marvell, Andrew
English poet whose political reputation overshadowed that of his poetry until the 20th century. He is considered to be one of the best secular Metaphysical poets.

▸ Suckling, Sir John
English Cavalier poet, dramatist, and courtier, best known for his lyrics.

▸ More Web Sites

Britannica Student Encyclopedia

Results 1-5 of 1173

▸ Cavalier poets
The so-called Cavalier poets were an informal group of English lyric poets during the reign of Charles I (1625–49). They followed classical models of elegance and wrote witty lyrics in praise of wine, women, and the carefree life.

The Metaphysical and the Cavalier Poets
from the English literature article
An important group of 17th-century writers were the metaphysical poets. Metaphysical poetry makes use of conceits—that is, of farfetched similes and metaphors intended to startle the reader into an awareness of the relationships among things ordinarily not associated.

Suckling, John
(1609–42). An English Cavalier poet and dramatist, Sir John Suckling is best known for his charming lyrics. He also was a prominent figure in the court of King Charles I.

Herrick, Robert
(1591–1674). A leading Cavalier poet of 17th-century England, Robert Herrick is read for the diversity and perfection of his works, which range from odes and folk songs to epigrams and love lyrics. Herrick excels in the kind of poetry that comes closest to music, by its "concord of sweet sounds," ...

▸ More Web Sites

The Web's Best Sites

Results 1-2 of 1925

Thomas Carew (1594-1640)
Luminarium
Information on the life and works of this English poet and first of the Cavalier song writers. Contains critical writings and essays. Covers links.

Richard Lovelace (1618-1657)
Luminarium
"Information on the life and works of this English poet, soldier, and Royalist whose graceful lyrics made him the prototype of the perfect Cavalier. Contains critical essays and links."

This site description tells you that this article contains critical essays as well as links to more information.

Additional Content
Expand your search on Cavalier Poets with these databases:
Journals and magazines
Britannica Concise Encyclopedia
Britannica Elementary Encyclopedia

Video & Media
Results 1-2 of 10.
Poetry: Great Haiku Poets (00:54)

Haiku has boasted many renowned poets.

These links take you to articles in journals and magazines, and to additional encyclopedia entries.

Differentiated Instruction — Solutions for All Learners

Strategy for Less Proficient Readers
Remind students that no one screens the materials that are posted on the Internet, and that students must rely on their own skills of evaluation to decide which sites are reliable. Do an online search using the keywords "Cavalier Poets." Print out the search results page and pages from one or two of the sites listed on that page. Show students how to identify the sources of the information on the linked pages, the sponsors of the pages, and the dates when the materials were last updated.

Strategy for Gifted/Talented
Challenge students to work alone or in small groups to generate an original Web page that links to useful and reliable sources about British Cavalier Poets. Have students evaluate online search results to locate and select several informational sites. Students should then create links to these sites on their page. Ask students to show their Web pages to the class and to give students a guided tour of the page and its links.

Reading Online Search Engine Results

• Tell students that their keyword searches are likely to yield a page of results like the one shown here. Students should notice the formatting of the search results page and the order in which the results are listed. Have students read the annotations to the search engine results page.

• **Ask** students to identify the features of a page of search engine results. **Answer:** The search engine results include a navigation bar, links to Web pages that contain the keywords, information about how many Web sites using the keywords are available, and descriptions of available pages.

• **Ask** students to predict which pages, based on their descriptions, will be the most useful and reliable. **Answer:** Students should select the pages that are most clearly devoted to the Cavalier poets. They should avoid pages that are not prepared or sponsored by academic institutions.

continued on p. 632

631

Reading Online Search Engine Results (cont.)

- **Ask** students to explain what the page shown here is and to identify the features it contains.

  Answer: The second page is an article that was listed on the search results page shown on p. 631. It contains information about the subject that was searched using keywords. It also provides information on bibliographic formatting and additional links.

- Remind students that it is important for them to evaluate sources that are listed in search engine results. First, they can evaluate a source based on the information that appears on the results page. If a link looks good, they should click on it. Then, they should read the information on the Web page. Again they should evaluate it after checking on the source of the page and when it was last updated.

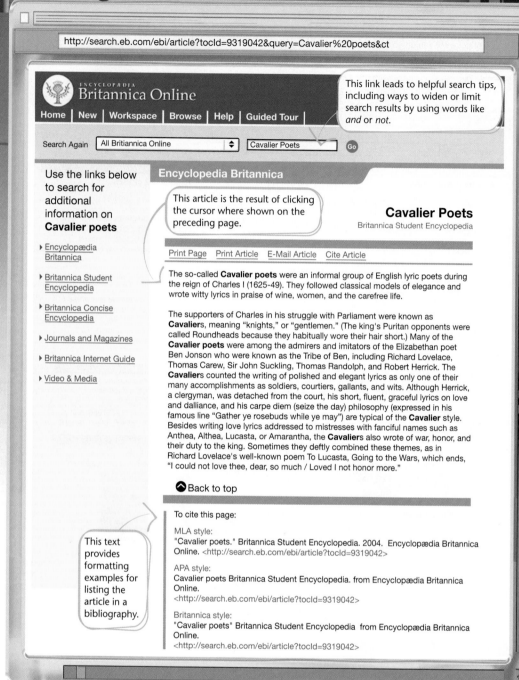

http://search.eb.com/ebi/article?tocId=9319042&query=Cavalier%20poets&ct

ENCYCLOPÆDIA Britannica Online

Home | New | Workspace | Browse | Help | Guided Tour

Search Again | All Britannica Online ▲▼ | Cavalier Poets | Go

This link leads to helpful search tips, including ways to widen or limit search results by using words like *and* or *not*.

Encyclopedia Britannica

Use the links below to search for additional information on **Cavalier poets**

▸ Encyclopædia Britannica

▸ Britannica Student Encyclopedia

▸ Britannica Concise Encyclopedia

▸ Journals and Magazines

▸ Britannica Internet Guide

▸ Video & Media

This article is the result of clicking the cursor where shown on the preceding page.

Cavalier Poets
Britannica Student Encyclopedia

Print Page   Print Article   E-Mail Article   Cite Article

The so-called **Cavalier poets** were an informal group of English lyric poets during the reign of Charles I (1625-49). They followed classical models of elegance and wrote witty lyrics in praise of wine, women, and the carefree life.

The supporters of Charles in his struggle with Parliament were known as **Cavalier**s, meaning "knights," or "gentlemen." (The king's Puritan opponents were called Roundheads because they habitually wore their hair short.) Many of the **Cavalier poets** were among the admirers and imitators of the Elizabethan poet Ben Jonson who were known as the Tribe of Ben, including Richard Lovelace, Thomas Carew, Sir John Suckling, Thomas Randolph, and Robert Herrick. The **Cavalier**s counted the writing of polished and elegant lyrics as only one of their many accomplishments as soldiers, courtiers, gallants, and wits. Although Herrick, a clergyman, was detached from the court, his short, fluent, graceful lyrics on love and dalliance, and his carpe diem (seize the day) philosophy (expressed in his famous line "Gather ye rosebuds while ye may") are typical of the **Cavalier** style. Besides writing love lyrics addressed to mistresses with fanciful names such as Anthea, Althea, Lucasta, or Amarantha, the **Cavalier**s also wrote of war, honor, and their duty to the king. Sometimes they deftly combined these themes, as in Richard Lovelace's well-known poem To Lucasta, Going to the Wars, which ends, "I could not love thee, dear, so much / Loved I not honor more."

🔺 Back to top

This text provides formatting examples for listing the article in a bibliography.

To cite this page:

MLA style:
"Cavalier poets." Britannica Student Encyclopedia. 2004. Encyclopædia Britannica Online. <http://search.eb.com/ebi/article?tocId=9319042>

APA style:
Cavalier poets Britannica Student Encyclopedia. from Encyclopædia Britannica Online.
<http://search.eb.com/ebi/article?tocId=9319042>

Britannica style:
"Cavalier poets" Britannica Student Encyclopedia from Encyclopædia Britannica Online.
<http://search.eb.com/ebi/article?tocId=9319042>

632 ■ *A Turbulent Time (1625–1798)*

Reading: Evaluating the Appropriateness of a Search Result

Directions: *Choose the letter of the best answer to each question about online search engines.*

1. Which of the articles below might provide the most general overview of the research topic Cavalier poets?
   A "Cavalier Poets"
   B "Marvell, Andrew"
   C "The Metaphysical and the Cavalier Poets"
   D "Great Haiku Poets"

2. Based on the search engine results, which medium lends itself best to the topic of Cavalier poets?
   A videos and media
   B surveys
   C case studies
   D encyclopedia articles

3. Which link might you use for research comparing the Cavaliers with another group of poets?
   A "Jonson and the Cavalier Poets"
   B "vers de societe"
   C "The Metaphysical and the Cavalier Poets"
   D "Links to Poets"

Reading: Comprehension and Interpretation

Directions: *Write your answers on a separate sheet of paper.*

4. What might you learn about Cavalier poets, in general, by reading a few of the biographies in the search results?

5. **(a)** Which sites in the encyclopedia search results contain examples of the poetry of the Cavalier poets? **(b)** What search keywords might result in samples of Cavalier poetry?

6. **(a)** Identify three advantages to conducting research online. **(b)** What disadvantages might come with trusting information found via online resources?

Timed Writing: Explanation

Using the chart on page 630 as a model, create a chart for a new research topic related to British literature. First, identify a topic. Then, explain why you chose each search keyword. Next, explain why some types of Web sites and information would be best suited for your research topic. *(25 minutes)*

Reading Informational Materials: Online Search Engines ▪ 633

Reading: Evaluating the Appropriateness of a Search Result

1. A
2. D
3. C
4. Students might learn who the Cavalier poets were, when the poets wrote, what historical events influenced their writing, and what themes were common in their poetry.
5. (a) The Luminarium sites for Thomas Carew and Richard Lovelace contain examples of the poetry of the Cavalier poets. (b) Students may find poems online by searching for the names of specific poets or titles of specific poems.
6. (a) Advantages include access to hundreds if not thousands of pertinent sites, quick access to general information such as encyclopedia articles, and easy access to in-depth information including visuals. (b) Disadvantages may include the lack of older scholarship that has not been posted; the presence of unreliable sources; and difficulty in identifying reliable sources.

Timed Writing: Explanation

- Before students begin, refer them to the chart on p. 630. Suggest that students list at least five or six possible search key words in their charts.
- Suggest that students give 5 minutes to planning, 10 minutes to writing, and 5 minutes to reviewing and revising.

Tips for
Using Technology

Remind students that there are many search engines available to them, and that each one may yield different results even if students use the same keywords. Ask students to identify search engines they have used. If students have access to computers, ask them to experiment with using the same keywords on at least two different search engines. As a class, discuss the results of the different searches. Point out which Web sites were identified by more than one search engine.

 **Writing About Literature**

Students will

1. write a comparison-and-contrast essay about the use of language in two literary works.

2. identify, compare, and contrast the ways in which writers use language to express their ideas.

3. use writing strategies to generate ideas and to plan, organize, evaluate, and revise writing.

Compare and Contrast Literary Themes

Words are the tools that a writer uses to communicate, but not every writer looks at words in the same way. Some writers use words to describe the world as accurately as possible. Samuel Johnson produced a dictionary that precisely defined words so that they could be used as tools for this purpose. Other writers, however, use words to redefine the world. They stretch the meanings of words to show the reader a new perspective, as when John Donne describes the parting of two lovers as an ìexp ansion" of their love ("A Valediction," p. 438). In an essay, compare and contrast the ways that two writers from the seventeenth and eighteenth centuries viewed words.

See the box to the right for the details of the assignment.

Assignment: Words at Work

Write an essay comparing the ways two seventeenth- or eighteenth-century writers treat words, whether as tools to describe the world accurately or as the means to see the world from an unusual perspective.

Criteria:
- Include a thesis statement that summarizes the main point of your comparison.
- Thoroughly analyze two writers' views of words by carefully discussing representative works.
- Approximate length: 700 words

Prewriting

Find a focus. Review the literature in the unit. Use a chart like the one below to help you analyze how writers look at words. As you take notes, consider these questions to narrow your focus:

- Is the writer using words in a direct, descriptive way?
- Does the writer use words playfully or satirically?
- Does the writer use a given set of words to describe a situation with which such words are not typically associated?
- Does the writer take a situation and transform it by redescribing it as another type of situation?
- Does the writer report facts with precision?

Model: Taking Notes to Focus on a Theme

Work	Key Words	Writer's Attitude Toward Words
"A Valediction: Forbidding Mourning" by Donne	"breach," "expansion," "twin compasses"	Donne uses the language of science to redefine parting.
A Journal of the Plague Year by Defoe	"pit. . . . forty feet in length," "1114 bodies"	Defoe uses words with journalistic precision to make his fiction seem real.

Gather details. Select two works to compare, and analyze each text carefully. Note the words and phrases that best capture the way each writer looks at words.

Write a working thesis. Write a thesis sentence identifying the key similarities or differences between the works you will compare. Use this sentence to guide you as you gather additional details.

Read to Write

Review at least four writers and their work before choosing two to compare. Choose two works that show a strong contrast in the writer's view of words.

634 ■ A Turbulent Time (1625–1798)

Prewriting

- To give students guidance in developing this assignment, give them the **Writing About Literature,** pages 222–223 in *Unit 3 Resources*.

- Lead the class in a discussion on the different ways in which writers in this unit use words to express their perspectives on the world. The discussion should help students find two works to compare in their essays.

- Suggest that students take notes on two writers whose use of language they will compare and contrast in their essays. They can record their notes in a Three-column Chart like the one on p. 282 of *Graphic Organizer Transparencies.*

- When constructing their thesis statements, students should focus on the differences in the ways in which the two authors use language.

Tips for Test Taking

A writing prompt on a standardized test may ask students to compare and contrast elements of two reading passages. In a test situation, it is particularly important for students to organize their ideas clearly and logically. Suggest that students use a simple graphic organizer such as an outline or chart to identify elements to compare and contrast. Students should write an introductory sentence that clearly identifies the comparisons or contrasts, and should use clue words and phrases (*similarly, in contrast, likewise, on the other hand*) to help guide readers through the essay.

Teaching Resources

The following resources can be used to extend or enrich the Instruction for Writing About Literature.

Unit 3 Resources
Writing About Literature, pp. 222–223

General Resources
Rubrics for Comparison-and-Contrast Essay, pp. 69–70

Graphic Organizer Transparencies
Three-column Chart, p. 282

Drafting

Organize. A logical and clear organization matches the needs of your essay. In the outline below, the writer chose to discuss Defoe first because his use of words is straightforward, whereas Donne uses words to create a new perspective. Even though Defoe's work is chronologically later, it makes sense to discuss it first in this essay.

Elaborate with specific examples. As you plan and structure your ideas, make sure that you have adequate support for each statement. Use an informal outline to keep track of the examples you plan to use.

 **Write to Learn**

The gaps in your outline may help you identify weaknesses in your analysis. If you are having trouble finding examples to include, consider looking in a different passage or choosing a different selection to discuss.

Model: Including Examples in an Informal Outline

II. In *A Journal of the Plague Year,* Defoe uses words to describe the world accurately:

    A. He includes detailed descriptions: a pit is "about forty feet in length, and about fifteen or sixteen feet broad, . . ."

    B. Words are journalistic, even when reporting emotions: "This was a mournful scene indeed. . . ."

III. In "Valediction," Donne uses words to show a new perspective:

    A. Crying is renamed as "tear-floods" and "sigh-tempests."

    B. Separating is not a "breach, but an expansion."

Revising and Editing

Review content: Eliminate contradictions. Comparing works can create a confusing draft. Make sure that you have not included any contradictions or unnecessary details that detract from your argument.

> **Contradictory Statement:** Fiction always invents a new world, so Defoe uses the plain-spoken language of journalism to present a realistic description of the plague.
>
> **Logical Statement:** Even though he is writing fiction, Defoe uses the plain-spoken language of journalism to present realistic descriptions.

Review style: Analyze your own word choice. Review your word choices to make sure that they are effective and say what you mean. Replace flat or repetitive language with active and striking words.

Write to Explain

Establish clear contrasts with words like *however, instead,* and *whereas* or phrases like *on the other hand* and *on the contrary.*

Publishing and Presenting

Submit your work to a literary magazine. Prepare your essay for a school literary magazine, adding background information for readers.

WG *Prentice Hall Writing and Grammar Connection: Chapter 14*

Drafting

Make sure that students have equal amounts of evidence from each of their authors and that they organize the information logically. They should discuss the work of one author before beginning discussion of the other.

Revising and Editing

Student partners may want to exchange papers and suggest revisions. Partners can help identify problems, such as contradictions in the essay's main argument or ways to clarify the contrasts.

Publishing and Presenting

Suggest that students prepare their essays for submission to a literary magazine by printing them out in the approved format of the magazine's submission department.

WG **Writing and Grammar, Diamond Level**

Students will find additional instruction on writing a comparison-and-contrast essay in Chapter 9.

Writing and Grammar Interactive Textbook CD-ROM

Students can use the following tools as they compare their comparison-and-contrast essays:

- Topic Bank
- Comparison and Contrast
- Unity and Coherence

Six Traits Focus

✔	Ideas	✔	Word Choice
✔	Organization		Sentence Fluency
	Voice		Conventions

Assessing the Essay

To evaluate students' essays, use the rubrics for a Comparison-and-Contrast Essay, pp. 69–70 in *General Resources.*

Differentiated Instruction   Solutions for All Learners

Strategy for Less Proficient Writers
Work with students to gather details to support the two examples that they are comparing and contrasting. Encourage them to list ways in which each work uses language. If students are having difficulty, encourage them to break down the work sentence by sentence or to ask of each sentence: *How are these words being used?*

Strategy for Advanced Writers
Advanced readers may enjoy the challenge of comparing the language of three authors represented in the unit. To do this, they will have to find a third author whose use of language contrasts with or complements the other two. Students might also select a modern writer and compare his or her use of language to the writers of the previous centuries.

 Meeting Your Standards

Students will

1. write a reflective essay.

2. use writing strategies to generate ideas and to plan, organize, evaluate, and revise the composition.

3. apply grammar skills.

 From the Author's Desk

Richard Rodriguez

Show students segment 3 on Richard Rodriguez on *From the Author's Desk DVD*. Discuss the writer's approach to reflective writing.

Writing Genres

Using the Form Point out that reflective essays are incorporated into other types of writing. Mention these examples:

- Friendly letters often include reflection. Adding reflection makes a letter more personal and meaningful for the recipient.

- Standardized tests and application forms may ask for a personal narrative—for example, an event that changed your life or an incident that helped you choose a profession.

Writing Workshop
Work in Progress

If students have done the Work-in-Progress assignments throughout Part 2, suggest that they examine their recorded ideas as they begin prewriting. They may have an idea in their portfolios that they wish to develop into a reflective essay.

Narration: Reflective Essay

In this unit, thought-provoking essays by Samuel Johnson and Joseph Addison offer revealing glimpses of each writer's personality. These **reflective essays** also encourage readers to reflect more deeply on the significance of personal experiences. Follow the steps outlined in this workshop to write your own reflective essay.

Assignment Write a reflective essay to describe an event from your personal experience, and then share insights about its significance.

What to Include Your reflective essay should feature the following elements:

- a statement of a general view that you have gained from experience
- descriptions of the incidents that helped shape that general view
- a balance between individual incidents and more general ideas
- clear connections between beliefs and events
- a consistent, personal tone

To preview the criteria on which your reflective essay may be assessed, see the rubric on page 643.

Using the Form
You may use elements of a reflective essay in these writing situations:

- friendly letters
- political speeches
- autobiographical anecdotes
- personal narratives

Reading **Writing** *Connection*

To get a feel for the reflective essay, read "On Spring" by Samuel Johnson, page 594.

636 ■ *A Turbulent Time (1625–1978)*

Teaching Resources

The following resources can be used to enrich or extend the instruction for the Writing Workshop.

Unit 3 Resources
  Writing Workshop, pp. 224–225

General Resources
  Reflective Essay Rubrics, pp. 47–48

From the Author's Desk DVD
  Richard Rodriguez, Segments 3 and 4

Graphic Organizer Transparencies
  Rubric for Self-Assessment, p. 123

Prewriting

Choosing Your Topic

To write a strong reflective essay, you need to tie two elements together: a belief that you hold about life, and an event or events that led you to that belief. Use one of the following strategies to choose a suitable topic:

- **Freewrite** for five minutes, nonstop, on important events or experiences in your life, or on beliefs that you hold strongly. Jot down as many ideas as you can. Then, review your freewriting for connections between general beliefs and specific incidents, and choose a topic.

- **Top Five List.** Make a list of times in your life when you discovered something wonderful. For example, maybe you discovered a family of chipmunks in your yard, or you finally mastered a new sport. For each key event, note what you learned, and think about the ways it broadened your horizons.

Narrowing Your Topic

Once you have some general ideas for events, beliefs, or experiences to include in your essay, focus your topic. For example, if you wrote down a series of events that happened to you in your first year of high school, write a sentence that describes the insight you want your reflective essay to reveal. Then, prepare to focus on what you gained from these experiences.

Gathering Details

Create a chart like the one shown to gather details for your essay. If you find that the connections among your ideas are still vague, freewrite again until you have a clearer grasp of their relationship.

Then, review your chart and write three focus statements.

- First, sum up your central *insight* in a single, clear sentence.

- Then, write another sentence summarizing the *experiences* leading to this insight.

- Finally, write a sentence explaining the *connection* between the insight and the experiences. Refer to these three focus statements as you draft.

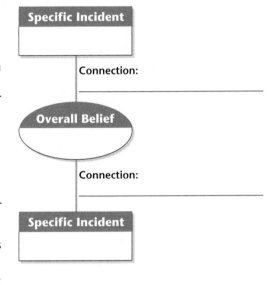

Prewriting

- Have students choose topics either from their Work-in-Progress ideas or by using the freewriting or listing strategies described on this page. Remind students that their potential topics should cover events or experiences that students would wish to share with others. Students should avoid sharing experiences that are too personal.

- After students have completed their freewriting and listing, ask them to work in small groups. Students should share their ideas with their groups and ask for feedback. Group members should ask clarifying questions, such as "Why was this event or experience important?" or "What did you learn from this experience?"

- Tell students to use the graphic organizer on this page to make connections between their freewriting ideas and the overall beliefs those ideas support.

- Encourage students to spend time creating thoughtful summary sentences. After students summarize their insights, experiences, and connections, explain that their summary statements can be used as the topic sentences for sections of the essay.

Six Traits Focus

✔	Ideas		Word Choice
✔	Organization		Sentence Fluency
	Voice		Conventions

Writing and Grammar, Diamond Level

Students will find additional instruction on prewriting for a reflective essay in Chapter 4, Section 2.

Writing and Grammar Interactive Textbook CD-ROM

Students can use the following tools as they complete their reflective essays:

- Customizable Outline
- Descriptive Word Bin
- Vague Adjectives Revising Tool
- Editing

Tips for Using Rubrics

- Before students begin work on this assignment, have them preview the Rubric for Self-Assessment (p. 643) to know what is expected. You may show them this rubric on transparency (*Graphic Organizer Transparencies,* p. 123).

- Review the Assessment criteria in class. Before students use the Rubric for Self-Assessment, work with them to rate the Student Model on p. 640 by applying one or two criteria to it.

- If you wish to assess students' reflective essays with either a 4-point, 5-point, or 6-point scoring rubric, see *General Resources,* pp. 47 and 48.

Drafting

- Remind students that their opening paragraph should include mention of the specific incident that spurred a more general insight.

- Explain that it is essential that students write with a consistent tone in their essays and to resist deviating from that tone.

- It may help students to think of the body of their essays as the story of the incident that led them to a moment of insight. Suggest that students use time lines or a storyboard to plot out the incident.

- Encourage students to elaborate on the important details in their essays. The details they mention can be descriptions that help readers imagine the scene, dialogue that makes an incident come to life, or even an internal monologue revealing the writer's thoughts. Challenge students to elaborate on or explode at least three details in their writing.

Drafting

Shaping Your Writing

Decide where to start. A well-organized reflective essay alternates between generalizations and specific incidents. Your opening paragraph should include both a statement of the overall belief on which the essay is based and a brief indication of how you arrived at that position.

Experiment with ways to present these two elements effectively. For instance, you might open with a statement of belief but include only one or two tantalizing details about the incidents that led you to it.

Establish a tone. Introduce a recognizable tone for your essay, from the beginning, and stay with it throughout. A serious, straightforward tone is certainly acceptable, but you might consider using one of these:

- **Ironic tone:** a good tone to use when your details show that things do not always work out as expected or intended
- **Humorous tone:** a logical choice when your examples are amusing

Model: Experimenting with Specific Tones

Ironic Tone
I welcomed my coach's criticism as warmly as any self-centered ten-year-old might. I was quite comfortable postponing any action until the following year, by which time I expected the matter would be forgotten.

Humorous Tone
Having a little brother is not as big a pain as people say. It's worse. Yet after years of his tattling and tagging along, one incident brought home to me how important family is—even little brothers. I no longer want to sell him to the circus.

Providing Elaboration

Incorporate details. Flesh out your reflective essay by incorporating the details you gathered earlier as well as new details that come to mind as you write. Bring your reflections to life for your readers by including details that reveal not only what happened but what you thought and felt about it.

Explode a moment. After you draft, expand any descriptions in your essay by telling more about what happened, what something looked like, or how the people involved—including you—reacted. Then, write the details you want to add.

To read the complete student model from which this example is taken, see page 642.

Student Model: Exploding a Moment

Julie was cute and dated the most popular boys in our school.

She was a Student Council member. She was also the most

confident person I knew, and she welcomed an understudy.

a cheerleader and

These additional details provide more description.

Six Traits Focus

✔ Ideas	✔ Word Choice
✔ Organization	Sentence Fluency
✔ Voice	Conventions

WG **Writing and Grammar,** Diamond Level

Students will find additional instruction on drafting a reflective essay in Chapter 4, Section 3.

Tips for *Using a Graphic Organizer*

If students have trouble adopting a tone in their essays, suggest that they try writing a few sentences of the essay in two different ways, using two different tones. Challenge students to model their writing on the excerpts that appear in the graphic organizer on this page. Students should write a few sentences of their essays in a straightforward tone, and a few sentences using a humorous or ironic tone. Tell students to show their sentences to a partner and ask for feedback about which tone is more effective.

Richard Rodriguez

These paragraphs appear in *Days of Obligation,* a philosophical travel book of mine that ranges over several centuries and back and forth across the U.S.–Mexico border. Each chapter, like the fragment below, is autobiographical. But that is only to say, memory is my guide throughout; memory forces me to reflect on the lessons within my life.

"In my reflective essays, the 'I' moves freely."

— *Richard Rodriguez*

Professional Model:

From *Days of Obligation*

Our last house on "Eye" Street was across from an old cemetery. No memory attached to it. The grass was watered and cut once a month by the city. There were no scrolls or wrought-iron fences; no places to put flowers. There were granite plaques level with the ground. Early dates. Solitary names. Men. Men who had come early to California and died young.

No grandsons or granddaughters came forward in the 1950s when Sacramento needed the land to build a school, a new Sutter Junior High School. A plywood fence was hammered up around the cemetery and, within that discretionary veil, bulldozers chugged and grunted, pulling up moist hairy mounds of what had once been the light of day; trucks came to carry it all away.

In early November, white tulle fog rises from the valley floor. My father is easy with this ancient weather reminiscent of the sea. My father is whistling this morning as he scrambles two eggs. My mother turns away from the window, pulling her blue bathrobe closer around her throat. I am sitting at the kitchen table. I am sixteen years old. I am pouring milk onto Sugar Frosted Flakes, watching milk rise in the bowl. My parents will die. I will die. Everyone I know will someday be dead. The blue parakeet my mother has taught to say "pretty boy" swings upon his little trapeze, while my mother pours coffee.

Each paragraph is about remembrance or the refusal to remember: civic amnesia; the forgetfulness of ancestors; the middle-aged writer's teenage discovery of death; the adult's inability to remember winter.

Images of nature are everywhere in this meditation on death — the parakeet, winter fog, clumps of grass upturned by bulldozers. As the contending images suggest: Death is the end of life yet also part of nature.

Notice here how the most astonishing ideas of life can come not with a drumbeat or violin, but in an instant of a Saturday morning, between spoonfuls of cereal.

Writing Workshop ■ *639*

Tips for
Reflective Writing

Give students these suggestions for revising their reflective writing:

1. Look for places in your draft where you can include a detail that helps make a scene complete. For example, in the excerpt from *Days of Obligation,* Rodriguez includes the detail of his mother pulling her robe tighter around her throat. The detail is a small one, but it gives the reader a vivid picture.

2. Include details that appeal to all of the senses, as Rodriguez does. He appeals to a sense of taste and smell (father cooking eggs), sound (parakeet saying "Pretty boy"), touch (mother and her robe), and sight (milk rising in a cereal bowl). Sensory details help writing come alive.

3. Remember that the event or moment at the center of your reflective essay does not have to be an important one. Notice how Rodriguez manages to capture his teenage self's realization that life is short as he was eating cereal on an ordinary morning.

Richard Rodriquez

- Show students Segment 4 on Richard Rodriguez on **From the Author's Desk DVD**. Discuss Rodriguez's idea that literature shows readers that they are connected to people who are not like them. Ask students how writing about their own lives may connect them to others.

- Point out that Rodriguez was inspired by many writers but does not believe that writers should be role models. He suggests instead that readers should learn from a writer's words not from a writer's life. Ask students to think about what their own writing, particularly their reflective essays, might teach readers.

- Discuss Rodriguez's comments on the excerpt from *Days of Obligation.* Talk about how he acknowledges how memory is faulty and how, as a mature writer, he realizes how different he is from his younger self. Ask students to consider how distance from an event in their lives affects how they remember it. Challenge students, as they write their reflective essays, to be aware of how they have changed since the time they are writing about.

- Have a volunteer read aloud the annotation next to the third paragraph of the model on p. 639. Point out how Rodriguez manages to find a meaningful idea about life during an ordinary moment. Challenge students to do the same in their reflective essays.

Revising

- Encourage students to review their drafts for any places that are "narrative heavy" or "narrative light" and to incorporate additional information to balance their reflective essays.

- Remind students of the strategy of "exploding a moment" as they revise. If a section of the essay needs more details, they can consider how to explode a moment and add more description or dialogue.

- Remind students that they can brainstorm and use other idea-generating strategies when revising, especially when they are adding new details.

- It may help students to think of the connection between incident and insight as a cause-and-effect relationship. Students can use transitional words and phrases that convey cause and effect, such as *therefore, because,* or *as a result,* to help the reader see the connections.

- Suggest that student partners share their drafts and consider any suggestions the other makes. Remind students to look for tone, clarity of ideas, and connections at this stage, rather than proofreading issues.

Six Traits Focus

✔ Ideas	✔ Word Choice	
✔ Organization	Sentence Fluency	
✔ Voice	Conventions	

Writing and Grammar, Diamond Level

Students will find additional instruction on revising a reflective essay in Chapter 4, Section 4.

Writing Workshop

Revising

Revising Your Overall Structure

Balance narration with reflection. Review your writing to make sure that you balance the specifics of the incidents you narrate with your general ideas.

1. Bracket any segments of the essay that describe specific incidents.
2. Mark in blue any points at which you have included a detail that does not set a scene or advance ideas.
3. Use a different color to mark the points where you provide your interpretation of events.

Student Model: Balancing Narration with Reflection

[I giggled and flirted my way through the next two years.] ~~[During that time, my Dad got a new job and we moved to a different neighborhood.]~~ Through it all, I felt as if I was putting on an act. [In the middle of my junior year, I received my first ACT results.] I was not happy with my scores.

> Ashley deleted this incident because it did not contribute toward her insight or provide necessary background.

Revising Your Word Choice

Strengthen your connections. Examine the connections in your essay between events and the generalizations to which they have led you. Sometimes these connections can be clarified simply by the use of appropriate transitional words or phrases:

Examples:

> And that is how . . .
> Suddenly I understood that . . .
> After this happened, . . .
> As a result, . . .

Peer Review: Ask a partner to identify places in your essay where your connections could be stronger.

- Together, discuss connections that make the relationships between your ideas clear.

- Then, make your revisions and share your work with your partner.

To read the complete student model, see page 642.

Tips for
Improving Word Choice

Give students the following suggestions for revising word choice:

1. Look for places in your draft where an added detail can expand a moment or bring an idea to life.

2. Circle "to be" verbs—such as *am, is, are, was, were, be, being, been.* Challenge yourself to change some of them to more vivid action verbs. You may need to rewrite the sentences when you change the verb.

3. Replace clichéd expressions with more precise and original phrases. For example, replace the trite phrase "My feet were as cold as ice" with "my feet were so cold I thought they would crack into tiny pieces when I walked."

Developing Your Style
Moving From Personal to Universal

Life-Lessons A reflective essay should move from personal experiences to broader meanings. These meanings usually involve life-lessons that everybody can understand: for example, the importance of taking a stand on an issue involving your core beliefs, or the necessity to keep in touch with the feelings and viewpoints of others. As you write, draw legitimate, sound generalizations from your experiences, and comment on your general views and beliefs in an accessible, personal way.

The Sense of an Ending If you have made your points well, a reflective essay does not need an elaborate conclusion. Nevertheless, the ending is the part of your essay that leaves the reader with a final impression. This chart offers some ideas for effective endings:

Effective Endings	
Write an Epilogue	Tell what has happened, if anything, to reinforce or to modify your belief since the events that originally led up to it.
Sum Up	Sum up your feelings or insights about your experience.
Pose a Question	Leave the reader with a question, especially if your essay explores the conflict in a situation or relationship.

Find It in Your Reading Read or review Samuel Johnson's essay "On Spring" on page 594.

1. Find two personal experiences that Johnson discusses in the essay.
2. Identify and evaluate the general lessons that Johnson draws from these experiences.

Try It in Your Writing Review the draft of your reflective essay. For each paragraph in your draft, follow these steps:

1. Underline the specific events and details that you have included.
2. Circle the broader, more general lessons, observations, or beliefs about life to which these events and details have led you. Consider the universality of the lessons and whether your audience would understand and agree with them.
3. Revise your essay, as necessary, to make your lessons more accessible to your audience.

 Prentice Hall Writing and Grammar Connection: Chapter 4, Section 4

Developing Your Style

- Make sure that students understand that one of the purposes for writing a reflective essay is to discuss an idea that they believe in or value. Students' essays will have more value if they articulate why their ideas or beliefs are important.
- Review with students the options for effective endings that appear in the chart on this page. Discuss how a lackluster conclusion to an otherwise interesting essay can leave readers disappointed.
- Discuss how Samuel Johnson blends the personal and the universal in his essay "On Spring."

1. **Possible answers:** Johnson conversed with a man who looked forward with hope to every spring; Johnson describes men who amuse themselves with card games, dinners, and conversation rather than natural beauty.

2. **Possible answers:** From the man who looked forward to spring, Johnson learned to appreciate spring and poetic descriptions of spring more fully. By thinking about men who do not enjoy nature, Johnson realized that such men are running away from grief or fear.

- Remind students that their essays should be accessible to many readers. Students are relating an experience that has personal meaning, but they should remember that their readers may never have had such an experience. Describing the experience well and explaining its meaning clearly will be essential.

Writing and Grammar, Diamond Level

Students will find additional instruction on writing the ending to a reflective essay in Chapter 4, Section 4.

Differentiated Instruction
Solutions for All Learners

Strategy for Special Needs Students
During the revision stage, it may help students to articulate the message they hope their essay imparts. Allow student partners to talk about the lessons at the center of their essays. The partners should take turns making notes, as precisely as possible, of what their partners say. Then students should review their essays to see whether that message comes through clearly in the essay.

Strategy for Advanced Writers
Tell students that the connections they draw between an incident and a general insight should challenge their readers. While they should provide plenty of details and information for their readers, they should not feel as though they have to "connect all the dots" for them. Readers will appreciate having to make inferences. It will make reading the essay a more interesting experience.

Student Model

- Explain that the Student Model is a sample, and that essays may be longer.
- **Ask** students to identify the specific incident or topic of Ashley's essay and how she connects it to something more general. **Answer:** The incident Ashley chooses is learning that a writer set stories in a place he'd never visited; her general insight is that she had been attempting something foreign in her own life, and it was better to be true to herself.
- Discuss with students what details make Ashley's account seem balanced between individual and general ideas.
- Point out how Ashley keeps her prose energetic with a consistent tone and vivid details and imagery.
- Show students how Ashley reports incidents that lead to her realization and how she states her central insight in her conclusion.

Writing Genres

Reflective Writing in the Real World Explain that good reflective writing offers readers or listeners an insight into the writer's mind and life. Tell students that reflective writing is often used in speeches, introductions, or toasts to honor friends, family, or co-workers. Managers use it in memos and meetings; religious leaders use it in sermons and lectures; and teachers and coaches use it to communicate what they have learned to their students and protégés.

Student Model: Ashley Philips
Ruston, LA

Coming Home

North Carolina novelist T. R. Pearson told me recently that when he was a teenager, he had set his stories in New York City, though he had never been there. "I thought New York was where it was," he laughed, adding that the fiction he had produced during this period was uniformly bad. Almost accidentally, he had begun to write about the life he really knew—life in little towns like Reidsville, North Carolina. It was only then that he succeeded at what he was attempting. Pearson's remarks set me thinking about my own life. Like Tom Pearson, I had spent a part of my life attempting something foreign and feeling unhappy with the result.

When I was in grade school, I read through every book in our classroom and did special reports. Research thrilled me. Books were the most important part of my life. I knew who I was. And I was happy.

In freshman year, though, I decided that my own life paled compared with that of my older friend Julie. Julie was popular and dated the most popular boys in our school. She was a cheerleader and a Student Council member. She was also the most confident person I knew, and she welcomed an understudy. I borrowed Julie's clothes and copied her hairstyles, right down to the huge hair bows that were her signature. By the end of the year I had decided to run for cheerleader.

I giggled and flirted my way through the next two years. Through it all, I felt as if I was putting on an act. In the middle of my junior year, I received my first ACT results. I was not happy with my scores. I began to reevaluate my life. I decided not to run for cheerleader. I paid less attention to who was popular and concentrated on friendships that were comfortable and fun. I threw myself into my science project and was exhilarated when I took top honors at the state science fair. By the end of the year, a teacher had invited me to serve as editor of a literary magazine. I felt that I was home again.

This December, as I sat listening to T. R. Pearson discuss the path that had led him to his true subject, I felt I knew exactly what he was talking about. It was a warm December day. A late fall sun filtered through the pine trees onto my English teacher's deck. Four other students and I sat in deck chairs and listened to Pearson speak about writing. It all felt so natural. This, I thought, is the kind of world I want to live in. I realized then that you can never get anywhere if you leave your true self behind. At that moment, I could not, for all the world, remember why cheerleading or Julie's boys or big hair bows had ever mattered.

> Ashley sets up a clear connection between the narrative that follows and her general point: Success depends on being true to oneself.

> By carefully selecting details, Ashley includes just enough incidents to support and balance her general insight.

> Ashley's short, decisive self-descriptions establish a consistent tone.

> Ashley reports incidents that clearly lead to her realization.

> In her conclusion, Ashley clearly states her general insight. (See Developing your style, p. 641.)

642

Editing and Proofreading

Review your essay to eliminate errors in grammar, spelling, or punctuation.

Focus on Complete Sentences: In formal writing, avoid incomplete sentences, or fragments. In your reflective essay, use them only for style. Review your essay, and correct sentence fragments by joining them with complete sentences.

Publishing and Presenting

Consider one of the following ways to share your writing:

Create a radio broadcast. Use your reflective essay as the basis for an opinion piece for the radio. Rehearse your presentation so that you can deliver it without awkward pauses, matching your voice to the tone of your essay. Record your presentation so that you can critique it later. **Publish on the Internet.** Post your reflective essay on a Web site for student writing. Invite feedback from other writers, using both conventional and electronic modes of correspondence.

Reflecting on Your Writing

Writer's Journal Jot down your thoughts on the experience of writing a reflective essay. Begin by answering these questions:

- What have you learned about moving from the particular to the general, and back again, in your writing?
- What new aspects of the topic did you discover as you developed plans for your essay?

WG Prentice Hall Writing and Grammar Connection: Chapter 4

Rubric for Self-Assessment

Evaluate your reflective essay using the following criteria and rating scale, or, with your classmates, determine your own reasonable evaluation criteria.

Criteria	Rating Scale
	not very *very*
Focus: How clearly do you state your general view?	1 2 3 4 5
Organization: How logical is your organization?	1 2 3 4 5
Support/Elaboration: How well do you describe incidents that support your beliefs?	1 2 3 4 5
Style: How well do you establish a personal tone?	1 2 3 4 5
Conventions: How correct is your grammar, especially your use of complete sentences?	1 2 3 4 5

Writing Workshop ■ *643*

Editing and Proofreading

- Have students go through their essays and identify any errors in comma usage. As a class, review some common comma errors and their solutions.
- Suggest that students read their essays aloud in a soft voice as a way to find any run-on sentences or sentences that are incorrectly punctuated.

Six Traits Focus

Ideas		Word Choice	
Organization	✔	Sentence Fluency	
Voice		Conventions	✔

ASSESS

Publishing and Presenting

- Ask students to reread their essays, considering which elements might appeal to an audience. Writing containing vivid descriptions and snappy dialogue might come across well on the radio. An essay with a controversial or unusual insight might prompt discussion on a Web site.
- Encourage students to practice delivering their radio presentations to a friend or into a tape recorder. Students should ask for feedback or listen to the recordings, paying particular attention to the tone of voice.

Reflecting on Your Writing

- Have students use the questions on p. 643 as the starting point for their journal entries. Encourage students to write more about what they learned from the experience of preparing their essays.
- Ask volunteers to share what they learned from the experience of presenting or publishing their essays.

WG **Writing and Grammar, Diamond Level**

Students will find additional guidance for editing and proofreading, publishing and presenting, and reflecting on a reflective essay in Chapter 4, Section 5.

Tips for Test Taking

When taking a test that includes a reflective writing prompt, students should be careful not to write an essay about an experience without making a connection to a larger theme, issue, or insight. Most reflective essay prompts encourage students to tell about an experience from their lives that has taught them an important lesson. Encourage students to estimate how much of the essay they should spend retelling the event and how much they should spend explaining its significance. Remind students to balance the two elements as much as possible.

Knowing Your Terms: Analyzing Information

Explain that the terms listed under Terms to Learn will be used in standardized-test situations when students are asked to discuss facts or ideas in a text and explain the relationships among them.

Terms to Learn

- Review *differentiate.* Tell students that differentiating is similar to contrasting two items in a comparison-and-contrast essay. Suggest that when asked to differentiate, students ask, "How are the items *not* alike?" For example, if they were asked to differentiate between metaphors and similes, students should focus on how the two literary terms differ.

- Review *analyze.* Emphasize that analysis is separating something into parts and then explaining the parts and how they are related. When analyzing information, students should include details that help explain each concept.

- Review *infer* and *inference.* Remind students that to infer is to draw a conclusion based on information in a text and on their own knowledge and experience.

 For: An Interactive Crossword Puzzle
Visit: www.PHSchool.com
Web Code: Esj-5301

ASSESS

Answers

1. Johnson's dictionary included all the words in the English language, not just the difficult

644

High-Frequency Academic Words

High-frequency academic words are words that appear often in textbooks and on standardized tests. Though you may already know the meaning of many of these words, they usually have a more specific meaning when they are used in textbooks and on tests.

Know Your Terms: Analyzing Information

Each of the words listed is a verb that tells you to show that you recognize the significance of text details and the relationships among them. The words indicate the kinds of details and information you should provide in your answer.

Terms to Learn

Differentiate Identify and explain the qualities that distinguish two items or ideas.

> Sample test item: *Differentiate* between foreshadowing and flashback.

Analyze Break down a topic or an issue into parts and explain them.

> Sample test item: In an essay, *analyze* Romantic theories of nature and the imagination.

Infer Show that you have used text details to figure out what is not stated.

> Sample test item: What can you *infer* from Pepys's *Diary* about medicine in 1660?

Practice

Directions: *Questions 1–3 refer to the passage.*

Johnson's Firsts Johnson set himself the task of making a different kind of dictionary, one of the first to include all the words in the English language, not just the difficult ones. In addition, he would show not only how to divide the words into syllables, but also where words came from. He would draw from his own gigantic learning to provide, for the first time in any dictionary, illustrative quotations from famous writers. Johnson's lexicon would report on the way writers actually used the English language.

Underfunded and working almost alone, Johnson defined some 43,000 words and included more than 114,000 supporting quotations drawn from every area of literature. Laboring for almost nine years, he captured the majesty of the English language and gave it a dignity that was long overdue.

1. *Differentiate* Johnson's dictionary from dictionaries that had come before.

2. *Analyze* Johnson's approach to dictionary writing and explain the significance of his dictionary.

3. What can you *infer* from this passage about Johnson's purpose for writing his dictionary?

Answers continued

ones. It also showed syllabification, word history, and quotations from famous writers, which had not been done before.

2. Johnson's approach to dictionary writing was to define a word, explain its history and the way it should be used, and to illuminate its meaning with quotations.

Johnson's approach was more rigorous and accurate than that used in previous dictionaries.

3. **Possible response:** Johnson's purpose was to create a dictionary that accurately explained the history and proper usage of the English language.

Critical Reading:
Writer's Point of View

In the reading sections of certain tests, you may be required to read a passage to interpret the writer's point of view. Use the following strategies to help you answer questions testing this skill.

- As you read, look for clues to the writer's attitude toward the subject. Try to differentiate this attitude from other possible points of view.

- Remember that a writer can reveal his or her attitude in direct statements, or in an indirect manner, through choice of words or details.

- As you read the passage, consider the writer's tone. Is it positive, negative, humorous, or serious?

- Look for changes in the writer's point of view within the passage.

Practice

Directions: *Read the passages, then answer the questions that follow.*

A. The nine African Americans who were the first to integrate Central High School in Little Rock, Arkansas, are among the heroes of the civil rights movement. On their first day at school, they were turned away by a violent mob. Only after President Dwight Eisenhower sent troops to protect the courageous "Little Rock Nine" were they able to attend classes.

B. A blaze caused by an unattended campfire destroyed 3,500 acres of Balsam Forest. Since 1984, more than 300 fires have burned there, causing one death and the destruction of acres of prime forest. Campfires are simply impossible to control, especially in dry months. Tell your legislator, today, to vote for a ban on campfires in Balsam Forest.

1. In Passage A, what is the writer's attitude toward the nine students?

A envy   **C** distaste

B admiration   **D** fear

2. In Passage B, which statement best expresses the writer's point of view?

A Campfires should be permitted in Balsam Forest.

B Preserving forest land is desirable.

C Camping should be banned in Balsam Forest.

D Campfires should not be allowed in Balsam Forest.

3. Which program would the author of Passage B most likely support?

A fire safety training for campers   **C** camper orientation

B a study of fire damage   **D** a ban on camping in Balsam Forest

Test-Taking Strategies

- As you read, ask yourself what other viewpoint the writer might have taken.

- Look for charged words that indicate feelings or opinions, whether negative or positive.

Assessment Workshop ■ 645

Tips for
Test Taking

To answer questions about point of view on a standardized test, students should compare each answer option to the information in the passage. Remind students that the author's point of view will be the main idea of a persuasive passage and should sum up the writer's ideas. Suggest that students restate the writer's point of view in their own words before reading the answer options. Then they should select the answer option closest to the writer's ideas.

✓ **Meeting Your Standards**

Students will

1. identify a writer's attitude toward his or her subject.

2. look for words, phrases, or ideas that express the writer's tone.

3. recognize a writer's point of view.

Critical Reading

- Remind students that a writer's attitude and tone are expressed through the language he or she uses to present ideas. Students should look for words that appeal to the reader's emotions.

- Explain that a person's "tone of voice" describes the way his or her words sound. Similarly, in writing, tone is the way a piece of writing sounds. The tone can often be summed up in one word, such as *ironic, playful, witty,* or *sentimental.*

- Remind students that if an author's point of view is not directly stated, they may have to use the passage's details and tone to determine the author's intention.

- Have students read the Practice passage and then answer the questions.

- Point out that in question 1, answers A, C, and D imply negative emotions. Students should examine the passage for words that indicate a positive or negative attitude about the subject.

- In question 2, answers A and D are opposites. One or both of them will probably be incorrect. Students should read the statements carefully to avoid confusion.

- Point out that in question 3, answer A suggests an idea that the author has said is not possible. Answer B has already been done. Answer C does not address the problem of fires. Only D mentions an idea that would solve the problem addressed in the passage.

ASSESS
Answers

1. B
2. D
3. D

645

Four Types of Persuasive Speeches

- Review with students the four types of persuasive speeches and the purposes of each: *proposition of fact, proposition of value, proposition to create concern,* and *proposition of policy.*

- Have students discuss the different ways in which these types of persuasive speech are supported.

- Review the chart on this page with students, and encourage them to copy it into their notebooks for future study.

Persuasive Techniques

- Review with students the various persuasive techniques and their characteristics, including *deductive arguments, inductive arguments, emotional appeals, effective diction,* and *rhetorical devices.*

- After students complete the Activity on the student page, have them discuss which types of persuasive speech and which persuasive techniques seemed especially effective.

Assess the Activity

To evaluate students' analyses, use the Analyzing Persuasive Techniques rubric, p. 83 in *General Resources.*

Analyzing Persuasive Techniques

In a **persuasive speech**, the speaker's goal is to change the audience's attitudes, beliefs, or actions. The techniques that a speaker uses to achieve this general goal depend on the speaker's specific focus. To analyze a persuasive speech, consider the four major focuses for a persuasive speech and the various types of persuasive devices used by a speaker.

Four Types of Persuasive Speeches

Persuasive speeches can be categorized by the type of proposition, or central point, for which they argue.

Persuasive Techniques

Persuasive speakers use a wide variety of techniques and elements, depending on the type of proposition they are advocating and their audience. Some techniques address the listener's mind, some address the heart, while others address the ear. Techniques include the following:

Type	Purpose	Support
Proposition of Fact	To prove a claim about facts	Expert opinions; research findings; inductive arguments
Proposition of Value	To apply values to facts	Appeals to widely shared values; deductive arguments; factual claim
Proposition to Create Concern	To establish that a situation is an important problem	Appeals to widely shared values; expert opinions; research findings; powerful images and comparisons
Proposition of Policy	To support a course of action	Appeals to widely shared values; expert opinions; research findings; inductive arguments; powerful images and comparisons

- **Deductive arguments** apply a general principle to a specific case to reach a conclusion.

- **Inductive arguments** make a generalization based on a selection of representative cases.

- **Emotional appeals** are statements intended to move a listener to feel a certain way about a situation.

- **Effective diction,** or word choice, ensures clarity and vivid, memorable formulations of main points.

- **Rhetorical devices**—such as repetition, rhetorical questions (questions to which the expected answer is obvious), and vivid comparisons—add force and make points memorable.

Not all persuasive techniques are suitable for each type of proposition. For instance, emotional appeals can be an effective element for a proposition of value but would not be effective if used for a proposition of fact.

Activity ❯ *Listen and Analyze* ❯ Evaluate the effectiveness of a formal or informal persuasive presentation such as a radio editorial or a classmate's speech. Identify the type of speech and the persuasive techniques used. As you listen, note the speaker's perspective on the topic, and offer supportive feedback.

Differentiated Instruction   Solutions for All Learners

Strategy for Less Proficient Readers

These students may have unusual difficulty distinguishing among the four kinds of persuasive speeches. Encourage students when they're listening to a persuasive speech on television, on the radio, or in a lecture or town hall meeting to consider what it is that the speaker is trying to achieve by persuading his or her audience. By using the list of common purposes for persuasive speaking and the list of common supports, less proficient students can determine what kind of speech it is. For example, if the speech treats the need for crosswalks to enable people to cross a busy street and the speaker appeals to widely shared values or powerful images, students might say the persuasive speech is a proposition to create concern or a proposition of policy.

Featured Titles:

Moll Flanders
Daniel Defoe
Signet Classic, 1981

Fiction Moll Flanders, the first-person narrator of this novel, starts out in life as "a poor desolate girl without friends, without clothes, without help or helper in the world." Gradually, she claws her way up from the gutter to a life of wealth and security, often making mistakes along the way. Defoe, however, does not condemn her. He sees her more as a victim of society's evils than as an evildoer herself. By the end of the novel, Moll feels "sincere penitence" for the wrongs she has done. Readers, however, may not experience any regret for their fascinating literary adventures in England's criminal underworld.

Works Presented in Unit Three:
If sampling a portion of the following texts has built your interest, treat yourself to the full works.

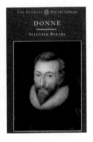

Donne: Selected Poetry
John Donne, edited by John Hayward
Penguin Books, 1950

Paradise Lost and Paradise Regained
John Milton
Signet Classic, 1968

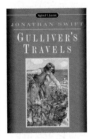

Gulliver's Travels
Jonathan Swift
Signet Classic, 1999

The Life of Samuel Johnson
James Boswell, edited by Christopher Hibbert
Penguin Books, 1986

Many of these titles are available in the Prentice Hall/Penguin Literature Library. Consult your teacher before choosing one.

Continued from Right Column

incestuous marriage, readers should remember that Moll is unaware of the situation at first and ends it immediately upon discovering the truth.

Lexile: 1390L

Life of Samuel Johnson by James Boswell This book occasionally depicts attitudes that would have been common during the eighteenth century but that would be considered sexist by today's standards.

Lexile: Appropriate for high school students

Planning Students' Further Reading

Discussions of literature can raise sensitive and often controversial issues. Before you recommend further reading to your students, consider the values and sensitivities of your community as well as the age, ability, and sophistication of your students. It is also good policy to preview literature before you recommend it to students. The notes below offer some guidance on specific titles.

Selected Poetry by John Donne
Some of the satires and elegies, such as "Love's Progress," contain overt sexual references as well as sexual innuendos.

Lexile: NP

Paradise Lost and ***Paradise Regained*** by John Milton
Paradise Lost and *Paradise Regained* present a poet's interpretation of biblical events, which may offend some students. Also, some may be offended by the fact that Satan is portrayed somewhat sympathetically in *Paradise Lost* and is considered by some scholars to be the poem's epic hero. Other potentially offensive subjects include Adam and Eve's nakedness, the description of Death as the product of an incestuous union between Satan and Sin, and expressions of sexist attitudes.

Lexile: NP

Gulliver's Travels by Jonathan Swift
Some students may be offended by Swift's satire of religion and politicians. Other sensitive issues include references to prostitution, a beheading, accusations of adultery, drinking, urinating, defecating, and sexist attitudes. Also, it is suggested that the Emperor of Japan required foreigners to trample on a crucifix. The book satirizes religious and political disputes, doctors and lawyers, and many other aspects of society. It makes insensitive remarks about dwarfs and portrays the emperor of Japan as anti-Christian.

Lexile: Appropriate for high school students

Moll Flanders by Daniel Defoe
Sensitive issues include Moll's numerous sexual relationships out of wedlock, her life of crime, and her marriage to her brother. Point out that Defoe's purpose in including such sordid situations is to show how difficult life was for women in Moll's day and how depraved a widowed mother with no means of support could easily become. With regard to Moll's

647

INDEX OF AUTHORS AND TITLES

Note: Nonfiction selections and informational text appear in red. Page numbers in italic text refer to background or biographical information.

INDEX OF SKILLS

Note: Page numbers in **boldface** refer to pages where terms are defined.

Vocabulary

Grammar and Style

Report
> investigative, **203**
> research, **992**

Script, multimedia presentation of
poem, 1293

Sequel, 1100

Short story, **R21**

Speech, persuasive, 413, 447, 1129
> welcome, 325

Style, imitating author's, 553

Summary, 135

Timed writing. *See* **Timed Writing
Applications,** above

Workplace writing, 836, **R23**

Writing Strategies

Prewriting

Choosing topic by
> charting, 211, 255
> checking available sources,
> 993
> discussion group, 407
> freewriting, 637
> itemizing, 1331
> listing, 208, 211, 637, 1331
> media flip-through, 1331
> news scan, 407
> reviewing notebooks, journals,
> and textbooks, 993
> sentence starters, 211

Narrowing topic by, 211, 637,
993
> assessing values, 834
> charting, 404, 990
> finding focus, 208, 404, 407,
> 634, 834, 990, 1328
> finding relevant media, 1331
> generating questions to identify
> necessary background, 787
> note-taking for summary, 247
> note-taking to focus on theme,
> 634
> testing ideas, 404

Gathering details, 208, 211, 404, 407,
634, 637, 990
> analyzing voice for parody,
> 1249
> analyzing sources for reliability,
> 977
> charting, 939, 1199
> > cause-and-effect
> > relationships, 881
> > to compare definitions, 571
> > to comparing viewpoints, 959
> > for evaluation, 1328
> examples from literature, 834
> matching information to job,
> 837
> note cards, source and note,
> 993

organizing details, 699
organizing materials, 1331
research in, 993
work history for résumé, 837

Writing working thesis, 208, 404, 634,
990

Drafting

Shaping writing by
> being concise, 838
> character in starting out strong,
> 212
> creating call for action, 408
> deciding where to start, 638
> developing thesis statement, 994
> dialogue, 212
> establishing organizational plan,
> 994
> establishing tone, 638
> focusing thesis statement, 991
> logical organization, 209
> outlining, 405, 838
> pacing, 212
> playing to strengths, 838, 1329
> positioning media sources,
> 1332
> relating broad themes to
> personal experience, 500
> selecting and following format,
> 838
> selecting media sources, 1332
> setting, 212
> showcasing thesis statement, 408
> tying together points in effective
> conclusion, 1329
> using parallelism and antithesis,
> 553
> writing powerful introduction,
> 994

Elaborating by
> appeals, 408
> arguments, 408
> citing specific examples, 405, 835
> clarifying media references,
> 1332
> conflict, 212
> considering variety and flow,
> 1332
> drafting annotations for primary
> sources, 921
> explode a moment, 638
> framing media references, 1332
> handling sources, 994
> including examples in informal
> outline, 635
> including references and
> citations, 397
> including quotations, 209
> incorporating specific details,
> 638
> outlining
> > examples, 635

ideas, 835
using reactions to develop
situation, 187
word banks, 1224

ending well, 212

following script format, 1293

organizing, 835, 991, 1329

organizing critical response, 1115

Revising

adding rhetorical devices, 1129

adding support
> by connecting general to specific,
> 457
> with precise details, 1273
> for audience, 833
> knowledge level of readers,
> 1035

clarifying
> connections of ideas, 32, 65
> connections with transitions,
> 1283
> time and place, 214
> to connect personal and general,
> 585

content
> to assess emotional language,
> 1329
> for beginning and ending, 835
> to check connections, 991
> for contradictions, 635
> for logical connections, 405
> for persuasive language, 821
> to enhancing subtlety of
> interpretation, 721
> for purpose, 833
> for thoroughness, 209

elaborating, 1053
> on critical insights, 89
> for precision, 1154

eliminating contradictions, 635

improving persuasive impact, 1311

indicating cause-and-effect transition,
896

organizing
> for logic, 203, 405

outlining
> post-draft, 447

overall structure, 214
> arranging arguments in logical
> order, 410
> to balance specific and general,
> 603
> balancing narrative with
> reflection, 640
> to deepen analysis, 1323
> improving media handling, 1334
> reviewing format, 840
> unified support for, 803

paragraphs, 996

parallelism to create persuasive tone,
279

INDEX OF FEATURES

Note: Page numbers in **boldface** refer to pages where terms are defined.

ACKNOWLEDGMENTS

Harcourt, Inc. and Faber and Faber Limited

"The Hollow Men" from *Collected Poems 1909-1962* by T.S. Eliot, copyright © 1936 by Harcourt Inc., copyright © 1964, 1963 by T.S. Eliot, reprinted by permission of the publisher. "Journey of the Magi" from *Collected Poems 1909–1962* by T. S. Eliot, copyright 1936 by Harcourt Brace & Company, copyright © 1964, 1963 by T. S. Eliot.

Harcourt, Inc.

"The Lady in the Looking Glass: A Reflection" from *A Haunted House And Other Short Stories* by Virginia Woolf, copyright 1944 and renewed 1972 by Harcourt, Inc.

Harcourt, Inc. and A M Heath & Company Limited, Authors' Agents

"Shooting an Elephant" from *Shooting An Elephant And Other Essays* by George Orwell (copyright © George Orwell, 1936).

Harlan Davidson/Forum Press, Inc.

Excerpt from *Book I* of *Utopia* by Thomas More, translated and edited by N.V.S. Ogden. Copyright © 1949 by Harlan Davidson, Inc. Reprinted by permission.

HarperCollins Publishers, Inc. and William Heinemann, Ltd.

"A Devoted Son" from *Games At Twilight And Other Stories* by Anita Desai. Copyright © 1978 by Anita Desai. Reprinted by permission of HarperCollins Publishers, Inc..

David Higham Associates Limited

"On the Patio" from *Poems 1954–1987* by Peter Redgrove. Copyright © Peter Redgrove, 1959, 1961, 1963, 1966, 1972, 1973, 1975, 1977, 1979, 1981, 1985, 1986, 1987. Reprinted by permission.

Kensington Publishing

"The Lorelei" by Heinrich Heine from *The Poetry and Prose of Heinrich Reine*, edited by Frederic Ewen. Copyright © 1948, 1976 by The Citadel Press. All rights reserved. Reprinted by arrangement with Kensington Publishing Corp. www.kensingtonbooks.com

Alfred A. Knopf, Inc.

"The Demon Lover," from *The Collected Stories Of Elizabeth Bowen* by Elizabeth Bowen, copyright © 1981 by Curtis Brown Ltd., Literary Executors of the Estate of Elizabeth Bowen. "The Negro Speaks of Rivers," copyright © 1926 by Alfed A. Knopf, Inc. and renewed 1954 by Langston Hughes, from *Selected Poems of Langston Hughes* by Langston Hughes. Used by permission of Alfred A. Knopf, a division of Random House, Inc.

Liveright Publishing Corporation

"anyone lived in a pretty how town" copyright © 1940, 1968, 1991 by the Trustees for the E.E. Cummings Trust, from *Complete Poems: 1904–1962* by E.E. Cummings, edited by George J. Firmage. Used by permission of Liveright Publishing Corporation.

Michelin Travel Publications

"Tintern Abbey" from *The Green Guide*. Copyright © Michelin et Cie, proprietaires-editeurs, 2001. Reprinted by permission.

The National Gallery

"The Gallery's Role and Objectives" by *The National Gallery, London*. Used with permission.

New Beacon Books Ltd.

"Time Removed" from *Fractured Circles* by James Berry, published by New Beacon Books Ltd. Copyright © 1979, James Berry. "Freedom" from *Fractured Circles* by James Berry, published by New Beacon Books Ltd. Copyright © 1979, James Berry. From "Lucy: Englan' Lady" from *Lucy's Letter and Loving* by James Berry. Copyright © 1982 by James Berry, first published by New Beacon Books Ltd in 1982. Reprinted by permission.

New Directions Publishing Corporation

"Fern Hill" by Dylan Thomas, from *The Poems of Dylan Thomas*. Copyright © 1945 by The Trustees for the Copyrights of Dylan Thomas. "Do Not Go Gentle Into That Good Night" by Dylan Thomas, from *The Poems of Dylan Thomas*. Copyright © 1952 by Dylan Thomas. "Anthem for Doomed Youth" by Wilfred Owen, from *The Collected Poems of Wilfred Owen*. Copyright © 1963 by Chatto & Windus, Ltd. "Not Waving But Drowning" by Stevie Smith, from *Collected Poems of Stevie Smith*. Copyright © 1972 by Stevie Smith. Reprinted by permission of New Directions Publishing Corp.

Oxford University Press, Inc.

"The Wanderer," from *An Anthology of Old English Poetry*, edited by Charles W. Kennedy, translated by Charles W. Kennedy, copyright © 1960 by Oxford University Press, Inc. Used by permission of Oxford University Press, Inc.

Oxford University Press, UK

"To Lucasta, Going To the Wars" from *The Poems Of Richard Lovelace*, edited by C.H. Wilkinson, copyright © 1953. "To the Virgins, to Make Much of Time" from *The Poems Of Robert Herrick*, edited by L.C. Martin.

Penguin Books Ltd. (London)

From *A History Of The English Church And People* by Bede, translated by Leo Sherley-Price, revised by R.E. Latham (Penguin Classics 1955, Revised edition 1968). Copyright © Leo Sherley-Price, 1955, 1968. Used with permission of Penguin Group (UK).

From "The Canterbury Tales: The Wife of Bath's Tale" by Geoffrey Chaucer translated by Nevill Coghill from *The Canterbury Tales*. From "The Pardoner's Tale" by Geoffrey Chaucer translated by Nevill Coghill from *The Canterbury Tales*.

Random House, Inc.

"Homeless," copyright © 1987 by Anna Quindlen, from *Living Out Loud* by Anna Quindlen. "In Memory of W. B. Yeats" copyright © 1940 & renewed 1968 by W.H. Auden, from *W. H. Auden: Collected Poems* by W. H. Auden, edited by Edward Mendelson. "Musée des Beaux Arts" from *W. H. Auden: Collected Poems* by W. H. Auden, edited by Edward Mendelson. Copyright 1940 and renewed 1968 by W. H. Auden. Used by permission of Random House, Inc.

Random House, Inc. and Faber and Faber Ltd.

"Not Palaces" by Stephen Spender. In the UK, from *Collected Poems 1928–1985*. Copyright © 1986 by Stephen Spender. Copyright © 1934 by The Modern Library, Inc. and renewed 1962, 1964, 1986 by Stephen Spender.

Russell & Volkening, Inc.

"The Train from Rhodesia" from *Selected Stories* by Nadine Gordimer copyright © 1950 by Nadine Gordimer, renewed in 1978 by Nadine Gordimer. Reprinted by the permission of Russell & Volkening as agents for the author.

Salisbury Post

"Shakespearean expert brings skills to Rowan County" by Cortney L. Hill from *www.salisburypost.com*. Reprinted by permission.

Dr. Anne Savage

Excerpt from *The Anglo-Saxon Chronicle*, translated and collated by Anne Savage. Copyright © 1983 by Phoebe Phillips.

Scovil Chichak Galen Literary Agency, Inc.

"We'll Never Conquer Space" by Arthur C. Clarke, from *Science Digest, June 1960*, Copyright © 1960 by Popular Mechanics Company.

Simon & Schuster, Inc and Jonathan Clowes Ltd.

"No Witchcraft for Sale," from *African Short Stories* by Doris Lessing. Copyright © 1951 by Doris Lessing. Reprinted by kind permission of Jonathan Clowes, Ltd., London, on behalf of Doris Lessing.

Scribner, an imprint of Simon & Schuster Adult Publishing Group

"The Second Coming" from *The Collected Works of W.B. Yeats, Volume I: The Poems, Revised*, edited by Richard J. Finneran. Copyright © 1924 by The Macmillan Publishing Company, copyright renewed © 1952 by Bertha Georgie Yeats. Reprinted with the permission of Scribner, an imprint of Simon & Schuster Adult Publishing Group.

Taylor & Francis Group

Lines from *An Essay on Man, Canto III* and lines from *Canto V* from *The Rape Of The Lock*, from *The Poems* of Alexander Pope edited by John Butt. Published by Methuen & Co., Ltd, London.

The University of Chicago Press

Excerpt from *The Iliad Of Homer*, translated by Richmond Lattimore. Copyright © 1951, The University of Chicago. Reprinted by permission.

University of Texas Press

"Sonnet LXIX" on page 147 from *100 Love Sonnets: Cien Sonetos De Amor* by Pablo Neruda, translated by Stephen Tapscott, Copyright © Pablo Neruda 1959 and Fundacion Pablo Neruda, Copyright © 1986 by the University of Texas Press. "Sonnet LXXXIX" on page 189 from *100 Love Sonnets: Cien Sonetos De Amor*, by Pablo Neruda, translated by Stephen Tapscott, Copyright © Pablo Neruda 1959 and Fundacion Pablo Neruda, Copyright © 1986 by the University of Texas Press. Reprinted by permission of the University of Texas Press.

Viking Penguin, Inc.

"The Book of Sand" from *Collected Fictions*, by Jorge Luis Borges, translated by Andrew Hurley, copyright © 1998 by Maria Kodama; translation copyright © 1998 by Penguin Putnam, Inc. "The Rocking-Horse Winner", copyright © 1933 by the Estate of D. H. Lawrence, renewed © 1961 by Angelo Ravagli and C. M. Weekley, Executors of the Estate of Frieda Lawrence, from *Complete Short Stories Of D.H. Lawrence* by D.H. Lawrence. "Araby", from *Dubliners* by James Joyce, copyright 1916 by B. W. Heubsch. Definitive text Copyright © 1967 by The Estate of James Joyce. From *In Athens Once*, from *Days Of Obligation* by Richard Rodriguez, copyright © 1992 by Richard Rodriguez. Used by permission of Viking Penguin, a division of Penguin Group (USA) Inc.

Viking Penguin, Inc. and Barbara Levy, Literary Agency

"Wirers" from *Collected Poems Of Siegfried Sasson* by Siegfried Sassoon, copyright 1918, 1920 by E. P. Dutton. Copyright 1936, 1946, 1947, 1948 by Siegfried Sassoon.

Viking Penguin, Inc. and David Higham Associates Ltd.

"A Shocking Accident", copyright © 1957 by Graham Greene, from *Collected Stories Of Graham Greene* by Graham Greene.

Wake Forest University Press

"Carrick Revisited" from *Selected Poems Of Louis Macneice*, edited by Michael Longley. Copyright © Wake Forest University Press, 1990. Reprinted by permission.

The Arthur Waley Estate

Excerpts from *The Analects Of Confucious*, translated and annotated by Arthur Waley. Copyright © 1938 by George Allen and Unwin Ltd. Reprinted by permission of The Arthur Waley Estate.

Stanley Weintraub

"Queen Victoria's Empire" from *Victoria. An Intimate Biography* by Stanley Weintraub. Used with permission of Stanley Weintraub.

W. W. Norton & Company, Inc.

"Outside History" from *Outside History: Selected Poems, 1980–1990* by Eavan Boland. Copyright © 1990 by Eavan Boland. From *Sir Gawain And The Green Knight: A New Verse Translation* translated by Marie Borroff. Copyright © 1967 by W.W. Norton & Company, Inc. Used by permission of W.W. Norton & Company, Inc.

Yale University Press

"The Seafarer" from *Poems From The Old English*, translated by Burton Raffel. Copyright © 1960, 1964; renewed 1988, 1922 by The University of Nebraska Press. Copyright © 1994 by Burton Raffel. From *Mary Chesnut's Civil War*, edited by C. Vann Woodward. Copyright © 1981 by C. Vann Woodward, Sally Bland Metts, Barbara G. Carpenter, Sally Bland Johnson, and Katherine W. Herbert. Reprinted by permission.

Note: Every effort has been made to locate the copyright owner of material reproduced on this component. Omissions brought to our attention will be corrected in subsequent editions.

CREDITS

Gallery of Art, Washington; **458: (m.):** The Granger Collection, New York; **458: (t.):** The Granger Collection, New York; **458: (b.):** New York Public Library; **460:** *The Interrupted Sleep*, oil on canvas. Oval 29–1/2 × 25–1/2 in., Francois Boucher, The Metropolitan Museum of Art, The Jules Bache Collection, 1949. (49.7.46) Photograph © 1984 The Metropolitan Museum of Art; **464:** *Young Man Writing*, Joos van Craesbeeck (follower of), Musee des Beaux-Arts, Nantes, France, Giraudon/The Bridgeman Art Library, London/New York; **469:** Mary Evans Picture Library; **470: (b.):** Bildarchiv Preussischer Kulturbesitz; **470: (t.):** Astrolabe, Museum fur Kunst and Gewerbe, Hamburg; **472:** Bettmann/CORBIS; **474:** Russell Illig/Getty Images; **476:** The Granger Collection, New York; **478:** Courtesy of the Trustees of British Library; **481:** Courtesy of the Trustees of British Library; **483:** Courtesy of the Trustees of British Library; **484: (r.):** Getty Images; **484: (l.):** Corel Professional Photos CD-ROM™; **490:** The Granger Collection, New York; **492:** Bildarchiv Preussischer Kulturbesitz; **495:** Fitzwilliam Museum, Cambridge; **501:** The Granger Collection, New York; **502: (r.):** The Granger Collection, New York; **502: (l.):** The Granger Collection, New York; **504:** Last page of Samuel Pepys's Diary 31 May 1669 , Pepys Library, Magdalene College, Cambridge, England; **506:** The Granger Collection, New York; **508–509:** *The Great Fire, 1666*, (coloured engraving) by Marcus Willemsz Doornik (17th century), Guildhall Library, Corporation of London/Bridgeman Art Library, London/New York; **512:** Courtesy of the Trustees of British Library; **515:** The Granger Collection, New York; **520:** The Granger Collection, New York; **524:** The Granger Collection, New York; **527:** The Granger Collection, New York; **531:** The Granger Collection, New York; **536:** The Granger Collection, New York; **538:** Corel Professional Photos CD-ROM™; **541:** *The Barge*, 1895–1896, (detail), Aubrey Beardsley from "The Rape of the Lock," Smithers, 1896 from The Best of Beardsley, Collected and edited by R.A. Walker, ©1948 by The Bodley Head, Published in the U.S.A. by Excalibur Books, plate 63; **542:** *The Rape of the Lock*, 1895–1896, Aubrey Beardsley, from "The Rape of the Lock," Smithers, 1896 from The Best of Beardsley, Collected and edited by R.A. Walker, ©1948 by The Bodley Head, Published in the U.S.A. by Excalibur Books, plate 64; **545: (r.):** Getty Images; **545: (l.):** Corel Professional Photos CD-ROM™; **547:** *The Battle of the Beaux and the Belles*, drawing for the eighth illustration from Rape of the Lock by Alexander Pope (1688–1744) pub. by Leonard Smithers, 1896 (pen & ink on paper) by Aubrey Beardsley (1872–98), The Barber Institute of Fine Arts, University of Birmingham/Bridgeman Art Library, London/New York; **548:** Historical Picture Archive/CORBIS; **554: (r.):** The Granger Collection, New York; **554: (l.):** The Granger Collection, New York; **557:** The Granger Collection, New York; **565:** ©British Museum; **572: (r.):** The Granger Collection, New York; **572: (l.):** The Granger Collection, New York; **574:** Lenore Weber/Omni-Photo Communications, Inc.; **578:** Lenore Weber/Omni-Photo Communications, Inc.; **580:** *Cottage and Pond, Moonlight*, Thomas Gainsborough, Art Resource, NY/Victoria and Albert Museum, London; **586:** Jack Hollingsworth/Getty Images; **587:** AP/Wide World Photos; **588:** The Granger Collection, New York; **589:** *Girl Writing by Lamplight*, c. 1850, by William Henry Hunt (1790–1864), The Maas Gallery London/Bridgeman Art Library, London/New York; **592: (r.):** The Granger Collection, New York; **592: (l.):** The Granger Collection, New York; **594:** Corel Professional Photos CD-ROM™; **599:** Corel Professional Photos CD-ROM™; **604:** Prentice Hall; **605:** The Granger Collection, New York; **607:** Royalty-Free/CORBIS; **608:** CORBIS; **610:** Lake County Museum/CORBIS; **612:** The Granger Collection, New York; **614:** ©Sotheby's/akg-images; **616:** The Granger Collection, New York; **621:** ©The Trustees of The British Museum; **626:** Bob Kramer/Stock, Boston; **628:** Mary Kate Denny/PhotoEdit/PNI; **629:** John Barrett/Globe Photos; **631: (r.):** © National Portrait Gallery, London;

631: (l.): The Granger Collection, New York; **636:** Getty Images; **639:** Prentice Hall; **648–649:** *Two Men Observing the Moon*, Caspar David Friedrich, oil on canvas, 35 × 44.5 cm, (1819–1820), Staatl, Kunstsammlungen, Neue Meister, Dresden, Germany, Erich Lessing/Art Resource, NY; **650: (m.):** Prentice Hall; **650: (b.):** *Portrait of Dr. Erasmus Darwin* (1731–1802) scientist, inventor and poet, grandfather of Charles Darwin, c. 1770, Joseph Wright of Derby (1734–97)/Darwin College, Cambridge, UK/Bridgeman Art Library, NY; **650: (t.):** Astrolabe, Museum fur Kunst und Gewerbe, Hamburg; **652: (t.):** The Granger Collection, New York; **652: (b.):** The Granger Collection, New York; **652: (m.r.):** The Granger Collection, New York; **652: (m.l.):** Corel Professional Photos CD-ROM™; **652: (t.):** Astrolabe, Museum fur Kunst und Gewerbe, Hamburg; **653: (t.l.):** ©Barson Collection/Archive Photos; **653: (t.r.):** The Granger Collection, New York; **653: (m.):** The Granger Collection, New York; **654:** The Granger Collection, New York; **654: (t.):** Astrolabe, Museum fur Kunst und Gewerbe, Hamburg; **655:** Corel Professional Photos CD-ROM™; **656: (b.):** *Power loom weaving*, 1834 (engraving) by Thomas Allom (1804–72) (after), Private Collection/Bridgeman Art Library, London/New York; **656: (t.):** Astrolabe, Museum fur Kunst und Gewerbe, Hamburg; **657:** Tea Time, David Emil, Christie's, London/SuperStock; **658: (m.):** ©Hulton/Archive; **658: (t.):** Astrolabe, Museum fur Kunst und Gewerbe, Hamburg; **658: (b.):** Corel Professional Photos CD-ROM™; **659:** Corel Professional Photos CD-ROM™; **660:** Astrolabe, Museum fur Kunst und Gewerbe, Hamburg; **661:** *Sketch for Hadleigh Castle*, John Constable, Oil on canvas, c1829, The Granger Collection, New York; **663:** *Hummingbird Hunters*, 1884, James Farrington Gookins, Collection of the Shelden Swope Art Museum, Terre Haute, Indiana; **664: (l.):** *Robert Burns*, Alexander Nasmyth, by courtesy of the National Portrait Gallery, London; **664: (r.):** The Granger Collection, New York; **666:** ©R. IJ. Erwin/Photo Researchers, Inc.; **669:** *The Bow*, Talbot Hughes, Warrington Museum and Art Gallery, Cheshire, UK/Bridgeman Art Library; **670: (r.):** Getty Images; **670: (l.):** Corel Professional Photos CD-ROM™; **673:** *The Village Wedding*, detail, by Sir Luke Fildes (1844–1927), Christopher Wood Gallery, London/Bridgeman Art Library, London/New York; **678:** The Granger Collection, New York; **680:** From a Manuscript of "The Lamb" by William Blake, Lessing J. Rosenwald Collection, Courtesy of the Library of Congress, Washington, D.C.; **681:** The Granger Collection, New York; **683:** ©Archive Photos; **688: (b.):** The Granger Collection, New York; **688: (t.):** Prentice Hall; **689:** Getty Images; **690:** *Mary Shelley* (detail), c.1840, Richard Rothwell, by courtesy of the National Portrait Gallery, London; **692–693:** *A View of Chamonix and Mt. Blanc*, Ludwig Ferdinand Schnorr von Carolsfeld, Austrian Gallery, Vienna; **701:** *Elizabeth Beale Bordley*, ca. 1797, Gilbert Stuart, Oil on canvas, 29 1/4 × 24", 1886.2, Courtesy of the Museum of American Art of the Pennsylvania Academy of the Fine Arts, Philadelphia. Bequest of Elizabeth Mifflin.; **702:** Bettmann/CORBIS; **703:** *The Wanderer Over the Sea of Clouds*, 1818, by Caspar-David Friedrich (1774–1840), Kunsthalle, Hamburg/Bridgeman Art Library, London/New York; **706:** The Granger Collection, New York; **708:** The Granger Collection, New York; **711: (l.):** Corel Professional Photos CD-ROM™; **711: (r.):** Getty Images; **712:** *Tintern Abbey*, J.M.W. Turner, ©British Museum; **715:** *Storming of the Bastille, 14 July 1789*, Anonymous, Chateau, Versailles, France, Giraudon/Art Resource, NY; **717:** Corel Professional Photos CD-ROM™; **723:** Michael Jenner/Robert Harding World Imagery; **724:** Rights and Permissions will add to their acknowledgements; **726:** Astrolabe, Museum fur Kunst und Gewerbe, Hamburg; **727:** Colin Raw/Getty Images; **728:** *Samuel Taylor Coleridge* (detail), Peter Vandyke, by courtesy of the National Portrait Gallery, London; **730:** Engraving by Gustáve Doré for The Rime of the Ancient Mariner by Samuel Taylor Coleridge ©1970 by Dover Publications, Inc.; **733:** Engraving by Gustáve Doré

Communications, Inc.; **978: (r.):** E.O. Hoppé/CORBIS; **978: (l.):** The Granger Collection, New York; **980:** *Bird's Nest*, W. Jenkins. Warrington Museum and Art Gallery, Cheshire, UK/Bridgeman Art Library; **983:** Bettmann/CORBIS; **989:** Courtesy of the Library of Congress; **992:** Bob Daemmrich/PhotoEdit Inc.; **995:** gezette.de Buro fur Fotografie; **1006–1007:** *The City Rises*, 1911 (tempera on card), Umberto Boccioni (1882–1916), Jesi Collection, Milan, Italy/Bridgeman Art Library, London/New York; **1008: (m.):** Colin McPherson/CORBIS; **1008: (b.):** Hulton-Deutsch Collection/CORBIS; **1008: (t.):** Astrolabe, Museum fur Kunst und Gewerbe, Hamburg; **1010: (l.):** Imperial War Museum, London; **1010: (t.r.):** Corel Professional Photos CD-ROM™; **1010: (b.r.):** Corbis-Bettmann; **1010: (m.):** The National Archives/CORBIS; **1011: (r.):** ©Peter Marlow/Sygma; **1011: (l.):** NASA; **1011: (m.):** Michael St. Maur Shell/CORBIS; **1012: (b.):** *Head of a Woman*, Pablo Picasso, Prado, Madrid, Spain/Fitzwilliam Museum, University of Cambridge,UK/ The Bridgeman Art Library, London/New York, ©2004Estate of Pablo Picasso/Artists Rights Society (ARS), New York; **1012: (t.):** Astrolabe, Museum fur Kunst und Gewerbe, Hamburg; **1012: (m.):** Corel Professional Photos CD-ROM™; **1013:** Musée de Verdun/Luc Joubert/Tallandier; **1014: (b.):** Culver Pictures, Inc.; **1014: (t.):** Astrolabe, Museum fur Kunst und Gewerbe, Hamburg; **1015:** CORBIS; **1016: (t.):** Astrolabe, Museum fur Kunst und Gewerbe, Hamburg; **1016: (b.):** Corel Professional Photos CD-ROM™; **1017:** David Hockney, *The Crossword Puzzle*, Minneapolis, Jan. 1983, photographic collage, 33 × 46", ©David Hockney; **1018: (r.):** Martin Jones/CORBIS; **1018: (l.):** Astrolabe, Museum fur Kunst und Gewerbe, Hamburg; **1019:** Corel Professional Photos CD-ROM™; **1021:** *The Children enter the Palace of Luxury*, probably from "The Bluebird" by Maeterlinck, 1911 (oil on card) by Frederick Cayley Robinson, (1862–1927), The Fine Art Society, London/Bridgeman Art Library, London/New York; **1022:** Hulton-Deutsch Collection/CORBIS; **1024:** *Her Signal*, c. 1892, Norman Garstin (1847–1926), The Royal Cornwall Museum, Truro/Bridgeman Art Library, London/New York; **1027:** Dennis Stock/Magnum Photos, Inc.; **1029:** Peter Johnson/CORBIS; **1031:** *Ravenna: City and port of Classis*. Mosaic, late 6th century AD from Basilicia of St. Apollinare Nuovo., The Granger Collection, New York; **1036: (b.):** Chuck Carlton/Index Stock Photography, Inc.; **1036: (t.):** Astrolabe, Museum fur Kunst und Gewerbe, Hamburg; **1038:** *T. S. Elliot* (detail), 1888–1965, Sir Gerald Kelly, National Portrait Gallery, Smithsonian Institution, Art Resource, New York; **1044:** Astrolabe, Museum fur Kunst und Gewerbe, Hamburg; **1049: (r.):** Getty Images; **1049: (l.):** Corel Professional Photos CD-ROM™; **1054: (t.r.):** *Louis MacNeice* (detail), Howard Loster, by Courtesy of the National Portrait Gallery, London; **1054: (b.):** The Granger Collection, New York; **1054: (t.l.):** Bettmann/CORBIS; **1056:** The Granger Collection, New York; **1060:** *The Fall of Icarus*, Pieter Brueghel, Musées Royaux des Beaux-Arts de Belgique, Bruxelles; **1062–1063:** Simon Wilkinson/Getty Images; **1065:** Richard Nowitz/CORBIS; **1071: (inset)** ©Kim Sayer/CORBIS; **1071: (border)** istockphoto.com; **1072:** Jeremy Homer/CORBIS; **1072: (border)** istockphoto.com; **1074:** The Granger Collection, New York; **1076–1077:** ©Gregory C. Dimijian/Photo Researchers, Inc.; **1079:** Alinari/Art Resource, NY; **1082–1083:** ©Orwell Archive; **1088:** Alfred A. Knopf; **1090:** Corel Professional Photos CD-ROM™; **1092:** *Portrait of N. Pietrunkevic*, Nikolai Ge, Scala/Art Resource, NY; **1093: (r.):** Getty Images; **1093: (l.):** Corel Professional Photos CD-ROM™; **1095:** *Sleepless Night*, Nikolai Romadin, Scala/Art Resource, NY; **1101:** *A Balloon Site, Coventry*, 1940, Dame Laura Knight, Imperial War Museum, London; **1102: (t.r.):** The Granger Collection, New York; **1102: (b.r.):** The Granger Collection,

New York; **1102: (b.l.):** *Siefried Sassoon* (detail), Bassano, by Courtesy of the National Portrait Gallery, London; **1102: (t.l.):** Getty Images; **1104:** Photri; **1106:** Photri; **1107:** The Granger Collection, New York; **1108:** ©S.C. Fried/Photo Researchers, Inc.; **1110:** Bettmann/CORBIS; **1116: (r.):** The Granger Collection, New York; **1116: (l.):** *Winston Churchill* (detail), National Portrait Gallery, Smithsonian Institution, Washington, D.C./Art Resource, NY; **1118:** Snark/Art Resource, NY; **1124:** Culver Pictures, Inc.; **1130: (l.):** Thomas Victor; **1130: (r.):** The Irish Times; **1132–1133:** ©D'Lynn Waldron; **1137:** *Starry Night over the Rhone River*, Vincent van Gogh, Musee d'Orsay, Paris, France, Giraudon/Art Resource, NY; **1142:** Thomas Victor; **1144–1145:** Peter Dublin/Stock, Boston; **1147:** Terry Madison/Getty Images; **1150–1151:** Peter Dublin/Stock, Boston; **1155:** Josephine Trotter/SuperStock; **1157:** Getty Images; **1158: (r.):** The Granger Collection, New York; **1158: (l.):** *Joseph Conrad* (detail), Walter Tittle, by Courtesy of the National Portrait Gallery, London; **1161:** Dieter & Mary Plage/Bruce Coleman, Inc.; **1163:** Emma Lee/Getty Images; **1166–1167:** Michael Freidel/Woodfin Camp & Associates; **1170–1171:** Tony Arruza/CORBIS; **1175:** *St. Patrick's Close*, Walter Osborne, National Gallery of Ireland; **1177: (r.):** Getty Images; **1177: (l.):** Corel Professional Photos CD-ROM™; **1182: (r.):** Photo by Jerry Bauer; **1182: (l.):** The Granger Collection, New York; **1185:** *The Garden of Love*, Walter Richard Sickert, Fitzwilliam Museum, Cambridge; **1186:** Stephen Johnson/Getty Images; **1188:** Getty Images; **1190:** Getty Images; **1192:** The Granger Collection, New York; **1194:** Culver Pictures, Inc.; **1200: (l.):** *D. H. Lawrence* (detail), Jan Juta, by Courtesy of the National Portrait Gallery, London; **1200: (r.):** Getty Images; **1203:** Bettmann/CORBIS; **1209:** Culver Pictures, Inc.; **1212–1213:** Aaron Horowitz/CORBIS; **1217:** Hans Neleman/Getty Images; **1227:** Steve Dunwell/Getty Images; **1228:** Susan Meiselas/Magnum Photos, Inc.; **1229:** *Political World*, ©Kenneth Eward/BioGrafz—Science Source/Photo Researchers, Inc.; **1230: (r.):** Thomas Victor; **1230: (l.):** Getty Images; **1232:** *Fishermen at Sea off the Needles*, J.M.W. Turner, Tate Gallery (on loan)/e.t.archive; **1234:** James P. Blair/Getty Images; **1236–1237:** Dann Coffey/Getty Images; **1239:** © J. B. Lafitte/Photo Researchers, Inc.; **1243:** Jim Ballard/Getty Images; **1250: (r.):** *Stevie Smith* (detail), photo for the National Photographic Record, by Courtesy of the National Portrait Gallery, London; **1250: (b.l.):** Nicolas Elder/Globe Photos; **1250: (t.l.):** Getty Images; **1252:** *Tombstones of Tiberius Julius Rufus and his son, Petronius Rufus and their wives*, Erich Lessing/Art Resource, NY; **1256:** Ross M. Horowitz/Getty Images; **1262:** Ian Berry/Magnum Photos, Inc.; **1265:** *Man from the Village*, Carlton Murrell, Courtesy of the artist; **1266:** Getty Images; **1268:** *The Red House*, Carlton Murrell, Courtesy of the artist; **1274:** Time Life Pictures/Getty Images; **1276–1277:** Richard A Cooke III/Getty Images; **1284:** Eugene Richards/Magnum Photos, Inc.; **1286:** ©Bettmann/CORBIS; **1288:** StockTrek/Getty Images; **1289:** Siede Preis/Getty Images; **1294: (b.):** Jim Erickson/CORBIS; **1294: (t.):** Colin McPherson/CORBIS; **1295:** Sue Ann Miller/Getty Images; **1296:** Thomas Victor; **1300–1301:** Dinodia/Omni-Photo Communications, Inc.; **1304:** Grace Davies/Omni-Photo Communications, Inc.; **1312:** Bettmann/CORBIS; **1314:** NASA/Omni-Photo Communications, Inc.; **1317:** NASA/Omni-Photo Communications, Inc.; **1318:** NASA/Omni-Photo Communications, Inc.; **1319: (r.):** Getty Images; **1319: (l.):** Corel Professional Photos CD-ROM™; **1324:** NASA; **1327:** AP/Wide World Photos; **1330:** David Young-Wolff/PhotoEdit Inc.; **1333:** Colin McPherson/CORBIS

Map and Art Credits: All graphic organizer: In-House Pros; All maps by Mapping Specialist, except where noted

STAFF CREDITS

Staff Credits: Ernie Albanese, Diane Alimena, **Rosalyn Arcilla,** Jasjit Arneja, **Nancy Barker, Amy Baron,** Rachel Beckman, Betsy Bostwick, **Ellen Bowler,** Jennifer Brady, Evonne Burgess, Rui Camarinha, **Pam Carey,** Lisa Carrillo, Jaime Cohen, Allison Cook, **Irene Ehrmann,** Leanne Esterly, Steve Frankel, Philip Fried, **Maggie Fritz,** Michael Ginsberg, **Elaine Goldman,** Patricia Hade, **Monduane Harris, Martha Heller,** Beth Hyslip, Vicki A. Kane, **Kate Krimsky,** Mary Sue Langan, Monica Lehmann, **Mary Luthi, George Lychock,** Gregory Lynch, Daniela Mastria, Kathleen Mercandetti, Karyl Murray, Jim McDonough, Kerrie Miller, Ken Myett, Kim Ortell, Carolyn Pallof, Sal Pisano, Jackie Regan, Erin Rehill-Seker, Bruce Rolff, Laura Ross, Carolyn Sapontzis, **Melissa Shustyk, Robert Siek, Rita Sullivan, Cynthia Summers,** Patrice Titterington, Jane S. Traulsen.

Additional Credits: Susan C. Ball, William Bingham, Andrea Brescia, Pradeep Byram, Donna Chappelle, Jennifer Ciccone, Jason Cuoco, Phillip Gagler, Judith Gaelick, Florrie Gadson, James Garratt, Allen Gold, Kristan Hoskins, Lisa Iozzia, Mohamed Kaptan, Barbara Kehr, Terry Kim, Stuart Kirschenbaum, Linda Latino, Julian Liby, Karen Mancinelli, Ginidir Marshall, Bill McAllister, John McClure, Patrick J. McCarthy, Caroline McDonnell, Meg Montgomery, Gita NadasLesley Pierson, Rachel Ross, Lloyd Sabin, James Savakis, Donna Schindler, Debi Taffet, Elizabeth Torjussen, Ryan Vaarsi, Gina M. Wangrycht.